T0238661

Lecture Notes in Computer Science   **9035**

Commenced Publication in 1973
Founding and Former Series Editors:
Gerhard Goos, Juris Hartmanis, and Jan van Leeuwen

Advanced Research in Computing and Software Science

Subline of Lecture Notes in Computer Science

More information about this series at http://www.springer.com/series/7407

Lecture Notes in Computer Science 9035

Commenced Publication in 1973
Founding and Former Series Editors:
Gerhard Goos, Juris Hartmanis, and Jan van Leeuwen

Advanced Research in Computing and Software Science

Subline of Lecture Notes in Computer Science

More information about this series at http://www.springer.com/series/7407

Christel Baier · Cesare Tinelli (Eds.)

Tools and Algorithms for the Construction and Analysis of Systems

21st International Conference, TACAS 2015
Held as Part of the European Joint Conferences
on Theory and Practice of Software, ETAPS 2015
London, UK, April 11–18, 2015
Proceedings

 Springer

Editors
Christel Baier
Technical University of Dresden
Dresden
Germany

Cesare Tinelli
The University of Iowa
Iowa City
Iowa
USA

ISSN 0302-9743
Lecture Notes in Computer Science
ISBN 978-3-662-46680-3
DOI 10.1007/978-3-662-46681-0

ISSN 1611-3349   (electronic)

ISBN 978-3-662-46681-0   (eBook)

Library of Congress Control Number: 2015934133

LNCS Sublibrary: SL1 – Theoretical Computer Science and General Issues

Springer Heidelberg New York Dordrecht London

Printed on acid-free paper

Springer-Verlag GmbH Berlin Heidelberg is part of Springer Science+Business Media
(www.springer.com)

Foreword

ETAPS 2015 was the 18th instance of the European Joint Conferences on Theory and Practice of Software. ETAPS is an annual federated conference that was established in 1998, and this year consisted of six constituting conferences (CC, ESOP, FASE, FoSSaCS, TACAS, and POST) including five invited speakers and two tutorial speakers. Prior to and after the main conference, numerous satellite workshops took place and attracted many researchers from all over the world.

ETAPS is a confederation of several conferences, each with its own Program Committee and its own Steering Committee (if any). The conferences cover various aspects of software systems, ranging from theoretical foundations to programming language developments, compiler advancements, analysis tools, formal approaches to software engineering, and security. Organizing these conferences into a coherent, highly synchronized conference program enables the participation in an exciting event, having the possibility to meet many researchers working in different directions in the field, and to easily attend talks at different conferences.

The six main conferences together received 544 submissions this year, 152 of which were accepted (including 10 tool demonstration papers), yielding an overall acceptance rate of 27.9%. I thank all authors for their interest in ETAPS, all reviewers for the peer-reviewing process, the PC members for their involvement, and in particular the PC Co-chairs for running this entire intensive process. Last but not least, my congratulations to all authors of the accepted papers!

ETAPS 2015 was greatly enriched by the invited talks by Daniel Licata (Wesleyan University, USA) and Catuscia Palamidessi (Inria Saclay and LIX, France), both unifying speakers, and the conference-specific invited speakers [CC] Keshav Pingali (University of Texas, USA), [FoSSaCS] Frank Pfenning (Carnegie Mellon University, USA), and [TACAS] Wang Yi (Uppsala University, Sweden). Invited tutorials were provided by Daniel Bernstein (Eindhoven University of Technology, the Netherlands and the University of Illinois at Chicago, USA), and Florent Kirchner (CEA, the Alternative Energies and Atomic Energy Commission, France). My sincere thanks to all these speakers for their inspiring talks!

ETAPS 2015 took place in the capital of England, the largest metropolitan area in the UK and the largest urban zone in the European Union by most measures. ETAPS 2015 was organized by the Queen Mary University of London in cooperation with the following associations and societies: ETAPS e.V., EATCS (European Association for Theoretical Computer Science), EAPLS (European Association for Programming Languages and Systems), and EASST (European Association of Software Science and Technology). It was supported by the following sponsors: Semmle, Winton, Facebook, Microsoft Research, and Springer-Verlag.

The organization team comprised:

- General Chairs: Pasquale Malacaria and Nikos Tzevelekos
- Workshops Chair: Paulo Oliva
- Publicity chairs: Michael Tautschnig and Greta Yorsh
- Members: Dino Distefano, Edmund Robinson, and Mehrnoosh Sadrzadeh

The overall planning for ETAPS is the responsibility of the Steering Committee. The ETAPS Steering Committee consists of an Executive Board (EB) and representatives of the individual ETAPS conferences, as well as representatives of EATCS, EAPLS, and EASST. The Executive Board comprises Gilles Barthe (satellite events, Madrid), Holger Hermanns (Saarbrücken), Joost-Pieter Katoen (Chair, Aachen and Twente), Gerald Lüttgen (Treasurer, Bamberg), and Tarmo Uustalu (publicity, Tallinn). Other members of the Steering Committee are: Christel Baier (Dresden), David Basin (Zurich), Giuseppe Castagna (Paris), Marsha Chechik (Toronto), Alexander Egyed (Linz), Riccardo Focardi (Venice), Björn Franke (Edinburgh), Jan Friso Groote (Eindhoven), Reiko Heckel (Leicester), Bart Jacobs (Nijmegen), Paul Klint (Amsterdam), Jens Knoop (Vienna), Christof Löding (Aachen), Ina Schäfer (Braunschweig), Pasquale Malacaria (London), Tiziana Margaria (Limerick), Andrew Myers (Boston), Catuscia Palamidessi (Paris), Frank Piessens (Leuven), Andrew Pitts (Cambridge), Jean-Francois Raskin (Brussels), Don Sannella (Edinburgh), Vladimiro Sassone (Southampton), Perdita Stevens (Edinburgh), Gabriele Taentzer (Marburg), Peter Thiemann (Freiburg), Cesare Tinelli (Iowa City), Luca Vigano (London), Jan Vitek (Boston), Igor Walukiewicz (Bordeaux), Andrzej Wąsowski (Copenhagen), and Lenore Zuck (Chicago).

I sincerely thank all ETAPS SC members for all their hard work to make the 18th edition of ETAPS a success. Moreover, thanks to all speakers, attendants, organizers of the satellite workshops, and to Springer for their support. Finally, many thanks to Pasquale and Nikos and their local organization team for all their efforts enabling ETAPS to take place in London!

January 2015   Joost-Pieter Katoen

Preface

This volume contains the proceedings of the 21st International Conference on Tools and Algorithms for the Construction and Analysis of Systems (TACAS 2015). The conference took place during April 13–17, 2015 in the lecture halls of Queen Mary University of London as part of the 18th European Joint Conferences on Theory and Practice of Software (ETAPS 2015).

TACAS is a forum for researchers, developers, and users interested in rigorously based tools and algorithms for the construction and analysis of systems. The conference aims to bridge the gaps between different communities with this common interest and support them in their quest to improve the utility, reliability, flexibility, and efficiency of tools and algorithms for building systems. The research areas covered by TACAS 2015 include specification and verification techniques, software and hardware verification, analytical techniques for real-time, hybrid and stochastic systems, analytical techniques for safety, security and dependability, model checking, theorem proving, SAT and SMT solving, static and dynamic program analysis, testing, abstraction techniques for modeling and verification, compositional and refinement-based methodologies, system construction and transformation techniques, tool environments and tool architectures, as well as applications and case studies.

As in former years, TACAS 2015 solicited four types of submissions:

- research papers, identifying and justifying a principled advance to the theoretical foundations for the construction and analysis of systems, where applicable supported by experimental validation;
- case-study papers, reporting on case studies and providing information about the system being studied, the goals of the study, the challenges the system poses to automated analysis, research methodologies and approaches used, the degree to which goals were attained, and how the results can be generalized to other problems and domains;
- regular tool papers, presenting a new tool, a new tool component, or novel extensions to an existing tool, with an emphasis on design and implementation concerns, including software architecture and core data structures, practical applicability, and experimental evaluations;
- short tool-demonstration papers, focussing on the usage aspects of tools.

This year, TACAS attracted a total of 164 paper submissions, divided into 105 research papers, 11 case-study papers, 31 regular tool papers, and 17 tool-demonstration papers. Each submission was refereed by at least three reviewers. In total, 45 papers were accepted for presentation at the conference: 27 research papers, 2 case-study papers, 7 regular tool papers, and 9 tool-demonstration papers, with an overall acceptance rate of 27 %. The acceptance rate for full papers (research, case-study, or regular tool papers) was 17 %.

TACAS 2015 hosted the 4th International Competition on Software Verification (SV-COMP), chaired and organized by Dirk Beyer. The competition had a record number of participants: 22 verification tools from 13 countries were submitted for the systematic comparative evaluation. This volume includes an overview of the competition results, and short papers describing 15 of the participating tools. These papers were reviewed by a separate Program Committee and each of them was refereed by four reviewers. A session in the TACAS program was assigned for the presentation of the results, by the SV-COMP Chair, and of the participating tools, by the developer teams.

Besides the presentation of the submitted contributions, the program included an invited talk by Wang Yi (Uppsala University, Sweden) on *Scalable Timing Analysis by Refinement* and two plenary invited talks by ETAPS unifying speakers Daniel Licata (Wesleyan University, US) and Catuscia Palamidessi (Inria Saclay and LIX, France).

We would like to thank all the authors who submitted papers to TACAS 2015, the Program Committee members and their subreviewers, the TACAS Tool Chair Jaco van de Pol and the SV-COMP Chair Dirk Beyer. We thank the competition teams for participating and show casing their tools to the TACAS community. We benefited greatly from the EasyChair conference management system, which we used to handle the submission, review, discussion, and proceedings preparation processes. Special thanks go to Joachim Klein and Dirk Beyer for their assistance in the preparation of these proceedings. Finally, we would like to thank the TACAS Steering Committee and the ETAPS Steering Committee for their guidance, and the ETAPS 2015 Organizing Committee, chaired by Pasquale Malacaria and Nikos Tzevelekos, for their assistance.

January 2015   Christel Baier
                                                            Cesare Tinelli

Organization

TACAS Program Committee

Erika Ábrahám	RWTH Aachen University, Germany
Christel Baier	Technical University of Dresden, Germany
Nathalie Bertrand	Inria Rennes Bretagne-Atlantique, France
Armin Biere	Johannes Kepler University, Austria
Patricia Bouyer	LSV, CNRS and ENS Cachan, France
Marsha Chechik	University of Toronto, Canada
Alessandro Cimatti	Fondazione Bruno Kessler, Italy
Rance Cleaveland	University of Maryland, USA
Cindy Eisner	IBM Haifa Research Lab, Israel
Uli Fahrenberg	IRISA Rennes, France
Hubert Garavel	Inria Grenoble Rhône-Alpes, France
Patrice Godefroid	Microsoft Research, USA
Susanne Graf	Université Joseph Fourier/CNRS/VERIMAG, France
Orna Grumberg	Technion - Israel Institute of Technology, Israel
Arie Gurfinkel	Software Engineering Institute, Carnegie Mellon University, USA
Klaus Havelund	Jet Propulsion Laboratory, California Institute of Technology, USA
Holger Hermanns	Saarland University, Germany
Reiner Hähnle	Technische Universität Darmstadt, Germany
Daniel Kroening	Oxford University, UK
Kim Larsen	Aalborg University, Denmark
Tiziana Margaria	University of Limerick and Lero, the Irish Software Research Center, Ireland
Ken Mcmillan	Microsoft Research, USA
Tobias Nipkow	Technische Universität München, Germany
David Parker	University of Birmingham, UK
Corina Pasareanu	CMU/NASA Ames Research Center, USA
Ruzica Piskac	Yale University, USA
Jean-Francois Raskin	Université Libre de Bruxelles, Belgium
Philipp Ruemmer	Uppsala University, Sweden
Sriram Sankaranarayanan	University of Colorado, USA
Scott Smolka	Stony Brook University, USA
Bernhard Steffen	Technische Universität Dortmund, Germany
Cesare Tinelli	The University of Iowa, USA

Jaco van de Pol   University of Twente, The Netherlands
Helmut Veith   Vienna University of Technology, Austria
Willem Visser   Stellenbosch University, South Africa
Heike Wehrheim   University of Paderborn, Germany
Lenore Zuck   University of Illinois at Chicago, USA

SV-COMP Program Committee

Dirk Beyer   University of Passau, Germany
Franck Cassez   NICTA Sydney, Australia
Matthias Dangl   University of Passau, Germany
Bernd Fischer   Stellenbosch University, South Africa
Arie Gurfinkel   Software Engineering Institute Carnegie
     Mellon University, USA
Matthias Heizmann   University of Freiburg, Germany
Ton-Chanh Le   National University of Singapore, Singapore
Ondrej Lengal   Brno University of Technology, Czech Republic
Jeremy Morse   University of Bristol, UK
Vadim Mutilin   ISP RAS, Russia
Alexander Nutz   University of Freiburg, Germany
Gennaro Parlato   University of Southampton, UK
Zvonimir Rakamarić   University of Utah, USA
Herbert Oliveira Rocha   Federal University of Amazonas, Brazil
Pablo Sánchez   University of Cantabria, Spain
Thomas Ströder   RWTH Aachen University, Germany
Michael Tautschnig   Queen Mary University of London, UK
Salvatore La Torre   Università degli Studi di Salerno, Italy
Ming-Hsien Tsai   Academia Sinica, China
Caterina Urban   École normale supérieure Paris, France
Tomas Vojnar   Brno University of Technology, Czech Republic
Dexi Wang   Tsinghua University, China
Wei Wang   New York University, USA

Additional Reviewers

Abdelkader, Karam
Albarghouthi, Aws
Aleksandrowicz, Gadi
Ashok, Vikas
Arbel, Eli
Axelsson, Emil
Bacci, Giorgio
Bacci, Giovanni
Backeman, Peter
Barbot, Benoît

Basset, Nicolas
Bauer, Oliver
Beneš, Nikola
Bodden, Eric
Bogomolov, Sergiy
Boichut, Yohan
Bollig, Benedikt
Bolosteanu, Iulia
Boudjadar, Jalil
Bozzano, Marco

Brenguier, Romain
Brihaye, Thomas
Bruns, Daniel
Bubel, Richard
Butkova, Yuliya
Caillaud, Benoît
Cattaruzza, Dario
Chakarov, Aleksandar
Chaki, Sagar
Chen, Xin
Corzilius, Florian
Csallner, Christoph
D'Souza, Deepak
David, Cristina
DeFrancisco, Richard
Dehnert, Christian
Delaune, Stephanie
Dimitrova, Rayna
Din, Crystal Chang
Doko, Marko
Doyen, Laurent
Eckhardt, Jonas
Egly, Uwe
Estievenart, Morgane
Evrard, Hugues
Fedyukovich, Grigory
Fernandes Pires, Anthony
Ferrer Fioriti, Luis María
Filieri, Antonio
Filiot, Emmanuel
Flores Montoya, Antonio E.
Fournier, Paulin
Frehse, Goran
Fröhlich, Andreas
Gardy, Patrick
Gario, Marco
Gay, Simon
Geldenhuys, Jaco
Gibson-Robinson, Thomas
Given-Wilson, Thomas
Golden, Bat-Chen
Graf-Brill, Alexander
Grebing, Sarah
Griggio, Alberto
Grinchtein, Olga
Gu, Ronghui

Haddad, Axel
Haesaert, Sofie
Hahn, Ernst Moritz
Hanazumi, Simone
Hartmanns, Arnd
Hashemi, Vahid
Hatefi, Hassan
Hentschel, Martin
Heule, Marijn
Hoenicke, Jochen
Holík, Lukáš
Holzer, Andreas
Hostettler, Steve
Howar, Falk
Irfan, Ahmed
Isberner, Malte
Islam, Md. Ariful
Ivrii, Alexander
Jansen, Nils
Jeffrey, Alan
Jegourel, Cyrille
Jimborean, Alexandra
Jobstmann, Barbara
Joshi, Saurabh
Kahsai, Temesghen
Keidar-Barner, Sharon
Khamespanah, Ehsan
Kim, Jin Hyun
Kinder, Johannes
King, Tim
Kloos, Johannes
Komuravelli, Anvesh
Konnov, Igor
Kopetzki, Dawid
Kotek, Tomer
Krčál, Jan
Kremer, Gereon
Kremer, Steve
Krishna, Siddharth
Křetínský, Jan
Lampka, Kai
Lang, Frédéric
Legay, Axel
Lengal, Ondrej
Leucker, Martin
Markey, Nicolas

Contents

Tool Demonstrations

Stochastic Models

SAT and SMT

Partial Order Reduction, Bisimulation and Fairness

Competition on Software Verification

Parameter Synthesis

Program Synthesis

Program and Runtime Verification

Temporal Logic and Automata

Model Checking

Invited Talk

Scalable Timing Analysis with Refinement

Nan Guan[1], Yue Tang[1], Jakaria Abdullah[2], Martin Stigge[2], and Wang Yi[1,2]

[1] Northeastern University, China
[2] Uppsala University, Sweden

Abstract. Traditional timing analysis techniques rely on composing system-level worst-case behavior with local worst-case behaviors of individual components. In many complex real-time systems, no single local worst-case behavior exists for each component and it generally requires to enumerate all the combinations of individual local behaviors to find the global worst case. This paper presents a scalable timing analysis technique based on abstraction refinement, which provides effective guidance to significantly prune away state space and quickly verify the desired timing properties. We first establish the general framework of the method, and then apply it to solve the analysis problem for several different real-time task models.

Keywords: Real-time systems, timing analysis, scalability, digraph real-time task model.

1 Introduction

A real-time system is often described by a collection of recurring tasks, each of which repeatedly activates workload with fixed periods [10]. The analysis problem of this simple task model has been well-studied and efficient techniques exist. The key idea is to identify the worst-case behavior of each single task, and the system-level worst-case behavior is composed by the local worst-case behaviors of individual tasks.

To meet the increasing requirements on functionality and quality of service, real-time systems become more and more complex. For example, the workload activation pattern of a task may change from time to time depending on the system state. A major challenge is that there is no single local worst-case behavior of each task. Several candidate behaviors of a task may be incomparable, and it is generally necessary to enumerate and analyze all the combinations of the candidate behaviors of all tasks to figure out which particular combination is the worst. This leads to combinatorial state space explosion. It has been proved that the analysis problem of even very simple task models is strongly coNP-hard [14], as long as each task has multiple candidate behaviors that can potentially lead to the system-level worst case. Existing analysis techniques for such systems all suffer serious combinatorial state space explosion and are highly non-scalable.

This paper presents a timing analysis technique based on refinement to address the above challenge. For each task, we construct a tree-like structural state

© Springer-Verlag Berlin Heidelberg 2015
C. Baier and C. Tinelli (Eds.): TACAS 2015, LNCS 9035, pp. 3–18, 2015.
DOI: 10.1007/978-3-662-46681-0_1

space, where each leave corresponds to a concrete behavior of the task and each node in the tree over-approximates its children. Then the analysis is performed with the tree structures of all tasks in a top-down manner, starting with the combination of roots, i.e., the most coarse approximation, and being iteratively refined by moving down to the leaves. This provides us effective guidance to significantly prune away state space and quickly find the exact system-level worst-case behavior. This method is applicable to timing analysis problems for a wide range of real-time task models. In this paper, we first establish the general framework of refinement-based analysis, then apply it to three different real-time task models, namely the rate-adaptive real-time task model [4], the digraph real-time task model [12] and its extension with synchronization. We also present a tool suit currently under development, which is used for complex real-time systems modeling and efficient analysis based on techniques presented in this paper.

2   Behaviors, Abstractions and Refinement

A *system* Sys consists of a finite number of components, $\mathsf{Sys} = \langle \mathsf{C}_1, \cdots, \mathsf{C}_n \rangle$. Each component is defined as a finite set of *concrete behaviors* over domain $\mathcal{D}$. Semantically, a component C_i is a subset of $\mathcal{D}$. We use $\pi_i, \pi'_i, \cdots \in \mathsf{C}_i$ to represent the *concrete* behaviors of component C_i. A *concrete system behavior* $\Pi = \langle \pi_1, \cdots, \pi_n \rangle$ is a combination of concrete behaviors of individual components, and thus system Sys is defined by a subset of domain $\mathcal{D}^n$.

We analyze the *performance* of the system (or a particular component in the system), which is defined over a set of performance metrics $\mathcal{P}$ that forms a total order $\langle \mathcal{P}, \unrhd \rangle$. For two elements $\omega, \omega' \in \mathcal{P}$, $\omega \unrhd \omega'$ means that performance ω is at least as bad as ω'. For example, if we use "worst-case response time" as the performance metrics, then the performance is defined over the real number set, $\mathcal{P} = \mathbb{R}$, and the total order relation $\unrhd$ is the numerical comparison "$\geq$". Moreover, we use $\omega \rhd \omega'$ to denote that performance ω is strictly worse than ω' (e.g., the numerical comparison "$>$"). Given a concrete system behavior Π, the evaluation function $\mathsf{Evl}(\Pi)$ returns the performance of interest for Π.

We aim at hard real-time systems, for which we are interested in the *worst-case* performance $\overline{\omega}$ of the system:

$$\overline{\omega} = \max_{\forall \Pi \in \mathsf{Sys}} \{\mathsf{Evl}(\Pi)\} \tag{1}$$

where "max" denotes the maximum element of a set according to total order $\unrhd$, i.e., $p = \max(p, p')$ if and only if $p \unrhd p'$. If the worst-case performance meets the required timing properties, the system is guaranteed to honor the timing constraints under any circumstance at runtime.

Directly using Equation (1) to calculate the worst-case performance, we shall enumerate $\prod_{i=1}^{n} |\mathsf{C}_i|$ different system behaviors, which is highly intractable except for very small task systems.

2.1   Abstraction Tree

We define a superset of the concrete behaviors of each task and conduct the analysis with these supersets. The supersets, though lead to a even larger state space, have certain structure that helps us to effectively prune away a large portion of the state space and quickly come to the desired worst-case behavior.

Formally, for each component defined by C_i in the system $\langle C_1, \cdots, C_n \rangle$, we construct a join-semilattice $\langle \widetilde{C}_i, \succcurlyeq, \sqcup \rangle$, where $\widetilde{C}_i$ is a superset of C_i within domain $\mathcal{D}$, i.e., $C_i \subseteq \widetilde{C}_i \subseteq \mathcal{D}$. We call elements in $\widetilde{C}_i \setminus C_i$ the *abstract behaviors* of C_i. The partial order $\succcurlyeq$ is defined as follows: For any $\pi_i, \pi_i' \in \mathcal{D}$, $\pi_i \succcurlyeq \pi_i'$ (called π_i *dominates* π_i') if and only if

$$\forall \langle \pi_1, \cdots, \pi_{i-1}, \pi_{i+1}, \cdots, \pi_n \rangle \in \mathcal{D}^n :$$
$$\mathsf{Evl}(\langle \pi_1, \cdots, \pi_i, \cdots, \pi_n \rangle) \trianglerighteq \mathsf{Evl}(\langle \pi_1, \cdots, \pi_i', \cdots, \pi_n \rangle)$$

The $\sqcup$ operator gets an upper bound of the two operands according to $\succcurlyeq$, and thus $p \sqcup q \succcurlyeq p$ and $p \sqcup q \succcurlyeq q$.

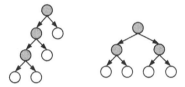

Fig. 1. Two possible abstraction trees of a component, where white nodes are concrete behaviors and grey nodes are abstract behaviors

Within the join-semilattice $\langle \widetilde{C}_i, \succcurlyeq, \sqcup \rangle$, we can construct a binary *abstraction tree* according to the following rules:

- Each concrete behavior corresponds to one leave in the tree.
- The parent is the join (by $\sqcup$) of its two children.

Note that the abstraction tree of a component is in general *not* unique, i.e., the abstraction tree for a task can be constructed in different ways, as long as the above rules are satisfied. For example, Figure 1 shows two possible abstraction trees of a component with 4 concrete behaviors. Different abstraction trees may lead to different efficiency of the analysis procedure in the following.

2.2   Refinement-Based Analysis

The refinement-based analysis uses the abstraction tree of each component, and a prioritized working list $\mathcal{Q}$. Each element in the working list records a system behavior, i.e., a combination of behaviors from different abstraction trees. The priority is ordered according to the evaluation result of the system behavior: the worse performance the higher priority. The pseudo-code of the analysis algorithm is shown in Figure 2. The analysis procedure is performed in a top-down manner, starting with the combination of the root of each abstraction tree. Each time we take and remove the highest-priority system behavior, i.e., the first element, from $\mathcal{Q}$, and generate two new system behaviors by replacing one component's behavior by its children in the corresponding abstraction tree (the $refine(\Pi)$ routine). Then we evaluate these new system behaviors and add them to $\mathcal{Q}$, with proper order according to the evaluation results. This procedure iterates, until the highest priority element in $\mathcal{Q}$ is a combination of leaves. Then the evaluation result of this concrete system behavior is the desired worst-case performance.

```
1: Q ← ∅
2: Q.add(Π, Evl(Π))
3: while Π is abstract do
4:    (Π′, Π″) ← refine(Π)
5:    Q.add(Π′, Evl(Π′))
6:    Q.add(Π″, Evl(Π″))
7:    Π ← Q.pophead()
8: end while
9: return  Evl(Π)
```

Fig. 2. Pseudo-code of the refinement-based analysis algorithm

In the refinement routine $refine(\Pi)$, Π is replaced by new system behaviors in which some component behavior is replaced by a node that is one step further from the root in the corresponding tree. So after a finite number steps of refinement, all elements in $\mathcal{Q}$ consist of only concrete behaviors (leaves), up on which the algorithm must terminate.

At any step of the algorithm, for a concrete system behavior Π that leads to the worst-case performance ($\mathsf{Evl}(\Pi) = \overline{\omega}$), there exists an element Π' in $\mathcal{Q}$ such that each behavior in Π' is an ascent of the corresponding concrete behavior in Π, so we have $\mathsf{Evl}(\Pi') \trianglerighteq \overline{\omega}$. On the other hand, due to the ordering rule of elements in $\mathcal{Q}$, the evaluation result ω of the head element in $\mathcal{Q}$ satisfies $\omega \trianglerighteq \mathsf{Evl}(\Pi')$, and thus $\omega \trianglerighteq \overline{\omega}$. When the algorithm terminates, the return value ω is the evaluation result of a concrete system behavior, which implies $\overline{\omega} \trianglerighteq \omega$. In summary, we have $\omega = \overline{\omega}$, i.e., the return value of the algorithm is the exact worst-case performance.

2.3   Early Termination

At any step during the execution of the algorithm in Figure 2, the evaluation result of the head of $\mathcal{Q}$ is an over-approximation of $\overline{\omega}$, and as the algorithm continues the result becomes more and more precise. In the design procedure, it is possible that the designer realized that the worst-case performance is guaranteed to satisfy the requirement even with an over-approximated estimation. For example, in schedulability analysis one can safely claim the system is valid when the over-approximate estimation of the worst-case response times are already smaller than the deadlines. In this case, we add the following codes

```
1: if Evl(Π) is satisfactory then
2:    return Evl(Π)
3: end if
```

before line 4 in the algorithm of Figure 2 to let the algorithm terminate earlier.

3   Rate-Adaptive Tasks

In some real-time systems, task activation may depend on the system state. For example, in automotive applications, some tasks are linked to rotation, thus their activation rate is proportional to the angular velocity of a specific device [4,11,5]. To avoid overload, a common practice adopted in automotive applications is to let tasks execute less functionality with higher activation rates, which is formulated as the *rate-adaptive task system* in the following section.

3.1   Rate-Adaptive Task Model

We consider a task set τ of n independent rate-adaptive tasks (components) $\{T_1, T_2, \cdots, T_n\}$. Each task T_i has m_i different configurations, and it is character-ized by a worst-case execution time (WCET) vector $e_i = \{e_i^1, \cdots, e_i^{m_i}\}$, a period vector $p_i = \{p_i^1, \cdots, p_i^{m_i}\}$, and a relative deadline vector $d_i = \{d_i^1, \cdots, d_i^{m_i}\}$. We assume tasks have constrained deadlines, i.e., $\forall a \in [1, m_i] : d_i^a \leq p_i^a$. At runtime a task may use one of these m_i configurations, i.e., use $\langle e_i^a, p_i^a, d_i^a \rangle$, $a \in [1, m_i]$, and behaves like a regular periodic task with this particular parameter setting. Note that we do *not* consider dynamic transition among different configurations.

We use the static-priority scheduling algorithm to schedule jobs released by all tasks. Each task is assigned a static priority in a priori, and each of its released job inherits this priority. We assume tasks are ordered in decreasing priority order, i.e., T_i's priority is higher than T_j's iff $i < j$. At each time instant at runtime, the job with the highest priority among all the jobs that have been released but not finished yet is selected for execution. The performance metric we are interested in is the *worst-case response time*, i.e., the maximal delay between the release and the finishing time of a job, of each task with each configuration.

3.2   Analysis of Worst-Case Response Times

The worst-case response time of each task with each configuration can be an-alyzed independently. Therefore, without loss of generality, in the following we focus on the analysis of task T_i and only consider one configuration $\langle e_i, p_i, d_i \rangle$ (superscript omitted for simplicity).

Given a configuration $\langle e_j^a, p_j^a, d_i^a \rangle$, the maximal workload released by task T_j during time interval of size t can be precisely represented by function $rf_a(t)$ [8]:

$$rf_a(t) := \lceil t/p_j^a \rceil \times e_j^a$$

We use $rf_a(t)$ as a concrete behavior of task T_j (a leave in the abstraction tree) corresponding to configuration $\langle e_j^a, p_j^a, d_j^a \rangle$.

The partial order $\succcurlyeq$ among behaviors is defined as follows:

$$rf_a \succcurlyeq rf_{a'} \iff \forall t > 0, rf_a(t) \geq rf_{a'}(t)$$

The join operator $\sqcup$ is is defined as:

$$rf_a = rf_{a'} \sqcup rf_{a''} \iff \forall t > 0, rf_a(t) = \max(rf_{a'}(t), rf_{a''}(t))$$

We use $rf = \langle rf_{a_1} \cdots rf_{a_n} \rangle$ to denote a behavior of the system (only considering higher-priority tasks). The evaluation function $\mathsf{Evl}(rf)$ is defined as

$$\mathsf{Evl}(rf) = \min_{t>0} \left\{ t \,\middle|\, e_i + \sum_{rf_{a_j} \in rf} rf_{a_j}(t) \leq t \right\}$$

With the join operator and the evaluation function defined above, we can thus construct the abstraction tree of each task and perform refinement-based analysis by the algorithm in Figure 2, to calculate the worst-case response time of the task and the configuration under analysis.

4 Graph-Based Real-Time Tasks

Many real-time systems may have different workload activation states and switch among them at runtime. State transition systems can usually be modeled by graphs. In this section we consider a very general real-time workload representation, the Digraph Real-Time (DRT) task model [12], which models workload activation patterns by arbitrary directed graphs.

4.1 The DRT Task Model

A task system consists of n independent DRT tasks (components) $\{T_1, \cdots, T_n\}$. A task T is represented by a directed graph $G(T) = (V(T), E(T))$ with $V(T)$ denoting the set of vertices and $E(T)$ the set of edges of the graph. The vertices $V(T) = \{v_1, \cdots, v_n\}$ represent the types of all jobs that can be released by T. Each vertex v is labeled with a tuple $\langle e(v), d(v) \rangle$, where $e(v) \in \mathbb{N}$ denotes the worst-case execution time (WCET), $d(v) \in \mathbb{N}$ denotes the relative deadline. We implicitly assume the relation $e(v) \leq d(v)$ for all job types v. The edges of $G(T)$ represent the order in which jobs generated by T are released. Each edge $(u, v) \in E(T)$ is labeled with $p(u, v) \in \mathbb{N}$ denoting the minimum inter-release separation time between u and v. Deadlines are constrained, i.e., for each vertex u we have $d(u) \leq p(u, v)$ for all edges (u, v).

A job J is represented by a tuple (r, e) consisting of an absolute release time r and an execution time e. The semantics of a DRT task system is defined as the set of *job sequences* it may generate: $\sigma = [(r_0, e_0), (r_1, e_1), ...]$ is a job sequence if all jobs are monotonically ordered by release times, i.e., $r_i \leq r_j$ for $i \leq j$. A job sequence $\sigma = [(r_0, e_0), (r_1, e_1), ...]$ is generated by T if $\pi = (v_0, v_1, \cdots)$ is a path in $G(T)$ and for all $i \geq 0$:

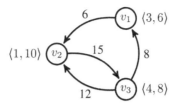

Fig. 3. A DRT task

1. $r_{i+1} - r_i \geq p(v_i, v_{i+1})$ and
2. $e_i \leq e(v_i)$

Combining the job sequences of individual tasks results in a job sequence of the task set.

Figure 3 shows an example to illustrate the semantics of DRT tasks. When the system starts, T releases its first run-time job by an arbitrary vertex. Then the released sequence corresponds to a particular direct path through $G(T)$. Consider the job sequence $\sigma = [(2,3),(10,1),(25,4),(37,1)]$ which corresponds to path $\pi = (v_1, v_2, v_3, v_2)$ in $G(T)$. Note that this example demonstrates the "sporadic" behavior allowed by the semantics of the DRT model. The first job in σ (corresponds to v_1) is released at time 2, and the second job in σ (v_2) is released 2 time units later than its earliest possible release time, while the job of v_3 and the second job of v_2 are released as early as possible.

We still use the static-priority scheduling algorithm to schedule jobs. The performance metric we are interested in is the *worst-case response time* of each vertex (job type) of each task.

4.2   Analysis of Worst-Case Response Time

Since the relative deadline of each vertex is no larger than the inter-release separation of all of its outgoing edges, in any feasible task system each vertex must be finished before the release of its successor vertices. Therefore, the analysis of each vertex within one task can be performed independently. In the following, we focus on the analysis of a particular vertex v of task T.

The response time of a vertex v is decided by the job sequences released by higher-priority tasks and the workload of itself. Therefore, to calculate the worst-case response time of v, conceptually, we should enumerate all the possible combinations of job sequences from each higher-priority task. Among the job sequences of a task, only the ones with minimal release separation and maximal execution demand (WCET) of vertices can possibly lead to the worst-case response time, each of which corresponds to a path in the task graph.

The workload of a path π can be abstracted with a *request function* [15], which for each t returns the maximal accumulated execution requirement of all jobs that π may release until time t (suppose the first job of π is released at time 0). For a path $\pi = (v_0, \cdots, v_l)$ through the graph $G(T)$ of a task T, we define its *request function* as

$$rf_\pi(t) := \max\{ e(\pi') \mid \pi' \text{ is prefix of } \pi \text{ and } p(\pi') < t \}$$

where $e(\pi) := \sum_{i=0}^{l} e(v_i)$ and $p(\pi) := \sum_{i=0}^{l-1} p(v_i, v_{i+1})$. We use $rf_\pi(t)$ as a concrete behavior of task T_j (a leave in the abstraction tree) corresponding to path π. Note that to analyze the worst-case response time of vertex v, we only need to look into time intervals of size up to $d(v)$, since otherwise v deems to be unschedulable. The number of different paths that can be generated by $G(T)$ in a bounded time interval is finite, so there are only finite number of concrete behaviors of a task.

The partial order $\succeq$ among behaviors is defined as follows:

$$rf_\pi \succeq rf_{\pi'} \Leftrightarrow \forall t \in (0, d(v)], rf_\pi(t) \geq rf_{\pi'}(t)$$

The join operator $\sqcup$ is is defined as:

$$rf_\pi = rf_{\pi'} \sqcup rf_{\pi''} \Leftrightarrow \forall t \in (0, d(v)], rf_\pi(t) = \max(rf_{\pi'}(t), rf_{\pi''}(t))$$

We use $rf = \langle rf_{\pi_1} \cdots rf_{\pi_n} \rangle$ to denote a behavior of the system (only considering higher-priority tasks). The evaluation function $\mathsf{Evl}(rf)$ is defined as

$$\mathsf{Evl}(rf) = \min_{t>0} \left\{ t \,\middle|\, e(v) + \sum_{rf_{\pi_i} \in rf} rf_{\pi_i}(t) \leq t \right\}$$

where $e(v)$ is the WCET of the analyzed vertex itself.

With the join operator and the evaluation function, we can thus construct the abstraction tree of each task and perform refinement-based analysis by the algorithm in Figure 2, to calculate the worst-case response time of v.

5   Digraph Tasks with Synchronization

In last two sections, tasks are assumed to be independent from each other, so it is easy to compose the system behaviors with individual component behaviors and can easily fit into the refinement-based analysis framework. In this section, we extend the DRT task model with synchronization. We show that the refinement-based analysis framework can also be applied to systems where strong inter-component dependency exists. The key is to construct proper behavior representation to capture interactions among components in the abstract domain.

5.1   DRT with Synchronization

Assume a finite number of communication channels $\{\mathsf{ch}_1, \cdots \mathsf{ch}_x\}$, through which tasks can send or receive signals and thus synchronize with each other. Sending a signal through channel ch is denoted by $\mathsf{ch}!$, while receiving a signal is denoted by $\mathsf{ch}?$. We call both sending and receiving operations *synchronization operations*.

We call ch! the *dual operation* of ch? and vice versa. We use $dual(a)$ to denote the dual operation of a, e.g. $dual(ch!) = ch?$. We use OP to denote the set of all synchronization operations in the system, which includes a pair of both sending and receiving operations for each channel and an null operation φ denoting that a vertex does not synchronize with others.

Each vertex v in a task graph is marked by a single synchronization operation (either sending or receiving), denoted by $op(v)$. The release of a job by vertex v is synchronized with other jobs (from other tasks) marked with the dual operation of $op(v)$, i.e., v can release a job only if another vertex marked with $dual(op(v))$ is also eligible to release a job.

Figure 4 gives an example illustrating the semantics of the synchronization operations. The vertical dashed lines denote the time points at which the minimal inter-release separation constraints are satisfied. During the shadowed time intervals, a vertex waits for its dual operation to release a job. The vertical arrows denote actual job release times. Note that inter-release separation is counted relative to the actual release time of the previous job (the vertical arrows), rather than the time points when the previous inter-release separation constraint is satisfied (the dashed lines). It is allowed that at some time point a vertex v can synchronize with multiple vertices from different tasks. In this case, v non-deterministically chooses one of them for synchronization. In the example of Figure 4, at time 11 both task T_2 and T_3 can synchronize with T_1. The figure shows one possible running sequence where task T_1 chooses to synchronize with T_2, and the third vertex of T_3 continues to wait.

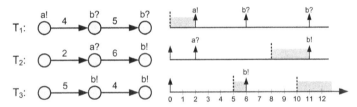

Fig. 4. An example illustrating the semantics of synchronization operations

5.2   Analysis of Worst-Case Response Time

Similar to Section 4, the analysis of each vertex within one task can be performed independently, so in the following we focus on the analysis of a particular vertex v of task T. Recall that in an independent DRT task system, the response time of a vertex only depends on higher-priority tasks and its own workload. However, when synchronization is added, the response time of a vertex also depends on lower-priority tasks, which can affect the execution of higher-priority tasks by synchronization operations.

We define the behavior corresponding to a path π in task graph $G(T)$ as a pair $bhv_\pi = \langle erf_\pi, pst_\pi \rangle$, where

$$erf_\pi(t, o) = \begin{cases} rf_\pi(t) & \text{if } o = op(fv(\pi, t)) \\ 0 & \text{otherwise} \end{cases} \quad , \quad pst_\pi(t, o) = \begin{cases} \{\pi\} & \text{if } o = op(fv(\pi, t)) \\ \emptyset & \text{otherwise} \end{cases}$$

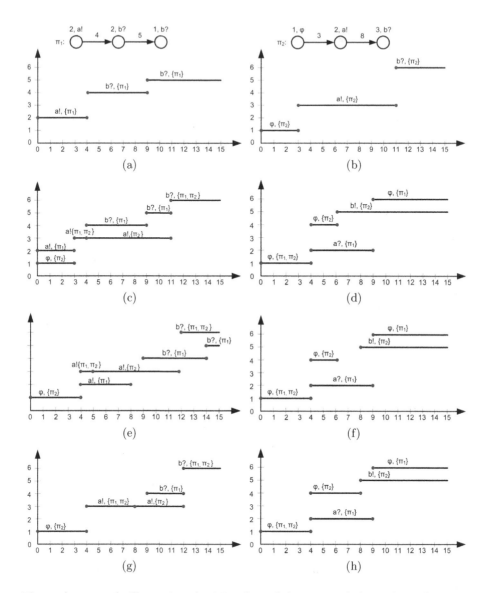

Fig. 5. An example illustrating the join of two behaviors and the update of system behaviors. (a) and (b) are two paths (of the same task) and the graphical representation of their behaviors; (c) shows the join of behaviors in (a) and (b); (d) is an (abstract) behavior of another task; (e) and (f) are the results of Update of (c) and (d); (g) and (h) are the results of fixing the inconsistency and redundancy in (e) and (f) by Set2Func.

$fv(\pi, t)$ returns the last vertex v_i along path $\pi = \{v_0, v_1, \cdots\}$ that is possible to release a job at time t (the path starts at time 0 and $t > 0$):

$$fv(\pi, t) = v_m \text{ s.t. } \left(\sum_{i=0}^{m} p(v_{i-1}, v_i) < t \wedge \sum_{i=0}^{m+1} p(v_{i-1}, v_i) \geq t \right).$$

where we let $p(v_{-1}, v_0) = 0$ for consistency. Figure 5-(a) and (b) show the graphical representation of the behaviors of two paths π_1 and π_2.

The partial order $\succcurlyeq$ among behaviors is defined as follows:

$$\langle erf_\pi, pst_\pi \rangle \succcurlyeq \langle erf_{\pi'}, pst_{\pi'} \rangle \Leftrightarrow$$
$$\forall t \in (0, d(v)], \forall o \in \mathsf{OP} : erf_\pi(t, o) \geq erf_{\pi'}(t, o) \wedge pst_\pi(t, o) \supseteq pst_{\pi'}(t, o)$$

The join operator $\sqcup$ is defined as:

$$\langle erf_\pi, pst_\pi \rangle = \langle erf_{\pi'}, pst_{\pi'} \rangle \sqcup \langle erf_{\pi''}, pst_{\pi''} \rangle \Leftrightarrow$$
$$\forall t \in (0, d(v)], \forall o \in \mathsf{OP} : \begin{cases} erf_\pi(t, o) = \max\left(erf_{\pi'}(t, o), erf_{\pi''}(t, o)\right) \\ pst_\pi(t, o) = pst_{\pi'}(t, o) \cup pst_{\pi''}(t, o) \end{cases}$$

Figure 5-(c) shows the resulting abstract behavior of joining the two concrete behaviors in Figure 5-(a) and (b). Graphically, a behavior $\langle erf_\pi, pst_\pi \rangle$ can also be represented by a set of segments, each segment $s = \langle start, end, o, pst \rangle$ having a start time $start$, an ending time end, a synchronization operation o and a path set pst. Let $bhv = \{bhv_1, \cdots, bhv_n\}$ be the function representation of a system behavior. Then bhv can be converted to the corresponding segment-set representation by $S = \mathsf{Func2Set}(bhv)$, and the inverse conversion is $bhv = \mathsf{Set2Func}(S)$.

1: $S \leftarrow \mathsf{Func2Set}(bhv)$
2: $\mathsf{Update}(S)$
3: $bhv \leftarrow \mathsf{Set2Func}(S)$
4: $\overline{erf} \leftarrow$ the subset of behaviors in $bhv.erf$ of higher priority tasks.
5: $R \leftarrow \min_{t>0}\{t | e(v) + sum(t)\}$, where

$$sum(t) \leftarrow \sum_{erf_T \in \overline{erf}} \left\{ \max_{\forall o \in \mathsf{OP}} \{erf_T(t, o)\} \right\}$$

6: **return** R

Fig. 6. Pseudo-code of $\mathsf{Evl}(bhv)$

If bhv consists of only concrete behaviors, the evaluation with bhv can be performed by "simulating" the release and execution sequence of the corresponding paths, which will not be further discussed here. The interesting case is when bhv is an abstract system behavior, the evaluation function for which is defined by the algorithm in Figure 6. The release of vertices may wait for extra delay due to synchronization operations. If we use individual task behaviors to calculate the maximal possible workload of each task independently and sum them up as the total system workload (as in last section), the evaluation result will be very pessimistic. To improve evaluation precision with abstract behaviors, we use the Update function to also consider the extra release delay due to synchronization in abstract behaviors, the pseudo-code of which is shown in Figure 7.

```
 1: S' ← ∅
 2: while S ≠ S' do
 3:     S' ← S
 4:     for all S_{T_i} ∈ S do
 5:         for all s ∈ S_{T_i} : s.o ≠ ∅ do
 6:             Φ = {ss | T_j ∈ τ \ {T_i} ∧ ss ∈ S_{T_j} ∧ ss.o = dual(s.o)}
 7:             if Φ = ∅ then
 8:                 t' = +∞
 9:             else
10:                 t' = min_{ss∈Φ}{ss.start}
11:             end if
12:             △ ← max(t' − s.start, 0)
13:             for all s' ∈ S_{T_i} : s'.start ≥ s.start ∧ s'.pst ⊆ s.pst do
14:                 s'.start = s'.start + △
15:                 s'.end = s'.end + △
16:             end for
17:         end for
18:     end for
19: end while
20: return
```

Fig. 7. Pseudo-code of Update(S)

Update(S) iteratively updates the abstract behavior of each task. At each step, the algorithm tries to shift a segment s to right by looking for the earliest eligible time point t' of $dual(s.o)$ in all other tasks. If t' is later than the start time of s, s should be shifted to start at t', and all later segments that depend on s in concrete behaviors also shift rightwards correspondingly. This procedure repeats until a global fixed point is reached. Figure 5-(e) and (f) show the resulting segment sets by applying the above procedure to the segment sets in Figure 5-(c) and (d).

Shifting some of the segments in S may lead to inconsistency and redundancy regarding the represented concrete behaviors. For example, in Figure 5-(e) there is no segment covering time interval $[3, 4)$. This is because segment $\langle 3, 4, a!, \{\pi_1, \pi_2\}\rangle$ is shifted to right. To resolve this, we shall extend segment $\langle 0, 4, \phi, \{\pi_2\}\rangle$ to cover $[3, 4)$. Also in Figure 5-(e), time interval $[13, 15)$ is covered by two segments both with $b?$ and path π_1. In this case, the lower segment is redundant and should be merged into the upper one. Function Set2Func addresses these inconsistencies and redundancies and transfer the segment sets to well-defined function representations of behaviors.

6   Experiments

In this section, we briefly report some experiment results with the DRT task model described in Section 4. Experiments are conducted with randomly generated DRT task sets. To generate a task, a random number of vertices is created with edges connecting them according to a specified branching degree. The following table gives details of the used parameter ranges, where p denotes inter-release separation between two vertices, e and d denotes the WCET and relative deadline of a vertex, respectively.

Table 1. Parameter ranges

vertices	out-degree	p	d/p	e/d
$[5, 10]$	$[1, 3]$	$[100, 300]$	$[0.5, 1]$	$[0, 0.07]$

Feasible task sets created by this method have sizes up to about 20 tasks with over 100 individual job types in total. For evaluating the effectiveness of the abstraction refinement scheme, we capture for each call to the refinement-base analysis how many system behaviors have been analyzed. We compare this number with the total number of system behaviors, i.e., all the combinations of individual task behaviors. This ratio indicates how much computational work the refinement scheme saves, compared to a naive brute-force style test.

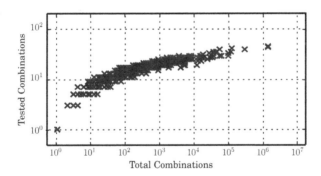

Fig. 8. Tested versus total number of system behaviors

We capture 105 samples and show our results in Figure 8. We see that the combinatorial abstraction refinement scheme saves work in the order of several magnitudes. More details of the experiments can be found in [13].

7   Tool

TIMES [1] is a tool suit for schedulability analysis of complex real-time systems, in which task systems are modeled with task automata [6] that are essentially timed automata [3], and the analysis problems are solved using the UPPAAL model checker [9]. The TIMES modeling language based on timed automata provides powerful expressiveness, but also limits the scalability of the tool due to the high complexity of verification problems for timed automata.

Currently we are developing a new version of TIMES based on the less expressive DRT task model and several scalable timing analysis techniques developed recently (including the refinement-based analysis in this paper). Note that a DRT task is in fact a task automaton with one clock, where only lower bounds on the clock are allowed to use in expressing timing constraints on job releases. The new TIMES is expected to have much higher analysis efficiency and can deal with large-scale realistic systems. The tool offers the following main features:

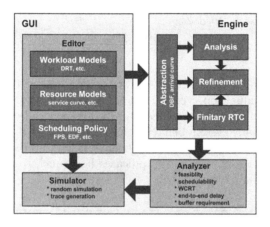

Fig. 9. Tool Architecture

- **Editor** to graphically model a system and the abstract behaviour of its environment. Workload is modeled as a set of DRT tasks, and different DRT tasks can synchronize with each other by communication channels and/or semaphores. System resource is modeled with a topology of processing and communication units, and each unit is associated with a service curve [16]. The users can choose the scheduling policy on each unit.
- **Simulator** to visualize the system behavior as Gant charts and message sequence charts. The simulator can be used to randomly generate possible execution traces, or alternatively the user can control the execution by selecting the transitions to be taken. The simulator can also be used to visualize error traces produced in the analysis phase.
- **Analyzer** to check various properties of the system model, including feasibility, scheduability, worst-case response time (WCRT), end-to-end delay and buffer requirement.

The tool architecture is depicted in Figure 9. The tool consists of two main parts, a Graphical User Interface (GUI) and an analysis engine. The GUI consists of editors, simulator and analyzer as described above, and uses XML to represent the system descriptions both internally and externally. The analysis engine consists of four parts. The *Abstraction* module transform the DRT workload models into abstract representations such as demand bound functions (DBF) [2] and request bound functions (RBF) [15]. The transformation is very efficient, based on the path abstraction technique proposed in [12]. The *Refinement* module is the core of the engine, which uses the framework in this paper to iteratively obtain tighter and tighter analysis results until the property of interest is proved/disproved. At each step of the analysis, it invokes either the *Analysis* module for traditional WCRT analysis and schedulability test, or invokes the *Finitary RTC* module for efficient system-wide performance analysis using Finitary Real-Time Calculus [7] in the presence of a distributed platform.

Acknowledgement. This work is partially supported by NSF of China (No. 61300022 and 61370076).

References

1. Amnell, T., Fersman, E., Mokrushin, L., Pettersson, P., Yi, W.: TIMES - A tool for modelling and implementation of embedded systems. In: Katoen, J.-P., Stevens, P. (eds.) TACAS 2002. LNCS, vol. 2280, pp. 460–464. Springer, Heidelberg (2002)
2. Baruah, S.K., Mok, A., Rosier, L.: Preemptively scheduling hard-real-time sporadic tasks on one processor. In: Proceedings of the 11th Real-Time Systems Symposium (RTSS) (1990)
3. Bengtsson, J.E., Yi, W.: Timed automata: Semantics, algorithms and tools. In: Desel, J., Reisig, W., Rozenberg, G. (eds.) ACPN 2003. LNCS, vol. 3098, pp. 87–124. Springer, Heidelberg (2004)
4. Buttazzo, G.C., Bini, E., Buttle, D.: Rate-adaptive tasks: Model, analysis, and design issues. Technical Report (2013)
5. Davis, R.I., Feld, T., Pollex, V., Slomka, F.: Schedulability tests for tasks with variable rate-dependent behaviour under fixed priority scheduling. In: the 20th IEEE Real-Time and Embedded Technology and Applications Symposium (RTAS) (2014)
6. Fersman, E., Krcal, P., Pettersson, P., Yi, W.: Task automata: Schedulability, decidability and undecidability. Information and Computation (2007)
7. Guan, N., Yi, W.: Finitary real-time calculus: Efficient performance analysis of distributed embedded systems. Proceedings of the IEEE 34th Real-Time Systems Symposium (RTSS) (2013)
8. Joseph, M., Pandya, P.K.: Finding response times in a real-time system. The Computer Journal (1986)
9. Larsen, K.G., Pettersson, P., Yi, W.: Uppaal in a nutshell. International Journal on Software Tools for Technology Transfer, STTT (1997)
10. Liu, C.L., Layland, J.W.: Scheduling algorithms for multiprogramming in a hard-real-time environment. Journal of the ACM (1973)
11. Pollex, V., Feld, T., Slomka, F., Margull, U., Mader, R., Wirrer, G.: Sufficient real-time analysis for an engine control unit with constant angular velocities. In: Design, Automation and Test Conference in Europe (DATE) (2013)

12. Stigge, M., Ekberg, P., Guan, N., Yi, W.: The digraph real-time task model. In: Proceedings of the 17th IEEE Real-Time and Embedded Technology and Applications Symposium (RTAS), pp. 71–80. IEEE (2011)
13. Martin, Stigge, N.G., Yi, W.: Refinement-based exact response-time analysis. In: the 26th EUROMICRO Conference on Real-Time Systems (ECRTS) (2014)
14. Martin Stigge and Wang Yi. Hardness results for static priority real-time scheduling. In: Proceedings of the 24th Euromicro Conference on Real-Time Systems (ECRTS), pp. 189–198. IEEE (2012)
15. Stigge, M., Yi, W.: Combinatorial abstraction refinement for feasibility analysis. In: Procedings of the 34th IEEE Real-Time Systems Symposium (RTSS), pp. 340–349 (2013)
16. Thiele, L., Chakraborty, S., Naedele, M.: Real-time calculus for scheduling hard real-time systems. In: Proc. Inti. Symposium on Circuits and Systems (2000)

Hybrid Systems

A Formally Verified Hybrid System for the Next-Generation Airborne Collision Avoidance System*

Jean-Baptiste Jeannin[1], Khalil Ghorbal[1], Yanni Kouskoulas[2], Ryan Gardner[2], Aurora Schmidt[2], Erik Zawadzki[1], and André Platzer[1]

[1] Carnegie Mellon University
[2] The Johns Hopkins University Applied Physics Laboratory

Abstract. The *Next-Generation Airborne Collision Avoidance System* (ACAS X) is intended to be installed on all large aircraft to give advice to pilots and prevent mid-air collisions with other aircraft. It is currently being developed by the Federal Aviation Administration (FAA). In this paper we determine the geometric configurations under which the advice given by ACAS X is safe under a precise set of assumptions and formally verify these configurations using hybrid systems theorem proving techniques. We conduct an initial examination of the current version of the real ACAS X system and discuss some cases where our safety theorem conflicts with the actual advisory given by that version, demonstrating how formal, hybrid approaches are helping ensure the safety of ACAS X. Our approach is general and could also be used to identify unsafe advice issued by other collision avoidance systems or confirm their safety.

1 Introduction

With growing air traffic, the airspace becomes more crowded, and the risk of airborne collisions between aircraft increases. In the 1970s, after a series of mid-air collisions, the Federal Aviation Administration (FAA) decided to develop an onboard collision avoidance system: the Traffic Alert and Collision Avoidance System (TCAS). This program had great success, and prevented many mid-air collisions over the years. Some accidents still happened; for example, a collision over Überlingen in 2002 occurred due to conflicting orders between TCAS and air traffic control. Airspace management will evolve significantly over the next decade with the introduction of the next-generation air traffic management system; this will create new requirements for collision avoidance. To meet these new requirements, the FAA has decided to develop a new system: the Next-Generation Airborne Collision Avoidance System, known as ACAS X [4,9,13].

Like TCAS, ACAS X avoids collisions by giving vertical guidance to an aircraft's pilot. A typical scenario involves two aircraft: the *ownship* where ACAS X is installed, and another aircraft called the *intruder* that is at risk of colliding with the ownship.

---

* This research was conducted under the sponsorship of the Federal Aviation Administration Traffic Alert & Collision Avoidance System (TCAS) Program Office (PO) AJM-233 under contract number DTFAWA-11-C-00074. Additionally, support for the basic verification technology used as a foundation for this research was provided by the National Science Foundation under NSF CAREER Award CNS-1054246.

C. Baier and C. Tinelli (Eds.): TACAS 2015, LNCS 9035, pp. 21–36, 2015.
DOI: 10.1007/978-3-662-46681-0_2

Table 1. Sample advisories and their modeling variables; full table in Technical Report [10]

	ACAS X Specification [12]				Our model	
	Vertical Rate Range		Strength	Delay	Sign	Advisory
Advisory	Min (ft/min)	Max (ft/min)	a_r	d_p (s)	w	$\dot{h}_f$ (ft/min)
DNC	$-\infty$	0	g/4	5	-1	0
MCL	current	$+\infty$	g/4	5	$+1$	current
CL1500	$+1500$	$+\infty$	g/4	5	$+1$	$+1500$
SCL2500	$+2500$	$+\infty$	g/3	3	$+1$	$+2500$
COC	$-\infty$	$+\infty$	Not applicable			

ACAS X is designed to avoid *Near Mid-Air Collisions* (*NMACs*), situations where two aircraft come within $r_p = 500$ ft horizontally and $h_p = 100$ ft vertically [13] of each other. The NMAC definition describes a volume centered around the ownship, shaped like a hockey *puck* of radius r_p and half-height h_p.

In order to be accepted by pilots, and thus operationally suitable, ACAS X needs to strike a balance between giving advice that helps pilots avoid collisions but also minimizes interruptions. These goals oppose each other, and cannot both be perfectly met in the presence of unknown pilot behavior. This paper focuses on precisely characterizing the circumstances in which ACAS X gives advice that is safe. An integral part of the ACAS X development process, this work is intended to help ensure that the design of ACAS X is correct, potentially by identifying ways it should be adjusted.

Airborne Collision Avoidance System ACAS X. In order to prevent an NMAC with other aircraft, ACAS X uses various sensors to determine the position of the ownship, as well as the positions of any intruders [5]. It computes its estimate of the best pilot action by linearly interpolating a precomputed *table* of actions, and, if appropriate, issuing an *advisory* to avoid potential collisions [6] through a visual display and a voice message.

An advisory is a request to the pilot of the ownship to alter or maintain her vertical speed. ACAS X advisories are strictly vertical, and never request any horizontal maneuvering. Table 1 shows a sample of the advisories ACAS X can issue. For example, Do-Not-Climb (DNC) requests that the pilot not climb, and Climb-1500 (CL1500) requests that the pilot climb at more than 1500 ft/min. ACAS X can issue a total of 16 different advisories plus Clear-of-Conflict (COC), which indicates that no action is necessary. To comply with an advisory, the pilot must adjust her vertical rate to fall within the corresponding vertical rate range. Based on previous research [12], the pilot is assumed to do so using a vertical acceleration of strength at least a_r starting after a delay of at most d_p after the advisory has been announced by ACAS X.

At the heart of ACAS X is a table whose domain describes possible configurations for the current state of an encounter, and whose range is a set of scores for each possible action [12,14]. The table is obtained from a Markov Decision Process (MDP) approximating the dynamics of the system in a discretization of the state-space, and optimized using dynamic programming to maximize the expected value of events over all future paths for each action [12]. Near Mid-Air Collision events, for example, are associated with large negative values and issuing an advisory is associated with a small negative value. The policy is to choose the action with the highest expected value from a multi-linear interpolation of grid points in this table. ACAS X uses this table, along with some heuristics, to determine the best action to take for the geometry in which it finds itself.

Identifying Formally Verified Safe Regions. Since ACAS X involves both *discrete* advisories to the pilot and *continuous* dynamics of aircraft, it is natural to formally verify it using hybrid systems. However the complexity of ACAS X, which uses at its core a large lookup table—defining 29,212,664 interpolation regions within a 5-dimensional state-space—makes the direct use of hybrid systems verification techniques intractable. Our approach is different. It identifies *safe regions* in the state space of the system where the current positions and velocities of the aircraft ensure that a particular advisory, if followed, prevents all possible NMACs. Then it *compares* these regions to the configurations where the ACAS X table returns this same advisory. Moreover our safe regions are *symbolic* in their parameters, and can thus be easily adapted to new parameters.

Our results provide independent characterizations of the ACAS X behavior to provide a clear and complete picture of its performance. Our method can be used by the ACAS X development team in two ways. It provides a mathematical proof—with respect to a model—that ACAS X is absolutely safe for some configurations of the aircraft. Additionally, when ACAS X is not safe, it is able to identify unsafe or unexpected behaviors and suggests ways of correcting them.

Our approach of formally deriving safe regions then comparing them to the behavior of an industrial system is, as far as we are aware, the first of its kind in the formal verification of hybrid systems. The approach may be valuable for verifying or assessing properties of other systems with similar complexities, or also using large lookup tables, which is a common challenge in practice. Finally, the constraints we identified for safety are fairly general and could be used to analyze other collision avoidance systems.

The paper is organized as follows. After an overview of the method in Sect. 2, we start with a simple two-dimensional model assuming immediate reaction of the pilot in Sect. 3. We extend the model to account for the reaction time of the pilot in Sect. 4, and extend the results to a three-dimensional model in Sect. 5. In Sect. 6, we conduct an initial analysis of ACAS X whereby we compare the advisory recommended by a core component of ACAS X with our safe regions, identifying the circumstances where safety of those ACAS X advisories is guaranteed within our model.

2   Overview of the ACAS X Modelling Approach

To construct a safe region of an advisory for an aircraft, imagine following all allowable trajectories of the ownship relative to the intruder, accounting for every possible position of the ownship and its surrounding puck at every future moment in time. The union of all such positions of the puck describes a potentially unsafe region; for each point there exists a trajectory that results in an NMAC. Dually, if the intruder is outside this set, i.e., in the safe region, an NMAC cannot occur in the model.

Fig. 1 depicts an example of a head-on encounter and its associated safe region for the advisory CL1500, projected in a vertical plane with both aircraft. It is plotted in a *frame fixed to the intruder* and centered at the initial position of the ownship. The ownship, surrounded by the puck, starts at position 1 and traces out a trajectory following

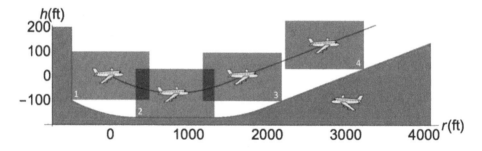

Fig. 1. Trajectory of ownship (red) and safe region for the intruder (green), immediate response

the red curve. It first accelerates vertically with $g/4$ until reaching the desired vertical velocity of $+1500$ ft/min at position 3. It then climbs at $+1500$ ft/min, respecting the specification of Table 1. The green safe-region indicates starting points in the state space for which the aircraft will remain safe for the duration of the encounter. Note that no safe region exists above the trajectory since the ownship could accelerate vertically at greater than $g/4$ or climb more than $+1500$ ft/min, in accordance with Table 1.

Model of Dynamics. Let us consider an encounter between two planes—ownship O and intruder I, as portrayed in Fig. 2. Following the notation of the ACAS X community [12], let r be the horizontal distance between the aircraft and h the height of the intruder relative to the ownship. We assume that the relative horizontal velocity $\vec{r_v}$ of the intruder with respect to the ownship is constant throughout the encounter. I.e., from a top view, the planes follow straight-line trajectories. Let θ_v be the non-directed angle between $\vec{r_v}$ and the line segment $\vec{r}$. In the vertical dimension, we assume that the ownship's vertical velocity $\dot{h}_0$ can vary at any moment, while the intruder's vertical velocity $\dot{h}_1$ is fixed throughout the encounter. Moreover, we assume that the magnitude of the vertical acceleration of the ownship cannot exceed a_d in absolute value.

For a typical encounter, r varies between 0 nmi and 7 nmi,[1] h between $-4,000$ ft and $4,000$ ft, r_v between 0 kts and 1,000 kts, and $\dot{h}_0$ and $\dot{h}_1$ between $-5,000$ ft/min and $+5,000$ ft/min. The acceleration a_d is usually $g/2$, where g is Earth's gravitational acceleration. The NMAC *puck* has radius $r_p = 500$ ft and half-height $h_p = 100$ ft.

Model of Advisories. Recall that ACAS X prevents NMACs by giving advisories to the ownship's pilot. Every advisory, except COC, has a vertical rate range of the form $(-\infty, \dot{h}_f]$ or $[\dot{h}_f, +\infty)$ for some vertical rate $\dot{h}_f$ (Table 1), which we call the *target vertical velocity*. We model any advisory by its corresponding target vertical velocity $\dot{h}_f$, and a binary variable w for its orientation, whose value is -1 if the vertical rate range of the advisory is $(-\infty, \dot{h}_f]$ and $+1$ if it is $[\dot{h}_f, +\infty)$. This symbolic encoding can represent many advisories and is robust to changes in the ACAS X advisory set.

---

[1] We use units most common in the aerospace community, even though they are not part of the international system, including nautical miles nmi (1,852 metres), knots kts (nautical miles per hour), feet ft (0.3048meter) and minutes min (60seconds).

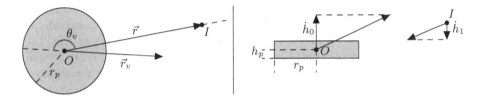

Fig. 2. Top view (left) and side view (right) of an encounter, with NMAC puck in gray

Following ACAS X design work [12], we assume that the ownship pilot complies with each advisory within d_p seconds, and that she accelerates with acceleration at least a_r to reach the target vertical velocity.

3   Safe Region for an Immediate Pilot Response

We present in this section a simplified version of the dynamics from Sect. 2. We give a hybrid model for this simplified system and prove its safety. The new assumptions will be relaxed in later sections to achieve the safety verification of the full model of Sect. 2.

Model. In this section, we assume that the ownship and intruder are flying head-on ($\theta_v = 180°$). We also assume that the pilot reacts immediately to any advisory ($d_p = 0$ s), and that the advisory COC is not allowed. These assumptions will be relaxed in Sect. 4 and Sect. 5. We assume that r is a scalar: if $r \geq 0$ then the ownship is flying towards the intruder, otherwise it is flying away from it. Both cases could require an advisory. Since the ownship and intruder are flying head-on with straight line trajectories, there exists a vertical plane containing both their trajectories. In this plane, the puck becomes a rectangle centered around the ownship, of width $2r_p$ and height $2h_p$, and there is an NMAC if and only if the intruder is in this rectangle (in gray on Fig. 1).

Differential Dynamic Logic and KeYmaera. We model our system using Differential Dynamic Logic d$\mathcal{L}$ [17,18,19], a logic for reasoning about hybrid programs. The logic d$\mathcal{L}$ allows discrete assignments, control structures, and execution of differential equations. It is implemented in the theorem prover KeYmaera [21], that we use to verify our safe regions with respect to our models. All the KeYmaera models and proofs of this paper can be found at `http://www.ls.cs.cmu.edu/pub/acasx.zip`, and statistics in Technical Report [10].

The d$\mathcal{L}$ formula for the model that we use in this section is given in Eq. (1).

$$
\begin{aligned}
&{}_1 \; r_p \geq 0 \wedge h_p > 0 \wedge r_v \geq 0 \wedge a_r > 0 \wedge (w = -1 \vee w = 1) \wedge C_{\mathsf{impl}}(r, h, \dot{h}_0) \rightarrow \\
&{}_2 \; [(\; (\; ?\mathsf{true}\; \cup\; \dot{h}_f := *; (w := -1 \cup w := 1); ?C_{\mathsf{impl}}(r, h, \dot{h}_0); \mathsf{advisory} := (w, \dot{h}_f)\;); \\
&{}_3 \quad a := *; \{r' = -r_v, h' = -\dot{h}_0, \dot{h}_0' = a \;\&\; w\dot{h}_0 \geq w\dot{h}_f \vee wa \geq a_r\} \\
&{}_4 \;)^*]\, (|r| > r_p \vee |h| > h_p)
\end{aligned}
\tag{1}
$$

This formula of the form $p \rightarrow [\alpha]q$ says all executions of program α starting in a state satisfying logical formula p end up in a state satisfying q. It is akin to the Hoare triple $\{p\}\alpha\{q\}$ with precondition p and postcondition q. The precondition in Eq. (1) imposes constraints on several constants, as well as the formula $C_{\mathsf{impl}}(r, h, \dot{h}_0)$ (defined below) that forces the intruder to be in a safe region for an initial advisory $(w, \dot{h}_f)$. We cannot guarantee safety if the intruder starts initially in an unsafe region. The postcondition encodes absence of NMAC. Line 2 expresses the action of the ACAS X system. The nondeterministic choice operator $\cup$ expresses that the system can either continue with the same advisory by doing nothing—just testing ?true—this ensures it always has a valid choice and cannot get stuck. Otherwise it can choose a new advisory $(w, \dot{h}_f)$ that passes the safety condition $C_{\text{impl}}(r, h, \dot{h}_0)$—advisory will be the next message to the pilot. Line 3 expresses the action of the ownship, first nondeterministically choosing an arbitrary acceleration $(a := *)$ then following the continuous dynamics. The evolution of the variables r, h and $\dot{h}_0$ is expressed by a differential equation, and requires (using the operator $\&$) that the ownship evolves towards its target vertical velocity $\dot{h}_f$ at acceleration a_r (condition $wa \geq a_r$), unless it has already reached vertical velocity $\dot{h}_f$ (condition $w\dot{h}_0 \geq w\dot{h}_f$). Finally, the star $*$ on line 4 indicates that the program can be repeated any number of times, allowing the system to go through several advisories.

Implicit Formulation of the Safe Region. As explained in Sect. 2, we use a frame fixed to the intruder and with its origin at the initial position of the ownship (see Fig. 1).

First case: if $w = +1$ and $\dot{h}_f \geq \dot{h}_0$. Fig. 1 shows, in red, a possible trajectory of an ownship following exactly the requirements of ACAS X. This *nominal* trajectory of the ownship is denoted by $\mathcal{N}$. The pilot reacts immediately, and the ownship starts accelerating vertically with acceleration a_r until reaching the target vertical velocity $\dot{h}_f$—describing a parabola—then climbs at vertical velocity $\dot{h}_f$ along a straight line. Horizontally, the relative velocity r_v remains constant. Integrating the differential equations in Eq. (1) line 3, the ownship position (r_t, h_t) at time t along $\mathcal{N}$ is given by:

$$(r_t, h_t) = \begin{cases} \left(r_v t, \ \frac{a_r}{2} t^2 + \dot{h}_0 t \right) & \text{if } 0 \leq t < \frac{\dot{h}_f - \dot{h}_0}{a_r} \quad (a) \\ \left(r_v t, \ \dot{h}_f t - \frac{(\dot{h}_f - \dot{h}_0)^2}{2a_r} \right) & \text{if } \frac{\dot{h}_f - \dot{h}_0}{a_r} \leq t \quad (b) \end{cases} \quad (2)$$

Recall that in the ACAS X specification, the ownship moves vertically with acceleration of *at least* a_r, then continues with vertical velocity of *at least* $\dot{h}_f$. Therefore all possible future positions of the ownship are *above* the red nominal trajectory. An intruder is safe if its position is always either to the side of or under any puck centered on a point in $\mathcal{N}$, that is:

$$\forall t. \forall r_t. \forall h_t. \big((r_t, h_t) \in \mathcal{N} \rightarrow |r - r_t| > r_p \vee h - h_t < -h_p \big) \quad (3)$$

We call this formulation the *implicit formulation of the safe region*. It does not give explicit equations for the safe region border, but expresses them instead implicitly with respect to the nominal trajectory.

Generalization. The reasoning above is generalized to the case where $\dot{h}_f < \dot{h}_0$, and symmetrically to the case $w = -1$. The most general implicit formulation of the safe region is C_{impl} in Fig. 3, and verified to be safe in KeYmaera:

Theorem 1 (Correctness of implicit safe regions). *The $d\mathcal{L}$ formula given in Eq. (1) is valid. That is as long as the advisories obey formula C_{impl} there will be no NMAC.*

Implicit formulation

$$A(t, h_t, \dot{h}_0) \equiv \left(\begin{array}{l} 0 \leq t < \dfrac{\max(0, w(\dot{h}_f - \dot{h}_0))}{a_r} \wedge h_t = \dfrac{wa_r}{2}t^2 + \dot{h}_0 t \\[3ex] \vee \quad t \geq \dfrac{\max(0, w(\dot{h}_f - \dot{h}_0))}{a_r} \wedge h_t = \dot{h}_f t - \dfrac{w\max(0, w(\dot{h}_f - \dot{h}_0))^2}{2a_r} \end{array} \right)$$

$$C_{\mathsf{impl}}(r, h, \dot{h}_0) \equiv \forall t. \forall r_t. \forall h_t. \Big(r_t = r_v t \wedge A(t, h_t, \dot{h}_0)$$
$$\rightarrow (|r - r_t| > r_p \vee w(h - h_t) < -h_p) \Big)$$

Explicit formulation

$$\mathsf{case}_1(r, \dot{h}_0) \equiv -r_p \leq r < -r_p - \dfrac{r_v \min(0, w\dot{h}_0)}{a_r}$$

$$\mathsf{bound}_1(r, h, \dot{h}_0) \equiv wr_v^2 h < \dfrac{a_r}{2}(r + r_p)^2 + wr_v \dot{h}_0(r + r_p) - r_v^2 h_p$$

$$\mathsf{case}_2(r, \dot{h}_0) \equiv -r_p - \dfrac{r_v \min(0, w\dot{h}_0)}{a_r} \leq r \leq r_p - \dfrac{r_v \min(0, w\dot{h}_0)}{a_r}$$

$$\mathsf{bound}_2(r, h, \dot{h}_0) \equiv wh < -\dfrac{\min(0, w\dot{h}_0)^2}{2a_r} - h_p$$

$$\mathsf{case}_3(r, \dot{h}_0) \equiv r_p - \dfrac{r_v \min(0, w\dot{h}_0)}{a_r} < r \leq r_p + \dfrac{r_v \max(0, w(\dot{h}_f - \dot{h}_0))}{a_r}$$

$$\mathsf{bound}_3(r, h, \dot{h}_0) \equiv wr_v^2 h < \dfrac{a_r}{2}(r - r_p)^2 + wr_v \dot{h}_0(r - r_p) - r_v^2 h_p$$

$$\mathsf{case}_4(r, \dot{h}_0) \equiv r_p + \dfrac{r_v \max(0, w(\dot{h}_f - \dot{h}_0))}{a_r} < r$$

$$\mathsf{bound}_4(r, h, \dot{h}_0) \equiv (r_v = 0) \vee \left(wr_v h < w\dot{h}_f(r - r_p) - \dfrac{r_v \max(0, w(\dot{h}_f - \dot{h}_0))^2}{2a_r} - r_v h_p \right)$$

$$\mathsf{case}_5(r, \dot{h}_0) \equiv -r_p \leq r < -r_p + \dfrac{r_v \max(0, w(\dot{h}_f - \dot{h}_0))}{a_r}$$

$$\mathsf{bound}_5(r, h, \dot{h}_0) \equiv wr_v^2 h < \dfrac{a_r}{2}(r + r_p)^2 + wr_v \dot{h}_0(r + r_p) - r_v^2 h_p$$

$$\mathsf{case}_6(r, \dot{h}_0) \equiv -r_p + \dfrac{r_v \max(0, w(\dot{h}_f - \dot{h}_0))}{a_r} \leq r$$

$$\mathsf{bound}_6(r, h, \dot{h}_0) \equiv (r_v = 0 \wedge r > r_p)$$
$$\vee \left(wr_v h < w\dot{h}_f(r + r_p) - \dfrac{r_v \max(0, w(\dot{h}_f - \dot{h}_0))^2}{2a_r} - r_v h_p \right)$$

$$C_{\mathsf{expl}}(r, h, \dot{h}_0) \equiv \left(w\dot{h}_f \geq 0 \rightarrow \bigwedge_{i=1}^{4}(\mathsf{case}_i(r, \dot{h}_0) \rightarrow \mathsf{bound}_i(r, h, \dot{h}_0)) \right)$$
$$\wedge \left(w\dot{h}_f < 0 \rightarrow \bigwedge_{i=5}^{6}(\mathsf{case}_i(r, \dot{h}_0) \rightarrow \mathsf{bound}_i(r, h, \dot{h}_0)) \right)$$

Fig. 3. Implicit and explicit formulations of the safe region for an immediate response

Explicit Formulation of the Safe Region. The implicit formulation of the safe region gives an intuitive understanding of where it is safe for the intruder to be. However, because it still contains quantifiers, its use comes at the extra cost of eliminating the quantifiers. An efficient comparison with the ACAS X table, as described in Sect. 6, can only be achieved with a quantifier-free, *explicit formulation*, that we present in this section. We show that both formulations are equivalent. As for the implicit formulation, we derive the equations for one representative case before generalizing them.

First case: if $w = +1$, $r_v > 0$, $\dot{h}_0 < 0$ and $\dot{h}_f \geq 0$. We are in the case shown in Fig. 1 and described in detail above. The nominal trajectory $\mathcal{N}$ is given by Eq. (2)(a) and Eq. (2)(b). The boundary of the (green) safe region in Fig. 1 is drawn by either the bottom left hand corner, the bottom side or the bottom right hand corner of the puck. This boundary can be characterized by a set of equations:

0. positions left of the puck's initial position ($r < -r_p$) are in the safe region;
1. then the boundary follows the bottom left hand corner of the puck as it is going down the parabola of Eq. (2)(a); therefore for $-r_p \leq r < -r_p - \frac{r_v \dot{h}_0}{a_r}$, the position (r, h) is safe if and only if $h < \frac{a_r}{2r_v^2}(r + r_p)^2 + \frac{\dot{h}_0}{r_v}(r + r_p) - h_p$;
2. following this, the boundary is along the bottom side of the puck as it is at the bottom of the parabola of Eq. (2)(a); therefore for $-r_p - \frac{r_v \dot{h}_0}{a} \leq r \leq r_p - \frac{r_v \dot{h}_0}{a_r}$, the position (r, h) is in the safe region if and only if $h < -\frac{\dot{h}_0^2}{2a_r} - h_p$;
3. then the boundary follows the bottom right hand corner of the puck as it is going up the parabola of Eq. (2)(a); therefore for $r_p - \frac{r_v \dot{h}_0}{a_r} < r \leq r_p + \frac{r_v(\dot{h}_f - \dot{h}_0)}{a_r}$, the position (r, h) is safe if and only if $h < \frac{a_r}{2r_v^2}(r - r_p)^2 + \frac{\dot{h}_0}{r_v}(r - r_p) - h_p$;
4. finally the boundary follows the bottom right hand corner of the puck as it is going up the straight line of Eq. (2)(b); therefore for $r_p + \frac{r_v(\dot{h}_f - \dot{h}_0)}{a_r} < r$, the position (r, h) is in the safe region if and only if $h < \frac{\dot{h}_f}{r_v}(r - r_p) - \frac{(\dot{h}_f - \dot{h}_0)^2}{2a_r} - h_p$.

Generalization. The general case is given in the formula C_{expl} of Fig. 3. The cases 1-4 and their associated bounds are for the case $w\dot{h}_f \geq 0$, whereas cases 5 and 6 and associated bounds are for $w\dot{h}_f < 0$. We again use KeYmaera to formally prove that this explicit safe region formulation is equivalent to its implicit counterpart.

Lemma 1 (Correctness of explicit safe regions). *If $w = \pm 1$, $r_p \geq 0$, $h_p > 0$, $r_v \geq 0$ and $a_r > 0$, then the conditions $C_{\text{impl}}(r, h, \dot{h}_0)$ and $C_{\text{expl}}(r, h, \dot{h}_0)$ are equivalent.*

4   Safe Region for a Delayed Pilot Response

We generalize the model of Sect. 3 to account for a non-deterministic, non-zero pilot delay, and for periods of time where the system does not issue an advisory (i.e., COC).

Model. In this section, we still assume that the ownship and intruder are flying head-on ($\theta_v = 180°$). We use the same conventions as in Sect. 3 for r and r_v. The model includes an initial period where there is no compliance with any advisory—the ownship accelerates non-deterministically (within limits) in the vertical direction. As before, we derive the safe regions by considering all possible positions of the ownship's puck in all possible trajectories that might evolve in the encounter. To represent pilot delay for an advisory, the model assumes an immediate advisory, and period of non-compliance d_p, representing the time it takes the pilot to respond. To represent COC, the model looks for a safe advisory it can issue d_ℓ in the future if necessary, (d_ℓ being the system delay, and shortest COC) so the period of non-compliance is $d_p + d_\ell$.

$$
\begin{aligned}
&{}_1 \; r_p \geq 0 \wedge h_p > 0 \wedge r_v \geq 0 \wedge a_r > 0 \wedge a_d \geq \wedge d_p \geq 0 \wedge d_\ell \geq 0 \\
&{}_2 \; \wedge(w = -1 \vee w = 1) \wedge D_{\mathsf{impl}}(r, h, \dot{h}_0, d) \rightarrow \\
&{}_3 \; [(\; (\text{?true} \; \cup \; \dot{h}_f := *; (w := -1 \cup w := 1); \\
&{}_4 \; \qquad\qquad (\boldsymbol{d := d_p}; \text{?}D_{\mathsf{impl}}(r, h, \dot{h}_0, d); \text{advisory} := (w, \dot{h}_f) \; \cup \\
&{}_5 \; \qquad\qquad\quad \boldsymbol{d := d_p + d_\ell}; \text{?}D_{\mathsf{impl}}(r, h, \dot{h}_0, d); \text{advisory} := \mathsf{COC} \;)); \qquad (4) \\
&{}_6 \; \quad a := *; \text{?}(\boldsymbol{wa \geq -a_d}); t_\ell := 0; \\
&{}_7 \; \quad \{r' = -r_v, h' = -\dot{h}_0, \dot{h}'_0 = a, d' = -1, t'_\ell = 1 \; \& \\
&{}_8 \; \quad (t_\ell \leq d_\ell) \wedge (d \leq 0 \rightarrow w\dot{h}_0 \geq w\dot{h}_f \vee wa \geq a_r)\} \\
&{}_9 \;)^*] \, (|r| > r_p \vee |h| > h_p)
\end{aligned}
$$

We modify the model of Eq. (1) to capture these new ideas, and obtain the model of Eq. (4), highlighting the differences in **bold**. The structure, precondition (lines 1 and 2) and postcondition (line 9) are similar. The clock d, if positive, represents the amount of time until the ownship pilot must respond to the current advisory to remain safe. Lines 3 to 5 represent the actions of the ACAS X system. As before, the system can continue with the same advisory (?true). Otherwise it can select a safe advisory $(w, \dot{h}_f)$ to be applied after at most delay d_p; or it can safely remain silent, displaying COC, if it knows an advisory $(w, \dot{h}_f)$ that is safe if applied after delay $d_p + d_\ell$. In line 6, the pilot non-deterministically chooses an acceleration ($a := *$), within some limit ($wa \geq -a_d$). The set of differential equations in line 7 describes the system's dynamics, and the conditions in line 8 use the clock t_ℓ to ensure that continuous time does not evolve longer than system delay d_ℓ without a system response ($t_\ell \leq d_\ell$). Those conditions also ensure that when $d \leq 0$ the pilot starts complying with the advisory. The model is structured so that the pilot can safely delay responding to an advisory for up to d_p, and to an advisory associated with COC for up to $d_p + d_\ell$—considering upper bounds on the reaction delay is necessary to get a formal proof of safety. Because of the loop in our model (line 9), the safety guarantees of this theorem apply to encounters whose advisories change as the encounter evolves, encounters with periods of no advisory, and encounters where the pilot exhibits some non-deterministic behavior.

In the rest of the section we use the same approach as in Sect. 3: we first derive an implicit formulation, then an equivalent explicit formulation of the safe region, and prove that the safe region guarantees that the intruder cannot cause an NMAC.

Formulations of the Safe Region. As in Sect. 3, let us place ourselves in the referential centered on the current position of the ownship and where the intruder is fixed, and let us

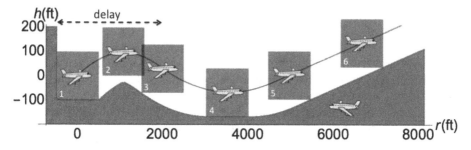

Fig. 4. Trajectory of the ownship (red) and safe region for the intruder (green), delayed response

first assume that the ownship receives an advisory $(w, \dot{h}_f)$ such that $w = +1$, and that $d \geq 0$. Let us focus on the period of time before the pilot reacts, which we henceforth call delay. During the delay, the ownship can take any vertical acceleration less than a_d in absolute value, therefore its nominal trajectory $\mathcal{N}_d$ is to accelerate the opposite way of the advisory, at acceleration $-a_d$. Horizontally, its speed is constant at r_v. It thus describes a *delay parabola*, in red on Fig. 4, and its position (r_t, h_t) along the nominal trajectory for $0 \leq t < d$ is given by $(r_t, h_t) = \left(r_v t, -\frac{a_d}{2}t^2 + \dot{h}_0 t\right)$.

After the delay, i.e., after time d, the nominal trajectory $\mathcal{N}_d$ is the same as a nominal trajectory $\mathcal{N}$ from Sect. 3, translated by time d and by its position at time d given by $r_d = r_t(d)$ and $h_d = h_t(d)$, and starting with vertical velocity $\dot{h}_d = \dot{h}_0 - a_d d$. As in Sect. 3, we can now express the implicit formulation of the safe region:

$$\forall t. \forall r_t. \forall h_t. \big((r_t, h_t) \in \mathcal{N}_d \to |r - r_t| > r_p \vee h - h_t < -h_p\big)$$

Symmetrically, the reasoning of this section extends to the case where $w = -1$. Moreover, we can handle cases where $d < 0$, i.e., after the pilot has reacted, by replacing d by $\max(0, d)$. The generalized implicit formulation of the safe region is given as D_{impl} in Fig. 5. Note that it involves the expression $A(t - \max(0, d), h_t - h_d, \dot{h}_d)$ from Fig. 3 capturing the implicit safe region of Sect. 3 translated by time $\max(0, d)$, vertical height h_d, and starting at vertical speed $\dot{h}_d$. It is proved correct in KeYmaera.

Theorem 2 (Correctness of delayed safe regions). *The dℒ formula given in Eq. (4) is valid. That is as long as the advisories obey formula D_{impl} there will be no NMAC.*

Similarly as in Sect. 4, we determine an explicit formulation of the safe region, called D_{expl} in Fig. 5 based on Fig. 3, and prove it correct in KeYmaera.

Lemma 2 (Correctness of delayed explicit safe regions). *If $w = -1$ or $w = +1$, $r_p \geq 0$, $h_p > 0$, $r_v \geq 0$, $a_r > 0$, $a_d \geq 0$, $d_p \geq 0$ and $d_\ell \geq 0$ then the two conditions $D_{\mathsf{impl}}(r, h, \dot{h}_0, d)$ and $D_{\mathsf{expl}}(r, h, \dot{h}_0, d)$ are equivalent.*

5   Reduction from 3D Dynamics to 2D Dynamics

In this section, we show that, with respect to our assumptions, any 3-dimensional encounter (Sect. 2) can be reduced to a 2-dimensional encounter (Sect. 3) without loss of generality. This is done using a change of reference frame and a dimension reduction.

Implicit formulation

$$B(t, h_t, \dot{h}_0, d) \equiv 0 \le t < \max(0, d) \wedge h_t = -\frac{wa_d}{2}t^2 + \dot{h}_0 t$$

$$\text{const} \equiv h_d = -\frac{wa_d}{2}\max(0, d)^2 + \dot{h}_0 \max(0, d) \wedge \dot{h}_d - \dot{h}_0 = -wa_d \max(0, d)$$

$$D_{\text{impl}}(r, h, \dot{h}_0, d) \equiv \forall t. \forall r_t. \forall h_t. \forall h_d. \forall \dot{h}_d.$$

$$\left(r_t = r_v t \wedge (B(t, h_t, \dot{h}_0, d) \vee \text{const} \wedge A(t - \max(0, d), h_t - h_d, \dot{h}_d)) \right.$$

$$\left. \rightarrow (|r - r_t| > r_p \vee w(h - h_t) < -h_p) \right)$$

Explicit formulation

$$r_d = r_v \max(0, d) \qquad\qquad \dot{h}_d = \dot{h}_0 - wa_d \max(0, d)$$

$$h_d = -\frac{wa_d}{2}\max(0, d)^2 + \dot{h}_0 \max(0, d)$$

$$\text{case}_7(r) \equiv -r_p \le r \le r_p \qquad\qquad \text{bound}_7(r, h) \equiv wh < -h_p$$

$$\text{case}_8(r) \equiv r_p < r \le r_d + r_p \qquad\qquad \text{case}_9(r) \equiv -r_p \le r < r_d - r_p$$

$$\text{bound}_8(r, h) \equiv wr_v^2 h < -\frac{a_d}{2}(r - r_p)^2 + wr_v \dot{h}_0(r - r_p) - r_v^2 h_p$$

$$\text{bound}_9(r, h) \equiv wr_v^2 h < -\frac{a_d}{2}(r + r_p)^2 + wr_v \dot{h}_0(r + r_p) - r_v^2 h_p$$

$$D_{\text{expl}}(r, h, \dot{h}_0, d) \equiv \left(\bigwedge_{i=7}^{9} (\text{case}_i(r) \rightarrow \text{bound}_i(r, h)) \right) \wedge C_{\text{expl}}(r - r_d, h - h_d, \dot{h}_d)$$

Fig. 5. Implicit and explicit formulations of the safe region for a delayed response

For the sake of clarity, let us use a reference frame $(O, \vec{i}, \vec{j}, \vec{k})$ fixed to the ownship (O). In this reference frame, the position of an intruder I is represented by the tuple (x, y, h), and the differential equation system that governs its motion is given by $\dot{x} = r_x$, $\dot{y} = r_y$, $\dot{h} = a$, where r_x, r_y and a remain constant as time evolves. Therefore, the motion of the encounter can be decoupled into a 2-dimensional horizontal encounter in the reference frame $(O, \vec{i}, \vec{j})$ (horizontal plane) and a 1-dimensional vertical encounter in the reference frame $(O, \vec{k})$. In what follows, we reduce the horizontal encounter from a 2-dimensional motion to a 1-dimensional motion, thereby simplifying the problem conceptually and computationally by reducing its number of variables.

Fig. 6 depicts a top view of a generic encounter. We denote by $\vec{r}$ the position, and $\vec{r}_v$ the velocity, of the intruder relative to the ownship, and by $r_v \ge 0$ the norm of $\vec{r}_v$.

First suppose $r_v > 0$. The idea is to choose a reference frame $(O', \vec{i'}, \vec{j'})$ in which one axis $\vec{i'}$ is aligned with $\vec{r}_v$, such that no relative motion happens in the other direction $\vec{j'}$. Its fixed center O' is defined as the orthogonal projection of point

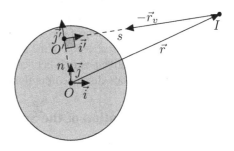

Fig. 6. Top view of the two reference frames

O on the direction of $\vec{r}_v$. The unit vector $\vec{i'}$ is defined as $\frac{\vec{r}_v}{r_v}$, and $\vec{j'}$ is a unit such that $(O', \vec{i'}, \vec{j'})$ is positively oriented.

Let $\vec{v}_{|O}$ (resp. $\vec{v}_{|O'}$) denote the coordinates of a vector $\vec{v}$ relative to the reference frame $(O, \vec{i}, \vec{j})$ (resp. $(O', \vec{i'}, \vec{j'})$). Then, the coordinates for $\vec{r}$ and $\vec{r}_v$ are: $\vec{r}_{|O} = (x, y)$, $\vec{r}_{v|O} = (r_x, r_y)$, $\vec{r}_{|O'} = (s, n)$ and $\vec{r}_{v|O'} = (-r_v, 0)$. The scalar product $\vec{r} \cdot \vec{r}_v$ and the cross product $\vec{r} \times \vec{r}_v$ are independent of the horizontal reference frame, therefore:

$$xr_x + yr_y = -sr_v \qquad xr_y - yr_x = nr_v \qquad (5)$$

Given r_x and r_y, Eqns. (5) imply that the coordinates (x, y) are uniquely determined by the choice of (s, n), as long as $r_v \neq 0$ (using $r_v^2 = r_x^2 + r_y^2$). For any 2-dimensional configuration, the encounter can thus be considered a head-on encounter where s plays the role of r and where a new puck radius, denoted s_p, plays the role of r_p.

Let us now determine the radius s_p of the dimension-reduced encounter, and prove that the absence of NMAC in $(O, \vec{i}, \vec{j})$—characterized by $r^2 > r_p^2$—is equivalent to the absence of NMAC in $(O', \vec{i'}, \vec{j'})$—characterized by $s^2 > s_p^2$. Using (5):

$$r_v^2 r^2 = r_v^2(x^2 + y^2) = (xr_x + yr_y)^2 + (xr_y - yr_x)^2 = r_v^2(s^2 + n^2) \ .$$

Since $r_v \neq 0$, this implies $r^2 = s^2 + n^2$. Therefore, $r^2 > r_p^2$ if and only if $s^2 + n^2 > r_p^2$ or equivalently $s^2 > r_p^2 - n^2$. If $r_p^2 - n^2 < 0$, the direction of the vector $\vec{r}_v$ does not intersect the puck, the inequality $s^2 > r_p^2 - n^2$ is trivially true, and the encounter is safe. If $r_p^2 - n^2 \geq 0$, we choose the new puck radius s_p for the dimension-reduced encounter as $s_p = \sqrt{r_p^2 - n^2} \geq 0$, and the safety condition in $(O', \vec{i'}, \vec{j'})$ becomes $s^2 \geq s_p^2$. When $\theta_v = 180°$, one has $s = r$, $n = 0$ and $s_p = r_p$ as in Sect. 3–4.

As the encounter evolves in $(O, \vec{i}, \vec{j})$ along $\dot{x} = r_x, \dot{y} = r_y$, its dimension-reduced version evolves in $(O', \vec{i'}, \vec{j'})$ along the differential equations $\dot{s} = -r_v, \dot{n} = 0$, obtained by differentiating Eqns. (5) and canceling r_v. The following proposition, proved in KeYmaera, combines both dynamics and shows that the absence of an NMAC of radius r_p in $(O, \vec{i}, \vec{j})$ is equivalent to the absence of an NMAC of radius s_p in $(O', \vec{i'}, \vec{j'})$.

Proposition 1 (Horizontal Reduction). *The following dℒ formula is valid*

$$\left(xr_x + yr_y = -sr_v \wedge xr_y - yr_x = nr_v \wedge x^2 + y^2 = n^2 + s^2 \wedge r_v^2 = r_x^2 + r_y^2\right)$$
$$\rightarrow [\dot{x} = r_x, \dot{y} = r_y, \dot{s} = -r_v, \dot{n} = 0] \left(x^2 + y^2 > r_p^2 \leftrightarrow s^2 > r_p^2 - n^2\right) \quad (6)$$

Observe that the horizontal NMAC condition in $(O', \vec{i'}, \vec{j'})$ only depends on the change of one variable rather than two. The proposition also applies to the special case $r_v = 0$. In this case the origin O' is no longer defined, and Eqns. (5) are trivially true. The variables s and n are constants ($\dot{s} = 0, \dot{n} = 0$), their initial values are only restricted by the condition $n^2 + s^2 = x^2 + y^2$ in the assumption of the proposition, but they are not unique. When the relative position between the two aircraft does not evolve over time, if the intruder is at a safe distance initially, the encounter is still safe for all time.

6   Initial Examination of the Safety of ACAS X

In this section, we use Theorem 1 to check the safety of advisories given by ACAS X. We focus on Run 12 (July 2014) of the optimized logic tables, a core component of

Table 2. Summary of the points of the state space at which we examined ACAS X

	Range r (ft)	Relative speed r_v (ft/s)	Angle θ_v (degrees)	Relative altitude h (ft)	Vertical rates $\dot{h}_0, \dot{h}_1$ (ft/s)	Previous advisory
Min value	1,500	100	180°	-4,000	-41.67	None
Max value	200,000	2,200	180°	4,000	41.67	None
Number of values	80	10	1	33	13^2	1

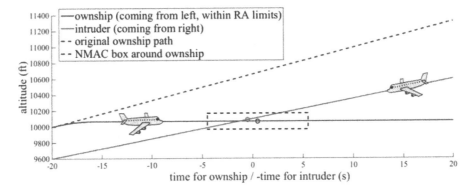

Fig. 7. Original ownship path (cyan) and intruder path (red) vs. ownship responding to a do-not-climb (DNC) advisory issued by the ACAS X tables in starting state: $r = 4{,}000$ ft, $r_v = 200$ ft/s, $\theta_v = 180°$, $h = 600$ ft, $\dot{h}_0 = 1{,}980$ ft/min, $\dot{h}_1 = -1{,}500$ ft/min.

ACAS X. The full policy of the system is built on these lookup tables and incorporates additional components to handle various operational scenarios. We compare the ACAS X table to the explicit regions where the pilot reacts immediately (Sect. 3). For a given initial state of an encounter, we query the *first* advisory issued by ACAS X and check its safety as identified in Theorem 1. In a real scenario, ACAS X could later strengthen or reverse the first advisory as the encounter evolves. But the safety of the first advisory is critical from an operational prospective as later changes are undesirable.

Our initial analysis considers a nominal set of discrete states—summarized in Table 2—of the ACAS X MDP model where no advisory has yet been issued. All compared states are head-on encounters: in a sense, they are the most obviously dangerous configurations. For those states, the ACAS X advisories are compared against the safe regions stated in Fig. 3. Overall, 4,461,600 discrete states were examined, among which 44,306 states (1.2%) did not meet the conditions of Fig. 3: 11,524 of these were unresolvable, i.e., the intruder was too close for any advisory to avoid NMAC; while 32,782 could have been resolved with a different safe advisory that satisfies Theorem 1.

Our analysis led to the identification of unexpected behavior in the ACAS X lookup tables. In some cases, the ACAS X advisory seems to *induce* an NMAC (Fig. 7), i.e., if the initial advisory is not strengthened or reverted later, an NMAC will occur. In other cases, the advisory does not seem to have any benefit, that is flying at vertical rates disallowed by the advisory would actually avoid NMAC while not all allowed vertical rates are safe. Of course, such unsafe advisories would be disallowed by our safe regions. Notice that these behaviors are not necessarily all deemed undesirable, as ACAS X tries to minimize alerting the pilot unless it has to do so; for some cases, ACAS X will strengthen the advisory later and hence does not issue a disruptive alert immediately. Fig. 7 depicts a typical example where the ACAS X advisory induces an NMAC. The ownship is flying from the left and the intruder from the right. As time counts down, the intruder evolves towards the ownship and an NMAC happens at $t = 0$. The original path of the ownship does not lead to an NMAC. However, ACAS X gives a Do-Not-Climb advisory. If the pilot, following this advisory, decides to stop climbing, its trajectory will cause an NMAC. (Other examples are in Technical Report [10].)

The development of the safe regions gave an insight into possible improvements for the ACAS X system. Although we are not analyzing the complete system, nor the subsequent advisories, we automatically pointed out some subregions of the state space worth looking at. Some of those problems were independently identified by the ACAS X team using simulation-based testing, and will be addressed in subsequent revisions of the system. When extended to check contiguous regions of the state space, our approach will have the potential for a complete analysis of the system over all potential encounter configurations, thereby reducing vulnerability to the sampling of encounter scenarios.

7 Related Work

Kochenderfer and Chryssanthacopoulos [12] describe the design of the ACAS X lookup-tables. Their principled approach, based on optimizing an MDP, guarantees the selection of optimal advisories according to a cost model. The state space and dynamics are discretized. Their notion of optimality depends on costs assigned to various events.

Von Essen and Giannakopoulou [3] use probabilistic model-checking to analyze an MDP based on [12]. They investigate the probability of several undesirable events occurring. Because they ostensibly analyze an MDP, their work inherits many of the assumptions of ACAS X, including discretized dynamics. Their analysis depends heavily on the MDP considered and thus needs to be redone on every version of ACAS X.

Lygeros and Lynch [16] use hybrid techniques to formally verify the TCAS conflict resolution algorithms. They assume—rather than prove—that TCAS ends up in a state where one aircraft has a climbing advisory and the other a descending advisory. They then prove (by hand) a lower bound on the vertical separation of both aircraft at the point of closest approach. In contrast, we do not assume anything on ACAS X's advisories.

Holland et al. [9] and Chludzinski [1] simulate large numbers of encounters, including tracks from recorded flight data, to evaluate the performance of ACAS X. These simulations account for high-fidelity details of an encounter, but they only cover a finite set of the continuous state space with no formal guarantees.

Tomlin et al. [22], Platzer and Clarke [20], Loos et al. [15] and more recently Ghorbal et al. [8] use hybrid systems approaches to design safe horizontal maneuvers for collision avoidance. Dowek et al. [2] and Galdino et al. [7] describe and verify in the PVS theorem prover a collision avoidance system of their design called KB3D.

Overall, our approach is different from previous complementary work in that:

- unlike [3,12], we rely on an independent model from the one used to design ACAS X;
- unlike [2,7,8,15,20,22] we analyze an independent industrial system and not a safe-by-design system;

- unlike [2,3,7] our analysis uses realistic, continuous dynamics;
- unlike [16,22] we provide universal safe regions that can be reused for new versions of ACAS X or even for new systems;
- unlike [1,9,11,16,22], we provide mechanized proofs of correctness of our model.

8   Conclusion and Future Work

We developed a general strategy for analyzing the safety of complicated, real-world collision avoidance systems, and applied it to ACAS X. Our strategy identifies safe regions where an advisory is proved to always keep the aircraft clear of NMAC, under some assumptions. We identified states where ACAS X is provably safe, and fed others showing unexpected behaviors back to the ACAS X development team. The identified safe regions are independent from the version of ACAS X and can thus be reused for future versions. In future work, we plan to extend our hybrid model to account for curved trajectories of both aircraft as well as vertical acceleration of the intruder.

Acknowledgments. The authors would like to warmly thank Stefan Mitsch and Jan-David Quesel for their support of the KeYmaera tool. The authors would also like to thank Jeff Brush, Jessica Holland, Robert Klaus, Barbara Kobzik-Juul, Mykel Kochenderfer, Ted Londner, Sarah Loos, Ed Morehouse, Wes Olson, Michael Owen, Joshua Silbermann, Neal Suchy, and the ACAS X development team for interesting remarks.

References

1. Chludzinski, B.J.: Evaluation of TCAS II version 7.1 using the FAA fast-time encounter generator model. Tech. Rep. ATC-346, MIT Lincoln Laboratory (April 2009)
2. Dowek, G., Muñoz, C., Carreño, V.: Provably safe coordinated strategy for distributed conflict resolution. In: AIAA Guidance Navigation, and Control Conference and Exhibit (2005)
3. von Essen, C., Giannakopoulou, D.: Analyzing the next generation airborne collision avoidance system. In: Ábrahám, E., Havelund, K. (eds.) TACAS 2014 (ETAPS). LNCS, vol. 8413, pp. 620–635. Springer, Heidelberg (2014)
4. Federal Aviation Administration: Introduction to TCAS II, version 7.1 (February 2011)
5. Federal Aviation Administration TCAS Program Office: Algorithm design description for the surveillance and tracking module of ACAS X, run12 (July 2014)
6. Federal Aviation Administration TCAS Program Office: Algorithm design description for the threat resolution module of ACAS X, version 3 Rev. 1 (May 2014)
7. Galdino, A.L., Muñoz, C., Ayala-Rincón, M.: Formal verification of an optimal air traffic conflict resolution and recovery algorithm. In: Leivant, D., de Queiroz, R. (eds.) WoLLIC 2007. LNCS, vol. 4576, pp. 177–188. Springer, Heidelberg (2007)
8. Ghorbal, K., Jeannin, J.-B., Zawadzki, E., Platzer, A., Gordon, G.J., Capell, P.: Hybrid theorem proving of aerospace systems: Applications and challenges. Journal of Aerospace Information Systems (2014)
9. Holland, J.E., Kochenderfer, M.J., Olson, W.A.: Optimizing the next generation collision avoidance system for safe, suitable, and acceptable operational performance. Air Traffic Control Quarterly (2014)

10. Jeannin, J.B., Ghorbal, K., Kouskoulas, Y., Garnder, R., Schmidt, A., Zawadzki, E., Platzer, A.: A formally verified hybrid system for the next-generation airborne collision avoidance system. Tech. Rep. CMU-CS-14-138, School of Computer Science, Carnegie Mellon University, Pittsburgh, PA (2014), http://reports-archive.adm.cs.cmu.edu/anon/2014/CMU-CS-14-138.pdf KeYmaera files available at http://www.ls.cs.cmu.edu/pub/acasx.zip
11. Kochenderfer, M.J., Espindle, L.P., Kuchar, J.K., Griffith, J.D.: Correlated encounter model for cooperative aircraft in the national airspace system version 1.0. Tech. Rep. ATC-344, MIT Lincoln Laboratory (October 2008)
12. Kochenderfer, M.J., Chryssanthacopoulos, J.P.: Robust airborne collision avoidance through dynamic programming. Tech. Rep. ATC-371, MIT Lincoln Laboratory (January 2010)
13. Kochenderfer, M.J., Holland, J.E., Chryssanthacopoulos, J.P.: Next generation airborne collision avoidance system. Lincoln Laboratory Journal 19(1), 17–33 (2012)
14. Kochenderfer, M.J., Monath, N.: Compression of optimal value functions for Markov decision processes. In: Data Compression Conference, Snowbird, Utah (2013)
15. Loos, S.M., Renshaw, D.W., Platzer, A.: Formal verification of distributed aircraft controllers. In: HSCC, pp. 125–130. ACM (2013)
16. Lygeros, J., Lynch, N.: On the formal verification of the TCAS conflict resolution algorithms. In: IEEE Decision and Control, vol. 2, pp. 1829–1834. IEEE (1997)
17. Platzer, A.: Differential dynamic logic for hybrid systems. J. Autom. Reas. 41(2), 143–189 (2008)
18. Platzer, A.: Logical Analysis of Hybrid Systems: Proving Theorems for Complex Dynamics. Springer (2010)
19. Platzer, A.: Logics of dynamical systems. In: LICS, pp. 13–24. IEEE (2012)
20. Platzer, A., Clarke, E.M.: Formal verification of curved flight collision avoidance maneuvers: A case study. In: Cavalcanti, A., Dams, D.R. (eds.) FM 2009. LNCS, vol. 5850, pp. 547–562. Springer, Heidelberg (2009)
21. Platzer, A., Quesel, J.-D.: KeYmaera: A hybrid theorem prover for hybrid systems (System description). In: Armando, A., Baumgartner, P., Dowek, G. (eds.) IJCAR 2008. LNCS (LNAI), vol. 5195, pp. 171–178. Springer, Heidelberg (2008)
22. Tomlin, C., Pappas, G.J., Sastry, S.: Conflict resolution for air traffic management: A study in multiagent hybrid systems. IEEE Transactions on Automatic Control 43(4), 509–521 (1998)

Verified Reachability Analysis
of Continuous Systems

Fabian Immler*

Institut für Informatik, Technische Universität München
immler@in.tum.de

Abstract. Ordinary differential equations (ODEs) are often used to model the dynamics of (often safety-critical) continuous systems.

This work presents the formal verification of an algorithm for reachability analysis in continuous systems. The algorithm features adaptive Runge-Kutta methods and rigorous numerics based on affine arithmetic. It is proved to be sound with respect to the existing formalization of ODEs in Isabelle/HOL. Optimizations like splitting, intersecting and collecting reachable sets are necessary to analyze chaotic systems. Experiments demonstrate the practical usability of our developments.

Keywords: Numerical Analysis, Rigorous Numerics, Validated Numerics, Ordinary Differential Equation, Continuous System, Interactive Theorem Proving.

1   Introduction

Many real-world systems with continuous dynamics can be modeled with ordinary differential equations (ODEs). An important task is to determine for a set of initial states all reachable states. This requires to compute enclosures for solutions of ODEs, which is done by tools for guaranteed integration (e.g., VNODE-LP [21] or COSY [5]) and also by tools for reachability analysis of hybrid systems (with the state-of-the-art tool for linear dynamics SpaceEx [13] and tools supporting non-linear dynamics like Flow* [9], HySAT/iSAT [12], or Ariadne [4]). Such tools aim at computing safe overapproximations, an intended use is often the analysis of safety-critical systems. Therefore any effort to improve the level of rigor is valuable, and such efforts have been undertaken already: Nedialkov [21] implemented VNODE-LP using literate programming such that correctness of the code can be examined by human experts. Taylor models, which are used to represent reachable sets in COSY, Flow*, and Ariadne, have been formalized in theorem provers in the context of Ariadne [10] but also as a generic means for validated numerics [8,25].

Here we present the formal verification of an algorithm for reachability analysis of continuous systems. The algorithm splits, reduces and collects reachable

---

* Supported by the DFG RTG 1480 (PUMA).

C. Baier and C. Tinelli (Eds.): TACAS 2015, LNCS 9035, pp. 37–51, 2015.
DOI: 10.1007/978-3-662-46681-0_3

sets during the analysis, crucial features for being able to analyze chaotic systems. Propagation of reachable sets is implemented using higher-order Runge-Kutta methods with adaptive step size control. The formal verification of all those algorithms is a novel contribution and a qualitative improvement on the level of trust that can be put into reachability analysis of continuous systems. Experiments show that our algorithms allow to analyze low-dimensional, non-linear systems that are out of reach for many of the existing tools. Nevertheless, our work should not be considered a rival to the existing tools or concepts, which are more mature and flexible. We would rather like to demonstrate that formal verification does not exclude competitive performance.

We build on our formalization of affine arithmetic and the Euler method [15]. The verification is carried out with respect to the theory of ODEs in the interactive theorem prover Isabelle/HOL [22]. Every definition and theorem we display in this document possesses a formally proved and mechanically checked counterpart. The development is available in the Archive of Formal Proofs [18].

1.1 Related Work: ODEs and ITPs

In addition to the previously mentioned work on analysis of continuous systems, there also exists related work on differential equations formalized in theorem provers: Spitters and Makarov [20] implement Picard iteration to calculate solutions of ODEs in the interactive theorem prover Coq, but restricted to relatively short existence intervals. Boldo *et al.* [6] approximate the solution of one particular partial differential equation with a C-program and verify its correctness in Coq. Platzer [23] uses a different approach in that he does not do numerical analysis but uses differential invariants to reason symbolically about dynamical systems in a proof assistant.

2 Main Ideas

In what follows, we consider the problem of computing reachable sets for systems defined by an autonomous ODE $\dot{x} = f(x)$ with $f : \mathbb{R}^n \to \mathbb{R}^n$. We denote the solution depending on initial condition x_0 and time t with $\varphi(x_0, t)$. Reachability analysis aims at computing (or overapproximating) all states of the system that are reachable from some set of initial states $X_0 \subseteq \mathbb{R}^n$ within a time horizon $T \subseteq \mathbb{R}$, i.e., the set $\varphi(X_0, T)$.

We will start by illustrating the main ingredients of our algorithm for reachability analysis. We do not claim originality for those ideas, however combining all of them for numerically solving ODEs and especially formally verifying them is, to the best of our knowledge, a novel contribution.

Rigorous Numerics. First of all, in any numerical computation, continuous, real-valued quantities are approximated with finite precision. One therefore needs to cope with round-off errors. Reasoning about them explicitly gets very tedious. We therefore take the approach of set-based computing, or *rigorous numerics*:

The idea is to compute with sets instead of single values and abstract all kinds of errors (including round-off) by including them into the set. The data structure we choose is *affine forms*, they represent sets called *zonotopes* and have been successfully applied in hybrid systems analysis [14].

Guaranteed Runge-Kutta Methods with Step Size Adaptation. Bouissou *et al.* [7] presented the idea to turn "classical" numerical Algorithms into guaranteed methods by using affine arithmetic. They illustrated their approach on a *stiff* (i.e., numerical approximations requiring very small step sizes in parts of the state space) ODE, which makes adaptive step size control necessary. In general, automatic step size adaptation improves the performance of any numerical method, as it avoids wasting computational time on "easy" parts of the solution and maintains high accuracy on "hard" parts of the solution.

Splitting. Zonotopes are convex sets, this leads of course to loss of precision when non-convex sets need to be enclosed. But non-linear dynamics produce non-convex sets, which is why a purely zonotope based approach is likely to fail because of more and more increasing overapproximations. The immediate approach is to split the sets before they grow too large, and have the union of smaller sets represent the larger non-convex set.

Reduction. While splitting sets allows to maintain precision in the presence of non-convex sets, it leads to problems when the dynamics produce large sets. Especially when analyzing chaotic systems, small initial sets expand rapidly – due to the dynamics of the system, not necessarily because of inaccurate computations. This may produce a prohibitively large number of split sets. Any possibility to reduce the size of reachable sets therefore is a valuable improvement because it helps to reduce the number of sets. Our method is based on the idea that whenever a reachable set flows through a hyperplane, it can be reduced to the intersection with that hyperplane. We got the idea of reducing to transversal hyperplanes from Tucker's [24] algorithm, which reduces reachable sets after every step to axis-perpendicular hyperplanes. Bak [3] also proposed to perform reductions transversal to the flow. But in his setting, the user needs to come up with suitable reductions.

3   Verification

We formalize all of the previous "main ideas" using the interactive theorem prover Isabelle/HOL [22]. We build on Isabelle/HOL's library for multivariate analysis and the formalization of ODEs [17]. Our algorithms are formalized as monadic programs using Lammich's [19] framework. In such programs, we write $x \leftarrow y$ to bind x to the result of y, which may also fail. We write $x \in X$ to choose an arbitrary element x from the set X.

3.1   Reachability in Continuous Systems

In order to verify our algorithms, we need of course a specification. We assume a continuous system where the evolution is governed by a continuous *flow* $\varphi(x, t)$, i.e., $\varphi(\varphi(x_0, t), s) = \varphi(x_0, t + s)$. We formalize reachability with the ternary predicate $\curvearrowright$, where $X \curvearrowright_{C_X} Y$ holds if the evolution flows every point of $X \subseteq \mathbb{R}^n$ to $Y \subseteq \mathbb{R}^n$ and does not leave the set C_X in the meantime.

$$X \curvearrowright_{C_X} Y := \forall x \in X.\ \exists t \geq 0.\ \varphi(t, x_0) \in Y \wedge (\forall 0 \leq s \leq t.\ \varphi(s, x_0) \in C_X)$$

C_X can therefore be used to describe safety properties during the reachability analysis. This predicate allows to easily combine steps in reachability analysis according to the rule $X \curvearrowright_{C_X} Y \wedge Y \curvearrowright_{C_Y} Z \implies X \curvearrowright_{(C_X \cup C_Y)} Z$.

3.2   Rigorous Numerics: Affine Arithmetic

Rigorous (or *guaranteed*) numerics means computing with sets that guarantee to enclose the quantities of interest. The most basic data structure to represent sets is intervals, but those suffer from the wrapping effect – enclosing rotated boxes with boxes leads to large overapproximations. Moreover dependencies between variables are lost, e.g. for an enclosure $x \in [-1; 1]$, the term $x - x$ evaluates to $[-2; 2]$ in interval arithmetic.

Affine arithmetic [11] improves over interval arithmetic by tracking linear dependencies. For this one utilizes affine forms, represented by a list of *generators* $\langle a_0, \ldots, a_k \rangle$ with $a_i \in \mathbb{R}^n$. An affine form is the formal expression $a_0 + \sum_{0 < i \leq k} \varepsilon_i \cdot a_i$ where the formal variables ε_i are called *noise symbols*. The set $\gamma\langle a_0, \ldots, a_k \rangle$ represented by an affine form is called a *zonotope* and is given as the set of all elements when the formal variables ε_i range over $[-1; 1]$: $\gamma\langle a_0, \ldots, a_k \rangle = \{a_0 + \sum_{0 < i \leq k} \varepsilon_i \cdot a_i \mid -1 \leq \varepsilon_i \leq 1\}$

Affine forms track linear dependencies, because the formal variables are treated symbolically. Examining the dependency problem from before, if we have the affine form $1 \cdot \varepsilon_1$ representing the enclosure $x \in \gamma(1 \cdot \varepsilon_1) = [-1; 1]$, then evaluating $x - x$ in affine arithmetic yields $1 \cdot \varepsilon_1 - 1 \cdot \varepsilon_1 = 0 \cdot \varepsilon_1$. The result represents therefore the exact quantity $\{0\}$. Any linear operation $A : \mathbb{R}^n \to \mathbb{R}^n$ can be represented exactly, as it distributes over the generators of the affine form: $A(\gamma(\langle a_0, \ldots, a_k \rangle)) = \gamma\langle Aa_0, \ldots, Aa_k \rangle$. Nonlinear operations like multiplication or division are linearized, adding the linearization error as a new noise symbol. Provided with safe estimations on round-off errors, those can be included in computations with affine forms as well. In general, all kinds of uncertainties can be added using Minkowski addition $X \oplus Y = \{x + y \mid x \in X \wedge y \in Y\}$, which can be implemented efficiently for affine forms by taking a disjoint union of the generators.

3.3   Guaranteed Runge-Kutta Methods

Having presented the background on rigorous numerics, we will now concentrate on solving ODEs numerically. A classical approach is given by Runge-Kutta methods, which approximate the solution in a series of discrete steps in time. We assume from now on an autonomous ODE $\dot{x} = f(x)$ and $f \in \mathcal{C}^2(\mathbb{R}^n, \mathbb{R}^n)$ twice continuously differentiable. Recall that we denote the solution for initial value x_0 at time t with $\varphi(x_0, t)$. Runge-Kutta methods are one-step methods: they discretize the time into a *grid* of times $t_0, \ldots, t_i, \ldots$ with step size $h_i = t_{i+1} - t_i$ and compute a series of steps $x_i \approx \varphi(x_0, t_i)$. The *discretization error* $|\varphi(x_i, h_i) - x_i|$ is obtained via Taylor series expansions of the solution and the Runge-Kutta method.

Runge-Kutta methods can be turned into guaranteed methods by evaluating the approximate steps using rigorous numerics, e.g., in affine arithmetic. To be guaranteed, it is necessary to explicitly include the discretization error in the set representation. In order to obtain a safe estimate for the discretization error, one first needs to prove that the solution exists for the desired step and find an a-priori bound on the solution.

A unique solution for an initial value x_0 exists for stepsize h if the iteration given by the Picard operator $P_h : \mathcal{C}^\infty([0;h], \mathbb{R}^n) \to \mathcal{C}^\infty([0;h], \mathbb{R}^n)$ with $P_h(\varphi) = (t \mapsto x_n + \int_0^t f(\varphi(s))\mathrm{d}s)$ has a unique fixed point, which can be reduced to finding a post fixed point for an overapproximating operator $Q_h : \mathcal{P}(\mathbb{R}^n) \to \mathcal{P}(\mathbb{R}^n)$ with $Q_h(X) = X_n + [0;h] \cdot f(X)$.

cert-stepsize is defined to choose a step size h and iterate Q_h until a post fixed point C is reached, i.e., $Q_h(C) \subseteq C$. If that does not succeed, the iteration restarts with a smaller step size. *cert-stepsize* returns the chosen step size and the post fixed point, which certifies the existence of a unique solution for the chosen step size. The post fixed point also gives an *a-priori* bound on the solution:

Theorem 1 (Certification of Step). *If $x_0 \in X_0$ and cert-stepsize$(X_0) = (h, C)$, then there exists a unique solution $\varphi(x_0, [0;h]) \subseteq C$.*

The most basic Runge-Kutta method is the method of Euler, it approximates the solution $\varphi(x_0, h)$ with the linear function with the slope given by the ODE f at instant t: $\varphi(x_0, h) \approx x_0 + h \cdot f(x_0)$. The right-hand side of this approximation is exactly the first two terms of a Taylor series expansion of the solution φ. When evaluating f at different points, one can achieve that the Taylor series expansions match up to higher order, which is the idea of Runge-Kutta methods.

We verified a generic two-stage Runge-Kutta method $rk2_h(x) = x + h \cdot \psi_h(x)$, with $\psi_h(x) = (1 - \frac{1}{2p})f(x) + \frac{1}{2p}f(x + hpf(x))$. Then $rk2_h(x_0)$ approximates the solution: $|\varphi(x_0, h) - rk2_h(x_0)| \in \mathcal{O}(h^3)$. We assume $0 < p \le 1$ for the parameter p, one can choose e.g., $p = 1$, to obtain the classical method of Heun.

For non-guaranteed methods, it suffices to show via Taylor series expansions of φ and $rk2_h$ that the solution and Runge-Kutta approximation differ by some remainder term in $\mathcal{O}(h^3)$. For a guaranteed method, an explicit estimate for the remainder term is needed, which requires higher derivatives of f. We denote by $f'(x) : \mathbb{R}^n \to \mathbb{R}^n$ the derivative (the linear mapping given by the Jacobian matrix) of f at x and with $f''(x) : \mathbb{R}^n \to \mathbb{R}^n \to \mathbb{R}^n$ the derivative of f' (a bilinear mapping).

Algorithm 1. Step of Runge-Kutta method

1: **function** $rkstep(X_0)$
2:     $(h, C) \leftarrow cert\text{-}stepsize(X_0)$
3:     $R \leftarrow rk2\text{-}remainder_h(X_0, C)$
4:     $C' \leftarrow rk2\text{-}remainder_{[0;h]}(X_0, C)$
5:     $X_1 \leftarrow rk2_h(X_0) \oplus R$
6:     $X_C \leftarrow rk2_{[0;h]}(X_0) \oplus C'$
7:     $\varepsilon \leftarrow width(R)$
8:     **return** $(h, \varepsilon, X_1, X_C)$

When we set $I = [0; 1]$ and $T = [0; h]$ as enclosures for the occurring mean values, the following expression for the remainder term can be deduced and proved correct:

$$rk2\text{-}remainder_h(X, X_C) := \frac{h^3}{6} f''(X_C)\big(f(X_C)\big)\big(f(X_C)\big)+$$

$$+ \frac{h^3}{6} f'(X_C)\big(f'(X_C)(f(X_C))\big) - \frac{h^3 p}{4} f''(X + hpIf(X))\big(f(X)\big)\big(f(X)\big)$$

Theorem 2 (Remainder of Two-Stage Runge-Kutta). *If $\varphi(x_0, t) \in X$ and $\varphi(x_0, T) \subseteq X_C$, then $\varphi(x_0, h) - rk2_h(X) \in rk2\text{-}remainder_h(X, X_C)$.*

With Algorithm 1, *rkstep*, we compute one step of the guaranteed Runge-Kutta method: C is a first, rough enclosure for the solution over the interval $[0; h]$, which is used to compute a tighter enclosure X_C over the interval and an even tighter one X_1 at the time instant h. The algorithm then satisfies the following specification, which follows from Theorems 1 and 2.

Theorem 3 (Step of Runge-Kutta Method). *Assume $x_0 \in X_0$ and $rkstep(X_0) = (h, \varepsilon, X_1, X_C)$. Then there exists a unique solution $\varphi(x_0, [0; h]) \subseteq X_C$ with $\varphi(x_0, h) \in X_1$, or in terms of the reachability predicate $X_0 \curvearrowright_{X_C} X_1$.*

Note that the computation (in particular for *rk2-remainder*) requires the higher derivatives f', f'' of f, which Isabelle/HOL can automatically derive from the symbolic representation of f. The quantity ε did not occur in the specification. It gives the size of the remainder term, the discretization error. We can therefore use ε to guide step size control in section 3.7.

3.4 Splitting

In the previous section we had developed the analysis of the discretization error, which is unfortunately not the only source of error. Errors are introduced due to linearization of operations on affine forms: non-convex sets are enclosed in the convex zonotopes. These errors are quadratic in the size of the zonotope, acceptable precision can therefore be maintained if the size of the zonotopes is kept small. Zonotopes generated by $\langle a_0, \ldots, a_n \rangle$ can be split

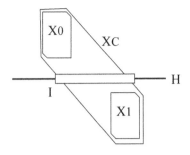

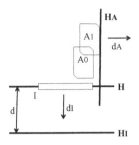

Fig. 1. Idealized reduction   **Fig. 2.** Selection of hyperplanes

by halving one of the generators a_i, i.e., setting $split\,(\langle a_0, \ldots, a_n\rangle, i) = (\langle a_0 - a_i/2, a_1, \ldots, a_{i-1}, a_i/2, a_{i+1}, \ldots, a_n\rangle, \langle a_0 + a_i/2, a_1, \ldots, a_{i-1}, a_i/2, a_{i+1}, \ldots, a_n\rangle)$
The range of the resulting zonotopes encloses the range of the argument, which follows from the definition of γ.

Theorem 4 (Splitting). $split(X) = (Y, Z) \implies \gamma(X) \subseteq \gamma(Y) \cup \gamma(Z)$.

3.5 Reduction of Reachable Sets

Too many splits impair performance, which is why the size of the reachable sets must be reduced whenever possible. The idea is to reduce reachable sets by looking at how the flow passes through a given hyperplane H.

The general idea is to start with a reachable set X_0 above the hyperplane and perform one Runge-Kutta step $rkstep(X_0) = (h, \varepsilon, X_1, X_C)$ towards a reachable set X_1 below the hyperplane, see Figure 1. The enclosure for the flow between X_0 and X_1 is given by X_C, which means that every flow that eventually reaches X_1 has to pass through the intersection $I := X_C \cap H$. Therefore the computation of reachable sets can continue with I instead of X_1, which is of advantage if I is smaller than X_1.

However, the situation is in general a bit more complicated because X_1 cannot be guaranteed to lie below H, or only with very large step sizes. Also the dynamics might just "scratch" the hyperplane, i.e., not completely passing through it. To cope with those difficulties, Algorithm 2 is used to compute the intersection of the flow from reachable set X_0 with the hyperplane H: it iterates Runge-Kutta steps until the set has passed through H. It also allows to *abort* the iteration if e.g., the flow has changed its dominating direction during the iteration.

The relation between the reachable set and the computed intersection can be expressed with the reachability predicate $X \curvearrowright_{C_X} Y$. In addition, we write $H^{\geq}$ for the half-plane above H. This allows to specify the outcome of *intersect-flow*. Every flow starting from X above the half-plane reaches the intersection.

Theorem 5 (Intersection of Flow from X with Hyperplane H).
intersect-flow$(X, H) = (A, \mathcal{X}, \mathcal{I}) \implies (X \cap H^{\geq}) \curvearrowright_{\mathcal{X}} (A \cup \bigcup_{I \in \mathcal{I}} I)$

Algorithm 2. Intersection of Flow from X with Hyperplane H

1: **function** *intersect-flow*(X, H)
2:     $\mathcal{I}, \mathcal{X} = \emptyset$
3:     **while** $\neg(X$ below $H) \wedge \neg abort(X)$ **do**
4:         $(h, \varepsilon, X_1, X_C) \leftarrow rkstep(X)$
5:         $\mathcal{I} \leftarrow \mathcal{I} \cup \{X_C \cap H\}$ ▷ intersection of zonotope with hyperplane
6:         $\mathcal{X} \leftarrow \mathcal{X} \cup \{X_C\}$
7:         $X \leftarrow X_1$
8:     **return** $(X, \mathcal{X}, \mathcal{I})$

The crucial step of Algorithm 2 is the computation of the intersection of the zonotope X_C with the hyperplane H in line 5, which can only be done approximately. The verification of this is a nontrivial task [16].

3.6 Summarization of Intersections

When the intersection is computed by flowing the reachable set through the hyperplane step by step, we get a set $\mathcal{I}$ consisting of individual intersections I_i. Many of the sets I_i usually overlap, in order to avoid redundant enclosures, it is desirable to remove the overlaps. Ideally, this could be done using set difference, an operation under which zonotopes are not closed. Therefore an overapproximation has to suffice. The overapproximation lays a grid of (hyper-)rectangles $R_k = [r_k^-; r_k^+]$ over the interval enclosure $[I^-; I^+]$ of $\bigcup_{I \in \mathcal{I}} I: [I^-; I^+] = \bigcup_k R_k$. Then we shrink every element R_k to R_k' such that the union still encloses I: $R_k' = R_k \cap [r_k'^-; r_k'^+]$ where $[r_k'^-; r_k'^+]$ is the interval enclosure of $\bigcup_{i.\ I_i \cap R_k \neq \emptyset} I_i$, i.e. the union of all I_i that overlap with R_k. This process might even remove some of the sets R_k'.

The only important proposition to prove is that the so computed collection is a safe overapproximation, i.e., we have the following theorem:

Theorem 6 (Summarization of Intersections). $\bigcup_{I \in \mathcal{I}} I \subseteq \bigcup_k R_k'$

3.7 Reachability Analysis

Up to now, we only considered single steps of the reachability analysis, either a Runge-Kutta step, or reducing a reachable set onto a hyperplane. In order to compute reachable sets for larger time intervals, these steps need to be iterated.

The whole reachability analysis algorithm consists again of several parts: The first part, *flow-towards-plane*, iterates Runge-Kutta steps to flow a collection of reachable sets towards a given hyperplane. This iteration includes step-size adaption, splitting of zonotopes, and finally the intersection. *flow-towards-plane* takes place in a loop of *reach* that decides which plane to flow to next.

Flowing towards One Plane. The loop of Algorithm 3, *flow-towards-plane*, maintains three kinds of sets: Flowing sets $\mathcal{F}$, intersected sets $\mathcal{I}$ and aborted

---

Algorithm 3. Flowing Towards one Plane

1: **function** *flow-towards-plane*($\mathcal{F}_0, H$)
2:     $\mathcal{F} \leftarrow \mathcal{F}_0, \mathcal{I} \leftarrow \emptyset, \mathcal{A} \leftarrow \emptyset$
3:     **while** $\mathcal{F} \neq \emptyset$ **do**
4:         $(X, h) \in \mathcal{F}$
5:         $\mathcal{F} \leftarrow \mathcal{F} \setminus \{X\}$
6:         **if** *width*(X) $\geq$ *max-width* **then**   ▷ splitting is needed
7:             $(X, Y) \leftarrow$ *split*(X)
8:             $\mathcal{F} \leftarrow \mathcal{F} \cup \{(X, h), (Y, h)\}$
9:         **else**
10:            $(h, \varepsilon, X_1, X_C) \leftarrow$ *rkstep*(X)
11:            **assert**(*safe*(X_C))
12:            **if** *reject*(ε) **then** $\mathcal{F} \leftarrow \mathcal{F} \cup \{(X, h/2)\}$ ▷ step size control
13:            **else if** $X_C \cap H \neq \emptyset$ **then**
14:                $(A, \mathcal{X}, \mathcal{I}') \leftarrow$ *intersect-flow*(X, H)
15:                **assert**(*safe*($\mathcal{X}$))
16:                $\mathcal{A} \leftarrow \mathcal{A} \cup \{A\}$; $\mathcal{I} \leftarrow \mathcal{I} \cup \mathcal{I}'$
17:            **else if** *abort*(X) **then**   ▷ abort when direction of flow changes
18:                $\mathcal{A} \leftarrow \mathcal{A} \cup \{X\}$
19:            **else** $\mathcal{F} \leftarrow \mathcal{F} \cup \{(X, \textit{adapt-stepsize}(h, \varepsilon))\}$ ▷ step size control
20:     **return** $(\mathcal{A}, \mathcal{I})$

---

sets $\mathcal{A}$, all reachable sets are checked to be *safe* with respect to some given specification in the loop (lines 12,17). The sets in $\mathcal{F}$ are associated with a step size h. All sets are supposed to flow towards a given plane H. Inside the loop, *flow-towards-plane* decides if sets need to be split (line 7), it performs a Runge-Kutta step in line 11 and decides from the discretization error ε whether the step size was too large and needs to be rejected (line 13). If close to the hyperplane, an intersection is performed. Sets may also be aborted when the direction of the flow changes (line 19). If otherwise successful, the step size is allowed to grow in line 22, depending on the discretization error.

Assuming that $\bigcup_{F \in \mathcal{F}_0} F \subseteq H^{\geq}$, the invariant that the algorithm maintains in its while loop is given in the following theorem.

Theorem 7 (Invariant of *flow-towards-plane*).

$$\left(\bigcup_{F \in \mathcal{F}_0} F \right) \curvearrowright_{\textit{safe}} \left(\left(\bigcup_{X \in (\mathcal{A} \cup \mathcal{F})} X \cap H^{\geq} \right) \cup \left(\bigcup_{I \in \mathcal{I}} I \cap H \right) \right)$$

The flows ending in $\mathcal{A}$ or $\mathcal{F}$ can be restricted to the half-space above, because the parts of the sets below the plane is taken care of by the intersection. They need to be restricted because it cannot be guaranteed that they are always above H (splitting might introduce overapproximations). The flows to the intersections I need to be restricted to the plane, because the computed sets can also be overapproximations.

Flowing from Plane to Plane. Algorithm *flow-towards-plane*($\mathcal{F}_0, H$) flows reachable sets from $\mathcal{F}_0$ towards a plane H and returns sets $\mathcal{I}$ that intersect the

---

Algorithm 4. Reachability from Plane to Plane

1: **function** $reach(\mathcal{F}_0)$
2:     $H \leftarrow choose\text{-}plane(\mathcal{F}_0, d), \mathcal{X} \leftarrow \emptyset, \mathfrak{F} \leftarrow \{(\mathcal{F}_0, H)\}$
3:     **while** $\mathfrak{F} \neq \emptyset$ **do**
4:         $(\mathcal{F}, H) \in \mathfrak{F}$
5:         $\mathfrak{F} \leftarrow \mathfrak{F} \setminus \{\mathcal{F}\}$
6:         $(\mathcal{A}, \mathcal{I}) \leftarrow flow\text{-}towards\text{-}plane(\mathcal{F}, H)$
7:         $H_\mathcal{A} \leftarrow choose\text{-}plane(\mathcal{A}, 0)$ ▷ aborted sets – collect as soon as possible
8:         $H_\mathcal{I} \leftarrow choose\text{-}plane(\mathcal{I}, d)$ ▷ regular intersection – collect after distance d
9:         **if** $abort(H)$ **then** $\mathcal{X} \leftarrow \mathcal{X} \cup \mathcal{I}$
10:        **else** $\mathfrak{F} \leftarrow \mathfrak{F} \cup (\mathcal{I}, H_\mathcal{I})$
11:        $\mathfrak{F} \leftarrow \mathfrak{F} \cup (\mathcal{A}, H_\mathcal{A})$
12:        **return** $\mathcal{X}$

---

plane H and sets $\mathcal{A}$ that have been aborted before. Then *choose-plane* selects different planes that determine where the sets in $\mathcal{I}$ and $\mathcal{A}$ supposed to flow next. We sketch *choose-plane* only informally: For the sets in $\mathcal{I}$, one determines the strongest direction $d_\mathcal{I}$ imposed by the dynamics and has them flow towards a plane located a certain distance d in the strongest direction and perpendicular to that direction (Figure 2). For the aborted sets in $\mathcal{A}$, one similarly determines the strongest direction $d_\mathcal{A}$, but places the plane directly next to the sets. Reducing the sets with intersections directly after switching the direction of the flow turned out to be an effective means to keep the reachable sets small. For simplicity, we only choose axis-perpendicular hyperplanes: experiments have suggested that arbitrary hyperplanes do not necessarily lead to better performance.

The final result for our reachability Algorithm 4 reads as follows: if the algorithm $reach(\mathcal{F}_0)$ returns $\mathcal{X}$, then the sets from $\mathcal{F}_0$ flow towards $\mathcal{X}$, passing only through safe sets:

Theorem 8. $reach(\mathcal{F}_0) = \mathcal{X} \implies \left(\bigcup_{F \in \mathcal{F}_0} F\right) \curvearrowright_{safe} \left(\bigcup_{X \in \mathcal{X}} X\right).$

4   Implementation

We presented our algorithms on an abstract level, but refined them (still verified in Isabelle/HOL) towards an executable specification, using Lammich's [19] framework. From the executable specification, Isabelle/HOL allows to generate Standard ML code. When executing it, we have to trust the (mostly syntactic) translation from terms in Isabelle/HOL to Standard ML. We also trust the compiler (PolyML 5.5.2) together with its library for big integers.

The working sets $\mathcal{I}, \mathcal{F}, \mathcal{A}, \mathfrak{F}$ in Algorithms 2, 3, and 4 for example are implemented using lists. Their elements, the reachable sets X, A, I are represented by affine forms, which are represented by the list of their generators $\langle a_0, \ldots, a_k \rangle$. Most of the generators of an affine form are zero, which is why affine forms are represented more efficiently as sparse lists. Moreover we keep the invariant that the sparse lists are sorted, which allows for efficient implementation of binary

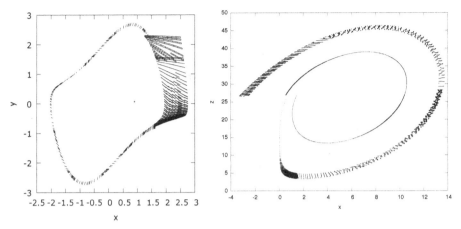

Fig. 3. Van-der-Pol, $w = 175$

Fig. 4. Least (inner) and most (outer) chaotic IVP of the Lorenz system under study

operations like addition or multiplication. Real numbers are implemented using pairs of integers $m, e \in \mathbb{Z}$, which represent the real number $m \cdot 2^e$. For these idealized floating point numbers, rounding is performed explicitly.

The abstract algorithms we presented here consist of roughly 300 lines of code in our abstract formalization. Including the library for affine arithmetic and real numbers, the generated code consists of more than 5500 lines. The verification of the algorithms presented here can be estimated with approximately 4500 lines of code, but this number does not include the mathematical background theory about ODEs, which consists of about 6000 lines.

5   Experiments

We evaluate the performance and capabilities of our algorithm on small, classical examples of nonlinear ODEs and compare our implementation with VNODE-LP (version 0.3) and the Taylor model based tool Flow* (version 1.2). Both tools perform neither splitting nor some sort of reduction. We also try to do comparisons with Bak's [3] approach, which we call Flow*-PI: Bak experiments in Flow* with manually declaring hyperplanes ("pseudo-invariants") for reduction. Recall that in contrast to Flow*-PI, our algorithm determines the hyperplanes for reductions automatically.

Van-der-Pol. For the Van-der-Pol oscillator (Figure 3, plotted from the output of our verified algorithm), which is given by the ODE $\dot{x} = y$; $\dot{y} = (1 - x^2)y - x$, we consider initial value problems $x_0 \in 1.25 + w \cdot [0, 0.01], y_0 \in [2.28; 2.32]$ and vary the size of the initial set with the parameter w. For $w = 30$, Althoff [1] reports a run-time of 23 seconds. Since different parameters (e.g., step size, order of Taylor models, error tolerance) can be chosen for the different tools, it is hard to perform an objective comparison. We tried to be fair by setting the parameters to result

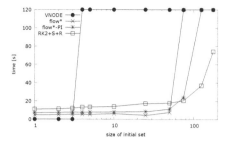 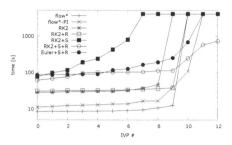

Fig. 5. Run-time for growing initial sets of the Van-der-Pol system

Fig. 6. Run-time for increasingly chaotic initial value problems of the Lorenz system

in comparable step sizes (0.01) for Flow* and our algorithm. An adaptive order of 4-6 seemed like the best compromise between performance and accuracy for Flow*, a further parameter is 10^{-5} for the remainder estimation.

Figure 5 summarizes the results of our experimentation: it shows the run-time for VNODE-LP, Flow*, Flow*-PI and our tool RK2+S+R (splitting and reduction enabled). Failed attempts are set to 120 seconds. VNODE-LP can only handle small initial sets. The tool Flow* can handle initial sets up to size $w = 50$, and takes between 3 and 8 seconds. For the same problems, our tool takes between 10 and 18 seconds. It scales with larger initial sets and is the only one that can handle $w \in \{125, 175\}$. This is due to the very effective reduction taking place at $x \approx 1.5$, when $y \approx -1$, as can be seen in Figure 3. Manually inserting hyperplanes for reduction at $y = 0$ and $x = 1.5$ allows Flow*-PI to integrate $w = 75$ in 24 seconds. We were unable to come up with hyperplanes that would allow Flow*-PI integration for larger values of w.

Lorenz. Consider the classical Lorenz system $\dot{x} = 11.8x - 0.29(x + y)z$; $\dot{y} = -22.8y + 0.29(x + y)z$; $\dot{z} = -2.67z + (x + y)(2.2x - 1.3y)$ in Jordan normal form. We experiment with 13 initial sets of width 0.005 along the line segment between $(0.74, 2.21, 27)$ and $(1.5, 2.25, 27)$. The dynamics exhibits with smaller values for x more and more chaotic behavior. Enclosures of the least and most chaotic problem (computed with our verified algorithm) are depicted in Figure 4.

We toggle the different optimizations of our tool in order to study their respective effects. Moreover we compare our tool with Flow* and Flow*-PI (VNODE-LP fails to integrate any of those problems). For Flow*-PI, we chose to reduce at $x = 2, z = 27$, and $x = 6$, which gives reductions similar to our algorithm: compare Figure 4, where one can see reductions at $x \approx 1.5$ (at $z \approx 5$) and $z = 27$ (at $x \approx 13$). The results are summarized in Figure 6 and we interpret them as follows. Flow* is fastest, but fails on the three most chaotic problems. Flow*-PI allows to solve one additional problem. The Runge-Kutta method with reduction and splitting (RK2+S+R) allows to solve all of the problems, utilizing the Euler-method (Euler+S+R) shows similar scaling behavior but is less efficient. Just RK2 and RK2 with reduction (RK2+R) are more efficient when the dynamics is less chaotic, but promptly fail (similar to Flow*) when chaos takes over. In

Table 1. Comparison for two particular IVPs of the Lorenz system

IVP	method	step size	time [s]	error(x)
#8: $(0.94, 2.16, 27)$	$rk2, 10^{-5}$	$7 \cdot 10^{-4}$	194	0.14
	$rk2, 2 \cdot 10^{-4}$	$2 \cdot 10^{-3}$	67	0.24
	$rk2, 2 \cdot 10^{-2}$	$5 \cdot 10^{-4}$	286	0.9
	Flow*	$5 \cdot 10^{-3}$	13	0.02
	Flow*-PI	$5 \cdot 10^{-3}$	16	0.3
#10: $(0.79, 2.14, 27)$	$rk2, 10^{-5}$	$2 \cdot 10^{-4}$	595	0.3
	$rk2, 2 \cdot 10^{-4}$	$6 \cdot 10^{-4}$	241	0.5
	$rk2, 2 \cdot 10^{-2}$	$1 \cdot 10^{-4}$	1648	1.3
	Flow*	$5 \cdot 10^{-4}$	121	5.8
	Flow*-PI	$5 \cdot 10^{-4}$	106	0.5

summary, this shows that splitting is essential for handling chaotic systems, but (as can be seen at RK2+S) does not scale without reduction.

For another comparison, we study the effect of different strategies for step-size adaptation: we vary the threshold of discretization error for rejecting steps between $10^{-5}, 10^{-4}, 10^{-2}$. Table 1 shows that (at least for good performance) a compromise needs to be found: small local errors require more, smaller steps, but allowing for too large local errors results in larger sets, therefore more splitting and worse performance.

Comparing the performance of $rk2, 2 \cdot 10^{-4}$ with Flow* and Flow*-PI in Table 1, we can see that on the easier problem #8, Flow* is very efficient: it achieves better precision despite larger step size. On the more complicated problem #10, Flow* fails to achieve the same accuracy, because the reachable sets grow too large. This problem is successfully addressed by the reductions performed in Flow*-PI and our method. Compared with Flow*-PI, our method achieves with slightly larger step sizes the same accuracy, it is a bit more than twice as slow, but it does not need manual interaction for choosing the reductions.

6   Conclusion

We presented a formally verified analyzer for continuous systems given by ODEs. Its performance is in the range of other, non-verified tools, and even scales better than them in the presence of large initial sets and chaotic dynamics. More importantly, our algorithm introduces a new level of mathematical rigor and therefore trust to analyzers for continuous systems.

Discussion. There is no single best approach to reachability analysis of ODEs, therefore many of our design decisions were guided heuristically. Optimizations like splitting and reduction to hyperplanes are only effective for low-dimensional systems. Concerning splitting of reachable sets, an alternative could be to use a more complex data structure like Taylor models that directly represent non-convex sets. It seems, however, that splitting is also necessary for Taylor model based analysis tools, as could be seen in section 5. Another possibility to reduce the reachable sets without geometric intersections has been proposed by Althoff [2], but it depends on the problem at hand which one is more efficient and/or precise.

Future work. Since we support intersection of reachable sets with hyperplanes, we should be able to generalize the approach to handle switching surfaces of hybrid systems. Moreover we aim to propagate more topological information (e.g. partial derivatives) of the flow in order to be able to certify the computations for the existence of the Lorenz-attractor [24].

Acknowledgements. I would like to thank the anonymous reviewers for their helpful feedback and in particular for pointing me to Bak's work [3].

References

1. Althoff, M.: Reachability analysis of nonlinear systems using conservative polynomialization and non-convex sets. In: Proceedings of the 16th International Conference on Hybrid Systems: Computation and Control, HSCC 2013, pp. 173–182. ACM, New York (2013)
2. Althoff, M., Krogh, B.H.: Avoiding geometric intersection operations in reachability analysis of hybrid systems. In: Proceedings of the 15th ACM International Conference on Hybrid Systems: Computation and Control, HSCC 2012, pp. 45–54. ACM, New York (2012)
3. Bak, S.: Reducing the wrapping effect in flowpipe construction using pseudo-invariants. In: Proceedings of the 4th ACM SIGBED International Workshop on Design, Modeling, and Evaluation of Cyber-Physical Systems, CyPhy 2014, pp. 40–43. ACM, New York (2014)
4. Balluchi, A., Casagrande, A., Collins, P., Ferrari, A., Villa, T., Sangiovanni-Vincentelli, A.L.: Ariadne: a framework for reachability analysis of hybrid automata. In: Proceedings of the 17th International Symposium on Mathematical Theory of Networks and Systems (MTNS 2006), Kyoto, Japan (July 2006)
5. Berz, M., Makino, K.: Verified integration of ODEs and flows using differential algebraic methods on high-order Taylor models. Reliable Computing 4(4), 361–369 (1998)
6. Boldo, S., Clment, F., Fillitre, J.C., Mayero, M., Melquiond, G., Weis, P.: Wave equation numerical resolution: A comprehensive mechanized proof of a C program. Journal of Automated Reasoning 50(4), 423–456 (2013)
7. Bouissou, O., Chapoutot, A., Djoudi, A.: Enclosing temporal evolution of dynamical systems using numerical methods. In: Brat, G., Rungta, N., Venet, A. (eds.) NFM 2013. LNCS, vol. 7871, pp. 108–123. Springer, Heidelberg (2013)
8. Brisebarre, N., Joldeş, M., Martin-Dorel, É., Mayero, M., Muller, J.-M., Paşca, I., Rideau, L., Théry, L.: Rigorous polynomial approximation using Taylor models in CoQ. In: Goodloe, A.E., Person, S. (eds.) NFM 2012. LNCS, vol. 7226, pp. 85–99. Springer, Heidelberg (2012)
9. Chen, X., Ábrahám, E., Sankaranarayanan, S.: Flow*: An analyzer for non-linear hybrid systems. In: Sharygina, N., Veith, H. (eds.) CAV 2013. LNCS, vol. 8044, pp. 258–263. Springer, Heidelberg (2013)

10. Collins, P., Niqui, M., Revol, N.: A validated real function calculus. Mathematics in Computer Science 5(4), 437–467 (2011)
11. de Figueiredo, L., Stolfi, J.: Affine arithmetic: Concepts and applications. Numerical Algorithms 37(1-4), 147–158 (2004)
12. Fränzle, M., Herde, C., Ratschan, S., Schubert, T., Teige, T.: Efficient solving of large non-linear arithmetic constraint systems with complex boolean structure. Journal on Satisfiability, Boolean Modeling and Computation 1, 209–236 (2007)
13. Frehse, G., Le Guernic, C., Donzé, A., Cotton, S., Ray, R., Lebeltel, O., Ripado, R., Girard, A., Dang, T., Maler, O.: SpaceEx: Scalable verification of hybrid systems. In: Gopalakrishnan, G., Qadeer, S. (eds.) CAV 2011. LNCS, vol. 6806, pp. 379–395. Springer, Heidelberg (2011)
14. Girard, A.: Reachability of uncertain linear systems using zonotopes. In: Morari, M., Thiele, L. (eds.) HSCC 2005. LNCS, vol. 3414, pp. 291–305. Springer, Heidelberg (2005)
15. Immler, F.: Formally verified computation of enclosures of solutions of ordinary differential equations. In: Badger, J.M., Rozier, K.Y. (eds.) NFM 2014. LNCS, vol. 8430, pp. 113–127. Springer, Heidelberg (2014)
16. Immler, F.: A verified algorithm for geometric zonotope/hyperplane intersection. In: Proceedings of the 2015 Conference on Certified Programs and Proofs, CPP 2015, pp. 129–136. ACM, New York (2015)
17. Immler, F., Hölzl, J.: Numerical analysis of ordinary differential equations in Isabelle/HOL. In: Beringer, L., Felty, A. (eds.) ITP 2012. LNCS, vol. 7406, pp. 377–392. Springer, Heidelberg (2012)
18. Immler, F., Hölzl, J.: Ordinary differential equations. Archive of Formal Proofs (February 2015), Formal proof development, http://afp.sf.net/devel-entries/Ordinary_Differential_Equations.shtml
19. Lammich, P.: Refinement for monadic programs. Archive of Formal Proofs (2012), Formal proof development, http://afp.sf.net/entries/Refine_Monadic.shtml
20. Makarov, E., Spitters, B.: The Picard algorithm for ordinary differential equations in Coq. In: Blazy, S., Paulin-Mohring, C., Pichardie, D. (eds.) ITP 2013. LNCS, vol. 7998, pp. 463–468. Springer, Heidelberg (2013)
21. Nedialkov, N.: Implementing a rigorous ODE solver through literate programming. In: Rauh, A., Auer, E. (eds.) Modeling, Design, and Simulation of Systems with Uncertainties, Mathematical Engineering, vol. 3, pp. 3–19. Springer, Heidelberg (2011)
22. Nipkow, T., Paulson, L.C., Wenzel, M.: Isabelle/HOL. LNCS, vol. 2283. Springer, Heidelberg (2002)
23. Platzer, A.: The complete proof theory of hybrid systems. In: Proceedings of the 2012 27th Annual IEEE/ACM Symposium on Logic in Computer Science, LICS 2012, pp. 541–550. IEEE Computer Society, Washington, DC (2012)
24. Tucker, W.: A rigorous ODE solver and Smale's 14th problem. Foundations of Computational Mathematics 2(1), 53–117 (2002)
25. Zumkeller, R.: Formal global optimisation with Taylor models. In: Furbach, U., Shankar, N. (eds.) IJCAR 2006. LNCS (LNAI), vol. 4130, pp. 408–422. Springer, Heidelberg (2006)

HYCOMP: An SMT-Based Model Checker
for Hybrid Systems*

Alessandro Cimatti, Alberto Griggio, Sergio Mover, and Stefano Tonetta

Fondazione Bruno Kessler
{cimatti,griggio,mover,tonettas}@fbk.eu

Abstract. HYCOMP is a model checker for hybrid systems based on Satisfiability Modulo Theories (SMT). HYCOMP takes as input networks of hybrid automata specified using the HyDI symbolic language. HYCOMP relies on the encoding of the network into an infinite-state transition system, which can be analyzed using SMT-based verification techniques (e.g. BMC, K-induction, IC3). The tool features specialized encodings of the automata network and can discretize various kinds of dynamics.

HYCOMP can verify invariant and LTL properties, and scenario specifications; it can also perform synthesis of parameters ensuring the satisfaction of a given (invariant) property. All these features are provided either through specialized algorithms, as in the case of scenario or LTL verification, or applying off-the-shelf algorithms based on SMT. We describe the tool in terms of functionalities, architecture, and implementation, and we present the results of an experimental evaluation.

1 Introduction

Embedded systems (e.g. control systems for railways, avionics, and space) feature the interaction of discrete systems with the environment by means of controlled and monitored variables that evolve continuously in time. The validation and verification of embedded systems designs must often take into account a model of the continuous evolution of such variables. Hybrid systems [26] are a clean modeling framework for embedded systems because they exhibit both continuous transitions ruled by flow conditions and discrete changes represented with logical formulas.

A fundamental step in the design of these systems is the validation and verification of the models, performed by checking specifications expressed e.g. as invariants, temporal-logic formulas, or scenarios. In spite of the undecidability of these problems, several verification techniques have been developed and have proved to be applicable in a wide number of cases. An emerging approach to the verification of hybrid systems is the application of techniques based on Satisfiability Modulo Theories (SMT). The hybrid system is encoded into a symbolic transition system and reachability problems are represented by means of first-order formulas, which can then be solved with SMT-based techniques. Thanks to the strong progress in the field of SMT, these approaches are increasingly applied in real settings.

---

* This work was carried out within the D-MILS project, which is partially funded under the European Commission's Seventh Framework Programme (FP7).

C. Baier and C. Tinelli (Eds.): TACAS 2015, LNCS 9035, pp. 52–67, 2015.
DOI: 10.1007/978-3-662-46681-0_4

In this paper we present HYCOMP, a symbolic model checker for hybrid systems. HYCOMP is built on top of the NUXMV model checker [9], and implements various verification techniques based on SMT. HYCOMP takes as input networks of hybrid automata specified using the HyDI symbolic language [15]. HYCOMP relies on the encoding of the network into an infinite-state transition system, which can then be analyzed using various SMT-based verification techniques provided by NUXMV (e.g. BMC, K-induction, IC3). The tool features specialized encodings of the automata network and can discretize various kinds of dynamics. HYCOMP can verify invariant and LTL properties [14], and scenario specifications [16]; it can also perform synthesis of parameters ensuring the satisfaction of a given (invariant) property [12]. The tool has been used as a research platform for developing novel verification techniques, both for hybrid systems [8,16,14,33,17] as well as for more general infinite-state systems [12,13]. Moreover, it has been used in different projects, both industrial and research-oriented ones (such the ESA-funded projects IRONCAP and HASDEL, and the FP7 project MISSA). In these projects HYCOMP turned out to be really useful to support the analysis of asynchronous systems (also in the discrete case, as a front-end to NUXMV) and to solve expressive verification problems (e.g. to verify temporal properties of real-time systems). The tool is freely available for non-commercial use and can be downloaded at http://hycomp.fbk.eu. In this paper, we focus on the technical details about HYCOMP as a tool.

Related tools. There exist several related tools and languages for the verification of hybrid systems. These tools are mainly focused on the verification of invariants and most of them compute an overapproximation of the set of the reachable states. HYTECH [24] is a model checker for linear hybrid automata, which represents the continuous part of the reachable states using polyhedra. PHAVER [21] and SPACEEX [22] model affine continuous dynamics with inputs. They check invariant properties computing an approximation of the set of the reachable states using different techniques (polyhedra and support functions). Other model checkers, HSOLVER [36], D/DT [3] and ARIADNE [6], FLOW* [10], verify invariants of non-linear hybrid systems.

KEYMAERA [35] is a theorem prover for hybrid systems. It can handle non-linear hybrid systems, with symbolic parameters and an unbounded number of components. Opposed to HYCOMP, it may require a manual user intervention during the proof process and it supports a subset of LTL properties.

HybridSAL [37] is very similar to HYCOMP. The tool encodes linear hybrid systems as infinite-state transition systems, which can be verified using the SAL [32] model checker. HybridSAL also implements other abstraction techniques (e.g. See [40]), but it does not implement the quantifier free encoding for polynomial hybrid systems. The tool cannot prove LTL properties, it does not provide verification algorithms that exploit the hybrid automata network, and is not integrated with the efficient invariant verification algorithms of NUXMV (e.g. *IC3*).

In the fragment of timed automata, the reference tool is UPPAAL [5]. It supports the model checking of a subset of TCTL (Timed Computation Tree Logic) properties. The reachability is explicit in the discrete states of the automata. The tool does not handle hybrid systems and LTL properties. Moreover, UPPAAL does not allow the user to model parametric designs.

ATMOC is an SMT-based model checker for invariant [30], LTL [28] and MITL [29] properties for symbolic timed automata.

MCMT [23] and PASSEL [27] are two other SMT-based tools for verifying parameterized systems composed by timed or linear hybrid automata. They differ since the focus is on systems with an infinite number of processes, which HYCOMP cannot handle. They cannot verify LTL and scenario specification, while only MCMT can synthesize parameters. Neither of them can analyze systems with complex dynamics.

Outline. In §2, we give a brief overview of the HyDI modeling language. In §3 we describe the tool functionalities; we provide implementation details in §4, and in §5 we present results of an empirical evaluation of HYCOMP wrt. related state-of-the-art tools. We conclude the paper in §6.

2 Modeling Language

Overview. The input language of HYCOMP is HYDI [15] (Hybrid automata with DIscrete interaction). A HYDI program describes a network of hybrid automata interacting with standard discrete synchronizations. HYDI extends the language of the NUXMV model checker (which in turn extends the language of the NUSMV model checker with infinite domain types) with specific constructs related to the hybrid semantics and to the synchronization of asynchronous processes. The network is defined in the *main* module, which declares a set of processes (defined by instantiations of modules) and a set of synchronizations. The modules contain the definition of the hybrid behavior. The discrete-time part is described with a set of discrete variables (e.g., Boolean, integer, real) and a set of formulas representing the initial states, the invariant conditions, and transition relation. The continuous-time part is described with continuous variables, flow and urgent conditions.

A simple example. Figure 1 shows a small example of communicating tanks specified in HYDI. Each tank has an input and output flow of water. The input water flows only in one of the tanks and when this tank is full, a valve switches the water flow to the other tank. While one tank is being filled with new water, the other is being emptied since there is always a flow of water that goes out of each tank.

More specifically, *tank1* and *tank2* are two instances of the module *Tank*, which is instantiated with different values of the parameters. These are a flag *initial*, which chooses which tank initially takes the incoming water, the maximum input flow, and the minimum output flow. The synchronizations connect the event *noflowin* of *tank1*, which represents the stop of flow in *tank1*, with the event *flowin*, which starts the flow in *tank2*, and vice versa.

The discrete state space of each tank is described with two variables: *state* and *flow*. The *state* variable represents the condition of the tank to be *empty*, *full*, or *half-empty/full* (either filling or emptying). The *flow* variable is a Boolean that represents if there is or not an input flow of water. The continuous variables q, inq, $outq$ represent the quantity of water that is present in the tank, the incoming quantity and the outgoing quantity, respectively.

```
MODULE main
VAR   tank1: Tank(TRUE,2,1);
      tank2: Tank(FALSE,2,1);
SYNC tank1,tank2
      EVENTS flowin,noflowin;
SYNC tank1,tank2
      EVENTS noflowin,flowin;

MODULE Tank(initial, maxin, minout)
EVENT flowin, noflowin, tau;
VAR state: {empty, half, full};
      flow: boolean; inq: continuous;
      q: continuous; outq: continuous;

INIT q=0 & (initial <-> flow)
INVAR   q>=0 & q<=100 &
      (state=empty -> q=0) &
      (state=full -> q=100)
```

```
TRANS
(EVENT=flowin -> (next(flow)=TRUE &
                  next(state)=state))&
(EVENT=noflowin -> (state=full &
                  next(flow)=FALSE &
                  next(state)=state))&
(EVENT=tau -> (next(flow)=flow)) &
  next(q)=q

FLOW
((state=empty & !flow) -> der(q)=0) &
(!(state=empty & !flow) ->
                  der(q)=der(inq)-der(outq));
FLOW
(!flow -> (der(inq)=0)) &
(flow -> (der(inq)>0 &
                  der(inq)<=maxin))&
der(outq)>=minout
```

Fig. 1. A small HYDI example

Any transition satisfying the transition and invariant conditions is valid. Therefore, the *state* variable can change only with an internal *tau* event; when q is 0 then it can pass from *half* to *empty* and backwards, while when q is 100 the state can pass from *half* to *full* and backwards; when the tank receives the event *flowin* the *flow* variable becomes true; when the tank is full, it triggers the event *noflowin* switching the *flow* variable to false. Note how the symbolic representation allows a compact definition of discrete states (there are implicitly six discrete states in the example) and discrete transitions (six in the example).

The derivative of q is always given by the difference between the rate of water flowing in and the rate of water

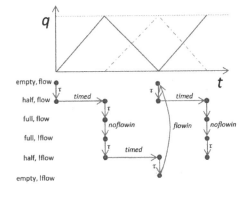

Fig. 2. A possible execution of the *tank1* process in the tank example. The lower part shows the sequence of transitions and discrete states. In the upper part, the quantity q is plotted against time (the dash line represents the quantity in the other tank).

flowing out. The water flowing in the tank is zero if the *flow* variable is false, otherwise it is positive and not greater than a *maxin* value that is passed as parameter to the *tank* module. The rate of water flowing out is instead always greater than another parameter named *maxout*.

Intuitively, the system performs discrete and continuous transitions. In the former case, the variables evolve according to the invariant and transition conditions. In the latter case, the discrete variables do not change, while the continuous variables change according to the invariant and flow conditions (with an implicit elapsing of time).

For example, Figure 2 shows a trace of *tank1* that starts from the state *empty* with *flow=TRUE* and $q=0$; then a *tau* transition changes the state into *half*; then a *timed* transition makes q reach the value *100* and another *tau* transition changes the state into *full*; in this state, *tank1* can synchronize with *tank2* switching *flow* into *FALSE*. Now a *tau* transition change the state to *half*, and another *timed* transition makes q reach the value *0*. The trace continues in this way oscillating the quantity q between *0* and *100*.

Supported continuous dynamics. HYCOMP supports different types of flow conditions. Each type enables different kinds of verification. In particular, we distinguish among the following classes of hybrid systems:

- Hybrid systems with linear constraints (see [26]), also known as *linear hybrid automata*, where the flow condition is given by symbolic constraints over the derivatives of continuous variables.
- Hybrid systems with linear ODE (see [31,22]), also known as *linear hybrid systems* where the flow condition is defined by a system of linear Ordinary Differential Equations (ODE).
- Hybrid systems with polynomial dynamics (see [20]): hybrid systems such that the continuous evolution is described with a function over time, thus without using derivatives.

In the first two cases, the flow condition is in the form $\phi(V_D) \to \psi(V_C, \dot{V}_C)$ where $\phi(V_D)$ is a formula over the discrete variables defining where the flow is valid, while $\psi(V_C, \dot{V}_C)$ is a formula over the continuous variables and their derivatives defining the actual dynamics. Both ϕ and ψ are restricted to linear arithmetic.

In the case of hybrid systems with linear constraints, ψ is a conjunction of equalities or inequalities over derivatives only (thus, without occurrences of continuous variables). The tank example falls in this class. In the case of hybrid systems with linear ODEs, ψ is a conjunction of equalities over both derivatives and continuous variables. The case of hybrid systems with polynomial dynamics, are supported with another keyword **EXPLICIT_FLOW**, which must be followed by an equality defining the next value of a continuous variable after a timed transition as a polynomial of the *delta* variable representing the elapsed time.

Supported synchronizations. Synchronizations specify if two events of two processes must happen at the same time. If two events are not synchronized, they interleave. Such synchronization is quite standard in automata theory and process algebra. It has been generalized with guards to restrict when the synchronization can happen.

Processes can share variables through the passage of parameters in the instantiations. However, they are limited to read the variables of other processes. This permits an easy identification of when the variables do not change even if the transitions are described with a generic relation (compared to a more restrictive functional description).

In order to capture the semantics of some design languages, it is necessary to enrich the synchronization with further constraints that specify a particular policy scheduling the interaction of the processes. For this reason, it is possible to specify a *scheduler* in the main module of the HYDI program in terms of state variables, initial and transition conditions. These conditions may predicate over the events of the processes.

Fig. 3. Encoding process

3 Description of Tool Functionalities

3.1 Encodings

HYCOMP implements the encoding of a hybrid automata network into *Infinite-state Transition Systems* (*ITSs*). The encoding process, shown in Figure 3, is constituted of two main phases: the *discretization* and the *interleaving encoding*. The input of this process is a HYDI program, while the resulting transition system can be exported into the NUXMV format. If the input HYDI program is purely discrete, HYCOMP supports an alternative flow in the encoding process, which can parse a discrete HYDI file into a discrete asynchronous network of components, thus bypassing the discretization phase. The *discretization* phase encodes the continuous variables, the flow and urgent conditions of the hybrid automata network into a network of discrete *ITSs*. In the *interleaving encoding*, the tool translates the interleaving of the transition systems of the network and their synchronization constraints into a synchronous composition. We refer the reader to [15,34] for the formalizaion with proofs of correctness of the encoding process.

Discretization of a process. The discretization phase translates each HYDI process P_c into a discrete HYDI process P_d (a process with no continuous variables, no flow and urgent conditions). Continuous variables are converted into discrete real variables and an additional real variable *delta* is introduced to represent the amount of time elapsed in the continuous transition. Moreover, P_c defines an additional event value *timed*, which labels the discrete transition of P_c that encodes the continuous transition of P_d.

The definition of the timed transition ensures that all the discrete variables of P_c do not change, that the amount of time elapsed is non-negative, and that the continuous variables evolve according to the flow condition and the *delta* variable. The different types of supported dynamics described in Section 2 are handled in different ways.

In the linear hybrid automata case, the predicate of the flow condition are a linear combination of the first derivatives of the continuous variables (i.e. $\sum_{x \in X} \dot{x} + a \leq 0$). The discretization encodes a linear combination as a formula P_d that relates the change of values of the variables to the amount of time elapsed `delta`. For the tank example, we have the following discretization:

```
TRANS (EVENT = timed) -> (
(delta=0 -> (next(q)=q & next(inq)=inq & next(outq)=outq)) &
((state=empty & !flow) -> next(q)=q) &
(!(state=empty & !flow) -> (
          next(q)-q=next(inq)-inq-next(outq)+outq)) &
(!flow -> (next(inq)=inq)) &
(flow -> (next(inq)-inq > 0 & next(inq)-inq <= delta*maxin)) &
next(outq)-outq >= delta*minout)
```

In the linear hybrid automata we just encode the invariant condition of P_c as **INVAR** in P_d. The encoding is correct due to the convexity of invariant conditions (that is enforced in the HYDI syntax).

In the polynomial hybrid system case, the input model already defines an explicit solution in function of `delta`. HYCOMP can also compute a polynomial explicit solution in `delta` for some linear hybrid systems. The capabilities of the tool are limited to a very simple case, where the explicit solution can be obtained by substitution (e.g. given $\dot{x} = y, \dot{y} = 1$ we can easily compute $y(t) = t + y(0)$ and $x(t) = \frac{1}{2}t^2 + y(0)t + x(0)$). Due to the possible non-linearity of the solution the invariant may be violated for some value $0 < \epsilon < delta$, even if the invariant is convex and it holds on the interval points (0 and *delta*). For this reason, HYCOMP implements a specialized encoding [17], which limits the duration of the timed transition in order to always observe the points where the invariant changes its truth value.

For linear hybrid systems, HYCOMP implements the time-aware relational abstraction encoding of [33]. The idea of relational abstraction is to obtain a formula $R(X, X')$ such that, if there is a trajectory from v to v' in the linear system, then v, v' is a model for $R(X, X')$. $R(X, X')$ over-approximates the original hybrid system and thus the resulting encoding can be used to prove safety properties.

The discretization process encodes the **URGENT** conditions that can be expressed in HYDI. An **URGENT** condition is a formula $U(V)$, where V are discrete variables, such that if $U(V)$ holds time cannot elapse. HYCOMP encodes the urgent condition as **TRANS** U(V) -> delta = 0.

The discretization process can be controlled by two additional options. The first option automatically adds a clock variable *time* that keeps track of the total amount of time elapsed in the system. The variable may complicate some verification algorithms (e.g. the *BMC* algorithm for LTL properties is completely unuseful when using this encoding, since in the transition system there are no more infinite paths where the value of the time diverges), but it may be necessary for other algorithms (e.g. the one based on local-time semantic and *K-zeno*). The second option removes from the encoding the possibility to have a path with two consecutive continuous transitions[1]. In this case the encoding adds an additional Boolean variable b, which records if the last transition was the time elapse (**EVENT** = timed -> **next**(b)) and forbids two consecutive time elapses (**EVENT** = timed -> !b).

Discretization of the network. HYCOMP can perform two different encodings of hybrid automata networks, one based on *global-time semantics* and the other on *local-time semantics* [4]. The global-time semantic captures the standard semantic of a network of hybrid automata: time elapses in all the automata in the network and for the same duration. Instead, in the local-time semantic each automaton keeps the total amount of time elapsed in a local clock variable, which is incremented *independently* by each automaton. In this way, time may elapse in one automaton but not in the others. The encoding also forces that, when automata synchronize, they must also agree on the value of their local time clocks. The same condition on clocks is also required at the end of a run.

---

[1] The option is not sound for the encoding of polynomial hybrid systems.

Global-time and local-time semantic are encoded using synchronization constraints. For the global-time semantic, HYCOMP adds a strong synchronization constraint between each pair of automata in the network. For the tank example, it would add the following **SYNC** constraint:

```
SYNC tank1,tank2  EVENTS timed, timed
   CONDITION tank1.delta = tank2.delta;
```

The **CONDITION** constraint must hold when there is the synchronization.

HYCOMP encodes the local-time semantic changing each synchronization condition and invariant property of the system. The encoding forces that the local time variable of the automata must have the same value when there is a synchronization. In the tank example, HYCOMP would create the following **SYNC** constraints:

```
SYNC tank1, tank2  EVENTS flowin, noflowin
   CONDITION tank1.time = tank2.time;
SYNC tank1, tank2 EVENTS noflowin, flowin
   CONDITION tank1.time = tank2.time;
```

The same condition about time has to be enforced also on **INVARSPEC** properties. HYCOMP encodes each property **INVARSPEC** P as **INVARSPEC** S -> P, where S encodes the equality of all the local time variables of the network processes.

Interleaving encoding. In order to convert the asynchronous composition of the processes into a synchronous composition, HYCOMP adds to each process an additional event, *stutter*. This represents an additional transition where the process remains in the same state while the other processes move. Then, HYCOMP encodes the synchronization constraints as an additional global **TRANS** constraints. The encoding of the first **SYNC** declaration of the tank example is:

```
TRANS tank1.EVENT = flowin <-> tank2.EVENT = noflowin
```

HYCOMP provides two additional options. The *step semantic* relaxes the interleaving encoding allowing to execute in parallel several independent transitions. The other option allows to generate an encoding partitioned by the values of the **EVENT** variable.

3.2 Verification

HYCOMP provides the possibility to verify different kinds of properties, namely invariants, LTL, and scenario specifications. These are based on different verification algorithms, which work either directly on the network of asynchronous ITSs (scenario verification, *BMC* using shallow synchronization) or on the synchronous transition system (*BMC, IC3, K-induction*).

Invariant Properties. HYCOMP implements several algorithms to verify invariant properties. The property is expressed as a first-order formula over the state variables of the hybrid automata network. The tool can either prove or falsify the property and, in the latter case, construct a finite path that witnesses the violation.

HYCOMP verifies invariant properties by using several SMT-based algorithms implemented in NUXMV: *IC3*, *K-induction*, their combination with implicit predicate abstraction [38,13] and Bounded Model Checking (BMC). HYCOMP implements specialized BMC encodings for networks of hybrid automata: the tool implements a BMC encoding that alternates continuous and discrete transitions [1] and the *shallow synchronization* encoding [8], which exploits local-time semantic to obtain shorter counterexample paths.

We note that all the verification algorithms are enabled when the encoding is expressed in *Linear Real Arithmetic Theory*. This is the case if the hybrid automaton is linear or when using time-aware relational abstraction, but it is not the case for polynomial hybrid systems. The limitation is due to the integration of an SMT solver supporting the *Theory of Reals* (i.e. support for polynomials), since the tool only provides an experimental implementation of BMC that uses the Z3 or ISAT [2] SMT-solvers[3].

LTL Properties. The tool allows the user to verify LTL properties interpreted over discrete sequences of states. It implements a specialized algorithm, *K-zeno* [14], which is based on a reduction of liveness to the reachability of an accepting condition and excludes Zeno paths (unrealistic paths where time does not diverge) from the analysis.

HYCOMP allows the user to call the NUXMV BMC algorithms for LTL verification to find a violation to the LTL property. However, in this case the Zeno paths of the hybrid automata are excluded in the encoding of the hybrid automata network using a fairness condition (i.e. a condition that holds infinitely often) that enforces the divergence of time. Note that the BMC algorithms will only find lasso-shaped paths.

Scenario Specifications. The last kind of specification verified by HYCOMP are scenarios: a scenario allows a user to specify the exchange of messages in a network of hybrid automata. The scenario specifications supported by HYCOMP are a variant of Message Sequence Charts (MSC). For all the automata in the network, an MSC defines a sequence of events (i.e. labels of the automata) and constraints evaluated when an event happens (e.g. the system must execute an event within a given amount of time). The MSC is *feasible* if there exists a path in the hybrid automata network that simulates it and that also satisfies the MSC constraints. Otherwise, the MSC is *unfeasible*.

HYCOMP implements two different approaches to verify scenario specifications. In one approach, the tool reduces the problem of scenario verification to a reachability problem, using an automaton to monitor the MSC feasibility. The other approach [16] exploits local-time semantic and consists of a specialized BMC encoding of the problem. The approach may either find a witness of feasibility or prove that a scenario is not feasible, using a variant of *K-induction*.

3.3 Parameter Synthesis

The tool allows the user to synthesize the set of parameter values of the system that guarantee its safe behavior. For example, the tool may be used to automatically syn-

---

[2] http://z3.codeplex.com, http://projects.avacs.org/projects/isat

[3] HYCOMP does not link or distribute Z3 or ISAT, which should be installed by the end user.

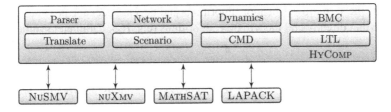

Fig. 4. HYCOMP architecture

thesize timeout values or deadlines that the system must guarantee (e.g. the maximum timeout to send a packet in a communication protocol).

In our framework, parameters are specified as **FROZENVAR** (a variable that never change its value during the system execution) and the safe behavior as an invariant property. The tool returns a formula of the parameters that represents the (possibly non-convex) feasible region of parameters.

HYCOMP uses the parameter synthesis algorithm implemented in NUXMV [12].

4 Tool Architecture and Implementation Details

4.1 Architecture

In Figure 4 we show the architecture of the tool. HYCOMP uses as libraries the model checkers NUSMV and NUXMV [9] and the MathSAT [18] SMT solver.

HYCOMP uses several data structures and functions from NUSMV: its formula representation and manipulation package, its type system, its functions for flattening of hierarchical modules and its representation of transition systems.

HYCOMP uses the SMT-based algorithms implemented in NUXMV (e.g. *IC3*, *K-induction*, BMC, parameter synthesis) and also the NUXMV front-end to MathSAT. The front-end exposes the MathSAT functionalities (satisfiability check, incremental interface, extraction of unsat cores and interpolants), provides an automatic declaration of the variables in the solver and an automatic conversion from different formula representations (NUXMV and MathSAT representations). Finally HYCOMP also uses the linear algebra library LAPACKE[4] for the computation of relational abstractions.

The internal architecture of the tool is represented in the upper part of Figure 4. The tool is divided in packages that clearly separate different functionalities. The *parser* package is used to parse and type check a HYDI file. The results of this phase is a network of hybrid automata. The data structures that represent networks of hybrid automata and of transition systems are defined in the *network* package. All the encoding process is contained in the *translate* package, which also provides the functions to discretize continuous dynamics. Different representations of a continuous system and functions used to manipulate them are defined in the *dynamics* package. The verification algorithms for LTL verification is implemented in the *ltl* package, while the specialized BMC algorithms are implemented in the *bmc* package. Finally, the package *scenario*

---

[4] http://www.netlib.org/lapack/

implements the scenario verification algorithms and the *cmd* package provides the user commands that directly call the NUXMV algorithms (e.g. *IC3*, parameter synthesis).

4.2 Implementation Details

Network representation. HYCOMP represents asynchronous network of processes, which can be either hybrid automata or transition systems. The data structure is agnostic of the process type and provides common functionalities to represent and manipulate synchronization constraints. One of these is the computation of the transitive closure of synchronizations (in HYDI, if there is a synchronization between the event a of p_1 and the event b of p_2, and another synchronization between the event b of p_2 and the event c of p_3, then there is an implicit synchronization between a of p_1 and c of p_3). HYCOMP represents the graph of synchronizations, where nodes are processes and undirected edges are synchronizations, and computes its transitive closure.

Mapback of results. While the user is aware of the existence of the various encoding phases, the tool hides all the artifacts of the encoding. This is important to avoid misunderstanding and allows for modifying the encoding in the future. The encoding phases keep a map from a symbol in the source model to its correspondent symbol in the encoding (e.g. a continuous variable is mapped to the real variable used in the discrete encoding). Since we have several transformations (discretization and encoding of interleaving) we have several maps, which can be composed and inverted, to map the results obtained during verification (e.g. counterexample paths) to the original model.

Symbolic enumeration of discrete locations. The discretization in the case of linear hybrid systems requires to reason on a system of ODEs. Since the input is symbolic, HYCOMP has to enumerate the set of discrete locations and, for each one of them, compute the correspondent system of ODEs. For example, consider the following **FLOW**:

```
FLOW der(x) = x & (b -> der(y) = 1) & (!b -> der(y) = 0);
```

If b is true, then the linear system is `der(x) = x & der(y) = 1`, otherwise we have `der(x) = x & der(y) = 0`. HYCOMP enumerates all the possible disjoint subsets of discrete locations using MathSAT. The idea is to use an additional Boolean variable for each discrete condition in the flow declarations (e.g. the variable `f0` for TRUE, `f1` for `b` and `f2` for `!b`), encoding that the variable is true if and only if the condition is true (e.g. `f0 <-> TRUE && f1 <-> b && f2 <-> !b`). Then, MathSAT enumerates all the possible satisfying partial models formed by the Boolean variables (in the example they are `f0 & f1 & !f2` and `f0 & !f1 & f2`). Each partial model identifies a symbolic discrete location where the **FLOW** is a system of ODEs.

5   Experimental Evaluation

We show an experimental comparison on the verification of invariant properties on timed and linear hybrid automata. This comparison is novel and complements the comparisons for LTL, scenario verification, and parameter synthesis presented in previous papers [14,16,12].

	IC3-IA		IC3-IA-ALT		UPPAAL		UPPAAL-RED	
	#p	time	#p	time	#p	time	#p	time
Csma-cd	12	2608.94	14	258.22	6	18.50	6	251.96
Fischer	8	1466	14	476.88	11	312.48	11	401.67
FischerSAL	6	258.15	5	463.92	11	356.49	11	451.35
HDDI	14	220.77	14	224.55	14	2.21	14	3.07
Lynch-Mahata	8	1710.81	6	494.12	11	416.69	11	534.05
All instances	48	6265	53	1918	**53**	**1106**	53	1642

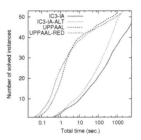

Fig. 6. Cumulative plot on mutex properties

Fig. 5. Results on mutual exclusion properties. **#p** is the total number of instances solved and **time** the time in seconds took to solve them.

The main goal of the experimental evaluation is to position the tool with respect to the existing state of the art and not to evaluate the algorithms. For the latter goal, one would need more benchmarks and properties.

All the experiments have been performed on a cluster of 64-bit Linux machines with a 2.7 Ghz Intel Xeon X5650 CPU, with a memory limit of 4Gb and a time limit of 900 seconds. The HYCOMP tool and the benchmarks used in the experiments are available at https://es.fbk.eu/people/mover/tests/tacas15hycomp.tar.bz2.

5.1 Timed Automata

We compared HYCOMP with UPPAAL [5] on timed automata benchmarks obtained either from the UPPAAL or the MCMT [23] distributions, converting the benchmark in the HYDI language. We selected the following benchmarks: the *Fischer* protocol, one of its variant, *FischerSAL*, the *Csma-cd* protocol, the *HDDI* protocol and the *Lynch-Mahata* protocol. For each benchmark we checked the mutual exclusion property and we generated several invariant properties, which specify that a specific configuration of locations in the network is not reachable. We generated several instances of the benchmarks increasing the number of processes.

For HYCOMP, we run *IC3* with implicit predicate abstraction (*IC3-IA*), the BMC implementation that alternates timed and discrete transitions (*BMC*) and *IC3* on the encoding that avoids two consecutive timed transition (*IC3-IA-ALT*). In all the cases, we used the global-time semantic. For UPPAAL, we used two different configurations[5]: in the first one (UPPAAL) we used Different Bounded Matrices representation, while in the second one (UPPAAL-RED) we used the minimal constraint systems representation.

In Figure 6 and Table 5 we show the comparison on the mutual exclusion properties. We see that UPPAAL is generally faster than *IC3-IA-ALT* and *IC3-IA*. In detail, *IC3-IA* and *IC3-IA-ALT* outperform UPPAAL on two benchmarks, while they are worse on the other three: there are several instances that can be solved by UPPAAL and not by HYCOMP and vice-versa.

In Figure 7 we show the results verifying the automatically generated properties. UPPAAL solves more instances (325 in 14581 sec.) than *IC3-IA-ALT* (290 in 4776 sec).

---

[5] In both cases we used the version 4.0.14 of UPPAAL with the options "*-n 0, -o 0, -s 1*".

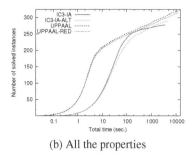 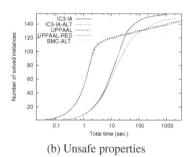

(b) All the properties   (b) Unsafe properties

Fig. 7. Cumulative plot on the automatically generated properties

	IC3-IA		IC3-IA-ALT		SPACEEX	
	#p	time	#p	time	#p	time
Distributed Controller	**14**	402.56	14	451.08	1	0.69
Fischer	5	905.82	**5**	558.49	3	74.73
Nuclear Reactor	14	783.02,	**14**	96.67	1	26.99
Navigation safe	28	1823.25	28	1768.78	**28**	43.76
Navigation-double safe	**17**	3213.59	16	3198.29	13	1599.16
Navigation unsafe	28	3280.17	28	4525.07	**28**	43.74
Navigation-double unsafe	**17**	4722.68	13	2438.36	14	2496.69
All instances	**123**	15131	118	13037	46	1745

Fig. 8. Results on LHA benchmarks. **#p** is the total number of instances solved and **time** the time in seconds took to solve them.

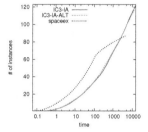

Fig. 9. Cumulative plot for LHA benchmarks

If we focus on unsafe properties, we see that *IC3-IA* (155 in 983 sec.) and *IC3-IA-ALT* (149 in 2274 sec.) are more effective than UPPAAL (146 in 3426 sec.).

5.2   Linear Hybrid Automata

We compared HYCOMP and SPACEEX [22] on the verification of invariant properties of the following linear hybrid automata benchmarks: an LHA version of the *Fischer* protocol [2], the control of nuclear reactor of [39] (*Nuclear Reactor*), the model of a robot controller [25] (*Distributed Controller*) and two LHA variants (*Navigation, Navigation-double*) of the navigation benchmark [19]. *Navigation* models describe the movement of an object in an $n \times n$ grid of square cells, which will eventually reach a stable region. *Navigation-double* is a variant with two grids and two objects.

For all the benchmarks, except the navigation ones, we checked a mutual exclusion property and we generated several instances increasing the number of components in the network. For *Navigation* and *Navigation-double*, we increased the number of cells in the grid and considered a safe and an unsafe property (the object is in the stability region after or before a given time).

For HYCOMP, we run *IC3-IA* and *IC3-IA-ALT*, while for SPACEEX we used the *phaver* scenario. We show the results of the comparison in Figure 9 and Table 8.

6 Conclusion

We presented HYCOMP, an SMT-based model checker for hybrid systems. The tool features an expressive input language and a rich set of functionalities, such as verification of invariant and LTL properties, verification of scenario specifications and parameter synthesis. We demonstrated the potential of the tool, showing its competitiveness with the state of the art.

We plan to develop HYCOMP in several directions, adding algorithms for abstraction-refinement in presence of complex dynamics, integrating more expressive specifications such as HRELTL and improving the underlying SMT-based verification algorithms. We also have plans to integrate HYCOMP in analysis tools for safety assessment (XSAP [7]) and contract-based design (OCRA [11]).

References

1. Ábrahám, E., Becker, B., Klaedtke, F., Steffen, M.: Optimizing bounded model checking for linear hybrid systems. In: Cousot, R. (ed.) VMCAI 2005. LNCS, vol. 3385, pp. 396–412. Springer, Heidelberg (2005)
2. Alur, R., Dang, T., Ivancic, F.: Counterexample-guided predicate abstraction of hybrid systems. Theor. Comput. Sci. 354(2), 250–271 (2006)
3. Asarin, E., Dang, T., Maler, O.: The d/dt Tool for Verification of Hybrid Systems. In: Brinksma, E., Larsen, K.G. (eds.) CAV 2002. LNCS, vol. 2404, pp. 365–370. Springer, Heidelberg (2002)
4. Bengtsson, J.E., Jonsson, B., Lilius, J., Yi, W.: Partial order reductions for timed systems. In: Sangiorgi, D., de Simone, R. (eds.) CONCUR 1998. LNCS, vol. 1466, pp. 485–500. Springer, Heidelberg (1998)
5. Bengtsson, J., Larsen, K.G., Larsson, F., Pettersson, P., Yi, W.: Uppaal - a tool suite for automatic verification of real-time systems. In: Alur, R., Sontag, E.D., Henzinger, T.A. (eds.) HS 1995. LNCS, vol. 1066, pp. 232–243. Springer, Heidelberg (1996)
6. Benvenuti, L., Bresolin, D., Collins, P., Ferrari, A., Geretti, L., Villa, T.: Assume guarantee verification of nonlinear hybrid systems with ariadne. International Journal of Robust and Nonlinear Control 24(4), 699–724 (2014)
7. Bozzano, M., Villafiorita, A.: The FSAP/NuSMV-SA Safety Analysis Platform. STTT 9(1), 5–24 (2007)
8. Bu, L., Cimatti, A., Li, X., Mover, S., Tonetta, S.: Model checking of hybrid systems using shallow synchronization. In: Hatcliff, J., Zucca, E. (eds.) FMOODS/FORTE 2010. LNCS, vol. 6117, pp. 155–169. Springer, Heidelberg (2010)
9. Cavada, R., Cimatti, A., Dorigatti, M., Griggio, A., Mariotti, A., Micheli, A., Mover, S., Roveri, M., Tonetta, S.: The NUXMV Symbolic Model Checker. In: Biere, A., Bloem, R. (eds.) CAV 2014. LNCS, vol. 8559, pp. 334–342. Springer, Heidelberg (2014)
10. Chen, X., Ábrahám, E., Sankaranarayanan, S.: Flow*: An analyzer for non-linear hybrid systems. In: Sharygina, N., Veith, H. (eds.) CAV 2013. LNCS, vol. 8044, pp. 258–263. Springer, Heidelberg (2013)
11. Cimatti, A., Dorigatti, M., Tonetta, S.: OCRA: A tool for checking the refinement of temporal contracts. In: ASE, pp. 702–705 (2013)
12. Cimatti, A., Griggio, A., Mover, S., Tonetta, S.: Parameter synthesis with IC3. In: FMCAD, pp. 165–168 (2013)

13. Cimatti, A., Griggio, A., Mover, S., Tonetta, S.: IC3 modulo theories via implicit predicate abstraction. In: Ábrahám, E., Havelund, K. (eds.) TACAS 2014 (ETAPS). LNCS, vol. 8413, pp. 46–61. Springer, Heidelberg (2014)
14. Cimatti, A., Griggio, A., Mover, S., Tonetta, S.: Verifying LTL properties of hybrid systems with K-LIVENESS. In: Biere, A., Bloem, R. (eds.) CAV 2014. LNCS, vol. 8559, pp. 424–440. Springer, Heidelberg (2014)
15. Cimatti, A., Mover, S., Tonetta, S.: Hydi: A language for symbolic hybrid systems with discrete interaction. In: EUROMICRO-SEAA, pp. 275–278 (2011)
16. Cimatti, A., Mover, S., Tonetta, S.: Smt-based scenario verification for hybrid systems. Formal Methods in System Design 42(1), 46–66 (2013)
17. Cimatti, A., Mover, S., Tonetta, S.: Quantifier-free encoding of invariants for hybrid systems. Formal Methods in System Design 45(2), 165–188 (2014)
18. Cimatti, A., Griggio, A., Schaafsma, B.J., Sebastiani, R.: The mathSAT5 SMT solver. In: Piterman, N., Smolka, S. (eds.) TACAS 2013. LNCS, vol. 7795, pp. 93–107. Springer, Heidelberg (2013)
19. Fehnker, A., Ivančić, F.: Benchmarks for hybrid systems verification. In: Alur, R., Pappas, G.J. (eds.) HSCC 2004. LNCS, vol. 2993, pp. 326–341. Springer, Heidelberg (2004)
20. Fränzle, M.: What Will Be Eventually True of Polynomial Hybrid Automata? In: Kobayashi, N., Babu, C. S. (eds.) TACS 2001. LNCS, vol. 2215, pp. 340–359. Springer, Heidelberg (2001)
21. Frehse, G.: PHAVer: algorithmic verification of hybrid systems past HyTech. STTT 10(3), 263–279 (2008)
22. Frehse, G., Le Guernic, C., Donzé, A., Cotton, S., Ray, R., Lebeltel, O., Ripado, R., Girard, A., Dang, T., Maler, O.: SpaceEx: Scalable verification of hybrid systems. In: Gopalakrishnan, G., Qadeer, S. (eds.) CAV 2011. LNCS, vol. 6806, pp. 379–395. Springer, Heidelberg (2011)
23. Ghilardi, S., Ranise, S.: MCMT: A model checker modulo theories. In: Giesl, J., Hähnle, R. (eds.) IJCAR 2010. LNCS, vol. 6173, pp. 22–29. Springer, Heidelberg (2010)
24. Henzinger, T.A., Ho, P., Wong-Toi, H.: HYTECH: A Model Checker for Hybrid Systems. STTT 1(1-2), 110–122 (1997)
25. Henzinger, T.A., Ho, P.H.: Hytech: The cornell hybrid technology tool. In: Antsaklis, P.J., Kohn, W., Nerode, A., Sastry, S.S. (eds.) HS 1994. LNCS, vol. 999, pp. 265–293. Springer, Heidelberg (1995)
26. Henzinger, T.A.: The theory of hybrid automata. In: LICS, pp. 278–292 (1996)
27. Johnson, T.T., Mitra, S.: A small model theorem for rectangular hybrid automata networks. In: Giese, H., Rosu, G. (eds.) FMOODS/FORTE 2012. LNCS, vol. 7273, pp. 18–34. Springer, Heidelberg (2012)
28. Kindermann, R., Junttila, T., Niemelä, I.: Beyond Lassos: Complete SMT-Based Bounded Model Checking for Timed Automata. In: Giese, H., Rosu, G. (eds.) FORTE 2012 and FMOODS 2012. LNCS, vol. 7273, pp. 84–100. Springer, Heidelberg (2012)
29. Kindermann, R., Junttila, T.A., Niemelä, I.: Bounded Model Checking of an MITL Fragment for Timed Automata. In: ACSD, pp. 216–225 (2013)
30. Kindermann, R., Junttila, T.A., Niemelä, I.: Smt-based induction methods for timed systems. In: Jurdziński, M., Ničković, D. (eds.) FORMATS 2012. LNCS, vol. 7595, pp. 171–187. Springer, Heidelberg (2012)
31. Lafferriere, G., Pappas, G.J., Yovine, S.: Symbolic Reachability Computation for Families of Linear Vector Fields. J. Symb. Comput. 32(3), 231–253 (2001)
32. de Moura, L., Owre, S., Rueß, H., Rushby, J., Shankar, N., Sorea, M., Tiwari, A.: SAL 2. In: Alur, R., Peled, D.A. (eds.) CAV 2004. LNCS, vol. 3114, pp. 496–500. Springer, Heidelberg (2004)

33. Mover, S., Cimatti, A., Tiwari, A., Tonetta, S.: Time-aware relational abstractions for hybrid systems. In: EMSOFT, pp. 1–10 (2013)
34. Mover, S.: Verification of Hybrid Systems using Satisfiability Modulo Theories. Ph.D. thesis, University of Trento (2014)
35. Platzer, A., Quesel, J.-D.: KeYmaera: A Hybrid Theorem Prover for Hybrid Systems (System Description). In: Armando, A., Baumgartner, P., Dowek, G. (eds.) IJCAR 2008. LNCS (LNAI), vol. 5195, pp. 171–178. Springer, Heidelberg (2008)
36. Ratschan, S., She, Z.: Safety verification of hybrid systems by constraint propagation-based abstraction refinement. ACM Trans. Embedded Comput. Syst. 6(1) (2007)
37. Tiwari, A.: HybridSAL Relational Abstracter. In: Madhusudan, P., Seshia, S.A. (eds.) CAV 2012. LNCS, vol. 7358, pp. 725–731. Springer, Heidelberg (2012)
38. Tonetta, S.: Abstract model checking without computing the abstraction. In: Cavalcanti, A., Dams, D.R. (eds.) FM 2009. LNCS, vol. 5850, pp. 89–105. Springer, Heidelberg (2009)
39. Wang, F.: Symbolic parametric safety analysis of linear hybrid systems with bdd-like data-structures. IEEE Trans. Software Eng. 31(1), 38–51 (2005)
40. Zutshi, A., Sankaranarayanan, S., Tiwari, A.: Timed Relational Abstractions for Sampled Data Control Systems. In: Madhusudan, P., Seshia, S.A. (eds.) CAV 2012. LNCS, vol. 7358, pp. 343–361. Springer, Heidelberg (2012)

C2E2: A Verification Tool for Stateflow Models

Parasara Sridhar Duggirala[1], Sayan Mitra[2], Mahesh Viswanathan[1],
and Matthew Potok[2]

[1] Department of Computer Science, University of Illinois at Urbana Champaign
{duggira3,vmahesh}@illinois.edu
[2] Department of Electrical and Computer Engineering,
University of Illinois at Urbana Champaign
mitras@illinois.edu

Abstract. Mathworks' Stateflow is a predominant environment for modeling embedded and cyber-physical systems where control software interacts with physical processes. We present Compare-Execute-Check-Engine (C2E2)—a verification tool for continuous and hybrid Stateflow models. It checks bounded time invariant properties of models with nonlinear dynamics, and discrete transitions with guards and resets. C2E2 transforms the model, generates simulations using a validated numerical solver, and then computes reachtube over-approximations with increasing precision. For this last step it uses annotations that have to be added to the model. These annotations are extensions of proof certificates studied in Control Theory and can be automatically obtained for linear dynamics. The C2E2 algorithm is sound and it is guaranteed to terminate if the system is robustly safe (or unsafe) with respect to perturbations of guards and invariants of the model. We present the architecture of C2E2, its workflow, and examples illustrating its potential role in model-based design, verification, and validation.

1 Introduction

Cyber-physical systems (CPS) are systems that involve the close interaction between a software controller and a physical plant. The state of the physical plant evolves continuously with time and is often modeled using ordinary differential equations (ODE). The software controller, on the other hand, evolves through discrete steps and these steps influence the evolution of the physical process. This results in a "hybrid" behavior of discrete and continuous steps that makes the formal analysis of these models particularly challenging, so much so, that even models that are mathematically extremely simple are computationally intractable. In addition, many physical plants have complicated continuous dynamics that are described by nonlinear differential equations. Such plants, even without any interaction with a controlling software, are often unamenable to automated analysis.

On the other hand, the widespread deployment of CPS in safety critical scenarios like automotives, avionics, and medical devices, have made formal, automated analysis of such systems necessary. This is evident from the extensive activity in the research community [20,19,7]. Given the challenges of formally verifying CPS, the sole analysis technique that is commonly used to analyze nonlinear systems is numerical simulation. However, given the large, uncountable space of behaviors, using numerical simulations

© Springer-Verlag Berlin Heidelberg 2015
C. Baier and C. Tinelli (Eds.): TACAS 2015, LNCS 9035, pp. 68–82, 2015.
DOI: 10.1007/978-3-662-46681-0_5

to discover design flaws is like searching for a needle in the proverbial haystack. In this paper we present a tool C2E2 (Compare-Execute-Check-Engine) that leverages the power of numerical simulations to formally prove or disprove the safety of CPS over a bounded time interval.

Systems analyzed by C2E2 are described using Mathworks™ Stateflow™ diagrams. Stateflow is the predominant, even de facto standard, environment for designing and developing embedded and CPS both in the industry and in academia. C2E2 interprets Stateflow designs as hybrid automata [14], which is a popular mathematical model, with precise semantics, for describing CPS. The models given as input to C2E2 must be *annotated*. The annotations here are similar in spirit to code assertions and contracts used in the software verification domain. Each mode in the Stateflow diagram has to be annotated with what we call a *discrepancy function* by the user. Discrepancy functions are a generalization of several proof certificates used in control theory for analyzing convergence and divergence of trajectories. In [8] we define discrepancy functions and discuss how they can be computed automatically for a reasonably expressive class of models. C2E2 transforms the input model and compiles it with a numerical simulation library to produce a validated simulator for the model. This simulator is then used for computing increasingly precise reach set over-approximations until it proves or disproves the bounded time safety property.

Our simulation based verification approach underlying C2E2, was first presented in [8] and was subsequently used for a significant case study in [9]. The current paper outlines several enhancements to the C2E2 tool that have been made since then. First the verification algorithm presented in [8] only worked for *switched systems* [1] where the time of mode switches is explicitly given in the input. In this paper, we extend the algorithm to analyze "full hybrid automata", i.e., continuous variables can be reset on mode switches, and mode switches take place based on enabling guards rather than explicitly given times. These theoretical improvements enable us to use C2E2 on a new set of examples. We report our experience in using C2E2 on these examples and its performance as experimental results. Next, C2E2 has been engineered to be more robust, moving from an in-house prototype, to something that can be used by the wider academic community. Finally, the tool now has a few additional features that make for a better user experience. First, it has been integrated with Stateflow, to make it useful for a wider community. Second, it can be used through a graphical user interface. And lastly, visualization tools have been added to enable users to plot various aspects of the reachable state space.

1.1   Related Work

Tools for verifying CPS vary widely based on the complexity of the complexity of the continuous dynamics. Uppaal [15], HyTech [11], and SpaceEx [10] are tools verifying timed automata, rectangular hybrid automata and linear hybrid automata respectively. Current tools available for verifying nonlinear dynamics are d/dt [2], Flow* [5] and Ariadne [3]. Typically these tools use symbolic methods for computing reachable set

---

[1] Switched system here refers to a design where the state of the physical plant does not change when a discrete transition is taken.

of states (or their overapproximations) from a given initial set for inferring safety of the system. Such tools provide formal soundness guarantees, however, do not provide relative completeness. Further, these tools do not analyze Stateflow models and hence a user has to specify model in the a specific input language, which requires additional learning curve for using these tools.

Given the popularity of Simulink-Stateflow framework to model CPS, there are several MATLAB based tools which verify such models. Breach [7] uses sensitivity analysis for analyzing MTL properties of systems using simulations. This analysis is sound and relatively complete for linear systems, but does not provide formal guarantees for nonlinear systems. S-Taliro [19] is a falsification engine that searches for counterexamples using Monte-Carlo techniques and hence provides only probabilistic guarantees. STRONG [6] uses robustness analysis for coverage of all executions from the initial set, using Lyapunov functions, however cannot handle nonlinear systems. C2E2, although requires additional annotations, can handle nonlinear systems specified in Stateflow and provide rigorous soundness and completeness guarantees. The simulation based verification algorithm in [8] has been extended for more general properties in [9] and to networked input output systems in [13].

2   Hybrid Models and Safety Verification

Hybrid automata is a convenient and widely used mathematical framework for modeling CPS. One of its key features is that it combines two distinct modeling styles, namely, differential equations and automata. For CPS, this enables the physical environment to be modeled by differential equations and software and communication to modeled by discrete state transitions.

Figure 1(a) shows an example of a simplified hybrid model of cardiac cell with a pacemaker created using Mathworks' Stateflow. The pacemaker has two modes or *locations* of operation: in the *stimOn* mode the cell is electrically stimulated by the pacemaker, and in *stimOff* the stimulus is absent. The continuous variables u and v model certain electrical properties of the cell. The stimulus is applied to the cell at regular time intervals as measured by the clock t. The resulting evolution of one of the continuous variables over time is shown in Figure 1(b).

Although there is no published formal semantics of Stateflow models, it is standard to consider them as hybrid automata [17,12,7]. Let us denote the set of all the variables (both continuous and discrete) in the model as the set V. This set includes a special variable *loc* to denote the current location. In this case, *loc* can be either *stimOff* or *stimOn*. The rest of the variables in V are continuous and real-valued. The set of all possible valuations of all variables in V is denoted as $val(V)$—this defines the set of states of the model. The continuous evolution of the variables is modeled by *trajectories*. A single trajectory τ is a function $\tau : [0, t] \rightarrow val(V)$, where $t \geq 0$ is the duration τ. The state of the system at a given time t in τ is $\tau(t)$, and the value of a particular variable $v \in V$ at that state is denoted by $\tau(t).v$. A set of trajectories is specified by differential equations involving the continuous variables (see, for example, Figure 1). A trajectory τ satisfies an ordinary differential equation (ODE) $\dot{v} = f(v)$ if at each time

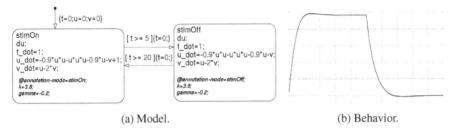

(a) Model.   (b) Behavior.

Fig. 1. (a) Simplified Stateflow™ model of a cardiac cell and a pacemaker. (b) A simulation of the model from an initial state.

t in the domain of the trajectory, $\frac{d(\tau(t).v)}{dt} = f(\tau(t).v)$. When f is a nice[2] function, the ODE has a unique solution for a given initial state and a duration. With different initial states and time bounds, an ODE defines a set of trajectories.

The discrete transitions between the two locations are specified by a set A of actions (see Figure 1). An action $a \in A$ is enabled at a state whenever the state satisfies a special predicate $Guard_a$ that is associated with the action. The discrete transition from the location *stimOn* to *stimOff* is enabled only when $t >= 5$, that is the clock has counted 5 units in *stimOn*. When the system takes a discrete transition, the new state of the system after the transition is defined by a function $Reset_a$ that maps the old state to a new state (and possibly a new location). For example, the reset function for *stimOn* to *stimOff* sets $t = 0$, $loc = stimOff$, and leaves the other continuous variables u and v unchanged. All of these components together defines the behavior of the hybrid automaton in terms of a sequence of alternating trajectories and transitions.

Definition 1. *A Hybrid Automaton (HA) $\mathcal{A}$ is a tuple $\langle V, Loc, A, \mathcal{D}, \mathcal{T} \rangle$ where*

(a) $V = X \cup \{loc\}$ is a set of variables. Here loc is a discrete variable of finite type Loc. Valuations of loc are called locations. *Each $x \in X$ is a continuous variable of type $\mathbb{R}$. Elements of $val(V)$ are called* states.

(b) A is a finite set of actions *or transition labels.*

(c) $\mathcal{D} \subseteq val(V) \times A \times val(V)$ is the set of discrete transitions. *A discrete transition $(\mathbf{v}, a, \mathbf{v}') \in \mathcal{D}$ is written as $\mathbf{v} \xrightarrow{a} \mathbf{v}'$. The discrete transitions are specified by finitely many guards and reset maps involving V.*

(d) $\mathcal{T}$ is a set of trajectories for X which is closed under suffix, prefix and concatenation (see [14] for details). For each $l \in Loc$, a set of trajectories $\mathcal{T}_l$ for location l are specified by differential equations E_l and an invariant $I_l \subseteq val(X)$. Over any trajectory $\tau \in \mathcal{T}_l$, loc remains constant and the variables in X evolve according to E_l such that for all at each time in the domain of τ, $\tau(t)$ satisfies the invariant I_l.

An execution of a hybrid automaton $\mathcal{A}$ records all the information (about variables) over a particular run. Formally, an *execution* is an alternating sequence of trajectories

---

[2] For example, Lipschitz continuous or smooth. A continuous function $f : \mathbb{R}^n \times \mathbb{R} \to \mathbb{R}$ is *smooth* if all its higher derivatives and partial derivatives exist and are also continuous. It has a Lipschitz constant $K \geq 0$ if for every $x_1, x_2 \in \mathbb{R}^n$, $||f(x_1) - f(x_2)|| \leq K||x_1 - x_2||$.

and actions $\sigma = \tau_0 a_1 \tau_1 \ldots$ where each τ_i is a closed trajectory and $\tau_i(t) \overset{a_{i+1}}{\rightsquigarrow} \tau_{i+1}(0)$, where t is the last time point in τ_i. The *duration* of an execution is the total duration of all the trajectories. The set of all executions is denoted as $execs(\mathcal{A})$. In this paper, we only consider executions with bounded number of switches and with bounded duration. Given a set of initial states $\Theta \subseteq val(V)$, the set of *executions from* Θ are those executions in $execs(\mathcal{A})$ with their first state, $\tau_0(0)$, in Θ. The set of executions starting from Θ of duration at most T and with at most N transitions will be denoted as $execs(\mathcal{A}, \Theta, T, N)$.

Definition 2 (Safe and Unsafe). *Given a hybrid automaton $\mathcal{A}$ with an initial set Θ, unsafe set U, time bound T, and transition bound N, it is said to be unsafe, if there exists an execution $\tau_0 a_1 \ldots \tau_k \in execs(\mathcal{A}, \Theta, T, N)$ such that $\tau_k(t) \in U$, where t is the last time point in τ_k. Otherwise, $\mathcal{A}$ is said to be* safe.

Our algorithm for safety verification as well as its analysis relies heavily on the notion of distance between continuous states and trajectories of the automaton. To state our results formally, we need to introduce a we notations first. For a vector $x \in \mathbb{R}^n$, $||x||$ denotes the ℓ^2 norm. For $x_1, x_2 \in \mathbb{R}^n$, $||x_1 - x_2||$ is the Euclidean distance between the points. For $\delta > 0$, $B_\delta(x_1) \subseteq \mathbb{R}^n$ denotes the set of points that is a closed ball of radius δ centered at x_1. For a set $S \subseteq \mathbb{R}^n$, $B_\delta(S) = \cup_{x \in S} B_\delta(x)$. $B_\delta(S)$ expands S by δ. We will find it convenient to also define the notion of shrinking S by δ: For $\delta < 0$, and $S \subseteq \mathbb{R}^n$, $B_\delta(S) = \{x \in S \mid B_{-\delta}(x) \subseteq S\}$. For a bounded set S, a δ-cover of S is a finite collection of balls $\mathcal{X} = \{B_\delta(x_i)\}_{i=1}^m$ such that $S \subseteq \bigcup_{i=1}^m B_\delta(x_i)$. Its diameter $dia(S) \overset{\Delta}{=} \sup_{x_1, x_2 \in S} ||x_1 - x_2||$.

Definition 3 (Perturbing a Hybrid Automaton). *Given a hybrid automaton $\mathcal{A} = \langle V, Loc, A, \mathcal{D}, \mathcal{T} \rangle$, we define an ϵ-perturbation of $\mathcal{A}$ as a new automaton $\mathcal{A}_\epsilon$ that has identical components as $\mathcal{A}$, except, (a) for each location $\ell \in Loc$, $I_\ell^{\mathcal{A}_\epsilon} = B_\epsilon(I_\ell^{\mathcal{A}})$ and (b) for each action $a \in A$, $Guard_a^{\mathcal{A}_\epsilon} = B_\epsilon(Guard_a^{\mathcal{A}})$.*

Here $I_{loc}^{\mathcal{A}}$ is the invariant of the location of a hybrid automaton $\mathcal{A}$ and $Guard_a^{\mathcal{A}}$ denotes the guard set for action a. The definition permits $\epsilon < 0$ for perturbation of a hybrid automaton. Informally, a positive perturbation of a hybrid automaton $\mathcal{A}$ bloats the invariants and guard sets and therefore enlarges the set of executions. A negative perturbation on the other hand, shrinks the invariants and the guards and therefore reduces the set of executions.

Definition 4 (Robust Safety and Unsafety). *Given a hybrid automaton $\mathcal{A}$ with an initial set Θ, unsafe set U, time bound T, and bound on discrete transitions N, it is said to be* robustly safe *if and only if $\exists \epsilon > 0$, such that $\mathcal{A}_\epsilon$, with initial set Θ_ϵ, unsafe set U_ϵ, time bound T, and transition bound N is safe. It is said to be* robustly unsafe *if and only if $\exists \epsilon < 0$ such that $\mathcal{A}_\epsilon$, with initial set Θ_ϵ, unsafe set U_ϵ, time bound T, and transition bound N, is unsafe.*

For safety verification C2E2 expects the users to provide annotations for the ODEs defining the trajectories of the hybrid automaton in question. These annotations are called discrepancy function. For a differential equation $\dot{x} = f(x, t)$, the general definition of discrepancy function is given in [8]. In this paper, we consider a special form of discrepancy function given in Definition 5.

Definition 5. *Given a differential equation $\dot{x} = f(x)$, the tuple $\langle K, \gamma \rangle$ is called an exponential discrepancy function for the dynamics, if and only if for any two trajectories τ_1, τ_2 satisfying the differential equation, it holds that:*

$$||\tau_1(t) - \tau_2(t)|| \leq K||\tau_1(0) - \tau_2(0)||e^{\gamma t} \tag{1}$$

We call K as the multiplicity factor and γ as the exponential factor of the annotation.

Along with the input models, we expect the user to specify the discrepancy function by providing values for $\langle K, \gamma \rangle$. Also, if the differential equation is Lipschitz continuous with constant L, then $\langle K, \gamma \rangle = \langle 1, L \rangle$ would be a valid annotation. In Figure 1, the annotations for both the locations are provided as $\langle K, \gamma \rangle = \langle 3.8, -0.2 \rangle$.

3   Verifying Hybrid Systems from Simulations

We give an overview of the verification algorithm implemented in C2E2. In brief, the algorithm generates a cover of the initial set (a collection of regions) and then performs four steps repeatedly until it reaches a safe/unsafe decision for each region in the cover or its refinement. In making this decision, it generates a simulation from the center of the region and then bloats this simulation by a factor computed from the given annotation to compute an over-approximation of the reachable states. If the over-approximation decides safe/unsafe then it moves on to another region in the cover, otherwise, it refines the cover to obtain better over-approximation of the reachable states. These operations are performed by several subroutines which we describe next.

3.1   Building Blocks

The first building block for the algorithm is a subroutine called *valSim* that generates validated simulations for the individual dynamical systems or locations of the hybrid automaton. Given a trajectory τ starting from a given state, *valSim* subroutine computes overapproximation of τ with specific error.

Definition 6 (Validated Simulation). *Given an error bound $\epsilon > 0$, a time step $h > 0$, a time bound $T = (k+1)h$, and an initial state x_0, an (x_0, ϵ, h, T)-simulation of the differential equation $\dot{x} = f(x)$ is a sequence of sets of continuous states $\rho = R_0, R_1, \ldots, R_k$ such that (a) for any i in the sequence $dia(R_i) \leq \epsilon$, and (b) for any time t in the interval $[ih, (i+1)h]$, the solution from x_0 at time t is in R_i, i.e., $\tau(t) \in R_i$.*

The subroutine $valSim(x_0, h, T, f)$ returns a tuple $\langle \rho, \epsilon \rangle$ such that ρ is an (x_0, ϵ, h, T)-simulation. In C2E2, validated simulation engines such as VNODE-LP [18] and CAPD [4] are used for implementing *valSim*. For the completeness of our algorithm, we require that the error ϵ can be made arbitrarily small by decreasing h. In systems with finite precision arithmetic, simulation engines produce accurate simulations up to the order of 10^{-7}, and also there are libraries supporting arbitrary precision integration for some differential equations. Next, the *computeReachTube* subroutine: it uses simulations to compute over-approximations of a set of trajectories from a set of initial states.

Definition 7 (Overapproximate Reach Tube). *For a set of initial states S, error bound $\epsilon > 0$, time step $h > 0$, and $T = (k+1)h$, an (S, ϵ, h, T)-reachtube of the differential equation $\dot{x} = f(x)$ is a sequence $\psi = R_0, R_1, \ldots, R_k$ such that (a) for any i in the sequence $dia(R_i) \le \epsilon$, (b) for any trajectory starting τ from S and for each time $t \in [ih, (i+1)h]$, $\tau(t) \in R_i$.*

If S is large and ϵ is small then the strict inclusion may preclude a (S, ϵ, h, T)-reachtube from existing. To compute reachtubes from a compact set S centered at x_0, *computeReachTube* performs the following three steps:

1. $\langle \rho, \epsilon_1 \rangle \leftarrow valSim(x_0, h, T, f)$, let $\rho = R_0, \ldots, R_k$.
2. $\epsilon_2 = \sup\{K\|x_1 - x_2\|e^{\gamma t} \mid x_1, x_2 \in S, t \in [0, T]\}$, where $\langle K, \gamma \rangle$ is the annotation for the dynamics given by f.
3. $\psi = B_{\epsilon_2}(R_1), \ldots, B_{\epsilon_2}(R_k)$.

From Definition 5 it follows that ψ is a $(S, \epsilon_1 + \epsilon_2, h, T)$-reachtube. It can be shown [8] that $\epsilon \to 0$ as $\delta \to 0$ and $h \to 0$. In summary, the subroutine call *computeReachTube* (S, h, T, f) returns $\langle \psi, \epsilon \rangle$ using the above steps. To provide formal guarantees from reachtube over-approximations, we need to distinguish when a given reachtube *must* satisfy a predicate P from when it *may* satisfy it. The next subroutine *tagRegion* tags each region in a reachtube with respect to a given predicate.

Definition 8 (Tagging). *Given two sets $R, P \subseteq \mathbb{R}^n$ the subroutine tagRegion(R, P) returns must, may or $\bot$ such that, (a) if $R \subseteq P$, then return must, (b) if $R \cap P \ne \emptyset$ and $R \not\subseteq P$ then return may, and (c) otherwise ($R \cap P = \emptyset$), return tag $= \bot$.*

The above subroutines are used for over-approximating reach sets and deciding safety for individual differential equations of individual locations of a hybrid automaton. In order to reason about invariants, guards, and resets which are essential for capturing the hybrid behavior of mode switches, we have to (a) detect the reachable states that satisfy the respective location invariants and (b) identify the states from which location switches or transitions can occur. The next subroutine *invariantPrefix*(ψ, S) takes a reachtube and a set S and returns the longest contiguous prefix of ψ that intersects with S. This is later used in solving problem (a).

Definition 9 (Invariant Prefix). *Given a reachtube $\psi = R_0, \ldots, R_k$ and a set S, invariantPrefix(ψ, S) returns the longest sequence $\phi = \langle R_0, tag_0 \rangle \ldots \langle R_m, tag_m \rangle$, such that $\forall 0 \le i \le m$, $tag_i = $ must when $\forall j \le i$, $tagRegion(R_j, S) = $ must and $tag_i = $ may when $\forall j \le i$, $tagRegion(R_j, S) \ne \bot$ and $\exists l \le i$, $tagRegion(R_l, S) = $ may. That is, if $m < k$, then $tagRegion(R_{m+1}, S) = \bot$.*

Intuitively, a region R_i is tagged *must* in an invariant prefix, if all the regions before R_i (including itself) are contained within the set S. It is tagged *may* if all the regions before it have nonempty intersection with S, and at least one of them (including itself) is not contained within the set S. Given a reachtube ψ from a set Q, $\phi = invariantPrefix(\psi, Inv_{loc})$ returns the over-approximation of the valid set of trajectories from Q that respect the invariant of the location loc of the hybrid automaton. If a region R_i in ϕ is tagged *must*, then there exists at least one trajectory from Q that can reach R_i. Also, the set of all reachable states from Q that satisfy the invariant are contained in ϕ. Subroutine *checkSafety* checks whether such an invariant prefix ϕ is safe with respect to an unsafe set U. It defined as:

$$checkSafety(\phi, U) = \begin{cases} safe, & \text{if } \forall \langle R, \cdot \rangle \in \phi, \bot = tagRegion(R, U) \\ unsafe, & \text{if } \exists \langle R, must \rangle \in \phi, must = tagRegion(R, U) \\ unknown, & \text{otherwise} \end{cases}$$

Notice that ϕ is inferred to be *safe* only when all the regions in the invariant prefix are tagged $\bot$ with respect to U (i.e. empty intersection). It is *unsafe* only when there is a *must* region in the invariant prefix is contained within U. This is the core of the soundness argument for the verification algorithm, i.e., if $checkSafety(\phi, U)$ returns *safe* or *unsafe*, then indeed that is the correct answer for the set of initial states covered by ϕ.

The final subroutine *nextRegions* computes over-approximation of the reachable states that serve as the initial states in a new location after a transition to it. A discrete transition a is enabled at the instance trajectory τ satisfies the guard condition $Guard_a$ and the state after the discrete transition is obtained by applying the reset map $Reset_a$. Given a sequence of tagged regions, the subroutine *nextRegions* returns the tagged set of reachable regions after a discrete transition.

Definition 10 (Next Regions). *Given* $\phi = \langle R_0, tag_0 \rangle, \ldots, \langle R_m, tag_m \rangle$, *a sequence of tagged regions, the subroutine* $nextRegions(\phi)$ *returns a set of tagged regions* **R**. $\langle R', tag' \rangle \in \mathbf{R}$ *if and only if there exists an action* a *of the automaton and a region* R_i *in* ϕ *such that* $R' = Reset_a(R_i)$ *and one of the following conditions hold:*

(a) $R_i \subseteq Guard_a, tag_i = must, tag' = must.$
(b) $R_i \cap Guard_a \neq \emptyset, R_i \nsubseteq Guard_a, tag_i = must, tag' = may.$
(c) $R_i \cap Guard_a \neq \emptyset, tag_i = may, tag' = may.$

A tagged region $\langle R', tag' \rangle \in \mathbf{R}$ is labeled *must* only when the region R_i is a *must* region and is contained within the $Guard_a$. In all other cases, the region is tagged *may* when $R_i \cap Guard_a \neq \emptyset$. This ensures that a regions tagged *must* are indeed reachable after the discrete transition, and all the regions tagged *may* contain the reachable states after the discrete transition.

3.2 Verification Algorithm

The C2E2 algorithm for verification is given in Algorithm 1. Lines 4 - 17 implement the main loop that computes a cover of the initial set, computes the overapproximation of reachtube, checks safety, and refines the cover if needed. The subroutine *taggedCover* (line 3), first computes a cover of S (Θ in the first iteration) with sets of δ diameter and tags them (with *tagRegion*) with respect to S. The resulting tagged sets are collected in $\mathcal{X}$. We add additional attributes to each tagged region: $Time$ tracks the time of the trajectory leading to a region, Loc tracks its current location, and $Switches$ tracks the number of discrete transitions taken. Although not explicitly mentioned in the algorithm, we update the tags for regions in the reachtube based on the time taken by trajectories and the discrete transitions encountered during verification. The algorithm checks whether all the executions of hybrid automaton from the regions in the cover of the initial set are safe or unsafe. If it is safe, then the region is removed from the set S (line 13); if it is unsafe, then the algorithm returns unsafe (line 10); and if it is neither then the cover is refined (line 15).

For each of the regions in the tagged δ-cover of the initial set, the inner loop (lines 6 - 11) computes over-approximations of the reachable states. The subroutine *computeReachTube* (line 7) computes an overapproximation of all the trajectories starting from the tagged region in the initial set cover. Subroutine *invariantPrefix* (line 8) computes ϕ, an overapproximation of the valid set of trajectories which respect the invariant of the current location. Safety of ϕ is checked using the subroutine *checkSafety* (line 9). The regions in ϕ where discrete transitions are enabled and the initial states for the trajectories in the next location are computed in subroutine *nextRegions* (line 10). This loop continues until either the time bound for verification or the bound for number of discrete transitions is satisfied.

The reachtubes computed in lines 7, 8 are an overapproximation of all the reachable states of hybrid automaton $\mathcal{A}$, given in Lemma 1. The regions in the reachtubes are *must* only when they satisfy the invariant of each location and completely contained within the guard set it follows that these regions are reachable by at least one execution of $\mathcal{A}$, given as Lemma 2. For the set of regions $\mathcal{R}$ tagged *may*, it follows that $\epsilon = max\{dia(R)|R \in \mathcal{R}\}$ bloating of the invariants and guard sets would ensure that these regions are also reachable, given in Lemma 3. As the reachtubes can be made arbitrarily precise by decreasing the time step and the initial partitioning, it follows that given any ϵ, the precision of reachtubes can be bounded by ϵ by using small values for δ and h. Lemma 1 helps in proving soundness and Lemmas 2 and 3 help in proving relative completeness. This guarantees that if the system is robustly safe, then the algorithm terminates and returns safe, and if the system is robustly unsafe, then the algorithm terminates and returns unsafe, given in Theorem 1.

Lemma 1. *All the regions R tagged may or must in ϕ (line 7 of algorithm 1) contains the reachable set of states of hybrid automaton $\mathcal{A}$ starting from Θ within T time and N discrete transitions.*

Lemma 2. *If a region R is tagged must in ϕ (line 7 of algorithm 1), then there exists at least one execution of $\mathcal{A}$ from the initial set Θ that reaches R within T time and N discrete transitions.*

Lemma 3. *Let $\mathcal{R}$, be the set of all regions tagged may in ϕ (line 7 of algorithm 1) and $\epsilon = max\{dia(R)|R \in \mathcal{R}\}$. Given any region $R \in \mathcal{R}$, there exists at least one execution of $\mathcal{A}_\epsilon$ from the initial set Θ_ϵ that reaches R within T time and N discrete transitions.*

Theorem 1 (Soundness and Relative Completeness). *Given initial set Θ, unsafe set U, time bound T, bound on discrete transitions N, and hybrid automaton $\mathcal{A}$, if the algorithm 1 returns safe or unsafe, then the system $\mathcal{A}$ is safe or unsafe. The algorithm will always terminate whenever the system is either robustly safe or robustly unsafe.*

---

input : $\mathcal{A}, \Theta, U, T, N$
output: System is $safe$ or $unsafe$

1 $S \leftarrow \Theta; h \leftarrow h_0; \delta \leftarrow \delta_0;$
2 **while** $S \neq \emptyset$ **do**
3      $\mathcal{X} \leftarrow taggedCover(S, \delta)$;
4   **for** $elem \in \mathcal{X}$ **do**
5          $Q_C \leftarrow \{elem\};$
6   **for** $e \in Q_C \wedge e.Time < T \wedge e.Switches < N$ **do**
7              $\langle \psi, \epsilon \rangle \leftarrow computeReachTube(e.R, e.Loc, h, T - e.Time)$;
8              $\phi \leftarrow invariantPrefix(\psi, Inv_{e.Loc})$;
9              $result \leftarrow checkSafety(\phi, U)$;
10   **if** $result == safe$ **then** $Q_C \leftarrow Q_C \cup nextRegions(\phi)$ **else if**
               $result == unsafe \wedge elem.tag == must$ **then return** $unsafe$ **else break**

11   **end**
12   **if** $result == safe$ **then**
13         $S \leftarrow S \setminus elem.R$;
14   **else**
15         $\delta \leftarrow \delta/2; h \leftarrow h/2$;
16   **end**
17   **end**
18 **end**
19 **return** $safe$;

Algorithm 1. Algorithm for safety verification of hybrid automata using simulations and annotations.

4 C2E2: Internals and User Experience

4.1 Architecture of C2E2

The architecture for C2E2 is shown in Figure 2. The front end parses the input models, connects to the verification engine, provides a property editor and a plotter. It is developed in Python and vastly extends the Hylink parser [17] for Stateflow models. The verification algorithm (Algorithm 1) is implemented in C++. The front end parses the input model file (.mdl or .hyxml) into an intermediate format and generates the simulation code. The properties are obtained from the input file or from the user through the front end's GUI. The simulation code is compiled using a validated simulation engine provided by Computer Assisted Proofs in Dynamic Groups (CAPD) library [4]. This compiled code and the property are read by the C2E2 verification algorithm which also uses the GLPK libraries. The verification result and the computed reachable set are read by the front end for display and visualization. This modular architecture allows us to extend the functionality of the tool to new types of models (such as Simulink, DAEs), different simulation engines (for example, Boost, VNODE-LP), and alternative checkers (such as Z3).

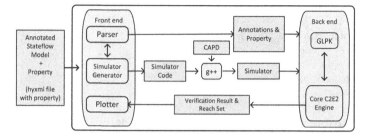

Fig. 2. Architecture of C2E2

4.2 Models, Properties, and Annotations

C2E2[3] takes as input annotated Stateflow models (such as in Figure 1(a)) with ODEs (possibly nonlinear) and discrete transitions defined by guards and resets. The guards have to be conjunctions of polynomial predicates over the state variables and the reset maps have to be polynomial real-valued functions. The properties can be specified in the .hyxml model files or using the GUI. C2E2 can verify bounded time safety properties specified by a time bound, a polyhedral set of initial states and another set of unsafe states.

Annotations. The user has to write annotations for each ODE in the model. This is done by specifying the multiplicity factor K and the exponential factor γ as comments in the Stateflow model, shown in Figure 1(a). For a broad range of nonlinear systems such annotations can be found. We illustrate with some examples.

Example 1. Consider a linear system $\dot{x} = Ax$, where all the eigenvalues of matrix A is nonzero. Let λ_m be the maximum among the real parts of all the eigenvalues of A. Then, for any two trajectories τ_1 and τ_2 of the linear system $||\tau_1(t) - \tau_2(t)|| \leq ||A||e^{\lambda_m t}||\tau_1(0) - \tau_2(0)||$ is an annotation. Here the matrix norm $||A||$ is defined as $\sup\{x^T A x \mid ||x|| = 1\}$ and it can be computed using semidefinite programming. The input format would be $K = ||A||$ and $\gamma = \lambda_m$.

Example 2. Consider the differential equation in *stimOn* mode of the cardiac cell example: $\dot{u} = (0.1 - u)(u - 1)u - v$ and $\dot{v} = u - 2v$. By computing the maximum eigenvalues of the Jacobian matrix of the differential equation and the maximum norm of the contraction metric [16], we get that $||\tau_1(t) - \tau_2(t)|| \leq 3.8e^{-0.2t}||\tau_1.(0) - \tau_2.(0)||$ as an annotation. The input is specified as $K = 3.8$ and $\gamma = -0.2$.

Example 3. Consider the differential equation $\dot{x} = 1 + x^2y - 2.5x$; $\dot{y} = 1.5x - x^2y - y$. By analyzing the auxiliary system (x_1, y_1) and (x_2, y_2), using the incremental stability [1], we have that

$$\frac{d}{dt}[(x_1 - x_2)^2 + 2(x_1 - x_2)(y_1 - y_2) + (y_1 - y_2)^2] = -2(x_1 - x_2 + y_1 - y_2)^2 < 0.$$

---
[3] https://publish.illinois.edu/c2e2-tool/

Therefore, for trajectories τ_1 and τ_2 of the differential equations it hence follows that $(\tau_1(t).x - \tau_2(t).x)^2 + 2(\tau_1(t).x - \tau_2(t).x)(\tau_1(t).y - \tau_2(t).y) + (\tau_1(t).y - \tau_2(t).y)^2 \leq (x_1 - x_2)^2 + 2(x_1 - x_2)(y_1 - y_2) + (y_1 - y_2)^2$ where (x_1, y_1) and (x_2, y_2) are the initial states of τ_1 and τ_2 respectively. The function $||\tau_1(t) - \tau_2(t)|| \leq 2||\tau_1(0) - \tau_2(0)||e^{0 \times t}$ is an annotation and is specified as $K = 2, \gamma = 0$.

4.3   User Experience

In this section, we discuss the C2E2 interface for handling verification, properties and visualization. The users can add, edit, copy, delete or verify several properties. As each property is edited, the *smart parser* provides real-time feedback about syntax errors and unbounded initial sets (Figure 3(b)). Once properties are edited the verifier can be launched. Visual representation of reachable states and locations can aid debugging process. To this end, we have integrated a visualizer into C2E2 for plotting the projections of the reachable states. Once a property has been verified, the user can plot the valuations of variables against time or valuations of pairs of variables (phase plots). The unsafe set is projected on the set of plotting variables. The property parser and visualizer uses the Parma Polyhedra Library[4] and matplotlib[5]. Example plot for the cardiac cell is shown in Figure 3(c).

(a) Model.   (b) Property.   (c) Reachable Set.

Fig. 3. Figure showing a snippet of cardiac cell model in (a), property dialog for specifying properties in (b), plot of reachable set for cardiac cell model in (c)

4.4   Stateflow Model Semantics

The annotated Stateflow models when given as input are interpreted as hybrid automaton as C2E2. Nondeterminism, which is allowed in hybrid automata framework is prohibited in Stateflow models. All the discrete transitions in Stateflow models are deterministic and are interpreted as "urgent" i.e. a transition is taken by the system *as soon as* it is enabled. In our front end, we construct hybrid automaton for Stateflow models respecting the "urgent" semantics. Under such interpretation, the guard sets are only allowed

---

[4] http://bugseng.com/products/ppl/
[5] http://matplotlib.org/

to be hyperplanes. In general, the verification algorithm in Section 3 may not terminate for such guard conditions. We therefore use a heuristic and verify an ϵ perturbed model of the Stateflow model to ensure termination of verification algorithm.

4.5   Experiments

Simulation based verification approach for annotated models has been demonstrated to outperform other verification tool such as Flow* and Ariadne in [8]. In this paper, we present the verification results for some of the nonlinear and linear hybrid automata benchmarks in Table 1. The annotations for each of these benchmarks have been obtained by procedures given in Section 4.2. All the experiments have been performed on Intel i-7 Quad core processor with 8GB ram running Ubuntu 11.10.

Table 1. Experimental Results for benchmark examples. Vars: Number of Variables, Num. Loc. : Number of discrete locations in hybrid automata, TH: Time Horizon for Verification, VT (sec) : Verification time for C2E2 in seconds, Result: Verification result of C2E2.

Benchmark	Vars.	Num. Loc.	TH	VT (sec)	Result
Cardiac Cell	3	2	15	17.74	safe
Cardiac Cell	3	2	15	1.91	unsafe
Nonlinear Navigation	4	4	2.0	124.10	safe
Nonlinear Navigation	4	4	2.0	4.94	unsafe
Inverted Pendulum	2	1	10	1.27	safe
Inverted Pendulum	2	1	10	1.32	unsafe
Navigation Benchmark	4	4	2.0	94.35	safe
Navigation Benchmark	4	4	2.0	4.74	unsafe

This early termination strategy for unsafe behavior of the system (Algorithm 1, line 10) when the system is unsafe is reflected in Table 1. On standard examples C2E2 can successfully verify these systems within the order of minutes and also handle nonlinear differential equations with trigonometric functions of inverted pendulum.

5   Conclusions and Future Work

C2E2 presented in this paper is a tool for verifying a broad class of hybrid and dynamical systems models. It uses validated simulations and model annotations to prove the most commonly encountered type of properties, namely bounded-time invariants. It can handle models created using the Stateflow environment that is the de facto standard in embedded control design and implementation. The improvements presented in this paper beyond the version of [8], include the complete support for hybrid models implemented in a new algorithm and the supporting theory, the new user interface for editing properties, and the reachtube plotting function. The tool is freely available for academic and research use from https://publish.illinois.edu/c2e2-tool/.

Our future plans include implementation of features to support temporal precedence properties [9] and compositional reasoning [13,12]. Another avenue of work leverages the "embarrassing parallelism" in the simulation-based approach. We anticipate that the C2E2's architecture and its open interfaces, for example, the .hyxml input format, text-based representation of reachtubes, will support research and eduction in embedded and hybrid systems community by helping explore new ideas in modeling, verification, synthesis, and and testing.

Acknowledgements. The authors were supported by the National Science Foundation research grant CSR 1016791.

References

1. Angeli, D.: A lyapunov approach to incremental stability properties. IEEE Transactions on Automatic Control (2000)
2. Asarin, E., Dang, T., Maler, O.: The d/dt tool for verification of hybrid systems. In: Brinksma, E., Larsen, K.G. (eds.) CAV 2002. LNCS, vol. 2404, pp. 365–370. Springer, Heidelberg (2002)
3. Balluchi, A., Casagrande, A., Collins, P., Ferrari, A., Villa, T., Sangiovanni-Vincentelli, A.: Ariadne: a framework for reachability analysis of hybrid automata. In: International Symposium on Mathematical Theory of Networks and Systems, MNTS (2006)
4. CAPD. Computer assisted proofs in dynamic groups, http://capd.ii.uj.edu.pl/index.php
5. Chen, X., Ábrahám, E., Sankaranarayanan, S.: Flow*: An analyzer for non-linear hybrid systems. In: Sharygina, N., Veith, H. (eds.) CAV 2013. LNCS, vol. 8044, pp. 258–263. Springer, Heidelberg (2013)
6. Deng, Y., Rajhans, A., Julius, A.A.: STRONG: A trajectory-based verification toolbox for hybrid systems. In: Joshi, K., Siegle, M., Stoelinga, M., D'Argenio, P.R. (eds.) QEST 2013. LNCS, vol. 8054, pp. 165–168. Springer, Heidelberg (2013)
7. Donzé, A.: Breach, A toolbox for verification and parameter synthesis of hybrid systems. In: Touili, T., Cook, B., Jackson, P. (eds.) CAV 2010. LNCS, vol. 6174, pp. 167–170. Springer, Heidelberg (2010)
8. Duggirala, P.S., Mitra, S., Viswanathan, M.: Verification of annotated models from executions. In: International Conference on Embedded Software, EMSOFT (2013)
9. Duggirala, P.S., Wang, L., Mitra, S., Viswanathan, M., Muñoz, C.: Temporal precedence checking for switched models and its application to a parallel landing protocol. In: Jones, C., Pihlajasaari, P., Sun, J. (eds.) FM 2014. LNCS, vol. 8442, pp. 215–229. Springer, Heidelberg (2014)
10. Frehse, G., Le Guernic, C., Donzé, A., Cotton, S., Ray, R., Lebeltel, O., Ripado, R., Girard, A., Dang, T., Maler, O.: SpaceEx: Scalable verification of hybrid systems. In: Gopalakrishnan, G., Qadeer, S. (eds.) CAV 2011. LNCS, vol. 6806, pp. 379–395. Springer, Heidelberg (2011)
11. Henzinger, T.A., Ho, P.-H., Wong-Toi, H.: HyTech: A model checker for hybrid systems. In: Grumberg, O. (ed.) CAV 1997. LNCS, vol. 1254, pp. 460–463. Springer, Heidelberg (1997)
12. Huang, Z., Fan, C., Mereacre, A., Mitra, S., Kwiatkowska, M.: Invariant verification of nonlinear hybrid automata networks of cardiac cells. In: Biere, A., Bloem, R. (eds.) CAV 2014. LNCS, vol. 8559, pp. 373–390. Springer, Heidelberg (2014)

13. Huang, Z., Mitra, S.: Proofs from simulations and modular annotations. In: International Conference on Hybrid Systems: Computation and Control, pp. 183–192 (2014)
14. Kaynar, D.K., Lynch, N., Segala, R., Vaandrager, F.: The Theory of Timed I/O Automata. Synthesis Lectures on Computer Science. Morgan Kaufmann (November 2005)
15. Larsen, K.G., Pettersson, P., Yi, W.: Uppaal in a nutshell. International Journal on Software Tools for Technology Transfer (STTT) 1(1), 134–152 (1997)
16. Lohmiller, W., Slotine, J.J.E.: On contraction analysis for non-linear systems. Automatica (1998)
17. Manamcheri, K., Mitra, S., Bak, S., Caccamo, M.: A step towards verification and synthesis from simulink/stateflow models. In: International Conference on Hybrid Systems: Computation and Control, HSCC (2011)
18. Nedialkov, N.: VNODE-LP: Validated solutions for initial value problem for ODEs. Technical report, Department of Computing and Software, McMaster University (2006)
19. Nghiem, T., Sankaranarayanan, S., Fainekos, G., Ivancic, F., Gupta, A., Pappas, G.: Montecarlo techniques for falsification of temporal properties of non-linear hybrid systems. In: International Conference on Hybrid Systems: Computation and Control HSCC (2010)
20. Zou, L., Zhan, N., Wang, S., Franzle, M., Qin, S.: Verifying simulink diagrams via a hybrid hoare logic prover. In: International Conference on Embedded Software EMSOFT (2013)

Program Analysis

Non-cumulative Resource Analysis

Elvira Albert[1], Jesús Correas Fernández[1], and Guillermo Román-Díez[2]

[1] DSIC, Complutense University of Madrid, Spain
[2] DLSIIS, Technical University of Madrid, Spain

Abstract. Existing cost analysis frameworks have been defined for cumulative resources which keep on increasing along the computation. Traditional cumulative resources are execution time, number of executed steps, amount of memory allocated, and energy consumption. Non-cumulative resources are acquired and (possibly) released along the execution. Examples of non-cumulative cost are memory usage in the presence of garbage collection, number of connections established that are later closed, or resources requested to a virtual host which are released after using them. We present, to the best of our knowledge, the first generic static analysis framework to infer an *upper bound* on the *peak cost* for non-cumulative types of resources. Our analysis comprises several components: (1) a pre-analysis to infer when resources are being used simultaneously, (2) a *program-point* resource analysis which infers an upper bound on the cost at the points of interest (namely the points where resources are acquired) and (3) the elimination from the upper bounds obtained in (2) of those resources accumulated that are not used simultaneously. We report on a prototype implementation of our analysis that can be used on a simple imperative language.

1 Introduction

Cost analysis (a.k.a. resource analysis) aims at statically (without executing the program) inferring *upper bounds* on the resource consumption of the program as functions of the input data sizes. Traditional resources (e.g., time, steps, memory allocation, number of calls) are *cumulative*, i.e., they always increase along the execution. Ideally, a cost analysis framework is *generic* on the type of resource that the user wants to measure so that the resource of interest is a parameter of the analysis. Several generic cost analysis frameworks have been defined for cumulative resources using different formalisms. In particular, the classical framework based on recurrence relations has been used to define a cost analysis for a Java-like language [2]; approaches based on program invariants are defined in [11,14]; type systems have been presented in [15].

Non-cumulative resources are first acquired and then released. Typical examples are memory usage in the presence of garbage collection, maximum number of connections established simultaneously, the size of the stack of activation records, etc. The problem is nowadays also very relevant in *virtualized* systems, as in cloud computing, in which resources are acquired when needed and released after being used. It is recognized that non-cumulative resources introduce new

© Springer-Verlag Berlin Heidelberg 2015
C. Baier and C. Tinelli (Eds.): TACAS 2015, LNCS 9035, pp. 85–100, 2015.
DOI: 10.1007/978-3-662-46681-0_6

challenges in resource analysis [5,12]. This is because the resource consumption can increase and decrease along the computation, and it is not enough to reason on the final state of the execution, but rather the upper bound on the cost can happen at any intermediate step. We use the term *peak cost* to denote such maximum cost of the program execution for non-cumulative resources.

While the problem of inferring the peak cost has been studied in the context of memory usage for specific models of garbage collection [5,8,12], a generic framework to estimate the non-cumulative cost does not exist yet. The contribution of this paper is a generic resource analysis framework for a today's imperative language enriched with instructions to acquire and release resources. Thus, our framework can be instantiated to measure any type of non-cumulative resource that is acquired and (optionally) freed. The analysis is defined in two steps which are our main contributions: (1) We first infer the sets of resources which can be in use simultaneously (i.e., they have been both acquired and none of them released at some point of the execution). This process is formalized as a static analysis that (over-)approximates the sets of acquire instructions that can be in use simultaneously, allowing us to capture the simultaneous use of resources in the execution. (2) We then perform a *program-point* resource analysis which infers an upper bound on the cost at the points of interest, namely the points at which the resources are acquired. From such upper bounds, we can obtain the peak cost by just eliminating the cost due to acquire instructions that do not happen simultaneously with the others (according to the analysis information gathered at step 1). Additionally, we describe an extension of the framework which can improve the accuracy of the upper bounds by accounting only once the cost introduced at program points where resources are allocated and released repeatedly. Finally, we illustrate how the framework can be extended to get upper bounds for programs that allocate different kinds of resources.

We demonstrate the accuracy and feasibility of our approach by implementing a prototype analyzer for a simple imperative language. Preliminary experiments show that the non-cumulative resource analysis achieves gains up to 92.9% (on average 53.9%) in comparison to a cumulative resource analysis. The analysis can be used online from a web interface at `http://costa.ls.fi.upm.es/noncu`.

2   The Notion of Peak Cost

We start by defining the notion of peak cost that we aim at over-approximating by means of static analysis in the concrete setting.

2.1   The Language

The framework is developed on a language which is deliberately simple to define the analysis in a clear way. Complex features of modern languages like mutable variables, class, inheritance, exceptions, etc. must be considered by the underlying resource analysis used as a black box by our approach (and there are a number of approaches to handle them [2,5,11]). Thus they are handled implicitly in our setting. For the sake of simplicity, the set *Types* is defined as {int}.

$$(1) \quad \frac{r = eval(\mathsf{e}, tv), tr' = tr[y \mapsto \langle r, a_{pp}\rangle], H' = H \cup \{\!\{\langle id, y, a_{pp}, r\rangle\}\!\}}{\langle id, m, pp \equiv \mathsf{y} = \mathsf{acquire} \; (\mathsf{e}); s, tv, tr\rangle \cdot A; H \; \leadsto \; \langle id, m, s, tv, tr'\rangle \cdot A; H'}$$

$$(2) \quad \frac{\langle r, a_{pp'}\rangle = tr(y), tr' = tr[y \mapsto \bot], H' = H \setminus \{\!\{\langle id, y, a_{pp'}, r\rangle\}\!\}}{\langle id, m, pp \equiv \mathsf{release} \; \mathsf{y}; s, tv, tr\rangle \cdot A; H \; \leadsto \; \langle id, m, s, tv, tr'\rangle \cdot A; H'}$$

Fig. 1. Language Semantics for resource allocation and release

We have *resource* variables used to refer to the resources allocated by an acquire instruction. A program consists of a set of methods whose definition takes the form $t \; m \; (t_1 v_1, \ldots t_n v_n)\{s\}$ where $t \in$ *Types* is the type returned by the method, $v_1, \ldots, v_n$ are the input parameters of types $t_1, \ldots, t_n \in$ *Types* and s is a sequence of instructions that adheres to the following grammar:

$$e ::= x \mid n \mid e + e \mid e * e \mid e - e \qquad b ::= e > e \mid e == e \mid b \wedge b \mid b \vee b \mid !b \qquad s ::= i \mid i; s$$
$$i ::= x{=}e \mid x{=}m(\overline{z}) \mid \mathsf{return} \; x \mid \mathsf{if} \; b \; \mathsf{then} \; s_1 \; \mathsf{else} \; s_2 \mid \mathsf{while} \; b \; \{s\} \mid \mathsf{y} = \mathsf{acquire} \; (e) \mid \mathsf{release} \; y$$

We assume that resource variables, named y, are local to methods and they cannot be passed as input parameters nor returned by methods (otherwise tracking such references is more complex, while it is not relevant to the main ideas in the paper). We assume that the program includes a main($\overline{x}$) method, where $\overline{x}$ are the input parameters, from which the execution starts. The instruction y = acquire (e) allocates the amount of resources stated by the expression e. The instruction release y releases the resources allocated at the last acquire associated to y. If a resource variable is reused without releasing its resources, the reference to such resources is lost and they cannot be released any longer.

Example 1. Fig. 2 shows to the left a method m (abbreviation of main) that allocates resources at lines 2 (L2 for short) and L4. The resources allocated at L2 are released at L5. In addition, method m invokes method q at L3 and L6. For simplicity, we assume that m is called using positive values for n and s and the expressions k_1, k_2, k_3 are constant integer values. As it is not relevant, we do not include the return instruction at the end of the methods. Method q executes a while loop where k_2 units are allocated at L10 and such resources are not released. Thus, these resources *escape* from the scope of the loop and the method, i.e., they *leak* upon exit of the loop and return of the method. Besides, the program allocates w units at L11. As we have two calls to q, the input parameter w will take the value s or s+4. The resources allocated at L11 are released at L12 and do not escape from the loop execution. In addition, at L15 we have an additional, non-released, acquire of k_3 units.

A *program state* is of the form $AS;H$, where AS is a stack of *activation records* and H is a *resource handler*. Each activation record is of the form $\langle id, m, s, tv, tr\rangle$, where id is a unique identifier, m is the name of the method, s is the sequence of instructions to be executed, tv is a variable mapping and tr is a resource variable mapping. When resources are allocated in m, tr maps the corresponding resource variable to a tuple of the form $\langle r, a_{pp}\rangle$, where r is the amount of resources allocated and a_{pp} is the program point of the instruction where the resources have been allocated. The resource handler H is a multiset which stores

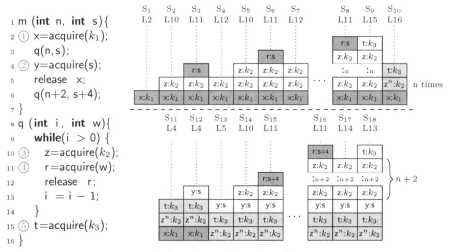

Fig. 2. Running Example

the resources allocated so far, containing elements of the form $\langle id, y, a_{pp}, r \rangle$, where id is the activation record identifier, y is the variable name, a_{pp} is the program point of the acquire and r is the amount of resources allocated. Fig. 1 shows, in a rewriting-based style, the rules that are relevant for the resource consumption. The semantics of the remaining instructions is standard. Intuitively, rule (1) evaluates the expression e and adds a new element to H. As H stores the resources allocated so far, it might contain identical tuples. Moreover, the resource variable mapping tr is updated with variable y linked to $\langle r, a_{pp} \rangle$. Rule (2) takes the information stored in tr for y, i.e. $\langle r, a_{pp} \rangle$, and removes from H one instance of the corresponding element. In addition, variable y is updated to point to $\bot$, which means that y does not have any resources associated. When the execution performs a release on a variable that maps to $\bot$ (because no acquire has been performed or because it has already been released), the resources state is not modified. Execution starts from a main method and an initial state $S_0 = \langle 0, \mathsf{main}, body(\mathsf{main}), tv(\overline{x}), \emptyset \rangle; \emptyset$, where $tv(\overline{x})$ is the variable mapping initialized with the values of the input parameters. Complete executions are of the form $S_0 \rightsquigarrow S_1 \rightsquigarrow \ldots \rightsquigarrow S_n$ where S_n corresponds to the last state. Infinite traces correspond to non-terminating executions.

Example 2. To the right of Fig. 2 we depict the evolution of the resources accumulated in H. We use S_i, to refer to the execution state i and, below each state, we include the program line which is executed at such state. For each state we show the elements stored in H but, for simplicity, we do not include in the figure the id nor a_{pp}. At S_1, H accumulates k_1 units due to the acquire at L2. S_2, S_3 and S_4 depict H along the first iteration of the loop, where k_2 units are acquired and not released from z. Moreover, within the loop, s units are acquired at L11 and released from r at L12. At S_5, which corresponds to the second iteration of the loop, we reuse the resource variable z and we have two identical elements in H. As the loop iterates n times, at the last iteration (S_9)

we have $(n-1)*k_1$ units that have lost their reference. Additionally, k_3 extra units pointed by t are allocated at S_9. At S_{10}, which corresponds to the end of the execution of the method, $n*k_2+k_3$ units escape from the first execution of q and they are no longer available to be released. We represent such escaped resources with light grey color. For brevity, we use $z^n{:}k_2$ to represent n instances of the element $z{:}k_2$. At S_{12} we acquire s resources and we release the k_1 units pointed by x at S_{13}. At S_{14} we start a new execution of method q.

2.2   Definition of Peak Cost

Let us formally define the notion of *peak cost* in the concrete setting. The peak cost corresponds to the maximum amount of resources that are used simultaneously. We use H_i to refer to the multiset H at S_i, and we use R_i to denote the amount of resources contained in H_i, i.e., $R_i = \sum\{r \mid \langle \_, \_, \_, r \rangle \in H_i\}$. By '$\_$', we mean any possible value. In the next definition, we use R_i to define the notion of *peak cost* for an execution trace.

Definition 1 (Concrete Peak Cost). *The* peak cost *of an execution trace* $t{\equiv}S_0 \leadsto S_n$ *of a program P on input values $\overline{x}$ is defined as* $\mathcal{P}(\overline{x}){=}max(\{R_i \mid S_i{\in}t\})$.

Example 3. According to the evolution of H shown to the right of Fig. 2, the maximum value of R_i could be reached at four different states, S_8, S_{12}, S_{16} and S_{18}. We ignore those states where H is subsumed by other states as they cannot be maximal. For instance, states S_1 to S_7 or S_9 are subsumed by S_8; or S_{12} contains S_{10}, S_{11} and S_{13}. Thus, $\mathcal{P}(n, s){=}max(R_8, R_{12}, R_{16}, R_{18})$, where $R_8 = k_1+n*k_2+s$, $R_{12} = k_1+n*k_2+k_3+s$, $R_{16} = n*k_2+k_3+s+(n+2)*k_2+(s+4)$, and $R_{18}{=}n*k_2+k_3+s+(n+2)*k_2+k_3$. Thus, the peak cost of the example depends not only on the input parameters n, s, but also on the values of k_1, k_2, k_3.

3   Simultaneous Resource Analysis

The *simultaneous resource analysis* (SRA) is used to infer the sets of acquire instructions that can be simultaneously in use. The abstract state of the SRA consists of two sets $\mathcal{C}$ and $\mathcal{H}$. The set $\mathcal{C}$ contains elements of the form $y{:}a_{pp}$ indicating that the resource variable y is linked to the acquire instruction at program point pp. Since it is not always possible to relate the acquire instruction to its corresponding resource variable, we use $\star{:}a_{pp}$ to represent that some resources have been acquired at a_{pp} but the analysis has lost the variable linked to a_{pp}. The set $\mathcal{H}$ is a set of sets, such that each set contains those a_{pp} that are simultaneously alive in an abstract state of the analysis. Let us introduce some notation. We use $\ddot{m}$ to refer to the program point after the return instruction of method m. We use $\mathcal{C}_{pp}$ (resp. $\mathcal{H}_{pp}$) to denote the value of $\mathcal{C}$ (resp. $\mathcal{H}$) after processing the instruction at program point pp. $\mathcal{A}(\mathcal{C})$ is the set $\{a_{pp} \mid \_{:}a_{pp} \in \mathcal{C}\}$ that contains all a_{pp} in $\mathcal{C}$. The operation $\mathcal{H}_1 \uplus \mathcal{H}_2$, where $\mathcal{H}_1$ and $\mathcal{H}_2$ are sets of sets, first applies $\mathcal{H} = \mathcal{H}_1 \cup \mathcal{H}_2$, and then removes those sets in $\mathcal{H}$ that are contained in another set in $\mathcal{H}$.

The analysis of each method m abstractly executes its instructions, by applying the transfer function τ in Fig. 3, such that the abstract state at each

(1) $\tau(pp : y\!=\!\mathsf{acquire}(\_), \langle \mathcal{C}, \mathcal{H} \rangle) = \langle \mathcal{C}[y\!:\!a_{pp'}/\star\!:\!a_{pp'}] \cup \{y\!:\!a_{pp}\}, \mathcal{H} \uplus \{\mathcal{A}(\mathcal{C}) \cup \{a_{pp}\}\} \rangle$

(2) $\tau(pp : \mathsf{release}\ y, \langle \mathcal{C}, \mathcal{H} \rangle) = \langle \mathcal{C} \setminus \{y\!:\!a_{pp}\}, \mathcal{H} \rangle$

(3) $\tau(pp : \mathsf{m}(\_), \langle \mathcal{C}, \mathcal{H} \rangle) = \langle \mathcal{C} \cup \mathcal{C}_{\dot{m}}[x\!:\!a_{pp'}/\star\!:\!a_{pp'}], \mathcal{H} \uplus \{\mathcal{A}(\mathcal{C}) \cup M \mid M \in \mathcal{H}_{\dot{m}}\} \rangle$

(4) $\tau(pp : b, \langle \mathcal{C}, \mathcal{H} \rangle) = \langle \mathcal{C}, \mathcal{H} \rangle$

Fig. 3. Transfer Function of the Simultaneous Resource Analysis

program point describes the status of all acquire instructions executed so far. The set $\mathcal{C}$ is used to infer the local effect of the acquire and release instructions within a method. The set $\mathcal{H}$ is used to accumulate the information of the acquire instructions that might have been in use simultaneously. Let us explain the different cases of the transfer function τ. The execution of acquire, case (1), links the acquire to the resource variable y by adding $\{y\!:\!a_{pp}\}$ to $\mathcal{C}$. As a resource variable can only point to one acquire instruction, in (1) we update any existing $y\!:\!a_{pp'}$ by removing the previous link to y and replacing it by $\star$. In addition, rule (1) performs the operation $\{\mathcal{A}(\mathcal{C}) \cup \{a_{pp}\}\} \uplus \mathcal{H}$ to capture in $\mathcal{H}$ the acquired resources simultaneously in use at this point. In (2) we remove the last acquire instruction pointed to by the resource variable y. When a method is invoked (rule (3)), we add to $\mathcal{C}$ those resources that might escape from m ($\mathcal{C}_{\dot{m}}$) but replacing their resource variables in m by $\star$ (as resource variables are local). Additionally, at (3), all sets in $\mathcal{H}_{\dot{m}}$ are joined with $\mathcal{A}(\mathcal{C})$ to capture the resources that might have been simultaneously alive in the execution of m. The resulting sets of such operation are added to $\mathcal{H}$. We define the $\sqcup$ operation between two abstract states $\langle \mathcal{C}_1, \mathcal{H}_1 \rangle \sqcup \langle \mathcal{C}_2, \mathcal{H}_2 \rangle$ as $\langle \mathcal{C}_1 \cup \mathcal{C}_2, \mathcal{H}_1 \uplus \mathcal{H}_2 \rangle$. The analysis of while loops requires iterating until a fixpoint is reached. As the number of acquire instructions and the number of resource variables in the program are finite, widening is not needed.

Example 4. Let us apply the SRA to the running example. To avoid cluttering the expressions, instead of the line numbers, we use a_i to refer to the acquire at the program point marked with ⓘ in Fig. 2. For instance, a_1 refers to the acquire marked with ① at L2. We use $\mathcal{C}_l$ (resp. $\mathcal{H}_l$) to denote the set $\mathcal{C}$ (resp. $\mathcal{H}$) at line l. Let us see the results of the SRA for some selected program points.

$\mathcal{C}_2 = \{x\!:\!a_1\}$ $\mathcal{H}_2 = \{\{a_1\}\}$

$\mathcal{C}_3 = \{x\!:\!a_1, \star\!:\!a_3, \star\!:\!a_5\}$ $\mathcal{H}_3 = \{\{a_1, a_3, a_4\}, \{a_1, a_3, a_5\}\}$

$\mathcal{C}_4 = \{x\!:\!a_1, \star\!:\!a_3, \star\!:\!a_5, y\!:\!a_2\}$ $\mathcal{H}_4 = \{\{a_1, a_3, a_4\}, \{a_1, a_3, a_5, a_2\}\}$

$\mathcal{C}_5 = \{\star\!:\!a_3, \star\!:\!a_5, y\!:\!a_2\}$ $\mathcal{H}_5 = \{\{a_1, a_3, a_4\}, \{a_1, a_3, a_5, a_2\}\}$

$\mathcal{C}_6 = \mathcal{C}_{\dot{m}} = \{\star\!:\!a_3, \star\!:\!a_5, y\!:\!a_2\}$ $\mathcal{H}_6 = \mathcal{H}_{\dot{m}} = \{\{a_1, a_3, a_4\}, \{a_1, a_3, a_5, a_2\}, \{a_2, a_3, a_4, a_5\}^{\circledast}\}$

$\mathcal{C}_{10} = \{\star\!:\!a_3, z\!:\!a_3\}$ $\mathcal{H}_{10} = \{\{a_3, a_4\}\}$

$\mathcal{C}_{11} = \{\star\!:\!a_3, z\!:\!a_3, r\!:\!a_4\}$ $\mathcal{H}_{11} = \{\{a_3, a_4\}\}$

$\mathcal{C}_{12} = \mathcal{C}_{14} = \{\star\!:\!a_3, z\!:\!a_3\}$ $\mathcal{H}_{12} = \mathcal{H}_{14} = \{\{a_3, a_4\}\}$

$\mathcal{C}_{15} = \mathcal{C}_{\ddot{q}} = \{\star\!:\!a_3, z\!:\!a_3, t\!:\!a_5\}$ $\mathcal{H}_{15} = \mathcal{H}_{\ddot{q}} = \{\{a_3, a_4\}, \{a_3, a_5\}\}$

We can see that $\mathcal{C}_{11}$ is the only program point where a_4 is alive as it is released at L12. On the contrary, as a_3 is not released within the loop, we include $\star\!:\!a_3$ in $\mathcal{C}_{10}$–$\mathcal{C}_{14}$, and it escapes from the loop and from q. As $\mathcal{H}$ gathers all a_{pp} that might be alive at any program point, when the fixpoint is reached, $\mathcal{H}_{10} - \mathcal{H}_{14}$ contain the set $\{a_3, a_4\}$. The computation of $\mathcal{H}_{\ddot{q}}$ is done by means of the operation $\mathcal{A}(\mathcal{C}_{\ddot{q}}) \uplus \mathcal{H}_{14}$, that is, $\mathcal{H}_{\ddot{q}} = \{\{a_3, a_5\}\} \uplus \{\{a_3, a_4\}\} = \{\{a_3, a_5\}, \{a_3, a_4\}\}$, capturing that a_3, a_4, a_5 are not simultaneously in use at any state of q. Moreover, we can see in $C_{\ddot{q}}$ that the resources allocated at a_3 and a_5 escape from the execution of q. Let us continue with the computation of C_3 and $\mathcal{H}_3$. Firstly, $\star{:}a_3$ and $\star{:}a_5$ are added to C_3. Secondly, $\mathcal{H}_3$ is computed by adding $C_2{=}\{a_1\}$ to all sets in $\mathcal{H}_{\ddot{q}}$. To compute C_4, the analysis adds $y{:}a_2$ to C_3. The computation of $\mathcal{H}_4$ adds $\{a_1, a_3, a_5, a_2\}$ to $\mathcal{H}_3$, and replaces $\{a_1, a_3, a_5\}$ because it is a subset of $\{a_1, a_3, a_5, a_2\}$. Finally, to obtain $\mathcal{H}_6$, the set $\mathcal{A}(C_6){=}\{a_3, a_5, a_2\}$ is added to the sets in $\mathcal{H}_{\ddot{q}}$, resulting in the set $T = \{\{a_2, a_3, a_4, a_5\}, \{a_2, a_3, a_5\}\}$. Then $\mathcal{H}_6$ is obtained by computing $\mathcal{H}_5 \uplus T$. Note that $\{a_2, a_3, a_5\}$ is not in $\mathcal{H}_6$ as it is contained in a set of $\mathcal{H}_5$.

Theorem 1 (Soundness). *Given an execution trace $t \equiv S_0 {\rightsquigarrow} \ldots {\rightsquigarrow} S_n$ of a program P on input values $\overline{x}$, for any state $S_i \in t$, we have that:*
(a) $\exists\, \mathbb{H} \in \mathcal{H}_{\ddot{main}}.\ A(H_i) \subseteq \mathbb{H}$ where $A(H_i) = \{a_{pp} \mid \langle \text{-}, \text{-}, a_{pp}, \text{-} \rangle \in H_i\}$;
(b) if $\exists\langle \text{-}, \text{-}, a_{pp}, \text{-} \rangle \in H_n$ then $\text{-}{:}a_{pp} \in C_{\ddot{main}}$

4   Non-cumulative Resource Analysis

In this section we present our approach to use the information obtained in Sec. 3 to infer the peak cost of the execution. The first part, Sec. 4.1, consists in performing a program-point resource analysis in which we are able to infer the resources acquired at the points of interest. In Sec. 4.2, we discard from the upper bound obtained before those resources which are not used simultaneously.

4.1   Program-Point Resource Analysis

Our goal is to distinguish within the upper bounds (UB) obtained by resource analysis the amount of resources acquired at a given program point. To do so, we rely on the notion of *cost center* (CC) [1]. Originally, CCs were introduced for the analysis of distributed systems, such that, each CC is a symbolic expression of the form $c(o)$ where o is a location identifier used to separate the cost of each distributed location. Essentially, the resource analysis assigns the cost of an instruction *inst* to the distributed location o by multiplying the cost due to the execution of the instruction, denoted *cost(inst)* in a generic way, by the cost center of the location $c(o)$, i.e., $cost(inst){*}c(o)$. This way, the UBs that the analysis obtains are of the form $\sum c(o_i){*}C_i$, where each o_i is a location identifier and C_i is the total cost accumulated at this location.

Importantly, the notion of CC can be used in a more general way to define the granularity of a cost analyzer, i.e., the kind of separation that we want to observe in the UBs. In our concrete application, the expressions of the cost centers o_i will refer to the program points of interest. Thus, we are defining a resource analyzer that provides the resource consumption at program point level, i.e., a *program point* resource analysis. In particular, we define a CC for each acquire instruction in the program. Thus, CCs are of the form $c(a_{pp})$ for each instruction $pp{:}\mathsf{acquire}(e)$. In essence, the analyzer every time that accounts for the cost of executing an acquire instruction multiplies such cost by its corresponding cost center. The amount of resources allocated at the instruction $pp{:}\mathsf{acquire}(e)$ is accumulated as an expression of the form $c(a_{pp}) * \mathsf{nat}(e)$, where $\mathsf{nat}(e)$ is a function that returns e if $e > 0$ and 0 otherwise. We wrap the expression e with nat because this way the analyzer treats it as a non-negative expression whose cost we want to maximize, and computes the worst case of such expression (technical details can be found in [2]). The cost analyzer computes an *upper bound* for the total cost of executing P as an expression of the form $\mathcal{U}_P(\bar{x}) = \sum_{i=1}^{n} c(a_i) * C_i$, where C_i is a cost expression that bounds the resources allocated by the $\mathsf{acquire}$ instructions of the program. We omit the subscript in $\mathcal{U}$ when it is clear from the context. If one is interested in the amount of resources allocated by one particular $\mathsf{acquire}$ instruction a_{pp}, denoted $\mathcal{U}(\bar{x})|_{a_{pp}}$, we simply replace all $c(a_{pp'})$ with $pp \neq pp'$ by 0 and $c(a_{pp})$ by 1. We extend it to sets as $\mathcal{U}(\bar{x})|_S = \sum_{a_{pp} \in S} \mathcal{U}(\bar{x})|_{a_{pp}}$.

Example 5. The program point UB for the running example is:

$$\mathcal{U}(n, s) = \overbrace{c(a_1) * k_1}^{e_1} + \overbrace{c(a_2) * \mathsf{nat}(s)}^{e_2} + \overbrace{\mathsf{nat}(n) * (c(a_3) * k_2 + c(a_4) * \mathsf{nat}(s)) + c(a_5) * k_3}^{e_3} + \underbrace{\mathsf{nat}(n+2) * (c(a_3) * k_2 + c(a_4) * \mathsf{nat}(s+4)) + c(a_5) * k_3}_{e_4}$$

We have a CC for each $\mathsf{acquire}$ instruction in the program multiplied by the amount of resources allocated by the corresponding $\mathsf{acquire}$. In the examples, we do not wrap constants in nat because constant values do not need to be maximized, e.g. in the subexpression e_1 which corresponds to the cost of L2. The subexpression e_2 corresponds to L4 where s units are allocated. Expression e_3 corresponds to the first call to q, where the loop iterates $\mathsf{nat}(n)$ times and consumes $c(a_3) * k_2$ ($L10$) and $c(a_4) * \mathsf{nat}(s)$ ($L11$) resources for each iteration, plus the final $\mathsf{acquire}$ at $L15$, which allocates $c(a_5) * k_3$ resources. The cost of the second call to q is captured by e_4, where the number of iterations is bounded by $\mathsf{nat}(n+2)$ and $\mathsf{nat}(s+4)$ resources are allocated. e_4 also includes the cost allocated at L15. Let us continue by using $\mathcal{U}(n, s)$ to compute the resources allocated at a particular location, e.g. a_4, denoted by $\mathcal{U}(n, s)|_{a_4}$. To do so, we replace $c(a_4)$ by 1 and the rest of $c(\_)$ by 0. Thus, $\mathcal{U}(n, s)|_{a_4} = \mathsf{nat}(n) * \mathsf{nat}(s) + \mathsf{nat}(n+2) * \mathsf{nat}(s+4)$. Similarly, given the set of program points $\{a_3, a_5\}$, we have $\mathcal{U}(n, s)|_{\{a_3, a_5\}} = \mathcal{U}(n, s)|_{\{a_3\}} + \mathcal{U}(n, s)|_{\{a_5\}} = \mathsf{nat}(n) * k_2 + k_3 + \mathsf{nat}(n+2) * k_2 + k_3$.

4.2   Inference of Peak Cost

We can now put all pieces together. The SRA described in Sec. 3 allows us to infer the $\mathsf{acquire}$ instructions which could be allocated simultaneously. Such information is gathered in the set $\mathcal{H}$ of the SRA. In fact, the set $\mathcal{H}$ at the last program point of the program, namely main, collects all possible states of the resource allocation during program execution. Using this set we define the notion of *peak cost* as the maximum of the UBs computed for each possible set in $\mathcal{H}_{\mathsf{main}}$.

Definition 2 (Peak Cost). *The* peak cost *of a program* $P(\bar{x})$, *denoted* $\widehat{\mathcal{P}}(\bar{x})$, *is defined as* $\widehat{\mathcal{P}}(\bar{x}) = max(\{\mathcal{U}(\bar{x})|_{\mathbb{H}} \mid \mathbb{H} \in \mathcal{H}_{\mathsf{main}} \})$.

Intuitively, for each $\mathbb{H}$ in $\mathcal{H}_{\mathsf{main}}$, we compute its restricted UB, $\mathcal{U}(\bar{x})|_{\mathbb{H}}$, by removing from $\mathcal{U}(\bar{x})$ the cost due to $\mathsf{acquire}$ instructions that are not in $\mathbb{H}$, i.e., those $\mathsf{acquire}$ that were not active simultaneously with the elements in h.

Example 6. By using $\mathcal{H}_{\tilde{m}} = \{\{a_1, a_3, a_4\}, \{a_1, a_3, a_5, a_2\}, \{a_2, a_3, a_4, a_5\}\}$, the peak cost of m is the maximum of the expressions:

$$\mathcal{U}(n, s)|_{\{a_1, a_3, a_4\}} = k_1 + \mathsf{nat}(n)*(k_2 + \mathsf{nat}(s)) + \mathsf{nat}(n{+}2)*(k_2 + \mathsf{nat}(s{+}4))$$
$$\mathcal{U}(n, s)|_{\{a_1, a_3, a_5, a_2\}} = k_1 + \mathsf{nat}(s) + \mathsf{nat}(n)*k_2 + k_3 + \mathsf{nat}(n{+}2)*k_2 + k_3$$
$$\mathcal{U}(n, s)|_{\{a_2, a_3, a_4, a_5\}} = \mathsf{nat}(s) + \mathsf{nat}(n)*(k_2{+}\mathsf{nat}(s)) + k_3 + \mathsf{nat}(n{+}2)*(k_2{+}\mathsf{nat}(s{+}4)){+}k_3$$

Each UB expression over-approximates the value of R for the different states seen in Ex. 3 that could determine the concrete peak cost, namely $\mathcal{U}(n, s)|_{\{a_1, a_3, a_4\}}$ over-approximates the resource consumption at state S_8, $\mathcal{U}(n, s)|_{\{a_1, a_3, a_5, a_2\}}$ corresponds to S_{12}, and $\mathcal{U}(n, s)|_{\{a_2, a_3, a_4, a_5\}}$ bounds S_{16} and S_{18}.

Theorem 2 (Soundness). $\mathcal{P}(\overline{x}) \leq \widehat{\mathcal{P}}(\overline{x})$.

5 Extensions of the Basic Framework

In this section we discuss several extensions to our basic framework. First, Sec. 5.1 discusses how context-sensitive analysis can improve the accuracy of the results. Sec. 5.2 describes an improvement for handling *transient* acquire instructions, i.e., those resources which are allocated and released repeatedly but only one of all allocations is in use at a time. Finally, Sec. 5.3 introduces the extension of the framework to handle several kinds of resources.

5.1 Context-Sensitivity

Establishing the granularity of the analysis at the level of program points may lead to a loss of precision. This is because the computation of the SRA and the resource analysis are not able to distinguish if an acquire instruction is executed multiple times from different contexts. As a consequence, all resource usage associated to a given a_{pp} is accumulated in a single CC.

Example 7. The set $\mathcal{H}_{\tilde{m}}$ computed in Ex. 4 includes a_4 in two different sets. The first set corresponds to the first call to q (L3), where s units are allocated, whereas the second set corresponds to the second call (L6), and where s+4 units are allocated. Observe that the SRA of m does not distinguish such situation as both executions of L11 are represented as a single program point a_4. The same occurs in the computation of the UBs. In Ex. 6 we have computed $\mathcal{U}(n, s)|_{a_4} = \mathsf{nat}(n)*\mathsf{nat}(s){+}\mathsf{nat}(n{+}2)*\mathsf{nat}(s{+}4)$, which accounts for the resources acquired at L11. Note that $\mathcal{U}(n, s)|_{a_4}$ does not separate the cost of the different calls to q.

Intuitively, this loss of precision can be detected by checking if the *call graph* of the program contains convergence nodes, i.e., methods that have more than one incoming edge because they are invoked from different contexts. In such case, we can use standard techniques for context-sensitive analysis [16], e.g., method replication. In particular, the program can be rewritten by creating a different copy of the method for each incoming edge. Method replication guarantees that the calling contexts are not merged unless they correspond to a method call within a loop (or transitively from a loop). In the latter case, we indeed need to merge them and obtain the worst-case cost of all iterations, as the underlying resource analysis [2] already does.

Example 8. As q is called at L3 and L6, the application of the context-sensitive replication builds up a program with two methods: q_1 (from the call at L3) and q_2 (from L6). In addition, the modified version of m, denoted m', calls q_1 at L3 and q_2 at L6. We use a_{31} (resp. a_{32}) to refer to the acquire at L10 for the replica q_1 (resp. q_2). The SRA for m' returns: $\mathcal{H}_{\tilde{m}'} = \{\{a_1, a_{31}, a_{41}\}, \{a_1, a_{31}, a_{51}, a_2\}, \{a_{31}, a_{51}, a_2, a_{32}, a_{42}\}, \{a_{31}, a_{51}, a_2, a_{32}, a_{52}\}\}$ and $\mathcal{C}_{\tilde{m}'} = \{a_2, a_{31}, a_{32}, a_{51}, a_{52}\}$. Observe that the set marked with ⊙ in Ex. 4 is now split in two different sets, which precisely capture the states S_{16} and S_{18} of Fig. 2. Moreover, we distinguish a_{41}, a_{42} and a_{51}, a_{52} that allow us to separate the different calls to q, which is crucial for accounting the peak cost more accurately. The UB for m' is:

$$\mathcal{U}_{m'}(n, s) = c(a_1)*k_1 + c(a_2)*\text{nat}(s) + \text{nat}(n)*(c(a_{31})*k_2 + c(a_{41})*\text{nat}(s)) + c(a_{51})*k_3 +$$
$$\text{nat}(n+2)*(c(a_{32})*k_2 + c(a_{42})*\text{nat}(s+4)) + c(a_{52})*k_3$$

In contrast to $\mathcal{U}_m(n, s)|_{a_4}$, shown in Ex. 5, now we can compute $\mathcal{U}_{m'}(n, s)|_{a_{41}} = \text{nat}(n)*\text{nat}(s)$ and $\mathcal{U}_{m'}(n, s)|_{a_{42}} = \text{nat}(n+2)*\text{nat}(s+4)$. $\widehat{\mathcal{P}}_{m'}(n, s)$ is the maximum of:

$$\mathcal{U}_{m'}(n, s)|_{\{a_1, a_{31}, a_{41}\}} = k_1 + \text{nat}(n)*(k_2 + \text{nat}(s)) \qquad [S_8]$$
$$\mathcal{U}_{m'}(n, s)|_{\{a_1, a_{31}, a_{51}, a_2\}} = k_1 + \text{nat}(s) + \text{nat}(n)*k_2 + k_3 \qquad [S_{12}]$$
$$\mathcal{U}_{m'}(n, s)|_{\{a_{31}, a_{51}, a_2, a_{32}, a_{42}\}} = \text{nat}(s) + \text{nat}(n)*k_2 + k_3 + \text{nat}(n+2)*(k_2 + \text{nat}(s+4)) \quad [S_{16}]$$
$$\mathcal{U}_{m'}(n, s)|_{\{a_{31}, a_{51}, a_2, a_{32}, a_{52}\}} = \text{nat}(s) + \text{nat}(n)*k_2 + k_3 + \text{nat}(n+2)*k_2 + k_3 \qquad [S_{18}]$$

To the right of the UB expressions above we show their corresponding state of Fig. 2. In contrast to Ex. 6, now we have a one-to-one correspondence, and thus $\widehat{\mathcal{P}}_{m'}(n, s)$ is more accurate than $\widehat{\mathcal{P}}_m(n, s)$ in Ex. 6.

5.2   Handling Transient Resource Allocations

A complementary optimization with that in Sec. 5.1 can be performed when resources are acquired and released multiple times along the execution of the program within loops (or recursion). We use the notion of *transient* acquire to refer to an acquire(e) instruction at a_{pp} that is executed and released repeatedly but in such a way that the resources allocated by different executions of a_{pp} never coexist. As the UBs of Sec. 4 are computed by multiplying the number of times that each acquire instruction is executed by the worst case cost of each execution, the fact that the allocations of a transient acquire do not coexist is not accurately captured by the UB.

Example 9. Let us focus on the acquire a_4 of the running example. Although a_4 is executed multiple times within the loop, each allocation does not escape from the corresponding iteration because it is released at L12. To the right of Fig. 2 we can see that states S_3, S_6, S_8, S_{15} and S_{16} include the cost allocated by a_4 only once (elements in dark grey). Thus, a_4 is a transient acquire. In spite of this, we compute $\mathcal{U}_{m'}(n, s)|_{a_{41}} = \text{nat}(n)*\text{nat}(s)$, which accounts for the cost allocated at a_{41} as many times as a_{41} might be executed. Certainly, $\mathcal{U}_{m'}(n, s)|_{a_{41}}$ is a sound but imprecise approximation for the cost allocated by a_{41}.

We can improve the accuracy of the UBs for a transient acquire a_{pp} by including its worst case cost only once. We start by identifying when a_{pp} is transient in the concrete setting. Intuitively, if a_{pp} is transient the resources allocated at a_{pp} do not leak. Thus, in the last state of the execution, S_n, no resource allocated at a_{pp} remains in H_n (see the semantics at Fig. 1).

Definition 3 (Transient Acquire). *Given a program P, an acquire instruction a_{pp} is transient if for every execution trace of P, $S_1 \leadsto \ldots \leadsto S_n$, $\langle \_, \_, a_{pp}, \_ \rangle \notin H_n$.*

Example 10. In Fig. 2 we can see that a_1 and a_4 (shown in dark grey) are transient because their resources are always released at L5 and L12, resp.

In order to count the cost of a transient acquire only once, we use a particular instantiation of the cost analysis described in Sec. 4.1 to determine an UB on the number of times that such acquire might be executed. We use $\mathcal{U}^c$ to denote such UB which is computed by replacing the expression C_i (see Sec. 4.1) by 1 in the computation of $\mathcal{U}$. Assuming that $\mathcal{U}$ and $\mathcal{U}^c$ have been approximated by the same cost analyzer, we gain precision by obtaining the cost associated to a transient acquire instruction using its *singleton cost*.

Definition 4 (Singleton Cost). *Given a_{pp} we define its singleton cost as $\widetilde{\mathcal{U}}(\overline{x})|_{a_{pp}} = \mathcal{U}(\overline{x})|_{a_{pp}} / \mathcal{U}^c(\overline{x})|_{a_{pp}}$ if $\_ : a_{pp} \notin \mathcal{C}_{\ddot{main}}$ and $\widetilde{\mathcal{U}}(\overline{x})|_{a_{pp}} = \mathcal{U}(\overline{x})|_{a_{pp}}$, otherwise.*

Intuitively, when a_{pp} is transient, its singleton cost is obtained dividing the accumulated UB by the number of times that a_{pp} is executed. If it is not transient, we must keep the accumulated UB. According to Def. 3 and Th. 1(b), if $a_{pp} \notin \mathcal{C}_{main}$, then a_{pp} is transient, and so we can perform the division. We use $\widetilde{\mathcal{P}}$ to refer to the peak cost obtained by using $\widetilde{\mathcal{U}}$ instead of $\mathcal{U}$. In general, given a set of a_{pp}, we use $\widetilde{\mathcal{U}}_{m'}|_S$ to refer to the UBs computed using the singleton cost of each $a_{pp} \in S$.

Example 11. Let us continue with the context-sensitive replica of the running example, m'. We start by computing $\mathcal{U}^c_{m'}(n,s)|_{a_{41}} = \mathsf{nat}(n)$ and $\mathcal{U}_{m'}(n,s)|_{a_{41}} = \mathsf{nat}(n) * \mathsf{nat}(s)$. As we can see in Ex. 8, $a_{41}, a_{42} \notin \mathcal{C}_{\ddot{m}'}$, then $\widetilde{\mathcal{U}}_{m'}(n,s)|_{a_{41}} = \mathsf{nat}(s)$ which is the worst case of executing a_{41} only once. For a_{42} we have $\widetilde{\mathcal{U}}_{m'}(n,s)|_{a_{42}} = \mathsf{nat}(s+4)$. Regarding the remaining acquire instructions, either they cannot be divided, or can be divided by 1. Thus, we have that $\widetilde{\mathcal{P}}_{m'}(n,s)$ is the maximum of the following expressions:

$$\widetilde{\mathcal{U}}_{m'}(n,s)|_{\{a_1, a_{31}, a_{41}\}} = k_1 + \mathsf{nat}(n) * k_2 + \mathsf{nat}(s) \qquad [S_8]$$
$$\widetilde{\mathcal{U}}_{m'}(n,s)|_{\{a_1, a_{31}, a_{51}, a_2\}} = k_1 + \mathsf{nat}(s) + \mathsf{nat}(n) * k_2 + k_3 \qquad [S_{12}]$$
$$\widetilde{\mathcal{U}}_{m'}(n,s)|_{\{a_{31}, a_{51}, a_2, a_{32}, a_{42}\}} = \mathsf{nat}(s) + \mathsf{nat}(n) * k_2 + k_3 + \mathsf{nat}(s+4) \qquad [S_{16}]$$
$$\widetilde{\mathcal{U}}_{m'}(n,s)|_{\{a_{31}, a_{51}, a_2, a_{32}, a_{52}\}} = \mathsf{nat}(s) + \mathsf{nat}(n) * k_2 + k_3 + \mathsf{nat}(n+2) * k_2 + k_3 \qquad [S_{18}]$$

Theorem 3 (Soundness). *Given a program $P(\overline{x})$ and its context-sensitive replica $P'(\overline{x})$, we have that $\mathcal{P}_P(\overline{x}) \leq \widetilde{\mathcal{P}}_{P'}(\overline{x})$.*

5.3   Handling Different Resources Simultaneously

Our goal is now to allow allocation of different types of resources in the program (e.g., we want to infer the heap space usage and the number of simultaneous connections to a database). To this purpose, we extend the instruction acquire(e) (see Sec. 2.1) with an additional parameter which determines the kind of resource to be allocated, i.e., acquire(res,e). Such extension does not require any modification to the semantics. We define the function $type(a_{pp})$ which returns the type of resource allocated at a_{pp}. Now, we extend Def. 1 to consider the resource of interest. We use $R_i(\mathsf{res})$ to refer to the following value $R_i(\mathsf{res}) = \sum \{ r \mid \langle \_, \_, a_{pp}, r \rangle \in H_i \wedge type(a_{pp}) = \mathsf{res} \}$.

Definition 5 (Concrete Peak Cost). *Given a resource* res, *the* peak cost *of an execution trace* t *of program* $P(\overline{x}, res)$ *is* $\mathcal{P}(\overline{x}, res) = max(\{R_i(res)|S_i \in t\})$.

Interestingly, such extension does not require any modification neither to the SRA of Sec. 3 nor to the program point resource analysis of Sec. 4. This is due to the fact that the analysis works at the level of program points and one program point can only allocate one particular type of resource. We define $\mathcal{R}(res)$ as the set of program points that allocate resources of type res, i.e., $\mathcal{R}(res)=\{a_{pp} \mid type(a_{pp})=res\}$. Thus, we extend the notion of peak cost of Def. 2 with the type of resource, i.e., $\widehat{\mathcal{P}}(\overline{x}, res)=max(\{\mathcal{U}(\overline{x})|_{\mathbb{H}\cap\mathcal{R}(res)} \mid \mathbb{H} \in \mathcal{H}_{\ddot{m}ain}\})$. Observe that the only difference with Def. 2 is in the intersection $\mathbb{H} \cap \mathcal{R}(res)$ which restricts the considered acquire when computing the UBs. One relevant aspect is that by computing the UB only once, we are able to obtain the peak cost for different types of resources by restricting the UB for each resource of interest. The extension of Th. 2 and Th. 3 to include a particular resource is straightforward.

Example 12. Let us modify the acquire instructions of the running example in Fig. 2 to add the resource to be allocated. Now we have that L2 is $x =$ acquire(hd,k_1) and L11 is $r =$ acquire(hd,w), where hd is a type of resource. We assume that L4, L10, L15 allocate a different type of resource, e.g. a resource of type mem. Then, using the context-sensitive replica of the program, we have that $\mathcal{R}(hd) = \{a_1, a_{41}, a_{42}\}$, and $\mathcal{R}(mem) = \{a_2, a_{31}, a_{32}, a_{51}, a_{52}\}$. Now, using the UB from Ex. 11, we have that $\widehat{\mathcal{P}}(n, s, hd)_{m'}$ is the maximum of the expressions:

$$\widetilde{\mathcal{U}}_{m'}(n, s, hd)|_{\{a_1, a_{31}, a_{41}\}\cap\mathcal{R}(hd)} = k_1+\mathsf{nat}(s) \quad [S_8]$$
$$\widetilde{\mathcal{U}}_{m'}(n, s, hd)|_{\{a_1, a_{31}, a_{51}, a_2\}\cap\mathcal{R}(hd)} = k_1 \quad [S_{12}]$$
$$\widetilde{\mathcal{U}}_{m'}(n, s, hd)|_{\{a_{31}, a_{51}, a_2, a_{32}, a_{42}\}\cap\mathcal{R}(hd)} = \mathsf{nat}(s+4) \quad [S_{16}]$$
$$\widetilde{\mathcal{U}}_{m'}(n, s, hd)|_{\{a_{31}, a_{51}, a_2, a_{32}, a_{52}\}\cap\mathcal{R}(hd)} = 0 \quad [S_{18}]$$

6   Experimental Evaluation

We have implemented a prototype peak cost analyzer for simple sequential programs that follow the syntax of Sec. 2.1, but that besides use a functional language to define data types (the use of functions does not require any conceptual modification to our basic analysis). This language corresponds to the sequential sublanguage of ABS [13], a language which besides has concurrency features that are ignored by our analyzer. To perform the experiments, our analyzer has been applied to some programs written in ABS: BBuffer, a bounded-buffer for communicating producers and consumers; MailServer, a client-server system; Chat, a chat application; DistHT, an implementation of a hash table; BookShop, a book shop application; and PeerToPeer, a peer-to-peer network.

The non-cumulative resource that we measure is the peak of the size of the stack of activation records. For each method executed, an activation record is created, and later removed when the method terminates. The size might depend on the arguments used in the call, as due to the use of functional data structures, when a method is invoked, the data structures (used as parameters) are passed and stored. This aspect is interesting because we can measure the peak size, not

Table 1. Experimental Evaluation (times in seconds)

Benchmark	$\#_l$	$\#_e$	$\mathbf{T}_n$	$\mathbf{T}_c$	$\%_n$	$\%_c$	$\%_s$	$\%_{cn}$	$\%_{sn}$	$\%_{sc}$
BBuffer	105	3125	0.93	1.07	4.9	35.7	43.9	32.1	40.6	15.7
MailServer	115	3375	9.58	1.23	16.0	42.4	58.2	30.2	47.1	27.6
Chat	302	2500	0.58	0.58	69.9	69.9	92.9	0.0	74.8	74.8
DistHT	353	2500	0.68	2.27	40.2	82.8	84.8	71.2	74.6	10.7
BookShop	353	4096	2.22	2.41	6.5	6.5	32.4	0.0	27.9	27.9
PeerToPeer	240	4.09	5.62	11.86	0.4	8.8	11.4	8.5	11.1	3.0
					23.0	41.0	53.9	23.7	46.0	26.6

only due to activation records whose size is constant, but also measure the size of the data structures used in the invocations, and take them into account.

In order to evaluate our analysis we have obtained different UBs on the size of the stack of activation records and compared their precision. In particular, we have compared the UBs obtained by the resource analysis of [2] (a cumulative cost analyzer), our basic non-cumulative approach (Sec. 4.2), the context-sensitive extension of Sec. 5.1 and the UBs obtained by using the singleton cost of each acquire as described in Sec. 5.2. In order to obtain concrete values for the gains, we have evaluated the UB expressions for different combinations of the input arguments and computed the average. For a concrete input arguments $\overline{x}$, we compute the gain of $\widehat{\mathcal{P}}(\overline{x})$ w.r.t. $\mathcal{U}(\overline{x})$ using the formula $(1 - \widehat{\mathcal{P}}(\overline{x})/\mathcal{U}(\overline{x})) * 100$. In order to compute the sizes of the activation records of the methods, we have modified each method of the benchmarks by including in the beginning of the method one acquire and one release at the end of each method to free it. Let us illustrate it with an example, if we have a method Int m (Data d,Int i) {Int j=i+1}, we modify it to {x=acquire(1+1+d+1+1); Int j=i+1; release x;}. The addends of the expression 1+1+d+1+1 correspond to: the pointer to the activation record, the size of the returned value (1 unit), the size of the information received through d (d units), the size of i (1 unit), and the size of j (1 unit). The instruction release(x) releases all resources. Experiments have been performed on an Intel Core i5 (1.8GHz, 4GB RAM), running OSX 10.8.

Table 1 summarizes the results obtained. Columns $\#_l$ and $\#_e$ show, resp., the number of lines of code and the number of input argument combinations evaluated. Columns $\mathbf{T}_n$, $\mathbf{T}_c$ show, resp., the time (in seconds) to perform the basic non-cumulative analysis and the context-sensitive non-cumulative analysis. Columns $\%_n$, $\%_c$, $\%_s$ show, resp., the gain of the non-cumulative resource analysis, its context-sensitive extension and the singleton cost extension w.r.t. the cumulative analysis. Column $\%_{cn}$ shows the gain of $\widehat{\mathcal{P}}$ applied to the context sensitive replica of the program w.r.t. its application to the original program. Columns $\%_{sn}$ and $\%_{sc}$ show, resp., the gain of $\widetilde{\mathcal{P}}$ w.r.t. $\widehat{\mathcal{P}}$, and w.r.t. $\widehat{\mathcal{P}}$ applied to the context sensitive replica of the program. The last row shows the average of the results. As regards analysis times, we argue that the time taken by the analyzer is reasonable and the context-sensitive approach although more expensive is feasible. As regards precision, we can observe that the gains obtained by the non-cumulative analyses are significant w.r.t. the cumulative resource analysis. As it can be expected, $\widetilde{\mathcal{P}}$ shows the best results with gains from 11% to 93%.

The non-cumulative analysis and its context-sensitive version also present significant gains, on average 23% and 41% respectively. The improvement gained by applying non-cumulative analysis to the context-sensitive extension is also relevant, a gain of 23.7%. As resources are released in all methods, we achieve a significant improvement with $\widetilde{\mathcal{P}}$, from 46% to 26.6% on average. All in all, we argue that the experimental evaluation shows the accuracy of non-cumulative resource analysis and the precision gained with its extensions.

7   Conclusions and Related Work

To the best of our knowledge, this is the first generic framework to infer the peak of the resource consumption of sequential imperative programs. The crux of the framework is an analysis to infer the resources that might be used simultaneously along the execution. This analysis is formalized as a data-flow analysis over a finite domain of sets of resources. The inference is followed by a program-point resource analysis which defines the resource consumption at the level of the program points at which resources are acquired.

Previous work on non-cumulative cost analysis of sequential imperative programs has been focused on the particular resource of memory consumption with garbage collection, while our approach is generic on the kind of non-cumulative cost that one wants to measure. Our framework can be used to redefine previous analyses of heap space usage [5] into the standard cost analysis setting. Depending on the particular garbage collection strategy, the release instruction will be placed at one point or another. For instance, if one uses scope-based garbage collection, all release instructions are placed just before the method return instruction and our framework can be applied. If one wants to use a liveness-based garbage collection, then the liveness analysis determines where the release instructions should go, and our analysis is then applied. The important point to note is that these analyses [5] provided a solution based on the generation of non-standard cost relations specific to the problem of memory consumption. It thus cannot be generalized to other kind of non-cumulative resources. Non-cumulative resource analysis, by means of the use of malloc and free, is studied at [9], but the approach is limited to constant resource consumption. Several analyses around the RAML tool [12] also assume the existence of acquire and release instructions and the application of our framework to this setting is an interesting topic for further research. The differences between amortized cost analysis and a standard cost analysis are discussed in [6,10]. Also, we want to study the recasting of [7] into our generic framework.

Recent work defines an analysis to infer the peak cost of distributed systems [3]. There are two fundamental differences with our work: (1) [3] is developed for cumulative resources, and the extension to non-cumulative resources is not studied there and (2) [3] considers a concurrent distributed language, while our focus is on sequential programs. There is nevertheless a similarity with our work in the elimination from the total cost of elements that do not happen simultaneously. However, in the case of [3] this information is gathered by a complex may-happen-in-parallel analysis [4] which infers the interleavings that may occur during the execution followed by a post-process in which a graph is built and its cliques are used to detect when several tasks can be executing concurrently. In our case, we are able to detect when resources are used simultaneously by means of a simpler analysis defined as a standard data-flow analysis on a finite domain. Besides, the upper bounds in [3] are obtained by a task-level resource analysis since in their case they want to obtain the resource consumption at the granularity of tasks rather than at program point granularity. As in our case, the use of context sensitive analysis [16] can improve the accuracy of the results.

Acknowledgments. This work was funded partially by the EU project FP7-ICT-610582 ENVISAGE: Engineering Virtualized Services (http://www.envisage-project.eu), by the Spanish project TIN2012-38137, and by the CM project S2013/ICE-3006.

References

1. Albert, E., Arenas, P., Flores-Montoya, A., Genaim, S., Gómez-Zamalloa, M., Martin-Martin, E., Puebla, G., Román-Díez, G.: SACO: Static Analyzer for Concurrent Objects. In: Ábrahám, E., Havelund, K. (eds.) TACAS 2014 (ETAPS). LNCS, vol. 8413, pp. 562–567. Springer, Heidelberg (2014)
2. Albert, E., Arenas, P., Genaim, S., Puebla, G., Zanardini, D.: Cost analysis of java bytecode. In: De Nicola, R. (ed.) ESOP 2007. LNCS, vol. 4421, pp. 157–172. Springer, Heidelberg (2007)
3. Albert, E., Correas, J., Román-Díez, G.: Peak Cost Analysis of Distributed Systems. In: Müller-Olm, M., Seidl, H. (eds.) Static Analysis. LNCS, vol. 8723, pp. 18–33. Springer, Heidelberg (2014)
4. Albert, E., Flores-Montoya, A.E., Genaim, S.: Analysis of May-Happen-in-Parallel in Concurrent Objects. In: Giese, H., Rosu, G. (eds.) FORTE 2012 and FMOODS 2012. LNCS, vol. 7273, pp. 35–51. Springer, Heidelberg (2012)
5. Albert, E., Genaim, S., Gómez-Zamalloa, M.: Parametric Inference of Memory Requirements for Garbage Collected Languages. In: ISMM 2010, pp. 121–130 (2010)
6. Alonso-Blas, D.E., Genaim, S.: On the Limits of the Classical Approach to Cost Analysis. In: Miné, A., Schmidt, D. (eds.) SAS 2012. LNCS, vol. 7460, pp. 405–421. Springer, Heidelberg (2012)
7. Braberman, V., Fernández, F., Garbervetsky, D., Yovine, S.: Parametric Prediction of Heap Memory Requirements. In: ISMM 2008, pp. 141–150. ACM (2008)
8. Braberman, V.A., Garbervetsky, D., Hym, S., Yovine, S.: Summary-based inference of quantitative bounds of live heap objects. SCP 92, 56–84 (2014)
9. Cook, B., Gupta, A., Magill, S., Rybalchenko, A., Simsa, J., Singh, S., Vafeiadis, V.: Finding heap-bounds for hardware synthesis. In: FMCAD 2009, pp. 205–212 (2009)
10. Flores-Montoya, A., Hähnle, R.: Resource analysis of complex programs with cost equations. In: Garrigue, J. (ed.) APLAS 2014. LNCS, vol. 8858, pp. 275–295. Springer, Heidelberg (2014)
11. Gulwani, S., Mehra, K.K., Chilimbi, T.M.: Speed: Precise and Efficient Static Estimation of Program Computational Complexity. In: POPL 2009, pp. 127–139. ACM (2009)
12. Hofmann, M., Jost, S.: Static prediction of heap space usage for first-order functional programs. In: POPL 2013, pp. 185–197. ACM (2003)

13. Johnsen, E.B., Hähnle, R., Schäfer, J., Schlatte, R., Steffen, M.: ABS: A Core Language for Abstract Behavioral Specification. In: Aichernig, B.K., de Boer, F.S., Bonsangue, M.M. (eds.) Formal Methods for Components and Objects. LNCS, vol. 6957, pp. 142–164. Springer, Heidelberg (2011)
14. Sinn, M., Zuleger, F., Veith, H.: A simple and scalable static analysis for bound analysis and amortized complexity analysis. In: Biere, A., Bloem, R. (eds.) CAV 2014. LNCS, vol. 8559, pp. 745–761. Springer, Heidelberg (2014)
15. Trinder, P.W., Cole, M.I., Hammond, K., Loidl, H.W., Michaelson, G.: Resource analyses for parallel and distributed coordination. CCPE 25(3), 309–348 (2013)
16. Whaley, J., Lam, M.S.: Cloning-based context-sensitive pointer alias analysis using binary decision diagrams. In: PLDI, pp. 131–144. ACM (2004)

Value Slice: A New Slicing Concept
for Scalable Property Checking

Shrawan Kumar[1,*], Amitabha Sanyal[2], and Uday P. Khedker[2]

[1] Tata Consultancy Services Ltd, Pune, India
shrawan.kumar@tcs.com
[2] IIT Bombay, Mumbai 400076, India
{as,uday}@cse.iitb.ac.in

Abstract. A backward slice is a commonly used preprocessing step for scaling property checking. For large programs though, the reduced size of the slice may still be too large for verifiers to handle. We propose an aggressive slicing method that, apart from slicing out the same statements as backward slice, also eliminates computations that only decide whether the point of property assertion is reachable. However, for precision, we also carefully identify and retain *all* computations that influence the values of the variables in the property. The resulting slice, called *value slice*, is smaller and scales better for property checking than backward slice.

We carry experiments on property checking of industry strength programs using three comparable slicing techniques: backward slice, value slice and an even more aggressive slicing technique called thin slice that retains only those statements on which the variables in the property are data dependent. While backward slicing enables highest precision and thin slice scales best, value slice based property checking comes close to the best in both scalability and precision. This makes value slice a good compromise between backward and thin slice for property checking.

1 Introduction

Given a program and a set of variables at a program point of interest, *program slicing* [19] pares the program to contain only those statements that are likely to influence the values of the variables at that program point. The set of variables and the program point, taken together, is called the *slicing criterion*. Several variants of the original slicing technique, called *backward slicing*, have since been proposed [16]. These have been used for program understanding, debugging, testing, maintenance, software quality assurance and reverse engineering. A survey of applications of program slicing appears in [5]. This paper focuses on the use of slicing for scaling up property checking.

Among slicing techniques, backward slicing is the natural choice for property checking. While computation of backward slice is efficient and scalable, the size of the slice is a matter of concern. Empirical studies [11] have shown that the size of the backward slice on an average is about 30% of the program size. This size is still too large for the analysis of large programs. In addition, the statements sliced out are irrelevant

---

* Also research scholar at IIT Bombay. This work is part of his doctoral dissertation.

© Springer-Verlag Berlin Heidelberg 2015
C. Baier and C. Tinelli (Eds.): TACAS 2015, LNCS 9035, pp. 101–115, 2015.
DOI: 10.1007/978-3-662-46681-0_7

```
 1 int main()
 2 {
 3   int i,j,k,st;
 4   int t,u;
 5   t=i=j=k=0;
 6   st = fn3();
 7   while (i<1000)
 8   {
 9    i= i+ fn2();
10    t = fn1(i,j);
11    if (t>100)
12    {
13     if (st ==1)
14     { j++; k++; }
15     else
16     {j+=2; k+=1;}
17     u = j-k;
18     assert
19       (u==0||u==k);
20    }
21   }
22   return 0;
23 }
24 int fn1();
25 int fn2();
26 int fn3();
```
(a) Backward slice

```
 1 int main()
 2 {
 3   int i,j,k,st;
 4   int u;
 5   j=k=0;
 6   st = fn3();
 7   while (*)
 8   {
 9
10
11    if (*)
12    {
13     if (st ==1)
14     { j++; k++; }
15     else
16     {j+=2; k+=1;}
17     u = j-k;
18     assert
19       (u==0||u==k);
20    }
21   }
22   return 0;
23 }
24 // fn1 removed
25 // fn2 removed
26 int fn3();
```
(b) Value slice

```
 1 int main()
 2 {
 3   int i,j,k;
 4   int u;
 5   j=k=0;
 6
 7   while (*)
 8   {
 9
10
11    if (*)
12    {
13     if (*)
14     { j++; k++; }
15     else
16     {j+=2; k+=1;}
17     u = j-k;
18     assert
19       (u==0||u==k);
20    }
21   }
22   return 0;
23 }
24 // fn1 removed
25 // fn2 removed
26 // fn3 removed
```
(c) Thin slice

Fig. 1. Usual backward slice, value slice and thin slice

to the asserted property and their elimination does not reduce the load on the verifier significantly. To remedy this, we propose an alternate notion of slicing based on the observation that a backward slice consists of two categories of statements (i) statements that decide whether the slicing criterion will be reached during execution, and (ii) statements that decide the values of variables in the slicing criterion. Our results show that the second category of statements, called *value-impacting*, are often enough for property checking. We also show that the size of the slice consisting of value-impacting statements, called a *value slice*, is about half the size of the backward slice.

An attempt similar to ours called *thin slicing* [17] retains only those statements on which the variables in the slicing criterion are data-dependent. In particular, *all* conditional statements are eliminated. While this does bring down the size of the slice, unlike our method it also eliminates some conditional statements that are value-impacting and thus crucial for property checking.

As a motivating example, Figure 1(a) shows an `assert` involving u at line 18. The functions `fn1` and `fn2` are large and complex but without side effects. Clearly, a backward slice with the slicing criterion $\langle 18, u \rangle$ does not eliminate any statement from the program. SATABS (version 3.0) [8], a robust and scalable predicate abstraction based property checking tool, times out on this program on a limit of 20 minutes.

Observe however that the value of u does not depend on the values of i or t. Since these variables merely decide the reachability of line 18 during execution, the statements computing them are non-value-impacting and thus considered irrelevant. Issues related to reachability are being addressed in an ongoing work and are beyond the scope of this paper.

Figure 1(b) shows a slice of the program that captures the computation of every value of u in the original program. Conditional statements that do not value-impact u are replaced by a ∗ standing for a randomly chosen boolean value. The resulting slice is much smaller in comparison to the backward slice (the entire program). SATABS succeeds in showing that the property is indeed satisfied on the sliced program, and, by implication, on the original program. On the other hand, the thin slice shown in Figure 1(c), while smaller in size, is not useful since the property does not hold on the sliced program. Thus any verifier will produce counterexamples on this slice that will be spurious on the original program.

The contributions of this paper are:

1. We define a new notion of slicing called value slice and propose a worklist based algorithm for its computation. The algorithm is shown to be correct by construction.
2. We describe the results of experiments on property checking based on the three comparable slicing methods—backward, value and thin slices. We show that on both criteria, scalability and precision, value slice based property checking yields results that are close to the best among the three slicing methods.

We conclude that as a slicing technique for increasing the scalability of property checking, value slice represents a sweet spot between backward and thin slice.

2   Background

We shall present our ideas in the context of imperative programs made of assignments, conditional statements (the conditions being without side-effects), *while* loops, and function calls. We allow *break* and *continue* statements in loops. However, we restrict ourselves to goto-less programs with single-entry loops and two-way branching conditional statements; it makes for an easier formal treatment of our method without losing expressibility. We also allow the full range of C-types including arrays and pointers.

Our analysis will be based on a model of the program called the control flow graph (CFG) [1]. A CFG is a pair $\langle N, E \rangle$, where N is a set of nodes representing atomic statements, i.e. assignment statements and conditions (also called predicates) of the program[1]. Further, $(n_1, n_2) \in E$, if there is a possible flow of control from n_1 to n_2 without any intervening node. We use $n_1 \to n_2$ and $n_1 \overset{b}{\to} n_2$ to denote unconditional and conditional edges, where $b \in \{true, false\}$ indicates the branch outcome. Each statement (or node) is associated with a unique label l that represents the program point just before the statement. Often we shall refer to a node by its label. In addition, each CFG is assumed to have two distinguished nodes with labels $ENTRY$ and $EXIT$. Except for $ENTRY$ and $EXIT$, there is a one-to-one correspondence between the nodes

---

[1] For the rest of the paper, a statement will mean an atomic statement.

of the CFG and the statements of the program. Thus we shall use the terms statement and node interchangeably.

2.1   Program States and Traces

Let Var be the set of variables in a program P and Val be the set of possible values which the variables in Var can take. A *program state* is a map $\sigma : Var \to Val$ such that $\sigma(v)$ denotes the value of v in the program state σ. Given $X \subseteq Var$, a X-restriction of σ, denoted as $\lfloor \sigma \rfloor_X$, is a map $X \to Val$ such that $\forall x \in X.\lfloor \sigma \rfloor_X(x) = \sigma(x)$. Finally, an *execution state* is a pair $\langle l, \sigma \rangle$, where σ is a program state and l is the label of a CFG node. The execution of a program is a sequence of execution states starting with $\langle ENTRY, \sigma_0 \rangle$, where σ_0 is the initial program state. We assume that the next state is given by a function $\mathcal{T}$, i.e. for each execution state $\langle l, \sigma \rangle$, the next state is $\mathcal{T}(\langle l, \sigma \rangle)$.

A *trace* is a (possibly infinite) sequence of execution states $[\langle l_i, \sigma_i \rangle]$, $i \geq 0$, where $l_0 = ENTRY$, σ_0 is an initial program state, and $\langle l_{i+1}, \sigma_{i+1} \rangle = \mathcal{T}(\langle l_i, \sigma_i \rangle)$ for all $i \geq 0$. When the trace sequence is finite and ends with an execution state $\langle EXIT, \sigma \rangle$, it is called a *terminating trace*. We shall only consider terminating traces in the rest of the paper.

2.2   Data and Control Dependence

A definition d of a variable v in a node n is said to be a *reaching definition* [1] for a label l, if there is a control flow path from n to l devoid of any other definition of v. A variable x at label l is said to be *data dependent* on a definition d of x, if d is a *reaching definition* for l. Given a set of variables X and a label l, the set of definitions that the variables in X are dependent on is denoted by $DU(l, X)$.

Backward slicing algorithms are implemented efficiently using post-dominance and control dependence [10,12]. A node n_2 *post-dominates* a node n_1 if every path from n_1 to *EXIT* contains n_2. If, in addition, $n_1 \neq n_2$, then n_2 is said to *strictly post-dominate* n_1. A node n is *control dependent* on an edge $c \xrightarrow{b} n'$, denoted $c \xrightarrow{b} n$, if n post-dominates n', and n does not strictly *post-dominate* c. If the label b is not important in a context, it is elided.

The transitive closure of control dependences, i.e. a chain of control dependences starting with the predicate c and edge b and ending with the node n is denoted as $c \overset{b}{\leadsto} n$. Note that because of return and break statements, it is possible to have both $c \overset{b}{\leadsto} n$ and $c \overset{b'}{\leadsto} n$, where $b \neq b'$.

2.3   Subprogram and Backward Slice

The basis for slicing is a *slicing criterion* defined as a pair $\Upsilon = \langle l, V \rangle$, where l is a statement label and $V \subseteq Var$ is a set of variables. The slicing criterion represents our interest in the values of the variables in V just before the execution of the statement at l. Let $REF(s)$ denote the set of variables referred in a node s. Given a statement s with label l', we will use $LV(s)$ to denote the slicing criterion $\langle l', REF(s) \rangle$.

A *subprogram* of P is a program formed by deleting some statements from P while retaining its structure. This means if a statement enclosed by a predicate c in P is included in the subprogram, then so is c itself. Given a program P and a slicing criterion with location l, an *augmented program* is obtained by inserting a $SKIP$ (do nothing) statement at l. Clearly, an augmented program has the same behavior as the original program. In the sequel, we shall assume that our programs are augmented. Finally, we shall assume that program points of the same statement in the original program and the slice are represented by the same label.

Assume for the rest of this section that the slicing criterion is $\Upsilon = \langle l, V \rangle$. Given a program P, we define *SC-execution states* to be the execution states of P with label l. For a subprogram to be called a backward slice, there should be a relation between the traces of the program and the slice on the same input when we restrict the traces to their SC-execution states. We call a trace thus restricted as a *sub-trace*. We say that the two sub-traces $[(l, \sigma_i)], 1 \leq i \leq k$ and $[(l, \sigma_i')], 1 \leq i \leq k'$ are *SC-equivalent* wrt Υ, if $k = k'$, and for each i between 1 and k, $\lfloor \sigma_i \rfloor_V = \lfloor \sigma_i' \rfloor_V$.

Let $Tr(P, I, \Upsilon)$ denote the sub-trace of a program P on input I for the slicing criterion Υ. We now define P' to be a *backward slice* of P with respect to Υ, if for all inputs I, $Tr(P, I, \Upsilon)$ and $Tr(P', I, \Upsilon)$ are SC-equivalent. As we shall see later, for the same input the sub-traces of the program and its value-slice may not be of the same length. We therefore need a weaker notion of SC-equivalence. We say that a pair of sub-traces $[(l, \sigma_i)], 1 \leq i \leq k$ and $[(l, \sigma_i')], 1 \leq i \leq k'$ are *weak-SC-equivalent* wrt Υ, if for each i between 1 and $min(k, k')$, $\lfloor \sigma_i \rfloor_V = \lfloor \sigma_i' \rfloor_V$. The value $min(k, k')$ is called the *trace observation window* for the pair of sub-traces.

3   Value Slice

Given a slicing criterion $\langle l, V \rangle$, a value slice is the answer to the question: "Which statements can possibly influence the values of the variables in V observed at l"?

The answer to this question for $P1$ in Figure 2 for the slicing criterion $\langle 17, \{y\} \rangle$ is as follows: y at 17 gets its value from x through the assignment at 15. x, in turn, gets its value from the definitions at 14 and 8, and both of these can reach 15. Thus 8, 14 and 15 are in the value slice. The predicate c2 at 13 is also in the value slice, since, of the values generated at 14 and 8, the value that actually reaches line 15 is decided by c2. Finally, line 10, where c2 itself is computed, is also in the value slice. The resulting program is $P2$ without the lines shaded gray.

Although $P2$ (ignoring gray lines) contains all statements required to answer the question posed earlier for the slicing criterion $\langle 17, \{y\} \rangle$, it is not suitable for property checking. The reason is that apart from the statements that decide the values of variables at the slicing criterion, we also need to explicate the CFG paths along which the computations of these values take place. Therefore, if a statement in the slice is control dependent on a predicate that, by itself, does not influence values of the variables in the slicing criterion, the predicate is retained in the slice in an abstract form. This brings the predicates at lines 16 and 11 into the value slice but replaced by '*' indicating a non-deterministic branch. We call such predicates *abstract predicates*. Note, however, that if none of the statements that are transitively control dependent on a predicate are included in the slice, the predicate itself can be eliminated.

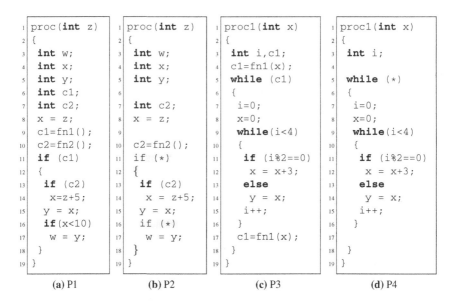

Fig. 2. Various forms of value slices

In the context of property checking, the inclusion of c2 in a concrete form at line 13 is a crucial difference between value slice and thin-slice[2]. As an example, assume that when $P1$ is executed with v as the initial value of z, c2 evaluates to *false* and the value reaching y at 17 is also v. For the same initial value of z, the value slice $P2$ will also assign the same value v to y. However, if we abstract c2 as '*', the resulting program may produce a trace which assigns the value $v+5$ to y at line 17. To avoid such spurious counterexamples, we retain the predicate c2 at line 13 in a concrete form.

To generalize this point, consider the execution of $P3$ in Figure 2. Assuming that the outer loop executes twice for an input, the sub-trace for $\langle 14, \{x\}\rangle$ is $[\langle 14, 3\rangle, \langle 14, 6\rangle, \langle 14, 3\rangle, \langle 14, 6\rangle]$. However, if the predicates of both the whiles are abstracted, then one of the sub-traces generated is $[\langle 14, 3\rangle, \langle 14, 3\rangle]$. The two sub-trace do not match in that they are not weak-SC-equivalent. On the other hand, program $P4$ in which only the outer loop predicate is abstracted, produces as a sub-trace zero or more repetitions of $[\langle 14, 3\rangle, \langle 14, 6\rangle]$. We therefore include the predicate i<4 in the value slice for the slicing criterion $\langle 14, \{x\}\rangle$. The predicate i%2==0 is also in the value slice by a similar argument. In summary, for the same input, the sub-traces of a value-slice and the original program are required to be weak-SC-equivalent. Based on these considerations, we now specify the conditions to be satisfied by a value slice.

Definition 1. (Value-slice) *A value slice P^V of a program P for a slicing criterion $\langle l, V\rangle$ satisfies the following conditions:*
1. P^V is a subprogram of P with some predicates in abstract form.

---

[2] For comparison in the context of property checking, predicate c2, which would have been eliminated in the thin-slice, is retained in an abstract form.

2. If P terminates with trace τ on an input, then there should exist a trace τ' of P^V on the same input which is SC-equivalent *to τ.*

3. If P terminates with trace τ on an input, then every trace τ' of P^V on the same input should be weak-SC-equivalent *to τ.*

3.1 Value-Impacting Statements

While the trace-based definition is good from a semantic point of view, we present a definition that will enable us to statically identify the set of statements that should necessarily be in the value slice in concrete form. We call such statements *value-impacting* and define the term shortly. As mentioned in the background section, we shall use the term "node" to also mean atomic statements.

Definition 2. (Value-impacting Node) *A node s value-impacts $\Upsilon = \langle l, V \rangle$, if any of the following conditions hold:*

1. s is an assignment in $DU(\Upsilon)$.

2. s is an assignment, and there exists a node t such that t value-impacts Υ and s is in $DU(LV(t))$.

3. s is a predicate c from which there exist paths π_1 and π_2 starting with the out-edges of c and ending at the first occurrence of l. Further, there exists a node $t \neq c$ such that t value-impacts Υ, and (a) t is the first value-impacting node along π_1 (b) t is not the first value-impacting node along π_2.

A triplet $\langle \pi_1, \pi_2, t \rangle$ due to which a predicate c satisfies rule (3) will be called a *witness* for c being value-impacting. As an illustration, consider the slicing criterion $\langle 14, \{x\} \rangle$ for $P3$ in Figure 2. Statements 12 and 8 are value-impacting because of rules 1 and 2. Interestingly, the predicates i%2==0 and i<4 are value-impacting because of rule 3 with witnesses $\langle \pi_1\colon 11 \xrightarrow{t} 12 \rightarrow 15 \rightarrow 9 \xrightarrow{t} 11 \xrightarrow{f} 14, \pi_2\colon 11 \xrightarrow{f} 14, 12 \rangle$ and $\langle \pi_1\colon 9 \xrightarrow{t} 11 \xrightarrow{f} 14, \pi_2\colon 9 \xrightarrow{f} 17 \rightarrow 5 \xrightarrow{t} 7 \rightarrow 8 \rightarrow 9 \xrightarrow{t} 11 \xrightarrow{f} 14, 11 \rangle$. Clearly, if a node s *value-impacts* Υ then there is a path from s to l.

Let $VI(\Upsilon)$ be the set of value-impacting nodes of Υ. Let the set of abstract predicates $AP(\Upsilon)$ consist of predicates that are not by themselves *value-impacting*, but on which other value-impacting nodes are transitively control dependent. We construct a subprogram P^{VS} of P by choosing the statements in $VI(\Upsilon) \cup AP(\Upsilon)$ along with *SKIP* and *ENTRY*. The predicates in $AP(\Upsilon)$ appear in P^{VS} in abstract form. We claim that P^{VS} is a *value slice*. Clearly condition 1 of Definition 1 is satisfied. To show that P^{VS} satisfies conditions 2 and 3, we shall first prove a lemma which shows that if the traces of the original program and the value slice on the same input are restricted to executions states involving value-impacting statements, then they match each other when compared to the extent of the trace with the smaller length. In the lemmas below, AVI denotes the set of concrete statements in P^{VS}. Further, for $s \in AVI$, $AREF(s)$ denotes $REF(s)$ when $s \in VI(\Upsilon)$, V when s is *SKIP* and $\emptyset$ when s is *ENTRY*.

Lemma 1. *Let τ and τ' be traces of the programs P and P^{VS} for an input I. Assume that $\tau_s = [\langle l_i, \sigma_i \rangle]$, $i \geq 1$ and and $\tau'_s = [\langle l'_j, \sigma'_j \rangle]$, $j \geq 1$ are restrictions of τ and τ' to the statements in AVI. Let k be the minimum of the number of elements in τ_s and τ'_s. Then for all $i \leq k$, $l_i = l'_i$ and $\lfloor \sigma_i \rfloor_{Z_i} = \lfloor \sigma'_i \rfloor_{Z_i}$, where $Z_i = AREF(l_i)$.*

Proof. We shall prove the lemma by induction on the common label index i of the two traces. Obviously $i \leq k$, else the lemma is vacuously true.

Base step : $i = 1$. The lemma holds trivially as $l_1 = l_1' = ENTRY$ and $\sigma_1 = \sigma_1' = I$.

Induction step: Let the hypothesis be true for i. Since $\lfloor \sigma_i \rfloor_{Z_i} = \lfloor \sigma_i' \rfloor_{Z_i}$, the edges followed from l_i and l_i' in τ and τ' are the same. Assume $l_{i+1} \neq l_{i+1}'$. This is only possible if (a) there is a predicate c in the original program which has been abstracted in the value slice, (b) the path from l_i to l_{i+1} goes through one of the out-edges b_1 of c, and (c) the path from l_i' to l_{i+1}' goes through the other out-edge b_2 of c. Obviously, there are paths π_1 and π_2 from c to l through b_1 and c to l through b_2, and l_{i+1} and l_{i+1}' are the first value-impacting statements on π_1 and π_2 respectively. Therefore, the predicate c is value-impacting and cannot be abstracted in the value-slice, a contradiction. Therefore, $l_{i+1} = l_{i+1}'$.

Now suppose that for some variable $x \in Z_{i+1}$, $\sigma_{i+1}(x) \neq \sigma_{i+1}'(x)$. Then there must be a statement d which provides the value of x at l_{i+1}; x does not get its value from the input I. This implies d is a value-impacting statement. Clearly, d occurs before l_{i+1} and thus it either also occurs before l_i or is l_i itself. By induction hypothesis, d must also be there in τ' and therefore $\sigma_{i+1}(x) = \sigma_{i+1}'(x)$. ∎

The following lemma implies that condition 2 of Definition 1 holds for P^{VS}.

Lemma 2. *Let τ be a finite trace for program P for an input I. Let $\tau' = [\langle l_i, \sigma_i \rangle]$, $1 \leq i \leq k$, be the sub-sequence of τ restricted to the nodes in P^{VS}. Then for every prefix of τ' there is a prefix $\tau'' = [\langle l_i', \sigma_i' \rangle]$ of some trace of P^{VS} for the same input I, such that for all i, $1 \leq i \leq k$, (a) $l_i = l_i'$, (b) if l_i is in $AVI(\Upsilon)$, then $\lfloor \sigma_i \rfloor_{Z_i} = \lfloor \sigma_i' \rfloor_{Z_i}$, where $Z_i = AREF(l_i)$.*

Proof. Consider a sub-sequence τ' of an arbitrary trace. Let the length of the sub-sequence be k. Let τ_i' be the prefix of τ' with length i. The proof is by induction on the length i of the prefix τ_i'.

Base step: $i = 1$ The lemma holds trivially as $[\langle ENTRY, I \rangle]$ is the only prefix of length 1 for any trace of P as well as P^{VS}.

Induction step: Assume that the statement of the lemma holds for prefixes of τ' of length up to i. Consider a prefix τ_{i+1}' of length $i+1 \leq k$. By induction hypothesis, there exists a trace of P^{VS}, which has a prefix τ_i'' of length i and for which statement of the lemma holds with respect to the prefix τ_i'. If the node l_i in τ_{i+1}' (and in τ_i') is an abstract predicate in $AP(\Upsilon)$, then program control reaching the predicate can take either branch. Otherwise $l_i \in AVI(\Upsilon)$, and $\lfloor \sigma_i \rfloor_{Z_i} = \lfloor \sigma_i' \rfloor_{Z_i}$ by the induction hypothesis. Thus for any edge taken out of l_i in τ', l_i' in τ_i'' can be made to take the same edge out. Assume this edge extends τ_i'' to τ_{i+1}'' by taking l_i' to l_{i+1}'.

We claim that there exists a trace of P^{VS}, having τ_{i+1}'' as its prefix, such that $l_{i+1} = l_{i+1}'$. If not, the divergence must be because of some condition c after l_i and before l_{i+1} in τ'. But then $c \rightsquigarrow l_{i+1}$ and therefore $c \in P^{VS}$. This means that there is a trace of P^{VS} such that $l_{i+1} = l_{i+1}'$. Further, by Lemma 1, if $l_{i+1} \in AVI(\Upsilon)$, $\lfloor \sigma_{i+1} \rfloor_{Z_{i+1}} = \lfloor \sigma_{i+1}' \rfloor_{Z_{i+1}}$. ∎

Now consider sub-traces of P and P^{VS} for an arbitrary input I. Using Lemma 1, it is easy to show by an induction on the length of the trace observation window that

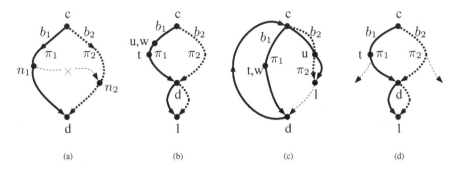

Fig. 3. (a) A property of CFG paths. (b)-(d) Situations that make a predicate value-impacting. In Fig (c), path π_1 is $c \rightarrow t \rightarrow d \rightarrow c \rightarrow u \rightarrow l$.

the sub-traces of P and P^{VS} are weak-SC-equivalent. Therefore the third condition in Definition 1 holds, and we claim that:

Theorem 1. *The abstract subprogram* P^{VS} *is a value slice.*

3.2 Relating Value-Impacting Statements to Data and Control Dependences

Figure 3 shows certain situations that we shall refer to in subsequent discussions. c denotes a predicate having two outgoing edges b_1 and b_2 that start the paths π_1 (solid line) and π_2 (thick dashed line). l denotes the node of the slicing criterion. We begin by mentioning a property of the programs under consideration. In figure (a), d is the first node common to π_1 and π_2. Since our program model does not allow arbitrary jumps, the following property, illustrated in Figure 3 (a), holds:

Prop: Let π_1 and π_2 be disjoint paths from a predicate c to a node d, and let n_1 and n_2 be nodes on these paths distinct from d. Then there cannot exist a path from n_1 to n_2.

It is clear that the most challenging part of value slice computation is the computation of value-impacting predicates. Given a predicate c, we now identify necessary and sufficient conditions for c to value-impact $\Upsilon = \langle l, V \rangle$.

Consider P1 of Fig. 2. The predicate c2 is value-impacting for the slicing criterion $\langle 15, \{x\} \rangle$. Observe in this case that line 15 is not control dependent on c2 while the value-impacting assignment at line 14 is control dependent on c2. We generalize this observation, illustrated in Figure 3 (b), to obtain the first necessary condition for a predicate c to be value-impacting:

$cond_1$: If l is not transitively control dependent on c, then a value-impacting node $t \neq c$ is control dependent on c.

Notice that $cond_1$ is also corroborated for the slicing criterion $\langle 17, \{y\} \rangle$, with predicate c1 as c and the predicate at line 13 as t.

Now consider P3 in which i<4 is value-impacting for $\langle 14, \{x\} \rangle$. In this case line 14 is transitively control dependent on i<4 through the true out-edge. The value-impacting assignment for this criterion at line 8 is reachable through the false-edge of predicate i<4, as both are in a cycle $9 \xrightarrow{f} 17 \to 5 \xrightarrow{t} 7 \to 8 \to 9$. The predicate i%2==0 is also value-impacting for $\langle 14, \{x\}\rangle$, and line 14 is control dependent on i%2==0 through the false out-edge. Moreover, the value-impacting assignment at line 12 is control dependent on predicate i%2==0 through the true out-edge. This observation, generalized in Figure 3 (c), gives the second necessary condition for c to be value-impacting:

$cond_2$: If l is transitively control dependent on c through only one out-edge, say b_2, then there is a value-impacting node $t \neq c$ such that t is not transitively control dependent on c through b_2 and c and t are in a cycle.

There is a third condition $cond_3$ which covers the case when l is transitively control dependent on c through both out-edges, as shown through Figure 3 (d). As mentioned earlier, this happens when some of the branches emanating from a predicate do not merge back due to return statements.

$cond_3$: If l is transitively control dependent on c through both edges, then there is a value-impacting node $t \neq c$ which is transitively control dependent on c through exactly one edge.

Note that the antecedent of exactly one of the three conditions $cond_1$, $cond_2$ and $cond_3$ always holds. Therefore, for the conjunction of these conditions to hold, only the condition with true antecedent needs to hold; the other two will hold vacuously. We will now show that conjunction of $cond_1$, $cond_2$ and $cond_3$ is a necessary and sufficient condition for c to be value-impacting and can thus be used for obtaining a sound and precise value slice. But we first prove a property of the witness of a value-impacting predicate.

Lemma 3. *Let c be a value-impacting node for the slicing criterion $\langle l, V\rangle$ with a witness $\langle \pi_1, \pi_2, u\rangle$. Then, at least one of π_1 or π_2 must have a value-impacting node before any common node appearing on both π_1 and π_2.*

Proof. Let π_1' and π_2' be the disjoint prefixes of π_1 and π_2 ending with a common node d (possibly l itself). Assume that both π_1' and π_2' have no value-impacting statements before d. Obviously, $u \neq d$ otherwise, contrary to our assumption, c will not be value-impacting. Since u is not the first value-impacting on π_2, π_2 must diverge from π_1 after d but before u. The divergence point will have to be a predicate, say c'. It is easy to see that c' will be a value impacting node on π_1 before u, a contradiction.   ∎

We now show that the conjunction of $cond_1$, $cond_2$ and $cond_3$ is a necessary criterion for a predicate c to be value-impacting.

Lemma 4. *Given a slicing criterion $\Upsilon = \langle l, V\rangle$ and a value-impacting predicate c, conditions $cond_1$, $cond_2$ and $cond_3$ hold.*

Proof.

1. Let $\langle \pi_1, \pi_2, u\rangle$ be the witness for c to be a value-impacting statement for l. Since l is not transitively control dependent on c, the situation must be as depicted in Figure 3 (b), where d is the immediate post-dominator of c. By Lemma 3, at least

one of π_1 or π_2 must have the first value-impacting node w before d. First assume that w lies on the segment of π_1. Obviously, $w = u$ and w must post-dominate the out-edge b_1. In addition, by *Prop*, w can not strictly post-dominate the out-edge b_2. Thus w is the required t. The case of w lying on the segment of π_2 can be argued similarly.

2. Assume that l is transitively control dependent on c through the out-edge b_2 only. Since c is value-impacting, by *Prop*, the situation resembles Figure 3 (c) and the witness is either $\langle \pi_1, \pi_2, w \rangle$ or $\langle \pi_2, \pi_1, u \rangle$. If the witness is $\langle \pi_2, \pi_1, u \rangle$, then there must be a value-impacting node $t \neq u$ in the looping segment c to c of π_1. If the witness is $\langle \pi_1, \pi_2, w \rangle$, then $t = w$ and t must once again be in the c to c segment of π_2. In both cases, t is not transitively control dependent on c through b_2 and is in a cycle with c.

3. Assume that l is transitively control dependent on c through both out-edges b_1 and b_2. Since c is value-impacting, there will be a witness with paths π_1 and π_2 as shown in Figure 3 (d). By Lemma 3, there is a value-impacting statement t on π_1 or π_2 before d. Without loss of generality, we assume that t is on π_1 and it is first value impacting statement on π_1. By *Prop*, t has to be transitively control dependent on c through b_1 and only through b_1. ■

We now show that the conjunction of $cond_1$, $cond_2$ and $cond_3$ is also a sufficient condition.

Lemma 5. *Given a slicing criterion $\Upsilon = \langle l, V \rangle$ and a predicate c such that the conditions $cond_1$, $cond_2$ and $cond_3$ hold, c is value-impacting for Υ.*

Proof. In each case we shall identify a witness for c to be value-impacting for Υ.

1. Assume that l is not transitively control dependent on c and t is control dependent on c through the b_1 edge. Clearly, t post-dominates edge b_1. Consider the first value-impacting statement u between c and t (u may be the same as t). Then the required witness is $\langle \pi_1, \pi_2, u \rangle$ as shown in Figure 3 (b).

2. Assume l is transitively control dependent on c through only one of the edges, say b_2. Also assume that there is a node t that is not transitively control dependent on c through b_2 and that c and t are in a cycle. Then the witness is $\langle \pi_1, \pi_2, t \rangle$, as shown in Figure 3 (c).

3. Now assume that l is transitively control dependent on c through both edges and t is transitively control dependent on c through the b_1 edge only. Then the witness is $\langle \pi_1, \pi_2, t' \rangle$, as shown in Figure 3 (d), where t' is first value impacting node on π_1 and may be same as t. ■

4 Value Slice Computation

Given a program dependence graph (PDG) [10], representing data and control dependences in the program, it is easy to compute value-impacting assignments using Definition 2. In addition, Lemmas 4 and 5 can be used to identify value-impacting predicates. These value-impacting assignments and predicates are augmented with abstract predicates to obtain the value-slice. A minor implementation detail is that a predicate with

```
1: function compVI(l, V)                      1: function iConds(t, lct, lcf)
2: begin                                      2: begin
3:   lct = tcd(l, true)                       3:   tct = tcd(t, true)
4:   lcf = tcd(l, false)                      4:   tcf = tcd(t, false)
5:   vi = ∅                                   5:   dc = cd(t)
6:   wl = DU(l, V)                            6:   cnd₁ = dc \ (lct ∪ lcf)
7:   while wl is not empty do                 7:   cnd₂ᵗ = (lct \ tct) ∩ incycle(t)
8:     choose an element t from wl            8:   cnd₂ᶠ = (lcf \ tcf) ∩ incycle(t)
9:     ic = iConds(t, lct, lcf)               9:   cnd₃ᵗ = lct ∩ lcf ∩ (tct \ tcf)
10:    vi = vi ∪ {t}                          10:  cnd₃ᶠ = lct ∩ lcf ∩ (tcf \ tct)
11:    wl = (wl \ {t}) ∪                      11:  return (cnd₁ ∪ cnd₂ᵗ ∪ cnd₂ᶠ ∪
12:       ((ic ∪ DU(LV(t))) \ vi)            12:        cnd₃ᵗ ∪ cnd₃ᶠ)
13:  end while                                13: end
14:  return vi
15: end
```

Fig. 4. Algorithm to compute VI

the reaching definitions of all its variables in VI is retained in concrete form, even if the predicate itself is not in VI. Abstracting the predicate in this case would not result in a decrease in the size of the slice. Note that the precision of the slice depends on the precision of the PDG; given a precise PDG, the value slice exactly matches P^{VS}.

Figure 4 gives an algorithm to compute $VI(\langle l, V \rangle)$. We use $tcd(t, b)$ to denote $\{c \mid c \overset{b}{\rightsquigarrow} t\}$ and $cd(t)$ to denote $\{c \mid c \rightarrowtail t\}$. We compute tcd and cd from the PDG of the program. In addition, $incycle(t)$ is the set of predicates which are in a cycle with t. The worklist wl in the algorithm contains value-impacting statements which have not been explored, i.e. they have not been used to find other value-impacting statements. vi contains value-impacting statements which have been explored. Given a value-impacting statement t, ic is the set of predicates and $DU(LV(t))$ the set of assignments that become value-impacting because of t. ic is computed using the function $iConds$ which encodes $cond_1$, $cond_2$ and $cond_3$ in a straightforward manner. As an example, cnd_1, the encoding of $cond_1$, computes the set of predicates c which become value-impacting because t is directly control dependent on c and l is not transitively control dependent on c.

Assume there are E edges and N nodes in the CFG of which C are predicates. Since a node goes into the worklist at most once, the while loop in $compVI$ iterates at most N times. Further, let there be E_d data dependence and E_c control dependence edges in the PDG, adding to $E_p = E_d + E_c$ edges. The sets lct and lcf can be pre-computed in $O(C)$ time and stored in $O(C)$ space, so that membership of these sets can be checked in constant time. Further, Tarjan's algorithm [18] can be used to find all strongly connected components (SCCs) in a CFG in $O(E + N)$ time, from which we can pre-compute $incycle(t)$. This takes $O(N \times C)$ time and $O(N \times C)$ space. Thus $c \in incycle(t)$ can also be checked in constant time.

It is clear that each data dependent edge will be traversed at most once during the entire run of $compVI$. Similarly, because of dc and cnd_1, each control dependent edge will also be visited at most once during execution of $compVI$. The computation of tct, tcf, cnd_2 and cnd_3 all require $O(C)$ time. So the overall complexity of the algorithm is $O(E+N)+O(N \times C)+O(E_c+E_d) \approx O(N \times C)+O(E_p)$. Note that backward slice

Prg	KLOC	Asserts	Backward Slice			Value Slice				Thin Slice				Scale up (%)			Precision loss (%)	
			Y	N	?	Y	N	N_S	?	Y	N	N_S	?	Back.	Value	Thin	Value	Thin
(a)	(b)	(c)	(d)	(e)	(f)	(g)	(h)	(i)	(j)	(k)	(l)	(m)	(n)	(o)	(p)	(q)	(r)	(s)
$icecast$	18	27	3	0	24	8	9	0	10	0	21	8	6	11	63	78	0	38
$navi1$	41	58	39	0	19	38	5	3	15	25	14	10	19	67	74	67	7	26
$navi2$	52	68	44	0	24	52	4	2	12	40	16	10	12	65	82	82	4	18
$navi3$	50	80	59	7	14	55	16	6	9	31	43	32	6	83	89	93	8	43
$navi4$	166	70	17	0	53	28	4	0	38	27	24	7	19	24	46	73	0	14
$navi5$	156	70	16	2	52	24	5	0	41	25	24	10	21	26	41	70	0	20
$navi6$	162	70	25	0	45	42	1	0	27	15	32	26	23	36	61	67	0	55
$navi7$	350	60	11	0	49	18	0	0	42	11	25	3	24	18	30	60	0	8
$navi8$	366	56	20	2	34	38	2	0	16	27	20	12	9	39	71	84	0	26
$navi9$	159	50	13	0	37	22	1	0	27	13	22	13	15	26	46	70	0	37
Average														39	60	74	2	29

Fig. 5. Scalability and precision of property checking based on different kinds of slices. Y and N stand for 'yes' and 'no' answers returned by the property checker. ? stands for 'no decision' and N_S stands for a 'no' that is known to be spurious.

computation has a complexity of $O(E_p)$. Since in the worst case $O(E_p) = O(N \times N)$, the worst case complexity is the same for backward slice and value slice.

5   Implementation and Measurements

We have built a scalable property checking tool based on value slicing[3]. Our implementation supports full version of C including pointers, structures, arrays, heap allocation and function calls. Following custom, the heap is abstracted in terms of allocation points and arrays are summarized to a single abstract element. However, structures are field sensitive: x.a and x.b are treated as separate entities. Pointers are handled using a flow sensitive but context insensitive points-to analysis. We first construct an intraprocedural PDG for each function, using the algorithm of Billardi and Pingali [4] to construct the control dependence graph. The PDGs are then linked and interprocedurally valid data and control dependences computed using the method by Horwitz et. al. [12].

We carried out our experiments on 3.0 GHz Intel Core2Duo processor with 2 GB RAM and 32 bit OS. We chose SATABS (version 3.0) [8] as the verifier for its robustness and its scalability. We experimented on one open source application, $icecast$, and 60 modules of varying sizes of a proprietary code base of a large automotive navigation system, grouped into nine groups: $navi1$ to $navi9$. Average size of individual modules in these groups varied from 6 KLOC to 61 KLOC. We checked for the "array index out of bounds" property on these programs. The size and the number of asserts for each group of program are shown in the table. For each chosen instance, we computed backward slice, value slice and thin slice. All three slices were submitted to SATABS, with a time-out limit of three minutes and three kinds of outcomes were recorded: Property

---

[3] Implemented on top of PRISM, a static analyzer generator developed at TRDDC, Pune [14,7].

satisfied (Y), property failed (N), and no decision(?). The possible reasons for the last outcome are time-out, too many iterations, or SATABS failing due to some other causes.

The Y answers of all three slices are correct by construction of the slice. Similarly, an N answer for the backward slice is also correct. However, in case of a value or thin slice, if an assert with an N answer is also recorded as a Y during property checking with the other two slices, it is also recorded as being a spurious N (N_S in the table). Scalability, given by $(Y + N)/(Y + N+?)$ is the ratio of definite outcomes over all outcomes. Loss of precision is the ratio of outcomes that are known to be spurious over all definite outcomes ($N_S/(Y + N)$). The results are presented in Figure 5.

From the results, it is obvious that both value and thin slice help in scaling up property checking, with thin slice having a small advantage (14%) over value slice. However, compared to the backward slice, the precision drops considerably (29%) in the case of thin slice, while there is only a marginal drop (2%) for value slice. This implies that refinement will be required in many more cases with thin slice as compared to value slice. We also expect refinement cycles to be shorter for value slice because of fewer abstractions. This shows that value slice is a good compromise between backward and thin slices as it provides considerable scalability with only a marginal loss in precision.

6 Related Work

Following the introduction of backward slicing by Weiser [19], several variations of slicing have been proposed. Notable among these are forward slicing [3], chopping [13], and assertion based slicing [6,9,2]. Restricted to the slicing criterion, all these techniques produce slices with behaviours equivalent to the original program. Dynamic slice [15] matches the behaviour of the original program for a run over a specific input.

Thin slicing [17], used for debugging, is the first approach that produces a slice whose behaviour differs from the original program with respect to the slicing criterion. A thin slice retains only those statements that the variables in the slicing criterion are data dependent on and abstracts out all predicates. This approach comes closest to our method. While this results in smaller slices, our experiments show that the slices are too imprecise for property checking. Interestingly, the authors do mention the importance of identifying the predicates that we include in the value slice in a concrete form. However it is done manually during debugging.

7 Conclusion

Slicing is an obvious pre-processing step before submitting a program to a verifier for property checking. For this purpose, backward slice has been the choice so far, since its behaviour exactly matches the behaviour of the original program with respect to the property being checked. In this paper, we have suggested a more aggressive form of slicing called value slice which slices out statements affecting reachability of the assertion point and retains just those statements which influence the values of the property variables. Property checking with value slice is more scalable than backward slice. However, our method also carefully identifies and retains certain predicates due to which property checking with value slice is more precise than an even more aggressive form of slicing called thin slice. Indeed, our experiments show that on both axes of comparison, scalability and precision, value slice based property checking comes close to the best performer of the three comparable forms of slicing that we have considered.

An overall property checking process could include refinement steps on getting a failure answer. If the counterexample generated by the verifier turns out to be spurious, one can use its trace to choose an abstract predicate that can be concretized. At worst, the refinement process could end in a backward slice. An alternate single step refinement process could use the backward slice directly to determine whether the negative answer is genuine. Our experiments also show that the size of the value slice is on the average about 50% of the size of the backward slice. Thus value slices can also be used for program understanding and debugging.

References

1. Aho, A.V., Lam, M.S., Sethi, R., Ullman, J.D.: Compilers: Principles, Techniques, & Tools. Pearson Education, Inc. (2006)
2. Barros, J.B., da Cruz, D., Henriques, P.R., Pinto, J.S.: Assertion-based slicing and slice graphs. In: Proceedings of SEFM (2010)
3. Bergeretti, J.-F., Carré, B.A.: Information-flow and data-flow analysis of while-programs. ACM Trans. Program. Lang. Syst. 7(1), 37–61 (1985)
4. Bilardi, G., Pingali, K.: A framework for generalized control dependence. In: Proceedings of PLDI (1996)
5. Binkley, D.W., Gallagher, K.B.: Program slicing. Advances in Computers 43, 1–50 (1996)
6. Canfora, G., Cimitile, A., De Lucia, A.: Conditioned program slicing. Information & Software Technology 40(11-12), 595–607 (1998)
7. Chimdyalwar, B., Kumar, S.: Effective false positive filtering for evolving software. In: Proceedings of ISEC (2011)
8. Clarke, E., Kroning, D., Sharygina, N., Yorav, K.: SATABS: SAT-based predicate abstraction for ANSI-C. In: Halbwachs, N., Zuck, L.D. (eds.) TACAS 2005. LNCS, vol. 3440, pp. 570–574. Springer, Heidelberg (2005)
9. Comuzzi, J.J., Hart, J.M.: Program slicing using weakest preconditions. In: Gaudel, M.-C., Wing, J.M. (eds.) FME 1996. LNCS, vol. 1051, pp. 557–575. Springer, Heidelberg (1996)
10. Ferrante, J., Ottenstein, K.J., Warren, J.D.: The program dependence graph and its use in optimization. ACM Trans. Program. Lang. Syst. 9(3), 319–349 (1987)
11. Gold, N., Harman, M.: An empirical study of static program slice size. ACM Trans. on Software Engineering and Methodology (TOSEM) 16 (2007)
12. Horwitz, S., Reps, T., Binkley, D.: Interprocedural slicing using dependence graphs. SIGPLAN Not. 23, 35–46 (1988)
13. Jackson, D., Rollins, E.J.: Chopping: A generalization of slicing. Technical report, Pittsburgh, PA, USA (1994)
14. Khare, S., Saraswat, S., Kumar, S.: Static program analysis of large embedded code base: an experience. In: Proceedings of ISEC (2011)
15. Korel, B., Laski, J.: Dynamic program slicing. Inf. Process. Lett. 29(3), 155–163 (1988)
16. Silva, J.: A vocabulary of program slicing-based techniques. ACM Comput. Surv. 44(3), 1–41 (2012)
17. Sridharan, M., Fink, S.J., Bodik, R.: Thin slicing. In: Proceedings of PLDI (2007)
18. Tarjan, R.E.: Depth-first search and linear graph algorithms. SIAM J. Comput. 1(2), 146–160 (1972)
19. Weiser, M.: Program slicing. In: Proceedings of ICSE (1981)

A Method for Improving the Precision and Coverage of Atomicity Violation Predictions

Reng Zeng, Zhuo Sun, Su Liu, and Xudong He

School of Computing and Information Sciences
Florida International University
Miami, Florida 33199, USA
{rzeng001,zsun003,sliu002,hex}@cis.fiu.edu

Abstract. Atomicity violations are the most common non-deadlock concurrency bugs, which have been extensively studied in recent years. Since detecting the actual occurrences of atomicity violations is extremely hard and exhaustive testing of a multi-threaded program is in general impossible, many predictive methods have been proposed, which make error predictions based on a small number of instrumented interleaved executions. Predictive methods often make tradeoffs between precision and coverage. An over-approximate predictive method ensures coverage but lacks precision and thus may report a large number of false bugs. An under-approximate predictive method ensures precision but lacks coverage and thus can miss significant real bugs. This paper presents a post-prediction analysis method for improving the precision of the prediction results obtained through over-approximation while achieving better coverage than that obtained through under-approximation. Our method analyzes and filters the prediction results of over-approximation by evaluating a subset of read-after-write relationships without enforcing all of them as in existing under-approximation methods. Our post-prediction method is a static analysis method on the predicted traces from dynamic instrumentation of C/C++ executable, and is faster than dynamic replaying methods for ensuring precision.

1 Introduction

Multi-threaded programs are prone to bugs due to concurrency. Concurrency bugs are hard to find and reproduce due to the large number of interleavings. Most non-deadlock concurrency bugs are atomicity violation bugs due to the unprotected accesses of shared variables by multiple threads. Existing approaches for detecting atomicity violation can be static or dynamic. Static approaches [6] usually suffer from a large number of false positives due to concurrency and pointer aliasing. Dynamic approaches include monitor based methods that require atomicity violations to manifest during monitored runs [11][5][19], and predictive methods that explore atomicity violations in alternative interleavings extracted from some sample instrumented runs [17][18][4][1].

Predictive methods use either (1) under-approximate models ([15][16][1][14]): the set of extracted interleavings with the exact same read-after-write relationships as in the instrumented runs, which are a subset of all feasible interleavings;

© Springer-Verlag Berlin Heidelberg 2015
C. Baier and C. Tinelli (Eds.): TACAS 2015, LNCS 9035, pp. 116–130, 2015.
DOI: 10.1007/978-3-662-46681-0_8

or (2) over-approximate models ([21][17][8][7][20]): the set of all possible inter-leavings extracted from the instrumented runs, which may not be feasible in the original program due to data constraints and ad-hoc synchronization. Hence predictive methods based on under-approximate models have inadequate cover-age and predictive methods based on over-approximate models lack precision. Many predictive methods mentioned above made tradeoffs between precision and coverage. Figure 1 shows the relationships between various predictive meth-ods in terms of precision and coverage. Although precise coverage captures the exact bugs in a multi-threaded program and thus is ideal, it cannot be achieved practically. Our method AVFilter and replaying methods are not independent predictive methods, but post-prediction analysis methods. A replaying method can eliminate false bugs, but incurs heavy runtime overhead and may not be able to produce the exact same execution sequence as an instrumented run due to nondeterminism [2][9][10].

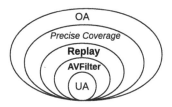

Fig. 1. Relationships of predictive methods on coverage and precision, in which a larger circle shows more coverage and the circles within the precise coverage do not contain false predictions.
UA - Under-approximate methods [15][16][1][14].
OA - Over-approximate methods [21][17][8][7][20], e.g. Figures 2, and 6.
AVFilter - Post-prediction analysis method in this paper.
Replay - Methods in [17] of rescheduling violation traces predicted by OA methods
Precise Coverage - Precise coverage [18] captures the exact bugs in a multi-threaded program.

This paper presents a post-prediction analysis method AVFilter for improv-ing the precision of the prediction results obtained through over-approximation while achieving better coverage than that obtained from under-approximation methods. The method checks and filters the results of over-approximation by evaluating a subset of critical read-after-write relationships without enforcing all of them as in under-approximation methods.

2   Preliminaries

A multi-threaded program P has a set of threads and a set of shared vari-ables. An instrumented execution $\sigma = s_1, ..., s_n$ of P is a sequence of executed

Table 1. Limited coverage of prediction using under-approximate (UA) models for two threads (Superscript denotes the thread number T1 or T2)

	Observed Execution	Possible Alternative Execution	Description of Unserializability or Missed Reason
Covered	$R^1R^1W^2$	$R^1W^2R^1$	Two reading accesses read from different writes
	$R^1W^1W^2$	$R^1W^2W^1$	Forwarded writing access in T2 is overwritten
	$W^1W^1W^2$	$W^1W^2W^1$	Forwarded writing access in T2 is overwritten
	$R^2W^1W^2$	$W^1R^2W^2$	An intermediate value is read
	$W^2W^1W^1$	$W^1W^2W^1$	Forwarded writing access in T1 is overwritten
Missed	$W^1R^1W^2$	$W^1W^2R^1$	Intra-thread read-after-write in T1 prohibits interleaved writing in T2
	$W^1W^1R^2$	$W^1R^2W^1$	Inter-thread read-after-write prohibits forwarded reading in T2
	$W^2R^1R^1$	$R^1W^2R^1$	Inter-thread read-after-write prohibits forwarded reading in T1
	$W^2W^1R^1$	$W^1W^2R^1$	Intra-thread read-after-write in T1 prohibits interleaved writing in T2
	$W^2R^1W^1$	$R^1W^2W^1$	Inter-thread read-after-write prohibits forwarded reading in T1

statements. A trace is the projection of an execution to a sequence of annotated shared variable accesses and synchronization events. Formally, a trace, $\tau = e_1, ..., e_m$ is a sequence of events where each event $e_i (1 \leq i \leq m)$ is a tuple $\langle seq_i, tid_i, action_i, br_i \rangle$ in which seq_i is an increasing sequence number, tid_i is a thread handle, $action_i$ is either an atomic shared variable access or a synchronization event, and br_i is the number of branches between e_i and its immediate preceding event within the same thread. Given a trace $\tau = e_1, ..., e_m$, a partial order thread model $(E_\tau, \prec)$ can be defined, where E_τ is the set of events occurring in τ and $\prec$ is a causal relation on E_τ. The causal relation $\prec$ respects all constraints of synchronization primitives and program orders within individual threads. Thus $(E_\tau, \prec)$ captures a set of alternative interleaving traces derived from the original trace τ. A trace τ' in $(E_\tau, \prec)$ is feasible if and only if it is a projection of a feasible execution σ' of P. The strength of the causal relation $\prec$ affects the number of possible interleaved traces in $(E_\tau, \prec)$.

Definition 1. *(Under-approximate models) When the exact same read-after-write relation on all shared variables in τ is enforced in $\prec$, every trace $\tau' \in (E_\tau, \prec)$ is feasible. Such a partial order thread model $(E_\tau, \prec)$ is called under-approximate.*

Definition 2. *(Over-approximate models) When not the exact same read-after-write relation on all shared variables in τ is enforced in $\prec$, some trace $\tau' \in (E_\tau, \prec)$ may not be feasible. Such a partial order thread model $(E_\tau, \prec)$ is called over-approximate.*

An atomicity violation bug is caused by a broken order of accesses to a shared variable x within one thread by another thread. Most atomicity violation bugs involve only three accesses to a shared variable within two threads based on the study in [11], in which 101 out of 105 bugs involved only two threads. Thus existing methods for atomicity violation detection and prediction work on every shared variable within every pair of threads incrementally. Furthermore, these methods assume sequential consistent memory such that the logic order of the program execution is respected in physical machine execution. Table 1 shows ten interleaving scenarios of three accesses to a shared variable between two threads that result in atomicity violations, among which only five can be predicted by methods using under-approximate models while other five are missed due to some broken read-after-write relationship within three accesses. Our method can predict each of scenarios above.

3   AVFilter: Performing Post-prediction Static Analysis

AVFilter works on over-approximate models from a given trace τ to remove false predictions so that the remaining atomicity violation predictions are all feasible. These remaining feasible atomicity violation predictions cover all the predictions obtained from predictive methods using under-approximate models of τ. This analysis method is general and is applicable to the prediction results from many existing predictive methods using over-approximate models. The only information needed is an instrumented trace τ and three memory accesses in τ that forms an atomicity violation pattern [21][18].

3.1   Data Constraints Causing False Predictions

Data constraints are data dependencies that can make a predicted atomicity violation trace infeasible. Typical data constraints include branch conditions dependent on shared variables and queue accesses dependent on shared indexing variables. In real-world applications, data dependency can be quite complicated and appear in various obscure ways. Figure 2 shows a reformatted code snippet from Apache web server, which gives an example of data constraints. Figure 2(a)

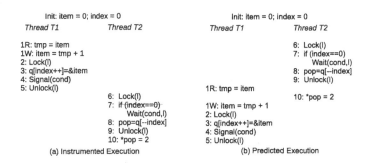

Fig. 2. A false positive due to a data constraint (reformatted code snippet from Apache web server)

shows a trace of an instrumented execution, in which shared variable *index* is read in line 7 and line 8 after its writing in line 3, and hence there are data dependencies in two pairs of accesses to *index*: line 3 and line 7, line 3 and line 8. Figure 2(b) shows a trace with a predicted atomicity violation pattern in which line 10 has a writing access to the shared memory *item* in Thread T2 between the reading access (line 1R) and the writing access (line 1W) in Thread T1. However, both pairs of accesses to *index* above are broken, which make the memory access in line 10 in the predicted trace infeasible.

A solution to deal with data constraints requires a precise and complete partial order thread model extracted from an instrumented trace. The precision ensures the feasibility of any predicted atomicity violation in the partial order thread model, and the completeness requires any feasible atomicity violation be captured in the partial order thread model. Enforcing all the exact read-after-write relationships of the instrumented trace in the partial order thread model can ensure the precision of the partial order thread model. Several methods [16][14] introduced the exact read-after-write relationships as a simple solution to ensure the precision. However, the data constraints imposed by the exact read-after-write relationships are too strong, thus make the resulting partial order thread model over restrictive and under-approximate.

3.2   Problem Formulation

During post-prediction analysis, any predicted atomicity violation trace is an alternative interleaving respecting the same causal relations imposed by the synchronization events as the original instrumented trace. Thus we can view a trace as a sequence of atomic (reading or writing) accesses without synchronization events to simplify the discussion. Let $\tau = a_1^{t_1}, a_2^{t_2}, ..., a_n^{t_n}$ be a sequence of atomic accesses to share variables in an interleaved execution of two threads, in which a superscript indicates the thread an event belongs to, thus $t_i \in \{1, 2\}$ for $1 \le i \le n$; and a subscript indicates the occurrence position of an event in the interleaving trace.

Over-approximate predictive methods in [21][11][17] are based on three-access atomicity violation patterns. Table 1 gives all possible atomicity violation patterns after reordering the event in thread 2 to occur between the two events in thread 1. Although the above methods check only a pair of threads, they are applicable to many threads by checking every pair of threads on every shared variable one at a time.

A predicted atomicity violation trace is $\tau' = ..., a_{i'}^1, ..., a_{j'}^2, ..., a_{k'}^1, ...$ with atomicity violation pattern $a_{i'}^1, a_{j'}^2, a_{k'}^1$ which are three consecutive accesses to a shared variable x. τ' is the result of reordering some accesses in a given original instrumented trace τ where (1) $\tau = ..., a_i^1, ..., a_k^1, ..., a_j^2, ...$ or (2) $\tau = ..., a_j^2, ..., a_i^1, ..., a_k^1, ...$. Events $a_{i'}^1, a_{j'}^2, a_{k'}^1$ in τ' correspond to the exact same events a_i^1, a_j^2, a_k^1 in τ. Accesses other than $a_{i'}^1, a_{j'}^2, a_{k'}^1$ are not explicitly identified in τ' but may also be reordered due to the reordering of a_i^1, a_j^2, a_k^1 in τ. τ' may not be feasible due to the violation of some read-after-write relationship in

τ. τ' is feasible if its prefix up to $a_{k'}^1$ is feasible since anything happens after $a_{k'}^1$ does not affect the feasibility of τ'.

3.3   Our Method

Our method works on the predicted traces that already contained all synchronization information. The underlying idea of our method is to check whether any reordered event inside the violation pattern $a_{i'}^1, ..., a_{j'}^2, ..., a_{k'}^1$ in τ' can break some critical read-after-write relationship inside the subsequence $a_i^1, ..., a_k^1, ..., a_j^2$ in situation (1) or the subsequence $a_j^2, ..., a_i^1, ..., a_k^1$ in situation (2) in the instrumented trace τ. Before reordering, a_j^2 may happen after a_k^1 as in situation (1), or before a_i^1 as in situation (2). Let $a \dashrightarrow b$ denote event a occurs before event b, We explain our checking idea for situation (1), i.e. $a_i^1 \dashrightarrow a_k^1 \dashrightarrow a_j^2$ (the checking idea for situation (2) is similar). In Figures 3, 4 and 5, w and r are used to describe a read-after-write relationship with regard to either a different shared variable or the same shared variable accessed in $a_{i'}^1, a_{j'}^2, a_{k'}^1$. In Figure 3, a reading event r^2 is moved forward due to the reordering of a_j^2, thus breaking the read-after-write relationship between w^1 and r^2.

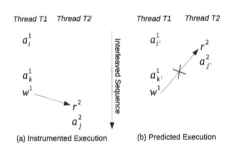

(a) Instrumented Execution   (b) Predicted Execution

Fig. 3. Read-after-write relationship is broken, assuming $a_i^1 \dashrightarrow a_k^1 \dashrightarrow a_j^2$ and a moved forward reading event r^2 before $a_{k'}^1$, $r^2 \in \tau(a_k^1, a_j^2)$

    In Figures 4 and 5, $Prev(a_j^2)$ denotes the immediate preceding access to the same shared variable as a_j^2. In Figure 4, due to the reordered $a_{i'}^1, a_{j'}^2, a_{k'}^1$, $Prev(a_j^2)$ is moved forward to happen before $a_{i'}^1$, thus r^2 is moved forward to happen before w^1, causing the breaking of the read-after-write relationship between w^1 and r^2.

    In Figure 5, due to the reordered $a_{i'}^1, a_{j'}^2, a_{k'}^1$, $Prev(a_j^2)$ is moved forward to happen before $a_{i'}^1$, thus w^2 is moved forward to happen before r^1, causing the breaking of the read-after-write relationship between r^1 and its original defining writing access.

    Lemmas 1 and 2 identify all the cases in which a reordered event may affect the feasibility of τ'. Let $\tau(a,b)$ be accesses in τ that occur after a and before b, $\tau[a,b)$ be accesses in $\tau(a,b)$ including a, and $\tau(a,b]$ be accesses in $\tau(a,b)$

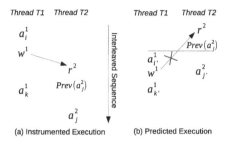

Fig. 4. Read-after-write relationship is broken, assuming $a_i^1 \dashrightarrow a_k^1 \dashrightarrow a_j^2$ and a moved forward reading event before $a_{i'}^1, r^2 \in \tau(a_i^1, Prev(a_j^2)]$

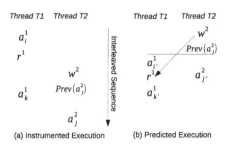

Fig. 5. Read-after-write relationship is broken, assuming $a_i^1 \dashrightarrow a_k^1 \dashrightarrow a_j^2$ and a moved forward writing event w^2, $w^2 \in \tau(a_i^1, Prev(a_j^2)]$

including b, $Prev(a^i)$ denote the immediate preceding atomic access to the same shared variable as a in thread i, and $Next(a^i)$ denote the immediate succeeding atomic access to the same shared variable as a in thread i.

Lemma 1. *Given a predicted atomicity violation trace* $\tau' = ..., a_{i'}^1, ..., a_{j'}^2, ...,$ $a_{k'}^1, ...$ *with atomicity violation pattern* $a_{i'}^1, a_{j'}^2, a_{k'}^1$ *with regard to a shared variable* x, *and the original instrumented trace* $\tau = ..., a_i^1, ..., a_k^1, ..., a_j^2, ...$ τ' *can be infeasible due to a violated data constraint caused by only one of the following cases* *(1) a moved forward reading event in thread 2:* $r^2 \in \tau(a_k^1, a_j^2)$ *and* $r^2 \dashrightarrow a_{k'}^1$; *(2) a moved forward reading event in thread 2:* $r^2 \in \tau(a_i^1, Prev(a_j^2)]$ *and* $r^2 \dashrightarrow a_{i'}^1$; *or* *(3) a moved forward writing event in thread 2:* $w^2 \in \tau(a_i^1, Prev(a_j^2)]$, $w^2 \dashrightarrow a_{i'}^1$ *and the existence of a branch instruction between* $\tau[a_i^1, a_k^1)$.

The proof of the lemma is omitted due to limited space. Note a moved forward writing event in thread 2: $w^2 \in \tau[Prev(a_j^2), a_k^1)$ and $w^2 \dashrightarrow a_{k'}^1$ can break some read-after-write relationship after $a_{k'}^1$, but does not affect the feasibility of τ'.

Figure 2 shows an example of case (1) in Lemma 1, where the predicted atomicity violation trace τ' in (b) is infeasible. In (b) line 1R is $a_{i'}^1$, line 10 is $a_{j'}^2$, line 1W is $a_{k'}^1$, and line 7 is the moved forward reading r. The read-after-write relationship with line 3 is broken. As a result, the condition in line 7 is true and *Wait* is executed that makes τ' infeasible.

Lemma 2. *Given a predicted atomicity violation trace* $\tau' = ..., a^1_{i'}, ..., a^2_{j'}, ...,$ $a^1_{k'}, ...$ *with atomicity violation pattern* $a^1_{i'}, a^2_{j'}, a^1_{k'}$ *with regard to a shared variable* x, *and the original instrumented trace* $\tau = ..., a^2_j, ..., a^1_i, ..., a^1_k, ...$ τ' *can be infeasible due to a violated data constraint caused by only one of the following cases (1) a moved forward reading event in thread 1:* $r^1 \in \tau(a^2_j, a^1_i]$ *and* $r^1 \dashrightarrow a^2_{j'}$; *(2) a moved forward reading event in thread 1:* $r^1 \in \tau(Next(a^2_j), a^1_k)]$, $r^1 \dashrightarrow Next(a^2_{j'})$, *and the existence of some branch instruction between* $\tau[a^1_i, a^1_k)$.

The proof of this lemma is omitted due to limited space. Note any moved forward writing event in thread 1 does not affect the feasibility of τ'.

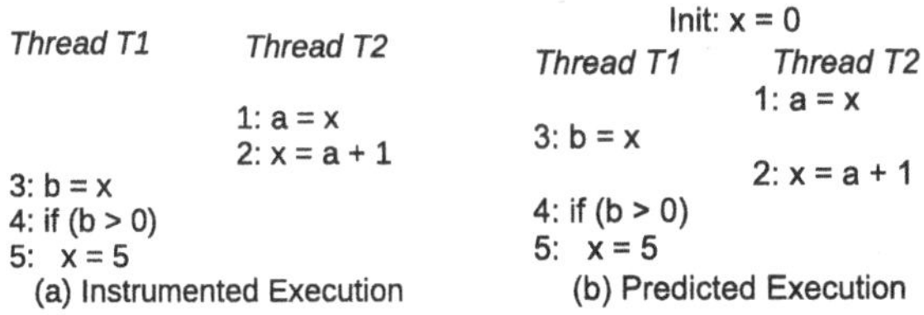

Fig. 6. A false positive due to local dependency

Figure 6 shows an example of case (1) in Lemma 2, where the predicted atomicity violation trace τ' in (b) is infeasible. In (b), line 3 is $a^1_{i'}$, line 2 is $a^2_{j'}$, line 5 is $a^1_{k'}$, and line 3 is the moved forward reading $r^1 \in \tau(a^2_j, a^1_i]$. The broken read-after-write relationship from line 2 now reads a new value 0 in line 3. As a result, $b^1_{k'}$ cannot be executed and thus τ' is infeasible.

Our method is realized in the following Algorithm 1. An instrumented trace contains a sequence of events, and each event is defined by a thread identifier tid, a memory access type (read or write) rw, a shared variable var, and the number br of branches between this event and its immediate preceding event within the same thread. Other fields in an instrumented trace are omitted here without affecting the post-prediction analysis. An atomicity violation prediction is based on an atomicity violation pattern $a^1_{i'}, a^2_{j'}, a^1_{k'}$ involving two threads 1 and 2. The algorithm analyzes the feasibility of a predicted violation according to Lemmas 1 and 2. The complexity is linear to the size of trace, and note the algorithm only needs to check the subsequence containing the three accesses a^1_i, a^2_j, a^1_k. Five true returns in the algorithm correspond to the five cases in Lemmas 1 and 2.

3.4 Comparison with Precise Coverage and the Coverage of Under-Approximate Methods

As shown in Figure 1, the coverage of our method AVFilter is a subset of the precise coverage and a superset of the coverage of under-approximate methods.

Algorithm 1. Algorithm of post-prediction analysis

Input: $\tau : seq \rightarrow (tid_{seq}, rw_{seq}, var_{seq}, br_{seq})$, and three seq: $...a_i^1..., ...a_j^2..., ...a_k^1...$
that contain accesses relevant to a violation pattern $a_{i'}^1, a_{j'}^2, a_{k'}^1$ in τ'.

Output: Whether a predicted violation maybe infeasible.

1: **if** $a_j^2 > a_i^1$ **then**
2:     $prev \leftarrow max(seq)$ where $tid_{seq} = 2 \wedge var_{seq} = var_{a_j^2} \wedge seq < a_j^2$
3:     **for** $r \in (a_i^1, prev] \cup (a_k^1, a_j^2) \wedge rw_r = read \wedge tid_r = 2$ **do**
4:         $w = max(seq)$ where $rw_{seq} = write \wedge var_{seq} = var_r \wedge seq < r$
5:         **if** $r \in (a_i^1, prev] \wedge w > a_i^1 \wedge tid_w = 1$ **then**
6:             **return** $True$
7:         **end if**
8:         **if** $r \in (a_k^1, a_j^2) \wedge w > a_k^1 \wedge tid_w = 1$ **then**
9:             **return** $True$
10:        **end if**
11:    **end for**
12:    **for** $r \in [a_i^1, a_k^1) \wedge rw_r = read \wedge tid_r = 1$ **do**
13:        $w = min(seq)$ where $rw_{seq} = write \wedge var_{seq} = var_r \wedge seq > r \wedge tid_w = 2$
14:        **if** $w \leq prev \wedge \exists seq . (r < seq < a_k^1) \wedge (tid_{seq} = 1) \wedge br_{seq} > 0$ **then**
15:            **return** $True$
16:        **end if**
17:    **end for**
18: **end if**
19: **if** $a_j^2 < a_i^1$ **then**
20:     **for** $r \in (a_j^2, a_i^1] \wedge rw_r = read \wedge tid_r = 1$ **do**
21:         $w = max(seq)$ where $rw_{seq} = write \wedge var_{seq} = var_r \wedge seq < r$
22:         **if** $w \geq a_j^2 \wedge tid_w = 2$ **then**
23:             **return** $True$
24:         **end if**
25:     **end for**
26:     $next \leftarrow min(seq)$ where $tid_{seq} = 2 \wedge var_{seq} = var_{a_j^2} \wedge seq > a_j^2$
27:     **for** $r \in (a_i^1, a_k^1) \wedge rw_r = read \wedge tid_r = 1$ **do**
28:         $w = max(seq)$ where $rw_{seq} = write \wedge var_{seq} = var_r \wedge seq < r \wedge tid_w = 2$
29:         **if** $w > next \wedge \exists seq . (r < seq < a_k^1) \wedge (tid_{seq} = 1) \wedge br_{seq} > 0$ **then**
30:             **return** $True$
31:         **end if**
32:     **end for**
33: **end if**
34: **return** $False$

No False Positives with Better Coverage than Under-Approximate Methods. Lemmas 1 and 2 define the necessary conditions that a violated data constraint can cause a predicted atomicity violation trace infeasible. Thus Lemmas 1 and 2 have ensured that any surviving predicted atomicity violation trace is a feasible one, assuming a predictive method such as [21] preserved all control constraints. Under-approximate methods ensure precision by eliminating all traces breaking any read-after-write relationships. Our post-prediction analysis method ensures precision while eliminating only a subset of predicted atomicity violation traces breaking certain read-after-write relationships in the original instrumented trace.

Potential False Negatives. The false prediction shown in Figure 6 becomes a real one if the initial value of variable x is changed to 1, which is treated as infeasible by our method. The predicted traces often only contain the access information on shared variables while omitting the access information of local variables and the potential dependencies between shared and local variables. It is not possible to determine with certainty whether a trace with some broken read-after-write relationship is feasible or not without exploring the complex inter-variable dependencies in the actual program. Therefore, we treat those traces containing broken read-after-write relationship as infeasible to ensure the soundness of our method.

4   Experiments and Evaluation

We have implemented the proposed algorithm in a prototype tool based on the tool in [21] and conducted several experiments on a PC with dual core 2.33GHz CPU and 2GB memory. In the following subsections, we show the benefits of AVFilter in terms of improving precision, ensuring coverage, and achieving scalability.

Improving Precision

We evaluate our algorithm using as many benchmarks as available from the existing state of the art works [11][17][18]. [11] uses C based Apache web server and C++ based MySQL database, [17] uses small Java programs and Java based Apache ftp server, and [18] uses a few small C programs. We first run our tool [21] on three C/C++ benchmark programs to obtain predictive atomicity violations. Since our tool [21] implements an over-approximate method, the number of predicted atomicity violations should be representative in other over-approximate methods such as [11][17]. We then run AVFilter on the predicted atomicity violations obtained from [21] to eliminate potential false positives.

The experiment results using Apache web server, FFmpeg, and MySQL database are shown in Table 2, and the experiment results using the benchmarks in [18] are shown in Table 3. The experiment result of Apache ftp server of [17] is listed in the table for comparison purpose that shows our method is

Table 2. Experimental results using real world programs

	Program Size	Events in Trace	OA	AVFilter	AVFilter-time	Replay-time
Apache web server 2.0.48 (C)	1.5 MB	140532	155	1	12.1 sec	-
Apache ftp server (Java) [17]	53 KB	-	109	-	-	2.27 hrs
FFmpeg 2.0 (C)	41 MB	550352	29	0	11.6 sec	-
MySQL 4.0.12 (C++)	7 MB	3273281	5202	1	4322 sec	-

much faster than using replaying methods to achieve precision. Our algorithm has shown tremendous improvement on prediction precision.

In Table 2, both Apache web server and MySQL have a known atomicity violation bug but FFmpeg does not. The first column *Program Size* gives the size of the executable, the second column *Events in Trace* lists the number of events in the instrumented trace; the third column *OA* contains the number of predicted atomicity violations using the over-approximate method in [21]; the fourth column *AVFilter* is the number of predicted atomicity violations after the post-prediction analysis using AVFilter; the fifth column *AVFilter-time* is the time in seconds to perform post-prediction analysis; the last column shows the replaying time in hours to replay all predictions.

Ensuring Coverage

In Table 3, Programs *atom001* and *atom002* have atomicity violations that are extracted from a real bug [12]. Their modified versions without atomicity violations are *atom001a* and *atom002a*. Other programs are Linux/Pthreads/C implementation of the parameterized bank example [3], in which program *bank-av-8* has atomicity violations; program *bank-sav-8* adds a condition variable as a partial fix without avoiding all atomicity violations for any shared variable; and program *bank-nav-8* adds a transaction lock to remove all atomicity violations. The first three columns provide the statistics of programs, in which *svars-causing-av* is the number of shared variables causing predicted atomicity violations. The next two columns provide the statistics of our method, which uses the results of an over-approximate method in [21]. *OA-svars* is the number of shared variables causing predicted atomicity violations using over-approximate methods, *AVFilter-svars* is the number of shared variables causing predicted atomicity violations after post-prediction analysis using AVFilter. Note that a single shared variable may generate many possible atomicity violation traces, which can often be eliminated by a single fix. We count shared variables in *AVFilter-svars* that have at least one feasible predicted violation trace. The last column *UA-avs* is the number of predicted atomicity violation traces generated by under-approximate methods that enforce the exact same read-after-write relation on all shared variables in an instrumented trace.

One shared variable in *atom002* is missed due to read-after-write relationships on other shared variables. Our method cannot decide whether it is feasible because the value of a shared variable or a local variable depends on the value

Table 3. Experimental results on precision and coverage using the benchmark in [18]

Program			Our method		UA methods
name	threads	svars-causing-av	OA-svars	AVFilter-svars	UA-avs
atom001	3	1	1	1	0
atom001a	3	0	1	0	0
atom002	3	1	1	0	0
atom002a	3	0	1	0	0
bank-av-8	9	8	8	8	0
bank-sav-8	9	8	8	8	0
bank-nav-8	9	0	8	0	0

of another shared variable. [18] collects and encodes all program information in CTP and thus can detect it. From the experiment results in Table 3, It can be seen that under-approximate methods miss feasible atomicity violations.

Achieving Scalability

We compare the running time to CTP [18] in Figure 7, based on statistics provided in [18] as CTP is not publicly available.

The running times, under negligible hardware differences, in Figure 7 show that our method's scalability is promising compared to those of the symbolic method CTP [18]. When the size of programs grows, e.g. *bank-nav-8* containing more code than others, the formulas built in CTP also grow bigger and require more time to be solved. Our method stops as soon as a broken read-after-write relationship defined in Lemmas 1 or 2 is detected, and incurs insignificant time increase when the size of a program grows and thus can handle much larger programs.

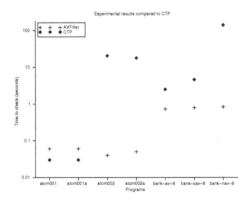

Fig. 7. Performance compared to CTP [18]

Our method is also evaluated using the complete Apache web server, MySQL database and FFmpeg audio/video codec library, as shown in Table 2, and is applicable to large scale programs.

5   Related Works

Predictive methods based on under-approximate models such as [16][1][14] admit only interleaving traces with the exact same read-after-write relations on all shared variables as in the instrumented executions to achieve precision; however, the constraints imposed by the read-after-write relations are too strong, which make the derived partial order thread models over restrictive and thus exclude many feasible alternative interleaving traces. Predictive methods based on over-approximate models such as [21][17][8][7][20] admit not only all feasible interleaving traces but also infeasible interleaving traces due to data constraints and ad-hoc synchronization, and thus can make imprecise false predictions. [15] allows broken read-after-write relations but prohibits the thread with such a read event to continue, hence can be considered as using under-approximate model.

CTP [18] is an analysis tool applicable to the predicted atomicity violation traces generated by over-approximate methods, thus is the most relevant work to ours. CTP achieves precision and complete coverage by using the values of shared variables and local variables in the predicted atomicity violation trace, which requires heavy instrumentation and the static analysis of the complete source code. Our method explores ways to improve precision and to ensure coverage while avoiding heavy instrumentation and the static analysis of source code.

Some tools use replaying methods to ensure precision. Penelope [17] instruments the scheduler to follow a predicted schedule, from which it gets a set of threads and the number of steps that each thread should take before the next context switch. Only after execution reaches the point of the violation pattern, the scheduler releases all threads to their normal execution. Before the execution reaches the violation point, it incurs the same overhead as an instrumented execution, in addition to the overhead of instrumenting scheduler. CHESS [13] is a systematic and deterministic testing tool for concurrent programs, which takes complete control over scheduling of threads; however, its scheduler is non-preemptive and therefore cannot model the behavior of a real scheduler that may preempt a thread at any point during its execution. Following the exact same schedule of a predicted atomicity violation trace still cannot guarantee perfect replaying since perfect replaying is impossible without capturing all sources of nondeterminism, as demonstrated in [2][9][10].

6   Conclusion

Predictive methods for atomicity violations need to consider the tradeoffs between precision and coverage. This paper presents a post-prediction analysis method AVFilter to improve the precision of predicted atomicity violation traces generated from over-approximate methods and to achieve better coverage than that obtained from under-approximate methods. AVFilter covers all ten scenarios in Table 1. AVFilter is general and is applicable to the prediction results from many existing predictive methods using over-approximate models. AVFilter does not rely on the instrumentation of local variables and the analysis of source code, and thus is scalable and applicable to large programs.

Acknowledgements. This work was partially supported by the NSF of U.S. under award HRD-0833093. Reng has also been supported by a Dissertation Year Fellowship of Florida International University.

References

1. Chen, F., Serbanuta, T.F., Rosu, G.: jPredictor: a predictive runtime analysis tool for java. In: Proceedings of the 30th International Conference on Software Engineering (ICSE 2008), Leipzig, Germany, pp. 221–230 (2008)
2. Dunlap, G.W., King, S.T., Cinar, S., Basrai, M.A., Chen, P.M.: ReVirt: enabling intrusion analysis through virtual-machine logging and replay. In: Proceedings of the 5th Symposium on Operating Systems Design and Implementation (OSDI 2002), Boston, MA, USA, pp. 211–224 (2002)
3. Farchi, E., Nir, Y., Ur, S.: Concurrent bug patterns and how to test them. In: Proceedings of the 17th International Symposium on Parallel and Distributed Processing, IPDPS 2003 (2003)
4. Farzan, A., Madhusudan, P.: The complexity of predicting atomicity violations. In: Kowalewski, S., Philippou, A. (eds.) TACAS 2009. LNCS, vol. 5505, pp. 155–169. Springer, Heidelberg (2009)
5. Flanagan, C., Freund, S.N., Yi, J.: Velodrome: a sound and complete dynamic atomicity checker for multithreaded programs. In: Proceedings of the 2008 ACM SIGPLAN Conference on Programming Language Design and Implementation (PLDI 2008), Tucson, AZ, USA, pp. 293–303 (2008)
6. Flanagan, C., Qadeer, S.: A type and effect system for atomicity. In: Proceedings of the 2003 ACM SIGPLAN Conference on Programming Language Design and Implementation (PLDI 2003), San Diego, CA, USA, pp. 338–349 (2003)
7. Ganai, M.K.: Scalable and precise symbolic analysis for atomicity violations. In: Proceedings of the 2011 26th IEEE/ACM International Conference on Automated Software Engineering (ASE 2011), Lawrence, KS, USA, pp. 123–132 (2011)
8. Kahlon, V., Wang, C.: Universal causality graphs: A precise happens-before model for detecting bugs in concurrent programs. In: Touili, T., Cook, B., Jackson, P. (eds.) CAV 2010. LNCS, vol. 6174, pp. 434–449. Springer, Heidelberg (2010)
9. Konuru, R., Srinivasan, H., Choi, J.D.: Deterministic replay of distributed java applications. In: Proceedings of 14th International Parallel and Distributed Processing Symposium (IPDPS 2000), Cancun, Mexico, pp. 219–227 (2000)
10. Liu, X., Lin, W., Pan, A., Zhang, Z.: WiDS checker: combating bugs in distributed systems. In: Proceedings of the 4th USENIX Conference on Networked Systems Design and Implementation (NSDI 2007), Cambridge, MA, USA, pp. 19–19 (2007)
11. Lu, S., Park, S., Zhou, Y.: Finding Atomicity-Violation bugs through unserializable interleaving testing. IEEE Transactions on Software Engineering 38(4), 844–860 (2011)

12. Lu, S., Tucek, J., Qin, F., Zhou, Y.: AVIO: detecting atomicity violations via access interleaving invariants. In: Proceedings of the 12th International Conference on Architectural Support for Programming Languages and Operating Systems (ASPLOS 2006), San Jose, CA, USA, pp. 37–48 (2006)
13. Musuvathi, M., Qadeer, S., Ball, T., Basler, G., Nainar, P.A., Neamtiu, I.: Finding and reproducing heisenbugs in concurrent programs. In: Proceedings of the 8th USENIX Conference on Operating Systems Design and Implementation (OSDI 2008), San Diego, CA, USA, pp. 267–280 (2008)
14. Sen, K., Roşu, G., Agha, G.: Detecting errors in multithreaded programs by generalized predictive analysis of executions. In: Steffen, M., Zavattaro, G. (eds.) FMOODS 2005. LNCS, vol. 3535, pp. 211–226. Springer, Heidelberg (2005)
15. Şerbănuţă, T.F., Chen, F., Roşu, G.: Maximal causal models for sequentially consistent systems. In: Qadeer, S., Tasiran, S. (eds.) RV 2012. LNCS, vol. 7687, pp. 136–150. Springer, Heidelberg (2013)
16. Sinha, A., Malik, S., Wang, C., Gupta, A.: Predictive analysis for detecting serializability violations through trace segmentation. In: Proceedings of the 9th International Conference on Formal Methods and Models for Codesign (MEMOCODE 2011), Cambridge, UK, pp. 99–108 (2011)
17. Sorrentino, F., Farzan, A., Madhusudan, P.: Penelope: weaving threads to expose atomicity violations. In: Proceedings of the 18th ACM SIGSOFT International Symposium on Foundations of Software Engineering (FSE 2010), Santa Fe, NM, USA, pp. 37–46 (2010)
18. Wang, C., Limaye, R., Ganai, M., Gupta, A.: Trace-based symbolic analysis for atomicity violations. In: Esparza, J., Majumdar, R. (eds.) TACAS 2010. LNCS, vol. 6015, pp. 328–342. Springer, Heidelberg (2010)
19. Wang, L., Stoller, S.D.: Runtime analysis of atomicity for multithreaded programs. IEEE Transactions on Software Engineering 32, 93–110 (2006)
20. Yi, J., Sadowski, C., Flanagan, C.: SideTrack: generalizing dynamic atomicity analysis. In: Proceedings of the 7th Workshop on Parallel and Distributed Systems: Testing, Analysis, and Debugging (PADTAD 2009), Chicago, IL, USA, pp. 8:1–8:10 (2009)
21. Zeng, R., Sun, Z., Liu, S., He, X.: McPatom: A predictive analysis tool for atomicity violation using model checking. In: Donaldson, A., Parker, D. (eds.) SPIN 2012. LNCS, vol. 7385, pp. 191–207. Springer, Heidelberg (2012)

Commutativity of Reducers[*]

Yu-Fang Chen[1], Chih-Duo Hong[1], Nishant Sinha[2], and Bow-Yaw Wang[1]

[1] Institute of Information Science, Academia Sinica, Taiwan
[2] IBM Research, India

Abstract. In the Map-Reduce programming model for data parallel computation, a reducer computes an output from a list of input values associated with a key. The inputs however may not arrive at a reducer in a fixed order due to nondeterminism in transmitting key-value pairs over the network. This gives rise to the *reducer commutativity* problem, that is, is the reducer computation independent of the order of its inputs? In this paper, we study the reducer commutativity problem formally. We introduce a syntactic subset of integer programs termed *integer reducers* to model real-world reducers. In spite of syntactic restrictions, we show that checking commutativity of integer reducers over unbounded lists of exact integers is undecidable. It remains undecidable even with input lists of a fixed length. The problem however becomes decidable for reducers over unbounded input lists of bounded integers. We propose an efficient reduction of commutativity checking to conventional assertion checking and report experimental results using various off-the-shelf program analyzers.

1 Introduction

Map-Reduce is a widely adopted programming model for data-parallel computation such as those in a cloud computing environment. The computation consists of two key phases: *map* and *reduce*. Each phase is carried out by a number of map and reduce instances called mappers and reducers respectively. A mapper takes a key-value pair as input and produces zero or more output key-value pairs. The output pairs produced by all mappers are *shuffled* by a load-balancing algorithm and delivered to appropriate reducers. A reducer iterates through the input values associated with a particular key and produces an output key-value pair. Consider the example which counts frequencies of each word in a distributed file system. A mapper takes an input pair (*filename, content*) and produces an output pair $(w, 1)$ for each word w in *content*. A reducer then receives an input pair $(w, [1; 1; \cdots ; 1])$ and returns an output pair (w, n) where n is the sum of values associated with the word w, equivalently, the frequency of the word w.

Due to the deployment of mappers/reducers, load-balancing algorithm and network latency, the order of values received by a reducer is not fixed. If a reducer computes different outputs for different input orders (namely, it is *not commutative*), the Map-Reduce program may yield different results on different runs. This makes such programs hard to debug and even cause errors. The commutativity problem for a reducer

---

[*] This work was partially supported by the Ministry of Science and Technology of Taiwan (102-2221-E-001 -016 -MY3, 103-2221-E-001 -019 -MY3, and 103-2221-E-001 -020 -MY3).

© Springer-Verlag Berlin Heidelberg 2015
C. Baier and C. Tinelli (Eds.): TACAS 2015, LNCS 9035, pp. 131–146, 2015.
DOI: 10.1007/978-3-662-46681-0_9

program R is to check if the computation of R is commutative over its (possibly unbounded) list of inputs. A recent study [19] found that the majority of analyzed real-life reducers are in fact non-commutative. Somewhat surprisingly, the problem of formally checking commutativity of reducers however has attracted little attention.

At a first glance, the commutativity problem for arbitrary reducers appears to be undecidable by the Rice's theorem. Yet reducers are seldom Turing machines in practice. Most real-world reducers simply iterate through their input list and compute their outputs; they do not have complicated control or data flows. Therefore, one wonders if the commutativity problem for such reducers can be decided for practical purposes.

On the other hand, because real-world reducers have a simple structure, perhaps manual inspection is enough to decide if a reducer is commutative? Consider the two sample reducers dis and rangesum shown below (in C syntax, simplified by omitting the *key* input). Both reducers compute the average of a selected set of elements from the input array x of length N and are very similar structurally. However, note that dis is commutative while rangesum is not: dis selects elements from x which are greater than 1000, while rangesum selects elements at index more than 1000. Checking commutativity of such reducers manually can be tricky. Automated tool support is required.

```
int dis (int x[N]) {              int rangesum (int x[N]) {
  int i = 0, ret = 0, cnt = 0;      int i, ret = 0, cnt = 0;
  for (i = 0; i < N; i++) {         for (i = 0; i < N; i++) {
    if (x[i] > 1000){                 if (i > 1000){
      ret = ret + x[i];                 ret = ret + x[i];
      cnt = cnt + 1;                     cnt = cnt + 1;
    }                                 }
  }                                 }
  if (cnt !=0) return ret / cnt;    if (cnt !=0) return ret / cnt;
  else return 0;                    else return 0;
}                                 }
```

In this paper, we investigate the problem of reducer commutativity checking formally. To model real-world reducers, we introduce *integer reducers*, a syntactically restricted class of loopy programs over integer variables. In addition to assignments and conditional branches, a reducer contains an iterator to loop over inputs. Two operations are allowed on the iterator: *next*, which moves the iterator to the subsequent element in the input list; and *initialize*, which moves the iterator to the beginning of input list. Integer reducers do not allocate memory and are assumed to always terminate. In spite of these restrictions, we believe that integer reducers can capture the core computation of real-world reducers faithfully. The paper makes the following contributions:

- Via a reduction from solving Diophantine equations, we first show that checking the commutativity of integer reducers over exact integers with unbounded lengths of input lists is *undecidable*. The problem remains undecidable even with a bounded number of input values.
- Most reducer programs do not use exact integers in practice. We investigate the problem of checking reducer commutativity over bounded integers but with unbounded lengths of input lists. This problem turns out to be *decidable*. Using automata- and group-theoretic constructions, we reduce the commutativity checking problem to the language equivalence problem over two-way deterministic finite automata.
- Finally, we reduce the reducer commutativity problem to program assertion checking. The reduction applies to arbitrary reducers instances with input lists of a bounded

length. It enables checking the commutativity of real-world reducers automatically using off-the-shelf program analyzers. We present an evaluation of different program analysis techniques for checking reducer commutativity.

Related Work. Previous work on commutativity [17,15,6] has focused on checking if interface operations on a shared data structure commute, often to enable better parallelization. Their approach is *event*-centric, that is, it checks for independence of operations on data with arbitrary shapes. In contrast, our approach is *data*-centric: we use group-theoretic reductions on ordered data collections for efficient checking.

A recent survey [19] points out the abundance of non-commutative reducers in industrial Map-Reduce deployments. Previous approaches to checking reducer commutativity use black-box testing [20] and symbolic execution [4]. They generate large number of tests using permutations of the input and verify that the output is same. This does not scale even for small input sizes. Checking commutativity of reducers may be seen as a specific form of regression checking [10,7] where the two versions are identical except permuting the input order. The work in [11] proposes a static analysis technique to check re-orderings in the data-flow architecture consisting of multiple map and reduce phases using read or write conflicts between different phases. It does not consider the data commutativity problem.

The paper is organized as follows. We review basic notions in Sec. 2. Sec. 3 presents a formal model for reducers and a definition of the commutativity problem. It is followed by the undecidability result (Sec. 4). We then consider reducers with only bounded integers in Sec. 5. Sec. 6 shows the commutativity problem for bounded integer reducers is decidable. Sec. 7 gives the experimental results. We conclude in Sec. 8.

2 Preliminaries

Let $\mathbb{Z}, \mathbb{Z}^+, \mathbb{N}$ denote the set of integers, positive integers, and non-negative integers respectively. Define $\underline{n} = \{1, 2, \ldots, n\}$ when $n \in \mathbb{Z}^+$. A *permutation* on $\underline{n}$ is a one-to-one and onto mapping from $\underline{n}$ to $\underline{n}$. The set of permutations on $\underline{n}$ is denoted by S_n. It can be shown that S_n is a group (called the *symmetric group on n letters*) under the functional composition. Let $l_1, l_2, \ldots, l_m \in \mathbb{Z}$. We write $[l_1; l_2; \cdots ; l_m]$ to denote the integer list consisting of the elements $l_1, l_2, \ldots, l_m$. For an integer list ℓ, the notations $|\ell|$, $\mathsf{hd}(\ell)$, and $\mathsf{tl}(\ell)$ denote the length, head, and tail of ℓ respectively. The function $\mathsf{empty}(\ell)$ returns 1 if ℓ is empty; otherwise, it returns 0. For instance, $\mathsf{hd}([0; 1; 2]) = 0$, $\mathsf{tl}([0; 1; 2]) = [1; 2]$, and $\mathsf{empty}(\mathsf{tl}([0; 1; 2])) = 0$.

We define the semantics of reducer programs using transition systems. A *transition system* $\mathcal{T} = \langle S, \longrightarrow \rangle$ consists of a (possibly infinite) set S of *states* and a *transition relation* $\longrightarrow \subseteq S \times S$. For $s, t \in S$, we write $s \to t$ for $(s, t) \in \to$.

A *two-way deterministic finite automaton (2DFA)* $M = \langle Q, \Sigma, \Delta, q_0, F \rangle$ consists of a finite *state set* Q, a finite *alphabet* Σ, a *transition function* $\Delta : Q \times \Sigma \to Q \times \{L, R, -\}$, an *initial state* $q_0 \in Q$, and an *accepting set* $F \subseteq Q$. A 2DFA has a read-only *tape* and a *read head* to indicate the current symbol on the tape. If $\Delta(q, a) = (q', \gamma)$, M at the state q reading the symbol a transits to the state q'. It then moves its read head to the left, right, or same position when γ is L, R, or $-$ respectively. A *configuration* of M is of the form wqv where $w \in \Sigma^*$, $v \in \Sigma^+$, and $q \in Q$; it indicates that M is at the state q and reading the first symbol of v. The *initial configuration of M on input w* is $q_0 w$. For any $q_f \in F$, $a \in \Sigma$, and $w \in \Sigma^*$, $wq_f a$ is an *accepting configuration*. M *accepts* a string $w \in \Sigma^*$ if M starts from the initial configuration on input w and reaches an accepting configuration. Define $L(M) = \{w : M \text{ accepts } w\}$. A 2DFA can be algorithmically translated to a classical deterministic finite automata accepting the same language [16]. It hence recognizes a regular language.

Theorem 1. *Let $M = \langle Q, \Sigma, \Delta, q_0, F \rangle$ be a 2DFA. $L(M)$ is regular.*

2.1 Facts about Symmetric Groups

We will need notations and facts from basic group theory. Let $x_1, x_2, \ldots, x_k \in \underline{n}$ be distinct. The notation $(x_1 \ x_2 \ \cdots \ x_k)$ denotes a permutation function on $\underline{n}$ such that $x_1 \mapsto x_2, x_2 \mapsto x_3, \ldots, x_{k-1} \mapsto x_k$, and $x_k \mapsto x_1$. Define $\tau_k = (1 \ 2 \ \cdots \ k)$.

Theorem 2 ([12]). *For every $\sigma \in S_n$, σ is equal to a composition of τ_2 and τ_n.*

For $\ell = [l_1; l_2; \cdots; l_m]$ and $\sigma \in S_m$, define $\sigma(\ell) = [l_{\sigma(1)}; l_{\sigma(2)}; \cdots; l_{\sigma(m)}]$. For example, $\tau_3([3; 2; 1]) = [2; 1; 3]$. The following proposition will be useful.

Proposition 1. *Let A be a set of lists. The following are equivalent:*

1. *for every $\ell \in A$ with $|\ell| > 1$, both $\tau_2(\ell)$ and $\tau_{|\ell|}(\ell)$ are in A;*
2. *for every $\ell \in A$ and $\sigma \in S_{|\ell|}$, $\sigma(\ell)$ is in A.*

In other words, to check whether all permutations of a list belong to a set, it suffices to check two specific permutations by Proposition 1.

3 Integer Reducers

Map-Reduce is a programming model for data parallel computation. Programmers can choose to implement map and reduce phases in a programming language of their choice. In order to analyze real-world reducers, we give a formal model to characterize the essence of reducers. Our model allows to describe the computation of reducers and investigate their commutativity.

A reducer receives a key k and a non-empty list of values associated with k as input; it returns a key-value pair as an output. We are interested in checking whether the output is independent of the order of input list. Since both input and output keys are not essential, they are ignored in our model. Most data parallel computation moreover deals with numerical values [19] We assume that both input and output values are integers. To access values in a input list, our model has iterators adopted from modern programming languages. A reducer performs its core computation by iterating over the input list.

Reducers are represented by control flow graphs. Let $\mathtt{Var}$ denote the set of integer variables. Define the syntax of commands $\mathtt{Cmd}$ as follows.

$$v \in \mathtt{Var} \stackrel{\triangle}{=} \mathtt{x} \mid \mathtt{y} \mid \mathtt{z} \mid \cdots$$
$$e \in \mathtt{Exp} \stackrel{\triangle}{=} e = e \mid e > e \mid !\, e \mid e \,\&\&\, e \mid \cdots \mid -2 \mid -1 \mid 0 \mid 1 \mid 2 \mid \cdots \mid v \mid e{+}e \mid e{\times}e \mid$$
$$\qquad \mathtt{cur}() \mid \mathtt{end}()$$
$$c \in \mathtt{Cmd} \stackrel{\triangle}{=} v := e \mid \mathtt{init}() \mid \mathtt{next}() \mid \mathtt{assume}\ e \mid \mathtt{return}\ e$$

In addition to standard expressions and commands, the command `assume` e blocks the computation when e evaluates to false. The command `init()` initializes the iterator by pointing to the first input value in the list. The expression `cur()` returns the current input value pointed to by the iterator. The `next()` command updates the iterator by pointing to the next input value. The expression `end()` returns 1 if the iterator is at the end of the list; it returns 0 otherwise.

A *control flow graph (CFG)* $G = \langle N, E, \text{cmd}, n_s, n_e \rangle$ consists of a finite set of *nodes* N, a set of *edges* $E \subseteq N \times N$, a *command labeling function* $\text{cmd} : E \to \text{Cmd}$, a *start* node $n_s \in N$, and an *end* node $n_e \in N$. The start node has no incoming edges. The end node has no outgoing edges and exactly one incoming edge. The only incoming edge of the end node is the only edge labeled with a `return` command. Without loss of generality, we assume that the first command is always `init()` and all variables are initialized to 0. Moreover, edges with the same source must all be labeled `assume` commands; the Boolean expressions in these `assume` commands must be exhaustive and exclusive. In other words, we only consider deterministic reducers.

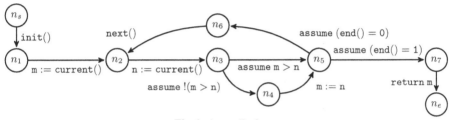

Fig. 1. A max Reducer

Figure 1 shows the CFG of a reducer. After the iterator is initialized, the reducer stores the first input value in the variable m. For each input value, it stores the value in n. If m is not greater than n, the reducer updates the variable m. It then checks if there are more input values. If so, the reducer performs a `next()` command and examines the next input value. Otherwise, m is returned. The reducer thus computes the maximum value of the input list.

In order to define the semantics of reducers, we assume a set of *reserved variables* $\mathbf{r} = \{\text{vals}, \text{iter}, \text{result}\}$. The reserved variable `vals` contains the list of input values; `result` contains the output value. The reserved variable `iter` is a list; it is used to model the iterator for input values. A *reserved valuation* maps each reserved variable to a value. $Val[\mathbf{r}]$ denotes the set of reserved valuations.

In addition to reserved variables, a reducer has a finite set of program variables $\mathbf{x}$. A *program valuation* assigns integers to program variables. $Val[\mathbf{x}]$ is the set of program valuations. For $\rho \in Val[\mathbf{r}]$, $\eta \in Val[\mathbf{x}]$, and $e \in \text{Exp}$, define $\llbracket e \rrbracket_{\rho,\eta}$ as follows.

$$\llbracket n \rrbracket_{\rho,\eta} \overset{\triangle}{=} n \qquad\qquad \llbracket x \rrbracket_{\rho,\eta} \overset{\triangle}{=} \eta(x)$$

$$\llbracket e_0 + e_1 \rrbracket_{\rho,\eta} \overset{\triangle}{=} \llbracket e_0 \rrbracket_{\rho,\eta} + \llbracket e_1 \rrbracket_{\rho,\eta} \qquad\qquad \llbracket e_0 \times e_1 \rrbracket_{\rho,\eta} \overset{\triangle}{=} \llbracket e_0 \rrbracket_{\rho,\eta} \times \llbracket e_1 \rrbracket_{\rho,\eta}$$

$$\llbracket !e \rrbracket_{\rho,\eta} \overset{\triangle}{=} \neg \llbracket e \rrbracket_{\rho,\eta} \qquad\qquad \llbracket e_0 \,\&\&\, e_1 \rrbracket_{\rho,\eta} \overset{\triangle}{=} \llbracket e_0 \rrbracket_{\rho,\eta} \wedge \llbracket e_1 \rrbracket_{\rho,\eta}$$

$$\llbracket e_0 = e_1 \rrbracket_{\rho,\eta} \overset{\triangle}{=} \llbracket e_0 \rrbracket_{\rho,\eta} = \llbracket e_1 \rrbracket_{\rho,\eta} \qquad\qquad \llbracket e_0 > e_1 \rrbracket_{\rho,\eta} \overset{\triangle}{=} \llbracket e_0 \rrbracket_{\rho,\eta} > \llbracket e_1 \rrbracket_{\rho,\eta}$$

$$\llbracket \text{cur}() \rrbracket_{\rho,\eta} \overset{\triangle}{=} \text{hd}(\rho(\text{iter})) \qquad\qquad \llbracket \text{end}() \rrbracket_{\rho,\eta} \overset{\triangle}{=} \text{empty}(\text{tl}(\rho(\text{iter})))$$

Let $G = \langle N, E, \mathrm{cmd}, n_s, n_e \rangle$ be a CFG. Define $\mathrm{Cmd}_G = \{\mathrm{cmd}(m,n) : (m,n) \in E\}$. We first define the exact integer semantics of G. $\mathrm{IntReducer}_G$ is a transition system $\langle Q, \longrightarrow \rangle$ where $Q = N \times Val[\mathbf{r}] \times Val[\mathbf{x}]$ and $\longrightarrow$ is defined as follows.

$$(m, \rho, \eta) \to (n, \rho, \eta[x \mapsto [\![e]\!]_{\rho,\eta}]) \qquad \text{if } \mathrm{cmd}(m,n) \text{ is } x := e$$
$$(m, \rho, \eta) \to (n, \rho[\mathtt{iter} \mapsto \rho(\mathtt{vals})], \eta) \qquad \text{if } \mathrm{cmd}(m,n) \text{ is } \mathtt{init}()$$
$$(m, \rho, \eta) \to (n, \rho[\mathtt{iter} \mapsto \mathrm{tl}(\rho(\mathtt{iter}))], \eta) \qquad \text{if } \mathrm{cmd}(m,n) \text{ is } \mathtt{next}()$$
$$(m, \rho, \eta) \to (n, \rho[\mathtt{result} \mapsto [\![e]\!]_{\rho,\eta}], \eta) \qquad \text{if } \mathrm{cmd}(m,n) \text{ is } \mathtt{return}\ e$$
$$(m, \rho, \eta) \to (n, \rho, \eta) \qquad \text{if } \mathrm{cmd}(m,n) \text{ is } \mathtt{assume}\ e \text{ and } [\![e]\!]_{\rho,\eta} = \mathtt{tt}$$

On an $\mathtt{init}()$ command, $\mathrm{IntReducer}_G$ re-initializes the reserved variable $\mathtt{iter}$ with the input values in $\mathtt{inputs}$. The head of $\mathtt{iter}$ is the current input value of the iterator. On a $\mathtt{next}()$ command, $\mathtt{iter}$ discards the head and hence moves to the next input value. If $\mathtt{iter}$ is the empty list, no more input values remain to be read. Finally, he reserved variable $\mathtt{result}$ records the output value on the $\mathtt{return}$ command.

For $(n, \rho, \eta), (n', \rho', \eta') \in Q$, we write $(n, \rho, \eta) \xrightarrow{*} (n', \rho', \eta')$ if there are states (n_i, ρ_i, η_i) such that $(n, \rho, \eta) = (n_1, \rho_1, \eta_1)$, $(n', \rho', \eta') = (n_{k+1}, \rho_{k+1}, \eta_{k+1})$, and for every $1 \leq i \leq k$, $(n_i, \rho_i, \eta_i) \to (n_{i+1}, \rho_{i+1}, \eta_{i+1})$. Since variables are initialized to 0, let $\rho_0 \in Val[\mathbf{r}]$ and $\eta_0 \in Val[\mathbf{x}]$ be constant 0 valuations. For any non-empty list ℓ of integers, $\mathrm{IntReducer}_G$ *returns* r on ℓ if $(n_s, \rho_0[\mathtt{vals} \mapsto \ell], \eta_0) \xrightarrow{*} (n_e, \rho', \eta')$ and $\rho'(\mathtt{result}) = r$. The elements in ℓ are the *input values*. The returned value r is an *output value*. We will also write $\mathrm{IntReducer}_G(\ell)$ for the output value on ℓ.

The *commutativity problem for integer reducers* is the following: given an integer reducer $\mathrm{IntReducer}_G$, decide whether $\mathrm{IntReducer}_G(\ell)$ is equal to $\mathrm{IntReducer}_G(\sigma(\ell))$ for every non-empty list ℓ of input values and every permutation $\sigma \in S_{|\ell|}$.

4   Undecidability of Commutativity for Integer Reducers

By Rice's theorem, the commutativity problem for Turing machines is undecidable. In practice, reducers must terminate and are often simple processes running on commodity machines. In this section, we show that the commutativity problem is undecidable even for a very restricted class of integer reducers which can iterate through each input value at most once. Such reducers are called *single-pass integer reducers*.

Undecidability is obtained by a reduction from the Diophantine problem. Let $x_1, x_2, \ldots, x_m$ be variables. A *Diophantine equation over* $x_1, x_2, \ldots, x_m$ is of the form

$$p(x_1, x_2, \ldots, x_m) = \sum_{\delta=0}^{D} \sum_{\delta_1 + \delta_2 + \cdots + \delta_m = \delta} c_{\delta_1, \delta_2, \ldots, \delta_m} x_1^{\delta_1} x_2^{\delta_2} \cdots x_m^{\delta_m} = 0$$

where $\delta_i \in \mathbb{N}$ for every $1 \leq i \leq m$ and D is a constant. A *system of k Diophantine equations $S(x_1, x_2, \ldots, x_m)$ over* $x_1, x_2, \ldots, x_m$ consists of k Diophantine equations $p_j(x_1, x_2, \ldots, x_m) = 0$ where $1 \leq j \leq k$. A *solution* to a system of k Diophantine equations $S(x_1, x_2, \ldots, x_m)$ is a tuple of integers $i_1, i_2, \ldots, i_m$ such that $p_j(i_1, i_2, \ldots, i_m) = 0$ for every $1 \leq j \leq k$. The *Diophantine problem* is to determine whether a given system of Diophantine equations has a solution.

Theorem 3 ([13]). *The Diophantine problem is undecidable.*

Given a system of Diophantine equations, it is straightforward to construct a single-pass integer reducer to check whether the input list of integers is a solution to the system. If the input list is indeed a solution, the reducer returns 1; otherwise, it returns 0. Hence if the given system has no solution, the reducer always returns 0 on any permutation of an input list. Note that the reducer is also commutative when the given system is trivially solved. Our construction introduces two additional variables to make the reducer not commutative on any solvable systems of Diophantine equations.

Theorem 4. *Commutativity problem for single-pass integer reducers is undecidable.*

4.1 Single-Pass Reducers over Fixed-Length Inputs

The commutativity problem for single-pass integer reducers is undecidable. It is therefore impossible to verify whether an arbitrary integer reducer produces the same output on the same input values in different orders. In the hope of identifying a decidable subproblem, we consider the commutativity problem with a fixed number of input values. The m-*commutativity problem* for integer reducers is the following: given an integer reducer IntReducer_G, determine whether $\text{IntReducer}_G(\ell) = \text{IntReducer}_G(\sigma(\ell))$ for every list of input values ℓ of length m and $\sigma \in S_m$. Because solving Diophantine equations with 9 non-negative variables is undecidable [12], the m-commutativity problem is undecidable when $m \geq 11$.

Theorem 5. *The m-commutativity problem of single-pass integer reducers is undecidable when $m \geq 11$.*

4.2 From m-Commutativity to Program Analysis

Since it is impossible to solve the m-commutativity problem completely, we propose a sound but incomplete solution to the problem. For any m input values, the naïve solution is to check whether an integer reducer returns the same output value on all permutations of the m input values. Since the number of permutations grows exponentially, the solution clearly is impractical. A more effective technique is needed.

```
l₁ := *; l₂ := *; ... lₘ := *;

x₁ := l₁; x₂ := l₂; ... xₘ := lₘ;
ret :=IntReducerG([x₁; x₂; ...; xₘ]);

x₁ := l₂; x₂ := l₁; x₃ := l₃; ... xₘ := lₘ;
ret₂ :=IntReducerG([x₁; x₂; ...; xₘ]);
assert (ret = ret₂);

x₁ := l₂; x₂ := l₃; ... xₘ₋₁ := lₘ; xₘ := l₁;
retₘ:=IntReducerG([x₁; x₂; ...; xₘ]);
assert (ret = retₘ);
```

Fig. 2. Checking m-Commutativity

Our idea is to apply the group-theoretic reduction from Proposition 1. Figure 2 shows a program that realizes the idea. In the program, the expression $*$ denotes a non-deterministic value. The program starts with m non-deterministic integer values in $l_1, l_2, \ldots, l_m$. It stores the result of $\text{IntReducer}_G([l_1; l_2; \ldots; l_m])$ in ret. The program then computes the results of $\texttt{IntReducer}_G(\tau_2([l_1; l_2; \ldots; l_m]))$ and $\texttt{IntReducer}_G(\tau_m([l_1; l_2; \ldots; l_m]))$. If both results are equal to $\texttt{ret}$ for every input values, $\texttt{IntReducer}_G$ is m-commutative.

Theorem 6. *If assertions in Figure 2 hold for all computation, $\texttt{IntReducer}_G$ is m-commutative.*

Theorem 6 gives a sound but incomplete technique for the m-commutativity problem. Using off-the-shelf program analyzers, we can verify whether the assertions in Figure 2 always hold for all computation. If program analyzers establish both assertions, we conclude that $\texttt{IntReducer}_G$ is m-commutativity.

5   Bounded Integer Reducers

The commutativity problem for integer reducers is undecidable (Theorem 4). Undecidability persists even if the number of input values is fixed (Theorem 5). One may conjecture that the number of input values is irrelevant to undecidability of the commutativity problem. What induces undecidability of the problem then?

Exact integers induce undecidability in computational problems such as the Diophantine problem. However, in most programming languages, exact integers are not supported natively. Consequently, real-world reducers seldom use exact integers. It is thus more faithful to consider reducers with only bounded integers.

Fix $d \in \mathbb{Z}^+$. Define $\mathbb{Z}_d = \{0, 1, \ldots, d-1\}$. Recall that $\mathbf{r} = \{\texttt{vals}, \texttt{iter}, \texttt{result}\}$ are reserved variables. A *bounded reserved valuation* assigns the reserved variables $\texttt{vals}, \texttt{iter}$ lists of values in $\mathbb{Z}_d$, and $\texttt{result}$ a value in $\mathbb{Z}_d$; a *bounded program valuation* maps $\mathbf{x}$ to $\mathbb{Z}_d$. We write $BVal[\mathbf{r}]$ and $BVal[\mathbf{x}]$ for the sets of bounded reserved valuations and bounded program valuations respectively. For every $\rho \in BVal[\mathbf{r}]$, $\eta \in BVal[\mathbf{x}]$, and $e \in \texttt{Exp}$, define $\lVert e \rVert_{\rho,\eta}$ as follows.

$$\lVert n \rVert_{\rho,\eta} \stackrel{\triangle}{=} n \bmod d \qquad\qquad \lVert x \rVert_{\rho,\eta} \stackrel{\triangle}{=} \eta(x)$$

$$\lVert e_0 + e_1 \rVert_{\rho,\eta} \stackrel{\triangle}{=} \lVert e_0 \rVert_{\rho,\eta} + \lVert e_1 \rVert_{\rho,\eta} \bmod d$$

$$\lVert e_0 \times e_1 \rVert_{\rho,\eta} \stackrel{\triangle}{=} \lVert e_0 \rVert_{\rho,\eta} \times \lVert e_1 \rVert_{\rho,\eta} \bmod d$$

$$\lVert !e \rVert_{\rho,\eta} \stackrel{\triangle}{=} \neg \lVert e \rVert_{\rho,\eta} \qquad \lVert e_0 \mathbin{\&\&} e_1 \rVert_{\rho,\eta} \stackrel{\triangle}{=} \lVert e_0 \rVert_{\rho,\eta} \wedge \lVert e_1 \rVert_{\rho,\eta}$$

$$\lVert e_0 = e_1 \rVert_{\rho,\eta} \stackrel{\triangle}{=} \lVert e_0 \rVert_{\rho,\eta} = \lVert e_1 \rVert_{\rho,\eta} \qquad \lVert e_0 > e_1 \rVert_{\rho,\eta} \stackrel{\triangle}{=} \lVert e_0 \rVert_{\rho,\eta} > \lVert e_1 \rVert_{\rho,\eta}$$

$$\lVert \texttt{cur}() \rVert_{\rho,\eta} \stackrel{\triangle}{=} \mathsf{hd}(\rho(\texttt{iter})) \qquad \lVert \texttt{end}() \rVert_{\rho,\eta} \stackrel{\triangle}{=} \mathsf{empty}(\mathsf{tl}(\rho(\texttt{iter})))$$

Let $G = \langle N, E, \texttt{cmd}, n_s, n_e \rangle$ be a CFG over program variables $\mathbf{x}$. We now define the bounded integer semantics of G. $\texttt{BoundedReducer}_G$ is a transition system $\langle Q, \longrightarrow \rangle$ where $Q = N \times BVal[\mathbf{r}] \times BVal[\mathbf{x}]$ and the following transition relation $\longrightarrow$:

$$\begin{aligned}
(m, \rho, \eta) &\hookrightarrow (n, \rho, \eta[x \mapsto \lVert e \rVert_{\rho,\eta}]) && \text{if } \mathrm{cmd}(m, n) \text{ is } x := e \\
(m, \rho, \eta) &\hookrightarrow (n, \rho[\texttt{iter} \mapsto \rho(\texttt{vals})], \eta) && \text{if } \mathrm{cmd}(m, n) \text{ is } \texttt{init}() \\
(m, \rho, \eta) &\hookrightarrow (n, \rho[\texttt{iter} \mapsto \mathsf{tl}(\rho(\texttt{iter}))], \eta) && \text{if } \mathrm{cmd}(m, n) \text{ is } \texttt{next}() \\
(m, \rho, \eta) &\hookrightarrow (n, \rho[\texttt{result} \mapsto \lVert e \rVert_{\rho,\eta}], \eta) && \text{if } \mathrm{cmd}(m, n) \text{ is } \texttt{return } e \\
(m, \rho, \eta) &\hookrightarrow (n, \rho, \eta) && \text{if } \mathrm{cmd}(m, n) \text{ is } \texttt{assume } e \text{ and } \lVert e \rVert_{\rho,\eta} = \mathsf{tt}
\end{aligned}$$

Except that expressions are evaluated in modular arithmetic, BoundedReducer$_G$ behaves exactly the same as the integer reducer IntReducer$_G$. We write $(n, \rho, \eta) \overset{*}{\hookrightarrow} (n', \rho', \eta')$ if there are $(n_1, \rho_1, \eta_1) = (n, \rho, \eta)$ and $(n_{k+1}, \rho_{k+1}, \eta_{k+1}) = (n', \rho', \eta')$ such that $(n_i, \rho_i, \eta_i) \hookrightarrow (n_{i+1}, \rho_{i+1}, \eta_{i+1})$ for every $1 \leq i \leq k$. For any non-empty list ℓ of values in $\mathbb{Z}_d$, the bounded integer reducer BoundedReducer$_G$ *returns r on ℓ* if $(n_s, \rho_0[\text{vals} \mapsto \ell], \eta_0) \overset{*}{\hookrightarrow} (n_e, \rho', \eta')$ and $\rho'(\text{result}) = r$. BoundedReducer$_G(\ell)$ denotes the output value r returned by BoundedReducer$_G$ on the list ℓ of input values.

Note that the number of input values is unbounded. BoundedReducer$_G$ is an infinite-state transition system due to the reserved variables vals and iter. On the other hand, all program variables and the reserved variable result can only have finitely many different values. We will exploit this fact to attain our decidability result.

6   Deciding Commutativity of Bounded Integer Reducers

We present an automata-theoretic technique to solve the commutativity problem for bounded integer reducers. Although bounded integer reducers receive input lists of arbitrary lengths, their computation can be summarized by 2DFA exactly. Based on the 2DFA characterizing the computation of a bounded integer reducer, we construct another 2DFA to summarize the computation of the reducer on permuted input values. Using Proposition 1, we reduce the commutativity problem for bounded integer reducers to the language equivalence problem for 2DFA. Since language equivalence problem of 2DFA is decidable, checking bounded integer reducer commutativity is decidable.

More precisely, let G be a CFG, $m > 0$, and $l_1, l_2, \ldots, l_m, r \in \mathbb{Z}_d$. We construct a 2DFA A_G such that it accepts the string $\triangleleft l_1 l_2 \cdots l_m \triangleright r$ exactly when the bounded integer reducer BoundedReducer$_G$ returns r on the list $[l_1; l_2; \ldots; l_m]$. For clarity, we say l_i is the i-th input value of A_G, which is in fact the i-th input value of BoundedReducer$_G$. We use the read-only tape as the reserved vals variable. Two additional reserved variables cur and end are introduced for the cur() and end() expressions. On a return command, A_G stores the returned value in the reserved result variable. If the last symbol r of the input string is equal to result, A_G accepts the input. Otherwise, it rejects the input. More concretely, let $\mathbf{s} = \{\text{cur}, \text{end}, \text{result}\}$ be reserved variables and $G = \langle N, E, \text{cmd}, n_s, n_e \rangle$ a CFG over program variables $\mathbf{x}$. A *finite reserved valuation* maps $\mathbf{s}$ to $\mathbb{Z}_d$; a *finite program valuation* maps $\mathbf{x}$ to $\mathbb{Z}_d$. We write $FVal[\mathbf{s}]$ and $FVal[\mathbf{x}]$ for the sets of finite reserved valuations and finite program valuations respectively. Note that $FVal[\mathbf{s}]$ and $FVal[\mathbf{x}]$ are finite sets since $\mathbf{s}, \mathbf{x}, \mathbb{Z}_d$ are finite. For every $\rho \in FVal[\mathbf{s}]$, $\eta \in FVal[\mathbf{x}]$, and $e \in \text{Exp}$, define $\{\!| e |\!\}_{\rho, \eta}$ as follows.

$$\{\!| n |\!\}_{\rho,\eta} \overset{\triangle}{=} n \bmod d \qquad\qquad \{\!| x |\!\}_{\rho,\eta} \overset{\triangle}{=} \eta(x)$$

$$\{\!| e_0 + e_1 |\!\}_{\rho,\eta} \overset{\triangle}{=} \{\!| e_0 |\!\}_{\rho,\eta} + \{\!| e_1 |\!\}_{\rho,\eta} \bmod d$$

$$\{\!| e_0 \times e_1 |\!\}_{\rho,\eta} \overset{\triangle}{=} \{\!| e_0 |\!\}_{\rho,\eta} \times \{\!| e_1 |\!\}_{\rho,\eta} \bmod d$$

$$\{\!| !e |\!\}_{\rho,\eta} \overset{\triangle}{=} \neg \{\!| e |\!\}_{\rho,\eta} \qquad\qquad \{\!| e_0 \,\&\&\, e_1 |\!\}_{\rho,\eta} \overset{\triangle}{=} \{\!| e_0 |\!\}_{\rho,\eta} \wedge \{\!| e_1 |\!\}_{\rho,\eta}$$

$$\{\!| e_0 = e_1 |\!\}_{\rho,\eta} \overset{\triangle}{=} \{\!| e_0 |\!\}_{\rho,\eta} = \{\!| e_1 |\!\}_{\rho,\eta} \qquad\qquad \{\!| e_0 > e_1 |\!\}_{\rho,\eta} \overset{\triangle}{=} \{\!| e_0 |\!\}_{\rho,\eta} > \{\!| e_1 |\!\}_{\rho,\eta}$$

$$\{\!| \text{cur}() |\!\}_{\rho,\eta} \overset{\triangle}{=} \rho(\text{cur}) \qquad\qquad \{\!| \text{end}() |\!\}_{\rho,\eta} \overset{\triangle}{=} \rho(\text{end})$$

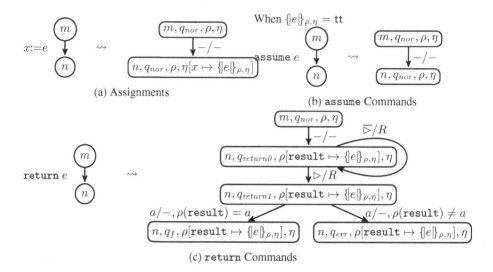

(a) Assignments

(b) assume Commands

(c) return Commands

Fig. 3. Construction of A_G

A state of A_G is a quadruple (n, q, ρ, η) where n is a node in G, q is a control state, ρ is a finite reserved valuation, and η is a finite program valuation. The control state q_{nor} means the "normal" operation mode. For an assignment command in G, A_G simulates the assignment in its finite states (Figure 3a). For an assume command, A_G has a transition exactly when the assumed expression evaluated to tt (Figure 3b). For a return command, A_G stores the returned value in result and enters the control state $q_{return0}$. A_G then moves its read head to the right until it sees the $\triangleright$ symbol (Figure 3c)[2]. On the $\triangleright$ symbol, A_G enters the control state $q_{return1}$ and compares the last symbol a with the returned value. It enters the accepting state q_f if they are equal.

For an init() command, A_G initializes the iterator at the control state q_{rewind} by moving its read head to the left until the $\triangleleft$ symbol is read. A_G then moves its read head to the first input value, sets end to 0 and enters the control state q_{next0} to update the reserved variable current (Figure 4a). For the next() command, A_G enters q_{next0} to update the value of current (Figure 4b). At the control state q_{next0}, the symbol under its read head is the next input value. If end is 1, A_G enters the error control state q_{err} immediately. Otherwise, it updates the reserved variable cur, moves its read head to the right, and checks if there are more input values at the control state q_{next1}. If the symbol is $\triangleright$, A_G sets end to 1 and enters the normal operation mode (Figure 4c).

Lemma 1. *Let* BoundedReducer$_G$ *be a bounded integer reducer for a CFG* $G = \langle N, E, \text{cmd}, n_s, n_e \rangle$, $m > 0$, *and* $l_1, l_2, \ldots, l_m, r \in \mathbb{Z}_d$. *Then*

$$L(A_G) = \{\triangleleft l_1 l_2 \cdots l_m \triangleright r : \text{BoundedReducer}_G([l_1; l_2; \cdots ; l_m]) = r\}.$$

The commutativity problem for bounded integer reducers asks us to check whether a given bounded integer reducer returns the same output value on any permutation of

---

[2] $\overline{\alpha}$ denotes any symbol other than α.

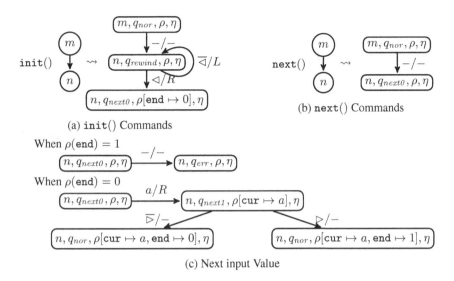

(a) init() Commands

(b) next() Commands

(c) Next input Value

Fig. 4. Construction of A_G (continued)

input values. Applying Proposition 1, it suffices to consider two particular permutations. We have shown that the computation of a bounded integer reducer can be summarized by a 2DFA. Our proof strategy hence is to summarize the computation of the given bounded integer reducer on permuted input values by two 2DFA. We compare the computation of a bounded integer reducer on original and permuted input values by checking if the two 2DFA accept the same language.

We will generalize the construction of A_G to define another 2DFA named $A_G^{\tau_2}$ for the computation on permuted input values. Consider a non-empty list of input values $\ell = [l_1; l_2; \cdots; l_m]$ with $m > 1$. The 2DFA $A_G^{\tau_2}$ will accept the string $\lhd l_1 l_2 \cdots l_m \rhd r$ where r is $\texttt{BoundedReducer}_G(\tau_2(\ell))$ and $\texttt{BoundedReducer}_G$ is the bounded integer reducer for the CFG G. Our construction uses additional reserved variables to store the first two input values. $A_G^{\tau_2}$ also has two new control states to indicate whether the first two input values are to be read. Since the construction of $A_G^{\tau_2}$ is more complicated, we skip its description due to page limit.

Lemma 2. *Let* $\texttt{BoundedReducer}_G$ *be a bounded integer reducer for a CFG* $G = \langle N, E, \mathrm{cmd}, n_s, n_e \rangle$, $m > 0$, *and* $l_1, l_2, \ldots, l_m, r \in \mathbb{Z}_d$. *Then*

$$L(A_G^{\tau_2}) = \{\lhd l_1 l_2 \cdots l_m \rhd r : \texttt{BoundedReducer}_G(\tau_2([l_1; l_2; \cdots; l_m])) = r\}.$$

Lemma 3. *Let* $\texttt{BoundedReducer}_G$ *be a bounded integer reducer for a CFG* $G = \langle N, E, \mathrm{cmd}, n_s, n_e \rangle$. *The languages* $L(A_G^{\tau_2}) = L(A_G)$ *if and only if* $\texttt{BoundedReducer}_G(\ell) = \texttt{BoundedReducer}_G(\tau_2(\ell))$ *for every non-empty list* ℓ *of values in* $\mathbb{Z}_d$.

Based on the construction of A_G, we construct another 2DFA named $A_G^{\tau_*}$ which characterizes the computation of the given bounded integer reducer $\texttt{BoundedReducer}_G$ on input values in a different permutation. More precisely, for any non-empty list of input values $\ell = [l_1; l_2; \cdots; l_{|\ell|}]$, $A_G^{\tau_*}$ accepts the string $\lhd l_1 l_2 \cdots l_{|\ell|} \rhd r$ where r is

BoundedReducer$_G(\tau_{|\ell|}(\ell))$. For the string $\lhd l_1 l_2 \cdots l_{|\ell|} \rhd r$ on $A_G^{\tau*}$'s tape, we want to summarize the computation of BoundedReducer$_G$ on $[l_2; l_3; \cdots ; l_{|\ell|}; l_1]$. Observe that l_2 is the *2nd input value* of $A_G^{\tau*}$ and the *1st input value* of BoundedReducer$_G$ on $\tau_{|\ell|}(\ell)$.

A state of $A_G^{\tau*}$ is a quadruple (n, q, ρ, η) where n is a node in G, q is a control state, ρ is a finite reserved valuation, and η is a finite program valuation. In addition to s, $A_G^{\tau*}$ has the reserved variable fst to memorize the first input value of $A_G^{\tau*}$. It also has three new control states: q_0 for initialization, q_{nor} for the normal operation mode, and q_{last} for the case where the last input value of BoundedReducer$_G$ on $\tau_{|\ell|}(\ell)$ has been read.

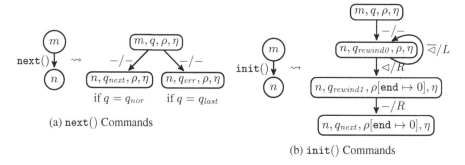

(a) next() Commands

(b) init() Commands

Fig. 5. Construction of $A_G^{\tau*}$

$A_G^{\tau*}$ starts by storing its first input value in the reserved variable fst and moving to the normal operation mode q_{nor}. To initialize the iterator, $A_G^{\tau*}$ moves its read head and stores the first input value of BoundedReducer$_G$ on $\tau_{|\ell|}(\ell)$ in the reserved variable cur. Retrieving the next input value of BoundedReducer$_G$ on $\tau_{|\ell|}(\ell)$ is slightly different. If there are more input values, $A_G^{\tau*}$ moves its read head to the right and updates cur accordingly. Otherwise, the first input value of $A_G^{\tau*}$ is the last input value of BoundedReducer$_G$ on $\tau_{|\ell|}(\ell)$. $A_G^{\tau*}$ sets cur to the value of fst and enters q_{last}.

More concretely, $A_G^{\tau*}$ transits to the control state q_{next} if it is in the normal operation mode q_{nor} for a next() command. It enters the error state q_{err} when the last input value of BoundedReducer$_G$ on $\tau_{|\ell|}(\ell)$ has been read (Figure 5a). For an init() command, $A_G^{\tau*}$ moves its read head to the second input value of $A_G^{\tau*}$. Since the second input value of $A_G^{\tau*}$ is the first input value of BoundedReducer$_G$ on $\tau_{|\ell|}(\ell)$, $A_G^{\tau*}$ sets end to 0 and enters the control state q_{next} to update the reserved variable cur (Figure 5b).

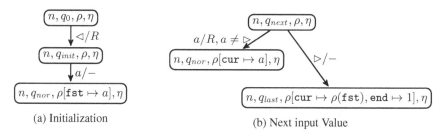

(a) Initialization

(b) Next input Value

Fig. 6. Construction of $A_G^{\tau*}$ (continued)

Figure 6a shows the initialization step. $A_G^{\tau_*}$ simply stores its first input value in the reserved variable fst and transits to the normal operation model q_{nor}. The auxiliary control state q_{next} retrieves the next input value of BoundedReducer$_G$ on $\tau_{|\ell|}(\ell)$ (Figure 6b). If there are more input values of $A_G^{\tau_*}$, $A_G^{\tau_*}$ updates cur, moves its read head to the right, and transits to the normal operation mode q_{nor}. If $A_G^{\tau_*}$ reaches the end of its input values, the first input value of $A_G^{\tau_*}$ is the last input value of BoundedReducer$_G$ on $\tau_{|\ell|}(\ell)$. $A_G^{\tau_*}$ hence updates cur to the value of fst, sets end to 1, and transits to q_{last}.

Lemma 4. *Let* BoundedReducer$_G$ *be a bounded integer reducer for a CFG* $G = \langle N, E, \mathrm{cmd}, n_s, n_e \rangle$, $m > 0$, *and* $l_1, l_2, \ldots, l_m, r \in \mathbb{Z}_d$. *Then*

$$L(A_G^{\tau_*}) = \{ \triangleleft l_1 l_2 \cdots l_m \triangleright r : \mathtt{BoundedReducer}_G(\tau_m([l_1; l_2; \cdots ; l_m])) = r \}.$$

Lemma 5. *Let* BoundedReducer$_G$ *be a bounded integer reducer for a CFG* $G = \langle N, E, \mathrm{cmd}, n_s, n_e \rangle$. *The languages* $L(A_G) = L(A_G^{\tau_*})$ *if and only if* BoundedReducer$_G(\ell) = $ BoundedReducer$_G(\tau_{|\ell|}(\ell))$ *for every non-empty list* ℓ *of values in* $\mathbb{Z}_d$.

By Proposition 1, Lemma 3 and 5, we have the following theorem:

Theorem 7. *Let* BoundedReducer$_G$ *be a bounded integer reducer for a CFG* $G = \langle N, E, \mathrm{cmd}, n_s, n_e \rangle$. $L(A_G) = L(A_G^{\tau_2}) = L(A_G^{\tau_*})$ *if and only if* BoundedReducer$_G(\ell) = $ BoundedReducer$_G(\sigma(\ell))$ *for every non-empty list* ℓ *of values in* $\mathbb{Z}_d$ *and* $\sigma \in S_{|\ell|}$.

The next result follows from decidability of 2DFA language equivalence problem.

Theorem 8. *The commutativity problem for bounded integer reducers is decidable.*

7   Experiments

The reduction in Sec. 4.2 allows us to use any off-the-shelf program analyzer to check commutativity of reducers. Given a reducer, we construct a program by the reduction and verify its assertions by program analyzers. This section evaluates the performance of state-of-the-art program analyzers for checking commutativity.

We compare CBMC [3], KLEE [2], CPACHECKER [1], and our prototype tool, SYMRED. Two configurations of CPACHECKER are used: predicate abstraction automated with interpolation and abstract interpretation using octagon domain. CBMC is a bounded model checker for C programs over bounded machine integers. The tools KLEE and SYMRED implement symbolic execution techniques: KLEE symbolically executes one path at-a-time while SYMRED constructs multi-path reducer summaries using symbolic execution and precise data-flow merging [18]. The tool KLEE uses STP [8] while SYMRED uses Z3 [5] as the underlying solver.

All experiments were conducted on a Xeon 3.07GHz Linux Ubuntu workstation with 16GB memory (Table 1). The symbol (TO) denotes timeout (5 minutes). The symbol (F) denotes that an incorrect result is reported. We found that KLEE cannot handle programs with division on some benchmarks; such cases are shown with the symbol -.

Our benchmarks consist of a set of 5 reducer programs in C, parameterized over the length of the input list (from 5 to 100). All the benchmark reducers but rangesum are commutative. The first three sets of benchmarks compute respectively the sum, average, and max value of the list. The benchmark `sep` computes the difference of the occurrences of even and odd numbers in the list. The example `dis` computes the average of input values greater than 100000. The example `rangesum` computes the average of input values of index greater than a half of the list length. We model input lists as bounded arrays and the iteration as a while loop with an index variable.

CPACHECKER with predicate abstraction generates predicates by interpolating incorrect error traces to separate reachable states and bad states. Benchmark sets such as `sum` and `avg` contain no branch conditions and has only one symbolic trace. Here, it suffices to check the satisfiability and compute interpolant of the single trace formula. Still, the verifier cannot scale to large input lists for these examples.

CPACHECKER with abstract interpretation over octagon domain finishes in seconds on all benchmarks but reports false positives on all commutative ones. We observe that a suitable abstract domain for checking commutativity should simultaneously support (a) permutations of the input list (b)

Table 1. Experimental Results

	CBMC	CPA-Pred.	CPA-Oct.	SYMRED	KLEE
sum5.c	43	64	3(F)	0.2	0.02
sum10.c	TO	TO	3(F)	0.4	0.02
sum20.c	TO	TO	3(F)	1	0.03
sum40.c	TO	TO	3(F)	1	0.04
sum60.c	TO	TO	4(F)	2	0.1
avg5.c	TO	TO	3(F)	0.3	-
avg10.c	TO	TO	3(F)	0.4	-
avg20.c	TO	TO	3(F)	0.8	-
avg40.c	TO	TO	3(F)	1	-
avg60.c	TO	TO	3(F)	2	-
max5.c	3	TO	3(F)	0.5	6
max10.c	215	TO	5(F)	7	102
max20.c	TO	TO	6(F)	103	TO
max40.c	TO	TO	7(F)	288	TO
max60.c	TO	TO	9(F)	TO	TO
sep5.c	0.2	21	4(F)	0.5	0.1
sep10.c	0.3	TO	8(F)	2	5
sep20.c	2	TO	202(F)	22	TO
sep40.c	26	TO	TO	21	TO
sep60.c	TO	TO	TO	22	TO
dis5.c	TO	3	4(F)	1	-
dis10.c	TO	TO	5(F)	3	-
dis20.c	TO	TO	9(F)	TO	-
dis40.c	TO	TO	24(F)	TO	-
dis60.c	TO	TO	67(F)	TO	-
rangesum5.c	0.1	5	3	0.3	-
rangesum10.c	0.1	8	3	0.5	-
rangesum20.c	2	18	3	0.9	-
rangesum40.c	4	25	4	2	-
rangesum60.c	5	TO	4	2	-

numerical properties such as the sum of the input list, and (c) equivalence between numerical values. Although individual domains for numerical properties of lists [9] and program equivalence [14] exist, we are not aware of any domain combining both simultaneously.

Reducers with addition and division operations in general are difficult for CBMC. The `avg` and `div` benchmarks use divisions and the tool cannot handle cases with input lists of length more than 5. The `sep` benchmark does not use divisions. CBMC scales better on this benchmark. For `rangesum`, CBMC catches the bug in seconds.

The two symbolic execution based approaches, KLEE and SYMRED, seem to be more effective for commutativity checking. SYMRED performs better than KLEE on `sep` and `max`, both containing branches. We believe this is because SYMRED avoids KLEE-like path enumeration using precise symbolic merges with *ite* (if-then-else) expressions at join locations. Loop iterations produce nested *ite* expressions. Although simplification of such expressions reduces the actual solver time on most benchmarks, it fails to curb the blowup for the `dis` benchmark. Therefore, better heuristics are needed to check reducer commutativity for unbounded input sizes.

8 Conclusions

We present tractability results on the commutativity problem for reducers by analyzing a syntactically restricted class of integer reducers. We show that deciding commutativity of single-pass reducer over exact integers is undecidable via a reduction from solving Diophantine equation. Undecidability holds even if reducers receive only a bounded number of input values. We further show that the problem is decidable for reducers over unbounded input list over bounded integers via a reduction to language equivalence checking of 2DFA. A practical solution to commutativity checking is provided via a reduction to assertion checking using group-theoretic reduction. We evaluate the performance of multiple program analyzers on parameterized problem instances. In future, we plan to investigate better heuristics and exploit more structural properties of real-world reducers for solving the problem for unbounded inputs over exact integers.

References

1. Beyer, D., Keremoglu, M.E.: CPACHECKER: A tool for configurable software verification. In: Gopalakrishnan, G., Qadeer, S. (eds.) CAV 2011. LNCS, vol. 6806, pp. 184–190. Springer, Heidelberg (2011)
2. Cadar, C., Dunbar, D., Engler, D.R.: KLEE: Unassisted and automatic generation of high-coverage tests for complex systems programs. In: OSDI, pp. 209–224. ACM (2008)
3. Clarke, E., Kroning, D., Lerda, F.: A tool for checking ANSI-C programs. In: Jensen, K., Podelski, A. (eds.) TACAS 2004. LNCS, vol. 2988, pp. 168–176. Springer, Heidelberg (2004)
4. Csallner, C., Fegaras, L., Li, C.: New ideas track: testing MapReduce-style programs. In: FSE, pp. 504–507 (2011)
5. de Moura, L., Bjørner, N.S.: Z3: An efficient SMT solver. In: Ramakrishnan, C.R., Rehof, J. (eds.) TACAS 2008. LNCS, vol. 4963, pp. 337–340. Springer, Heidelberg (2008)
6. Dimitrov, D., Raychev, V., Vechev, M., Koskinen, E.: Commutativity race detection. In: PLDI, p. 33. ACM (2014)
7. Felsing, D., Grebing, S., Klebanov, V., Rummer, P., Ulbrich, M.: Automating regression verification. In: ASE, pp. 349–360 (2014)
8. Ganesh, V., Dill, D.L.: A decision procedure for bit-vectors and arrays. In: Damm, W., Hermanns, H. (eds.) CAV 2007. LNCS, vol. 4590, pp. 519–531. Springer, Heidelberg (2007)
9. Halbwachs, N., Peron, M.: Discovering properties about arrays in simple programs. In: PLDI (2008)
10. Hawblitzel, C., Kawaguchi, M., Lahiri, S.K., Rebêlo, H.: Towards modularly comparing programs using automated theorem provers. In: Bonacina, M.P. (ed.) CADE 2013. LNCS, vol. 7898, pp. 282–299. Springer, Heidelberg (2013)
11. Hueske, F., Peters, M., Sax, M.J., Rheinländer, A., Bergmann, R., Krettek, A., Tzoumas, K.: Opening the black boxes in data flow optimization. VLDB Endowment 5(11) (2012)
12. Hungerford, T.W.: Algebra. Graduate Texts in Mathematics, vol. 73. Springer (2003)
13. Jones, J.P.: Universal diophantine equation. Journal of Symbolic Logic 47(3) (1982)
14. Kovacs, M., Seidl, H., Finkbeiner, B.: Relational abstract interpretation for the verification of 2-hypersafety properties. In: CCS, pp. 211–222. ACM (2013)
15. Kulkarni, M., Nguyen, D., Prountzos, D., Sui, X., Pingali, K.: Exploiting the commutativity lattice. ACM SIGPLAN Notices 46(6) (2011)

16. Rabin, M.O., Scott, D.: Finite automata and their decision problems. IBM Journal Res. Dev. 3(2) (1959)
17. Rinard, M., Diniz, P.C.: Commutativity analysis: A new analysis technique for parallelizing compilers. TOPLAS 19(6), 942–991 (1997)
18. Sinha, N., Singhania, N., Chandra, S., Sridharan, M.: Alternate and learn: Finding witnesses without looking all over. In: Madhusudan, P., Seshia, S.A. (eds.) CAV 2012. LNCS, vol. 7358, pp. 599–615. Springer, Heidelberg (2012)
19. Xiao, T., Zhang, J., Zhou, H., Guo, Z., McDirmid, S., Lin, W., Chen, W., Zhou, L.: Nondeterminism in MapReduce considered harmful? an empirical study on non-commutative aggregators in MapReduce programs. In: Companion Proceedings of ICSE, pp. 44–53 (2014)
20. Xu, Z., Hirzel, M., Rothermel, G.: Semantic characterization of MapReduce workloads. In: IISWC, pp. 87–97 (2013)

Verification and Abstraction

Inferring Simple Solutions to Recursion-Free Horn Clauses via Sampling⋆

Hiroshi Unno[1] and Tachio Terauchi[2]

[1] University of Tsukuba, Tsukuba, Japan
uhiro@cs.tsukuba.ac.jp
[2] JAIST, Nomi, Japan
terauchi@jaist.ac.jp

Abstract. Recursion-free Horn-clause constraints have received much recent attention in the verification community. It extends Craig interpolation, and is proposed as a unifying formalism for expressing abstraction refinement. In abstraction refinement, it is often desirable to infer "simple" refinements, and researchers have studied techniques for inferring simple Craig interpolants. Drawing on the line of work, this paper presents a technique for inferring simple solutions to recursion-free Horn-clause constraints. Our contribution is a constraint solving algorithm that lazily samples fragments of the given constraints whose solution spaces are used to form a simple solution for the whole. We have implemented a prototype of the constraint solving algorithm in a verification tool, and have confirmed that it is able to infer simple solutions that aid the verification process.

1 Introduction

In program verification, Craig interpolation [3] is a technique for discovering predicates that can be used to prove the correctness of the given program. For example, in predicate abstraction, interpolants from the formula representing the counterexample are used as predicates to refute the counterexample [7], and in lazy abstraction via interpolation, interpolants from the formula representing the program unwinding are used to construct sufficient loop invariants [12]. In general, there is more than one interpolant that can be inferred from the same formula, and which interpolant is inferred can significantly affect the performance of the client verifier. The "goodness" of an interpolant is an elusive characteristic, and while there is not yet a definite measure, it has been suggested that *simple* interpolants often work better (perhaps justified by the belief that correct programs tend to be correct for simple reasons, per Occam's razor). Recently, researchers have proposed to infer simple interpolants between a pair of formulas by *sampling* conjunctions of atoms from each formula, inferring their interpolant, and repeating the process until the interpolant for the whole

---

⋆ This work was supported by MEXT Kakenhi 23220001, 26330082, 25280023, and 25730035.

C. Baier and C. Tinelli (Eds.): TACAS 2015, LNCS 9035, pp. 149–163, 2015.
DOI: 10.1007/978-3-662-46681-0_10

is found [17,1]. By inferring simple interpolants for the samples that are likely to generalize, the method efficiently infers a simple interpolant for the whole.

In this paper, we extend the idea to inferring simple solution to recursion-free Horn-clause constraints. Recently, recursion-free Horn-clause constraints have received much attention in the verification community as they generalize interpolation and can express the predicate discovery process of a wide variety of software verifiers (imperative, procedural, higher-order functional, concurrent, etc. [20,18,6,5,4,14,2,19]).[1] We emphasize that inferring a simple solution to recursion-free Horn-clause constraints is non-trivial and *cannot be done by simply applying the methods for interpolation*, because one must look simultaneously for simple predicates to be assigned to each predicate variable in the given constraints that together satisfy the constraints (e.g., it cannot be done by just iteratively applying interpolation as a blackbox process [20,18]).

The key ideas in our approach are to 1.) maintain as samples *conjunctive* recursion-free Horn-clause constraint that only contain clauses whose formula part is a conjunction of atoms, 2.) infer a simple solution to the samples via a novel decompositional approach (cf. Sections 3.1–3.3), and 3.) check if the solution inferred for the samples is also a solution for the whole, and if not, obtain a new sample as a counterexample and repeat the process. Finally, 4.) instead of computing a concrete solution for each subproblem, we compute an *abstract solution space* representing a possibly infinite set of solutions, thereby making the process more likely to be able to find a simple solution for the whole.

Related Work. Besides the above sampling-based approaches to inferring simple interpolants that inspired this work, previous research has proposed to infer simple interpolants by post-processing the proof (of $\models \phi_1 \Rightarrow \phi_2$) in a proof-based interpolation [8].

To our knowledge, this paper is the first work on inferring simple solutions to recursion-free Horn-clause constraints. Existing approaches to solving recursion-free Horn-clause constraints can be classified into two types: the *iterative approach* that uses interpolation as a blackbox process to solve the constraints one predicate variable at a time [20,18], and the *constraint-expansion approach* that reduces the problem to tree interpolation (equivalently, solving "tree-like" constraints) [11,13,14]. As remarked above, the iterative approach is unsuited for inferring simple solutions because a solution inferred for one predicate variable can affect the rest and block the discovery of a simple solution for the whole. The constraint-expansion approach is also unsuited for inferring simple solutions because it makes exponentially many copies of predicate variables whose solutions are conjuncted to form the solution for the original, thereby resulting in a complex solution (see also the discussion in Section 3.1).

Paper Organization. The rest of the paper is organized as follows. Section 2 presents preliminary definitions. Section 3 and its subsections describe the new constraint solving algorithm in a top-down manner. We first present the top-

---

[1] Interpolation between ϕ_1 and ϕ_2 is equivalent to solving the Horn-clause constraint $\{P(\widetilde{x}) \Leftarrow \phi_1, \bot \Leftarrow P(\widetilde{x}) \land \neg\phi_2\}$ where $\{\widetilde{x}\} = fvs(\phi_1) \cap fvs(\phi_2)$.

level process in Section 3. Section 3.1 describes the sub-algorithm for inferring simple solutions for samples. As we explain there in more detail, inferring simple solutions to samples requires its own innovations as simply applying the existing approaches can produce complex solutions. To this end, we present a novel approach where the problem is decomposed into smaller subproblems for which simple solutions can be found easily and combined to form a simple solution for the whole sample set. We describe the approach in detail in Sections 3.1–3.3. We report on a preliminary implementation and experiment results in Section 4, and conclude the paper in Section 5. The extended report [21] contains extra materials and omitted proofs.

2 Preliminaries

A *formula* ϕ in the signature of quantifier-free linear rational arithmetic (QFLRA) is a Boolean combination of atoms. An *atom* (or *literal*) p is an inequality of the form $t_1 \geq t_2$ or $t_1 > t_2$ where t_i are terms. A *term* t is either a *variable* x, a *rational constant* r, a multiplication of a term by a rational constant $r \cdot t$, or a summation of terms $t_1 + t_2$. We write $\bot$ and $\top$ respectively for contradiction and tautology. A *predicate variable application* a is of the form $P(\tilde{t})$ where P is a *predicate variable* of the arity $|\tilde{t}|$. We write $ar(P)$ for the arity of P.

A *Horn clause* (or simply *clause*) hc is defined to be of the form $a_0 \Leftarrow a_1 \wedge \cdots \wedge a_n \wedge \phi$. We call a_0 (resp. $a_1 \wedge \cdots \wedge a_n \wedge \phi$) the *head* (resp. *body*) of hc. We write $fvs(hc)$ (resp. $fvs(\phi)$) for the set of term variables in hc (resp. ϕ). We write $pvL(hc)$ for the predicate variable occurring on the left hand side of $\Leftarrow$ and $pvsR(hc)$ for the set of predicate variables occurring in the right hand side of $\Leftarrow$. We write $pvs(hc)$ for the set of predicate variables occurring in hc (i.e., $pvs(hc) = \{pvL(hc)\} \cup pvsR(hc)$).

We define a *Horn clause constraint set* (HCCS) to be a pair $(\mathcal{H}, P_\bot)$ where $\mathcal{H}$ is a finite set of clauses and $P_\bot$ is a predicate variable in $\mathcal{H}$ with $ar(P_\bot) = 0$ (intuitively, $P_\bot$ is implicitly constrained by the clause $\bot \Leftarrow P_\bot()$). We define $fvs(\mathcal{H}) = \bigcup_{hc \in \mathcal{H}} fvs(hc)$. We define $pvs(\mathcal{H}) = \bigcup_{hc \in \mathcal{H}} pvs(hc)$, $pvsL(\mathcal{H}) = \{pvL(hc) \mid hc \in \mathcal{H}\}$, $pvsR(\mathcal{H}) = \bigcup_{hc \in \mathcal{H}} pvsR(hc)$, $roots(\mathcal{H}) = pvsL(\mathcal{H}) \backslash pvsR(\mathcal{H})$, $inters(\mathcal{H}) = pvsL(\mathcal{H}) \cap pvsR(\mathcal{H})$, and $leaves(\mathcal{H}) = pvsR(\mathcal{H}) \setminus pvsL(\mathcal{H})$. We say that $\mathcal{H}$ is *single-root* if $roots(\mathcal{H})$ is singleton, and write $root(\mathcal{H})$ for P such that $\{P\} = roots(\mathcal{H})$.

Concrete and Abstract Solutions. A predicate substitution θ is a finite map from predicate variables P to predicates of the form $\lambda(x_1, \ldots, x_{ar(P)}).\phi$ such that $fvs(\phi) \subseteq \{x_1, \ldots, x_{ar(P)}\}$. Given an HCCS $(\mathcal{H}, P_\bot)$, a predicate substitution θ with $pvs(\mathcal{H}) \subseteq dom(\theta)$ is called a *solution* of $\mathcal{H}$ if $\models \theta(hc)$ for each $hc \in \mathcal{H}$ and $\models \bot \Leftarrow \theta(P_\bot)()$. We write $\theta \models (\mathcal{H}, P_\bot)$ when θ is a solution of $(\mathcal{H}, P_\bot)$.

We define *abstract solution space* that represents a possibly infinite set of solutions. To this end, we define *formula template* ψ to be a formula but with the grammar extended to include terms of the form $c \cdot t$ where c is an *unknown coefficient variable*. We define an *abstract solution space* S to be a pair (Θ, ϕ) where Θ is a finite map from predicate variables P to *predicate templates* of the form $\lambda(x_1, \ldots, x_{ar(P)}).\psi$ and ϕ is a (non-template) QFLRA formula over unknowns. For $S = (\Theta, \phi)$ and $P \in dom(\Theta)$, we write $S(P)$ for $\Theta(P)$. We say that a concrete solution θ is an *instance* of an abstract solution space (Θ, ϕ), written $\theta \succeq (\Theta, \phi)$, if $dom(\theta) = dom(\Theta)$ and there exists a map σ from unknowns to rationals such that $\models \sigma(\phi)$ and for all $P \in dom(\theta)$, $\theta(P) = \sigma(\Theta(P))$. We write $S' \succeq S$ if for all θ, $\theta \succeq S'$ implies $\theta \succeq S$. We write $S' \succeq_P S$ if $S' \succeq S$ and $S'(P)$ contains no unknowns.

Horn Clause Constraint Kinds. The *dependency relation* $\lhd_{\mathcal{H}}$ is defined to be the relation that, for all $P, Q \in pvs(\mathcal{H})$, $Q \lhd_{\mathcal{H}} P$ if and only if $Q(\tilde{t}_1) \Leftarrow a \wedge \cdots \wedge P(\tilde{t}_2) \wedge \cdots \wedge \phi \in \mathcal{H}$. We write $\lhd_{\mathcal{H}}^*$ for the reflexive transitive closure of $\lhd_{\mathcal{H}}$ and $\lhd_{\mathcal{H}}^+$ for the transitive closure of $\lhd_{\mathcal{H}}$. We say that P is *recursive* if $P \lhd_{\mathcal{H}}^+ P$. We say that P is *head-joining* (resp. *body-joining*) if P occurs more than once in the left (resp. right) hand sides of clauses in $\mathcal{H}$. We write $recpvs(\mathcal{H})$, $hjnpvs(\mathcal{H})$, and $bjnpvs(\mathcal{H})$ respectively for the set of recursive, head-joining, and body-joining predicate variables in $\mathcal{H}$. We say that $\mathcal{H}$ is *recursion-free* if $recpvs(\mathcal{H}) = \emptyset$, is *body-disjoint* if $bjnpvs(\mathcal{H}) = \emptyset$, and is *head-disjoint* if $hjnpvs(\mathcal{H}) = \emptyset$.[2] We say that $\mathcal{H}$ is *conjunctive* if for each $hc \in \mathcal{H}$, the formula part of hc is a conjunction of literals. We say that a single-root $\mathcal{H}$ is *connected* if for any $P \in pvs(\mathcal{H})$, $root(\mathcal{H}) \lhd_{\mathcal{H}}^* P$. We extend the notions to HCCSs in the obvious way (e.g., $(\mathcal{H}, P_\perp)$ is recursion-free if $\mathcal{H}$ is recursion-free).

Any Horn clause set in this paper will be recursion-free. Therefore, in what follows, we restrict ourselves to recursion-free Horn clause sets and HCCSs and omit the redundant qualifier "recursion-free".

Example 1. Consider the HCCS $(\mathcal{H}_{ex1}, P_\perp)$ where $\mathcal{H}_{ex1}$ is the set of clauses below.

$$P(x, y, z) \Leftarrow x \geq z \wedge y \geq 2 - z$$
$$Q(x, y) \Leftarrow P(x, y, z) \wedge (z = 0 \vee z = 1 \vee z = 2)$$
$$P_\perp() \Leftarrow Q(x, y) \wedge Q(-x, -y)$$

We have $recpvs(\mathcal{H}_{ex1}) = \emptyset$, $hjnpvs(\mathcal{H}_{ex1}) = \emptyset$, and $bjnpvs(\mathcal{H}_{ex1}) = \{Q\}$, and so the HCCS is recursion-free and head-disjoint but neither conjunctive nor body-disjoint. (An equality $t_1 = t_2$ is $t_1 \geq t_2 \wedge t_2 \geq t_1$.)

A solution for the HCCS, θ_{ex1}, and an abstract solution space for the HCCS, $(\Theta_{ex1}, \phi_{ex1})$ are shown below. Note that $\theta_{ex1} \succeq (\Theta_{ex1}, \phi_{ex1})$.

$$\theta_{ex1}(P) = \lambda(x, y, z).x + y \geq 2$$
$$\theta_{ex1}(Q) = \lambda(x, y).x + y \geq 1$$
$$\theta_{ex1}(P_\perp) = \lambda().\perp$$

$$\Theta_{ex1}(P) = \lambda(x, y, z).c_0 + c_1 \cdot x + c_2 \cdot y \geq 0$$
$$\Theta_{ex1}(Q) = \lambda(x, y).x + y \geq 1$$
$$\Theta_{ex1}(P_\perp) = \lambda().\perp$$
$$\phi_{ex1} \equiv 0 < c_1 = c_2 \leq -c_o \leq 2 \cdot c_1$$

3   The Top-Level Procedure

Figure 1 shows the top-level procedure of the constraint solving algorithm $\mathcal{A}_{solve}$ which takes as input an HCCS $(\mathcal{H}, P_\perp)$ and returns its solution or detects that it

---

[2] The terminologies are adopted from [14,13].

is unsolvable. As remarked in Section 1, the algorithm looks for a simple solution of the given HCCS by lazy sampling. $\mathcal{A}_{solve}$ initializes the sample set *Samples* to $\emptyset$ (line 2), and repeats the loop (lines 3-12) until convergence. The loop first calls the sub-algorithm $\mathcal{A}_{samp}$ on the HCCS (*Samples*, $P_\perp$) to find an abstract space of solutions to the current sample set. If no solution is found for the samples, then no solution exists for the whole constraint set $(\mathcal{H}, P_\perp)$ either, and we exit the loop (line 5). Otherwise, an abstract solution space S for the samples is inferred, and we pick a concrete instance θ of S (line 7) as the *candidate* solution. If θ is a solution for the whole then we return it as the inferred solution (line 8). Otherwise, there is a clause in $\mathcal{H}$, say $P(\tilde{t}) \Leftarrow \bigwedge \tilde{a} \wedge \phi$, that is unsatisfied and a model σ in which the clause is invalid with θ. From the clause and σ, we obtain the conjunctive clause $P(\tilde{t}) \Leftarrow \bigwedge \tilde{a} \wedge \bigwedge C(\phi, \sigma)$ as the new sample to be added to the sample set (line 12). Here, $C(\phi, \sigma)$ is the set of atoms representing the part of ϕ where σ holds true, and is defined as follows.

$$C(\phi, \sigma) = \{p \mid p \text{ occurs in } \phi \text{ and } \sigma \models p\} \cup \{\neg p \mid p \text{ occurs in } \phi \text{ and } \sigma \models \neg p\}$$

Intuitively, the added sample clause represents a portion of the input HCCS that is not yet covered by the solution found for the current sample set.

By construction, the sample HCCS (*Samples*, $P_\perp$) is always conjunctive. The sub-algorithm $\mathcal{A}_{samp}$, whose details are deferred to Section 3.1, takes the conjunctive HCCS (*Samples*, $P_\perp$) and infers an abstract space of solutions for it. Next, we show the correctness of $\mathcal{A}_{solve}$, assuming that $\mathcal{A}_{samp}$ works correctly (i.e., it returns a nonempty abstract solution space to the input conjunctive HCCS if it is solvable and otherwise

```
01: 𝒜_solve((ℋ, P⊥)) =
02:    Samples := ∅;
03:    while true do
04:       match 𝒜_samp((Samples, P⊥)) with
05:          NoSol → return NoSol
06:       | Sol(S) →
07:          let θ ⪰ S in
08:          if θ ⊨ (ℋ, P⊥) then
09:             return Sol(θ)
10:          else
11:             let σ, P(t̃) ⇐ ⋀ã ∧ φ ∈ ℋ
                where σ ⊭ θ(⋀ã ∧ φ ⇒ P(t̃)) in
12:             Samples :=
                Samples ∪ {P(t̃) ⇐ ⋀ã ∧ ⋀C(φ,σ)}
```

Fig. 1. The Top-Level Procedure

returns *NoSol*). Let $D(\phi) = \{C(\phi, \sigma) \mid \sigma \models \phi\}$. Let $(D(\mathcal{H}), P_\perp)$ be the conjunctive HCCS obtained by replacing each clause $a \Leftarrow \bigwedge \tilde{a} \wedge \phi$ in $\mathcal{H}$ with the clauses $\{a \Leftarrow \bigwedge \tilde{a} \wedge \bigwedge C \mid C \in D(\phi)\}$. Note that, because $D(\phi)$ is finite, $D(\mathcal{H})$ is also finite and $(D(\mathcal{H}), P_\perp)$ is an HCCS. Also, the following can be shown from the fact that $\models \phi \Leftrightarrow \bigvee_{C \in D(\phi)} \bigwedge C$.

Lemma 1. θ *is a solution of* $(\mathcal{H}, P_\perp)$ *if and only if it is a solution of* $(D(\mathcal{H}), P_\perp)$.

We can also show that, in each loop iteration, the added sample is not in the current sample set, and therefore the sample set grows monotonically as the loop progresses, as stated in the following lemma.

Lemma 2. *Suppose* $\theta \models (Samples, P_\perp)$, $\sigma \models \bigwedge \theta(\tilde{a}) \wedge \phi$, *and* $\sigma \not\models \theta(P)(\tilde{t})$. *Then,* $P(\tilde{t}) \Leftarrow \tilde{a} \wedge \bigwedge C(\phi, \sigma) \notin Samples$.

From the lemmas, we show the correctness of $\mathcal{A}_{solve}$, stated in the theorem below.

Theorem 1 (Correctness of $\mathcal{A}_{solve}$). *Given an $HCCS(\mathcal{H}, P_\perp)$, $\mathcal{A}_{solve}((\mathcal{H}, P_\perp))$ returns a solution of $(\mathcal{H}, P_\perp)$ if $(\mathcal{H}, P_\perp)$ is solvable, and otherwise returns NoSol.*

A reader may wonder why $\mathcal{A}_{solve}$ does not directly check if there exists a solution to the input HCCS from the entire abstract solution space S returned by $\mathcal{A}_{samp}$ (i.e., check $\exists \theta \succeq S.\theta \models (\mathcal{H}, P_\perp)$) and infer new samples by using the entire S if not. We opt against the approach because checking $\exists \theta \succeq S.\theta \models (\mathcal{H}, P_\perp)$ requires an expensive non-linear constraint solving. Instead, we let $\mathcal{A}_{solve}$ choose a concrete solution from S to be used as a candidate.[3]

Example 2. Consider running $\mathcal{A}_{solve}$ on the HCCS $(\mathcal{H}_{ex1}, P_\perp)$ from Example 1. Suppose that at some iteration, $Samples = \{P(x,y,z) \Leftarrow x \geq z \wedge y \geq 2 - z, Q(x,y) \Leftarrow P(x,y,z) \wedge z = 0, P_\perp() \Leftarrow Q(x,y) \wedge Q(-x,-y)\}$, and $\mathcal{A}_{samp}$ returned some abstract solution space S given $(Samples, P_\perp)$.

Let $\theta \succeq S$ be the candidate solution chosen at line 7 where $\theta = \{P \mapsto \lambda(x,y,z).y \geq 2 - z, Q \mapsto \lambda(x,y).y \geq 2, P_\perp \mapsto \lambda().\perp\}$. Because $\theta \not\models (\mathcal{H}_{ex1}, P_\perp)$, we obtain a new sample. A possible sample obtained here is $Q(x,y) \Leftarrow P(x,y,z) \wedge z = 2$. Adding the new sample to $Samples$, in the next loop iteration, as we shall detail in Example 3, $\mathcal{A}_{samp}$ returns an abstract solution space containing the solution θ_{ex1} shown in Example 1.   ▲

3.1   The Sub-Algorithm $\mathcal{A}_{samp}$

$\mathcal{A}_{samp}$ takes as input a conjunctive HCCS, and returns a non-empty abstract space of its solutions if it is solvable and otherwise returns *NoSol*. As remarked before, $\mathcal{A}_{samp}$ looks for *simple* solutions that are likely to generalize when given to the upper-procedure $\mathcal{A}_{solve}$ to be used as a candidate solution for the whole.

The internal workings of $\mathcal{A}_{samp}$ are quite intricate. The subtlety comes from body-joining predicate variables and head-joining predicate variables. Indeed, as we shall show in Section 3.3, inferring

```
01: 𝒜_samp((ℋ, P⊥)) =
02:   S := ({P⊥ ↦ λ().⊥} ∪ {P ↦ λx̃.⊤ | P ∈ 𝒬}, ⊤)
        where 𝒬 = roots(ℋ) \ {P⊥};
03:   WorkSet := initWS(ℋ);
04:   while WorkSet ≠ ∅ do
05:     let ℋ′ ∈ WorkSet
          where root(ℋ′) ∉ ⋃_{ℋ∈WorkSet} pvsR(ℋ) in
06:     WorkSet := WorkSet \ {ℋ′};
07:     let S′ ⪰_{root(ℋ′)} S in S := S′;
08:     let 𝒞,LMap = MkCnsts(ℋ′, S, ℋ) in
09:     for each (ℋ″, P′⊥) ∈ 𝒞 do
10:       match 𝒜_hj((ℋ″, P′⊥)) with
11:         NoSol → return NoSol
12:         | Sol(S′) →
13:             S := combSol∧(S′, S, LMap)
14:   return Sol(S)
```

Fig. 2. The Sub-Algorithm $\mathcal{A}_{samp}$

---

[3] Perhaps a somewhat subtle aspect of $\mathcal{A}_{solve}$ is that it is guaranteed to terminate and return a correct result despite only considering one concrete solution from the set of solutions returned by $\mathcal{A}_{samp}$ in each iteration.

a simple solution to a conjunctive body-and-head-disjoint HCCS is easy in that such an HCCS has either no solution or a simple solution where each predicate contains just one atom. $\mathcal{A}_{samp}$ decomposes the problem into easily solvable parts and combines their solutions to obtain a simple solution for the whole. The key to the success is to do a *coarse* decomposition so that there are few subproblems to be solved and the solutions to be combined, thereby resulting in a simple solution for the whole sample set.

Figure 2 shows the overview of $\mathcal{A}_{samp}$. Given the input conjunctive HCCS $(\mathcal{H}, P_\perp)$, we initialize the abstract solution space S to map $P_\perp$ to $\lambda().\perp$ and the other root predicate variables $P \in roots(\mathcal{H}) \setminus \{P_\perp\}$ to $\lambda(x_1, \ldots, x_{ar(P)}).\top$ (line 2), and initialize the work set $WorkSet$ to $initWS(\mathcal{H})$ which is the coarsest connected sets of clauses that partition $\mathcal{H}$ and are body-joined only at the roots and the leaves (informally, $initWS(\mathcal{H})$ partitions $\mathcal{H}$ into body-disjoint "trees"). Formally, $initWS(\mathcal{H}) = \{\{hc \in \mathcal{H} \mid P \blacktriangleleft^*_{(\mathcal{H},\mathcal{R}\setminus\{P\})} pvL(hc)\} \mid P \in \mathcal{R}\}$ where $\mathcal{R} = (bjnpvs(\mathcal{H}) \cap pvsL(\mathcal{H})) \cup roots(\mathcal{H})$, and $Q \blacktriangleleft_{(\mathcal{H},\mathcal{R}')} R$ if and only if $Q \vartriangleleft_\mathcal{H} R$ and $Q \notin \mathcal{R}'$. As we show in the lemma below, $initWS(\mathcal{H})$ is indeed the coarsest connected partition of $\mathcal{H}$ that is body-joined only at the roots and the leaves.

Lemma 3. $initWS(\mathcal{H})$ *is the smallest set* X *that satisfies:* 1. $\mathcal{H} = \bigcup X$, 2. $\forall \mathcal{H}_1, \mathcal{H}_2 \in X.\mathcal{H}_1 \cap \mathcal{H}_2 = \emptyset$, 3. $\forall \mathcal{H}' \in X.$ $\mathcal{H}'$ *is connected, and* 4. $\forall \mathcal{H}' \in X. bjnpvs(\mathcal{H}) \cap inters(\mathcal{H}') = \emptyset$.

Then, we solve each element of $WorkSet$ by calling $\mathcal{A}_{hj}$, starting from the root-most one that contains $P_\perp$, and recording the inferred solutions in S (lines 4-13). $\mathcal{A}_{hj}$ is a sub-algorithm that, given a conjunctive body-disjoint (but possibly head-joined) HCCS, infers its solution if it is solvable and otherwise returns *NoSol*. The detailed description of $\mathcal{A}_{hj}$ is deferred to Section 3.2.

To invoke $\mathcal{A}_{hj}$ on an element $\mathcal{H}' \in WorkSet$, $\mathcal{A}_{samp}$ first partially concretizes the current abstract solution space S so that it maps $root(\mathcal{H}')$ to a concrete predicate (line 7), and then uses $MkCnsts$ to convert $\mathcal{H}'$ into the set of the conjunctive body-disjoint HCCSs $\mathcal{C}$ (line 8). $MkCnsts$ also returns $LMap$ that maps the copied leaf predicate variables in $\mathcal{C}$ to the originals in $\mathcal{H}'$. Formally, $MkCnsts(\mathcal{H}', S, \mathcal{H})$ constructs $\mathcal{C}$ and $LMap$ as follows. Let $\mathcal{H}'_{lcpy}$ be $\mathcal{H}'$ with each leaf predicate variable application $P(\widetilde{t})$ replaced by $P_{cpy}(\widetilde{t})$ for a fresh predicate variable P_{cpy}. $LMap$ is the map from the fresh predicate variable P_{cpy} to the original P that it replaced. Let $P_{rt} = root(\mathcal{H}')$ and $S(P_{rt}) = \lambda\widetilde{x}.\neg \bigvee_{i=1}^n \phi_i$ where each ϕ_i is a conjunction of literals. Then, $\mathcal{C}$ is the set of HCCSs $\{(\mathcal{H}'_{lcpy} \cup \mathcal{H}_{lcsts} \cup \{P'_\perp() \Leftarrow P_{rt}(\widetilde{x}) \wedge \phi_i\}, P'_\perp) \mid i \in \{1, \ldots, n\}\}$ where $P'_\perp$ is a fresh predicate variable and $\mathcal{H}_{lcsts}$ is the set of clauses below.

$$\{P(\widetilde{x}) \Leftarrow \phi_i \mid P \in dom(LMap)$$
$$lsol(\mathcal{H}, LMap(P)) = \lambda\widetilde{x}. \bigvee_{i=1}^m \phi_i \text{ where each } \phi_i \text{ is conjunction of literals}\}$$

Here, $lsol(\mathcal{H}, P)$ is the predicate expressing the "lower-bound" solution of P that is implied by $\mathcal{H}$, and it is defined recursively as follows.

$$lsol(\mathcal{H}, P) = \lambda\widetilde{x}. \bigvee \left\{\phi \wedge \bigwedge_{i=1}^m lsol(\mathcal{H}, R_i)(\widetilde{t_i}) \mid P(\widetilde{x}) \Leftarrow \phi \wedge \bigwedge_{i=1}^m R_i(\widetilde{t_i}) \in \mathcal{H}\right\}$$

Intuitively, $MkCnsts(\mathcal{H}', S, \mathcal{H})$ substitutes the solution $S(root(\mathcal{H}'))$ for $root(\mathcal{H}')$ in $\mathcal{H}'$, adds the constraints required for the leaf predicate variables, and expands the constraint so that the result is a set of conjunctive body-disjoint HCCSs.

The solution inferred for each constraint in $\mathcal{C}$ is combined and recorded in the abstract solution space S (line 12). The solution combination operation $combSol_\wedge$ combines the abstract solutions by conjuncting the constraints over the unknowns and conjuncting the predicate templates point-wise, using $LMap$ to conjunct the solutions for the copied leaf predicates into the original. Formally, $combSol_\wedge((\Theta, \psi), (\Theta', \psi'), LMap) = (combL(\Theta, LMap) \wedge \Theta', \psi \wedge \psi')$ where

$$combL(\Theta, LMap) = \{P \mapsto \Theta(P) \mid P \notin ran(LMap)\}$$
$$\cup \{P \mapsto \bigwedge_{LMap(P')=P} \Theta(P') \mid P \in ran(LMap)\}$$

We show the correctness of $\mathcal{A}_{samp}$ assuming that $\mathcal{A}_{hj}$ works correctly (i.e., it returns a non-empty abstract solution space to the input conjunctive body-disjoint HCCS if it is solvable and otherwise returns $NoSol$).

Theorem 2 (Correctness of $\mathcal{A}_{samp}$). *Given a conjunctive HCCS $(\mathcal{H}, P_\perp)$, $\mathcal{A}_{samp}((\mathcal{H}, P_\perp))$ returns a non-empty abstract solution space of $(\mathcal{H}, P_\perp)$ if $(\mathcal{H}, P_\perp)$ is solvable, and otherwise it returns NoSol.*

We note that it is possible to solve a conjunctive (or non-conjunctive) HCCS more directly by expanding the HCCS to eliminate body-joining and head-joining predicate variables so that it is reduced to a tree-like form [11,13,14]. However, the approach makes exponentially many copies of predicate variables whose solutions are conjuncted to form the solution of the original, which often results in complex solutions. $\mathcal{A}_{samp}$ avoids complicating the solution by only making linearly many copies of predicate variables and only copying body-joining predicate variables (assuming that simple solutions are inferred for the root and body-joining predicate variables), and is therefore more likely to infer simple solutions for the whole.[4] In Section 4, we compare our approach with the constraint-expansion approach and show that our approach infers simpler solutions that aid the verification process.[5]

Also, in the implementation, we optimize the solution combination operation $combSol_\wedge$ so that instead of always taking the conjunction of the inferred solutions as described above, we eagerly apply constraint solving to reduce the number of atoms in the combined abstract solution space whenever possible (cf. Example 3).

Example 3. Let $(\mathcal{H}_{ex2}, P_\perp)$ be the HCCS $(Samples, P_\perp)$ given to $\mathcal{A}_{samp}$ in the last iteration of $\mathcal{A}_{solve}$ in Example 2. S is initialized to $(\{P_\perp \mapsto \lambda().\perp\}, \top)$.

---

[4] Our approach still exponentially expands the constraints, due to $lsol(\cdot)$. It only avoids (always) making exponentially many copies of the predicate variables.

[5] The comparison is with $\mathcal{A}_{solve}$ for solving the whole HCCS and not with $\mathcal{A}_{samp}$ that is just used to solve a sample set.

Because, $bjnpvs(\mathcal{H}_{ex2}) = \{P, Q\}$, $initWS(\mathcal{H}_{ex2}) = \{\mathcal{H}_1, \mathcal{H}_2, \mathcal{H}_3\}$ where

$$\mathcal{H}_1 = \{P_\perp() \Leftarrow Q(x, y) \wedge Q(-x, -y)\}$$
$$\mathcal{H}_2 = \{Q(x, y) \Leftarrow P(x, y, z) \wedge z = 0, Q(x, y) \Leftarrow P(x, y, z) \wedge z = 2\}$$
$$\mathcal{H}_3 = \{P(x, y, z) \Leftarrow x \geq z \wedge y \geq 2 - z\}$$

$\mathcal{H}_1$ is chosen as the first element to be solved from the workset, and we have $MkCnsts(\mathcal{H}_1, S, \mathcal{H}) = (\{(\mathcal{H}_{ex3}, P'_\perp)\}, LMap)$ where $LMap = \{Q_1 \mapsto Q, Q_2 \mapsto Q\}$ and $\mathcal{H}_{ex3}$ is the set of clauses below.

$$\{Q_i(x, y) \Leftarrow x \geq 0 \wedge y \geq 2, Q_i(x, y) \Leftarrow x \geq 2 \wedge y \geq 0 \mid i = 1, 2\} \cup$$
$$\{P_\perp() \Leftarrow Q_1(x, y) \wedge Q_2(-x, -y), P'_\perp \Leftarrow P_\perp() \wedge \neg\perp\}$$

$\mathcal{A}_{samp}$ then applies $\mathcal{A}_{hj}$ to $(\mathcal{H}_{ex3}, P'_\perp)$ and obtains an abstract solution space $S_1 = (\Theta_{ex3}, \phi_{ex3})$ (see Example 4 for details) where

$$\Theta_{ex3} = \begin{aligned} &\{Q_i \mapsto \lambda(x, y).c_{i,0} + c_{i,1} \cdot x + c_{i,2} \cdot y \geq 0 \mid i = 1, 2\} \cup \\ &\{P_\perp \mapsto \lambda().\perp, P'_\perp \mapsto \lambda().\perp\} \end{aligned}$$
$$\phi_{ex3} \equiv \begin{aligned} &c_{1,0} + c_{2,0} < 0 \wedge c_{1,1} = c_{2,1} \geq 0 \wedge c_{1,2} = c_{2,2} \geq 0 \wedge \\ &\bigwedge_{i=1,2}(c_{i,0} \geq -2 \cdot c_{i,2} \wedge c_{i,0} \geq -2 \cdot c_{i,1}) \end{aligned}$$

$\mathcal{A}_{samp}$ then combines the solution space to update S to $combSol_\wedge(S_1, S, LMap) = (\{P_\perp \mapsto \lambda().\perp, Q \mapsto \lambda(x, y).c_{1,0} + c_{1,1} \cdot x + c_{1,2} \cdot y \geq 0 \wedge c_{2,0} + c_{2,1} \cdot x + c_{2,2} \cdot y \geq 0\}, \phi_{ex3})$. In the implementation, we eagerly apply constraint solving to reduce the number of atoms in the combined solution space. In this example, we check if $\sigma_{uni}(\phi_{ex3})$ is satisfiable where $\sigma_{uni} = \{c_{2,i} \mapsto c_{1,i} \mid i = 0, 1, 2\}$, and if so updates S to $(\{P_\perp \mapsto \lambda().\perp, Q \mapsto \lambda(x, y).c_{1,0} + c_{1,1} \cdot x + c_{1,2} \cdot y \geq 0\}, \sigma_{uni}(\phi_{ex3}))$ instead. Here, $\sigma_{uni}(\phi_{ex3}) = c_{1,0} < 0 \wedge c_{1,1} \geq 0 \wedge c_{1,2} \geq 0 \wedge c_{1,0} \geq -2 \cdot c_{1,2} \wedge c_{1,0} \geq -2 \cdot c_{1,1}$ which is satisfiable.

Next, $\mathcal{A}_{samp}$ chooses $\mathcal{H}_2$ to solve. It updates the space S so that $S(Q)$ is concrete. For example, $S(Q) = \lambda(x, y).x + y \geq 1$. Then, it solves $\mathcal{H}_2$ and updates S by proceeding similarly to the case for $\mathcal{H}_1$. Lastly, $\mathcal{H}_3$ is solved, and $\mathcal{A}_{samp}$ returns the solution space $(\theta_{ex1}, \top)$ from Example 1.   ▲

3.2   The Sub-Algorithm $\mathcal{A}_{hj}$

$\mathcal{A}_{hj}$ takes as input a conjunctive body-disjoint (but possibly head-joined) HCCS. To infer simple solutions to the given HCCS, $\mathcal{A}_{hj}$ first checks if the given HCCS has a solution in the simplest space that maps each predicate variable to a predicate consisting of a single atom, that we call an *atomic solution*, and decomposing the HCCS into smaller subparts containing less head-joining predicate variables if no atomic solution is found. $\mathcal{A}_{hj}$ calls itself recursively to do the decomposition until a solution is found, and the solution spaces of the decomposed subparts are combined to form the solution space for the whole. The key observation here is that, as we shall show in Lemma 4, a conjunctive body-disjoint HCCS with no head-joining predicate variable (i.e., is head-disjoint) is guaranteed to either has an atomic solution or no solution at all. Therefore, the decomposition process is guaranteed to converge to either find a solution or detect that the input HCCS is unsolvable.

Figure 3 shows the overview of $\mathcal{A}_{hj}$. $\mathcal{A}_{hj}$ first calls $\mathcal{A}_{atom}$, whose details are deferred to Section 3.3, to check if there exists an atomic solution to the given HCCS. If so, then it returns the inferred space of atomic solutions (line 3). Otherwise, it checks if the given HCCS is head-disjoint. If so, then there can be no

```
01:  𝒜_hj((ℋ, P⊥)) =
02:    match 𝒜_atom((ℋ, P⊥)) with
03:      Sol(S) → return Sol(S)
04:    | NoSol →
05:      if hjnpvs(ℋ) = ∅ then
06:        return NoSol
07:      else
08:        let ℋ₁, ℋ₂ = Decomp(ℋ) in
09:        match 𝒜_hj((ℋ₁, P⊥)), 𝒜_hj((ℋ₂, P⊥)) with
10:          NoSol, _ | _, NoSol → return NoSol
11:        | Sol(S₁), Sol(S₂) → Sol(combSol∨(S₁, S₂))
```

Fig. 3. The Sub-Algorithm $\mathcal{A}_{hj}$

solution to the given HCCS, and we return *NoSol* (line 6). Otherwise, we pick a head-joining predicate variable, say P, and decompose the $\mathcal{H}$ into $\mathcal{H}_1$ and $\mathcal{H}_2$ such that $\mathcal{H}_1$ and $\mathcal{H}_2$ split the clauses in $\mathcal{H}$ whose head is P (along with their "subtree" clauses). (The details of the decomposition is quite intricate and deferred to later in the section.) Then, we call $\mathcal{A}_{hj}$ recursively to infer the solutions for the subparts $\mathcal{H}_1$ and $\mathcal{H}_2$. If either part is found to be unsolvable, then we return *NoSol* (line 10). Otherwise, we combine the returned solution spaces for the subparts to obtain the solution space for the whole (line 11). The combination operation *combSol*$_\vee$ is analogous to *combSol*$_\wedge$ used in $\mathcal{A}_{samp}$ except that we take a point-wise disjunction of the solutions as opposed to taking a conjunction (and that there is no management of the copied leaf predicate variables). More formally, $combSol_\vee((\Theta, \psi), (\Theta', \psi')) = (\Theta \vee \Theta', \psi \wedge \psi')$ where $\Theta \vee \Theta'$ is the point-wise disjunction of Θ and Θ'. As with *combSol*$_\wedge$, in the implementation, we eagerly apply constraint solving to reduce the number of atoms in the combined solution space instead of always taking the disjunction.

We describe the details of the decomposition operation *Decomp*. As remarked above, the role of *Decomp* is to decompose the input HCCS into parts that contain fewer clauses that are head-joined. This is done by selecting some head-joining predicate variable and making two copies of the original that split the portion of the subtrees reachable from the selected predicate variable. More formally, given a non-head-disjoint $\mathcal{H}$, $Decomp(\mathcal{H})$ returns $(\mathcal{H}_1, \mathcal{H}_2)$ as follows. We pick some head-joining predicate variable $P \in hjnpvs(\mathcal{H})$. Let $\mathcal{H}_P$ be the set of clauses in $\mathcal{H}$ having P as the head. We partition $\mathcal{H}_P$ into non-empty disjoint subsets $\mathcal{H}_1'$ and $\mathcal{H}_2'$. For each $\mathcal{H}_i'$ ($i \in \{1, 2\}$), let $\mathcal{H}_i''$ be the set of clauses in $\mathcal{H}$ whose head is Q where $R \vartriangleleft_{\mathcal{H}}^* Q$ for some predicate variable R that appears in the body of a clause in $\mathcal{H}_i'$. Then, we set $\mathcal{H}_i = \mathcal{H} \setminus (\mathcal{H}_i' \cup \mathcal{H}_i'')$.

We show the correctness of $\mathcal{A}_{hj}$, assuming that the sub-algorithm $\mathcal{A}_{atom}$ works correctly. As we show in Section 3.3, $\mathcal{A}_{atom}$ checks if there exists an atomic solution to the conjunctive body-disjoint (but possibly head-joined) HCCS given as the input, and it is guaranteed to return a non-empty abstract solution space if the given HCCS is solvable and head-disjoint. Then, the following theorem follows from the property of *Decomp* and *combSol*$_\vee$ and the fact that the recursive decompositions may happen only as many times as the number of head-joined clauses in the input HCCS.

Theorem 3 (Correctness of $\mathcal{A}_{hj}$). *Given a conjunctive body-disjoint HCCS $(\mathcal{H}, P_\perp)$, $\mathcal{A}_{hj}((\mathcal{H}, P_\perp))$ returns a non-empty abstract solution space of $(\mathcal{H}, P_\perp)$ if $(\mathcal{H}, P_\perp)$ is solvable, and otherwise it returns NoSol.*

The above description of *Decomp* leaves freedom on how to actually do the decomposition, that is, which head-joining predicate variable to select and how to split the subtrees reachable from the selected predicate variable. While Theorem 3 holds true regardless of how the decomposition is done, choosing a coarse decomposition is important for inferring a simple solution. To this end, in the implementation described in Section 4, we choose the decomposition by analyzing the reason for $\mathcal{A}_{atom}$'s failure on finding an atomic solution (cf. line 2) which is returned as an unsatisfiable core of the constraints that $\mathcal{A}_{atom}$ attempted to solve. In addition, instead of doing the recursive decompositions independently for the parts $\mathcal{H}_1$ and $\mathcal{H}_2$ as in Figure 3, we synchronize the decompositions in the recursive call branches to minimize the unnecessary decompositions.[6]

Example 4. Recall $(\mathcal{H}_{ex3}, P'_\perp)$ from Example 3. $(\mathcal{H}_{ex3}, P'_\perp)$ has an atomic solution, and therefore, the first call to $\mathcal{A}_{atom}$ by $\mathcal{A}_{hj}$ (line 3) immediately succeeds and returns an abstract solution space. Here, the returned abstraction solution space is $(\mathcal{H}_{ex3}, P'_\perp)$ from Example 3 (see Example 5 for details).

3.3 The Sub-Algorithm $\mathcal{A}_{atom}$

As remarked in Section 3.2, $\mathcal{A}_{atom}$ decides if there exists an atomic solution to the given conjunctive body-disjoint HCCS, and returns a non-empty abstract solution space of atomic solutions if so. Given the input HCCS $(\mathcal{H}, P_\perp)$, $\mathcal{A}_{atom}$ prepares the *atomic solution template* $\Theta_\mathcal{H}$ that maps each predicate variable $P \in pvs(\mathcal{H})$ to the formula template of the form $\lambda(x_1, \ldots, x_{ar(P)}).c_0 + \Sigma_{i=1}^{ar(P)} c_i \cdot x_i \geq 0$ where c_i's are fresh unknowns.[7] Then, it generates the constraint $\phi_\mathcal{H} = constr(\Theta_\mathcal{H}, (\mathcal{H}, P_\perp)) = c < 0 \wedge \bigwedge_{hc \in \mathcal{H}} constr(\Theta_\mathcal{H}, hc)$ where $\Theta_\mathcal{H}(P_\perp) = \lambda().c \geq 0$ and $constr(\Theta_\mathcal{H}, hc)$ is defined as follows; for $hc = a_0 \Leftarrow \bigwedge_{i=1}^{\ell} a_i \wedge \bigwedge_{i=1}^{q} p_i$ with $fvs(hc) = \{x_1, \ldots, x_m\}$,

$$constr(\Theta_\mathcal{H}, hc) = \bigwedge_{i=1}^{q} \alpha_i \geq 0 \wedge \bigwedge_{j=0}^{m} t_{0,j} = (\Sigma_{i=1}^{\ell} t_{i,j}) + (\Sigma_{i=1}^{q} \alpha_i \cdot r_{i,j})$$

where $\alpha_1, \ldots, \alpha_q$ are fresh unknowns, and $\Theta_\mathcal{H}(a_i)$ and p_i are respectively $t_{i,0} + \Sigma_{j=1}^{m} t_{i,j} \cdot x_j \geq 0$ (for $i \in \{0, \ldots, \ell\}$) and $r_{i,0} + \Sigma_{j=1}^{m} r_{i,j} \cdot x_j \geq 0$ (for $i \in \{1, \ldots, q\}$) for some linear terms over unknowns $t_{i,j}$ and rational constants $r_{i,j}$. Note that $\phi_\mathcal{H}$ is a QFLRA formula over unknowns (i.e., it contains no variable or product of unknowns).

---

[6] *Decomp* is similar in spirit to the sample set "split" operation from [1].

[7] For simplicity, in this section, we only consider non-strict inequality atoms. Strict inequalities can be handled similarly by using the Motzkin's transposition theorem instead of the Farkas' lemma (cf. the extended report [21]).

Then, $\mathcal{A}_{atom}$ checks if $\phi_{\mathcal{H}}$ is satisfiable, that is, if there exists an assignment σ to the unknowns such that $\models \sigma(\phi_{\mathcal{H}})$, and if so, returns $(\Theta_{\mathcal{H}}, \phi_{\mathcal{H}})$ as the abstract solution space. Otherwise, it detects that $(\mathcal{H}, P_\perp)$ has no atomic solution and returns *NoSol*. We state and prove the correctness of $\mathcal{A}_{atom}$.

Theorem 4 (Correctness of $\mathcal{A}_{atom}$). *Given a conjunctive body-disjoint HCCS $(\mathcal{H}, P_\perp)$, $\mathcal{A}_{atom}((\mathcal{H}, P_\perp))$ returns a non-empty abstract atomic solution space S of $(\mathcal{H}, P_\perp)$ if $(\mathcal{H}, P_\perp)$ has an atomic solution, and otherwise returns NoSol.*

Also, the following holds by the Farkas' lemma [16].

Lemma 4. *A conjunctive body-disjoint and head-disjoint HCCS either has an atomic solution or no solution.*

Therefore, $\mathcal{A}_{atom}$ completely decides the solvability of a conjunctive body-disjoint head-disjoint HCCS. In general, a solvable conjunctive body-disjoint (but not head-disjoint) HCCS may not be atomically solvable. For example, $(\mathcal{H}, P_\perp)$ where $\mathcal{H} = \{P(x,y) \Leftarrow x \leq 0 \wedge y \leq 1, P(x,y) \Leftarrow x \leq 1 \wedge y \leq 0, P_\perp() \Leftarrow P(x,y) \wedge x > 0 \wedge y > 0\}$ is solvable but has no atomic solution. Thus, when $\mathcal{A}_{atom}$ fails to find an atomic solution to such an HCCS, the information is propagated back to $\mathcal{A}_{hj}$ to decompose some head-joined clauses.

Example 5. Consider the HCCS $(\mathcal{H}_{ex3}, P'_\perp)$ from Example 3 (note that it is head-disjoint). $\mathcal{A}_{atom}$ prepares the atomic solution template $\Theta_{\mathcal{H}_{ex3}} = \{Q_i \mapsto \lambda(x,y).c_{i,0} + c_{i,1} \cdot x + c_{i,2} \cdot y \geq 0 \mid i = 1, 2\} \cup \{P_\perp \mapsto \lambda().c_{3,0} \geq 0, P'_\perp \mapsto \lambda().c_{4,0} \geq 0\}$ and generates the constraint $constr(\Theta_{\mathcal{H}_{ex3}}, (\mathcal{H}_{ex3}, P'_\perp))$:

$$c_{4,0} < 0 \wedge \alpha_1, \alpha_2 \geq 0 \wedge c_{4,0} = c_{3,0} + \alpha_1 \wedge c_{3,0} = c_{1,0} + c_{2,0} + \alpha_2 \wedge$$
$$0 = c_{1,1} - c_{2,1} \wedge 0 = c_{1,2} - c_{2,2} \wedge$$
$$\bigwedge_{i=1,2} \left(\begin{array}{l} \alpha_{i,1}, \alpha_{i,2}, \alpha_{i,3} \geq 0 \wedge c_{i,0} = -2 \cdot \alpha_{i,2} + \alpha_{i,3} \wedge c_{i,1} = \alpha_{i,1} \wedge c_{i,2} = \alpha_{i,2} \wedge \\ \alpha_{i,4}, \alpha_{i,5}, \alpha_{i,6} \geq 0 \wedge c_{i,0} = -2 \cdot \alpha_{i,4} + \alpha_{i,6} \wedge c_{i,1} = \alpha_{i,4} \wedge c_{i,2} = \alpha_{i,5} \end{array} \right)$$

In the constraint generation, we add the tautology $1 \geq 0$ to the body of each clause. This often widens the obtained solution space. After satisfiability checking and simplification, $\mathcal{A}_{atom}$ returns the abstract solution space $(\Theta_{ex3}, \phi_{ex3})$ given in Example 3.   ▲

4   Implementation and Experiments

We have implemented a prototype of the new constraint solving algorithm $\mathcal{A}_{solve}$. We use the linear programming tool GLPK (http://www.gnu.org/software/glpk) for the linear constraint solving that is used to operate on abstract solution spaces, and Z3 (http://z3.codeplex.com) for the unsat core generation in $\mathcal{A}_{hj}$ and for checking the candidate solution against the whole HCCS in $\mathcal{A}_{solve}$. We use the objective function in linear programming to find a model with small valuations to further bias towards simple solutions.

We use the constraint solver as the backend of the MoCHi software model checker [9]. MoCHi verifies assertion safety of OCaml programs via predicate

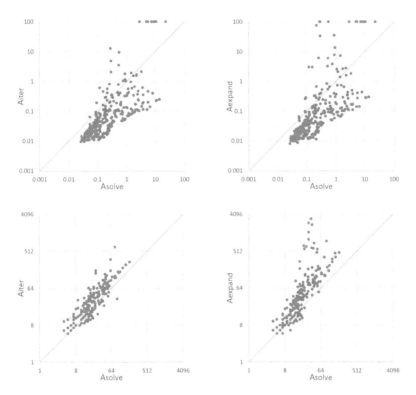

Fig. 4. Run time (upper) and solution size (lower) comparisons of the HCCS solving algorithms on benchmarks HCCSs

abstraction, higher-order model checking, and CEGAR. MoCHi is a good platform for experimenting with the constraint solver because the Horn-clause constraints solved there often have a complex structure. (Intuitively, this is because the constraints express the flow of data in the program to be verified, and data often flow in a complex way in a functional program, e.g., passed to and returned from recursive functions, captured in closures, etc.)

We compare the new algorithm $\mathcal{A}_{solve}$ with two other algorithms, $\mathcal{A}_{iter}$ and $\mathcal{A}_{expand}$. $\mathcal{A}_{iter}$ is an implementation of the iterative approach to solving HCCS [20,18], and is also used in the previous work on MoCHi [9,15,22,10]. $\mathcal{A}_{expand}$ is an implementation of the constraint-expansion approach [4,14] in which the given HCCS is first expanded into a body-disjoint head-disjoint HCCS and the iterative algorithm is used to solve the resulting HCCS. (See also **Related Work** in Section 1.)

We have ran the three algorithms on 327 HCCSs generated by running MoCHi with $\mathcal{A}_{solve}$ on 139 benchmark programs, most of which are taken from the previous work on MoCHi [9,15,22,10]. We measured the time spent on solving each HCCS by each algorithm as well as the size of the inferred solution (the sum of the syntactic sizes of the predicates). We also compare the overall verification speed of MoCHi when using the three algorithms on the 139 benchmark

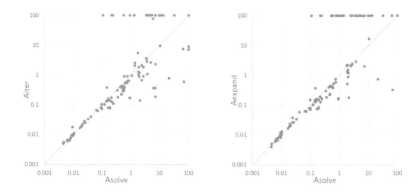

Fig. 5. Run time comparison of the HCCS solving algorithms on benchmarks programs

programs. The experiments were conducted on a machine with 2.69 GHz i7-4600U processor with 16 GB of RAM, with the time limit of 100 seconds. The benchmark programs, the benchmark HCCSs and the experiment results are available online [21].

Figure 4 shows the scatter plots that compare the run times and the solution sizes of $\mathcal{A}_{solve}$, $\mathcal{A}_{iter}$, and $\mathcal{A}_{expand}$ on each of the 318 benchmark HCCSs. The run time plots show that, on most instances, $\mathcal{A}_{solve}$ is slower than $\mathcal{A}_{iter}$ and $\mathcal{A}_{expand}$ due to the additional effort to find a simple solution. The plots also show that $\mathcal{A}_{solve}$ is sometimes faster than the other two. The behavior is attributed to the fact that $\mathcal{A}_{solve}$ is sometimes able to find a solution for the whole by sampling a very small fraction of the given HCCS, and the fact that $\mathcal{A}_{iter}$ and $\mathcal{A}_{expand}$ (after the expansion) uses the iterative approach which can be sometimes slow on large instances. The solution size plots show that $\mathcal{A}_{solve}$ is able to compute smaller solutions than the other two on most instances.

Figure 5 shows the plots comparing the run times of the overall verification process on each of the 139 benchmark programs for each constraint solving algorithm. The plots show that, with the new algorithm $\mathcal{A}_{solve}$, MoCHi is able to verify significantly more programs within the time limit than with the other two algorithms. The plots also show that the heavier cost of constraint solving in the new algorithm is often compensated by the better predicates inferred, thereby allowing the overall verification speed to match those of the other algorithms even on instances that the other algorithms were able to verify in time.

5   Conclusion

We have presented a new approach to solving recursion-free Horn-clause constraints. Our approach is inspired by the sampling-based approach to inferring simple interpolants [17,1] and is geared toward inferring simple solutions. We have shown that the new approach is effective at inferring simple solutions that are useful to program verification.

References

1. Albarghouthi, A., McMillan, K.L.: Beautiful interpolants. In: Sharygina, N., Veith, H. (eds.) CAV 2013. LNCS, vol. 8044, pp. 313–329. Springer, Heidelberg (2013)
2. Bjørner, N., McMillan, K., Rybalchenko, A.: On solving universally quantified horn clauses. In: Logozzo, F., Fähndrich, M. (eds.) Static Analysis. LNCS, vol. 7935, pp. 105–125. Springer, Heidelberg (2013)
3. Craig, W.: Linear reasoning. a new form of the herbrand-gentzen theorem. The Journal of Symbolic Logic 22(03), 250–268 (1957)
4. Grebenshchikov, S., Lopes, N.P., Popeea, C., Rybalchenko, A.: Synthesizing software verifiers from proof rules. In: PLDI, pp. 405–416. ACM (2012)
5. Gupta, A., Popeea, C., Rybalchenko, A.: Predicate abstraction and refinement for verifying multi-threaded programs. In: POPL, pp. 331–344. ACM (2011)
6. Gupta, A., Popeea, C., Rybalchenko, A.: Solving recursion-free horn clauses over LI+UIF. In: Yang, H. (ed.) APLAS 2011. LNCS, vol. 7078, pp. 188–203. Springer, Heidelberg (2011)
7. Henzinger, T.A., Jhala, R., Majumdar, R., McMillan, K.L.: Abstractions from proofs. In: POPL, pp. 232–244. ACM (2004)
8. Hoder, K., Kovács, L., Voronkov, A.: Playing in the grey area of proofs. In: POPL, pp. 259–272. ACM (2012)
9. Kobayashi, N., Sato, R., Unno, H.: Predicate abstraction and CEGAR for higher-order model checking. In: PLDI, pp. 222–233. ACM (2011)
10. Kuwahara, T., Terauchi, T., Unno, H., Kobayashi, N.: Automatic termination verification for higher-order functional programs. In: Shao, Z. (ed.) ESOP 2014 (ETAPS). LNCS, vol. 8410, pp. 392–411. Springer, Heidelberg (2014)
11. McMillan, K., Rybalchenko, A.: Computing relational fixed points using interpolation. Technical Report MSR-TR-2013-6 (January 2013)
12. McMillan, K.L.: Lazy abstraction with interpolants. In: Ball, T., Jones, R.B. (eds.) CAV 2006. LNCS, vol. 4144, pp. 123–136. Springer, Heidelberg (2006)
13. Rümmer, P., Hojjat, H., Kuncak, V.: Classifying and solving horn clauses for verification. In: Cohen, E., Rybalchenko, A. (eds.) VSTTE 2013. LNCS, vol. 8164, pp. 1–21. Springer, Heidelberg (2014)
14. Rümmer, P., Hojjat, H., Kuncak, V.: Disjunctive interpolants for horn-clause verification. In: Sharygina, N., Veith, H. (eds.) CAV 2013. LNCS, vol. 8044, pp. 347–363. Springer, Heidelberg (2013)
15. Sato, R., Unno, H., Kobayashi, N.: Towards a scalable software model checker for higher-order programs. In: PEPM, pp. 53–62. ACM (2013)
16. Schrijver, A.: Theory of linear and integer programming. Wiley (1998)
17. Sharma, R., Nori, A.V., Aiken, A.: Interpolants as classifiers. In: Madhusudan, P., Seshia, S.A. (eds.) CAV 2012. LNCS, vol. 7358, pp. 71–87. Springer, Heidelberg (2012)
18. Terauchi, T.: Dependent types from counterexamples. In: POPL, pp. 119–130. ACM (2010)
19. Terauchi, T., Unno, H.: Relaxed stratification: A new approach to practical complete predicate refinement. In: ESOP (2015) (to appear)
20. Unno, H., Kobayashi, N.: Dependent type inference with interpolants. In: PPDP, pp. 277–288. ACM (2009)
21. Unno, H., Terauchi, T.: Inferring simple solutions to recursion-free horn clauses via sampling. In: 2015, http://www.cs.tsukuba.ac.jp/~uhiro
22. Unno, H., Terauchi, T., Kobayashi, N.: Automating relatively complete verification of higher-order functional programs. In: POPL, pp. 75–86. ACM (2013)

Analysis of Dynamic Process Networks

Kedar S. Namjoshi[1,*] and Richard J. Trefler[2,**]

[1] Bell Laboratories, Alcatel-Lucent, Murray Hill, NJ, USA
kedar@research.bell-labs.com
[2] University of Waterloo, Waterloo, Ontario, Canada
trefler@cs.uwaterloo.ca

Abstract. We formulate a method to compute global invariants of dynamic process networks. In these networks, inter-process connectivity may be altered by an adversary at any point in time. Dynamic networks serve as models for ad-hoc and sensor-network protocols. The analysis combines elements of compositional reasoning, symmetry reduction, and abstraction. Together, they allow a small "cutoff" network to represent arbitrarily large networks. A compositional invariant computed on the small network generalizes to a parametric invariant of the shape "for all networks and all processes: property p holds of each process and its local neighborhood." We illustrate this method by showing how to compute useful invariants for a simple dining philosophers protocol, and the latest version of the ad-hoc routing protocol AODV (version 2).

1 Introduction

For communication protocols, model checking is typically applied to small network instances to detect errors. Full correctness requires analyzing networks of arbitrary size. This is, in general, an undecidable problem. Our work considers the question of analyzing the behavior of a *dynamic* process network. In a dynamic network, an adversary can modify the structure of the network at any time by adding or dropping nodes and connections. Dynamic process networks are practically relevant, as they may be used to model ad-hoc and sensor-network protocols, which usually operate under adversarial conditions.

The analysis question is mathematically challenging, as verification of a dynamic network requires showing correctness for an unbounded family of networks. Consider, say, a dynamic ring network. Starting with a two-node ring, dynamic changes result in rings of arbitrary size. It is interesting that showing

---

* Supported, in part, by DARPA under agreement number FA8750-12-C-0166. The U.S. Government is authorized to reproduce and distribute reprints for Governmental purposes notwithstanding any copyright notation thereon. The views and conclusions contained herein are those of the authors and should not be interpreted as necessarily representing the official policies or endorsements, either expressed or implied, of DARPA or the U.S. Government.
** Supported in part by Natural Sciences and Engineering Research Council of Canada Discovery and Collaborative Research and Development Grants.

© Springer-Verlag Berlin Heidelberg 2015
C. Baier and C. Tinelli (Eds.): TACAS 2015, LNCS 9035, pp. 164–178, 2015.
DOI: 10.1007/978-3-662-46681-0_11

parametric correctness (i.e., for all fixed rings) does not suffice. For instance, consider a valid state of a dining philosophers' protocol where eating philosophers are separated by a non-eating philosopher. Removing the middle node and collapsing the ring creates an invalid state with adjacent eating philosophers. Protocols on dynamic networks typically incorporate recovery actions to be taken on adjacency changes so as to avoid such erroneous outcomes.

In this work, we propose a new approach to this challenging verification question. Our analysis method combines elements of compositional reasoning, symmetry reduction and abstraction. To motivate these ingredients, consider that in a dynamic network, global invariants must be maintained in the face of adversarial, unpredictable changes. Hence, the coupling between process states is likely to be weak, which is just the situation where compositional analysis is most effective. In order to obtain a uniform invariant which applies to all nodes, it is necessary to abstract from differences between node neighborhoods (such as the number of neighbors). This is achieved by neighborhood abstraction, which induces local symmetries between nodes. Local symmetries suffice to ensure that compositional invariants are isomorphic across all nodes in a network family.

In a nutshell, the method works as follows: First, one picks a small representative instance R, and sets up a collection of local (i.e., neighborhood) symmetries between nodes from arbitrary instances and nodes of R. Next, a compositional invariant is calculated for R. Local symmetries guarantee that the compositional invariant for R generalizes appropriately to all instances. Dynamic changes are handled by showing that they do not violate the compositional invariant. For a property P that is preserved by the symmetries, it follows that P holds of all instances if it holds for R. The result is a universally quantified, inductive invariant, of the form "for all networks and all processes: property P holds of each process and its local neighborhood."

The method is only partly automated. The specification of symmetries is done manually, while the compositional calculation on R is automatic. As the symmetries concern only the neighborhood of a node, in our experience, it is not too difficult to determine a good set of symmetries. We illustrate this through two protocols: the first is a Dining Philosophers protocol, modified to operate over dynamic graphs; the second is a model of the AODV protocol used for routing in ad-hoc networks (we analyze the latest version, AODVv2 [2]).

Known methods for analyzing dynamic networks operate with sets of graphs of arbitrary size. Termination is ensured either through heuristics which recognize graph patterns [27] or through results from the theory of well quasi ordering (WQO) [13]. Our method is rather different, simpler to implement and, we believe, closer to intuition. Many interesting parametric verification questions are undecidable on general graphs and ad-hoc networks [14]. The AODV protocol has gone through several versions. Earlier analyses targeted AODV [1] and DYMO [27]. We analyze the latest version (AODV version 2), which is quite different from the original. In the course of constructing a formal model, we noticed a correctness issue, which has been acknowledged by the authors. Our proofs apply to the corrected protocol.

2 Dynamic Networks and Compositional Reasoning

We define the computational model of a dynamic process network, focusing on dynamic changes. We then define the rules to validate a proposed compositional invariant. Abstraction and symmetry properties are treated in Section 3.

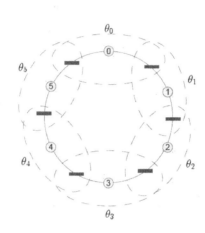

Fig. 1. A ring network. Nodes are represented by circles, edges by boxes, and links by lines connecting them. The neighborhood of a node is shown as a dashed ellipse.

We begin with an informal overview. A process network is defined by a process template and a way of instantiating the template on a communication graph. Every node of the graph is associated with a process. The transitions of a process depend on its internal state and the state on its adjacent edges. Hence, processes communicate by reading and modifying state on shared edges. In a dynamic setting, at any point in time, an adversary can modify the network by adding or deleting a node-edge link, or by adding or removing isolated nodes and edges. A process has the capability to react instantaneously and atomically to a change in the neighborhood of its node. In the following, we define these concepts precisely.

2.1 Networks, Assignment, and States

A *network*, G, is defined as the tuple (N, E, L), where N is a set of *nodes*, E is a set of *edges*, and $L \subseteq (N \times E) \cup (E \times N)$ is a set of node-edge *links*. (Note that an edge is not just a pair of nodes, but an element in its own right.) The network in Figure 1 shows a ring system. Each element has a color. Edge e is an *output edge* for node m if (m, e) is a link, and an input edge if (e, m) is a link. In either case, we say that e is adjacent to m. The *neighborhood* of a node

m, written $nbd(G, m)$, is formed by m together with its adjacent edges. Node m *points to* node n if an output edge of m is adjacent to n.

An *assignment* to a network specifies a domain of values for each edge, and a process for each node. A *process* assigned to a node n with k adjacent edges has the structure (S, S^0, T), where S is a set of states defined as the Cartesian product $S_I \times E_1 \times \ldots E_k$, where S_I is the internal state set, and $E_1, \ldots, E_k$ are the domains of the adjacent edges, S^0 is a set of initial states, and T is a transition relation, a subset of $S \times S$. We refer to several types of states:

- A *global state* is a vector formed by specifying an internal state for the process on each node and by a value from the domain of each edge
- A *local state* for node n with adjacent edges $e_1, \ldots, e_K$ is a vector formed by specifying an internal state for the process assigned to n, and by a value from the domain of each of the edges $e_1, \ldots, e_K$
- An *internal state* for node n is an internal state of the process assigned to n
- A *joint state* for nodes m, n is written as a pair $[a, b]$ where a is a local state for m, and b is a local state for n, and a and b have identical values for every edge e that is adjacent to both m and n. Joint states are used to formulate interference between processes.

For a global state s, we write $s[n]$ for the internal state of node n, $s[nbd(G, n)]$ for the local state of node n, and $s[e]$ for the value on edge e.

2.2   Semantics: Static and Dynamic

A network can transition from a global state s to global state t by the action of a single process, say at node n. This action may change at most the local state of node n, so T_n relates $s[nbd(G, n)]$ to $t[nbd(G, n)]$. Moreover, $t[e] = s[e]$ for every edge that is not adjacent to n, and $t[m] = s[m]$ for every node $m \neq n$. The set of *initial global states* is denoted I. For a family of networks, we assume that there is an initial global state for every network in the family. The projection of states in I on m, the set of *initial local states* for m, is denoted by I_m, which must be a subset of the initial states of that process. The global transition graph is induced by interleaving transitions from individual processes, starting from an initial state.

Adversarial actions change the underlying network graph. We consider the following actions:

- addition or removal of a link
- addition or removal of an isolated node (i.e., one without adjacent edges)
- addition or removal of an isolated edge (i.e., one without adjacent nodes)

To allow a process to react to a link addition or removal, we specify transitions $link(n, e)$ (link addition) and $unlink(n, e)$ (link removal) for node n and edge e. These transitions operate on the local state of node n after the change.

To account for graph (and hence, state vector) changes, we introduce the concept of a *configuration*, which is a pair (G, s), where G is the network graph and s is a global state of G. In a static transition, the graph stays constant, so the corresponding change is from a configuration (G, s) to (G, t). For a dynamic change, the graph also changes as does the global state. This is detailed below for two representative changes, the other cases are similar.

- *Addition of a link* (n, e) *in a graph* $G = (N, E, L)$ *and state* s. The new configuration is (G', s'). The new network G' is given by $N' = N$, $E' = E$, and $L' = L \cup \{(n, e)\}$. The new state s' is the successor of s by the $link(n, e)$ transition at node n, taken in the configuration (G', s).
- *Addition of an isolated node* n *in a graph* $G = (N, E, L)$ *and state* s. The new configuration is (G', s'). The new network G' has node set $N' = N \cup \{n\}$, edge set $E' = E$ and links $L' = L$. The new state s' is such that $s'[x] = s[x]$ for each element (node or edge) of G, and $s'[n]$ is an initial state of the process assigned to n.

2.3   Inductive and Compositional Invariants

An *invariant* for a dynamic network is a set of configurations which includes all the configurations reachable from a set of initial configurations. This set is *inductive* if it is closed under all transitions. A *compositional invariant* is an inductive invariant of a special shape and satisfying a special set of constraints. It is formed as the conjunction of a number of local invariants, one for each process in a network. Thus, we use (G, n) to identify the process at node n in network G, and write $\theta(G, n)$ as the set of local states for (G, n) which form its local invariant. These sets (viewed equivalently as predicates) must satisfy the following conditions. For all (G, n):

- (Initiality) All initial states of the process at (G, n) are in $\theta(G, n)$
- (Step) $\theta(G, n)$ is closed under transitions of the process at (G, n)
- (Non-interference) If node m points to node n in G, for any joint state $[b, a]$ of (m, n) where $a \in \theta(G, n)$ and $b \in \theta(G, m)$: if $T_{(G,m)}$ transforms $[b, a]$ to $[b', a']$, then $a' \in \theta(G, n)$.

Remark 1. Notational conventions are inspired by [15]. Sets are represented as predicates. The notation $[\varphi]$ indicates that the formula φ is valid.

In addition, there are conditions to be met for dynamic changes. Let G be the original network and let G' be the network obtained by adding a (fresh) link between node n and edge e. Two constraints arise from link addition (similar constraints arise for other dynamic actions):

- θ is preserved by the action $link(n, e)$ at n. I.e., for any valuation a for $nbd(G, n)$ and any value v for edge e: if $a \in \theta(G, n)$ and $link(n, e)$ transforms (a, v) to (a', v'), then $(a', v') \in \theta(G', n)$.
- Interference due to the *link* action must preserve θ for any node m that is pointed to by n. I.e., for any joint state $[b, a]$ of (m, n) where $a \in \theta(G, n)$ and $b \in \theta(G, m)$, and any valuation v for edge e: if $link(n, e)$ transforms $([b, a], v)$ to $([b', a'], v')$, then $b' \in \theta(G', m)$.

Theorem 1. *If the compositional constraints hold, the assertion $\xi = (\forall G, n : \theta(G, n))$ is an inductive invariant of the dynamic network.*

Consider θ as a vector (or a map) from network-node pairs (G, n) to sets of local states. The set of vectors forms a complete lattice, with vectors ordered point-wise by the subset relation. The constraints form a set of simultaneous implications of the form $[F_{(G,n)}(\theta) \Rightarrow \theta(G, n)]$, where F is monotonic in θ. Hence, there is a least solution by the Knaster-Tarski theorem. The least solution to the first three constraints alone is the strongest "non-dynamic" compositional invariant, denoted Σ^*. The least solution to all constraints is the strongest dynamic compositional invariant, which we denote by Δ^*. Note that Δ^* is weaker than Σ^* as it must satisfy the non-dynamic constraints.

3   Symmetry Reduction

We show how to define and use localized neighborhood symmetries to reduce the computation of a compositional invariant to a small set of representative processes. This technique applies equally well to a single network or to a family of networks.

3.1   Fixed Networks

Fix a network G and a process assignment. The local symmetries of the network are defined as a relation B with entries of the form (m, β, n), where β is itself a relation between the local state spaces of processes m and n. Intuitively, β relates similar neighborhood states. The relation B should satisfy some structural properties:

- (Identity) For every m, there is an entry (m, β, m) in B. For every such entry, β is an equivalence relation
- (Symmetry) If $(m, \beta, n) \in B$ then $(n, \beta^{-1}, m) \in B$
- (Transitivity) if (m, β, n) and (n, γ, k) are in B, then $(n, \beta; \gamma, k)$ is in B

It follows that the *orbit relation* $m \sim n$, which holds if (m, β, n) is in B for some β, is an equivalence.

Definition 1. *Local Symmetry*

A relation B satisfying the structural conditions forms a local symmetry if, for every (m, β, n) in B, any step or interference transition of m can be simulated by a step or interference transition of n. More precisely, the following forward-simulation properties hold.

- (initial match) For every initial state x of the process at m, there is an initial state y of the process at n such that $(x, y) \in \beta$.
- (local simulation) If $(x, y) \in \beta$ and there is a transition (x, x') in T_m, then either there is y' such that (y, y') is in T_n and $(x', y') \in \beta$, or there is a neighbor j of n and a state b of j which is reachable by j-steps alone such that there is a joint (j, n) transition $([b, y], [b', y'])$ due to T_j and $(x', y') \in \beta$.

- (interference simulation) If $(x, y) \in \beta$, and i is a neighbor of m, and there is a joint (i, m) transition $([a, x], [a', x'])$ due to T_i, then either there is a neighbor j of n for which (i, γ, j) is in B and for every b such that $(a, b) \in \gamma$, there is a joint (j, n) transition $([b, y], [b', y'])$ due to T_j, such that $(x', y') \in \beta$, or there is a transition (y, y') in T_n such that $(x', y') \in \beta$.

Remark 2. We refer to this notion as a symmetry as it is the semantic form of a structural local symmetry definition formulated in [23]. The earlier formulation is in terms of network structure, as a *groupoid*, a set of tuples of the form (m, β, n), where β is an isomorphism on the graph neighborhoods of nodes m and n. While that is more obviously a structural symmetry, it is limiting since it does not allow defining symmetries up to an abstraction.

Definition 2. *For a relation R and a set Y, let $\langle R \rangle Y$ be the set of elements which have an R-successor in Y. I.e., $\langle R \rangle Y = \{x \mid xRy \text{ for some } y \text{ in } Y\}$.*

Theorem 2. (Symmetry Theorem) *Let B be a local symmetry on G. Let θ^* be the strongest compositional invariant on G. Then, for every m, n such that (m, β, n) is in B, it is the case that $[\theta_m^* \Rightarrow \langle \beta \rangle \theta_n^*]$.*

Proof: From the chaotic iteration theorem [9], every fair schedule of updates computes the least fixpoint. We use a schedule where the initialization is done first; then the schedule alternates a single transition step for all processes, and a single interference step for all processes. This proof applies to a non-dynamic network.

The proof is by induction on fixpoint stages. Assume that the statement is true for every state in θ^k. Now consider m, n such that (m, β, n) is in B and let x' be in θ_m^{k+1} but not in θ_m^k.

[Basis] If x' is an initial state of m, the claim holds by the initial match condition.

[Induction: Step] Suppose that x' is a successor of a state x in θ_m^k. By the inductive hypothesis, there is a state y in θ_n^* such that $x\beta y$. In the first case of local simulation, there is a transition (y, y') in T_n such that $x'\beta y'$. In that case, y' is also in θ_n^* by its closure under step transitions. In the other case, there is a neighbor j of n and a reachable state b of j such that there is a joint transition $([b, y], [b', y'])$ of T_j and $(x', y') \in \beta$. As b is reachable through step transitions alone, it must be in θ_j^*, so that $[b, y]$ is a joint state which satisfies θ_j^* and θ_n^*. By closure of θ^* under interference, the state y' is in θ_n^*.

[Induction: Interference] Now suppose that x' is obtained through interference. I.e., there is a transition T_i, for some neighbor i of m, from a joint state $[a, x]$ to joint state $[a', x']$, where $a \in \theta_i^k$ and x is in θ_m^k. By the inductive hypothesis, there is a state y in θ_n^* such that $x\beta y$. The first case of interference simulation ensures that there is a neighbor j of n such that (i, γ, j) is in B, and for all b such that $(a, b) \in \gamma$, there is a transition $([b, y], [b', y'])$ due to T_j where $(x', y') \in \beta$. By the induction hypothesis, as $a \in \theta_i^k$, there is some $b \in \theta_j^*$ which is related to a by γ. For that b, the joint state $[b, y]$ satisfies θ_j^* and θ_n^* so, by closure under interference, y' is in θ_n^*. The other case of interference simulation ensures that there is a transition (y, y') in T_n such that $(x', y') \in \beta$; in that case, y' is in θ_n^* by closure under step transitions. **EndProof.**

Note that the claim holds also if single-step conditions are replaced with stuttering (i.e., where a single step is matched by a possibly empty path). We will use this relaxation for the examples.

Corollary 1. *Let P be a property of local states. If (m, β, n) is in symmetry B, and P is invariant under β, then $[\theta_m^* \Rightarrow P]$ if, and only if, $[\theta_n^* \Rightarrow P]$.*

Equivalence reduction. From the structural properties of B, the relation $\sim$ is an equivalence relation. Hence, in order to check a property that is invariant under all the β-relations in B, by Corollary 1, it suffices to compute the θ components for a representative of each equivalence class of $\sim$. Therefore, for a fixed network, the use of local symmetries can substantially reduce the number of fixpoint computations. (We show in an earlier work [23] that for a ring network with K nodes, it suffices to compute only one component of the fixpoint instead of all K.) Moreover, it suggests that, for a parameterized or dynamic network, symmetries that span members of a network family can be used to reduce the problem of checking a property for all instances to checking it for a small, fixed-size set of representative instances. We consider this next.

3.2   Parameterized and Dynamic Network Families

We apply the local symmetry definitions to a family of networks by redefining the symmetry relation to relate two nodes in (possibly) different networks. I.e., the relation consists of triples $((G, m), \beta, (H, n))$. We immediately obtain the analogues of Theorem 2 and Corollary 1 for a parametric network family.

Theorem 3. *Let B be a local symmetry on a parametric network family. Let θ^* be the strongest compositional invariant. Then, for every (G, m) and (H, n) such that $((G, m), \beta, (H, n))$ is in B, it is the case that $[\theta^*(G, m) \Rightarrow \langle \beta \rangle \theta^*(H, n)]$.*

Corollary 2. *Let P be a property of local states. If $((G, m), \beta, (H, n))$ is in symmetry B, and P is invariant under β, then $[\theta^*(G, m) \Rightarrow P]$ if, and only if, $[\theta^*(H, n) \Rightarrow P]$.*

An example of this reduction is as follows. Consider a family of ring networks $\{R_i\}$, where the process at each node is the same regardless of ring size. Then the relation β connects (R_k, m) with (R_l, n) precisely if the local state of m in the ring R_k is identical to the local state of n in ring R_l. For any property P which depends only on local states, the two nodes will satisfy P in the same way, by Corollary 2. Moreover, as any two nodes are connected by a local symmetry, all nodes in the family fall into a single equivalence class. Hence, it suffices to compute a compositional invariant for a 2-node ring instance and check the property P for that instance in order to deduce that it holds for the entire family.

We would like to extend this form of reasoning to dynamic networks. In order to do so, we make the following assumption:

- (React) Any reaction to a dynamic change preserves the *non-dynamic* invariant. Formally, let Σ^* be the strongest *non-dynamic* compositional invariant.

Consider a node (G, m) and a dynamic change at m or at one of its neighbors which changes the graph to G'. If, before the reaction, (G, m) and its neighbors have local states in Σ^*, then the local state of m after the reaction is in $\Sigma^*(G', m)$.

We believe that this is a reasonable assumption. A protocol designer must place a node in a "safe" local state after a dynamic change. It is reasonable to imagine that this safe state is one that is known to be a locally reachable state and, therefore, belongs to Σ^*. As we show in the following section, our example protocols satisfy this assumption.

Theorem 4. *Under the React assumption, the strongest compositional invariant for the non-dynamic and the dynamic systems are identical.*

Proof Sketch: Recall that Σ^* denotes the strongest non-dynamic compositional invariant, and Δ^* the strongest dynamic compositional invariant. As the initial configurations cover all graphs, $\Sigma^*(G, m)$ and $\Delta^*(G, m)$ are non-empty for all nodes (G, m).

The constraints defining validity of a compositional invariant for the dynamic case are an extension of those for the non-dynamic case. Hence, Δ^* is also a non-dynamic compositional invariant. Therefore, Σ^* is below Δ^* (point-wise).

We use React to show the other direction. The proof is by induction on the fixpoint stages. The claim is that, at stage k, Δ^k is below Σ^* for all components. This is true initially as Δ^0 is the set of initial states. Assume that it is true at stage k. The step and interference updates are common to both and, as the update function is monotonic, the hypothesis continues to hold at the next stage. In the dynamic setting, Δ^{k+1} is also updated as the result of reactions to network changes at node (G, m) or at one of its neighbors. By the induction hypotheses, the originating states are in Δ^k, and therefore in Σ^*. By the React assumption, the resulting local state for (G', m) is also in $\Sigma^*(G', m)$. Hence, the hypothesis continues to hold at stage $k + 1$. A newly added node begins at an initial state, which is already covered in Σ^*; a deleted node has no effect. **EndProof.**

This theorem lets us reduce the dynamic case to the non-dynamic, parameterized case. I.e., we can apply symmetry reductions as illustrated by the ring network example. We show in the following section how this applies to the two protocols we consider in this work.

4   Applications

In this section, we show how two dynamic protocols may be analyzed using the following procedure, based on the theory laid out in the previous sections:

1. Define a symmetry B for the entire network family, with finitely many equivalence classes
2. Find a representative network instance, R, whose nodes cover all of the equivalence classes
3. Compute the strongest non-dynamic compositional invariant for R.

4. Check that the React assumption is satisfied for all nodes in the family. In order to do so, it suffices to show that every reaction which results in a state of (G', m) is related to a state in the invariant of the representative instance.

Let property P be invariant under the symmetries in B. By Corollary 2, if P holds of $\Sigma^*(R, k)$ for all nodes k in R, it holds of all nodes in the entire family.

The first two steps are not automated, but one may consider some guidelines. If the network family has graphs with nodes of arbitrary degree, the symmetry relation must abstract from the degree of the node. A localized abstraction of the state space may be needed if the space is large or unbounded. The symmetry and React conditions could be checked with an SMT solver or a theorem prover. The fixpoint computation of Σ^* for the representative network can be done automatically if the local state space is finite.

4.1   Dynamic Dining Philosophers Protocol

A non-dynamic version which operates on arbitrary networks was analyzed in [24]; here, we consider modifications to respond to dynamic network changes.

The basic protocol. The protocol has a number of similar processes operating on an arbitrary network. Every edge on the network models a shared "fork". The edge between nodes i and j is called f_{ij} or, equivalently, f_{ji}. Its value is one of $\{i, j, \perp\}$. Node i is said to *own* the fork f_{ij} if $f_{ij} = i$; node j owns this fork if $f_{ij} = j$; and the fork is available if $f_{ij} = \perp$. The process at node i goes through the internal states T (thinking), H (hungry), E (eating), and R (release). Let $nbr(i, j, G)$ be a predicate true for nodes i, j in network G if the two nodes share an edge. The transitions for the process at node i are as follows.

- A transition from T to H is always enabled.
- In state H, the process acquires forks, but may also choose to release them
  - (acquire fork) if $nbr(i, j, G)$ and $f_{ij} = \perp$, set $f_{ij} := i$,
  - (release fork) if $nbr(i, j, G)$ and $f_{ij} = i$, set $f_{ij} := \perp$, and
  - (to-eat) if $(\forall j : nbr(i, j, G) : f_{ij} = i)$, then change state to E.
- A transition from E to R is always enabled.
- In state R, the process releases its owned forks.
  - (release fork) if $nbr(i, j, G)$ and $f_{ij} = i$, set $f_{ij} := \perp$
  - (to-think) if $(\forall j : nbr(i, j, G) : f_{ij} \neq i)$, change state to T

The initial state of the system is one where all processes are in state T and all forks are available (i.e., have value $\perp$). The desired safety property is that there is no reachable global state where neighboring processes are in the state E.

Responding to Dynamic Network Changes. The protocol is safe for a fixed network. It is, however, unsafe under dynamic changes. For instance, the addition of a fresh link changes the nbr relation, and can cause two processes both of which are in their eating (E) state to become adjacent, violating safety. To avoid this possibility, the *link* transition is defined so that if a process is eating, it moves back to hungry (H), without releasing its forks; otherwise, the state is unchanged. The removal of a link cannot violate safety; in fact, it may make a hungry process eligible to eat, if all remaining edges are owned by that process. Hence, the *unlink* transition keeps the local state unchanged. The initial state of a newly added node is thinking (T).

Symmetry Reduction. We show (informally) how to carry out the steps described previously. Define the symmetry B with entries $((G, m), \beta, (H, n))$ for all G, H and nodes m in G and n in H, where β is defined as follows. Local states x of (G, m) and y of (H, n) are related by β if they have the same internal state (i.e., one of T, H, E, R), and node m owns all of its neighboring forks if, and only if, node n owns all of its neighboring forks. This meets the structural conditions on B, and there is a single equivalence class for the orbit relation (as every node is related to every other node).

We now sketch the check for simulation, which holds under stuttering. For instance, state x of (G, m) may be one where node m is hungry and has acquired 2 out of 4 neighboring forks, while state y of (H, n) is a state where node n is hungry and has acquired 6 out of 7 neighboring forks. An interference transition of m which results in it being granted one additional fork is matched by y (i.e., by a stuttering step), while an interference transition of n which results in it being granted the last remaining fork is matched by a sequence of two interference transitions from x.

The representative system consists of the smallest instance, a two-node ring. Its strongest compositional invariant can be calculated automatically. This asserts (cf. [24]) that, for each node, if the node is in state E, it owns all neighboring forks. By Theorem 3, this assertion holds for *all* nodes in the family.

Finally, we have to check the React assumption which allows a reduction from dynamic to parametric analysis. As outlined earlier in this section, we consider dynamic transitions where the origin state is related to the invariant of the representative system. For a link removal, the local state does not change. The interesting case is where the local state is E. Since the origin state of node m is related to the representative invariant, node m must own all forks. Removing one fork does not change this property, and the resulting state is also in the representative invariant. For link addition, the protocol moves to a non-E internal state, which trivially belongs to the representative invariant.

It follows by Theorem 4 that the same invariant holds for the dynamic system. It follows that neighboring nodes cannot be in state E, as that would imply (from the invariant) the existence of a shared edge which is owned by both nodes, a contradiction.

4.2   Analyzing the AODV Protocol

AODV is used to establish routes in a mobile ad-hoc network. The first version of this protocol [1] was analyzed in [6] with theorem proving, model checking and (manual) abstraction, in [10], using predicate abstraction on the global state (although this version omits sequence numbering, which is used to handle dynamic changes) and recently in [19], using process algebra. The property of interest is whether the protocol can be put into a state where there is a routing loop. We analyzed the latest version of AODV, called AODVv2 [2]. Enough has changed that these earlier proofs are no longer applicable to the new version. In the course of our modeling, we discovered an error in the AODVv2 protocol (in the handling of broken routes) and suggested a fix. The authors have acknowledged the error, and accepted the fix. The following analysis is for the corrected protocol.

The AODV protocol is used in a network where nodes are mobile, so that connectivity between two nodes may change at any time. The protocol is used to establish a route from a source node S to a target node T. The source floods the network with RREQs (route requests). When an RREQ reaches T, it responds with an RREP (route reply) message, which makes its way back to S through the request tree created during the RREQ flood. Unlike the earlier version, AODVv2 maintains two entries for each route: one pointing back to S, the other pointing back to T. Each entry has a next-hop field, a hop-count (more generally, a route cost), and a sequence number. The intuition is that higher sequence numbers indicate newer routes, while lower hop-counts indicate shorter routes. Thus, there is a natural way to compare routes. We say that a route x is "better than" a route y if $(seq_x, -hop_x)$ is lexicographically strictly greater than $(seq_y, -hop_y)$. I.e., if $seq_x > seq_y$ or if $seq_x = seq_y$ and $hop_x < hop_y$. In this situation, we also say that route y is "worse" than route x. We write this relationship as $y \prec x$.

The methodology developed so far considers a node as the focal point. One could as well consider a pair of adjacent nodes as the focal point, so that the invariant assertions have the form $\theta(G, (m, e, n))$ where m and n are adjacent in G with a single shared edge e. The concepts, compositional constraints, and theorems carry over in a straightforward way. For instance, a local state of (m, e, n) is interfered with by transitions at nodes which are adjacent to m and n.

As sequence numbers and hop-count are both unbounded, we need to compute compositional invariants under an abstraction. The natural abstraction, given the intuition, is to relate routes using the better-than relation, and to keep track of whether m is the next-hop of n. We define a relation β between $(G, (m, e, n))$ and $(H, (k, f, l))$ as follows. Local states x and y are related in β if, and only if, the internal states are the same, and corresponding pairs of route entries (e.g., those for (m, n) and (k, l); and for (m, e) and (k, f)) are related in the same way using the better-than relation, and next-hop relations are also comparable. For a small, 3 process network, the compositional invariant shows that $r_m \succeq r_e$, and if m is the next-hop for n, then $r_m \succ r_n$. (The notation r_i represents the route entry for node or edge i.)

We then check that the symmetry simulation conditions hold, limiting attention to states which are related by β to states in the compositional invariant for the representative. The React conditions also hold, as the only reaction of the protocol to a deleted edge is to mark a route which follows that edge as being broken, and to send RERR (error) messages to adjacent nodes. As the reactions do not modify the actual route entries, they preserve the compositional invariant. From the symmetry theorem, the invariant for the representative network extends to the entire dynamic system.

5   Related Work and Conclusions

Compositional analysis has a long history and a large literature (cf. [11]); we refer here only to the most directly related work. The fixpoint definition used in this paper is a fully compositional (i.e., assume-guarantee) form of the Owicki-Gries method [25]. Parameterized verification is undecidable in general [5], but decidability results are known (cf. [18,16]), and several semi-decision procedures have been developed. Typically, these approximate the infinite family of networks with finitary objects, for instance, the finite basis for upward-closed sets from well-quasi-orderings [3] and finite-state transducers [20]. These objects are, however, complex: mathematically and in terms of practical manipulation. A number of recent papers [26,22,23,24,4] have shown that the substantially simpler methods of localized analysis can be used to show parametric correctness for a number of non-trivial protocols.

The new contribution of this work is to provide a localized method to show the correctness of protocols which operate on dynamic networks. This requires two key steps. First, it is necessary to define new compositional constraints which correspond to actions taken by a protocol in response to dynamic changes. Second, as the set of possible networks is infinite, it is necessary to collapse the reasoning on to a representative network through the use of localized symmetries, induced by abstractions. The result of compositional analysis on the representative generalizes to a quantified inductive invariant which holds for the entire dynamic network family.

There are several other approaches to the analysis of dynamic and ad-hoc networks. The work in [7] shows that Hoare triples for restricted logics are decidable. Work in [14,12] applies well-quasi-ordering (wqo) theory to ad-hoc networks, while the algorithm of [13] relies on symbolic forward exploration. Reasoning with these approaches is in terms of global states. The methods given here are localized in nature, which ensures simple representation and calculations, carried out with a small number of abstract processes. Also, as argued in the introduction, the dynamic nature of the changes contributes to the effectiveness of compositional reasoning.

The single abstract process view is also found in the network grammar method [28] and the environment abstraction method [8] for analysis of parametric protocols. In [21], the techniques in [17] are extended to dynamically changing systems represented with graph grammars. Despite the high-level similarities to these methods, our approach differs in being grounded in compositional analysis and in its ability to analyze dynamic changes.

In this work, we put forward a straightforward analysis framework for dynamic network protocols, and show that it suffices to construct correctness proofs for two non-trivial protocols, over an infinite set of possible networks. This strengthens the conjecture which originally inspired this work: that dynamic network protocols must be loosely coupled, and hence especially amenable to compositional analysis. The simplicity and naturalness of the symmetry relations for the two protocols lead us to believe that there is much scope for heuristic methods which automatically determine an appropriate symmetry relation.

References

1. Ad Hoc On-Demand Distance Vector (AODV) Routing. Internet Draft, IETF Mobile Ad hoc Networks Working Group
2. Dynamic MANET On-demand (AODVv2) Routing. Internet Draft, IETF Mobile Ad hoc Networks Working Group,
   `http://datatracker.ietf.org/doc/draft-ietf-manet-aodvv2/`
3. Abdulla, P.A., Cerans, K., Jonsson, B., Tsay, Y.-K.: General decidability theorems for infinite-state systems. In:.LICS, pp. 313–321. IEEE Computer Society (1996)
4. Abdulla, P.A., Haziza, F., Holík, L.: All for the price of few. In: Giacobazzi, R., Berdine, J., Mastroeni, I. (eds.) VMCAI 2013. LNCS, vol. 7737, pp. 476–495. Springer, Heidelberg (2013)
5. Apt, K.R., Kozen, D.: Limits for automatic verification of finite-state concurrent systems. Inf. Process. Lett. 22(6), 307–309 (1986)
6. Bhargavan, K., Obradovic, D., Gunter, C.A.: Formal verification of standards for distance vector routing protocols. J. ACM 49(4), 538–576 (2002)
7. Bouajjani, A., Jurski, Y., Sighireanu, M.: A generic framework for reasoning about dynamic networks of infinite-state processes. In: Grumberg, O., Huth, M. (eds.) TACAS 2007. LNCS, vol. 4424, pp. 690–705. Springer, Heidelberg (2007)
8. Clarke, E.M., Talupur, M., Veith, H.: Environment abstraction for parameterized verification. In: Emerson, E.A., Namjoshi, K.S. (eds.) VMCAI 2006. LNCS, vol. 3855, pp. 126–141. Springer, Heidelberg (2006)
9. Cousot, P., Cousot, R.: Automatic synthesis of optimal invariant assertions: mathematical foundations. In: ACM Symposium on Artificial Intelligence & Programming Languages, vol. 12(8), pp. 1–12. ACM, Rochester (1977)
10. Das, S., Dill, D.L.: Counter-example based predicate discovery in predicate abstraction. In: Aagaard, M.D., O'Leary, J.W. (eds.) FMCAD 2002. LNCS, vol. 2517, pp. 19–32. Springer, Heidelberg (2002)
11. de Roever, W.-P., de Boer, F., Hannemann, U., Hooman, J., Lakhnech, Y., Poel, M., Zwiers, J.: Concurrency Verification: Introduction to Compositional and Noncompositional Proof Methods. Cambridge University Press (2001)
12. Delzanno, G., Sangnier, A., Traverso, R., Zavattaro, G.: On the complexity of parameterized reachability in reconfigurable broadcast networks. In: FSTTCS. LIPIcs, vol. 18, pp. 289–300. Schloss Dagstuhl - Leibniz-Zentrum fuer Informatik (2012)
13. Delzanno, G., Sangnier, A., Zavattaro, G.: Parameterized verification of safety properties in ad hoc network protocols. In: PACO. EPTCS, vol. 60, pp. 56–65 (2011)
14. Delzanno, G., Sangnier, A., Zavattaro, G.: Verification of ad hoc networks with node and communication failures. In: Giese, H., Rosu, G. (eds.) FORTE 2012 and FMOODS 2012. LNCS, vol. 7273, pp. 235–250. Springer, Heidelberg (2012)
15. Dijkstra, E., Scholten, C.: Predicate Calculus and Program Semantics. Springer (1990)

16. Emerson, E., Namjoshi, K.: Reasoning about rings. In: ACM Symposium on Principles of Programming Languages (1995)
17. Emerson, E.A., Trefler, R.J., Wahl, T.: Reducing model checking of the few to the one. In: Liu, Z., Kleinberg, R.D. (eds.) ICFEM 2006. LNCS, vol. 4260, pp. 94–113. Springer, Heidelberg (2006)
18. German, S., Sistla, A.: Reasoning about systems with many processes. Journal of the ACM (1992)
19. Höfner, P., van Glabbeek, R.J., Tan, W.L., Portmann, M., McIver, A., Fehnker, A.: A rigorous analysis of aodv and its variants. In: MSWiM, pp. 203–212. ACM (2012)
20. Kesten, Y., Maler, O., Marcus, M., Pnueli, A., Shahar, E.: Symbolic model checking with rich ssertional languages. In: Grumberg, O. (ed.) CAV 1997. LNCS, vol. 1254, pp. 424–435. Springer, Heidelberg (1997)
21. Langari, Z., Trefler, R.: Symmetry for the analysis of dynamic systems. In: NASA Formal Methods 2011, pp. 252–266 (2011)
22. Namjoshi, K.S.: Symmetry and completeness in the analysis of parameterized systems. In: Cook, B., Podelski, A. (eds.) VMCAI 2007. LNCS, vol. 4349, pp. 299–313. Springer, Heidelberg (2007)
23. Namjoshi, K.S., Trefler, R.J.: Local symmetry and compositional verification. In: Kuncak, V., Rybalchenko, A. (eds.) VMCAI 2012. LNCS, vol. 7148, pp. 348–362. Springer, Heidelberg (2012)
24. Namjoshi, K.S., Trefler, R.J.: Uncovering symmetries in irregular process networks. In: Giacobazzi, R., Berdine, J., Mastroeni, I. (eds.) VMCAI 2013. LNCS, vol. 7737, pp. 496–514. Springer, Heidelberg (2013)
25. Owicki, S.S., Gries, D.: Verifying properties of parallel programs: An axiomatic approach. Commun. ACM 19(5), 279–285 (1976)
26. Pnueli, A., Ruah, S., Zuck, L.D.: Automatic deductive verification with invisible invariants. In: Margaria, T., Yi, W. (eds.) TACAS 2001. LNCS, vol. 2031, pp. 82–97. Springer, Heidelberg (2001)
27. Saksena, M., Wibling, O., Jonsson, B.: Graph grammar modelling and verification of ad hoc routing protocols. LNCS, pp. 18–32 (2008)
28. Shtadler, Z., Grumberg, O.: Network grammars, communication behaviors and automatic verification. In: Sifakis, J. (ed.) CAV 1989. LNCS, vol. 407, pp. 151–165. Springer, Heidelberg (1990)

Tool Demonstrations

MULTIGAIN: A Controller Synthesis Tool for MDPs with Multiple Mean-Payoff Objectives

Tomáš Brázdil[1], Krishnendu Chatterjee[2], Vojtěch Forejt[3], and Antonín Kučera[1]

[1] Faculty of Informatics, Masaryk University, Brno, Czech Republic
[2] IST Austria
[3] Department of Computer Science, University of Oxford, UK

Abstract. We present MULTIGAIN, a tool to synthesize strategies for Markov decision processes (MDPs) with multiple mean-payoff objectives. Our models are described in PRISM, and our tool uses the existing interface and simulator of PRISM. Our tool extends PRISM by adding novel algorithms for multiple mean-payoff objectives, and also provides features such as (i) generating strategies and exploring them for simulation, and checking them with respect to other properties; and (ii) generating an approximate Pareto curve for two mean-payoff objectives. In addition, we present a new practical algorithm for the analysis of MDPs with multiple mean-payoff objectives under memoryless strategies.

1 Introduction

Markov decision processes (MDPs) are a standard model for analysis of probabilistic systems with non-determinism [12], with a wide range of applications [5]. In each state of an MDP, a controller chooses one of several actions (the nondeterministic choices), and the current state and action gives a probability distribution over the successor states. One classical objective used to study quantitative properties of systems is the *limit-average (or mean-payoff)* objective, where a reward (or cost) is associated with each transition and the objective assigns to every run the average of the rewards over the run. MDPs with single mean-payoff objectives have been well studied in the literature (see, e.g., [14]). However, in many modeling domains, there is not a single goal to be optimized, but multiple, potentially interdependent and conflicting goals. For example, in designing a computer system, the goal is to maximize average performance while minimizing average power consumption. Similarly, in an inventory management system, the goal is to optimize several dependent costs for maintaining each kind of product. The complexity of MDPs with multiple mean-payoff objectives was studied in [6].

In this paper we present MULTIGAIN, which is, to the best of our knowledge, the first tool for synthesis of controller strategies in MDPs with multiple mean-payoff objectives. The MDPs and the mean-payoff objectives are specified in the well-known PRISM modelling language. Our contributions are as follows: (1) we extend PRISM with novel algorithms for multiple mean-payoff objectives from [6]; (2) develop on the results of [6] to synthesize strategies, and explore

© Springer-Verlag Berlin Heidelberg 2015
C. Baier and C. Tinelli (Eds.): TACAS 2015, LNCS 9035, pp. 181–187, 2015.
DOI: 10.1007/978-3-662-46681-0_12

them for simulation, and check them with respect to other properties (as done in PRISM-games [9]); and (3) for the important special case of two mean-payoff objectives we provide the feature to visualize the approximate Pareto curve (where the Pareto curve represents the "trade-off" curve and consists of solutions that are not strictly dominated by any other solution). Finally, we present a new practical approach for analysis of MDPs with multiple mean-payoff objectives under memoryless strategies: previously an NP bound was shown in [8] by guessing all bottom strongly connected components (BSCCs) of the MDP graph for a memoryless strategy and this gave an exponential enumerative algorithm; in contrast, we present a linear reduction to solving a boolean combination of linear constraints (which is a special class of mixed integer linear programming where the integer variables are binary).

2   Definitions

MDPs and Strategies. An MDP $G = (S, A, Act, \delta)$ consists of (i) a *finite* set S of states; (ii) a *finite* set A of actions, (iii) an action enabledness function $Act : S \to 2^A \setminus \{\emptyset\}$ that assigns to each state s the set $Act(s)$ of actions enabled at s, and (iv) a transition function $\delta : S \times A \to dist(S)$ that given a state s and an action $a \in Act(s)$ gives a probability distribution over the successor states ($dist(S)$ denotes all probability distributions over S). W.l.o.g. we assume that every action is enabled in exactly one state, and we denote this state $Src(a)$. Thus, we will assume that $\delta : A \to dist(S)$. *Strategies* describe how to choose the next action given a finite path (of state and action pairs) in the MDP. A strategy consists of a set of memory elements to remember the history of the paths. The memory elements are updated stochastically in each transition, and the next action is chosen probabilistically (among enabled actions) based on the current state and current memory [6]. A strategy is *memoryless* if it depends only on the current state.

Multiple Mean-payoff Objectives. A single mean-payoff objective consists of a reward function r that assigns a real-valued reward $r(s, a)$ to every state s and action a enabled in s, and the mean-payoff objective $\mathsf{mp}(r)$ assigns to every infinite path (or run) the long-run average of the rewards of the path, i.e., for $\pi = (s_0 a_0 s_1 a_1 \dots)$ we have $\mathsf{mp}(r)(\pi) = \liminf_{n \to \infty} \frac{1}{n} \cdot \sum_{i=0}^{n-1} r(s_i, a_i)$. In multiple mean-payoff objectives, there are k reward functions $r_1, r_2, \dots, r_k$, and each reward function r_i defines the respective mean-payoff objective $\mathsf{mp}(r_i)$. Given a strategy σ and a random variable X, we denote by $\mathbb{E}_s^\sigma[X]$ the expectation of the σ w.r.t. X, given a starting state s. Thus for a mean-payoff objective $\mathsf{mp}(r)$, the expected mean-payoff is $\mathbb{E}_s^\sigma[\mathsf{mp}(r)]$.

Synthesis Questions. The relevant questions in analysis of MDPs with multiple objectives are as follows: (1) *(Existence)*. Given an MDP with k reward functions, starting state s_0, and a vector $\boldsymbol{v} = (v_1, v_2, \dots, v_k)$ of k real-values, the existence question asks whether there exists a strategy σ such that for all $1 \le i \le k$ we have $\mathbb{E}_{s_0}^\sigma[\mathsf{mp}(r_i)] \ge v_i$. (2) *(Synthesis)*. If the answer to the existence question is yes, the synthesis question asks for a witness strategy to satisfy the existence question. An optimization question related to multiple objectives is the computation of the Pareto-curve (or the trade-off curve), where the Pareto curve consists of vectors $\boldsymbol{v}$ such that the answer to the existence question is yes, and for all vectors $\boldsymbol{v}'$ that strictly dominate $\boldsymbol{v}$ (i.e., $\boldsymbol{v}'$ is at least $\boldsymbol{v}$ in all dimensions and strictly greater in at least one dimension) the answer to the existence question is no.

3   Algorithms and Implementation

We first recall the existing results for MDPs with multiple mean-payoff objectives [6], and then describe our implementation and extensions. Before presenting the existing results, we first recall the notion of maximal end-components in MDPs.

Maximal End-components. A pair (T, B) with $\emptyset \neq T \subseteq S$ and $B \subseteq \bigcup_{t \in T} Act(t)$ is an *end component* of G if (1) for all $a \in B$, whenever $\delta(a)(s') > 0$ then $s' \in T$; and (2) for all $s, t \in T$ there is a finite path from s to t such that all states and actions that appear in the path belong to T and B, respectively. An end component (T, B) is a *maximal end component (MEC)* if it is maximal wrt. pointwise subset ordering. An MDP is *unichain* if for all $B \subseteq A$ satisfying $B \cap Act(s) \neq \emptyset$ for any $s \in S$ we have that (S, B) is a MEC. Given an MDP, we denote S_{MEC} the set of states s that are contained within a MEC.

Result From [6]. The results of [6] showed that (i) the existence question can be answered in polynomial time, by reduction to linear programming; (ii) if there exists a strategy for the existence problem, then there exists a witness strategy with only two-memory states. It also established that if the MDP is unichain, then memoryless strategies are sufficient. The polynomial-time algorithm is as follows: it was shown in [6] that the answer to the existence problem is yes iff there exists a non-negative solution to the system of linear inequalities given in Fig. 1.

Syntax and Semantics. Our tool accepts PRISM MDP models as input, see [1] for details. The multi-objective properties are expressed as `multi(list)` or `mlessmulti(list)` where *list* is a comma separated list of mean-payoff reward properties, which can be *boolean*, e.g. `R{'r1'}>=0.5 [S]`, and in the case of

$$\mathbf{1}_{s_0}(s) + \sum_{a \in A} y_a \cdot \delta(a)(s) = \sum_{a \in Act(s)} y_a + y_s \qquad \text{for all } s \in S \quad (1)$$

$$\sum_{s \in S_{MEC}} y_s = 1 \qquad (2)$$

$$\sum_{s \in C} y_s = \sum_{a \in A \cap C} x_a \qquad \text{for all MECs } C \text{ of } G \quad (3)$$

$$\sum_{a \in A} x_a \cdot \delta(a)(s) = \sum_{a \in Act(s)} x_a \qquad \text{for all } s \in S \quad (4)$$

$$\sum_{a \in A} x_a \cdot \boldsymbol{r}_i(a) \geq \boldsymbol{v}_i \qquad \text{for all } 1 \leq i \leq k \quad (5)$$

Fig. 1. System L of linear inequalities (here $\mathbf{1}_{s_0}(s)$ is 1 if $s=s_0$, and 0 otherwise) `multi` also *numerical*, e.g. `R{'r2'}min=?` `[S]`. In the reward properties, `S` stands for steady-state, following PRISM's terminology.

If all properties in the list are boolean, the multi-objective property `multi`(*list*) is also boolean and is true iff there is a strategy under which all given reward properties in the list are simultaneously satisfied. If there is a single numerical query, the multi-objective query intuitively asks for the maximal achievable reward of the numerical reward query, subject to the restriction given by the boolean queries. We also allow two numerical queries; in such case MULTI-GAIN generates a Pareto curve. The semantics of `mlessmulti` follows the same pattern, the only difference being that only memoryless (randomised) strategies are being considered. The reason we don't allow numerical reward properties in `mlessmulti` is that the supremum among all memoryless strategies might not be realised.

Implementation of Existence Question. We have implemented the algorithm of [6]. Our implementation takes as input an MDP with multiple mean-payoff objectives and a value vector v, and computes the linear inequalities of Fig. 1 or a *mixed integer linear programming* (MILP) extension in case of memoryless strategies. The system of linear inequalities is solved with LPsolve [2] or Gurobi [3].

Implementation of the Synthesis Question. We now describe how to obtain witness strategies. Assume that the linear program from Fig. 1 has a solution, where a solution to a variable z is denoted by $\bar{z}$. We construct a new linear program, comprising Eq. 1 together with the equations $y_s = \sum_{a \in Act(s)} \bar{x}_a$ for all $s \in S_{MEC}$.

Let $\hat{z}$ denote a solution to variables z in this linear program. The stochastic-update strategy is defined to have 2 memory states ("transient" and "recurrent"), with the transition function defined to be $\sigma_t(s)(a) = \hat{y}_a / \sum_{b \in Act(s)} \hat{y}_b$ and $\sigma_r(s)(a) = \bar{x}_a / \sum_{b \in Act(s)} \bar{x}_b$, and the probability of switching from "transient" to "recurrent" state upon entering s being $\hat{y}_s / (\sum_{a \in Act(s)} \hat{y}_a + \hat{y}_s)$. The correctness of the witness construction follows from [6].

MILP for Memoryless Strategies. For memoryless strategies, the current upper bound is NP [8] and the previous algorithm enumerates all possible BSCCs under a memoryless strategy. We present a polynomial-time reduction to solving a boolean combination of linear constraints, that can be easily encoded using MILP with binary variables [16]. The key requirement for memoryless strategies is that a state can either be recurrent or transient. For the existence question restricted to memoryless strategies we modify the linear constraints from Fig. 1 as follows: (i) we add constraints; for all states s and actions $b \in Act(s)$: $y_b > 0 \implies (x_b > 0 \vee \sum_{a \in Act(Src(b))} x_a = 0)$; (ii) we replace constraint (3) from Fig. 1 by constraints that for all states s: $y_s = \sum_{a \in Act(s)} x_a$. The constraint (ii) is a strengthening of constraint (3), as the above constraint implies constraint (3). Further details are in [7].

Approximate Pareto Curve for Two Objectives. To generate a Pareto curve, we successively compute solutions to several linear programs for a single

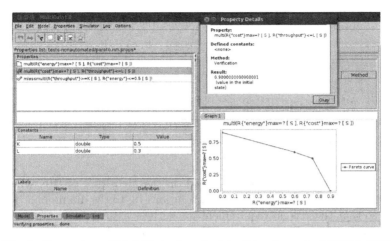

Fig. 2. Screenshot of MultiGain (largely inheriting from the PRISM GUI)

mean-payoff objective, where every time the objective is obtained as a weighted sum of the objectives for which the Pareto curve is generated. The weights are selected in a way similar to [11], allowing us to obtain the approximation of the curve.

Unlike the PRISM implementation for multi-objective cumulative rewards, our tool is able to generate the Pareto curve for objectives of the form `multi(R{'r1'}max=?[S], R{'r2'}max=? [S], R{'r3'}>=0.5 [S])` where the objectives to be optimised are subject to restrictions given by other rewards.

Features of Our Tool. In summary, our tool extends PRISM by developing algorithms to solve MDPs with multiple mean-payoff objectives. Along with the algorithm from [6] we have also implemented a visual representation of the Pareto curve for two-dimensional objectives. The implementation utilises a multi-objective visualisation available in PRISM for cumulative reward and LTL objectives.

In addition, we adapted a feature from PRISM-games [9] which allows the user to generate strategies, so that they can be explored and investigated by simulation. A product (Markov chain) of an MDP and a strategy can be constructed, allowing the user to employ it for verification of other properties.

The tool is available at `http://qav.cs.ox.ac.uk/multigain/`, and the source code is provided under GPL. For licencing reasons, Gurobi is not included with the download, but it can be added manually by following provided steps.

4 Experimental Results: Case Studies

We have evaluated our tool on two standard case studies, adapted from [1], and also mention other applications where our tool could be used.

Table 1. Experimental results. For space reasons, the [S] argument to R is omitted

model	para.	property (A: multi(...), B: mlessmulti(...))	MDP states	LP vars (binary)	rows	total time (s)	solving time (s)	value
phil	3	A:R{"think"}max=?,R{"eat"}>=0.3	956	6344	1915	0.23	0.08	2.119
	3	B:R{"think"}>=2.11,R{"eat"}>=0.3	956	12553 (6344)	11773	209.9	209.7	true
	3	B:R{"think"}>=2.12,R{"eat"}>=0.3	956	12553 (6344)	11773	20.9	20.7	false
	4	A:R{"think"}max=?,R{"eat"}>=1	9440	80368	18883	4.4	3.8	2.429
	5	A:R{"think"}max=?,R{"eat"}>=1	93068	967168	186139	616.0	606.4	3.429
mutex	3	A:R{"try"}max=? [S],R{"crit"}>=0.2	27766	119038	55535	214.9	212.7	2.679
	4	A:R{"try"}max=? [S],R{"crit"}>=0.3	668836	3010308	1337675	t/o	t/o	t/o
	4	A:R{"try"}>=3.5 [S],R{"crit"}>=0.3	668836	3010308	1337676	4126	4073	true

Dining philosophers is a case study based on the algorithm of [10], which extends Lehmann and Rabin's randomised solution [13] to the dining philosophers problem so that there is no requirement for fairness assumptions. The constant N gives the number of philosophers. We use two reward structures, think and eat for the number of philosophers currently thinking and eating, respectively.

Randomised Mutual Exclusion models a solution to the mutual exclusion problem by [15]. The parameter N gives the number of processes competing for the access to the critical section. Here we defined reward structures try and crit for the number of processes that are currently trying to access the critical section, and those which are in it, currently (the latter number obviously never being more than 1).

Evaluation. The statistics for some of our experiments are given in Table 1 (the complete results are available from the tool's website). The experiments were run on a 2.66GHz PC with 4GB RAM, the LP solver used was Gurobi and the timeout ("t/o") was set to 2 hours. We observed that our approach scales to mid-size models, the main limitation being the LP solver.

Other Applications. We mention two applications which are solved using MDPs with multiple mean-payoff objectives. (A) The problem of synthesis from incompatible specifications was considered in [17]. Given a set of specifications $\varphi_1, \varphi_2, \ldots, \varphi_k$ that cannot be all satisfied together, the goal is to synthesize a system such that for all $1 \leq i \leq k$ the distance to specification φ_i is at most v_i. In adversarial environments the problem reduces to games and for probabilistic environments to MDPs, with multiple mean-payoff objectives [17]. (B) The problem of synthesis of steady state distributions for ergodic MDPs was considered in [4]. The problem can be modeled with multiple mean-payoff objectives by considering indicator reward functions r_s, for each state s, that assign reward 1 to every action enabled in s and 0 to all other actions. The steady state distribution synthesis question of [4] then reduces to the existence question for multiple mean-payoff MDPs.

Concluding Remarks. We presented the first tool for analysis of MDPs with multiple mean-payoff objectives. The limiting factor is the LP solver, and so an interesting direction would be to extend the results of [18] to multiple objectives.

Acknowledgements. The authors were in part supported by Austrian Science Fund (FWF) Grant No P23499- N23, FWF NFN Grant No S11407-N23 (RiSE), ERC Start grant (279307: Graph Games) and the research centre Institute for Theoretical Computer Science (ITI), grant No. P202/12/G061.

References

1. http://www.prismmodelchecker.org/
2. http://sourceforge.net/projects/lpsolve/
3. http://www.gurobi.com
4. Akshay, S., Bertrand, N., Haddad, S., Hélouët, L.: The steady-state control problem for markov decision processes. In: Joshi, K., Siegle, M., Stoelinga, M., D'Argenio, P.R. (eds.) QEST 2013. LNCS, vol. 8054, pp. 290–304. Springer, Heidelberg (2013)
5. Baier, C., Katoen, J.-P.: Principles of model checking. MIT Press (2008)
6. Brázdil, T., Brožek, V., Chatterjee, K., Forejt, V., Kučera, A.: Two views on multiple mean-payoff objectives in Markov decision processes. In: LICS 2011, pp. 33–42. IEEE Computer Society (2011)
7. Brázdil, T., Chatterjee, K., Forejt, V., Kučera, A.: MultiGain: A controller synthesis tool for mdps with multiple mean-payoff objectives. CoRR, abs/1501.03093 (2015)
8. Chatterjee, K.: Markov decision processes with multiple long-run average objectives. In: FSTTCS, pp. 473–484 (2007)
9. Chen, T., Forejt, V., Kwiatkowska, M., Parker, D., Simaitis, A.: PRISM-games: A model checker for stochastic multi-player games. In: Piterman, N., Smolka, S.A. (eds.) TACAS 2013 (ETAPS 2013). LNCS, vol. 7795, pp. 185–191. Springer, Heidelberg (2013)
10. Duflot, M., Fribourg, L., Picaronny, C.: Randomized dining philosophers without fairness assumption. Distributed Computing 17(1), 65–76 (2004)
11. Forejt, V., Kwiatkowska, M., Parker, D.: Pareto curves for probabilistic model checking. In: Chakraborty, S., Mukund, M. (eds.) ATVA 2012. LNCS, vol. 7561, pp. 317–332. Springer, Heidelberg (2012)
12. Howard, R.A.: Dynamic Programming and Markov Processes. MIT Press (1960)
13. Lehmann, D., Rabin, M.: On the advantage of free choice: A symmetric and fully distributed solution to the dining philosophers problem. In: POPL 1981 (1981)
14. Puterman, M.L.: Markov Decision Processes. J. Wiley and Sons (1994)
15. Rabin, M.: N-process mutual exclusion with bounded waiting by $4 \log_2 N$-valued shared variable. Journal of Computer and System Sciences 25(1), 66–75 (1982)
16. Schrijver, A.: Theory of Linear and Integer Programming. John Wiley & Sons (1998)
17. Černý, P., Gopi, S., Henzinger, T.A., Radhakrishna, A., Totla, N.: Synthesis from incompatible specifications. In: EMSOFT, pp. 53–62 (2012)
18. Wimmer, R., Braitling, B., Becker, B., Hahn, E.M., Crouzen, P., Hermanns, H., Dhama, A., Theel, O.E.: Symblicit calculation of long-run averages for concurrent probabilistic systems. In: QEST, pp. 27–36. IEEE Computer Society Press (2010)

syntMaskFT: A Tool for Synthesizing Masking Fault-Tolerant Programs from Deontic Specifications

Ramiro Demasi[1,*], Pablo F. Castro[3,4,**], Nicolás Ricci[3,4,**],
Thomas S.E. Maibaum[2], and Nazareno Aguirre[3,4,**]

[1] Fondazione Bruno Kessler, Trento, Italy
demasi@fbk.eu
[2] Department of Computing and Software, McMaster University, Hamilton,
Ontario, Canada
tom@maibaum.org
[3] Departamento de Computación, FCEFQyN, Universidad Nacional de Río Cuarto,
Río Cuarto, Córdoba, Argentina
{pcastro,nricci,naguirre}@dc.exa.unrc.edu.ar
[4] Consejo Nacional de Investigaciones Científicas y Técnicas (CONICET), Argentina

Abstract. In this paper we introduce syntMaskFT, a tool that synthesizes fault-tolerant programs from specifications written in a fragment of branching time logic with deontic operators, designed for specifying fault-tolerant systems. The tool focuses on producing masking tolerant programs, that is, programs that during a failure mask faults in such a way that they cannot be observed by the environment. It is based on an algorithm we have introduced in previous work, and shown to be sound and complete. syntMaskFT takes a specification and automatically determines whether a masking fault-tolerant component is realizable; in such a case, a description of the component is produced together with the maximal set of faults that can be supported for this level of tolerance. We present the ideas behind the tool by means of a simple example, and also report the result of experiments realized with more complex case studies.

Keywords: Fault-tolerance, Program synthesis, Temporal logics, Deontic logics.

1 Introduction

Critical systems, i.e., systems that are involved in serious or vital activities such as medical procedures (e.g., software for medical devices) or the control of vehicles (e.g., software controllers in the automotive and the avionics industries) are

---

* My contribution to this paper was made during my PhD studies at McMaster University, supported by a Fellowship from the IBM Canada Centre for Advanced Studies, in support of the Automotive Partnership Canada funded project NECSIS.
** This work was partially supported by the Argentinian Agency for Scientific and Technological Promotion (ANPCyT), through grants PICT 2012 No. 1298 and PICT 2013 No. 0080; and by the MEALS project (EU FP7 programme, grant agreement No. 295261).

C. Baier and C. Tinelli (Eds.): TACAS 2015, LNCS 9035, pp. 188–193, 2015.
DOI: 10.1007/978-3-662-46681-0_13

subject to a variety of potential failures. In many cases, these failures are not the result of software defects; instead, these may be the result of environmental conditions, such as power outages, electronic noise, or the physical failure of devices, that are not straightforward to avoid. The seriousness of the activities in which critical systems are involved makes it necessary to mitigate the effect of such failures. Therefore, the problem of guaranteeing through verification a certain degree of *fault-tolerance*, ensuring that systems will not be corrupted or degraded below a certain level despite the occurrence of faults, has gained considerable attention in recent years. Moreover, given the complexity of these systems and their properties, *automated* verification techniques for fault-tolerant systems are becoming increasingly important. While verification is (usually) *a posteriori*, a related automated alternative is *synthesis*. Various automated system analysis techniques (e.g., SAT and automata based techniques) have been recently adapted for *system synthesis*, i.e., the task of automatically obtaining a correct-by-construction implementation from a system specification [1,2].

Despite the growing research on system synthesis, the availability of tools for fault-tolerant system synthesis is still low. In this paper we present syntMaskFT, a tool for synthesizing masking fault-tolerant programs from deontic logic specifications. The theoretical foundations of the tool were put forward in [4,5]. In this paper, we concentrate on *masking fault-tolerance* which intuitively corresponds to the case in which the system is able to completely mask faults, not allowing these to have any observable consequences for the users. Roughly speaking, our synthesis algorithm takes as input a component specification, and automatically determines whether a component with masking fault-tolerance is realizable or not. In case such a fault-tolerant component is feasible, its implementation, together with the maximal set of faults supported for this level of tolerance, are automatically computed. A distinguishing feature of the tool is the use of Deontic Logic. These logics enrich standard (temporal) modalities with operators such as *obligation* and *permission*, making it possible to distinguish between normal and abnormal system behavior. In our approach, the logical specification of the component is given in dCTL-, a fragment of a branching time temporal logic with deontic operators [3], especially designed for fault-tolerant component specification. Let us emphasize that in our approach faults are declaratively embedded in the logical specification, where these are understood as violations to the obligations prescribing the behavior of the system. Thereby, we can inject faults automatically from deontic formula violations. Regarding the engine of our tool, it is based on a tableau-based method for deriving a finite state model from a dCTL- specification, with simulation algorithms for calculating masking fault-tolerance. Finally, we have conducted a series of experiments to test the performance of syntMaskFT in practice.

2   dCTL

The logic dCTL is an extension of Computation Tree Logic (CTL), with its novel part being the deontic operators $\mathbf{O}(\psi)$ (obligation) and $\mathbf{P}(\psi)$ (permission), which are applied to a path formula ψ. Most importantly, the deontic operators allow us to declaratively distinguish the normative (correct, without faults) part of the system from its non-normative (faulty) part; an example of its use is shown below. The tool deals with a fragment of dCTL (named dCTL-), described in the following BNF style grammar:

$$\Phi ::= \top \mid p_i \mid \neg\Phi \mid \Phi \to \Phi \mid \mathsf{A}(\Psi) \mid \mathsf{E}(\Psi) \mid \mathbf{O}(\Psi) \mid \mathbf{P}(\Psi)$$
$$\Psi ::= \mathsf{X}\Phi \mid \Phi\,\mathcal{U}\,\Phi \mid \Phi\,\mathcal{W}\,\Phi$$

The standard boolean operators and the CTL quantifiers A and E have the usual semantics. Deontic operators have the following meaning: $\mathbf{O}(\psi)$: *the path formula ψ is obliged in every future state, reachable via non-faulty transitions*; $\mathbf{P}(\psi)$: *there exists a normal execution, i.e., not involving faults, starting from the current state and along which the path formula ψ holds*. These operators allow one to capture the intended behavior of the system when no faults are present. We present a simple example to illustrate the use of this logic to specify systems. The semantics of the logic is given via colored Kripke structures. A *colored Kripke structure* is a 5-tuple $\langle S, I, R, L, \mathcal{N} \rangle$, where S is a finite set of states, $I \subseteq S$ is a set of initial states, $R \subseteq S \times S$ is a transition relation, $L : S \to \wp(AP)$ is a labeling function indicating which propositions are true in each state, and $\mathcal{N} \subseteq S$ is a set of *normal*, or "green" states. The complement of $\mathcal{N}$ is the set of "red", abnormal or faulty, states. Arcs leading to abnormal states can be thought of as faulty transitions, or simply *faults* (see Fig.1).

Example 1. Consider a memory cell that stores a bit of information and supports reading and writing operations. A state in this system maintains the current value of the memory cell, writing allows one to change this value, and reading returns the stored value. A property that one might associate with this model is that the value read from the cell coincides with that of the last writing performed in the system. Moreover, a potential fault occurs when a cell unexpectedly loses its charge, and its stored value turns into another one. A typical technique to deal with this situation is *redundancy*: use three memory bits instead of one. Writing operations are performed simultaneously on the three bits. Reading, on the other hand, returns the value that is repeated at least twice in the memory bits; this is known as *voting*, and the value read is written back to the three bits.

We take the following approach to model this system: each state is described by variables r and w, which record the value stored in the system (taking *voting* into account) and the last writing operation performed, respectively. First, note that variable w is only used to enable the verification of properties of the model, thus this variable will not be present in any implementation of the memory. The state also maintains the values of the three bits that constitute the system, captured by boolean variables c_0, c_1 and c_2. Part of the specification together with the associated intuition, is shown below:

- $\mathbf{O}(r \leftrightarrow w)$, *the value read from the cell ought to coincide with the last writing performed.*
- $\mathbf{O}((c_0 \wedge c_1 \wedge c_2) \vee (\neg c_0 \wedge \neg c_1 \wedge \neg c_2))$, a safety property of the system: *the three bits should coincide,*

- $\mathsf{AG}(\neg r \leftrightarrow ((\neg c_0 \wedge \neg c_1) \vee (\neg c_0 \wedge \neg c_2) \vee (\neg c_1 \wedge \neg c_2)))$, *the reading of a 0 corresponds to the value read in the majority.*

We also note that we consider variables r, w as the *interface* of our memory cell, that is, the observable information of this specification. In particular, note the deontic formula given above; the first one states that we should read the same value that was written, and the second one says that, when no faults are present, the three bits of the cell coincide, otherwise a fault has occurred.

3   Masking Fault-Tolerance

Intuitively, a system is said to be *masking fault-tolerant* when the faulty behavior is masked in such a way that it cannot be observed by the user. In [6], Gärtner gives a more rigorous definition of masking fault-tolerance: a system is *masking tolerant* when it continues satisfying its specification even under the occurrence of faults. In [4], we propose to capture the notion of masking by means of simulation relations; here we introduce this idea by means of the memory example. Consider the colored Kripke structure in Figure 1 (where red states and arrows

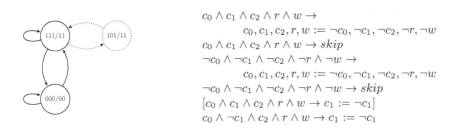

$$c_0 \wedge c_1 \wedge c_2 \wedge r \wedge w \to$$
$$c_0, c_1, c_2, r, w := \neg c_0, \neg c_1, \neg c_2, \neg r, \neg w$$
$$c_0 \wedge c_1 \wedge c_2 \wedge r \wedge w \to skip$$
$$\neg c_0 \wedge \neg c_1 \wedge \neg c_2 \wedge \neg r \wedge \neg w \to$$
$$c_0, c_1, c_2, r, w := \neg c_0, \neg c_1, \neg c_2, \neg r, \neg w$$
$$\neg c_0 \wedge \neg c_1 \wedge \neg c_2 \wedge \neg r \wedge \neg w \to skip$$
$$[c_0 \wedge c_1 \wedge c_2 \wedge r \wedge w \to c_1 := \neg c_1]$$
$$c_0 \wedge \neg c_1 \wedge c_2 \wedge r \wedge w \to c_1 := \neg c_1$$

Fig. 1. Colored Structure and Guarded Program for Memory Cell

are depicted using dotted lines), this structure is a model of the system described in Example 1, where the circle labeled with $111/11$ represents the state where all the bits are on, and r and w are set to *true*, and similarly for the other states. In this example a fault changing one bit is taken into account (the faulty state is drawn using dotted lines). Note that this model can also be described by using a simple guarded language; this is illustrated on the right in the same figure; note that in this case the faulty action is enclosed within brackets. We said that this structure is making fault-tolerant, since the faulty state is masked by the nonfaulty ones. Indeed, taking into account the variables in the interface (r, w in this case), one cannot observe any difference in comparison to the normal behavior of the program (the fault is masked by the redundancy of bits).

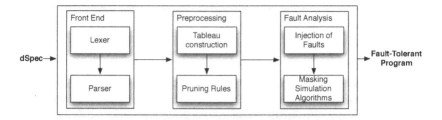

Fig. 2. The Architecture of syntMaskFT

4   The Tool syntMaskFT

The main goal of syntMaskFT is, given a specification, to return the description of a system that masks a maximum number of faults. The description of the system can be given in two ways: a colored Kripke structure, or a simple description using a guarded command language in the style shown in the figure above. To this end, the tool uses a SAT method for dCTL- together with a simulation relation to prune the state space. The architecture of syntMaskFT is illustrated in Figure 2. The input of syntMaskFT is a deontic specification *dSpec*, composed of an *interface*, an *init-spec*, and a *normal-spec*. *interface* is described by a subset of the state variables, which, intuitively, form the visible part of the system; *init-spec* and *normal-spec* are dCTL- formulas, where the former specifies the initial states of the system, and the latter specifies properties that are required to hold in all states that are reachable from the initial states. Initially, syntMaskFT reads a deontic specification *dSpec* as an input file, which is then tokenized (Lexer) and parsed to obtain abstract syntax trees according to the dCTL- expression grammar (Parser). The abstract syntax trees are stored as elements of a set of dCTL- formulas. The preprocessing component constructs an initial tableau T_N for the input *dSpec* based on a dCTL- SAT procedure. Pruning rules are applied to the the tableau T_N in order to remove all nodes that are either propositionally inconsistent, do not have enough successors, or are labeled with a CTL or deontic eventuality formula which is not fulfilled. This process returns as a result *true*, if *dSpec* is satisfiable, or *false*, in the case *dSpec* is unsatisfiable. If *dSpec* is satisfiable, it has a finite model that is embedded in the tableau T_N. Assuming a positive result from the dCTL- decision procedure for *dSpec*, the next step is to perform a fault analysis. In this phase, faults are injected into the tableau in the first place, where faults are understood as (all possible) violations to the deontic obligations imposed in the description of the correct behavior of the system. Subsequently, a masking simulation algorithm (taking into account the input interface) is executed in order to remove those nodes from the tableau that cannot be masked. Finally, the tableau T_F is unravelled into a masking fault-tolerant program implementing *dSpec*.

Table 1. Experimental results

Name	Faults Injected	faults unmasked/removed	Time in sec
Byzantine Agreement	7	4	0.20
Token Ring	220	150	111.85
N-Modular-Redundancy	410	260	535.91
Memory Cell	100	70	10.13

5 Implementation and Evaluation

The syntMaskFT tool is implemented in Java. All experiments have been conducted on a computer with a 2.9 Ghz Intel Core i5 with 4 GB of memory.

We have performed experiments to test the performance of our tool in practice. A well-known case study in the fault-tolerant community is the *Byzantine agreement problem*, formalized in [7]. We have specified this example in dCTL-and synthesized a solution for one general and three lieutenants. Another experiment that we have performed is *N-Modular-Redundancy* (NMR), a form of modular redundancy in which N systems perform a process whose results are processed by a majority-voting system to produce a single output. An NMR system can tolerate up to n module failures, where $n = (N-1)/2$. For this case study, we have evaluated 5-modular-redundancy using our tool. Our third experiment involves an adaptation of a case study from [2], a token ring for solving distributed mutual exclusion, where processes $0 \ldots N$ are organized in a ring with the token being circulated along the ring in a fixed direction. We have synthesized a token ring for four processes and an identical result to that reported in [2]. Finally, our last experiment is the memory cell presented in Example 1. Table 1 summarizes the experimental results on these models, reporting the number of faults injected and removed to achieve masking tolerance, and running times.

syntMaskFT is free software. Documentation and installation instructions can be found at `https://code.google.com/p/synt-mask-ft/`.

References

1. Attie, P.C., Arora, A., Emerson, E.A.: Synthesis of fault-tolerant concurrent programs. ACM Trans. Program. Lang. Syst. 26(1) (2004)
2. Bonakdarpour, B., Kulkarni, S., Abujarad, F.: Symbolic synthesis of masking fault-tolerant distributed programs. Distributed Computing 25(1) (2012)
3. Castro, P.F., Kilmurray, C., Acosta, A., Aguirre, N.: dCTL: A Branching Time Temporal Logic for Fault-Tolerant System Verification. In: Proc. of SEFM (2011)
4. Demasi, R., Castro, P.F., Maibaum, T.S.E., Aguirre, N.: Characterizing Fault-Tolerant Systems by Means of Simulation Relations. In: Proc. of IFM (2013)
5. Demasi, R., Castro, P.F., Maibaum, T.S.E., Aguirre, N.: Synthesizing Fault-Tolerant Systems from Deontic Specifications. In: Proc. of ATVA (2013)
6. Gärtner, F.: Fundamentals of Fault-Tolerant Distributed Computing in Asynchronous Environments. ACM Comput. Surv. 31(1) (1999)
7. Lamport, L., Merz, S.: Specifying and Verifying Fault-Tolerant Systems. In: Proc. of FTRTFT (1994)

νZ - An Optimizing SMT Solver

Nikolaj Bjørner[1], Anh-Dung Phan[2], and Lars Fleckenstein[3]

[1] Microsoft Research, Redmond, WA, USA
[2] DTU Compute, Technical University of Denmark
[3] Microsoft Dynamics, Vedbæk, Denmark
nbjorner@microsoft.com, padu@dtu.dk, LarsFleckenstein@outlook.com

Abstract. νZ is a part of the SMT solver Z3. It allows users to pose and solve optimization problems modulo theories. Many SMT applications use models to provide satisfying assignments, and a growing number of these build on top of Z3 to get *optimal* assignments with respect to objective functions. νZ provides a portfolio of approaches for solving linear optimization problems over SMT formulas, MaxSMT, and their combinations. Objective functions are combined as either Pareto fronts, lexicographically, or each objective is optimized independently. We describe usage scenarios of νZ, outline the tool architecture that allows dispatching problems to special purpose solvers, and examine use cases.

1 An Invitation to νZ

νZ extends the functionality of Z3 [7] to include optimization objectives. It allows users to solve SMT constraints and at the same time formulate optimality criteria for the solutions. It relieves users of Z3 from writing their own loops around the solver to find optimal values. The solver integrates state-of-the-art algorithms for optimization, and it extends some of these algorithms with its own twists: For example, it includes direct support for difference logic solvers, it uses Simplex over non-standard numbers to find unbounded constraints, and it applies an incremental version of the MaxRes [11] algorithm for MaxSAT solving.

To give a first idea, we can ask to optimize the term $x+y$ under the constraints $y < 5 \wedge x < 2$ and $y - x < 1$ using the SMT query to the right. The optimal answer is given as 2 and νZ returns a model where $x = y = 1$. The example shows the `maximize` command that is added to the SMT-LIB [13] syntax.

```
(declare-fun x () Int)
(declare-fun y () Int)
(assert (and (< y 5) (< x 2)))
(assert (< (- y x) 1))
(maximize (+ x y))
(check-sat)
(get-model)
```

1.1 Optimization Commands

The full set of commands νZ adds to SMT-LIB are:

© Springer-Verlag Berlin Heidelberg 2015
C. Baier and C. Tinelli (Eds.): TACAS 2015, LNCS 9035, pp. 194–199, 2015.
DOI: 10.1007/978-3-662-46681-0_14

```
(declare-fun x () Int)              (declare-fun x () Int)
(declare-fun y () Int)              (declare-fun y () Int)
(define-fun a1 () Bool (> x 0))     (assert (= (+ x y) 10))
(define-fun a2 () Bool (< x y))     (assert (>= x 0))
(assert (=> a2 a1))                 (assert (>= y 0))
(assert-soft a2    :dweight 3.1)    (maximize x)
(assert-soft (not a1) :weight 5)    (maximize y)
(check-sat)                         (set-option :opt.priority box)
(get-model)                         (check-sat)
```

Fig. 1. Maximize $3.1 \cdot a2 + 5 \cdot \overline{a1}$. νZ finds a solution where $y \leq x \leq 0$

Fig. 2. νZ produces two independent optima $x = 10$, respectively $y = 10$

- (maximize t) - instruct the solver to maximize t. The type of the term t can be either Integer, Real or Bit-vector.
- (minimize t) - instruct the solver to minimize t.
- (assert-soft F [:weight n | :dweight d] [:id id]) - assert soft constraint F, optionally with an integral weight n or a decimal weight d. If no weight is given, the default weight is 1 (1.0). Decimal and integral weights can be mixed freely. Soft constraints can be furthermore tagged with an optional name id. This enables combining multiple different soft objectives. Fig. 1 illustrates a use with soft constraints.

1.2   Combining Objectives

Multiple objectives can be combined using lexicographic, Pareto fronts or as independent box objectives.

Lexicographic Combinations: By default, νZ maximizes objectives t_1, t_2 subject to the constraint F using a lexicographic combination. It finds a model M, such that M satisfies F and the pair $\langle M(t_1), M(t_2) \rangle$ is lexicographically maximal. In other words, there is no model M' of F, such that either $M'(t_1) > M(t_1)$ or $M'(t_1) = M(t_1)$, $M'(t_2) > M(t_2)$.

Pareto Fronts: Again, given two maximization objectives t_1, t_2, the set of Pareto fronts under F are the set of models $M_1, \ldots, M_i, \ldots, M_j, \ldots$, such that either $M_i(t_1) > M_j(t_1)$ or $M_i(t_2) > M_j(t_2)$, and at the same time either $M_i(t_1) < M_j(t_1)$ or $M_i(t_2) < M_j(t_2)$; and for each M_i, there is no M' that dominates M_i. νZ uses the Guided Improvement Algorithm [14] to produce multiple objectives. Fig. 3 illustrates a use where Pareto combination is specified.

Boxes: Box objectives, illustrated in Fig.2 are used to specify independent optima subject to a formula F. They are used in the Symba tool [9]. The box combination of objectives t_1, t_2 requires up to two models M_1, M_2 of F, such that $M_1(t_1)$ is the maximal value of t_1 and $M_2(t_2)$ is the maximal value for t_2.

1.3   Programming Optimization

The optimization features are available over Z3's programmatic APIs for C, C++, Java, .NET, and Python. There is furthermore a library available as an example that plugs into the Microsoft Solver Foundation (MSF). Fig. 3 shows an example using the Python API to generate Pareto optimal solutions. Fig. 4 shows an OML model used by MSF.

```
x, y = Ints('x y')
opt = Optimize()
opt.set(priority='pareto')
opt.add(x + y == 10, x >= 0, y >= 0)
mx = opt.maximize(x)
my = opt.maximize(y)
while opt.check() == sat:
    print mx.value(), my.value()
```

```
Model[
  Decisions[
    Reals[-Infinity, Infinity], xs, xl],
  Constraints[
    limits -> 0 <= xs & 0 <= xl,
    BoxWood -> xs + 3 * xl <= 200,
    Lathe -> 3 * xs + 2 * xl <= 160],
  Goals[
    Maximize[$ -> 5 * xs + 20 * xl]]]
```

Fig. 3. Pareto optimization in Python.
νZ produces all 11 Pareto fronts.

Fig. 4. OML model used by MSF

1.4   MILP, MaxSAT, CP and SMT

Efficient mixed integer linear solvers are backbones of several highly tuned tools, such as CPLEX and Gurobi, used in operations research contexts. Being able to state and solve optimization objectives in the context of logical constraints has also been well recognized in the SMT community [12,5,15,8] and it is a recurring feature request for Z3 as well. We briefly outline a use case in Section 4, and through this experience we observed a need for more abstract and flexible ways of modeling problems than exposed by OML used by the Microsoft Solver Foundation (MSF), where flexible Boolean combinations of constraints, which empower end-users to refine models, are afterthoughts. By making νZ generally available, we hope to make it easier for existing users to use Z3, for instance [2], and to fuel further applications that benefit from the flexibility and expressive power of Z3's SMT engines, including theory support and quantifiers, with the convenience of built-in support for (reasonably tuned) optimization algorithms. In return, we anticipate that new applications from SMT users can inspire advances in areas such as non-linear arithmetic, mixed symbolic/numerical algorithms, and combinations with Horn clauses.

1.5   Resources

The full source code of νZ is available with Z3 from `http://z3.codeplex.com`, the sources compile on all main platforms, there is an online tutorial on `http://rise4fun.com/z3opt/tutorial/`, and a companion paper [3] describes details of algorithms used in νZ.

2   Architecture

Fig. 5 gives an architectural overview of νZ. The input SMT formulas and objectives are rewritten and simplified using a custom strategy that detects 0-1 integer variables and rewrites these into Pseudo-Boolean Optimization (PBO) constraints. Objective functions over 0-1 variables are rewritten as MaxSAT problems[1]. If there are multiple objectives, then νZ orchestrates calls into the SMT or SAT cores. For box constraints over reals, νZ combines all linear arithmetic objectives and invokes a single instance of the OptSMT engine; for lexicographic combinations of soft constraints, νZ invokes the MaxSAT engine using multiple calls.

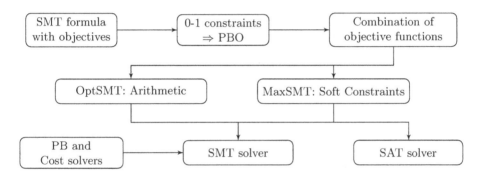

Fig. 5. νZ system architecture

3   Internals

OptSMT: We have augmented Z3's dual Simplex core with a primal phase that finds maximal assignments for reals. It also improves bounds on integers as long as the improvements are integral. It is used, similarly to [15,9], to improve values of objective functions. A similar primal Simplex solver is also accessible to Z3's difference logic engines. νZ discovers unbounded objectives by using non-standard arithmetic: It checks if $t \geq \infty$ is feasible, over the extension field $R \cup \{\epsilon, \infty := 1/\epsilon\}$. This contrasts the approach proposed in [9] that uses a search through hyper-planes extracted from inequalities.

νZ also contains a Pseudo-Boolean theory solver. It borrows from [4,1] for simplification, generating conflict clauses, and incrementally compiling into small sorting circuits. It also adds an option to prune branches using dual simplex.

MaxSMT: νZ implements several engines for MaxSAT. These include WMax [12], MaxRes [11], BCD2 [10], MaxHS [6]. WMax uses a specialized theory solver of *costs*, also explored in [5]. The solver associates penalties with a set of tracked propositional variables. It then monitors the truth assignments to these variables, as given

---

[1] Using the correspondence: *maximize* $c_1 \cdot x_1 + c_2 \cdot x_2 \equiv$ *(assert-soft x_1 :weight c_1)*, *(assert-soft x_2 :weight c_2)*.

by the SAT solver. The cost is incremented when a tracked variable is assigned to *false*. The solver creates a conflict clause when the cost exceeds the current optimal value. WMax can be interrupted at any point with a current upper bound. Our implementation of MaxRes generally performs much better than WMax. MaxRes increments a lower bound when there is an unsatisfiable core of the soft constraints. It then replaces the core $F_1, \ldots, F_k$ with new soft constraints $F_1', F_2', \ldots, F_{k-1}'$ using the equations:

$$F_1' = F_2 \vee F_1, \ F_2' = F_3 \vee (F_1 \wedge F_2), \ \ldots, \ F_{k-1}' = F_k \vee ((F_1 \wedge F_2) \wedge \ldots \wedge F_{k-1}) \ .$$

SAT: νZ reduces Pseudo-Boolean formulas to propositional SAT by converting cardinality constraints using sorting circuits, using a Shannon decomposition (BDDs) of simple PB inequalities and falling back to bit-vector constraints on inequalities where the BDD conversion is too expensive. This transformation is available by ensuring that the option `:opt.enable_sat` is `true`. For benchmarks that can be fully reduced to propositional SAT, MaxRes uses Z3's SAT solver.

4   A Use for νZ

As a driving scenario for νZ we used an experimental warehouse manager in the context of Microsoft Dynamics AX. The objective is to reduce cost by optimizing how shipments are distributed on trucks, reducing the number of trucks, the distance traveled by the truck while maximizing the amount of goods delivered. AX can deliver the standard constraints and cost functions, e.g., weight and volume of a truck, but users often want to be more specific. For example, frozen foods need to be in a cooled truck and cannot be packed together with chemicals. The expressive power and convenience of SMT is useful: these constraints can be formulated as a Boolean combination of linear constraints over 0-1 variables, while the objective functions we considered could be expressed as lexicographic combinations of a couple of cost functions. Such cost functions are expected to evolve when users learn more about their usages. The abstraction layer of the models provides this flexibility.

Table 1. Evaluation of νZ on selected examples

Source	Category	Solved instances	Time
MaxSAT 2014 wpms industrial track	MaxSAT	361/410	0.5-1800s
MaxSAT 2014 pms industrial track	MaxSAT	406/568	0.5-1800s
Longest Paths	MaxSAT	bb 8/8	<0.05s
Longest Paths	MaxSAT	chat 34/34	1-36s
DAL Allocation challenge	PBO	SampleA&B 96/96	0.02-6s
Symba [9]	LRA	2435/2435	0.2s-36s
OptiMathSAT [15]	LRA	9 non-random	0.5-20s

4.1 Experience

We evaluated νZ on a cross-section of benchmarks used in MaxSAT competitions, from Z3 users, and from recent publications. Table 1 summarizes a selected evaluation. Motivating examples from users included strategy scheduling for Vampire (MaxSAT) that are easy with the new MaxSAT engine, but used to be hard for the bisection search used by Vampire. Likewise, Cezary Kaliszyk has used Z3 to tune his portfolio solver using linear arithmetic constraints. His systems are significantly more challenging (take days to run). In this case WMax offers partial solutions during search. Elvira Albert tried using Z3 for finding longest paths, her benchmarks are called bb ($\approx$300 clauses), chat ($\approx$3K clauses) and p2p ($\approx$30K clauses), and we summarize timing for bb and chat below; the p2p category times out.

References

1. Abío, I., Nieuwenhuis, R., Oliveras, A., Carbonell, E.R.: A parametric approach for smaller and better encodings of cardinality constraints. In: CP (2013)
2. Becker, K., Schätz, B., Armbruster, M., Buckl, C.: A formal model for constraint-based deployment calculation and analysis for fault-tolerant systems. In: SEFM, pp. 205–219 (2014)
3. Bjørner, N., Phan, A.-D.: νZ - Maximal Satisfaction with Z3. In: SCSS (2014)
4. Chai, D., Kuehlmann, A.: A fast pseudo-boolean constraint solver. IEEE Trans. on CAD of Integrated Circuits and Systems 24(3), 305–317 (2005)
5. Cimatti, A., Franzén, A., Griggio, A., Sebastiani, R., Stenico, C.: Satisfiability modulo the theory of costs: Foundations and applications. In: TACAS (2010)
6. Davies, J., Bacchus, F.: Postponing optimization to speed up MAXSAT solving. In: CP, pp. 247–262 (2013)
7. de Moura, L.M., Bjørner, N.: Z3: An Efficient SMT Solver. In: TACAS (2008)
8. Larraz, D., Nimkar, K., Oliveras, A., Rodríguez-Carbonell, E., Rubio, A.: Proving Non-termination Using Max-SMT. In: CAV, pp. 779–796 (2014)
9. Li, Y., Albarghouthi, A., Kincaid, Z., Gurfinkel, A., Chechik, M.: Symbolic optimization with SMT solvers. In: POPL, pp. 607–618 (2014)
10. Morgado, A., Heras, F., Marques-Silva, J.: Improvements to Core-Guided Binary Search for MaxSAT. In: SAT, pp. 284–297 (2012)
11. Narodytska, N., Bacchus, F.: Maximum Satisfiability Using Core-Guided MaxSAT Resolution. In: AAAI, pp. 2717–2723 (2014)
12. Nieuwenhuis, R., Oliveras, A.: On SAT Modulo Theories and Optimization Problems. In: SAT, pp. 156–169 (2006)
13. Ranise, S., Tinelli, C.: The SMT Library, SMT-LIB (2006), http://www.SMT-LIB.org
14. Rayside, D., Estler, H.-C., Jackson, D.: The Guided Improvement Algorithm. Technical Report MIT-CSAIL-TR-2009-033. MIT (2009)
15. Sebastiani, R., Tomasi, S.: Optimization in SMT with $\mathcal{LA}(\mathbf{Q})$ Cost Functions. In: IJCAR, pp. 484–498 (2012)

dReach: δ-Reachability Analysis for Hybrid Systems

Soonho Kong, Sicun Gao, Wei Chen, and Edmund Clarke

Computer Science Department, Carnegie Mellon University, USA

Abstract. dReach is a bounded reachability analysis tool for nonlinear hybrid systems. It encodes reachability problems of hybrid systems to first-order formulas over real numbers, which are solved by delta-decision procedures in the SMT solver dReal. In this way, dReach is able to handle a wide range of highly nonlinear hybrid systems. It has scaled well on various realistic models from biomedical and robotics applications.

1 Introduction

dReach is a bounded reachability analysis tool for hybrid systems. It encodes bounded reachability problems of hybrid systems as first-order formulas over the real numbers, and solves them using δ-decision procedures in the SMT solver dReal [12]. dReach is able to handle a wide range of highly nonlinear hybrid systems [16,13,15,3]. Figure 1 highlights some of its features: on the left is an example of some nonlinear dynamics that dReach can handle, and on the right a visualized counterexample generated by dReach on this model.

It is well-known that the standard bounded reachability problems for simple hybrid systems are already highly undecidable [2]. Instead, we work in the framework of δ-reachability of hybrid systems [10]. Here δ is an arbitrary positive rational number, provided by the user to specify the bound on numerical errors that can be tolerated in the analysis. For a hybrid system H and an unsafe region unsafe (both encoded as logic formulas), the δ-reachability problem asks for one of the following answers:

- safe: H cannot reach unsafe.
- δ-unsafe: H^δ can reach unsafe$^\delta$.

Here, H^δ and unsafe$^\delta$ encode (δ-bounded) overapproximations of H and unsafe, defined explicitly as their syntactic variants.It is important to note that the definition makes the answers no weaker than standard reachability: When safe is the answer, we know for certain that H does not reach the unsafe region (no δ is involved); when δ-unsafe is the answer, we know that there exists some δ-bounded perturbation of the system that can render it unsafe. Since δ can be chosen to be very small, δ-unsafe answers in fact discover robustness problem in the system, which should be regarded as unsafe indeed. We have proved that bounded δ-reachabilty is decidable for a wide range of nonlinear hybrid systems, even

© Springer-Verlag Berlin Heidelberg 2015
C. Baier and C. Tinelli (Eds.): TACAS 2015, LNCS 9035, pp. 200–205, 2015.
DOI: 10.1007/978-3-662-46681-0_15

$$\frac{dx}{dt} = \left(\alpha_x \left(k_1 + \frac{(1-k_1)z}{z+k_2} \right) - \beta_x \left(k_3 + \frac{(1-k_3)z}{z+k_4} \right) - m_1 \left(1 - \frac{z}{z_0} \right) \right) x$$

$$\frac{dy}{dt} = m_1 \left(1 - \frac{z}{z_0} \right) x + \left(\alpha_y \left(1 - d \frac{z}{z_0} \right) - \beta_y \right) y$$

$$\frac{dz}{dt} = \frac{z_0 - z}{\tau}$$

$$\frac{dv}{dt} = \left(\alpha_x \left(k_1 + \frac{(1-k_1)z}{z+k_2} \right) - \beta_x \left(k_3 + \frac{(1-k_3)z}{z+k_4} \right) - m_1 \left(1 - \frac{z}{z_0} \right) \right) x$$

$$+ m_1 \left(1 - \frac{z}{z_0} \right) x + \left(\alpha_y \left(1 - d \frac{z}{z_0} \right) - \beta_y \right) y$$

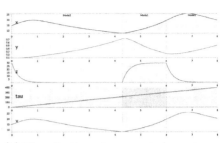

(a) An example of nonlinear hybrid system model: off-treatment mode of the prostate cancer treatment model [16]

(b) Visualization of a generated counterexample. Change in the shade of colors represents discrete mode changes.

Fig. 1. An example of nonlinear dynamics and counterexample-generation

with reasonable complexity bounds [10]. This framework provides the formal correctness guarantees of dReach.

Apart from solving δ-reachability, the following key features of dReach distinguish it from other existing tools in this domain [7,9,1,8,14,5,6].

1. Expressiveness. dReach allows the user to describe hybrid systems using first-order logic formulas over real numbers with a wide range of nonlinear functions. This allows the user to specify the continuous flows using highly nonlinear differential equations, and the jump and reset conditions with complex Boolean combinations of nonlinear constraints. dReach also faithfully translates mode invariants into ∃∀ logic formulas, which can be directly solved under certain restrictions on the invariants.

2. Property-guided search. dReach maintains logical encodings (the same approach as [6]), whose size is linear in the size of the inputs, of the reachable states of a hybrid system [10]. The tool searches for concrete counterexamples to falsify the reachability properties, instead of overapproximating the full reachable states. This avoids the usual state explosion problem in reachable set computation, because the full set of states does not need to be explicitly stored. This change is analogous to the difference between SAT-based model checking and BDD-based symbolic model checking.

3. Tight integration of symbolic reasoning and numerical solving. dReach delegates the reasoning on discrete mode changes to SAT solvers, and uses numerical constraint solving to handle nonlinear dynamics. As a result, it can combine the full power of both symbolic reasoning and numerical analysis algorithms. In particular, all existing tools for reachable set computation can be easily plugged-in as engines for solving the continuous part of the dynamics, while logic reasoning tools can overcome the difficulty in handling complex mode transitions.

The paper is structured as follows. We describe the system architecture in Section 2, and give some details about the logical encoding in the tool in Section 3. We then explain the input format and usage in Section 4.

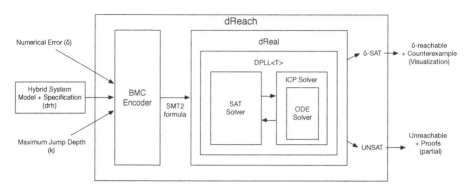

Fig. 2. Architecture of dReach: It consists of an bounded model-checking module and an SMT solver, dReal. In the first phase, the Encoder module translates an input hybrid system into a logic formula. In the second phase, an SMT solver, dReal, solves the encoded δ-reachability problem using a solving framework that combines DPLL(T), Interval Constraint Propagation, and reliable (interval-based) numerical integration.

2   System Description

The system architecture of dReach is given in Figure 2. We ask the user to provide the following input file and two parameters:

- The input file specifies the hybrid system, the reachability properties in question, and some time bounds on the continuous flow in each mode. The grammar is described in Section 4.1.
- A bound on the number of mode changes.
- A numerical error bound δ.

From these inputs, dReach generates a logical encoding that involves existential quantification and universal quantification on the time variables. The logical encoding is compact, always linear in the size of the inputs. The tool then makes iterative calls to the underlying solver dReal [12] to decide the reachability properties. When the answer is δ-reachable, dReach generates a counterexample and its visualization. When the answer is unreachable, no numerical error is involved and a (partial, for now) logical proof of unsatisfiability can be provided [11].

3   Logical Encoding of Reachability

The details of our encoding scheme is given in [10]. Here we focus on explaining how differential equations and the universal quantifications generated by mode invariants are encoded, as an extension of the SMT-LIB [4] standard. Although such formulas are automatically generated by dReach from the hybrid system descrpition, the explanation below can be helpful for understanding the inner mechanism of our solver.

Encoding Integrations. In each mode of a hybrid system, we need to specify continuous flows defined by systems of ordinary differential equations. We extend SMT-LIB with a command `define-ode` to define such systems. For instance, we use `define-ode` as follows to assign a name $flow_1$ to a group of ODE, $\frac{dx}{dt} = v$ and $\frac{dv}{dt} = -x^2$.

```
(define-ode flow1 ((= d/dt[x] v) (= d/dt[v] (- 0 (^ x 2)))))
```

We then allow integration terms in the formula. We view the solution of system of differential equations as a constraint between the initial-state variables, time duration, and the end-state variables. We can then write

```
(= [x_t_1 ... x_t_n] (integral 0 t [x_0_1 ... x_0_n] flow_i)),
```

to represent $x = x_0 + \int_0^t flow_i(x(s))ds$. Note that we do not need to explicitly mention $x(s)$ as a function in the encoding, which can be inferred by the solver.

Universal Quantification for Mode Invariant Constraints. To encode mode invariants in hybrid systems, we need $\exists\forall^t$-formulas [13] which is a restricted form of $\exists\forall$ formula where the universal quantifications are limited to the time variables. In drh, we introduce a new keyword `forall_t` to encode $\exists\forall^t$ formulas. Given a time bound $[0, time_i]$, mode invariant f at mode n is encoded into (`forall_t n [0 time_i] f`).

4 Using dReach

4.1 Input Format

The input format for describing hybrid systems and reachability properties consists of five sections: macro definitions, variable declarations, mode definitions, and initial condition, and goals. We focus on intuitive explanations here. Figure 3 shows how to describe a small example hybrid system, an inelastic bouncing ball with air resistance.

- In macro definitions, we allows users to define macros in C preprocessor style which can be used in the following sections. Macro expansions occur before the other parts are processed.
- A variable declaration specifies a real variable and its domain in a real interval. dReach requires special declaration for *time* variable, to specify the upperbound of time duration.
- A mode definition consists of mode id, mode invariant, flow, and jump. *id* is a unique positive interger assigned to a mode. An invariant is a conjuction of logic formulae which must always hold in a mode. A flow describes the continuous dynamics of a mode by providing a set of ODEs. The first formula of *jump* is interpreted as a guard, a logic formula specifying a condition to make a transition. Note that this allows a transition but does not force it. The second argument of *jump*, n denotes the target mode-id. The last one is *reset*, a logic formula connecting the old and new values for the transition.

```
1    #define D 0.45
2    #define K 0.9
3    [0, 15] x; [9.8] g; [-18, 18] v; [0, 3] time;
4    {    mode 1;
5         invt: (v <= 0);   (x >= 0);
6         flow: d/dt[x] = v; d/dt[v] = -g - (D * v ^ 2);
7         jump: (x = 0) ==> @2 (and (x' = x) (v' = - K * v)); }
8    {    mode 2;
9         invt: (v >= 0);   (x >= 0);
10        flow: d/dt[x] = v; d/dt[v] = -g + (D * v ^ 2);
11        jump: (v = 0) ==> @1 (and (x' = x) (v' = v)); }
12   init: @1 (and (x >= 5) (v = 0));
13   goal: @1 (and (x >= 0.45));
```

Fig. 3. An example of drh format: Inelastic bouncing ball with air resistance. Lines 1 and 2 define a drag coefficient $D = 0.45$ and an elastic coefficient $K = 0.9$. Line 3 declares variables x, g, v, and *time*. At lines 4 - 7 and 8 - 11, we define two modes – the falling and the bouncing-back modes respectively. At line 12, we specify the hybrid system to start at mode 1 (@1) with initial condition satisfying $x \geq 5 \wedge v = 0$. At line 13, it asks whether we can have a trajectory ending at mode 1 (@1) while the height of the ball is higher than 0.45.

- *initial-condition* specifies the initial mode of a hybrid system and its initial configuration. *goal* shares the same syntactic structure of *initial-condition*.

4.2   Command Line Options

dReach follows the standard unix command-line usage:

dReach <options> <drh file>

It has the following options:

- If -k <N> is used, set the unrolling bound k as N (Default: 3). It also provides -u <N> and -l <N> options to specify upper- and lower-bounds of unrolling bound.
- If --precision <p> is used, use precision p (Default: 0.001).
- If --visualize is set, dReach generates extra visualization data.

We have a web-based visualization toolkit[1] which processes the generated visualization data and shows the counterexample trajectory. It provides a way to navigate and zoom-in/out trajectories which helps understand and debug the target hybrid system better.

---

[1] The detailed instructions are available at https://github.com/dreal/dreal/blob/master/doc/ode-visualization.md

References

1. Althoff, M., Krogh, B.H.: Reachability analysis of nonlinear differential-algebraic systems. IEEE Trans. Automat. Contr. 59(2), 371–383 (2014)
2. Alur, R., Courcoubetis, C., Henzinger, T.A., Ho, P.-H.: Hybrid automata: An algorithmic approach to the specification and verification of hybrid systems. In: Grossman, R.L., Ravn, A.P., Rischel, H., Nerode, A. (eds.) HS 1991 and HS 1992. LNCS, vol. 736, pp. 209–229. Springer, Heidelberg (1993)
3. Asad, H.U., Jones, K.D., Surre, F.: Verifying robust frequency domain properties of non linear oscillators using SMT. In: 17th International Symposium on Design and Diagnostics of Electronic Circuits Systems, pp. 306–309 (April 2014)
4. Barrett, C., Stump, A., Tinelli, C.: The SMT-LIB Standard: Version 2.0. In: Gupta, A., Kroening, D. (eds.) Proceedings of the 8th International Workshop on Satisfiability Modulo Theories, Edinburgh, UK (2010)
5. Chen, X., Ábrahám, E., Sankaranarayanan, S.: Taylor model flowpipe construction for non-linear hybrid systems. In: RTSS, pp. 183–192 (2012)
6. Cimatti, A., Mover, S., Tonetta, S.: Smt-based verification of hybrid systems. In: Proceedings of the Twenty-Sixth AAAI Conference on Artificial Intelligence, Toronto, Ontario, Canada, July 22-26 (2012)
7. Fränzle, M., Teige, T., Eggers, A.: Engineering constraint solvers for automatic analysis of probabilistic hybrid automata. J. Log. Algebr. Program. 79(7), 436–466 (2010)
8. Frehse, G.: PHAVer: Algorithmic verification of hybrid systems past hyTech. In: Morari, M., Thiele, L. (eds.) HSCC 2005. LNCS, vol. 3414, pp. 258–273. Springer, Heidelberg (2005)
9. Frehse, G., Le Guernic, C., Donzé, A., Cotton, S., Ray, R., Lebeltel, O., Ripado, R., Girard, A., Dang, T., Maler, O.: SpaceEx: Scalable verification of hybrid systems. In: Gopalakrishnan, G., Qadeer, S. (eds.) CAV 2011. LNCS, vol. 6806, pp. 379–395. Springer, Heidelberg (2011)
10. Gao, S., Kong, S., Chen, W., Clarke, E.M.: Delta-complete analysis for bounded reachability of hybrid systems. CoRR, abs/1404.7171 (2014)
11. Gao, S., Kong, S., Clarke, E.: Proof generation from delta-decisions. In: SYNASC (2014)
12. Gao, S., Kong, S., Clarke, E.M.: dReal: An SMT solver for nonlinear theories over the reals. In: CADE, pp. 208–214 (2013)
13. Gao, S., Kong, S., Clarke, E.M.: Satisfiability modulo ODEs. In: FMCAD, pp. 105–112 (2013)
14. Herde, C., Eggers, A., Fränzle, M., Teige, T.: Analysis of hybrid systems using hysat. In: ICONS, pp. 196–201 (2008)
15. Kapinski, J., Deshmukh, J.V., Sankaranarayanan, S., Arechiga, N.: Simulation-guided lyapunov analysis for hybrid dynamical systems. In: HSCC 2014, Berlin, Germany, April 15-17, pp. 133–142 (2014)
16. Liu, B., Kong, S., Gao, S., Zuliani, P., Clarke, E.: Parameter identification using delta-decisions for biological hybrid systems. In: CMSB (2014)

Uppaal Stratego[*]

Alexandre David, Peter Gjøl Jensen, Kim Guldstrand Larsen,
Marius Mikučionis, and Jakob Haahr Taankvist

Department of Computer Science, Aalborg University,
Selma Lagerlöfs Vej 300, 9220 Aalborg Øst, Denmark

Abstract. Uppaal Stratego is a novel tool which facilitates generation, optimization, comparison as well as consequence and performance exploration of strategies for stochastic priced timed games in a user-friendly
manner. The tool allows for efficient and flexible "strategy-space" exploration before adaptation in a final implementation by maintaining strategies as first class objects in the model-checking query language. The paper
describes the strategies and their properties, construction and transformation algorithms and a typical tool usage scenario.

1 Introduction

Model checking may be used to verify that a proposed controller prevents an
environment from causing dangerous situations while, at the same time, operating in a desirable manner. This approach has been successfully pursued in the
setting of systems modeled as finite-state automata, timed automata, and probabilistic automata of various types with nuSMV [7], FDR [11], Uppaal [3] and
PRISM [13] as prime examples of model checking tools supporting the above
mentioned formalisms. Most recently the simulation-based method of *statistical*
model checking has been introduced in Uppaal SMC [4], allowing for highly
scaleable analysis of *fully* stochastic Sriced Timed Automata with respect to a
wide range of performance properties. For instance, expected waiting-time and
cost, and time-bounded and cost reachability probabilities, may be estimated
(and tested) with an arbitrary precision and high degree of confidence. Combined with the symbolic model checking of Uppaal this enables an adequate
analysis of mixed critical systems, where certain (safety) properties must hold
with absolute certainty, whereas for other quantitative (performance) properties
a reasonably good estimation may suffice, see e.g. [10].

Rather than verifying a *proposed* controller, synthesis – when possible – allows
an algorithmic construction of a controller which is guaranteed to ensure that the
resulting systems will satisfy the desired correctness properties. The extension
of controller synthesis to timed and hybrid games started in the 90s with the
seminal work of Pnueli et al. [1,14] on controller synthesis for timed games where

---

[*] The research has received funding from the European FET projects SENSATION
and CASSTING, the ARTEMIS project MBAT as well as the Sino-Danish Basic
Research Center IDEA4CPS.

© Springer-Verlag Berlin Heidelberg 2015
C. Baier and C. Tinelli (Eds.): TACAS 2015, LNCS 9035, pp. 206–211, 2015.
DOI: 10.1007/978-3-662-46681-0_16

the synthesis problem was proven decidable by a symbolic dynamic programming technique. In UPPAAL TIGA [2,5] an efficient on-the-fly algorithm for synthesis of reachability and safety objectives for timed games has been implemented, with a number of successful industrial applications having been made including zone-based climate control for pig-stables [12] and controllers for hydraulic pumps with 60% improvement in energy-consumption compared with industrial practice at the time [6,15].

However, once a strategy has been synthesized for a given objective no further analysis has been supported so far. In particular it has not been possible to make a deeper examination of a synthesized strategy in terms of other additional properties that may or may not hold under the strategy. Neither has it been possible to optimize a synthesized non-deterministic safety strategy with respect to desired performance measures. Both of these issues have been addressed by the authors in recent work [8,9], and in this paper we present the tool UPPAAL STRATEGO which combines these techniques to generate, optimize, compare and explore consequences and performance of strategies synthesized for stochastic priced timed games in a user-friendly manner. In particular, the tool allows for efficient and flexible "strategy-space" exploration before adaptation in a final implementation.

UPPAAL STRATEGO[1] integrates UPPAAL and the two branches UPPAAL SMC [4] (statistical model checking), UPPAAL TIGA [2] (synthesis for timed games) and the method proposed in [9] (synthesis of near optimal schedulers) into one tool suite. UPPAAL STRATEGO comes with an extended query language where strategies are first class objects that may be constructed, compared, optimized and used when performing (statistical) model checking of a game under the constraints of a given synthesized strategy.

Consider the jobshop scheduling problem shown in Fig. 1 which models a number of persons sharing a newspaper. Each task process reads a section of the paper, whereas only one person can read a particular section at a time. Each reader wants to read the newspaper in different orders, and the stochastic environment chooses how long it takes to read each section. This makes the problem a problem of finding a strategy, rather than finding a static scheduler as in the classical jobshop scheduling problem.

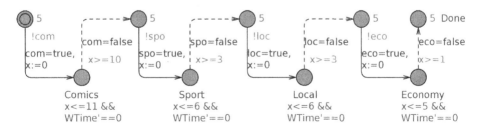

Fig. 1. UPPAAL STRATEGO template of a single person reading a newspaper

---

[1] UPPAAL STRATEGO is available at http://people.cs.aau.dk/~marius/stratego/

Figure 1 shows a stochastic priced timed game (SPTG) which models one person reading the newspaper. The circles are locations and the arrows are transitions. The solid arrows are transitions controlled by the controller and the dashed are transitions controlled by the stochastic environment. The model reflects the reading of the four sections in the preferred order (here comics, sport, local and economy) for the preferred amount of time. In the top locations the person is waiting for the next section to become available; here four Boolean variables are used to ensure mutex on the reading of a section. In the bottom locations, the person is reading the particular section for a duration given by a uniform distribution on the given interval, e.g. [10,11] for our person's reading of sport. The stopwatch WTime is only running in the waiting locations thus effectively measuring the accumulated time when the person is waiting to read. Given a complete model with several persons constantly competing for the sections, we are interested in synthesizing strategies for several multi-objectives, e.g. synthesize a strategy ensuring that all persons have completed reading within 100 minutes, and then minimize the expected waiting time for our preferred person.

2   Games, Automata and Properties

Using the features of UPPAAL STRATEGO we can analyze the SPTG in Fig. 1. Internally, UPPAAL STRATEGO has different models and representations of strategies, an overview of these and their relations are given in Fig. 2. The model seen in Fig. 1 is a SPTG, as WTime is a cost function or price with location dependent rate (here 0 or 1), and we assume that environment takes transitions according to a uniform distribution over time.

As shown in Fig. 2 we can abstract a SPTG into a timed game (TGA). This abstraction is obtained simply by ignoring the prices and stochasticity in the model. Note that since prices are observers, this abstraction does not affect the possible behavior of the model, but merely forgets the likelihood and cost of various behaviors. The abstraction maps a $1^1/_2$-player game, where the opponent is stochastic into a 2-player game with an antagonistic opponent.

Given a TGA ($\mathcal{G}$) we can use UPPAAL TIGA to synthesize a strategy σ (either deterministic or non-deterministic). This strategy can, when put in parallel with the TGA, $\mathcal{G}|\sigma$, be model-checked in the same way as usual in UPPAAL. We

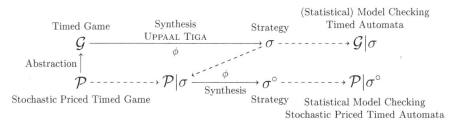

Fig. 2. Overview of models and their relations. The lines show different actions. The dashed lines show that we use the object.

can also use the strategy in a SPTG $\mathcal{P}$, and obtain $\mathcal{P}|\sigma$. Under a strategy it is possible to do statistical model checking (estimation of probability and cost, and comparison), which enables us to observe the behavior and performance of the strategy when we assume that the environment is purely stochastic. This also allows us to use to use prices under σ, even though they were not considered in the synthesis of σ. From both $\mathcal{P}$ and $\mathcal{P}|\sigma$ learning is possible using the method proposed in [9]. The learning algorithm uses a simulation based method for learning near-optimal strategies for a given price metric. If σ is the most permissive strategy guaranteeing some goal, then the learning algorithm can optimize under this strategy, and we will get a strategy σ° which is near-optimal but still has the guarantees of σ. As the last step we can construct $\mathcal{P}|\sigma^\circ$, which we can then do statistical model checking on.

3 Strategies

In UPPAAL STRATEGO we operate three different kinds of strategies, all memoryless. *Non-deterministic strategies* are strategies which give a *set* of actions in each state, with the most permissive strategy – when it exists – offering the largest set of choices. In the case of timed games, most permissive strategies exist for safety and time-bounded reachability objectives. *Deterministic strategies* give *one* action in each state. *Stochastic strategies* give a *distribution* over the set of actions in each state. Fig. 3 shows how strategies are generated and used. For generating strategies, we can use UPPAAL TIGA or the method proposed in [9] on SPTGs. UPPAAL TIGA generates (most permissive) *non-deterministic* or *deterministic* strategies. The method proposed in [9] generates strategies which are deterministic. A strategy generated with UPPAAL STRATEGO can undergo different investigations: model checking, statistical model checking and learning. Learning consume non-deterministic strategies (potentially multiple actions per state) and may produce a deterministic one by selecting a single action for each state, such that the final deterministic strategy is optimized towards some goal. Figure 3 shows that currently it is possible to model check only under symbolically synthesized strategies (as opposed to optimized ones) as symbolic model checking requires the strategy to be represented entirely in terms of zones (constraint systems over clock values and their differences). Statistical model checking can only be done under stochastic strategies. All deterministic strategies can be thought of as stochastic by assigning a probability of 1 to the *one* choice.

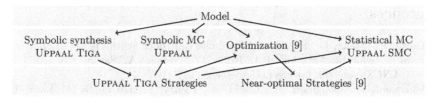

Fig. 3. Overview of algorithms and data structures in UPPAAL STRATEGO

To evaluate non-deterministic strategies statistically we applying a stochastic uniform distribution over the non-deterministic choices.

4   Query Language

We let strategies become first class citizens by introducing strategy assignment **strategy S =** and strategy usage **under S** where **S** is an identifier. These are applied to the queries already used in UPPAAL, UPPAAL TIGA and UPPAAL SMC as well as those proposed in [9]. An overview of these queries is given in Table 1. Notice that we changed the syntax of the queries presented in [9]. Recall the example with the four authors sharing a newspaper as presented in Fig. 1. We compute a strategy for Kim to reach his plane within one hour on line 1 in Fig. 4. Respecting this, we find that Marius cannot join, as the query on line 2 is not satisfied. Instead, we optimize that Peter joins in on line 3 ([<=60] is a bound on how long the simulations we learn from used can be). Finally, line 4 estimates that Jakob is done with probability ≥0.9 under Peter's optimizations.

Table 1. Types of queries

UPPAAL	Safety	`A[] prop under NS`
	Liveness	`A<> prop under NS`
TIGA	Guarantee objective	`strategy NS = control: A<> prop`
	Guarantee objective	`strategy NS = control: A[] prop`
SMC	Evaluation	`Pr[bound](<> prop) under SS`
	Expected	`value E[bound;int](min: prop) under SS`
	Simulations	`simulate int [bound]{expr1,expr2} under SS`
[9]	Minimize objective	`strategy DS = minE (expr) [bound]: <> prop under NS`
	Maximize objective	`strategy DS = maxE (expr) [bound]: <> prop under NS`

```
strategy Travel = control: A<> Kim.Done && time <= 60
E<> Marius.Done && time <= 60 under Travel
strategy PeterTravel = minE (time) [<=60] : <>Peter.Done under Travel
Pr[<=60] (<> Jakob.Done) under PeterTravel                      ≥ 0.901855
```

Fig. 4. UPPAAL STRATEGO queries and results for the model in Fig. 1

References

1. Asarin, E., Maler, O., Pnueli, A.: Symbolic controller synthesis for discrete and timed systems. In: Antsaklis, P.J., Kohn, W., Nerode, A., Sastry, S.S. (eds.) HS 1994. LNCS, vol. 999, Springer, Heidelberg (1995)
2. Behrmann, G., Cougnard, A., David, A., Fleury, E., Larsen, K.G., Lime, D.: UPPAAL-tiga: Time for playing games! In: Damm, W., Hermanns, H. (eds.) CAV 2007. LNCS, vol. 4590, pp. 121–125. Springer, Heidelberg (2007)

3. Behrmann, G., David, A., Larsen, K.G., Håkansson, J., Pettersson, P., Yi, W., Hendriks, M.: Uppaal 4.0. In: Proceedings of the 3rd International Conference on the Quantitative Evaluation of Systems, QEST 2006, IEEE Computer Society, Washington, DC (2006)

4. Bulychev, P.E., David, A., Larsen, K.G., Mikučionis, M., Poulsen, D.B., Legay, A., Wang, Z.: UPPAAL-SMC: statistical model checking for priced timed automata. In: Proceedings 10th Workshop on Quantitative Aspects of Programming Languages and Systems, QAPL 2012, Tallinn, Estonia. EPTCS, vol. 85 (March 2012)

5. Cassez, F., David, A., Fleury, E., Larsen, K.G., Lime, D.: Efficient on-the-fly algorithms for the analysis of timed games. In: Abadi, M., de Alfaro, L. (eds.) CONCUR 2005. LNCS, vol. 3653, pp. 66–80. Springer, Heidelberg (2005)

6. Cassez, F., Jessen, J.J., Larsen, K.G., Raskin, J.-F., Reynier, P.-A.: Automatic synthesis of robust and optimal controllers – an industrial case study. In: Majumdar, R., Tabuada, P. (eds.) HSCC 2009. LNCS, vol. 5469, pp. 90–104. Springer, Heidelberg (2009)

7. Cimatti, A., Clarke, E., Giunchiglia, E., Giunchiglia, F., Pistore, M., Roveri, M., Sebastiani, R., Tacchella, A.: NuSMV 2: An openSource tool for symbolic model checking. In: Brinksma, E., Larsen, K.G. (eds.) CAV 2002. LNCS, vol. 2404, p. 359. Springer, Heidelberg (2002)

8. David, A., Fang, H., Larsen, K.G., Zhang, Z.: Verification and performance evaluation of timed game strategies. In: Legay, A., Bozga, M. (eds.) FORMATS 2014. LNCS, vol. 8711, pp. 100–114. Springer, Heidelberg (2014)

9. David, A., Jensen, P.G., Larsen, K.G., Legay, A., Lime, D., Sørensen, M.G., Taankvist, J.H.: On time with minimal expected cost! In: Cassez, F., Raskin, J.-F. (eds.) ATVA 2014. LNCS, vol. 8837, pp. 129–145. Springer, Heidelberg (2014)

10. David, A., Larsen, K.G., Legay, A., Mikučionis, M.: Schedulability of herschelplanck revisited using statistical model checking. In: Margaria, T., Steffen, B. (eds.) ISoLA 2012, Part II. LNCS, vol. 7610, pp. 293–307. Springer, Heidelberg (2012)

11. Gibson-Robinson, T., Armstrong, P., Boulgakov, A., Roscoe, A.W.: FDR3 — A modern refinement checker for CSP. In: Ábrahám, E., Havelund, K. (eds.) TACAS 2014 (ETAPS). LNCS, vol. 8413, pp. 187–201. Springer, Heidelberg (2014)

12. Jessen, J.J., Rasmussen, J.I., Larsen, K.G., David, A.: Guided controller synthesis for climate controller using UPPAAL TIGA. In: Raskin, J.-F., Thiagarajan, P.S. (eds.) FORMATS 2007. LNCS, vol. 4763, pp. 227–240. Springer, Heidelberg (2007)

13. Kwiatkowska, M., Norman, G., Parker, D.: PRISM 4.0: Verification of probabilistic real-time systems. In: Gopalakrishnan, G., Qadeer, S. (eds.) CAV 2011. LNCS, vol. 6806, pp. 585–591. Springer, Heidelberg (2011)

14. Maler, O., Pnueli, A., Sifakis, J.: On the synthesis of discrete controllers for timed systems. In: Mayr, E.W., Puech, C. (eds.) STACS 1995. LNCS, vol. 900, Springer, Heidelberg (1995)

15. Zhao, H., Zhan, N., Kapur, D., Larsen, K.G.: A "hybrid" approach for synthesizing optimal controllers of hybrid systems: A case study of the oil pump industrial example (2012)

BINSEC: Binary Code Analysis
with Low-Level Regions*

Adel Djoudi and Sébastien Bardin

CEA, LIST, Gif-sur-Yvette, F-91191, France
first.name@cea.fr

Abstract. This article presents the open source BINSEC platform for (formal) binary-level code analysis. The platform is based on an extension of the DBA Intermediate Representation, and it is composed of three main modules: a front-end including several syntactic disassembly algorithms and heavy simplification of the resulting IR, a simulator supporting the recent low-level region-based memory model, and a generic static analysis module.

1 Introduction

Binary-level program analysis has gained interest in these last years in order to address the problems of analyzing closed-source software or mobile code (including malware) and detecting compiler-induced bugs. Not requiring source code makes such analysis widely applicable.

The goal of BINSEC is to ease the development of binary code analyzers by providing an open formal model for binary programs and an open-source platform allowing to share front-ends and ISA support. Like other platforms such as BAP [7], GDSL [12], Jakstab [11] or OSMOSE [3,4], our platform disassembles binary code and translates the resulting machine instructions into an intermediate language, which is then analyzed. The main novelties of BINSEC are the following:

- an extended Intermediate Representation (IR) providing abstraction and specification mechanisms (Section 2), contrary to the very operational nature of previous proposals [5,7,9,13];
- a low-level region-based semantics [2], allowing both an abstract view of the memory and the ability to simulate correctly many native codes (Section 3.3);
- a simplification engine able to remove a large part of flag operations (Section 3.2).

BINSEC is open-source (lgpl), it is written in OCaml and it is available at
http://sebastien.bardin.free.fr/binsec/.

2 Intermediate Representation: Extended DBA

DBA Model. Dynamic Bit-vector Automata (DBA) [5] have been proposed as a generic and concise formal model for low-level programs. They offer the following advantages:

---

* Work partially funded by French ANR (project BINSEC, grant ANR-12-INSE-0002).

© Springer-Verlag Berlin Heidelberg 2015
C. Baier and C. Tinelli (Eds.): TACAS 2015, LNCS 9035, pp. 212–217, 2015.
DOI: 10.1007/978-3-662-46681-0_17

(1) an architecture-independent formalism, (2) a very concise set of instructions and operators, and (3) a simple semantics, without any implicit side-effect. They have been used for modeling PowerPC and a few other architectures in previous binary-level analyzers [3,4,6]. Note that floating-point arithmetic, multi-thread and self-modification are currently outside of the scope of DBA.

The key ingredients of the formalism are the following: a DBA program manipulates a finite set of global variables ranging over bitvectors (registers) and an array of bitvectors of size 8 (memory); all bitvector sizes are statically known; a single machine instruction is decoded into a *block* of DBA instructions - including intermediate computations and temporary variables.

Extended DBA Model. While DBA have shown to be useful in the analysis of safety-critical systems [1], they lack abstraction and specification mechanisms in order to handle binary-level analysis over large non-critical codes [1]. We propose the following improvements:

- more abstract operations (`malloc`, `nondet`) together with basic specification mechanisms (`assume`, `assert`), see Figure 1;
- a more abstract low-level region-based semantics [2], representing memory as a dynamic collection of disjoint arrays (`constant`, `stack`, `malloc(id)`) while being able to simulate precisely many low-level programs, see Section 4;
- access permissions for `read`, `write` and `execute` operations; permissions are defined on *region zones*, i.e. region partitions defined by (user-given) predicates;
- tags on instructions and variables for embedding useful information available at decoding, such as `<tmp>` or `<flag>` for variables and `<call>` or `<ret>` for jumps.

Instructions	Expressions
- lhs := rhs, goto addr	- e{i .. j}, $\text{ext}_{u,s}$(e,n), e :: e
- goto addr < call, ret, none >	- @(expr, $\overrightarrow{k}$), @(expr, $\overleftarrow{k}$)
- goto expr < call, ret, none >	- e $\{+,-,\times,/_{u,s},\%_{u,s}\}$ e
- ite(cond)? goto addr : goto addr'	- e $\{<_{u,s},\leq_{u,s},=,\neq,\geq_{u,s},>_{u,s}\}$ e
- lhs := malloc(size), goto addr	- e $\{\wedge,\vee,\oplus,<<,>>_{u,s}\}$ e, !e
- free(expr), goto addr	
- lhs := nondet(size), goto addr	
- assert(cond), goto addr	
- assume(cond), goto addr	
- stop < ok, ko, none >	

Fig. 1. Extended DBA instructions

3   Platform Overview

BINSEC is designed around three basic services, depicted in Figure 2: (1) a front-end translating executable codes into DBA programs (loading, decoding, syntactic disassembly, support of DBA stubs) and simplifying them; (2) a simulator for extended DBA, supporting three different memory models (flat, standard regions [8], low-level regions [2]); and finally (3) a generic static analysis engine (in progress) allowing safe CFG recovery.

---

[1] This drawback is common to other formal IRs such as REIL [9], RREIL [13] and BAP [7].

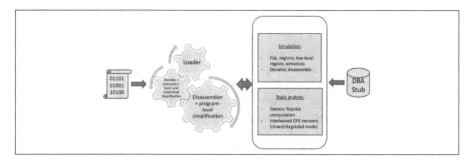

Fig. 2. BINSEC platform

3.1   Front-End

Loading and Decoding. The main service here is a decoding function taking a (virtual) address and returning a block of DBA instructions simulating the semantics of the corresponding machine code instruction. The platform currently supports the ELF format (a PE loader is in progress) and a decoder for x86-32 is provided. The following features are supported: all prefixes but wait and lock, all basic instructions (380 instr.) and all mmx instructions not involving floating-point registers (100 instr.).

Disassembly. The goal of disassembly is to give the semantics of the whole executable file. This is a very hard problem because of dynamic jumps [6,10,11]. We provide implementations of the most common solutions: (1) recursive disassembly, with the possibility to specify some jump targets; (2) linear sweep disassembly (typically used by objdump) with instruction-wise or byte-wise granularity, the later allowing to disassemble overlapping instructions; (3) a combination of recursive and linear sweep disassembly, mimicking the approach of IDA pro; and finally (4) a combination of recursive disassembly with dynamic execution, where jump targets are discovered through simulation.

Formal Stubs. A formal stub is a block of DBA instructions that will be inserted at some address of the retrieved program, either in place of the result of the decoder (@replace) or in combination with it (@insert). This feature is useful either when the corresponding code is not available (analysis of object files rather than executable files), or for abstracting parts of the code (typically, library functions). A stub for libc/malloc function is described in Figure 3.

```
@replace : 0xb7fff414 {
      tmp<32> := nondet (32);                          // abstracting a failure condition, typically out of memory
      if (tmp = 0<32>) goto l1 else goto l2 ;
  l1 : eax<32> := 0<32>;   goto l3 ;                    // failure, result is NULL
  l2 : eax<32> := malloc (@[esp + 4<32>,<−,4]);         // DBA malloc, with size read on stack
      assume ((eax modu 4<32>) = 0<32>);               // alignment constraint
  l3 : esp<32> := esp + 4<32>;                          // stack cleanup
      goto @[esp − 4<32>,<−,4];                         // jump to return address (call-site) retrieved from the stack
}
```

Fig. 3. A stub for libc/malloc

3.2 Simplifications

Simplifications discard unused DBA instructions, typically those instructions modeling flag updates. The goal is to help later analyzes, either automatic or human-based. We essentially try to simplify temporary variables and flag variables, identified through DBA tags. We rely on rewriting rules (instruction-wise), constant propagation and elimination of temporary variables (block-wise), and liveness analysis for flag elimination (inter-block). The method removes up to 75% of flag operations (cf. Section 4).

3.3 Memory Model and Simulation

Memory Models. We provide a partitioned memory model in the vein of CompCert [8], with values of the form (r, val) where r is a region symbol - the base, and val is a bitvector - the offset (Cst being a special region symbol acting as 0). This modeling is very adapted for managing dynamically allocated memory and allows robust formal analyzes thanks to implicit partitioning of memory. However, most operations are illegal with pure regions [8], e.g. $(r_1, v_1) - (r_2, v_2)$ is undefined when $r_1 \neq r_2$ and $r_2 \neq Cst$. Unfortunately, undefined patterns are found in common libc programs, such as memmove or memcopy, and, even worst, they can also be introduced at compile-time. For instance, an instruction x = if (!x) then 1 else 0; can be compiled as follows (assuming x is stored in eax):

```
neg eax            // eax := -eax.  CF := 0 if source operand (eax) is 0; otherwise CF := 1
sbb eax, eax       // eax := eax - (eax + CF) = -CF
inc eax            // eax := eax + 1 = -CF + 1
```

The compiler performs here an optimization called *branchless conditional* in order to optimize instruction pipelining. In a region-based model, the result of the first neg instruction is undefined when the input is a pointer value, i.e. $r \neq Cst$. Low-level region-based models [2] have been introduced recently to address this issue by allowing some reasoning over region symbols.

Simulation. We provide simulation and random testing modes supporting all features of extended DBA. Three different memory models can be selected: (a) flat model (memory as a single array), (b) standard region-based model and (c) low-level region-based model. Interestingly, all models are implemented in a unified way, pure regions and flat model being viewed as restrictions of low-level regions.

3.4 Static Analysis Interface

We provide a generic fixpoint computation for abstract domains given as lattices, allowing one to quickly prototype binary-level analyzers. The current implementation offers the following advantages: (1) tight interleaving of syntactic disassembly with value analysis [6,11], allowing sound resolution of indirect jumps; (2) the possibility to restrict a priori the set of possible jump targets (closed mode) by providing a finite set of acceptable targets; (3) a degraded mode, in the vein of [10], where the analyzer switches to an unsound analysis whenever a jump or a memory operation cannot be resolved precisely enough. The interface is currently limited to non-relational abstract domains. We plan to extend it quickly to relational domains and to provide implementations of the most common domains.

4 Experiments

We evaluate our implementation on two main criteria: the impact of low-level regions and the effectiveness of our simplifications. Simplifications are performed over standard Unix programs, while experiments on low-level regions are carried upon a collection of small- to medium-size procedures (up to 5,000 machine instructions) from libc and the VeriSec benchmark[2]. All experiments are performed on an Intel Core i5 3.20Ghz.

Benefits of Simplifications. Results are presented in Table 1 and summarized in Table 2. Simplifications allow a global reduction of instructions of 24%, and (most important) flag assignments are reduced by about 73%, which is interesting because these operations are complex to handle in analyzers. Simplified DBA programs are in average 2.5x larger than native codes (3.3x larger without simplifications)[3]. This is pretty close to the minimal ratio between DBA and machine code, since an inter-block goto is added to each DBA block.

Table 1. Evaluating DBA optimization

program	native	DBA		simplified DBA		
	loc	loc	† ko	loc	time	red
bash	166K	558K	5	402K	10.65m	27.95%
cat	7303	23K	0	18K	16.62s	20.55%
echo	3345	10K	0	8181	6.39s	22.38%
less	23K	80K	5	56K	89.31s	29.03%
ls	18K	63K	6	45K	83.42s	27.38%
mkdir	7329	24K	5	18K	23.65s	27.08%
netstat	16K	50K	3	41K	68.48s	17.43%
ps	11125	36K	0	28K	47.90s	21.38%
pwd	3581	11K	0	8942	9.77s	21.47%
rm	9186	30K	16	23K	31.13s	22.52%
sed	9993	32K	0	24K	37.50s	24.24%
tar	64K	212K	7	159K	5.2m	25.26%
touch	7944	26K	0	19K	30.02s	25.75%
uname	3271	10K	0	8131	8.89s	21.68%

† ko: # unsupported instructions

Table 2. Average reductions

DBA vs asm (no simpl)		3.3x
reduction	dba instr	24.00%
	tmp assign	21.89%
	flag assign	73.17%
DBA vs asm (simpl)		2.5x

DBA vs asm: ratio between # DBA instructions and # machine instructions

Benefits of Low-level Regions. We compare both memory models on their ability to provide defined concrete semantics on the benchmark programs. These programs contain some patterns that illustrate illegal operations in standard region-based model. Results are summarized in Table 3, where we also provide time information w.r.t. the flat memory model. The standard region-based model succeeds in only 1/20 example, while low-level regions succeed in 20/20 examples. It seems that low-level regions are absolutely necessary in order to give a (useful) non-flat semantics to binary programs.

---

[2] Available at https://se.cs.toronto.edu/index.php/Verisec_Suite

[3] Simon *et al.* report a 7x size increase for GDSL/RREIL, and a 3.5x size increase after simplifications [12].

Table 3. Simulation with three different memory models

program	standard regions	low-level regions	flat
aligned_calloc	x	✓ 4.73s	0.0003s
llpointer_arithmetic	x	✓ 3.51s	0.01s
malloc	x	✓ 0.62s	0.008s
memcpy	x	✓ 0.001s	0.003
memmove	x	✓ 0.49s	0.01s
mmap	x	✓ 0.03s	0.02s
neg_sbb_inc	x	✓ 2.81s	2.82s
pointer_arithmetic	x	✓ 0.02s	0.02s
pointer_logical	x	✓ 0.12s	0.001
pointer_or_int	x	✓ 0.07s	0.0006s
success	0/10	10/10	10/10

program	standard regions	low-level regions	flat
test_or_pointer	1.08s	✓ 1.09s	1.09s
loops	x	✓ 1.006s	1.07s
full	x	✓ 5.76s	5.73s
istrstr	x	✓ 5.54s	5.77s
istrstr_loops	x	✓ 5.40s	5.61s
istrstr2_loops	x	✓ 5.27s	5.64s
parse_config	x	✓ 3.83s	4.12s
guard_random_index	x	✓ 0.14s	0.13
guard_strstr	x	✓ 5.53s	5.53s
guard_strchr	x	✓ 2.98s	3.02s
success	1/10	10/10	10/10

5 Future Work

We plan to extend very quickly our framework with more decoders (`PowerPC`, `ARM`) and loaders (`PE`). We also plan to extend the static analysis interface and add basic facilities for symbolic execution, taking low-level memory regions into account.

References

1. Bardin, S., Baufreton, P., Cornuet, N., Herrmann, P., Labbé, S.: Binary-level Testing of Embedded Programs. In: QSIC 2013. IEEE, Los Alamitos (2013)
2. Besson, F., Blazy, S., Wilke, P.: A Precise and Abstract Memory Model for C Using Symbolic Values. In: Garrigue, J. (ed.) APLAS 2014. LNCS, vol. 8858, pp. 449–468. Springer, Heidelberg (2014)
3. Bardin, S., Herrmann, P.: Structural Testing of Executables. In: ICST 2008. IEEE, Los Alamitos (2013)
4. Bardin, S., Herrmann, P.: OSMOSE: Automatic Structural Testing of Executables. Softw. Test., Verif. Reliab. 21(1), 29–54 (2011)
5. Bardin, S., Herrmann, P., Leroux, J., Ly, O., Tabary, R., Vincent, A.: The BINCOA Framework for Binary Code Analysis. In: Gopalakrishnan, G., Qadeer, S. (eds.) CAV 2011. LNCS, vol. 6806, pp. 165–170. Springer, Heidelberg (2011)
6. Bardin, S., Herrmann, P., Védrine, F.: Refinement-Based CFG Reconstruction from Unstructured Programs. In: Jhala, R., Schmidt, D. (eds.) VMCAI 2011. LNCS, vol. 6538, pp. 54–69. Springer, Heidelberg (2011)
7. Brumley, D., Jager, I., Avgerinos, T., Schwartz, E.J.: BAP: A Binary Analysis Platform. In: Gopalakrishnan, G., Qadeer, S. (eds.) CAV 2011. LNCS, vol. 6806, pp. 463–469. Springer, Heidelberg (2011)
8. Leroy, X., Appel, A.W., Blazy, S., Stewart, G.: The CompCert memory model. In: Program Logics for Certified Compilers. Cambridge University Press (2014)
9. Dullien, T., Porst, S.: REIL: A platform-independent intermediate representation of disassembled code for static code analysis. In: CanSecWest 2009 (2009)
10. Kinder, J., Kravchenko, D.: Alternating Control Flow Reconstruction. In: Kuncak, V., Rybalchenko, A. (eds.) VMCAI 2012. LNCS, vol. 7148, pp. 267–282. Springer, Heidelberg (2012)
11. Kinder, J., Veith, H.: Jakstab: A static analysis platform for binaries. In: Gupta, A., Malik, S. (eds.) CAV 2008. LNCS, vol. 5123, pp. 423–427. Springer, Heidelberg (2008)
12. Simon, A., Kranz, J.: The GDSL toolkit: Generating Frontends for the Analysis of Machine Code. In: PPREW 2014. ACM, New York (2014)
13. Sepp, A., Mihaila, B., Simon, A.: Precise Static Analysis of Binaries by Extracting Relational Information. In: WCRE 2011, IEEE, Los Alamitos (2011)

Insight: An Open Binary Analysis Framework

Emmanuel Fleury[1], Olivier Ly[1], Gérald Point[2], and Aymeric Vincent[3]

LaBRI, UMR 5800, Talence, France
[1]Université de Bordeaux, Talence, France
[2]CNRS, Talence, France
[3]INP Bordeaux Aquitaine, Talence, France
{emmanuel.fleury,olivier.ly,gerald.point,aymeric.vincent}@labri.fr

Abstract. We present INSIGHT, a framework for binary program analysis and two tools provided with it: CFGRECOVERY and iii.

INSIGHT is intended to be a full environment for analyzing, interacting and verifying executable programs. INSIGHT is able to translate x86, x86-64 and msp430 binary code to our intermediate representation and execute it symbolically in an abstract domain where each variable (register, memory cell) is substituted by a formula representing all its possible values along the current execution path.

CFGRECOVERY aims at automatically rebuilding the program control flow based only on the executable file. It heavily relies on SMT solvers.

iii provides an interactive and a (Python) programmable interface to a coherent set of features from the INSIGHT framework. It behaves like a debugger except that the execution traces that are examined are symbolic and cover a collection of possible concrete executions at once. For example, iii allows to perform an interactive reconstruction of the CFG.

Keywords: binary analysis, CFG recovery, symbolic debugging.

1 Introduction

Nowadays, finding complex bugs automatically has become fruitful and useful. Yet, most of software analysis techniques rely on the fact that a complete blueprint of the program is available (full specifications, formal design documents, source code) at a level of abstraction suitable for analysis.

A recent interest has been shown in analyzing executable programs with no prior knowledge of their internals [11,2,4]. These efforts have been essentially pushed forward by the need to get some trust on external binary-only software, or analyzing potentially malicious software.

But, one of the main problems of binary analysis is to rebuild a correct control flow graph of the program which can be made difficult to recover because of data-entanglement, self-modifying code, or other binary specific effects (intentional or not) linked to this specific format. It is needed because most, if not all, the analysis techniques require the control flow graph to operate, which means that the recovery of the control flow comes before any other usual analysis. Moreover,

© Springer-Verlag Berlin Heidelberg 2015
C. Baier and C. Tinelli (Eds.): TACAS 2015, LNCS 9035, pp. 218–224, 2015.
DOI: 10.1007/978-3-662-46681-0_18

depending on the completeness and the accuracy of the recovery, the analysis may succeed or fail. Thus, in order to leverage existing techniques on higher-level code, the first step will be to recover the control flow as accurately as possible.

A few pioneers of binary analysis already made advances on recovery techniques [7,12]. But, recent works [11,2,4] led to new approaches for both recovery and/or analysis on binary programs and the design of new tools: McVeto [14], CodeSurfer/x86 [1], OSMOSE [4], Jakstab [10], or frameworks: BitBlaze [13], BAP [6], Otawa [3]. Yet, few of these tools are actually open platforms which could be used by the community to ease the cumbersome steps of working on binary programs for new researchers in this field.

INSIGHT is a framework, including a library and tools, aiming to provide an environment to perform binary analysis for verification purposes. Yet, even if our first intent was binary verification, one may use the framework for other goals such as program control flow extraction, reverse engineering, decompilation, ... As a first step, we built a complete chain of modules that can be used to extract concrete or symbolic traces of the binary program in a simulated environment, translate it into our intermediate representation and perform analyses on it.

These modules have been combined into two tools that are now part of the framework: CFGRECOVERY, an automated tool to recover the control flow of the binary program and the INSIGHT Interactive Inspector (iii), an interactive tool working as a debugger to execute and interact with both the original binary program and its intermediate representation.

INSIGHT was started during the BINCOA ANR-funded project [5]. The framework is not currently focused on performance, and on small programs of a few kilobytes, a couple of minutes of computation on an Intel Core i5 laptop are to be expected to recover the control flow graph using Mathsat [8] as the SMT solver. Starting stepping through a program of any size under iii is immediate. INSIGHT, CFGRECOVERY and iii are freely available with an open source 2-clause BSD license (visit http://insight.labri.fr).

In the following we first present the library, then the tools, and we conclude with future research directions.

2   The Insight Library

The INSIGHT library gathers all the functions, data structures and algorithms that allow to build tools for binary analysis. It includes primitives to handle our intermediate representation, which is called the *microcode*, the functions used to extract and translate the original assembly into microcode and a way to execute it within a simulated environment on a given abstract domain.

2.1   Insight's Microcode

Binary instructions are translated into an architecture-independent representation called *microcode*. Fig. 1 gives an example of *microcode*. The *microcode* is an

oriented graph whose nodes are labelled with addresses (*e.g.* [0x0,0]) and edges
with a guard (≪...≫) and an instruction (*e.g.* an assignment var:=expr).

The addresses which label nodes are composed of two parts: a global address
which corresponds to the address as seen by the binary program, and a local
sub-address which allows to translate one assembly instruction into a sub-graph.
The guards are formulae with a boolean value, and the edge can exist in the
semantics of the microcode in a given context only if the guard evaluates to true
in that context.

There are three types of instructions: a **skip** instruction which does
nothing but go to its successor (*e.g.*
at [0x1,0] a conditional jump); all
static jumps are implemented with
a skip instruction. An **assignment**
which assigns the value of an expression to a l-value (*e.g.* eax is assigned to at [0x5,0]). And, a **dynamic jump** which has no successor in the graph but provides an expression determining the global address where execution should continue (*eg.* at [0x3,0] a jump to the
value of eax).

Expressions can use a variety of
bitvector operators (addition, bits
extraction, ...), and base operands
are made of constants, variables,
and memory references. Every sub-

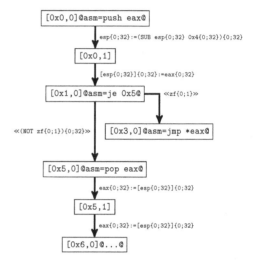

Fig. 1. Microcode example (from x86 asm)

expression includes the possibility of extracting a bitvector. This way, sub-
bitvectors of variables and memory references constitute acceptable l-values and
are legitimate expressions.

2.2   Microcode Providers and Handling

One of the very appealing features of INSIGHT is its ability to load a binary
program and translate it into microcode. This feature is provided thanks to
GNU's libbfd which allows to open almost any executable container format (*e.g.*
ELF, PE-COFF). Translation from binary assembly instructions into microcode
is provided by INSIGHT itself, but uses the GNU libopcodes as a first step.
This translation is currently implemented almost fully for 32-bit x86, 64-bit x86
and 16-bit MSP430. Yet, it is important to notice that only integer datatypes
are supported (no floating point, SIMD, ...) as is the case of the other binary
analysis software that we know of.

A handful of classes are used to represent a microcode program. In order to
ease creation of microcode and thus the writing of decoders, a very simple API is
provided to add microcode instructions to a program. Furthermore, a very useful

feature is the ability to annotate almost any object of microcode. For example, a microcode node corresponding to a given address can be annotated by the textual representation of the assembly instruction at that address; dynamic jumps can be annotated by their potential targets; and so on. This gives a homogeneous place for analyses to store their results and helps provide the end-user with information related to a given microcode part.

2.3   Simulation on Domains

Mainly, two domains are provided: a "*concrete*" domain which allows computations of a single value per l-value and provides the usual operations on bitvectors. And, a "*symbolic*" domain which represents sets of values thanks to assertions constraining variables and memory elements. Two additional toy domains are also provided: the "*sets*" domain which uses sets of concrete values to represent possible values, and the "*intervals*" domain which uses a pair of integers to represent an interval of concrete values.

The simulation on the symbolic domain is the one we massively rely on for recovering the control flow of the program. Indeed, we use symbolic execution to collect program traces and build a microcode program from it. This technique has already been used for many other purposes like automatic software testing [4] or processor microcode verification [9].

More precisely, *symbolic execution* is performed by the simulation engine that will execute every step of the program assuming symbolic values for inputs rather than concrete ones. Our symbolic domain is the set of all the (quantifier free) bitvector arithmetic formulae, which allows to represent exactly the semantics of assembly instructions.

3   CFGRecovery

CFGRECOVERY is a tool dedicated to the recovery of the control flow of an executable program in the most accurate way, only based on the binary form of the program. Several classical disassembly strategies may be chosen (*linear sweep*, *recursive traversal*). But, our main disassembly method is to use an underapproximation strategy using *symbolic execution* in order to avoid spurious execution traces and to output a possibly incomplete but trusted control flow graph. A very simple example is given in Fig. 2, it shows the disassembly of code with instruction overlapping obfuscation using `objdump` on the left, and with CFGRECOVERY on the right. Note that CFGRECOVERY is accurate.

4   Insight's Interactive Inspector (iii)

INSIGHT's interactive inspector (iii) is a cross-debugger using an abstract domain to represent memory and register values. The iii tool is a Python interpreter enriched with INSIGHT library features. As for CFGRECOVERY, it can

```
instruction_overlapping-i386: file format elf32-i386
Disassembly of section .text:

08048098 <_start>:
 8048098:  b8 00 03 c1 bb    mov    $0xbbc10300,%eax
 804809d:  b9 00 00 00 05    mov    $0x5000000,%ecx
 80480a2:  01 c8             add    %ecx,%eax
 80480a4:  eb f4             jmp    804809a <_start+0x2>
 80480a6:  01 d8             add    %ebx,%eax
 80480a8:  bb 00 00 00 00    mov    $0x0,%ebx
 80480ad:  b8 01 00 00 00    mov    $0x1,%eax
 80480b2:  cd 80             int    $0x80
```

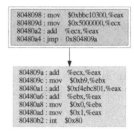

1a. objdump (linear sweep) disassembly.   1b. CFGRECOVERY disassembly.

Fig. 2. Example of code disassembled by objdump (1a) and CFGRECOVERY (1b)

load binary executable files and simulate them over any domain supported by the framework.

The basic principle of operation of iii is that a microcode program is continuously maintained in memory and is enriched by explicit loading of microcode, or by exploring a binary executable using symbolic execution. At each step, an edge of the microcode is followed, and any location which is encountered and not yet part of the microcode will be added to it.

Many usual debugger commands are available in iii, possibly adapted to its specificities. For example, the step() function follows the microcode edges associated with a full assembly instruction, but also the microstep() function follows just one edge of the microcode. Another example is the cont() function which will continue until one of the usual conditions occurs (breakpoint or "end of program") or when non-determinism is encountered, in which case the user is asked to select which edge to follow.

It is also possible to load microcode stubs at any address in the code prior to reaching that address. We usually use stubs to replace a call to an external procedure by a simplified model of it. These stubs can be loaded at a given address and "folded" into this global address by letting the stub loader replace all other global addresses by local addresses. This allows to preserve global address space whose usage is dictated by the binary program.

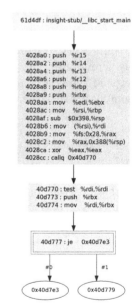

Fig. 3. iii CFG exploration

At any moment, the (symbolic) content of memory and registers can be displayed similarly to what can be done in a debugger. The current microcode can also be displayed graphically with the current microcode node in the simulation trace highlighted, and hotkeys allow to call functions like step() to extend the trace from within the graph. See Fig. 3.

5   Future Directions

INSIGHT has now reached a level of achievement that allows to extract a coherent microcode model from possibly complex software and interact with it. Many new ideas can be explored with the framework and we hope the community will take advantage of this massive open source code base. We intend to further research on topics such as self-modifying code, loop summarization, and verification. Also practical usage of the framework for reverse engineering purposes is a promising lead.

Acknowledgments. We would like to thank all the contributors, and especially R. Tabary for his work on INSIGHT and also for the `crackme` example used in the demo.

References

1. Balakrishnan, G., Gruian, R., Reps, T., Teitelbaum, T.: CodeSurfer/x86—A platform for analyzing x86 executables. In: Bodik, R. (ed.) CC 2005. LNCS, vol. 3443, pp. 250–254. Springer, Heidelberg (2005)
2. Balakrishnan, G., Reps, T.: WYSINWYX: What You See Is Not What You eXecute. Journal of ACM Transactions on Programming Languages and Systems (TOPLAS) 32 (2010)
3. Ballabriga, C., Cassé, H., Rochange, C., Sainrat, P.: OTAWA: An open toolbox for adaptive WCET analysis. In: Min, S.L., Pettit, R., Puschner, P., Ungerer, T. (eds.) SEUS 2010. LNCS, vol. 6399, pp. 35–46. Springer, Heidelberg (2010)
4. Bardin, S., Herrmann, P.: OSMOSE: automatic structural testing of executables. Software Testing, Verification and Reliability 21(1), 29–54 (2011)
5. Bardin, S., Herrmann, P., Leroux, J., Ly, O., Tabary, R., Vincent, A.: The BINCOA framework for binary code analysis. In: Gopalakrishnan, G., Qadeer, S. (eds.) CAV 2011. LNCS, vol. 6806, pp. 165–170. Springer, Heidelberg (2011)
6. Brumley, D., Jager, I., Avgerinos, T., Schwartz, E.J.: BAP: A binary analysis platform. In: Gopalakrishnan, G., Qadeer, S. (eds.) CAV 2011. LNCS, vol. 6806, pp. 463–469. Springer, Heidelberg (2011)
7. Cifuentes, C.: Reverse Compilation Techniques. Ph.D. thesis, Queensland University of Technology, Department of Computer Science (1994)
8. Cimatti, A., Griggio, A., Schaafsma, B.J., Sebastiani, R.: The mathSAT5 SMT solver. In: Piterman, N., Smolka, S.A. (eds.) TACAS 2013 (ETAPS 2013). LNCS, vol. 7795, pp. 93–107. Springer, Heidelberg (2013)
9. Franzn, A., Cimatti, A., Nadel, A., Sebastiani, R., Shalev, J.: Applying SMT in symbolic execution of microcode. In: Proc. of Int. Conf. on Formal Methods in Computer-Aided Design (FMCAD 2010), pp. 121–128. IEEE (2010)
10. Kinder, J., Veith, H.: Jakstab: A static analysis platform for binaries. In: Gupta, A., Malik, S. (eds.) CAV 2008. LNCS, vol. 5123, pp. 423–427. Springer, Heidelberg (2008)
11. Kinder, J., Zuleger, F., Veith, H.: An abstract interpretation-based framework for control flow reconstruction from binaries. In: Jones, N.D., Müller-Olm, M. (eds.) VMCAI 2009. LNCS, vol. 5403, pp. 214–228. Springer, Heidelberg (2009)

12. Mycroft, A.: Type-based decompilation (or program reconstruction via type reconstruction). In: Swierstra, S.D. (ed.) ESOP 1999. LNCS, vol. 1576, pp. 208–223. Springer, Heidelberg (1999)
13. Song, D., Brumley, D., Yin, H., Caballero, J., Jager, I., Zhenkai, K.M.G.a.L., James, N., Pongsin, P., Prateek, S.: BitBlaze: A new approach to computer security via binary analysis. In: Proc. of Int. Conf. on Information Systems Security (ICISS). LNCS, pp. 1–25. Springer, Heidelberg (2008)
14. Thakur, A., Lim, J., Lal, A., Burton, A., Driscoll, E., Elder, M., Andersen, T., Reps, T.: Directed proof generation for machine code. In: Touili, T., Cook, B., Jackson, P. (eds.) CAV 2010. LNCS, vol. 6174, pp. 288–305. Springer, Heidelberg (2010)

SAM: The Static Analysis Module of the MAVERIC Mobile App Security Verification Platform

Alessandro Armando[1,2], Gianluca Bocci[3], Giantonio Chiarelli[3], Gabriele Costa[1], Gabriele De Maglie[1], Rocco Mammoliti[3], and Alessio Merlo[1]

[1] DIBRIS, University of Genova, Italy
name.surname@unige.it
[2] Bruno Kessler Foundation, Trento, Italy
armando@fbk.eu
[3] Poste Italiane, Roma, Italy
{boccigi2,chiare96,mammoliti.rocco}@posteitaliane.it

Abstract. The tremendous success of the mobile application paradigm is due to the ease with which new applications are uploaded by developers, distributed through the application markets (e.g. Google Play), and finally installed by the users. Yet, the very same model is causing serious security concerns, since users have no or little means to ascertain the trustworthiness of the applications they install on their devices. To protect their customers, Poste Italiane has defined the Mobile Application Verification Cluster (MAVERIC), a process for the systematic security analysis of third-party mobile apps that leverage the online services provided by the company (e.g. home banking, parcel tracking). We present SAM, a toolkit that supports this process by automating a number of operations including reverse engineering, privilege analysis, and automatic verification of security properties. We introduce the functionalities of SAM through a demonstration of the platform applied to real Android applications.

1 Introduction

Mobile devices are becoming the main access point for many security-critical online services (e.g., e-Banking). Handling valuable resources and data, they are appealing targets for security attacks. In this context, mobile applications represent a major threat. Smartphones retrieve and install software packages from unknown, possibly malicious sources. However, most of the modern mobile operating systems try to regulate the software distribution, therefore mitigating the associated risk, by means of trusted repositories, called application stores, e.g., Google Play and Apple Store. Major service providers, including Poste Italiane, participate in this ecosystem both *directly*, i.e., by publishing their Apps, and *indirectly*, i.e., through third-party apps that access web services offered by Poste Italiane. The ability to tell apart benign applications from malicious or flawed ones is therefore a primary goal for Poste Italiane. In fact,

© Springer-Verlag Berlin Heidelberg 2015
C. Baier and C. Tinelli (Eds.): TACAS 2015, LNCS 9035, pp. 225–230, 2015.
DOI: 10.1007/978-3-662-46681-0_19

the latter malicious or flawed application run on the customer's mobile devices may severely affect the security of the transactions as well as the privacy of the customer. To tackle the challenge Poste Italiane is developing the *Mobile Application Verification Cluster* (MAVERIC), a unified verification framework that provides automated support to a number of key activities ranging from mobile app verification to legal analysis. Security experts at the Poste Italiane Computer Emergency Response Team (CERT) are already using MAVERIC to systematically assess the security of the Poste Italiane mobile apps ecosystem.

In this paper we introduce the *Static Analysis Module* (SAM), a core component of the MAVERIC architecture. SAM integrates some state-of-the-art static analysis techniques for mobile application packages (APKs) and produces a detailed security assessment report containing statistics, properties of the analyzed application, and a number of additional artefacts.

The paper is structured as follows. Section 2 presents the architecture of the SAM, Section 3 describes the components of the module and Section 4 provides a brief overview of the MAVERIC web application. Finally, Section 5 concludes the paper.

2   MAVERIC and SAM

Static software analysis is a complex and multifaceted task. In most cases, static analysis methods have a precise scope. For instance, *malware detection* [6] aims at discovering whether an application carries malicious code. Instead, *code review* [7] applies to software sources for finding flaws in implementations. As they target different aspects and resources, the available static analysis techniques are often complementary and can be combined to extend their potential to new emerging scenarios. SAM integrates different static analysis approaches to support the automatic assessment of Android applications.

The architecture of MAVERIC is depicted in Fig. 1. MAVERIC leverages AppVet [9] to orchestrate a number of fully automated security analysis techniques. AppVet is open-source web service developed by NIST that supports the integration of mobile application analysis tools. It must be noted that AppVet supports basic logging and data management functionalities, but it does not include any analysis component. MAVERIC extends AppVet with several new modules and tools. Among them, SAM implements a set of components supporting the systematic security assessment of Android applications. In the near future, MAVERIC will be extended with further modules targeting other aspects of the security analysis of mobile applications such as the dynamic and legal analyses. Below, we briefly introduce the SAM sub-modules and their role.

Reverse Engineering. It gets the APK file containing the Android app and retrieves general information about the APK and its content (i.e., developer, version, release date, etc.). Moreover, it rebuilds the source code and computes metrics and statistics on it.

Permission Checking. It infers permission requests and usage from both the manifest file and the application code.

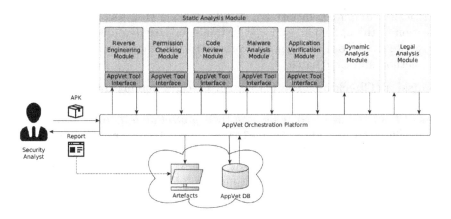

Fig. 1. Architecture of the MAVERIC platform

Code Review. It verifies whether the APK code contains some common vulnerabilities by comparing it with a list of known ones.

Malware Analysis. It processes the APK looking for malware components and known, malicious patterns.

Application Verification. It checks whether the APK complies with a security policy (specified by the analyst).

The results of the analysis are provided back to the analysts in the form of artefacts (e.g. analysis reports). In the next section, we detail the SAM submodules and we report their development status.

3   Static Analysis Techniques

In this section we present the techniques supported by SAM.

Reverse Engineering. The reverse engineering module relies on few tools for APK inspection and Java bytecode decompilation. Used software include Androguard (https://code.google.com/p/androguard/), APKTool (https://code.google.com/p/android-apktool/), DEX2JAR (https://code.google.com/p/dex2jar/) and CFR (http://www.benf.org/other/cfr/). This module recreates the resources that the developer used to build the APK. They include source code, configuration files and other resources (multimedia contents, binary data, etc.).

The extracted code is processed for finding whether the application uses *native libraries*, *dynamic class loading* or *code reflection*. Although not always dangerous, these features might cause a security breach. For instance, native code can evade VM security checks (as it is directly executed by the OS).

For each class file, the reverse engineering module returns the size in KB, the number of methods and fields. Also, it assigns an obfuscation score $o \in [0, 1]$

heuristically computed. Intuitively, o indicates the ease to perform a manual inspection of the app code, e.g., $o = 1$ stands for heavily obfuscated code. The heuristic function considers syntactic properties like length and variation of variable, method and class names.

Permission Checking. The permission checking module retrieves and processes the sets of permissions *requested* (R) and *used* (U) by the APK. The elements of R and U are listed along with their *protection level* (obtained from the API specification, see http://developer.android.com/training/articles/security-tips.html). The protection level ranges over {*SignatureOrSystem*, *System*, *Dangerous*, *Normal*}. Typically, higher values, e.g., *SignatureOrSystem*, denote permissions needed to access valuable resources or critical functionalities.

The module also computes the relation between U and R. Ideally, applications should statically declare exactly all the permissions they need at runtime, i.e., $U = R$. Instead, if $R \setminus U \neq \emptyset$ some permissions are requested but not used. This means that the application is somehow over-privileged. Although not necessarily dangerous, this case is in contrast with the *least privilege* principle [5]. Finally, if $U \setminus R \neq \emptyset$ some permissions used by the code are not declared. This condition can lead to runtime issues. As a matter of fact, when an unprivileged piece of code attempts an access, a security error is fired. The application carrying these instructions[1], is terminated with a security exception. Although the permissions could be obtained dynamically, e.g., granted by a another app, the application is behaving differently from what is declared in its manifest.

Malware Analysis. Malware detection has a long standing tradition and several approaches exist. A common technique is the *signature-based detection*, consisting in a comparison between application fingerprints against large databases of known malware [8]. Other methods include analysis of program semantics [3] and runtime behavioural checking [10]. These techniques consider different perspectives and can be applied to a single APK for obtaining a multi-dimensional malware profile. The malware analysis module can interact with third-party online malware detection services to do this. For instance, *VirusTotal* (https://www.virustotal.com/) is a state-of-the-art web application orchestrating several malware analysis tools and listing their output. Other, similar services are *NVISO ApkScan* (http://apkscan.nviso.be/) and *MARBLE Scan* (http://www.marblesecurity.com/).

Application Verification. The application verification module exploits *model checking* [4] to verify that an APK complies with a policy defined as a temporal property. The module proceeds by extracting a model of the app and verifying whether it satisfies the policy or not. Models are generated by extracting control flow graphs and by translating them into labeled transition systems. Policies are specified through a specification language called ConSpec [1], i.e., a policy language already exploited in both verification and monitoring frameworks. ConSpec uses a Java-like syntax for defining an abstract security controller.

---

[1] Notice that if such code is unreachable, the application includes unneeded elements which is often suspect.

The controller consists of a sequence of event-guarded rules. When one of the events takes place, the controller changes its state (defined through a set of variables) according to a statement associated to the rule. Model checking is carried out by SPIN (`http://spinroot.com/`), a state-of-the-art model checker. A similar application verification approach was used in [2] where a prototype implementation analysed hundreds of Android applications against a BYOD policy of the US Government.

Secure Code Review. Code review aims at discovering known vulnerabilities and dangerous code patterns. A source of such patterns is provided by the *OWASP top ten* (available at `https://www.owasp.org/`). Although some of the reported vulnerabilities cannot be detected by only considering a mobile application, e.g., *M1: Weak Server Side Controls*, part of them are localized in the APK code. For instance, *M2: Insecure Data Storage* describes how certain APIs can be misused by applications storing critical data in the file system. The dangerous behaviour can be encoded and verified with techniques analogous to those used for application verification (see above). For the time being, four of the OWASP top ten vulnerabilities have been encoded in ConSpec and are checked against the target applications.

4 MAVERIC Web Application

The MAVERIC platform is available at `https://130.251.1.32:80/maveric`. Anonymous users can log in through the credentials `username: guest` and `password: guest`. After user authentication, the application shows the main screen as depicted in Figure 2.

Fig. 2. The main screen of the MAVERIC web application

From the main screen, users can read the existing reports (accessible from the right panel after selecting an entry from the list). Moreover, users can submit new APKs for the analysis. After submitting a new app, the web application displays the progress of the analyses. When one of the sub-modules terminates, its report is accessible through the *Result* link next to the module name.

5 Conclusion

This paper presented SAM, the static analysis module of the MAVERIC platform. SAM provides security analysts with several functionalities for the security assessment of mobile applications. We described each of the components participating in the module and showed how they contribute to the integrated analysis process. Although it is still under development, SAM can be already applied to the security analysis of mobile code.

References

1. Aktug, I., Naliuka, K.: ConSpec – A formal language for policy specification. Science of Computer Programming 74(1-2), 2–12 (2008) Special Issue on Security and Trust
2. Armando, A., Costa, G., Merlo, A., Verderame, L.: Enabling BYOD Through Secure Meta-market. In: Proceedings of the 2014 ACM Conference on Security and Privacy in Wireless & Mobile Networks, WiSec 2014, pp. 219–230. ACM, New York (2014)
3. Christodorescu, M., Jha, S., Seshia, S.A., Song, D., Bryant, R.E.: Semantics-Aware Malware Detection. In: Proceedings of the 2005 IEEE Symposium on Security and Privacy, SP 2005, pp. 32–46. IEEE Computer Society, Washington, DC (2005)
4. Clarke, E.M., Emerson, E.A., Sistla, A.P.: Automatic verification of finite-state concurrent systems using temporal logic specifications. ACM Trans. Program. Lang. Syst. 8(2), 244–263 (1986)
5. Denning, P.J.: Fault tolerant operating systems. ACM Comput. Surv. 8(4), 359–389 (1976)
6. Idika, M.: A Survey of Malware Detection Techniques. Technical report, Purdue University (February 2007)
7. McGraw, G.: Automated Code Review Tools for Security. Computer 41(12), 108–111 (2008)
8. McGraw, G., Morrisett, G.: Attacking malicious code: A report to the infosec research council. IEEE Softw. 17(5), 33–41 (2000)
9. Quirolgico, S., Voas, J., Kuhn, R.: Vetting Mobile Apps. IT Professional 13(4), 9–11 (2011)
10. Sekar, R., Gupta, A., Frullo, J., Shanbhag, T., Tiwari, A., Yang, H., Zhou, S.: Specification-based Anomaly Detection: A New Approach for Detecting Network Intrusions. In: Proceedings of the 9th ACM Conference on Computer and Communications Security, CCS 2002, pp. 265–274. ACM, New York (2002)

Symbolic Model-Checking Using ITS-Tools

Sorbonne Universités, UPMC Univ. Paris 6, LIP6, and CNRS UMR 7606,
4 place Jussieu, F-75252 Paris Cedex 05, France
`yann.thierry-mieg@lip6.fr`

Abstract. We present verification toolset ITS-tools, featuring a symbolic model-checking back-end engine based on hierarchical set decision diagrams (SDD) that supports reachability, CTL and LTL model-checking and a user-friendly eclipse based front-end. Using model transformations to a Guarded Action Language (GAL) as intermediate format, ITS-tools can analyze third party (Uppaal, Spin, Divine...) specifications.

1 Introduction

ITS-tools is a symbolic model-checker relying on state of the art decision diagram (DD) technology. It offers model-checking (CTL, LTL) of large concurrent specifications expressed in a variety of formalisms: communicating process (Promela, DVE), timed specifications (Uppaal timed automata, time Petri nets) and high-level Petri nets. We are focused on verification of (large) globally asynchronous locally synchronous specifications, an area where DD naturally excel due to independent variations of (small) parts of the state signature.

We leverage model transformation technology to support model-checking of domain specific languages (DSL). Models are transformed to the Guarded Action Language (GAL), a simple yet expressive language with finite Kripke structure semantics.

Most of this paper is a discussion of the elements visible in Fig. 1. The top of the figure corresponds to the front-end (sections 2, 3), and is embedded in Eclipse, while the bottom of the figure corresponds to the back end (sections 4, 5).

2 Guarded Action Language

We define GAL as a pivot language that essentially describes a generator for a labeled finite Kripke structure using a C like syntax. This simple yet expressive language makes no assumptions on the existence of high-level concepts such as processes or channels. While direct modeling in GAL is possible (and a rich eclipse based editor is provided), the language is mainly intended to be the target of a model transformation from a (high-level) language closer to the end-users.

A **GAL** model contains a set of integer variables and fixed size integer arrays defining its state, and a set of guarded transitions bearing a label chosen from a finite set. We use C 32 bit signed integer semantics, with overflow effects; this ensures all variables have a finite (if large 2^{32}) domain. GAL offers a rich signature consisting of all C operators for manipulation of the int and `boolean` data type and of arrays (including nested

© Springer-Verlag Berlin Heidelberg 2015
C. Baier and C. Tinelli (Eds.): TACAS 2015, LNCS 9035, pp. 231–237, 2015.
DOI: 10.1007/978-3-662-46681-0_20

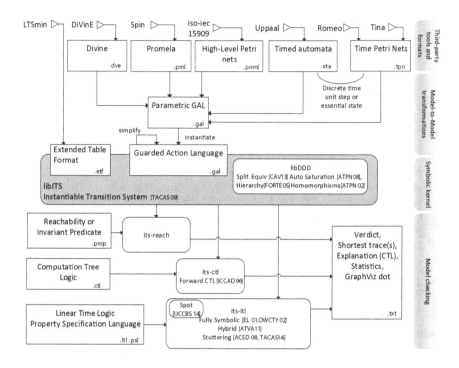

Fig. 1. Architecture of ITS-tools. Square boxes are files, rounded boxes are tools

array expressions). There is no explicit support for pointers, though they can be simulated with an array *heap* and indexes into it. In any state (i.e. an assignment of values to the variables and array cells of the GAL) a transition whose boolean guard predicate is true can fire executing the statements of its body in a single atomic step. The body of the transition is a sequence of statements, assigning new values to variables using an arithmetic expression on current variable values. A special $call(\lambda)$ statement allows to execute the body of any transition bearing label λ, modeling non-determinism as a label based synchronization of behaviors. A special fixpoint instruction is provided allowing to express modal μ-calculus least and greatest fixpoints thus giving the language a potent expressive power.

Parametric GAL specifications may contain parameters, that are defined over a finite range. These parameters can be used in transition definitions, compactly representing similar alternatives. They can also be used to define finite iterations (for loop), and as symbolic constants where appropriate. Parameters do not increase expressive power, the symbolic kernel does not know about them, as specifications are instantiated before model-checking. The tool applies rewriting strategies on parametric transitions before instantiation, in many cases avoiding the polynomial blowup in size resulting from a naive parameter instantiation. Rewriting rules that perform static simplifications (constant identification...) of a GAL benefit all input formalisms.

Model to Model Transformations. Model-driven engineering (MDE) proposes to define domain specific languages (DSL), which contain a limited set of domain concepts [28]. This input is then transformed using model transformation technology to produce executable artifacts, tests, documentation or to perform specific validations. In this context GAL is designed as a convenient target formally expressing model semantics. We thus provide an EMF [1] compliant meta-model of GAL that can be used to leverage standard meta-modeling tools to write model to model transformations. This reduces the adoption cost of using formal validation as a step of the software engineering process.

3 Third-Party Support

We have implemented translations to GAL for several popular formalisms used by third party tools. We rely on XText for several of these: with this tool we define the grammar and meta-model of an existing formalisms, and it generates a rich code editor (context sensitive code completion, on the fly error detection,...) for the target language. The editor obtained after some customization is then often superior to that of the original tool. We applied this approach for the DVE language of DiVinE [5], the Promela language of Spin [3] and the Timed Automata of Uppaal [4] (in Uppaal's native XTA syntax).

The translation for DVE (succinctly presented in [13]) is quite direct, since the language has few syntactic constructs, and they are almost all covered by GAL. Channels are modeled as arrays, process give rise to a variable that reflects the state they are in. Similarly, the translation for Promela presents no real technical difficulty, although a first analysis of Promela code is necessary to build the underlying control flow graph (giving an automaton for each process). We currently do not support functions and the C fragment of Promela.

Discrete Time. The support for TA and TPN uses discrete time assumptions. Note that analysis in the discrete setting has been shown to be equivalent to analysis in a dense time setting provided all constraints in the automata are of the form $x \leq k$ but not $x < k$ [21,8]. For both of these formalisms, we build a transition that represents a one time unit delay and updates clocks appropriately. This transition is in fact a sequence of tests for each clock, checking if an urgent time constraint is reached (time cannot elapse), if the clock is active (increment its counter) or if it is inactive either because it will be reset before being read again, or because it has reached a value greater than any it could be tested against before a reset (do nothing).

A translation from high-level Petri nets (HLPN) conforming with the recent iso standard (thus produced by a variety of tools) is also available. HLPN are roughly to Place/Transition nets what parametric GAL are to GAL: they are not more expressive (if all data types are finite) but they are much more compact and readable. Interestingly, the instantiation of GAL parameters is often much less explosive than the translation from HLPN to P/T nets: synchronizations of independent behaviors (e.g. interaction between a server S and a client C) can be represented using a sequence of *call*(λ) in GAL, where the P/T net must explicitly have a transition for each possible synchronization choice.

4 Symbolic Kernel

ITS-tools use symbolic representations of sets of states using decision diagrams to face the combinatorial state space explosion of finite concurrent systems. Its kernel is **lib-DDD**, a C++ decision diagram library supporting Data Decision Diagrams (DDD [15]) and hierarchical Set Decision Diagrams (SDD [16]). Operations on these decision diagrams are encoded using homomorphisms [15], giving a user great flexibility and expressive power. The library can automatically and dynamically rewrite these operations to produce saturation effects in least fixpoint computations [20]. The Split-equiv algorithm introduced in [13] enables efficient evaluation of complex expressions including array subscripts and arithmetic, a feature heavily used to symbolically encode the semantics of GAL.

libITS is a C++ library built on top of libDDD, offering a simple and uniform API to write symbolic model checking algorithms for any system that can be described as an Instantiable Transition System (ITS). An ITS is essentially a labeled transition system with successor and predecessor functions described as operating on sets of states, and a boolean predicate function enabling state based logic reasoning. The tool supports compositions of labeled transition systems by directly using hierarchy in the state representation reflecting the composition [27]. libITS has native adapters for several formalisms (not represented on the figure), we focus in this paper on GAL.

ETF Support. A native ETF to ITS adapter is provided with libITS, supporting this output format of LTSmin. ETF files [10] represent the semantics of a finite Kripke structure in a format adapted to symbolic manipulation. This allows to analyze (CTL, LTL) models expressed in the many formalisms that LTSmin supports, provided generation of ETF succeeds (essentially if LTSmin can compute all reachable states).

5 Model-Checking

Using the ITS API we have built several model-checking tools. The tool **its-reach** can compute reachable states, and shortest witness paths (one or more if so desired) to target states designated by a boolean predicate. In a discrete time setting, this can be used to compute best or worst case time bounds on runs. It can also perform bounded depth exploration of a state space (a.k.a. bounded model-checking). It implements several heuristics to compute a static variable order for the input model.

The tool **its-ctl** performs verification of CTL properties (though fairness constraints are currently not supported). It reuses a component of VIS [11], a model-checking tool for verification and synthesis of gate level specifications, to transform input formulae into forward CTL form [22]. Forward CTL often allows (but not always) to use the forward transition relation alone, which is easier to compute than the backward (predecessor) transition relation. Hence forward CTL verification is more efficient in general, and furthermore many subproblems can be solved using least fixpoints (e.g. Forward Until) that benefit from automatic saturation at DD level.

The tool **its-ltl** performs hybrid (i.e. that build an explicit graph in which each node stores a set of states as a decision diagram) or fully symbolic verification of LTL and

PSL properties. The transformation of the formula into a (variant of) Büchi automaton and the emptiness checks of the product for hybrid approaches rely on Spot [24,17], a library for LTL and PSL model-checking. Fully symbolic model-checking uses forward variants of Emerson-Lei [19] or One-Way Catch Them Young [26]. The hybrid approaches efficiently exploit saturation and often outperform fully symbolic ones [18]. When the property is stuttering invariant (e.g. $LTL \setminus X$) we also offer optimized hybrid [23] and fully symbolic [7] algorithms that exploit saturation.

Other prototypes for solving games [29] and to exploit symmetries [14] on top of decision diagrams have been built, showing the versatility of the ITS API, but these tools are not part of the current release.

6 Case Studies and Experiments

In [6] ITS-tools were used to analyze compositions of time Petri nets produced from a DSL VeriSensor dedicated to wireless sensor network modeling. The specification analyzed contained around 50 clocks, many of which are concurrently enabled, preventing analysis by explicit tools such as Tina. With "its-reach" functional properties could be checked as well as quantitative measures such as worst-case lifetime analysis. In the Neoppod project [12] the CTL component was used to verify response and consistency properties of a protocol for a distributed database. Inria's Atsyra project [25] computes attack defense trees from a DSL using a model-to-model transformation to GAL.

In terms of raw benchmark power, ITS-tools participated in several editions of the model-checking contest at Petri nets conference, ranking first place in several categories [2]. It is compared favorably to LTSmin and to SAT solver Superprove on the benchmark BEEM[13]. It outperformed the symbolic tool Smart using its own benchmark models in [27]. On timed models, comparisons to Uppaal show that we tend to scale better in number of clocks, but are more sensitive to large bounds on clocks, something that was reported in previous similar experiments [9].

7 Conclusion

The ITS-tools are freely available from the webpage `http://ddd.lip6.fr`, offering easy access to efficient symbolic model-checking for a wide range of formalisms thanks to the general purpose Guarded Action Language.

Acknowledgements. The ITS-tools is the result of many years of collaborative development with both colleagues and students at LIP6, without whom this tool presentation would not be possible.

References

1. Eclipse Modeling Framework, `http://www.eclipse.org/modeling/emf/`
2. Model checking contest @ petri nets home page, `http://mcc.lip6.fr/`
3. Spin model checker home page, `http://spinroot.com/`

 4. Uppaal home page, http://www.uppaal.org
 5. Barnat, J., Brim, L., Havel, V., Havlíček, J., Kriho, J., Lenčo, M., Ročkai, P., Štill, V., Weiser, J.: DiVinE 3.0 – An Explicit-State Model Checker for Multithreaded C & C++ Programs. In: Sharygina, N., Veith, H. (eds.) CAV 2013. LNCS, vol. 8044, pp. 863–868. Springer, Heidelberg (2013)
 6. Ben Maïssa, Y., Kordon, F., Mouline, S., Thierry-Mieg, Y.: Modeling and Analyzing Wireless Sensor Networks with VeriSensor: an Integrated Workflow. Transactions on Petri Nets and Other Models of Concurrency (ToPNoC) VIII, 24–47 (2013)
 7. Ben Salem, A.E., Duret-Lutz, A., Kordon, F., Thierry-Mieg, Y.: Symbolic model checking of stutter-invariant properties using generalized testing automata. In: Ábrahám, E., Havelund, K. (eds.) TACAS 2014 (ETAPS). LNCS, vol. 8413, pp. 440–454. Springer, Heidelberg (2014)
 8. Beyer, D.: Improvements in BDD-based reachability analysis of timed automata. In: Oliveira, J.N., Zave, P. (eds.) FME 2001. LNCS, vol. 2021, p. 318. Springer, Heidelberg (2001)
 9. Beyer, D., Lewerentz, C., Noack, A.: Rabbit: A tool for BDD-based verification of real-time systems. In: Hunt Jr., W.A., Somenzi, F. (eds.) CAV 2003. LNCS, vol. 2725, pp. 122–125. Springer, Heidelberg (2003)
10. Blom, S., van de Pol, J., Weber, M.: LTSMIN: distributed and symbolic reachability. In: Touili, T., Cook, B., Jackson, P. (eds.) CAV 2010. LNCS, vol. 6174, pp. 354–359. Springer, Heidelberg (2010)
11. Brayton, R.K., et al.: VIS: A System for Verification and Synthesis. In: Alur, R., Henzinger, T.A. (eds.) CAV 1996. LNCS, vol. 1102, pp. 428–432. Springer, Heidelberg (1996)
12. Choppy, C., Dedova, A., Evangelista, S., Hong, S., Klai, K., Petrucci, L.: The NEO protocol for large-scale distributed database systems: Modelling and initial verification. In: Lilius, J., Penczek, W. (eds.) PETRI NETS 2010. LNCS, vol. 6128, pp. 145–164. Springer, Heidelberg (2010)
13. Colange, M., Baarir, S., Kordon, F., Thierry-Mieg, Y.: Towards distributed software model-checking using decision diagrams. In: Sharygina, N., Veith, H. (eds.) CAV 2013. LNCS, vol. 8044, pp. 830–845. Springer, Heidelberg (2013)
14. Colange, M., Kordon, F., Thierry-Mieg, Y., Baarir, S.: State Space Analysis using Symmetries on Decision Diagrams. In: Application of Concurrency to System Design (ACSD), pp. 164–172. IEEE Computer Society (2012)
15. Couvreur, J.M., Encrenaz, E., Paviot-Adet, E., Poitrenaud, D., Wacrenier, P.A.: Data decision diagrams for Petri net analysis. In: Application and Theory of Petri Nets (ICATPN), pp. 129–158 (2002)
16. Couvreur, J.M., Thierry-Mieg, Y.: Hierarchical decision diagrams to exploit model structure. In: Formal Techniques for Networked and Distributed Systems (FORTE), pp. 443–457 (2005)
17. Duret-Lutz, A.: LTL translation improvements in Spot 1.0. International Journal on Critical Computer-Based Systems 5(1/2), 31–54 (2014)
18. Duret-Lutz, A., Klai, K., Poitrenaud, D., Thierry-Mieg, Y.: Self-loop aggregation product — A new hybrid approach to on-the-fly LTL model checking. In: Bultan, T., Hsiung, P.-A. (eds.) ATVA 2011. LNCS, vol. 6996, pp. 336–350. Springer, Heidelberg (2011)
19. Emerson, E.A., Lei, C.L.: Modalities for model checking: Branching time logic strikes back. Science of Computer Programming 8(3), 275–306 (1987)
20. Hamez, A., Thierry-Mieg, Y., Kordon, F.: Hierarchical Set Decision Diagrams and Automatic Saturation. In: van Hee, K.M., Valk, R. (eds.) PETRI NETS 2008. LNCS, vol. 5062, pp. 211–230. Springer, Heidelberg (2008)
21. Henzinger, T.A., Manna, Z., Pnueli, A.: What good are digital clocks? In: Kuich, W. (ed.) ICALP 1992. LNCS, vol. 623, pp. 545–558. Springer, Heidelberg (1992)

22. Iwashita, H., Nakata, T., Hirose, F.: Ctl model checking based on forward state traversal. In: Computer-Aided Design (ICCAD). pp. 82–87. IEEE/ACM (1996)

23. Klai, K., Poitrenaud, D.: MC-SOG: An LTL model checker based on symbolic observation graphs. In: van Hee, K.M., Valk, R. (eds.) PETRI NETS 2008. LNCS, vol. 5062, pp. 288–306. Springer, Heidelberg (2008)

24. Spot, L.R.D.E.: a library for LTL model-checking, http://spot.lip6.fr/

25. Pinchinat, S., Acher, M., Vojtisek, D.: Towards synthesis of attack trees for supporting computer-aided risk analysis. In: Workshop on Formal Methods in the Development of Software (co-located with SEFM) (2014)

26. Somenzi, F., Ravi, K., Bloem, R.: Analysis of symbolic SCC hull algorithms. In: Aagaard, M.D., O'Leary, J.W. (eds.) FMCAD 2002. LNCS, vol. 2517, pp. 88–105. Springer, Heidelberg (2002)

27. Thierry-Mieg, Y., Poitrenaud, D., Hamez, A., Kordon, F.: Hierarchical set decision diagrams and regular models. In: Kowalewski, S., Philippou, A. (eds.) TACAS 2009. LNCS, vol. 5505, pp. 1–15. Springer, Heidelberg (2009)

28. Voelter, M., Benz, S., Dietrich, C., Engelmann, B., Helander, M., Kats, L.C.L., Visser, E., Wachsmuth, G.: DSL Engineering - Designing, Implementing and Using Domain-Specific Languages. dslbook.org (2013)

29. Zhang, Y., Bérard, B., Kordon, F., Thierry-Mieg, Y.: Automated Controllability and Synthesis with Hierarchical Set Decision Diagrams. In: Workshop on Discrete Event Systems (WODES). pp. 291–296. IFAC/Elsevier, Berlin, Germany (September 2010)

Stochastic Models

Semantic Importance Sampling for Statistical Model Checking*

Jeffery P. Hansen, Lutz Wrage, Sagar Chaki, Dionisio de Niz, and Mark Klein

Carnegie Mellon University, Pittsburgh, PA, USA
{jhansen,lwrage,chaki,dio,mk}@sei.cmu.edu

Abstract. Statistical Model Checking (SMC) is a technique, based on Monte-Carlo simulations, for computing the bounded probability that a specific event occurs during a stochastic system's execution. Estimating the probability of a "rare" event accurately with SMC requires many simulations. To this end, Importance Sampling (IS) is used to reduce the simulation effort. Commonly, IS involves "tilting" the parameters of the original input distribution, which is ineffective if the set of inputs causing the event (i.e., input-event region) is disjoint. In this paper, we propose a technique called Semantic Importance Sampling (SIS) to address this challenge. Using an SMT solver, SIS recursively constructs an abstract indicator function that over-approximates the input-event region, and then uses this abstract indicator function to perform SMC with IS. By using abstraction and SMT solving, SIS thus exposes a new connection between the verification of non-deterministic and stochastic systems. We also propose two optimizations that reduce the SMT solving cost of SIS significantly. Finally, we implement SIS and validate it on several problems. Our results indicate that SIS reduces simulation effort by multiple orders of magnitude even in systems with disjoint input-event regions.

1 Introduction

As systems become more complex, there is a growing demand for efficient and precise techniques to verify correctness of their behavior. In this paper, we target a common probabilistic verification problem – estimating the probability of an event Φ (e.g., some sort of failure) during the execution of a system $\mathcal{M}$ that takes stochastic inputs (e.g., sensor readings, task execution times, etc.) Analytic solutions to this problem (e.g., probabilistic model checking, see Section 2) do not scale to many real-world systems due to complexity. We focus on an alternate approach called Statistical Model Checking (SMC) [16], which relies on Monte-Carlo-based simulations to solve this verification task more scalably.

---

* This material is based upon work funded and supported by the Department of Defense under Contract No. FA8721-05-C-0003 with Carnegie Mellon University for the operation of the Software Engineering Institute, a federally funded research and development center. This material has been approved for public release and unlimited distribution. DM-0002083.

© Springer-Verlag Berlin Heidelberg 2015
C. Baier and C. Tinelli (Eds.): TACAS 2015, LNCS 9035, pp. 241–255, 2015.
DOI: 10.1007/978-3-662-46681-0_21

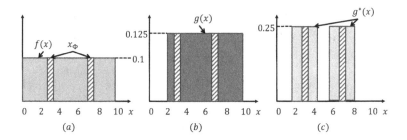

Fig. 1. Example of SIS; f = original input distribution; g = tilted distribution; g^* = distribution produced by SIS

SMC produces two results – the estimate $\hat{p}$ of the probability p of Φ and a measure of precision e. The key challenge in SMC is "simulation explosion" – the number of simulations required to achieve a high e becomes prohibitively large if p is small (i.e., Φ is rare). Importance Sampling [11,14] (IS) has been shown to address this challenge. Suppose the random input x to $\mathcal{M}$ has distribution f. In IS, we first perform SMC under a different input distribution g that makes Φ more likely (i.e., increases p), and then adjust the result back to f.

Traditionally, importance Sampling is implemented by "tilting" the parameters of the input distributions to increase the likelihood of Φ. However, tilting is less effective if the set of inputs that cause Φ, i.e., the input-event region denoted x_Φ, is disjoint. For instance, this happens when analyzing a program where Φ only occurs if the execution follows one of several control-flow paths, each triggered by a distinct input range. Figure 1(a) shows such a case. The actual input distribution f is uniform in the range $[0, 10]$, and $x_\Phi = [2.99, 3.01] \cup [6.99, 7.01]$. Figure 1(b) shows a tilted distribution g uniform in the range $[2, 10]$. While g makes Φ more likely than f, it still assigns positive weight to large parts – e.g., $(3.01, 6.99)$ – of the input space that do not belong to x_Φ.

In this paper, we address this challenge, and make three specific contributions. First, we develop a new technique to construct more precise input distributions for IS – such as g^* shown in Figure 1(c) – even when the input-event region is disjoint. This technique, which we call Semantic Importance Sampling (SIS), takes as input a description of $\mathcal{M}$ and f, and recursively computes a precise "over-approximation" of x_Φ in the form of an abstract indicator function (AIF). In each step of the recursion, SIS constructs a verification condition using $\mathcal{M}$ and f and checks its satisfiability with an SMT solver to eliminate parts of the input space that are not in x_Φ. The algorithm outputs an AIF represented by a set of "input cubes", i.e., a disjunction of intervals [7] over the input variables of $\mathcal{M}$. Subsequently, SIS uses the AIF to construct a precise input distribution, and perform SMC with IS. By using the semantics of $\mathcal{M}$, SIS successfully applies concepts and techniques used widely in the verification of non-deterministic systems (such as abstraction, SMT solving, and verification conditions) to the analysis of stochastic systems, building new bridges between the two disciplines.

The most expensive component of SIS are the calls to the SMT solver. Our second contribution is two optimizations to SIS that reduce the number of SMT calls while maintaining correctness. Finally, we implement SIS in a tool called OSMOSIS and use it to verify a number of stochastic systems with rare events. Our results indicate that SIS reduces the number of simulations significantly, in some cases by a factor of over 600, and verification time by an order of magnitude or more. Furthermore, our optimizations reduce both the number of SMT calls and overall SMT solving time, typically by a factor of 2. All our tools and examples are available at `andrew.cmu.edu/~schaki/misc/osmosis.zip`.

2 Related Work

Probabilistic model checking [15] (PMC) is an automated, algorithmic approach for computing numerical properties of stochastic systems. In PMC, the system is modeled as a finite state probabilistic automaton, e.g., a discrete time Markov chain (DTMC), a continuous time Markov chain (CTMC), or a Markov decision process (MDP) which is exhaustively explored in the analysis. The property is expressed as formula in a temporal logic, e.g., probabilistic Computation Tree Logic (PCTL) [8]. Verification consists of exhaustive exploration of the statespace to construct equations which are then solved numerically. In contrast, we follow the SMC approach, which is based on Monte-Carlo simulations. An excellent comparison between PMC and SMC is provided by Younes et al. [17].

SMC [16,2] has been applied to a wide variety of systems including stochastic hybrid automata [4], and real time systems [5]. Methods proposed to increase SMC performance include importance splitting [10], and importance sampling [14]. Importance sampling, upon which our approach is based, has been long known in the statistics literature[11] and has recently come to the attention of the SMC community[3]. Approaches proposed to finding the importance sampling bias function include Cross-Entropy Method[2,9] and Coupling [1].

Borges et al., [13] proposes a technique for estimating failure probabilities in software based on stratified sampling. Their technique differs from ours in that they partition the input space based on path conditions in the model, whereas we use an approach that modifies the input distribution.

Luckow et al. [12] have developed techniques for exact and approximate analysis of stochastic systems with non-determinism. They use symbolic execution and learning to iteratively construct schedulers under which worst-case (or best-case) behavior of the system is observed. This approach can be seen as an extension of statistical model checking to concurrent systems. They do not use importance sampling, and could benefit from our techniques.

3 Background

Consider a system $\mathcal{M}$ with finite vector of random inputs x. Assume that $\mathcal{M}$ is deterministic, i.e., its behavior is fixed for a fixed value of x. The SMC problem is to estimate the probability that $\mathcal{M}$ satisfies a property Φ, denoted $\mathcal{M} \models \Phi$, given a joint probability distribution f on x, i.e., to estimate $p = Pr[\mathcal{M} \models \Phi]$. We assume that whether $\mathcal{M} \models \Phi$ under input x can be determined by simulating $\mathcal{M}$ for finite time. Specifically, we assume that $\mathcal{M}$ is a program that terminates under all inputs, and $\mathcal{M} \models \Phi$ under input x iff the execution of $\mathcal{M}$ under input x violates an assertion (representing a desired safety property) in $\mathcal{M}$.

Let us write $x \sim f$ to mean x is distributed by f. SMC involves a series of Bernoulli trials, modeling each trial as a Bernoulli random variable having value 1 with probability p, and 0 with probability $1 - p$. For each trial i, a random vector $x_i \sim f$ is generated, and the system $\mathcal{M}$ is simulated with input x_i to generate a trace σ_i. The trial's outcome is 1 if Φ holds on σ_i, and 0 otherwise.

Define an indicator function $I_{\mathcal{M} \models \Phi} : x \rightarrow \{0, 1\}$ that returns 1 if $\mathcal{M} \models \Phi$ under input x, and 0 otherwise. Then, when $x \sim f$, the probability that $\mathcal{M} \models \Phi$ holds will be $p = E[I_{\mathcal{M} \models \Phi}(x)] = \int I_{\mathcal{M} \models \Phi}(x)f(x)dx$ which can be estimated as:

$$\hat{p} = \sum_{i=1}^{N} I_{\mathcal{M} \models \Phi}(x_i) \tag{1}$$

where N is the number of trials and $x_i \sim f$. We will refer to this estimator as the Crude Monte-Carlo (CMC) estimator. The precision of $\hat{p}$ is quantified by its "relative error" $RE(\hat{p}) = \frac{\sqrt{Var(\hat{p})}}{E[\hat{p}]}$ where $Var(\hat{p})$ is the variance of the estimator. It is known[2] that for Bernoulli trials, relative error is related to the number of trials N and the probability of the event p as:

$$RE(\hat{p}) = \sqrt{\frac{1 - p}{pN}} \approx \frac{1}{\sqrt{pN}} \qquad N = \frac{1 - p}{pRE^2(\hat{p})} \approx \frac{1}{pRE^2(\hat{p})} \tag{2}$$

Importance Sampling. From (2) we see that the number of simulations needed to achieve a fixed precision with SMC increases rapidly as the target event becomes rarer. Importance Sampling [14] (IS) has been applied [2] to address this challenge effectively by reducing $Var(\hat{p})$. The key idea behind IS is to first simulate $\mathcal{M}$ under a different input distribution g to reduce the variance of the estimator, and then mathematically adjust the result back to the original distribution f as:

$$p = \int I_{\mathcal{M} \models \Phi}(x) \frac{f(x)}{g(x)} g(x)dx = \int I_{\mathcal{M} \models \Phi}(x)W(x)g(x)dx \tag{3}$$

where $W : x \rightarrow \frac{f(x)}{g(x)}$ is a *weight function*. The estimator for this form is:

$$\hat{p} = \sum_{i=1}^{N} I_{\mathcal{M} \models \Phi}(x_i)W(x_i) \tag{4}$$

where the $x_i \sim g$. The biggest challenge in applying IS effectively is choosing a "good" g that will reduce $Var(\hat{p})$. Typically this is done by "tilting" f by changing its distribution parameters (mean, variance etc.) However, as discussed, tilting is not effective if Φ is disjoint in the input space. In effect, SIS constructs a good g even in such cases. We describe SIS in detail in the next section.

4   Semantic Importance Sampling

To explain SIS, we begin with a known result [2] that there always exists an optimal IS distribution:

$$g^\circ(x) = \frac{I_{\mathcal{M}\models\Phi}(x)f(x)}{p} \tag{5}$$

for which $Var(\hat{p}) = 0$, i.e., if IS is done with $g = g^\circ$, then a single sample is sufficient to compute $\hat{p}$. However, there are two challenges to using g° for IS: (i) g° depends on p, the answer we are actually looking for; and (ii) g° also depends on the indicator function $I_{\mathcal{M}\models\Phi}$, but since this function represents $\mathcal{M} \models \Phi$ itself, it may be too complex to represent analytically.

The key insight behind SIS is to construct an *abstract indicator function* (AIF) $I^*_{\mathcal{M}\models\Phi} : x \to \{0,1\}$ such that: (i) $\forall x \; I_{\mathcal{M}\models\Phi}(x) = 1 \Rightarrow I^*_{\mathcal{M}\models\Phi}(x) = 1$; and (ii) $I^*_{\mathcal{M}\models\Phi}$ is simple enough to represent analytically. Note that $\{x \mid I^*_{\mathcal{M}\models\Phi}(x) = 1\}$ is an over-approximation of the set of inputs under which $\mathcal{M} \models \Phi$. This AIF induces the following IS distribution and weight function:

$$g^*(x) = \frac{I^*_{\mathcal{M}\models\Phi}(x)f(x)}{p^*} \tag{6}$$

$$W^*(x) = \frac{f(x)}{g^*(x)} = \frac{f(x)p^*}{I^*_{\mathcal{M}\models\Phi}(x)f(x)} = \frac{p^*}{I^*_{\mathcal{M}\models\Phi}(x)} \tag{7}$$

where $p^* = E[I^*_{\mathcal{M}\models\Phi}(x)]$ is the probability that for an input $x \sim f$, $I^*_{\mathcal{M}\models\Phi}(x) = 1$. Note that as the function $I^*_{\mathcal{M}\models\Phi}$ approaches $I_{\mathcal{M}\models\Phi}$, g^* also approaches g°. In the limit, $I^*_{\mathcal{M}\models\Phi} = I_{\mathcal{M}\models\Phi}$ implies $g^* = g^\circ$.

Probability Estimation and Relative Error in SIS. Substituting $W^*(x)$ from (7) into (4), we get the SIS estimator for $p = E[I_{\mathcal{M}\models\Phi}(x)]$ given $x \sim f$ as:

$$\hat{p} = \frac{1}{N}\sum_{i=1}^{N} I_{\mathcal{M}\models\Phi}(x_i)W^*(x_i) = \frac{1}{N}\sum_{i=1}^{N} I_{\mathcal{M}\models\Phi}(x_i)\frac{p^*}{I^*_{\mathcal{M}\models\Phi}(x_i)} \tag{8}$$

with $x_i \sim g^*$ used in this importance sampled estimator. Note from (6) that $I^*_{\mathcal{M}\models\Phi}(x_i)$ is always 1 when $x_i \sim g^*$, thus this term can be dropped from the summation. Also, since p^* is a constant (8) simplifies to:

$$\hat{p} = \frac{p^*}{N}\sum_{i=1}^{N} I_{\mathcal{M}\models\Phi}(x_i) \tag{9}$$

This can be split into a raw part and a scalar part as $\hat{p} = p^* \times \hat{p}_{\text{raw}}$, where:

$$\hat{p}_{\text{raw}} = \frac{1}{N}\sum_{i=1}^{N} I_{\mathcal{M}\models\Phi}(x_i) \tag{10}$$

Since $\hat{p}_{\text{raw}}$ is an unweighted average of Bernoulli random variables, its relative error can be estimated [2] as:

$$RE(\hat{p}_{\text{raw}}) \approx \frac{1}{\sqrt{p_{\text{raw}}N}} \tag{11}$$

Furthermore, since $\hat{p} = p^* \times \hat{p}_{\text{raw}}$, and p^* is a constant, the relative error for $\hat{p}$ is the same as the relative error of $\hat{p}_{\text{raw}}$, i.e., $RE(\hat{p}) = RE(\hat{p}_{\text{raw}})$.

4.1   The SIS Algorithm

The SIS algorithm involves the following steps:

1. Recursively construct the AIF $I^*_{\mathcal{M}\models\Phi}$.
2. Calculate p^*.
3. Use SMC to estimate $\hat{p}_{\text{raw}}$ with desired $RE(\hat{p}) = RE(\hat{p}_{\text{raw}})$, using $I^*_{\mathcal{M}\models\Phi}$ to draw random inputs from g^*. Output $\hat{p} = p^* \times \hat{p}_{\text{raw}}$.

The core of SIS is Step 1, the generation of the AIF. We describe this in the following sections by first discussing our representation of the AIF, then describing the recursive algorithm.

AIF as a Cube Set. We assume that the input x to $\mathcal{M}$ is a vector of M independent[1], but not necessarily identically distributed random variables. For each dimension x_j in x, let F_j be the Cumulative Distribution Function (CDF), F_j^{-1} be the inverse CDF (or quantile function), and $u_j = F_j(x_j)$ be the quantile domain variable. Now let ξ be an M-dimensional axis-aligned input domain hypercube defining an interval $[l_j, h_j]$ on each input variable x_j for $1 \leq j \leq M$. We also define the quantile domain hypercube c defined by the ranges $[F_j(l_j), F_j(h_j)]$ for each dimension. We use the notation $c = F(\xi)$ and $\xi = F^{-1}(c)$ to transform cubes between the input and quantile domains. We will use the terms *input cube* and *quantile cube* to refer to cubes in the input and quantile domains, respectively. When the term *cube* is used without qualification we will assume quantile cubes. We can now represent the AIF in terms of a quantile cube set C^* as:

$$I^*_{\mathcal{M}\models\Phi}(x) = \begin{cases} 1 \text{ if } \exists c \in C^* \mid F(x) \in c \\ 0 \text{ otherwise} \end{cases} \tag{12}$$

where $(\forall x\ I_{\mathcal{M}\models\Phi}(x) = 1) \Rightarrow (\exists c \in C^*|F(x) \in c)$ (i.e., all inputs where $\mathcal{M} \models \Phi$ holds are covered by some cube in C^*).

Cube Splitting. Let ξ_U be the input cube defining the support of the input distribution function f. The corresponding quantile domain cube $c_U = F(\xi_U)$ will have a range of $[0, 1]$ on each dimension. We call this the level-0 cube. We write c/j to mean the cube formed by splitting the interval on u_j in c in half, and retaining only the upper half. Similarly, $c/\bar{j}$ is the result of a similar operation where the lower half of the interval is retained. Note that we can split on the same variable multiple times. A level-k cube is the result of k splits on the level-0 cube. For example if c_U is the level-0 cube, then $c_U/1/\bar{1}$ is the level-2 cube in which the interval for u_1 is $[0.5, 0.75]$. After each split, the probability that an input drawn from f falls in the result is halved. Thus, the probability of an input drawn from f falling in a level-k cube is $\frac{1}{2^k}$.

---

[1] Non-independent random inputs y are replaced by a function $h(x)$ of independent random variables x, which is folded into $I_{\mathcal{M}\models\Phi}(y)$ to yield $I_{\mathcal{M}\models\Phi}(h(x))$.

```
(1)    CubeSet aifGen(SMT φ,Cube c)
(2)    {
(3)        if (Solve(φ, F⁻¹(c)) == UNSAT) return ∅;
(4)        if (level(c) == Lmax) return {c};
(5)        int j = (level(c)/G)  % M;
(6)        Cube c₀ = c/j̄; Cube c₁ = c/j;
(7)        return aifGen(φ, c₀) ∪ aifGen(φ, c₁);
(8)    }
```

Fig. 2. Basic AIF Generation Algorithm; G=variable grouping factor, M=number of inputs, L_{max}=recursion depth limit, `Solve` = satisfiability check via SMT solver

Recursive AIF Construction. Generation of the AIF $I^*_{\mathcal{M}\models\Phi}$ is performed recursively through the hierarchical use of an SMT solver. The basic algorithm `aifGen` is shown in Figure 2. It takes as input the SMT representation φ of the indicator function $I_{\mathcal{M}\models\Phi}(x)$, and the input cube c over which to generate an abstraction. It is assumed that φ is constructed so as to be SAT for inputs x iff $I_{\mathcal{M}\models\Phi}(x) = 1$. Constant L_{max} is the maximum recursion depth. `aifGen` returns the subset of level-L_{max} cubes in C^* within cube c. C^* representing the AIF as defined in (12) can then be determined by calling `aifGen`, and passing the level-0 cube c_U as c.

The algorithm works as follows. At Line 3, the SMT solver is applied to the model φ over the cube $\xi = F^{-1}(c)$. The cube is applied to the model by modifying the assertions in the model corresponding to the intervals on the input variables. The SMT solver can return SAT, UNSAT or UNKNOWN (e.g., if it times out). If the result is UNSAT, then $\mathcal{M} \models \Phi$ does not hold in the input space described by c, and so it returns the empty set. If the result is SAT or UNKNOWN, we continue with the rest of the algorithm. While an UNKNOWN result will reduce the efficiency of the algorithm, the result will still be sound.

At Line 4, the level of the current cube c is checked against the specified maximum recursion depth L_{max}. If we are at that maximum recursion depth, we simply return the set containing just the cube c.

At Line 5, we choose an input variable index on which to split the current cube. In our current implementation, we simply cycle through the variables round-robin by using the current level modulo the total number of input variables M. Integer division by a variable grouping factor G allows us to choose the same variable G levels in a row before moving to the next variable. It is possible that other methods of choosing the splitting order may lead to more efficient abstractions, however we have not yet explored this area.

At Lines 6-7, we split the cube c around the selected variable u_j forming the cubes c_0, and c_1 for the lower and upper half of the CDF interval on variable u_j in c. We then recursively call the generation algorithm on those two sub-cubes and return the union of the cube sets returned by each call.

Calculation of p^*. Recall that $p^* = E[I^*_{\mathcal{M}\models\Phi}(x)]$ given $x \sim f$. Since: (i) all cubes in the set C^* returned by `aifGen` are level-L_{max}, (ii) they are non-overlapping, (iii) there are $2^{L_{max}}$ level-L_{max} cubes, and (iv) each cube covers equal probability in f, then p^* can be calculated from the ratio of the number of cubes in C^* to the total number of level-L_{max} cubes as:

$$p^* = \frac{|C^*|}{2^{L_{\max}}} \qquad (13)$$

4.2 Optimized AIF Generation

The most expensive component of `aifGen` are the calls to `Solve`. We now present two optimizations that can reduce the number of calls.

Optimization 1: Skip on UNSAT. Consider the algorithm in Figure 2. Notice that at the point where we split the cube at Line 6, we already know that cube c is not UNSAT. The means that if one of the child cubes c_0 or c_1 is UNSAT, the other one must be SAT[2]. To take advantage of this, we modify the algorithm to take an additional boolean argument `assumeSAT` indicating we should skip the call to `Solve` and assume it returns SAT when `assumeSAT` is true. Then we make the first recursive call on c_0 with `assumeSAT` set to false. If this call returns the empty set, then the result for that half was UNSAT, and we pass true for `assumeSAT` when making the recursive call on c_1, otherwise we make the recursive call with `assumeSAT` set to false and execute `Solve` as normal.

Optimization 2: Counter-Example Reuse. A second optimization is possible by making use of the counter-example returned by `Solve` when the result is SAT. In this case, we assume that `Solve` returns, as counter-example, a cube ξ_d containing a satisfying solution. We convert ξ_d to a quantile cube $c_d = F(\xi_d)$. If c_d is completely contained by one of the child cubes in the recursive call, we can skip the call to `Solve` for that call. We require c_d to be completely contained since the counter-example cube ξ_d returned by `Solve` is a cube in which there *exists* a solution to the SMT formula, but *not all* points in the cube are necessarily a solution. In most cases c_d will be contained by one or the other of the child cubes in the recursive calls, but it is possible that c_d could fall on an edge and thus not be applicable to either recursive call. In this case, it is still possible that Optimization 1 can apply. We assume that `Solve` will return the empty cube $\emptyset$ when the result is UNKNOWN which will suppress use of this optimization for the child invocations. It can be shown that if there are k calls to `Solve` without this optimization, that there will be $\lfloor \frac{k}{2} \rfloor + 1$ with this optimization as long as: (i) `Solve` never returns UNKNOWN, and (ii) the counter-example c_d returned by `Solve` always falls in one of the two sub-cubes. This sets an upper bound of $1/2$ on the amount by which calls to `Solve` can be reduced.

Optimized AIF Generation Algorithm. Figure 3 shows the fully optimized abstract indicator function incorporating both of the optimizations discussed above. Line 3 tests for conditions that allow us to skip the SMT check. In the case that we are skipping a check, we can pass the existing c_d to the child recursive calls since it may apply to one of those calls as well. When doing the SMT check with `Solve` at Line 4, we include an additional return parameter ξ_d in which the counter-example cube is returned. We assume that the empty cube $\emptyset$ is returned if the result is not SAT. At Line 5 we convert the input cube ξ_d

---

[2] It could be UNKNOWN if result from cube c is UNKNOWN, but without loss of soundness we treat an UNKNOWN as SAT for the purpose of this optimization.

```
(1)     CubeSet aifGen(SMT I,Cube c,boolean assumeSAT,Cube c_d)
(2)     {
(3)       if (!assumeSAT && c_d != ∅ && !(c_d ⊆ c)) {
(4)         if (Solve(I, F^{-1}(c), &xi_d) == UNSAT) return ∅;
(5)         c_d = F(ξ_d);
(6)       }
(7)       if (level(c) == L_max) return {c};
(8)       int j = (level(c)/G) % M;
(9)       Cube c_0 = c/j̄; Cube c_1 = c/j;
(10)      CubeSet s_0 = aifGen(I, c_0, false, c_d);
(11)      CubeSet s_1 = ∅;
(12)      if (s_0 == ∅) s_1 = aifGen(I, c_1, true, c_d);
(13)      else s_1 = aifGen(I, c_1, false, c_d);
(14)      return s_0 ∪ s_1;
(15)    }
```

Fig. 3. Optimized Abstract Indicator Function (AIF) Generation Algorithm; G=variable grouping factor, M=number of input, L_{max}=recursion depth limit

to a quantile cube c_d. Lines 12 to 13 implement Optimization 1. If $s_0 = \emptyset$, then the result of the test for c_0 was UNSAT and we can assume that the test for c_1 will be SAT.

4.3 Statistical Model Checking

After generating the AIF $I^*_{\mathcal{M}\models\Phi}$, and computing p^* with (13), the last step in SIS is the actual SMC. As previously mentioned, we draw samples from the distribution g^* as defined in (6), then use (10) to estimate the raw probability $\hat{p}_{raw}$ and scale this by p^*.

Random Input Generation. To generate a random input from g^*, we recognize that this is the equivalent of generating an input x from f and accepting only those for which $I^*_{\mathcal{M}\models\Phi}(x) = 1$. We do this by first randomly selecting a cube c from C^* with uniform probability since each cube has equal probability of containing a sample drawn from f. We then choose a uniform vector $u \in c$ and use the inverse CDF to generate the input vector as $x = F^{-1}(u)$.

No. Of Samples. From (2), the number of samples N^* needed to estimate $\hat{p}_{raw}$ is:

$$N^* = \frac{1 - p_{raw}}{p_{raw}RE^2(\hat{p}_{raw})} = \frac{1 - p/p^*}{p/p^*RE^2(\hat{p}_{raw})} \tag{14}$$

From (9), we know that $RE(\hat{p}) = RE(\hat{p}_{raw})$. Assuming small p and $p^* \gg p$, the speedup due to SIS can be estimated as:

$$\frac{N}{N^*} = \frac{\frac{1-p}{pRE^2(\hat{p})}}{\frac{1-p/p^*}{p/p^*RE^2(\hat{p}_{raw})}} = \frac{1-p}{p^* - p} \approx \frac{1}{p^*} \tag{15}$$

5   Osmosis

We implemented SIS in a tool called OSMOSIS. The input to OSMOSIS is a description of $\mathcal{M}$ in an annotated version of C, with the target property Φ defined as

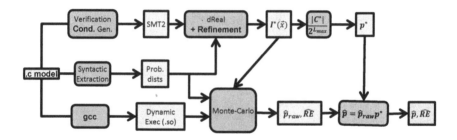

Fig. 4. Architecture of OSMOSIS Tool

`ASSERT()` statements. OSMOSIS calculates the probability of an `ASSERT()` failure via SIS, using dReal[6] as the back-end SMT solver.

Osmosis Architecture. Figure 4 shows the architecture of OSMOSIS. The input model is processed by: (i) `gcc` to generate a dynamic executable; (ii) a syntactic extractor which looks for `//@dist` declarations to determine the input space and distributions; and (iii) a verification condition generator that generates an SMT formula corresponding to the C model. Then `aifGen` (from Figure 2 or Figure 3) is used to build the AIF $I^*_{\mathcal{M}\models\Phi}$. This AIF is used to calculate p^*, and in conjunction with the dynamically loaded executable for $\mathcal{M}$ to estimate $\hat{p}_{\mathrm{raw}}$ and $RE(\hat{p}_{\mathrm{raw}})$. Finally, $\hat{p}$ is calculated using p^* and $\hat{p}_{\mathrm{raw}}$.

Osmosis Input Format. Figure 5(a) shows an example OSMOSIS input model. The annotations at Lines 4 and 5 indicate the inputs to the model. Line 4 defines a random input named "a" with a uniform distribution between 0 and 5. Line 5 defines a random input named "b" with a normal distribution with mean 3, standard deviation 1 which has been censored to be between 0 and 5. Where appropriate, we refer to the model input collectively as the vector x.

There are two special functions/macros in OSMOSIS models: (i) `ASSERT()` defines a condition that is expected to be true; and (ii) `INPUT_D()` accesses a random input declared in an annotation. The suffix `_D` on `INPUT_D()` indicates the return type of `double`. In Figure 5(a), Lines 8 and 9 access inputs "a" and "b" and place them in C variables also named "a" and "b". Some computations are performed on lines 10 and 11, then finally an assertion is made on Line 13. The `#include` on Line 1, allows the model include the special OSMOSIS functions to be compiled by a standard compiler such as `gcc` for use in the SMC phase.

SMT Generation. In order to implement `Solve`, OSMOSIS translates the C model into a verification condition represented as an SMT formula φ, which is in essence, a representation of the indicator function $I_{\mathcal{M}\models\Phi}$, i.e., any input value x satisfies φ iff $I_{\mathcal{M}\models\Phi}(x) = 1$. In constructing φ, stochastic inputs defined by the `//@dist` annotations in the C model use the same variable name as the declaration. The model is also converted to single-static-assignment form so that each local variable is assigned once. A generation number is appended to each variable name and is incremented for each assignment to that variable.

Conditional (`if`) statements are translated by generating a variable for the condition, then translating both branches as consequences of implications of the

```
(1)   #include "osmosis_model.h"
(2)
(3)        .
(4)   //@dist a=uniform(min=0,max=5)
(5)   //@dist b=normal(mean=3,std=1,
                       min=0,max=5)
(6)   void model()
(7)   {
(8)      double a = INPUT_D("a");
(9)      double b = INPUT_D("b");
(10)     double c = a + b;
(11)     double d = (a - b)/2.0;
(12)
(13)     ASSERT(sin(c)*cos(d) <= 0.999);
(14) }
```

(a)

```
(1)   (set-logic QF_NRA)
(2)   (declare-fun a () Real)
(3)   (declare-fun b () Real)
(4)   (declare-fun a_1 () Real)
(5)   (declare-fun b_1 () Real)
(6)   (declare-fun c_1 () Real)
(7)   (declare-fun d_1 () Real)
(8)   (assert (>= a 0))
(9)   (assert (<= a 5))
(10)  (assert (>= b 0))
(11)  (assert (<= b 5))
(12)  (assert (= a_1 a))
(13)  (assert (= b_1 b))
(14)  (assert (= c_1 (+ a_1 b_1)))
(15)  (assert (= d_1 (/ (- a_1 b_1) 2)))
(16)  (assert (not (<= (* (sin c_1)
                          (cos d_1)) 0.999)))
(17)  (check-sat)
(18)  (exit)
```

(b)

```
if (a > b)
   a = cos(a*b);
```

(c)

```
(assert (= _C1 (> a_1 b_1)))
(assert (or (not _C1) (= a_2 (cos (* a_1 b_1)))))
(assert (or _C1 (= a_2 a_1)))
```

(d)

Fig. 5. (a) OSMOSIS Input Example; (b) SMT for OSMOSIS Input Example; (c) a conditional statement; and (d) its translation to SMT

condition, or the compliment of the condition. If there are differing numbers of assignments to a variable in the branches, then an additional assertion is added to reconcile the generation numbers of the variables. For example, the C statement in Figure 5(c) generates the SMT assertions in Figure 5(d). Loop (`while` and `for`) statements are unrolled and must include an annotation to indicate the maximum loop count. Note that the construction of φ is effective and linear in the size of the model.

Finally, `ASSERT()` conditions are negated since we are interested in testing if there are any inputs that can result in an assertion failure. All `ASSERT()` statements are merged into a single SMT assertion comprised of a disjunction of the compliments of the expressions in the C input model.

Figure 5(b) shows the φ generated from the $\mathcal{M}$ given in Figure 5(a). Line 8 through 11 define the intervals in the stochastic inputs. Lines 12 and 13 are the assignments from the stochastic inputs to the local C variables from Lines 8 and 9 of the input model. Lines 14 and 15 correspond to the local variables assignments in Lines 10 and 11 of the C model. Finally, Line 16 is derived from the `ASSERT()` statement on Line 13 of the C model.

Monte-Carlo Simulation. The final step of OSMOSIS is Monte-Carlo simulation to estimate $\hat{p}_{\mathrm{raw}}$ using (10). Each Bernoulli trial in this simulation is conducted by directly executing the dynamically loadable executable of the model. The model source file is compiled by `gcc`, dynamically loaded, then repeatedly called for each trial. Before each execution a random vector $x \sim g^*$ is generated as described above and used to initialize a global array. A global flag variable indicating success/failure is also cleared. The function `INPUT_D()` indexes and returns a value from the input array. The `ASSERT()` statement tests the condition,

Table 1. AIF Generation Results; In=number of inputs; L_{max}=recursion depth limit; G=variable grouping factor, Time=generation time in seconds; none, 1, 2 and 1+2 indicate which optimizations were used

Name	In	L_{max}/G	p^*	$1/p^*$	dReal Calls none	1	2	1+2	Time none	1+2
simple	2	10/1	5.859×10^{-3}	169	49	38	26	26	0.15	0.1
		12/1	2.197×10^{-3}	455	73	57	40	40	0.21	0.1
hockey	2	10/1	3.516×10^{-2}	28.4	255	213	142	137	315	228
		12/1	1.148×10^{-2}	87.1	391	328	214	211	364	255
backoff	6	10/4	1.797×10^{-1}	5.6	479	451	240	240	33	14
		12/4	1.797×10^{-1}	5.6	1583	1551	792	792	61	28
bounce	2	10/1	2.997×10^{-2}	33	117	86	59	59	91	53
		12/1	1.221×10^{-2}	81	221	163	111	111	150	84

and if the condition fails it sets the global flag to `true` and returns. Success or failure of the trial is recorded based on the value of the flag variable. Trials resulting in an `ASSERT()` fail correspond to inputs x_i where $I_{\mathcal{M}\models\Phi}(x_i) = 1$, and those where the `ASSERT()` does not fail correspond to inputs where $I_{\mathcal{M}\models\Phi}(x_i) = 0$. Trials are conducted until a target relative error is met.

6   Results

To evaluate our technique, we tried OSMOSIS on the following problems:

Simple. The example problem from Figure 5a.

Hockey. An air hockey puck is given a random impulse from a random direction. We test if it stops on a target after zero or more bounces.

Backoff. An exponential backoff problem in which two senders attempt up to 3 communications. Failure occurs if transmission for either exceeds a deadline.

Bounce. A ball is launched at a random initial angle and velocity. We test if it falls in a small hole after potentially bouncing a number of times.

Each of these problems has the characteristic that the failure region is disjoint in the input space. For example, in the hockey problem there are multiple paths by which the puck can reach the target. All experiments were performed under Linux Ubuntu 12.04 on a 2.2GHz Intel Core i7 machine with 16 Gb of RAM. We used a 60 second timeout for each call to dReal (after which it returns UNKNOWN). However, we experienced no timeouts on any of our test problems.

Table 1 shows the results for AIF generation. For each example, we adjust the recursion depth limit and the variable grouping factor (number of successive times each input is split while recursing). We used a larger G for the "backoff" example because we observed that a higher G improves performance for models with many inputs. Recall from (15) that $1/p^*$ is an estimate for the expected speedup $\frac{N}{N^*}$ of SIS versus Crude Monte-Carlo (CMC). Note that while we use L_{max} to limit the recursion depth while generating the AIF, a breadth-first implementation of `aifGen` could potentially use p^*, terminating when we have achieved a sufficient gain, or when there is insufficient improvement from one level to the next. The four columns under "dReal Calls" show the number of calls that were made to dReal using no optimization, using Optimization 1 only, using Optimization 2 only and using both optimizations (see Section 4.2).

We see that both optimizations are effective at reducing the number of calls, but that Optimization 2 performs better, reducing the number of calls as well as total SMT solving time by half in most cases. Also, while there is some benefit to using both optimizations together, the additional advantage is relatively small. This is because when using both optimizations together, Optimization 1 can only be applied when the counter-example employed by Optimization 2 falls on a cube boundary, or when analysis of a parent cube timed out and is UNKNOWN.

Finally, the "Time" column shows the time to generate $I^*_{\mathcal{M}\models\Phi}$ in seconds. Times using no optimization (none), and using both optimizations $(1+2)$ are shown to demonstrate the impact of the optimization techniques. Note that in our current implementation, we do not parallelize the calls to dReal, which could lead to additional gains.

Table 2. SMC Results; $RE = RE(\hat{p})$=target relative error; G=grouping factor

Name	RE	$L_{\max}/G$	$\hat{p}$	N	N/N^*	Time (sec.) SMC	total
simple		CMC	5.95×10^{-4}	1.68×10^7	–	6	6
	0.01	10/1	5.89×10^{-4}	8.95×10^4	187	<0.1	0.1
		12/1	6.03×10^{-4}	2.64×10^4	636	<0.1	0.1
		CMC	5.910×10^{-4}	1.69×10^9	–	580	580
	0.001	10/1	5.910×10^{-4}	8.92×10^6	189	4	4.1
		12/1	5.910×10^{-4}	2.72×10^6	304	1	1.1
hockey		CMC	6.18×10^{-4}	1.58×10^7	–	6.8	6.8
	0.01	10/1	6.18×10^{-4}	5.59×10^5	28.3	0.3	228.3
		12/1	6.22×10^{-4}	1.74×10^5	90.1	0.1	255.1
		CMC	6.215×10^{-4}	1.61×10^9	–	687	687
	0.001	10/1	6.214×10^{-4}	5.56×10^7	29.0	25	253
		12/1	6.212×10^{-4}	1.74×10^7	92.5	8	263
backoff		CMC	1.21×10^{-4}	8.24×10^7	–	25	25
	0.01	10/4	1.20×10^{-4}	1.50×10^7	5.5	6	20
		12/4	1.21×10^{-4}	1.50×10^7	5.5	6	34
		CMC	1.193×10^{-4}	8.38×10^9	–	2,593	2,593
	0.001	10/4	1.190×10^{-4}	1.51×10^9	5.5	553	567
		12/4	1.194×10^{-4}	1.50×10^9	5.6	543	571
bounce		CMC	2.96×10^{-5}	3.337×10^8	–	133	133
	0.01	10/4	3.00×10^{-5}	8.464×10^6	39	4.1	57.1
		12/4	2.97×10^{-5}	4.104×10^6	81	2.0	86.1
		CMC	2.989×10^{-5}	3.345×10^{10}	–	13,619	13,619
	0.001	10/4	2.993×10^{-5}	8.474×10^8	39.5	432	485
		12/4	2.994×10^{-5}	4.068×10^8	82	209	293

Table 2 shows the results from the SMC phase of OSMOSIS. For each sample problem, we show the results for target relative errors (RE) of 0.01 and 0.001. At each target RE, we compare CMC with SIS using two different recursion depth limits as shown in the L_{max}/G column. The probability estimate for each experiment is shown in the $\hat{p}$ column. We see that the estimates for CMC and SIS are very close for each problem, and that as expected the agreement for those at a relative error of 0.001 are closest.

The column labeled N shows the number of samples needed to achieve the target relative error for each experiment, and the column labeled N/N^* shows the improvement of SIS over CMC. We can see improvements ranging from a factor of 5 to a factor of over 600. When we compare the measured N/N^* to the values predicted by $1/p^*$ in Table 1, we see good agreement. For example, in the "hockey" problem with a recursion depth of 10, we got 28.4 as the predicted improvement, compared to measured improvements of 28.3 for a target RE of 0.01 and 29.0 for a target RE of 0.001. Note our predictor is based on the assumption that $p^* \gg p$, and so is slightly less accurate for examples such as "simple" where this does not hold.

That last two columns show the verification time for the SMC phase alone, and for the total time including the abstract indicator function generation time shown in Table 1. We see that SIS outperforms CMC in all cases where verification is expensive, often by an order of magnitude or more. Also since the cost for generating the abstract indicator function is fixed regardless of the target RE, there will always be some target RE for which SIS outperforms CMC.

7   Conclusion

Statistical model checking (SMC) is a prominent approach for rigorous analysis of stochastic systems using Monte-Carlo simulations. In this paper, we developed a new technique, called Semantic Importance Sampling (SIS), to advance the state-of-the art in applying SMC to compute the probability of a rare event using a small number of simulations. SIS uses the semantics of the target system to recursively compute an abstract indicator function (AIF), which is subsequently employed to perform SMC. We also present two optimizations to SIS that reduce the number of calls to SMT solvers needed to compute the AIF. We have implemented SIS in a tool called OSMOSIS, and experimented with a number of examples. Our results indicate that SIS reduces cost of SMC by orders of magnitude, and our optimizations, in combination, reduce the cost of SMT solving by half. We believe that extending SIS to analyze stochastic systems compositionally, and combining it with symbolic simulation techniques, are important directions for future research.

References

1. Barbot, B., Haddad, S., Picaronny, C.: Coupling and importance sampling for statistical model checking. In: Flanagan, C., König, B. (eds.) TACAS 2012. LNCS, vol. 7214, pp. 331–346. Springer, Heidelberg (2012)
2. Clarke, E.M., Zuliani, P.: Statistical model checking for cyber-physical systems. In: Bultan, T., Hsiung, P.-A. (eds.) ATVA 2011. LNCS, vol. 6996, pp. 1–12. Springer, Heidelberg (2011)
3. Reijsbergen, D., et al.: Rare event simulation for highly dependable systems with fast repairs. In: Proceedings of the 7th International Conference on Quantitative Evaluation of Systems (2010)
4. David, A., Du, D., Guldstrand Larsen, K., Legay, A., Mikučionis, M.: Optimizing Control Strategy Using Statistical Model Checking. In: Brat, G., Rungta, N., Venet, A. (eds.) NFM 2013. LNCS, vol. 7871, pp. 352–367. Springer, Heidelberg (2013)
5. David, A., Larsen, K.G., Legay, A., Mikučionis, M., Wang, Z.: Time for Statistical Model Checking of Real-Time Systems. In: Gopalakrishnan, G., Qadeer, S. (eds.) CAV 2011. LNCS, vol. 6806, pp. 349–355. Springer, Heidelberg (2011)
6. Gao, S., Kong, S., Clarke, E.M.: dReal: An SMT Solver for Nonlinear Theories over the Reals. In: Bonacina, M.P. (ed.) CADE 2013. LNCS, vol. 7898, pp. 208–214. Springer, Heidelberg (2013)
7. Gurfinkel, A., Chaki, S.: BOXES: A Symbolic Abstract Domain of Boxes. In: Cousot, R., Martel, M. (eds.) SAS 2010. LNCS, vol. 6337, pp. 287–303. Springer, Heidelberg (2010)
8. Hansson, H., Jonsson, B.: A Logic for Reasoning about Time and Reliability. Formal Aspects of Computing (FACJ) 6(5), 512–535 (1994)
9. Jegourel, C., Legay, A., Sedwards, S.: Cross-entropy optimisation of importance sampling parameters for statistical model checking. In: Madhusudan, P., Seshia, S.A. (eds.) CAV 2012. LNCS, vol. 7358, pp. 327–342. Springer, Heidelberg (2012)
10. Jegourel, C., Legay, A., Sedwards, S.: Importance Splitting for Statistical Model Checking Rare Properties. In: Sharygina, N., Veith, H. (eds.) CAV 2013. LNCS, vol. 8044, pp. 576–591. Springer, Heidelberg (2013)
11. Kahn, H.: Stochastic (monte carlo) attenuation analysis. Tech. Rep. P-88, Rand Corp. (1949)
12. Luckow, K.S., Pasareanu, C.S., Dwyer, M.B., Filieri, A., Visser, W.: Exact and approximate probabilistic symbolic execution for nondeterministic programs. In: Proc. of ASE (2014)
13. Borges, M., et al.: Compositional solution space quantification for probabilistics software analysis. In: Proceedings of PLDI: Programming Language Design and Implementation (June 2014)
14. Srinivasan, R.: Importance Sampling: Applications in Communications and Detection. Engineering online library, Springer (2002)
15. Stoelinga, M.: Alea jacta est: verification of probabilistic, real-time and parametric systems. Ph.D. thesis, University of Nijmegen, the Netherlands (2002)
16. Younes, H.L.S.: Verification and planning for stochastic processes with asynchronous events. Ph.D. thesis, Carnegie Mellon University (2004)
17. Younes, H.L.S., Kwiatkowska, M.Z., Norman, G., Parker, D.: Numerical vs. statistical probabilistic model checking. STTT 8(3), 216–228 (2006)

Strategy Synthesis for Stochastic Games with Multiple Long-Run Objectives

Nicolas Basset[1], Marta Kwiatkowska[1], Ufuk Topcu[2], and Clemens Wiltsche[1]

[1] Department of Computer Science, University of Oxford, United Kingdom
[2] Department of Electrical and Systems Engineering,
University of Pennsylvania, USA

Abstract. We consider turn-based stochastic games whose winning conditions are conjunctions of satisfaction objectives for long-run average rewards, and address the problem of finding a strategy that almost surely maintains the averages above a given multi-dimensional threshold vector. We show that strategies constructed from Pareto set approximations of expected energy objectives are ε-optimal for the corresponding average rewards. We further apply our methods to compositional strategy synthesis for multi-component stochastic games that leverages composition rules for probabilistic automata, which we extend for long-run ratio rewards with fairness. We implement the techniques and illustrate our methods on a case study of automated compositional synthesis of controllers for aircraft primary electric power distribution networks that ensure a given level of reliability.

1 Introduction

Reactive systems must continually interact with the changing environment. Since it is assumed that they should never terminate, their desirable behaviours are typically specified over infinite executions. Reactive systems are naturally modelled using games, which distinguish between the controllable and uncontrollable events. Stochastic games [13], in particular, allow one to specify uncertainty of outcomes by means of probability distributions. When such models are additionally annotated by rewards that represent, e.g., energy usage and time passage, quantitative objectives and analysis techniques are needed to ensure their correctness. Often, not just a single objective is under consideration, but several, potentially conflicting, objectives must be satisfied, for example maximising both throughput and latency of a network.

In our previous work [6,7], we formulated multi-objective expected total reward properties for stochastic games with certain terminating conditions and showed how ε-optimal strategies can be approximated. Expected total rewards, however, are unable to express long-run average (also called mean-payoff) properties of reactive systems. Another important class of properties are ratio rewards, with which one can state, e.g., speed (distance per time unit) or fuel efficiency (distance per unit of fuel). In this paper we consider controller synthesis for the general class of turn-based stochastic games whose winning conditions are conjunctions of satisfaction objectives for long-run average rewards. We represent the controllable and uncontrollable actions by Player $\lozenge$ and Player $\square$, respectively, and address the problem of finding a strategy to satisfy such long-run objectives almost surely for Player $\lozenge$ against all choices of Player $\square$. These objectives can be used to specify behaviours that guarantee that the probability density is above a threshold, in several dimensions, and the executions actually satisfy the objective we are interested in, which is important for, e.g., reliability and availability analysis. In contrast, expected rewards average the reward over different probabilistic outcomes, possibly with arbitrarily high variance, and thus it may be the case that none of the paths actually satisfy the objective.

Satisfaction Objectives. The specifications we consider are quantitative, in the sense that they are required to maintain the rewards above a certain threshold, and we are interested in almost sure satisfaction, that is, this condition on the rewards is satisfied with probability one. The problem we study generalises the setting of stopping games with multiple satisfaction objectives, which for LTL specifications can be solved via reduction to expected total rewards [7], while our methods are applicable to general turn-based stochastic games. In stopping games, objectives defined using total rewards are appropriate, since existence of the limits is ensured by termination; however, total rewards may diverge for reactive systems, and hence we cannot reduce our problem to total rewards.

Strategy Synthesis. Stochastic games with multiple objectives have been studied in [9], where determinacy under long-run objectives (including ours) is shown (but without strategy construction). However, in general, the winning strategies are history-dependent, requiring infinite memory, which is already the case for Markov decision processes [4]. We restrict to finite memory strategies and utilise the stochastic memory update representation of [6]. For approximating expected total rewards in games, one can construct strategies (in particular, their memory update representation) after finitely many iterations from the difference between achievable values of successive states [7], but long-run properties erase all transient behaviours, and so, in general, we cannot use the achievable values for strategy construction. Inspired by [5], we use expected energy objectives to compute the strategies. These objectives are meaningful in their own right to express that, at every step, the average over some resource requirement does not exceed a certain budget, i.e. some sequences of operations are allowed to violate the budget constraint, as long as they are balanced by other sequences of operations. Consider, for example, sequences of stock market transactions: it is desirable that the expected capital never drops below zero (or some higher value), which can be balanced by credit for individual transactions below the threshold. Synthesis via expected energy objectives yields strategies that not only achieve the required target, but we also obtain a bound on the maximum expected deviation at any step by virtue of the bounded energy. Then, given an achievable target v for mean-payoff, the target 0 is ε-achievable by an energy objective with rewards shifted by $-v$, and the same strategy achieves $v - \varepsilon$ for the mean-payoff objective under discussion.

Compositional Synthesis. In our previous work [3], we proposed a synchronising parallel composition for stochastic games that enables a compositional approach to controller synthesis that significantly outperforms the monolithic method. The strategy for the composition of games is derived from the strategies synthesised for the individual components. To apply these methods for a class of objectives (e.g. total rewards), one must (i) show that the objectives are defined on traces, i.e. synchronisation of actions is sufficient for information sharing; (ii) provide compositional verification rules for probabilistic automata (e.g. assume-guarantee rules); and (iii) provide synthesis methods for single component games. We address these points for long-run average objectives, extending [10] for (ii), enabling compositional synthesis for ratio rewards. A key characteristic of the rules is the use of fairness, which requires that no component is prevented from making progress. The methods of [3] were presented with total rewards, where (trivial) fairness was only guaranteed through synchronised termination.

Case Study. We implement the methods and demonstrate their scalability and usefulness via a case study that concerns the control of the electric power distribution on aircraft [11]. In avionics, the transition to more-electric aircraft has been brought about by advances in electronics technology, reducing take-off weight and power consumption. We extend the (non-quantitative) game-theoretic approach of [16] to the stochastic games setting with multiple long-run satisfaction objectives, where the behaviour of generators is described stochastically. We demonstrate how our approach yields controllers that ensure given reliability levels and higher uptimes than those reported in [16].

Contributions. Our main contributions are as follows.

- We show that expected energy objectives enable synthesis of ε-optimal finite-memory strategies for almost sure satisfaction of average rewards (Theorem 2).
- We propose a semi-algorithm to construct ε-optimal strategies using stochastically updated memory (Theorem 1).
- We extend compositional rules to specifications defined on traces, and hence show how to utilise ratio rewards in compositional synthesis (Theorem 3).
- We demonstrate compositional synthesis using long-run objectives via a case study of an aircraft electric power distribution network.

Related Work. For Markov decision processes (MDPs), multi-dimensional long-run objectives for satisfaction and expectation were studied in [4], and expected ratio rewards in [15]. Satisfaction for long-run properties in stochastic games is the subject of [9]; in particular, they present algorithms for combining a single mean-payoff with a Büchi objective, which rely on the non-quantitative nature of the Büchi objective, and hence cannot be straightforwardly extended to several mean-payoff objectives that we consider. Non-stochastic games with energy objectives have been considered, for example, in [5], where it is assumed that Player □ plays deterministically, in contrast to our approach that permits the use of stochasticity. Our almost sure satisfaction objectives are related to the concept of quantiles in [1], in that they correspond to 1-quantiles, but here we consider mean-payoff objectives for games. An extended version of this paper, including proofs, can be found in [2].

2   Preliminaries

Notation. A *discrete probability distribution* (or *distribution*) over a (countable) set Q is a function $\mu : Q \to [0,1]$ such that $\sum_{q \in Q} \mu(q) = 1$; its *support* $\mathsf{supp}(\mu)$ is $\{q \in Q \mid \mu(q) > 0\}$. We denote by $\mathcal{D}(Q)$ the set of all distributions over Q with finite support. A distribution $\mu \in \mathcal{D}(Q)$ is *Dirac* if $\mu(q) = 1$ for some $q \in Q$, and if the context is clear we just write q to denote such a distribution μ.

We work with the usual metric-space topology on $\mathbb{R}^n$. The *downward closure* of a set X is defined as $\mathsf{dwc}(X) \stackrel{\text{def}}{=} \{y \mid \exists x \in X . y \le x\}$. A set $X \subseteq \mathbb{R}^n$ is *convex* if for all $x_1, x_2 \in X$, and all $\alpha \in [0,1]$, $\alpha x_1 + (1 - \alpha) x_2 \in X$; its *convex hull* $\mathsf{conv}(X)$ is the smallest convex set containing X. Given a set X, $\alpha \times X$ denotes the set $\{\alpha \cdot x \mid x \in X\}$. The *Minkowski sum* of sets X and Y is $X + Y \stackrel{\text{def}}{=} \{x + y \mid x \in X, x \in Y\}$. We refer to the sth component of a vector v by v_s and $[v]_s$. We write ε to denote the vector $(\varepsilon, \varepsilon, \ldots, \varepsilon)$. For a vector x (resp. vector of sets Z) and a scalar ε, define $x + \varepsilon$ by $[x + \varepsilon]_s = x_s + \varepsilon$ (resp. $[Z + \varepsilon]_s \stackrel{\text{def}}{=} Z_s + \varepsilon$) for all components s of x (resp. Z), where, for a set X, let $X + \varepsilon \stackrel{\text{def}}{=} \{x + \varepsilon \mid x \in X\}$. For vectors x and y, $x \cdot y$ denotes their dot-product, and $x \bullet y$ denotes component-wise multiplication.

Stochastic Games. We consider turn-based action-labelled stochastic two-player games (henceforth simply called *games*), which distinguish two types of nondeterminism, each controlled by a separate player. Player $\Diamond$ represents the controllable part for which we want to synthesise a strategy, while Player $\square$ represents the uncontrollable environment.

Definition 1. *A game G is a tuple $\langle S, (S_\Diamond, S_\square), \varsigma_0, \mathcal{A}, \longrightarrow \rangle$, where S is a finite set of* states *partitioned into* Player $\Diamond$ states $S_\Diamond$ *and* Player $\square$ states $S_\square$; $\varsigma_0 \in S$ *is an* initial state; $\mathcal{A}$ *is a finite set of* actions; *and* $\longrightarrow \subseteq S \times (\mathcal{A} \cup \{\tau\}) \times \mathcal{D}(S)$ *is a* transition relation, *such that, for all s, $\{(s, a, \mu) \in \longrightarrow\}$ is finite.*

We write $s \stackrel{a}{\longrightarrow} \mu$ for a *transition* $(s, a, \mu) \in \longrightarrow$. The action labels $\mathcal{A}$ on transitions model observable behaviours, whereas τ can be seen as internal: it cannot be used in winning conditions and is not synchronised in the composition. We denote the set of *moves* (also called *stochastic states*) by $S_\bigcirc \stackrel{\text{def}}{=} \{(a, \mu) \in \mathcal{A} \times \mathcal{D}(S) \mid \exists s \in S . s \stackrel{a}{\longrightarrow} \mu\}$, and let $\overline{S} = S \cup S_\bigcirc$. Let the set of *successors* of $s \in \overline{S}$ be $\mathsf{succ}(s) \stackrel{\text{def}}{=} \{(a, \mu) \in S_\bigcirc \mid s \stackrel{a}{\longrightarrow} \mu\} \cup \{t \in S \mid \mu(t) > 0 \text{ with } s = (a, \mu)\}$. A *probabilistic automaton* (PA, [12]) is a game with $S_\Diamond = \emptyset$, and a *discrete-time Markov chain* (DTMC) is a PA with $|\mathsf{succ}(s)| = 1$ for all $s \in S$.

A finite (infinite) *path* $\lambda = s_0(a_0, \mu_0)s_1(a_1, \mu_1)s_2 \ldots$ is a finite (infinite) sequence of alternating states and moves, such that for all $i \ge 0$, $s_i \stackrel{a_i}{\longrightarrow} \mu_i$ and $\mu_i(s_{i+1}) > 0$. A finite path λ ends in a state, denoted $\mathsf{last}(\lambda)$. A finite (infinite) *trace* is a finite (infinite) sequence of actions. Given a path, its trace is the sequence of actions along λ, with τ projected out. Formally, $\mathsf{trace}(\lambda) \stackrel{\text{def}}{=}$

PROJ$_{\{\tau\}}(a_0 a_1 \ldots)$, where, for $\alpha \subseteq \mathcal{A} \cup \{\tau\}$, PROJ$_\alpha$ is the morphism defined by PROJ$_\alpha(a) = a$ if $a \notin \alpha$, and ϵ (the empty trace) otherwise.

Strategies. Nondeterminism for each player is resolved by a strategy, which maps finite paths to distributions over moves. For PAs, we do not speak of player strategies, and implicitly consider strategies of Player $\square$. Here we use an alternative, equivalent formulation of strategies using stochastic memory update [4].

Definition 2. *A Player $\diamond$ strategy π is a tuple $\langle \mathfrak{M}, \pi_u, \pi_c, \alpha \rangle$, where $\mathfrak{M}$ is a countable set of memory elements; $\pi_u \colon \mathfrak{M} \times S \to \mathcal{D}(\mathfrak{M})$ is a memory update function; $\pi_c \colon S_\diamond \times \mathfrak{M} \to \mathcal{D}(S)$ is a next move function s.t. $\pi_c(s, m)(t) > 0$ only if $t \in \mathsf{succ}(s)$; and $\alpha \colon S \to \mathcal{D}(\mathfrak{M})$ defines for each state of G an initial memory distribution. A Player $\square$ strategy σ is defined in an analogous manner.*

A strategy is *finite-memory* if $|\mathfrak{M}|$ is finite. Applying a strategy pair (π, σ) to a game G yields an *induced DTMC* $G^{\pi,\sigma}$ [7]; an induced DTMC contains only reachable states and moves, but retains the entire action alphabet of G.

Probability Measures and Expectations. The *cylinder set* of a finite path λ (resp. finite trace $w \in \mathcal{A}^*$) is the set of infinite paths (resp. traces) with prefix λ (resp. w). For a finite path $\lambda = s_0(a_0, \mu_0) s_1 (a_1, \mu_1) \ldots s_n$ in a DTMC D we define $\mathrm{Pr}_{D,s_0}(\lambda)$, the measure of its cylinder set, by $\mathrm{Pr}_{D,s_0}(\lambda) \overset{\text{def}}{=} \prod_{i=0}^{n-1} \mu_i(s_{i+1})$, and write $\mathrm{Pr}_{G,s}^{\pi,\sigma}$ for $\mathrm{Pr}_{G^{\pi,\sigma},s}$. For a finite trace w, $\mathsf{paths}(w)$ denotes the set of minimal finite paths with trace w, i.e. $\lambda \in \mathsf{paths}(w)$ if $\mathsf{trace}(\lambda) = w$ and there is no path $\lambda' \neq \lambda$ with $\mathsf{trace}(\lambda') = w$ and λ' being a prefix of λ. The measure of the cylinder set of w is $\tilde{\mathrm{Pr}}_{D,s}(w) \overset{\text{def}}{=} \sum_{\lambda \in \mathsf{paths}(w)} \mathrm{Pr}_{D,s}(\lambda)$, and we call $\tilde{\mathrm{Pr}}_{D,s}$ the *trace distribution* of D. The measures uniquely extend to infinite paths due to Carathéodory's extension theorem. We denote the set of infinite paths of D starting at s by $\Omega_{D,s}$. The *expectation* of a function $\boldsymbol{\rho} \colon \Omega_{D,s} \to \mathbb{R}_{\pm\infty}^n$ over infinite paths in a DTMC D is $\mathbb{E}_{D,s}[\boldsymbol{\rho}] \overset{\text{def}}{=} \int_{\lambda \in \Omega_{D,s}} \boldsymbol{\rho}(\lambda) d\mathrm{Pr}_{D,s}(\lambda)$.

Rewards. A *reward structure* (with n-dimensions) of a game is a partial function $r \colon \overline{S} \to \mathbb{R}$ ($r \colon \overline{S} \to \mathbb{R}^n$). A reward structure r is *defined on actions* $\mathcal{A}_r$ if $r(a, \mu) = r(a, \mu')$ for all moves $(a, \mu), (a, \mu') \in S_\bigcirc$ such that $a \in \mathcal{A}_r$, and $r(s) = 0$ otherwise; and if the context is clear we consider it as a total function $r \colon \mathcal{A}_r \to \mathbb{R}$ for $\mathcal{A}_r \subseteq \mathcal{A}$. Given an n-dimensional reward structure $\boldsymbol{r} \colon \overline{S} \mapsto \mathbb{R}^n$, and a vector $\boldsymbol{v} \in \mathbb{R}^n$, define the reward structure $\boldsymbol{r} - \boldsymbol{v}$ by $[\boldsymbol{r} - \boldsymbol{v}]_s \overset{\text{def}}{=} \boldsymbol{r}(s) - \boldsymbol{v}$ for all $s \in \overline{S}$. For a path $\lambda = s_0 s_1 \ldots$ and a reward structure r we define $\mathrm{rew}^N(r)(\lambda) \overset{\text{def}}{=} \sum_{i=0}^{N} r(s_i)$, for $N \geq 0$; the *average reward* is $\mathrm{mp}(r)(\lambda) \overset{\text{def}}{=} \liminf_{N \to \infty} \frac{1}{N+1} \mathrm{rew}^N(r)(\lambda)$; given a reward structure c such that, for all $s \in \overline{S}$, $c(s) \geq 0$ and, for all bottom strongly connected components (BSCCs) $\mathcal{B}$ of D, there is a state s in $\mathcal{B}$ such that $c(s) > 0$, the *ratio reward* is $\mathrm{ratio}(r/c)(w) \overset{\text{def}}{=} \liminf_{N \to \infty} \mathrm{rew}^N(r)(w)/(1 + \mathrm{rew}^N(c)(w))$. If D has finite state space, the lim inf of the above rewards can be replaced by the true limit in the expectation, as it is almost surely defined. Further, the above rewards straightforwardly extend to multiple dimensions using vectors.

Specifications and Objectives. A *specification* φ is a predicate on path distributions, and we write $D \models \varphi$ if $\varphi(\mathrm{Pr}_{D,s_0})$ holds. We say that a Player $\diamond$ strategy π *wins* for a specification φ in a game G, written $\pi \models \varphi$, if, for all Player $\square$

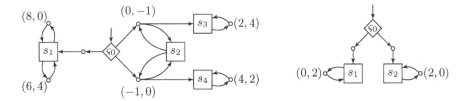

Fig. 1. Example games. Moves and states for Player $\lozenge$ and Player $\square$ are shown as $\circ$, $\lozenge$ and $\square$ resp.; two-dimensional rewards shown where non-zero.

strategies σ, $G^{\pi,\sigma} \models \varphi$, and say that φ is *achievable* if such a winning strategy exists. A specification φ is *defined on traces of* $\mathcal{A}$ if $\varphi(\tilde{\text{Pr}}_{D,\varsigma_0}) = \varphi(\tilde{\text{Pr}}_{D',\varsigma_0'})$ for all DTMCs D, D' such that $\tilde{\text{Pr}}_{D,\varsigma_0}(w) = \tilde{\text{Pr}}_{D',\varsigma_0'}(w)$ for all traces $w \in \mathcal{A}^*$.

A DTMC D satisfies an *expected energy* specification $\text{EE}_s(\boldsymbol{r})$ if there exists $\boldsymbol{v}_0$ such that $\mathbb{E}_{D,s}[\text{rew}^N(\boldsymbol{r})] \geq \boldsymbol{v}_0$ for all $N \geq 0$; D satisfies $\text{EE}(\boldsymbol{r})$ if, for every state s of D, D satisfies $\text{EE}_s(\boldsymbol{r})$. An *almost sure average* (resp. *ratio*) *reward objective* for target v is $\text{Pmp}_s(\boldsymbol{r})(\boldsymbol{v}) \equiv \text{Pr}_{D,s}(\text{mp}(\boldsymbol{r}) \geq \boldsymbol{v}) = 1$ (resp. $\text{Pratio}_s(\boldsymbol{r})(\boldsymbol{v}) \equiv \text{Pr}_{D,s}(\text{ratio}(\boldsymbol{r}/\boldsymbol{c}) \geq \boldsymbol{v}) = 1$). If the rewards $\boldsymbol{r}$ and $\boldsymbol{c}$ are understood, we omit them and write just $\text{Pmp}_s(\boldsymbol{v})$ and $\text{Pratio}_s(\boldsymbol{v})$. By using n-dimensional reward structures, we require that a strategy achieves the *conjunction* of the objectives defined on the individual dimensions. Minimisation is supported by inverting signs of rewards. Given an objective φ with target vector $\boldsymbol{v}$, denote by $\varphi[\boldsymbol{x}]$ the objective φ with $\boldsymbol{v}$ substituted by $\boldsymbol{x}$. A target $\boldsymbol{v} \in \mathbb{R}^n$ is a *Pareto vector* if $\varphi[\boldsymbol{v} - \varepsilon]$ is achievable for all $\varepsilon > 0$, and $\varphi[\boldsymbol{v} + \varepsilon]$ is not achievable for any $\varepsilon > 0$. The downward closure of the set of all such vectors is called a *Pareto set*.

Example. Consider the game in Figure 1 (left), showing a stochastic game with a two-dimensional reward structure. Player $\lozenge$ can achieve $\text{Pmp}_{\varsigma_0}(3,0)$ if going left at ς_0, and $\text{Pmp}_{\varsigma_0}(1,1)$ if choosing either move to the right, since then s_3 and s_4 are almost surely reached. Furthermore, achieving an expected mean-payoff does not guarantee achieving almost-sure satisfaction in general: the Player $\lozenge$ strategy going up right from ς_0 achieves an expected mean-payoff of at least $(1,1.5)$, which by the above argument cannot be achieved almost surely. Also, synthesis in MDPs [4,15] can utilise the fact that the strategy controls reachability of end-components; e.g., if all states in the game of Figure 1 (left) are controlled by Player $\lozenge$, $(3,2)$ is almost surely achievable.

3 Strategy Synthesis for Average Rewards

We consider the problem of computing ε-optimal strategies for almost sure average reward objectives $\text{Pmp}_{\varsigma_0}(\boldsymbol{v})$. Note that, for any $\boldsymbol{v} \geq 0$, the objective $\text{Pmp}_{\varsigma_0}(\boldsymbol{r})(\boldsymbol{v})$ is equivalent to $\text{Pmp}_{\varsigma_0}(\boldsymbol{r} - \boldsymbol{v})(\boldsymbol{0})$, i.e. with the rewards shifted by $-\boldsymbol{v}$. Hence, from now on we assume w.l.o.g. that the objectives have target $\boldsymbol{0}$.

3.1 Expected Energy Objectives

We show how synthesis for almost sure average reward objectives reduces to synthesis for expected energy objectives. Applying finite-memory strategies to games results in finite induced DTMCs. Infinite memory may be required for winning strategies of Player $\Diamond$ [4]; here we synthesise only finite-memory strategies for Player $\Diamond$, in which case only finite memory for Player $\Box$ is sufficient:

Lemma 1. *A finite-memory Player $\Diamond$ strategy is winning for the objective* $\mathrm{EE}(\boldsymbol{r})$ *(resp.* $\mathrm{Pmp}_{\varsigma_0}(\boldsymbol{r})(\boldsymbol{v})$*) if it wins against all finite-memory Player $\Box$ strategies.*

We now state our key reduction lemma to show that almost sure average reward objectives can be ε-approximated by considering EE objectives.

Lemma 2. *Given a finite-memory strategy π for Player $\Diamond$, the following hold:*

   (i) if π satisfies $\mathrm{EE}(\boldsymbol{r})$, then π satisfies $\mathrm{Pmp}_{\varsigma_0}(\boldsymbol{r})(\boldsymbol{0})$; and
   (ii) if π satisfies $\mathrm{Pmp}_{\varsigma_0}(\boldsymbol{r})(\boldsymbol{0})$, then, for all $\varepsilon > 0$, π satisfies $\mathrm{EE}(\boldsymbol{r} + \boldsymbol{\varepsilon})$.

Our method described in Theorem 2 below allows us to compute $\mathrm{EE}(\boldsymbol{r} + \boldsymbol{\varepsilon})$, and hence, by virtue of Lemma 2(i), derive ε-optimal strategies for $\mathrm{Pmp}_{\varsigma_0}(\boldsymbol{0})$. Item (ii) of Lemma 2 guarantees completeness of our method, in the sense that, for any vector $\boldsymbol{v}$ such that $\mathrm{Pmp}_{\varsigma_0}(\boldsymbol{r})(\boldsymbol{v})$ is achievable, we compute an ε-optimal strategy; however, if $\boldsymbol{v}$ is not achievable, our algorithm does not terminate.

3.2 Strategy Construction

We define a value iteration method that in k iterations computes the sets X_s^k of shortfall vectors at state s, so that for any $\boldsymbol{v}_0 \in X_s^k$, Player $\Diamond$ can keep the expected energy above $\boldsymbol{v}_0$ during k steps of the game. Moreover, if successive sets X_s^{k+1} and X_s^k satisfy $X_s^k \sqsubseteq X_s^{k+1} + \varepsilon$, where $A \sqsubseteq B \Leftrightarrow \mathrm{dwc}(A) \subseteq \mathrm{dwc}(B)$, then we can construct a finite-memory strategy for $\mathrm{EE}(\boldsymbol{r} + \boldsymbol{\varepsilon})$ using Theorem 1.

Value Iteration. Let $\mathrm{Box}_M \overset{\text{def}}{=} [-M, 0]^n$. The *M-downward closure* of a set X is $\mathrm{Box}_M \cap \mathrm{dwc}(X)$. Let $\mathcal{P}_c^M(X)$ be the set of convex closed M-downward-closed subsets of X. Let $\mathcal{L}_M \overset{\text{def}}{=} (\mathcal{P}_c^M(\mathrm{Box}_M))^{|\overline{S}|}$, endow it with the partial order $X \subseteq Y \Leftrightarrow \forall s \in \overline{S} . X_s \subseteq Y_s$, and add the *top element* $\top \overset{\text{def}}{=} \mathrm{Box}_M^{|\overline{S}|}$. For a fixed M, define the operator $F_M : \mathcal{L}_M \to \mathcal{L}_M$ by $[F_M(X)]_s \overset{\text{def}}{=} \mathrm{Box}_M \cap \mathrm{dwc}(Y_s)$, where

$$Y_s \overset{\text{def}}{=} \boldsymbol{r}(s) + \begin{cases} \mathrm{conv}(\bigcup_{t \in \mathrm{succ}(s)} X_t) & \text{if } s \in S_\Diamond \\ \bigcap_{t \in \mathrm{succ}(s)} X_t & \text{if } s \in S_\Box \\ \sum_{t \in \mathrm{supp}(\mu)} \mu(t) \times X_t & \text{if } s = (a, \mu) \in S_\bigcirc. \end{cases}$$

The operator F_M reflects what Player $\Diamond$ can achieve in the respective state types. In $s \in S_\Diamond$, Player $\Diamond$ can achieve the values in successors (union), and can randomise between them (convex hull). In $s \in S_\Box$, Player $\Diamond$ can achieve only values that are in all successors (intersection), since Player $\Box$ can pick arbitrarily.

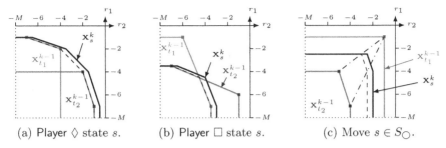

(a) Player $\Diamond$ state s.   (b) Player $\Box$ state s.   (c) Move $s \in S_{\bigcirc}$.

Fig. 2. Value iteration and strategy construction, for state s with successors t_1, t_2, and reward $r_1(s) = 0.5$, $r_2(s) = 0$. The Pareto set under-approximation X_s^k is computed from $X_{t_1}^{k-1}$ and $X_{t_2}^{k-1}$. To achieve a point $\boldsymbol{p} \in C_s^k$, the strategy updates its memory as follows: for $s \in S_{\Box}$, for all $t \in \mathsf{succ}(s)$, $\boldsymbol{p} - \boldsymbol{r}(s) \in \mathsf{conv}(C_t^{k-1})$; for $s \in S_{\Diamond} \cup S_{\bigcirc}$, there exist successors $t \in \mathsf{succ}(s)$ and a distribution α s.t. $\boldsymbol{p} - \boldsymbol{r}(s) \in \sum_t \alpha(t) \times \mathsf{conv}(C_t^k)$, where, for $s = (a, \mu) \in S_{\bigcirc}$, we fix $\alpha = \mu$. As F is order preserving, it is sufficient to use X_t^l instead of X_t^k for any $l \geq k$.

Lastly, in $s \in S_{\bigcirc}$, Player $\Diamond$ can achieve values with the prescribed distribution. F_M is closely related to our operator for expected total rewards in [6], but here we cut off values above zero with Box_M, similarly to the controllable predecessor operator of [5] for computing energy in non-stochastic games. Box_M ensures that the strategy we construct in Theorem 1 below never allows the energy to diverge in any reachable state. For example, in Figure 1 (right), for $\boldsymbol{v} = (\frac{1}{2}, \frac{1}{2})$, $\mathrm{EE}_{\varsigma_0}(\boldsymbol{r} - \boldsymbol{v})$ is achievable while, for the states $s \in \{s_1, s_2\}$, $\mathrm{EE}_s(\boldsymbol{r} - \boldsymbol{v})$ is not. Since one of s_1 or s_2 must be reached, $\mathrm{EE}(\boldsymbol{r} - \boldsymbol{v})$ is not achievable, disallowing the use of Lemma 2(i); and indeed, $\mathrm{Pmp}_{\varsigma_0}(\boldsymbol{v})$ is not achievable. Bounding with M allows us to use a geometric argument in Lemma 3 below, replacing the finite lattice arguments of [5], since our theory is more involved as it reflects the continuous essence of randomisation.

We show in the following proposition that F_M defines a monotonic fixpoint computation and that it converges to the greatest fixpoint of F_M. Its proof relies on Scott-continuity of F_M, and invokes the Kleene fixpoint theorem.

Proposition 1. *F_M is order-preserving, $\top \supseteq F_M(\top) \supseteq F_M^2(\top) \supseteq \cdots$, and the greatest fixpoint $\mathit{fix}(F_M)$ exists and is equal to $\lim_{k \to \infty} F_M^k(\top) = \cap_{k \geq 0} F_M^k(\top)$.*

Further, we use F_M to compute the set of shortfall vectors required for Player $\Diamond$ to win for $\mathrm{EE}_s(\boldsymbol{r})$ via a value iteration with relative stopping criterion defined using ε, see Lemma 3 below. Denote $X^k \stackrel{\text{def}}{=} F_M^k(\top)$. The value iteration is illustrated in Figure 2: at iteration k, the set X_s^k of possible shortfalls until k steps is computed from the corresponding sets X_t^{k-1} for successors $t \in \mathsf{succ}(s)$ of s at iteration $k-1$. The values are restricted to be within Box_M, so that obtaining an empty set at a state s in the value iteration is an indicator of divergence at s. Any state that must be avoided by Player $\Diamond$ yields an empty set. For instance, in Figure 1 (left), with target $(1, 1)$ the value iteration diverges at s_1 for any $M \geq 0$, but at ς_0,

Player $\diamondsuit$ can go to the right to avoid accessing s_1. The following proposition ensures completeness of our method, stated in Theorem 2 below.

Proposition 2. *If* $\mathrm{EE}(\boldsymbol{r})$ *is achievable then* $[fix(F_M)]_{\varsigma_0} \neq \emptyset$ *for some* $M \geq 0$.

Proof (Sketch). First, we consider the expected enrgy of finite DTMCs, where, at every step, we cut off the positive values. This entails that the sequence of the resulting truncated non-positive expected energies decreases and converges toward a limit vector $\boldsymbol{u}$ whose coordinates are finite if $\mathrm{EE}(\boldsymbol{r})$ is satisfied. We show that, when $\mathrm{EE}(\boldsymbol{r})$ is satisfied by a strategy π, there is a global lower bound $-M$ on every coordinate of the limit vector $\boldsymbol{u}$ for the DTMC $G^{\pi,\sigma}$ induced by any Player $\square$ strategy σ. We show that, for this choice of M, the fixpoint of F_M for the game G is non-empty in every state reachable under π. We conclude that $[fix(F_M)]_{\varsigma_0} \neq \emptyset$ for some $M \geq 0$ whenever $\mathrm{EE}(\boldsymbol{r})$ is achievable.

Lemma 3. *Given M and ε, for every non-increasing sequence (X^i) of elements of $\mathcal{L}_M$ there exists $k \leq k^{**} \stackrel{\text{def}}{=} \left[2n((\lceil \frac{M}{\varepsilon} \rceil + 2)^2 + 2)\right]^{|\overline{S}|}$ such that $X^k \sqsubseteq X^{k+1} + \varepsilon$.*

Proof (Sketch). We first consider a single state s, and construct a graph with vertices from the sequence of sets (X^i), and edges indicating dimensions where the distance is at least ε. Interpreting each dimension as a colour, we use a Ramseyan argument to find the bound $k^* \stackrel{\text{def}}{=} n \cdot ((\lceil \frac{M}{\varepsilon} \rceil + 2)^2 + 2)$ for a single state. To find the bound $k^{**} \stackrel{\text{def}}{=} (2k^*)^{|\overline{S}|}$, which is for *all* states, we extract successive subsequences of $\{1, 2, \ldots, k^{**}\} \stackrel{\text{def}}{=} I_0 \supseteq I_1 \supseteq \cdots \supseteq I_{|\overline{S}|}$, where going from I_i to I_{i+1} means that one additional state has the desired property, and such that the invariant $|I_{i+1}| \geq |I_i|/(2k^*)$ is satisfied. At the end $I_{|\overline{S}|}$ contains at least one index $k \leq k^{**}$ for which all states have the desired property.

Strategy Construction. The strategies are constructed so that their memory corresponds to the extreme points of the sets computed by $F_M^k(\top)$. The strategies stochastically update their memory, and so the expectation of their memory elements corresponds to an expectation over such extreme points.

Let C_s^k be the set of *extreme points* of $\mathsf{dwc}(X_s^k)$, for all $k \geq 0$ (since $X^k \in \mathcal{L}_M$, the sets X_s^k are closed). For any point $\boldsymbol{p} \in X_s^k$, there is some $\boldsymbol{q} \geq \boldsymbol{p}$ that can be obtained by a convex combination of points in C_s^k, and so the strategy we construct uses C_s^k as memory, randomising to attain the convex combination $\boldsymbol{q}$. Note that the sets C_s^k are finite, yielding finite-memory strategies.

If $X_{\varsigma_0}^{k+1} \neq \emptyset$ and $X^k \sqsubseteq X^{k+1} + \varepsilon$ for some $k \in \mathbb{N}$ and $\varepsilon \geq 0$, we can construct a Player $\diamondsuit$ strategy π for $\mathrm{EE}(\boldsymbol{r} + \varepsilon)$. Denote by $\overline{T} \subseteq \overline{S}$ the set of states s for which $X_s^{k+1} \neq \emptyset$. For $l \geq 1$, define the *standard l-simplex* by $\Delta^l \stackrel{\text{def}}{=} \{B \in [0,1]^l \mid \sum_{\beta \in B} \beta = 1\}$. The memory $\mathfrak{M} \stackrel{\text{def}}{=} \bigcup_{s \in \overline{T}} \{(s, \boldsymbol{p}) \mid \boldsymbol{p} \in C_s^k\}$ is initialised according to α, defined by $\alpha(s) \stackrel{\text{def}}{=} [(s, \boldsymbol{q}_0^s) \mapsto \beta_0^s, \ldots, (s, \boldsymbol{q}_n^s) \mapsto \beta_n^s]$, where $\boldsymbol{\beta}^s \in \Delta^n$, and, for all $1 \leq i \leq n$, $\boldsymbol{q}_i^s \in C_s^k$. The update π_u and next move function π_c are defined as follows: at state s with memory $(s, \boldsymbol{p})$, for all $t \in \mathsf{succ}(s)$, pick n vectors $\boldsymbol{q}_i^t \in C_t^k$ for $1 \leq i \leq n$, with coefficients $\boldsymbol{\beta}^t \in \Delta^n$, such that

---
Algorithm 1. PMP Strategy Synthesis

1: **function** SYNTHPMP(G, r, v, ε)
2:   Set the reward structure to $r - v + \frac{\varepsilon}{2}$; let $k \leftarrow 0$; $M \leftarrow 2$; $X^0 \leftarrow \top$;
3:   **while** true **do**
4:     **while** $X^k \not\sqsubseteq X^{k+1} + \frac{\varepsilon}{2}$ **do**
5:       $k \leftarrow k + 1$; $X^{k+1} \leftarrow F_M(X^k)$;
6:     **if** $X^k_{\varsigma_0} \neq \emptyset$ **then**
7:       Construct π for $\frac{\varepsilon}{2}$ and any $v_0 \in C^k_{\varsigma_0}$ using Theorem 1; **return** π
8:     **else**
9:       $k \leftarrow 0$; $M \leftarrow M^2$;

- **for** $s \in S_\Diamond$, there is $\gamma \in \Delta^{|\mathsf{succ}(s) \cap \overline{T}|}$, such that $\sum_t \gamma_t \cdot \sum_i \beta_i^t \cdot q_i^t \geq p - r(s) - \varepsilon$;
- **for** $s \in S_\Box$, for all $t \in \mathsf{succ}(s)$, $\sum_i \beta_i^t \cdot q_i^t \geq p - r(s) - \varepsilon$; and
- **for** $s = (a, \mu) \in S_\bigcirc$, we have $\sum_{t \in \mathsf{supp}(\mu)} \mu(t) \cdot \sum_i \beta_i^t \cdot q_i^t \geq p - r(s) - \varepsilon$;

and, for all $t \in \mathsf{succ}(s)$, let $\pi_u((s,p),t)(t,q_i^t) \stackrel{\text{def}}{=} \beta_i^t$ for all i, and $\pi_c(s,(s,p))(t) \stackrel{\text{def}}{=} \gamma_t$ if $s \in S_\Diamond$.

Theorem 1. *If $X^{k+1}_{\varsigma_0} \neq \emptyset$ and $X^k \sqsubseteq X^{k+1} + \varepsilon$ for some $k \in \mathbb{N}$ and $\varepsilon \geq 0$, then the Player $\Diamond$ strategy constructed above is finite-memory and wins for* $\mathrm{EE}(r + \varepsilon)$.

Proof (Sketch). We show the strategy is well-defined, i.e. the relevant extreme points and coefficients exist, which is a consequence of $X^k \sqsubseteq X^{k+1} + \varepsilon$. We then show that, when entering a state s_o with a memory p_o, the expected memory from this state after N steps is above $p_o - \mathbb{E}_{D,s_o}[\mathrm{rew}^N(r)] - N\varepsilon$. As the memory is always non-positive, this implies that $\mathbb{E}_{D,s_o}[\mathrm{rew}^N(r + \varepsilon)] \geq p_o \geq -M$ for every state s_o with memory p_o, for every N. We conclude that $\mathrm{EE}(r + \varepsilon)$ holds.

3.3   Strategy Synthesis Algorithm

Given a game G, a reward structure r with target vector v, and $\varepsilon > 0$, the semi-algorithm given in Algorithm 1 computes a strategy winning for $\mathrm{Pmp}_{\varsigma_0}(r)(v - \varepsilon)$.

Theorem 2. *Whenever v is in the Pareto set of $\mathrm{Pmp}_{\varsigma_0}(r)$, then Algorithm 1 terminates with a finite-memory ε-optimal strategy.*

Proof (Sketch). Since v is in the Pareto set of the almost sure average reward objective, by Lemma 2(*ii*) the objective $\mathrm{EE}(r - v + \frac{\varepsilon}{2})$ is achievable, and, by Proposition 2, there exists an M such that $fix(F_M)$ is nonempty. The condition in Line 6 is then satisfied as $\emptyset \neq [fix(F_M)]_{\varsigma_0} \subseteq X^k_{\varsigma_0}$. Further, due to the bound M on the size of the box Box_M in the value iteration, the inner loop terminates after a finite number of steps, as shown in Lemma 3. Then, by Theorem 1, the strategy constructed in Line 7 (with degradation factor $\frac{\varepsilon}{2}$ for the reward $r - v + \frac{\varepsilon}{2}$) satisfies $\mathrm{EE}(r - v + \varepsilon)$, and hence, using Lemma 2(*i*), $\mathrm{Pmp}_{\varsigma_0}(r)(v - \varepsilon)$.

4   Compositional Synthesis

In order to synthesise strategies compositionally, we introduced in [3] a composition of games, and showed that assume-guarantee rules for PAs can be applied in synthesis for games: whenever there is a PA verification rule, the corresponding game synthesis rule has the same form and side-conditions (Theorem 1 of [3]). We present a PA assume-guarantee rule for ratio rewards. The PA rules in [10] only support total expected rewards, while our rule works with any specification defined on traces, and in particular with ratio rewards (Proposition 4).

Ratio Rewards. Ratio rewards $\text{ratio}(\boldsymbol{r}/\boldsymbol{c})$ generalise average rewards $\text{mp}(\boldsymbol{r})$, since, to express the latter, we let $\boldsymbol{c}(s) = 1$ for all $s \in \overline{S}$. The following proposition states that to solve $\text{Pratio}_{\varsigma_0}(\boldsymbol{r}/\boldsymbol{c})(\boldsymbol{v})$ it suffices to solve $\text{Pmp}_{\varsigma_0}(\boldsymbol{r})(\boldsymbol{v} \bullet \boldsymbol{c})$.

Proposition 3. *A finite-memory Player* $\Diamond$ *strategy* π *satisfies* $\text{Pratio}_{\varsigma_0}(\boldsymbol{r}/\boldsymbol{c})(\boldsymbol{v})$ *if and only if it satisfies* $\text{Pmp}_{\varsigma_0}(\boldsymbol{r})(\boldsymbol{v} \bullet \boldsymbol{c})$.

Fairness. Given a composed PA $\mathcal{M} = \|_{i \in I} M^i$, a strategy σ is *fair* if at least one action of each component $\mathcal{M}_i$ is chosen infinitely often with probability 1. We write $\mathcal{M} \models^f \varphi$ if, for all fair strategies σ, $\mathcal{M}^\sigma \models \varphi$.

Theorem 3. *Given compatible PAs* $\mathcal{M}_1$ *and* $\mathcal{M}_2$, *specifications* φ^{G_1} *and* φ^{G_2} *defined on traces of* $\mathcal{A}_{G_i} \subseteq \mathcal{A}_i$ *for* $i \in \{1, 2\}$, *then the following is sound:*

$$\frac{\mathcal{M}_1 \models^f \varphi^{G_1} \quad \mathcal{M}_2 \models^f \varphi^{G_2}}{\mathcal{M}_1 \| \mathcal{M}_2 \models^f \varphi^{G_1} \wedge \varphi^{G_2}}.$$

To use Theorem 3, we show that objectives using total or ratio rewards are defined on traces over some subset of actions.

Proposition 4. *If* n-*dimensional reward structures* $\boldsymbol{r}$ *and* $\boldsymbol{c}$ *are defined on actions* $\mathcal{A}_{\boldsymbol{r}}$ *and* $\mathcal{A}_{\boldsymbol{c}}$, *respectively, then objectives using ratio rewards* $\text{ratio}(\boldsymbol{r}/\boldsymbol{c})$ *are defined on traces of* $\mathcal{A}_{\boldsymbol{r}} \cup \mathcal{A}_{\boldsymbol{c}}$.

Note that average rewards are not defined over traces in general, since its divisor counts the transitions, irrespective of whether the specification takes them into account. In particular, when composing systems, the additional transitions in between those originally counted skew the value of the average rewards. Moreover, τ-transitions are counted, but do not appear in the traces.

5   A Case Study: Aircraft Power Distribution

We demonstrate our synthesis methods on a case study for the control of the electrical power system of a more-electric aircraft [11], see Figure 3(a). Power is to be routed from generators to buses (and loads attached to them) by controlling the contactors (i.e. controllable switches) connecting the network nodes. Our models are based on a game-theoretic study of the same control problem in [16], where the control objective is to ensure the buses are powered, while avoiding

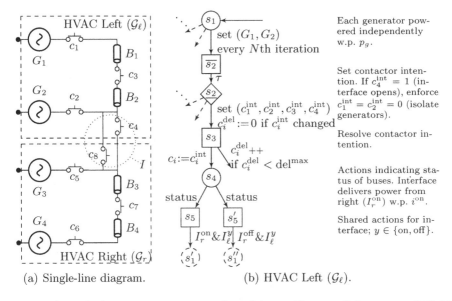

(a) Single-line diagram.   (b) HVAC Left ($\mathcal{G}_\ell$).

Fig. 3. Aircraft electric power system, adapted from a Honeywell, Inc. patent [11]. The single-line diagram of the full power system (a) shows how power from the generators (G_i) can be routed to the buses (B_i) through the contactors (c_i). The left HVAC subsystem model $\mathcal{G}_\ell$ is shown in (b), and $\mathcal{G}_r$ is symmetric. I_ℓ^x and I_r^y is the interface status on the left and right side, resp., where x, y stand for either "on" or "off". One iteration of the reactive loop goes from s_1 to s_5 and starts again at s_1, potentially with some variables changed, indicated as s_1' or s_1''.

unsafe configurations. The controllers have to take into account that contactors have delays, and the generators available in the system may be reconfigured, or even exhibit failures. We show that, by incorporating stochasticity in the models derived from the reliability statistics of the generators, controllers synthesised from ratio rewards achieve better uptimes compared to those reported in [16].

5.1 Model

The system comprises several components, each consisting of buses and generators, and we consider the high-voltage AC (HVAC) subsystem, shown in Figure 3(a), where the dashed boxes represent the components set out in [11]. These components are physically separated for reliability, and hence allow limited interaction and communication. Since the system is reactive, i.e. the aircraft is to be controlled continually, we use long-run properties to specify correctness.

The game models and control objectives in [16] are specified using LTL properties. We extend their models to stochastic games with quantitative specifications, where the contactors are controlled by Player ◊ and the contactor dynamics and the interfaces are controlled by Player □, and compose them by means of the synchronising parallel composition of [3]. The advantage of stochasticity is that the reliability specifications desired in [16] can be faithfully encoded. Further, games allow us to model truly adversarial behaviour (e.g. uncontrollable contactor dynamics), as well as nondeterministic interleaving in the composition.

Contactors, Buses and Generators. We derive the models based on the LTL description of [16]: the status of the buses and generators are kept in Boolean variables $B_1, \ldots, B_4$ and $G_1, \ldots, G_4$ resp., and their truth value represents whether the bus or generator is powered; the contactor status is kept in Boolean variables $c_1, \ldots, c_8$, and their truth value represents if the corresponding contactor lets the current flow. For instance, if in $\mathcal{G}_\ell$ the generator G_1 is on but G_2 is off, the controller needs to switch the contactors c_1 and c_3 on, in order to power both buses B_1 and B_2. At the same time, short circuits from connecting generators to each other must be avoided, e.g. contactors c_1, c_2 and c_3 cannot be on at the same time, as this configuration connects G_1 and G_2. The contactors are, for example, solid state power controllers [14], which typically have non-negligible reaction times with respect to the times the buses should be powered. Hence, as in [16], we model that Player $\Diamond$ can only set the *intent* c_i^{int} of contactor i, and only after some delay is the contactor status c_i set to this intent. For the purposes of this demonstration, we only model a delayed turn-off time, as it is typically larger than the turn-on time (e.g. 40 ms, the turn-off time reported in [8]). Whether or not a contactor is delayed is controlled by Player $\square$.

Interface. The components can deliver power to each other via the interface I, see Figure 3(a), which is bidirectional, i.e. power can flow both ways. The original design in [11] does not include connector c_8, and so c_4 has to ensure that no short circuits occur over the interface: if B_3 is powered, c_4 may only connect if B_2 is unpowered, and vice versa; hence, c_4 can only be on if both B_2 and B_3 are unpowered. By adding c_8, we break this cyclic dependence.

Actions shared between components model transmission of power. The actions I_r^x and I_ℓ^y for $x, y \in \{\mathrm{on, off}\}$ model whether power is delivered via the interface from the right or left, respectively, or not. Hence, power flows from left to right via c_8, and from right to left via c_4; and we ensure via the contactors that power cannot flow in the other direction, preventing short circuits.

Reactive Loop. We model each component as an infinite loop of Player $\square$ and Player $\Diamond$ actions. One iteration of the loop, called *time step*, represents one time unit T, and the system steps through several stages, corresponding to the states in $\mathcal{G}_\ell$ (and $\mathcal{G}_r$): in s_1 the status of the generators is set every Nth time step; in s_2 the controller sets the contactors; in s_3 the delay is chosen nondeterministically; in s_4 actions specify whether both buses are powered, and whether a failure occurs; and in s_5 information is transmitted over the interface. The τ-labelled Dirac transitions precede all Player $\Diamond$ states to enable composition [3].

Generator Assumptions. We assume that the generator status remains the same for N time steps, i.e. after $0, N, 2N, \ldots$ steps the status may change, with the generators each powered with probability p_g, independently from each other. N and p_g can be obtained from the mean-time-to-failure of the generators. This is in contrast to [16], where, due to non-probabilistic modelling, the strongest assumption is that generators do not fail at the same time.

Table 1. Performance statistics, for various choices of b (bus uptime), f (failure rate), i^{on} (interface uptime), and model and algorithm parameters. A minus $(-)$ for i^{on} means the interface is not used. The Pareto and Strategy columns show the times for EE Pareto set computation and strategy construction, respectively.

Target			Model Params.				Algorithm Params.		Runtime [s]	
b	f	i^{on}	N	$\text{del}^{\max}$	p_g	$\lvert S\rvert$	ε	k	Pareto	Strategy
0.90	0.01	$-$	0	0	0.8	1152	0.001	20	25	0.29
0.85	0.01	$-$	3	1	0.8	15200	0.001	65	1100	2.9
0.90	0.01	$-$	3	1	0.8	15200	0.001	118	2100	2.1
0.90	0.01	0.6	0	0	0.8	2432	0.01	15	52	0.53
0.95	0.01	0.6	0	0	0.8	2432	0.01	15	49	0.46
0.90	0.01	0.6	2	1	0.8	24744	0.01	80	4300	4.80

5.2 Specifications and Results

The main objective is to maximise uptime of the buses, while avoiding failures due to short circuits, as in [16]. Hence, the controller has to react to the generator status, and cannot just leave all contactors connected. The properties are specified as ratio rewards, since we are interested in the proportion of time the buses are powered. To use Theorem 3, we attach all rewards to the status actions or the synchronised actions I_ℓ^x and I_r^y. Moreover, every time step, the reward structure t attaches T to these actions to measure the progress of time.

The reward structure "buses$_\ell$" (resp. "buses$_r$") assigns T for each time unit both buses of $\mathcal{G}_\ell$ (resp. $\mathcal{G}_r$) are powered; and the reward structure "fail$_\ell$" (resp. "fail$_r$") assigns 1 for every time unit a short circuit occurs in $\mathcal{G}_\ell$ (resp. $\mathcal{G}_r$). Since the synchronised actions I_r^{on} and I_ℓ^{on} are taken whenever power is delivered over the interface, we attach reward structures, with the same name, assigning T whenever the corresponding action is taken. For each component $x \in \{\ell, r\}$, the objectives are to keep the uptime of the buses above b, i.e. $P_x^{\text{bus}} \equiv \text{Pratio}_{\varsigma_0}(\text{buses}_x/t)(b)$; to keep the failure rate below f, i.e. $P_x^{\text{safe}} \equiv \text{Pratio}_{\varsigma_0}(-\text{fail}_x/t)(-f)$, where minimisation is expressed using negation; and, if used, to keep the interface uptime above i^{on}, i.e. $P_x^{\text{int}} \equiv \text{Pratio}_{\varsigma_0}(I_x^{\text{on}}/t)(i^{\text{on}})$. We hence consider the specification $P_x^{\text{bus}} \wedge P_x^{\text{safe}} \wedge P_x^{\text{int}}$, for $x \in \{\ell, r\}$. Using the rule from Theorem 3 in Theorem 1 of [3], we obtain the strategy composed of the individual strategies to control the full system, satisfying $P_\ell^{\text{bus}} \wedge P_\ell^{\text{safe}} \wedge P_r^{\text{bus}} \wedge P_r^{\text{safe}}$, i.e. both components are safe and the buses are powered.

Strategy Synthesis. We implement the algorithms of this paper as an extension of our multi-objective strategy synthesis tool of [7], using a compact representation of the polyhedra $F_M^k(\top)$. Table 1 shows, for several parameter choices, the experimental results, which were obtained on a 2.8 GHz PC with 32 GB RAM. In [16], the uptime objective was encoded in LTL by requiring that buses are powered at least every Kth time step, yielding an uptime for the buses of $1/K$, which translates to an uptime of 20% (by letting $K = 5$). In contrast, using stochastic games we can utilise the statistics of the generator reliability, and obtain bus uptimes of up to 95% for generator health $p_g = 0.8$. For the models without delay, the synthesised strategies approximate memoryless deterministic strategies but when adding delay, randomisation is introduced in the memory updates. The model will be included in a forthcoming release of our tool.

6 Conclusion

We synthesise strategies for almost sure satisfaction of multi-dimensional average and ratio objectives, and demonstrate their application to assume-guarantee controller synthesis. It would be interesting to study the complexity class of the problem considered here. Satisfaction for arbitrary thresholds is subject to further research. Solutions involving an oracle computing the almost-sure winning region [9] would need to be adapted to handle our ε-approximations. Moreover, we are interested in strategies for disjunctions of satisfaction objectives.

Acknowledgements. Part of this work was sponsored by ERC AdG-246967 VERIWARE, and AFOSR grant FA9550-12-1-0302, ONR grant N000141310778.

References

1. Baier, C., Dubslaff, C., Klüppelholz, S., Leuschner, L.: Energy-utility analysis for resilient systems using probabilistic model checking. In: Ciardo, G., Kindler, E. (eds.) PETRI NETS 2014. LNCS, vol. 8489, pp. 20–39. Springer, Heidelberg (2014)
2. Basset, N., Kwiatkowska, M., Topcu, U., Wiltsche, C.: Strategy synthesis for stochastic games with multiple long-run objectives. Technical Report RR-14-10, University of Oxford (2014)
3. Basset, N., Kwiatkowska, M., Wiltsche, C.: Compositional controller synthesis for stochastic games. In: Baldan, P., Gorla, D. (eds.) CONCUR 2014. LNCS, vol. 8704, pp. 173–187. Springer, Heidelberg (2014)
4. Brázdil, T., Brozek, V., Chatterjee, K., Forejt, V., Kucera, A.: Two views on multiple mean-payoff objectives in Markov decision processes. LMCS 10(1) (2014)
5. Chatterjee, K., Randour, M., Raskin, J.F.: Strategy synthesis for multi-dimensional quantitative objectives. Acta Inf. 51(3-4), 129–163 (2014)
6. Chen, T., Forejt, V., Kwiatkowska, M., Simaitis, A., Wiltsche, C.: On stochastic games with multiple objectives. In: Chatterjee, K., Sgall, J. (eds.) MFCS 2013. LNCS, vol. 8087, pp. 266–277. Springer, Heidelberg (2013)
7. Chen, T., Kwiatkowska, M., Simaitis, A., Wiltsche, C.: Synthesis for multi-objective stochastic games: An application to autonomous urban driving. In: Joshi, K., Siegle, M., Stoelinga, M., D'Argenio, P.R. (eds.) QEST 2013. LNCS, vol. 8054, pp. 322–337. Springer, Heidelberg (2013)
8. Automation Direct. Part number AD-SSR610-AC-280A, Relays and Timers, Book 2 (14.1), eRL-45 (2014)
9. Gimbert, H., Horn, F.: Solving simple stochastic tail games. In: SODA, pp. 847–862. SIAM (2010)
10. Kwiatkowska, M., Norman, G., Parker, D., Qu, H.: Compositional probabilistic verification through multi-objective model checking. I&C, 232:38–65 (2013)
11. Michalko, R.G.: Electrical starting, generation, conversion and distribution system architecture for a more electric vehicle, US Patent 7,439,634 (2008)

12. Segala, R.: Modelling and Verification of Randomized Distributed Real Time Systems. PhD thesis, Massachusetts Institute of Technology (1995)
13. Shapley, L.S.: Stochastic games. Proc. Natl. Acad. Sci. USA 39(10), 1095 (1953)
14. Sinnett, M.: 787 no-bleed systems: saving fuel and enhancing operational efficiencies. Aero Quarterly, 6–11 (2007)
15. von Essen, C.: Quantitative Verification and Synthesis. PhD thesis, VERIMAG (2014)
16. Xu, H., Topcu, U., Murray, R.M.: Reactive protocols for aircraft electric power distribution. In: CDC. IEEE (2012)

FAUST²: Formal Abstractions of Uncountable-STate STochastic Processes

Sadegh Esmaeil Zadeh Soudjani[1], Caspar Gevaerts[1], and Alessandro Abate[2,1,*]

[1] Delft Center for Systems and Control (DCSC),
TU Delft – Delft University of Technology, Delft, The Netherlands
S.EsmaeilZadehSoudjani@tudelft.nl
[2] Department of Computer Science, University of Oxford, Oxford, United Kingdom
alessandro.abate@cs.ox.ac.uk

Abstract. FAUST² is a software tool that generates formal abstractions of (possibly non-deterministic) discrete-time Markov processes (dtMP) defined over uncountable (continuous) state spaces. A dtMP model is specified in MATLAB and abstracted as a finite-state Markov chain or a Markov decision process. The abstraction procedure runs in MATLAB and employs parallel computations and fast manipulations based on vector calculus, which allows scaling beyond state-of-the-art alternatives. The abstract model is formally put in relationship with the concrete dtMP via a user-defined maximum threshold on the approximation error introduced by the abstraction procedure. FAUST² allows exporting the abstract model to well-known probabilistic model checkers, such as PRISM or MRMC. Alternatively, it can handle internally the computation of PCTL properties (e.g. safety or reach-avoid) over the abstract model. FAUST² allows refining the outcomes of the verification procedures over the concrete dtMP in view of the quantified and tunable error, which depends on the dtMP dynamics and on the given formula. The toolbox is available at
http://sourceforge.net/projects/faust2/

1 Models: Discrete-Time Markov Processes

We consider a discrete-time Markov process (dtMP) $s(k), k \in \mathbb{N} \cup \{0\}$ defined over a general state space, such as a finite-dimensional Euclidean domain [1] or a hybrid state space [2]. The model is denoted by the pair $\mathfrak{S} = (\mathcal{S}, T_\mathfrak{s})$. $\mathcal{S}$ is a continuous (uncountable) but bounded state space, e.g. $\mathcal{S} \subset \mathbb{R}^n, n < \infty$. We denote by $\mathcal{B}(\mathcal{S})$ the associated sigma algebra and refer the reader to [2, 3] for details on measurability and topological considerations. The conditional stochastic kernel $T_\mathfrak{s} : \mathcal{B}(\mathcal{S}) \times \mathcal{S} \to [0, 1]$ assigns to each point $s \in \mathcal{S}$ a probability measure $T_\mathfrak{s}(\cdot|s)$, so that for any set $A \in \mathcal{B}(\mathcal{S}), k \in \mathbb{N} \cup \{0\}$,

$$\mathbb{P}(s(k+1) \in A | s(k) = s) = \int_A T_\mathfrak{s}(d\bar{s}|s).$$

* This work has been supported by the European Commission STREP project MoVeS 257005 and IAPP project AMBI 324432, and by the John Fell OUP Research Fund.

C. Baier and C. Tinelli (Eds.): TACAS 2015, LNCS 9035, pp. 272–286, 2015.
DOI: 10.1007/978-3-662-46681-0_23

We refer to the code or to the case study for a modeling example. The software allows handling the relevant instance of Stochastic Hybrid Systems (SHS). SHS are discrete-time Markov processes evolving over hybrid state spaces. The hybrid state $s = (q, x)$ of SHS has two components: $q \in \mathcal{Q}$ is the discrete part, and $x \in \mathbb{R}^{n_q}$ is the continuous part. The state space of the SHS is the (disjoint) union of continuous spaces associated to the discrete locations $\mathcal{S} \subset \cup_{q \in \mathcal{Q}}\{q\} \times \mathbb{R}^{n_q}$. The formal definition and characterization of the conditional stochastic kernel of a SHS, along its theoretical analysis and formal verification, are discussed in detail in [2, 4–9].

Implementation: FAUST^2 in implemented in MATLAB and its user interaction is enhanced by a Graphical User Interface as in Figure 1. A dtMP model is fed into FAUST^2 as follows. Select the Formula free option in the box Problem selection ① in Figure 1, and enter the bounds on the state space $\mathcal{S}$ as a $n \times 2$ matrix in the prompt Domain in box ⑧. Alternatively if the user presses the button Select ⑧, a pop-up window prompts the user to enter the lower and upper values of the box-shaped bounds of the state space. The transition kernel $T_\mathfrak{s}$ can be specified by the user (select User-defined ②) in an m-file, entered in the text-box Name of kernel function, or loaded by pressing the button Search for file ⑦. Please open the files ./Templates/SymbolicKernel.m for a template and ExampleKernel.m for an instance of kernel $T_\mathfrak{s}$. As a special case, the class of affine dynamical systems with additive Gaussian noise is described by the difference equation $s(k+1) = \mathtt{A}s(k) + \mathtt{B} + \eta(k)$, where $\eta(\cdot) \sim \mathcal{N}(0, \mathtt{Sigma})$. (Refer to the Case Study on how to express the difference equation as a stochastic kernel.) For this common instance, the user can select the option Linear Gaussian model in the box Kernel distribution ②, and input properly-sized matrices $\mathtt{A}, \mathtt{B}, \mathtt{Sigma}$ in the MATLAB workspace. FAUST^2 also handles Gaussian dynamical models $s(k + 1) = f(s(k)) + g(s(k))\eta(k)$ with nonlinear drift and variance: select the bottom option in box ② and enter the symbolic function [f g] via box ⑦. □

The software also handles models with non-determinism [9], here regarded as *external* and as such accessible: a *controlled* dtMP is a tuple $\mathfrak{S} = (\mathcal{S}, \mathcal{U}, T_\mathfrak{s})$, where $\mathcal{S}$ is as before, $\mathcal{U}$ is a continuous control space (e.g. a bounded set in $\mathbb{R}^m$), and $T_\mathfrak{s}$ is a Borel-measurable stochastic kernel $T_\mathfrak{s} : \mathcal{B}(\mathcal{S}) \times \mathcal{S} \times \mathcal{U} \to [0, 1]$, which assigns to any state $s \in \mathcal{S}$ and input $u \in \mathcal{U}$ a probability measure $T_\mathfrak{s}(\cdot|s, u)$.

Implementation: In order to specify a non-deterministic model in FAUST^2, tick the relevant check Controlled/non-deterministic model ③, and enter the bounds on the space $\mathcal{U}$ as a $m \times 2$ matrix in the window Input set ⑧. □

2   Formal Finite-State Abstractions of dtMP Models

This section discusses the basic procedure to approximate a dtMP $\mathfrak{S} = (\mathcal{S}, T_\mathfrak{s})$ as a finite-state Markov chain (MC) $\mathfrak{P} = (\mathcal{P}, T_p)$, as implemented in FAUST^2. $\mathcal{P} = \{z_1, z_2, \ldots, z_p\}$ is a finite set of abstract states of cardinality p, and $T_p : \mathcal{P} \times \mathcal{P} \to [0, 1]$ is a transition probability matrix over the finite space $\mathcal{P}$: $T_p(z, z')$ characterizes the probability of transitioning from state z to state z'. The finite

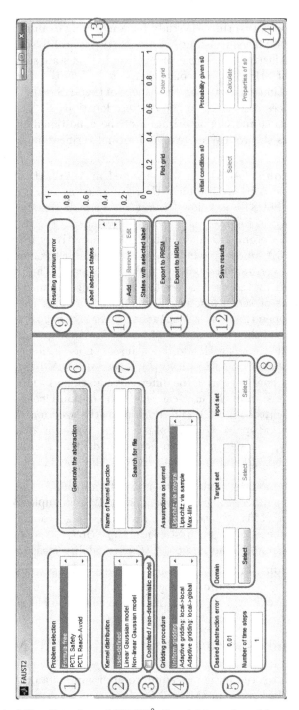

Fig. 1. Graphical User Interface of FAUST^2. Overlaid numbered boxes refer to specific description in the text.

state space of $\mathfrak{P}$ is constructed by (arbitrarily) partitioning the state space of $\mathfrak{S}$ and selecting a representative point in each partition set to make up the states in $\mathcal{P}$. The probability of transitioning from (abstract) state z to state z', $T_p(z, z')$, is computed by marginalizing the stochastic kernel $T_{\mathfrak{s}}$ of $\mathfrak{S}$, namely computing the probability of jumping from state z to any point in the (concrete) partition set corresponding to the (abstract) state z'. Algorithm 1 describes the abstraction of model $\mathfrak{S}$ as a finite-state MC $\mathfrak{P}$ [6]. In Algorithm 1, $\Xi : \mathcal{P} \to 2^{\mathcal{S}}$ represents a set-valued map that associates to any point $z_i \in \mathcal{P}$ the corresponding partition set $A_i \subseteq \mathcal{S}$, whereas the map $\xi : 2^{\mathcal{S}} \to \mathcal{P}$ relates any point s or set in $\mathcal{S}$ to the corresponding discrete state in $\mathcal{P}$.

Algorithm 1. Abstraction of dtMP $\mathfrak{S}$ by MC $\mathfrak{P}$

Require: input dtMP $\mathfrak{S} = (\mathcal{S}, T_{\mathfrak{s}})$
 1: Select a finite partition of the state space $\mathcal{S}$ as $\mathcal{S} = \cup_{i=1}^{p} A_i$ (A_i are non-overlapping)

 2: For each A_i, select an arbitrary representative point $z_i \in A_i, \{z_i\} = \xi(A_i)$
 3: Define $\mathcal{P} = \{z_i, i = 1, ..., p\}$ as the finite state space of the MC $\mathfrak{P}$
 4: Compute the transition probability matrix $T_p(z, z') = T_{\mathfrak{s}}(\Xi(z')|z)$ for all $z, z' \in \mathcal{P}$
Ensure: output MC $\mathfrak{P} = (\mathcal{P}, T_p)$

Consider the representation of the kernel $T_{\mathfrak{s}}$ by its density function $t_{\mathfrak{s}} : \mathcal{S} \times \mathcal{S} \to \mathbb{R}^{\geq 0}$, namely $T_{\mathfrak{s}}(ds'|s) = t_{\mathfrak{s}}(s'|s)ds'$ for any $s, s' \in \mathcal{S}$. The abstraction error over the next-step probability distribution introduced by Algorithm 1 depends on the regularity of function $t_{\mathfrak{s}}$: assuming that $t_{\mathfrak{s}}$ is Lipschitz continuous, namely that there is a finite positive constant $h_{\mathfrak{s}}$ such that

$$|t_{\mathfrak{s}}(\bar{s}|s) - t_{\mathfrak{s}}(\bar{s}|s')| \leq h_{\mathfrak{s}} \|s - s'\|, \quad \forall s, s', \bar{s} \in \mathcal{S}, \tag{1}$$

then the next-step error is $E = h_{\mathfrak{s}} \delta_{\mathfrak{s}} \mathscr{L}(\mathcal{S})$, where $\delta_{\mathfrak{s}}$ is the max diameter of the state-space partition sets and $\mathscr{L}(\mathcal{S})$ is the volume of the state space [6]. When interested in working over a finite, N-step time horizon, the error results in the quantity EN. Notice that the error can be reduced via $\delta_{\mathfrak{s}}$ by considering a finer partition, which on the other hand results in a MC $\mathfrak{P}$ with a larger state space. It is evidently key to obtain error bounds that are as tight as possible: the error bounds on the abstraction can be improved in three different ways [8, 10]. First, by computing a local version of the error; second, by leveraging continuity requirements that go beyond the Lipschitz condition raised in (1); and, finally, by normalizing possibly ill-conditioned dynamics operating on heterogeneous spatial scales.

Implementation: FAUST^2 enables the user to enter the time horizon N of interest (box **Number of time steps** ⑤), and a threshold on the maximum allowed error (box **Desired abstraction error** ⑤). The software generates a Markov chain with the desired accuracy by pressing the button **Generate the abstraction** ⑥. Among other messages, the user is prompted with an estimated running time, which is based on an over-approximation of the Lipschitz constant of the kernel, on a uniform partitioning of the space $\mathcal{S}^1$, and on the availability of parallelization procedures in MATLAB, and is asked whether to proceed.   □

In the case of a non-deterministic dtMP, the input space is also partitioned as $\mathcal{U} = \cup_{i=1}^{q} U_i$, and arbitrary points $u_i \in U_i$ are selected. The dtMP $\mathfrak{S}$ is abstracted as a Markov decision process (MDP) $\mathfrak{P} = (\mathcal{P}, \mathcal{U}_p, T_p)$, where now the finite input space is $\mathcal{U}_p = \{u_1, u_2, \ldots, u_q\}$, and $T_p(u, z, z') = T_{\mathfrak{s}}(\Xi(z')|z, u)$ for all $z, z' \in \mathcal{P}, u \in \mathcal{U}_p$. The abstraction error can be formally quantified as $E = 2(h_{\mathfrak{s}} \delta_{\mathfrak{s}} + h_u \delta_u) \mathscr{L}(\mathcal{S})$, where δ_u is the max diameter of the input-space partitions and h_u is the Lipschitz constant of the density function with respect to the inputs, that is $|t_{\mathfrak{s}}(\bar{s}|s, u) - t_{\mathfrak{s}}(\bar{s}|s, u')| \leq h_u \|u - u'\|$, $\forall u, u' \in \mathcal{U}, s, \bar{s} \in \mathcal{S}$.

Implementation: The user may tick the check in ③ to indicate that the dtMP is controlled (non-deterministic), specify a box-shaped domain for the input in box Input set ⑧, enter a time horizon in box Number of time steps ⑤, and require an error threshold in box Desired abstraction error ⑤. FAUST² automatically generates an MDP according to the relevant formula on the error.

Notice that the quantification of the abstraction error requires state and input spaces to be bounded. In the case of an unbounded state space, the user should truncate it to a bounded, box-shaped domain: selecting the Formula free option in the box Problem selection ①, the domain is prompted in box Domain ⑧. Algorithm 1 is automatically adjusted by assigning an absorbing abstract state to the truncated part of the state space. For details please see [10, 11].

The user may select one of two options in the box Gridding procedure ④, dealing with adaptive gridding. FAUST² generates partition sets based on local computation of the error, as follows: a rather course partition of the state space is initially selected and the corresponding local errors are computed; the partition is sequentially refined by splitting the sets if the maximum local error is greater than the threshold entered by the user in box ⑤. In the step, the partition can be refined by splitting the partition set with the largest local error, which results in an abstraction with the least number of states but requires a larger computational time (cf. [10, Algorithm 3]); alternatively, FAUST² obtains faster generation time by splitting all the sets with local errors greater than threshold (cf. [10, Algorithm 4]). Both procedures are guaranteed to result, after a finite number of steps, in the desired selected error. We plan to implement an *anytime algorithm* option, as possible for the discussed adaptive gridding procedures. This option enables the user to externally interrupt the refinement procedure at any time, and returns the last computed abstract model together with its associated error bound.   □

The states of the abstract model $\mathfrak{P}$ may be labeled. The state labeling map $\mathsf{L} : \mathcal{P} \to \Sigma$, where Σ is a finite alphabet, is defined by a set of linear inequalities: for any $\alpha \in \Sigma$ the user characterizes the set of states $\mathsf{L}^{-1}(\alpha)$ as the intersection of half-planes (say, as a box or a simplex): the software automatically determines

---

[1] At the moment we assume to have selected options Uniform gridding and Lipschitz via integral among the lists in box ④. Comments on further options are in Section 3.

all points $z \in \mathcal{P}$ belonging to set $\mathsf{L}^{-1}(\alpha)$. The obtained labeled finite-state model can be automatically exported to well-known model checkers, such as PRISM and MRMC [12, 13], for further analysis. In view of the discussed error bounds, the outcomes of the model checking procedures over the abstract model $\mathfrak{P}$ may be refined over the concrete dtMP $\mathfrak{G}$ – more details can be found in [6, 11].

Implementation: Labels are introduced in FAUST^2 as follows: suppose that the intersection of half-planes $A_\alpha z \leq B_\alpha$ (where A_α, B_α are properly-sized matrices) tags states z by label $\alpha \in \Sigma$. The user may add such a label by pressing button Add ⑩ and subsequently entering symbol α and matrices A_α, B_α in the pop-up window. The user can also edit or remove any previously defined label using buttons Edit, Remove in ⑩, respectively. The button States with selected label ⑩ shows the sets associated to the active label over the plot in ⑬ .

The user may click the buttons in ⑪ to export the abstracted model to PRISM or to MRMC. Alternatively, FAUST^2 is designed to automatically check or optimize over quantitative, non-nested PCTL properties, without relying on external model checkers: Section 3 elaborates on this capability.   □

3   Formula-Dependent Abstractions for Verification

Algorithm 1, presented in Section 2, can be employed to abstract a dtMP as a finite-state MC/MDP, and to directly check it against properties such as probabilistic invariance or reach-avoid, that is over (quantitative, non-nested) bounded-until specifications in PCTL [14]. Next, we detail this procedure for the finite-horizon probabilistic invariance (a.k.a. safety) problem, which can be formalized as follows. Consider a bounded continuous set $A \in \mathcal{B}(\mathcal{S})$ representing the set of safe states. Compute the probability that an execution of $\mathfrak{G}$, associated with an initial condition $s_0 \in \mathcal{S}$ remains within set A during the finite time horizon $[0, N]$, that is $p_{s_0}(A) := \mathbb{P}\{s(k) \in A \text{ for all } k \in [0, N]|s(0) = s_0\}$.

The quantity $p_{s_0}(A)$ can be employed to characterize the satisfiability set of a corresponding bounded-until PCTL formula, namely

$$s_0 \models \mathbb{P}_{\sim\epsilon}\{\text{true } \mathsf{U}^{\leq N}(\mathcal{S}\backslash A)\}   \Leftrightarrow   p_{s_0}(A) \sim 1 - \epsilon,$$

where $\mathcal{S}\backslash A$ is the complement of A over $\mathcal{S}$, true is a state formula valid everywhere on $\mathcal{S}$, the inequality operator $\sim \in \{>, \geq, <, \leq\}$, and $\sim$ represents its complement.

FAUST^2 formally approximates the computation of $p_{s_0}(A), \forall s_0 \in \mathcal{S}$, as follows. $\mathfrak{G}$ is abstracted as an MC $\mathfrak{P}$ via Algorithm 1: the bounded safe set A is partitioned as $A = \cup_{i=1}^{p-1} A_i$; representative points $z_i \in A_i$ are selected and, along with an extra absorbing variable ϕ for $\mathcal{S}\backslash A$, make up the state space $\mathcal{P}$; the transition probability matrix T_p is obtained by marginalizing the concrete kernel $T_\mathfrak{s}$. Given the obtained discrete-time MC $\mathfrak{P} = (\mathcal{P}, T_p)$ and considering the finite safe set $A_p = \{z_1, \ldots, z_{p-1}\} \subset \mathcal{P}$, FAUST^2 internally computes the safety probability over $\mathfrak{P}$ via dynamic programming [6], along with the associated abstraction error which is now tailored over the PCTL formula of interest.

Implementation: The user may select option PCTL Safety in the list within box ①, enter the boundaries of the Safe set within box ⑧, and press button ⑥ to proceed obtaining the abstraction and computing the probability of the selected formula. The computed value of $p_{s_0}(A)$ is displayed in box Probability given s0 ⑭, for any user-selected initial state s_0 that is input in box Initial condition s0 ⑭. The user can optionally press button Properties of s0 ⑭ to get more information about the concrete state s_0, including the related discrete state $z = \xi(\Xi(s))$ of the MC, as well as the associated labels. Furthermore, the quantity $p_{s_0}(A)$ can be plotted, as a function of the initial state s_0, by pressing buttons Plot grid and Color grid in ⑬. Clearly these outputs are exclusively available for models of dimensions $n = 1, 2, 3$.   □

It is of interest to obtain tight bounds on the error associated to the abstraction procedure since, given a user-defined error threshold, tighter bounds would generate abstract models $\mathfrak{P}$ with fewer states. The abstraction error bound in FAUST^2, tailored around the discussed safety problem, can be efficiently decreased under different types of regularity assumptions on the conditional density function of the dtMP $\mathfrak{S}$ [10]. For instance, in contrast to the global continuity assumption in (1), if $t_\mathfrak{s}$ is locally Lipschitz continuous as

$$|t_\mathfrak{s}(\bar{s}|s) - t_\mathfrak{s}(\bar{s}|s')| \leq h(i,j) \|s - s'\|, \quad \forall \bar{s} \in A_j, \forall s, s' \in A_i, \tag{2}$$

(here sets A_i form a partition of A, as from Algorithm 1) then the error is

$$|p_{s_0}(A) - p_{p_0}(A_p)| \leq \max\{\gamma_i \delta_i | i = 1, ..., p\}, \tag{3}$$

where $p_{p_0}(A_p)$ is initialized at the discrete state $p_0 = \xi(s_0) \in A_p$. Here δ_i is the diameter of the set $A_i \subset A$, and the constants γ_i are given by $\gamma_i = N \sum_{j=1}^{m} h(i,j) \mathscr{L}(A_j)$. Since $h(i,j) \leq h_\mathfrak{s}$, the obtained error in (3) is smaller than the older quantity $N h_\mathfrak{s} \delta_\mathfrak{s} \mathscr{L}(\mathcal{S})$. Notice that the structure of the error in (3) leads to gridding algorithms for abstraction that are adapted to the formula and can be made sequential [10]: FAUST^2 initializes the procedure with coarse partition sets (resulting in a small MC abstraction but with a large approximation error), and sequentially refines the partitions adaptively where the local errors are high (leading to an MC abstraction with increasing state space), until the global error becomes less than a user-defined threshold.

Implementation: FAUST^2 allows the user to select three different gridding procedures in box Gridding procedure ④: the reader is referred to [10] for the details of these three options. The Uniform gridding option leads to a one-shot (non sequential) procedure, as already discussed in Section 2, whereas the two Adaptive gridding options result in sequential and adaptive procedures leading to better errors and to smaller abstractions, but in general requiring more computation time. The error bound quantification hinges on the constant in the right-hand side of (2), which can be computed differently as in box Assumptions on kernel ④: tighter errors lead to longer computations [10]. In order to provide full control on the chosen inputs, for any possible selection of gridding procedure, desired abstraction error, and error bound computation, the user is prompted in a pop-up window with an estimated running time, and asked whether to proceed.

This range of algorithms and procedures are also implemented for probabilistic reach-avoid (constrained reachability) problems, which are encompassed by general bounded-until PCTL formulas $\mathbb{P}_{\sim\epsilon}\{\Phi \, \mathsf{U}^{\leq N}\Psi\}$. The user can select this option in box Problem selection ①, and is asked to input sets Φ, Ψ as safe and target sets in the texts in box ⑧.

Let us remark that the described abstraction algorithms and procedures are also available for the formula-free abstraction discussed in Section 2.   □

The safety problem for a controlled dtMP [9] is defined as follows. Consider the class of deterministic Markov policies $\pi = (\mu_0, \mu_1, \ldots)$, where the functions $\mu_k : \mathcal{S} \to \mathcal{U}$ are properly measurable deterministic functions. The safety probability for a controlled dtMP under a given policy π is given by

$$p_{s_0}^{\pi}(A) := \mathbb{P}\{s(k) \in A \text{ for all } k \in [0, N] | s(0) = s_0, u(k+1) = \mu_k(s(k))\}.$$

The safety problem deals with the computation of the *maximally safe* deterministic Markov policy π^*, such that $p_{s_0}^{\pi^*}(A) = \sup_{\pi} p_{s_0}^{\pi}(A)$, $\forall s_0 \in A$. Similarly we can compute the *minimally safe* policy, or an optimal policy related to the reach-avoid problem (defined with the bounded-until operator).

Implementation: FAUST^2 computes a suboptimal policy for a given problem over an MDP, with a given threshold on the distance to the optimal safety probability, and quantifies the corresponding approximate quantity $p_{s_0}^{\pi^*}(A)$. The approximate optimal policy can be stored by pushing button Save results ⑫, which provides the user with two options: either storing it in the disk as a .mat file, or loading it to the workspace.   □

4   Accessing and Testing **FAUST^2**

The toolbox is available at

http://sourceforge.net/projects/faust2/

We have successfully tested the toolbox with MATLAB R2012a, R2012b, R2013a, R2013b, on machines running Windows 7, Apple OSX 10.9, and Linux Open-SUSE. FAUST^2 exploits the command integral of MATLAB (introduced in version R2012a) for numerical integrations. (The previous versions of MATLAB contain instruction quad and its variations, which will be removed in the future versions of MATLAB – we have thus opted for the most up-to-date version.) Optimization and symbolic computation toolboxes of MATLAB are necessary. FAUST^2 automatically checks the presence of these packages and displays an error to the user in their absence. The software also takes the advantage of the MATLAB parallel computation toolbox if present. The use of parallel computation toolbox is currently disabled for Apple operating systems due to a conflict.

Please download FAUST^2 from Sourceforge. The files are organized in the main folder as follows: the sub-folder Autonomous Models contains the codes for deterministic systems (without input); the sub-folder Controlled Models

includes the codes for non-deterministic systems (input dependent); the sub-
folder `Templates` contains templates and examples for the definition of symbolic
conditional density functions; the sub-folder `Case Study` contains the files used
in the next Section to test the software on a practical study. The file `README` can
be opened with your preferred text editor and contains instructions on how to
set up and run the software. Alternatively, FAUST^2 can be tested on a case study
as elaborated in the next Section. Please set the current directory of MATLAB
to the folder where the software is stored and run `FAUST2.m` from the MATLAB
command line.

5   Case Study

In this section we apply FAUST^2 to compute optimal control strategies for the
known room temperature regulation benchmark [15]. Probabilistic models for
the underlying dynamics are based on [16] and on [2]. We consider the temperature regulation in multiple rooms via cooling water circulation. The amount
of extracted heat is changed via a flow-control valve. Then the input signal is
the percentage of the valve in the open position. The dynamics of the room
temperature evolve in discrete time according to the equations

$$s_1(k+1) = s_1(k) + \frac{\Delta}{C_{ra}}((s_2(k) - s_1(k))k_{cw}u(k) + (T_a - s_1(k))k_{out}) + \eta_{ra}(k),$$

$$s_2(k+1) = s_2(k) + \frac{\Delta}{C_{cw}}((s_1(k) - s_2(k))k_{cw}u(k) + Q) + \eta_{cw}(k), \qquad (4)$$

where s_1 is the air temperature inside the room, s_2 is the cooling water temperature, T_a is the ambient temperature, Δ is the discrete sampling time [min],
and $\eta_{ra}(\cdot), \eta_{cw}(\cdot)$ are stationary, independent random processes with normal
distributions $\mathcal{N}(0, \sigma_{ra}^2 \Delta)$ and $\mathcal{N}(0, \sigma_{cw}^2 \Delta)$, respectively. Equations (4) can be
encompassed in the condensed two-dimensional model

$$s(k+1) = f(s(k), u(k)) + \eta(k), \quad \eta(\cdot) \sim \mathcal{N}(0, \Sigma_\eta),$$

which results in a stochastic kernel that is a Gaussian conditional distribution
$\mathcal{N}(f(s, u), \Sigma_\eta)$, where $\Sigma_\eta = diag(\Delta[\sigma_{ra}^2, \sigma_{cw}^2])$. The file `Chiller_Kernel_2d.m`
appearing with the release of the software, provides numerical values and phys-
ical interpretations of the parameters in equations (4), as well as the symbolic
structure of the conditional density function. The dynamical model in (4) can be
as well extended to a two-room temperature control (which results in a three-
dimensional model), and its conditional density function can be found in file
`Chiller_Kernel_3d.m`. We will run FAUST^2 on both 2D and 3D setups.

   We are interested in keeping the temperature of the room(s) within a given
temperature interval over a fixed time horizon: this can be easily stated as a
(probabilistic) safety problem, where we maximize over the feasible inputs to
the model. We instantiate and compute this problem over the model above as
described in the main text, while providing a step-by-step guide to the user.

In order to select the problem and import the model in FAUST^2, please follow these steps: select PCTL Safety in box ①, choose User-defined in box ②, tick the check-box ③ to indicate a controlled model, and write the name Chiller_Kernel_2d.m in the text of box ⑦ to load the density function of the two-dimensional model (④).

In the next stage we perform the abstraction and compute the quantity of interest (maximal safety probability). Select the most straightforward (but coarsest) abstraction algorithm, by choosing options Uniform gridding and Lipschitz via integral in ④. Proceed entering the problem parameters as follows: input the number of time steps as 3 and select a desired abstraction error equal to 0.5 in box ⑤; enter the safe temperature interval A as [19.7,20.3; 4.7,5.3], as well as the input space $\mathcal{U}$ as [0,1] in the text within box ⑧.

At this point the software can proceed with the main computations. Please press the button in box ⑥, in order to generate the abstract MDP, to compute the optimal policy and the related maximal safety probability. When the computation is complete, let us proceed with some post-processing: press the buttons Plot grid and Color grid in box ⑬, to generate Figure 2 (left) representing the maximal safety probability. The result of the computation can be stored for further analysis by pressing button ⑫: for instance Figure 2 (right) is generated by retrieving the optimal state-dependent Markov policy at step $N-1$. The obtained abstract MDP has 144 states and 33 input actions. The experiment has been run in MATLAB 8.4 (R2014b) equipped with parallel computation toolbox on a 12-core Intel Xeon 3.47 GHz PC with 24 GB of memory and Windows 7 operating system. The initial estimate of the required time and the actual simulation time were 5.2 and 3.5 minutes, respectively. The simulation time includes both the generation of the abstract MDP and optimization over the input action.

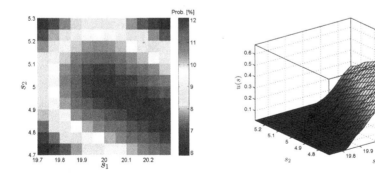

Fig. 2. Room temperature control problem. Left: obtained uniform partition of the safe set, along with optimal safety probability for each partition set (color bar on the right). The safety probability is equal to zero over the complement of the safe set. Right: optimal Markov policy at step $N-1$, as a function of the model states.

A similar procedure can be followed to study the same probabilistic safety problem over a two-room temperature control, instantiated via the density function `Chiller_Kernel_3d.m`. Figure 3 presents the outcomes obtained using the Adaptive gridding and Lipschitz via integral options, selected in box ④. The abstraction parameters used in this problem is as follows: number of time steps 3, safe temperature interval [19.5,20.5; 19.5,20.5; 4.5,5.5], input space [0,1; 0,1]. We have selected a large abstraction error equal to 12 in box ⑤ to be able to visualize the adaptive grid generated by the software. The obtained abstract MDP has 45 states and 64 input actions. The experiment has been run on the same computer. The initial estimate of the required time and the actual simulation time were 20.7 and 26.2 minutes, respectively. The user can select a smaller error, at the likely cost of a larger computation time. For this case study, the implemented approach allows for the applicability of the abstraction technique at least to models with dimension 6 (that is, with 6 continuous variables), which is beyond the performance of currently available discretization-based approaches. The reader interested in detailed computational benchmarks for the presented techniques is referred to [8, 10].

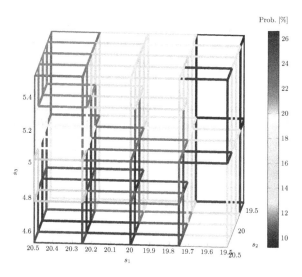

Fig. 3. Two-room temperature control problem. Obtained partition of the safe set, together (bar) with optimal safety probability.

6   Summary of the Commands in the Graphical User Interface

We provide a summary of the commands of the GUI in FAUST[2], as they appear in the boxes highlighted in Figure 1.

① The box Problem selection provides a list with three options: select Formula free to obtain an abstraction of the model which can be exported to PRISM or to MRMC for further analysis; choose PCTL Safety in order to abstract the model and compute a safety probability; or opt for PCTL Reach-Avoid to get the abstraction tailored around the computation of the reach-avoid probability.

② The box Kernel distribution gives three options in a list: select Linear Gaussian model if the model belongs to the class of Linear Gaussian difference equations (cf. Section 1) and define matrices A,B,Sigma in the MATLAB workspace; choose Non-linear Gaussian model if the process noise is Gaussian and the drift and variance are non-linear (cf. Section 1), enter the drift and variance as a single symbolic function with two outputs via box ⑦; otherwise choose User-defined and enter your kernel as a symbolic function using ⑦.

③ Check this box if the model is non-deterministic (controlled).

④ Box Gridding procedure provides three options: select Uniform gridding to generate a grid based on global Lipschitz constant h (cf. Section 2), where the state space is partitioned uniformly along each dimension; choose Adaptive gridding: local->local to generate the grid adaptively based on local Lipschitz constants $h(i,j)$ (cf. Section 3), where the size of partition sets is smaller where the local error is higher; select Adaptive gridding: local->global to generate the grid adaptively based on local Lipschitz constants $h(i)$ (cf. [10]). The first option is likely to generate the largest number of partition sets and to be the fastest in the generation of the grid. The second option is likely to generate the smallest number of partition sets but to be the slowest in the grid generation. For the detailed comparison of these gridding procedures, please see [10].

The box Assumptions on kernel provides three choices: option Lipschitz via integral requires the density function $t_\mathfrak{s}(\bar{s}|s)$ to be Lipschitz continuous with respect to the current state s, and the quantity $T_p(z,z') = T_\mathfrak{s}(\Xi(z')|z)$ is used in the marginalization (integration) step; option Lipschitz via sample requires the density function $t_\mathfrak{s}(\bar{s}|s)$ to be Lipschitz continuous with respect to both current and the next states $s, \bar{s}$, and the quantity $T_p(z,z') = T_\mathfrak{s}(z'|z)\mathscr{L}(\Xi(z'))$ is used in the marginalization step; option Max-Min does not require any continuity assumption, but takes longer time in the computation of the error.

⑤ The time horizon of the desired PCTL formula or of the problem of interest, and the required upper bound on the abstraction error should be input in these two boxes. For the case of formula-free abstraction you may enter 1 as the number of time steps.

⑥ Press this button after entering the necessary data to generate the abstraction: this runs the main code. First, various checks are done to ensure the correctness of the inputed data. Then the partition sets are generated via gridding, the transition matrix is calculated, and the probability and the optimal policy are computed if applicable.

⑦ This box is activated for options User-defined and Non-linear Gaussian model in ②. For the first option, the conditional density function must be an m-file that generates $t_s(\bar{s}|s,u)$ symbolically. Please refer to `SymbolicKernel.m` for a template and `ExampleKernel.m` for an example. The name of kernel function should be entered in the text-box or the function should be loaded by pressing the button Search for file. For the option Non-linear Gaussian model, the non-linear drift and variance must be specified as a single symbolic function with two outputs. Please refer to `NonLinKernel.m` for a template and `NonLinKernelExample.m` for an example.

⑧ If the Formula-free option is selected in ①, the user can enter the bounds of the state space in the first of the boxes, named Domain. In case any of the additional two options in ① are selected, the boundaries of the safe set should be entered in the first text-box named Safe set. If the PCTL Reach-Avoid option in ① is selected, the second box is activated and the boundaries of the target set should be entered in the text-box named Target set. If the model is non-deterministic and the check in box ③ is ticked, the third box is also activated and the boundaries of the Input space may be entered in the box named Input set. In all cases the boundaries are to be given as a matrix with two columns, where the first and second columns contain lower and upper bounds, respectively. Alternatively, the user can press the Select button and separately enter the lower and upper bounds in the pop-up window.

⑨ The resulting error of the abstraction procedure, which is less than or equal to the desired abstraction error introduced in ⑤. This box shows the error associated to the abstracted model.

⑩ The user can add, remove, or edit labels associated to the abstract states. The set of states with any label $\alpha \in \Sigma$ can be represented by the intersection of half-planes $A_\alpha z \leq B_\alpha$. In order to tag these states with the associated label, the user presses button Add and subsequently enters symbol α and matrices A_α, B_α in a pop-up window. The user can also edit or remove any previously defined label by activating its symbol in the static-box and using buttons Edit, Remove. The button States with selected label will show the set of states associated with the active label in ⑬. Adding labels is essential in particular for exporting the result to PRISM or to MRMC.

⑪ The abstracted Markov chain or MDP can be exported to PRISM or to MRMC using these buttons. FAUST[2] enables two ways of exporting the result to PRISM: as a `.prism` format that is suitable for its GUI, or as the combination of `.tra` and `.sta` files, which are appropriate for the command line.

⑫ Use this button to store the results. A pop-up window appears after pushing the button and the user can opt for storing the date over the workspace, or in memory as an `.mat` file.

⑬ The user can plot the generated grid for the state space using the first button. Pressing this button opens a new window showing the partitioned input space for the controlled model. The solution of the safety and of the reach-avoid probability can also be visualized by pressing the second button. This option obviously works exclusively for dimensions $n = 1, 2, 3$.

(14) The user can enter any initial state s_0 in the first box and calculate the safety or the reach-avoid probability of the model starting from that initial state, by pressing the button Calculate. The button Properties of s0 gives the abstracted state associated to s_0, namely $z = \xi(\Xi(s_0))$ (cf. Algorithm 1), and all the labels assigned to this state.

7   Extensions and Outlook

There are a number of enticing extensions we are planning to work on, with the objective of rendering FAUST^2 widely useful and easily deployable.

FAUST^2 is presently implemented in MATLAB, which is the modeling software of choice in a number of engineering areas. We plan to improve part of its functionalities employing a faster, lower-level programming language, and to enhance the seamless integration with model checking tools.

Furthermore, we plan to extend the functionality of FAUST^2 by allowing for general label-dependent partitioning, and we are exploring the implementation with differently shaped partitioning sets [10]. We moreover plan to extend the applicability of FAUST^2 to models with discontinuous and degenerate [17, 18] kernels, to implement higher-order approximations [19], to include abstraction techniques specialized for stochastic max-plus linear systems [20], to embed formal truncations of the model dynamics [21], and to refine techniques and algorithms for non-deterministic (control-dependent) models. Finally, we plan to look into implementing in the tool bounds for infinite horizon properties, as currently investigated theoretically.

References

1. Meyn, S., Tweedie, R.: Markov chains and stochastic stability. Springer (1993)
2. Abate, A., Prandini, M., Lygeros, J., Sastry, S.: Probabilistic reachability and safety for controlled discrete time stochastic hybrid systems. Automatica 44(11), 2724–2734 (2008)
3. Bertsekas, D., Shreve, S.: Stochastic Optimal Control: The Discrete-Time Case. Athena Scientific (1996)
4. Abate, A., Amin, S., Prandini, M., Lygeros, J., Sastry, S.: Computational approaches to reachability analysis of stochastic hybrid systems. In: Bemporad, A., Bicchi, A., Buttazzo, G. (eds.) HSCC 2007. LNCS, vol. 4416, pp. 4–17. Springer, Heidelberg (2007)
5. Summers, S., Lygeros, J.: Verification of discrete time stochastic hybrid systems: A stochastic reach-avoid decision problem. Automatica 46(12), 1951–1961 (2010)
6. Abate, A., Katoen, J.P., Lygeros, J., Prandini, M.: Approximate model checking of stochastic hybrid systems. European Journal of Control 6, 624–641 (2010)
7. Abate, A., Katoen, J.P., Mereacre, A.: Quantitative automata model checking of autonomous stochastic hybrid systems. In: ACM Proceedings of the 14th International Conference on Hybrid Systems: Computation and Control, Chicago, IL, pp. 83–92 (2011)

 8. Esmaeil Zadeh Soudjani, S., Abate, A.: Adaptive gridding for abstraction and verification of stochastic hybrid systems. In: Proceedings of the 8th International Conference on Quantitative Evaluation of Systems, pp. 59–69 (September 2011)
 9. Tkachev, I., Mereacre, A., Katoen, J., Abate, A.: Quantitative automata-based controller synthesis for non-autonomous stochastic hybrid systems. In: Proceedings of the 16th international conference on Hybrid Systems: Computation and Control, HSCC 2013, pp. 293–302 (2013)
10. Esmaeil Zadeh Soudjani, S., Abate, A.: Adaptive and sequential gridding procedures for the abstraction and verification of stochastic processes. SIAM Journal on Applied Dynamical Systems 12(2), 921–956 (2013)
11. Tkachev, I., Abate, A.: Formula-free Finite Abstractions for Linear Temporal Verification of Stochastic Hybrid Systems. In: Proceedings of the 16th International Conference on Hybrid Systems: Computation and Control, Philadelphia, PA, pp. 283–292 (April 2013)
12. Hinton, A., Kwiatkowska, M., Norman, G., Parker, D.: PRISM: A tool for automatic verification of probabilistic systems. In: Hermanns, H., Palsberg, J. (eds.) TACAS 2006. LNCS, vol. 3920, pp. 441–444. Springer, Heidelberg (2006)
13. Katoen, J.P., Khattri, M., Zapreev, I.S.: A Markov reward model checker. In: IEEE Proceedings of the International Conference on Quantitative Evaluation of Systems, Los Alamos, CA, USA, pp. 243–244 (2005)
14. Hansson, H., Jonsson, B.: A logic for reasoning about time and reliability. Formal Aspects of Computing 6(5), 512–535 (1994)
15. Fehnker, A., Ivančić, F.: Benchmarks for hybrid systems verification. In: Alur, R., Pappas, G.J. (eds.) HSCC 2004. LNCS, vol. 2993, pp. 326–341. Springer, Heidelberg (2004)
16. Malhamé, R., Chong, C.: Electric load model synthesis by diffusion approximation of a high-order hybrid-state stochastic system. IEEE Transactions on Automatic Control 30(9), 854–860 (1985)
17. Esmaeil Zadeh Soudjani, S., Abate, A.: Probabilistic invariance of mixed deterministic-stochastic dynamical systems. In: ACM Proceedings of the 15th International Conference on Hybrid Systems: Computation and Control, Beijing, PRC, pp. 207–216 (April 2012)
18. Esmaeil Zadeh Soudjani, S., Abate, A.: Probabilistic reach-avoid computation for partially-degenerate stochastic processes. IEEE Transactions on Automatic Control 59(2), 528–534 (2014)
19. Esmaeil Zadeh Soudjani, S., Abate, A.: Higher-Order Approximations for Verification of Stochastic Hybrid Systems. In: Chakraborty, S., Mukund, M. (eds.) ATVA 2012. LNCS, vol. 7561, pp. 416–434. Springer, Heidelberg (2012)
20. Adzkiya, D., Esmaeil Zadeh Soudjani, S., Abate, A.: Finite Abstractions of Stochastic Max-Plus-Linear Systems. In: Norman, G., Sanders, W. (eds.) QEST 2014. LNCS, vol. 8657, pp. 74–89. Springer, Heidelberg (2014)
21. Esmaeil Zadeh Soudjani, S., Abate, A.: Precise Approximations of the Probability Distribution of a Markov Process in Time: An Application to Probabilistic Invariance. In: Ábrahám, E., Havelund, K. (eds.) TACAS 2014 (ETAPS). LNCS, vol. 8413, pp. 547–561. Springer, Heidelberg (2014)

SAT and SMT

Linearly Ordered Attribute Grammar Scheduling Using SAT-Solving

Jeroen Bransen[1], L. Thomas van Binsbergen[2,1], Koen Claessen[3], and Atze Dijkstra[1]

[1] Utrecht University, Utrecht, The Netherlands
{J.Bransen,atze}@uu.nl
[2] Royal Holloway, University of London, Egham, UK
ltvanbinsbergen@acm.org
[3] Chalmers University of Technology, Gothenburg, Sweden
koen@chalmers.se

Abstract. Many computations over trees can be specified using attribute grammars. Compilers for attribute grammars need to find an evaluation order (or *schedule*) in order to generate efficient code. For the class of *linearly ordered attribute grammars* such a schedule can be found statically, but this problem is known to be NP-hard.

In this paper, we show how to encode linearly ordered attribute grammar scheduling as a SAT-problem. For such grammars it is necessary to ensure that the dependency graph is cycle free, which we approach in a novel way by transforming the dependency graph to a chordal graph allowing the cycle freeness to be efficiently expressed and computed using SAT solvers.

There are two main advantages to using a SAT-solver for scheduling: (1) the scheduling algorithm runs faster than existing scheduling algorithms on real-world examples, and (2) by adding extra constraints we obtain fine-grained control over the resulting schedule, thereby enabling new scheduling optimisations.

Keywords: Attribute Grammars, static analysis, SAT-solving.

1 Introduction

Attribute Grammars [Knuth, 1968] are a formalism for describing the semantics of context-free languages, thereby making them suitable for the construction of compilers. Examples of compilers written using attribute grammars are the Java compiler JastAddJ [Ekman and Hedin, 2007], and the Haskell compiler UHC [Dijkstra et al., 2009]. The use of attribute grammars in the UHC motivates this paper and as such UHC is a real world test case for evaluating the effectiveness of the given approach.

An attribute grammar essentially describes computations over trees, also known as folds or catamorphisms. Although the attribute grammar defines exactly *what* should be computed, it does not define *when* values should be computed. It is therefore up to the attribute grammar compiler (the compiler that

© Springer-Verlag Berlin Heidelberg 2015
C. Baier and C. Tinelli (Eds.): TACAS 2015, LNCS 9035, pp. 289–303, 2015.
DOI: 10.1007/978-3-662-46681-0_24

translates the attribute grammar definition into a runtime evaluator) to find an evaluation order. Such an evaluation order or schedule should satisfy the dependencies induced by the specification of attribute computations in the attribute grammar definition and must be found statically, which means that for the given grammar an evaluation order should be found such that for every finite abstract syntax tree of the grammar the evaluation order should compute all values in a finite number of steps. Specifically, no cyclic data dependencies may occur at runtime for any given parse tree.

The class of *ordered attribute grammars* [Kastens, 1980] is a well-known subclass of attribute grammars for which a polynomial time scheduling algorithm exists. However, despite what the name suggests there exist attribute grammars for which a static evaluation order can be found that do not belong to the class of ordered attribute grammars. In our work on compiler construction we often encountered such grammars, giving rise to the need of other scheduling algorithms [Bransen et al., 2012, Van Binsbergen et al., 2015]. We therefore look at the class of *linearly ordered attribute grammars* in this paper, which is the largest class of attribute grammars for which a static evaluation order can be found. The problem of statically finding such evaluation order is known to be NP-complete [Engelfriet and Filè, 1982].

1.1   Summary

We solve the linearly ordered attribute grammar scheduling problem by translating it into the Boolean satisfiability problem (SAT), the standard NP-complete problem [Cook, 1971]. Even though the worst case runtime of all known SAT-solving algorithms is exponential in the input size, many SAT-solvers work very well in practice [Claessen et al., 2009]. By translating into the SAT problem we can therefore use an efficient existing SAT-solver to solve our problem, and even benefit from future improvements in the SAT-community. In our implementation we use MiniSat[1] [Eén and Sörensson, 2004].

The core of the scheduling problem consists of finding a total order on the nodes of a set of dependency graphs (directed acyclic graphs) such that all direct dependencies, which are coming from the input grammar, are satisfied. However, there is interplay between the different dependency graphs caused by the order that is found in one dependency graph resulting in indirect dependencies that need to be satisfied in another dependency graph. This interplay of dependencies, which is explained later in detail, is what makes the problem hard.

To encode this problem in SAT we represent each edge in the dependency graphs as a Boolean variable, with its value indicating the direction of the edge. For the direct dependencies the value is already set, but for the rest of the variables the SAT-solver may choose the direction of the edge. Ensuring cycle-freeness requires us to encode transitivity with SAT-constraints, which in the straight-forward solution leads to a number of extra constraints cubic in the number of variables. To avoid that problem we make our graphs *chordal*

---

[1] http://minisat.se

[Dirac, 1961]. In a chordal graph every cycle of size > 3 contains an edge between two non-adjacent nodes in the cycle. In other words, if there exists a cycle in the graph, there must also exist a cycle of at most three nodes. This allows us to encode cycle freeness more efficiently by only disallowing cycles of length three. Chordality has been used previously to encode equality logic in SAT using undirected graphs [Bryant and Velev, 2002]; to our knowledge this is the first application of chordality to express cycle-freeness of directed graphs.

Apart from the fact that this translation into the SAT problem helps in efficiently (in practice) solving the scheduling problem, there also is another benefit: it is now possible to encode extra constraints on the resulting schedule. We show two scheduling optimisations that are interesting from an attribute grammar point of view, for which the optimal schedule can be found efficiently by expressing the optimisation in the SAT problem.

1.2 Overview

In this paper we make the following main contributions:

- We show how to encode the problem of scheduling linearly ordered attribute grammars as a SAT problem
- We show that chordal graphs can be used to encode cycle-freeness in SAT problems
- We show how certain attribute grammar optimisations can be encoded as part of the formulation of the SAT problem

Furthermore, we have implemented the described techniques in the UUAGC[2] [Swierstra et al., 1999] and show that the technique works well in practice for the UHC.

The outline of the paper is as follows. We start in Section 2 and Section 3 by explaining linearly ordered attribute grammars and the difficulties in scheduling in more detail. We then describe the translation into the SAT problem in Section 4 and show the effectiveness of our approach in Section 5. In Section 6 we describe the two attribute grammar optimisations and finally in Section 7 we discuss some problems and conclude.

2 Attribute Grammars

An attribute grammar consists of three parts: a context-free grammar, a set of attribute definitions and a set of semantic functions. Instead of a context-free grammar describing the concrete syntax of the language, we feel that it is more intuitive to visualise the grammar as describing the abstract syntax tree of the language. We therefore say that an attribute grammar consists of a set of algebraic data types describing the abstract syntax, a set of attribute definitions and a set of semantic functions. The attribute definitions and semantic functions describe how values should be computed over the abstract syntax tree.

---

[2] http://www.cs.uu.nl/wiki/HUT/AttributeGrammarSystem

In the rest of this paper we stick to the usual attribute grammar terminology, so with a *nonterminal* we mean a type, and a *production* is a constructor of that type. Furthermore, the name *lhs* (short for left-hand side) refers to the constructor itself, while the children of a production have separate names. As this paper is about scheduling and data dependencies, we do not explain the syntax of the semantic functions here, but it is important to remark that these functions define how the value of a certain attribute can be computed from other attributes.

There are two types of attributes: *inherited* attributes with values that are passed from a parent to its children, and *synthesized* attributes with values that are passed from the children to their parents. In the pictures we draw inherited attributes on the left side of a node, and the synthesized attributes on its right side.

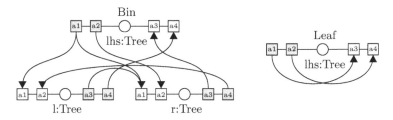

Fig. 1. Example attribute grammar for binary trees with two inherited and two synthesized attributes

In Figure 1 we show an example attribute grammar with one nonterminal *Tree* which has two productions: *Bin* and *Leaf*. The *Bin* production has two children named *l* and *r*, both of the type *Tree*, and *Leaf* has no children. The *Tree* nonterminal has four attributes: two inherited attributes a1 and a2 and two synthesized attributes a3 and a4.

The figure shows *production dependency graphs*, one for every production of the grammar. A set of semantic function definitions are given by the programmer for every production. The definitions specify how the synthesized attributes of a nonterminal are calculated in each of the different productions of that nonterminal. In semantic function definitions the inherited attributes of the nonterminal can be used as well as the synthesized attributes of its children. The attributes that are available to use, coloured gray in the picture, we call the *input* attributes. Besides the semantic functions of the synthesized attributes of the parent node, the semantic functions of the inherited attributes of the children need to be defined. The attributes that require a definition, coloured white in the picture, we call the *output* attributes. Note that with a semantic function definition for all output attributes we know how to compute all attributes as every input attribute is an output attribute of another node[3].

---

[3] Except for the inherited attributes of the root node. Its values need to be given as an argument to the semantic evaluator.

Although we talk about dependency graphs in the context of scheduling, we actually draw the edges in the other direction. The edges in the picture represent data flow, which from an attribute grammar perspective is much more intuitive. For example, in the *Bin* production the attribute a1 of the child r is computed from a1 from the parent and a3 from the child l. The edges are thus always directed from an input attribute to an output attribute, and the actual dependency graph can be obtained by reversing all edges. The edges that follow directly from the source code are the *direct dependencies*.

3   Linearly Ordered Attribute Grammars

Given an attribute grammar definition the attribute grammar compiler generates a runtime evaluator that takes an abstract syntax tree as input and computes all attribute values. There are two approaches for doing the scheduling: at runtime (dynamic) or at compile time (static).

For dynamic scheduling one could rely on existing machinery for lazy evaluation, for example in Haskell, which is the approach taken by [Saraiva, 1999]. There the attribute grammar definitions are translated into lazy Haskell functions in a straightforward way by producing functions that take the inherited attributes as argument and return the synthesized attributes. Whenever an inherited attribute (indirectly) depends on the value of a synthesized attribute, this means the function has a cyclic definition, which is no problem for languages with lazy semantics, and can actually result in efficient code [Bird, 1984].

There are two problems with dynamic scheduling. First, whenever the attribute grammar contains a true cyclic definition, the evaluator enters an infinite loop at runtime. However, these cycles could have been detected at compile time! Furthermore, the code needs lazy functions while with the static scheduling strict evaluators can be generated, leading to more efficient code in practice.

For static scheduling efficient evaluators can be generated, but the problem is that static scheduling is hard. In [Kastens, 1980] a polynomial time algorithm is given for static scheduling of the class of ordered attribute grammars, but unfortunately we often encounter attribute grammars outside of that class. All our attribute grammars do however fall in the class of linearly ordered attribute grammars, which is the largest class of attribute grammars for which a static schedule can be found. Although the scheduling is NP-complete, we have implemented a backtracking algorithm in earlier work [Van Binsbergen et al., 2015] that is feasible in practice. However, in this paper we show that we can do better by creating an algorithm that is faster and allows for different optimisations on the resulting schedule.

Conceptually, static scheduling of linearly ordered attribute grammars is not very complex. For each nonterminal a total order should be found on its attributes, such that all production dependency graphs all cycle free. However, because a nonterminal can have multiple productions and a production can have children of different types, choices made on the order of attributes of one nonterminal can influence the order of attributes in another nonterminal.

In order to encode this we also construct a *nonterminal dependency graph*. This graph contains all attributes that are defined for the corresponding nonterminal and the edges in this graph must define a total order on the attributes. Furthermore, the edges in the nonterminal dependency graph should agree with the (indirect) dependencies from the production dependency graphs such that no cycles exist.

The nonterminal dependency graphs and production dependency graphs are consistent if 1) whenever there is a path from attribute a to b in a production dependency graph then there needs to be an edge from a to b in the nonterminal dependency graph in which a and b occur[4] and 2) if there is an edge from a to b in a nonterminal dependency graph then there needs to be an edge from a to b for all occurrences of a and b in the production dependency graphs.

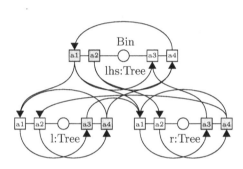

Fig. 2. Production dependency graph for Bin for the order a2 → a4 → a1 → a3

Figure 2 shows the production dependency graph of the production *Bin* with a complete order on the attributes. In this case there is only a single nonterminal so both the parent and the child nodes have the same attribute order, made explicit by extra edges from the nonterminal dependency graph. Because this dependency graph is still cycle free after adding the edges for the complete order and the same holds for the *Leaf* production, the order a2 → a4 → a1 → a3 is a valid schedule for the nonterminal *Tree*.

To find the total order we add edges to the nonterminal dependency graph and rely on the SAT-solver to determine their direction. Instead of adding an edge for all possible pairs of attributes it is sufficient to add an edge for all pairs of inherited and synthesized attributes. The order described by an assignment to these variables is not (always) total as there might be pairs of attributes, which attributes are either both inherited or both synthesized, without a relative ordering. This is not a problem as the evaluation order for such pairs can be chosen arbitrarily.

---

[4] There is no such nonterminal dependency graph if the two attributes belong to different nodes.

4   Translation into SAT

To represent the scheduling problem as a Boolean formula we introduce a variable for each edge, indicating the direction of the edge. The direct dependencies coming from the source code are constants, but for the rest of the edges the SAT-solver can decide on the direction. However, the encoding has been chosen in such way that a valid assignment of the variables corresponds to a valid schedule.

Our algorithm has the following steps:

1. Construct a nonterminal dependency graph for each nonterminal and add an edge between all pairs of inherited and synthesized attributes
2. Construct a production dependency graph for each production and add an edge for every direct dependency
3. Make all graphs chordal
4. Introduce a SAT variable for each edge in any of the graphs including the chords added in step 3. Variables of edges between attributes of the same nonterminal must be shared between nonterminal dependency graphs and production dependency graphs
5. Set the value of all variables corresponding to direct dependencies
6. Exclude all cycles of length three by adding constraints
7. Optionally add extra constraints for optimisations

The first two steps have been explained in the previous sections. Step 3 is explained below, step 4 is trivial, and step 5 and 6 follow from the explanation below. Finally step 7 is explained in Section 6.

4.1   Chordal Graphs

A chordal graph is an undirected graph in which each cycle of length > 3 contains a *chord*. A chord is an edge between two nodes in the cycle that are not adjacent. As a consequence each cycle of length > 3 can be split up into two smaller cycles, so if a chordal graph contains a cycle it must also contain a cycle of size three. Chordal graphs are therefore sometimes also referred to as *triangulated graphs*.

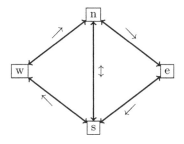

Fig. 3. There can not exists a cycle w-n-e-s without either a cycle n-s-w or n-e-s

In our case the graphs are directed, but we can still apply the same trick! In Figure 3 we illustrate how to use chordal graphs to exclude cycles. If there exists a cycle of length four, then it is not possible to choose a direction for the edge between n and s without introducing a cycle of length three. Hence, if we make our graph chordal by adding edges which may have an arbitrary direction and explicitly exclude all cycles of length three, we ensure that no cycles can exist at all.

4.2   Chordal Graph Construction

There are several algorithms for making a graph chordal. We use an algorithm based on the following alternative definition of a chordal graph:

Definition 1. *An undirected graph G is* chordal *if and only if it has a perfect elimination order. A perfect elimination order is an ordering $v_1, \ldots, v_n$ `of the vertices of G such that in the graph $G[v_1, \ldots, v_i]$, $\forall(i)$ $(1 \leq i \leq n)$, the vertex v_i is* simplicial. *A vertex v is called simplicial in a graph G if the neighbourhood of v forms a connected component in G. The neighbourhood of v are all vertices w such that there exists an edge between v and w. The graph $G[v_1, \ldots, v_i]$ is the induced subgraph of G containing only the vertices $v_i, \ldots, v_i$ and the edges between these vertices.*

From this definition we can construct the following algorithm for making a graph chordal:

1. While the graph still contains vertices:
   (a) Select a vertex v from the graph
   (b) For every pair (a, b) of unconnected vertices in the neighbourhood of v:
       i. Add the edge $(a \leftrightarrow b)$ to the graph
   (c) Remove v, and all edges connected to v, from the graph.

One important open question in this algorithm is the order in which the vertices should be chosen. In Section 5.1 we show the results for several heuristics that we have implemented and tried on the UHC. We would like to remark that regardless of the heuristic used, this approach always leads to much smaller SAT problems than encoding transitivity in the SAT problem for ruling out cycles.

4.3   Finding the Schedule

When the constructed Boolean formula is given to the SAT-solver, the result is either that the formula is not satisfiable, meaning that no schedule can been found, or satisfiable, meaning that there is a schedule. It is not hard to see that the formula is satisfiable if and only if there exists a valid schedule for the given attribute grammar definition, and in this paper we give no formal proof of this claim.

In the case where the formula is satisfiable, we obviously want to find the result. From the SAT solver we can ask for the truth value of each variable in the solution, so when our algorithm keeps the connection between edges and variables we can complete our directed graph and trivially find the complete order for all attributes from that. The constraints guarantee that this graph contains no cycles.

4.4   Shared Edges

One important implementation detail is that of shared edges. As explained, the nonterminal dependency graphs and the production dependency graphs share the edges that define the order of the attributes. Because each edge is represented by a variable in the SAT problem we can simply encode this by assigning the same variable to the shared edges.

However, as we also make both graphs chordal, the edges added to make the graphs chordal can also be shared. This is exactly what our implementation does, such that the SAT problem is kept as small as possible. The implementation is therefore slightly more complicated than explained in the previous sections.

5   Empirical Results

We use the Utrecht Haskell Compiler (UHC) [Dijkstra et al., 2009] as the main test case for our work. The source code of the UHC consists of several attribute grammar definitions together with Haskell code. The biggest attribute grammar in the UHC, called *MainAG*, consists of 30 nonterminals, 134 productions, 1332 attributes (44.4 per nonterminal) and 9766 dependencies and is the biggest attribute grammar we know of.

We have compiled several attribute grammars using the Utrecht University Attribute Grammar Compiler (UUAGC) [Swierstra et al., 1999], in which we have implemented our approach. Apart from our SAT approach there are three other scheduling algorithms that have been implemented to which we can compare our approach:

- *Kastens*: the algorithm from [Kastens, 1980] which only works for ordered attribute grammars, of which most examples are not a member.
- *Kennedy-Warren*: The algorithm from [Kennedy and Warren, 1976] that we have implemented in the UUAGC before [Bransen et al., 2012] is an algorithm that schedules all absolutely noncircular attribute grammars, an even larger class than the linearly ordered attribute grammars. However, the scheduling is not completely static so the generated evaluator also does part of the scheduling at runtime.
- *LOAG-backtrack*: we have also implemented a backtracking algorithm for linearly ordered attribute grammars [Van Binsbergen et al., 2015], based on Kastens' algorithm. This algorithm solves exactly the same scheduling problem as the SAT approach described in this paper and uses exponential time in worst case. In case of the *MainAG* no backtracking is required to find a schedule.

Table 1. Comparison of the four scheduling algorithms

Algorithm	Kastens'	Kennedy-Warren	LOAG-backtrack	LOAG-SAT
UHC MainAG	-	33s	13s	9s
Asil Test	-	1.8s	4.4s	3.4s
Asil ByteCode	-	0.6s	29.4s	2.8s
Asil PrettyTree	-	390ms	536ms	585ms
Asil InsertLabels	-	314ms	440ms	452ms
UUAGC CodeGeneration	-	348ms	580ms	382ms
Pigeonhole principle	-	107ms	1970ms	191ms
Helium TS_Analyse	190ms	226ms	235ms	278ms

In Table 1 we show the compilation times for the examples for the four different algorithms. All times include parsing of the attribute grammar description, code generation and adding chords, which is what takes most time in the SAT approach. The SAT-solver takes less than a second to find a solution in all cases.

The other test cases we have used for testing are the UUAGC itself, *Asil* [Middelkoop et al., 2012] which is a byte code instrumenter, the *Helium* compiler [Heeren et al., 2003] which is a Haskell compiler specifically intended for students learning Haskell, and an encoding of the Pigeonhole principle. We removed one clause in such way there exists exactly one valid schedule, resulting in an artificial attribute grammar that is hard to schedule.

5.1   Chordal Graph Heuristics

As explained in Section 4.2 we need to find an order in which to handle the vertices such that the resulting SAT problem is as small as possible. In Table 2 we show the results of different heuristics for the MainAG of the UHC. In this table we use three different sets: $\mathcal{D}$ is the set of direct dependencies (step 2, Section 4), $\mathcal{C}$ is the set of edges that are added to make the graph chordal (step 3, Section 4) and $\mathcal{S}$ is the set of edge between all inherited and synthesized pairs (step 1, Section 4). For each of the sets we take only the edges in the neighbourhood of v for comparison.

6   Optimisations

We have shown that expressing the scheduling problem as a SAT problem and using an existing SAT-solver can improve the running time of the scheduling, but that is not the only advantage. In the SAT problem one can easily add extra constraints to further influence the resulting schedule. In Section 6.2 and Section 6.3 we show two of such optimisations that are useful from an attribute grammar perspective. These optimisations have not been implemented in the release version of the UUAGC, but we have run preliminary experiments to verify that they work as expected.

Table 2. Table showing the number of clauses and variables required for solving the MainAG of the UHC, selecting the next vertex in the elimination order based on different ways to compare neighbourhoods

Order	#Clauses	#Vars	Ratio
$(\mid \mathcal{D} \mid, \mid \mathcal{S} \mid, \mid \mathcal{C} \mid)$	21,307,812	374,792	57.85
$(\mid \mathcal{D} \mid, \mid \mathcal{C} \mid, \mid \mathcal{S} \mid)$	8,301,557	220,690	37.62
$(\mid \mathcal{S} \mid, \mid \mathcal{D} \mid, \mid \mathcal{C} \mid)$	12,477,519	287,151	43.45
$(\mid \mathcal{S} \mid, \mid \mathcal{C} \mid, \mid \mathcal{D} \mid)$	8,910,379	241,853	36.84
$(\mid \mathcal{C} \mid, \mid \mathcal{D} \mid, \mid \mathcal{S} \mid)$	3,004,705	137,277	21.89
$(\mid \mathcal{C} \mid, \mid \mathcal{S} \mid, \mid \mathcal{D} \mid)$	3,359,910	156,795	21.43
$(\mid \mathcal{D} \mid + \mid \mathcal{S} \mid, \mid \mathcal{C} \mid)$	12,424,635	386,323	32.16
$(\mid \mathcal{D} \mid, \mid \mathcal{S} \mid + \mid \mathcal{C} \mid)$	8,244,600	219,869	37.50
$(\mid \mathcal{D} \mid + \mid \mathcal{C} \mid, \mid \mathcal{S} \mid)$	2,930,922	135,654	21.61
$(\mid \mathcal{S} \mid, \mid \mathcal{D} \mid + \mid \mathcal{C} \mid)$	8,574,307	236,348	36.28
$(\mid \mathcal{S} \mid + \mid \mathcal{C} \mid, \mid \mathcal{D} \mid)$	3,480,866	157,089	22.16
$(\mid \mathcal{C} \mid, \mid \mathcal{D} \mid + \mid \mathcal{S} \mid)$	3,392,930	157,568	21.53
$(\mid \mathcal{C} \mid + \mid \mathcal{D} \mid + \mid \mathcal{S} \mid)$	3,424,001	148,724	23.02
$(3* \mid \mathcal{S} \mid *(\mid \mathcal{D} \mid + \mid \mathcal{C} \mid) + (\mid \mathcal{D} \mid * \mid \mathcal{C} \mid)^2)$	2,679,772	127,768	20.97

6.1   Interacting with the Solver

Instead of directly expressing all constraints in the initial SAT problem, we use a different trick for implementing the two optimisations: interacting with the solver. After the initial scheduling problem has been solved, we can ask for the truth value of all variables to construct the schedule. MiniSat also keeps some state in memory that allows us to add extra constraints to the problem, and ask for a new solution. In this way we can start with an initial solution and interact with the solver until some optimum has been reached.

6.2   Minimising Visits

The result of the static scheduling is a runtime evaluator that computes the values of the attributes for a given abstract syntax tree. The total order for each nonterminal defines in what order attributes should be computed, but in the implementation of the evaluator we make use of a slightly bigger unit of computation: a *visit*.

A visit is an evaluation step in the runtime evaluator that takes the values of a (possibly empty) set of inherited attributes and produces a (non-empty) set of synthesized attributes. In order to compute these values, visits to the child nodes may happen, and at the top of the tree the wrapping code invokes all visits of the top node one by one.

Because invoking a visit at runtime may have a certain overhead, we would like the number of visits to be as small as possible. In other words, in the total order on the attributes we would like to minimise the number of places where a synthesized attribute is followed by an inherited attribute, because that is the location where a new visit needs to be performed.

It is theoretically impossible to minimise the total number of visits performed for the full abstract syntax tree, because at compile-time we do not have a concrete abstract syntax tree at hand and only know about the grammar. We therefore try to minimise the maximum number of visits for any nonterminal, which is the number of alternating pairs of inherited and synthesized attributes in the total order.

In our algorithm, we use efficient counting constraints, expressed in the SAT solver using sorting networks [Swierstra et al., 1999]. This enables us to count the number of true literals in a given set of literals, and express constraints about this number. A standard procedure for finding a solution for which the minimal number of literals in such a set is true can be implemented on top of a SAT-solver using a simple loop.

We use the following algorithm for minimising the maximal number of visits:

1. Construct the initial SAT problem and solve
2. Construct the set of all production rules P
3. Construct counting networks that count the number of visits $V(p)$ for all production rules p in P
4. Count the number of visits for each production rule in the current solution; let M be the maximum value
5. Repeat while $M > 0$:
   (a) Add constraints that express that for all productions p in P: $V(p) \leq M$
   (b) Construct a counting network that counts how many production rules p have $V(p) = M$
   (c) Compute a solution for which this number is minimised using the loop described above
   (d) Remove all p in P for which now $V(p) = M$ from the set P
   (e) Compute the new maximum value M of $V(p)$ for all p left in P

The above algorithm features a complicated combination of counting networks; one network for each production rule, and one network for each corresponding output of these networks. Still, the procedure finds optimal solutions very quickly in practice, in times that are negligible and not practically measurable compared to the time of generating the initial SAT-problem. The number of iterations for the minimisation loops has never been more than 5 in any of our problems.

The algorithm is guaranteed to find the global optimum. For our largest example, the solution found had a total of 130 visits, which was 29 visits less in total than the previously known optimum, found using backtracking heuristics.

One could criticise the usefulness of this particular optimisation for attribute grammars. Indeed, details in how one should optimise the number of visits depend very much on the kind of trees we are going to run the compiled code on. Our point is that we can easily express variants of optimisations. For example, we can also minimise the sum of all visits using a similar (but simpler) procedure to the one above. Again, the running time of that procedure is very short.

6.3   Eager Attributes

Another optimisation is the ability to define *eager attributes*. Eager attributes are
attributes that should be computed as soon as possible, and must be annotated
by the attribute grammar programmer as such. We would like our scheduling
algorithm then to schedule them as early as possible in the total order.

As an example, in a typical compiler there is an attribute containing the
errors that occur in compilation. When running the compiler one is typically
first interested in knowing if there are any errors; if so they must be printed to
the screen and the compiler can stop its compilation. If there are no errors, then
all other work that is not strictly necessary for the generation of errors can be
done to complete the compilation.

In order to schedule a given attribute as early as possible, we are going to
partition all attributes contained in the grammar into two sets E (for early) and
L (for late). The idea is that E contains all attributes that may be needed to
be computed before the eager attribute (i.e. there exist production rules which
require this), and L contains all attributes that we can definitely compute after
knowing the eager attribute (i.e. no production rule requires any attribute in L
for computing the eager attribute). We want to find a schedule for which the
size of E is minimal.

To compute this, we introduce a SAT variable $E(a)$ for every attribute a, that
expresses whether or not a is in E or not. We set $E(a)$ to be true for the initial
eager attribute a. We go over the graphs for the nonterminals and production
rules, and generates constraints that express that whenever a points to b and we
have $E(b)$, then we also need $E(a)$.

Finally, we use a counting network for all literals $E(a)$, and ask for a solution
that minimises the number of literals in E.

We have run this algorithm on every output attribute of the top-level nonterminal of all our examples. For our largest grammar, the hardest output to
compute took 1 second. So, while a harder optimisation than the previous one,
it is very doable in practice.

One can imagine other variants of this optimisation, where we have a set of
eager attributes, or a combination of eager and late attributes. At the time of
the writing of this paper, we have not experimented with such variants yet.

7   Discussion and Conclusion

We have explained the difficulties in attribute grammar scheduling and shown
how to solve this problem using a SAT-solver. The given approach has been
implemented and tested on a full-scale compiler built using attribute grammars.
Results show that the algorithm works faster than other approaches.

In the translation into the SAT-problem we have used a novel technique for
ruling out cycles in the SAT problem using chordal graphs. Existing work on
chordality for expressing equality logic [Bryant and Velev, 2002] was the inspi-
ration for this technique. Using chordal graphs makes the problems much smaller

than directly ruling out cycles, while encoding the same restrictions. We believe that this technique is applicable in other problems using SAT-solvers as well.

Furthermore, we have shown that expressing the problem as a SAT problem has the advantage that extra constraints can be added. We illustrated this with two possible properties of the resulting schedule that an attribute grammar programmer may want to influence. Even though this makes the scheduling problem potentially harder, as the algorithm is left fewer choices, the solution is found very fast in all practical cases we have tried.

Another benefit of this approach that the attribute grammar scheduling can benefit from breakthroughs in the SAT community. The more efficient SAT solvers become, the better the attribute grammar scheduling becomes leading to larger and larger attribute grammars that are feasible to schedule.

One problem with the current approach in contrast to most other scheduling algorithms is the unpredictability. SAT-solvers use certain heuristics to quickly find solutions in many applications, but it can theoretically happen that for a certain attribute grammar the SAT problem that is generated is not suitable for these heuristics. A seemingly innocent change in the attribute grammar definition could therefore theoretically lead to a large increase in compile time. However, we have not encountered this problem and we believe that this situation is unlikely to happen because of the maturity of the SAT-solvers.

All in all, we believe that this approach fully solves the basic scheduling problem in an elegant way. There are ample possibilities for improving the resulting schedules based on attribute grammar knowledge like the two discussed in Section 6, so we have also made room for future improvements in the scheduling and compilation of attribute grammars.

References

[van Binsbergen et al., 2015] van Binsbergen, L.T., Bransen, J., Dijkstra, A.: Linearly ordered attribute grammars: With automatic augmenting dependency selection. In: Proceedings of the 2015 Workshop on Partial Evaluation and Program Manipulation, PEPM 2015, pp. 49–60. ACM, New York (2015)

[Bird, 1984] Bird, R.S.: Using circular programs to eliminate multiple traversals of data. Acta Informatica 21, 239–250 (1984)

[Bransen et al., 2012] Bransen, J., Middelkoop, A., Dijkstra, A., Swierstra, S.D.: The Kennedy-Warren algorithm revisited: Ordering attribute grammars. In: Russo, C., Zhou, N.-F. (eds.) PADL 2012. LNCS, vol. 7149, pp. 183–197. Springer, Heidelberg (2012)

[Bryant and Velev, 2002] Bryant, R.E., Velev, M.N.: Boolean satisfiability with transitivity constraints. ACM Trans. Comput. Logic 3(4), 604–627 (2002)

[Claessen et al., 2009] Claessen, K., Een, N., Sheeran, M., Sörensson, N., Voronov, A., Åkesson, K.: Sat-solving in practice. Discrete Event Dynamic Systems 19(4), 495–524 (2009)

[Swierstra et al., 1999] Codish, M., Zazon-Ivry, M.: Pairwise cardinality networks. In: Clarke, E.M., Voronkov, A. (eds.) LPAR-16 2010. LNCS, vol. 6355, pp. 154–172. Springer, Heidelberg (2010)

[Cook, 1971] Cook, S.A.: The complexity of theorem-proving procedures. In: Proceedings of the Third Annual ACM Symposium on Theory of Computing, STOC 1971, pp. 151–158. ACM, New York (1971)

[Dijkstra et al., 2009] Dijkstra, A., Fokker, J., Swierstra, S.D.: The architecture of the Utrecht Haskell Compiler. In: Proceedings of the 2nd ACM SIGPLAN Symposium on Haskell, Haskell 2009, pp. 93–104. ACM, New York (2009)

[Dirac, 1961] Dirac, G.A.: On rigid circuit graphs. Abh. Math. Sem. Univ. Hamburg 25, 71–76 (1961)

[Eén and Sörensson, 2004] Eén, N., Sörensson, N.: An extensible SAT-solver. In: Giunchiglia, E., Tacchella, A. (eds.) SAT 2003. LNCS, vol. 2919, pp. 502–518. Springer, Heidelberg (2004)

[Ekman and Hedin, 2007] Ekman, T., Hedin, G.: The JastAdd extensible Java compiler. In: Proceedings of the 22nd Annual ACM SIGPLAN Conference on Object-Oriented Programming Systems and Applications, OOPSLA 2007, pp. 1–18. ACM, New York (2007)

[Engelfriet and Filè, 1982] Engelfriet, J., Filè, G.: Simple multi-visit attribute grammars. Journal of Computer and System Sciences 24(3), 283–314 (1982)

[Heeren et al., 2003] Heeren, B., Leijen, D., van IJzendoorn, A.: Helium, for learning haskell. In: Proceedings of the 2003 ACM SIGPLAN Workshop on Haskell, Haskell 2003, pp. 62–71. ACM, New York (2003)

[Kastens, 1980] Kastens, U.: Ordered attributed grammars. Acta Informatica 13(3), 229–256 (1980)

[Kennedy and Warren, 1976] Kennedy, K., Warren, S.K.: Automatic generation of efficient evaluators for attribute grammars. In: Proceedings of the 3rd ACM SIGACT-SIGPLAN Symposium on Principles on Programming Languages, POPL 1976, pp. 32–49. ACM, New York (1976)

[Knuth, 1968] Knuth, D.E.: Semantics of context-free languages. Mathematical Systems Theory 2(2), 127–145 (1968)

[Middelkoop et al., 2012] Middelkoop, A., Elyasov, A.B., Prasetya, W.: Functional instrumentation of actionscript programs with asil. In: Gill, A., Hage, J. (eds.) IFL 2011. LNCS, vol. 7257, pp. 1–16. Springer, Heidelberg (2012)

[Saraiva, 1999] Saraiva, J.: Purely Functional Implementation of Attribute Grammars: Zuiver Functionele Implementatie Van Attributengrammatica's. IPA dissertation series. IPA (1999)

[Swierstra et al., 1999] Swierstra, S.D., Alcocer, P.R.A.: Designing and implementing combinator languages. In: Swierstra, S.D., Oliveira, J.N. (eds.) AFP 1998. LNCS, vol. 1608, pp. 150–206. Springer, Heidelberg (1999)

On Parallel Scalable Uniform SAT Witness Generation[*,**]

Supratik Chakraborty[1], Daniel J. Fremont[2], Kuldeep S. Meel[3],
Sanjit A. Seshia[2], and Moshe Y. Vardi[3]

[1] Indian Institute of Technology, Bombay
[2] University of California, Berkeley
[3] Department of Computer Science, Rice University

Abstract. Constrained-random verification (CRV) is widely used in industry for validating hardware designs. The effectiveness of CRV depends on the uniformity of test stimuli generated from a given set of constraints. Most existing techniques sacrifice either uniformity or scalability when generating stimuli. While recent work based on random hash functions has shown that it is possible to generate almost uniform stimuli from constraints with 100,000+ variables, the performance still falls short of today's industrial requirements. In this paper, we focus on pushing the performance frontier of uniform stimulus generation further. We present a random hashing-based, easily parallelizable algorithm, UniGen2, for sampling solutions of propositional constraints. UniGen2 provides strong and relevant theoretical guarantees in the context of CRV, while also offering significantly improved performance compared to existing almost-uniform generators. Experiments on a diverse set of benchmarks show that UniGen2 achieves an average speedup of about 20× over a state-of-the-art sampling algorithm, even when running on a single core. Moreover, experiments with multiple cores show that UniGen2 achieves a near-linear speedup in the number of cores, thereby boosting performance even further.

1 Introduction

Functional verification is concerned with the verification and validation of a *Design Under Verification* (DUV) with respect to design specifications. With

---

[*] The full version is available at http://www.cs.rice.edu/CS/Verification/Projects/UniGen/

[**] The authors would like to thank Suguman Bansal and Karthik Murthy for valuable comments on the earlier drafts, Armando Solar-Lezama for benchmarks, and Mate Soos for tweaking CMS to support UniGen2. This work was supported in part by NSF grants CNS 1049862, CCF-1139011, CCF-1139138, by NSF Expeditions in Computing project "ExCAPE: Expeditions in Computer Augmented Program Engineering", by BSF grant 9800096, by a gift from Intel, by a grant from Board of Research in Nuclear Sciences, India, by the Shared University Grid at Rice funded by NSF under Grant EIA-0216467 and a partnership between Rice University, Sun Microsystems, and Sigma Solutions, Inc., and by TerraSwarm, one of six centers of STARnet, a Semiconductor Research Corporation program sponsored by MARCO and DARPA.

© Springer-Verlag Berlin Heidelberg 2015
C. Baier and C. Tinelli (Eds.): TACAS 2015, LNCS 9035, pp. 304–319, 2015.
DOI: 10.1007/978-3-662-46681-0_25

the increasing complexity of DUVs, functional verification has become one of the most challenging and time-consuming steps in design validation [3]. In view of the high computational cost of formal verification, simulation-based techniques have been extensively employed in industrial practice. The success of such techniques depends on the *quality* of input stimuli with which the design is simulated. The generation of high-quality stimuli that uncover hidden bugs continues to be a challenging problem even today [21].

The problem of high-quality stimulus generation has led to the emergence of *constrained-random simulation*, also known as *constrained-random verification* (CRV) [22]. In CRV, a verification engineer is tasked with the construction of verification scenarios, expressed as constraints over stimuli. Typically, constructing these scenarios involves applying past user experience, inputs from design engineers, and domain-specific knowledge. A constraint solver is then invoked to generate random stimuli satisfying the constraints. Since the distribution of errors in the design is not known *a priori*, each random stimulus is just as likely to produce an error as any other. Therefore, achieving a uniformly random distribution over stimuli satisfying the constraints is highly desirable.

While constraint-solving technologies have witnessed significant advancements over the last decade, methods of generating uniformly distributed solutions still face huge scalability hurdles. This has been observed repeatedly in the literature [6] and by industry practitioners[1]. In this paper, we take a step towards remedying the current situation by proposing an easily parallelizable sampling algorithm for Boolean constraints that provides strong theoretical guarantees (similar to those provided by an almost-uniform generator) in the context of CRV, and also runs significantly faster than current state-of-the-art techniques on a diverse set of benchmark problems.

Since constraints arising in CRV can often be encoded as propositional formulae in conjunctive normal form (CNF), we focus on almost-uniform sampling of satisfying assignments of CNF formulae (known as SAT *witnesses*). This problem has been extensively studied in both theoretical and practical contexts, and has many applications, including probabilistic reasoning, approximate model counting, and Markov logic networks [4]. Until recently, approaches to solving this problem belonged to one of two classes: those which provide strong guarantees of uniformity but scale poorly [2,24], and those which scale to large problem instances but rely on heuristics and hence offer very weak or no uniformity guarantees [11,16,14].

Recently, Chakraborty, Meel, and Vardi [4] proposed a new algorithmic approach to bridge the gap between these two extremes. The main idea behind their approach is to use universal hashing in order to partition the space of witnesses into roughly equal "cells". Under an appropriate partitioning scheme, choosing a random witness from a randomly chosen cell provides strong uniformity guarantees. The most recent instance of this approach is called UniGen [6]. While UniGen scales to formulae much larger than those that can be handled

---

[1] Private Communication: R. Kurshan.

by previous state-of-the-art techniques, the runtime performance of UniGen still falls short of industry requirements.

Since the end of Dennard scaling, there has been a strong revival of interest in parallelizing a wide variety of algorithms to achieve improved performance [10]. One of the main goals in parallel-algorithm design is to achieve a speedup nearly linear in the number of processors, which requires the avoidance of dependencies among different parts of the algorithm [8]. Most of the sampling algorithms used for uniform witness generation fail to meet this criterion, and are hence not easily parallelizable. In contrast, the algorithm proposed in this paper is inherently parallelizable, and achieves a near-linear speedup.

Our primary contribution is a new algorithm, UniGen2, that addresses key performance deficiencies of UniGen. Significantly, UniGen2 generates many more samples (witnesses) per iteration compared to UniGen, thereby reducing the number of SAT calls required per sample to a *constant*. While this weakens the guarantee of independence among samples, we show that this does not hurt the primary objective of CRV. Specifically, we prove that UniGen2 provides almost as strong guarantees as UniGen with respect to discovery of bugs in a CRV setting. On the practical front, we present an implementation of UniGen2, and show by means of extensive experiments that it significantly outperforms existing state-of-the-art algorithms, while generating sample distributions that are indistinguishable from those generated by an ideal uniform sampler. UniGen2 is also inherently parallelizable, and we have implemented a parallel version of it. Our experiments show that parallel UniGen2 achieves a near-linear speedup with the number of cores.

2   Notation and Preliminaries

Let F denote a Boolean formula in conjunctive normal form (CNF), and let X be the set of variables appearing in F. The set X is called the *support* of F. Given a set of variables $S \subseteq X$ and an assignment σ of truth values to the variables in X, we write $\sigma_{\downarrow S}$ for the projection of σ onto S. A *satisfying assignment* or *witness* of F is an assignment that makes F evaluate to true. We denote the set of all witnesses of F by R_F and the projection of R_F on S by $R_{F \downarrow S}$. For the rest of the paper, we use S to denote the *sampling set*, the set of variables on which we desire assignments to be projected. Even when no projection is desired explicitly, S can often be restricted to a small subset of X, called an *independent support* (see [6] for details) such that $|R_F| = |R_{F \downarrow S}|$. For notational simplicity, we omit mentioning F and S when they are clear from the context.

We use $\Pr[X]$ to denote the probability of event X. We say that a set of events $\{X_1, X_2, \ldots, X_n\}$ are (l, u) *almost-independent almost-identically distributed* (henceforth, called (l, u)-*a.a.d.*) if $\forall i \in \{1, \ldots n\}$, $l \leq \Pr[X_i] \leq u$ and $l \leq \Pr[X_i | (\{X_1, \ldots, X_n\} \setminus X_i)] \leq u$. Note that this notion is similar to that of independently identically distributed (i.i.d.) events, but somewhat weaker.

Given a Boolean formula F and sampling set S, a *probabilistic generator* of witnesses of F is a probabilistic algorithm that generates a random element of

$R_{F\downarrow S}$. A *uniform generator* $\mathcal{G}^u(\cdot, \cdot)$ is a probabilistic generator that guarantees $\Pr[\mathcal{G}^u(F, S) = y] = 1/|R_{F\downarrow S}|$, for every $y \in R_{F\downarrow S}$. An *almost-uniform generator* $\mathcal{G}^{au}(\cdot, \cdot, \cdot)$ relaxes the above guarantees, ensuring only that $1/((1+\varepsilon)|R_{F\downarrow S}|) \leq \Pr[\mathcal{G}^{au}(F, S, \varepsilon) = y] \leq (1+\varepsilon)/|R_{F\downarrow S}|$ for every $y \in R_{F\downarrow S}$ and tolerance ε (> 0). Probabilistic generators are allowed to occasionally "fail" by returning no witness although $R_{F\downarrow S} \neq \emptyset$. The failure probability must be bounded by a constant strictly less than 1.

A special class of hash functions, called *r-wise independent* hash functions, play a crucial role in our work. Let n, m and r be positive integers, and let $H(n, m, r)$ denote a family of r-wise independent hash functions mapping $\{0, 1\}^n$ to $\{0, 1\}^m$. We use $h \xleftarrow{R} H(n, m, r)$ to denote the probability space obtained by choosing a hash function h uniformly at random from $H(n, m, r)$. The property of r-wise independence guarantees that for all $\alpha_1, \ldots \alpha_r \in \{0, 1\}^m$ and for all distinct $y_1, \ldots y_r \in \{0, 1\}^n$, $\Pr[\bigwedge_{i=1}^r h(y_i) = \alpha_i : h \xleftarrow{R} H(n, m, r)] = 2^{-mr}$. For every $\alpha \in \{0, 1\}^m$ and $h \in H(n, m, r)$, let $h^{-1}(\alpha)$ denote the set $\{y \in \{0, 1\}^n \mid h(y) = \alpha\}$. Given $R_{F\downarrow S} \subseteq \{0, 1\}^{|S|}$ and $h \in H(|S|, m, r)$, we use $R_{F\downarrow S, h, \alpha}$ to denote the set $R_{F\downarrow S} \cap h^{-1}(\alpha)$. If we keep h fixed and let α range over $\{0, 1\}^m$, the corresponding sets $R_{F\downarrow S, h, \alpha}$ form a partition of $R_{F\downarrow S}$.

We use a particular class of hash functions from $\{0, 1\}^m$ to $\{0, 1\}^n$, denoted by $H_{xor}(n, m)$, which is defined as follows. Let $h : \{0, 1\}^m \to \{0, 1\}^n$ be a hash function, y be a vector in $\{0, 1\}^m$ and $h(y)[i]$ be the ith component of the vector $h(y)$. The family $H_{xor}(n, m)$ is defined as $\{h \mid h(y)[i] = a_{i,0} \oplus (\bigoplus_{k=1}^n a_{i,k} \cdot y[k]), a_{i,j} \in \{0, 1\}, 1 \leq i \leq m, 0 \leq j \leq n\}$, where $\oplus$ denotes XOR. By choosing values of $a_{i,j}$ randomly and independently, we can choose a random function from $H_{xor}(n, m)$. It was shown in [12] that the family $H_{xor}(n, m)$ is 3-wise independent.

3   Related Work

Uniform generation of SAT witnesses was studied by Jerrum, Valiant, and Vazirani [15], who showed that the problem can be solved in probabilistic polynomial time, given access to a Σ_2^P oracle. In addition, they showed that almost-uniform generation is polynomially inter-reducible with approximate model counting. Bellare, Goldreich, and Petrank [2] improved this result and provided an algorithm in BPP^{NP}. Unfortunately, their algorithm fails to scale beyond few tens of variables in practice [4]. A completely different approach to uniform generation of SAT witnesses is due to Yuan et al. [24], wherein a sample is generated by performing a random walk over a weighted binary decision diagram (WBDD). The high space requirement of this technique limits its applicability in practice.

In several settings (some industrial), generation of stimuli for CRV is typically done via heuristic methods that provide very weak or no guarantees of uniformity. One of the earliest such approaches was to randomly seed a SAT solver [19]. While this is simple in principle, the distributions generated by random seeding have been shown to be highly skewed in practice [17]. An alternative approach focusing on the generation of "diverse" solutions was proposed by Nadel [20], but it also fails to provide theoretical guarantees of coverage.

Markov Chain Monte Carlo (MCMC) algorithms, such as those based on simulated annealing or the Metropolis-Hastings algorithm, have been studied extensively in the literature [18] in the context of generating samples from a probability space. The eventual convergence to the target distribution for MCMC methods is often impractically slow in practice under mild requirements. Most MCMC-based sampling tools therefore use heuristic adaptations [17,16] to improve performance and reduce correlation between samples. Unfortunately, these heuristics significantly weaken or even destroy the theoretical guarantees.

Interval propagation [14] has been used extensively in industrial practice to achieve scalable stimulus generation. Techniques based on interval propagation, however, generate highly non-uniform distributions. Recent efforts via the conversion of constraints into belief networks [11,7] have also failed to achieve the desired balance between performance and guarantees of uniformity.

Recently, several random hashing-based techniques have been proposed to bridge the wide gap between scalable algorithms and those that give strong guarantees of uniformity when sampling witnesses of propositional constraints [4,6,9]. Hashing-based sampling techniques were originally pioneered by Sipser [23] and further used by Jerrum et al [15], and Bellare et al [2]. The key idea in hashing-based techniques is to first partition the space of satisfying assignments into small "cells" of roughly equal size using r-wise independent hash functions (for a suitable value of r), and then randomly choose a solution from a randomly picked cell. Bellare et al. showed that by choosing $r = n$ (where the propositional constraint has n variables), we can guarantee uniform generation. The resulting algorithm, however, does not scale in practice. Chakraborty, Meel, and Vardi [4] subsequently showed that with $r = 3$, a significantly more scalable near-uniform generator named UniWit can be designed. Building on the principle underlying UniWit, Ermon et al. [9] suggested further algorithmic improvements to uniform generation of witnesses.

Recently, Chakraborty et al. proposed a new algorithm named UniGen [5], which improves upon the ideas of UniWit. In particular, UniGen provides stronger guarantees of uniformity by exploiting a deep connection between approximate counting and almost-uniform sampling [15]. Furthermore, UniGen has been shown to scale to formulae with hundreds of thousands of variables. Even so, UniGen is typically 2-3 orders of magnitude slower than a single call to a SAT solver and therefore, its runtime performance falls short of the performance of heuristic methods commonly employed in industry to generate stimuli for CRV [2]. In this paper, we offer several improvements to UniGen and obtain an algorithm with substantially improved performance that can be further scaled by parallelization to match the requirements of industry.

---

[2] A random-constrained test case generator is typically allowed to be 10× slower than a constraint solver (private communication with industry expert W. Hung).

4   A Parallel SAT Sampler

In this section, we first motivate the need for sampling solutions of constraints in parallel, and then provide technical details of our algorithm, named UniGen2.

Parallelization. While simulation-based verification typically involves running in parallel many simulations with different input stimuli, the generation of these stimuli is often done sequentially. This is because existing approaches to stimulus generation are not efficiently parallelizable without degrading guarantees of uniformity. For example, approaches based on random seeding of a SAT solver maintain information about which regions of the solution space have already been explored, since choosing random seeds is often not good enough to steer the solver towards new regions of the solution space [17]. Different threads generating solutions must therefore communicate with each other, impeding efficient parallelization. In MCMC-based approaches, to generate independent samples in parallel, each thread has to take a random walk until a stationary distribution is reached. The length of this walk is often impractically long in the case of combinatorial spaces with complex internal structure [9]. Heuristics to speed up MCMC-based techniques destroy guarantees of uniformity even in the sequential case [17]. Methods based on random walks on WBDDs are amenable to parallelization, but they are known not to scale beyond a few hundred variables. The lack of techniques for sampling solutions of constraints in parallel while preserving guarantees of effectiveness in finding bugs is therefore a major impediment to high-performance CRV.

The algorithm UniGen2 presented in this section takes a step forward in addressing the above problem. It has an initial preprocessing step that is sequential but low-overhead, followed by inherently parallelizable sampling steps. It generates samples (stimuli) that are provably nearly as effective as those generated by an almost-uniform sampler for purposes of detecting a bug. Furthermore, our experiments demonstrate that a parallel implementation of UniGen2 achieves a near-linear speedup in the number of processor cores. Given that current practitioners are forced to trade guarantees of effectiveness in bug hunting for scalability, the above properties of UniGen2 are significant. Specifically, they enable a new paradigm of CRV wherein parallel stimulus generation and simulation can provide the required runtime performance while also providing theoretical guarantees.

Algorithm. Our algorithm, named UniGen2, bears some structural similarities with the UniGen algorithm proposed earlier in [6]. Nevertheless, there are key differences that allow UniGen2 to outperform UniGen significantly. Like UniGen, UniGen2 takes a CNF formula F, a sampling set S and a tolerance ε (that is chosen to be at least 6.84 for technical reasons). Note that the formula F and set S uniquely define the solution set $R_{F\downarrow S}$.

Similarly to UniGen, UniGen2 works by partitioning $R_{F\downarrow S}$ into "cells" using random hash functions, then randomly selecting a cell by adding appropriate constraints to F. If the chosen cell has the right size (where the acceptable size range depends on the desired tolerance ε), we can enumerate all the solutions in it and return a uniform random sample from among them. Unlike UniGen, however, UniGen2 samples multiple times from the same cell. This decreases the generation time per sample by a large factor (about $10\times$ in our experiments), while preserving strong guarantees of effectiveness of the samples in finding bugs.

Algorithm 1. EstimateParameters(F, S, ε)

/* Returns (hashBits, loThresh, hiThresh) as required by GenerateSamples */
1: Find $\kappa \in (0, 1)$ such that $\varepsilon = (1 + \kappa)(7.44 + \frac{0.392}{(1-\kappa)^2}) - 1$
2: pivot $\leftarrow \left\lceil 4.03 \left(1 + \frac{1}{\kappa}\right)^2 \right\rceil$
3: hiThresh $\leftarrow \left\lceil 1 + \sqrt{2}(1 + \kappa)\text{pivot} \right\rceil$; loThresh $\leftarrow \left\lfloor \frac{1}{\sqrt{2}(1+\kappa)}\text{pivot} \right\rfloor$
4: $i \leftarrow 0$
5: **while** $i < n$ **do**
6:     $i \leftarrow i + 1$
7:     Choose h at random from $H_{xor}(|S|, i)$
8:     Choose α at random from $\{0, 1\}^i$
9:     $Y \leftarrow \text{BSAT}(F \wedge (h(S) = \alpha), 61, S)$
10:     **if** $1 \leq |Y| \leq 60$ **then**
11:         **return** (round $(\log |Y| + i + \log 1.8 - \log \text{pivot})$, loThresh, hiThresh)
12: **return** $\bot$

Algorithm 2. GenerateSamples($F, S, \text{hashBits}, \text{loThresh}, \text{hiThresh}$)

1: Pick an order V of the values $\{\text{hashBits} - 2, \text{hashBits} - 1, \text{hashBits}\}$
2: **for** $i \in V$ **do**
3:     Choose h at random from $H_{xor}(|S|, i)$
4:     Choose α at random from $\{0, 1\}^i$
5:     $Y \leftarrow \text{BSAT}(F \wedge (h(S) = \alpha), \text{hiThresh}, S)$
6:     **if** (loThresh $\leq |Y| <$ hiThresh) **then**
7:         **return** loThresh distinct random elements of Y
8: **return** $\bot$

UniGen2 is an algorithmic framework that operates in two stages: the first stage, EstimateParameters (Algorithm 1), performs low-overhead one-time pre-processing for a given F, S, and ε to compute numerical parameters 'hashBits', 'loThresh', and 'hiThresh'. The quantity hashBits controls how many cells $R_{F\downarrow S}$ will be partitioned into, while loThresh and hiThresh delineate the range of acceptable sizes for a cell. In the second stage, GenerateSamples (Algorithm 2) uses these parameters to generate loThresh samples. If more samples are required, GenerateSamples is simply called again with the same parameters. Theorem 3 below shows that invoking GenerateSamples multiple times does not cause the loss of any theoretical guarantees. We now explain the operation of the two subroutines in detail.

Lines 1–3 of EstimateParameters compute numerical parameters based on the tolerance ε which are used by GenerateSamples. The variable 'pivot' can be thought of as the ideal cell size we are aiming for, while as mentioned above 'loThresh' and 'hiThresh' define the allowed size range around this ideal. For simplicity of exposition, we assume that $|R_{F\downarrow S}| > \max(60, \text{hiThresh})$. If not, there are very few solutions and we can do uniform sampling by enumerating all of them as in UniGen [6].

Lines 4–11 of EstimateParameters compute 'hashBits', an estimate of the number of hash functions required so that the corresponding partition of $R_{F\downarrow S}$ (into 2^{hashBits} cells) has cells of the desired size. This is done along the same lines as in UniGen, which used an approximate model counter such as ApproxMC [5]. The procedure invokes a SAT solver through the function $\text{BSAT}(\phi, m, S)$. This returns a set, consisting of models of the formula ϕ which all differ on the set of variables S, that has size m. If there is no such set of size m, the function returns a maximal set. If the estimation procedure fails, EstimateParameters returns $\perp$ on line 12. In practice, it would be called repeatedly until it succeeds. Theorem 1 below shows that on average few repetitions are needed for EstimateParameters to succeed, and this is borne out in practice.

The second stage of UniGen2, named GenerateSamples, begins on lines 1–2 by picking a hash count i close to hashBits, then selecting a random hash function from the family $H_{xor}(|S|, i)$ on line 3. On line 4 we pick a random output value α, so that the constraint $h(S) = \alpha$ picks out a random cell. Then, on line 5 we invoke BSAT on F with this additional constraint, obtaining at most hiThresh elements Y of the cell. If $|Y| <$ hiThresh then we have enumerated every element of $R_{F\downarrow S}$ in the cell, and if $|Y| \geq$ loThresh the cell is large enough for us to get a good sample. So if loThresh $\leq |Y| <$ hiThresh, we randomly select loThresh elements of Y and return them on line 7.

If the number of elements of $R_{F\downarrow S}$ in the chosen cell is too large or too small, we choose a new hash count on line 2. Note that line 1 can pick an arbitrary order for the three hash counts to be tried, since our analysis of UniGen2 does not depend on the order. This allows us to use an optimization where if we run GenerateSamples multiple times, we choose an order which starts with the value of i that was successful in the previous invocation of GenerateSamples. Since hashBits is only an estimate of the correct value for i, in many benchmarks on which we experimented, UniGen2 initially failed to generate a cell of the right size with $i =$ hashBits-2, but then succeeded with $i =$ hashBits-1. In such scenarios, beginning with $i =$ hashBits-1 in subsequent iterations saves considerable time. This heuristic is similar in spirit to "leapfrogging" in ApproxMC [5] and UniWit [4], but does not compromise the theoretical guarantees of UniGen2 in any way.

If all three hash values tried on line 2 fail to generate a correctly-sized cell, GenerateSamples fails and returns $\perp$ on line 8. Theorem 1 below shows that this happens with probability at most 0.38. Otherwise, UniGen2 completes by returning loThresh samples.

Parallelization of UniGen2. As described above, UniGen2 operates in two stages: EstimateParameters is initially called to do one-time preprocessing, and then GenerateSamples is called to do the actual sampling. To generate N samples, we can invoke EstimateParameters once, and then GenerateSamples N/loThresh times, since each of the latter calls generates loThresh samples (unless it fails). Furthermore, each invocation of GenerateSamples is completely independent of the others. Thus if we have k processor cores, we can just perform $N/(k \cdot \text{loThresh})$ invocations of GenerateSamples on each. There is no need for any inter-thread communication: the "leapfrogging" heuristic for choosing the order on line 1 can simply be done on a per-thread basis. This gives us a linear speedup in the number of cores k, since the per-thread work (excluding the initial preprocessing) is proportional to $1/k$. Furthermore, Theorem 3 below shows that assuming each thread has its own source of randomness, performing multiple invocations of GenerateSamples in parallel does not alter its guarantees of uniformity. This means that UniGen2 can scale to an arbitrary number of processor cores as more samples are desired, while not sacrificing any theoretical guarantees.

5   Analysis

In this section, we present a theoretical analysis of the uniformity, effectiveness in discovering bugs, and runtime performance of UniGen2. For lack of space, we defer all proofs to the full version. For technical reasons, we assume that $\varepsilon > 6.84$. Our first result bounds the failure probabilities of EstimateParameters and GenerateSamples.

Theorem 1. EstimateParameters *and* GenerateSamples *return* $\bot$ *with probabilities at most* 0.009 *and* 0.38 *respectively.*

Next we show that a single invocation of GenerateSamples provides guarantees nearly as strong as those of an almost-uniform generator.

Theorem 2. *For given* F, S, *and* ε, *let* L *be the set of samples generated using* UniGen2 *with a single call to* GenerateSamples. *Then for each* $y \in R_{F\downarrow S}$, *we have*

$$\frac{\text{loThresh}}{(1+\varepsilon)|R_{F\downarrow S}|} \leq \Pr[y \in L] \leq 1.02 \cdot (1+\varepsilon)\frac{\text{loThresh}}{|R_{F\downarrow S}|}.$$

Now we demonstrate that these guarantees extend to the case when GenerateSamples is called multiple times, sequentially or in parallel.

Theorem 3. *For given* F, S, *and* ε, *and for* hashBits, loThresh, *and* hiThresh *as estimated by* EstimateParameters, *let* GenerateSamples *be called* N *times with these parameters in an arbitrary parallel or sequential interleaving. Let* $E_{y,i}$ *denote the event that* $y \in R_{F\downarrow S}$ *is generated in the* i^{th} *call to* GenerateSamples. *Then the events* $E_{y,i}$ *are* (l, u)*-a.a.d. with* $l = \frac{\text{loThresh}}{(1+\varepsilon)|R_{F\downarrow S}|}$ *and* $u = \frac{1.02 \cdot (1+\varepsilon)\text{loThresh}}{|R_{F\downarrow S}|}$.

Next we show that the above result establishes very strong guarantees on the effectiveness of UniGen2 in discovering bugs in the CRV context. In this context, the objective of uniform generation is to maximize the probability of discovering a bug by using a diverse set of samples. Let us denote the fraction of stimuli that trigger a bug by f, i.e. if B is the set of stimuli that trigger a bug, then $f = |B|/|R_{F\downarrow S}|$. Furthermore, if N is the desired number of stimuli we wish to generate, we want to minimize the failure probability, i.e. the probability that the N randomly generated stimuli fail to intersect the set B. If the stimuli are generated uniformly, the failure probability is $(1 - f)^N$. Using binomial expansion, the failure probability can be shown to decrease exponentially in N, with decay rate of f (henceforth denoted as *failure decay rate*). We can evaluate the effectiveness of a stimulus-generation method by comparing the failure decay rate it achieves to that of a uniform generator. Alternatively, given some $\delta > 0$, we can ask how many samples are needed to ensure that the failure probability is at most δ. Normalizing by the number of samples needed by an ideal uniform generator gives the *relative number of samples needed* to find a bug. Our next theorem shows that UniGen2 is as effective as an almost-uniform generator according to both of these metrics but needs many fewer SAT calls.

Theorem 4. *Given F, S, ε, and $B \subseteq R_{F\downarrow S}$, let $f = |B|/|R_{F\downarrow S}| < 0.8$, $\nu = \frac{1}{2}(1 + \varepsilon)f$, and $\hat{\nu} = 1.02 \cdot \text{loThresh} \cdot \nu < 1$. Then we have the following bounds:*

generator type	*uniform*	UniGen	UniGen2
failure decay rate	f	$\frac{f}{1+\varepsilon}$	$(1 - \hat{\nu})\frac{f}{1+\varepsilon}$
relative # of samples needed	1	$(1 + \nu)(1 + \varepsilon)$	$\frac{1+\hat{\nu}}{1-\hat{\nu}}(1 + \varepsilon)$
relative expected # of SAT calls	1	$\frac{3 \cdot \text{hiThresh}(1+\nu)(1+\varepsilon)}{0.52}$	$\frac{3 \cdot \text{hiThresh}}{0.62 \cdot \text{loThresh}}\frac{1+\hat{\nu}}{1-\hat{\nu}}(1 + \varepsilon)$

If $8.09 \le \varepsilon \le 242$ and $f \le 1/1000$, then UniGen2 *uses fewer SAT calls than* UniGen *on average.*

Thus under reasonable conditions such as occur in industrial applications, UniGen2 is more efficient than UniGen at finding bugs. We illustrate the significance of this improvement with an example. Suppose 1 in 10^4 inputs causes a bug. Then to find a bug with probability $1/2$, we would need approximately $6.93 \cdot 10^3$ uniformly generated samples. To achieve the same target, we would need approximately $1.17 \cdot 10^5$ samples from an almost-uniform generator like UniGen, and approximately $1.20 \cdot 10^5$ samples from UniGen2, using a tolerance (ε) of 16 in both cases. However, since UniGen2 picks multiple samples from each cell, it needs fewer SAT calls. In fact, the expected number of calls made by UniGen2 is only $3.38 \cdot 10^6$, compared to $4.35 \cdot 10^7$ for UniGen – an order of magnitude difference! Therefore, UniGen2 provides as strong guarantees as UniGen in terms of its ability to discover bugs in CRV, while requiring far fewer SAT calls. Note that while the rest of our results hold for $\varepsilon > 6.84$, our guarantee of fewer expected SAT calls in UniGen2 holds for a subrange of values of ε, as indicated in Theorem 4.

Finally, since the ratio of hiThresh to loThresh can be bounded from above, we have the following result.

Theorem 5. *There exists a fixed constant* $\lambda = 40$ *such that for every F, S, and ε, the expected number of* SAT *queries made by* UniGen2 *per generated sample is at most* λ.

In contrast, the number of SAT calls per generated sample in UniGen is proportional to hiThresh and thus to ε^{-2}. An upper bound on the expected number of SAT queries makes it possible for UniGen2 to approach the performance of heuristic methods like random seeding of SAT solvers, which make only one SAT query per generated sample (but fail to provide any theoretical guarantees).

6   Evaluation

To evaluate the performance of UniGen2, we built a prototype implementation in C++ that employs the solver CryptoMiniSAT [1] to handle CNF-SAT augmented with XORs efficiently[3]. We conducted an extensive set of experiments on diverse public domain benchmarks, seeking to answer the following questions:

1. How does UniGen2's runtime performance compare to that of UniGen, a state-of-the-art almost-uniform SAT sampler?
2. How does the performance of parallel UniGen2 scale with the # of cores?
3. How does the distribution of samples generated by UniGen2 compare with the ideal distribution?
4. Does parallelization affect the uniformity of the distribution of the samples?

Our experiments showed that UniGen2 outperforms UniGen by a factor of about $20\times$ in terms of runtime. The distribution generated by UniGen2 is statistically indistinguishable from that generated by an ideal uniform sampler. Finally, the runtime performance of parallel UniGen2 scales linearly with the number of cores, while its output distribution continues to remain uniform.

6.1   Experimental Setup

We conducted experiments on a heterogeneous set of benchmarks used in earlier related work [6]. The benchmarks consisted of ISCAS89 circuits augmented with parity conditions on randomly chosen subsets of outputs and next-state variables, constraints arising in bounded model checking, bit-blasted versions of SMTLib benchmarks, and problems arising from automated program synthesis. For each benchmark, the sampling set S was either taken to be the independent support of the formula or was provided by the corresponding source. Experiments were conducted on a total of 200+ benchmarks. We present results for only a subset of representative benchmarks here. A detailed list of all the benchmarks is available in the Appendix.

For purposes of comparison, we also ran experiments with UniGen [6], a state-of-the-art almost-uniform SAT witness generator. We employed the Mersenne

---

[3] The tool (with source code) is available at
http://www.cs.rice.edu/CS/Verification/Projects/UniGen/

Twister to generate pseudo-random numbers, and each thread was seeded independently using the C++ class random_device. Both tools used an overall timeout of 20 hours, and a BSAT timeout of 2500 seconds. All experiments used $\varepsilon = 16$, corresponding to loThresh = 11 and hiThresh = 64. The experiments were conducted on a high-performance computer cluster, where each node had a 12-core, 2.83 GHz Intel Xeon processor, with 4GB of main memory per core.

6.2   Results

Runtime Performance. We compared the runtime performance of UniGen2 with that of UniGen for all our benchmarks. For each benchmark, we generated between 1000 and 10000 samples (depending on the size of the benchmark) and computed the average time taken to generate a sample on a single core. The results of these experiments for a representative subset of benchmarks are shown in Table 1. The columns in this table give the benchmark name, the number of variables and clauses, the size of the sampling set, the success probability of UniGen2, and finally the average runtime per sample for both UniGen2 and UniGen in seconds. The success probability of UniGen2 was computed as the fraction of calls to GenerateSamples that successfully generated samples.

Table 1. Runtime performance comparison of UniGen2 and UniGen (on a single core)

					UniGen2	UniGen
Benchmark	#vars	#clas	|S|	Succ. Prob	Runtime(s)	Runtime(s)
s1238a_3_2	686	1850	32	1.0	0.3	7.17
s1196a_3_2	690	1805	32	1.0	0.23	4.54
s832a_15_7	693	2017	23	1.0	0.04	0.51
case_1_b12_2	827	2725	45	1.0	0.24	6.77
squaring16	1627	5835	72	1.0	4.16	79.12
squaring7	1628	5837	72	1.0	0.79	21.98
doublyLinkedList	6890	26918	37	1.0	0.04	1.23
LoginService2	11511	41411	36	1.0	0.05	0.55
Sort	12125	49611	52	1.0	4.15	82.8
20	15475	60994	51	1.0	19.08	270.78
enqueue	16466	58515	42	1.0	0.87	14.67
Karatsuba	19594	82417	41	1.0	5.86	80.29
lltraversal	39912	167842	23	1.0	0.18	4.86
llreverse	63797	257657	25	1.0	0.73	7.59
diagStencil_new	94607	2838579	78	1.0	3.53	60.18
tutorial3	486193	2598178	31	1.0	58.41	805.33
demo2_new	777009	3649893	45	1.0	3.47	40.33

Table 1 clearly shows that UniGen2 significantly outperforms UniGen on all types of benchmarks, even when run on a single core. Over the entire set of 200+ benchmarks, UniGen2's runtime performance was about 20× better than that of UniGen on average (using the geometric mean). The observed performance gain can be attributed to two factors. First, UniGen2 generates loThresh (11 in our experiments) samples from every cell instead of just 1 in the case of UniGen. This provides a speedup of about 10×. Second, as explained in Section 4, UniGen2 uses "leapfrogging" to optimize the order in which the values of i in line 2 of Algorithm 2 are chosen. In contrast, UniGen uses a fixed order. This provides an additional average speedup of $2\times$ in our experiments. Note also that the success probability of UniGen2 is consistently very close to 1 across the entire set of benchmarks.

Parallel Speedup. To measure the effect of parallelization on runtime performance, we ran the parallel version of UniGen2 with 1 to 12 processor cores on our benchmarks. In each experiment with C cores, we generated 2500 samples per core, and computed the C-core resource usage as the ratio of the average individual core runtime to the total number of samples (i.e. $C \times 2500$). We averaged our computations over 7 identical runs. The speedup for C cores was then computed as the ratio of 1-core resource usage to C-core resource usage. Figure 1 shows how the speedup varies with the number of cores for a subset of our benchmarks. The figure illustrates that parallel UniGen2 generally scales almost linearly with the number of processor cores.

To obtain an estimate of how close UniGen2's performance is to real-world requirements (roughly $10\times$ slowdown compared to a simple SAT call), we measured the slowdown of UniGen2 (and UniGen) running on a single core relative to a simple SAT call on the input formula. The (geometric) mean slowdown for UniGen2 turned out to be 21 compared to 470 for UniGen. This shows that UniGen2 running in parallel on 2–4 cores comes close to matching the requirements of CRV in industrial practice.

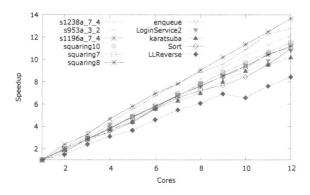

Fig. 1. Effect of parallelization on the runtime performance of UniGen2

Uniformity Comparison. To measure the quality of the distribution generated by UniGen2 and parallel UniGen2 in practice, we implemented an *ideal sampler*, henceforth denoted as IS. Given a formula F, the sampler IS first enumerates all witnesses in $R_{F\downarrow S}$, and then picks an element of $R_{F\downarrow S}$ uniformly at random. We compared the distribution generated by IS with that generated by UniGen2 run sequentially, and with that generated by UniGen2 run in parallel on 12 cores.

In the last case, the samples generated by all the cores were aggregated before comparing the distributions. We had to restrict the experiments for comparing distributions to a small subset of our benchmarks, specifically those which had less than $100,000$ solutions. We generated a large number N ($\geq 4 \times 10^6$) of samples for each benchmark using each of IS, sequential UniGen2, and parallel UniGen2. Since we chose N much larger than $|R_{F\downarrow S}|$, all witnesses occurred multiple times in the list of samples. We then computed the frequency of generation of individual witnesses, and grouped witnesses appearing the same number of times together. Plotting the distribution of frequencies — that is, plotting points (x, y) to indicate that each of x distinct witnesses were generated y times — gives a convenient way to visualize the distribution of the samples. Figure 2 depicts this for one representative benchmark (case110, with 16,384 solutions). It is clear from Figure 2 that the distribution generated by UniGen2 is practically indistinguishable from that of IS. Furthermore, the quality of the distribution is not affected by parallelization. Similar observations also hold for the other benchmarks for which we were able to enumerate all solutions. For the example shown in Fig. 2, the Jensen-Shannon distance between the distributions from sequential UniGen2 and IS is 0.049, while the corresponding figure for parallel UniGen2 and IS is 0.052. These small Jensen-Shannon distances make the distribution of UniGen2 (whether sequential or parallel) indistinguishable from that of IS (See Section IV(C) of [13]).

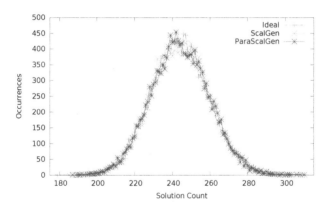

Fig. 2. Uniformity comparison between an ideal sampler (IS), UniGen2, and parallel UniGen2. Results from benchmark 'case110' with $N = 4 \cdot 10^6$.

7   Conclusion

Constrained-random simulation has been the workhorse of functional verification for the past few decades. In this paper, we introduced a new algorithm, UniGen2, that outperforms state-of-the-art techniques by a factor of about $20\times$. UniGen2 trades off independence of samples for speed while still providing strong guarantees of discovering bugs with high probability. Furthermore, we showed that the parallel version of UniGen2 achieves a linear speedup with increasing number of cores. This suggests a new paradigm for constrained-random verification, wherein we can obtain the required runtime performance through parallelization without losing guarantees of effectiveness in finding bugs.

References

1. CryptoMiniSAT, http://www.msoos.org/cryptominisat2/
2. Bellare, M., Goldreich, O., Petrank, E.: Uniform generation of NP-witnesses using an NP-oracle. Information and Computation 163(2), 510–526 (2000)
3. Bening, L., Foster, H.: Principles of verifiable RTL design – A functional coding style supporting verification processes. Springer (2001)
4. Chakraborty, S., Meel, K.S., Vardi, M.Y.: A scalable and nearly uniform generator of SAT witnesses. In: Sharygina, N., Veith, H. (eds.) CAV 2013. LNCS, vol. 8044, pp. 608–623. Springer, Heidelberg (2013)
5. Chakraborty, S., Meel, K.S., Vardi, M.Y.: A scalable approximate model counter. In: Schulte, C. (ed.) CP 2013. LNCS, vol. 8124, pp. 200–216. Springer, Heidelberg (2013)
6. Chakraborty, S., Meel, K.S., Vardi, M.Y.: Balancing scalability and uniformity in SAT-witness generator. In: Proc. of DAC, pp. 1–6 (2014)
7. Dechter, R., Kask, K., Bin, E., Emek, R.: Generating random solutions for constraint satisfaction problems. In: AAAI, pp. 15–21 (2002)
8. Eager, D.L., Zahorjan, J., Lazowska, E.D.: Speedup versus efficiency in parallel systems. IEEE Trans. on Computers 38(3), 408–423 (1989)
9. Ermon, S., Gomes, C.P., Sabharwal, A., Selman, B.: Embed and project: Discrete sampling with universal hashing. In: Proc. of NIPS (2013)
10. Esmaeilzadeh, H., Blem, E., Amant, R.S., Sankaralingam, K., Burger, D.: Dark silicon and the end of multicore scaling. In: Proc. of ISCA, pp. 365–376 (2011)
11. Gogate, V., Dechter, R.: A new algorithm for sampling CSP solutions uniformly at random. In: Benhamou, F. (ed.) CP 2006. LNCS, vol. 4204, pp. 711–715. Springer, Heidelberg (2006)
12. Gomes, C.P., Sabharwal, A., Selman, B.: Near uniform sampling of combinatorial spaces using XOR constraints. In: Proc. of NIPS, pp. 670–676 (2007)
13. Grosse, I., Bernaola-Galván, P., Carpena, P., Román-Roldán, R., Oliver, J., Stanley, E.: Analysis of symbolic sequences using the Jensen-Shannon divergence. Physical Review E 65(4), 41905 (2002)
14. Iyer, M.A.: Race: A word-level ATPG-based constraints solver system for smart random simulation. In: Proc. of ITC, pp. 299–308. Citeseer (2003)
15. Jerrum, M.R., Valiant, L.G., Vazirani, V.V.: Random generation of combinatorial structures from a uniform distribution. TCS 43(2-3), 169–188 (1986)
16. Kitchen, N.: Markov Chain Monte Carlo Stimulus Generation for Constrained Random Simulation. PhD thesis, University of California, Berkeley (2010)
17. Kitchen, N., Kuehlmann, A.: Stimulus generation for constrained random simulation. In: Proc. of ICCAD, pp. 258–265 (2007)
18. Madras, N.: Lectures on Monte Carlo Methods. Fields Institute Monographs, vol. 16. AMS (2002)

19. Moskewicz, M.W., Madigan, C.F., Zhao, Y., Zhang, L., Malik, S.: Chaff: Engineering an efficient SAT solver. In: Proc. of DAC, pp. 530–535. ACM (2001)
20. Nadel, A.: Generating diverse solutions in SAT. In: Sakallah, K.A., Simon, L. (eds.) SAT 2011. LNCS, vol. 6695, pp. 287–301. Springer, Heidelberg (2011)
21. Naveh, R., Metodi, A.: Beyond feasibility: CP usage in constrained-random functional hardware verification. In: Schulte, C. (ed.) CP 2013. LNCS, vol. 8124, pp. 823–831. Springer, Heidelberg (2013)
22. Naveh, Y., Rimon, M., Jaeger, I., Katz, Y., Vinov, M., Marcus, E., Shurek, G.: Constraint-based random stimuli generation for hardware verification. In: Proc. of AAAI, pp. 1720–1727 (2006)
23. Sipser, M.: A complexity theoretic approach to randomness. In: Proc. of STOC, pp. 330–335 (1983)
24. Yuan, J., Aziz, A., Pixley, C., Albin, K.: Simplifying Boolean constraint solving for random simulation vector generation. TCAD 23(3), 412–420 (2004)

Approximate Counting in SMT
and Value Estimation for Probabilistic Programs

Dmitry Chistikov, Rayna Dimitrova, and Rupak Majumdar

Max Planck Institute for Software Systems (MPI-SWS), Germany
{dch,rayna,rupak}@mpi-sws.org

Abstract. #SMT, or model counting for logical theories, is a well-known hard problem that generalizes such tasks as counting the number of satisfying assignments to a Boolean formula and computing the volume of a polytope. In the realm of satisfiability modulo theories (SMT) there is a growing need for model counting solvers, coming from several application domains (quantitative information flow, static analysis of probabilistic programs). In this paper, we show a reduction from an approximate version of #SMT to SMT.

We focus on the theories of integer arithmetic and linear real arithmetic. We propose model counting algorithms that provide approximate solutions with formal bounds on the approximation error. They run in polynomial time and make a polynomial number of queries to the SMT solver for the underlying theory, exploiting "for free" the sophisticated heuristics implemented within modern SMT solvers. We have implemented the algorithms and used them to solve a value estimation problem for a model of loop-free probabilistic programs with nondeterminism.

1 Introduction

Satisfiability modulo theories (SMT) is nowadays ubiquitous, and the research landscape is not only enjoying the success of existing SMT solvers, but also generating demand for new features. In particular, there is a growing need for *model counting* solvers; for example, questions in quantitative information flow and in static analysis of probabilistic programs are naturally cast as instances of model counting problems for appropriate logical theories [15,25,28].

We define the #SMT problem that generalizes several model counting questions relative to logical theories, such as computing the number of satisfying assignments to a Boolean formula (#SAT) and computing the volume of a bounded polyhedron in a finite-dimensional real vector space. Specifically, to define model counting modulo a *measured theory*, first suppose every variable in a logical formula comes with a domain which is also a measure space. Assume that, for every logical formula φ in the theory, the set of its models $[\![\varphi]\!]$ is measurable with respect to the product measure; the *model counting (or #SMT)* problem then asks, given φ, to compute the measure of $[\![\varphi]\!]$, called the *model count* of φ.

In our work we focus on the model counting problems for theories of bounded integer arithmetic and linear real arithmetic. These problems are complete for the complexity class #**P**, so fast exact algorithms are unlikely to exist.

© Springer-Verlag Berlin Heidelberg 2015
C. Baier and C. Tinelli (Eds.): TACAS 2015, LNCS 9035, pp. 320–334, 2015.
DOI: 10.1007/978-3-662-46681-0_26

We extend to the realm of SMT the well-known hashing approach from the world of #SAT, which reduces *approximate* versions of counting to decision problems. From a theoretical perspective, we solve a model counting problem with a resource-bounded algorithm that has access to an oracle for the decision problem. From a practical perspective, we show how to use unmodified existing SMT solvers to obtain approximate solutions to model-counting problems. This reduces an approximate version of #SMT to SMT.

Specifically, for integer arithmetic (not necessarily linear), we give a randomized algorithm that approximates the model count of a given formula φ to within a multiplicative factor $(1+\varepsilon)$ for any given $\varepsilon > 0$. The algorithm makes $O(\frac{1}{\varepsilon} |\varphi|)$ SMT queries of size at most $O(\frac{1}{\varepsilon^2} |\varphi|^2)$ where $|\varphi|$ is the size of φ.

For linear real arithmetic, we give a randomized algorithm that approximates the model count with an additive error γN, where N is the volume of a box containing all models of the formula, and the coefficient γ is part of the input. The number of steps of the algorithm and the number of SMT queries (modulo the combined theory of integer and linear real arithmetic) are again polynomial.

As an application, we show how to solve the value estimation problem [28] for a model of loop-free probabilistic programs with nondeterminism.

Techniques. Approximation of #**P** functions by randomized algorithms has a rich history in complexity theory [31,34,21,20]. Jerrum, Valiant, and Vazirani [21] described a hashing-based **BPP$^{\mathbf{NP}}$** procedure to approximately compute any #**P** function, and noted that this procedure already appeared implicitly in previous papers by Sipser [30] and Stockmeyer [31]. The procedure works with encoded computations of a Turing machine and is thus unlikely to perform well in practice. Instead, we show a direct reduction from approximate model counting to SMT solving, which allows us to retain the structure of the original formula. An alternate approach could eagerly encode #SMT problems into #SAT, but experience with SMT solvers suggests that a "lazy" approach may be preferable for some problems.

For the theory of linear real arithmetic, we also need an ingredient to handle continuous domains. Dyer and Frieze [11] suggested a discretization that introduces bounded additive error; this placed approximate volume computation for polytopes—or, in logical terms, approximate model counting for quantifier-free linear real arithmetic—in #**P**. Motivated by the application in the analysis of probabilistic programs, we extend this technique to handle formulas with existentially quantified variables. To this end, we prove a geometric result that bounds the effect of projections: this gives us an approximate model counting procedure for existentially quantified linear arithmetic formulas. Note that applying quantifier elimination as a preprocessing step may make the resulting formula exponential; instead, our approach works directly on the original formula that contains existentially quantified variables.

We have implemented our algorithm on top of the Z3 SMT solver and applied it to formulas encoding the value estimation problem for probabilistic programs. Our initial experience suggests that simple randomized algorithms using off-the-shelf SMT solvers can be reasonably effective.

Related Work. #SMT is a well-known hard problem whose instances have been studied before, e. g., in volume computation [11], in enumeration of lattice points in integer polyhedra [1], and as #SAT [17]. Indeed, very simple subproblems, such as counting the number of satisfying assignments of a Boolean formula or computing the volume of a union of axis-parallel rectangles in $\mathbb{R}^n$ are already #**P**-hard (see Section 2 below).

Existing techniques for #SMT either incorporate model counting primitives into propositional reasoning [26,35] or are based on enumerative combinatorics [23,25,15]. Typically, exact algorithms [23,26,15] are exponential in the worst case, whereas approximate algorithms [25,35] lack provable performance guarantees. In contrast to exact counting techniques, our procedure is easily implementable and uses "for free" the sophisticated heuristics built in off-the-shelf SMT solvers. Although the solutions it produces are not exact, they provably meet user-provided requirements on approximation quality. This is achieved by extending the hashing approach from SAT [16,17,7,13] to the SMT context.

A famous result of Dyer, Frieze, and Kannan [12] states that the volume of a convex polyhedron can be approximated with a multiplicative error in probabilistic polynomial time (without the need for an SMT solver). In our application, analysis of probabilistic programs, we wish to compute the volume of a projection of a Boolean combination of polyhedra; in general, it is, of course, non-convex. Thus, we cannot apply the volume estimation algorithm of [12], so we turn to the "generic" approximation of #**P** using an **NP** oracle instead. Our #SMT procedure for linear real arithmetic allows an additive error in the approximation; it is unknown if the exact volume of a polytope has a small representation [11].

An alternative approach to approximate #SMT is to apply Monte Carlo methods for volume estimation. They can easily handle complicated measures for which there is limited symbolic reasoning available. Like the hashing technique, this approach is also exponential in the worst case [20]: suppose the volume in question, p, is very small and the required precision is a constant multiple of p. In this case, Chernoff bound arguments would suggest the need for $\Omega(\frac{1}{p})$ samples; the hashing approach, in contrast, will perform well. So, while in "regular" settings (when p is non-vanishing) the Monte Carlo approach performs better, "singular" settings (when p is close to zero) are better handled by the hashing approach. The two techniques, therefore, are complementary to each other.

Contributions. We extend, from SAT to SMT, the hashing approach to approximate model counting:

1. We formulate the notion of a measured theory (Section 2) that gives a unified framework for model-counting problems.
2. For the theory of bounded integer arithmetic, we provide a direct reduction (Theorem 1 in Section 2) from approximate counting to SMT.
3. For the theory of bounded linear real arithmetic, we give a technical construction (Lemma 1 in subsection 3.2) that lets us extend the results of Dyer and Frieze to the case when the polytope is given as a projection of a Boolean combination of polytopes; this leads to an approximate model counting procedure for this theory (Theorem 2 in Section 2).

4. As an application, we solve the value estimation problem for small loop-free probabilistic programs with nondeterminism (Section 4).

An extended version of the paper is available as [8].

2   The #SMT Problem

We present a framework for a uniform treatment of model counting both in discrete theories like SAT (where it is literally counting models) and in linear real arithmetic (where it is really volume computation for polyhedra). We then introduce the notion of approximation and show an algorithm for approximate model counting by reduction to SMT.

Preliminaries: Counting Problems and #P. A relation $R \subseteq \Sigma^* \times \Sigma^*$ is a *p-relation* if (1) there exists a polynomial $p(n)$ such that if $(x, y) \in R$ then $|y| = p(|x|)$ and (2) the predicate $(x, y) \in R$ can be checked in deterministic polynomial time in the size of x. Intuitively, a p-relation relates inputs x to solutions y. It is easy to see that a decision problem L belongs to **NP** if there is a p-relation R such that $L = \{x \mid \exists y.R(x, y)\}$.

A *counting problem* is a function that maps Σ^* to $\mathbb{N}$. A counting problem $f \colon \Sigma^* \to \mathbb{N}$ belongs to the class #**P** if there exists a p-relation R such that $f(x) = |\{y \mid R(x, y)\}|$, i.e., the class #**P** consists of functions that count the number of solutions to a p-relation [33]. *Completeness* in #**P** is with respect to Turing reductions; the same term is also (ab)used to encompass problems that reduce to a fixed number of queries to a #**P** function (see, e.g., [11]).

#SAT is an example of a #**P**-complete problem: it asks for the number of satisfying assignments to a Boolean formula in CNF [33]. Remarkably, #**P** characterizes the computational complexity not only of "discrete" problems, but also of problems involving real-valued variables: approximate volume computation (with additive error) for bounded rational polyhedra in $\mathbb{R}^k$ is #**P**-complete [11].

Measured Theories and #SMT. Suppose $\mathcal{T}$ is a logical theory. Let $\varphi(x)$ be a formula in this theory with free first-order variables $x = (x_1, \ldots, x_k)$. Assume that $\mathcal{T}$ comes with a fixed interpretation, which specifies domains of the variables, denoted $D_1, \ldots, D_k$, and assigns a meaning to predicates and function symbols in the signature of $\mathcal{T}$. Then a tuple $a = (a_1, \ldots, a_k) \in D_1 \times \ldots \times D_k$ is called a *model* of φ if the sentence $\varphi(a_1, \ldots, a_k)$ holds, i.e., if $a \models_{\mathcal{T}} \varphi(x)$. We denote the set of all models of a formula $\varphi(x)$ by $\llbracket \varphi \rrbracket$; the *satisfiability problem* for $\mathcal{T}$ asks, for a formula φ given as input, whether $\llbracket \varphi \rrbracket \neq \emptyset$.

Consider the special cases of (propositional) SAT and linear real arithmetic. For SAT, atomic predicates are of the form $x_i = b$, for $b \in \{0, 1\}$, the domain D_i of each x_i is $\{0, 1\}$, and formulas are propositional formulas in conjunctive normal form. For linear real arithmetic, atomic predicates are of the form $c_1 x_1 + \ldots + c_k x_k \leqslant d$, for $c_1, \ldots, c_k, d \in \mathbb{R}$, the domain D_i of each x_i is $\mathbb{R}$, and formulas are conjunctions of atomic predicates. Sets $\llbracket \varphi \rrbracket$ in these cases are the set of satisfying assignments and the polyhedron itself, respectively.

Suppose the domains $D_1, \ldots, D_k$ given by the fixed interpretation are measure spaces: each D_i is associated with a σ-algebra $\mathcal{F}_i \subseteq 2^{D_i}$ and a measure $\mu_i \colon \mathcal{F}_i \to$

$\mathbb{R}$. This means, by definition, that $\mathcal{F}_i$ and μ_i satisfy the following properties: $\mathcal{F}_i$ contains $\emptyset$ and is closed under complement and countable unions, and μ_i is non-negative, assigns 0 to $\emptyset$, and is σ-additive.

In our special cases, these spaces are as follows. For SAT, each $\mathcal{F}_i$ is the set of all subsets of $D_i = \{0, 1\}$, and $\mu_i(A)$ is simply the number of elements in A. For linear real arithmetic, each $\mathcal{F}_i$ is the set of all Borel subsets of $D_i = \mathbb{R}$, and μ_i is the Lebesgue measure.

Assume that each measure μ_i is σ-finite, that is, the domain D_i is a countable union of measurable sets (i.e., of elements of $\mathcal{F}_i$, and so with finite measure associated with them). This condition, which holds for both special cases, implies that the Cartesian product $D_1 \times \ldots \times D_k$ is measurable with respect to a unique *product measure* μ, defined as follows. A set $A \subseteq D_1 \times \ldots \times D_k$ is *measurable* (that is, μ assigns a value to A) if and only if A is an element of the smallest σ-algebra that contains all sets of the form $A_1 \times \ldots \times A_k$, with $A_i \in \mathcal{F}_i$ for all i. For all such sets, it holds that $\mu(A_1 \times \ldots \times A_k) = \mu_1(A_1) \ldots \mu_k(A_k)$.

In our special cases, the product measure $\mu(A)$ of a set A is the number of elements in $A \subseteq \{0, 1\}^k$ and the volume of $A \subseteq \mathbb{R}^k$, respectively.

We say that the theory $\mathcal{T}$ is *measured* if for every formula $\varphi(x)$ in $\mathcal{T}$ with free (first-order) variables $x = (x_1, \ldots, x_k)$ the set $[\![\varphi]\!]$ is measurable. We define the *model count* of a formula φ as $\mathsf{mc}(\varphi) = \mu([\![\varphi]\!])$. Naturally, if the measures in a measured theory can assume non-integer values, the model count of a formula is not necessarily an integer. With every measured theory we associate a *model counting problem*, denoted $\#\mathrm{SMT}[\mathcal{T}]$: the input is a logical formula $\varphi(x)$ in $\mathcal{T}$, and the goal is to compute the value $\mathsf{mc}(\varphi)$.

The $\#\mathrm{SAT}$ and volume computation problems are just special cases as intended, since $\mathsf{mc}(\varphi)$ is equal to the number of satisfying assignments of a Boolean formula and to the volume of a polyhedron, respectively.

Approximate Model Counting. We now introduce *approximate* $\#\mathrm{SMT}$ and show how approximate $\#\mathrm{SMT}$ reduces to SMT. For our purposes, a *randomized algorithm* is an algorithm that uses internal coin-tossing. We always assume, whenever we use the term, that, for each possible input x to $\mathcal{A}$, the overall probability, over the internal coin tosses r, that $\mathcal{A}$ outputs a wrong answer is at most $1/4$. (This error probability $1/4$ can be reduced to any smaller $\alpha > 0$, by taking the median across $O(\log \alpha^{-1})$ independent runs of $\mathcal{A}$.)

We say that a randomized algorithm $\mathcal{A}$ *approximates* a real-valued functional problem $\mathcal{C} \colon \Sigma^* \to \mathbb{R}$ *with an additive error* if $\mathcal{A}$ takes as input an $x \in \Sigma^*$ and a rational number $\gamma > 0$ and produces an output $\mathcal{A}(x, \gamma)$ such that

$$\Pr\big[|\mathcal{A}(x, \gamma) - \mathcal{C}(x)| \leqslant \gamma \mathcal{U}(x)\big] \geqslant 3/4,$$

where $\mathcal{U} \colon \Sigma^* \to \mathbb{R}$ is some specific and efficiently computable upper bound on the absolute value of $\mathcal{C}(x)$, i.e., $|\mathcal{C}(x)| \leqslant \mathcal{U}(x)$, that comes with the problem $\mathcal{C}$. Similarly, $\mathcal{A}$ *approximates* a (possibly real-valued) functional problem $\mathcal{C} \colon \Sigma^* \to \mathbb{R}$ *with a multiplicative error* if $\mathcal{A}$ takes as input an $x \in \Sigma^*$ and a rational number $\varepsilon > 0$ and produces an output $\mathcal{A}(x, \varepsilon)$ such that

$$\Pr\big[(1 + \varepsilon)^{-1}\mathcal{C}(x) \leqslant \mathcal{A}(x, \varepsilon) \leqslant (1 + \varepsilon)\mathcal{C}(x)\big] \geqslant 3/4.$$

The computation time is usually considered relative to $|x| + \gamma^{-1}$ or $|x| + \varepsilon^{-1}$, respectively (note the inverse of the admissible error). Polynomial-time algorithms that achieve approximations with a multiplicative error are also known as fully polynomial-time randomized approximation schemes (FPRAS) [21].

Algorithms can be equipped with *oracles* solving auxiliary problems, with the intuition that an external solver (say, for SAT) is invoked. In theoretical considerations, the definition of the running time of such an algorithm takes into account the preparation of *queries* to the oracle (just as any other computation), but not the answer to a query—it is returned within a single time step. Oracles may be defined as solving some specific problems (say, SAT) as well as any problems from a class (say, from **NP**). The following result is well-known.

Proposition 1 (generic approximate counting [21,31]). *Let* $C \colon \Sigma^* \to \mathbb{N}$ *be any member of* #**P**. *There exists a polynomial-time randomized algorithm* $\mathcal{A}$ *which, using an* **NP***-oracle, approximates* C *with a multiplicative error.*

In the rest of this section, we present our results on the complexity of model counting problems, #SMT$[\mathcal{T}]$, for measured theories. For these problems, we develop randomized polynomial-time approximation algorithms equipped with oracles, in the flavour of Proposition 1. We describe the proof ideas in Section 3. We relate the theories to value estimation problems of probabilistic programs later in Section 4; our implementation substitutes an appropriate solver for the oracle.

Integer arithmetic. By IA we denote the *bounded* version of integer arithmetic: each free variable x_i of a formula $\varphi(x_1, \ldots, x_k)$ comes with a bounded domain $D_i = [a_i, b_i] \subseteq \mathbb{Z}$, where $a_i, b_i \in \mathbb{Z}$. We use the counting measure $|\cdot| \colon A \subseteq \mathbb{Z} \mapsto |A|$, so the model count $\mathsf{mc}(\varphi)$ of a formula φ is the number of its models. In the formulas, we allow existential (but not universal) quantifiers at the top level. The model counting problem for IA is #**P**-complete.

Theorem 1. *The model counting problem for* IA *can be approximated with a multiplicative error by a polynomial-time randomized algorithm that has oracle access to satisfiability of formulas in* IA.

Linear real arithmetic. By RA we denote the *bounded* version of linear real arithmetic, with possible existential (but not universal) quantifiers at the top level. Each free variable x_i of a formula $\varphi(x_1, \ldots, x_k)$ comes with a bounded domain $D_i = [a_i, b_i] \subseteq \mathbb{R}$, where $a_i, b_i \in \mathbb{R}$. The associated measure is the standard Lebesgue measure, and the model count $\mathsf{mc}(\varphi)$ of a formula φ is the volume of its set of models. (Since we consider linear constraints, any quantifier-free formula defines a finite union of polytopes. It is an easy geometric fact that its projection on a set of variables will again be a finite union of bounded polytopes. Thus, existential quantification involves only finite unions.)

In the model counting problem for RA, the a priori upper bound $\mathcal{U}$ on the solution is $\prod_{i=1}^{k} (b_i - a_i)$; additive approximation of the problem is #**P**-complete.

Theorem 2. *The model counting problem for* RA *can be approximated with an additive error by a polynomial-time randomized algorithm that has oracle access to satisfiability of formulas in* IA + RA *(the combined theory of* IA *and* RA*).*

3 Proof Techniques

3.1 Approximate Discrete Model Counting

We now explain the idea behind Theorem 1. Let $\varphi(x)$ be an input formula in IA and $x = (x_1, \ldots, x_k)$ free variables of φ. Suppose M is a big enough integer such that all models of φ have components not exceeding M, i.e., $[\![\varphi]\!] \subseteq [0, M]^k$.

Our approach to approximating $\mathsf{mc}(\varphi) = |[\![\varphi]\!]|$ follows the construction in Jerrum et al. [21], which builds upon the following observation. Suppose our goal is to find a value v such that $v \leqslant \mathsf{mc}(\varphi) \leqslant 2v$, and we have an oracle $\mathcal{E}$, for "Estimate", answering questions of the form $\mathsf{mc}(\varphi) \geqslant^? N$. Then it is sufficient to make such queries to $\mathcal{E}$ for $N = N_m = 2^m$, $m = 0, \ldots, k \log(M + 1)$, and the overall algorithm design is reduced to implementing such an oracle efficiently.

It turns out that this can be done with the help of *hashing*. Suppose that a hash function h, taken at random from some family $\mathcal{H}$, maps elements of $[0, M]^k$ to $\{0, 1\}^m$. If the family $\mathcal{H}$ is chosen appropriately, then each potential model w is mapped by h to, say, 0^m with probability 2^{-m}; moreover, one should expect that any set $S \subseteq [0, M]^k$ of size d has roughly $2^{-m} \cdot d$ elements in $h^{-1}(0^m) = \{w \in [0, M]^k \mid h(w) = 0^m\}$. In other words, if $|S| \geqslant 2^m$, then $S \cap h^{-1}(0^m)$ is non-empty with high probability, and if $|S| \ll 2^m$, then $S \cap h^{-1}(0^m)$ is empty with high probability. Distinguishing between empty and non-empty sets is, in its turn, a satisfiability question and, as such, can be entrusted to the IA solver. As a result, we reduced the approximation of the model count of φ to a series of satisfiability questions in IA.

Our algorithm posts these questions as SMT queries of the form

$$\varphi(x) \wedge t(x, x') \wedge (h'(x') = 0^m), \tag{1}$$

where x and x' are tuples of integer variables, each component of x' is either 0 or 1, the formula $t(x, x')$ says that x' is binary encoding of x, and the IA formula $h'(x') = 0^m$ encodes the computation of the hash function h on input x'.

Algorithm 1 is the basis of our implementation. It returns a value v that satisfies the inequalities $(1 + \varepsilon)^{-1} \mathsf{mc}(\varphi) \leqslant v \leqslant (1 + \varepsilon) \, \mathsf{mc}(\varphi)$ with probability at least $1 - \alpha$. Algorithm 1 uses a set of parameters to discharge "small" values by enumeration in the SMT solver (parameters a, p) and to optimally query the solver for larger instances (parameters B, q, r). The procedure $\mathcal{E}$ given as Algorithm 2 asks the SMT solver for IA to produce a satisfying assignments (for a positive integer parameter a) to formulas of the form (1) by calling the procedure SMT. The constant B in the algorithm is defined by $B = ((\sqrt{a+1} + 1)/(\sqrt{a+1} - 1))^2$. To achieve the required precision with the desired probability, the algorithm makes q copies of the formula, constructing a formula with k' Boolean variables, and does a majority vote over r calls to the procedure $\mathcal{E}$, where

$$q = \left\lceil \frac{1 + \log B}{2 \log(1 + \varepsilon)} \right\rceil \quad \text{and} \quad r = \left\lceil 8 \ln \left(\frac{k' - \lfloor \log B - 2 \log(\sqrt{B} - 1) \rfloor - 3}{\alpha} \right) \right\rceil.$$

Algorithm 1. Approximate model counting for IA

Input: formula $\varphi(x)$ in IA
Output: value $v \in \mathbb{N}$
Parameters: $\varepsilon \in (0,1)$, /* approximation factor   */
                  $\alpha \in (0,1)$, /* error probability   */
                  $a \in \mathbb{N}$ /* enumeration limit for SMT solver   */
Pick B, q, p, r based on parameters (see text);
$\psi(x, x') = \varphi(x) \wedge t(x, x')$;
$\psi_q(\mathbf{x}, \mathbf{x}') = \psi(x^1, x'^1) \wedge \psi(x^2, x'^2) \wedge \ldots \wedge \psi(x^q, x'^q)$;
if $(e := \mathrm{SMT}(\psi_q, p+1)) \leq p$ then return $\sqrt[q]{e}$;
$k' :=$ number of bits in $\mathbf{x}'$;
for $m = 1, \ldots, k'+1$ do
$\quad$ $c := 0$; /* majority vote counter   */
$\quad$ for $j = 1, \ldots, r$ do
$\quad\quad$ $\lfloor$ if $\mathcal{E}(\psi_q, k', m, a)$ then $c := c+1$;
$\quad$ if $c \leq r/2$ then break;
return $\sqrt[q]{\dfrac{2^{(m+3/2)}\sqrt{B}}{(\sqrt{B}-1)^2}}$

Algorithm 2. Satisfiability "oracle" $\mathcal{E}$

Input: formula $\psi_q(\mathbf{x}, \mathbf{x}')$ in IA; $k', m, a \in \mathbb{N}$
Output: *true* or *false*
$h' := \mathrm{PICK\text{-}HASH}(k', m)$;
$\psi_{h'}(\mathbf{x}, \mathbf{x}') = \psi_q(\mathbf{x}, \mathbf{x}') \wedge (h'(\mathbf{x}') = 0^m)$;
return $(\mathrm{SMT}(\psi_{h'}, a) \geq a)$ /* check if $\psi_{h'}$ has at least a assignments */

For formulas φ with up to $p^{1/q}$ models, where $p = 2\lceil 4/(\sqrt{B}-1)^2\rceil$, Algorithm 1 returns precisely the model count $\mathrm{mc}(\varphi)$ computed by the procedure SMT which repeatedly calls the solver, counting the number of models up to $p+1$.

The family of hash functions $\mathcal{H}$ used by PICK-HASH needs to satisfy the condition of *pairwise independence*: for any two distinct vectors $x_1, x_2 \in [0, M]^k$ and any two strings $w_1, w_2 \in \{0,1\}^m$, the probability that a random function h from $\mathcal{H}$ satisfies $h(x_1) = w_1$ and $h(x_2) = w_2$ is equal to $1/2^{2m}$. There are several constructions for pairwise independent hash functions; we employ a commonly used family, that of random XOR constraints [34,2,17,6]. Given k' and m, the family contains (in binary encoding) all functions $h' = (h'_1, \ldots, h'_m) \colon \{0,1\}^{k'} \to \{0,1\}^m$ with $h'_i(x_1 \ldots, x_{k'}) = a_{i,0} + \sum_{j=1}^{k'} a_{i,j}x_j$, where $a_{i,j} \in \{0,1\}$ for all i and $+$ is the XOR operator (addition in $\mathrm{GF}(2)$). By randomly choosing the coefficients $a_{i,j}$ we get a random hash function from this family. The size of each query is thus bounded by $O(\frac{1}{\varepsilon^2}|\varphi|^2)$, where $|\varphi|$ is the size of the original formula φ, and there will be at most $O(\frac{1}{\varepsilon}|\varphi|)$ queries in total.

3.2   Approximate Continuous Model Counting

In this subsection we explain the idea behind Theorem 2. Let φ be a formula in RA; using appropriate scaling, we can assume without loss of generality that all the variables share the same domain. Suppose $[\![\varphi]\!] \subseteq [0, M]^k$ and fix some γ, with the prospect of finding a value v that is at most $\varepsilon = \gamma M^k$ away from $\mathsf{mc}(\varphi)$ (we take M^k as the value of the upper bound $\mathcal{U}$ in the definition of additive approximation). We show below how to reduce this task of continuous model counting to additive approximation of a model counting problem for a formula with a discrete set of possible models, which, in turn, will be reduced to that of multiplicative approximation.

We first show how to reduce our continuous problem to a discrete one. Divide the cube $[0, M]^k$ into s^k small cubes with side δ each, $\delta = M/s$. For each $y = (y_1, \ldots, y_k) \in \{0, 1, \ldots, s-1\}^k$, set $\psi'(y) = 1$ if at least one point of the cube $C(y) = \{y_j \delta \leqslant x_j \leqslant (y_j + 1) \, \delta, 1 \leqslant j \leqslant k\}$ satisfies φ; that is, if $C(y) \cap [\![\varphi]\!] \neq \emptyset$.

Imagine that we have a formula ψ such that $\psi(y) = \psi'(y)$ for all $y \in \{0, 1, \ldots, s-1\}^k$, and let ψ be written in a theory with a uniform measure that assigns "weight" M/s to each point $y_j \in \{0, 1, \ldots, s-1\}$; one can think of these weights as coefficients in numerical integration. From the technique of Dyer and Frieze [11, Theorem 2] it follows that for a quantifier-free φ and an appropriate value of s the inequality $|\mathsf{mc}(\psi) - \mathsf{mc}(\varphi)| \leqslant \varepsilon/2$ holds.

Indeed, Dyer and Frieze prove a statement of this form in the context of volume computation of a polyhedron, defined by a system of inequalities $Ax \leqslant b$. However, they actually show a stronger statement: given a collection of m hyperplanes in $\mathbb{R}^k$ and a set $[0, M]^k$, an appropriate setting of s will ensure that out of s^k cubes with side $\delta = M/s$ only a small number J will be *cut*, i.e., intersected by some hyperplane. More precisely, if $s = \lceil mk^2 M^k/(\varepsilon/2) \rceil$, then this number J will satisfy the inequality $\delta^k \cdot J \leqslant \varepsilon/2$. Thus, the total volume of cut cubes is at most $\varepsilon/2$, and so, in our terms, we have $|\mathsf{mc}(\psi) - \mathsf{mc}(\varphi)| \leqslant \varepsilon/2$ as desired.

However, in our case the formula φ need not be quantifier-free and may contain existential quantifiers at the top level. If $\varphi(x) = \exists u.\Phi(x, u)$ where Φ is quantifier-free, then the constraints that can "cut" the x-cubes are not necessarily inequalities from Φ. These constraints can rather arise from projections of constraints on variables x and, what makes the problem more difficult, their combinations. However, we are able to prove the following statement:

Lemma 1. *The number $\bar{J}$ of points $y \in \{0, 1, \ldots, s-1\}^k$ for which cubes $C(y)$ are cut satisfies $\bar{\delta}^k \cdot \bar{J} \leqslant \varepsilon/2$ if $\bar{\delta} = M/\bar{s}$, where $\bar{s} = \lceil 2^{\bar{m}+2k} k^2 M^k/(\varepsilon/2) \rceil = \lceil 2^{\bar{m}+2k} k^2/(\gamma/2) \rceil$ and $\bar{m}$ is the number of atomic predicates in Φ.*

A consequence of the lemma is that the choice of $\bar{s}$ ensures that the formula $\psi(y) = \exists x.(\varphi(x) \wedge x \in C(y))$ written in the combined theory $\mathsf{IA} + \mathsf{RA}$ satisfies the inequality $|\mathsf{mc}(\psi) - \mathsf{mc}(\varphi)| \leqslant \varepsilon/2$. Here we associate the domain of each free variable $y_j \in \{0, 1, \ldots, \bar{s}-1\}$ with the uniform measure $\mu_j(v) = M/\bar{s}$. Note that the value of $\bar{s}$ chosen in Lemma 1 will still keep the number of steps of our algorithm polynomial in the size of the input, because the number of bits needed to store the integer index along each axis is $\lceil \log(\bar{s}+1) \rceil$ and not $\bar{s}$ itself.

As a result, it remains to approximate $\mathsf{mc}(\psi)$ with additive error of at most $\varepsilon' = \varepsilon/2 = \gamma M^k/2$, which can be done by invoking the procedure from Theorem 1 that delivers approximation with multiplicative error $\beta = \varepsilon'/M^k = \gamma/2$.

4 Value Estimation for Probabilistic Programs

4.1 The Value Estimation Problem

We now describe an application of approximate model counting to probabilistic programs. Probabilistic programming models extend "usual" nondeterministic programs with the ability to sample values from a distribution and condition the behavior of the program based on observations [18]. Intuitively, probabilistic programs extend an imperative programming language like C with two constructs: a nondeterministic assignment to a variable from a range of values, and a probabilistic assignment that sets a variable to a random value sampled from a distribution. Designed as a modeling framework, probabilistic programs are typically treated as descriptions of probability distributions and not meant to be implemented as usual programs.

We consider a core loop-free imperative language extended with probabilistic statements and with nondeterministic choice:

$$s \ ::= \ x := e \mid x \sim \mathsf{Uniform}(a, b) \mid \mathsf{assume}(p) \mid s; s \mid s \| s \mid \mathsf{accept} \mid \mathsf{reject}.$$

The statement $x := e$ models (usual) assignment, $x \sim \mathsf{Uniform}(a, b)$ takes a value uniformly at random from $[a, b]$ and assigns it to x, $\mathsf{assume}(\varphi)$ models observations used to condition a distribution, $\|$ models nondeterministic choice between statements, and accept and reject are special accepting and rejecting statements.

Under each given assignment to the probabilistic variables, a program accepts (rejects) if there is an execution path that is compatible with the observations and goes from the initial state to an accepting (resp., rejecting) statement. Consider all possible outcomes of the probabilistic assignments in a program $\mathcal{P}$. Restrict attention to those that result in $\mathcal{P}$ reaching (nondeterministically) at least one of accept or reject statements—such elementary outcomes form the set Term (for "termination"); only these scenarios are compatible with the observations. Similarly, some of these outcomes may result in the program reaching (again, nondeterministically) an accept statement—they form the set Accept. Note that the sets Term and Accept are events in a probability space; define $\mathsf{val}(\mathcal{P})$, the *value* of $\mathcal{P}$, as the conditional probability $\Pr[\mathsf{Accept} \mid \mathsf{Term}]$, which is equal to the ratio $\frac{\Pr[\mathsf{Accept}]}{\Pr[\mathsf{Term}]}$ as $\mathsf{Accept} \subseteq \mathsf{Term}$. We assume that programs are well-formed in that $\Pr[\mathsf{Term}]$ is bounded away from 0.

Now consider a probabilistic program $\mathcal{P}$ *over a measured theory* $\mathcal{T}$, i.e., where the expressions and predicates come from $\mathcal{T}$. Associate a separate variable r with each probabilistic assignment in $\mathcal{P}$ and denote the corresponding distribution by $\mathsf{dist}(r)$. Let R be the set of all such variables r.

Proposition 2. *There exists a polynomial-time algorithm that, given a program $\mathcal{P}$ over $\mathcal{T}$, constructs logical formulas $\varphi_{\mathsf{acc}}(R)$ and $\varphi_{\mathsf{term}}(R)$ over $\mathcal{T}$ such that* $\mathsf{Accept} = [\![\varphi_{\mathsf{acc}}]\!]$ *and* $\mathsf{Term} = [\![\varphi_{\mathsf{term}}]\!]$, *where each free variable $r \in R$ is interpreted over its domain with measure* $\mathsf{dist}(r)$. *Thus,* $\mathsf{val}(\mathcal{P}) = \mathsf{mc}(\varphi_{\mathsf{acc}})/\mathsf{mc}(\varphi_{\mathsf{term}})$.

Proposition 2 reduces the *value estimation* problem—i.e., the problem of estimating $\mathsf{val}(\mathcal{P})$—to model counting. For the theories of integer and linear real arithmetic, we get a #**P** upper bound on the complexity of value estimation. On the other hand, value estimation is #**P**-hard, as it easily encodes #SAT. Finally, since the model counting problem can be approximated using a polynomial-time randomized algorithm with a satisfiability oracle, we also get an algorithm for approximate value estimation.

Proposition 3 (complexity of value estimation).
1. *The value estimation problem for loop-free probabilistic programs (over* IA *and* RA*) is* #**P***-complete. The problem is* #**P***-hard already for programs with Boolean variables only.*
2. *The value estimation problem for loop-free probabilistic programs over* IA *can be approximated with a multiplicative error by a polynomial-time randomized algorithm that has oracle access to satisfiability of formulas in* IA.
3. *The value estimation problem for loop-free probabilistic programs over* RA *can be approximated with an additive error by a polynomial-time randomized algorithm that has oracle access to satisfiability of formulas in* IA + RA.

4.2   Evaluation

We have implemented the algorithm from Subsection 3.1 in C++ on top of the SMT solver Z3 [10]. The SMT solver is used unmodified, with default settings.

Examples. For the evaluation we consider five examples. The first two are probabilistic programs that use nondeterminism. The remaining examples are Bayesian networks encoded in our language.

The Monty Hall problem [29] is a classic problem from probability theory. Imagine a television game show with two characters: the player and the host. The player is facing three doors, numbered 1, 2, and 3; behind one of them is a car, and behind the other two are goats. The player initially picks one of the doors, say door i, but does not open it. The host, who knows the position of the car, then opens another door, say door j with $j \neq i$, and shows a goat behind it. The player then gets to open one of the remaining doors. There are two available strategies: *stay* with the original choice, door i, or *switch* to the remaining alternative, door $k \notin \{i, j\}$. The Monty Hall problem asks, which strategy is better? It is widely known that, in the standard probabilistic setting of the problem, the switching strategy is the better one: it has payoff 2/3, i.e., it chooses the door with the car with probability 2/3; the staying strategy has payoff of only 1/3. We model this problem as a probabilistic program, where the host's actions are modelled using nondeterminism (for details see the extended version [8]).

Table 1. Input and algorithm parameters, and running time. The input parameter ε is the multiplicative approximation factor, α is the desired error probability and a is the number of satisfying assignments the SMT solver checks for; k' is the resulting number of bits and m_{acc} and m_{term} are the maximal hash sizes for φ_{acc} and φ_{term}.

Example	ε	α	a	k'	m_{acc}	m_{term}	time(s) for φ_{acc}	time(s) for φ_{term}
Monty Hall (1)	0.2	0.01	1	24	13	20	3.37	4.11
Three prisoners (2)	0.2	0.01	1	36	0	20	0.04	19.84
Alarm (3)	0.5	0.1	20	56	36	49	196.54	132.53
Grass model (4)	0.5	0.1	20	48	34	35	85.71	89.37
Sensitivity est. (5)	0.5	0.1	20	66	56	57	295.09	241.55

The three prisoners problem. Our second example is a problem that appeared in Martin Gardner's "Mathematical Games" column in the Scientific American in 1959. There, one of three prisoners (1, 2, and 3), who are sentenced to death, is randomly pardoned. The guard gives prisoner 1 the following information: If 2 is pardoned, he gives 1 the name of 3. If 3 is pardoned, he gives him the name of 2. If 1 is pardoned, he flips a coin to decide whether to name 2 or 3. Provided that the guard tells prisoner 1 that prisoner 2 is to be executed, determine what is prisoner 1's chance to be pardoned?

Pearl's burglar alarm and grass model. These two examples are classical Bayesian networks from the literature. Pearl's burglar alarm example is as given in [18, Figure 15]; the grass model is taken from [22, Figure 1].

Kidney disease eGFR sensitivity estimation. The last example is a probabilistic model of a medical diagnostics system with noisy inputs. We considered the program given in [18, Figure 11] using a simplified model of the input distributions. In our setting, we draw the value of the logarithm of the patient's creatinine level uniformly from the set $\{-0.16, -0.09, -0.08, 0, 0.08, 0.09, 0.16, 0.17\}$ (thus approximating the original lognormal distribution), regardless of the patient's gender, and the patient's age from the interval $[30, 80]$. The patient's gender and ethnicity are distributed in the same way as described in [28].

Results. For each program $\mathcal{P}$, we used our tool to estimate the model count of the formulas φ_{acc} and φ_{term}; the value $\mathsf{val}(\mathcal{P})$ of the program is approximated by v_{acc}/v_{term}, where v_{acc} and v_{term} are the approximate model counts computed by our tool. Table 1 shows input and algorithm parameters for the considered examples, as well as running time (in seconds) for computing v_{acc} and v_{term}. The approximation factor ε, the bound α on the error probability, and the enumeration limit a for the SMT solver are provided by the user. For examples (1) and (2), we choose ε to be 0.2, while for the remaining examples we take 0.5. The chosen value of ε has an impact on the number of copies q of the formula that we construct, an thus on the number k' of Boolean variables in the formula given to the solver. Furthermore, the more satisfying assignments a formula has, the larger dimension m of the hash function is reached during the run; m_{acc} and m_{term} are the maximal values of m reached on the runs on φ_{acc} and φ_{term}.

While our technique can solve these small instances in reasonable time, there remains much room for improvement. Although SAT solvers can scale to large instances, it is well known that even a small number of XOR constraints can quickly exceed the capabilities of state-of-the-art solvers [32]. Since for each m we add m parity constraints to the formula, we run into the SAT bottleneck: computing an approximation of $\mathsf{mc}(\varphi_{\mathsf{acc}})$ for example (4) with $\varepsilon = 0.3$ results in running time of several hours. (At the same time, exact counting by enumerating satisfying assignments is not a feasible alternative either: for the formula φ_{acc} in example (4), which has more than 400 000 of them, performing this task naively with Z3 also took several hours.) The efficiency of our approach can benefit from better handling of XOR constraints in the SMT solver. For example, SAT solvers such as CryptoMiniSat which deal with XOR constraints efficiently can scale to over 1K variables [6,5,17]. This, however, requires incorporating such a SAT solver within Z3.

The scalability needs improvement also in the continuous case, where our discretization procedure introduces a large number of discrete variables. For instance, a more realistic model of example (5) would be one in which the logarithm of the creatinine level is modeled as a continuous random variable. This would result, after discretization, in formulas with hundreds of Boolean variables, which appears to be beyond the limit of Z3's XOR reasoning.

5   Concluding Remarks

Static reasoning questions for probabilistic programs [18,28,19], as well as quantitative and probabilistic analysis of software [3,15,14,24], have received a lot of recent attention. There are two predominant approaches to these questions. The first one is to perform Monte Carlo sampling of the program [28,3,24,4,27]. To improve performance, such methods use sophisticated heuristics and variance reduction techniques, such as stratified sampling in [28,3]. The second approach is based on reduction to model counting [14,15,26,25], either using off-the-shelf #SMT solvers or developing #SMT procedures on top of existing tools. Another recent approach is based on data flow analysis [9]. Our work introduces a new dimension of approximation to this area: we reduce program analysis to #SMT, but carry out a randomized approximation procedure for the count.

By known connections between counting and uniform generation [21,2], our techniques can be adapted to generate (approximately) uniform random samples from the set of models of a formula in IA or RA. Uniform generation from Boolean formulas using hashing techniques was recently implemented and evaluated in the context of constrained random testing of hardware [6,5]. We extend this technique to the SMT setting, which was left as a future direction in [6] (previously known methods for counting integral points of polytopes [1,15] do not generalize to the nonlinear theory IA).

Further Directions.

Scalability. An extension of the presented techniques may be desirable to cope with larger instances of #SMT. As argued in subsection 4.2, incorporating XOR-aware reasoning into Z3 can be an important step in this direction.

Theories. Similar techniques apply to theories other than IA and RA. For example, our algorithm can be extended to the combined theory of string constraints and integer arithmetic. While SMT solvers can handle this theory, it would be nontrivial to design a model counting procedure using the previously known approach based on generating functions [25].

Distributions. Although the syntax of our probabilistic programs supports only Uniform, it is easy to simulate other distributions: Bernoulli, uniform with non-constant boundaries, (approximation of) normal. This, however, will not scale well, so future work may incorporate non-uniform distributions as a basic primitive. (An important special case covers weighted model counting in SAT, for which a novel extension of the hashing approach was recently proposed [5].)

Applications. A natural application of the uniform generation technique in the SMT setting would be a procedure that generates program behaviors uniformly at random from the space of possible behaviors. (For the model we studied, program behaviors are trees: the branching comes from nondeterministic choice, and the random variables are sampled from their respective distributions.)

References

1. Barvinok, A.: A polynomial time algorithm for counting integral points in polyhedra when the dimension is fixed. In: FOCS 1993. ACM (1993)
2. Bellare, M., Goldreich, O., Petrank, E.: Uniform generation of NP-witnesses using an NP-oracle. Inf. Comput. 163(2), 510–526 (2000)
3. Borges, M., Filieri, A., d'Amorim, M., Pasareanu, C., Visser, W.: Compositional solution space quantification for probabilistic software analysis. In: PLDI, p. 15. ACM (2014)
4. Chaganty, A., Nori, A., Rajamani, S.: Efficiently sampling probabilistic programs via program analysis. In: AISTATS. JMLR Proceedings, vol. 31, pp. 153–160. JMLR.org (2013)
5. Chakraborty, S., Fremont, D., Meel, K., Seshia, S., Vardi, M.: Distribution-aware sampling and weighted model counting for SAT. In: AAAI 2014, pp. 1722–1730 (2014)
6. Chakraborty, S., Meel, K.S., Vardi, M.Y.: A scalable and nearly uniform generator of SAT witnesses. In: Sharygina, N., Veith, H. (eds.) CAV 2013. LNCS, vol. 8044, pp. 608–623. Springer, Heidelberg (2013)
7. Chakraborty, S., Meel, K.S., Vardi, M.Y.: A scalable approximate model counter. In: Schulte, C. (ed.) CP 2013. LNCS, vol. 8124, pp. 200–216. Springer, Heidelberg (2013)
8. Chistikov, D., Dimitrova, R., Majumdar, R.: Approximate counting in SMT and value estimation for probabilistic programs. CoRR, abs/1411.0659 (2014)
9. Claret, G., Rajamani, S.K., Nori, A.V., Gordon, A.D., Borgström, J.: Bayesian inference using data flow analysis. In: ESEC/FSE 2013, pp. 92–102 (2013)
10. De Moura, L., Bjørner, N.S.: Z3: An efficient SMT solver. In: Ramakrishnan, C.R., Rehof, J. (eds.) TACAS 2008. LNCS, vol. 4963, pp. 337–340. Springer, Heidelberg (2008)
11. Dyer, M., Frieze, A.: On the complexity of computing the volume of a polyhedron. SIAM J. Comput. 17(5), 967–974 (1988)

12. Dyer, M., Frieze, A., Kannan, R.: A random polynomial time algorithm for approximating the volume of convex bodies. J. ACM 38(1), 1–17 (1991)
13. Ermon, S., Gomes, C., Sabharwal, A., Selman, B.: Taming the curse of dimensionality: Discrete integration by hashing and optimization. In: ICML (2), pp. 334–342 (2013)
14. Filieri, A., Pasareanu, C., Visser, W.: Reliability analysis in symbolic Pathfinder. In: ICSE, pp. 622–631 (2013)
15. Fredrikson, M., Jha, S.: Satisfiability modulo counting: A new approach for analyzing privacy properties. In: CSL-LICS, p. 42. ACM (2014)
16. Gomes, C., Hoffmann, J., Sabharwal, A., Selman, B.: From sampling to model counting. In: IJCAI, pp. 2293–2299 (2007)
17. Gomes, C., Sabharwal, A., Selman, B.: Model counting. In: Handbook of Satisfiability. Frontiers in Artificial Intelligence and Applications, vol. 185, pp. 633–654. IOS Press (2009)
18. Gordon, A., Henzinger, T., Nori, A., Rajamani, S., Samuel, S.: Probabilistic programming. In: FOSE 2014, pp. 167–181. ACM (2014)
19. Hur, C.-K., Nori, A., Rajamani, S., Samuel, S.: Slicing probabilistic programs. In: PLDI, p. 16. ACM (2014)
20. Jerrum, M., Sinclair, A.: The Markov chain Monte Carlo method: An approach to approximate counting and integration. In: Approximation Algorithms for NP-hard Problems, pp. 482–520. PWS Publishing (1996)
21. Jerrum, M., Valiant, L., Vazirani, V.: Random generation of combinatorial structures from a uniform distribution. TCS 43, 169–188 (1986)
22. Kiselyov, O., Shan, C.-C.: Monolingual probabilistic programming using generalized coroutines. In: UAI, pp. 285–292. AUAI Press (2009)
23. LattE tool, https://www.math.ucdavis.edu/~latte
24. Luckow, K.S., Pasareanu, C.S., Dwyer, M.B., Filieri, A., Visser, W.: Exact and approximate probabilistic symbolic execution for nondeterministic programs. In: ASE 2014, pp. 575–586 (2014)
25. Luu, L., Shinde, S., Saxena, P., Demsky, B.: A model counter for constraints over unbounded strings. In: PLDI, p. 57. ACM (2014)
26. Ma, F., Liu, S., Zhang, J.: Volume computation for boolean combination of linear arithmetic constraints. In: Schmidt, R.A. (ed.) CADE 2009. LNCS (LNAI), vol. 5663, pp. 453–468. Springer, Heidelberg (2009)
27. Sampson, A., Panchekha, P., Mytkowicz, T., McKinley, K., Grossman, D., Ceze, L.: Expressing and verifying probabilistic assertions. In: PLDI, p. 14. ACM Press (2014)
28. Sankaranarayanan, S., Chakarov, A., Gulwani, S.: Static analysis for probabilistic programs: inferring whole program properties from finitely many paths. In: PLDI, pp. 447–458. ACM (2013)
29. Selvin, S.: A problem in probability. American Statistician 29(1), 67 (1975)
30. Sipser, M.: A complexity-theoretic approach to randomness. In: STOC, pp. 330–335. ACM (1983)
31. Stockmeyer, L.: On approximation algorithms for $\#P$. SIAM J. of Computing 14, 849–861 (1985)
32. Urquhart, A.: Hard examples for resolution. J. ACM 34(1), 209–219 (1987)
33. Valiant, L.: The complexity of computing the permanent. Theoretical Computer Science 9, 189–201 (1979)
34. Valiant, L., Vazirani, V.: NP is as easy as detecting unique solutions. Theoretical Computer Science 47, 85–93 (1986)
35. Zhou, M., He, F., Song, X., He, S., Chen, G., Gu, M.: Estimating the volume of solution space for satisfiability modulo linear real arithmetic. Theory of Computing Systems 56(2), 347–371 (2015)

Pushing the Envelope of Optimization Modulo Theories with Linear-Arithmetic Cost Functions*

R. Sebastiani and P. Trentin

DISI, University of Trento, Italy

Abstract. In the last decade we have witnessed an impressive progress in the expressiveness and efficiency of Satisfiability Modulo Theories (SMT) solving techniques. This has brought previously-intractable problems at the reach of state-of-the-art SMT solvers, in particular in the domain of SW and HW verification. Many SMT-encodable problems of interest, however, require also the capability of finding models that are *optimal* wrt. some cost functions. In previous work, namely *Optimization Modulo Theory with Linear Rational Cost Functions – OMT($\mathcal{LRA} \cup \mathcal{T}$)*, we have leveraged SMT solving to handle the *minimization* of cost functions on linear arithmetic over the rationals, by means of a combination of SMT and LP minimization techniques.

In this paper we push the envelope of our OMT approach along three directions: first, we extend it to work with linear arithmetic on the mixed integer/rational domain, by means of a combination of SMT, LP and ILP minimization techniques; second, we develop a *multi-objective* version of OMT, so that to handle many cost functions simultaneously or lexicographically; third, we develop an *incremental* version of OMT, so that to exploit the incrementality of some OMT-encodable problems. An empirical evaluation performed on OMT-encoded verification problems demonstrates the usefulness and efficiency of these extensions.

1 Introduction

In many contexts including automated reasoning (AR) and formal verification (FV) important *decision* problems are effectively encoded into and solved as Satisfiability Modulo Theories (SMT) problems. In the last decade efficient SMT solvers have been developed, that combine the power of modern conflict-driven clause-learning (CDCL) SAT solvers with the expressiveness of dedicated decision procedures ($\mathcal{T}$-*solvers*) for several first-order theories of practical interest like, e.g., those of linear arithmetic over the rationals ($\mathcal{LRA}$) or the integers ($\mathcal{LIA}$) or their combination ($\mathcal{LRIA}$), those of non-linear arithmetic over the reals ($\mathcal{NLRA}$) or the integers ($\mathcal{NLIA}$), of arrays ($\mathcal{AR}$), of bit-vectors ($\mathcal{BV}$), and their combinations. (See [19,20,3] for an overview.) This has brought previously-intractable problems at the reach of state-of-the-art SMT solvers, in particular in the domain of software (SW) and hardware (HW) verification.

Many SMT-encodable problems of interest, however, may require also the capability of finding models that are *optimal* wrt. some cost function over arithmetical variables.

---

* This work is supported by Semiconductor Research Corporation (SRC) under GRC Research Project 2012-TJ-2266 WOLF. We thank Alberto Griggio for support with MATHSAT5 code.

C. Baier and C. Tinelli (Eds.): TACAS 2015, LNCS 9035, pp. 335–349, 2015.
DOI: 10.1007/978-3-662-46681-0_27

(See e.g. [22,16,21] for a rich list of such applications.) For instance, in SMT-based *model checking with timed or hybrid systems* (e.g. [2,1]) you may want to find executions which optimize the value of some parameter (e.g., a clock timeout value, or the total elapsed time) while fulfilling/violating some property (e.g., find the minimum time interval for a rail-crossing causing a safety violation).

Surprisingly, only few works extending SMT to deal with *optimization* problems have been presented in the literature [18,8,22,11,17,9,21,16,15,5] –most of which handle problems which are different to that addressed in this paper [18,8,11,17,9]. (We refer the reader to the related work section of [21] for a discussion on these approaches.)

Sebastiani and Tomasi [22,21] presented two procedures for adding to SMT($\mathcal{LRA} \cup \mathcal{T}$) the functionality of finding models minimizing some $\mathcal{LRA}$ cost variable $-\mathcal{T}$ being some (possibly empty) stably-infinite theory s.t. $\mathcal{T}$ and $\mathcal{LRA}$ are signature-disjoint. This problem is referred to as *Optimization Modulo Theories with linear cost functions on the rationals*, OMT($\mathcal{LRA} \cup \mathcal{T}$). (If $\mathcal{T}$ is the empty theory, then we refer to it as OMT($\mathcal{LRA}$).) [1] These procedures combine standard SMT and LP minimization techniques: the first, called *offline*, is much simpler to implement, since it uses an incremental SMT solver as a black-box, whilst the second, called *inline*, embeds the search for optimum within the CDCL loop schema, and as such it is more sophisticate and efficient, but it requires modifying the code of the SMT solver. In [22,21] these procedures have been implemented on top of the MATHSAT5 SMT solver [10] into a tool called OPTIMATHSAT, and an extensive empirical evaluation is presented.

Li et al. [16] extended the OMT($\mathcal{LRA}$) problem by considering *contemporarily* many cost functions for the input formula φ, namely $\{cost_1, ..., cost_k\}$, so that the problem consists in enumerating k independent models for φ, each minimizing one specific $cost_i$. In [16] they presented a novel offline algorithm for OMT($\mathcal{LRA}$), and implemented it into the tool SYMBA. Unlike with the procedures in [22,21], the algorithm described in [16] does not use a LP minimization procedure: rather, a sequence of blackbox calls to an underlying SMT solver (Z3) allows for finding progressively-better solutions along some objective direction, either forcing discrete jumps to some bounds induced by the inequalities in the problem, or proving such objective is unbounded. SYMBA is used as backend engine of the SW model checker UFO. [2] An empirical evaluation on problems derived from SW verification shows the usefulness of this multiple-cost approach.

Larraz et al. [15] present incomplete SMT($\mathcal{NLIA}$) and MaxSMT($\mathcal{NLIA}$) procedures, which use an OMT($\mathcal{LIA}$) tool as an internal component. The latter procedure, called BCLT, is described neither in [15] nor in any previous publication; however, it has been kindly made available to us by their authors upon request, together with a link to the master student's thesis describing it. [3]

Finally, we have been informed by a reviewer of an invited presentation given by Bjørner and Phan two months after the submission of this paper [5], describing general algorithms for optimization in SMT, including MaxSMT, incremental, multi-objective

---

[1] Importantly, both MaxSMT ([18,8,9]) and SMT with pseudo-Boolean constraints and costs [8] are straightforwardly encoded into OMT [22,21].

[2] https://bitbucket.org/arieg/ufo/

[3] http://upcommons.upc.edu/pfc/handle/2099.1/14204?locale=en

and lexicographic OMT, Pareto-optimality, which are implemented into the tool νZ on top of Z3. Remarkably, [5] presents specialized procedures for MaxSMT, and enriches the offline OMT schema of [22,21] with specialized algorithms for unbound-solution detection and for bound-tightening.

We are not aware of any other OMT tool currently available.

We remark a few facts about the OMT tools in [22,21,16,15]. First, none of them has an *incremental* interface, allowing for pushing and popping subformulas (including definitions of novel cost functions) so that to reuse previous search from one call to the other; in a FV context this limitation is relevant, because often SMT backends are called incrementally (e.g., in the previously-mentioned example of SMT-based bounded model checking of timed&hybrid systems). Second, none of the above tools supports mixed integer/real optimization, OMT($\mathcal{LRIA}$). Third, none of the above tools supports *both* multi-objective optimization and integer optimization. Finally, neither SYMBA nor BCLT currently handle combined theories.

In this paper we push the envelope of the OMT($\mathcal{LRA} \cup \mathcal{T}$) approach of [22,21] along three directions: (i) we extend it to work also with linear arithmetic on the mixed integer/rational domain, OMT($\mathcal{LRIA} \cup \mathcal{T}$), by means of a combination of SMT, LP and ILP minimization techniques; (ii) we develop a *multi-objective* version of OMT, so that to handle many cost functions simultaneously or lexicographically; (iii) we develop an *incremental* version of OMT, so that to exploit the incrementality of some OMT-encodable problems. We have implement these novel functionalities in OPTI-MATHSAT. An empirical evaluation performed on OMT-encoded formal verification problems demonstrates the usefulness and efficiency of these extensions.

Some more details can be found in an extended version of this paper. [4]

Content. The paper is organized as follows: in §2 we provide the necessary background knowledge on SMT and OMT; in §3 we introduce and discuss the above-mentioned novel extensions of OMT; in §4 we perform an empirical evaluation of such procedures.

2   Background

2.1   Satisfiability Modulo Theories

We assume a basic background knowledge on first-order logic and on CDCL SAT solving. We consider some first-order theory $\mathcal{T}$, and we restrict our interest to *ground* formulas/literals/atoms in the language of $\mathcal{T}$ ($\mathcal{T}$-formulas/literals/atoms hereafter).

A *theory solver for $\mathcal{T}$*, $\mathcal{T}$-*solver*, is a procedure able to decide the $\mathcal{T}$-satisfiability of a conjunction/set μ of $\mathcal{T}$-literals. If μ is $\mathcal{T}$-unsatisfiable, then $\mathcal{T}$-*solver* returns UNSAT and a set/conjunction η of $\mathcal{T}$-literals in μ which was found $\mathcal{T}$-unsatisfiable; η is called a $\mathcal{T}$-*conflict set*, and $\neg\eta$ a $\mathcal{T}$-*conflict clause*. If μ is $\mathcal{T}$-satisfiable, then $\mathcal{T}$-*solver* returns SAT; it may also be able to return some unassigned $\mathcal{T}$-literal $l \notin \mu$ from a set of all available $\mathcal{T}$-literals, s.t. $\{l_1, ..., l_n\} \models_{\mathcal{T}} l$, where $\{l_1, ..., l_n\} \subseteq \mu$. We call this process $\mathcal{T}$-*deduction* and $(\bigvee_{i=1}^{n} \neg l_i \vee l)$ a $\mathcal{T}$-*deduction clause*. Notice that $\mathcal{T}$-conflict and $\mathcal{T}$-deduction clauses are valid in $\mathcal{T}$. We call them $\mathcal{T}$-*lemmas*.

---

[4] Available at http://optimathsat.disi.unitn.it.

Given a $\mathcal{T}$-formula φ, the formula φ^p obtained by rewriting each $\mathcal{T}$-atom in φ into a fresh atomic proposition is the *Boolean abstraction* of φ, and φ is the *refinement* of φ^p. Notationally, we indicate by φ^p and μ^p the Boolean abstraction of φ and μ, and by φ and μ the refinements of φ^p and μ^p respectively.

In a lazy SMT($\mathcal{T}$) solver, the Boolean abstraction φ^p of the input formula φ is given as input to a CDCL SAT solver, and whenever a satisfying assignment μ^p is found s.t. $\mu^p \models \varphi^p$, the corresponding set of $\mathcal{T}$-literals μ is fed to the $\mathcal{T}$-*solver*; if μ is found $\mathcal{T}$-consistent, then φ is $\mathcal{T}$-consistent; otherwise, $\mathcal{T}$-*solver* returns a $\mathcal{T}$-conflict set η causing the inconsistency, so that the clause $\neg\eta^p$ is used to drive the backjumping and learning mechanism of the SAT solver. The process proceeds until either a $\mathcal{T}$-consistent assignment μ is found (φ is $\mathcal{T}$-satisfiable), or no more assignments are available (φ is $\mathcal{T}$-unsatisfiable).

Important optimizations are *early pruning* and $\mathcal{T}$-*propagation*. The $\mathcal{T}$-*solver* is invoked also when an assignment μ is still under construction: if it is $\mathcal{T}$-unsatisfiable, then the procedure backtracks, without exploring the (possibly many) extensions of μ; if it is $\mathcal{T}$-satisfiable, and if the $\mathcal{T}$-*solver* is able to perform a $\mathcal{T}$-deduction $\{l_1, ..., l_n\} \models_{\mathcal{T}} l$, then l can be unit-propagated, and the $\mathcal{T}$-deduction clause $(\bigvee_{i=1}^n \neg l_i \vee l)$ can be used in backjumping and learning. To this extent, in order to maximize the efficiency, most $\mathcal{T}$-solvers are *incremental* and *backtrackable*, that is, they are called via a push&pop interface, maintaining and reusing the status of the search from one call and the other.

The above schema is a coarse abstraction of the procedures underlying most state-of-the-art SMT tools. The interested reader is pointed to, e.g., [19,20,3] for details.

2.2   Optimization Modulo Theories

We recall the basic ideas about OMT($\mathcal{LRA} \cup \mathcal{T}$) and about the inline procedure in [22,21]. In what follows, $\mathcal{T}$ is some stably-infinite theory with equality s.t. $\mathcal{LRA}$ and $\mathcal{T}$ are signature-disjoint. ($\mathcal{T}$ can be a combination of theories.) We call an *Optimization Modulo $\mathcal{LRA} \cup \mathcal{T}$ problem, OMT($\mathcal{LRA} \cup \mathcal{T}$)*, a pair $\langle\varphi, cost\rangle$ such that φ is an SMT($\mathcal{LRA} \cup \mathcal{T}$) formula and $cost$ is an $\mathcal{LRA}$ variable occurring in φ, representing the cost to be minimized. The problem consists in finding a $\mathcal{LRA}$-model $\mathcal{M}$ for φ (if any) whose value of $cost$ is minimum. We call an *Optimization Modulo $\mathcal{LRA}$ problem (OMT($\mathcal{LRA}$))* an OMT($\mathcal{LRA} \cup \mathcal{T}$) problem where $\mathcal{T}$ is empty. If φ is in the form $\varphi' \wedge (cost < c)$ [resp. $\varphi' \wedge \neg(cost < c)$] for some value $c \in \mathbb{Q}$, then we call c an *upper bound* [resp. *lower bound*] for $cost$. If ub [resp. lb] is the minimum upper bound [resp. the maximum lower bound] for φ, we also call the interval [lb, ub[the *range* of $cost$.

Remark 1. [22,21] explain a general technique to encode an OMT($\mathcal{LRA}$) problem into OMT($\mathcal{LRA} \cup \mathcal{T}$) by exploiting the Delayed Theory Combination technique [6] implemented in MATHSAT5. It is easy to see that this holds also for $\mathcal{LIA}$ and $\mathcal{LRIA}$. Therefore, for the sake of brevity and readability, hereafter we consider the case where $\mathcal{T}$ is the empty theory (OMT($\mathcal{LRA}$), OMT($\mathcal{LIA}$) or OMT($\mathcal{LRIA}$)), referring the reader to [22,21] for a detailed explanation about how to handle the general case.

In the inline OMT($\mathcal{LRA}$) schema, the procedure takes as input a pair $\langle\varphi, cost\rangle$, plus optionally values for lb and ub (which are implicitly considered to be $-\infty$ and $+\infty$ if not present), and returns the model $\mathcal{M}$ of minimum cost and its cost $u \stackrel{\text{def}}{=} \mathcal{M}(cost)$; it returns the value ub and an empty model if φ is $\mathcal{LRA}$-inconsistent. The standard CDCL-based schema of the SMT solver is modified as follows.

Initialization. The variables l, u (defining the current range) are initialized to lb and ub respectively, the variable pivot (defining the pivot in binary search) is not initialized, the $\mathcal{LRA}$-atom PIV is initialized to $\top$ and the output model $\mathcal{M}$ is initialized to be an empty model.

Range Updating & Pivoting. Every time the search of the CDCL SAT solver gets back to decision level 0, the range $[l, u[$ is updated s.t. u [resp. l] is assigned the lowest [resp. highest] value u_i [resp. l_i] such that the atom $(cost < u_i)$ [resp. $\neg(cost < l_i)$] is currently assigned at level 0. Then the heuristic function BinSearchMode() is invoked, which decides whether to run the current step in binary- or in linear-search mode: in the first case (which can occur only if $l > -\infty$ and $u < \infty$) a value pivot $\in]l, u[$ is computed (e.g. pivot $= (l + u)/2$), and the (possibly new) atom PIV $\stackrel{\text{def}}{=} (cost < \text{pivot})$ is decided to be true (level 1) by the SAT solver. This temporarily restricts the cost range to $[l, \text{pivot}[$. Then the CDCL solver proceeds its search, as in §2.1.

Decreasing the Upper Bound. When an assignment μ is generated s.t. $\mu^p \models \varphi^p$ and which is found $\mathcal{LRA}$-consistent by $\mathcal{LRA}$-Solver, μ is also fed to $\mathcal{LRA}$-Minimize, returning the minimum cost min of μ; then the unit clause $C_\mu \stackrel{\text{def}}{=} (cost < \text{min})$ is learned and fed to the backjumping mechanism, which forces the SAT solver to backjump to level 0, then unit-propagating $(cost < \text{min})$. This restricts the cost range to $[l, \text{min}[$. $\mathcal{LRA}$-Minimize is embedded within $\mathcal{LRA}$-Solver –it is a simple extension of the LP algorithm in [12]– so that it is called incrementally after it, without restarting its search from scratch. Notice that the clauses C_μ ensure progress in the minimization every time that a new $\mathcal{LRA}$-consistent assignment is generated.

Termination. The procedure terminates when the embedded SMT-solving algorithm reveals an inconsistency, returning the current values of u and $\mathcal{M}$.

As a result of these modifications, we also have the following typical scenario.

Increasing the Lower Bound. In binary-search mode, when a conflict occurs and the conflict analysis of the SAT solver produces a conflict clause in the form $\neg\text{PIV} \vee \neg\eta'$ s.t. all literals in η' are assigned true at level 0 (i.e., $\varphi \wedge \text{PIV}$ is $\mathcal{LRA}$-inconsistent), then the SAT solver backtracks to level 0, unit-propagating $\neg\text{PIV}$. This case permanently restricts the cost range to $[\text{pivot}, u[$.

Notice that, to guarantee termination, binary-search steps must be interleaved with linear-search ones infinitely often. We refer the reader to [22,21] for details and for a description of further improvements to the basic inline procedure.

3   Pushing the Envelope of OMT

3.1   From OMT($\mathcal{LRA}$) to OMT($\mathcal{LRIA}$)

We start from the observation that the only $\mathcal{LRA}$-specific components of the inline OMT($\mathcal{LRA}$) schema of §2.2 are the $\mathcal{T}$-solving and minimizing procedures. Thus, under the assumption of having an efficient $\mathcal{LRIA}$-Solver already implemented inside the embedded SMT solver –like we have in MATHSAT5 [14]– the schema in §2.2 can be adapted to $\mathcal{LRIA}$ by invoking an $\mathcal{LRIA}$-specific minimizing procedure each time a truth-assignment μ s.t. $\mu^p \models \varphi^p$ is generated.

Remark 2. Notice that in principle in $\mathcal{LIA}$ the minimization step is not strictly necessary if the input problem is lower bounded. In fact, to find the optimum *cost* value it would be sufficient to iteratively enumerate and remove each solution found by the standard implementation of the $\mathcal{LIA}$-Solver, because each step guarantees an improvement of at least 1. Minimizing the *cost* value at each iteration of the SMT engine, however, allows for speeding up the optimization search by preventing the current truth assignment μ from being generated more than once. In addition, the availability of a specialized $\mathcal{LIA}$-Minimize procedure is essential to recognize unbounded problems.

The problem of implementing an efficient OMT($\mathcal{LRIA}$) tool reduces thus to that of implementing an efficient minimizer in $\mathcal{LRIA}$, namely $\mathcal{LRIA}$-Minimize, *which exploits and cooperates in synergy with the other components of the SMT solver.* In particular, it is advisable that $\mathcal{LRIA}$-Minimize is embedded into the $\mathcal{LRIA}$-Solver, so that it is called incrementally after the latter has checked the $\mathcal{LRIA}$-consistency of the current assignment μ. (Notice that, e.g., embedding into $\mathcal{LRIA}$-Minimize a MILP tool from the shelf would not match these requirements.) To this extent, we have investigated both theoretically and empirically three different schemas of Branch&Bound $\mathcal{LRIA}$-Minimize procedure, which we call *basic, advanced* and *truncated.*

The first step performed by $\mathcal{LRIA}$-Minimize is to check whether *cost* is lower bounded. Since a *feasible MILP* problem is unbounded if and only if its corresponding continuous relaxation is unbounded [7],[5] we run $\mathcal{LRA}$-Minimize on the relaxation of μ. If the relaxed problem if unbounded, then $\mathcal{LIA}$-Minimize returns $-\infty$; otherwise, $\mathcal{LRA}$-Minimize returns the minimum value of *cost* in the relaxed problem, which we set as the current *lower bound* lb for *cost* in the original problem. We also initialize the *upper bound* ub for *cost* to the value $\mathcal{M}(cost)$, where $\mathcal{M}$ is the model returned by the most recent call to the $\mathcal{LRIA}$-Solver on μ.

Then we explore the solution space by means of an LP-based Branch&Bound procedure that reduces the original MILP problem to a sequence of smaller sub-problems, which are solved separately.

Basic Branch&Bound. We describe first a naive version of the Branch&Bound minimization procedure. (Since it is very inefficient, we present it only as a baseline for the other approaches.) We first invoke $\mathcal{LRA}$-Minimize on the relaxation of the current $\mathcal{LRIA}$ problem. If the relaxation is found $\mathcal{LRA}$-unsatisfiable, then also the original problem is $\mathcal{LRIA}$-unsatisfiable, and the procedure backtracks. Otherwise, $\mathcal{LRA}$-Minimize returns a minimum-cost model $\mathcal{M}$ of cost min. If such solution is $\mathcal{LRIA}$-compliant, then we can return $\mathcal{M}$ and min, setting ub = min. (By "$\mathcal{LRIA}$-compliant solution" here we mean that the integer variables are all given integer values, whilst rational variables can be given fractional values.)

Otherwise, we select an integer variable x_j which is given a fractional value x_j^* in $\mathcal{M}$ as *branching variable*, and split the current problem into a pair of complementary sub-problems, by augmenting them respectively with the linear cuts $(x_j \leq \lfloor x_j^* \rfloor)$ and

---

[5] As in [7], by "continuous relaxation" –henceforth simply "relaxation"– we mean that the integrality constraints on the integer variables are relaxed, so that they can take fractional values.

$(x_j \geq \lceil x_j^* \rceil)$. Then, we separately explore each of these two sub-problems in a recursive fashion, and we return the best of the two minimum values of *cost* which is found in the two branches, with the relative model.

In order to make this exploration more efficient, as the recursive Branch&Bound search proceeds, we keep updating the upper bound ub to the current best value of *cost* corresponding to an $\mathcal{LRIA}$-compliant solution. Then, we can prune all sub-problems in which the $\mathcal{LRA}$ optimum *cost* value is greater or equal than ub, as they cannot contain any better solution.

Advanced Branch&Bound. Unlike the basic scheme, the advanced Branch&Bound is built on top of the $\mathcal{LRIA}$-Solver of MATHSAT5 and takes advantage of all the advanced features for performance optimization that are already implemented there [14]. In particular, we re-use its very-efficient internal Branch&Bound procedure for $\mathcal{LRIA}$-solving, which exploits historical information to drive the search and achieves higher pruning by *back-jumping* within the Branch&Bound search tree, driven by the analysis of unsatisfiable cores. (We refer the reader to [14] for details.)

We adapt the $\mathcal{LRIA}$-solving algorithm of [14] to minimization as follows. As before, the minimization algorithm starts by setting ub $= \mathcal{M}(cost)$, $\mathcal{M}$ being the model for μ which was returned by the most recent call to the $\mathcal{LRIA}$-Solver. Then the linear cut $(cost < \text{ub})$ is pushed on top of the constraint stack of the $\mathcal{LRIA}$-Solver, which forces the search to look for a better $\mathcal{LRIA}$-compliant solution than the current one.

Then, we use the internal Branch&Bound component of the $\mathcal{LRIA}$-Solver to seek for a new $\mathcal{LRIA}$-compliant solution. The first key modification is that we invoke $\mathcal{LRA}$-Minimize on each node of Branch&Bound search tree to ensure that x_{LP}^* is optimal in the $\mathcal{LRA}$ domain. The second modification is that, every time a new solution is found –whose cost ub improves the previous upper bound by construction– we empty the stack of $\mathcal{LRIA}$-Solver, push there a new cut in the form $(cost < \text{ub})$ and restart the search. Since the problem is known to be bounded, there are only a finite number of $\mathcal{LRIA}$-compliant solutions possible that can be removed from the search space. Therefore, the set of constraints is guaranteed to eventually become unsatisfiable, and at that point ub is returned as optimum *cost* value in μ to the SMT solver, which learns the unit clause $C_\mu \stackrel{\text{def}}{=} (cost < \text{ub})$.

Truncated Branch&Bound. We have empirically observed that in most cases the above scheme is effective enough that a single loop of advanced Branch&Bound is sufficient to find the optimal solution for the current truth assignment μ. However, the advanced Branch&Bound procedure still performs an additional loop iteration to prove that such solution is indeed optimal, which causes additional unnecessary overhead. Another drawback of advanced B&B is that for degenerate problems the Branch&Bound technique is very inefficient. In such cases, it is more convenient to interrupt the B&B search and simply return ub to the SMT solver, s.t. the unit clause $C_\mu \stackrel{\text{def}}{=} (cost < \text{ub})$ is learned; in fact, in this way we can easily re-use the entire stack of $\mathcal{LRIA}$-Solver routines in MATHSAT5 to find an improved solution more efficiently.

Therefore, we have implemented a "sub-optimum" variant of $\mathcal{LRIA}$-Minimize in which the inner $\mathcal{LRIA}$-Solver minimization procedure stops as soon as either it finds its first solution or it reaches a certain limit on the number of branching steps. The drawback of this variant is that, in some cases, it analyzes a truth assignment μ (augmented with the extra constraint $(cost < ub)$) more than once.

3.2   Multiple-objective OMT

We generalize the OMT($\mathcal{LRIA}$) problem to multiple cost functions as follows. A *multiple-cost OMT($\mathcal{LRIA}$) problem* is a pair $\langle \varphi, \mathcal{C} \rangle$ s.t $\mathcal{C} \stackrel{\text{def}}{=} \{cost_1, ..., cost_k\}$ is a set of $\mathcal{LRIA}$-variables occurring in φ, and consists in finding a set of $\mathcal{LRIA}$-models $\{\mathcal{M}_1, ..., \mathcal{M}_k\}$ s.t. each $\mathcal{M}_i$ makes $cost_i$ minimum. We extend the OMT($\mathcal{LRA}$) [OMT($\mathcal{LRIA}$)] procedures of §2.2 and §3.1 to handle multiple-cost problems. The procedure works in linear-search mode only.[6] It takes as input a pair $\langle \varphi, \mathcal{C} \rangle$ and returns a list of minimum-cost models $\{\mathcal{M}_1, ..., \mathcal{M}_k\}$, plus the corresponding list of minimum values $\{u_1, ..., u_k\}$. (If φ is $\mathcal{LRIA}$-inconsistent, it returns $u_i = +\infty$ for every i.)

Initialization. First, we set $u_i = +\infty$ for every i, and we set $\mathcal{C}^* = \mathcal{C}$, s.t. $\mathcal{C}^*$ is the list of currently-active cost functions.

Decreasing the Upper Bound. When an assignment μ is generated s.t. $\mu^p \models \varphi^p$ and which is found $\mathcal{LRIA}$-consistent by $\mathcal{LRIA}$-Solver, μ is also fed to $\mathcal{LRIA}$-Minimize. For each $cost_i \in \mathcal{C}^*$:

  (i) $\mathcal{LRIA}$-Minimize finds an $\mathcal{LRIA}$-model $\mathcal{M}$ for μ of minimum cost min_i;
 (ii) if min_i is $-\infty$, then there is no more reason to investigate $cost_i$, so that we set $u_i = -\infty$ and $\mathcal{M}_i = \mathcal{M}$, and $cost_i$ is dropped from $\mathcal{C}^*$;
(iii) if $min_i < u_i$, then we set $u_i = min_i$ and $\mathcal{M}_i = \mathcal{M}$.

As with the single-cost versions, $\mathcal{LRIA}$-Minimize is embedded within $\mathcal{LRIA}$-Solver, so that it is called incrementally after it, without restarting its search from scratch. After that, the clause

$$C_\mu \stackrel{\text{def}}{=} \bigvee_{cost_i \in \mathcal{C}^*} (cost_i < u_i) \tag{1}$$

is learned, and the CDCL-based SMT solving process proceeds its search. Notice that, since by construction $\mu \wedge C_\mu \models_{\mathcal{LRIA}} \bot$, a theory-driven backjumping step [3] will occur as soon as μ is extended to assign to true some literal of C_μ.

Termination. The procedure terminates either when $\mathcal{C}^*$ is empty or when φ is found $\mathcal{LRIA}$-inconsistent. (The former case is a subcase of the latter, because it would cause the generation of an empty clause C_μ (1).)

The clauses C_μ (1) ensure a progress in the minimization of one or more of the $cost_i$'s every time that a new $\mathcal{LRIA}$-consistent assignment is generated. We notice that, by construction, C_μ is such that $\mu \wedge C_\mu \models_{\mathcal{LRIA}} \bot$, so that each μ satisfying the original version of φ can be investigated by the minimizer only once. Since we have only a finite number of such candidate assignments for φ, this guarantees the

---

[6] Since the linear-search versions of the procedures in §2.2 and §3.1 differ only for the fact that they invoke $\mathcal{LRA}$-Minimize and $\mathcal{LRIA}$-Minimize respectively, here we do not distinguish between them. We only implicitly make the assumption that the $\mathcal{LRIA}$-Minimize does not work in truncated mode, so that it is guaranteed to find a minimum in one run. Such assumption is not strictly necessary, but it makes the explanation easier.

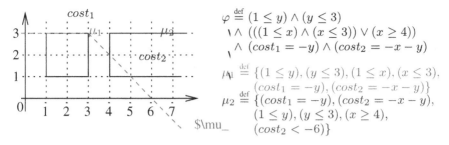

$$\varphi \overset{\text{def}}{=} (1 \leq y) \wedge (y \leq 3)$$
$$\wedge (((1 \leq x) \wedge (x \leq 3)) \vee (x \geq 4))$$
$$\wedge (cost_1 = -y) \wedge (cost_2 = -x - y)$$

$$\mu_1 \overset{\text{def}}{=} \{(1 \leq y), (y \leq 3), (1 \leq x), (x \leq 3),$$
$$(cost_1 = -y), (cost_2 = -x - y)\}$$
$$\mu_2 \overset{\text{def}}{=} \{(cost_1 = -y), (cost_2 = -x - y),$$
$$(1 \leq y), (y \leq 3), (x \geq 4),$$
$$(cost_2 < -6)\}$$

Fig. 1. In one possible execution over the $\mathcal{LRA}$-formula φ, the CDCL-based SMT engine finds the truth assignment μ_1 first, which is found $\mathcal{LRA}$-consistent by the $\mathcal{LRA}$-solver. (For the sake of readability, we've removed from the μ_i's the redundant literals like "$\neg(x \geq 4)$" from μ_1.) Then the minimizer finds the minima $\min_1 = -3$, $\min_2 = -6$, the upper bounds are updated to these values, and the clause $(cost_1 < -3) \vee (cost_2 < -6)$ is learned. The next $\mathcal{LRA}$-consistent assignment found is necessarily μ_2, from which the minimizer finds the minima $\min_1 = -3$, $\min_2 = -\infty$. Hence $cost_2$ is dropped from $\mathcal{C}^*$, and the unit clause $(cost_1 < -3)$ is learned, making φ $\mathcal{LRA}$-inconsistent, so that no more assignment is found and the procedure terminates. In a luckier execution $\mu_2 \setminus \{(cost_2 < -6)\}$ is found first, thus the minimizer finds directly the minima $\min_1 = -3$, $\min_2 = -\infty$ s.t. $(cost_1 < -3)$ is learned, and the procedure terminates without generating μ_1.

termination of the procedure. The correctness and completeness is guaranteed by these of $\mathcal{LRIA}$-Minimize, which returns the minimum values for each such assignment.

To illustrate the behaviour of our procedure, and to allow for a direct comparison wrt. the procedure described in [16], in Figure 1 we present its execution on the toy example $\mathcal{LRA}$-problem in [16]. Notice that, unlike the algorithm in [16], our procedure is driven by the Boolean search: each time a novel assignment is generated, it eagerly produces the maximum progress for as many $cost_i$'s as possible. The algorithm described in [16], instead, does not use a LP minimization procedure: rather, a sequence of blackbox calls to an underlying SMT solver (Z3) allows for finding progressively-better solutions along some objective direction, either forcing discrete jumps to some bounds induced by the inequalities in the problem, or proving such objective is unbounded.

The procedure is improved in various ways. First, we notice that the clause C_μ is strictly stronger than the clause $C_{\mu'}$ which was generated with the previous truth assignment μ', so that $C_{\mu'}$ can be safely dropped, keeping only one of such clauses at a time. This is as if we had only one such clause whose literals are progressively strengthened. Second, before step (i), the constraint $(cost_i < u_i)$ can be temporarily pushed into μ: if $\mathcal{LRIA}$-Minimize returns UNSAT, then there is no chance to improve the current value of u_i, so that the above constraint can be popped from μ and step (ii) and (iii) can be skipped for the current $cost_i$. Third, in case the condition in step (iii) holds, it is possible to learn also the $\mathcal{LRIA}$-valid clause $(cost_i < u_i) \rightarrow (cost_i < u_i')$ s.t. u_i' is the previous value of u_i. This allows for "activating" all previously-learned clauses in the form $\neg(cost_i < u_i') \vee C$ as soon as $(cost_i < u_i)$ is assigned to true.

Lexicographic Combination. As in [5], we easily extend our inline procedure to deal with the lexicographic combination of multiple costs $\{cost_1, ..., cost_k\}$. We start by looking for a minimum for $cost_1$: as soon as a minimum u_1 with its model $\mathcal{M}_1$ is found, if $u_1 = -\infty$ then we stop, otherwise we substitute inside φ the unit clause $(cost_1 < u_1)$ with $(cost_1 = u_1)$, we set $u_2 \stackrel{\text{def}}{=} \mathcal{M}_1(cost_2)$, and we look for the minimum of $cost_2$ in the resulting formula. This is repeated until all $cost_i$'s have been considered.

3.3 Incremental OMT

Many modern SMT solvers, including MATHSAT5, provide a *stack-based incremental interface*, by which it is possible to push/pop sub-formulas ϕ_i into a stack of formulas $\Phi \stackrel{\text{def}}{=} \{\phi_1, ..., \phi_k\}$, and then to check incrementally the satisfiability of $\bigwedge_{i=1}^{k} \phi_i$. The interface maintains the *status* of the search from one call to the other, in particular it records the *learned clauses* (plus other information). Consequently, when invoked on Φ, the solver can reuse a clause C which was learned during a previous call on some Φ' if C was derived only from clauses which are still in Φ.

In particular, in MATHSAT5 incrementality is achieved by first rewriting Φ into $\{A_1 \to \phi_1, ..., A_k \to \phi_k\}$, each A_i being a fresh Boolean variable, and then by running the SMT solver under the assumption of the variables $\{A_1, ..., A_k\}$, in such a way that every learned clause which is derived from some ϕ_i is in the form $\neg A_i \vee C$ [13]. Thus it is possible to safely keep the learned clause from one call to the other because, if ϕ_i is popped from Φ, then A_i is no more assumed, so that the clause $\neg A_i \vee C$ is inactive. (Such clauses can be garbage-collected from time to time to reduce the overhead.)

Since none of the OMT tools in [22,21,16,15] provides an incremental interface, nor such paper explains how to achieve it, here we address explicitly the problem of making OMT incremental.

We start noticing that if (i) the OMT tool is based on the schema in §2.1 or on its $\mathcal{LRIA}$ and multiple-cost extensions of §3.1 and §3.2, and (ii) the embedded SMT solver has an incremental interface, like that of MATHSAT5, then an OMT tool can be easily made incremental by exploiting the incremental interface of its SMT solver.

In fact, in our OMT schema all learned clauses are either $\mathcal{T}$-lemmas or they are derived from $\mathcal{T}$-lemmas and some of the subformulas ϕ_i's, *with the exception of the clauses* $C_\mu \stackrel{\text{def}}{=} (cost < \text{min})$ *(§2.2) [resp.* $C_\mu \stackrel{\text{def}}{=} (cost < \text{min})$ *(§3.1) and* $C_\mu \stackrel{\text{def}}{=} \bigvee_{cost_i \in \mathcal{C}^*}(cost_i < u_i)$ *(§3.2),]* which are "artificially" introduced to ensure progress in the minimization steps. (This holds also for the unit clauses (PIV) which are learned in an improved version, see [22,21].) Thus, in order to handle incrementality, it suffices to drop only these clauses from one OMT call to the other, while preserving all the others, as with incremental SMT.

In a more elegant variant of this technique, which we have used in our implementation, at each incremental call to OMT (namely the k-th call) a fresh Boolean variable $A^{(k)}$ is assumed. Whenever a new minimum min is found, the augmented clause $C_\mu^* \stackrel{\text{def}}{=} \neg A^{(k)} \vee (cost < \text{min})$ is learned instead of $C_\mu \stackrel{\text{def}}{=} (cost < \text{min})$. In the subsequent calls to OMT, $A^{(k)}$ is no more assumed, so that the augmented clauses C_μ^*'s which have been learned during the k-th call are no more active.

Notice that in this process reusing the clauses that are learned by the underlying SMT-solving steps is not the only benefit. In fact also the learned clauses in the form $\neg(cost < \text{min}) \vee C$ which may be produced after learning $C_\mu \stackrel{\text{def}}{=} (cost < \text{min})$ are preserved to the next OMT calls. (Same discourse holds for the C_μ's of §3.1 and §3.2.) In the subsequent calls such clauses are initially inactive, but they can be activated as soon as the current minimum, namely min$'$, becomes smaller or equal than min and the novel clause $(cost < min')$ is learned, so that $(cost < min)$ can be $\mathcal{T}$-propagated or $(\neg(cost < min') \vee (cost < min))$ can be $\mathcal{T}$-learned. This allows for reusing lots of previous search.

4 Experimental Evaluation

We have extended OPTIMATHSAT [22,21] by implementing the advanced and truncated B&B OMT($\mathcal{LRIA} \cup \mathcal{T}$) procedures described in §3.1. On top of that, we have implemented our techniques for multi-objective OMT (§3.2) —including the lexicographic combination— and incremental OMT (§3.3). Then, we have investigated empirically the efficiency of our new procedures by conducing two different experimental evaluations, respectively on OMT($\mathcal{LRIA}$) (§4.1) and on multi-objective and incremental OMT($\mathcal{LRA}$) (§4.2). All tests in this section were executed on two identical *8-core 2.20Ghz Xeon* machines with 64 GB of RAM and running Linux with 3.8-0-29 kernel, with an enforced timeout of 1200 seconds.

For every problem in this evaluation, the correctness of the minimum costs found by OPTIMATHSAT and its competitor tools, namely "min", have been cross-checked with the SMT solver Z3, by checking both the inconsistency of $\varphi \wedge (cost < min)$ and the consistency of $\varphi \wedge (cost = min)$. In all tests, when terminating, all tools returned the correct results. To make the experiments reproducible, the full-size plots, a Linux binary of OPTIMATHSAT, the input OMT problems, and the results are available. [7]

4.1 Evaluation of OMT($\mathcal{LRIA}$) Procedures

Here we consider three different configurations of OPTIMATHSAT based on the search schemas (linear vs. binary vs. adaptive, denoted respectively by "-LIN", "-BIN" and "-ADA") presented in §2.2; the adaptive strategy dynamically switches the search schemas between linear and binary search, based on the heuristic described in [21]. We run OPTIMATHSAT both with the advanced and truncated branch&bound minimization procedures for $\mathcal{LRIA}$ presented in §3.1, denoted respectively by "-ADV" and "-TRN".

In order to have a comparison of OPTIMATHSAT with both νZ and BCLT, in this experimental evaluation we restricted our focus on OMT($\mathcal{LIA}$) only. Here we do not consider SYMBA, since it does not support OMT($\mathcal{LIA}$). We used as benchmarks a set of 544 problems derived from SMT-based Bounded Model Checking and K-Induction on parametric problems, generated via the SAL model checker.[8]

The results of this evaluation are shown in Figure 2. By looking at the table, we observe that the best OPTIMATHSAT configuration on these benchmarks is -TRN-ADA, which uses the truncated branch&bound approach within the $\mathcal{LIA}$-Minimize procedure with adaptive search scheme. We notice that the differences in performances among the various configurations of OPTIMATHSAT are small on these specific benchmarks.

---

[7] http://disi.unitn.it/~trentin/resources/tacas15.tar.gz;   BCLT is available at http://www.lsi.upc.edu/~oliveras/bclt.gz; SYMBA is available at https://bitbucket.org/arieg/symba/src; νZ is available at http://rise4fun.com/z3opt.

[8] http://sal.csl.sri.com/

Tool:	#inst.	#solved	#timeout	time
BCLT	544	500	44	93040
νZ	544	544	0	36089
OptiM.-adv-lin	544	544	0	91032
OptiM.-adv-bin	544	544	0	99214
OptiM.-adv-ada	544	544	0	88750
OptiM.-trn-lin	544	544	0	91735
OptiM.-trn-bin	544	544	0	99556
OptiM.-trn-ada	544	544	0	88730

Fig. 2. A table comparing the performances of BCLT, νZ and different configurations of OPTI-MATHSAT on Bounded Model Checking problems

Comparing the OPTIMATHSAT versions against BCLT and νZ, we notice that OPTI-MATHSATand νZ solve all input formulas regardless of their configuration, νZ having better time performances, whilst BCLT timeouts on 44 problems.

4.2   Evaluation of Incremental and Multiple-objective OMT

As mentioned in Section §1, so far BCLT does not feature multi-objective OMT, and neither SYMBA nor BCLT implement incremental OMT. Thus, in order to test the efficiency of our multiple-objective OMT approach, we compared three versions of OP-TIMATHSAT against the corresponding versions of νZ and the two best-performing versions of SYMBA presented in [16], namely SYMBA(100) and SYMBA(40)+OPT-Z3.

So far SYMBA handles only OMT($\mathcal{LRA}$), without combinations with other theories. Moreover, it currently does not support strict inequalities inside the input formulas. Therefore for both comparisons we used as benchmarks the multiple-objective problems which were proposed in [16] to evaluate SYMBA, which were generated from a set of C programs used in the 2013 SW Verification Competition.[9] Also, SYMBA computes both the minimum and the maximum value for each *cost* variable, and there is no way of restricting its focus only on one direction. Consequently, in our tests we have forced also OPTIMATHSATand νZ to both minimize and maximize each objective. (More specifically, they had to minimize both $cost_i$ and $-cost_i$, for each $cost_i$.)

We tested three different configurations of νZ and OPTIMATHSAT:

- SINGLEOBJECTIVE: each tool is run singularly on the single-objective problems $\langle \varphi, cost_i \rangle$ and $\langle \varphi, -cost_i \rangle$ for each $cost_i$, and the cumulative time is taken;
- INCREMENTAL: as above, using the incremental version of each tool, each time popping the definition of the previous *cost* and pushing the new one;
- MULTIOBJECTIVE: each tool is run in multi-objective mode with $\bigcup_i \{cost_i, -cost_i\}$.

Figure 3 provides the cumulative plots and the global data of the performance of all procedures under test, whilst Figure 4 reports pairwise comparisons.

We first compare the different versions of OPTIMATHSAT (see Figure 3 and the first row of Figure 4). By looking at Figure 3 and at the top-left plot in Figure 4, we observe a uniform and relevant speedup when passing from non-incremental to incremental OMT.

---

[9] https://bitbucket.org/liyi0630/symba-bench

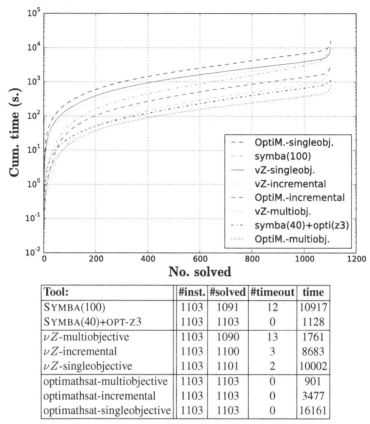

Tool:	#inst.	#solved	#timeout	time
SYMBA(100)	1103	1091	12	10917
SYMBA(40)+OPT-Z3	1103	1103	0	1128
νZ-multiobjective	1103	1090	13	1761
νZ-incremental	1103	1100	3	8683
νZ-singleobjective	1103	1101	2	10002
optimathsat-multiobjective	1103	1103	0	901
optimathsat-incremental	1103	1103	0	3477
optimathsat-singleobjective	1103	1103	0	16161

Fig. 3. Comparison of different versions of OPTIMATHSAT and SYMBA on the SW verification problems in [16]. (Notice the logarithmic scale of the vertical axis in the cumulative plots.)

This is explained by the possibility of reusing learned clauses from one call to the other, saving thus lots of search, as explained in §3.3.

By looking at Figure 3 and at the top-center plot in Figure 4, we observe a uniform and drastic speedup in performance –about one order of magnitude– when passing from single-objective to multiple-objective OMT. We also notice (top-right plot in Figure 4) that this performance is significantly better than that obtained with incremental OMT. Analogous considerations hold for νZ.

We see two main motivations for this improvement in performance with our multiple-objective OMT technique: first, every time a novel truth assignment is generated, the value of many cost functions can be updated, sharing thus lots of Boolean and $\mathcal{LRA}$ search; second, the process of certifying that there is no better solution, which typically requires a significant part of the overall OMT search [21], here is executed only once.

In the second row of Figure 4 we compare the performances of OPTIMATHSAT-MULTI-OBJECTIVE against the two versions of SYMBA and νZ-MULTI-OBJECTIVE. We observe that multi-objective OPTIMATHSAT performs much better than the default configuration of SYMBA, and significantly better than both SYMBA(40)+OPT-Z3 and νZ-MULTI-OBJECTIVE.

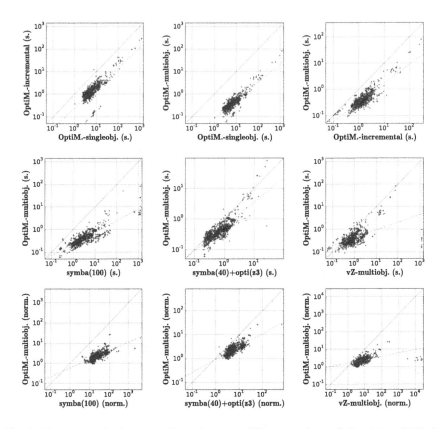

Fig. 4. First row: pairwise comparisons between different versions of OPTIMATHSAT. Second row: pairwise comparisons between OPTIMATHSAT-MULTIOBJECTIVE, the two versions of SYMBA and νZ-MULTIOBJECTIVE. Third row: "normalized" version of the plots in the second row.

We have also wondered how much the relative performances of OPTIMATHSAT, SYMBA and νZ depend on the relative efficiency of their underlying SMT solvers: MATHSAT5 for OPTIMATHSAT and Z3 for SYMBA and νZ. Thus we have run both MATHSAT5 and Z3 on the set of problems $\varphi \wedge (cost < \min)$ derived from the original benchmarks, and used their timings to divide the respective OPTIMATHSAT and SYMBA/νZ execution time values.[10] These "normalized" results, which are shown in the bottom row of Figure 4, seem to suggest that the better performances of OPTIMATHSAT are not due to better performances of the underlying SMT solver.

References

1. Audemard, G., Bozzano, M., Cimatti, A., Sebastiani, R.: Verifying Industrial Hybrid Systems with MathSAT. In: Proc. BMC 2004. ENTCS, vol. 119. Elsevier (2005)

---

[10] That is, each value represents the time taken by each OMT tool on $\langle \varphi, cost_i \rangle$ divided by the time taken by its underlying SMT solver to solve $\varphi \wedge (cost < \min)$.

2. Audemard, G., Cimatti, A., Korniłowicz, A., Sebastiani, R.: SAT-Based Bounded Model Checking for Timed Systems. In: Peled, D.A., Vardi, M.Y. (eds.) FORTE 2002. LNCS, vol. 2529, Springer, Heidelberg (2002)
3. Barrett, C., Sebastiani, R., Seshia, S.A., Tinelli, C.: Satisfiability Modulo Theories. In: Biere et al. [4], ch. 26, vol. 185, pp. 825–885 (February 2009)
4. Biere, A., Heule, M.J.H., van Maaren, H., Walsh, T. (eds.): Handbook of Satisfiability. IOS Press (February 2009)
5. Bjorner, N., Phan, A.-D.: νZ - Maximal Satisfaction with Z3. In: Proc. SCSS Invited Presentation, Gammart, Tunisia. EasyChair Proceedings in Computing, EPiC (December 2014), http://www.easychair.org/publications/?page=862275542
6. Bozzano, M., Bruttomesso, R., Cimatti, A., Junttila, T.A., Ranise, S., van Rossum, P., Sebastiani, R.: Efficient Theory Combination via Boolean Search. Information and Computation 204(10), 1493–1525 (2006)
7. Byrd, R.H., Goldman, A.J., Heller, M.: Technical Note– Recognizing Unbounded Integer Programs. Operations Research 35(1) (1987)
8. Cimatti, A., Franzén, A., Griggio, A., Sebastiani, R., Stenico, C.: Satisfiability modulo the theory of costs: Foundations and applications. In: Esparza, J., Majumdar, R. (eds.) TACAS 2010. LNCS, vol. 6015, pp. 99–113. Springer, Heidelberg (2010)
9. Cimatti, A., Griggio, A., Schaafsma, B.J., Sebastiani, R.: A Modular Approach to MaxSAT Modulo Theories. In: Järvisalo, M., Van Gelder, A. (eds.) SAT 2013. LNCS, vol. 7962, pp. 150–165. Springer, Heidelberg (2013)
10. Cimatti, A., Griggio, A., Schaafsma, B.J., Sebastiani, R.: The mathSAT5 SMT solver. In: Piterman, N., Smolka, S.A. (eds.) TACAS 2013. LNCS, vol. 7795, pp. 93–107. Springer, Heidelberg (2013)
11. Dillig, I., Dillig, T., McMillan, K.L., Aiken, A.: Minimum Satisfying Assignments for SMT. In: Madhusudan, P., Seshia, S.A. (eds.) CAV 2012. LNCS, vol. 7358, pp. 394–409. Springer, Heidelberg (2012)
12. Dutertre, B., de Moura, L.: A Fast Linear-Arithmetic Solver for DPLL(T). In: Ball, T., Jones, R.B. (eds.) CAV 2006. LNCS, vol. 4144, pp. 81–94. Springer, Heidelberg (2006)
13. Eén, N., Sörensson, N.: An extensible SAT-solver. In: Giunchiglia, E., Tacchella, A. (eds.) SAT 2003. LNCS, vol. 2919, pp. 502–518. Springer, Heidelberg (2004)
14. Griggio, A.: A Practical Approach to Satisfiability Modulo Linear Integer Arithmetic. Journal on Satisfiability, Boolean Modeling and Computation - JSAT 8, 1–27 (2012)
15. Larraz, D., Oliveras, A., Rodríguez-Carbonell, E., Rubio, A.: Minimal-Model-Guided Approaches to Solving Polynomial Constraints and Extensions. In: Sinz, C., Egly, U. (eds.) SAT 2014. LNCS, vol. 8561, pp. 333–350. Springer, Heidelberg (2014)
16. Li, Y., Albarghouthi, A., Kincad, Z., Gurfinkel, A., Chechik, M.: Symbolic Optimization with SMT Solvers. In: POPL. ACM Press (2014)
17. Manolios, P., Papavasileiou, V.: ILP modulo theories. In: Sharygina, N., Veith, H. (eds.) CAV 2013. LNCS, vol. 8044, pp. 662–677. Springer, Heidelberg (2013)
18. Nieuwenhuis, R., Oliveras, A.: On SAT Modulo Theories and Optimization Problems. In: Biere, A., Gomes, C.P. (eds.) SAT 2006. LNCS, vol. 4121, pp. 156–169. Springer, Heidelberg (2006)
19. Nieuwenhuis, R., Oliveras, A., Tinelli, C.: Solving SAT and SAT Modulo Theories: from an Abstract Davis-Putnam-Logemann-Loveland Procedure to DPLL(T). Journal of the ACM 53(6), 937–977 (2006)
20. Sebastiani, R.: Lazy Satisfiability Modulo Theories. Journal on Satisfiability, Boolean Modeling and Computation, JSAT 3(3-4), 141–224 (2007)
21. Sebastiani, R., Tomasi, S.: Optimization Modulo Theories with Linear Rational Costs. To Appear on ACM Transactions on Computational Logics, TOCL, http://optimathsat.disi.unitn.it/pages/publications.html
22. Sebastiani, R., Tomasi, S.: Optimization in SMT with LA(Q) Cost Functions. In: Gramlich, B., Miller, D., Sattler, U. (eds.) IJCAR 2012. LNCS (LNAI), vol. 7364, pp. 484–498. Springer, Heidelberg (2012)

Partial Order Reduction, Bisimulation and Fairness

Stateless Model Checking for TSO and PSO

Parosh Aziz Abdulla, Stavros Aronis, Mohamed Faouzi Atig,
Bengt Jonsson, Carl Leonardsson, and Konstantinos Sagonas

Dept. of Information Technology, Uppsala University, Sweden

Abstract. We present a technique for efficient stateless model checking of programs that execute under the relaxed memory models TSO and PSO. The basis for our technique is a novel representation of executions under TSO and PSO, called *chronological traces*. Chronological traces induce a partial order relation on relaxed memory executions, capturing dependencies that are needed to represent the interaction via shared variables. They are optimal in the sense that they only distinguish computations that are inequivalent under the widely-used representation by Shasha and Snir. This allows an optimal dynamic partial order reduction algorithm to explore a minimal number of executions while still guaranteeing full coverage. We apply our techniques to check, under the TSO and PSO memory models, LLVM assembly produced for C/pthreads programs. Our experiments show that our technique reduces the verification effort for relaxed memory models to be almost that for the standard model of sequential consistency. In many cases, our implementation significantly outperforms other comparable tools.

1 Introduction

Verification and testing of concurrent programs is difficult, since one must consider all the different ways in which instructions of different threads can be interleaved. To make matters worse, most architectures implement *relaxed memory models*, such as TSO and PSO [32,4], which make threads interact in even more and subtler ways than by standard interleaving. For example, a processor may reorder loads and stores by the same thread if they target different addresses, or it may buffer stores in a local queue.

A successful technique for finding concurrency bugs (i.e., defects that arise only under some thread schedulings), and for verifying their absence, is *stateless model checking* (SMC) [16], also known as *systematic concurrency testing* [21,35]. Starting from a test, i.e., a way to run a program and obtain some expected result, which is terminating and threadwisely deterministic (e.g. no data-nondeterminism), SMC systematically explores the set of all thread schedulings that are possible during runs of this test. A special runtime scheduler drives the SMC exploration by making decisions on scheduling whenever such decisions may affect the interaction between threads, so that the exploration covers all possible executions and detects any unexpected test results, program crashes, or assertion violations. The technique is completely automatic, has no false positives, does not suffer from memory explosion, and can easily reproduce the concurrency bugs it detects. SMC has been successfully implemented in tools such as VeriSoft [17], CHESS [25], and Concuerror [12].

There are two main problems for using SMC in programs that run under relaxed memory models (RMM). The first problem is that already under the standard model of

© Springer-Verlag Berlin Heidelberg 2015
C. Baier and C. Tinelli (Eds.): TACAS 2015, LNCS 9035, pp. 353–367, 2015.
DOI: 10.1007/978-3-662-46681-0_28

sequential consistency (SC) the number of possible thread schedulings grows exponentially with the length of program execution. This problem has been addressed by *partial order reduction* (POR) techniques that achieve coverage of *all* thread schedulings, by exploring only a representative subset [34,27,15,13]. POR has been adapted to SMC in the form of *Dynamic Partial Order Reduction* (DPOR) [14], which has been further developed in recent years [29,21,19,28,33,2]. DPOR is based on augmenting each execution by a *happens-before relation*, which is a partial order that captures dependencies between operations of the threads. Two executions can be regarded as equivalent if they induce the same happens-before relation, and it is therefore sufficient to explore one execution in each equivalence class (called a *Mazurkiewicz trace* [24]). DPOR algorithms guarantee to explore at least one execution in each equivalence class, thus attaining full coverage with reduced cost. A recent optimal algorithm [2] guarantees to explore *exactly* one execution per equivalence class.

The second problem is that in order to extend SMC to handle relaxed memory models, the operational semantics of programs must be extended to represent the effects of RMM. The natural approach is to augment the program state with additional structures, e.g., store buffers in the case of TSO, that model the effects of RMM [3,5,26]. This causes blow-ups in the number of possible executions, in addition to those possible under SC. However, most of these additional executions are equivalent to some SC execution. To efficiently apply SMC to handle RMM, we must therefore extend DPOR to avoid redundant exploration of equivalent executions. The natural definition of "equivalent" under RMM can be derived from the abstract representation of executions due to Shasha and Snir [31], here called *Shasha-Snir traces*, which is often used in model checking and runtime verification [18,20,10,11,7,8]. Shasha-Snir traces consist of an ordering relation between dependent operations, which generalizes the standard happens-before relation on SC executions; indeed, under SC, the equivalence relation induced by Shasha-Snir traces coincides with Mazurkiewicz traces. It would thus be natural to base DPOR for RMM on the happens-before relation induced by Shasha-Snir traces. However, this relation is in general cyclic (due to reorderings possible under RMM) and can therefore not be used as a basis for DPOR (since it is not a partial order). To develop an efficient technique for SMC under RMM we therefore need to find a different representation of executions under RMM. The representation should define an acyclic happens-before relation. Also, the induced trace equivalence should coincide with the equivalence induced by Shasha-Snir traces.

Contribution. In this paper, we show how to apply SMC to TSO and PSO in a way that achieves maximal possible reduction using DPOR, in the sense that redundant exploration of equivalent executions is avoided. A cornerstone in our contribution is a novel representation of executions under RMM, called *chronological traces*, which define a happens-before relation on the events in a carefully designed representation of program executions. Chronological traces are a succinct canonical representation of executions, in the sense that there is a one-to-one correspondence between chronological traces and Shasha-Snir traces. Furthermore, the happens-before relation induced by chronological traces is a partial order, and can therefore be used as a basis for DPOR. In particular, the Optimal-DPOR algorithm of [2] will explore exactly one execution per Shasha-Snir trace. In particular, for so-called *robust* programs that are not affected by RMM (these include data-race-free programs), Optimal-DPOR will explore as many executions under RMM as under SC: this follows from the one-to-one correspondence between chronological traces and Mazurkiewicz traces under SC. Furthermore, robustness can itself be considered a correctness criterion, which can also be automatically checked with our method (by checking whether the number of equivalence classes is increased when going from SC to RMM).

We show the power of our technique by using it to implement an efficient stateless model checker, which for C programs with pthreads explores all executions of a testcase or a program, up to some bounded length. During exploration of an execution, our implementation generates the corresponding chronological trace. Our implementation employs the source-DPOR algorithm [2], which is simpler than Optimal-DPOR, but about equally effective. Our experimental results for analyses under SC, TSO and PSO of number of intensely racy benchmarks and programs written in C/pthreads, shows that (i) the effort for verification under TSO and PSO is not much larger than the effort for verification under SC, and (ii) our implementation compares favourably against CBMC, a state-of-the-art bounded model checking tool, showing the potential of our approach.

2   Overview of Main Concepts

This section informally motivates and explains the main concepts of the paper. To focus the presentation, we consider mainly the TSO model. TSO is relevant because it is implemented in the widely used x86 as well as SPARC architectures. We first introduce TSO and its semantics. Thereafter we introduce Shasha-Snir traces, which abstractly represent the orderings between dependent events in an execution. Since Shasha-Snir traces are cyclic, we introduce an extended representation of executions, for which a natural happens-before relation is acyclic. We then describe how this happens-before relation introduces undesirable distinctions between executions, and how our new representation of chronological traces remove these distinctions. Finally, we illustrate how a DPOR algorithm exploits the happens-before relation induced by chronological traces to explore only a minimal number of executions, while still guaranteeing full coverage.

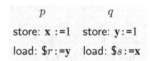

Fig. 1. A program implementing the classic idiom of Dekker's mutual exclusion algorithm

TSO — an Introduction. TSO relaxes the ordering between stores and subsequent loads to different memory locations. This can be explained operationally by equipping each thread with a *store buffer* [30], which is a FIFO queue that contains pending store operations. When a thread executes a store instruction, the store does not immediately affect memory. Instead it is delayed and enqueued in the store buffer. Nondeterministically, at some later point an *update* event occurs, dequeueing the oldest store from the store buffer and updating the memory correspondingly. Load instructions take effect immediately, without being delayed. Usually a load reads a value from memory. However, if the store buffer of the same thread contains a store to the same memory location, the value is instead taken from the store in the store buffer.

To see why this buffering semantics may cause unexpected program behaviors, consider the small program in Fig. 1. It consists of two threads p and q. The thread p first stores 1 to the memory location **x**, and then loads the value at memory location **y** into its register $\$r$. The thread q is similar. All memory locations and registers are assumed to have initial values 0.

```
p: store: x :=1  // Enqueue store
p: load: $r:=y   // Load value 0
  q: store: y:=1  // Enqueue store
  q: update       // y = 1 in memory
  q: load: $s:=x  // Load value 0
p: update        // x = 1 in memory
```

Fig. 2. An execution of the program in Fig. 1. Notice that $\$r = \$s = 0$ at the end.

It is easy to see that under the SC semantics, it is impossible for the program to terminate in a state where both registers $\$r$ and $\$s$ hold the value 0. However, under the buffering semantics of TSO, such a final state is possible. Fig. 2 shows one such program execution. We see that the store to **x** happens at the beginning of the execution, but does not take effect with respect to memory until the very end of the execution. Thus the store to **x** and the load to **y** appear to take effect in an order opposite to how they occur in the program code. This allows the execution to terminate with $\$r = \$s = 0$.

Shasha-Snir Traces for TSO. Partial order reduction is based on the idea of capturing the possible orderings between dependent operations of different threads by means of a happens-before relation. When threads interact via shared variables, two instructions are considered dependent if they access the same global variable, and at least one is a write. For relaxed memory models, Shasha and Snir [31] introduced an abstract representation of executions, here referred to as *Shasha-Snir traces*, which captures such dependencies in a natural way. Shasha-Snir traces induce equivalence classes of executions. Under sequential consistency, those classes coincide with the Mazurkiewicz traces. Under a relaxed memory model, there are also additional Shasha-Snir traces corresponding to the non-sequentially consistent executions.

A Shasha-Snir trace is a directed graph, where edges capture observed event orderings. The nodes in a Shasha-Snir trace are the executed instructions. For each thread, there are edges between each pair of subsequent instructions, creating a total order for each thread. For two instructions i and j in different threads, there is an edge $i \to j$ in a trace when i causally precedes j. This happens when j reads a value that was written by i, when i reads a memory location that is subsequently updated by j, or when i and j are subsequent writes to the same memory

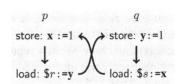

Fig. 3. The Shasha-Snir trace corresponding to the execution in Fig. 2

location. In Fig. 3 we show the Shasha-Snir trace for the execution in Fig. 2.

Making the Happens-Before Relation Acyclic. Shasha-Snir traces naturally represent the dependencies between operations in an execution, and are therefore a natural basis for applying DPOR. However, a major problem is that the happens-before relation induced by the edges is in general cyclic, and thus not a partial order. This can be seen already in the graph in Fig. 3. This problem can be addressed by adding nodes that represent explicit update events. That would be natural since such events occur in the representation of the execution in Fig. 2. When we consider the edges of the Shasha-Snir trace, we observe that although there is a conflict between p : load: $r:=y$ and q : store: $y:=1$, swapping their order in the execution in Fig. 2 has no observable effect; the load still gets the same value from memory. Therefore, we should only be concerned with the order of the load relative to the update event q : update.

These observations suggest to define a representation of traces that separates stores from updates. In Fig. 4 we have redrawn the trace from Fig. 3. Updates are separated from stores, and we order updates, rather than stores, with operations of other threads. Thus, there are edges between updates to and loads from the same memory location, and between two updates to the same memory location. In Fig. 4, there is an edge from each store to

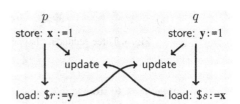

Fig. 4. A trace for the execution in Fig. 2 where updates are separated from stores

the corresponding update, reflecting the principle that the update cannot occur before the store. There are edges between loads and updates of the same memory location, reflecting that swapping their order will affect the observed values. However, notice that for this program there are no edges between the updates and loads of the same thread, since they access different memory locations.

Chronological Traces for TSO. Although the new representation is a valid partial order, it will in many cases distinguish executions that are semantically equivalent according to the Shasha-Snir traces. The reason for this is TSO buffer forwarding: When a thread executes a load to a memory location **x**, it will first check its store buffer. If the buffer contains a store to **x**, then the load returns the value of the newest such store buffer entry instead of loading the value from memory. This causes problems for a happens-before relation that orders all updates and loads of the same memory location.

For example, consider the program shown in Fig. 5. Any execution of this program will have two updates and one load to **x**. Those accesses can be permuted in six different ways. Fig. 6(a), 6(b) and 6(c) show three of the corresponding happens-before relations. In Fig. 6(a) and 6(b) the load is satisfied by buffer forwarding, and in 6(c) by a read from memory. These three relations all correspond to the same Shasha-Snir trace, shown in Fig. 7(a), and they all have the same observable behav-

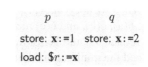

Fig. 5. A program illustrating buffer forwarding

ior, since the value of the load is obtained from the same store. Hence, we should find a representation of executions that does not distinguish between these three cases.

We can now describe *chronological traces*, our representation which solves the above problems, by omitting some of the edges, leaving some nodes unrelated. More precisely, edges between loads and updates should be omitted in the following cases.

1. A load is never related to an update originating in the same thread. This captures the intuition that swapping the order of such a load and update has no effect other

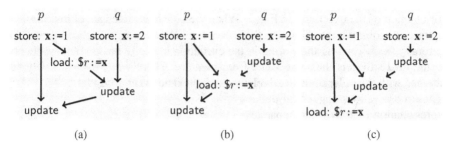

(a)   (b)   (c)

Fig. 6. Three redundant happens-before relations for Fig. 5

(a) A Shasha-Snir trace corresponding   (b) The three traces can be merged into this
to all three traces of Fig. 6   single trace

Fig. 7. Traces unifying the ones in Fig. 6

than changing a load from memory into a load of the same value from buffer, as seen when comparing Fig. 6(b) and 6(c).

2. A load ld from a memory location **x** by a thread p is never related to an update by an another thread q, if the update by q precedes some update to **x** originating in a store by p that precedes ld. This is because the value written by the update of q is effectively hidden to the load ld by the update to **x** by p. Thus, when we compare Fig. 6(a) and 6(b), we see that the order between the update by q and the load is irrelevant, since the update by q is hidden by the update by p (note that the update by p originates in a store that precedes the load).

When we apply these rules to the example of Fig. 5, all of the three representations in Fig. 6(a), 6(b), and 6(c) merge into a single representation shown in Fig. 7(b). In total, we reduce the number of distinguished cases for the program from six to three. This is indeed the minimal number of cases that must be distinguished by any representation, since the different cases result in different values being loaded by the load instruction or different values in memory at the end of the execution. Our proposed representation is optimal for the programs in Fig. 1 and 5. In Theorem 1 of Section 3 we will show that such an optimality result holds in general.

Chronological Traces for PSO. The TSO and PSO memory models are very similar. Adapting our techniques to PSO is done by slightly altering the definition of chronological traces. The details can be found in our technical report [1].

DPOR Based on Chronological Traces. Here, we illustrate how stateless model checking performs DPOR based on chronological traces, in order to explore one execution per chronological trace. As example, we use the small program of Fig. 5.

The algorithm initially explores an arbitrary execution of the program, and simultaneously generates the corresponding chronological trace. In our example, this execution can be the one shown in Fig. 8(a), along with its chronological trace. The algorithm then finds those edges of the chronological trace that can be reversed by changing the thread scheduling of the execution. In Fig. 8(a), the reversible edges are the ones from p : update to q : update, and from p : load: $\$r$:=**x** to q : update. For each such edge, the program is executed with this edge reversed. Reversing an edge can potentially lead to a completely different continuation of the execution, which must then be explored.

In the example, reversing the edge from p : load: $\$r$:=**x** to q : update will generate the execution and chronological trace in Fig. 8(b). Notice that the new execution is observably different from the previous one: the load reads the value 2 instead of 1.

The chronological traces in both Fig. 8(a) and 8(b) display a reversible edge from p : update to q : update. The algorithm therefore initiates an execution where q : update is performed before p : update. The algorithm will generate the execution and chronological trace in Fig. 8(c).

Notice that the only reversible edge in Fig. 8(c) is the one from q : update to p : update. However, executing p : update before q : update has already been explored in Fig. 8(a) and Fig. 8(b). Since there are no more edges that can be reversed, SMC terminates, having examined precisely the three chronological traces that exist for the program of Fig. 5.

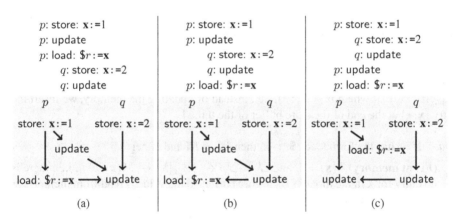

Fig. 8. How SMC with DPOR explores the program of Fig. 5

3 Formalization

In this section we summarize our formalization of the concepts of Section 2. We introduce our representation of program executions, define chronological traces, formalize Shasha-Snir traces for TSO, and prove a one-to-one correspondence between chronological traces and Shasha-Snir traces. The formalization is self-contained, but for lack of space, we sometimes use precise English rather than formal notation. A more fully formalized version, and theorem proofs, can be found in our technical report [1].

Parallel Programs. We consider parallel programs consisting of a number of threads that run in parallel, each executing a deterministic code, written in an assembly-like programming language. The language includes instructions store: $\mathbf{x}\colon\!=\$r$, load: $\$r\colon\!=\mathbf{x}$, and fence. Other instructions do not access memory, and their precise syntax and semantics are ignored for brevity. Here, and in the remainder of this text, $\mathbf{x}$, $\mathbf{y}$, $\mathbf{z}$ are used to name memory locations, u, v, w are used to name values, and $\$r$, $\$s$, $\$t$ are used to name processor registers. We use TID to denote the set of all thread identifiers.

Formal TSO Semantics. We formalize the TSO model by an operational semantics. Define a *configuration* as a pair $(\mathbb{L}, \mathbb{M})$, where $\mathbb{M}$ maps memory locations to values, and $\mathbb{L}$ maps each thread p to a local configuration of the form $\mathbb{L}(p) = (\mathbb{R}, \mathbb{B})$, where $\mathbb{R}$ is the state of local registers and program counter of p, and $\mathbb{B}$ is the contents of the store buffer of p. This content is a word over pairs $(\mathbf{x}, v)$ of memory locations and values. We let the notation $\mathbb{B}(\mathbf{x})$ denote the value v such that $(\mathbf{x}, v)$ is the rightmost pair in $\mathbb{B}$ of form $(\mathbf{x}, \_)$. If there is no such pair in $\mathbb{B}$, then $\mathbb{B}(\mathbf{x}) = \perp$.

In order to accommodate memory updates in our operational semantics, we assume that for each thread $p \in$ TID, there is an auxiliary thread $\mathrm{upd}(p)$, which nondeterministically performs memory updates from the store buffer of p. We use AuxTID $= \{\mathrm{upd}(p) | p \in \text{TID}\}$ to denote the set of auxiliary thread identifiers. We use p and q to refer to real or auxiliary threads in TID $\cup$ AuxTID as convenient.

For configurations $c = (\mathbb{L}, \mathbb{M})$ and $c' = (\mathbb{L}', \mathbb{M}')$, we write $c \xrightarrow{p} c'$ to denote that from configuration c, thread p can execute its next instruction, thereby changing the configuration into c'. Let $\mathbb{L}(p) = (\mathbb{R}, \mathbb{B})$, and $\mathbb{R}_{\mathsf{pc}}$ be obtained from $\mathbb{R}$ by advancing the program counter after p executes its next instruction. Depending on this next instruction op, we have the following cases.

Store: If op has the form store: $\mathbf{x}\colon\!=\$r$, then $c \xrightarrow{p} c'$ iff $\mathbb{M}' = \mathbb{M}$ and $\mathbb{L}' = \mathbb{L}[p \hookleftarrow (\mathbb{R}_{\mathsf{pc}}, \mathbb{B} \cdot (\mathbf{x}, v))]$ where $v = \mathbb{R}(\$r)$, i.e., instead of updating the memory, we insert the entry $(\mathbf{x}, v)$ at the end of the store buffer of the thread.

Load: If op has the form load: $\$r\colon\!=\mathbf{x}$, then $\mathbb{M}' = \mathbb{M}$ and either

1. **(From memory)** $\mathbb{B}(\mathbf{x}) = \perp$ and $\mathbb{L}' = \mathbb{L}[p \hookleftarrow (\mathbb{R}_{\mathsf{pc}}[\$r \hookleftarrow \mathbb{M}(\mathbf{x})], \mathbb{B})]$, i.e., there is no entry for $\mathbf{x}$ in the thread's own store buffer, so the value is read from memory, or
2. **(Buffer forwarding)** $\mathbb{B}(\mathbf{x}) \neq \perp$ and $\mathbb{L}' = \mathbb{L}[p \hookleftarrow (\mathbb{R}_{\mathsf{pc}}[\$r \hookleftarrow \mathbb{B}(\mathbf{x})], \mathbb{B})]$, i.e., p reads the value of $\mathbf{x}$ from its *latest* entry in its store buffer.

Fence: If op has the form fence, then $c \xrightarrow{p} c'$ iff $\mathbb{B} = \varepsilon$ and $\mathbb{M}' = \mathbb{M}$ and $\mathbb{L}' = \mathbb{L}[p \hookleftarrow (\mathbb{R}_{\mathsf{pc}}, \mathbb{B})]$. A fence can only be executed when the store buffer of the thread is empty.

Update: In addition to instructions which are executed by the threads, at any point when a store buffer is non-empty, an *update* event may nondeterministically occur. The memory is then updated according to the oldest (leftmost) letter in the store buffer, and that letter is removed from the buffer. To formalize this, we will assume that the auxiliary thread $\mathrm{upd}(p)$ executes a pseudo-instruction $\mathsf{u}(\mathbf{x})$. We then say that $c \xrightarrow{\mathrm{upd}(p)} c'$ iff $\mathbb{B} = (\mathbf{x}, v) \cdot \mathbb{B}'$ for some $\mathbf{x}$, v, $\mathbb{B}'$ and $\mathbb{M}' = \mathbb{M}[\mathbf{x} \hookleftarrow v]$ and $\mathbb{L}' = \mathbb{L}[p \hookleftarrow (\mathbb{R}, \mathbb{B}')]$.

Program Executions. A program execution is a sequence $c_0 \xrightarrow{p_1} c_1 \xrightarrow{p_2} \cdots \xrightarrow{p_n} c_n$ of configurations related by transitions labelled by actual or auxiliary thread IDs. Since each transition of each program thread (including the auxiliary threads of form $\mathsf{upd}(q)$) is deterministic, a program run is uniquely determined by its sequence of thread IDs. We will therefore define an *execution* as a word of *events*. Each event represents a transition in the execution as a triple (p, i, j), where p is a regular or auxiliary thread executing an instruction i (which can possibly be an update), and the natural number j is such that the event is the jth event of p in the execution.

Chronological Traces. We can now introduce the main conceptual contribution of the paper, viz. *chronological traces*. For an execution τ we define its chronological trace $\mathcal{T}_C(\tau)$ as a directed graph $\langle V, E \rangle$. The vertices V are all the events in τ (both events representing instructions and events representing updates). The edges are the union of six relations: $E = \rightarrow^{\mathsf{po}}_{\tau} \cup \rightarrow^{\mathsf{su}}_{\tau} \cup \rightarrow^{\mathsf{uu}}_{\tau} \cup \rightarrow^{\mathsf{src\text{-}ct}}_{\tau} \cup \rightarrow^{\mathsf{cf\text{-}ct}}_{\tau} \cup \rightarrow^{\mathsf{uf}}_{\tau}$. These edge relations are defined as follows, for two arbitrary events $e = (p, i, j), e' = (p', i', j') \in V$:

Program Order: $e \rightarrow^{\mathsf{po}}_{\tau} e'$ iff $p = p'$ and $j' = j + 1$, i.e., e and e' are consecutive events of the same thread.

Store to Update: $e \rightarrow^{\mathsf{su}}_{\tau} e'$ iff e' is the update event corresponding to the store e.

Update to Update: $e \rightarrow^{\mathsf{uu}}_{\tau} e'$ iff $i = \mathsf{u}(\mathbf{x})$ and $i' = \mathsf{u}(\mathbf{x})$ for some $\mathbf{x}$, and e and e' are consecutive updates to the memory location $\mathbf{x}$.

Source: $e \rightarrow^{\mathsf{src\text{-}ct}}_{\tau} e'$ iff e' is a load which reads the value of the update event e, which is from a different process. Notice that this definition excludes the possibility of $p = \mathsf{upd}(p')$; a load is never src-related to an update from the same thread.

Conflict: $e \rightarrow^{\mathsf{cf\text{-}ct}}_{\tau} e'$ iff e' is the update that overwrites the value read by e.

Update to Fence: $e \rightarrow^{\mathsf{uf}}_{\tau} e'$ iff $i = \mathsf{u}(\mathbf{x})$ for some $\mathbf{x}$, and $i' = \mathsf{fence}$ and $p = \mathsf{upd}(p')$ and e is the latest update by p which occurs before e' in τ. The intuition here is that the fence cannot be executed until all pending updates of the same thread have been flushed from the buffer. Hence the updates are ordered before the fence, and the chronological trace has an edge from the last of these updates to the fence event.

Shasha-Snir Traces. We will now formalize Shasha-Snir traces, and prove that chronological traces are equivalent to Shasha-Snir traces, in the sense that they induce the same equivalence relation on executions. We first recall the definition of Shasha-Snir traces. We follow the formalization by Bouajjani *et al.* [8].

First, we introduce the notion of a completed execution: An execution τ is *completed* when all stores have reached memory by means of a corresponding update event. In the context of Shasha-Snir traces, we will restrict ourselves to completed executions.

For a completed execution τ, we define the Shasha-Snir trace of τ as the graph $\mathcal{T}(\tau) = \langle V, E \rangle$ where V is the set of all non-update events (p, i, j) in τ (i.e., $i \neq \mathsf{u}(\mathbf{x})$ for all $\mathbf{x}$). The edges E is the union of four relations $E = \rightarrow^{\mathsf{po}}_{\tau} \cup \rightarrow^{\mathsf{st}}_{\tau} \cup \rightarrow^{\mathsf{src\text{-}ss}}_{\tau} \cup \rightarrow^{\mathsf{cf\text{-}ss}}_{\tau}$, where $\rightarrow^{\mathsf{po}}_{\tau}$ (program order) is the same as for Chronological traces, and where, letting $e = (p, i, j)$ and $e' = (p', i', j')$:

Store Order: $e \rightarrow_\tau^{st} e'$ iff i and i' are two stores, whose corresponding updates are consecutive updates to the same memory location. I.e., store order defines a total order on all the stores to each memory location, based on the order in which they reach memory.

Source: $e \rightarrow_\tau^{src-ss} e'$ iff e' is a load which reads its value from e, via memory or by buffer forwarding.

Conflict: $e \rightarrow_\tau^{cf-ss} e'$ iff e' is the store which overwrites the value read by e.

We are now ready to state the equivalence theorem.

Theorem 1. (Equivalence of Shasha-Snir Traces and Chronological Traces) *For a given program $\mathcal{P}$ with two completed executions τ, τ', it holds that $\mathcal{T}(\tau) = \mathcal{T}(\tau')$ iff $\mathcal{T}_C(\tau) = \mathcal{T}_C(\tau')$.*

DPOR for TSO. A DPOR algorithm can exploit Chronological traces to perform stateless model checking of programs that execute under TSO (and PSO), as illustrated at the end of Section 2. The explored executions follow the semantics of TSO in Section 3. For each execution, its happens-before relation, which is the transitive closure of the edge relation $E = \rightarrow_\tau^{po} \cup \rightarrow_\tau^{su} \cup \rightarrow_\tau^{uu} \cup \rightarrow_\tau^{src-ct} \cup \rightarrow_\tau^{cf-ct} \cup \rightarrow_\tau^{uf}$ of the corresponding chronological trace, is computed on the fly. This happens-before relation can in principle be exploited by any DPOR algorithm to explore at least one execution per equivalence class induced by Shasha-Snir traces. We state the following theorem of correctness.

Theorem 2. (Correctness of DPOR Algorithms) *The algorithms* Source-DPOR *and* Optimal-DPOR *of [2], based on the happens-before relation induced by chronological traces, explore at least one execution per equivalence class induced by Shasha-Snir traces. Moreover,* Optimal-DPOR *explores exactly one execution per equivalence class.*

4 Implementation

To show the effectiveness of our techniques we have implemented a stateless model checker for C programs. The tool, called Nidhugg, is available as open source at https://github.com/nidhugg/nidhugg. Major design decisions have been that Nidhugg: (i) should not be bound to a specific hardware architecture and (ii) should use an existing, mature implementation of C semantics, not implement its own. Our choice was to use the LLVM compiler infrastructure [23] and work at the level of its intermediate representation (IR). LLVM IR is low-level and allows us to analyze assembly-like but target-independent code which is produced after employing all optimizations and transformations that the LLVM compiler performs till this stage.

Nidhugg detects assertion violations and robustness violations that occur under the selected memory model. We implement the Source-DPOR algorithm from Abdulla *et al.* [2], adapted to relaxed memory in the manner described in this paper. Before applying Source-DPOR, each spin loop is replaced by an equivalent single load and assume statement. This substantially improves the performance of Source-DPOR, since a waiting spin loop may generate a huge number of improductive loads, all returning the same wrong value; all of these loads will cause races, which will cause the number of explored traces to explode. Exploration of program executions is performed by interpretation of LLVM IR, based on the interpreter lli which is distributed with LLVM. We support concurrency through the pthreads library. This is done by hooking calls to pthread functions, and executing changes to the execution stacks (adding new threads, joining, etc.) as appropriate within the interpreter.

5   Experimental Results

We have applied our implementation to several intensely racy benchmarks, all implemented in C/pthreads. They include classical benchmarks, such as Dekker's, Lamport's (fast) and Peterson's mutual exclusion algorithms. Others, such as indexer.c, are designed to showcase races that are hard to identify statically. Yet others (stack_safe.c) use pthread mutexes to entirely avoid races. Lamport's algorithm and stack_safe.c originate from the TACAS Competition on Software Verification (SV-COMP). Some benchmarks originate from industrial code: apr_1.c, apr_2.c, pgsql.c and parker.c.

We show the results of our tool Nidhugg in Table 1. For comparison we also include the results of two other analysis tools, CBMC [6] and goto-instrument [5], which also target C programs under relaxed memory. The techniques of goto-instrument and CBMC are described in more detail in Section 6.

All experiments were run on a machine equipped with a 3 GHz Intel i7 processor and 6 GB RAM running 64-bit Linux. We use version 4.9 of goto-instrument and CBMC. The benchmarks have been tweaked to work for all tools, in communication with the developers of CBMC and goto-instrument. All benchmarks are available at https://github.com/nidhugg/benchmarks_tacas2015.

Table 1 shows that our technique performs well compared to the other tools for most of the examples. We will briefly highlight a few interesting results.

We see that in most cases Nidhugg pays a very modest performance price when going from sequential consistency to TSO and PSO. The explanation is that the number of executions explored by our stateless model checker is close to the number of Shasha-Snir traces, which increases very modestly when going from sequential consistency to TSO and PSO for typical benchmarks. Consider for example the benchmark stack_safe.c, which is robust, and therefore has equally many Shasha-Snir traces (and hence also chronological traces) under all three memory models. Our technique is able to benefit from this, and has almost the same run time under TSO and PSO as under SC.

We also see that our implementation compares favourably against CBMC, a state-of-the-art bounded model checking tool, and goto-instrument. For several benchmarks, our implementation is several orders of magnitude faster.

The effect of the optimization to replace each spin loop by a load and assume statement can be seen in the pgsql.c benchmark. For comparison, we also include the benchmark pgsql_bnd.c, where the spin loop has been modified such that Nidhugg fails to automatically replace it by an assume statement.

The only other benchmark where Nidhugg is not faster is fib_true.c. The benchmark has two threads that perform the actual work, and one separate thread that checks the correctness of the computed value, causing many races, as in the case of spin loops.

Table 1. Analysis times (in seconds) for our implementation Nidhugg, as well as CBMC and goto-instrument under the SC, TSO and PSO memory models. Stars (*) indicate that the analysis discovered an error in the benchmark. A t/o entry means that the tool did not terminate within 10 minutes. An ! entry means that the tool crashed. ~~Struck-out~~ entries mean that the tool gave the wrong result. In the fence column, a dash (-) means that no fences have been added to the benchmark, a memory model indicates that fences have been (manually) added to make the benchmark correct under that and stronger memory models. The LB column shows the loop unrolling depth. Superior run times are shown in bold face.

			CBMC			goto-instrument			Nidhugg		
	fence	LB	SC	TSO	PSO	SC	TSO	PSO	SC	TSO	PSO
apr_1.c	-	5	t/o	t/o	t/o	t/o	!	!	**5.88**	**6.06**	**16.98**
apr_2.c	-	5	t/o	t/o	t/o	!	!	!	**2.60**	**2.20**	**5.39**
dcl_singleton.c	-	7	5.95	31.47	*18.01	5.33	5.36	*0.18	**0.08**	**0.08**	***0.08**
dcl_singleton.c	pso	7	5.88	30.98	29.45	5.20	5.18	5.17	**0.08**	**0.08**	**0.08**
dekker.c	-	10	2.42	*3.17	*2.84	1.68	*4.00	*220.11	**0.10**	***0.11**	***0.09**
dekker.c	tso	10	2.39	5.65	*3.51	1.62	297.62	t/o	**0.11**	**0.12**	***0.08**
dekker.c	pso	10	2.55	5.31	4.83	1.72	428.86	t/o	**0.11**	**0.12**	**0.12**
fib_false.c	-	-	*1.63	*3.38	*3.00	*1.60	*1.58	*1.56	*2.39	*5.57	*6.20
fib_false_join.c	-	-	*0.98	*1.10	*1.91	*1.31	*0.88	*0.80	***0.32**	***0.62**	***0.71**
fib_true.c	-	-	**6.28**	9.39	7.72	6.32	**7.63**	7.62	25.83	75.06	86.32
fib_true_join.c	-	-	6.61	8.37	10.81	7.09	5.94	5.92	**1.20**	**2.88**	**3.19**
indexer.c	-	5	193.01	210.42	214.03	191.88	70.42	69.38	**0.10**	**0.09**	**0.09**
lamport.c	-	8	7.78	*11.63	*10.53	6.89	t/o	t/o	**0.08**	***0.08**	***0.08**
lamport.c	tso	8	7.60	26.31	*15.85	6.80	513.67	t/o	**0.09**	**0.08**	***0.07**
lamport.c	pso	8	7.72	30.92	27.51	7.43	t/o	t/o	**0.08**	**0.08**	**0.08**
parker.c	-	10	12.34	*91.99	*86.10	11.63	~~9.70~~	9.65	**1.50**	***0.09**	***0.08**
parker.c	pso	10	12.72	141.24	166.75	11.76	10.66	10.64	**1.50**	**1.92**	**2.94**
peterson.c	-	-	0.35	*0.38	*0.35	0.18	*0.20	*0.21	**0.07**	***0.07**	***0.07**
peterson.c	tso	-	0.35	0.39	*0.35	0.19	0.18	~~0.56~~	**0.07**	**0.07**	***0.07**
peterson.c	pso	-	0.35	0.41	0.40	0.18	0.18	0.19	**0.07**	**0.07**	**0.08**
pgsql.c	-	8	19.80	60.66	*4.63	21.03	46.57	*296.77	**0.08**	**0.07**	***0.08**
pgsql.c	pso	8	23.93	71.15	121.51	19.04	t/o	t/o	**0.07**	**0.07**	**0.08**
pgsql_bnd.c	pso	(4)	**3.57**	**9.55**	**12.68**	3.59	t/o	t/o	89.44	106.04	112.60
stack_safe.c	-	-	44.53	516.01	496.36	45.11	42.39	42.50	**0.34**	**0.36**	**0.43**
stack_unsafe.c	-	-	*1.40	*1.87	*2.08	*1.00	*0.81	*0.79	***0.08**	***0.08**	***0.09**
szymanski.c	-	-	0.40	*0.44	*0.43	0.23	*0.89	*1.16	**0.07**	***0.13**	***0.07**
szymanski.c	tso	-	0.40	0.50	*0.43	0.23	0.23	~~2.48~~	**0.08**	**0.08**	***0.07**
szymanski.c	pso	-	0.39	0.50	0.49	0.23	0.24	0.24	**0.08**	**0.08**	**0.08**

We show with the benchmark fib_true_join.c that in this case, the problem can be alleviated by forcing the threads to join before checking the result.

Most benchmarks in Table 1 are small program cores, ranging from 36 to 118 lines of C code, exhibiting complicated synchronization patterns. To show that our technique is also applicable to real life code, we include the benchmarks apr_1.c and apr_2.c. They each contain approximately 8000 lines of code taken from the Apache Portable Runtime library, and exercise the library primitives for thread management, locking, and memory pools. Nidhugg is able to analyze the code within a few seconds. We notice that despite the benchmarks being robust, the analysis under PSO suffers a slowdown of about three times compared to TSO. This is because the benchmarks access a large number of different memory locations. Since PSO semantics require one store buffer per memory location, this affects analysis under PSO more than under SC and TSO.

6 Related Work

To the best of our knowledge, our work is the first to apply stateless model checking techniques to the setting of relaxed memory models; see e.g. [2] for a recent survey of related work on stateless model checking and dynamic partial order reduction techniques. There have been many works dedicated to the verification and checking of programs running under RMM (e.g., [18,20,22,3,10,11,7,8,9,36]). Some of them propose *precise* analyses for checking safety properties or robustness of finite-state programs under TSO (e.g., [3,8]). Others describe monitoring and testing techniques for programs under RMM (e.g., [10,11,22]). There are also a number of efforts to design bounded model checking techniques for programs under RMM (e.g., [36,9]) which encode the verification problem in SAT.

The two closest works to ours are those presented in [6,5]. The first of them [6] develops a bounded model checking technique that can be applied to different memory models (e.g., TSO, PSO, and Power). That technique makes use of the fact that the trace of a program under RMM can be viewed as a partially ordered set. This results in a bounded model checking technique aware of the underlying memory model when constructing the SMT/SAT formula. The second line of work reduces the verification problem of a program under RMM to verification under SC of a program constructed by a code transformation [5]. This technique tries to encode the effect of the RMM semantics by augmenting the input program with buffers and queues. This work introduces also the notion of Xtop objects. Although an Xtop object is a valid acyclic representation of Shasha-Snir traces, it will in many cases distinguish executions that are semantically equivalent according to the Shasha-Snir traces. This is never the case for chronological traces. An extensive experimental comparison with the corresponding tools [6,5] under the TSO and PSO memory models was given in Section 5.

7 Concluding Remarks

We have presented the first technique for efficient *stateless model checking* which is aware of the underlying relaxed memory model. To this end we have introduced *chronological traces* which are novel representations of executions under the TSO and PSO memory models, and induce a happens-before relation that is a partial order and can be used as a basis for DPOR. Furthermore, we have established a strict one-to-one correspondence between chronological and Shasha-Snir traces. Nidhugg, our publicly available tool, detects bugs in LLVM assembly code produced for C/pthreads programs and can be instantiated to the SC, TSO, and PSO memory models. We have applied Nidhugg to several programs, both benchmarks and of considerable size, and our experimental results show that our technique offers significantly better performance than both CBMC and goto-instrument in many cases.

We plan to extend Nidhugg to more memory models such as Power, ARM, and the C/C++ memory model. This will require to adapt the definition chronological traces to them in order to also guarantee the one-to-one correspondence with Shasha-Snir traces.

References

1. Abdulla, P.A., Aronis, S., Atig, M.F., Jonsson, B., Leonardsson, C., Sagonas, K.: Stateless model checking for TSO and PSO (2015) arXiv:1501.02069
2. Abdulla, P.A., Aronis, S., Jonsson, B., Sagonas, K.: Optimal dynamic partial order reduction. In: POPL, pp. 373–384. ACM (2014)
3. Abdulla, P.A., Atig, M.F., Chen, Y.-F., Leonardsson, C., Rezine, A.: Counter-example guided fence insertion under TSO. In: Flanagan, C., König, B. (eds.) TACAS 2012. LNCS, vol. 7214, pp. 204–219. Springer, Heidelberg (2012)
4. Adve, S.V., Gharachorloo, K.: Shared memory consistency models: A tutorial. Computer 29(12), 66–76 (1996)
5. Alglave, J., Kroening, D., Nimal, V., Tautschnig, M.: Software verification for weak memory via program transformation. In: Felleisen, M., Gardner, P. (eds.) ESOP 2013. LNCS, vol. 7792, pp. 512–532. Springer, Heidelberg (2013)
6. Alglave, J., Kroening, D., Tautschnig, M.: Partial orders for efficient bounded model checking of concurrent software. In: Sharygina, N., Veith, H. (eds.) CAV 2013. LNCS, vol. 8044, pp. 141–157. Springer, Heidelberg (2013)
7. Alglave, J., Maranget, L.: Stability in weak memory models. In: Gopalakrishnan, G., Qadeer, S. (eds.) CAV 2011. LNCS, vol. 6806, pp. 50–66. Springer, Heidelberg (2011)
8. Bouajjani, A., Derevenetc, E., Meyer, R.: Checking and enforcing robustness against TSO. In: Felleisen, M., Gardner, P. (eds.) ESOP 2013. LNCS, vol. 7792, pp. 533–553. Springer, Heidelberg (2013)
9. Burckhardt, S., Alur, R., Martin, M.M.K.: CheckFence: Checking consistency of concurrent data types on relaxed memory models. In: PLDI, pp. 12–21. ACM (2007)
10. Burckhardt, S., Musuvathi, M.: Effective program verification for relaxed memory models. In: Gupta, A., Malik, S. (eds.) CAV 2008. LNCS, vol. 5123, pp. 107–120. Springer, Heidelberg (2008)
11. Burnim, J., Sen, K., Stergiou, C.: Sound and complete monitoring of sequential consistency for relaxed memory models. In: Abdulla, P.A., Leino, K.R.M. (eds.) TACAS 2011. LNCS, vol. 6605, pp. 11–25. Springer, Heidelberg (2011)
12. Christakis, M., Gotovos, A., Sagonas, K.: Systematic testing for detecting concurrency errors in Erlang programs. In: ICST, pp. 154–163. IEEE (2013)
13. Clarke, E.M., Grumberg, O., Minea, M., Peled, D.: State space reduction using partial order techniques. STTT 2(3), 279–287 (1999)
14. Flanagan, C., Godefroid, P.: Dynamic partial-order reduction for model checking software. In: POPL, pp. 110–121. ACM (2005)
15. Godefroid, P.: Partial-Order Methods for the Verification of Concurrent Systems. LNCS, vol. 1032. Springer, Heidelberg (1996)

16. Godefroid, P.: Model checking for programming languages using VeriSoft. In: POPL, pp. 174–186. ACM (1997)
17. Godefroid, P.: Software model checking: The VeriSoft approach. Formal Methods in System Design 26(2), 77–101 (2005)
18. Krishnamurthy, A., Yelick, K.A.: Analyses and optimizations for shared address space programs. J. Parallel Distrib. Comput. 38(2), 130–144 (1996)
19. Lauterburg, S., Karmani, R.K., Marinov, D., Agha, G.: Evaluating ordering heuristics for dynamic partial-order reduction techniques. In: Rosenblum, D.S., Taentzer, G. (eds.) FASE 2010. LNCS, vol. 6013, pp. 308–322. Springer, Heidelberg (2010)
20. Lee, J., Padua, D.A.: Hiding relaxed memory consistency with a compiler. IEEE Trans. Computers 50(8), 824–833 (2001)
21. Lei, Y., Carver, R.: Reachability testing of concurrent programs. IEEE Trans. Softw. Eng. 32(6), 382–403 (2006)
22. Liu, F., Nedev, N., Prisadnikov, N., Vechev, M.T., Yahav, E.: Dynamic synthesis for relaxed memory models. In: PLDI, pp. 429–440. ACM (2012)
23. The LLVM compiler infrastructure, http://llvm.org
24. Mazurkiewicz, A.: Trace theory. In: Brauer, W., Reisig, W., Rozenberg, G. (eds.) APN 1986. LNCS, vol. 255, Springer, Heidelberg (1987)
25. Musuvathi, M., Qadeer, S., Ball, T., Basler, G., Nainar, P., Neamtiu, I.: Finding and reproducing heisenbugs in concurrent programs. In: OSDI, pp. 267–280. USENIX (2008)
26. Park, S., Dill, D.L.: An executable specification, analyzer and verifier for RMO (relaxed memory order). In: SPAA, pp. 34–41. ACM (1995)
27. Peled, D.: All from one, one for all, on model-checking using representatives. In: Courcoubetis, C. (ed.) CAV 1993. LNCS, vol. 697, pp. 409–423. Springer, Heidelberg (1993)
28. Saarikivi, O., Kähkönen, K., Heljanko, K.: Improving dynamic partial order reductions for concolic testing. In: ACSD. IEEE (2012)
29. Sen, K., Agha, G.: A race-detection and flipping algorithm for automated testing of multi-threaded programs. In: Bin, E., Ziv, A., Ur, S. (eds.) HVC 2006. LNCS, vol. 4383, pp. 166–182. Springer, Heidelberg (2007)
30. Sewell, P., Sarkar, S., Owens, S., Nardelli, F.Z., Myreen, M.O.: x86-TSO: A rigorous and usable programmer's model for x86 multiprocessors. Comm. of the ACM 53(7), 89–97 (2010)
31. Shasha, D., Snir, M.: Efficient and correct execution of parallel programs that share memory. ACM Trans. on Programming Languages and Systems 10(2), 282–312 (1988)
32. SPARC International, Inc. The SPARC Architecture Manual Version 9 (1994)
33. Tasharofi, S., Karmani, R.K., Lauterburg, S., Legay, A., Marinov, D., Agha, G.: TransDPOR: A novel dynamic partial-order reduction technique for testing actor programs. In: Giese, H., Rosu, G. (eds.) FORTE 2012 and FMOODS 2012. LNCS, vol. 7273, pp. 219–234. Springer, Heidelberg (2012)
34. Valmari, A.: Stubborn sets for reduced state space generation. In: Rozenberg, G. (ed.) APN 1990. LNCS, vol. 483, pp. 491–515. Springer, Heidelberg (1991)
35. Wang, C., Said, M., Gupta, A.: Coverage guided systematic concurrency testing. In: ICSE, pp. 221–230. ACM (2011)
36. Yang, Y., Gopalakrishnan, G., Lindstrom, G., Slind, K.: Nemos: A framework for axiomatic and executable specifications of memory consistency models. In: IPDPS. IEEE (2004)

GPU Accelerated Strong and Branching Bisimilarity Checking

Anton Wijs[1,2,*]

[1] RWTH Aachen University, Germany
[2] Eindhoven University of Technology, The Netherlands

Abstract. Bisimilarity checking is an important operation to perform explicit-state model checking when the state space of a model under verification has already been generated. It can be applied in various ways: reduction of a state space w.r.t. a particular flavour of bisimilarity, or checking that two given state spaces are bisimilar. Bisimilarity checking is a computationally intensive task, and over the years, several algorithms have been presented, both sequential, i.e. single-threaded, and parallel, the latter either relying on shared memory or message-passing. In this work, we first present a novel way to check strong bisimilarity on general-purpose graphics processing units (GPUs), and show experimentally that an implementation of it for CUDA-enabled GPUs is competitive with other parallel techniques that run either on a GPU or use message-passing on a multi-core system. Building on this, we propose, to the best of our knowledge, the first many-core branching bisimilarity checking algorithm, an implementation of which shows speedups comparable to our strong bisimilarity checking approach.

1 Introduction

Model checking [2] is a formal verification technique to ensure that a model satisfies desired functional properties. There are essentially two ways to perform it; *on-the-fly*, which means that properties are being checked while the model is being analysed, i.e. while its state space is explored, and *offline*, in which first the state space is fully generated and subsequently properties are checked on it. For the latter case, it is desirable to be able to compare and minimise state spaces, to allow for faster property checking. In action-based model checking, Labelled Transition Systems (LTSs) are often used to formalise state spaces, and (some flavour of) bisimilarity is used to compare and minimise them. Checking bisimilarity of LTSs is a computationally intensive operation, and over the years, several algorithms have been proposed, e.g. [17,20,15,19].

Graphics Processing Units (GPUs) have been used in recent years to dramatically speed up computations. For model checking, algorithms have been

---

* This work was sponsored by the NWO Exacte Wetenschappen, EW (NWO Physical Sciences Division) for the use of supercomputer facilities, with financial support from the Nederlandse Organisatie voor Wetenschappelijk Onderzoek (Netherlands Organisation for Scientific Research, NWO).

presented to use GPUs for several critical operations, such as on-the-fly state space exploration [4,23], offline property checking [3,8,9,22], counterexample generation [27], state space decomposition [24], but strong bisimilarity checking has not received much attention, and branching bisimilarity [14] has received none. In this paper, we propose new algorithms for these operations, in the latter case only assuming that the LTSs do not contain cycles of internal behaviour.

Structure of the paper. In Section 2, we present the basic notions used in this paper. Section 3 contains a discussion of the typical GPU setting, and explains how to encode the required input. In Section 4, we present our new algorithms, and Section 5 contains our experimental results. Finally, related work is discussed in Section 6, and Conclusions are drawn in Section 7.

2   Preliminaries

In this section, we discuss the basic notions involved to understand the problem, namely labelled transition systems, strong and branching bisimilarity, and the existing basic approaches to check strong and branching bisimilarity.

Labelled Transition Systems. We use Labelled Transition Systems (LTSs) to represent the semantics of finite-state systems. They are action-based descriptions, indicating how a system can change state by performing particular actions. An LTS $\mathcal{G}$ is a tuple $\langle \mathcal{S}, \mathcal{A}, \mathcal{T}, \underline{s} \rangle$, where $\mathcal{S}$ is a (finite) set of states, $\mathcal{A}$ is a set of actions or labels (including the invisible action τ), $\mathcal{T} \subseteq \mathcal{S} \times \mathcal{A} \times \mathcal{S}$ is a transition relation, and $\underline{s} \in \mathcal{S}$ is the initial state. Actions in $\mathcal{A}$ are denoted by a, b, c, etc. We use $s_1 \xrightarrow{a} s_2$ to denote $\langle s_1, a, s_2 \rangle \in \mathcal{T}$. If $s_1 \xrightarrow{a} s_2$, this means that in $\mathcal{G}$, an action a can be performed in state s_1, leading to state s_2. With $\mathcal{T}(s)$, we refer to the set of states that can be reached by following a single outgoing transition of s. Finally, the special action τ is used to denote internal behaviour of the system, and $s_1 \Rightarrow s_2$ indicates that it is possible to move from s_1 to s_2 via 0 or more τ-transition, i.e. $\Rightarrow$ is the reflexive, transitive closure of $\xrightarrow{\tau}$.

Strong Bisimilarity. The first equivalence relation between LTSs that we consider in this paper is strong bisimilarity.

Definition 1 (Strong Bisimulation). *A binary relation $R \subseteq \mathcal{S} \times \mathcal{S}$ is a* strong bisimulation *if R is symmetric and $s\ R\ t$ implies that if $s \xrightarrow{a} s'$ then $t \xrightarrow{a} t'$ with $s'R\ t'$.*

Two states s and t are *bisimilar*, denoted by $s \leftrightarrow t$, if there is a strong bisimulation relation R such that $s\ R\ t$.

In this paper, when trying to construct a bisimulation relation, we are always interested in the *largest* bisimulation. Strong bisimilarity is closed under arbitrary union, so this largest relation is the combination of all relations that can be constructed.

The problem of checking strong bisimilarity for LTSs when $|\mathcal{A}| = 1$ corresponds with the single function coarsest partition problem. The most widely known algorithms to solve this problem is by Paige & Tarjan (PT) [20] and by Kanellakis & Smolka (KS) [17], and both can be extended for the multiple functions coarsest partition problem, to handle LTSs with multiple actions.

A bisimilarity checking algorithm can be used both to minimise an LTS, by reducing all bisimilar states to a single state in the output LTS, and to compare two LTSs $\mathcal{G}_1 = \langle \mathcal{S}_1, \mathcal{A}_1, \mathcal{T}_1, \underline{s}_1 \rangle$, $\mathcal{G}_2 = \langle \mathcal{S}_2, \mathcal{A}_2, \mathcal{T}_2, \underline{s}_2 \rangle$. The latter boils down to checking whether $\underline{s}_1$ and $\underline{s}_2$ end up being bisimilar after checking bisimilarity on the combined LTS $\langle \mathcal{S}_1 \cup \mathcal{S}_2, \mathcal{A}_1 \cup \mathcal{A}_2, \mathcal{T}_1 \cup \mathcal{T}_2, \underline{s}_1 \rangle$ (for convenience, we assume that $\mathcal{S}_1 \cap \mathcal{S}_2 = \emptyset$).

We proceed with explaining the basic mechanism to check bisimilarity that we use in the remainder of this paper, which is partition refinement. In fact, this mechanism is the so-called "naive" reduction algorithm[1] mentioned by Kanellakis & Smolka [17], since it has been shown in the past to be suitable for parallelisation and, unlike PT, it can be extended straightforwardly for branching and weak bisimilarity [19]. We further motivate the use of this mechanism in Section 3 after the explanation of the GPU basics.

A *partition* of $\mathcal{S}$ is a set of m disjoint state sets called *blocks* B_i $(1 \leq i \leq m)$ such that $\bigcup_{1 \leq i \leq m} B_i = \mathcal{S}$. A partition refinement algorithm takes as input a partition, analyses it, and produces as output a *refinement* of that partition. A partition π' is a refinement of π iff every block of π' is contained in a block of π.

The idea behind using partition refinement for bisimilarity checking is that initially, a partition π consisting of a single block $B = \mathcal{S}$ is defined, which is then further refined on the criterion whether states in the same block can be distinguished w.r.t. π until no further refining can be done. The resulting partition then represents a bisimulation relation: two states s, t are bisimilar iff they are in the same block.

The problem of checking strong bisimilarity of LTSs with multiple transition labels, i.e. the multi-function coarsest partition problem, can now be formalised as follows:

Definition 2 (Strong Bisimilarity Checking Problem). *Given an LTS $\mathcal{G} = \langle \mathcal{S}, \mathcal{A}, \mathcal{T}, \underline{s} \rangle$ and an initial partition $\pi_0 = \{\mathcal{S}\}$, find a partition π such that:*

1. *$\forall B \in \pi$, $s, t \in B$, $a \in \mathcal{A}$, $B' \in \pi$. ($\exists s' \in B'.s \xrightarrow{a} s' \iff \exists t' \in B'.t \xrightarrow{a} t'$);*
2. *No partition $\pi' \neq \pi$ can be constructed which refines π and satisfies 1.*

Blom et al. [5,6,7] and Orzan [19] define the notion of a *signature* of a state, to reason about condition 1 in Def. 2. The signature $sig_\pi(s)$ of a state s in a partition π encodes which transitions can be taken from s and to which blocks in π they lead. In the following definition of $sig_\pi(s)$, we interpret a partition π as a function $\pi : \mathcal{S} \to \mathbb{N}$:

$$sig_\pi(s) = \{(a, \pi(s')) \mid s \xrightarrow{a} s'\}$$

In each iteration of a partition refinement algorithm, we can now check for each block $B \in \pi$ and each two states $s, t \in B$ whether $sig_\pi(s) = sig_\pi(t)$. If so, then

---

[1] In [17], some optimisations on this algorithm are presented. How well these are applicable in a GPU setting remains to be investigated.

Algorithm 1. Partition refinement with signatures

Require: $\mathcal{G} = \langle \mathcal{S}, \mathcal{A}, \mathcal{T}, \underline{s} \rangle$, $\pi = \{\mathcal{S}\}$
    $stable \leftarrow$ **false**
2: **while** $\neg stable$ **do**
    for all $B \in \pi$ **do**
4:      $\pi' \leftarrow (\pi \setminus \{B\}) \cup \{B_1, \ldots, B_m\}$,
        with $\bigcup_{1 \leq i \leq m} B_i = B \wedge \forall 1 \leq i, j \leq m.\forall s \in B_i, t \in B_j.(i = j \iff sig_\pi(s) = sig_\pi(t))$
6:    **if** $\pi \neq \pi'$ **then**
      $\pi \leftarrow \pi'$
8:    **else**
      $stable \leftarrow$ **true**

---

they should remain in the same block; if not, then B needs to be split. See Alg. 1 for this procedure.

Branching Bisimilarity. The second relation we consider is *branching bisimilarity* [14]. It is sensitive to internal behaviour while preserving the branching structure of an LTS, meaning that it preserves the potential to perform actions, even when internal behaviour is involved. It has several nice properties, among which are the facts that temporal logics such as the Hennessy-Milner logic with an until operator and CTL*-X characterise it [12].

Definition 3 (Branching Bisimulation). *A binary relation $R \subseteq \mathcal{S} \times \mathcal{S}$ is a branching bisimulation if R is symmetric and $s \, R \, t$ implies that if $s \xrightarrow{a} s'$ then*
- *either $a = \tau$ with $s' R \, t$;*
- *or $t \Rightarrow \hat{t} \xrightarrow{a} t'$ with $s \, R \, \hat{t}$ and $s' R \, t'$.*

Two states s and t are *branching bisimilar*, denoted by $s \underset{b}{\leftrightarrow} t$, if there is a branching bisimulation R such that $s \, R \, t$. Again, as in the case for strong bisimilarity, we are interested in the *largest* branching bisimulation when checking branching bisimilarity in an LTS.

A well-known property of branching bisimilarity is called *stuttering*, which plays an important role when constructing an algorithm to check branching bisimilarity of LTSs:

Definition 4 (Stuttering [14]). *Let R be the largest branching bisimulation relating states in $\mathcal{G} = \langle \mathcal{S}, \mathcal{A}, \mathcal{T}, \underline{s} \rangle$. If $s \xrightarrow{\tau} s_1 \xrightarrow{\tau} s_2 \xrightarrow{\tau} \cdots \xrightarrow{\tau} s_n \xrightarrow{\tau} s'$ $(n \geq 0)$ is a path such that there is a $t \in \mathcal{S}$ with $s \, R \, t$ and $s' R \, t$, then for all $1 \leq i \leq n$, we have $s_i \, R \, t$.*

Def. 4 defines the notion of an *inert τ-path*, or inert path, in which all intermediate states are branching bisimilar with each other. Alg. 1 can in principle be used directly for checking branching bisimilarity if we redefine $sig_\pi(s)$ as $sig_\pi^b(s)$, where $s \xRightarrow{\pi} \hat{s}$ expresses that there exists a τ-path between states $s, \hat{s}$ which is inert w.r.t. π:

$$sig_\pi^b(s) = \{(a, \pi(s')) \mid \exists \hat{s} \in \pi(s).s \xRightarrow{\pi} \hat{s} \xrightarrow{a} s' \wedge (a \neq \tau \vee \pi(s) \neq \pi(s'))\}$$

In the case of branching bisimilarity, τ-transitions are either *inert* (or *silent*) or not, depending on whether following the transitions results in losing potential behaviour. This defines whether the source and target states of a τ-transition are branching bisimilar or not. Consider the LTS shown in Fig. 2. From s_1, a τ-transition to s_7 can be done, in which we have a c-loop, and a τ-transition to state s_3. The latter transition is inert, since also in s_3, a τ-transition can be done to a state, s_6, which is branching bisimilar to s_7. In other words, s_3 can *simulate* the behaviour of s_1. However, in line with the stuttering property, inertness applies to transitive closures of τ-transitions. In the example, also $s_0 \xrightarrow{s}_1$ is inert, since the a-transition from s_0 can be simulated by s_3. Hence, we have $s_0 \leftrightarrow_b s_1 \leftrightarrow_b s_3$.

The definition of $sig_\pi^b(s)$ actually refers to π-*inertness* which means that both the source and target state of a τ-transition are in the same block in π. The added complication when checking branching bisimilarity w.r.t. strong is hence that closures of τ-transitions that are π-inert need to be taken into account. Because of this, the problem of checking branching bisimilarity is also known as the multiple functions coarsest partition with stuttering problem.

In the algorithm by Browne et al. [10] for checking stuttering equivalence, in every iteration, it needs to be checked whether for two states s and t the behaviour reachable via inert paths is equivalent, in order to establish that s and t are equivalent. This means that for each pair of possibly equivalent states, inert paths need to be reexplored. The complexity of the algorithm is $O(|\mathcal{S}|^5)$.

In the algorithm by Groote & Vaandrager (GV) [15], reexploration of inert paths is avoided, and its complexity is $O(|\mathcal{S}| \cdot (|\mathcal{S}| + |\mathcal{T}|))$. There, a pair of blocks (B, B') must be identified such that there both is a state in B with a transition to B', and there is no bottom state in B with a transition to B'. A state in B is a bottom state when it has no transition to a state in B. If such a pair of blocks can be found, then B must be split. This splitting criterion is directly based on the previously mentioned observation that a τ-path is inert iff it leads to a state which can simulate all behaviour of the intermediate states. Because of this, GV requires that no τ-cycles are present. This is not an important restriction, since compressing τ-cycles into individual states can be done in $O(|\mathcal{T}|)$ [1].

After the next section, explaining the basics of GPUs, we return to checking bisimilarity, focussing on existing approaches for many-core settings, and motivating our approach.

3   GPU Basics

In this paper, we focus on NVIDIA GPU architectures and the Compute Unified Device Architecture (CUDA) interface. However, our algorithms can be straight-forwardly applied to any architecture with massive hardware multithreading and the SIMT (Single Instruction Multiple Threads) model.

CUDA is NVIDIA's interface to program GPUs. It extends C and FORTRAN. We use the C extension. CUDA includes special declarations to explicitly place variables in the various types of memory (see Figure 1), predefined keywords to refer to the IDs of individual threads and blocks of threads, synchronisation statements, a run time API for memory management, and statements to define and launch GPU functions, known as *kernels.* In this section we give a brief overview of CUDA. More details can be found in, for instance, [9,23].

CUDA Programming Model. A CUDA program consists of a *host* program running on the Central Processing Unit (CPU) and a (collection of) CUDA kernels. Kernels describe the parallel parts of the program and are executed many times in parallel by different threads on the GPU device. They are launched from the host. Often at most one kernel can be launched at a time, but there are also GPUs that allow running multiple different kernels concurrently. When launching a kernel, the number of threads that should execute it needs to be specified. All those threads execute the same kernel, i.e. code. Each thread is executed by a streaming processor (SP), see Figure 1. In general, GPU threads are grouped in blocks of a predefined size, usually a power of two. A block of threads is assigned to a multiprocessor.

CUDA Memory Model. Threads have access to different kinds of memory. Each thread has a number of on-chip registers that allow fast access. Furthermore, threads within a block can together use the *shared memory* of a multiprocessor, which is also on-chip and fast. Finally, all blocks have access to the *global memory* which is large (currently up to 12 GB), but slow, since it is off-chip. Two caches called L1 and L2 are used to cache data read from the global memory. The host has read and write access to the global memory, which allows it to be used for communication between the host and the kernel.

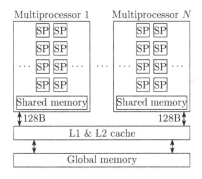

Fig. 1. Hardware model of CUDA GPUs

GPU Architecture. A GPU contains a set of streaming multiprocessors (SMs), and each of those contains a set of SPs. The NVIDIA KEPLER K20M, which we used for our experiments, has 13 SMs, each having 192 SPs, which is in total 2496 SPs. Furthermore, it has 5 GB global memory.

CUDA Execution Model. Threads are executed using the SIMT model. This means that each thread is executed independently with its own instruction address and local state (registers and local memory), but their execution is organised in groups of 32 called *warps.* The threads in a warp execute instructions in lock-step, i.e. they share a program counter. If the memory accesses of threads in a warp can be grouped together physically, i.e. if the accesses are coalesced, then the data can be obtained using a single fetch, which greatly improves the runtime compared to fetching physically separate data. When checking bisimilarity on state spaces, though, the required access to transitions is expected to be

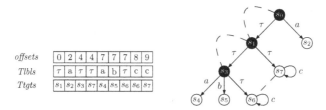

Fig. 2. An example LTS and its encoding in *offsets*, *Tlbls* and *Ttgts* arrays

irregular. This poses the challenge of reducing the number of irregular memory accesses despite of that fact.

LTS *Representation.* In order to check bisimilarity of LTSs on a GPU, we first need to find a suitable encoding of them to store the input data in the global memory. For this, we use a representation similar to those used to compactly describe sparse graphs. Fig. 2 shows an example of such an encoding of the LTS on the right. Three arrays are used to store the information. The first one, *offsets*, holds for every state i the start and end indices of its outgoing transitions in the other two arrays at *offsets*$[i]$ and *offsets*$[i + 1]$, respectively. Arrays *Tlbls* and *Ttgts* provide a list of the outgoing transitions, in particular their action labels and target states, respectively. In practice, actions are encoded by an integer, with $\tau = 0$, $a = 1$, etc. To give an example, the transitions of s_1 can be found from *offsets*$[1]$ up to *offsets*$[2]$, i.e. at positions 2 and 3, in *Tlbls* and *Ttgts*. Finally, it should be noted that the outgoing transitions of each state have been sorted by label lexicographically, with τ the smallest element. We will use this to our advantage later on, when we explain our multi-way splitting procedure.

Finally, we note that in the following, when we refer to an array entry as being *locked*, we mean that its highest bit has been set. In general, we use 32-bit integers to store data elements. Even if we reserve the highest bit of each entry, we can still refer to 2^{31} states. In a connected LTS, this means that we will also have at least $2^{31} - 1$ transitions. Since transitions take two integers to store each (in *Tlbls* and *Ttgts*), an LTS of that size would not fit in current GPUs anyway.

4   Many-Core Bisimilarity Checking

Strong Bisimilarity. The algorithm by Lee & Rajasekaran (LR) [18] is the first that has been proposed to check strong bisimilarity on SIMT architectures, and is based on KS. We discuss the main approach of it here since we will justify the choices we made for our algorithm w.r.t. LR, and since we have an experimental comparison between CUDA-implementations of LR (made by us) and the new algorithm in Section 5.

Table 1 shows an example situation when running LR on the LTS in Fig. 2. A number of arrays are used here. First of all, not listed in the table, a B

Table 1. Running LR on the LTS in Figure 2

P	$(0,s_0)$	$(0,s_3)$	$(0,s_4)$	$(1,s_1)$	$(1,s_6)$	$(2,s_2)$	$(2,s_5)$	$(2,s_7)$	-
V	0	1	2	0	1	0	1	2	-
$TSIZE$	2	3	0	2	1	0	0	1	-
$Lsrc$	$B[s_0]$	$B[s_0]$	$B[s_3]$	$B[s_3]$	$B[s_3]$	$B[s_1]$	$B[s_1]$	$B[s_6]$	$B[s_7]$
$Llbl$	τ	a	τ	a	b	τ	τ	c	c
$Lidx$	0	0	1	1	1	0	0	1	2
$Ltgt$	$B[s_1]$	$B[s_2]$	$B[s_6]$	$B[s_4]$	$B[s_5]$	$B[s_3]$	$B[s_7]$	$B[s_6]$	$B[s_7]$

array is maintained indicating to which block each state i belongs. With this, a partition array P is constructed consisting of tuples $(B[i], i)$, which is then sorted in parallel on $B[i]$ (initially, if we have a single block, no sorting is required). Next, a V array is filled assigning to each state i a block local ID between 0 and $|B[i]|$, i.e. an identifier local to the block it is in, which can be done using P. The order in which the states appear in P determines array $TSIZE$; the latter must be filled with the number of outgoing transitions of each corresponding state in P, which can be done in parallel using P and *offsets*. Finally, after obtaining absolute offsets using $TSIZE$, the L arrays are filled, listing the transitions in the LTS w.r.t. the current partition in the order of the states in P. Besides source and target block and the label, also the block local ID of the source is added in $Lidx$. Note that from L we can now directly learn the signature of each state.

Once L is filled, it is lexicographically sorted. Because the block local IDs have been included, this means that all transitions of a state are still next to each other, but now also sorted by label and target block. After removing duplicate entries in parallel, we have essentially made sure that the lists of outgoing transitions can be interpreted as sets. Then, the most interesting operation is performed, namely the comparison of signatures. For this, LR compares in parallel the signature of each state i with the one of state $i - V[i]$, i.e. of the state with block local ID 0 of the same block. This signature can directly be found using V. When the signatures are equal, nothing is done, but when they are not, a new block ID x is created and state i is assigned to it, i.e. $B[i]$ is set to x. How new block IDs should be chosen in parallel is not mentioned in [18], in fact, they split blocks sequentially, but we chose for the following mechanism: threads working on the same block and finding states that must be split off to select a new block ID first check whether $TSIZE[i - V[i]]$ is locked, i.e. whether its highest bit is set, and if not, lock it atomically. Only one thread will succeed in doing so, which will subsequently try to atomically increment a global ID counter. Once it succeeds, it stores the new value in $TSIZE[i - V[i]]$. After that, the other threads read this value and learn the new block ID.

LR is a typical SIMT application; all data is stored in arrays, and the threads manipulate these on a one-on-one basis, i.e. n threads work on arrays of size n. Moreover, LR uses a number of parallel operations, such as sorting and performing segmented scans, that are available in standard GPU libraries. For instance, we have implemented LR using the THRUST library. However, we chose to design an algorithm which is very different from this one, based on the following ideas:

1. Comparing states with a specific 'first' state is very suitable for a GPU, since it allows for threads to check locally whether their state needs to move to

another block, but we observe that this can be any state, and found a way to select such a first state, which we from now on will call a *representative*, without sorting. This allows for more coalesced memory access when threads can be assigned to consecutive states as opposed to consecutive elements of P. The order of states in P can be considered random.

2. Maintaining L requires many (expensive) memory accesses, and the involved reads and writes are not coalesced, due to the randomness imposed by the structure of the LTS. We chose to directly have each thread use the information from *Tlbls*, *Ttgts* and B concerning the involved transitions of both its assigned state and the associated representative, and construct the signatures in its local registers, which allows for fast comparisons, and reduces the memory requirements from $6 \cdot |\mathcal{S}| + 8 \cdot |\mathcal{T}|$ to $2 \cdot |\mathcal{S}| + 2 \cdot |\mathcal{T}|$.

3. If we start with a single block, which is not considered in [18], then each iteration except the last one produces exactly one new block. This does not scale well. In [16], a multi-way splitting procedure is proposed, but it is based on the entire signature of states, and not very suitable for our representative selection. We propose a multi-way splitting mechanism that is compatible.

The new algorithm. First, we will explain multi-way representative selection. In Fig. 3, part of the initial situation is shown when applying our algorithm on the LTS in Fig. 2. Initially, states are not in any block, indicated by $B[i] = $ '-'.

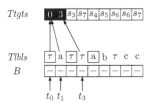

Ttgts

Tlbls
B

$t_0\ t_1\quad t_3$

Fig. 3. Representative selection

Each thread t_i checks if state s_i needs to move to a new block, which is indicated by the highest bit in *offsets*[i] being set. Then, they read a predetermined outgoing transition label of s_i. This is handled globally using variable *labelcounter*; if *labelcounter* $= j$, this means that every thread reads the label of the j-th transition. Let us call this label ℓ. Whenever $j > |\mathcal{T}(s_i)|$, we say that $\ell = 0$. Using $B[i]$ (interpreting '-' as 0) and ℓ, t_i computes a hash value $h = ((B[i] \cdot N) + \ell)$ mod $|\mathcal{T}|$, with N the number of different labels in the LTS. Next, *Ttgts* is temporarily reused to serve as a hash table, and thread i tries to atomically write a locked i to cell *Ttgts*[h]. Only one thread will succeed in doing so per cell. The one that does has now successfully promoted its state to representative of a new block, and the other threads, knowing that they have failed since they encountered a locked entry, read the representative ID from *Ttgts*[h] and store it in their B cells. Note that in general, h can be larger than $|Ttgts|$. Since we want no threads to meet in *Ttgts* that do not represent states from the same block, the selection procedure is actually done in several iterations, shifting the range of the hash table each iteration by $|Ttgts|$. This way of selecting allows using state IDs as block IDs, which is possible since the blocks are disjoint.

The selection procedure uses a form of multi-way splitting, i.e. splitting a block at once into more than two blocks, when possible, by ensuring that threads which encounter different transition labels try to atomically write to different cells in *Ttgts*. Note that in Section 3, we mentioned that the outgoing transitions of each state are in *Tlbls* sorted by label. This means that initially, if two states do not have the same first label, then they cannot be bisimilar, and can hence immediately be moved to different blocks. In the next iteration, we know that in each block B_i, all the states must have the same label on their first transition, so we focus on the second transition, and so on. Hence, in order for this to be effective, we use *labelcounter* to change the splitting criterion, which works as long as we have not reached the end of the transition list of at least one state.

Alg. 2 without the boxed code presents an overview of the entire strong bisimilarity checking procedure. We use the CUDA notation $\lll n \ggg$ to indicate that n threads execute a given kernel. Once new representatives have been selected at line 5, postprocessing is performed to recreate the original *Ttgts* array. This can be done efficiently, since the el-

---

Algorithm 2 Many-core bisimilarity checking

Require: $\mathcal{G} = \langle \mathcal{S}, \mathcal{A}, \mathcal{T}, \underline{s} \rangle$, $\pi = \{\mathcal{S}\}$

$\quad stable \leftarrow$ **false**

2: **while** $\neg stable$ **do**

$\quad\quad labelcounter \leftarrow (labelcounter + 1) \mod |\mathcal{T}|$

4: $\quad\quad device\_stable \leftarrow$ **true**

$\quad\quad selectRepresentatives \lll |\mathcal{S}| \ggg (labelcounter)$

6: $\quad\quad postprocessElection \lll |\mathcal{T}| \ggg ()$

$\quad\quad$ **while** *continue* **do**

8: $\quad\quad\quad device\_continue \leftarrow$ **false**

$\quad\quad\quad propagateBlockIDs \lll |\mathcal{S}| \ggg ()$

10: $\quad\quad\quad continue \leftarrow device\_continue$

$\quad\quad markNoninertTaus()$

12: $\quad\quad compareSignatures \lll |\mathcal{S}| \ggg ()$

$\quad\quad stable \leftarrow device\_stable$

---

ements that were removed during representative selection have been temporarily moved to the B array cells of the new representatives. At line 12, each block of threads fetches a consecutive tile of transitions from the global memory and stores it in the shared memory. Each thread i then does the following:

– It reads the outgoing transitions of s_i from the shared memory;
– It fetches $B[s_i]$ from the global memory;
– It employs its warp to fetch the transitions of $B[s_i]$ in a number of coalesced memory accesses, and stores all these transitions into its local registers;
– It looks up the block IDs of the corresponding target states;
– Finally, $sig_\pi(s_i)$ and $sig_\pi(B[s_i])$ are compared.

This procedure results in the highest bit of *offsets*$[i]$ being set, and the global variable *device_stable* being set to **false** iff the signatures are not equal. The content of *device_stable* is read by the host at line 13, after which another iteration is started or not, depending on its value.

Branching Bisimilarity. For branching bisimilarity, we need to handle the presence of inert paths, as mentioned in Section 2. Without doing so, Alg. 2 would after line 6 provide an incorrect representation of which blocks can be reached from each state, resulting in the signatures comparison at line 12 going wrong. To check branching bisimilarity, we therefore add a procedure to *propagate* block IDs over τ-transitions which can be considered inert at the current iteration. This is similar to the approach in the algorithm by Blom & Van de Pol [7].[2]

By definition, τ-transitions are inert w.r.t. a partition π iff their source and target states are in the same block. However, if we want threads to locally compare their state with the corresponding block representative, without looking beyond

---

[2] An alternative would be to try to port GV to GPUs, but GV requires several linked lists, and therefore dynamic memory allocation, making it less suitable for GPUs.

their outgoing transitions (which would lead to expensive searching through the global memory), then it cannot be ensured that source and target states are always in the same block. For example, consider the LTS in Fig. 2. Say we perform the initial representative selection without multiway splitting, and states s_1 and s_3 end up in the same block with s_1 as representative. Then a direct comparison of the two states would reveal that they have unequal signatures, even though transition $s_1 \xrightarrow{\tau} s_3$ is inert. On the other hand, $s_1 \xrightarrow{\tau} s_7$ is not inert, so these cases must be distinguishable by the checking algorithm.

To resolve this, we define the notion of a *visible* signature $\overline{sig}_\pi(s) = \{(a, \pi(s')) \mid s \xrightarrow{a} s' \wedge a \neq \tau\}$, and use the label $\bar{\tau}$ to denote a visible τ-transition. Visible τ-transitions are also included in a visible signature, but initially, all τ-transitions are invisible. This means that in our branching bisimilarity checking algorithm (for an overview, see Alg. 2 with the boxed code), we initially select representatives and compare signatures based on signatures without τ-transitions.

After representative selection, it must be checked whether τ-transitions are *possibly* π-inert, and if they are, the block IDs of their target states should be propagated to their source states, making the latter *propagating states*. The condition for a τ-transition to be possibly π-inert directly corresponds with the observation made in Section 2 that inert τ-paths must end in a state which can simulate all previously potential behaviour. The following is a relevant lemma.

Lemma 1. *A state can reach at most one block via π-inert τ-paths.*

Proof. Say that from a state s two blocks B_1, B_2 can be reached via π-inert τ-paths, leading to states $s' \in B_1$, $s'' \in B_2$. Since each subsequently discovered partition will be a refinement of π, we must have that $s' \not\bumpeq_b s''$. But then, we must have that $s \bumpeq_b s'$ and $s \bumpeq_b s''$. From the facts that $s' \not\bumpeq_b s''$ and that branching bisimilarity is an equivalence, we derive a contradiction. □

Definition 5 (Inertness condition and propagating state). *A transition $s \xrightarrow{\tau} s'$ is possibly π-inert, and s is a propagating state, iff*
  - *either s' is not propagating, and $(sig_\pi(s) \setminus \{(s, \tau, \pi(s'))\}) \subseteq \overline{sig}_\pi(s')$;*
  - *or s' is propagating, and $(sig_\pi(s) \setminus \{(s, \tau, \pi(s'))\}) \subseteq \overline{sig}_\pi(B[s'])$.*

The first alternative in Def. 5 refers to the case that the target state s' is not propagating. In that case, its visible signature should be a superset of $sig_\pi(s)$ minus τ-transitions leading to $\pi(s')$, i.e. s' should be able to simulate s. Note that this uses Lemma 1: all τ-transitions leading to blocks different from $\pi(s')$ in the signature of s are involved in the comparison, since a τ-transition to $\pi(s')$ can only be π-inert if all other τ-transitions to different blocks are not. The second alternative enables propagating results over τ-paths. If s' is propagating, then the signature of the representative $B[s']$ must be taken into account.

In Alg. 2, at lines 7-10, all possibly π-inert τ-transitions are detected, and we mark the source states as propagating using one bit. If a state s has multiple possibly π-inert τ-transitions to different blocks, we define $B[s] =$ '-' and mark s propagating. The latter is a conservative action; we refrain from propagating a block ID until we can detect a single block as being reachable via inert τ-paths.

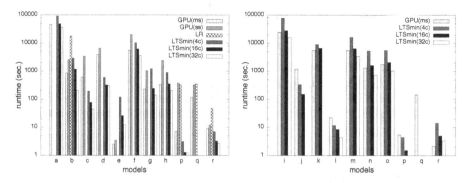

Fig. 4. Strong and branching bisimilarity checking runtimes (sec.)

When propagation finishes, τ-transitions that are not π-inert are relabelled to $\bar{\tau}$ at line 11, thereby adding them to the visible signatures. The signature comparison at line 12 now only concerns the non-propagating states.

Completeness of the algorithm follows from the inertness criterion (Section 2) and the fact that τ-transitions are conservatively marked visible (as long as we do not mark inert τ-transitions as visible, our partition has the largest branching bisimulation as a refinement). Finally, if in any iteration, a state must be moved from '-' to a block, then it must be added to a new block, i.e. one does not need to find an existing suitable block. That this is correct is shown next.

Lemma 2. *Say that state s has been marked non-propagating in iteration $i > 0$, when we have partition π. Then it should be added to a new block not in π.*

Proof. By reasoning towards a contradiction. Consider that when s is marked non-propagating, there already exists a block B' with representative t to which it should be added. Then, in iterations $j < i$, s still had at least one possibly π-inert τ-transition. Let us call the block reachable via that transition B'', and say that $sig_\pi(s) = T \cup \{(\tau, B'')\}$, with T some set of (action, block)-pairs. Because s should be added to B', we must have that t has the same signature as s, hence $sig_\pi(t) = T \cup \{(\tau, B'')\}$. But then, also t must have been propagating in $j < i$, contradicting the assumption that before i, t already represented a block.   □

Complexity of the algorithms. If we assume that we can launch $|\mathcal{S}|$ and $|\mathcal{T}|$ threads, then each kernel in Alg. 2 can be performed in $\mathrm{O}(1)$. Hence, strong bisimilarity checking can be done in $\mathrm{O}(|\mathcal{S}|)$, since worst-case, $|\mathcal{S}|$ iterations are required. In addition, branching bisimilarity checking requires worst-case a propagation procedure of $|\mathcal{S}|$ iterations, so its complexity is $\mathrm{O}(|\mathcal{S}|^2)$.

5   Experimental Results

In this section, we present some of our experimental comparisons of various GPU setups, and with the LTSMIN toolset, which is the only toolset we are aware of that offers parallel strong and branching bisimilarity checking, and therefore allows us to experimentally compare our implementations with the scalability of CPU approaches.[3] LTSMIN offers implementations of the algorithms by Blom et al. [5,6,7]. In this section, we report on a comparison with the algorithms from [5,6]. For the GPU experiments, we used an NVIDIA K20m with 5 GB memory on a machine with an INTEL E5-2620 2.0 GHz CPU running CENTOS LINUX. For the CPU experiments with LTSMIN 2.0, we used a machine with an AMD OPTERON 6172 processor with 48 cores, 192 GB RAM, running DEBIAN 6.0.7.

Table 2. Benchmark set

id	Model	#st.	#tr.	#ss	#sb
a	BRP250	219m	266m	101m	n.a.
b	coin8.3	87m	583m	20m	n.a.
c	cwi_33949	33m	165m	122k	n.a.
d	cwi_7838	8m	59m	1m	n.a.
e	diningcrypt14	18m	164m	18m	n.a.
f	firewire_dl800.36	129m	294m	34m	n.a.
g	mutualex7.13	76m	654m	76m	n.a.
h	SCSI_C_6	74m	404m	74m	n.a.
i	BRP250 h2	219m	266m	n.a.	19k
j	cwi_33949 h1	33m	165m	n.a.	12k
k	cwi_33949 h2	32m	158m	n.a.	3k
l	diningcrypt14 h2	2m	16m	n.a.	497k
m	firewire_dl800.36 h2	129m	294m	n.a.	26m
n	mutualex7.13 h1	76m	613m	n.a.	41m
o	mutualex7.13 h2	76m	562m	n.a.	32m
p	vasy_6020	6m	19m	7k	256
q	vasy_6120	6m	11m	6k	349
r	vasy_8082	8m	43m	408	290

Table 2 shows the characteristics of each LTS, namely 1) number of states, 2) number of transitions, 3) number of states in the strongly reduced LTS, and 4) number of states in the branching reduced LTS. Note that in some cases, no reduction can be achieved, which is an interesting worst-case scenario for our experiments. The models the LTSs stem from have been taken from various sources, namely the BEEM database [21], the CADP toolbox [13], the MCRL2 toolset [11], and the website of PRISM.[4] To produce cases for branching bisimilarity checking, we wrote a tool to automatically relabel a predefined number of transitions to τ. In the cases suffixed with h1 roughly 25% of the transitions have the label τ, while in the h2 LTSs this is 50%.

Fig. 4 presents the runtimes we measured (in seconds) for strong and branching bisimilarity checking, on the left and the right, respectively. We used the following setups: a CUDA implementation of our algorithms with (GPU(ms)) and without (GPU(ss)) multi-way splitting, a CUDA-version of LR, and the LTSMIN tool LTSMIN-REDUCE-DIST running with 4, 16, and 32 cores, which we refer to as LTSMIN from now on. In those cases where no result is given for a particular tool and model, the tool ran either out of memory (the CPU tools) or out of time (the GPU tools) on the aforementioned machine.

First of all, considering our algorithm, the positive effect of multiway splitting is apparent, it can speed up the checking by 2 to 50 times, and as expected, since it allows the checking to finish in fewer iterations. Second of all, notice that LR is clearly slower than our approach, in those cases that LR could actually be run, due to its higher memory requirements. These findings support

---

[3] For a list of all the experiments, and the relevant source code and models, see http://www.win.tue.nl/~awijs/GPUreduce

[4] http://www.prismmodelchecker.org

the hypothesis that our new approach performs better than LR on modern GPU architectures. In a number of cases, our tool achieves runtimes comparable to the 16-core LTSMIN setup. Given that LTSMIN scales nicely, this is encouraging. Since the multiway splitting in our approach is more limited to the one in LTSMIN, involving a specific transition label as opposed to entire signatures, our tool in particular performs worse when LTSMIN can aggressively use multiway splitting. Finally, it is worth noting that sometimes, LTSMIN runs out of memory. Storing signatures explicitly is more memory consuming than recreating them every time, but of course, one needs the parallel computation power for the recreation not to be a drawback. Since LTSMIN does not exploit shared memory, but keeps the memory separated per worker, this also means that increasing the number of workers tends to increase the presence of redundant information.

6 Related Work

Blom et al. [5,6,7,19] use the aforementioned signatures to distinguish states for distributed bisimilarity checking. In each iteration, the signatures are placed in a hash table, and used as block IDs to refine the partition. On GPUs, however, storing full signatures is very hard, requiring dynamic memory allocation.

Zhang & Smolka [28] propose a parallelisation of KS where threads communicate via message-passing. Such an approach cannot easily be migrated to the GPU setting, since message-passing among threads running on the same GPU does not naturally fit the GPU computation model. On the other hand, one could use message passing between GPUs that together try to check bisimilarity.

Jeong et al. [16] propose a parallel KS algorithm along the lines of [18] with multi-way splitting, but there is a probability that wrong results are obtained.

7 Conclusions

We presented new algorithms to perform strong and branching bisimilarity checking on GPUs. Experiments demonstrate that significant speedups can be achieved. As future work, we will try to further optimise the algorithms. There is still potential to avoid signature comparisons in specific cases. Furthermore, we will consider employing GPUs for other applications of model checking, for instance to find near-optimal schedules (e.g. [26]) and quantitative analysis (e.g. [25]).

References

1. Aho, A., Hopcroft, J., Ullman, J.: The Design and Analysis of Computer Algorithms. Addison-Wesley (1974)
2. Baier, C., Katoen, J.P.: Principles of Model Checking. The MIT Press (2008)
3. Barnat, J., Bauch, P., Brim, L., Češka, M.: Designing Fast LTL Model Checking Algorithms for Many-Core GPUs. J. Parall. Distrib. Comput. 72, 1083–1097 (2012)
4. Bartocci, E., DeFrancisco, R., Smolka, S.: Towards a GPGPU-parallel SPIN Model Checker. In: SPIN, pp. 87–96. ACM (2014)

5. Blom, S., Orzan, S.: Distributed Branching Bisimulation Reduction of State Spaces. In: FMICS. ENTCS, vol. 80, pp. 109–123. Elsevier (2003)
6. Blom, S., Orzan, S.: A Distributed Algorithm for Strong Bisimulation Reduction of State Spaces. STTT 7(1), 74–86 (2005)
7. Blom, S., van de Pol, J.: Distributed Branching Bisimulation Minimization by Inductive Signatures. In: PDMC. EPTCS, vol. 14, pp. 32–46. Open Publishing Association (2009)
8. Bošnački, D., Edelkamp, S., Sulewski, D., Wijs, A.: GPU-PRISM: An Extension of PRISM for General Purpose Graphics Processing Units. In: PDMC 2010, pp. 17–19. IEEE (2010)
9. Bošnački, D., Edelkamp, S., Sulewski, D., Wijs, A.: Parallel Probabilistic Model Checking on General Purpose Graphic Processors. STTT 13(1), 21–35 (2011)
10. Browne, M., Clarke, E.M., Grumberg, O.: Characterizing Finite Kripke Structures in Propositional Temporal Logic. TCS 59, 115–131 (1988)
11. Cranen, S., Groote, J.F., Keiren, J.J.A., Stappers, F.P.M., de Vink, E.P., Wesselink, W., Willemse, T.A.C.: An Overview of the mCRL2 Toolset and Its Recent Advances. In: Piterman, N., Smolka, S.A. (eds.) TACAS 2013. LNCS, vol. 7795, pp. 199–213. Springer, Heidelberg (2013)
12. De Nicola, R., Vaandrager, F.: Three Logics for Branching Bisimulation. Journal of the ACM 42(2), 458–487 (1995)
13. Garavel, H., Lang, F., Mateescu, R., Serwe, W.: CADP 2010: A Toolbox for the Construction and Analysis of Distributed Processes. In: Abdulla, P.A., Leino, K.R.M. (eds.) TACAS 2011. LNCS, vol. 6605, pp. 372–387. Springer, Heidelberg (2011)
14. van Glabbeek, R.J., Weijland, W.P.: Branching Time and Abstraction in Bisimulation Semantics. Journal of the ACM 43(3), 555–600 (1996)
15. Groote, J., Vaandrager, F.: An Efficient Algorithm for Branching Bisimulation and Stuttering Equivalence. In: Paterson, M. (ed.) ICALP 1990. LNCS, vol. 443, pp. 626–638. Springer, Heidelberg (1990)
16. Jeong, C., Kim, Y., Oh, Y., Kim, H.: A Faster Parallel Implementation of the Kanellakis-Smolka Algorithm for Bisimilarity Checking. In: ICS (1998)
17. Kanellakis, P., Smolka, S.: CCS Expressions, Finite State Processes, and Three Problems of Equivalence. In: PODC, pp. 228–240. ACM (1983)
18. Lee, I., Rajasekaran, S.: A Parallel Algorithm for Relational Coarsest Partition Problems and Its Implementation. In: Dill, D.L. (ed.) CAV 1994. LNCS, vol. 818, pp. 404–414. Springer, Heidelberg (1994)
19. Orzan, S.: On Distributed Verification and Verified Distribution. Ph.D. thesis, Free University of Amsterdam (2004)
20. Paige, R., Tarjan, R.: A Linear Time Algorithm to Solve the Single Function Coarsest Partition Problem. In: Paredaens, J. (ed.) ICALP 1984. LNCS, vol. 172, pp. 371–379. Springer, Heidelberg (1984)
21. Pelánek, R.: BEEM: Benchmarks for Explicit Model Checkers. In: Bošnački, D., Edelkamp, S. (eds.) SPIN 2007. LNCS, vol. 4595, pp. 263–267. Springer, Heidelberg (2007)
22. Wijs, A.J., Bošnački, D.: Improving GPU Sparse Matrix-Vector Multiplication for Probabilistic Model Checking. In: Donaldson, A., Parker, D. (eds.) SPIN 2012. LNCS, vol. 7385, pp. 98–116. Springer, Heidelberg (2012)
23. Wijs, A., Bošnački, D.: GPUexplore: Many-Core On-The-Fly State Space Exploration Using GPUs. In: Ábrahám, E., Havelund, K. (eds.) TACAS 2014. LNCS, vol. 8413, pp. 233–247. Springer, Heidelberg (2014)

24. Wijs, A., Katoen, J.-P., Bošnački, D.: GPU-Based Graph Decomposition into Strongly Connected and Maximal End Components. In: Biere, A., Bloem, R. (eds.) CAV 2014. LNCS, vol. 8559, pp. 310–326. Springer, Heidelberg (2014)
25. Wijs, A.J., Lisser, B.: Distributed Extended Beam Search for Quantitative Model Checking. In: Edelkamp, S., Lomuscio, A. (eds.) MoChArt IV. LNCS (LNAI), vol. 4428, pp. 166–184. Springer, Heidelberg (2007)
26. Wijs, A., van de Pol, J., Bortnik, E.: Solving Scheduling Problems by Untimed Model Checking - The Clinical Chemical Analyser Case Study. In: FMICS, pp. 54–61. ACM (2005)
27. Wu, Z., Liu, Y., Liang, Y., Sun, J.: GPU Accelerated Counterexample Generation in LTL Model Checking. In: Merz, S., Pang, J. (eds.) ICFEM 2014. LNCS, vol. 8829, pp. 413–429. Springer, Heidelberg (2014)
28. Zhang, S., Smolka, S.: Towards Efficient Parallelization of Equivalence Checking Algorithms. In: FORTE, North-Holland. IFIP Transactions, vol. C-10, pp. 121–135 (1992)

Fairness for Infinite-State Systems

Byron Cook[1], Heidy Khlaaf[1], and Nir Piterman[2]

[1] University College London, London, UK
[2] University of Leicester, Leicester, UK

Abstract. In this paper we introduce the first known tool for symbolically proving *fair*-CTL properties of (infinite-state) integer programs. Our solution is based on a reduction to existing techniques for fairness-free CTL model checking via the use of infinite non-deterministic branching to symbolically partition fair from unfair executions. We show the viability of our approach in practice using examples drawn from device drivers and algorithms utilizing shared resources.

1 Introduction

In model checking, fairness allows us to bridge between linear-time (*a.k.a.* trace-based) and branching-time (*a.k.a.* state-based) reasoning. Fairness is crucial, for example, to Vardi & Wolper's automata-theoretic technique for LTL verification [25]. Furthermore, when proving state-based CTL properties, we must often use fairness to model trace-based assumptions about the environment both in a sequential setting, and when reasoning about concurrent environments, where fairness is used to abstract away the scheduler.

In this paper we introduce the first-known fair-CTL model checking technique for (infinite-state) integer programs. Our solution reduces fair-CTL to fairness-free CTL using prophecy variables to encode a partition of fair from unfair paths. Cognoscenti may at first find this result surprising. It is well known that fair termination of Turing machines cannot be reduced to termination of Turing machines. The former is Σ_1^1-complete and the latter is RE-complete [18].[1] For similar reasons fair-CTL model checking of Turing machines cannot be reduced to CTL model checking of Turing machines. The key to our reduction is the use of infinite non-deterministic branching when model checking fairness-free CTL. As a consequence, in the context of infinite branching, fair and fairness-free CTL are equally difficult (and similarly for termination).

Motivation. Current techniques for model checking CTL properties provide no support for verification of fair-CTL, thus excluding a large set of branching-time liveness properties necessitating fairness. These properties are often imperative to verifying the liveness of systems such as Windows kernel APIs that acquire resources and APIs that release resources. Below are properties which can be expressed in fair-CTL, but not CTL nor LTL. We write these properties in CTL*,

---

[1] Sometimes termination refers to *universal termination*, which entails termination for *all* possible inputs. This is a harder problem and is co-RE^{RE}-complete.

© Springer-Verlag Berlin Heidelberg 2015
C. Baier and C. Tinelli (Eds.): TACAS 2015, LNCS 9035, pp. 384–398, 2015.
DOI: 10.1007/978-3-662-46681-0_30

a superset of both CTL and LTL[2]. For brevity, we write Ω for $\mathsf{GF}p \to \mathsf{GF}q$. A state property is indicated by φ (i.e., a combination of assertions on the states of the program) and p and q are subsets of program states, constituting our fairness requirement (infinitely often p implies infinitely often q).

The property $\mathsf{E}[\Omega \wedge \mathsf{G}\varphi]$ generalizes fair non-termination, that is, there exists an infinite fair computation all of whose states satisfy the property φ. The property $\mathsf{A}[\Omega \to \mathsf{G}[\varphi_1 \to \mathsf{A}(\Omega \to \mathsf{F}\varphi_2)]]$ indicates that on every fair path, every φ_1 state is later followed by a φ_2 state. We will later verify it for a Windows device driver, indicating that a lock will always eventually be released in the case that a call to a lock occurs, provided that whenever we continue to call a Windows API repeatedly, it will eventually return a desired value (fairness). Similarly, $\mathsf{A}[\Omega \to \mathsf{G}[\varphi_1 \to \mathsf{A}(\Omega \to \mathsf{FE}(\Omega \wedge \mathsf{G}\varphi_2))]]$ dictates that on every fair path whenever a φ_1 state is reached, on all possible futures there is a state which is a possible fair future and φ_2 is always satisfied. For example, one may wish to verify that there will be a possible active fair continuation of a server, and that it will continue to effectively serve if sockets are successfully opened.[3]

Furthermore, fair-CTL model checking is rudimentary to the well known technique of verifying LTL in the finite-state setting [25]. A fair-CTL model checker for infinite-state systems would thus enable us to implement the automata-theoretic approach to linear-time model checking by reducing it to fair-CTL model checking as is done in the finite-state setting.

Fairness is also crucial to the verification of concurrent programs, as well-established techniques such as [7] reduce concurrent liveness verification to a sequential verification task. Thread-modular reductions of concurrent to sequential programs often require a concept of fairness when the resulting sequential proof obligation is a progress property such as wait-freedom, lock-freedom, or obstruction-freedom. Moreover, obstruction freedom cannot be expressed in LTL without additional assumptions. With our technique we can build tools for automatically proving these sequential reductions using fair-CTL model checking.

Related Work. Support for fairness in finite and other decidable settings has been well studied. Tools for these settings (*e.g.* NuSMV for finite state systems [5,6], Moped and PuMoc for pushdown automata [23,24], Prism for probabilistic timed automata [19], and Uppaal for timed automata [15]) provide support for fairness constraints. Proof systems for the verification of temporal properties of fair systems (e.g., [3], [21]) also exist. However, such systems require users to construct auxiliary assertions and participate in the proof process.

Contrarily, we seek to automatically verify the undecidable general class of (infinite-state) integer programs supporting both control-sensitive and numerical properties. Additionally, some of these tools do not fully support CTL model checking, as they do not reliably support mixtures of nested universal/existential path quantifiers, etc. The tools which consider full CTL and the general class of

---

[2] These properties expressed in terms of the fair path quantifiers E_f and A_f are $\mathsf{E}_f \mathsf{G}\varphi, \mathsf{A}_f \mathsf{G}(\varphi_1 \to \mathsf{A}_f \mathsf{F}\varphi_2)$, and $\mathsf{A}_f \mathsf{G}(\varphi_1 \to \mathsf{A}_f \mathsf{F} \mathsf{E}_f \mathsf{G}\varphi_2)$, respectively.

[3] Notice that our definition of fair CTL considers finite paths. Thus, all path quantifications above range over finite paths as well.

integer programs as we do are [2], [10], and [12]. However, these tools provide no support for verifying fair-CTL.

When we consider the general class of integer programs, the use of infinite non-determinism to encode fairness policies has been previously utilized by Olderog *et al.* [1]. However, they do not rely on nondeterminism alone but require refinement of the introduced nondeterminism to derive concrete schedulers which enforce a given fairness policy. Thus, their technique relies on the ability to force the occurrence of fair events whenever needed by the reduction. We support general fairness constraints, rather than just fair scheduling. The ability to force the occurrence of fair events is too strong for our needs. Indeed, in the context of model checking we rely on the program continuing a normal execution until the "natural" fulfillment of the fairness constraint.

An analysis of fair discrete systems which separates reasoning pertaining to fairness and well-foundedness through the use of inductive transition invariants was introduced in [20]. Their strategy is the basis of the support for fairness added to TERMINATOR [8]. However, this approach relies on the computation of transition invariants [22], whereas our approach does not. We have recently shown that, in practice, state-based techniques that circumvent the computation of transition invariants perform significantly better [14]. Additionally, a technique utilized to reduce LTL model checking to fairness-free CTL model checking introduced by [11] is largely incomplete, as it does not sufficiently determinize all possible branching traces. Note that these methodologies are used to verify fairness and liveness constraints expressible within linear temporal logic, and are thus not applicable to verify fair branching-time logic or branching-time logic. Indeed, this was part of our motivation for studying alternative approaches to model checking with fairness.

2 Preliminaries

Transition Systems. A transition system is $M = (S, S_0, R, L)$, where S is a countable set of states, $S_0 \subseteq S$ a set of initial states, $R \subseteq S \times S$ a transition relation, and $L : S \to 2^{AP}$ a labeling function associating a set of propositions with every state $s \in S$. A *trace* or a *path* of a transition system is either a finite or infinite sequence of states. The set of infinite traces starting at $s \in S$, denoted by $\Pi_\infty(s)$, is the set of sequences $(s_0, s_1, \ldots)$ such that $s_0 = s$ and $\forall i \geq 0. (s_i, s_{i+1}) \in R$. The set of finite traces starting at $s \in S$, denoted by $\Pi_f(s)$, is the set of sequences $(s_0, s_1, \ldots, s_j)$ such that $s_0 = s$, $j \geq 0$, $\forall i < j. (s_i, s_{i+1}) \in R$, and $\forall s \in S. (s_j, s) \notin R$. Finally, the set of maximal traces starting at s, denoted by $\Pi_m(s)$, is the set $\Pi_\infty(s) \cup \Pi_f(s)$. For a path π, we denote the length of said path by $|\pi|$, which is ω in case that π is infinite.

Computation Tree Logic (CTL). We are interested in verifying state-based properties in computation tree logic (CTL). Our definition of CTL differs slightly from previous work, as it takes into account finite (maximal) paths. This semantics allows us to specify properties such as termination without requiring special

$$\frac{\alpha(s)}{M, s \models_m \alpha} \quad \frac{\neg\alpha(s)}{M, s \models_m \neg\alpha}$$

$$\frac{M, s \models \varphi_1 \quad M, s \models \varphi_2}{M, s \models_m \varphi_1 \wedge \varphi_2} \quad \frac{M, s \models \varphi_1 \vee M, s \models \varphi_2}{M, s \models_m \varphi_1 \vee \varphi_2}$$

$$\frac{\forall \pi = (s_0, s_1, \ldots) \in \Pi_m(s).\, M, s_1 \models \varphi}{M, s \models_m \mathsf{AX}\varphi} \quad \frac{\exists \pi = (s_0, s_1, \ldots) \in \Pi_m(s).\, M, s_1 \models \varphi}{M, s \models_m \mathsf{EX}\varphi}$$

$$\frac{\begin{array}{c}\forall \pi = (s_0, s_1, \ldots) \in \Pi_m(s).\, (\forall i \in [0, |\pi|).\, M, s_i \models \varphi_1) \vee \\ (\exists j \in [0, |\pi|).\, M, s_j \models \varphi_2 \wedge \forall i \in [0, j).\, M, s_i \models \varphi_1)\end{array}}{M, s \models_m \mathsf{A}[\varphi_1 \mathsf{W} \varphi_2]} \quad \frac{\begin{array}{c}\forall \pi = (s_0, s_1, \ldots) \in \Pi_m(s). \\ (\exists j \in [0, |\pi|).\, M, s_j \models \varphi)\end{array}}{M, s \models_m \mathsf{AF}\varphi}$$

$$\frac{\begin{array}{c}\exists \pi = (s_0, s_1, \ldots) \in \Pi_m(s). \\ (\exists j \in [0, |\pi|).\, M, s_j \models \varphi_2 \wedge \forall i \in [0, j).\, M, s_i \models \varphi_1)\end{array}}{M, s \models_m \mathsf{E}[\varphi_1 \mathsf{U} \varphi_2]} \quad \frac{\begin{array}{c}\exists \pi = (s_0, s_1, \ldots) \in \Pi_m(s). \\ (\forall i \in [0, |\pi|).\, M, s_i \models \varphi)\end{array}}{M, s \models_m \mathsf{EG}\varphi}$$

Fig. 1. Semantics of CTL: $\models_m$

atomic propositions to hold at program exit points, as proposed by Cook *et al.* in [13], and to reason about a transformation that introduces many finite paths.

A CTL formula is of the form:

$$\varphi ::= \alpha \mid \neg\alpha \mid \varphi \wedge \varphi \mid \varphi \vee \varphi \mid \mathsf{AX}\varphi \mid \mathsf{AF}\varphi \mid \mathsf{A}[\varphi \mathsf{W}\varphi] \mid \mathsf{EX}\varphi \mid \mathsf{EG}\varphi \mid \mathsf{E}[\varphi \mathsf{U}\varphi],$$

where $\alpha \in AP$ is an atomic proposition. We assume that formulae are written in negation normal form, in which negation only occurs next to atomic propositions. We introduce $\mathsf{AG}, \mathsf{AU}, \mathsf{EF}$, and EW as syntactic sugar as usual. A formula is in ACTL if it uses only universal operators, i.e., $\mathsf{AX}, \mathsf{AW}, \mathsf{AF}, \mathsf{AU}$, or AG.

Fig. 1 defines when a CTL property φ holds in a state $s \in S$ of a transition system M. We say that φ holds in M, denoted $M \models_m \varphi$, if $\forall s \in S_0.\, M, s \models_m \varphi$.

Fair CTL. For a transition system M, a fairness condition is $\Omega = (p, q)$, where $p, q \subseteq S$. When fairness is part of the transition system we denote it as $M = (S, S_0, R, L, \Omega)$. We still include Ω as a separate component in transformations and algorithms for emphasis. We freely confuse between assertions over program variables and sets of states that satisfy them. An infinite path π is unfair under Ω if states from p occur infinitely often along π but states from q occur finitely often. Otherwise, π is fair. The condition Ω denotes a strong fairness constraint. Weak fairness constraints can be trivially expressed by $\Omega = (\mathsf{true}, q)$, that is, states from q must occur infinitely often. Equivalently, π is fair if it satisfies the LTL formula $\pi \models (\mathsf{GF}p \rightarrow \mathsf{GF}q)$. For a transition system $M = (S, S_0, R, L, \Omega)$, an infinite path π, we denote $M, \pi \models \Omega$ if π is fair [17]. We consider strong fairness with one pair of sets of states. Extending our results to strong fairness over multiple pairs is simple and omitted for clarity of exposition.

For a transition system M and a CTL property φ, the definition of when φ holds in a state $s \in S$ is defined as in Fig. 1 except that $\Pi_m(s)$ is redefined to be $\Pi_f \cup \{\pi \in \Pi_\infty \mid M, \pi \models \Omega\}$. We use the notation $\models_{\Omega_+}$ when expressing fairness,

$$\textsc{Fair}((S, S_0, R, L), (p, q)) \triangleq (S_\Omega, S_\Omega^0, R_\Omega, L_\Omega) \text{ where}$$

$$
\begin{aligned}
S_\Omega &= S \times \mathbb{N} \\
R_\Omega &= \{((s, n), (s', n')) \mid (s, s') \in R\} \wedge \left(\begin{array}{c} (\neg p \wedge n' \leq n) \vee \\ (p \wedge n' < n) \vee \\ q \end{array}\right) \\
S_\Omega^0 &= S^0 \times \mathbb{N} \\
L_\Omega(s, n) &= L(s)
\end{aligned}
$$

Fig. 2. FAIR takes a system (S, S_0, R, L) and a fairness constraint (p, q) where $p, q \subseteq S$, and returns a new system $(S_\Omega, S_\Omega^0, R_\Omega, L_\Omega)$. Note that $n \geq 0$ is implicit, as $n \in \mathbb{N}$.

that is, we say that φ holds in M, denoted by $M \models_{\Omega_+} \varphi$, if $\forall s \in S_0. M, s \models_{\Omega_+} \varphi$. When clear from the context, we may omit M and simply write $s \models_{\Omega_+} \varphi$ or $s \models_m \varphi$.

3   Fair-CTL Model Checking

In this section we present a procedure for reducing fair-CTL model checking to CTL model checking. The procedure builds on a transformation of infinite-state programs by adding a prophecy variable that truncates unfair paths. We start by presenting the transformation, followed by a program's adaptation for using said transformation, and subsequently the model-checking procedure.

In Fig. 2, we propose a reduction $\textsc{Fair}(M, \Omega)$ that encodes an instantiation of the fairness constraint within a transition system. When given a transition system (S, S_0, R, L, Ω), where $\Omega = (p, q)$ is a strong-fairness constraint, $\textsc{Fair}(M, \Omega)$ returns a new transition system (without fairness) that, through the use of a prophecy variable n, infers all possible paths that satisfy the fairness constraint, while avoiding all paths violating the fairness policy. Intuitively, n is decreased whenever a transition imposing $p \wedge n' < n$ is taken. Since $n \in \mathbb{N}$, n cannot decrease infinitely often, thus enforcing the eventual invalidation of the transition $p \wedge n' < n$. Therefore, R_Ω would only allow a transition to proceed if q holds or $\neg p \wedge n' \leq n$ holds. That is, either q occurs infinitely often or p will occur finitely often. Note that a q-transition imposes no constraints on n', which effectively resets n' to an arbitrary value. Recall that extending our results to multiple fairness constraints is simple and omitted for clarity of exposition.

The conversion of M with fairness constraint Ω to $\textsc{Fair}(M, \Omega)$ involves the truncation of paths due to the wrong estimation of the number of p-s until q. This means that $\textsc{Fair}(M, \Omega)$ can include (maximal) finite paths that are prefixes of unfair infinite paths. So when model checking CTL we have to ensure that these paths do not interfere with the validity of our model checking procedure. Hence, we distinguish between maximal (finite) paths that occur in M and those introduced by our reduction. We do this by adding a proposition t to mark all original "valid" termination states prior to the reduction in Fig. 2 and by adjusting the CTL specification. These are presented in Section 3.3. We first provide high-level understanding of our approach through an example.

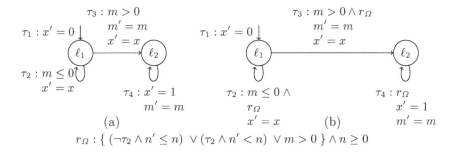

$$r_\Omega : \{ (\neg\tau_2 \wedge n' \leq n) \vee (\tau_2 \wedge n' < n) \vee m > 0 \} \wedge n \geq 0$$

Fig. 3. Reducing a transition system with the fair CTL property $\mathsf{AG}(x = 0 \to \mathsf{AF}(x = 1))$ and the fairness constraint $\mathsf{GF}\ \tau_2 \to \mathsf{GF}\ m > 0$. The original transition system is represented in (a), followed by the application of our fairness reduction in (b).

3.1 Illustrative Example

Consider the example in Fig. 3 for the fair CTL property $\mathsf{AG}(x = 0 \to \mathsf{AF}(x = 1))$ and the fairness constraint $\mathsf{GF}\ \tau_2 \to \mathsf{GF}\ m > 0$ for the initial transition system introduced in (a). We demonstrate the resulting transformation for this infinite-state program, which allows us to reduce fair model checking to model checking. By applying $\textsc{Fair}(M, \Omega)$ from Fig. 2, we obtain (b) where each original transition, τ_2, τ_3, and τ_4, are adjoined with restrictions such that $\{(\neg\tau_2 \wedge n' \leq n) \vee (\tau_2 \wedge n' < n) \vee m > 0 \} \wedge n \geq 0$ holds. That is, we wish to restrict our transition relations such that if τ_2 is visited infinitely often, then the variable m must be positive infinitely often. In τ_2, the unconstrained variable m indicates that the variable m is being assigned to a nondeterministic value, thus with every iteration of the loop, m acquires a new value. In the original transition system, τ_2 can be taken infinitely often given said non-determinism, however in (b), such a case is not possible. The transition τ_2 in (b) now requires that n be decreased on every iteration. Since $n \in \mathbb{N}$, n cannot be decreased infinitely often, causing the eventual restriction to the transition τ_2. Such an incidence is categorized as a finite path that is a prefix of some unfair infinite paths. As previously mentioned, we will later discuss how such paths are disregarded. This leaves only paths where the prophecy variable "guessed" correctly. That is, it prophesized a value such that τ_3 is reached, thus allowing our property to hold.

3.2 Prefixes of Infinite Paths

We explain how to distinguish between maximal (finite) paths that occur in M, and those that are prefixes of unfair infinite paths introduced by our reduction. Consider a transition system $M = (S, S_0, R, L, \Omega)$, where $\Omega = (p, q)$, and let φ be a CTL formula. Let t be an atomic proposition not appearing in L or φ. The transformation that marks "valid" termination states is $\textsc{Term}(M, t) = (S, S_0, R', L', \Omega')$, where $R' = R \cup \{(s, s) \mid \forall s'.(s, s') \notin R\}$, $\Omega' = (p, q \vee t)$ and for a state s we set $L'(s) = L(s) \cup \{t\}$ if $\forall s'\ .\ (s, s') \notin R$ and $L'(s) = L(s)$ otherwise.

$$\text{TERM}(\alpha, t) ::= \alpha$$
$$\text{TERM}(\varphi_1 \wedge \varphi_2, t) ::= \text{TERM}(\varphi_1, t) \wedge \text{TERM}(\varphi_2, t)$$
$$\text{TERM}(\varphi_1 \vee \varphi_2, t) ::= \text{TERM}(\varphi_1, t) \vee \text{TERM}(\varphi_2, t)$$
$$\text{TERM}(\text{EX}\varphi, t) ::= \neg t \wedge \text{EX}(\text{TERM}(\varphi, t))$$
$$\text{TERM}(\text{AX}\varphi, t) ::= t \vee \text{AX}(\text{TERM}(\varphi, t))$$
$$\text{TERM}(\text{EG}\varphi, t) ::= \text{EG}\,\text{TERM}(\varphi, t)$$
$$\text{TERM}(\text{AF}\varphi, t) ::= \text{AF}\,\text{TERM}(\varphi, t)$$
$$\text{TERM}(\text{A}[\varphi_1 \,\text{W}\, \varphi_2], t) ::= \text{A}[\text{TERM}(\varphi_1, t) \,\text{W}\, \text{TERM}(\varphi_2, t)]$$
$$\text{TERM}(\text{E}[\varphi_1 \,\text{U}\, \varphi_2], t) ::= \text{E}[\text{TERM}(\varphi_1, t) \,\text{U}\, \text{TERM}(\varphi_2, t)]$$

Fig. 4. Transformation $\text{TERM}(\varphi, t)$

That is, we eliminate all finite paths in $\text{TERM}(M, t)$ by instrumenting self loops and adding the proposition t on all terminal states. The fairness constraint is adjusted to include paths that end in such states. We now adjust the CTL formula φ that we wish to verify on M. Recall that t does not appear in φ. Now let $\text{TERM}(\varphi, t)$ denote the CTL formula transformation in Fig. 4.

The combination of the two transformations maintains the validity of a CTL formula in a given system.

Theorem 1. $M \models_{\Omega_+} \varphi \Leftrightarrow \text{TERM}(M, t) \models_{\Omega_+} \text{TERM}(\varphi, t)$

Proof Sketch (full proof in [9]). For every fair path of $\text{TERM}(M, t)$, we show that it corresponds to a maximal path in M and vice versa. The proof then proceeds by induction on the structure of the formula. For existential formulas, witnesses are translated between the models. For universal formulas, we consider arbitrary paths and translate them between the models.   □

After having marked the "valid" termination points in M by using the transformation $\text{TERM}(M, t)$, we must ensure that our fair-CTL model-checking procedure ignores "invalid" finite paths in $\text{FAIR}(M, \Omega)$. The finite paths that need to be removed from consideration are those that arise by wrong prediction of the prophecy variable n. The formula $\text{term} = \text{AFAX false}$ holds in a state s iff all paths from s are finite. We denote its negation EGEX true by $\neg\text{term}$. Intuitively, when considering a state (s, n) of $\text{FAIR}(M, \Omega)$, if (s, n) satisfies term, then (s, n) is part of a wrong prediction. If (s, n) satisfies $\neg\text{term}$, then (s, n) is part of a correct prediction. Further on, we will set up our model checking technique such that universal path formulas ignore violations that occur on terminating paths (which correspond to wrong predictions) and existential path formulas use only non-terminating paths (which correspond to correct predictions).

3.3   Fair-CTL Model Checking

We use $\text{FAIR}(M, \Omega)$ to handle fair-CTL model checking. Our procedure employs an existing CTL model checking algorithm for infinite-state systems. We assume that the CTL model checking algorithm returns an assertion characterizing all

```
1  let FAIRCTL(M, Ω, φ) : assertion =      22
2                                            23    | A Fφ₁ →
3      match(φ) with                        24        φ' = AF(a_φ₁ ∨ term)
4      | Q φ₁ OP φ₂                          25    | A Xφ₁ →
5      | φ₁ bool_OP φ₂ →                     26        φ' = AX(a_φ₁ ∨ term)
6          a_φ₁ = FAIRCTL(M, Ω, φ₁);         27    | φ₁ bool_OP φ₂ →
7          a_φ₂ = FAIRCTL(M, Ω, φ₂)          28        φ' = a_φ₁ bool_OP a_φ₂
8      | Q OP φ₁ →                           29    | α →
9          a_φ₁ = FAIRCTL(M, Ω, φ₁)          30        φ' = a_φ₁
10     | α →                                31
11         a_φ₁ = α                          32    M' = FAIR(M, Ω)
12                                           33    a = CTL(M', φ')
13     match(φ) with                        34
14     | E φ₁ U φ₂ →                         35    match(φ) with
15         φ' = E[a_φ₁ U(a_φ₂ ∧ ¬term)]      36    | E φ' →
16     | E Gφ₁ →                             37        return ∃n ≥ 0 . a
17         φ' = EG(a_φ₁ ∧ ¬term)             38    | A φ' →
18     | E Xφ₁ →                             39        return ∀n ≥ 0 . a
19         φ' = EX(a_φ₁ ∧ ¬term)             40    | _ →
20     | A φ₁ W φ₂ →                         41        return a
21         φ' = A[a_φ₁ W(a_φ₂ ∨ term)]
```

Fig. 5. Our procedure FAIRCTL(M, Ω, φ) which employs both an existing CTL model checker and the reduction FAIR(M, Ω). An assertion characterizing the states in which φ holds under the fairness constraint Ω is returned.

```
1  let VERIFY(M, Ω, φ) : bool =
2
3      a = FAIRCTL(TERM(M, t), Ω, TERM(φ, t))
4      return S₀ ⇒ a
```

Fig. 6. CTL model checking procedure VERIFY, which utilizes the subroutine in Fig. 5 to verify if a CTL property φ holds over M under the fairness constraints Ω

the states in which a CTL formula holds. Tools proposed by Beyene *et al.* [2] and Cook *et al.* [10] support this functionality. We denote such CTL verification tools by CTL(M, φ), where M is a transition system and φ a CTL formula.

Our procedure adapting FAIR(M, Ω) is presented in Fig. 5. Given a transition system M, a fairness constraint Ω, and a CTL formula φ, FAIRCTL returns an assertion characterizing the states in which φ fairly holds. Initially, our procedure is called by VERIFY in Fig. 6 where M and φ are initially transformed by TERM(M, t) and TERM(φ, t) discussed in Section 3.2. That is, TERM(M, t) marks all "valid" termination states in M to distinguish between maximal (finite) paths that occur in M and those introduced by our reduction. TERM(φ, t) allows us to disregard all aforementioned finite paths, as we only consider infinite paths, which correspond to a fair path in the original system.

Our procedure then begins by recursively enumerating over each CTL sub-property, wherein we attain an assertion characterizing all the states in which the sub-property holds under the fairness constraint Ω. These assertions will subsequently replace their corresponding CTL sub-properties as shown on lines 15,17,19, and so on. A new CTL formula φ' is then acquired by adding an appropriate termination or non-termination clause (lines 13-30). This clause allows us to ignore finite paths that are prefixes of unfair infinite paths. Recall that other finite paths were turned infinite and marked by the proposition t in TERM(M, t).

Ultimately, our reduction FAIR(M, Ω) is utilized on line 32, where we transform the input transition system M according to Fig. 2. With our modified CTL formula φ' and transition system M', we call upon the existing CTL model checking algorithm to return an assertion characterizing all the states in which the formula holds. The returned assertion is then examined on lines 35-39 to determine whether or not φ' holds under the fairness constraint Ω. If the property is existential, then it is sufficient that there exists at least one value of the prophecy variable such that the property holds. If the property is universal, then the property must hold for all possible values of the prophecy variable.

We state the correctness and completeness of our model checking procedure.

Theorem 2. *For every CTL formula φ and every transition system M with no terminating states we have $M \models_{\Omega_+} \varphi \Leftrightarrow S_0 \to$ FAIRCTL (M, Ω, φ).*

Proof Sketch (full proof in [9]). We show that every infinite path in FAIR(M, Ω) starting in (s, n) for some $n \in \mathbb{N}$ corresponds to an infinite path in M starting in s satisfying Ω, and vice versa. From this correspondence of fair paths in M and infinite paths in FAIR(M, Ω), we can safely disregard all the newly introduced finite paths given a transition system with no finite paths (i.e., TERM(M, t)). $\qquad\square$

We then proceed to show by induction on the structure of the formula that the assertion returned by FAIRCTL(M, Ω, φ) characterizes the set of states of M that satisfy φ. For a universal property, we show that if it holds from s in M then it(s modified form) holds from (s, n) for every n in FAIR(M, Ω) and vice versa. For an existential property, we show that if it holds from s in M then its modified form holds from (s, n) for some n in FAIR(M, Ω) and vice versa.

Corollary 1. *For every CTL formula φ and every transition system M we have $M \models_{\Omega_+} \varphi \Leftrightarrow$ VERIFY(M, Ω, φ) returns true.*

Proof. VERIFY calls FAIRCTL on TERM(M, t) and TERM(φ, t). It follows that TERM(M, t) has no terminating states and hence Theorem 2 applies to it. By Theorem 1, the mutual transformation of M to TERM(M, t) and φ to TERM(φ, t) preserves whether or not $M \models_{\Omega_+}$. The corollary follows. $\qquad\square$

4   Fair-ACTL Model Checking

In this section we show that in the case that we are only interested in universal path properties, i.e., formulas in ACTL, there is a simpler approach to fair-CTL model checking. In this simpler case, we can solely use the transformation FAIR(M, Ω). Just like in FAIRCTL, we still must ignore truncated paths that

$$\mathrm{NTERM}(\alpha) ::= \alpha$$
$$\mathrm{NTERM}(\varphi_1 \wedge \varphi_2) ::= \mathrm{NTERM}(\varphi_1) \wedge \mathrm{NTERM}(\varphi_2)$$
$$\mathrm{NTERM}(\varphi_1 \vee \varphi_2) ::= \mathrm{NTERM}(\varphi_1) \vee \mathrm{NTERM}(\varphi_2)$$
$$\mathrm{NTERM}(\mathsf{AX}\varphi) ::= \mathsf{AX}(\mathrm{NTERM}(\varphi) \vee \mathsf{term})$$
$$\mathrm{NTERM}(\mathsf{AF}\varphi) ::= \mathsf{AF}(\mathrm{NTERM}(\varphi) \vee \mathsf{term})$$
$$\mathrm{NTERM}(\mathsf{A}[\varphi_1 \mathsf{W} \varphi_2]) ::= \mathsf{A}[\mathrm{NTERM}(\varphi_1) \mathsf{W} (\mathrm{NTERM}(\varphi_2) \vee \mathsf{term})]$$

Fig. 7. Transformation NTERM( )

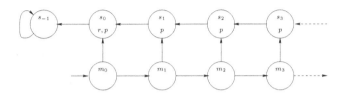

Fig. 8. A system showing that ECTL model checking is more complicated

correspond to wrong predictions. However, in this case, this can be done by a formula transformation.

Let $\mathrm{NTERM}(\varphi)$ denote the transformation in Figure 7. The transformation ensures that universal path quantification ignores states that lie on finite paths that are due to wrong estimations of the number of p-s until q. Using this transformation, it is possible to reduce fair-ACTL model checking to (A)CTL model checking over $\mathrm{FAIR}(M, \Omega)$. Formally, this is stated in the following theorem.

Theorem 3. *For every ACTL formula φ and every transition system M with no terminating states, we have $M \models_{\Omega_+} \varphi \Leftrightarrow \mathrm{FAIR}(M, \Omega) \models \mathrm{NTERM}(\varphi) \vee \mathsf{term}$.*

Proof Sketch (full proof in [9]). The proof proceeds by induction on the structure of the formula. We show that if the property holds from s in M then for every n the (modified) property holds from (s, n) in $\mathrm{FAIR}(M, \Omega)$ and vice versa. Note that the initial states of $\mathrm{FAIR}(M, \Omega)$ are all the initial states of M annotated by all possible options of $n \in \mathbb{N}$. It follows that the combination of all transformations reduce fair ACTL model checking to ACTL model checking. □

Corollary 2. *For every ACTL formula φ we have*

$$M \models_{\Omega_+} \varphi \Leftrightarrow \mathrm{FAIR}(\mathrm{TERM}(M, t), \Omega) \models \mathrm{NTERM}(\mathrm{TERM}(\varphi, t)) \vee \mathsf{term}$$

Proof. As $\mathrm{TERM}(M, t)$ produces a transition system with no terminating states and $\mathrm{TERM}(\varphi, t)$ converts an ACTL formula to an ACTL formula, the proof then follows from Theorem 1 and Theorem 3. □

The direct reduction presented in Theorem 3 works well for ACTL but does not work for existential properties. We now demonstrate why Fig. 2 is not sufficient to handle existential properties alone. Consider the transition system M in Figure 8, the fairness constraint $\Omega = \{(p, q)\}$, and the property

$\mathsf{EG}(\neg p \wedge \mathsf{EF}r)$. One can see that $M, m_0 \models_{\Omega_+} \mathsf{EG}(\neg p \wedge \mathsf{EF}r)$. Indeed, from each state s_i there is a unique path that eventually reaches s_0, where it satisfies r, and then continues to s_{-1}, where p does not hold. As the path visits finitely many p states it is clearly fair. So, every state m_i satisfies $\mathsf{EF}r$ by considering the path $m_i, s_i, s_{i-1}, \ldots, s_0, s_{-1}, \ldots$. Then the fair path $m_0, m_1, \ldots$ satisfies $\mathsf{EG}(\neg p \wedge \mathsf{EF}r)$. On the other hand, it is clear that no other path satisfies $\mathsf{EG}(\neg p \wedge \mathsf{EF}r)$.

Now consider the transformation $\mathrm{FAIR}(M, \Omega)$ and consider model checking of $\mathsf{EG}(\neg p \wedge \mathsf{EF}r)$. In $\mathrm{FAIR}(M, \Omega)$ there is no path that satisfies this property. To see this, consider the transition system $\mathrm{FAIR}(M, \Omega)$ and a value $n \in \mathbb{N}$. For every value of n the path $(m_0, n), (m_1, n), (m_2, n), \ldots$ is an infinite path in $\mathrm{FAIR}(M, \Omega)$ as it never visits p. This path does not satisfy $\mathsf{EG}(\neg p \wedge \mathsf{EF}r)$. Consider some state (m_j, n_j) reachable from (m_0, n) for $j > 2n$. The only infinite paths starting from (m_j, n_j) are paths that never visit the states s_i. Indeed, paths that visit s_i are terminated as they visit too many p states. Thus, for every $n \in \mathbb{N}$ we have $(m_0, n) \not\models \mathsf{EG}(\neg p \wedge \mathsf{EF}r)$. Finite paths in $\mathrm{FAIR}(M, \Omega)$ are those of the form $(m_0, n_0), \ldots, (m_i, n_i), (s_i, n_{i+1}), \ldots$. Such paths clearly cannot satisfy the property $\mathsf{EG}(\neg p \wedge \mathsf{EF}r)$ as the states s_i do satisfy p. Allowing existential paths to ignore fairness is clearly unsound. We note also that in $\mathrm{FAIR}(M, \Omega)$ we have $(m_0, n) \models \mathrm{NTERM}(\mathsf{AF}(p \vee \mathsf{AG}\neg r))$.

Reducing Fair Termination to Termination. Given the importance of termination as a system property, we emphasize the reduction of fair termination to termination. Note that termination can be expressed in ACTL as AFAX false, thus the results in Corollary 2 allow us to reduce fair termination to model checking (without fairness). Intuitively, a state that satisfies AX false is a state with no successors. Hence, every path that reaches a state with no successors is a finite path. Here, we demonstrate that for infinite-state infinite-branching systems, fair termination can be reduced to termination.

A transition system M terminates if for every initial state $s \in S_0$ we have $\Pi_\infty(s) = \emptyset$. System M fair-terminates under fairness Ω if for every initial state $s \in S_0$ and every $\pi \in \Pi_\infty(s)$ we have $\pi \not\models \Omega$, i.e., all infinite paths are unfair.

The following corollary follows from the proof of Theorem 3, where we establish a correspondence between fair paths of M and infinite paths of $\mathrm{FAIR}(M, \Omega)$.

Corollary 3. *M fair terminates iff* $\mathrm{FAIR}(M, \Omega)$ *terminates.*

Recall that the reduction relies on transition systems having an infinite branching degree. For transition systems with finite-branching degree, we cannot reduce fair termination of finite-branching programs to termination of finite-branching programs, as the former is Σ_1^1-complete and the latter is RE-complete [18].

5   Example

Consider the example in Fig. 9. We will demonstrate the resulting transformations which will disprove the CTL property $\mathsf{EG}\, x \leq 0$ under the weak fairness constraint GF true $\rightarrow \mathsf{GF}\, y \geq 1$ for the initial transition system introduced in (a). We begin by executing VERIFY in Fig. 6. In VERIFY the transition system in (a) is transformed

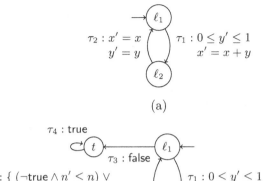

(a)

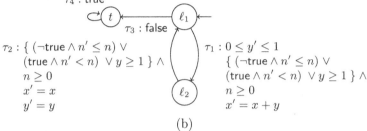

(b)

Fig. 9. Verifying a transition system with the CTL property EG $x \leq 0$ and the weak fairness constraint GF true → GF $y \geq 1$. The original transition system is represented in (a), followed by the application of our fairness reduction in (b).

according to $\text{TERM}(M, t)$ and the CTL formula EG $x \leq 0$ is transformed according to $\text{TERM}(M, t)$, as discussed in 3.2. Our main procedure FAIRCTL in Fig. 5 is then called. First, we recursively enumerate over the most inner sub-property $x \leq 0$, wherein $x \leq 0$ is returned as it is our base case. In lines 13-30, a new CTL formula φ' is then acquired by adding an appropriate termination or non-termination clause. This clause allows us to ignore finite paths that are prefixes of some unfair infinite paths, that is, those that have not been marked by $\text{TERM}(M, t)$. We then obtain (b) in Fig. 9 by applying $\text{FAIR}(M, \Omega)$ from Fig. 2 on line 32. Thus, we must restrict each transition such that $\{ (\neg \text{true} \wedge n' \leq n) \vee (\text{true} \wedge n' < n) \vee y \geq 1 \} \wedge n \geq 0$ holds. This can be seen in transitions τ_1 and τ_2.

Recall that $\text{FAIR}(M, \Omega)$ can include (maximal) finite paths that are prefixes of unfair infinite paths. We thus have to ensure that these paths do not interfere with the validity of our model checking procedure. We have shown how to distinguish between maximal (finite) paths that occur in M and those introduced by our transformation in Theorem 1. This is demonstrated by τ_3 and τ_4 in (b): in τ_3 we simply take the negation of the loop invariant (in this case it is false), as it would indicate a terminating path given that no other transitions follow the loop termination. In τ_4 we instrument a self loop and add the proposition t to eliminate all terminal states. Additionally, utilizing $\text{TERM}(\varphi, t)$ on EG $x \leq 0$ allows us to disregard all aforementioned marked finite paths, as we only consider infinite paths which correspond to a fair path in the original system.

On line 33, a CTL model checker is then employed with the transition system in (b) and the CTL formula φ'. We then apply tools provided by Beyene *et al.* [2] and Cook *et al.* [10] to the transformation introduced to verify CTL for infinite-state systems. An assertion characterizing the states in which φ' holds is returned

Program	LOC	Property	FC	Time(s)	Result
WDD1	20	AG(BlockInits() $\Rightarrow$ AF UnblockInits())	Yes	14.4	✓
WDD1	20	AG(BlockInits() $\Rightarrow$ AF UnblockInits())	No	2.1	χ
WDD2	374	AG(AcqSpinLock() $\Rightarrow$ AF RelSpinLock())	Yes	18.8	✓
WDD2	374	AG(AcqSpinLock() $\Rightarrow$ AF RelSpinLock())	No	14.1	χ
WDD3	58	AF(EnCritRegion() $\Rightarrow$ EG ExCritRegion())	Yes	12.5	χ
WDD3	58	AF(EnCritRegion() $\Rightarrow$ EG ExCritRegion())	No	9.6	✓
WDD4	302	AG(added_socket $> 0 \Rightarrow$ AFEG STATUS_OK)	Yes	30.2	✓
WDD4	302	AG(added_socket $> 0 \Rightarrow$ AFEG STATUS_OK)	No	72.4	χ
Bakery	37	AG(Noncritical $\Rightarrow$ AF Critical)	Yes	2.9	✓
Bakery	37	AG(Noncritical $\Rightarrow$ AF Critical)	No	16.4	χ
Prod-Cons	30	AG($p_i > 0 \Rightarrow$ AF $q_i <= 0$)	Yes	18.5	✓
Prod-Cons	30	AG($p_i > 0 \Rightarrow$ AF $q_i <= 0$)	No	5.5	χ
Chain	48	AG($x \geq 8 \Rightarrow$ AF $x = 0$)	Yes	1.8	✓
Chain	48	AG($x \geq 8 \Rightarrow$ AF $x = 0$)	No	4.7	χ

Fig. 10. Experimental evaluations of infinite-state programs such as Windows device drivers (WDD) and concurrent systems, which were reduced to non-deterministic sequential programs via [7]. Each program is tested for both the success of a branching-time liveness property with a fairness constraint and its failure due to a lack of fairness. A ✓ represents the existence of a validity proof, while χ represents the existence of a counterexample. We denote the lines of code in our program by LOC and the fairness constraint by FC. There exist no competing tools available for comparison.

and then further examined on lines 36 and 37, where it is discovered that this property does not hold due to the restrictive fairness constraint applied to the existential CTL property. The weak fairness constraint requires that infinitely often $y \geq 1$ holds, which interferes with the existential property that EG $x \leq 0$. This shows that for the existential fragment of CTL, fairness constraints restrict the transition relations required to prove an existential property. This can be beneficial when attempting to disprove systems and their negations.

6   Experiments

In this section we demonstrate the results of preliminary experiments with a prototype implementation. We applied our tool to several small programs: a classical mutual exclusion algorithm as well as code fragments drawn from device drivers. Our implementation is based on an extension to T2 [4], [14], [10].[4] As previously discussed, there are currently no known tools supporting fair-CTL for infinite-state systems, thus we are not able to make experimental comparisons.

Fig. 10 shows experimental evaluations of sequential Windows device drivers (WDD) and various concurrent systems[5]. WDD1 uses the fairness constraint GF(IoCreateDevice.exit{1}) $\Rightarrow$ GF(status = SUCCESS), while WDD2 and 3 utilize the same fairness constraint in relation to checking the acquisition and release of spin locks and the entrance and exit of critical regions, respectively.

---

[4] T2 can be acquired at http://research.microsoft.com/en-us/projects/t2/

[5] Benchmarks can be found at http://heidyk.com/experiments.html

WDD4 requires a weak fairness constraint indicating that STATUS_OK will hold a value of true infinitely often, that is, whenever sockets are successfully opened, the server will eventually return a successful status infinitely often.

Note that the initially concurrent programs are reduced to sequential programs via [7], which uses rely-guarantee reasoning to reduce multi-threaded verification to liveness. We verify the traditional Bakery algorithm, requiring that any thread requesting access to the critical region will eventually be granted the right to do so. The producer-consumer algorithm requires that any amount of input data produced, must be eventually consumed. The Chain benchmark consists of a chain of threads, where each thread decreases its own counter, but the next thread in the chain can counteract, and increase the counter of the previous thread, thus only the last thread in the chain can be be decremented unconditionally. These algorithms are verified on 2, 4, and 8 threads, respectively.

For the the existential fragment of CTL, fairness constraints can often restrict the transition relations required to prove an existential property, as demonstrated by WDD3. For universal CTL properties, fairness policies can assist in enforcing properties to hold that previously did not. Thus, our tool allows us to both prove and disprove the negation of each of the properties.

7 Discussion

We have described the first-known fair-CTL model checking technique for integer based infinite-state programs. Our approach is based on a reduction to existing techniques for fairness-free CTL model checking. The reduction relies on utilizing prophecy variables to introduce additional information into the state-space of the program under consideration. This allows fairness-free CTL proving techniques to reason only about fair executions. Our implementation seamlessly builds upon existing CTL proving techniques, resulting in experiments which demonstrate the practical viability of our approach.

Furthermore, our technique allows us to bridge between linear-time (LTL) and branching-time (CTL) reasoning. Not only so, but a seamless integration between LTL and CTL reasoning may make way for further extensions supporting CTL* verification of infinite-state programs [16]. We hope to further examine both the viability and practicality of such an extension.

We include the definition of fair-CTL considering only infinite paths and show how to change transition systems to use either definition in our technical report which can be acquired at [9]. Additionally, we show how to modify the proof system to incorporate an alternative approach to CTL verification advocated by Cook & Koskinen [12].

References

1. Apt, K., Olderog, E.: Fairness in parallel programs: The transformational approach. In: ACM TOPLAS, vol. 10 (1988)
2. Beyene, T.A., Popeea, C., Rybalchenko, A.: Solving existentially quantified horn clauses. In: Sharygina, N., Veith, H. (eds.) CAV 2013. LNCS, vol. 8044, pp. 869–882. Springer, Heidelberg (2013)
3. Bjørner, N., Browne, A., Colón, M., Finkbeiner, B., Manna, Z., Sipma, H., Uribe, T.: Verifying temporal properties of reactive systems: A step tutorial. FMSD 16(3) (2000)

4. Brockschmidt, M., Cook, B., Fuhs, C.: Better termination proving through cooperation. In: Sharygina, N., Veith, H. (eds.) CAV 2013. LNCS, vol. 8044, pp. 413–429. Springer, Heidelberg (2013)
5. Cimatti, A., Clarke, E., Giunchiglia, E., Giunchiglia, F., Pistore, M., Roveri, M., Sebastiani, R., Tacchella, A.: Nusmv 2: An opensource tool for symbolic model checking. In: Brinksma, E., Larsen, K.G. (eds.) CAV 2002. LNCS, vol. 2404, p. 359. Springer, Heidelberg (2002)
6. Clarke, E.M., Emerson, E.A., Sistla, A.P.: Automatic verification of finite-state concurrent systems using temporal logic specifications. ACM TOPLAS 8(2) (1986)
7. Cook, B., Gotsman, A., Parkinson, M., Vafeiadis, V.: Proving that non-blocking algorithms don't block. In: POPL. ACM (2009)
8. Cook, B., Gotsman, A., Podelski, A., Rybalchenko, A., Vardi, M.: Proving that programs eventually do something good. In: POPL. ACM (2007)
9. Cook, B., Khlaaf, H., Piterman, N.: Fairness for infinite-state systems. TR RN/14/11, UCL (2014)
10. Rybina, T., Voronkov, A.: Faster temporal reasoning for infinite-state programs. In: Baaz, M., Makowsky, J.A. (eds.) CSL 2003. LNCS, vol. 2803, pp. 546–573. Springer, Heidelberg (2003)
11. Cook, B., Koskinen, E.: Making prophecies with decision predicates. In: POPL. ACM (2011)
12. Cook, B., Koskinen, E.: Reasoning about nondeterminism in programs. In: PLDI. ACM (2013)
13. Cook, B., Koskinen, E., Vardi, M.: Temporal property verification as a program analysis task. In: Gopalakrishnan, G., Qadeer, S. (eds.) CAV 2011. LNCS, vol. 6806, pp. 333–348. Springer, Heidelberg (2011)
14. Cook, B., See, A., Zuleger, F.: Ramsey vs. lexicographic termination proving. In: Piterman, N., Smolka, S.A. (eds.) TACAS 2013. LNCS, vol. 7795, pp. 47–61. Springer, Heidelberg (2013)
15. David, A., Håkansson, J., Larsen, K.G., Pettersson, P.: Model checking timed automata with priorities using DBM subtraction. In: Asarin, E., Bouyer, P. (eds.) FORMATS 2006. LNCS, vol. 4202, pp. 128–142. Springer, Heidelberg (2006)
16. Emerson, E.A., Halpern, J.Y.: "Sometimes" and "not never" revisited: On branching versus linear time temporal logic. J. ACM 33(1) (January 1986)
17. Emerson, E.A., Lei, C.-L.: Temporal reasoning under generalized fairness constraints. In: Monien, B., Vidal-Naquet, G. (eds.) STACS 1986. LNCS, vol. 210, pp. 21–36. Springer, Heidelberg (1985)
18. Harel, D.: Effective transformations on infinite trees, with applications to high undecidability, dominoes and fairness. J. ACM 33, 224–248 (1986)
19. Kwiatkowska, M., Norman, G., Parker, D.: PRISM 4.0: Verification of probabilistic real-time systems. In: Gopalakrishnan, G., Qadeer, S. (eds.) CAV 2011. LNCS, vol. 6806, pp. 585–591. Springer, Heidelberg (2011)
20. Pnueli, A., Podelski, A., Rybalchenko, A.: Separating fairness and well-foundedness for the analysis of fair discrete systems. In: Halbwachs, N., Zuck, L.D. (eds.) TACAS 2005. LNCS, vol. 3440, pp. 124–139. Springer, Heidelberg (2005)
21. Pnueli, A., Sa'ar, Y.: All you need is compassion. In: Logozzo, F., Peled, D.A., Zuck, L.D. (eds.) VMCAI 2008. LNCS, vol. 4905, pp. 233–247. Springer, Heidelberg (2008)
22. Podelski, A., Rybalchenko, A.: Transition invariants. In: LICS (2004)
23. Schwoon, S.: Moped - A Model-Checker for Pushdown Systems (2002), http://www7.in.tum.de/~schwoon/moped
24. Song, F., Touili, T.: Pushdown model checking for malware detection. In: ESEC/FSE (2013)
25. Vardi, M.Y., Wolper, P.: Reasoning about infinite computations. I&C 115(1), 1–37 (1994)

Competition on Software Verification

Software Verification and Verifiable Witnesses
(Report on SV-COMP 2015)

Dirk Beyer

University of Passau, Germany

Abstract. SV-COMP 2015 marks the start of a new epoch of software verification: In the 4th Competition on Software Verification, software verifiers produced for each reported property violation a machine-readable error witness in a common exchange format (so far restricted to reachability properties of sequential programs without recursion). Error paths were reported previously, but always in different, incompatible formats, often insufficient to reproduce the identified bug, and thus, useless to the user. The common exchange format and the support by a large set of verification tools that use the format will make a big difference: One verifier can re-verify the witnesses produced by another verifier, visual error-path navigation tools can be developed, and here in the competition, we use witness checking to make sure that a verifier that claimed a found bug, had really found a valid error path. The other two changes to SV-COMP that we made this time were (a) the addition of the new property, a set of verification tasks, and ranking category for termination verification, and (b) the addition of two new categories for reachability analysis: Arrays and Floats. SV-COMP 2015, the fourth edition of the thorough comparative evaluation of fully-automatic software verifiers, reports effectiveness and efficiency results of the state of the art in software verification. The competition used 5 803 verification tasks, more than double the number of SV-COMP'14. Most impressively, the number of participating verifiers increased from 15 to 22 verification systems, including 13 new entries.

1 Introduction

The Competition on Software Verification (SV-COMP) [1] is a service to the verification community that consists of two parts: (a) the collection of verification tasks that the community of researchers in the area of software verification finds interesting and challenging, and (b) the systematic comparative evaluation of the relevant state-of-the-art tool implementations for automatic software verification with respect to effectiveness and efficiency.

Repository of Verification Tasks. The benchmark repository of SV-COMP [2] serves as collection of verification tasks that represent the current interest and abilities of tools for software verification. For the purpose of the competition, all verification tasks that are suitable for the competition are arranged into categories, according to the characteristics of the programs and the properties to be verified. The

---

[1] http://sv-comp.sosy-lab.org

[2] https://svn.sosy-lab.org/software/sv-benchmarks/trunk

© Springer-Verlag Berlin Heidelberg 2015
C. Baier and C. Tinelli (Eds.): TACAS 2015, LNCS 9035, pp. 401–416, 2015.
DOI: 10.1007/978-3-662-46681-0_31

assignment is discussed in the community, implemented by the competition chair, and finally approved by the competition jury. For the 2015 edition of SV-COMP, a total of 13 categories were defined, selected from verification tasks written in the programming language C. The SV-COMP repository also contains tasks written in Java[3] and as Horn clauses[4], but those were not used in SV-COMP.

Comparative Experimental Evaluation. This report concentrates on describing the rules, definitions, results, and on providing other interesting information about the setup and execution of the competition experiments. The main objectives that the community and organizer would like to achieve by running yearly competitions are the following:

1. provide an overview of the state of the art in software-verification technology and increase visibility of the most recent software verifiers,

2. establish a repository of software-verification tasks that can freely and publicly be used as standard benchmark suite for evaluating verification software,

3. establish standards that make it possible to compare different verification tools including a property language and formats for the results, and

4. accelerate the transfer of new verification technology to industrial practice.

The competition serves Objective (1) very well, which is witnessed by the past competition sessions at TACAS being among the best-attended ETAPS sessions, and by the large number of participating verification teams. Objective (2) is also served well: the repository was rapidly growing in the last years and reached a considerable size; many publications on algorithms for software verification base the experimental evaluation on the established verification benchmarks from the SV-COMP repository, and thus, it becomes a standard for evaluating new algorithms to use the SV-COMP collection. SV-COMP 2015 was a big step forward with respect to Objective (3). It was requested since long that **verification witnesses** should be given in a common format and can be accepted only if re-validated automatically by an independent witness checker. We have worked towards verifiable witnesses with success, but there is a lot of work left to be done. Whether or not SV-COMP serves well towards Objective (4) cannot be evaluated here.

Related Competitions. There are two other competitions in the field of software verification in general: RERS[5] and VerifyThis[6]. In difference to the RERS Challenges, SV-COMP is an experimental evaluation that is performed on dedicated machines, which provide the same *limited* amount of resources to each verification tool. In difference to the VerifyThis Competitions, SV-COMP focuses on evaluating tools for *fully-automatic* verification of program *source code* in a standard programming language. A more comprehensive list of other competitions was given in the previous report [3].

---

[3] https://svn.sosy-lab.org/software/sv-benchmarks/trunk/java

[4] https://svn.sosy-lab.org/software/sv-benchmarks/trunk/clauses

[5] http://rers-challenge.org

[6] http://etaps2015.verifythis.org

2   Procedure

The procedure for the competition organization was the same as in previous editions of SV-COMP [1, 2, 3], consisting of the three phases (1) *benchmark submission* (collect and classify new verification tasks), (2) *training* (teams inspect verification tasks and train their verifiers), and (3) *evaluation* (verification runs with all competition candidates and review of the system descriptions by the competition jury). Again, SV-COMP was an open competition, i.e., the verification tasks were known before the participating verifiers were submitted, such that there were no surprises and developers were able to train the verifiers. All systems and their descriptions have been archived on the SV-COMP web site and stamped for identification with SHA hash values. All teams received the preliminary results of their verifier for approval, before the results were publicly announced. This time, there was no demonstration category.

3   Definitions, Formats, and Rules

The specification of the various properties was streamlined last year, such that it was easy to extend the property language to express reachability using function calls instead of C labels in the source code of the verification tasks, which eliminates completely the need of C labels in the verification tasks. Most importantly, we introduced a *syntax for error witnesses* (more details are given below). The definition of verification task was not changed (taken from [3]).

Verification Tasks. A verification task consists of a C program and a property. A verification run is a non-interactive execution of a competition candidate on a single verification task, in order to check whether the following statement is correct: "The program satisfies the property." The result of a verification run is a triple (ANSWER, WITNESS, TIME). ANSWER is one of the following outcomes:

TRUE: The property is satisfied (i.e., no path that violates the property exists).

FALSE: The property is violated (i.e., there exists a path that violates the property) and a counterexample path is produced and reported as WITNESS.

UNKNOWN: The tool cannot decide the problem, or terminates abnormally, or exhausts the computing resources time or memory (i.e., the competition candidate does not succeed in computing an answer TRUE or FALSE).

WITNESS is explained below in an own sub-section. TIME is measured as consumed CPU time until the verifier terminates, including the consumed CPU time of all processes that the verifier started [4]. If the wall time was larger than the CPU time, then the TIME is set to the wall time. If TIME is equal to or larger than the time limit (15 min), then the verifier is terminated and the ANSWER is set to 'timeout' (and interpreted as UNKNOWN).

The verification tasks were partitioned into twelve separate categories and one category *Overall* that contains all verification tasks. The categories, their defining category-set files, and the contained programs are explained under *Verification Tasks* on the competition web site.

Table 1. Formulas used in the competition, together with their interpretation

Formula	Interpretation
G ! call(foo())	A call to function foo is not reachable on any finite execution of the program.
G valid-free	All memory deallocations are valid (counterexample: invalid free). More precisely: There exists no finite execution of the program on which an invalid memory deallocation occurs.
G valid-deref	All pointer dereferences are valid (counterexample: invalid dereference). More precisely: There exists no finite execution of the program on which an invalid pointer dereference occurs.
G valid-memtrack	All allocated memory is tracked, i.e., pointed to or deallocated (counterexample: memory leak). More precisely: There exists no finite execution of the program on which the program lost track of some previously allocated memory.
F end	All program executions are finite and end on proposition end (counterexample: infinite loop). More precisely: There exists no execution of the program on which the program never terminates.

Properties. The specification to be verified is stored in a file that is given as parameter to the verifier. In the repository, the specifications are available as .prp files in the respective directories of the benchmark categories.

The definition init(main()) gives the initial states of the program by a call of function main (with no parameters). The definition LTL(f) specifies that formula f holds at every initial state of the program. The LTL (linear-time temporal logic) operator G f means that f globally holds (i.e., everywhere during the program execution), and the operator F f means that f eventually holds (i.e., at some point during the program execution). The proposition call(foo) is true if a call to the function foo is reached, and the proposition end is true if the program execution terminates (e.g., return of function main, program exit, abort).

Call Unreachability. The reachability property p_{error} is encoded in the program source code using a call to function __VERIFIER_error(), expressed using the following specification (the interpretation of the LTL formula is given in Table 1):

CHECK(init(main()), LTL(G ! call(__VERIFIER_error())))

Memory Safety. The memory-safety property $p_{\text{memsafety}}$ (only used in one category) consists of three partial properties and is expressed using the following specification (interpretation of formulas given in Table 1):

CHECK(init(main()), LTL(G valid-free))
CHECK(init(main()), LTL(G valid-deref))
CHECK(init(main()), LTL(G valid-memtrack))

The verification result FALSE for the property $p_{\text{memsafety}}$ is required to include the violated partial property: FALSE(p), with $p \in \{p_{\text{valid-free}}, p_{\text{valid-deref}}, p_{\text{valid-memtrack}}\}$, means that the (partial) property p is violated. According to the requirements for verification tasks, all programs in category *MemorySafety* violate at most one (partial) property $p \in \{p_{\text{valid-free}}, p_{\text{valid-deref}}, p_{\text{valid-memtrack}}\}$. Per convention, functions `malloc` and `alloca` are assumed to always return a valid pointer, i.e., the memory allocation never fails, and function `free` always deallocates the memory and makes the pointer invalid for further dereferences. Further assumptions are explained under *Definitions and Rules* on the competition web site.

Program Termination. The termination property $p_{\text{termination}}$ (only used in one category) is based on the proposition **end** and expressed using the following specification (interpretation in Table 1):

```
CHECK( init(main()), LTL(F end) )
```

Verifiable Witnesses. For the first time in the history of software verification (of real-world, C programs),[7] we defined a formal, machine-readable format for error witnesses and required the verifiers to produce automatically-verifiable witnesses for the counterexample path that is part of the result triple as WITNESS. This new rule was applied to the categories with reachability properties and verification tasks of sequential programs without recursion. If an error path required recursive function calls or heap operations, the witness was not checked.

We represent witnesses as automata. Formally, a witness automaton consists of states and transitions, where each transition is annotated with data that can be used to match program executions. A data annotation can be (a) a token number (position in the token stream that the parser receives), (b) an assumption (for example, the assumption $a = 1$; means that program variable a has value 1), (c) a line number and a file name, (d) a function call or return, and (e) a piece of source-code syntax. More details are given on a web page.[8]

A witness checker is a software verifier that analyzes the synchronized product of the program with the witness automaton, where transitions are synchronized using program operations and transition annotations. This means that the witness automaton observes the program paths that the verifier wants to explore: if the operation on the program path does not match the transition of the witness automaton, then the verifier is forbidden to explore that path further; if the operation on the program path matches, then the witness automaton and the program proceed to the next state, possibly restricting the program's state such that the assumptions given in the data annotation are satisfied.

In SV-COMP, the time limit for a validation run was set to 10 % of the CPU time for a verification run, i.e., the witness checker was limited to 90 s. If the witness checker did not succeed in the given amount of time, then most likely the witness was not concrete enough (time for validation can be a quality indicator).

---

[7] There was research already on reusing previously computed error paths, but by the same tool and in particular, using tool-specific formats: for example, ESBMC was extended to reproduce errors via instantiated code [21], and CPACHECKER was used to re-check previously computed error paths by interpreting them as automata that control the state-space search [5]. The competition on termination uses CPF: `http://cl-informatik.uibk.ac.at/software/cpf`.

[8] `http://sv-comp.sosy-lab.org/2015/witnesses`

Table 2. Scoring schema for SV-COMP 2015 (penalties increased, cf. [3])

Reported result	Points	Description
UNKNOWN	0	Failure to compute verification result
FALSE correct	+1	Violation of property in program was correctly found
FALSE incorrect	−6	Violation reported but property holds (false alarm)
TRUE correct	+2	Correct program reported to satisfy property
TRUE incorrect	−12	Incorrect program reported as correct (wrong proofs)

Machine-readable witnesses in a common exchange format have the following advantages for the competition:

- Witness Validation: The answer FALSE is only accepted if the witness can be validated by an automatic witness checker.
- Witness Inspection: If a verifier found an error in a verification task that was previously assumed to have expected outcome TRUE, the witness that was produced could immediately be validated with two different verifiers (one explicit-value-based and one SAT-based).

Outside the competition, the following examples are among the many useful applications of witnesses in a common format:

- Witness Database: Witnesses can be stored in databases as later source of information.
- Bug Report: Witnesses can be a useful attachment for bug reports, in order to precisely report to the developers what the erroneous behavior is.
- Bug Confirmation: To gain more confidence that a bug is indeed present, the error witness can be re-confirmed with a different verifier, perhaps using a completely different technology.
- Re-Verification: If the result FALSE was established, the error witness can later be reused to re-establish the verification result with much less resources, for example, if the program source code is slightly changed and the developer is interested if the same bug still exists in a later version of the program [5].

Evaluation by Scores and Run Time. The scoring schema was changed in order to increase the penalty for wrong results (in comparison to the previous edition of the competition by a factor of 1.5). The overview is given in Table 2. The ranking is decided based on the sum of points and for equal sum of points according to success run time, which is the total CPU time over all verification tasks for which the verifier reported a correct verification result. *Opting-out from Categories* and *Computation of Score for Meta Categories* were defined as in SV-COMP 2013 [2]. The *Competition Jury* consists again of the chair and one member of each participating team. Team representatives of the jury are listed in Table 3.

Table 3. Competition candidates with their system-description references and representing jury members

Competition candidate	Ref.	Jury member	Affiliation
APROVE	[23]	Thomas Ströder	RWTH Aachen, Germany
BEAGLE		Dexi Wang	Tsinghua U, China
BLAST	[22]	Vadim Mutilin	ISP RAS, Russia
CASCADE	[26]	Wei Wang	New York U, USA
CBMC	[15]	Michael Tautschnig	Queen Mary U London, UK
CPACHECKER	[8]	Matthias Dangl	U Passau, Germany
CPAREC	[7]	Ming-Hsien Tsai	Academia Sinica, Taiwan
ESBMC	[17]	Jeremy Morse	U Bristol, UK
FOREST	[9]	Pablo Sanchez	U Cantabria, Spain
FORESTER	[13]	Ondřej Lengál	Brno UT, Czech Republic
FUNCTION	[25]	Caterina Urban	ENS Paris, France
HIPTNT+	[16]	Ton-Chanh Le	NUS, Singapore
LAZY-CSEQ	[14]	Gennaro Parlato	U Southampton, UK
MAP2CHECK		Herbert O. Rocha	FUA, Brazil
MU-CSEQ	[24]	Bernd Fischer	Stellenbosch U, South Africa
PERENTIE	[6]	Franck Cassez	Macquarie U/NICTA, Australia
PREDATORHP	[18]	Tomáš Vojnar	Brno UT, Czech Republic
SEAHORN	[10]	Arie Gurfinkel	SEI, USA
SMACK+CORRAL	[11]	Zvonimir Rakamarić	U Utah, USA
ULTIAUTOMIZER	[12]	Matthias Heizmann	U Freiburg, Germany
ULTIKOJAK	[20]	Alexander Nutz	U Freiburg, Germany
UNB-LAZY-CSEQ	[19]	Salvatore La Torre	U Salerno, Italy

4 Results and Discussion

The results of the competition experiments represent the state of the art in fully-automatic and publicly-available software-verification tools. The report shows the improvements of the last year, in terms of effectiveness (number of verification tasks that can be solved, correctness of the results, as accumulated in the score) and efficiency (resource consumption in terms of CPU time). The results that are presented in this article were approved by the participating teams.

Participating Verifiers. Table 3 provides an overview of the participating competition candidates and Table 4 lists the features and technologies that are used in the verification tools.

Technical Resources. The technical setup for running the experiments was similar to last year [3], except that we used eight, newer machines. All verification runs were natively executed on dedicated unloaded compute servers with a 3.4 GHz 64-bit Quad-Core CPU (Intel i7-4770) and a GNU/Linux operating system (x86_64-linux). The machines had 33 GB of RAM, of which exactly 15 GB (memory limit) were made available to the verifiers. The run-time limit for each verification run was 15 min of CPU time. The run-time limit for each witness check was set to 1.5 min of CPU time. The tables report the run time in seconds of CPU time; all measured values are rounded to two significant digits.

Table 4. Technologies and features that the verification tools offer

Verifier	CEGAR	Predicate Abstraction	Symbolic Execution	Bounded Model Checking	k-Induction	Property-Directed Reachability	Explicit-Value Analysis	Numerical Interval Analysis	Shape Analysis	Separation Logic	Bit-Precise Analysis	ARG-Based Analysis	Lazy Abstraction	Interpolation	Automata-Based Analysis	Concurrency Support	Ranking Functions
APRoVE			✓				✓	✓			✓						✓
BEAGLE	✓	✓		✓													
BLAST	✓	✓					✓					✓	✓	✓			
CASCADE			✓	✓							✓						
CBMC				✓	✓						✓					✓	
CPACHECKER	✓	✓	✓	✓	✓		✓	✓	✓		✓	✓	✓	✓			
CPAREC	✓	✓										✓	✓	✓			
ESBMC				✓	✓						✓					✓	
FOREST			✓	✓							✓						
FORESTER									✓						✓		
FUNCTION								✓									✓
HIPTNT+										✓							✓
LAZY-CSEQ				✓							✓					✓	
MAP2CHECK				✓							✓						
MU-CSEQ				✓							✓					✓	
PERENTIE	✓		✓				✓							✓	✓		
PREDATORHP									✓								
SEAHORN				✓		✓	✓					✓	✓	✓			
SMACK+CORRAL	✓			✓							✓						
ULTIAUTOMIZER	✓	✓											✓	✓	✓		✓
ULTIKOJAK	✓	✓											✓	✓	✓		
UNB-LAZY-CSEQ	✓	✓										✓	✓	✓		✓	

Table 5. Quantitative overview over all results Part 1 (score / CPU time)

Verifier Repr. jury member	Arrays 145 points 86 tasks	BitVectors 83 points 47 tasks	Concurrent 1222 points 1003 tasks	ContrFlow 3122 points 1927 tasks	DeviceDriv. 3097 points 1650 tasks	Floats 140 points 81 tasks	HeapManip. 135 points 80 tasks
APROVE T. Ströder, Germany							
BEAGLE D. Wang, China		4 58 s					
BLAST V. Mutilin, Russia				983 33 000 s	**2 736** 11 000 s		
CASCADE W. Wang, USA		52 16 000 s		537 43 000 s			70 6 000 s
CBMC M. Tautschnig, UK	-134 2 500 s	68 1 800 s	1 039 78 000 s	158 570 000 s	2 293 380 000 s	**129** 15 000 s	100 13 000 s
CPACHECKER M. Dangl, Germany	2 62 s	58 870 s	0 0 s	**2 317** 47 000 s	2 572 39 000 s	78 5 000 s	96 930 s
CPAREC M.-H. Tsai, Taiwan							
ESBMC J. Morse, UK	-206 5.5 s	**69** 470 s	1 014 13 000 s	1 968 59 000 s	2 281 36 000 s	-12 5 300 s	79 37 s
FOREST P. Sanchez, Spain							
FORESTER O. Lengál, Czechia							32 1.8 s
FUNCTION C. Urban, France							
HIPTNT+ T.-C. Le, Singapore							
LAZY-CSEQ G. Parlato, UK			**1 222** 5 600 s				
MAP2CHECK H. O. Rocha, Brazil							
MU-CSEQ B. Fischer, ZA			**1 222** 16 000 s				
PERENTIE F. Cassez, Australia							
PREDATORHP T. Vojnar, Czechia							**111** 140 s
SEAHORN A. Gurfinkel, USA	0 0.61 s	-80 550 s	-8 973 42 s	2 169 30 000 s	2 657 16 000 s	-164 5.9 s	-37 14 s
SMACK+CORRAL Z. Rakamarić, USA	**48** 400 s			1 691 78 000 s	2 507 72 000 s		109 820 s
ULTIAUTOMIZER M. Heizmann, Germany	2 6.4 s	5 170 s		1 887 54 000 s	274 850 s		84 460 s
ULTIKOJAK A. Nutz, Germany	2 5.9 s	-62 120 s		872 10 000 s	82 270 s		84 420 s
UNB-LAZY-CSEQ S. La Torre, Italy			984 36 000 s				

Table 6. Quantitative overview over all results Part 2 (score / CPU time)

Verifier Repr. jury member	MemSafety 361 points 205 tasks	Recursive 40 points 24 tasks	Sequential 364 points 261 tasks	Simple 68 points 46 tasks	Termination 742 points 393 tasks	Overall 9 562 points 5 803 tasks
APROVE T. Ströder, Germany					**610** 5 400 s	
BEAGLE D. Wang, China		6 22 s				
BLAST V. Mutilin, Russia				32 4 200 s		
CASCADE W. Wang, USA	**200** 82 000 s					
CBMC M. Tautschnig, UK	-433 14 000 s	0 10 000 s	-171 39 000 s	51 16 000 s		**1 731** 1 100 000 s
CPACHECKER M. Dangl, Germany	**326** 5 700 s	16 31 s	**130** 11 000 s	**54** 4 000 s	0 0 s	**4 889** 110 000 s
CPAREC M.-H. Tsai, Taiwan		18 140 s				
ESBMC J. Morse, UK			**193** 9 600 s	29 990 s		-2 161 130 000 s
FOREST P. Sanchez, Spain						
FORESTER O. Lengál, Czechia	22 25 s					
FUNCTION C. Urban, France					350 61 s	
HIPTNT+ T.-C. Le, Singapore					**545** 300 s	
LAZY-CSEQ G. Parlato, UK						
MAP2CHECK H. O. Rocha, Brazil	28 2 100 s					
MU-CSEQ B. Fischer, ZA						
PERENTIE F. Cassez, Australia						
PREDATORHP T. Vojnar, Czechia	**221** 460 s					
SEAHORN A. Gurfinkel, USA	0 0 s	-88 2.3 s	-59 5 800 s	**65** 1 400 s	0 0 s	-6 228 53 000 s
SMACK+CORRAL Z. Rakamarić, USA		**27** 2 300 s		51 5 100 s		
ULTIAUTOMIZER M. Heizmann, Germany	95 13 000 s	**25** 310 s	**15** 8 600 s	0 1 800 s	**565** 8 600 s	**2 301** 87 000 s
ULTIKOJAK A. Nutz, Germany	66 4 800 s	10 220 s	-10 7 000 s	3 140 s		231 23 000 s
UNB-LAZY-CSEQ S. La Torre, Italy						

Table 7. Overview of the top-three verifiers for each category (CPU time in s)

Rank	Candidate	Score	CPU Time	Solved Tasks	False Alarms	Wrong Proofs
Arrays						
1	SMACK+CORRAL	**48**	400	51	7	1
2	ULTIKOJAK	2	5.9	1		
3	ULTIAUTOMIZER	2	6.4	1		
BitVectors						
1	ESBMC	**69**	470	45		1
2	CBMC	68	1 800	44		1
3	CPACHECKER	58	870	40		1
Concurrency						
1	LAZY-CSEQ	**1 222**	5 600	1003		
2	MU-CSEQ	1 222	16 000	1003		
3	CBMC	1 039	78 000	848	1	1
ControlFlow						
1	CPACHECKER	**2 317**	47 000	1302	2	2
2	SEAHORN	2 169	30 000	1014	5	2
3	ESBMC	1 968	59 000	1212		36
DeviceDrivers64						
1	BLAST	**2 736**	11 000	1 481	5	9
2	SEAHORN	2 657	16 000	1 440	3	12
3	CPACHECKER	2 572	39 000	1 390	17	4
Floats						
1	CBMC	**129**	15 000	74		
2	CPACHECKER	78	5 100	54	2	
3	ESBMC	−12	5 300	27	7	2
HeapManipulation						
1	PREDATORHP	**111**	140	68		
2	SMACK+CORRAL	109	820	76	3	
3	CBMC	100	13 000	69		2
MemorySafety						
1	CPACHECKER	**326**	5 700	199	4	
2	PREDATORHP	221	460	134	1	
3	CASCADE	200	82 000	154	2	5
Recursive						
1	SMACK+CORRAL	**27**	2 300	23		1
2	ULTIAUTOMIZER	25	310	16		
3	CPAREC	18	140	12		
SequentializedConcurrency						
1	ESBMC	**193**	9 600	144	2	
2	CPACHECKER	130	11 000	113	1	
3	ULTIAUTOMIZER	15	8 600	51	9	
Simple						
1	SEAHORN	**65**	1 400	44		
2	CPACHECKER	54	4 000	32		
3	SMACK+CORRAL	51	5 100	43	2	
Termination						
1	APROVE	**610**	5 400	305		
2	ULTIAUTOMIZER	565	8 600	304	1	
3	HIPTNT+	545	300	290		
Overall						
1	CPACHECKER	**4 889**	110 000	3 211	29	7
2	ULTIAUTOMIZER	2 301	87 000	1 453	21	3
3	CBMC	1 731	1 100 000	4 056	77	453

One complete competition run (each candidate on all selected categories according to the opt-outs) consisted of 49 855 verification runs and 4 151 witness checks. The consumed total CPU time for one competition run required a total of 119 days of CPU time for the verifiers and 1 day for the witness checker. Each tool was executed at least twice, in order to make sure the results are accurate and not contradicting in any sense. Not counted in the above measures on the dedicated competition machines are the preparation runs that were required to find out if the verifiers are successfully installed and running. Other machines with a slightly different specification were used for those test runs while the eight dedicated machines were occupied by the official competition runs.

Quantitative Results. Tables 5 and 6 present a quantitative overview over all tools and all categories (FOREST and PERENTIE participated only in subcategory *Loops*). The format of the table is similar to those of previous SV-COMP editions [3]: The tools are listed in alphabetical order; every table cell for competition results lists the score in the first row and the CPU time for successful runs in the second row. We indicated the top-three candidates by formatting their score in bold face and in larger font size. An empty table cell means that the verifier opted-out from the respective category. For the calculation of the score and for the ranking, the scoring schema in Table 2 was applied, the scores for the meta categories *Overall* and *ControlFlow* (consisting of several sub-categories) were computed using normalized scores as defined in the report for SV-COMP'13 [2].

Table 7 reports the top-three verifiers for each category. The run time (column 'CPU Time') refers to successfully solved verification tasks (column 'Solved Tasks'). The columns 'False Alarms' and 'Wrong Proofs' report the number of verification tasks for which the tool reported wrong results: reporting an error path but the property holds (false positive) and claiming that the program fulfills the property although it actually contains a bug (false negative), respectively.

Score-Based Quantile Functions for Quality Assessment. Score-based quantile functions [2] are helpful for visualizing results of comparative evaluations. The competition web page [9] includes such a plot for each category; Fig. 1 illustrates only the category *Overall* (all verification tasks). Six verifiers participated in category *Overall*, for which the quantile plot shows the overall performance over all categories (scores for meta categories are normalized [2]).

Overall Quality Measured in Scores (Right End of Graph). CPACHECKER is the winner of this category: the x-coordinate of the right-most data point represents the highest total score (and thus, the total value) of the completed verification work (cf. Table 7; right-most x-coordinates match the score values in the table).

Amount of Incorrect Verification Work (Left End of Graph). The left-most data points of the quantile functions represent the total negative score of a verifier (x-coordinate), i.e., amount of incorrect and misleading verification work. Verifiers should start with a score close to zero; ULTIAUTOMIZER and CPACHECKER are best in this aspect (also the right-most columns of category *Overall* in Table 7

---

[9] http://sv-comp.sosy-lab.org/2015/results

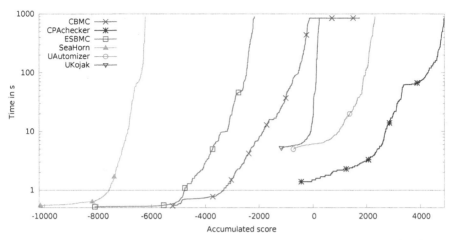

Fig. 1. Quantile functions for category *Overall*. We plot all data points (x, y) such that the maximum run time of the n fastest correct verification runs is y and x is the accumulated score of all incorrect results and those n correct results. A logarithmic scale is used for the time range from 1 s to 1000 s, and a linear scale is used for the time range between 0 s and 1 s.

report this: only 21 and 29 false alarms, respectively, and only 3 and 7 wrong proofs, for a total of 5 803 verification tasks).

Amount of Correct Verification Work (Length of Graph). The length of the graph indicates the amount of correct results: for example, CBMC and ESBMC both produce a large amount of correct results.

Characteristics of the Verification Tools. The plot visualizations also help understanding how the verifiers work internally: (1) The y-coordinate of the left-most data point refers to the 'easiest' verification task for the verifier. We can see that verifiers that are based on a Java virtual machine need some start-up time (CPACHECKER, ULTIAUTOMIZER, and ULTIKOJAK). (2) The y-coordinate of the right-most data point refers to the successfully solved verification task that the verifier spent most time on (this is mostly just below the time limit). We can read the ranking of verifiers in this category from right to left. (3) The area below a graph is proportional to the accumulated CPU time for successfully solved tasks. We can identify the most resource-efficient verifiers by looking at the right-most graphs and those closest to the x-axis. (4) Also the shape of the graph can give interesting insights: From CBMC's horizontal line just below the time limit at 850 s, we can see that this bounded model checker returns a result just before the time limit is reached. The quantile plot for CPACHECKER shows an interesting bend at 60 s of run time, where the verifier suddenly switches gears: it gives up with one strategy (without abstraction) performs an internal restart and proceeds using another strategy (with abstraction and CEGAR-based refinement).

Robustness, Soundness, and Completeness. The best tools of each category show that state-of-the-art verification technology is quite advanced already: Table 7 (last two columns) reports a low number of wrong verification results, with a few exceptions. CBMC and ESBMC are the two verifiers that produce the most wrong safety proofs (missed bugs): both of them are bounded model checkers. In three categories, the top-three verifiers did not report any wrong proof.

Verifiable Witnesses. One of the objectives of program verification is to provide a witness for the verification result. This was an open problem of verification technology: there was no commonly supported witness format yet, and the verifiers were not producing accurate witnesses that could be automatically assessed for validity. SV-COMP 2015 changed this (restricted to error witnesses for now): all verifiers that participated in categories that required witness validation supported the common exchange format for error witnesses, and produced error paths in that format. We used a witness checker to validate the obtained error paths.

5   Conclusion

The 4th edition of the Competition on Software Verification was successful in several respects: (1) We introduced *verifiable witnesses* (the verifiers produced error paths in a common exchange format, which made it possible to validate a given error path by using a separate witness checker). (2) We had a record number of *22 participating verification tools* from 13 countries. (3) The repository of verification tasks was extended by two new categories: *Arrays and Floats*. (4) The properties to be verified were extended by a liveness property: *Termination*. (5) The total number of verification tasks in the competition run was doubled (compared to SV-COMP'14) to a total of *5 803 verification tasks*. Besides the above-mentioned success measures, SV-COMP serves as a yearly overview of the state of the art in software verification, and witnesses an enormous pace of development of new theory, data structures and algorithms, and tool implementations that analyze real C code. As in previous years, the organizer and the jury made sure that the competition follows the high quality standards of the TACAS conference, in particular to respect the important principles of fairness, community support, transparency, and technical accuracy.

Acknowledgement.   We thank K. Friedberger for his support during the evaluation phase and for his work on the benchmarking infrastructure, the competition jury for making sure that the competition is well-grounded in the community, and the teams for making SV-COMP possible through their participation.

References

1. Beyer, D.: Competition on software verification (SV-COMP). In: Flanagan, C., König, B. (eds.) TACAS 2012. LNCS, vol. 7214, pp. 504–524. Springer, Heidelberg (2012)
2. Beyer, D.: Second competition on software verification. In: Piterman, N., Smolka, S.A. (eds.) TACAS 2013. LNCS, vol. 7795, pp. 594–609. Springer, Heidelberg (2013)

3. Beyer, D.: Status report on software verification. In: Ábrahám, E., Havelund, K. (eds.) TACAS 2014. LNCS, vol. 8413, pp. 373–388. Springer, Heidelberg (2014)
4. Beyer, D., Löwe, S., Wendler, P.: Benchmarking and resource measurement (2015) (unpublished manuscript)
5. Beyer, D., Wendler, P.: Reuse of verification results: Conditional model checking, precision reuse, and verification witnesses. In: Bartocci, E., Ramakrishnan, C.R. (eds.) SPIN 2013. LNCS, vol. 7976, pp. 1–17. Springer, Heidelberg (2013)
6. Cassez, F., Matsuoka, T., Pierzchalski, E., Smyth, N.: Perentie: Modular trace refinement and selective value tracking (Competition contribution). In: Baier, C., Tinelli, C. (eds.) TACAS 2015. LNCS, vol. 9035, pp. 438–441. Springer, Heidelberg (2015)
7. Chen, Y.-F., Hsieh, C., Tsai, M.-H., Wang, B.-Y., Wang, F.: CPArec: Verifying recursive programs via source-to-source program transformation (Competition contribution). In: Baier, C., Tinelli, C. (eds.) TACAS 2015. LNCS, vol. 9035, pp. 425–427. Springer, Heidelberg (2015)
8. Dangl, M., Löwe, S., Wendler, P.: CPACHECKER with support for recursive programs and floating-point arithmetic. In: Baier, C., Tinelli, C. (eds.) TACAS 2015. LNCS, vol. 9035, pp. 422–424. Springer, Heidelberg (2015)
9. Gonzalez-de-Aledo, P., Sanchez, P.: FramewORk for embedded system verificaTion (Competition contribution). In: Baier, C., Tinelli, C. (eds.) TACAS 2015. LNCS, vol. 9035, pp. 428–430. Springer, Heidelberg (2015)
10. Gurfinkel, A., Kahsai, T., Navas, J.A.: SeaHorn: A framework for verifying C programs (Competition contribution). In: Baier, C., Tinelli, C. (eds.) TACAS 2015. LNCS, vol. 9035, pp. 446–449. Springer, Heidelberg (2015)
11. Haran, A., Carter, M., Emmi, M., Lal, A., Qadeer, S., Rakamarić, Z.: SMACK+Corral: A modular verifier (Competition contribution). In: Baier, C., Tinelli, C. (eds.) TACAS 2015. LNCS, vol. 9035, pp. 450–453. Springer, Heidelberg (2015)
12. Heizmann, M., Dietsch, D., Leike, J., Musa, B., Podelski, A.: Ultimate Automizer with Array Interpolation (Competition contribution). In: Baier, C., Tinelli, C. (eds.) TACAS 2015. LNCS, vol. 9035, pp. 454–456. Springer, Heidelberg (2015)
13. Holík, L., Hruška, M., Lengál, O., Rogalewicz, A., Šimáček, J., Vojnar, T.: Forester: Shape analysis using tree automata large (Competition contribution). In: Baier, C., Tinelli, C. (eds.) TACAS 2015. LNCS, vol. 9035, pp. 431–434. Springer, Heidelberg (2015)
14. Inverso, O., Tomasco, E., Fischer, B., La Torre, S., Parlato, G.: Lazy-CSeq: A lazy sequentialization tool for C (Competition contribution). In: Ábrahám, E., Havelund, K. (eds.) TACAS 2014. LNCS, vol. 8413, pp. 398–401. Springer, Heidelberg (2014)
15. Kroening, D., Tautschnig, M.: CBMC: C bounded model checker (Competition contribution). In: Ábrahám, E., Havelund, K. (eds.) TACAS 2014 (ETAPS). LNCS, vol. 8413, pp. 389–391. Springer, Heidelberg (2014)
16. Le, T.C., Qin, S., Chin, W.-N.: Termination and non-termination specification inference In: PLDI 2015. ACM (2015) (unpublished manuscript)
17. Morse, J., Ramalho, M., Cordeiro, L., Nicole, D., Fischer, B.: ESBMC 1.22 (Competition contribution). In: Ábrahám, E., Havelund, K. (eds.) TACAS 2014. LNCS, vol. 8413, pp. 405–407. Springer, Heidelberg (2014)
18. Muller, P., Peringer, P., Vojnar, T.: Predator hunting party (Competition contribution). In: Baier, C., Tinelli, C. (eds.) TACAS 2015. LNCS, vol. 9035, pp. 442–445. Springer, Heidelberg (2015)

19. Nguyen, T.L., Fischer, B., La Torre, S., Parlato, G.: Unbounded Lazy-CSeq: A lazy sequentialization tool for C programs with unbounded context switches (Competition contribution). In: Baier, C., Tinelli, C. (eds.) TACAS 2015. LNCS, vol. 9035, pp. 460–462. Springer, Heidelberg (2015)

20. Nutz, A., Dietsch, D., Mohamed, M.M., Podelski, A.: Ultimate Kojak (Competition Contribution). In: Baier, C., Tinelli, C. (eds.) TACAS 2015. LNCS, vol. 9035, pp. 457–459. Springer, Heidelberg (2015)

21. Rocha, H., Barreto, R., Cordeiro, L., Neto, A.D.: Understanding programming bugs in ANSI-C software using bounded model checking counter-examples. In: Derrick, J., Gnesi, S., Latella, D., Treharne, H. (eds.) IFM 2012. LNCS, vol. 7321, pp. 128–142. Springer, Heidelberg (2012)

22. Shved, P., Mandrykin, M., Mutilin, V.: Predicate analysis with BLAST 2.7 (Competition contribution). In: Flanagan, C., König, B. (eds.) TACAS 2012. LNCS, vol. 7214, pp. 525–527. Springer, Heidelberg (2012)

23. Ströder, T., Aschermann, C., Frohn, F., Hensel, J., Giesl, J.: AProVE: Termination and memory safety of C programs (Competition contribution). In: Baier, C., Tinelli, C. (eds.) TACAS 2015. LNCS, vol. 9035, pp. 416–418. Springer, Heidelberg (2015)

24. Tomasco, E., Inverso, O., Fischer, B., La Torre, S., Parlato, G.: MU-CSeq 0.3: Sequentialization by read-implicit and coarse-grained memory unwindings (Competition contribution). In: Baier, C., Tinelli, C. (eds.) TACAS 2015. LNCS, vol. 9035, pp. 435–437. Springer, Heidelberg (2015)

25. Urban, C.: FuncTion: An abstract domain functor for termination (Competition contribution). In: Baier, C., Tinelli, C. (eds.) TACAS 2015. LNCS, vol. 9035, pp. 463–465. Springer, Heidelberg (2015)

26. Wang, W., Barrett, C.: Cascade (Competition contribution). In: Baier, C., Tinelli, C. (eds.) TACAS 2015. LNCS, vol. 9035, pp. 419–421. Springer, Heidelberg (2015)

AProVE: Termination and Memory Safety of C Programs[*]
(Competition Contribution)

Thomas Ströder, Cornelius Aschermann, Florian Frohn, Jera Hensel, and Jürgen Giesl

RWTH Aachen University, Germany

Abstract. AProVE is a system for automatic termination and complexity proofs of C, Java, Haskell, Prolog, and term rewrite systems. The particular strength of AProVE when analyzing C is its capability to reason about pointer arithmetic combined with direct memory accesses (as, e.g., in standard implementations of string algorithms). As a prerequisite for termination, AProVE also proves memory safety of C programs.

1 Verification Approach and Software Architecture

To analyze programs with explicit pointer arithmetic, one has to handle the interplay between addresses and the values they point to. AProVE uses an approach based on symbolic execution and abstraction to transform the input program into a *symbolic execution graph* that over-approximates all possible program runs. Language-specific features (such as pointer arithmetic in C) are handled when generating this graph. The nodes of the symbolic execution graph are abstract states that represent sets of actual program states, and paths in the graph correspond to evaluations in the program. To keep the graph finite, we use *abstraction* to replace several states at the same program location by a more general new state. To formalize abstract states, we introduce a novel abstract domain that can track allocated memory in detail. An important advantage of our domain is that although it is based on separation logic, standard integer SMT solving can be used for all reasoning needed in our approach. Thus, the rules for symbolic execution and generalization of states can easily be automated.

In C, violating *memory safety* (i.e., accessing non-allocated memory) leads to undefined (and possibly non-terminating) behavior. So to prove termination of C programs with low-level memory access, one must also ensure memory safety. Hence, during the construction of the symbolic execution graph, we also prove memory safety of the program. In a similar way, one could also prove other safety properties by checking that the graph has no path from initial to "unsafe" states.

After verifying memory safety, the graph is automatically transformed into an integer rewrite system (IRS) whose termination is analyzed afterwards. In this way, the same termination techniques in the *back-end* of AProVE are used for termination analysis of different programming languages in the *front-end*. A graphical overview of AProVE's architecture is shown on the next page. Details on

[*] Supported by DFG grant GI 274/6-1 and Research Training Group 1298 (*AlgoSyn*).

C. Baier and C. Tinelli (Eds.): TACAS 2015, LNCS 9035, pp. 417–419, 2015.
DOI: 10.1007/978-3-662-46681-0_32

our approach for analyzing C programs can be found in [9]. In [7], we explain the use of AProVE for other programming lan-

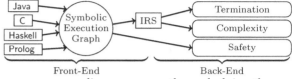

guages and give references to our corresponding papers on the underlying theory.

2   Strengths and Weaknesses

The strength of our approach for C is that it handles algorithms where the control flow depends on explicit pointer arithmetic and on detailed information about the contents of addresses, whereas most other tools fail for such algorithms. Moreover, in contrast to AProVE, most other termination provers ignore the problem of memory safety and just prove termination under the *assumption* that the program is memory safe. The success of AProVE at the annual international *Termination Competition*[1] shows that our rewriting-based approach is well suited for termination analysis of real-world programming languages. Here, AProVE won almost all categories related to termination of Java, Haskell, Prolog, and to termination or innermost runtime complexity of rewriting. Moreover, AProVE was the most powerful tool for termination analysis of C (the competition had such a category for the first time in 2014). At *SV-COMP*, AProVE already participated very successfully in 2014 when the competition featured a demonstration category for termination of C programs for the first time. This year, AProVE won the termination category of *SV-COMP* by proving termination for 305 of the 395 programs in this category (44 of the remaining programs are non-terminating, thus AProVE was successful on approx. 87% of the terminating ones).

On the other hand, since AProVE constructs symbolic execution graphs to prove memory safety and to infer suitable invariants needed for termination proofs, its runtime is often higher than that of other tools. Moreover, since symbolic execution graphs over-approximate the set of actual program runs, AProVE currently cannot *disprove* termination or memory safety.[2] A further weakness is that we only handle algorithms with integers and pointers, but no `struct` types yet, and that we assume integers to be unbounded. This is why AProVE currently only participates in the termination category, since this category assumes unbounded integers and the examples in this category do not contain `structs`. Finally, as our approach is targeted toward termination, up to now we did not implement support for other forms of safety besides memory safety.

3   Setup and Configuration

AProVE is developed by the *"Programming Languages and Verification"* group led by Jürgen Giesl at RWTH Aachen University. AProVE's main website is [1].

---

[1] http://www.termination-portal.org/wiki/Termination_Competition

[2] AProVE already proves non-termination of term rewriting and Java. We are currently working on adapting these techniques to the abstract domain used for C programs.

Here, AProVE can be downloaded as a command-line tool or as a plug-in for the popular Eclipse software development environment [5]. In this way, AProVE can already be applied during program construction. Moreover, AProVE can also be accessed directly via a web interface. The website [1] also contains a list of external tools used by AProVE and a list of present and past contributors.

The particular version for analyzing C programs according to the *SV-COMP* format can be downloaded from the following URL. In this version, we disabled the check for memory safety, since it was agreed that only memory safe programs will be included in the termination category of *SV-COMP*.

`http://aprove.informatik.rwth-aachen.de/eval/Pointer/AProVE.zip`

All files from this archive have to be extracted into one folder. AProVE is implemented in Java and needs a Java 7 Runtime Environment. To avoid handling the intricacies of C, we analyze programs in the platform-independent intermediate representation of the LLVM compilation framework [8] and AProVE requires the Clang compiler Version 2.9 [2] to translate C sources to LLVM. To solve the arising search problems in the back-end, AProVE needs the satisfiability checkers Z3 [3], Yices [4], and MiniSAT [6]. Moreover, extending the path environment is necessary so that AProVE can find the corresponding programs.

AProVE participated in the category *"Termination"*. It can be invoked for C files using the following call pattern. Here, `<problemFile>` is the C file to be analyzed for termination of the call `main()`, while `<outputFile>` is a file where AProVE should store its proof (or proof attempt).

`./AProVE.sh <problemFile> <outputFile>`

AProVE prints TRUE on the standard output if it can prove termination. Otherwise it prints UNKNOWN. As mentioned, currently, AProVE is not able to disprove termination for C programs, so AProVE does not print FALSE.

References

1. AProVE, `http://aprove.informatik.rwth-aachen.de/`
2. Clang, `http://clang.llvm.org/`
3. de Moura, L., Bjørner, N.: Z3: An efficient SMT solver. In: Ramakrishnan, C.R., Rehof, J. (eds.) TACAS 2008. LNCS, vol. 4963, pp. 337–340. Springer, Heidelberg (2008)
4. Dutertre, B., de Moura, L.: The Yices SMT solver (2006), `http://yices.csl.sri.com/tool-paper.pdf`
5. Eclipse, `http://www.eclipse.org/`
6. Eén, N., Sörensson, N.: An extensible SAT-solver. In: Giunchiglia, E., Tacchella, A. (eds.) SAT 2003. LNCS, vol. 2919, pp. 502–518. Springer, Heidelberg (2004)
7. Giesl, J., Brockschmidt, M., Emmes, F., Frohn, F., Fuhs, C., Otto, C., Plücker, M., Schneider-Kamp, P., Ströder, T., Swiderski, S., Thiemann, R.: Proving termination of programs automatically with AProVE. In: Demri, S., Kapur, D., Weidenbach, C. (eds.) IJCAR 2014. LNCS, vol. 8562, pp. 184–191. Springer, Heidelberg (2014)
8. Lattner, C., Adve, V.S.: LLVM: A compilation framework for lifelong program analysis & transformation. In: CGO 2004, pp. 55–88. IEEE (2004)
9. Ströder, T., Giesl, J., Brockschmidt, M., Frohn, F., Fuhs, C., Hensel, J., Schneider-Kamp, P.: Proving termination and memory safety for programs with pointer arithmetic. In: Demri, S., Kapur, D., Weidenbach, C. (eds.) IJCAR 2014. LNCS, vol. 8562, pp. 208–223. Springer, Heidelberg (2014)

Cascade
(Competition Contribution)

Wei Wang and Clark Barrett

New York University, New York, United States

Abstract. Cascade is a static program analysis tool developed at New York University. It uses bounded model checking to generate verification conditions and checks them using an SMT solver which either produces a proof of correctness or gives a concrete trace showing how an assertion can fail. It supports the majority of standard C features except for floating point. A distinguishing feature of Cascade is that its analysis uses a memory model which divides up memory into several partitions based on alias information.

1 Verification Approach

Bounded model checking (BMC) [4] is an efficient method to detect bugs automatically. The technique constructs a formula that encodes a program up to a user-specified bound. A *memory model* is a crucial part of the encoding in bounded model checking of programs, determining how the contents of and modifications to memory are represented. The most precise model is a *flat* model, which represents memory as a single array of bytes. However, this model typically does not scale well because the solver cannot easily infer which regions are disjoint.

Cascade uses a novel *partition* memory model. The main idea of this model is to split the memory according to the alias information acquired by incorporating a Steensgaard points-to analysis module [8]. This ensures that variables and dynamically allocated regions that may alias end up in the same partition. Each partition is modeled using a separate array. The memory partitioning significantly eases the burden of reasoning about disjointness and thus scales much better than the flat memory model, while the points-to-analysis approach ensures the soundness of modeling type-unsafe behaviors in C.

2 System Architecture

Cascade [9] is implemented in Java. The overall framework is illustrated in Figure 1. The C front-end converts a C program into an abstract syntax tree using a parser built using the xtc parser generator [6]. Both the core module and preprocessing module take the abstract syntax tree as input. In the preprocessing module, the points-to analysis is performed for each function in the C program without function-inlining or loop-unrolling. All the alias groups and the points-to relations among them are discovered here. The core module uses symbolic

© Springer-Verlag Berlin Heidelberg 2015
C. Baier and C. Tinelli (Eds.): TACAS 2015, LNCS 9035, pp. 420–422, 2015.
DOI: 10.1007/978-3-662-46681-0_33

execution [2, 3, 7] over the abstract syntax tree to build verification conditions as a SMT formula. Currently, it takes the approach of simple forward execution. The partition memory model is built based on the alias information generated at the preprocessing step. Verification conditions are discharged by an SMT solver. Cascade currently supports both CVC4 [1] and Z3 [5].

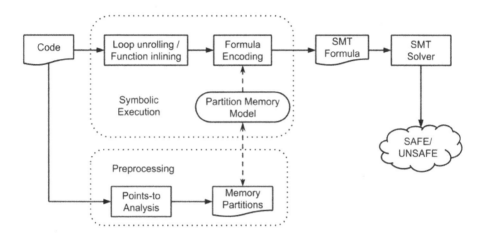

Fig. 1. Cascade framework

3   Strength and Weaknesses of the Approach

Cascade supports arbitrary user assertions, including reachability of labels in the C-code. Furthermore, it can detect bugs related to memory safety, including invalid memory accesses, invalid memory frees and memory leaks. In SV-COMP 2015, these checks are only enabled for the *MemorySafety* category. Cascade relies on loop unrolling and function inlining, and so it may perform poorly if either of these steps are required to be too large. In the competition, Cascade uses successively larger unrolls until a fixed bound of 1024 is reached, or a violation is detected, or a timeout is reached. Note that we set a timeout of 850 seconds. We also use a fixed function-inlining depth of 2. For memory safety checking, we use a different set of parameters: the maximum unroll is 200 and the inline depth is 5. If no error is found or the ERROR label cannot be reached within the maximum bounds, Cascade will report SAFE. Otherwise, it will report UNSAFE and the witness will be dumped in the GraphML format.

4   Tool Setup and Configuration

The version of Cascade submitted to SV-COMP 2015 can be downloaded at:

    http://cascade.cims.nyu.edu/bin/sv-comp-2015-4113-cvc4-patch.tar.gz

This version uses CVC4 as the back-end solver. Cascade requires JVM version 1.7.0. The archive unzips to a directory called `sv-comp-2015-4113-patch` which contains a script called `run_cascade_bmc`. The script should be run from the `sv-comp-2015-4113-patch` directory as follows:

```
run_cascade_bmc -trace <c-benchmark>
```

where `c-benchmark` is the name of the C file to be analyzed. The results are printed on stdout and should be interpreted as follows:

- if the last line printed is UNSAFE, this should be interpreted as FALSE;
- if the last line printed is UNSAFE:p_<prop> this should be intepreted as FALSE(<prop>);
- otherwise, if the last *word* printed is SAFE, this should be interpreted as TRUE;
- any other result should be interpreted as UNKNOWN.

For results that correspond to FALSE, a witness is dumped to the file:

```
out/<benchmark-name>/witness.graphml.
```

where `<benchmark-name>` is the filename of the C benchmark that was checked without the path prefix.

In the competition, Cascade will participate in the following categories: *Bit Vectors, Control Flow and Integer Variables, Heap Manipulation*, and *Memory Safety*. We will not participate in the others for various reasons including lack of support for function pointers and concurrency.

References

1. Barrett, C., Conway, C.L., Deters, M., Hadarean, L., Jovanović, D., King, T., Reynolds, A., Tinelli, C.: CVC4. In: Gopalakrishnan, G., Qadeer, S. (eds.) CAV 2011. LNCS, vol. 6806, pp. 171–177. Springer, Heidelberg (2011)
2. Biere, A., Cimatti, A., Clarke, E.M., Fujita, M., Zhu, Y.: Symbolic model checking using SAT procedures instead of BDDs. In: Proceedings of Design Automation Conference (DAC 1999), vol. 317, pp. 226–320 (1999)
3. Brand, D., Joyner, W.H.: Verification of protocols using symbolic execution. Comput. Networks 2, 351 (1978)
4. Clarke, E., Kroning, D., Lerda, F.: A tool for checking ANSI-C programs. In: Jensen, K., Podelski, A. (eds.) TACAS 2004. LNCS, vol. 2988, pp. 168–176. Springer, Heidelberg (2004)
5. de Moura, L.M., Bjørner, N.: Z3: An efficient SMT solver. In: TACAS, pp. 337–340 (2008)
6. Grimm, R.: Rats!, a parser generator supporting extensible syntax (2009)
7. King, J.C.: Symbolic execution and program testing. Communications of the ACM 385, 226–394 (1976)
8. Steensgaard, B.: Points-to analysis in almost linear time. In: ACM Symposium on Principles of Programming Languages, pp. 32–41 (1996)
9. Wang, W., Barrett, C., Wies, T.: Cascade 2.0. In: McMillan, K.L., Rival, X. (eds.) VMCAI 2014. LNCS, vol. 8318, pp. 142–160. Springer, Heidelberg (2014)

CPAchecker with Support for Recursive Programs and Floating-Point Arithmetic
(Competition Contribution)

Matthias Dangl, Stefan Löwe, and Philipp Wendler

University of Passau, Passau, Germany

Abstract. We submit to SV-COMP'15 the software-verification framework CPAchecker. The submitted configuration is a combination of seven different analyses, based on explicit-value analysis, k-induction, predicate analysis, and concrete memory graphs. These analyses use concepts such as CEGAR, lazy abstraction, interpolation, adjustable-block encoding, bounded model checking, invariant generation, and block-abstraction memoization. Found counterexamples are cross-checked by a bit-precise analysis. The combination of several different analyses copes well with the diversity of the verification tasks in SV-COMP.

1 Software Architecture

CPAchecker is a software verification framework built on the concept of CONFIGURABLE PROGRAM ANALYSIS (CPA). One of the main design goals of the framework is to ease the development of new analyses and verification approaches. The CPAs available in the framework can be recombined on a per-demand basis by only passing the according configuration parameters to CPAchecker, without the need of changes in the implementation. Commonly needed tasks, like tracking of program counter, call stack, and function-pointer values, are also implemented as separate CPAs, and may assist the main CPAs, such as the predicate analysis. The framework provides a front-end based on the C-parser of the Eclipse CDT project (http://www.eclipse.org/cdt/), and an interface to SMT solvers (MathSAT5 (http://mathsat.fbk.eu/) in our submission) for solving and interpolation.

2 Verification Approach

The configuration used by CPAchecker in this year's SV-COMP is conceptually similar to last year [4]: a sequential combination of five analyses [2], as shown in Fig. 1, with the addition of an analysis based on k-induction using continuously-refined auxiliary invariants [1] and the limitation of the predicate analysis to a single ABE-l configuration. Each analysis runs for a predefined time, and if it does not return a result within the time bounds, the next analysis is started. Whenever one of the analyses finds a counterexample, it is cross-checked and if deemed infeasible, the analysis that is currently running gets terminated and the next one takes over.

© Springer-Verlag Berlin Heidelberg 2015
C. Baier and C. Tinelli (Eds.): TACAS 2015, LNCS 9035, pp. 423–425, 2015.
DOI: 10.1007/978-3-662-46681-0_34

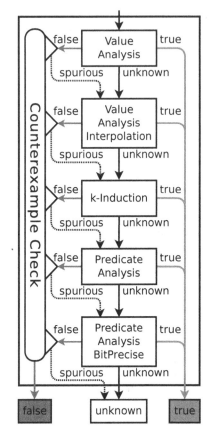

Fig. 1. Sequential combination to verify reachability properties

The time limit for each of the first three analyses is 60 s and the predicate analysis has no time limit. Similarly to last year, the counterexample checks are done by a bit-precise predicate analysis for the first four analyses, and the bounded model checker CBMC (http://www.cprover.org/cbmc) for the last analysis. In order to support the category "Floats", we have added support for precisely modeling the floating-point arithmetic to the predicate analysis (the value analysis cannot model non-deterministic values precisely enough to solve the programs in this category). This was made possible because the SMT solver MATHSAT5 now supports floating-point arithmetic as an SMT theory, and CPACHECKER leverages this by appropriately encoding most of the floating-point semantics of C in SMT formulae. Interpolation for floats is not yet supported, but not necessary for most programs in this category.

In two cases we deviate from the described configuration and use specialized approaches. As last year, we use a bounded analysis based on concrete memory graphs for verifying memory safety properties. For recursive programs, we use the predicate analysis with an extension of block-abstraction memoization [5], which uses two operators reduce and expand to remove information from the abstract state when entering a block (typically a function or loop body) if this information is not necessary inside the block, and restoring this information when leaving the block again. This allows a more efficient analysis and caching of the results for analyzed blocks. We extended this approach to support recursion (a recursive function call creates a new block). Together with an implementation of nested interpolation this allows the predicate analysis to analyze recursive programs with unbounded depth.

3   Strengths and Weaknesses

The sequential combination of several analyses covering different abstract domains allows CPACHECKER to be competitive on a wide range of benchmarks. The bit-precise analyses help to minimize the number of wrong answers to only 0.6 % of all programs. Improvements over last year's version include handling of floating-point arithmetic using MathSAT, the addition of an analysis based on k-induction with continuously-refined invariant generation [1], a novel interpolation routine for the value domain [3], and the use of an extension of block-abstraction memoization [5] as an analysis-independent framework for supporting recursive programs. Weaknesses of CPACHECKER are the missing support for concurrent programs and for checking termination. An abstraction technique for memory graphs would allow a more efficient analysis in the categories "Arrays" and "MemorySafety".

4 Setup and Configuration

CPACHECKER is available at `http://cpachecker.sosy-lab.org` and needs a Java 7 runtime environment. We submit version `1.3.10-svcomp15` for all categories. The command line for running CPACHECKER is

```
scripts/cpa.sh -sv-comp15 -disable-java-assertions -heap 10000m -spec property.prp program.i
```

Please add the parameter `-64` for C programs assuming a 64-bit environment, and `-setprop cpa.predicate.handlePointerAliasing=false` for the simple memory model. For machines with less RAM, the amount of memory given to the Java VM needs to be set accordingly by the parameter `-heap`. CPACHECKER will print the verification result and the name of the output directory to the console. In case CPACHECKER finds a property violation the witness is written to the file named `witness.graphml` within this directory.

5 Project and Contributors

CPACHECKER is an open-source project being developed by the members of the Software Systems Lab, led by Dirk Beyer, at the University of Passau. CPACHECKER is used and extended by the members of the Institute for System Programming of the Russian Academy of Sciences, the Universities of Paderborn, Darmstadt and Vienna, as well as at Verimag, Grenoble. We would like to thank all contributors for their work on CPACHECKER. The full list can be found at `http://cpachecker.sosy-lab.org`.

References

1. Beyer, D., Dangl, M., Wendler, P.: Combining k-induction with continuously-refined invariants. Technical Report MIP-1503, University of Passau. arXiv:1502.00096 (January 2015), `http://arxiv.org/abs/1502.00096`
2. Beyer, D., Henzinger, T.A., Keremoglu, M.E., Wendler, P.: Conditional model checking: A technique to pass information between verifiers. In: Proc. FSE 2012. ACM, NewYork (2012)
3. Beyer, D., Löwe, S., Wendler, P.: Domain-type-guided refinement selection based on sliced path prefixes. Technical Report MIP-1501, University of Passau. arXiv:1502.00045 (January 2015), `http://arxiv.org/abs/1502.00045`
4. Löwe, S., Mandrykin, M., Wendler, P.: CPACHECKER with sequential combination of explicit-value analyses and predicate analyses. In: Ábrahám, E., Havelund, K. (eds.) TACAS 2014 (ETAPS). LNCS, vol. 8413, pp. 392–394. Springer, Heidelberg (2014)
5. Wonisch, D., Wehrheim, H.: Predicate analysis with block-abstraction memoization. In: Aoki, T., Taguchi, K. (eds.) ICFEM 2012. LNCS, vol. 7635, pp. 332–347. Springer, Heidelberg (2012)

CPAREC: Verifying Recursive Programs via Source-to-Source Program Transformation
(Competition Contribution)

Yu-Fang Chen[1], Chiao Hsieh[1,2,*], Ming-Hsien Tsai[1],
Bow-Yaw Wang[1], and Farn Wang[2]

[1] Institute of Information Science, Academia Sinica, Taiwan
[2] Graduate Institute of Electrical Engineering, National Taiwan University, Taiwan
bridge@iis.sinica.edu.tw

Abstract. CPAREC is a tool for verifying recursive C programs via source-to-source program transformation. It uses a recursion-free program analyzer CPACHECKER as a black box and computes function summaries from the inductive invariants generated by CPACHECKER. Such function summaries enable CPAREC to check recursive programs.

1 Verification Approach

The CPAREC tool handles recursive programs by an iterative source-to-source transformation technique proposed in [2]. In each iteration, it transforms the original recursive program P into a non-recursive program P' that *under-approximates* the behaviors of P. The program P' will be sent to a black box program verifier V that does not support recursion. If an assertion violation in the program P' is found by the verifier V, it also indicates an assertion violation in the program P. Otherwise, the verifier should generate an *inductive invariant* as a proof for the unreachability of the assertion violation, from which CPAREC extracts candidates of *function summaries*.

Based on recursive rule of Hoare logic and fix-point theorem [3], CPAREC reduces the problem of checking the correctness of function summary candidates again to assertion checking. More specifically, it first replaces all function calls in P with the corresponding function summary candidates and obtain a new non-recursive program P''. Then it checks if all behaviors of P'' are included in the behaviors encoded in the function summary candidate of P. This step is again handled by a source-to-source program transformation with some additional assertions added. If the verifier V reports that all assertions are not violated, then CPAREC found correct function summaries and thus proved the correctness of P. Otherwise, it produces a more refined version of P by unwinding the function calls and proceeds to the next iteration of the verification procedure. The execution flow of CPAREC can be found in Figure 1.

---

* Corresponding author.

© Springer-Verlag Berlin Heidelberg 2015
C. Baier and C. Tinelli (Eds.): TACAS 2015, LNCS 9035, pp. 426–428, 2015.
DOI: 10.1007/978-3-662-46681-0_35

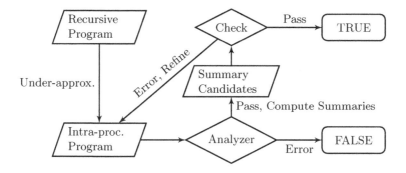

Fig. 1. The Execution Flow of CPAREC

2 Software Architecture

Currently, CPAREC uses CPACHECKER (over 140 thousands lines of JAVA code) as the underlying program analyzer [1]. CPAREC contains 1256 lines of OCAML code for syntactic source-to-source transformation using the CIL [4] library. The rest of the algorithm is implemented in 705 lines of PYTHON code. Among them only 270 lines are for extracting function summaries. Since syntactic transformation is independent of the underlying program analyzer, only about 14% of the code need to be rewritten should another analyzer be employed. When extracting summaries from inductive invariants, we sometimes need to quantify out additional variables that are neither formal parameters nor return variables. CPAREC uses the tool RedLog [5] for quantifier elimination.

3 Strengths and Weaknesses

Compared with other analysis algorithms for recursive programs, the one implemented in CPAREC is very *lightweight*. It only performs syntactic transformation and requires standard functionalities from underlying intraprocedure program analyzers. Moreover, our technique is very *modular*. Any intraprocedural analyzer providing proofs of inductive invariants can be employed by our tool. With the interface between CPAREC and the program analyzers described in the previous section, incorporating recursive analysis with existing program analyzers thus only requires minimal implementation efforts. Recursive analysis hence benefits from future advanced intraprocedural analysis with little cost through our lightweight and modular technique.

On the other hand, we suffer the same limitation as the black-box analyzer. For instance, using CPACHECKER, we can only produce *linear* summaries. However, in the recursive category of the competition, several examples require non-linear summaries for proving correctness. Moreover, we get the modularity for the price of losing some flexibility. For example, we cannot optimize the way that the underlying program analyzer constructs the trace formula and sends to SMT solver. This step potentially can reduce the number of variables that we need to quantify out and may improve performance.

4   Setup and Configuration

CPAREC is available at

https://github.com/fmlab-iis/cparec

The submitted version is v0.1-alpha. The simplest way to execute CPAREC is to first download the binary from the web-site. To setup the environment in Ubuntu 12.04 64-bit, JAVA Runtime, Python 2.7, the Python Networkx package, and the Python PyGraphviz package are required. Run following command to install above packages in Ubuntu 12.04 64-bit:

```
sudo apt-get install openjdk-7-jre python python-networkx python-pygraphviz
```

To process a benchmark example `program.c`, one should use the following script:

```
python <path_to_cparec>cparec/main.py program.c
```

No further parameters are needed. CPAREC will print the verification result to the console. We will only participate in the recursive category of the competition.

5   Software Project and Contributors

CPAREC is an open-source project from the programming language and formal method (PLFM) group at the Institute of Information Science, Academia Sinica, Taiwan. The main contributors are the authors of this paper. The programs are written by Chiao Hsieh and Ming-Hsien Tsai.

References

1. Beyer, D., Keremoglu, M.E.: CPACHECKER: A tool for configurable software verification. In: Gopalakrishnan, G., Qadeer, S. (eds.) CAV 2011. LNCS, vol. 6806, pp. 184–190. Springer, Heidelberg (2011)
2. Chen, Y.-F., Hsieh, C., Tsai, M.-H., Wang, B.-Y., Wang, F.: Verifying recursive programs using intraprocedural analyzers. In: Müller-Olm, M., Seidl, H. (eds.) Static Analysis. LNCS, vol. 8723, pp. 118–133. Springer, Heidelberg (2014)
3. Clarke, E.M.: Program invariants as fixed points. In: 18th Annual Symposium on Foundations of Computer Science, pp. 18–29. IEEE (1977)
4. Necula, G.C., McPeak, S., Rahul, S.P., Weimer, W.: CIL: Intermediate language and tools for analysis and transformation of C programs. In: Nigel Horspool, R. (ed.) CC 2002. LNCS, vol. 2304, p. 213. Springer, Heidelberg (2002)
5. Redlog, http://www.redlog.eu/

FramewORk for Embedded System verificaTion
(Competition Contribution)

Pablo Gonzalez-de-Aledo and Pablo Sanchez

University of Cantabria, Santander (Cantabria), Spain
{pabloga,sanchez}@teisa.unican.es

Abstract. FOREST is a bounded model checker that implements symbolic execution on top of the LLVM intermediate language and is able to detect errors in programs developed in C. FOREST transforms a program into a set of SMT formulas describing each feasible path and decides these formulas with an SMT solver. This enables it to prove the satisfiability of reachability conditions such as the ones presented in SV-COMP. FOREST implements different ways of representing SMT formulas: linear arithmetic, polynomials and generic bit-accurate and not bit-accurate representations.

1 Overview

As many bounded model checkers, to verify a property for a given piece of code, FOREST unfolds the execution of the code up to a certain depth and transforms each path into an SMT formula. Before this transformation, assertions and special functions are converted into conditions, so verification clauses can be expressed as reachability properties (in the SV-COMP framework, if a state can be reached from the start of the main procedure in which an LTL clause can be satisfied, then the program is unsafe). The transformation from source to SMT can be done using different theories (integers, linear formulas, polynomials, etc.), and formulas can be decided using different solvers (Boolector, Z3, CVC4 ...). For the competition, the theory of integers and real numbers has been chosen, and formulas are decided with Z3 [3]. This is a trade-off between accuracy and solving time.

2 Architecture

As a framework for automated program verification through symbolic execution, verification under FOREST comprises the following steps, which are illustrated in Figure 1.

1. **Configuration:** The 'forest' binary orchestrates the remaining tools and steps, and configures the framework according to command-line parameters or configuration files (xml files).

© Springer-Verlag Berlin Heidelberg 2015
C. Baier and C. Tinelli (Eds.): TACAS 2015, LNCS 9035, pp. 429–431, 2015.
DOI: 10.1007/978-3-662-46681-0_36

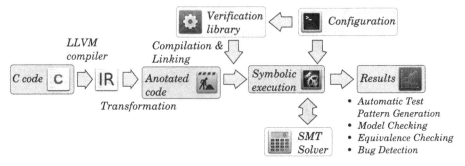

Fig. 1. FOREST architecture

2. **Front-End and intermediate representation:** As a front-end we use llvm-gcc, which transforms the source code to an llvm intermediate representation. In this representation, branch instructions are performed in two steps; first the result of the comparison is stored in a register. This register is then used in a jump instruction to implement the branch. This unifies comparisons so they can be handled as binary instructions.

3. **Annotation:** The intermediate representation is transformed via a transformation pass that instruments every operation with calls to back-end functions. These back-end functions dynamically compute the strongest postcondition from the 'start' state for every instruction so the effect of this instruction in the state can be considered when running the program.

4. **Static Heuristic:** The control-flow-graph of the intermediate representation is obtained and a heuristic is computed indicating possible paths from the entry point of the program to the destination. Yen's algorithm [1] is used to compute the k-shortest paths from entry to error location.

5. **Linking:** The transformed intermediate representation is linked with a verification library. This library implements the semantics of every operation in the intermediate representation and performs the symbolic execution as explained in the following step.

6. **Execution:** When executed, the program forks on every condition encountered in execution and the heuristic computed in step 4 is used to guide the exploration toward the error location. The A* algorithm [4] is used to search for paths between entry and error. While the program is run, the inserted functions from step 3 compute the strongest post-condition from the starting state, and this condition is passed to an SMT solver when a conditional branch is encountered. The effect of forking the execution on every branch instruction is that the program "unfolds" into a binary tree in which every process executes a different feasible path. Feasible paths are then added to A* set of candidate paths to continue exploration.

3   Strenghts and Weaknesses

As a bounded model checker, FOREST cannot generate proofs of correctness for unbounded programs. In these cases, we unfold the loops up to a certain depth, and check for satisfiability in an under-approximation of the program possible behaviours. This may be unsound in certain benchmarks such as `array_call3`, where FOREST fail to detect the error due to this limitation. Orthogonally to this problem, approximating the behavior of variables with integers and real types can also produce errors. This happens in the test 'verisec_sendmail', in which the reachability of the `error` state depends on an integer overflow. This bug is not detected using integer representation but can be spotted if we use the option `-solver bitvector`. The strengths of symbolic execution are its applicability in a wide spectrum of applications, the possibility of obtaining partial results and the speed of finding bugs when the program has some.

4 Tool Setup

The version of FOREST submitted to the competition can be downloaded executing the following command in a x86_64 Linux machine

```
wget teisa.unican.es/forest/images/install.sh -O - | bash
```

This should download and execute a script that installs the tool in the current path and performs some tests. A correct installation can be assessed if all tests are correct and terminate in time. The command-line options to be used in SV-COMP have been condensed to the '`-svcomp`' parameter. The file to analyse can be indicated with '`-file`'. Complete installation instructions can be obtained removing the tailing '`| bash`' from the previous command.

5 Software Project

FOREST is maintained by Pablo González de Aledo. This work has been supported by Project TEC2011-28666-C04-02 and grant BES-2012-055572, awarded by the Spanish Ministry of Economy and Competitivity. We gratefully acknowledge the help of Franck Cassez for the revision of this article and for his pertinent advice, and Fernando Herrera for testing the tool under different Linux distributions and machines.

References

1. Yen, J.Y.: An algorithm for finding shortest routes from all source nodes to a given destination in general networks. The Quarterly of Applied Mathematics 27, 526–530
2. Lattner, C., Adve, V.: LLVM: A compilation framework for lifelong program analysis & transformation. In: International Symposium on Code Generation and Optimization 2004, pp. 75–86 (2004)
3. de Moura, L., Bjørner, N.S.: Z3: An efficient SMT solver. In: Ramakrishnan, C.R., Rehof, J. (eds.) TACAS 2008. LNCS, vol. 4963, pp. 337–340. Springer, Heidelberg (2008)
4. Hart, P.E., Nilsson, N.J., Raphael, B.: A Formal Basis for the Heuristic Determination of Minimum Cost Paths. IEEE Transactions on Systems Science and Cybernetics SSC4 4, 100–107 (1968)

Forester: Shape Analysis Using Tree Automata
(Competition Contribution)

Lukáš Holík, Martin Hruška, Ondřej Lengál,
Adam Rogalewicz, Jiří Šimáček, and Tomáš Vojnar

FIT, Brno University of Technology, IT4Innovations Centre of Excellence, Czech Republic

Abstract. Forester is a tool for shape analysis of programs with complex dynamic data structures—including various flavours of lists (such as singly/doubly linked lists, nested lists, or skip lists) as well as trees and other complex data structures—that uses an abstract domain based on finite tree automata. This paper gives a brief description of the verification approach of Forester and discusses its strong and weak points revealed during its participation in SV-COMP'15.

1 Verification Approach

Forester is a tool for (sound) shape analysis of programs with complex dynamic data structures, such as various flavours of lists (including singly/doubly linked lists, nested lists, or skip lists) as well as trees and other complex data structures. The used abstract domain contains *forest automata*, a generalization of finite tree automata, described in [1,2]. The approach attempts to combine the strong points of two other approaches: (i) the scalability of *separation logic* [3], which is due to the concept of separation allowing local reasoning about disjoint parts of the program heap, and (ii) the flexibility of *abstract regular tree model checking* (ARTMC) [4], which uses finite tree automata for symbolic representation of the sets of reachable heap graphs.

The heap representation is based on the *forest decomposition* of the heap. This is a representation of the heap by a tuple of trees such that the roots of the trees correspond to the *cut-points* of the graph. A cut-point is a node that is either referenced from a program variable or that has more than one incoming edge. The trees in the tuple are free of cut-points and their leaves contain either non-pointer values or explicit references to roots of other trees. To represent *sets* of heaps—the elements of the concrete domain—instead of a tuple of trees Forester uses a tuple of tree automata, the so-called forest automaton. Each tree automaton represents a set of cut-point-free trees; the heap graphs represented by a forest automaton can be constructed from the forest automaton by taking a tree from the language of every tree automaton and connecting the references in the leaves of the trees to the roots of the referenced trees.

We associate an abstract transformer manipulating forest automata with every concrete operation. Joins are handled precisely (we split the execution and proceed in the verification run for each branch independently). The abstraction operator, called on loop points, is based on the *finite height abstraction* from ARTMC [4], and its main idea is to introduce loops in the tree automata to allow for a representation of infinite sets of trees with regular structure.

© Springer-Verlag Berlin Heidelberg 2015
C. Baier and C. Tinelli (Eds.): TACAS 2015, LNCS 9035, pp. 432–435, 2015.
DOI: 10.1007/978-3-662-46681-0_37

In order to be able to verify programs manipulating heaps where the number of cut-points is unbounded, we use *hierarchical* forest automata. These are forest automata that can use other (lower-level) forest automata as symbols, in a hierarchy of a finite height. These lower-level forest automata are called *boxes*. A box is essentially used to represent a repeated structure of the heap graph that contains some cut-points. The boxes to be used in a verification run are devised using the learning algorithm from [2].

In order to use Forester, it is necessary to properly model all external functions; Forester itself implements models of the two basic functions for memory allocation, `malloc` and `free`.

2   Tool Architecture

Forester is implemented in C++ as a GCC plugin that uses the Code Listener [5] infrastructure as the front-end for preprocessing the intermediate representation used in GCC (called GIMPLE) into a compiler-independent representation. Further, it uses the VATA library [6] as the back-end for manipulating tree automata. Forester translates the input program obtained from Code Listener into its internal representation, in which every program statement is represented by a sequence of abstract transformers that manipulate the symbolic representation of the program. The translated program is then subject to symbolic execution, during which Forester detects memory errors (invalid dereferences or frees, occurrence of garbage) and reachability of an error line.

3   Strengths and Weaknesses

The main strong point of Forester is that it gives sound results on all verification tasks that we run. In particular, Forester was able to find shape invariants for the most difficult programs in the Memory Safety category, i.e. programs manipulating 2 and 3 level skip lists, trees (including the Deutsch-Schorr-Waite tree traversal algorithm), and (nested) singly/doubly linked lists.

However, the overall performance of Forester on the benchmarks of SV-COMP'15 was significantly hindered by the following two causes. The first cause is the still quite high degree of immaturity of Forester in dealing with real-life C code with all its caveats—in the case Forester encounters some unsupported feature of C (such as the `union` data type, function pointers, or the use of arrays), it returns the UNKNOWN answer. The other cause is the incompleteness of the verification procedure and the current inability of the tool to distinguish spurious counterexamples from real ones; if a potentially spurious counterexample is found by Forester, it again returns UNKNOWN. However, it is possible to use the option `--false` to switch Forester into a mode in which it reports all found counterexamples and allows their subsequent analysis, either by a user or by e.g. a bug hunter.

4   Tool Setup and Configuration

An archive with the source code of the Forester competition release[1] can be down-loaded from the project web page. The file README-FORESTER-SVCOMP-2015 in the root directory of the archive contains information about how to build and run the tool. After Forester is successfully built, the fa_build directory contains a Python script sv_comp_run.py that executes the tool and transforms its output to the format expected by SV-COMP. The script expects the path to the file with the program under verification as an argument; further, the path to a file with a description of the properties to be verified can be specified using the --properties option. For the case the answer of Forester is **FALSE** (i.e. a real error is encountered in the program under verification), Forester returns the name of the property that has been violated. More-over, a mandatory --trace option is required to specify the path to the file where the witness leading from the entry point to the statement that caused the violation is to be saved. On the other hand, if Forester finds a shape invariant of the program without encountering a property violation, it returns **TRUE**.

Furthermore, if the --time option is given, Forester also writes to the standard output the CPU time that the verification run took. It is also possible to generate graph-ical representations of abstract program configurations at some line of code into a se-quence of files named according to the template filename-XXXX.dot by inserting the statement __VERIFIER_plot("filename") to the desired line of code in the processed program.

Forester participates in the following two categories of SV-COMP'15: Heap Manip-ulation and Memory Safety.

5   Software Project and Conclusion

Forester is developed by the VeriFIT group at Brno University of Technology and dis-tributed under the GNU General Public License version 3. The source code of Forester is in a git repository shared with Predator (a memory analyzer based on symbolic memory graphs [7]), which is developed in the same group.

This is the first submission of Forester to SV-COMP. In the future, we wish to focus on the following two points: (a) extending the set of the supported features of C, and (b) developing the ability to properly identify spurious counterexamples and to use them to refine the abstraction used.

Acknowledgement. This work was supported by the Czech Science Foundation (projects 14-11384S and 202/13/37876P), the BUT FIT project FIT-S-14-2486, and the EU/Czech IT4Innovations Centre of Excellence project CZ.1.05/1.1.00/02.0070.

---

[1] http://www.fit.vutbr.cz/research/groups/verifit/tools/
forester/download/forester-2014-10-31-9d3ad64.tar.gz

References

1. Habermehl, P., Holík, L., Rogalewicz, A., Šimáček, J., Vojnar, T.: Forest automata for verification of heap manipulation. Formal Methods in System Design 41(1) (2012)
2. Holík, L., Lengál, O., Rogalewicz, A., Šimáček, J., Vojnar, T.: Fully automated shape analysis based on forest automata. In: Sharygina, N., Veith, H. (eds.) CAV 2013. LNCS, vol. 8044, pp. 740–755. Springer, Heidelberg (2013)
3. Berdine, J., Calcagno, C., Cook, B., Distefano, D., O'Hearn, P.W., Wies, T., Yang, H.: Shape analysis for composite data structures. In: Damm, W., Hermanns, H. (eds.) CAV 2007. LNCS, vol. 4590, pp. 178–192. Springer, Heidelberg (2007)
4. Bouajjani, A., Habermehl, P., Rogalewicz, A., Vojnar, T.: Abstract regular (tree) model checking. International Journal on Software Tools for Technology Transfer 14(2) (2012)
5. Dudka, K., Peringer, P., Vojnar, T.: An easy to use infrastructure for building static analysis tools. In: Moreno-Díaz, R., Pichler, F., Quesada-Arencibia, A. (eds.) EUROCAST 2011, Part I. LNCS, vol. 6927, pp. 527–534. Springer, Heidelberg (2012)
6. Lengál, O., Šimáček, J., Vojnar, T.: VATA: A library for efficient manipulation of nondeterministic tree automata. In: Flanagan, C., König, B. (eds.) TACAS 2012. LNCS, vol. 7214, pp. 79–94. Springer, Heidelberg (2012)
7. Dudka, K., Peringer, P., Vojnar, T.: Byte-precise verification of low-level list manipulation. In: Logozzo, F., Fähndrich, M. (eds.) Static Analysis. LNCS, vol. 7935, pp. 215–237. Springer, Heidelberg (2013)

MU-CSeq 0.3: Sequentialization by Read-Implicit and Coarse-Grained Memory Unwindings[*]
(Competition Contribution)

Ermenegildo Tomasco[1][**], Omar Inverso[1], Bernd Fischer[2],
Salvatore La Torre[3], and Gennaro Parlato[1]

[1] Electronics and Computer Science, University of Southampton, UK
[2] Division of Computer Science, Stellenbosch University, South Africa
[3] Dipartimento di Informatica, Università di Salerno, Italy
et1m11@ecs.soton.ac.uk

Abstract. We describe a new CSeq module that implements improved algorithms for the verification of multi-threaded C programs with dynamic thread creation. It is based on sequentializing the programs according to a guessed sequence of write operations in the shared memory (memory unwinding, MU). The original algorithm (implemented in MU-CSeq 0.1) stores the values of all shared variables for each write (read-explicit fine-grained MU), which requires multiple copies of the shared variables. Our new algorithms store only the writes (read-implicit MU) or only a subset of the writes (coarse-grained MU), which reduces the memory footprint of the unwinding and so allows larger unwinding bounds.

1   Introduction

Sequentializations translate concurrent programs into sequential ones while preserving a given verification property (e.g., reachability). They reuse sequential verification tools and offer many advantages, such as the ability to focus on the concurrency aspects of a language, to quickly experiment with different approaches, and to build robust verification tools with less effort. We develop the CSeq tool as a modular sequentialization framework [1,2] for multi-threaded C programs with dynamic thread creation. It contains modules for the Lal/Reps scheme [5], a lazy sequentialization scheme aimed at bounded model checking [3,4], and a memory unwinding scheme [6].

A *memory unwinding* (MU) is an explicit representation of the write operations into the shared memory as a sequence that contains for each write the writing thread, the variable, and the written value. We can vary which writes are represented and thus exposed to the other threads, which leads to different strategies with different performance characteristics. In a *fine-grained* MU *every* write operation is represented explicitly and individually. In a *coarse-grained* MU we only represent a subset of the writes and group together multiple writes (by exposing for each group only the last write for each variable). In an *intra-thread* MU the writes in one group are all executed by one thread; the writes not represented can thus be seen as having been superseded by subsequent writes in the same context. In an *inter-thread* MU the writes in one group can come from different threads, thus summarizing the effect of multiple context switches.

[*] Partially supported by EPSRC EP/M008991/1, INDAM-GNCS 2014, and MIUR-FARB 2012-2014 grants.

[**] Corresponding author.

© Springer-Verlag Berlin Heidelberg 2015
C. Baier and C. Tinelli (Eds.): TACAS 2015, LNCS 9035, pp. 436–438, 2015.
DOI: 10.1007/978-3-662-46681-0_38

2   Verification Approach

Overview. Our approach can be seen as an *eager sequentialization* of the original concurrent program P over the unwound memory. We first guess an n-*memory unwinding* of P, i.e., a sequence $w_1 \ldots w_n$ identifying the threads, the shared variables and the values involved in the write operations of P. We then simulate all runs of P that are *compatible* with this guess. For the simulation, each thread is translated into a simulation function where write and read accesses over the shared memory are replaced by operations over the unwound memory. The simulation functions are executed sequentially, starting from the main function; each thread creation is translated into a call to the corresponding simulation function. All context switches are implicitly simulated through the MU. We adapt this general sequentialization scheme with different implementations, in particular for the functions to read from / write into the shared memory and for dynamic thread creation. The details can be found in [7].

Fine-Grained MU. In this approach, all the writes of a P run are considered meaningful to the other threads and thus exposed. We store each of them individually in the memory unwinding, with three arrays reporting respectively for each position the writing thread, the variable name and the written value. For an efficient implementation of the MU API functions, we also store some additional data such as the index of the last write performed in the simulation and a table containing, for each position and thread t, the position of next write of t in the memory unwinding.

We distinguish between the *read-explicit* and the *read-implicit* schemes. In the first case, all shared variables are replicated at each position of the sequence; we used this schema in MU-CSeq 0.1 [6]. Its main feature is that the value of each shared variable can be read directly at each step. It thus trades memory consumption for a simple logic in the implementation of the MU API. In the second scheme, at each position in the sequence, we copy only the shared variable that is modified by the corresponding write. The implementation of the MU API becomes more involved, but it yields an effective gain when the number of shared variables is large compared to the number of writes. We have also mixed the two schemes into a third one that is read-explicit for scalar variables and read-implicit for the arrays.

Coarse-Grained MU. In this approach, we store at each position of the sequence a partial mapping from the shared variables to values, with the meaning that the variables in the domain of the mapping are modified from the previous position and the value given by the mapping is their value at this position. A variable that is modified at position $i + 1$ could also be modified between positions i and $i + 1$ by other writes that are not exposed in the sequence. Thus, by exposing only some of the writes of a run (1) we restrict the number of possible runs that can match a MU (in fact, the unexposed writes cannot be read externally, and thus some possible interleavings of the threads are ruled out) and (2) we handle larger number of writes by nondeterministically deeming only some of them as interesting for the other threads.

In this approach we also distinguish between the cases in which either only one (*intra-thread coarse-grained* MU) or multiple (*inter-thread coarse-grained* MU) threads are allowed to modify the variables. Both variants can be realized as read-implicit, read-explicit and mixed schemes.

3   Architecture, Tool Setup, and Configuration

Architecture. MU-CSeq 0.3 is implemented as source-to-source transformations in Python, within the CSeq framework. This uses the `pycparser` (v2.10, `github.com/eliben/pycparser`) to parse a C program into an abstract syntax tree (AST), and then traverses the AST to construct a sequentialized version, as outlined above. The resulting program can be processed independently by any verification tool for C, but we have only tested MU-CSeq 0.3 with CBMC (v4.9 revision 4648, `www.cprover.org/cbmc/`). For the competition we use a wrapper script that bundles up the translation and calls CBMC for verification. The wrapper returns the output from CBMC.

We use a simple syntactic analysis of the program to determine which schema and parameters we use. In particular, if the program contains arrays we use the mixed fine-grained MU with parameters `-w25 -t10 -f2 -u2 -th10`; here w (resp., t) is the bound on the number of write operations (resp., of spawned threads), f is the unwind bound for `for` and u is the unwind bound for the remaining loops, and `thl` is the bound on the number of threads that are spawned in any *while*-loop. If the program contains more than 30 assignments but no loop, or a `pthread_create` inside a *for*-loop, we switch to the inter-thread coarse-grained MU, with parameters `-w2 -t52 -f52 -u1 -th10`. In all other cases we use again the first schema but with parameters `-w23 -t10 -f12 -u1 -th13`. We use a timeout of 850 seconds, and interpret the single case where this timeout applies as *true*.

Availability and Installation. MU-CSeq 0.3 is available at `http://users.ecs.soton.ac.uk/gp4/cseq/mu-cseq-0.3.zip`; it also requires installation of the `pycparser`. CBMC must be installed in the same directory as MU-CSeq.

Call. MU-CSeq should be called in the installation directory as follows: `mu-cseq.py -i file --spec specfile --witness logfile`.

Strengths and Weaknesses. MU-CSeq participates only in the concurrency category. It returns the correct answers for all problems in this category, but is slower than Lazy-CSeq, thus winning the Silver medal.

References

1. Fischer, B., Inverso, O., Parlato, G.: CSeq: A Sequentialization Tool for C. In: Piterman, N., Smolka, S.A. (eds.) TACAS 2013 (ETAPS 2013). LNCS, vol. 7795, pp. 616–618. Springer, Heidelberg (2013)
2. Fischer, B., Inverso, O., Parlato, G.: CSeq: A Concurrency Pre-Processor for Sequential C Verification Tools. In: ASE, pp. 710–713 (2013)
3. Inverso, O., Tomasco, E., Fischer, B., La Torre, S., Parlato, G.: Lazy-CSeq: A Lazy Sequentialization Tool for C. In: Ábrahám, E., Havelund, K. (eds.) TACAS 2014 (ETAPS). LNCS, vol. 8413, pp. 398–401. Springer, Heidelberg (2014)
4. Inverso, O., Tomasco, E., Fischer, B., La Torre, S., Parlato, G.: Bounded Model Checking of Multi-threaded C Programs via Lazy Sequentialization. In: Biere, A., Bloem, R. (eds.) CAV 2014. LNCS, vol. 8559, pp. 585–602. Springer, Heidelberg (2014)
5. Lal, A., Reps, T.W.: Reducing concurrent analysis under a context bound to sequential analysis. Formal Methods in System Design 35(1), 73–97 (2009)
6. Tomasco, E., Inverso, O., Fischer, B., La Torre, S., Parlato, G.: MU-CSeq: Sequentialization of C Programs by Shared Memory Unwindings. In: Ábrahám, E., Havelund, K. (eds.) TACAS 2014 (ETAPS). LNCS, vol. 8413, pp. 402–404. Springer, Heidelberg (2014)
7. Tomasco, E., Inverso, O., Fischer, B., La Torre, S., Parlato, G.: Verifying Concurrent Programs by Memory Unwinding. In: Baier, C., Tinelli, C. (eds.) TACAS 2015. LNCS, vol. 9035, pp. 551–565. Springer, Heidelberg (2015)

Perentie: Modular Trace Refinement and Selective Value Tracking
(Competition Contribution)

Franck Cassez[1,2], Takashi Matsuoka[1],
Edward Pierzchalski[1], and Nathan Smyth[1]

[1] NICTA*, Sydney, Australia
[2] Macquarie University and UNSW, Sydney, Australia

Abstract. PERENTIE is a software analysis tool based on iterative refinement of trace abstraction: if the refinement process terminates, the program is either declared correct or a counterexample is provided and the program is incorrect.

1 Overview

PERENTIE is a software analysis tool based on iterative refinement of trace abstraction [1,2], which is a CEGAR-like automata-based technique. The control flow graph (CFG) of a program is viewed as a finite automaton. The accepting states of the CFG are the states reached after a program assertion is violated. This finite automaton generates a language, the *trace abstraction*, of traces that are sequences of uninterpreted instructions. Consequently, all the (uninterpreted) traces accepted by the CFG are *error traces* leading to an error state.

Checking whether a program is correct amounts to determining whether the language of the CFG contains a *feasible* error trace. This is performed by an iterative refinement of the trace abstraction.

Our version of refinement of trace abstraction builds on top of our modular inter-procedural analysis algorithm [3]. Moreover, as the iterative refinement may not terminate, PERENTIE limits the number of iterations of the refinement phase and if it is inconclusive, it complements it with a second more precise refinement analysis, where it tracks the values of some variables that precisely

* NICTA is funded by the Australian Government through the Department of Communications and the Australian Research Council through the ICT Centre of Excellence Program. This material is based on research sponsored by Air Force Research Laboratory and the Defense Advanced Research Projects Agency (DARPA) under agreement number FA8750-12-9-0179. The U.S. Government is authorized to reproduce and distribute reprints for Governmental purposes notwithstanding any copyright notation thereon. The views and conclusions contained herein are those of the authors and should not be interpreted as necessarily representing the official policies or endorsements, either expressed or implied, of Air Force Research Laboratory, the Defense Advanced Research Projects Agency or the U.S. Government.

© Springer-Verlag Berlin Heidelberg 2015
C. Baier and C. Tinelli (Eds.): TACAS 2015, LNCS 9035, pp. 439–442, 2015.
DOI: 10.1007/978-3-662-46681-0_39

define some branching conditions. If this second phase is inconclusive as well, the overall analysis is inconclusive (output is UNKNOWN), otherwise the correctness status of the program is settled (TRUE, FALSE).

2   Software Architecture

PERENTIE's core engine is developed in SCALA. PERENTIE is flexible and can be configured from the command line by setting a maximum number of iterations for the first refinement phase, and a maximum state space size for the second phase. In this second phase, where some variable values are tracked, the state space may become infinite and this is why we set a bound to ensure termination.

Front end: The front end parser is built on top of the Edison Design Group (EDG) parser. It reads a C source file and generates an XML representation of the C program. The representation is passed on to our own XML parser (written in SCALA) that builds a CFG for every function in the source file.

Middle end: PERENTIE implements a library for manipulating automata including operations like product, union, (lazy) complement, DFS. This allows to extract candidate witness (uninterpreted) error traces from the CFG. Feasibility of a trace is checked using an SMT-solver by encoding the trace in static single assignment (SSA) form into a logical formula and checking for satisfiability. When the trace is infeasible, an *interpolant automaton* [1,3] is computed from a sequence of interpolants [1]. The standard construction requires an interpolating SMT-theorem prover to compute the interpolants from the infeasible trace. As those theorem provers are generally unable to produce interpolants for formulas containing arrays, we have implemented an alternative construction in the style of the weakest pre-condition computation that can compute inductive interpolants, and thus handle programs with arrays.

Back end: PERENTIE uses SMTInterpol [4] to check satisfiability of SSA formulas. When a program does not contain array variables, it is also used to generate inductive interpolants. Our software architecture is designed to accommodate any SMTLIB2 compliant solver and Z3 is currently being interfaced (although too late to be used for this competition).

3   Strengths and Weaknesses

This first version of PERENTIE has limited capabilities in terms of supported data structures. Pointers or structs, or arrays of non-integer type are not supported yet, and PERENTIE will abort the parsing phase with an inconclusive result. Moreover, data types such as `unsigned int` are treated as `int`, and we assume unbounded integers. Although our analysis is sound with unbounded integers, it may generate some false negatives when the actual data type is a bounded integer (overflows/underflows are ignored).

One of the major strengths PERENTIE is that it can discover loop invariants and prove correctness (generate Hoare triples) for programs with parameterised loop bounds (e.g., in the loop-new sub-category). The drawback is that to compute useful loop invariants, an interpolating SMT-solver is needed. For the time being, SMTINTERPOL [4] supports interpolants only for the theory of Linear Integer Arithmetic. This prevents us from automatically discovering good loop invariants when the SMT-solver theory does not support interpolation, e.g., when arrays or non-linear arithmetic expressions are used in the program[1]. Another nice feature of PERENTIE is its modular analysis [3] that avoids inlining function calls but this feature is not exercised in SV-COMP 2015.

4   Set Up and Configuration

Participation statement: PERENTIE opts-out from all categories (including Overall) and participates in the Loops.set sub-category of the *Control Flow and Integer Variables* category.

Set up and configuration: PERENTIE is available at http://ssrg.nicta.com.au/projects/software-verification/perentie/. The submitted version to SV-COMP 2015 is version 2014-10-31. The current version of PERENTIE requires a 64-bit (x86-64) Linux system, Java (JRE) 6 or higher and gcc. Command line usage is bash perentie.sh <c-file>. Usage, set up and configuration is described in the README.txt file in the tarball. For this competition, we use PERENTIE in sound[2] mode: when we can determine the result TRUE/FALSE, we output it, otherwise our analysis is inconclusive (parse errors, unsupported data types, theory not supported by the solver) and the output is UNKNOWN.

5   Software Project and Contributors

PERENTIE is developed and hosted by NICTA, Australia, and is currently closed source software. We would like to thank Pablo Gonzalez de Aledo Marugan, University of Cantabria, Spain, for helpful discussions.

References

1. Heizmann, M., Hoenicke, J., Podelski, A.: Refinement of trace abstraction. In: Palsberg, J., Su, Z. (eds.) SAS 2009. LNCS, vol. 5673, pp. 69–85. Springer, Heidelberg (2009)
2. Heizmann, M., Hoenicke, J., Podelski, A.: Software model checking for people who love automata. In: Sharygina, N., Veith, H. (eds.) CAV 2013. LNCS, vol. 8044, pp. 36–52. Springer, Heidelberg (2013)

---

[1] This happens only a handful of times in the Loop category.
[2] Due to our assumption that integers are unbounded, our analysis is sound only when no overflows occur. Two programs do have overflows related bugs and results in false negatives in our analysis.

3. Cassez, F., Müller, C., Burnett, K.: Summary-based inter-procedural analysis via modular trace refinement. In: FSTTCS 2014, LIPIcs, Schloss Dagstuhl - Leibniz-Zentrum fuer Informatik, New Dehli, India, December 15-17, vol. 29, pp. 545–556 (2014)
4. Christ, J., Hoenicke, J., Nutz, A.: SMTInterpol: An Interpolating SMT Solver. In: Donaldson, A., Parker, D. (eds.) SPIN 2012. LNCS, vol. 7385, pp. 248–254. Springer, Heidelberg (2012)

Predator Hunting Party (Competition Contribution)

Petr Muller, Petr Peringer, and Tomáš Vojnar

FIT, Brno University of Technology, IT4Innovations Centre of Excellence, Czech Republic

Abstract. This paper introduces PredatorHP (Predator Hunting Party), a program verifier built on top of the Predator shape analyser, and discusses its participation in the SV-COMP'15 software verification competition. Predator is a sound shape analyser dealing with C programs with lists implemented via low-level pointer operations. PredatorHP uses Predator to prove programs safe while at the same time using several bounded versions of Predator for bug hunting.

1 The Underlying Verification Approach

At the heart of PredatorHP there is the Predator shape analyser [2]. The main aim of Predator is *sound* shape analysis of sequential, non-recursive C programs that use low-level pointer operations for working efficiently with various kinds of linked lists. Predator supports many advanced uses of pointer arithmetics, address alignment, and block operations common in highly optimized system code, such as operating system kernels, drivers, memory allocators, and the like.

Predator is based on abstract interpretation with the abstract domain of *symbolic memory graphs* (SMGs) [2]. In a nutshell, SMGs consist of two kinds of nodes—namely, individual memory regions and uninterrupted list segments—and two kinds of edges, in particular, the so-called has-value and points-to edges. SMGs were inspired by separation logic with higher-order list predicates but with an added support for low-level memory operations. Moreover, all the needed algorithms for dealing with SMGs (symbolic execution of program statements, the join operator, widening in the form of abstraction, entailment checking) were newly designed to be as efficient as possible by leveraging the graph structure of SMGs. The most essential role is played by the join operator: both abstraction and entailment checking are built on top of it. Predator supports inter-procedural analysis by means of function summaries.

Recently, a new extension of Predator was implemented [1]. It uses the Predator kernel for transforming programs with list containers implemented by low-level pointer operations into equivalent programs with high-level container operations, which can be useful, e.g., for code understanding, easier verification, parallelisation, optimisation, etc.

2 From Predator to Predator Hunting Party

Predator is implemented as a GCC plug-in, which provides it with an industrial-strength compiler front-end. In particular, GCC is used to pre-process the input programs and to compile them into an intermediate representation (known as GIMPLE), which is further transformed into a bit more concise representation of the Code Listener framework [3] over which Predator runs. Predator is written in C++ with a use of the Boost libraries, mainly to enable using legacy compilers for building it.

© Springer-Verlag Berlin Heidelberg 2015
C. Baier and C. Tinelli (Eds.): TACAS 2015, LNCS 9035, pp. 443–446, 2015.
DOI: 10.1007/978-3-662-46681-0_40

Predator requires all external functions used in an analysed program to be properly modelled wrt. memory safety in order to exclude any side effects that could possibly break soundness of the analysis. The distribution of Predator includes models of some memory manipulating functions (like `malloc`, `free`, `memset`, `memcpy`, etc.).

PredatorHP is implemented as a Python script which runs several instances of Predator in parallel and composes the results they produce into the final verification verdict. In particular, PredatorHP first starts four Predators: One of them is the original Predator that soundly over-approximates the behaviour of the input program—we denote it as the *Predator verifier* below. Apart from that, three further Predators are started which are modified as follows: Their join operator is reduced to joining SMGs equal up to isomorphism, they use no list abstraction, and they use a bounded depth-first search to traverse the state space. They use bounds of 400, 700, and 1000 GIMPLE instructions, and so we call them as *Predator DFS hunters* 400, 700, and 1000, respectively.

If the Predator verifier claims a program correct, so does PredatorHP, and it kills all other Predators. If the Predator verifier claims a program incorrect, its verdict is ignored since it can be a false alarm (and, moreover, it is highly non-trivial to check whether it is false or not due to the involved use of list abstractions and joins). If one of the Predator DFS hunters finds an error, PredatorHP kills all other Predators and claims the program incorrect, using the trace provided by the DFS hunter who found the error.[1] If a DFS hunter claims a program correct, its verdict is ignored since it may be unsound.

In case the Predator verifier claims a program incorrect and no Predator DFS hunter finds an error within the appropriate bound, then PredatorHP starts one more Predator— a *Predator BFS hunter*. The BFS hunter does not use list abstraction and its join is reduced to equivalence up to isomorphism, but it performs an unlimited breadth-first search. If it manages to find an error within the SV-COMP'15 time budget, PredatorHP claims the program incorrect (note that without a time limit, the BFS hunter is guaranteed to find every error). If the BFS hunter finishes and does not find an error, the program is claimed correct. Otherwise, the verdict "unknown" is obtained.

3   Strengths and Weaknesses

The main strength of Predator lies in its sound treatment of heap manipulation. Unlike for various bounded model checkers, when Predator claims a program safe, all its possible behaviours are indeed safe. At the same time, Predator is also quite efficient. On the other hand, due to using over-approximation, it can easily generate false alarms. This danger was greatly reduced in PredatorHP by combining the sound Predator verifier with Predator hunters. This way, false alarms caused by abstraction are often suppressed, and a program claimed possibly unsafe by Predator can even be proved correct if its behaviour is bounded. Unfortunately, true error warnings can sometimes be also suppressed, resulting in a neutral "unknown" answer. However, overall, the balance is positive: about twice more false than true alarms were prevented on the SV-COMP benchmarks in the two categories where PredatorHP competes. The benefit is further

---

[1] The obtained trace can still be spurious due to the harsh abstraction of non-pointer data by Predator: All such data, apart from integers up to some fixed bound, are abstracted away.

amplified by the SV-COMP scoring scheme, which rewards preventing a wrong answer over keeping a correct one.

The improvement manifested mainly in the MemorySafety category, containing test-cases causing list abstractions in Predator to produce false alarms. By preventing all but a single one, while keeping all correct answers, PredatorHP is much more reliable than Predator alone. PredatorHP reduced false positives even for remaining SV-COMP categories, but unfortunately not enough to allow us to successfully participate in these.

The main weakness of PredatorHP is inherited from Predator, and it is the same as in previous years of SV-COMP. Namely, it is a rather weak support of non-pointer data and missing models of some library functions, which has not changed since SV-COMP'14. That is why, PredatorHP is participating in the MemorySafety and HeapManipulation categories only. Even within these categories, PredatorHP loses some points due to imprecise treatment of non-pointer data, leading to false alarms. The only other reason for Predator losing points in the MemorySafety and HeapManipulation categories is the fact that it cannot handle tree-like data structures and skip lists. In fact, it can handle them in a bounded way (i.e., in the same way as bounded model checkers)[2], but we have decided not to "harvest" easy points by sacrificing soundness of the verifier.

4 Tool Setup and Configuration

The source code of the PredatorHP release used in the competition can be downloaded from the project web page[3]. The file README-SVCOMP-2015 included in the archive describes how to build PredatorHP from source code and how to apply the tool on the competition benchmarks. After successfully building the tool from sources, a script named predatorHP.py can be invoked, once for each input program. The script takes a verification task file as a single positional argument. Paths to both the property file and the desired witness file are accepted via long options. The verification outcome is printed to the standard output. The script does not impose any resource limits other than terminating its child processes when they are no longer needed.

5 Software Project and Contributors

Predator is an open source software project developed at Brno University of Technology (BUT) and distributed under the GNU General Public License version 3. The main author of Predator is Kamil Dudka. Besides Kamil and the PredatorHP team, numerous external contributors are listed in the docs/THANKS file in the distribution of Predator. Collaboration on further development of Predator (e.g., better support of non-pointer data, handling of incomplete code, support of tree data structures, etc.) is welcome.

---

[2] According to our experiments, if we interpreted the fact that no error was found by any Predator DFS hunter such that the program is correct, we could successfully handle all programs manipulating trees and skip lists present in the SV-COMP'15 benchmark.

[3] http://www.fit.vutbr.cz/research/groups/verifit/tools/predator-hp

Acknowledgement. The work was supported by the Czech Science Foundation project 14-11384S, the internal BUT project FIT-S-14-2486, and the EU/Czech IT4Innovations Centre of Excellence project CZ.1.05/1.1.00/02.0070.

References

1. Dudka, K., Holík, L., Peringer, P., Trtík, M., Vojnar, T.: From Pointers to Containers. Under submission (2015)
2. Dudka, K., Peringer, P., Vojnar, T.: Byte-Precise Verification of Low-Level List Manipulation. In: Logozzo, F., Fähndrich, M. (eds.) Static Analysis. LNCS, vol. 7935, pp. 215–237. Springer, Heidelberg (2013)
3. Dudka, K., Peringer, P., Vojnar, T.: An Easy to Use Infrastructure for Building Static Analysis Tools. In: Moreno-Díaz, R., Pichler, F., Quesada-Arencibia, A. (eds.) EUROCAST 2011, Part I. LNCS, vol. 6927, pp. 527–534. Springer, Heidelberg (2012)

SeaHorn: A Framework for Verifying C Programs (Competition Contribution)*

Arie Gurfinkel[1], Temesghen Kahsai[2], and Jorge A. Navas[3]

[1] Software Engineering Institute / CMU, USA
[2] NASA Ames Research Center / CMU, USA
[3] NASA Ames Research Center / SGT, USA

Abstract. SEAHORN is a framework and tool for verification of safety properties in C programs. The distinguishing feature of SEAHORN is its modular design that separates how program semantics is represented from the verification engine. This paper describes its verification approach as well as the instructions on how to install and use it.

1 Verification Approach

SEAHORN is a framework and a tool for verification of safety properties for C programs. It is *parameterized* by the semantic representation of the program using Horn constraints and by the verification engine that leverages the latest advances made in constraint solving and Abstract Interpretation. The design of SEAHORN provides users with an extensible and customizable environment for experimenting and implementing with new software verification techniques.

Consider the simple program on the left. Using SEAHORN we encode it using, for instance, classical Hoare Logic:

```
int x = 1;
int y = 0;
while (*) {
    x = x + y;
    y = y + 1;
}
assert(x ≥ y);
```

$$(x = 1 \ \land \ y = 0) \rightarrow I(x, y)$$
$$(I(x, y) \ \land \ x' = x + y \ \land \ y' = y + 1) \rightarrow I(x', y')$$
$$(I(x, y) \ \land \ x < y) \rightarrow false$$

These logic formulas corresponding to the rule for while loops are indeed a set of recursive Horn clauses. Thus, the problem of proving whether the program is safe is reduced to checking whether these Horn clauses are satisfiable. Fortunately, they can be solved by a means of solvers (e.g., [5]), thus leveraging recent advances in Horn constraint solving.

* This material is based upon work funded and supported by NASA Contract No. NNX14AI09G, NSF Award No. 1422705 and by the Department of Defense under Contract No. FA8721-05-C-0003 with CMU for the operation of SEI, an FFRDC. Any opinions, findings and conclusions or recommendations expressed in this material are those of the author(s) and do not necessarily reflect the views of the United States Department of Defense. This material has been approved for public release and unlimited distribution. DM-0001865.

C. Baier and C. Tinelli (Eds.): TACAS 2015, LNCS 9035, pp. 447–450, 2015.
DOI: 10.1007/978-3-662-46681-0_41

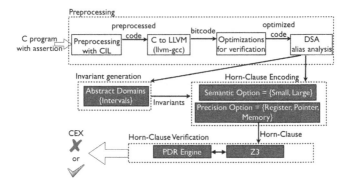

Fig. 1. Overview of SEAHORN architecture

2   Software Architecture

SEAHORN is implemented in C++ in the LLVM compiler infrastructure [6]. The overall approach is illustrated in Figure 1.

Preprocessing. To pre-process the competition benchmark, we utilize the front-end that was originally developed for UFO [1]. First, the input C program is pre-processed with CIL[1] to insert line markings for counterexamples, define missing functions, and initialize all local variables. Second, the result is translated into LLVM Intermediate Representation (IR), called *bitcode*, using llvm-gcc. Next, we perform compiler optimizations and preprocessing to simplify the verification task. As a preprocessing step, we further initialize any uninitialized registers using non-deterministic functions. This is used to bridge the gap between the verification semantics (which assumes a non-deterministic assignment) and compiler semantics, which tries to take advantage of the undefined behavior of uninitialized variables to perform code optimizations. We perform a number of program simplifications such as function inlining, static single assignment (SSA) form, dead code elimination, etc. Finally, we use a variant of Data Structure Analysis (DSA), an alias analysis that infers disjoint heap regions used to identify each memory access within a certain region.

Invariant Generation. Inductive invariants can be computed from the byte-code using a given abstract domain. SEAHORN uses the IKOS library [2] which is a collection of abstract domains and fixpoint iteration algorithms. SEAHORN runs in parallel with (using classical intervals) and without invariant generation.

Horn-Clause Encoding. Next, we translate bytecode to Horn constraints which acts as a very suitable intermediate representation for verification. SEAHORN is parametric on the semantics used for encoding. Currently, SEAHORN provides a Horn-clause style encoding based on small-step semantics [7] as well as a more efficient large-block encoding [3]. For the competition, we always use the

---

[1] http://www.cs.berkeley.edu/~necula/cil/

large-block encoding. The level of precision of the encoding can be also tuned. The options are: only registers (integer scalars), registers and pointer addresses (without content), and all of the above plus memory content (using theory of arrays). We use for the competition the latter which is the most precise level.

Horn-Clause Verification. SEAHORN is also parameterized by the solver. For the competition, SEAHORN uses PDR engine implemented in Z3 [4]. For the competition we improve PDR using invariants computed by IKOS. To motivate this decision, let us come back to our example described above. PDR alone can discover $x \geq y$ but it does not terminate, however, if populated with the inductive invariant $y \geq 0$, computed by IKOS, it proves it immediately.

3   Strength and Weaknesses

SEAHORN uses linear arithmetic to reason about scalars and pointer addresses, and theory of arrays for memory contents. However, SEAHORN provides little or no support for reasoning about dynamic linked data structures, bit-level precision, or concurrency. Another weakness of SEAHORN is inherited from the UFO front-end which relies on multiple tools: LLVM 2.6, LLVM 2.9, and CIL. The main strength of SEAHORN lies on its parameterized nature allowing experimenting with different encodings to model new semantics aspects, abstractions and verification algorithms.

4   Tool Setup

SEAHORN is available for download from `https://bitbucket.org/lememta/seahorn/wiki/Home`. SEAHORN is provided as a set of binaries and libraries for Linux x86-64 architecture. The options for running the tool are:

`./bin/seahorn-svcomp-par.py [-m64] [--cex=CEX] [--spec=SPEC] INPUT`

where -m64 turns on 64-bit model, CEX is the destination directory for the witness file, SPEC is the property file, and INPUT is a C file. If it terminates the output of SEAHORN is "`Result TRUE`" when the program is safe, "`Result FALSE`", when a counterexample is found or "`Result UNKNOWN`", otherwise.

References

1. Albarghouthi, A., Gurfinkel, A., Li, Y., Chaki, S., Chechik, M.: UFO: Verification with interpolants and abstract interpretation. In: Piterman, N., Smolka, S.A. (eds.) TACAS 2013 (ETAPS 2013). LNCS, vol. 7795, pp. 637–640. Springer, Heidelberg (2013)
2. Brat, G., Navas, J.A., Shi, N., Venet, A.: IKOS: A framework for static analysis based on abstract interpretation. In: Giannakopoulou, D., Salaün, G. (eds.) SEFM 2014. LNCS, vol. 8702, pp. 271–277. Springer, Heidelberg (2014)

3. Gurfinkel, A., Chaki, S., Sapra, S.: Efficient predicate abstraction of program summaries. In: Bobaru, M., Havelund, K., Holzmann, G.J., Joshi, R. (eds.) NFM 2011. LNCS, vol. 6617, pp. 131–145. Springer, Heidelberg (2011)
4. Hoder, K., Bjørner, N.: Generalized property directed reachability. In: Cimatti, A., Sebastiani, R. (eds.) SAT 2012. LNCS, vol. 7317, pp. 157–171. Springer, Heidelberg (2012)
5. Hoder, K., Bjørner, N., de Moura, L.: μZ– an efficient engine for fixed points with constraints. In: Gopalakrishnan, G., Qadeer, S. (eds.) CAV 2011. LNCS, vol. 6806, pp. 457–462. Springer, Heidelberg (2011)
6. Lattner, C., Adve, V.S.: LLVM: A compilation framework for lifelong program analysis & transformation. In: CGO. pp. 75–88 (2004)
7. Peralta, J.C., Gallagher, J.P., Saglam, H.: Analysis of imperative programs through analysis of constraint logic programs. In: Levi, G. (ed.) SAS 1998. LNCS, vol. 1503, pp. 246–261. Springer, Heidelberg (1998)

SMACK+Corral: A Modular Verifier*
(Competition Contribution)

Arvind Haran[1], Montgomery Carter[1], Michael Emmi[2],
Akash Lal[3], Shaz Qadeer[3], and Zvonimir Rakamarić[1]

[1] School of Computing, University of Utah, USA
zvonimir@cs.utah.edu
[2] IMDEA Software Institute, Spain
michael.emmi@imdea.org
[3] Microsoft Research, India & USA
akashl@microsoft.com

Abstract. SMACK and Corral are two components of a modular toolchain for verifying C programs. Together they exploit state-of-the-art compiler technologies and theorem provers to simplify and dispatch verification conditions.

1 Verification Approach

SMACK [3] is a translator from the LLVM compiler's intermediate representation (IR) into the Boogie intermediate verification language (IVL) [1]. Sourcing LLVM exploits a number of frontends, optimizations, and analyses. Targeting Boogie exploits a canonical platform which simplifies verifier implementations.

Corral [2] is a verifier for the Boogie IVL which views programs as control flow over any SMT-encodable expression language. Corral delegates semantic reasoning to SMT solvers, and in minimizing syntactic program assumptions, it is compatible with any theory supported by the underlying solvers.

SMACK+Corral leverages multiple theories to encode various C-language features. We can model memory in array theory, non-linear operations with uninterpreted functions, fixed-width words in bitvector theory, and arbitrary-length words in linear arithmetic. Though we make no attempt to generate inductive invariants, we can use any invariant generator as a pre-pass; if proved sound, the resulting invariants are injected into the program as assumptions which help Corral narrow its search.

2 Software Architecture

Figure 1 depicts the SMACK+Corral architecture. We leverage the LLVM[1] compiler's Clang C language family frontend to generate LLVM IR, an assembly-like language in *single static assignment* (SSA) form targeted by frontends for a diverse spectrum of languages (e.g., Java, JavaScript, Haskell, Erlang, Fortran) which is a convenient

---

* Partially supported by NSF award CCF 1346756 and a Microsoft Research SEIF award.
[1] http://llvm.org and http://clang.llvm.org

© Springer-Verlag Berlin Heidelberg 2015
C. Baier and C. Tinelli (Eds.): TACAS 2015, LNCS 9035, pp. 451–454, 2015.
DOI: 10.1007/978-3-662-46681-0_42

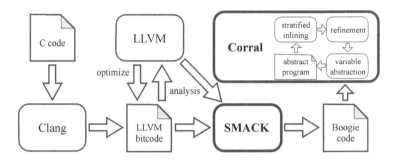

Fig. 1. The SMACK+Corral architecture

representation for code optimization. We then exploit LLVM to perform several code optimizations including control-flow graph simplification, constant propagation, and memory-to-register promotion. Collectively these optimizations can substantially simplify the source C program with fewer control locations and memory operations.

SMACK translates from the LLVM IR to the Boogie *intermediate verification language* (IVL). The Boogie IVL is a simple imperative language with well-defined, clean, and mathematically-focused semantics which is a convenient representation for software verifiers. Internally, SMACK leverages LLVM pointer-aliasing analyses to construct effective encodings of pointer and memory operations into Boogie, e.g., to avoid encoding program memory as one single array expression, which would be difficult for back-end verifiers to reason about.

Corral attempts to prove reachability of assertion violations in the Boogie program generated by SMACK *lazily*, in a goal-directed manner, to reduce pressure on the underlying theorem prover. Corral abstracts the input program via *variable abstraction*, attempting to identify a minimal set of global variables impacting the verification condition, and *stratified inlining*, attempting to identify a minimal unrolling of program loops and recursion impacting the verification condition. When necessary, Corral refines these abstractions by tracking additional global variables and further unrolling.

3 Strengths and Weaknesses of the Approach

Speaking generally, the main incentives of our approach are modularity and the exploitation of scalable technologies. Sourcing LLVM IR exploits a rapidly-growing frontier of LLVM frontends, encompassing a diverse set of languages including C/C++, Java, Haskell, Erlang, Python, Ruby, Ada, and Fortran. In addition, we benefit from code simplifications made by LLVM's optimizer, including constant propagation and CFG simplification, as well as readily-available analyses, including LLVM's pointer analyses. SMACK's translation to Boogie IVL exploits a canonical platform which simplifies the implementation of verifiers like Corral due to Boogie's minimal syntax and mathematically-focused expression language. Finally, by cleverly exploiting the power of efficient satisfiability modulo theories (SMT) solvers, Corral is able to scale up to complex verification queries on large programs. The general weaknesses of our approach are currently the limited support for proving programs correct, and the limited support for certain C-language features such as floating-point and bitwise operations.

4   Tool Setup and Configuration

Our SV-COMP 2015 submission[2] contains a prebuilt Linux binary without external dependencies, and is run by invoking the top-level script `smack-svcomp.sh`. The following command line options should be provided for SV-COMP benchmarks:

> `--outputdir` specifies a path where temporary files are generated;
> `--errorwitness` specifies the file name for an output error witness;
> `--m64` must be set on 64-bit benchmarks, such as Device Drivers Linux 64-bit.

For example, SMACK is invoked on a C benchmark file `b.c` by running

`smack-svcomp.sh b.c --outputdir /scratch --errorwitness /tmp/w.xml`

the result of which is either `TRUE`, `UNKNOWN`, or `FALSE(REACH)`, in which case an error witness is written to `/tmp/w.xml`.

SV-COMP Categories: Arrays, Control Flow and Integer Variables, Device Drivers Linux 64-bit, Heap Manipulation/Dynamic Data Structures, Recursive, and Simple.

Note: We preprocess SV-COMP benchmarks by removing `#N-source-lines`, `#pragma`, and `#line`, since tokenization breaks otherwise. The SV-COMP error witness checker must do the same for token numbers to match. We provide a simple Python script called `replacer.py` with our binary to perform this transformation.

5   Software Project and Contributors

SMACK is an MIT-licensed open-source project hosted by GitHub[3] developed and maintained by Michael Emmi of the IMDEA Software Institute and Zvonimir Rakamarić of the University of Utah, with additional contributions from Montgomery Carter, Arvind Haran, and Pantazis Deligiannis. SMACK is also hosted by Microsoft's rise4fun[4] website, which allows installation-free use. Corral is an Apache 2.0-licensed open-source project hosted by CodePlex[5] developed and maintained by Akash Lal and Shaz Qadeer of Microsoft Research. Corral is distributed with Microsoft's Static Driver Verifier, included in the Windows Driver Development Kit. Both SMACK and Corral are components of the Q modular verification-technology ecosystem[6].

---

[2] `http://soarlab.org/smack/smack-corral.tar.gz`
[3] `https://github.com/smackers/smack`
[4] `http://rise4fun.com/SMACK`
[5] `http://corral.codeplex.com`
[6] `http://research.microsoft.com/en-us/projects/verifierq`

References

1. DeLine, R., Leino, K.R.M.: BoogiePL: A typed procedural language for checking object-oriented programs. Technical Report MSR-TR-2005-70, Microsoft Research (2005)
2. Lal, A., Qadeer, S., Lahiri, S.K.: A solver for reachability modulo theories. In: Madhusudan, P., Seshia, S.A. (eds.) CAV 2012. LNCS, vol. 7358, pp. 427–443. Springer, Heidelberg (2012)
3. Rakamarić, Z., Emmi, M.: SMACK: Decoupling source language details from verifier implementations. In: Biere, A., Bloem, R. (eds.) CAV 2014. LNCS, vol. 8559, pp. 106–113. Springer, Heidelberg (2014)

Ultimate Automizer with Array Interpolation
(Competition Contribution)

Matthias Heizmann[1], Daniel Dietsch[1], Jan Leike[2], Betim Musa[1],
and Andreas Podelski[1]

[1] University of Freiburg, Germany
[2] The Australian National University

Abstract. Ultimate Automizer is a software verification tool that is
able to analyze reachability of an error label, memory safety, and termination of C programs. For all three tasks, our tool follows an automata-
based approach where interpolation is used to compute proofs for traces.
The interpolants are generated via a new scheme that requires only the
post operator, unsatisfiable cores and live variable analysis. This new
scheme enables our tool to use the SMT theory of arrays in combination
with interpolation.

1 Verification Approach

While analyzing a C program, Ultimate Automizer first applies several preprocessing steps and then executes an automata-based verification algorithm.

In a first step, the C program is translated into a Boogie program [7]. The
resulting Boogie program uses arrays to model the heap of the system, but does
not need any quantified axioms. Next, the Boogie program is translated into an
interprocedural control flow graph whose edges are labeled with code blocks of
the Boogie program.

Our verification algorithm [3] iteratively takes sample traces that lead to the
error location of the program and analyzes their feasibility. If the sample trace
is infeasible, we compute for this trace an infeasibility proof in form of a Hoare
annotation. Next, we take this proof and compute the largest set of traces whose
infeasibility can be proven with the assertions from the Hoare annotation [3]. We
continue until we find a sample trace that is a counterexample to the correctness
of the program or until we have shown infeasibility for all error traces.

For computations on sets of traces we use automata. We consider the control
flow graph of the program as an automaton and use the error location as an
accepting state. The search for new sample traces is implemented as an emptiness
check on the differences between all traces and the traces whose infeasibility has
been proven. The infeasibility of a trace is checked by an SMT solver and the
Hoare annotation for a trace is generated via interpolation. For programs with
several (possibly recursive) procedures we use automata over nested words and
nested interpolants [2].

Compared to last year's version, our tool received several improvements and
optimizations. We list two major innovations in the following paragraphs.

© Springer-Verlag Berlin Heidelberg 2015
C. Baier and C. Tinelli (Eds.): TACAS 2015, LNCS 9035, pp. 455–457, 2015.
DOI: 10.1007/978-3-662-46681-0_43

Array Interpolation. We generate sequences of interpolants for traces using a new interpolation scheme [8] that is theory-independent and can hence be applied for the AUFLIRA SMT theory which we use. Our interpolation scheme uses only the post operator and two additional modules. The first module uses an unsatisfiable core to abstract the trace to the core reason of its infeasibility. The second module uses a live variable analysis to project interpolants to the variables that are live at the corresponding position in the trace.

Termination Analysis. For termination analysis, we follow an automata-based approach [4] in which we consider infinite traces and use Büchi automata for computations on sets of traces. We use the tool ULTIMATE LASSORANKER[1] to analyze termination of lasso-shaped infinite traces. ULTIMATE LASSORANKER uses constraint solving to synthesize ranking functions as termination proofs [6] and infinite program executions as nontermination proofs [5]. In this competition we use a setting where the constraints are linear arithmetic SMT formulas and we use SMTINTERPOL [1] to check satisfiability of these constraints.

2   Strength and Weaknesses

Modeling the heap of the C program via arrays allows us to support a large number of C's language features in a sound way. However, e.g., if the C program contains casts of pointers, our tool yet often says "unsupported syntax". Because of our array interpolation, our main verification algorithm is able to handle all programs with the same interpolation-based technique. The price that we have to pay is that we are unable to infer certain kinds of invariants, e.g., we are unable to infer quantified invariants that state that all elements of a list are zero.

However, the modularity of our approach allows us to integrate different techniques while verifying a single program. We use our automata representation to decompose the program into sets of traces. For each set, the correctness proof can be constructed with a completely different technique or tool. The implementation of this integration is part of our current work.

3   Software Project

ULTIMATE AUTOMIZER is one toolchain of the ULTIMATE framework. ULTIMATE provides several plugins and libraries that allow one to build tools for program analysis. In the context of ULTIMATE AUTOMIZER, the most noteworthy components are: the above mentioned translation from C programs to Boogie programs, the above mentioned tool ULTIMATE LASSORANKER, an interface that allows plugins to communicate with any SMT-LIBv2 compatible SMT solver, and the ULTIMATE AUTOMATA LIBRARY. This library provides operations on (Büchi) nested word automata like, e.g., complementation, emptiness checking, or minimization.

The development of ULTIMATE was started at the University of Freiburg. Meanwhile, ULTIMATE received contributions from more than 30 developers. Several toolchains of ULTIMATE are available on our server via a web interface.

---

[1] http://ultimate.informatik.uni-freiburg.de/LassoRanker/

4   Tool Setup and Configuration

Our competition candidate requires that the SMT solver Z3[2] is installed and the Z3 binary is included in your PATH environment. Our competition candidate is available online[3] The zip archive in which Ultimate Automizer is shipped, contains the Python script `Ultimate.py`, which wraps input and output of our tool for the competition. In order to check if the C file `inputfile` satisfies the property specified by the SV-COMP property file `prop.prp`, you have to invoke the Python script as follows.

```
python Ultimate.py prop.prp inputfile 32bit|64bit simple|precise
```

The third argument defines the architecture for which the property is checked (either `32bit` or `64bit`). The fourth argument defines which SV-COMP memory model is assumed for the input file (either `simple` or `precise`).

The result is written to stdout and the output of Ultimate Automizer is written to the file `Ultimate.log`. If the checked property does not hold, a human readable counterexample is written to `UltimateCounterExample.errorpath` and an error witness (in the format defined in the SV-COMP rules) is written to `witness.graphml`. All three files are written to the working directory.

References

1. Christ, J., Hoenicke, J., Nutz, A.: SMTInterpol: An interpolating SMT solver. In: Donaldson, A., Parker, D. (eds.) SPIN 2012. LNCS, vol. 7385, pp. 248–254. Springer, Heidelberg (2012)
2. Heizmann, M., Hoenicke, J., Podelski, A.: Nested interpolants. In: Hermenegildo, M.V., Palsberg, J. (eds.) POPL, pp. 471–482. ACM (2010)
3. Heizmann, M., Hoenicke, J., Podelski, A.: Software model checking for people who love automata. In: Sharygina, N., Veith, H. (eds.) CAV 2013. LNCS, vol. 8044, pp. 36–52. Springer, Heidelberg (2013)
4. Heizmann, M., Hoenicke, J., Podelski, A.: Termination analysis by learning terminating programs. In: Biere, A., Bloem, R. (eds.) CAV 2014. LNCS, vol. 8559, pp. 797–813. Springer, Heidelberg (2014)
5. Leike, J., Heizmann, M.: Geometric series as nontermination arguments for linear lasso programs. In: WST, pp. 55–59 (2014)
6. Leike, J., Heizmann, M.: Ranking templates for linear loops. In: Ábrahám, E., Havelund, K. (eds.) TACAS 2014 (ETAPS). LNCS, vol. 8413, pp. 172–186. Springer, Heidelberg (2014)
7. Leino, K.R.M.: This is Boogie 2. Manuscript working draft. Microsoft Research, Redmond (June 2008),
   http://research.microsoft.com/en-us/um/people/leino/papers/krml178.pdf
8. Musa, B.: Trace abstraction with unsatisfiable cores. Bachelor's thesis, University of Freiburg, Germany (2013)

---

[2] https://z3.codeplex.com/ (We used the version z3-4.3.3.f50a8b0a59ff-x64.)
[3] https://ultimate.informatik.uni-freiburg.de/automizer/

ULTIMATE KOJAK with Memory Safety Checks
(Competition Contribution)

Alexander Nutz*, Daniel Dietsch, Mostafa Mahmoud Mohamed,
and Andreas Podelski

University of Freiburg
{nutz,dietsch,amin,podelski}@informatik.uni-freiburg.de

Abstract. ULTIMATE KOJAK is a symbolic software model checker implemented in the ULTIMATE framework. It follows the CEGAR approach and uses Craig interpolants to refine an overapproximation of the program until it can either prove safety or has found a real counterexample.

This year's version features a new refinement algorithm, a precise treatment of heap memory, which allows us to deal with pointer aliasing and to participate in the memsafety category, and an improved interpolants generator.

1 Verification Approach

ULTIMATE KOJAK starts verification by constructing a program graph for the input program. Nodes in the program graph are labelled with formulae that represent abstract program states, the edges are labelled with transition formulae. Procedure calls and returns are represented by special edges such that the program graph can be seen as a nested word automaton [4]. A failed emptiness check on this automaton yields an error path as a nested word. From the error path we build an SMT formula that is satisfiable if and only if the path is feasible. If the error path formula is satisfiable, we retrieve a model from the solver and translate the path together with the model back to an error witness. If the error path formula is unsatisfiable, we start our interpolant generator which uses an unsatisfiable core that the solver yields together with strongest post computation and live variable analysis to obtain a nested interpolant for the error path.

For refining the graph, we employ the IMPULSE (working title) algorithm [7]. In the first step of the refinement, we make a copy of each node on the error path, this copy's formula is conjoined with the interpolant formula we obtained for this position in the trace. We also make copies of the outgoing edges of each copied node. At first, we let them point to their original target. In the second step of the refinement, we attempt to redirect edges nodes with a stronger invariant formula such that, in the end, we may disconnect the initial location in the graph from the error location as soon as possible. These steps are depicted in Figure 1.

---

* Corresponding author.

© Springer-Verlag Berlin Heidelberg 2015
C. Baier and C. Tinelli (Eds.): TACAS 2015, LNCS 9035, pp. 458–460, 2015.
DOI: 10.1007/978-3-662-46681-0_44

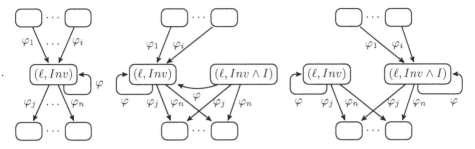

Fig. 1. The steps of the IMPULSE algorithm. Left: before refinement. Middle: after copying the node (ℓ, Inv). Right: after redirecting. Note that only edges corresponding to valid Hoare triples (in this picture: all) are redirected.

For dealing with memory safety properties, pointer aliasing and related problems, we make use of a simple but sufficient model of the heap used by C programs: A cell (byte) in the heap has its value stored in either an (SMT) integer array, an (SMT) real array or a pointer array. We use additional arrays to store which memory cells are allocated. Those are updated according to the specifications we introduce for malloc, free, and related procedures. Our memory safety checks are implemented by adding additional specifications to these procedures.

2 Software Architecture

ULTIMATE KOJAK is a toolchain in the ULTIMATE framework. ULTIMATE is a framework for program analysis and software model checking. It is kept modular such that all tools based on it may use a common infrastructure which, among others, consists of an interface to a SMT-LIBv2 compliant SMT solver, access to interpolation algorithms [2,6], a C parser and translator from C to Boogie [5], other parsers (for Boogie and AutomataScript, an language for describing automata), a plugin that builds a program graph from a Boogie program, a plugin which does large block encoding [1]. Furthermore, ULTIMATE provides an integration into Eclipse CDT that lets users verify their C programs directly from their IDE and also displays resulting error paths like a debugger.

3 Discussion – Strengths and Weaknesses

Our memory model is simple but sound. The solving algorithm is conceptually sound, too, so we expect to have only correct results. However, the memory model provides no further analysis of the heap, for instance for making restrictions on which pointers may be aliases. That may be a weakness with regards to scalability. Another disadvantage of the memory model is that it is only byte-precise. Thus we cannot deal with bitfields at the moment.

We hope that the new IMPULSE algorithm needs fewer solver calls and thus scales better than the refinement algorithm we used before which relied on splitting and slicing [3].

4   Tool Setup and Configuration

ULTIMATE KOJAK will compete in all categories of SV-COMP 2015 except *2. Bitvectors 3. Concurrency, 11. Floats* and *12. Termination.*
The competition version of ULTIMATE KOJAK is available from

> https://ultimate.informatik.uni-freiburg.de/kojak/

An installation of the SMT solver Z3 is required.[1]
The downloaded archive contains a Python script `Ultimate.py` that provides support for the SVCOMP-compatible input and output of the tool. The directory where the content of the archive lies has to be used as the working directory of the tool. The verification is started by the following command.

> `python Ultimate.py prop.prp inputfile 32bit|64bit simple|precise`

After a successful run, the script produces the following files:

– `Ultimate.log` A log file containing all output of ULTIMATE KOJAK during the verification run.
– `UltimateCounterExample.errorpath` If we found a counterexample, a human readable version of it will be written to this file.
– `witness.graphml` This file contains an error witness as specified by the SV-COMP rules[2] in GraphML.

References

1. Beyer, D., Cimatti, A., Griggio, A., Keremoglu, M.E., Sebastiani, R.: Software model checking via large-block encoding. In: FMCAD, pp. 25–32. IEEE (2009)
2. Christ, J., Hoenicke, J., Nutz, A.: SMTInterpol: An interpolating SMT solver. In: Donaldson, A., Parker, D. (eds.) SPIN 2012. LNCS, vol. 7385, pp. 248–254. Springer, Heidelberg (2012)
3. Ermis, E., Hoenicke, J., Podelski, A.: Splitting via interpolants. In: Kuncak, V., Rybalchenko, A. (eds.) VMCAI 2012. LNCS, vol. 7148, pp. 186–201. Springer, Heidelberg (2012)
4. Heizmann, M., Hoenicke, J., Podelski, A.: Nested interpolants. In: Hermenegildo, M.V., Palsberg, J. (eds.) POPL, pp. 471–482. ACM (2010)
5. Leino, K.R.M.: This is Boogie 2. Manuscript working draft. Microsoft Research, Redmond (2008),
http://research.microsoft.com/en-us/um/people/leino/papers/krml178.pdf
6. Musa, B.: Trace abstraction with unsatisfiable cores. Bachelor's thesis, University of Freiburg, Germany (2013)
7. Nutz, A.: Impulse: a new interpolating software model checker. Master's thesis, University of Freiburg, Germany (2011)

---

[1] We currently use version z3-4.3.3.f50a8b0a59ff-x64 from
http://z3.codeplex.com/downloads/get/924047, the directory .../z3/bin must be in the PATH.

[2] http://www.sosy-lab.org/~dbeyer/cpa-witnesses/

Unbounded Lazy-CSeq: A Lazy Sequentialization Tool for C Programs with Unbounded Context Switches[*]
(Competition Contribution)

Truc L. Nguyen[1], Bernd Fischer[2], Salvatore La Torre[3], and Gennaro Parlato[1]

[1] Electronics and Computer Science, University of Southampton, UK
[2] Division of Computer Science, Stellenbosch University, South Africa
[3] Dipartimento di Informatica, Università degli Studi di Salerno, Italy
tnl2g10@soton.ac.uk

Abstract. We describe a new CSeq module for the verification of multi-threaded C programs with dynamic thread creation. This module implements a variation of the *lazy sequentialization* algorithm implemented in Lazy-CSeq. The main novelty is that we now support an unbounded number of context switches and allow unbounded loops, while the number of allowed threads still remains bounded. This is achieved by a modified sequentialization transformation and the use of the CPAchecker as sequential verification backend.

1 Introduction

The tool CSeq [2,3] is a modular framework for the verification of multi-threaded C programs with dynamic thread creation that is based on sequentialization: the concurrent input program is translated into a corresponding sequential program, which is then verified using existing verification tools for sequential programs. Modules of CSeq implement different *eager* sequentialization schemes [2,3,7,8] and lazy sequentialization schemes targeted to bounded model checking [4,5].

The module Lazy-CSeq [5] implements a lazy sequentialization for bounded programs that avoids the recomputation of local states of the first lazy scheme [6]. It allows us to explore all runs of the original concurrent program up to a bounded number of context switches (arranged in rounds of a round-robin schedule). The new module UL-CSeq described here removes two limitations of this schema: it no longer bounds the number of rounds, and it can handle unbounded programs. In particular, while we still bound the number of threads in a run and the depth of the recursion in recursive function calls we keep the loops (i.e., we do not unroll them), as long as they do not contain thread creation statements. The resulting program has a finite control flow graph and thus is suitable for the tool CPAchecker [1] that we use in our experiments.

2 Verification Approach

Overview. Our sequentialization scheme bounds the number of possible threads in the program, which is achieved indirectly by finite unrolling of the loops that contain thread

---

[*] Partially supported by EPSRC grant no. EP/M008991/1, INDAM-GNCS 2014 grant and MIUR-FARB 2012-2014 grants.

© Springer-Verlag Berlin Heidelberg 2015
C. Baier and C. Tinelli (Eds.): TACAS 2015, LNCS 9035, pp. 461–463, 2015.
DOI: 10.1007/978-3-662-46681-0_45

creation statements. It runs the threads for an unbouded number of rounds, scheduling them in a round-robin fashion until all the threads terminate. The overall structure of the sequentialized program thus has a main driver and a simulation function for each thread. The purpose of the driver is to repeatedly call, in an infinite `while`-loop, the thread simulation functions according to a round-robin schedule. In each iteration an entire round of contexts (one for each thread) is executed.

For each thread, we maintain the program locations at which the previous round's context switch has happened and thus the computation must resume in the next round. To ensure the correctness of resuming from previous context switch, we also keep a global variable to store each thread's current mode (i.e., resume, execute, or suspend) in the simulation: To avoid the recomputation of the local states when a thread is resumed, we declare its local variables as `static` (i.e., persistent) and keep track of the program counter for each thread.

Heap allocation needs no special treatment during the sequentialization and can be delegated entirely to the backend model checker.

Thread Translation. The sequentialized program also contains a *thread simulation function* for each thread instance (including the original main). The code shared by multiple threads is duplicated for each of them such that each thread has its own code, and in particular, its own copy of the thread-local variables.

In the translation, we inject a guard for each statement to control the resumption, execution, and suspension of each thread. The injected code is

```
if (__cs_simulate == 1 ||          /* execute */
    (__cs_simulate == 0 && __cs_pc_1 == current_pc)){/*resume*/
    __cs_simulate = 1;
    if (__VERIFIER_nondet_bool()){ /* context switch guess  */
           __cs_pc_1 = current_pc;  /* save program location */
           __cs_simulate = 2;    }  /* suspend this thread   */
    else {   /* execute statement */  }
}
```

On resuming, this control code makes the function to skip all statements up to the program counter value at the last context switch. On positioning at the corresponding statement, the mode changes to execution, and the statements are executed until a context switch happens, and then the mode changes to suspend. In this mode, we skip the instructions until returning to the main driver. Context switches are nondeterministically guessed in the execution mode before each statement is executed. If- and while-statements also require the injection of similar code to guard the control flow conditions.

3   Architecture, Implementation, and Availability

Architecture. UL-CSeq is implemented as a source-to-source transformation tool in Python (v2.7.1). It uses the pycparser (v2.10, https://github.com/eliben/pycparser) to parse a C program into an abstract syntax tree (AST). The sequentialized program can then be processed independently by any sequential verification tool for C. UL-CSeq has been tested with CPAchecker (v1.3.4, http://cpachecker.sosy-lab.org/).

A small script bundles up translation and verification. The script first invokes the translation which sequentializes the concurrent program, and then calls the CPAchecker to analyze the sequentialized program as follows: `cpa.sh -timelimit 86400 -heap 12000M -preprocess -stats -predicateAnalysis -outputpath` *output*. The script returns TRUE (safe) or FALSE (unsafe) according to the analysis of CPAchecker.

Availability and Installation. UL-CSeq can be downloaded from this link `http://users.ecs.soton.ac.uk/gp4/cseq/ul-cseq-svcomp15.tar.gz`; it also requires installation of the `pycparser`. In the competition we used CPAchecker as a sequential verification backend; this must be installed in the directory of UL-CSeq. CPAchecker also requires the installation of Java Runtime Environment. For the competition, a compressed version of CPAchecker is included, and it can be used when unzipped.

Call. Since UL-CSeq is not a full verification tool but only a concurrency pre-processor, we only compete in the `Concurrency` category. Here, it should be called in the installation directory as follows: `./UL-CSeq.py -i` *file* `--spec` *specfile* `--witness` *logfile*.

Strengths and Weaknesses. UL-CSeq's main strength compared to Lazy-CSeq and MU-CSeq is that, due to the use of the CPAchecker as backed, a TRUE result now represents an actual correctness proof (at least if the number of threads in the program is bounded), and not just a failure to find an error. Its main weakness is that this is slower than the approach taken in Lazy-CSeq and MU-CSeq, resulting in a relatively large number of timeouts, and a lower overall score. Moreover, we still need to bound the number of threads a priori.

References

1. Beyer, D., Keremoglu, M.E.: CPACHECKER: A Tool for Configurable Software Verification. In: Gopalakrishnan, G., Qadeer, S. (eds.) CAV 2011. LNCS, vol. 6806, pp. 184–190. Springer, Heidelberg (2011)
2. Fischer, B., Inverso, O., Parlato, G.: CSeq: A Sequentialization Tool for C. In: Piterman, N., Smolka, S.A. (eds.) TACAS 2013 (ETAPS 2013). LNCS, vol. 7795, pp. 616–618. Springer, Heidelberg (2013)
3. Fischer, B., Inverso, O., Parlato, G.: CSeq: A Concurrency Pre-Processor for Sequential C Verification Tools. In: ASE, pp. 710–713 (2013)
4. Inverso, O., Tomasco, E., Fischer, B., La Torre, S., Parlato, G.: Lazy-CSeq: A Lazy Sequentialization Tool for C. In: Ábrahám, E., Havelund, K. (eds.) TACAS 2014 (ETAPS). LNCS, vol. 8413, pp. 398–401. Springer, Heidelberg (2014)
5. Inverso, O., Tomasco, E., Fischer, B., La Torre, S., Parlato, G.: Bounded Model Checking of Multi-threaded C Programs via Lazy Sequentialization. In: Biere, A., Bloem, R. (eds.) CAV 2014. LNCS, vol. 8559, pp. 585–602. Springer, Heidelberg (2014)
6. La Torre, S., Madhusudan, P., Parlato, G.: Reducing context-bounded concurrent reachability to sequential reachability. In: Bouajjani, A., Maler, O. (eds.) CAV 2009. LNCS, vol. 5643, pp. 477–492. Springer, Heidelberg (2009)
7. Tomasco, E., Inverso, O., Fischer, B., La Torre, S., Parlato, G.: MU-CSeq: Sequentialization of C Programs by Shared Memory Unwindings. In: Ábrahám, E., Havelund, K. (eds.) TACAS 2014 (ETAPS). LNCS, vol. 8413, pp. 402–404. Springer, Heidelberg (2014)
8. Tomasco, E., Inverso, O., Fischer, B., La Torre, S., Parlato, G.: Verifying Concurrent Programs by Memory Unwinding. In: Baier, C., Tinelli, C. (eds.) TACAS 2015. LNCS, vol. 9035, pp. 551–565. Springer, Heidelberg (2015)

FuncTion:
An Abstract Domain Functor for Termination*
(Competition Contribution)

Caterina Urban

ÉNS and CNRS and INRIA, France
urban@di.ens.fr

Abstract. FuncTion is a research prototype static analyzer designed for proving (conditional) termination of C programs. The tool automatically infers piecewise-defined ranking functions (and sufficient preconditions for termination) by means of abstract interpretation. It combines a variety of abstract domains in order to balance the precision and cost of the analysis.

1 Verification Approach

FuncTion is a prototype implementation of our analysis method and abstract domains described in [6,7,8].

Our analysis method follows the traditional approach for proving program termination by means of a well-founded argument or ranking function (i.e., a function from the states of a program to a well-ordered set whose value decreases during program execution). We build a ranking function for a program in an incremental way: we start from the program final states, where the function has value zero (and is undefined elsewhere); then, we add states to the domain of the function, retracing the program backwards and counting the maximum number of performed program steps as value of the function. In [2], Cousot and Cousot formalize this intuition into a sound and complete termination semantics, which is systematically derived by abstract interpretation of the program operational trace semantics.

In order to achieve an effective static analysis, we further abstract this semantics by means of piecewise-defined ranking functions. The analysis consists of two phases: a forward reachability analysis, followed by a backward termination analysis. Each phase proceeds by structural induction on the program syntax, iterating loops until stabilization. In case of nested loops, the analyses stabilize the inner loop for each iteration of the outer loop.

The forward analysis computes, at each program control point, an over-approximation of the set of program states that can be reached at these program points by considering all possible program executions. This provides a first over-approximation of the domain of the program ranking functions.

---

* The research leading to these results has received funding from the ARTEMIS Joint Undertaking under grant agreement no. 269335 (ARTEMIS project MBAT) (see Article II.9. of the JU Grant Agreement).

C. Baier and C. Tinelli (Eds.): TACAS 2015, LNCS 9035, pp. 464–466, 2015.
DOI: 10.1007/978-3-662-46681-0_46

The backward analysis computes, at each program control point, a piecewise-defined ranking function whose domain is (a subset of) the set of reachable states identified by the forward analysis, and whose value represents an upper bound on the number of program execution steps remaining before termination. The starting point is the constant function equal to zero at the program final control point. The piecewise-definition of the ranking functions is semantic-based and dynamic: during the analysis, pieces are split by tests, modified by assignments, and joined when merging control flows. In order to minimize the cost of the analysis, a widening limits the number of maintained pieces. The domain of the ranking function at the program initial control point provides a sufficient precondition for program termination: all program executions starting from a state in the domain of the ranking function are terminating.

2 Software Architecture

FuncTion is written in OCaml. For parsing C programs, we use our own ad-hoc parser generated using Menhir[1]. The available abstract domains for the forward reachability analysis are the numerical abstract domains of intervals [1], octagons [5], and convex polyhedra [3] provided by the APRON library [4]. The abstract domains used for the backward termination analysis are implemented on top of the APRON library: the piecewise-defined ranking functions are represented as decision trees [8]; the nodes of the decision trees are interval, octagonal, or polyhedral linear constraints, and the paths towards the leaves induce the piecewise-definition of the ranking functions; the leaves of the decision trees represent the value of the ranking functions as affine functions or ordinal-valued functions [7]. For the competition, we have chosen convex polyhedra for the reachability analysis and polyhedral linear constraints for the decision trees in the termination analysis.

3 Strengths and Weaknesses

A strength of FuncTion is its modular architecture: a variety of abstract domains are combined in order to balance the precision and cost of the analysis. An immediate consequence is the potential for improvements of the analysis by simply adding new abstract domains to the analyzer. However, FuncTion is still a research prototype, and so far it lacks any abstract domain for shape analysis: it provides only a limited support for arrays and pointers. Therefore, FuncTion is able to analyze only 83% of the SV-COMP 2015 benchmark test cases.

Moreover, the analyzer fails to prove termination of a significant number of terminating tests cases mainly due to a naïve widening operator [6,8]. We have yet to integrate state-of-the-art widening operators.

We emphasize the soundness of the analysis, which is confirmed by the absence of reported false negatives (i.e., reported termination for a non-terminating program) on the benchmark of SV-COMP 2015. On the other hand, FuncTion does

---

[1] http://cristal.inria.fr/~fpottier/menhir/

not report non-termination (i.e., it does not answer FALSE) for now, which causes a fair loss of score.

Finally, we argue that the ability of FuncTion to find significative preconditions for program termination is an important feature, which unfortunately is not taken into account in the competition.

4   Tool Setup and Configuration

The competition candidate for SV-COMP 2015 can be downloaded from:

http://www.di.ens.fr/~urban/sv-comp2015.zip.

FuncTion is only participating in the **Termination** category of SV-COMP 2015.

The competition candidate can be invoked using the following call pattern:

./function <file>

where <file> is the path to the C file to be analyzed for termination of the function main(). The analyzer prints TRUE on the standard output in case it can successfully prove termination. Otherwise, it prints UNKNOWN.

5   Software Project and Contributors

FuncTion has been developed as part of the author's PhD thesis. A web interface is available: http://www.di.ens.fr/~urban/FuncTion.html.

Grateful acknowledgements go to Antoine Miné for publishing the source code of his prototype[2], which helped to speed up the initial development of FuncTion.

References

1. Cousot, P., Cousot, R.: Static Determination of Dynamic Properties of Programs. In: International Symposium on Programming, pp. 106–130 (1976)
2. Cousot, P., Cousot, R.: An Abstract Interpretation Framework for Termination. In: POPL, pp. 245–258 (2012)
3. Cousot, P., Halbwachs, N.: Automatic Discovery of Linear Restraints Among Variables of a Program. In: POPL, pp. 84–96 (1978)
4. Jeannet, B., Miné, A.: APRON: A library of numerical abstract domains for static analysis. In: Bouajjani, A., Maler, O. (eds.) CAV 2009. LNCS, vol. 5643, pp. 661–667. Springer, Heidelberg (2009)
5. Miné, A.: The Octagon Abstract Domain. Higher-Order and Symbolic Computation 19(1), 31–100 (2006)
6. Urban, C.: The abstract domain of segmented ranking functions. In: Logozzo, F., Fähndrich, M. (eds.) Static Analysis. LNCS, vol. 7935, pp. 43–62. Springer, Heidelberg (2013)
7. Urban, C., Miné, A.: An abstract domain to infer ordinal-valued ranking functions. In: Shao, Z. (ed.) ESOP 2014 (ETAPS). LNCS, vol. 8410, pp. 412–431. Springer, Heidelberg (2014)
8. Urban, C., Miné, A.: A decision tree abstract domain for proving conditional termination. In: Müller-Olm, M., Seidl, H. (eds.) Static Analysis. LNCS, vol. 8723, pp. 302–318. Springer, Heidelberg (2014)

---

[2] http://www.di.ens.fr/~mine/banal/

Parameter Synthesis

Model Checking Gene Regulatory Networks*

Mirco Giacobbe[1], Călin C. Guet[1], Ashutosh Gupta[1,2], Thomas A. Henzinger[1],
Tiago Paixão[1], and Tatjana Petrov[1]

[1] IST Austria, Austria
[2] TIFR, India

Abstract. The behaviour of gene regulatory networks (GRNs) is typically analysed using simulation-based statistical testing-like methods. In this paper, we demonstrate that we can replace this approach by a formal verification-like method that gives higher assurance and scalability. We focus on Wagner's weighted GRN model with varying weights, which is used in evolutionary biology. In the model, weight parameters represent the gene interaction strength that may change due to genetic mutations. For a property of interest, we synthesise the constraints over the parameter space that represent the set of GRNs satisfying the property. We experimentally show that our parameter synthesis procedure computes the mutational robustness of GRNs –an important problem of interest in evolutionary biology– more efficiently than the classical simulation method. We specify the property in linear temporal logics. We employ symbolic bounded model checking and SMT solving to compute the space of GRNs that satisfy the property, which amounts to synthesizing a set of linear constraints on the weights.

1 Introduction

Gene regulatory networks (GRNs) are one of the most prevalent and fundamental type of biological networks whose main actors are genes regulating other genes. A topology of a GRN is represented by a graph of interactions among a finite set of genes, where nodes represent genes, and edges denote the type of regulation (activation or repression) between the genes, if any. In [21], Wagner introduced a simple but useful model for GRNs that captures important features of GRNs. In the model, a system state specifies the activity of each gene as a Boolean value. The system is executed in discrete time steps, and all gene values are synchronously and deterministically updated: a gene active at time n affects the value of its neighbouring genes at time $n+1$. This effect is modelled through two

---

* This research was supported by the European Research Council (ERC) under grant 267989 (QUAREM), the Austrian Science Fund (FWF) under grants S11402-N23 (RiSE) and Z211-N23 (Wittgenstein Award), the European Union's SAGE grant agreement no. 618091, ERC Advanced Grant ERC-2009-AdG-250152, the People Programme (Marie Curie Actions) of the European Union's Seventh Framework Programme (FP7/2007-2013) under REA grant agreement no. 291734, and the SNSF Early Postdoc.Mobility Fellowship, the grant number P2EZP2_148797.

© Springer-Verlag Berlin Heidelberg 2015
C. Baier and C. Tinelli (Eds.): TACAS 2015, LNCS 9035, pp. 469–483, 2015.
DOI: 10.1007/978-3-662-46681-0_47

kinds of parameters: *threshold* parameters assigned to each gene, which specify the strength necessary to sustain the gene's activity, and *weight* parameters assigned to pairs of genes, which denote the strength of their directed effect.

Some properties of GRNs can be expressed in linear temporal logic (LTL) (such as reaching a steady-state), where atomic propositions are modelled by gene values. A single GRN may or may not satisfy a property of interest. Biologists are often interested in the behavior of *populations of GRNs*, and in presence of environmental perturbations. For example, the parameters of GRNs from a population may change from one generation to another due to mutations, and the distribution over the different GRNs in a population changes accordingly. We refer to the set of GRNs obtained by varying parameters on a fixed topology as *GRN Space*. For a given population of GRNs instantiated from a GRN Space, typical quantities of interest refer to the long-run average behavior. For example, *robustness* refers to the averaged satisfiability of the property within a population of GRNs, after an extended number of generations. In this context, Wagner's model of GRN has been used to show that mutational robustness can gradually evolve in GRNs [10], that sexual reproduction can enhance robustness to recombination [1], or to predict the phenotypic effect of mutations [17]. The computational analysis used in these studies relies on explicitly executing GRNs, with the purpose of checking if they satisfy the property. Then, in order to compute the robustness of a population of GRNs, the satisfaction check must be performed repeatedly for many different GRNs. In other words, robustness is estimated by statistically sampling GRNs from the GRN Space and executing each of them until the property is (dis)proven. In this work, we pursue formal analysis of Wagner's GRNs which allows to avoid repeated executions of GRNs, and to compute mutational robustness with higher assurance and scalability.

In this paper, we present a novel method for synthesizing the space of parameters which characterize GRNs that satisfy a given property. These constraints eliminate the need of explicitly executing the GRN to check the satisfaction of the property. Importantly, the synthesized parameter constraints allow to efficiently answer questions that are very difficult or impossible to answer by simulation, e.g. emptiness check or parameter sensitivity analysis. In this work, we chose to demonstrate how the synthesized constraints can be used to compute the robustness of a population of GRNs with respect to genetic mutations. Since constraint evaluation is usually faster than executing a GRN, the constraints pre-computation enables faster computation of robustness. This further allows to compute the robustness with higher precision, within the same computational time. Moreover, it sometimes becomes possible to replace the statistical sampling with the exact computation of robustness.

In our method, for a given GRN Space and LTL property, we used SMT solving and bounded model checking to generate a set of constraints such that a GRN satisfies the LTL property if and only if its weight parameters satisfy the constraints. The key insight in this method is that the obtained constraints are complex Boolean combinations of linear inequalities. Solving linear constraints has been the focus of both industry and academia for some time. However, the technology for solving linear constraints with Boolean structure, namely SMT solving, has matured only in the last decade [3]. This technology has enabled us to successfully apply an SMT solver to generate the desired constraints.

We have built a tool which computes the constraints for a given GRN Space and a property expressed in a fragment of LTL. In order to demonstrate the effectiveness of our method, we computed the robustness of five GRNs listed in [8], and for three GRNs known to exhibit oscillatory behavior. We first synthesized the constraints and then we used them to estimate robustness based on statistical sampling of GRNs from the GRN space. Then, in order to compare the performance with the simulation-based methods, we implemented the approximate computation of robustness, where the satisfiability of the property is verified by executing the GRNs explicitly. The results show that in six out of eight tested networks, the pre-computation of constraints provides greater efficiency, performing up to three times faster than the simulation method.

Related Work. Formal verification techniques are already used for aiding various aspects of biological research [12,16,15,22]. In particular, the robustness of models of biochemical systems with respect to temporal properties has been studied [18,6,19]. Our work is, to the best of our knowledge, the first application of formal verification to studying the evolution of mutational robustness of gene regulatory networks and, as such, it opens up a novel application area for the formal verification community. As previously discussed, with respect to related studies in evolutionary biology, our method can offer a higher degree of assurance, more accuracy, and better scalability than the traditional, simulation-based approaches. In addition, while the mutational robustness has been studied only for invariant properties, our method allows to compute the mutational robustness for non-trivial temporal properties that are expressible in LTL, such as bistability or oscillations between gene states.

1.1 Motivating Example

In the following, we will illustrate the main idea of the paper on an example of a GRN Space T generated from the GRN network shown in Fig. 1(a). Two genes A and B inhibit each other, and both genes have a self-activating loop. The parameters (i_A, i_B) represent constant inputs, which we assume to be regulated by some other genes that are not presented in the figure. Each of the genes is assigned a threshold value (t_A, t_B), and each edge is assigned a weight $(w_{AA}, w_{AB}, w_{BA}, w_{BB})$. The dynamics of a GRN-individual chosen from T depends on these parameters. Genes are in either active or inactive state, which we represent with Boolean variables. For a given initial state of all genes, and for fixed values of weights and thresholds, the values of all genes evolve deterministically in discrete time-steps that are synchronized over all genes. Let a (resp. b) be the Boolean variable representing the activity of gene A (resp. B). We denote a GRN state by a pair (a, b). Let τ be the function that governs the dynamics of $\mathcal{G}$ (see Def. 3):

$$\tau(a, b) = (i_A + a w_{AA} - b w_{BA} > t_A,\ i_B + b w_{BB} - a w_{AB} > t_B)$$

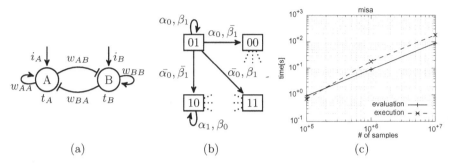

Fig. 1. Motivating example. a) The topology of a GRN with mutual inhibition of genes A and B. b) The labelled transition system where labels denote the linear constraints which enable the transition. α_0, α_1, β_0, and β_1 denote linear atomic formulas $i_A - w_{BA} \leq t_A$, $i_B + w_{BB} > t_B$, $i_B - w_{AB} \leq t_B$, and $i_A + w_{AA} > t_A$ respectively. c) Run-times comparison between execution method (dashed lines) and our evaluation method (solid lines).

The next state of a gene is the result of arithmetically adding the influence from other active genes.

The topology of mutually inhibiting pair of genes is known to be bistable: whenever one gene is highly expressed and the other is barely expressed, the system remains stable [13,19]. The bistability property can be written as the following LTL formula (see Def. 4):

$$(A \wedge \neg B \implies \Box(A \wedge \neg B)) \wedge (\neg A \wedge B \implies \Box(\neg A \wedge B)).$$

Let us fix values for parameters $t_A = t_B = 0.6$, $w_{AB} = w_{BA} = w_{BB} = 0.3$, and $i_A = i_B = \frac{2}{3}$. Then, we can check that a GRN is bistable by executing the GRN. Indeed, for the given parameter values, the states $(0,1)$ and $(1,0)$ are fixed points of τ. In other words, the GRN with those parameter values have two stable states: if they start in state $(0,1)$ (resp. $(1,0)$), they remain there. Now let us choose $i_A = \frac{2}{3}$, $i_B = \frac{1}{3}$. Again, by executing the GRN, we can conclude that it does not satisfy the property: at state $(0,1)$, B does not have sufficiently strong activation to surpass its threshold and the system jumps to $(0,0)$. Intuitively, since the external activation of B is too small, the phenotype has changed to a single stable state. In general, it is not hard to inspect that the bistability property will be met by any choice of parameters satisfying the following constraints:

$$\{i_A - w_{BA} \leq t_A,\ i_A + w_{AA} > t_A,\ i_B - w_{AB} \leq t_B,\ i_B + w_{BB} > t_B\}. \tag{1}$$

Let's now suppose that we want to compute the robustness of T in presence of variations on edges due to mutations. Then, for each possible value of parameters, one needs to verify if the respective GRN satisfies the property. Using the constraints (1), one may verify GRNs without executing them.

Our method automates this idea to any given GRN topology and any property specified in LTL. We first encode T as a parametrized labelled transition system, partly shown in Fig. 1(b). Our implementation does not explicitly construct this transition system, nor executes the GRNs (the implementation is described in Section 5). Then, we apply symbolic model checking to compute the constraints which represent the space of GRN's from T that satisfy the bi-stability property.

To illustrate the scalability of our method in comparison with the standard methods, in Fig. 1(c), we compare the performance of computing the mutational robustness with and without precomputing the constraints (referred to as *evaluation* and *execution* method respectively). We choose a mutation model such that each parameter takes 13 possible values distributed according to the binomial distribution (see Appendix in [14] for more details on the mutation model). We estimate the robustness value by statistical sampling of the possible parameter values. For a small number of samples, our method is slower because we spend extra time in computing the constraints. However, more samples may be necessary for achieving the desired precision. As the number of samples increases, our method becomes faster, because each evaluation of the constraints is two times faster than checking bistability by executing GRN-individuals. For 1.2×10^5 many simulations, execution and evaluation methods take same total time, and the robustness value estimated from these many samples lies in the interval $(0.8871, 0.8907)$ with 95% confidence. Hence, for this GRN, if one needs better precision for the robustness value, our method is preferred.

One may think that for this example, we may compute exact robustness because the number of parameter values is only 13^6 (four weights and two inputs). For simplicity of illustration, we chose this example, and we later present examples with a much larger space of parameters, for which exact computation of robustness is infeasible.

2   Preliminaries

In this section, we start by defining a *GRN Space*, which will serve to specify common features for GRNs from the same population. These common features are types of gene interactions (topology), constant parameters (thresholds), and ranges of parameter values that are subject to some environmental perturbation (weights). Then, we formally introduce a model of an individual GRN from the GRN Space and temporal logic to express its properties.

2.1   GRN Space

The key characteristics of the behaviour of a GRN are typically summarised by a directed graph where nodes represent genes and edges denote the type of regulation between the genes. A regulation edge is either *activation* (one gene's activity increases the activity of the other gene) or *repression* (one gene's activity decreases the activity of the other gene) [20]. In Wagner's model of a GRN, in addition to the activation types between genes, each gene is assigned a *threshold* and each edge (pair of genes) is assigned a *weight*. The threshold of a gene models the amount of activation level necessary to sustain activity of the gene. The weight on an edge quantifies the influence of the source gene on destination gene of the edge by means of a non-negative rational number.

We extend the Wagner's model by allowing a range of values for weight parameters. We call our model GRN Space, denoting that all GRNs instantiated from that space share the same topology, and their parameters fall into given ranges. We assume that each gene always has some minimum level of expression without any external influence. In the model, this constant input is incorporated by a special gene which is always active, and activates all other genes from the network. The weight on the edge between the special gene and some other gene represents the minimum level of activation. The minimal activation is also subject to perturbation.

Definition 1 (GRN Space). A gene regulatory network space is given by a tuple $T = (G, g_{in}, \rightarrow, \dashv, t, w^{max}, W)$, where

- $G = \{g_1, \ldots, g_d\}$ is a finite ordered set of genes,
- $g_{in} \in G$ is the special gene used to model the constant input for all genes,
- $\rightarrow \subseteq G \times G$ is the activation relation such that $\forall g \in G \setminus \{g_{in}\}\ (g_{in}, g) \in \rightarrow$ and $\forall g\ (g, g_{in}) \notin \rightarrow$,
- $\dashv \subseteq G \times G$ is the repression relation such that $\dashv \cap \rightarrow = \emptyset \wedge \forall g\ (g, g_{in}) \notin \dashv$,
- $t\colon G \to \mathbb{Q}$ is the threshold function such that $\forall g \in G \setminus \{g_{in}\}\ t(g) \geq 0$ and $t(g_{in}) < 0$,
- $w^{max}\colon (\rightarrow \cup \dashv) \to \mathbb{Q}_{\geq 0}$ is the maximum value of an activation/repression,
- $W = \mathcal{P}((\rightarrow \cup \dashv) \to \mathbb{Q}_{\geq 0})$ assigns a set of possible weight functions to each activation/inhibition relation, so that $w \in W \Rightarrow \forall (g, g') \in \rightarrow \cup \dashv\ w(g, g') \leq w^{max}(g, g')$.

2.2 GRN-individual

Definition 2 (GRN-individual). A GRN-individual $\mathcal{G}$ is a pair (T, w), where $w \in W$ is a weight function from the GRN Space.

A state $\sigma\colon G \to \mathbb{B}$ of a GRN-individual $\mathcal{G} = (T, w)$ denotes the activation state of each gene in terms of a Boolean value. Let $\Sigma(\mathcal{G})$ (resp. $\Sigma(T)$) denote the set of all states of $\mathcal{G}$ (resp. T), such that $\sigma(g_{in}) = true$. The GRN model executes in discrete time steps by updating all the activation states synchronously and deterministically according to the following rule: a gene is active at next time if and only if the total influence on that gene, from genes active at current time, surpasses its threshold.

Definition 3 (Semantics of a GRN-individual). A *run* of a GRN-individual $\mathcal{G} = (T, w)$ is an infinite sequence of states $\sigma_0, \sigma_1, \ldots$ such that $\sigma_n \in \Sigma(\mathcal{G})$ and $\tau(\sigma_n) = \sigma_{n+1}$ for all $n \geq 0$, where $\tau\colon \Sigma(\mathcal{G}) \to \Sigma(\mathcal{G})$ is a deterministic transition function defined by

$$\tau(\sigma) := \lambda g'.\left[\sum_{\{g|\sigma(g) \wedge (g,g') \in \rightarrow\}} w(g) \quad - \sum_{\{g|\sigma(g) \wedge (g,g') \in \dashv\}} w(g) \quad > t(g') \right]. \tag{2}$$

The language of $\mathcal{G}$, denoted by $[\![\mathcal{G}]\!]$, is a set of all possible runs of $\mathcal{G}$. Note that a GRN-individual does not specify the initial state. Therefore, $[\![\mathcal{G}]\!]$ may contain more than one run.

2.3   Temporal Properties

A GRN exists in a living organism to exhibit certain behaviors. Here we present a linear temporal logic (LTL) to express the expected behaviors of GRNs.

Definition 4 (Syntax of Linear Temporal Logic). The language of linear temporal logic fomulae is given by the grammar $\varphi ::= g \mid (\neg\varphi) \mid (\varphi \vee \varphi) \mid (\varphi \mathcal{U} \varphi)$, where $g \in G$ is a gene.

Linear temporal properties are evaluated over all (in)finite runs of states from $\Sigma(G)$. Let us consider a run $r = \sigma_1, \sigma_2, \sigma_3, \cdots \in \Sigma(G)^* \cup \Sigma(G)^\infty$. Let r^i be the suffix of r after i states and r_i is the ith state of r. The satisfaction relation $\models$ between a run and an LTL formula is defined as follows:

$$r \models g \text{ if } r_1(g), \qquad r \models \neg\varphi \text{ if } r \not\models \varphi, \qquad r \models \varphi_1 \vee \varphi_2 \text{ if } r \models \varphi_1 \text{ or } r \models \varphi_2,$$

$$r \models (\varphi_1 \mathcal{U} \varphi_2) \text{ if } \exists i.r^i \models \varphi_2 \text{ and } \forall j \leq i.r^j \models \varphi_1.$$

Note that if $|r| < i$ then r^i has no meaning. In such a situation, the above semantics returns *undefined*, i.e., r is too short to decide the LTL formula. We say a language $\mathcal{L} \models \varphi$ if for each run $r \in \mathcal{L}$, $r \models \varphi$, and a GRN $\mathcal{G} \models \varphi$ if $\mathcal{L}[\![\mathcal{G}]\!] \models \varphi$. Let $\Diamond\varphi$ be shorthand of $true\mathcal{U}\varphi$ and $\Box\varphi$ be shorthand of $\neg\Diamond\neg\varphi$.

Note that we did not include next operator in the definition of LTL. This is because a GRN does not expect something is to be done in strictly next cycle.

3   Algorithm for Parameter Synthesis

In this section we present an algorithm for synthesising the weights' space corresponding to a given property in linear temporal logic. The method combines LTL model checking [2] and satisfiability modulo theory (SMT) solving [4].

The method operates in two steps. First, we represent any GRN-individual from the GRN Space with a parametrized transition system: a transition exists between every two states, and it is labelled by linear constraints, that are necessary and sufficient constraints to enable that transition in a concrete GRN-individual (for example, see Fig. 1b). We say that a run of the parametrized transition system is *feasible* if the conjunction of all the constraints labelled along the run is satisfiable. Second, we search for all the feasible runs that satisfy the desired LTL property and we record the constraints collected along them. The disjunction of such run constraints fully characterises the regions of weights which ensure that LTL property holds in the respective GRN-individual.

Let $V = \{v_1, \ldots, v_n\}$ be a finite set of variable names. For some rationals $k_1, \ldots, k_n \in \mathbb{Q}$, let $k_1 v_1 + \cdots + k_n v_n + t > 0$ and $k_1 v_1 + \cdots + k_n v_n + t \geq 0$ be strict and non-strict linear inequalities over V, respectively. Let $polyhedra(V)$ be the set of all finite conjunctions of linear inequalities over V.

Definition 5 (Parametrized Transition System). For a given GRN Space T and a rational parameters map $v : G \to V$, the *parametrized transition system* (T, v) is a labelled transition system $(\Sigma(T), \Phi)$, where the labeling of the edges $\Phi : \Sigma(T) \times \Sigma(T) \to polyhedra(V)$ is defined as follows:

$$\Phi := \lambda\sigma\sigma'. \bigwedge_{g' \in G} \left[\sum_{\{g | \sigma(g) \wedge (g,g') \in \to\}} v(g) \quad - \sum_{\{g | \sigma(g) \wedge (g,g') \in \dashv\}} v(g) \; > \; t(g') \iff \sigma'(g') \right].$$

$\Phi(\sigma, \sigma')$ says that a gene g' is active in σ' iff the weighted sum of activation and suppression activity of the regulators of g' is above its threshold.

A *run* of (T, v) is a sequence of states $\sigma_0, \sigma_1, \ldots$ such that $\sigma_n \in \Sigma(T)$ for all $n \geq 0$, and $\Phi(\sigma_0, \sigma_1) \wedge \Phi(\sigma_1, \sigma_2) \wedge \ldots$ is said to be the *run constraint* of the run. A run is feasible if its run constraint is satisfiable. We denote by $[\![(T, v)]\!]$ the set of feasible traces for (T, v). For a weight function w, let $\Phi(\sigma, \sigma')[w/v]$ denote the formula obtained by substituting v by w and let $(T, v)[w/v] = (\Sigma(T), \Phi')$, where $\Phi'(\sigma, \sigma') = \Phi(\sigma, \sigma')[w/v]$ for each $\sigma, \sigma' \in \Sigma(T)$.

In the following text, we refer to the parametrized transition system (T, v) and an LTL property φ. Moreover, we denote the run constraint of run $r = \sigma_0, \sigma_1, \ldots \in [\![(T, v)]\!]$ by $cons(r)$.

Lemma 1. For a weight function w, the set of feasible runs of $(T, v)[w/v]$ is equal to $[\![(T, w)]\!]$.

The proof of the above lemma follows from the definition of the semantics for GRN-individual. Note that the run constraints are conjunctions of linear inequalities. Therefore, we apply efficient SMT solvers to analyze (T, v).

3.1 Constraint Generation via Model Checking

Now our goal is to synthesize the constraints over v which characterise exactly the set of weight functions w, for which (T, w) satisfies φ. Each feasible run violating φ reports a set of constraints which weight parameters should avoid. Once all runs violating φ are accounted for, the desired region of weights is completely characterized. More explicitly, the desired space of weights is obtained by conjuncting negations of run constraints of all feasible runs that satisfy $\neg\varphi$.

In Fig. 2, we present our algorithm GENCONS for the constraint generation. GENCONS unfolds (T, v) in depth-first-order manner to search for runs which satisfy $\neg\varphi$. At line 3, GENCONS calls recursive function GENCONSREC to do the unfolding for each state in $\Sigma(T)$. GENCONSREC takes six input parameters. The parameter $run.\sigma$ and $runCons$ are the states of the currently traced run and its respective run constraint. The third parameter are the constraints, collected due to the discovery of counterexamples, *i.e.*, runs which violate φ. The forth, fifth and sixth parameter are the description of the input transition system and the LTL property φ. Since GRN-individuals have deterministic transitions, we only need to look for the lassos upto length $|\Sigma(T)|$ for LTL model checking. Therefore, we execute the loop at line 7 only if the $run.\sigma$ has length smaller than $|\Sigma(T)|$.

function GENCONS$((T, v) = (\Sigma(T), \Phi), \varphi)$
begin
1   $goodCons := true$
2   **for** each $\sigma \in \Sigma(T)$ **do**
3    $goodCons :=$ GENCONSREC$(\sigma, true, goodCons, \Sigma(T), \Phi, \varphi)$
4   **done**
5   **return** $goodCons$
end

function GENCONSREC$(run.\sigma, runCons, goodCons, \Sigma(T), \Phi, \varphi)$
begin
6   **if** $|run.\sigma| < |\Sigma(T)|$ **then**
7   **for** each $\sigma' \in \Sigma(T)$ **do**
8 | $runCons' := runCons \wedge \Phi(\sigma, \sigma')$
9 | **if** $goodCons \wedge runCons'$ is sat **then**
10 | **if** $run.\sigma\sigma' \models \neg\varphi$ **then**   (∗ check may return undef ∗)
11 | $goodCons := goodCons \wedge \neg runCons'$
12 | **else**
13 | $goodCons :=$ GENCONSREC$(run.\sigma\sigma', runCons', goodCons, \Sigma(T), \Phi, \varphi)$
14   └ **done**
15   **return** $goodCons$
end

Fig. 2. Counterexample guided computation of the mutation space feasible wrt. φ. Let "." be an operator that appends two sequences. $run.\sigma\sigma' \models \neg\varphi$ can be implemented by converting $\neg\varphi$ into a Büchi automaton and searching for an accepting run over $run.\sigma\sigma'$. However, a finite path may be too short to decide whether φ holds or not. In that case, the condition at line 10 fails. Since (T, v) is finite, the finite runs are bound to form lassos within $|\Sigma(T)|$ steps. If a finite run forms a lasso, then the truth value of $run.\sigma\sigma' \models \neg\varphi$ will be determined.

The loop iterates over each state in $\Sigma(T)$. The condition at line 9 checks if $run.\sigma\sigma'$ is feasible and, if it is not, the loop goes to another iteration. Otherwise, the condition at line 10 checks if $run.\sigma\sigma' \models \neg\varphi$. Note that $run.\sigma\sigma' \models \neg\varphi$ may also return undefined because the run may be too short to decide the LTL property. If the condition returns true, we add negation of the run constraint in $goodCons$. Otherwise, we make a recursive call to extend the run at line 13. $goodCons$ tells us the set of values of v for which we have discovered no counterexample. GENCONS returns $goodCons$ at the end.

Since run constraints are always a conjunction of linear inequalities, $goodCons$ is a conjunction of clauses over linear inequalities. Therefore, we can apply efficient SMT technology to evaluate the condition at line 9. The following theorem states that the algorithm GENCONS computes the parameter region which satisfies property φ.

Theorem 1. For every weight function $w \in W$, the desired set of weight functions for which a GRN-individual satisfies φ equals the weight functions which satisfy the constraints returned by GENCONS:

$$(T, w) \models \varphi \text{ iff } w \models \text{GenCons}((T, v), \varphi).$$

Proof. The statement amounts to showing that the sets $A = \{w \mid (T, w) \models \varphi\}$ and $B = \bigcap_{r \in [\![(T,v)]\!] \wedge r \models \neg \varphi} \{w \mid w \models \neg cons(r)\}$ are equivalent. Notice that $W \setminus A = \bigcup_{r \in [\![(T,v)]\!] \wedge r \models \neg \varphi} \{w \mid w \models cons(r)\} = W \setminus B$.

We use the above presentation of the algorithm for easy readability. However, our implementation differs significantly from the presentation. We follow the encoding of [7] to encode the path exploration as a bounded-model checking problem. Further details about implementation are available in Section 5. The algorithm has exponential complexity in the size of T. However, one may view the above procedure as the clause learning in SMT solvers, where clauses are learnt when the LTL formula is violated [23]. Similar to SMT solvers, in practice, this algorithm may not suffer from the worst-case complexity.

Example 1. The GRN osc3 (shown in Fig. 3) was the model of a pioneering work in synthetic biology [11], and it is known to provide oscillatory behaviour: each gene should alternate its expression between 'on' and 'off' state:

$$\varphi_3 = \bigwedge_{v \in \{A, B, C\}} (v \Rightarrow \Diamond \neg v) \wedge (\neg v \Rightarrow \Diamond v).$$

The solutions are the constraints: $(T, w) \models \varphi_3$ iff $(i_A > t_A) \wedge (i_B > t_B) \wedge (i_C > t_C) \wedge (i_B - w_{AB} \leq t_B) \wedge (i_C - w_{BC} \leq t_C) \wedge (i_A - w_{CA} \leq t_A)$.

4   Computing Robustness

In this section, we present an application of our parameter synthesis algorithm, namely computing robustness of GRNs in presence of mutations. To this end, we formalize GRN-population and its robustness. Then, we present a method to compute the robustness using our synthesized parameters.

A GRN-population models a large number of GRN-individuals with varying weights. All the GRN-individuals are defined over the same GRN Space, hence they differ only in their weight functions. The GRN-population is characterised by the GRN Space T and a probability distribution over the weight functions. In the experimental section, we will use the range of weights W and the distribution π based on the mutation model outlined in the Appendix in [14].

Definition 6 (GRN-population). A GRN-population is a pair $\mathcal{Z} = (T, \pi)$, where $\pi : W \to [0, 1]$ is a probability distribution over all weight functions from the GRN Space T, i.e., $\sum_{w \in W} \pi(w) = 1$.

We write $\varphi(\mathcal{Z}) \in [0, 1]$ to denote an expectation that a GRN instantiated from a GRN-population $\mathcal{Z} = (T, \pi)$ satisfies φ. The value $\varphi(\mathcal{Z})$ is in the interval $[0, 1]$ and we call it robustness.

Definition 7 (Robustness). Let $\mathcal{Z} = (T, \pi)$ be a GRN-population, and φ be an LTL formula which expresses the desired LTL property. Then, the robustness of $\mathcal{Z}$ with respect to the property φ is given by

$$\varphi(\mathcal{Z}) := \sum_{\{w | [\![(T,w)]\!] \models \varphi\}} \pi(w)$$

The above definition extends that of [10], because it allows for expressing any LTL property as a phenotype, and hence it can capture more complex properties such as oscillatory behaviour. In the following, we will present an algorithm for computing the robustness, which employs algorithm GENCONS.

4.1   Evaluating Robustness

Let us suppose we get a GRN-population $\mathcal{Z} = (T, \pi)$ and LTL property φ as input to compute robustness. For small size of GRN Space T, robustness can be computed by explicitly enumerating all the GRN-individuals from T, and verifying each GRN-individual against φ. The probabilities of all satisfying GRN-individuals are added up. However, the exhaustive enumeration of the GRN Space is often intractable due to a large range of weight functions W in T. In those cases, the robustness is estimated statistically: a number of GRN-individuals are sampled from T according to the distribution π, and the fraction of satisfying GRN-individuals is stored. The sampling experiment is repeated a number of times, and the mean (respectively variance) of the stored values are reported as robustness (respectively precision).

Depending on how a sampled GRN-individual is verified against the LTL property, we have two methods:

- In the first method, which we will call *execution* method, each sampled GRN-individual is verified by executing the GRN-individual from all initial states and checking if each run satisfies φ;
- In the second method, which we will call *evaluation* method, the constraints are first precomputed with GENCONS, and each sampled GRN-individual is verified by evaluating the constraints.

Clearly, the time of computing the constraints initially renders the evaluation method less efficient. This cost is amortized when verifying a GRN-individual by constraint evaluation is faster than by execution. In the experimental section, we compare the overall performance of the two approaches on a number of GRNs from literature.

5   Experimental Results

We implemented a tool which synthesizes the parameter constraints for a given LTL property (see Section 3), and the methods for computing the mutational robustness (see Section 4.1). We ran our tool on a set of GRNs from the literature.

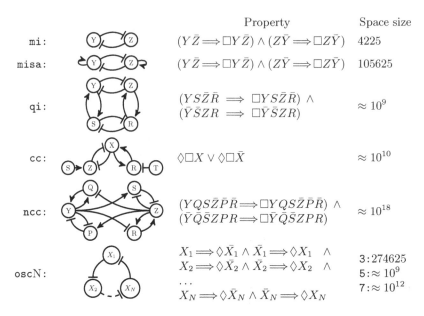

		Property	Space size
mi:		$(Y\bar{Z} \Longrightarrow \Box Y\bar{Z}) \wedge (Z\bar{Y} \Longrightarrow \Box Z\bar{Y})$	4225
misa:		$(Y\bar{Z} \Longrightarrow \Box Y\bar{Z}) \wedge (Z\bar{Y} \Longrightarrow \Box Z\bar{Y})$	105625
qi:		$(YS\bar{Z}\bar{R} \Longrightarrow \Box YS\bar{Z}\bar{R}) \wedge$ $(\bar{Y}\bar{S}ZR \Longrightarrow \Box \bar{Y}\bar{S}ZR)$	$\approx 10^9$
cc:		$\Diamond\Box X \vee \Diamond\Box\bar{X}$	$\approx 10^{10}$
ncc:		$(YQS\bar{Z}\bar{P}\bar{R} \Longrightarrow \Box YQS\bar{Z}\bar{P}\bar{R}) \wedge$ $(\bar{Y}\bar{Q}\bar{S}ZPR \Longrightarrow \Box \bar{Y}\bar{Q}\bar{S}ZPR)$	$\approx 10^{18}$
oscN:		$X_1 \Longrightarrow \Diamond\bar{X}_1 \wedge \bar{X}_1 \Longrightarrow \Diamond X_1 \quad \wedge$ $X_2 \Longrightarrow \Diamond\bar{X}_2 \wedge \bar{X}_2 \Longrightarrow \Diamond X_2 \quad \wedge$ $\ldots$ $X_N \Longrightarrow \Diamond\bar{X}_N \wedge \bar{X}_N \Longrightarrow \Diamond X_N$	3:274625 5:$\approx 10^9$ 7:$\approx 10^{12}$

Fig. 3. GRN benchmarks. mi, misa (mutual inhibition), qi (quad inhibition), and ncc (cell cycle switch) satisfy different forms of bistability. For the networks ci (cell cycle switch), the value of gene eventually stabilizes [9]. In osc3, also known as the *repressilator* [11], the gene values alternate. osc5 and osc7 (not shown) are generalizations of osc3, and also exhibit oscilating behavior.

5.1   Implementation

Our implementation does not explicitly construct the parametrised transition system described in Section 3 (Dfn. 5 and Alg. 2). Instead, we encode the bounded model-checking (Alg. 2) as a satisfiability problem, and we use an SMT solver to efficiently find *goodCons*. More concretely, we initially build a formula which encodes the parametrized transition system and it is satisfied if and only if some run of (T, v) satisfies $\neg\varphi$. If the encoding formula is satisfiable, the constraints $cons(r)$ along the run are collected, and $\neg cons(r)$ is added to *goodCons*. Then, we expand the encoding formula by adding $\neg cons(r)$, so as to rule out finding the same run again. We continue the search until no satisfying assignment of the encoding formula can be found. The algorithm always terminates because the validity of the property is always decided on finite runs (as explained in Section 3).

The implementation involves 8k lines of C++ and we use Z3 SMT solver as the solving engine. We use CUDD to reduce the size of the Boolean structure of the resulting formula. We ran the experiments on a GridEngine managed cluster system. The tool is available online[1].

---

[1] http://pub.ist.ac.at/~mgiacobbe/grnmc.tar.gz

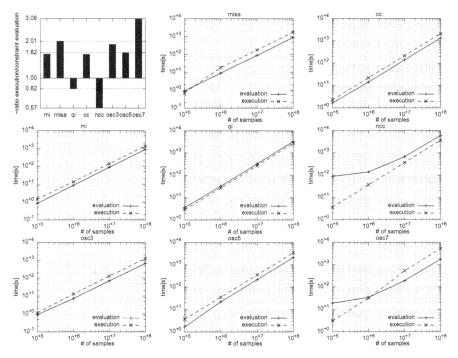

Fig. 4. The comparison in performance when mutational robustness is statistically estimated, and a property check is performed either by evaluation, or by execution (see Section 4.1 for the description of the two methods). The bar (top-left) shows the ratio of average times needed to verify the property of one sampled GRN-individual. For example, for osc7, the performance of evaluation method is more than three times faster. The other graphs show how the robustness computation time depends on the total number of sampled GRNs (in order to obtain robustness and to estimate the precision, we computed the mean of 100 experiments, each containing a number of samples ranging from 10^3 to 10^6). The graph is shown in log-log scale. The non-linear slope of the evaluation method is most notable in examples mcc and osc7, and it is due to the longer time used for compute the constraints.

5.2   Performance Evaluation

We chose eight GRN topologies as benchmarks for our tool. The benchmarks are presented in Fig. 3. The first five of the GRN topologies are collected from [8]. On these benchmarks we check for the steady-state properties. On the final three GRN topologies, we check for the oscillatory behavior. The results are presented in Fig. 4.

We ran the robustness computation by the evaluation and execution methods (the methods are described in Section 4.1). In order to obtain robustness and to estimate the precision, we computed the mean of 100 experiments, each containing a number of samples ranging from 10^3 to 10^6. The total computation time in the execution methods linearly depends on the number of samples used.

The total computation time in the evaluation method depends linearly on the number of samples, but initially needs time to compute the constraints. Technically, the time needed to compute robustness by execution method is $t_{ex} = k_{ex}p$, and the time needed to compute robustness by evaluation approach $t_{ev} = k_{ev}p + t_c$, where p represents the total number of samples used, t_c is the time to compute the constraints, and k_{ex} (resp. k_{ev}) is the time needed to verify the property by evaluation (resp. execution). We used linear regression to estimate the parameters k_{ex} and k_{ev}, and we present the ratio $\frac{k_{ex}}{k_{ev}}$ in top-left position of Fig. 4. The results indicate that on six out of eight tested networks, evaluation is more efficient than execution. For some networks, such as osc7, the time for computing the constraints is large, and the gain in performance becomes visible only once the number of samples is larger than 10^6.

6   Conclusion and Discussion

We pursued formal analysis of Wagner's GRN model, which allows symbolic reasoning about the behavior of GRNs under parameter perturbations. More precisely, for a given space of GRNs and a property specified in LTL, we have synthesized the space of parameters for which the concrete, individual GRN from a given space satisfies the property. The resulting space of parameters is represented by complex linear inequalities. In our analysis, we encoded a bounded model-checking search into a satisfiability problem, and we used efficient SMT solvers to find the desired constraints. We demonstrated that these constraints can be used to efficiently compute the mutational robustness of populations of GRNs. Our results have shown the cases in which the computation can be three times faster than the standard (simulation) techniques employed in computational biology.

While computing mutational robustness is one of the applications of our synthesized constraints, the constraints allow to efficiently answer many other questions that are very difficult or impossible to answer by executing the sampled GRNs. In our future work, we aim to work on further applications of our method, such as parameter sensitivity analysis for Wagner's model. Moreover, we plan to work on the method for exact computation of robustness by applying the point counting algorithm [5].

Wagner's GRN model is maybe the simplest dynamical model of a GRN – there are many ways to add expressiveness to it: for example, by incorporating multi-state expression level of genes, non-determinism, asynchronous updates, stochasticity. We are planning to study these variations and chart the territory of applicability of our method.

References

1. Azevedo, R.B.R., Lohaus, R., Srinivasan, S., Dang, K.K., Burch, C.L.: Sexual reproduction selects for robustness and negative epistasis in artificial gene networks. Nature 440(7080), 87–90 (2006)
2. Baier, C., Katoen, J.-P.: Principles of model checking, pp. 1–975. MIT Press (2008)

3. Barrett, C., Deters, M., de Moura, L., Oliveras, A., Stump, A.: 6 years of SMT-COMP. Journal of Automated Reasoning 50(3), 243–277 (2013)
4. Barrett, C.W., Sebastiani, R., Seshia, S.A., Tinelli, C.: Satisfiability modulo theories. Handbook of satisfiability 185, 825–885 (2009)
5. Barvinok, A., Pommersheim, J.E.: An algorithmic theory of lattice points in polyhedra. New perspectives in algebraic combinatorics 38, 91–147 (1999)
6. Batt, G., Belta, C., Weiss, R.: Model checking genetic regulatory networks with parameter uncertainty. In: Bemporad, A., Bicchi, A., Buttazzo, G. (eds.) HSCC 2007. LNCS, vol. 4416, pp. 61–75. Springer, Heidelberg (2007)
7. Biere, A., Cimatti, A., Clarke, E.M., Strichman, O., Zhu, Y.: Bounded model checking. Advances in computers 58, 117–148 (2003)
8. Cardelli, L.: Morphisms of reaction networks that couple structure to function. BMC Systems Biology 8(1), 84 (2014)
9. Cardelli, L., Csikász-Nagy, A.: The cell cycle switch computes approximate majority. Scientific reports 2 (2012)
10. Ciliberti, S., Martin, O.C., Wagner, A.: Robustness can evolve gradually in complex regulatory gene networks with varying topology. PLoS Computational Biology 3(2) (2007)
11. Elowitz, M.B., Leibler, S.: A synthetic oscillatory network of transcriptional regulators. Nature 403(6767), 335–338 (2000)
12. Fisher, J., Henzinger, T.A.: Executable cell biology. Nature Biotechnology 25(11), 1239–1249 (2007)
13. Gardner, T.S., Cantor, C.R., Collins, J.J.: Construction of a genetic toggle switch in escherichia coli. Nature 403(6767), 339–342 (2000)
14. Giacobbe, M., Guet, C.C., Gupta, A., Henzinger, T.A., Paixao, T., Petrov, T.: Model checking gene regulatory networks. arXiv preprint arXiv:1410.7704 (2014)
15. Jha, S.K., Clarke, E.M., Langmead, C.J., Legay, A., Platzer, A., Zuliani, P.: A bayesian approach to model checking biological systems. In: Degano, P., Gorrieri, R. (eds.) CMSB 2009. LNCS, vol. 5688, pp. 218–234. Springer, Heidelberg (2009)
16. Kwiatkowska, M., Norman, G., Parker, D.: Using probabilistic model checking in systems biology. ACM SIGMETRICS Performance Evaluation Review 35(4), 14–21 (2008)
17. MacCarthy, T., Seymour, R., Pomiankowski, A.: The evolutionary potential of the drosophila sex determination gene network. Journal of Theoretical Biology 225(4), 461–468 (2003)
18. Mateescu, R., Monteiro, P.T., Dumas, E., Jong, H.D.: Ctrl: Extension of ctl with regular expressions and fairness operators to verify genetic regulatory networks. Theoretical Computer Science 412(26), 2854–2883 (2011)
19. Rizk, A., Batt, G., Fages, F., Soliman, S.: A general computational method for robustness analysis with applications to synthetic gene networks. Bioinformatics 25(12), i169–i178 (2009)
20. Schlitt, T., Brazma, A.: Current approaches to gene regulatory network modelling. BMC Bioinformatics 8(Suppl 6), S9 (2007)
21. Wagner, A.: Does evolutionary plasticity evolve? Evolution, 50(3), 1008–1023 (1996)
22. Yordanov, B., Wintersteiger, C.M., Hamadi, Y., Kugler, H.: SMT-based analysis of biological computation. In: Brat, G., Rungta, N., Venet, A. (eds.) NFM 2013. LNCS, vol. 7871, pp. 78–92. Springer, Heidelberg (2013)
23. Zhang, L., Madigan, C.F., Moskewicz, M.H., Malik, S.: Efficient conflict driven learning in a boolean satisfiability solver. In: Computer Aided Verification, pp. 279–285. IEEE Press (2001)

Symbolic Quantitative Robustness Analysis of Timed Automata*

Ocan Sankur

Université Libre de Bruxelles, Brussels, Belgium

Abstract. We study the robust safety problem for timed automata under guard imprecisions which consists in computing an imprecision parameter under which a safety specification holds. We give a symbolic semi-algorithm for the problem based on a parametric data structure, and evaluate its performance in comparison with a recently published one, and with a binary search on enlargement values.

1 Introduction

Timed automata [2] are a well-established formal model for real-time systems. They can be used to model systems as finite automata, while using, in addition, a finite number of clocks to impose timing constraints on the transitions. Efficient model checking algorithms have been developed and implemented in tools such as Uppaal [6], IF [12]. Timed automata are, however, abstract models, and therefore make idealistic assumptions on timings, such as perfect continuity of clocks, infinite-precision time measures and instantaneous reaction times.

As for any abstract formalism, once desired properties of a system are proven on the model, a crucial question that remains is the *robustness* of these properties against the assumptions that have been made. What is the extent to which the assumptions behind the model can be relaxed while a given property still holds?

In this work, we are interested in the robustness against timing imprecisions. An important amount of work has been done in the timed automata literature to endow timed automata with a realistic semantics, and take imprecisions into account, *e.g.* [18,15,1]. The works [24] and [14] showed that perturbations on clocks, *i.e.* imprecisions or clock drifts, regardless of how small they are, may drastically change the behavior in some models. These observations mean that there is a need for verification tools to check the robustness of timed automata, that is, whether the behavior of a given timed automaton is preserved in the presence of perturbations, and to compute safe bounds on such perturbations.

We consider the robustness of timed automata for safety properties under timing imprecisions modeled by *guard enlargement*, consisting in relaxing each guard of the form $x \in [a, b]$ to $x \in [a - \delta, b + \delta]$ where δ is a parameter. Our goal is to decide if for some $\delta > 0$, the enlarged timed automaton satisfies its specification (Problem 1), and if this is the case, compute a safe upper bound

---

* Supported by the ERC starting grant inVEST (FP7-279499).

C. Baier and C. Tinelli (Eds.): TACAS 2015, LNCS 9035, pp. 484–498, 2015.
DOI: 10.1007/978-3-662-46681-0_48

on δ (Problem 2). We insist on the importance of both problems: while the first one decides the robustness of the model, the second one *quantifies* it by actually giving a bound under which the model is correct. This would allow one for instance to choose an appropriate hardware to implement the model [15,1].

Background. The formulation of Problem 1 has been studied starting with [24,14] for safety properties, and extended to LTL and richer specifications, *e.g.* [9,10] using region-based techniques which cannot be applied efficiently. A symbolic zone-based algorithm was given in [13] for *flat* timed automata, that is, without nested cycles by applying *acceleration* on its cycles. Problem 2 has been answered in [20] for flat timed automata, where the given algorithm computes the *largest* upper bound on δ satisfying the specification. The flatness is a rather restrictive hypothesis since, for instance, it is easily violated when the system is obtained by composition of timed automata that contain cycles. Recently, a zone-based algorithm and a tool to solve Problem 1 for *general* timed automata was given [21]; but the algorithm does not compute any bound on δ. The latter algorithm is based, roughly, on extending the standard forward exploration of the state space augmented with the acceleration of all cycles encountered during the search, with some tricks to optimize the computations. In [22], refinements between interfaces are studied in a game-based framework including syntactic enlargement to account for imprecisions. In [25,26] the authors use the fact that replacing all guards by closed ones allow one to verify *finite* paths (and the case of a periodic external synchronization) but this does not help in the analysis of the accumulation of imprecisions, nor can it allow one to compute a bound on δ.

Results. In this paper, we present a symbolic procedure to simultaneously solve Problems 1 and 2 for general timed automata; if the given model is robust, a safe upper bound on δ (which may not be the largest one) is output. The procedure is a semi-algorithm since we do not know whether it terminates although it did terminate on most of our experiments. It consists in a state-space exploration with an efficient parametric data structure which treats the enlargement δ as an unknown parameter, combined with an acceleration procedure for some of the cycles. We do not systematically accelerate cycles, but rather adopt a "lazy" approach: during the exploration, when the accumulated imprecisions go beyond a threshold, we accelerate some cycles that may be responsible for this accumulation. This greatly reduces the computation overhead compared to a systematic acceleration. We also adapt several abstraction operations such as LU abstraction [5], and closure inclusion [19] to the parametric setting to reduce the state space. We ran experiments to evaluate the performance of our procedure. Compared to [21], ours terminated faster in most cases, and sometimes with several orders of magnitude. To truly evaluate the gain of a parametric analysis, we also compared with a binary search on the values of δ using an exact model checker. Our procedure was often faster except against a low precision binary search (*i.e.* with few iterations). Section 6 contains a more detailed discussion.

2 Definitions

Given a finite set of clock $\mathcal{C}$, we call *valuations* the elements of $\mathbb{R}_{\geq 0}^{\mathcal{C}}$. For $R \subseteq \mathcal{C}$ and a valuation v, $v[R \leftarrow 0]$ is the valuation defined by $v[R \leftarrow 0](x) = v(x)$ for $x \in \mathcal{C} \setminus R$ and $v[R \leftarrow 0](x) = 0$ for $x \in R$. Given $d \in \mathbb{R}_{\geq 0}$ and a valuation v, $v + d$ is defined by $(v + d)(x) = v(x) + d$ for all $x \in \mathcal{C}$. We extend these operations to sets of valuations in the obvious way. We write $\mathbf{0}$ for the valuation that assigns 0 to every clock. An *atomic guard* is a formula of the form $k \leq x$ or $x \leq l$ where $x, y \in \mathcal{C}$, $k, l \in \mathbb{Q}$. A *guard* is a conjunction of atomic guards. A valuation v satisfies a guard g, denoted $v \models g$, if all atomic guards are satisfied when each $x \in \mathcal{C}$ is replaced by $v(x)$. We write $\Phi_{\mathcal{C}}$ for the set of guards built on $\mathcal{C}$.

A *timed automaton* $\mathcal{A}$ is a tuple $(\mathcal{L}, \mathsf{Inv}, \ell_0, \mathcal{C}, E)$, where $\mathcal{L}$ is a finite set of locations, $\mathsf{Inv} : \mathcal{L} \to \Phi_{\mathcal{C}}$ the invariants, $\mathcal{C}$ is a finite set of clocks, $E \subseteq \mathcal{L} \times \Phi_{\mathcal{C}} \times 2^{\mathcal{C}} \times \mathcal{L}$ is a set of edges, and $\ell_0 \in \mathcal{L}$ is the initial location. An edge $e = (\ell, g, R, \ell')$ is also written as $\ell \xrightarrow{g, R} \ell'$. For any location ℓ, let $E(\ell)$ denote the set of edges leaving ℓ. Following the literature on robustness in timed automata (e.g. [24,14]) we only consider timed automata with closed and rectangular guards (that is, we do not allow constraints of the form $x - y \leq k$). We also assume that all invariants contain an upper bound for all clocks.

A *run* of $\mathcal{A}$ is a sequence $q_1 e_1 q_2 e_2 \ldots q_n$ where $q_i \in \mathcal{L} \times \mathbb{R}_{\geq 0}^{\mathcal{C}}$, and writing $q_i = (\ell, v)$, we have $v \in \mathsf{Inv}(\ell)$, and either $e_i \in \mathbb{R}_{>0}$, in which case $q_{i+1} = (\ell, v + e_i)$, or $e_i = (\ell, g, R, \ell') \in E$, in which case $v \models g$ and $q_{i+1} = (\ell', v[R \leftarrow 0])$. We say that the run r is *along* $e_1 e_2 \ldots e_{n-1}$. A *path* is a sequence of edges whose endpoint locations are equal. Given a path $\rho = e_1 e_2 \ldots e_{n-1}$ and states q, q', we write $q \xrightarrow{\rho} q'$ if there is a run from q to q' along $e_1 e_2 \ldots e_{n-1}$. We write $q \Rightarrow q'$ if there is a path ρ with $q \xrightarrow{\rho} q'$. We also note $q \xrightarrow{\rho^+} q'$ if there is a run from q to q' along an arbitrary (positive) number of repetitions of ρ. A *cycle* of a timed automaton is a path that ends in the location it starts. As in [24,14], we assume that all cycles of considered timed automata reset all clocks at least once. Such cycles are called *progress cycles*.

Regions. The first decidability results on timed automata relied on a finite partition of the state space to so called *regions*, which can be defined using simple constraints on clocks [2]. We say that $\frac{1}{\eta}$ is the *granularity* of a timed automaton $\mathcal{A}$, if η is the smallest integer such that all constants of $\mathcal{A}$ are multiples of $\frac{1}{\eta}$. We generalize the definition of regions to arbitrary *granularities*. Let us denote $\mathbb{N}_\eta = \frac{1}{\eta}\mathbb{N}$. Consider a timed automaton $\mathcal{A}$, with granularity $\frac{1}{\eta}$, and consider a bound function $\alpha : \mathcal{C} \to \mathbb{N}_\eta$ mapping each clock to a bound. An α, η-*region* is defined by choosing

- for each clock $x \in \mathcal{C}$, a constraint among $\{x = k \mid k \in \mathbb{N}_\eta, k \leq \alpha(x)\} \cup \{k - \frac{1}{\eta} < x < k \mid k \in \mathbb{N}_\eta, \frac{1}{\eta} \leq k \leq \alpha(x)\} \cup \{x > \alpha(x)\}$.
- for each pair $x, y \in \mathcal{C}$ for which we chose the constraints $k - \frac{1}{\eta} < x < k$, and $l - \frac{1}{\eta} < y < l$, choose one constraint among $\mathsf{frac}(x) < \mathsf{frac}(y)$, $\mathsf{frac}(x) = \mathsf{frac}(y)$, or $\mathsf{frac}(x) > \mathsf{frac}(y)$, where $\mathsf{frac}(\cdot)$ denotes the fractional part.

It can be shown that α, η-regions finitely partition the state space $\mathbb{R}^{\mathcal{C}}$. For $\eta = 1$, this is the usual definition of regions. Given timed automata with rational constants, one often rescales the constants to work with integers. In the context of enlargement, however, it will be more convenient to work directly with rationals.

Difference-Bound Matrices. Because the number of regions is exponential in the input size, the region-based algorithms are not practical. Symbolic algorithms were rather given as an efficient solution based on *zones* which are convex subsets of the state space definable by clock constraints. Formally, a zone Z is a convex subset of $\mathbb{R}^{\mathcal{C}}$ definable by a conjunction of constraints of the form $x \leq k, l \leq x$, and $x - y \leq m$ where $x, y \in \mathcal{C}$, $k, l \in \mathbb{Q}_{\geq 0}$ and $m \in \mathbb{Q}$. Note that because all guards of the timed automata we consider are closed, all zones that appear during a state-space exploration are closed. Hence, we do not need to distinguish strict and non-strict inequalities as done for general timed automata.

We recall a few basic operations defined on zones. Let $\mathsf{Post}_{\geq 0}(Z)$ denote the zone describing the time-successors of Z, i.e., $\mathsf{Post}_{\geq 0}(Z) = \{v \in \mathbb{R}_{\geq 0}^{\mathcal{C}} \mid \exists t \geq 0, v - t \in Z\}$; and similarly $\mathsf{Pre}_{\geq 0}(Z) = \{v \in \mathbb{R}_{\geq 0}^{\mathcal{C}} \mid \exists t \geq 0, v + t \in Z\}$. Given $R \subseteq \mathcal{C}$, we let $\mathsf{Reset}_R(Z)$ be the zone $\{v \in \mathbb{R}_{\geq 0}^{\mathcal{C}} \mid \exists v' \in Z, v = v'[R \leftarrow 0]\}$, and $\mathsf{Free}_R(Z) = \{v \in \mathbb{R}_{\geq 0}^{\mathcal{C}} \mid \exists v' \in Z, v' = v[R \leftarrow 0]\}$. Intersection is denoted $Z \cap Z'$. Zones can be represented by *difference-bound matrices (DBM)* which are $|\mathcal{C}_0| \times |\mathcal{C}_0|$-matrices with values in $\mathbb{Q}$ [16]. Let us define $\mathcal{C}_0 = \mathcal{C} \cup \{0\}$, where 0 is seen as a clock whose value is always 0. Intuitively, each component $(x, y) \in \mathcal{C}_0^2$ of a DBM stores a bound on the difference $x - y$. For any DBM M, let $[\![M]\!]$ denote the zone it defines. DBMs admit *reduced forms* (a.k.a. normal form), and successor computation can be done efficiently (in $O(|\mathcal{C}|^3)$). We refer the reader to [7] for details. All of the above operations can be computed with DBMs. By a slight abuse of notation, we will use the same operations for DBMs as for zones, for instance, we will write $M' = \mathsf{Post}_{\geq 0}(M)$ where M and M' are reduced DBMs such that $[\![M']\!] = \mathsf{Post}_{\geq 0}[\![M]\!]$. We define an *extended zone* as a pair (ℓ, Z) where ℓ is a location and Z a zone. Given an edge $e = (\ell, g, R, \ell')$, and an extended zone (ℓ, Z), we define $\mathsf{Post}_e((\ell, Z)) = \mathsf{Inv}(\ell') \cap \mathsf{Post}_{\geq 0}(g \cap \mathsf{Reset}_R(Z))$, and $\mathsf{Pre}_e((\ell, Z)) = \mathsf{Pre}_{\geq 0}(g \cap \mathsf{Free}_R(\mathsf{Inv}(\ell') \cap Z))$. For a path $\rho = e_1 e_2 \ldots e_n$, we define Post_ρ and Pre_ρ by iteratively applying Post_{e_i} and Pre_{e_i} respectively.

Enlargement. We model timing imprecisions in timed automata by the *enlargements* of the guards and invariants of by rational values $\nu > 0$. The enlargement of an atomic guard $k \leq x$ (resp. $x \leq l$) is denoted $(k \leq x)_\nu = k - \nu \leq x$ (resp. $(x \leq l)_\nu = x \leq l + \nu$). The enlargement of a guard g, denoted $(g)_\nu$ is obtained by enlarging all its conjuncts. We denote by $\mathcal{A}_\nu$ the timed automaton obtained from $\mathcal{A}$ by enlarging all its guards and invariants by ν.

If ν is known, one could analyze $\mathcal{A}_\nu$ with known techniques, since this is still a timed automaton (with a possibly different granularity). Here, we are rather interesting in a parametric analysis. We thus consider a symbolic parameter δ. The *parametric enlargement* of a guard g, denoted $(g)_\delta$ is defined by replacing ν by the symbol δ in the above definition. We will always denote rational enlargement

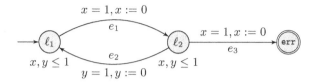

Fig. 1. A timed automaton representing the two processes P_1 and P_2 instantiated with period $p = 1$, and a buffer size of 1. The guard under the locations are the invariants. The edge e_1 represents the arrival of a token in the buffer (period of 1) while e_2 represents process P_2 reading a token from the buffer. The error state is reached via e_3 if two tokens are pushed to the buffer without any read in between. Without enlargement, any reachable state at location ℓ_2 satisfies $x = 0 \wedge y = 1$, so the error state is not reachable. Under enlargement by $\nu = \frac{1}{10}$, after the first transition, location ℓ_2 is reached by the set of states $1 - \nu \leq y \leq 1 + \nu \wedge 0 \leq x \leq 2\nu$ due to the enlargement of the guards and invariants. A simple calculation shows that the set of reachable states at location ℓ_2 after k cycles is $1 - (2k+1)\nu \leq y \leq 1 + \nu \wedge 0 \leq x \leq 2k\nu \wedge 1 - (2k+1)\nu \leq y - x \leq 1 + \nu$. Thus, for $k = 5$, we get $y \leq 1 + \nu \wedge x \leq 1 \wedge -\nu \leq y - x \leq 1 + \nu$, and $x = 1 \wedge y = 1$ is in this set, from which the error state is reachable.

values by ν, and the parameter symbol by δ. Similarly, *parametrically enlarged timed automata* are denoted $\mathcal{A}_\delta$. For $\nu > 0$, the *instantiation* of a parametrically enlarged guard $(g)_\delta$ by ν is denoted $(g)_\delta[\delta \leftarrow \nu]$ which is $(g)_\nu$.

Accumulation of Imprecisions. In some timed automata even the smallest enlargement can lead to drastically different behaviors due to the accumulation of the imprecisions over long runs [24]. As an example, consider the following simple problem. Two processes P_1, P_2 execute on different machines and communicate via a finite buffer. Every p time units, Process P_1 finishes a computation and pushes a token to the buffer; while P_2 reads a token from the buffer with the same period. We assume P_2 has an offset of p. The buffer will clearly not overflow in this system. However, assuming the slightest delay in the execution of P_2, or the slightest decrease in the execution time of P_1 leads to a buffer overflow since the delays will accumulate indefinitely. Figure 1 represents this system.

3   Accelerating Cycles

The original robust reachability algorithm of [24,14] consists in an exploration of the region graph, augmented with the addition of the images of all cycles *neighboring* reachable states. The idea is that when the guards are enlarged, these neighboring cycles become reachable, and they precisely capture all states that become reachable in the timed automaton for all values of δ. Thus, this algorithm computes the set $\cap_{\nu>0}\mathsf{Reach}(\mathcal{A}_\nu)$, where $\mathsf{Reach}(\mathcal{A}_\nu)$ denotes the states that are reachable in $\mathcal{A}_\nu$. A symbolic algorithm for this problem was given in [13] for *flat* timed automata, *i.e.* without nested cycles, and later improved in [20].

In this section, we summarize some of these results from [24,14,13,20] that we use in the rest of the paper. Let us fix a timed automaton $(\mathcal{L}, \mathsf{Inv}, \ell_0, \mathcal{C}, E)$, and a cycle ρ. The following lemma shows the effect of repeating cycles in enlarged timed automata, formalizing our observations on Fig. 1.

Lemma 1 ([20]). *Consider any extended zone* (ℓ, Z), *and a progress cycle* ρ *of* $\mathcal{A}$ *that starts in* ℓ. *If* $\mathsf{Pre}_\rho^*(\top) \cap Z \neq \emptyset$, *then starting from any state of* $\mathsf{Pre}_\rho^*(\top) \cap Z$, *for any* $\nu > 0$, *all states of* $\mathsf{Post}_{(\rho)_\nu}^*(\top)$ *are reachable in* $\mathcal{A}_\nu$, *by repeating* ρ.

As an example, consider Fig. 1. For the cycle $\rho = e_2 e_1$ that starts at ℓ_2, we have $\mathsf{Pre}_\rho^*(\top) = x, y \leq 1 \wedge x - y \leq 0$, and $\mathsf{Post}_{(\rho)_\nu}^*(\top) = x, y \leq 1 + \nu \wedge x - y \leq 0$. Since the point $(0, 1)$ is reachable and belongs to Pre_ρ^*, all states of $\mathsf{Post}_{(\rho)_\nu}^*(\top)$ are reachable, and in particular $(1, 1)$ from which the error state is reachable.

It is known that the above lemma does not hold for non-progress cycles; nevertheless, it was shown that in this case, $\mathsf{Post}_{(\rho)_\nu}^*(\top)$ is an *over-approximation* of the states reachable by repeating ρ under enlargement [11]. Thus, the algorithm of [24,14] may have false negatives (may answer "not robust" even though it is) but not false positives on timed automata with arbitrary cycles.

Conversely, it has been shown that any state that belongs to $\cap_{\nu > 0} \mathsf{Reach}(\mathcal{A}_\nu)$ is reachable along an alternation of exact runs and repetitions of enlarged cycles.

Lemma 2 ([14]). *Assume that* $q \to q'$ *in* $\mathcal{A}_\nu$ *for all* $\nu > 0$. *There exists a path* $\pi_0 \rho_0 \pi_1 \rho_0 \ldots \pi_n$ *of* $\mathcal{A}$ *and states* $q = q_0, q_0', q_1, q_1', \ldots, q_n = q'$, *such that for all* $0 \leq i \leq n - 1$, *and any* $\nu > 0$, $q_i \xrightarrow{\pi_i} q_i'$, $q_i' \in \mathsf{Pre}_{\rho_i}^*(\top)$, *and* $q_{i+1} \in \mathsf{Post}_{(\rho_i)_\nu}^*(\top)$.

Notice that the sequence of states $q_0, q_0', \ldots$ is independent of $\nu > 0$ in the above lemma, and that the enlargement is only used in $\mathsf{Post}_{((\rho)_i)_\nu}^*(\top)$.

The algorithms of [13,20] consist in a usual forward exploration on zones augmented with the application of Lemma 1, by enumerating *all* cycles in a *flat* timed automaton. This cannot be extended to general timed automata since the cycles that appear in Lemma 2 are not necessarily simple. This has been a major obstacle against general robust safety algorithms for timed automata.

4   Infinitesimally Enlarged DBMs

We define *infinitesimally enlarged DBMs (IEDBM)*, a parameterized extension of DBMs, which we will use to explore the state space of enlarged timed automata. These were first defined in [14] to be used solely as a proof technique. Here, we extend this data structure with additional properties and explicit computations of the bounds on parameter δ, and show how it can be used to efficiently explore the state space.

We fix a clock set $\mathcal{C}_0$ including the 0 clock. An *infinitesimally enlarged DBM (IEDBM)* is a pair $(M, P)_{\langle 0, \delta_0 \rangle}$ where M is a DBM and P is a $|\mathcal{C}_0| \times |\mathcal{C}_0|$ matrix over $\mathbb{N}$, called the *enlargement matrix*. The value $\delta_0 \in (0, \infty)$ is an upper bound on the unknown parameter δ. Intuitively, an IEDBM $(M, P)_{\langle 0, \delta_0 \rangle}$ represents the *set* of DBMs $M + \nu P$ where $\nu \in [0, \delta_0)$. Figure 2 shows an example. We often see, abusively, an IEDBM as a matrix over pairs $(m, p) \in \mathbb{Z} \times \mathbb{N}$. The component (x, y) is denoted by $(M, P)_{\langle 0, \delta_0 \rangle}[x, y]$. For simplicity, we always consider the half-open intervals of the form $[0, \delta_0)$ even though ν can be chosen equal to δ_0 in some cases. This is not a loss of generality since we are interested in the small values of ν.

IEDBMs will allow us to reason on the parametric state space of enlarged timed automata "for small values of δ", which means that our computations on the data structure will hold for all $\nu \in [0, \delta_0)$, where $\delta_0 > 0$ is bound that is possibly updated to a smaller value after each operation. For instance, given sets $Z_1 = 1 \leq x \leq 2 + 3\nu$ and $Z_2 = x \leq 3$, for unknown δ, and assume we want to compute their intersection. We will write $Z_1 \cap Z_2 = 1 \leq x \leq 2 + 3\delta$ and chose $\delta_0 \leq \frac{1}{3}$. To make these simplifications, we need to compare pairs of IEDBM components in a similar spirit. For instance, to make the above simplification, we write $(2,3)_{\langle 0, \frac{1}{3} \rangle} \leq (3,0)_{\langle 0, \frac{1}{3} \rangle}$, which means that $2 + 3\nu \leq 3$ for all $\nu \in [0, \frac{1}{3})$. We formalize this in the next subsection. To ease reading, we may omit δ_0 from IEDBMs if it is clear from the context.

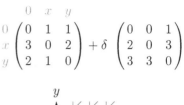

Fig. 2. An IEDBM (above) representing the parametric set $1 \leq x \leq 3 + 2\delta \wedge 1 - \delta \leq y \leq 2 + 3\delta$. The set is represented (below) for $\delta = 0.15$.

4.1   Operations on IEDBMs

We are now going to formalize the simplifications and the operations done on IEDBMs. In order to use our data structure for parametric exploration, we need to define basic operations on timed automata. Similar to DBMs, IEDBMs have *reduced forms*. To define the reduction operations, we define the + and min operations.

We define the sum as $(m, p)_{\langle 0, \delta_0 \rangle} + (n, q)_{\langle 0, \delta_1 \rangle} = (m + n, p + q)_{\langle 0, \min(\delta_0, \delta_1) \rangle}$. As an example of this operation, assume that we have the constraints $x - y \leq 2 + 3\delta$, and $y \leq 1 + \delta$ with the respective upper bounds δ_0 and δ_1. Then, by summation, we may deduce $x \leq 3 + 4\delta$ with the upper bound $\delta_2 = \min(\delta_0, \delta_1)$.

Lemma 3. *Given $(m_1, p_1)_{\langle 0, \delta_1 \rangle}, (m_2, p_2)_{\langle 0, \delta_2 \rangle}$, one can compute $i \in \{1, 2\}$, and δ_3 such that $\forall \nu \in [0, \delta_3)$, $m_i + \nu p_i = \min(m_1 + \nu p_1, m_2 + \nu p_2)$. We denote this by $(m_i, p_i)_{\langle 0, \delta_3 \rangle} = \min((m_1, p_1)_{\langle 0, \delta_1 \rangle}, (m_2, p_2)_{\langle 0, \delta_2 \rangle})$.*

We write $(m_1, p_1)_{\langle 0, \delta_1 \rangle} \leq (m_2, p_2)_{\langle 0, \delta_2 \rangle}$ iff $\min\left((m_1, p_1)_{\langle 0, \delta_1 \rangle}, (m_2, p_2)_{\langle 0, \delta_2 \rangle}\right) = (m_1, p_1)_{\langle 0, \delta_3 \rangle}$ for some δ_3; and $(m_1, p_1)_{\langle 0, \delta_1 \rangle} < (m_2, p_2)_{\langle 0, \delta_2 \rangle}$ if $m_1 \neq m_2 \vee p_1 \neq p_2$.

Intuitively, just like in regular DBMs, we will use the minimum operation to compute *conjunctions* of constraints. For instance, we already saw above that $x \leq 2 + 3\nu \wedge x \leq 3$ is simplified to $x \leq 2 + 3\nu$ given $\nu \in [0, \frac{1}{3})$. This will be written $\min\left((2, 3)_{\langle 0, \infty \rangle}, (3, 0)_{\langle 0, \infty \rangle}\right) = (2, 3)_{\frac{1}{3}}$. It should be clear that for any Boolean combination Φ of inequalities written between elements of the form $(m, p)_{\langle 0, \delta_1 \rangle}$, one can compute, by Lemma 3, a bound δ_0 such that either $\Phi[\delta \leftarrow \nu]$ holds for all $\nu \in [0, \delta_0)$, or $\neg \Phi[\delta \leftarrow \nu]$ holds for all $\nu \in [0, \delta_0)$.

If different upper bounds on δ are given for two elements to be compared, then we first update the bounds to the minimum of the two bounds. More generally, we assume that all components of an IEDBM have the same bound δ_0.

We say that an IEDBM $(M, P)_{\langle 0, \delta_0 \rangle}$ is *reduced* if for all $x, y, z \in \mathcal{C}_0$, $(M, P)_{\langle 0, \delta_0 \rangle}[x, y] \leq (M, P)_{\langle 0, \delta_0 \rangle}[x, z] + (M, P)_{\langle 0, \delta_0 \rangle}[z, y]$. IEDBMs can be reduced by the usual Floyd-Warshall algorithm, using the above min and $+$ operations:

Lemma 4. *Any IEDBM* $(M, P)_{\langle 0, \delta_0 \rangle}$ *can be reduced in time* $O(|\mathcal{C}_0|^3)$. *Moreover, if* $(M, P)_{\langle 0, \delta_0 \rangle}$ *is reduced, then for all* $\nu \in [0, \delta_0)$, $M + \nu P$ *is a reduced DBM.*

When we consider the complexity of minimization as in Lemma 3, we assume that operations on rationals are elementary operations (*i.e.* they can be performed in constant time). For a more precise analysis, one can incorporate the cost of these computations; for instance, the reduction operation in the previous lemma makes $O(|\mathcal{C}_0|^3)$ minimization operations, so as many operations on rationals.

We define the *parametric inclusion* by $(M, P)_{\langle 0, \delta_1 \rangle} \sqsubseteq (N, Q)_{\langle 0, \delta_2 \rangle}$ if, and only if for all $x, y \in \mathcal{C}$, $(M, P)[x, y] \leq (N, Q)[x, y]$.

Lemma 5. *One can compute, given* $(N_1, Q_1)_{\langle 0, \delta_1 \rangle}, (N_2, Q_2)_{\langle 0, \delta_2 \rangle}$, *and* $R \subseteq \mathcal{C}$, *and in time* $O(|\mathcal{C}|^3)$,

- *a reduced IEDBM* $(M, P)_{\langle 0, \delta_0 \rangle}$, *written* $(N_1, Q_1)_{\langle 0, \delta_1 \rangle} \sqcap (N_2, Q_2)_{\langle 0, \delta_2 \rangle}$, *such that* $M + \nu P = (N_1 + \nu Q_1) \cap (N_2 + \nu Q_2)$ *for all* $\nu \in [0, \delta_0)$,
- *a reduced IEDBM* $(M, P)_{\langle 0, \delta_0 \rangle}$, *written* $\mathtt{PReset}_R((N_1, Q_1)_{\langle 0, \delta_1 \rangle})$, *such that* $M + \nu P = \mathtt{Reset}_R(N_1 + \nu Q_1)$ *for all* $\nu \in [0, \delta_0)$,
- *a reduced IEDBM* $(M, P)_{\langle 0, \delta_0 \rangle}$, *written* $\mathtt{PPost}_{\geq 0}((N_1, Q_1)_{\langle 0, \delta_2 \rangle})$, *such that* $M + \nu P = \mathtt{Post}_{\geq 0}(N_1 + \nu Q_1)$ *for all* $\nu \in [0, \delta_0)$.

We are going to define the *parametric post* operation along an edge e. By a slight abuse of notation, we will see any (non-enlarged) guard g as the IEDBM $(g, \mathbf{0})_{\langle 0, \infty \rangle}$. When we consider the enlargement $(g)_\delta$ of a guard, this will also refer to the corresponding IEDBM with $\delta_0 = \infty$. By combining these operations, for a given edge e, we define $\mathtt{PPost}_e((M, P)_{\langle 0, \delta_0 \rangle}) = \mathtt{PPost}_{\geq 0}(\mathtt{PReset}_R(g \sqcap (M, P)_{\langle 0, \delta_0 \rangle}))$, where g is the guard of e, and R its reset set. By Lemma 5 this corresponds to $\mathtt{Post}_e(M + \delta P)$ for sufficiently small δ.

We refer to pairs of locations and IEDBMs as *symbolic states*. We extend the parametric post operator to symbolic states by $\mathtt{PPost}_e((\ell, Z)) = (\ell', Z')$ where $e = (\ell, g, R, \ell')$, and $Z' = \mathtt{PPost}_e(Z)$.

Lemma 6. *For any sequence of edges* $e_1 \ldots e_n$, *and symbolic state* (ℓ, Z), *if* $\mathtt{PPost}_{(e_1)_\delta (e_2)_\delta \ldots (e_{n-1})_\delta}((\ell, Z)) = (\ell', Z')$, *and* $(\ell', Z') \neq \emptyset$, *then there exists* $\delta_0 > 0$ *such that for all* $\nu \in [0, \delta_0)$, *and state* $q' \in (\ell', Z')[\delta \leftarrow \nu]$, *there exist* $q \in (\ell, Z)[\delta \leftarrow \nu]$ *such that* $(\ell_1, q) \xrightarrow{(e_1)_\nu \ldots (e_{n-1})_\nu} (\ell_n, q')$.

Let the *width* of $(M, P)_{\langle 0, \delta_0 \rangle}$ be defined as $\mathtt{width}(M, P) = \max_{x, y \in \mathcal{C}_0} P_{x, y}$.

4.2 Parametric Abstractions

We will first recall some abstractions applied on zones in a non-parametric setting, then generalize them to symbolic states described by IEDBMs.

Closures and LU-abstraction. Let $\alpha : \mathcal{C} \to \mathbb{N}$ be a bound function, and η a granularity. The α, η-*closure* of a zone Z is the union of the α, η-regions which intersects it. It is known that when α denotes the maximal constants to which each clock is compared in a timed automaton $\mathcal{A}$, and η the granularity of $\mathcal{A}$, a forward exploration based on α, η-closures is sound and complete [8]. However because closures are not convex, other abstractions have been in use in practical tools; one of them is *LU-abstraction*, where the idea is to relax some of the facets of a zone taking into consideration the maximal constants that appear in the guards of the timed automaton. We will recall the formal definition of LU-abstraction by adapting it to DBMs with only non-strict inequalities by a slight change. The correctness of the abstraction is preserved (proved in Lemma 7).

For a timed automaton $\mathcal{A}$ with granularity η, we define the two bound functions $L, U : \mathcal{C} \to \mathbb{N}_\eta$, called the *LU-bounds* where $L(x)$ (resp. $U(x)$) is the largest constant c such that the constraint $x \geq c$ (resp. $x \leq c$) appears in some guard or invariant. Given LU-bounds L, U, for any DBM M, we define $M' = \mathsf{Extra}^+_{LU}(M)$ as follows.

$$
M'_{x,y} = \begin{cases} \infty & \text{if } M_{x,y} > L(x), \text{ or } -M_{0,x} > L(x) \\ \infty & \text{if } -M_{0,y} > U(y), x \neq 0 \\ -U(y) - 1 & \text{if } -M_{0,y} > U(y), x = 0 \\ M_{x,y} & \text{otherwise.} \end{cases} \tag{1}
$$

We recall the correctness of LU-abstractions and closures for reachability properties. Given LU-bounds L, U we write $\alpha = \max(L, U)$ for the function $\alpha(x) = \max(L(x), U(x))$ for all $x \in \mathcal{C}$.

Lemma 7. *For any timed automaton $\mathcal{A}$ with granularity η, its LU-bounds L, U, and any path $e_1 e_2 \ldots e_n$ and extended zone (ℓ, Z), define $q_0 = q'_0 = q''_0 = (\ell, Z)$, and let for $0 \leq i < n$, $q_{i+1} = \mathsf{Post}_{e_i}(q_i)$, $q'_{i+1} = \mathsf{Extra}^+_{LU}(\mathsf{Post}_{e_i}(q'_i))$, and $q''_{i+1} = \mathsf{Closure}_{\alpha,\eta}(\mathsf{Extra}^+_{LU}(q''_i))$. Then, $q_n \neq \emptyset \Leftrightarrow q'_n \neq \emptyset \Leftrightarrow q''_n \neq \emptyset$.*

One can thus explore the state space of a timed automaton while systematically applying LU-abstraction at each step. In practice, one does not apply closures since they do not yield convex sets. Nevertheless, a $O(|\mathcal{C}|^2)$-time algorithm was given in [19] to decide whether $M \subseteq \mathsf{Closure}_\alpha(N)$. Thus, when the regular inclusion test is replaced with the latter one, the exploration becomes equivalent to an exploration using closures [19,8].

Parametric Closures and LU-abstraction. We would like to use these abstractions in our parametric setting. We will show how these sets can be computed parametrically using IEDBMs. Observe that when we consider parametrically enlarged timed automata, the LU-bounds also depend on δ. Let us denote the *parametric LU-bounds* by $L_\delta(x)$ (resp. $U_\delta(x)$) which is the maximum *parametric* constant, in the sense of Lemma 3, which appears in the guards of $\mathcal{A}_\delta$ as a lower bound (resp. upper bound) on x. We define the *parametric LU-abstraction*, for any IEDBM $(M, P)_{\langle 0, \delta_0 \rangle}$ by $(M', P')_{\langle 0, \delta_1 \rangle} = \mathsf{PExtra}^+_{L_\delta U_\delta}((M, P)_{\langle 0, \delta_0 \rangle})$ obtained by applying (1) where M is replaced by (M, P), L and U by L_δ and U_δ respectively. The new upper bound δ_1 is computed so that all comparisons in (1) hold.

Lemma 8. *Consider any enlarged timed automaton $\mathcal{A}_\delta$ and its parametric LU-bounds L_δ, U_δ. For any $(M, P)_{\langle 0, \delta_0 \rangle}$, if we write $(M', P')_{\langle 0, \delta_1 \rangle} = \mathtt{PExtra}^+_{L_\delta U_\delta}((M, P)_{\langle 0, \delta_0 \rangle})$, then for all $\nu \in [0, \delta_1)$, $M' + \nu P' = \mathtt{Extra}^+_{LU}(M + \nu P)$.*

Thus, LU-abstractions of enlarged zones have uniform representations for small δ.

For an enlarged timed automaton $\mathcal{A}_\delta$ we define $\alpha_\delta = \max(L_\delta, U_\delta)$. For $\nu > 0$, we will denote by α_ν the function obtained from α_δ by instantiating δ to ν. By a slight abuse of notation, we define the α_ν-*closure* of a zone as its (α_ν, η)-closure where η is the granularity of $\mathcal{A}_\nu$. Here $\mathcal{A}$ will be clear from the context, so there will be no ambiguity. We now adapt the inclusion algorithm of [19] to IEDBMs.

Lemma 9. *Given IEDBMs $Z = (M, P)_{\langle 0, \delta_0 \rangle}$ and $Z' = (N, Q)_{\langle 0, \delta_0 \rangle}$, we have $\forall \delta_0 > 0, \exists \nu \in [0, \delta_0), M + \nu P \not\subseteq \mathsf{Closure}_{\alpha_\nu}(N + \nu Q)$, iff, writing $Z' = N + \nu Q$, there exist $x, y \in \mathcal{C}$ such that*

1. $\left(Z'_{x,0} < Z_{x,0} \text{ and } Z'_{x,0} \leq \alpha_\delta(x)\right)$, or $\left(Z'_{0,x} < Z_{0,x} \text{ and } Z_{0,x} + \alpha_\delta(x) \geq 0\right)$,
2. or $Z_{0,x} + \alpha_\delta(x) \geq 0$, and $Z'_{y,x} < Z_{y,x}$, and $Z'_{y,x} \leq \alpha_\delta(y) + Z_{0,x}$.

Moreover, if this condition doesn't hold, then one can compute δ_1 under which we do have the inclusion $M + \nu P \subseteq \mathsf{Closure}_{\alpha_\nu}(N + \nu Q)$.

Notation 10. *We denote the successor operation followed by LU-abstraction as $\mathsf{ExPost}(\cdot) = \mathtt{Extra}^+_{LU}(\mathsf{Post}(\cdot))$. For the parametric version, we denote $\mathtt{PExPost}(\cdot) = \mathtt{PExtra}^+_{L_\delta U_\delta}(\mathtt{PPost}(\cdot))$, where the bounds L_δ, U_δ are implicit. We furthermore denote by $\sqsubseteq^c$ the parametric inclusion check defined by Lemma 9.*

We implicitly assume that when a parametric inclusion check $\sqsubseteq^c$ is performed, the upper bound δ_0 is globally updated to the new bound δ_1 given by Lemma 9.

4.3 Parametric Cycle Acceleration

In [20] a parametric data structure based on the *parameterized DBMs* of [3] was used to represent the state space under *all* values of δ rather than for small values. The corresponding algorithms are based on linear arithmetics of reals. This results in a more complicated data structure which is also more general. IEDBMs simplify this representation by storing the state space only for small values of δ, that is $\delta \in [0, \delta_0)$. To compute cycle accelerations, we recall a result of [20] which bounds the number of iterations to compute pre and post fixpoints of a given cycle.

Lemma 11 ([20]). *Let $N = |\mathcal{C}|^2$. For any cycle ρ, if $\mathtt{PPost}^*_{(\rho)_\delta}(\top) \neq \emptyset$ then $\mathtt{PPost}^*_{(\rho)_\delta}(\top) = \mathtt{PPost}^N_{(\rho)_\delta}(\top)$, and if $\mathtt{PPre}^*_\rho(\top) \neq \emptyset$ then $\mathtt{PPre}^*_\rho(\top) = \mathsf{Pre}^N_\rho(\top)$.*

Data: Timed automaton $\mathcal{A} = (\mathcal{L}, \mathsf{Inv}, \ell_0, \mathcal{C}, E)$, and target location ℓ_T.

1 Wait $:= \{(\ell_0, Z_0)_{\langle \infty \rangle}\}$, Passed $:= \emptyset$, $(\ell_0, Z_0).K := K_0$;
2 **while** $Wait \neq \emptyset$ **do**
3 | $(\ell, Z) := \mathsf{pop}(\text{Wait})$, Add (ℓ, Z) to Passed;
4 | **if** $\ell = \ell_T$ **then return** Unsafe;
5 | **if** $\mathsf{width}(Z) > (\ell, Z).K$ **then**
6 | | Let π denote the prefix that ends in (ℓ, Z), along edges $e_1 e_2 \ldots e_{|\pi|-1}$;
7 | | **foreach** *cycle* $\rho = e_i e_{i+1} \ldots e_j$ **do**
8 | | | **if** $\mathsf{PPre}_\rho^*(\top) \cap \pi_i \neq \emptyset$ *and* $\forall q \in$ Passed, $\mathsf{PPost}_{(\rho)_\delta}^*(\top) \not\sqsubseteq^c q$ **then**
9 | | | | Add $\mathsf{PPost}_{(\rho)_\delta}^*(\top)$ as a successor to π_j, and to Wait;
10 | | | **end**
11 | | **end**
12 | | **if** *no fixpoint was added* **then** $(\ell, Z).K = (\ell, Z).K + K_0$;
13 | | **foreach** $e \in E(\ell)$ s.t. $\forall q \in$ Passed, $\mathsf{PExPost}_{e_\delta}((\ell, Z)) \not\sqsubseteq^c q$ **do**
14 | | | $(\ell', Z') := \mathsf{PExPost}_{e_\delta}((\ell, Z))$;
15 | | | Add (ℓ', Z') to Wait;
16 | | | $(\ell', Z').\text{parent} := (\ell, Z)$;
17 | | | $(\ell', Z').K := (\ell, Z).K$;
18 | | **end**
19 **end**
20 **return** Safe;

Algorithm 1. Symbolic robust safety semi-algorithm. Here (ℓ_0, Z_0) is the initial state symbolic state, and K_0 is a positive constant. We have two containers *Wait* and *Passed* storing symbolic states. The search tree is formed by assigning to each visited state (ℓ, Z) a parent denoted $(\ell, Z).parent$ (Line 16). We also associate to each symbolic state a bound K on width, denoted $(\ell, Z).K$.

5 Symbolic Robust Safety

Our semi-algorithm consists of a zone-based exploration with IEDBMs using the parametric LU-abstraction and the inclusion algorithm $\sqsubseteq^c$ of Lemma 9. It is easy to see that an exploration based on IEDBMs may not terminate in general (see *e.g.* Fig. 1). Nevertheless, we apply acceleration on well chosen cycles while it is exploring the state space, and it terminated in most of our experiments. To choose the cycles to accelerate, we adopt a lazy approach: we fix a bound K, and run the forward search using IEDBMs until the target is reached or some symbolic state has width greater than K. In the latter case, we examine the prefix of the current state, and accelerate its cycles by Lemma 1. If no new state is obtained, then we increment the bound K for the current branch and continue the exploration. We thus interpret a large width as the accumulation of imprecisions due to cycles. No cycle may be responsible for a large width, in which case we increase the width threshold and continue the exploration.

We establish the correctness of our semi-algorithm in the following lemma. When it answers Unsafe, it has found a path that ends in the target state, and the proof shows that such a run exists in all $\mathcal{A}_\nu$ for $\nu > 0$. If it answers Safe, then it has terminated without visiting the target state. If δ_0 denotes the upper bound on δ after termination, the proof shows that for all $\nu \in [0, \delta_0)$, an exact exploration applied on $\mathcal{A}_\nu$ would visit the same symbolic states as our algorithm when the IEDBMs are instantiated with $\delta \leftarrow \nu$. In other words, the exploration search tree uniformly represents all the search trees that would be generated by an exact algorithm applied on $\mathcal{A}_\nu$ for $\nu \in [0, \delta_0)$.

Lemma 12 (Correctness). *For any timed automaton $\mathcal{A}$ and location ℓ_T, if Algorithm 1 answers Unsafe then for all $\nu > 0$, ℓ_T is reachable in $\mathcal{A}_\nu$ from the initial state. If it answers Safe, then if δ_0 denotes the upper bound on δ after termination, then for all $\nu \in [0, \delta_0)$, $\mathcal{A}_\nu$ does not visit ℓ_T.*

6   Experimental Evaluation

In this section, we evaluate the performance of our semi-algorithm on several benchmarks from the literature; most of which are available from www.uppaal.org, and have been considered in [21], with the exception of the scheduling tests (Sched *) which were constructed from the experiments of [17]. We implemented Alg. 1 in OCaml in a tool called Symrob (*sym*bolic *rob*ustness, available from www.ulb.ac.be/di/verif/sankur). We consider two other competing algorithms: the first one is the recently published tool Verifix [21] which solves the infinitesimal robust safety problem but does not output any bound on δ. The second algorithm is our implementation of a binary search on the values of δ which iteratively calls an exact model checker until a given precision is reached.

The exact model checking algorithm is a forward exploration with DBMs using LU extrapolation and the inclusion test of [19] implemented in Symrob. We do not use advanced tricks such as symmetry reduction, federations of zones, and clock decision diagrams; see *e.g.* [4]. The reason is that our goal here is to compare *algorithms* rather than *software tools*. These optimizations could be added to the exact model checker but also to our robust model checker (by adapting to IEDBMs), but we leave this for future work.

In Table 1, the number of visited symbolic states (as IEDBMs for Symrob and as DBMs for Verifix) and the running times are given. On most benchmarks Symrob terminated faster and visited less states. We also note that Symrob actually computed the *largest* δ below which safety holds for the benchmarks CSMA/CD and Fischer. One can indeed check that syntactically enlarging the guards by 1/3 (resp. 1/2) makes the respective classes of benchmarks unsafe (Recall that the upper bound δ_0 is always strict in IEDBMs). On one benchmark, Verifix wrongly classified the model as non-robust, which could be due to a bug or to the presence of non-progress cycles in the model (see [11]).

Table 2 shows the performance of the binary search for varying precision $\epsilon \in \{\frac{1}{10}, \frac{1}{20}, \frac{1}{40}\}$. With precision $\frac{1}{10}$, the binary search was sometimes faster than Symrob (*e.g.* on CSMA/CD), and sometimes slower (*e.g.* Fischer); moreover, the computed value of δ was underestimated in some cases (*e.g.* CSMA/CD and Fischer benchmarks). With precision $\frac{1}{20}$, more precision was obtained on δ but at a cost of an execution time that is often worse than that of Symrob

Table 1. Comparison between `Symrob` (breadth-first search, instantiated with $K_0 = 10$) and `Verifix` [21]. The running time of the exact model checking implemented in `Symrob` is given for reference in the column "Exact" (the specification was satisfied without enlargement in all models). Note that the visited number of states is not always proportional to the running time due to additional operations performed for acceleration in both cases. The experiments were performed on an Intel Xeon 2.67 GHz machine.

Benchmark	Robust − δ		Visited States		Time		
	Symrob	Verifix	Symrob	Verifix	Symrob	Verifix	Exact
CSMA/CD 9	Yes − 1/3	Yes	147,739	1,064,811	61s	294s	42s
CSMA/CD 10	Yes − 1/3	Yes	398,354	846,098	202s	276s	87s
CSMA/CD 11	Yes − 1/3	Yes	1,041,883	2,780,493	12m	26m	5m
Fischer 7	Yes − 1/2	Yes	35,029	81,600	11s	12s	6s
Fischer 8	Yes − 1/2	Yes	150,651	348,370	45s	240s	24s
Fischer 9	Yes − 1/2	Yes	627,199	1,447,313	4m	160m	2m20s
MutEx 3	Yes − 1000/11	Yes	37,369	984,305	3s	131s	3s
MutEx 4	No	No	195,709	146,893	16s	41s	4s
MutEx 4 fixed	Yes − 1/7	−	5,125,927	−	38m	>24h	7m
Lip Sync	−	No	−	29,647,533	>24h	14h	5s
Sched A	Yes − 1/4	No*	9,217	16,995	11s	248s	2s
Sched B	No	−	50,383	−	105s	>24h	40s
Sched C	No	No	5,075	5,356	3s	29s	2s
Sched D	No	No	15,075	928	2s	0.5s	0.5s
Sched E	No	No	31,566	317	5s	0.5s	0.5s

Table 2. Performance of binary search where the initial enlargement is 8, and the required precision ϵ is either 1/10, 1/20 or 1/40. Note that when the model is not robust, the binary search is inconclusive. Nonetheless, in these cases, we do know that the model is unsafe for the smallest δ for which we model-checked the model. In these experiments the choice of the initial condition (here, $\delta = 8$) wasn't significant since the first iterations always took negligible time compared to the case $\delta < 1$.

Benchmark	Robust − δ		Visited States		Time		
	$\epsilon = 1/10$	$\epsilon = 1/20$	$\epsilon = 1/10$	$\epsilon = 1/20$	$\epsilon = 1/10$	$\epsilon = 1/20$	$\epsilon = 1/40$
CSMA/CD 9	Yes − 1/4	Yes − 5/16	151,366	301,754	43s	85s	123s
CSMA/CD 10	Yes − 1/4	Yes − 5/16	399,359	797,914	142s	290s	428s
CSMA/CD 11	Yes − 1/4	Yes − 5/16	1,043,098	2,085,224	8m20s	17m	26m
Fischer 7	Yes − 3/8	Yes − 7/16	75,983	111,012	15s	21s	31s
Fischer 8	Yes − 3/8	Yes − 7/16	311,512	462,163	53s	80s	129s
Fischer 9	Yes − 3/8	Yes − 7/16	1,271,193	1,898,392	5m	7m30s	12m
MutEx 3	Yes − 8	Yes − 8	37,369	37,369	2s	2s	2s
MutEx 4	Inconclusive		1,369,963	1,565,572	1m5s	1m15s	1m30s
MutEx 4 fix'd	Yes − 5/8	Yes − 9/16	6,394,419	9,864,904	9m30s	17m	25m
Lip Sync	Inconclusive		−	−	>24h	>24h	>24h
Sched A	Yes − 7/16	Yes − 15/32	27,820	37,101	6s	9s	11s
Sched B	Inconclusive		109,478	336,394	35s	140s	20m
Sched C	Inconclusive		10,813	36,646	2s	6s	56s
Sched D	Inconclusive		27,312	182,676	2s	9s	60s
Sched E	Inconclusive		98,168	358,027	6s	17s	95s

and systematically more states to visit. Increasing the precision to $\frac{1}{40}$ leads to even longer execution times. On non-robust models, a low precision analysis is often fast, but since the result is inconclusive, one rather increases the precision, leading to high execution times. The binary search can be made complete by choosing the precision exponentially small [11] but this is too costly in practice.

7 Conclusion

We presented a symbolic procedure to solve the quantitative robust safety problem for timed automata based on infinitesimally enlarged DBMs. A good performance is obtained thanks to the abstraction operators we lifted to the parametric setting, and to the lazy approach used to accelerate cycles. Although no termination guarantee is given, we were able to treat several case studies from the literature, demonstrating the feasability of robustness verification, and the running time was often comparable to that of exact model checking. Our experiments show that binary search is often fast if run with low precision; however, as precision is increased the gain of a parametric analysis becomes clear. Thus, both approaches might be considered depending on the given model.

An improvement over binary search for a problem of refinement in timed games is reported in [23]; this might be extended to our problem as well. Both our tool and Verifix fail when a large number of cycles needs to be accelerated, and this is difficult to predict. An improvement could be obtained by combining our lazy acceleration technique using the combined computation of the cycles of [21]. An extension to LTL objectives could be possible using [9].

References

1. Altisen, K., Tripakis, S.: Implementation of timed automata: An issue of semantics or modeling? In: Pettersson, P., Yi, W. (eds.) FORMATS 2005. LNCS, vol. 3829, pp. 273–288. Springer, Heidelberg (2005)
2. Alur, R., Dill, D.L.: A theory of timed automata. Theoretical Computer Science 126(2), 183–235 (1994)
3. Annichini, A., Asarin, E., Bouajjani, A.: Symbolic techniques for parametric reasoning about counter and clock systems. In: Emerson, E.A., Sistla, A.P. (eds.) CAV 2000. LNCS, vol. 1855, pp. 419–434. Springer, Heidelberg (2000)
4. Behrmann, G., Bengtsson, J., David, A., Larsen, K.G., Pettersson, P., Yi, W.: Uppaal implementation secrets. In: Damm, W., Olderog, E.-R. (eds.) FTRTFT 2002. LNCS, vol. 2469, pp. 3–22. Springer, Heidelberg (2002)
5. Behrmann, G., Bouyer, P., Larsen, K.G., Pelanek, R.: Lower and upper bounds in zone-based abstractions of timed automata. Int. J. Softw. Tools Technol. Transf. 8(3), 204–215 (2006)
6. Behrmann, G., David, A., Larsen, K.G., Håkansson, J., Pettersson, P., Yi, W., Hendriks, M.: UPPAAL 4.0. In: QEST 2006, pp. 125–126 (2006)
7. Bengtsson, J., Yi, W.: Timed automata: Semantics, algorithms and tools. In: Desel, J., Reisig, W., Rozenberg, G. (eds.) Lectures on Concurrency and Petri Nets. LNCS, vol. 3098, pp. 87–124. Springer, Heidelberg (2004)

8. Bouyer, P.: Forward analysis of updatable timed automata. Formal Methods in System Design 24(3), 281–320 (2004)
9. Bouyer, P., Markey, N., Reynier, P.-A.: Robust model-checking of linear-time properties in timed automata. In: Correa, J.R., Hevia, A., Kiwi, M. (eds.) LATIN 2006. LNCS, vol. 3887, pp. 238–249. Springer, Heidelberg (2006)
10. Bouyer, P., Markey, N., Reynier, P.-A.: Robust analysis of timed automata via channel machines. In: Amadio, R.M. (ed.) FOSSACS 2008. LNCS, vol. 4962, pp. 157–171. Springer, Heidelberg (2008)
11. Bouyer, P., Markey, N., Sankur, O.: Robust model-checking of timed automata via pumping in channel machines. In: Fahrenberg, U., Tripakis, S. (eds.) FORMATS 2011. LNCS, vol. 6919, pp. 97–112. Springer, Heidelberg (2011)
12. Bozga, M., Graf, S., Mounier, L.: If-2.0: A validation environment for component-based real-time systems. In: Brinksma, E., Larsen, K.G. (eds.) CAV 2002. LNCS, vol. 2404, pp. 343–348. Springer, Heidelberg (2002)
13. Daws, C., Kordy, P.: Symbolic robustness analysis of timed automata. In: Asarin, E., Bouyer, P. (eds.) FORMATS 2006. LNCS, vol. 4202, pp. 143–155. Springer, Heidelberg (2006)
14. DeWulf, M., Doyen, L., Markey, N., Raskin, J.-F.: Robust safety of timed automata. Formal Methods in System Design 33(1-3), 45–84 (2008)
15. De Wulf, M., Doyen, L., Raskin, J.-F.: Almost ASAP semantics: From timed models to timed implementations. Formal Aspects of Computing 17(3), 319–341 (2005)
16. Dill, D.L.: Timing assumptions and verification of finite-state concurrent systems. In: Sifakis, J. (ed.) CAV 1989. LNCS, vol. 407, pp. 197–212. Springer, Heidelberg (1990)
17. Geeraerts, G., Goossens, J., Lindström, M.: Multiprocessor schedulability of arbitrary-deadline sporadic tasks: Complexity and antichain algorithm. Real-Time Systems. The International Journal of Time-Critical Computing Systems 48(2) (2013)
18. Gupta, V., Henzinger, T.A., Jagadeesan, R.: Robust timed automata. In: Maler, O. (ed.) HART 1997. LNCS, vol. 1201, pp. 331–345. Springer, Heidelberg (1997)
19. Herbreteau, F., Kini, D., Srivathsan, B., Walukiewicz, I.: Using non-convex approximations for efficient analysis of timed automata. In: FSTTCS 2011, pp. 78–89 (2011)
20. Jaubert, R., Reynier, P.-A.: Quantitative robustness analysis of flat timed automata. In: Hofmann, M. (ed.) FOSSACS 2011. LNCS, vol. 6604, pp. 229–244. Springer, Heidelberg (2011)
21. Kordy, P., Langerak, R., Mauw, S., Polderman, J.W.: A symbolic algorithm for the analysis of robust timed automata. In: Jones, C., Pihlajasaari, P., Sun, J. (eds.) FM 2014. LNCS, vol. 8442, pp. 351–366. Springer, Heidelberg (2014)
22. Larsen, K.G., Legay, A., Traonouez, L.-M., Wąsowski, A.: Robust specification of real time components. In: Fahrenberg, U., Tripakis, S. (eds.) FORMATS 2011. LNCS, vol. 6919, pp. 129–144. Springer, Heidelberg (2011)
23. Legay, A., Traonouez, L.-M.: PYECDAR: Towards open source implementation for timed systems. In: Van Hung, D., Ogawa, M. (eds.) ATVA 2013. LNCS, vol. 8172, pp. 460–463. Springer, Heidelberg (2013)
24. Puri, A.: Dynamical properties of timed automata. Discrete Event Dynamic Systems 10(1-2), 87–113 (2000)
25. Swaminathan, M., Franzle, M.: A symbolic decision procedure for robust safety of timed systems. In: TIME 2007, pp. 192–192 (2007)
26. Swaminathan, M., Fränzle, M., Katoen, J.-P.: The surprising robustness of (closed) timed automata against clock-drift. In: Ausiello, G., Karhumäki, J., Mauri, G., Ong, L. (eds.) IFIP TCS 2008. IFIP, vol. 273, pp. 537–553. Springer, Heidelberg (2008)

Program Synthesis

Pattern-Based Refinement of Assume-Guarantee Specifications in Reactive Synthesis*

Rajeev Alur, Salar Moarref, and Ufuk Topcu

University of Pennsylvania, Philadelphia, USA
{alur,moarref,utopcu}@seas.upenn.edu

Abstract. We consider the problem of compositional refinement of components' specifications in the context of compositional reactive synthesis. Our solution is based on automatic refinement of assumptions and guarantees expressed in linear temporal logic (LTL). We show how behaviors of the environment and the system can be inferred from counter-strategies and strategies, respectively, as formulas in special forms called patterns. Instantiations of patterns are LTL formulas which hold over all runs of such strategies, and are used to refine the specification by adding new input assumptions or output guarantees. We propose three different approaches for compositional refinement of specifications, based on how much information is shared between the components, and demonstrate and compare the methods empirically.

1 Introduction

Given a specification in a formal language such as linear temporal logic (LTL), reactive synthesis problem is to find a finite-state system that satisfies the specification, no matter how its environment behaves. The synthesis problem can be viewed as a game between two players: the system and its environment. The system attempts to satisfy the specification, while its environment tries to violate it. The specification is realizable, if there is a system that can satisfy it. Otherwise, a counter-strategy can be computed for the environment which describes the way it can behave so that no system can satisfy the specification.

The reactive synthesis problem is known to be intractable for general LTL specifications [1]. However, there are fragments of LTL, such as Generalized Reactivity(1) (GR(1)), for which the realizability and synthesis problems can be solved in polynomial time in the number of states of the reactive system [2]. Yet scalability is a big challenge as increasing the number of formulas in a specification may cause an exponential blowup in the size of its state space [2]. Compositional synthesis techniques can potentially address this issue by solving the synthesis problem for smaller components and merging the results such that the composition satisfies the specification. The challenge is then to find proper decompositions and assumptions-guarantees such that each component is realizable, its expectations of its environment can be discharged on the environment

---

* This research was partially supported by NSF Expedition in Computing project ExCAPE (grant CCF 1138996) and AFOSR (grant number FA9550-12-1-0302).

C. Baier and C. Tinelli (Eds.): TACAS 2015, LNCS 9035, pp. 501–516, 2015.
DOI: 10.1007/978-3-662-46681-0_49

and other components, and circular reasoning is avoided, so that the local controllers can be implemented simultaneously and their composition satisfies the original specification [3].

We study the problem of compositional refinement of components' specifications in the context of compositional reactive synthesis. We consider the special case in which the system consists of two components C_1 and C_2 and that a global specification is given which is realizable and decomposed into two local specifications, corresponding to C_1 and C_2, respectively. Furthermore, we assume that there is a serial interconnection between the components [3], i.e., only the output variables of C_2 depend on those of C_1. We are interested in computing refinements such that the refined local specifications are both realizable and when implemented, the resulting system satisfies the global specification.

Our solution is based on automated refinement of assumptions and guarantees expressed in LTL. In [4] we showed how an unrealizable specification can be refined by adding assumptions on its environment. The core of the method is the synthesis of a set of LTL formulas of special form, called patterns, which hold over all runs of an abstraction of the counter-strategy computed for the unrealizable specification. If the local specification for a component C_2 is unrealizable, we refine its environment assumptions, while ensuring that the other component C_1 can indeed guarantee those assumptions. To this end, it is sometimes necessary to refine C_1's specification by adding guarantees to it. We extend the methods in [4] to be able to refine guarantees as well as assumptions.

The main contributions of the paper are as follow. We extend our work in [4] in several aspects. We improve the scalability of the methods proposed in [4] by showing how a more compact abstraction can be constructed for counter-strategies and strategies. We extend the forms of patterns that can be synthesized, and show how a similar technique for refining unrealizable specifications can be used to refine the requirements of the system. We propose three different approaches that can be used to refine the specifications of the components in the context of compositional synthesis. Intuitively, these approaches differ in how much information about one component is shared with the other one. We show that providing more knowledge of one component's behavior for the other component can make it significantly easier to refine the local specifications, with the expense of increasing the coupling between the components. We illustrate and compare the methods with examples and a case study.

Related Work. The problem of refining the environment assumptions is also considered in [5,6]. Synthesizing distributed systems from global specification is a hard problem [7]. However, distributed controller synthesis algorithms exists for special architectures [8]. Assume-guarantee synthesis problem is considered in [9] and solved by computing secure-equilibrium strategies. We use a different approach for refining the specifications which is based on strategies and counter-strategies.

2   Preliminaries

Let P be the set of atomic propositions (Boolean variables) partitioned into input I and output O propositions. Linear temporal logic (LTL) is a formal specification language with two types of operators: logical connectives ($\neg$ (negation), $\vee$ (disjunction), $\wedge$ (conjunction), and $\rightarrow$ (implication)) and temporal operators (e.g., $\bigcirc$ (next), $\diamond$ (eventually), and $\square$ (always)). An LTL formula is interpreted over infinite words $w \in (2^P)^\omega$. The language of an LTL formula ϕ, denoted by $\mathcal{L}(\phi)$, is the set of infinite words that satisfy ϕ, i.e., $\mathcal{L}(\phi) = \{w \in (2^P)^\omega \mid w \models \phi\}$. We assume some familiarity of the reader with LTL. In this paper, We consider GR(1) specifications which are of the form $\phi = \phi_e \rightarrow \phi_s$, where ϕ_α for $\alpha \in \{e, s\}$ can be written as a conjunction of the following parts:

- ϕ_i^α: A Boolean formula over I if $\alpha = e$ and over $I \cup O$ otherwise, characterizing the initial state.
- ϕ_g^α: A formula of the form $\bigwedge_i \square\diamond B_i$ characterizing fairness/liveness, where each B_i is a Boolean formula over $I \cup O$.
- ϕ_t^α: An LTL formula of the form $\bigwedge_i \square\psi_i$ characterizing safety and transition relations, where ψ_i is a Boolean formula over expressions v and $\bigcirc v'$ where $v \in I \cup O$ and, $v' \in I$ if $\alpha = e$ and $v' \in I \cup O$ if $\alpha = s$.

Intuitively, ϕ_e indicates the assumptions on the environment and ϕ_s characterizes the requirements of the system. Any correct implementation that satisfies the specification guarantees to satisfy ϕ_s, provided that the environment satisfies ϕ_e.

A labeled transition system (LTS) is a tuple $\mathcal{T} = \langle Q, Q_0, \delta, \mathcal{L} \rangle$ where Q is a finite set of states, $Q_0 \subseteq Q$ is a set of initial states, $\delta \subseteq Q \times Q$ is a transition relation, and $\mathcal{L} : Q \rightarrow \phi$ is a labeling function which maps each state to a propositional formula $\phi = \bigwedge_i l_{p_i}$ expressed as a conjunction of literals l_{p_i} over propositions $p_i \in P$. The projection of a label ϕ with respect to a set of variables $U \subseteq P$ is defined as the propositional formula $\phi_{\downarrow U}$ where any literal ℓ_{p_i} over $p_i \in P\backslash U$ in ϕ is replaced by True, i.e., $\phi_{\downarrow U}$ only contains the variables from U. A *run* of an LTS is an infinite sequence of states $\sigma = q_0 q_1 q_2...$ where $q_0 \in Q_0$ and for any $i \geq 0$, $q_i \in Q$ and $(q_i, q_{i+1}) \in \delta$. The language of an LTS $\mathcal{T}$ is defined as the set $\mathcal{L}(\mathcal{T}) = \{w \in Q^\omega \mid w$ is a run of $\mathcal{T}\}$, i.e., the set of (infinite) words generated by the runs of $\mathcal{T}$.

A *Moore transducer* is a tuple $M = (S, s_0, \mathcal{I}, \mathcal{O}, \delta, \gamma)$, where S is a set of states, $s_0 \in S$ is an initial state, $\mathcal{I} = 2^I$ is the input alphabet, $\mathcal{O} = 2^O$ is the output alphabet, $\delta : S \times \mathcal{I} \rightarrow S$ is a transition function and $\gamma : S \rightarrow \mathcal{O}$ is a state output function. A *Mealy* transducer is similar, except that the state output function is $\gamma : S \times \mathcal{I} \rightarrow \mathcal{O}$. For an infinite word $w \in \mathcal{I}^\omega$, a run of M is an infinite sequence $\sigma \in S^\omega$ such that $\sigma_0 = s_0$ and for all $i \geq 0$ we have $\sigma_{i+1} = \delta(\sigma_i, w_i)$. The run σ on input word w produces an infinite word $M(w) \in (2^P)^\omega$ such that $M(w)_i = \gamma(\sigma_i) \cup w_i$ for all $i \geq 0$. The language of M is the set $\mathcal{L}(M) = \{M(w) \mid w \in \mathcal{I}^\omega\}$ of infinite words generated by runs of M.

An LTL formula ϕ is *satisfiable* if there exists an infinite word $w \in (2^P)^\omega$ such that $w \models \phi$. A Moore (Mealy) transducer M satisfies an LTL formula ϕ, written as $M \models \phi$, if $\mathcal{L}(M) \subseteq \mathcal{L}(\phi)$. An LTL formula ϕ is *Moore (Mealy) realizable* if there exists a Moore (Mealy, respectively) transducer M such that $M \models \phi$. The *realizability problem* asks whether there exists such a transducer for a given ϕ. Given an LTL formula ϕ over P and a partitioning of P into I and O, the *synthesis problem* is to find a Mealy transducer M with input alphabet $\mathcal{I} = 2^I$ and output alphabet $\mathcal{O} = 2^O$ that satisfies ϕ. A *counter-strategy* for the synthesis problem is a strategy for the environment that can falsify the specification, no matter how the system plays. Formally, a counter-strategy can be represented by a Moore transducer $M_c = (S', s'_0, \mathcal{I}', \mathcal{O}', \delta', \gamma')$ that satisfies $\neg \phi$, where $\mathcal{I}' = \mathcal{O}$ and $\mathcal{O}' = \mathcal{I}$ are the input and output alphabet for M_c which are generated by the system and the environment, respectively.

For a specification $\phi = \phi_e \rightarrow \phi_s$, we define an *assumption refinement* $\psi_e = \bigwedge_i \psi_{e_i}$ as a conjunction of a set of environment assumptions such that $(\phi_e \wedge \psi_e) \rightarrow \phi_s$ is realizable. Similarly, $\psi_s = \bigwedge_i \psi_{s_i}$ is a *guarantee refinement* if $\phi_e \rightarrow (\phi_s \wedge \psi_s)$ is realizable. An assumption refinement ψ_e is consistent with ϕ if $\phi_e \wedge \psi_e$ is satisfiable. Note that an inconsistent refinement $\phi_e \wedge \psi_e = \texttt{False}$, leads to an specification which is trivially realizable, but neither interesting nor useful.

3   Overview

Assume a global LTL specification is given which is realizable. Furthermore, assume the system consists of a set of components, and that a decomposition of the global specification into a set of local ones is given, where each local specification corresponds to a system component. The decomposition may result in components whose local specifications are unrealizable, e.g., due to the lack of adequate assumptions on their environment. The general question is how to refine the local specifications such that the refined specifications are all realizable, and when implemented together, the resulting system satisfies the global specification. In this paper we consider a special case of this problem. We assume the system consists of two components C_1 and C_2, where there is a serial interconnection between the components [3]. Intuitively, it means that the dependency between the output variables of the components is acyclic, as shown in Fig. 2. Let I be the set of input variables controlled by the environment and O be the set of output variables controlled by the system, partitioned into O_1 and O_2, the set of output variables controlled by C_1 and C_2, respectively. Formally, we define the problem as follows.

Problem Statement. Consider a realizable global specification $\phi = \phi_e \rightarrow \phi_s$. We assume ϕ is decomposed into two local specifications $\phi_1 = \phi_{e_1} \rightarrow \phi_{s_1}$ and $\phi_2 = \phi_{e_2} \rightarrow \phi_{s_2}$ such that $\phi_e \rightarrow (\phi_{e_1} \wedge \phi_{e_2})$ and $(\phi_{s_1} \wedge \phi_{s_2}) \rightarrow \phi_s$. We assume ϕ_e, ϕ_s, ϕ_{e_1}, ϕ_{s_1}, ϕ_{e_2}, and ϕ_{s_2} are GR(1) formulas which contain variables only from the sets I, $I \cup O$, I, $I \cup O_1$, $I \cup O_1$, and $I \cup O$, respectively. We would like to find refinements ψ and ψ' such that the refined specifications $\phi_1^{ref} = \phi_{e_1} \rightarrow (\phi_{s_1} \wedge \psi')$ and $\phi_2^{ref} = (\phi_{e_2} \wedge \psi) \rightarrow \phi_{s_2}$ are both realizable and $\psi' \rightarrow \psi$ is valid.

From Proposition 2 in [3] it follows that if such refinements exist, then the resulting system from implementing the refined specifications satisfies the global specification ϕ. We use this fact to establish the correctness of the decomposition and refinements in our proposed solutions. As ϕ is realizable, and C_1 is independent from C_2, it follows that ϕ_1 (in case it is not realizable) can become realizable by adding assumptions on its environment. Especially, providing all the environment assumptions of the global specification for C_1 is enough to make its specification realizable. However, it might not be the case for ϕ_2. In the rest of the paper, we assume that ϕ_1 is realizable, while ϕ_2 is not. We investigate how the strategy and counter-strategy computed for C_1 and C_2, respectively, can be used to find suitable refinements for the local specifications.

Our solution is based on an automated refinement of assumptions and guarantees expressed in LTL. In [4], we showed how an unrealizable specification can be refined by adding assumptions on the environment. The refinement is synthesized step by step guided by counter-strategies. When the specification is unrealizable, a counter-strategy is computed and a set of formulas of the forms $\Diamond\Box\psi$, $\Diamond\psi$, and $\Diamond(\psi \wedge \bigcirc\psi')$, which hold over *all* runs of the counter-strategy, is inferred. Intuitively, these formulas describe potentially "bad" behaviors of the environment that may cause unrealizability. Their complements form the set of *candidate* assumptions, and adding any of them as an assumption to the specification will prevent the environment from behaving according to the counter-strategy (without violating its assumptions). We say the counter-strategy is ruled out from the environment's possible behaviors. Counter-strategy-guided refinement algorithm in [4] iteratively chooses and adds a candidate assumption to the specification, and the process is repeated until the specification becomes realizable, or the search cannot find a refinement within the specified search depth. The user is asked to specify a subset of variables to be used in synthesizing candidate assumptions. This subset may reflect the designer's intuition on the source of unrealizability and help search for finding a proper refinement.

In this paper, we extend the algorithms in [4] to refine the guarantees of a specification. When the specification is realizable, a winning strategy can be computed for the system. We can use patterns to infer the behaviors of the strategies as LTL formulas. Formulas of the form $\Box\Diamond\psi$, $\Box\psi$, and $\Box(\psi \to \bigcirc\psi')$ can be used to infer *implicit* guarantees provided by the given strategy, i.e., they can be added to the original specification as guarantees, and the same strategy satisfies the new specification as well as the original one. These formulas can be seen as additional guarantees a component can provide in the context of compositional synthesis. Formulas of the form $\Diamond\Box\psi$, $\Diamond\psi$, and $\Diamond(\psi \wedge \bigcirc\psi')$ can be used to restrict the system by adding their complements to the specifications as guarantees. As a result, the current strategy is ruled out from system's possible strategies and hence, the new specification, if still realizable, will have a different strategy which satisfies the original specification, and also provides additional guarantees. Algorithm 1 shows how a set of additional guarantees $\mathcal{P}$ is computed for the specification ϕ and subset of variables U. For the computed strategy $\mathcal{M}_s$, the procedure **Infer-GR(1)-Formulas** synthesizes formulas of the forms $\Box\Diamond\psi, \Box\psi$, and $\Box(\psi \to \bigcirc\psi')$ which hold over all runs of the strategy. Similarly, the procedure **Infer-Complement-GR(1)-Formulas** synthesizes formulas of

---

Algorithm 1. FindGuarantees

Input: $\phi = \phi_e \rightarrow \phi_s$: a realizable specification, U: subset of variables
Output: $\mathcal{P}$: A set of formulas ψ such that $\phi_e \rightarrow (\phi_s \wedge \psi)$ is realizable
1 $\mathcal{M}_s = \textbf{ComputeStrategy}(\phi_1)$;
2 $\mathcal{P} := \textbf{Infer-GR(1)-Formulas}(\mathcal{M}_s, U)$;
3 $\mathcal{P}' := \textbf{Infer-Complement-GR(1)-Formulas}(\mathcal{M}_s, U)$;
4 **foreach** $\psi \in \mathcal{P}'$ **do**
5 | **if** $(\phi_e \rightarrow (\phi_s \wedge \neg\psi))$ *is realizable* **then**
6 | | $\mathcal{P} = \mathcal{P} \cup \neg\psi$;
7 return $\mathcal{P}$;

Fig. 3. Grid-world for the

Fig. 1. Room in Ex. 1   **Fig. 2.** Serial interconnection   case study

the form $\Diamond\Box\psi, \Diamond\psi$, and $\Diamond(\psi \wedge \bigcirc\psi')$. These procedures are explained in Sect. 4. In what follows, we will use *grid-world* examples commonly used in robot motion planning case studies to illustrate the concepts and techniques [10].

Example 1. Assume there are two robots, R_1 and R_2, in a room divided into eight cells as shown in Fig. 1. Both robots must infinitely often visit the goal cell 4. Besides, they cannot be in the same cell simultaneously (no collision). Finally, at any time step, each robot can either stay put or move to one of its neighbor cells. In the sequel, assume i ranges over $\{1, 2\}$. We denote the location of robot R_i with Loc_{R_i}, and cells by their numbers. Initially $Loc_{R_1} = 1$ and $Loc_{R_2} = 8$.

The global specification is realizable. Note that in this example, all the variables are controlled and there is no external environment. Assume that the specification is decomposed into ϕ_1 and ϕ_2, where $\phi_i = \phi_{e_i} \rightarrow \phi_{s_i}$ is the local specification for R_i. Assume $\phi_{e_1} = \texttt{True}$, and ϕ_{s_1} only includes the initial location of R_1, its transition rules, and its goal to infinitely often visit cell 4. ϕ_{s_2} includes the initial location of R_2, its transition rules, its objective to infinitely often visit cell 4, while avoiding collision with R_1. Here R_1 serves as the environment for R_2 which can play adversarially. ϕ_{e_2} only includes the initial location of R_1.

Inferring Formulas: ϕ_1 is realizable. A winning strategy $\mathcal{M}_{S_1}$ for R_1 is to move to cell 2 from the initial location, then to cell 3, and then to move back and forth between cells 4 and 3 forever. The following are examples of formulas inferred from this strategy: eventually always: $\Diamond\Box(Loc_{R_1} \in \{3, 4\})$, eventually: $\Diamond(Loc_{R_1} = 3)$, eventually next: $\Diamond(Loc_{R_1} = 3 \wedge \bigcirc Loc_{R_1} = 4)$, always eventually: $\Box\Diamond(Loc_{R_1} = 3)$, always: $\Box(Loc_{R_1} \in \{1, 2, 3, 4\})$, and always next: $\Box(Loc_{R_1} = 2 \rightarrow \bigcirc Loc_{R_1} = 3)$.

Refining Assumptions: Note that ϕ_2 includes no assumption on R_1 other than its initial location. Specifically, ϕ_2 does not restrict the way R_1 can move. The specification ϕ_2 is unrealizable. A counter-strategy for R_1 is to move from cell 1 to the goal cell 4, and stay there forever, preventing R_2 from fulfilling its requirements. Using the method of [4] for refining the assumptions on the environment, we find the refinements $\psi_1 = \Box\Diamond(Loc_{R_1} \neq 4)$, $\psi_2 = \Box(Loc_{R_1} \neq 4)$, and $\psi_3 = \Box(Loc_{R_1} = 4 \rightarrow \bigcirc Loc_{R_1} \neq 4)$. Intuitively, these refinements suggest that R_1 is not present in cell 4 at some point during the execution. Adding any of these formulas to the assumptions of ϕ_2 makes it realizable.

Refining Guarantees: Formula $\varphi = \Diamond\Box(Loc_{R_1} \in \{3,4\})$ is satisfied by $\mathcal{M}_{S_1}$, meaning that R_1 eventually reaches and stays at the cells 3 and 4 forever. An example of a guarantee refinement is to add the guarantee $\neg\varphi$ to ϕ_1. A winning strategy for the new specification is to move back and forth in the first row between initial and goal cells. That is, R_1 has the infinite run $(1,2,3,4,3,2)^\omega$.

We use these techniques to refine the interface specifications. We propose three different approaches for finding suitable refinements, based on how much information about the strategy of the realizable component is allowed to be shared with the unrealizable component. The first approach has no knowledge of the strategy chosen by C_1, and tries to find a refinement by analyzing counter-strategies. The second approach iteratively extracts some information from the strategies computed for ϕ_1, and uses them to refine the specifications. The third approach encodes the strategy as a conjunction of LTL formulas, and provides it as a set of assumptions for C_2, allowing it to have a full knowledge of the strategy. These approaches are explained in detail in Sect. 5.

Compositional Refinement: Assume $\mathcal{M}_{S_1}$ is the computed strategy for R_1. The first approach, computes a refinement for the unrealizable specification, then checks if the other component can guarantee it. For example, ψ_3 is a candidate refinement for ϕ_2. ϕ_1 can be refined by ψ_3 added to its guarantees. The strategy $\mathcal{M}_{S_1}$ still satisfies the new specification, and refined specifications are both realizable. Thus, the first approach returns ψ_3 as a possible refinement. Using the second approach, formula $\psi_4 = \Box\Diamond(Loc_{R_1} = 3)$ is inferred from $\mathcal{M}_{S_1}$. Refining both specifications with ψ_4 leads to two realizable specifications, hence ψ_4 is returned as a refinement. The third approach encodes $\mathcal{M}_{S_1}$ as conjunction of transition formulas $\psi_5 = \bigwedge_{i=1}^{3} \Box(Loc_{R_1} = i \rightarrow \bigcirc Loc_{R_1} = i+1) \wedge \Box(Loc_{R_1} = 4 \rightarrow \bigcirc Loc_{R_1} = 3)$. Refining assumptions of ϕ_2 with ψ_5 makes it realizable.

4   Inferring Behaviors as LTL Formulas

In this section we show how certain types of LTL formulas which hold over all runs of a counter-strategy or strategy can be synthesized. The user chooses the subset of variables U to be used in synthesizing the formulas. These formulas are computed as follows: First an LTS $\mathcal{T}$ is obtained from the given Moore (Mealy) transducer $\mathcal{M}$ which represents the counterstrategy (strategy, respectively). Next, using the set U, an abstraction $\mathcal{T}^a$ of $\mathcal{T}$ is constructed which is

Fig. 4. An LTS $\mathcal{T}$

Fig. 5. Abstract LTS $\mathcal{T}^a$ of $\mathcal{T}$

also an LTS. A set of patterns which hold over all runs of $\mathcal{T}^a$ is then synthesized. The instantiations of these patterns form the set of formulas which hold over all runs of the input transducer. Next we explain these steps in more detail.

4.1 Constructing the Abstract LTS

We briefly show how an abstraction of a given strategy or counter-strategy is obtained as an LTS. Given a Moore (Mealy) transducer $\mathcal{M}$, first an LTS $\mathcal{T} = (Q, \{q_0\}, \delta_{\mathcal{T}}, \mathcal{L})$ is obtained which keeps the structure of $\mathcal{M}$ while removing its input and output details. The states of $\mathcal{T}$ are labeled in a way that is consistent with the input/output valuations of $\mathcal{M}$. Next, using a user-specified subset of variables $U \subseteq I \cup O$, an abstraction $\mathcal{T}^a = (Q^a, Q_0^a, \delta_{\mathcal{T}^a}, \mathcal{L}^a)$ of $\mathcal{T}$ is computed based on the state labels $\mathcal{L}$. There is a surjective function $F : Q \rightarrow Q^a$ which maps each state of $\mathcal{T}$ to a unique state of $\mathcal{T}^a$. Intuitively, the abstraction $\mathcal{T}^a$ has a unique state for each maximal subset of states of $\mathcal{T}$ which have the same projected labels with respect to U, and if there is a transition between two states of $\mathcal{T}$, there will be a transition between their mapped states in $\mathcal{T}^a$. It can be shown that $\mathcal{T}^a$ simulates $\mathcal{T}$. Therefore, any formula φ which is satisfied by $\mathcal{T}^a$ is also satisfied by $\mathcal{T}$.

Remark 1. Patterns can be synthesized from either $\mathcal{T}$ or $\mathcal{T}^a$. It is sometimes necessary to use $\mathcal{T}^a$ due to the high complexity of the algorithms for computing certain types of patterns (e.g., eventually patterns), as $\mathcal{T}^a$ may have significantly less number of states compared to $\mathcal{T}$ which improves the scalability of the methods. However, abstraction may introduce additional non-determinism into the model, leading to refinements which are more "conservative." Besides, some of the formulas which are satisfied by $\mathcal{T}$, cannot be computed from $\mathcal{T}^a$. It is up to the user to choose techniques which serve her purposes better.

4.2 Synthesizing Patterns

Next we discuss how patterns of certain types can be synthesized from the given LTS $\mathcal{T}$. A pattern $\psi_{\mathcal{P}}$ is an LTL formula which is satisfied over all runs of $\mathcal{T}$, i.e., $\mathcal{T} \models \psi_{\mathcal{P}}$. We are interested in patterns of the forms $\Diamond\Box\psi_{\mathcal{P}}$, $\Diamond\psi_{\mathcal{P}}$, $\Diamond(\psi_{\mathcal{P}} \wedge \bigcirc\psi'_{\mathcal{P}})$, $\Box\Diamond\psi_{\mathcal{P}}$, $\Box\psi_{\mathcal{P}}$, and $\Box(\psi_{\mathcal{P}} \rightarrow \bigcirc\psi'_{\mathcal{P}})$, where $\psi_{\mathcal{P}}$ and $\psi'_{\mathcal{P}}$ are propositional formulas expressed as a disjunction of subset of states of $\mathcal{T}$. Patterns are synthesized using graph search algorithms which search for special *configurations*. For an LTS $\mathcal{T} = (Q, Q_0, \delta, \mathcal{L})$, a configuration $C \subseteq Q$ is a subset of states of $\mathcal{T}$. A configuration C is a $\bowtie$-configuration where $\bowtie \in \{\Box, \Box\Diamond, \Diamond, \Diamond\Box\}$ if $\mathcal{T} \models_{\bowtie} \bigvee_{q \in C} q$. For example, C is an $\Box\Diamond$-*configuration* if any run of $\mathcal{T}$ always eventually visits a state from C. A $\bowtie$-configuration C is minimal, if there is no configuration $C' \subset C$ which is an $\bowtie$-configuration, i.e., removing any state from C leads to a configuration which is not a $\bowtie$-configuration anymore. Minimal $\bowtie$-configurations are interesting since they lead to the *strongest* patterns of $\bowtie$-form [4]. Algorithms for computing $\Diamond\Box\psi_{\mathcal{P}}$, $\Diamond\psi_{\mathcal{P}}$, and $\Diamond(\psi_{\mathcal{P}} \wedge \bigcirc\psi'_{\mathcal{P}})$ patterns can be found in [4]. Here we give algorithms for computing patterns of the forms in GR(1).

$\Box\Diamond\psi_{\mathcal{P}}$ **Patterns**: The following theorem establishes the complexity of computing all minimal always eventually patterns over a given LTS.

Theorem 1. *Computing all minimal $\Box\Diamond$-configurations is NP-hard.*[1]

Consequently, computing all minimal (always) eventually patterns is infeasible in practice even for medium sized specifications. We propose an alternative algorithm which computes *some* of the always eventually patterns.[2] Although the algorithm has an exponential upper-bound, it is simpler and terminates faster in our experiments, as it avoids enumerating all configurations. It starts with the configuration $\{q_0\}$, and at each step computes the next configuration, i.e., the set of states that the runs of $\mathcal{T}$ can reach at the next step from the current configuration. A sequence $C_0, C_1, ..., C_j$ of configurations is discovered during the search, where $C_0 = \{q_0\}$ and $j \geq 0$. The procedure terminates when a configuration C_i is reached which is already visited, i.e., there exists $0 \leq j < i$ such that $C_j = C_i$. There is a cycle between C_j and C_{i-1} and thus, all the configurations in the cycle will always eventually be visited over all runs of $\mathcal{T}$.

$\Box\psi_{\mathcal{P}}$ **Pattern**: For a given LTS $\mathcal{T}$, a safety pattern of the form $\Box\psi$ is synthesized where ψ is simply the disjunction of all the states in $\mathcal{T}$, i.e., $\psi = \bigvee_{q \in Q} q$. It is easy to see that removing any state from ψ leads to a formula which is not satisfied by $\mathcal{T}$ anymore. The synthesis procedure is of complexity $O(|Q|)$.

$\Box(\psi_{\mathcal{P}} \to \bigcirc\psi'_{\mathcal{P}})$ **Patterns**: For a given LTS $\mathcal{T}$, a set of transition patterns of the form $\Box(\psi \to \bigcirc\psi')$ is synthesized. Each ψ consists of a single state $q \in Q$, for which the ψ' is disjunction of its successors, i.e. $\psi' = \bigvee_{q' \in Next(q)} q'$ where $Next(q) = \{q' \in Q \mid \delta(q) = q'\}$. Intuitively, each transition pattern states that always when a state is visited, its successors will be visited at the next step. The synthesis procedure is of complexity $O(|Q| + |\delta|)$.

4.3 Instantiating the Patterns

To obtain LTL formulas over a specified subset U of variables from patterns, we replace the states in patterns by their projected labels. For example, from an eventually pattern $\Diamond\psi_{\mathcal{P}} = \Diamond(\bigvee_{q \in Q_{\psi_{\mathcal{P}}}} q)$ where $Q_{\psi_{\mathcal{P}}} \subseteq Q$ is a configuration for $\mathcal{T} = (Q, \{q_0\}, \delta, \mathcal{L})$, we obtain the formula $\psi = \Diamond(\bigvee_{q \in Q_{\psi_{\mathcal{P}}}} \mathcal{L}(q)\downarrow_U)$.

Example 2. Let $\Sigma = \{a, b, c\}$ be the set of variables. Consider the LTS $\mathcal{T}$ shown in Fig. 4, where $\mathcal{L}(q_0) = \neg a \wedge \neg b \wedge \neg c$, $\mathcal{L}(q_1) = \neg a \wedge b \wedge \neg c$, $\mathcal{L}(q_2) = a \wedge \neg b \wedge \neg c$, $\mathcal{L}(q_3) = \neg a \wedge b \wedge \neg c$. Let $U = \{a, b\}$ be the set of variables specified by the

---

[1] Computing all minimal eventually patterns is also NP-hard
[2] We use a similar algorithm for computing *some* of the eventually patterns.

designer to be used in all forms of formulas. Figure 5 shows $\mathcal{T}^a$ which is an abstraction of $\mathcal{T}$ with respect to U, where the mapping function F is defined such that $F^{-1}(q_0^a) = \{q_0\}$, $F^{-1}(q_1^a) = \{q_1, q_3\}$, and $F^{-1}(q_2^a) = \{q_2\}$, and the labels are defined as $\mathcal{L}(q_0^a) = \neg a \wedge \neg b$, $\mathcal{L}(q_1^a) = \neg a \wedge b$, and $\mathcal{L}(q_2^a) = a \wedge \neg b$. A set of patterns are synthesized using the input LTS. For example, $\psi_{\mathcal{P}} = \Diamond(q_1^a)$ is an eventually pattern where $\mathcal{T}^a \models \psi_{\mathcal{P}}$, meaning that eventually over all runs of the $\mathcal{T}^a$ the state q_1^a is visited. An LTL formula is obtained using the patterns, labels and specified subset of variables. For example, $\psi = \Diamond(\neg a \wedge b)$ is obtained from the pattern $\psi_{\mathcal{P}}$, where the states q_1^a is replaced by its label. Note that the formula $\psi' = \Diamond((\neg a \wedge b) \wedge \bigcirc(a \wedge \neg b))$ can be synthesized from the pattern $\psi'_{\mathcal{P}} = \Diamond(q_1 \wedge \bigcirc q_2)$ from $\mathcal{T}$, however, $\mathcal{T}^a$ does not satisfy ψ'. A more conservative formula $\Diamond((\neg a \wedge b) \wedge \bigcirc((a \wedge \neg b) \vee (\neg a \wedge \neg b)))$ is obtained using the abstraction.

5   Compositional Refinement

We propose three approaches for compositional refinement of the specifications ϕ_1 and ϕ_2 in the problem stated in Sect. 3. These approaches differ mainly in how much information about the strategy of the realizable component is shared with the unrealizable component. All three approaches use bounded search to compute the refinements. The search depth (number of times the refinement procedure can be called recursively) is specified by the user. Note that the proposed approaches are not complete, i.e., failure to compute a refinement does not mean that there is no refinement.

Approach 1 ("No Knowledge of the Strategy of C_1"): One way to synthesize the refinements ψ and ψ' is to compute a refinement ψ' for the unrealizable specification ϕ_2 using the counter-strategy-guided refinement method in [4]. The specification ϕ_2 is refined by adding assumptions on its environment that rule out all the counter-strategies for ϕ_2, as explained in Sect. 3, and the refined specification $\phi_2^{ref} = (\phi_{e_1} \wedge \psi') \rightarrow \phi_{s_1}$ is realizable. We add $\psi = \psi'$ to guarantees of ϕ_1 and check if ϕ_1^{ref} is realizable. If ϕ_1^{ref} is not realizable, another assumption refinement for ϕ_2 must be computed, and the process is repeated for the new refinement. Note that if adding ψ to the guarantees of ϕ_1 does not make it realizable, there is no ψ'' such that $\psi'' \rightarrow \psi$, and adding ψ'' keeps ϕ_1 realizable. Therefore, a new refinement must be computed.

An advantage of this approach is that the assumption refinement ψ' for ϕ_2 is computed independently using the weakest assumptions that rule out the counter-strategies. Thus, ψ' can be used even if C_1 is replaced by another component C_1' with different specification, as long as C_1' can still guarantee ψ'.

Approach 2 ("Partial Knowledge of the Strategy of C_1"): For a given counter-strategy, there may exist many different candidate assumptions that can be used to refine the specification. Checking the satisfiability and realizability of the resulting refined specification is an expensive process, so it is more desirable to remove the candidates that are not promising. For example, a counter-strategy might represent a problem which cannot happen due to the strategy chosen by the other component. Roughly speaking, the more one component knows about the other one's implementation, the less number of scenarios it needs to consider and react to. The second approach shares information about the strategy synthesized for C_1 with C_2 as follows. It computes a set $\mathcal{P}$ of candidate LTL formulas which can be used to refine guarantees of ϕ_1. Then at each iteration, a formula $\psi \in \mathcal{P}$ is chosen, and it is checked if the counter-strategy for ϕ_2 satisfies $\neg\psi$ (similar to assumption mining in [5]). If it does and ψ is consistent with ϕ_2, it is checked if ψ is an assumption refinement for ϕ_2, in which case ψ can be used to refine the guarantees (assumptions) of ϕ_1 (ϕ_2, respectively), and ψ is returned as a suggested refinement. Otherwise, the local specifications are refined by ψ and the process is repeated with the new specifications. In this approach, some information about C_1's behavior is shared as LTL formulas extracted from the C_1's strategy. Only those formulas which completely rule out the counter-strategy are kept, hence reducing the number of candidate refinements, and keeping the more promising ones, while sharing as much information as needed from one component to the other one.

Approach 3 ("Full Knowledge of the Strategy of C_1") It might be preferred to refine the specification by adding formulas that are already satisfied by the current implementation of the realizable component in order not to change the underlying implementation. For example, assume a strategy $\mathcal{M}_S$ is already computed and implemented for ϕ_1, and the designer prefers to find a refinement ψ that is satisfied by $\mathcal{M}_S$. Yet in some cases, the existing strategy for C_1 must be changed, otherwise C_2 will not be able to fulfill its requirements. In this setting, the guarantees of C_1 can be refined to find a different winning strategy for it. The third approach is based on this idea. It shares the full knowledge of strategy computed for C_1 with C_2 by encoding the strategy as an LTL formula and providing it as an assumption for ϕ_2. Knowing exactly how C_1 plays might make it much easier for C_2 to synthesize a strategy for itself, if one exists. Furthermore, a counter-strategy produced in this case indicates that it is impossible for C_2 to fulfill its goals if C_1 sticks to its current strategy. Therefore, both specifications are refined and a new strategy is computed for the realizable component.

Algorithm 2 summarizes the third approach. Once a strategy is computed for the realizable specification, its corresponding LTS $\mathcal{T} = (Q, \{q_0\}, \delta, \mathcal{L})$ is obtained, and encoded as a conjunction of transition formulas as follows. We define a set of new propositions $\mathcal{Z} = \{z_0, z_1, \cdots, z_{\lceil log|Q|\rceil}\}$ which encode the states Q of $\mathcal{T}$. Intuitively, these propositions represent the memory of the strategy in generated transition formulas, and are considered as environment variables in the refined specification ϕ_2'. For ease of notation, let $|\mathcal{Z}|_i$ indicate the truth assignment to the propositions in $\mathcal{Z}$ which represents the state $q_i \in Q$. We encode $\mathcal{T}$ with the conjunctive formula $\psi = (|\mathcal{Z}|_0 \wedge \mathcal{L}(q_0) \wedge \bigwedge_{q_i \in Q} \square((|\mathcal{Z}|_i \wedge \mathcal{L}(q_i)) \rightarrow \bigcirc(\bigvee_{q_j \in \mathrm{Next}(q_i)} |\mathcal{Z}|_j \wedge \mathcal{L}(q_j)))$, where $\mathrm{Next}(q_i)$ is the set of states in $\mathcal{T}$ with a transition from q_i to them. We refer to ψ as *full encoding* of $\mathcal{T}$. Intuitively, ψ states that always when the strategy is in state $q_i \in Q$ with truth assignment to the variables given as $\mathcal{L}(q_i)$, then at next step it will be in one of the adjacent states $q_j \in \mathrm{Next}(q_i)$ with truth assignment $\mathcal{L}(q_j)$ to the variables, and initially it is in state q_0. The procedure **Encode-LTS** in Alg. 2 takes an LTS and returns a conjunctive LTL formula representing it.

The unrealizable specification ϕ_2 is then refined by adding the encoding of the strategy as assumptions to it. If the refined specification ϕ_2' is realizable, there exists a strategy for C_2, assuming the strategy chosen for C_1, and the encoding is returned as a possible refinement. Otherwise, the produced counter-strategy $\mathcal{CS}'$ shows how the strategy for C_1 can prevent C_2 from realizing its specification. Hence, the specification of both components need to be refined. Procedure **findCandidateAssumptions** computes a set $\mathcal{P}$ of candidate assumptions that can rule out $\mathcal{CS}'$, and at each iteration, one candidate is chosen and tested by both specifications for satisfiability and realizability. If any of these candidate formulas can make both specifications realizable, it is returned as a refinement. Otherwise, the process is repeated with only those candidates that are consistent with ϕ_2, and keep ϕ_1 realizable. As a result, the set of candidate formulas is pruned and the process is repeated with the more promising formulas. If no refinement is found within the specified search depth, `False` is returned.

Remark 2. Introducing new propositions representing the memory of the strategy $\mathcal{S}_1$ computed for ϕ_1 leads to assumptions that provide C_2 with full knowledge of how C_1 reacts to its environment. Therefore, if the new specification refined by these assumptions is not realizable, the counter-strategy would be an example of how $\mathcal{S}_1$ might prevent ϕ_2 from being realizable, giving the designer the certainty that a different strategy must be computed for C_1, or in other words both specifications must be refined. However, if introducing new propositions is undesirable, an *abstract encoding* of the strategy (without memory variables) can be obtained by returning conjunction of *all* transition formulas $\Box(\psi \to \bigcirc\psi')$ computed over the strategy. The user can specify the set of variables in which she is interested. This encoding represents an abstraction of the strategy that might be *non-deterministic*, i.e., for the given truth assignment to environment variables, there might be more than one truth assignment to outputs of C_1 that are consistent with the encoding. Such relaxed encoding can be viewed as sharing partial information about the strategy of C_1 with C_2.

As an example, consider the LTS $\mathcal{T}$ in Fig. 4 which can be encoded as $(q_0 \land \neg a \land \neg b \land \neg c) \land \Box((q_0 \land \neg a \land \neg b \land \neg c) \to \bigcirc(q_1 \land \neg a \land b \land \neg c)) \land \cdots \land \Box((q_3 \land \neg a \land b \land \neg c) \to \bigcirc(q_0 \land \neg a \land \neg b \land \neg c))$. An abstract encoding without introducing new variables and considering only a and b results in formula $\Box((\neg a \land \neg b) \to \bigcirc(\neg a \land b)) \land \Box((\neg a \land b) \to \bigcirc((\neg a \land \neg b) \lor (a \land \neg b))) \land \Box((a \land \neg b) \to \bigcirc(\neg a \land b))$.

6   Case Study

We now demonstrate the techniques on a robot motion planning case study. We use RATSY [11] for computing counter-strategies, JTLV [12] for synthesizing strategies, and Cadence SMV model checker [13] for model checking. The experiments are performed on a Intel core i7 3.40 GHz machine with 16GB memory.

Algorithm 2. CompositonalRefinement3

Input: $\phi_1 = \phi_{e_1} \to \phi_{s_1}$: a realizable specification, $\phi_2 = \phi_{e_2} \to \phi_{s_2}$: an
unrealizable specification, α: search depth, U: subset of variables

Output: ψ such that $\phi_{e_1} \to (\phi_{s_2} \wedge \psi)$ and $(\phi_{e_2} \wedge \psi) \to \phi_{s_2}$ are realizable

1 **if** $\alpha < 0$ **then**
2 | return **False**;
3 Let $\mathcal{S}$ be the strategy for ϕ_1;
4 $\psi := $ **Encode-LTS**$(\mathcal{S})$;
5 $\phi'_2 := (\psi \wedge \phi_{e_2}) \to \phi_{s_2}$;
6 **if** ϕ'_2 *is realizable* **then**
7 | return ψ;
8 **else**
9   Let $\mathcal{CS}'$ be a counter-strategy for ϕ'_2;
10    $\mathcal{P} := $ **findCandidateAssumptions**$(\mathcal{CS}', U)$;
11   **foreach** $\varphi \in \mathcal{P}$ **do**
12   Let ϕ''_2 be $(\varphi \wedge \phi_{e_2}) \to \phi_{s_2}$;
13   Let ϕ''_1 be $\phi_{e_1} \to (\phi_{s_1} \wedge \varphi)$;
14   **if** ϕ''_1 *is realizable and* ϕ''_2 *is satisfiable* **then**
15   **if** ϕ''_2 *is realizable* **then**
16 | return φ;
17   **else**
18             $\psi := $ compositionalRefinement3$(\phi''_1, \phi''_2, \alpha - 1, U)$;
19   **if** $\psi \neq$ **False** **then**
20 | return $\psi \wedge \varphi$;
21 return **False**;

Consider the robot motion planning example over the discrete workspace shown in Fig. 3. Assume there are two robots R_1 and R_2 initially in cells 1 and 25, respectively. Robots can move to one of their neighbor cells at each step. There are two rooms in bottom-left and the upper-right corners of the workspace protected by two doors D_1 (cell 10) and D_2 (cell 16). The robots can enter or exit a room through its door and only if it is open. The objective of R_1 (R_2) is to infinitely often visit the cell 5 (21, respectively). The global specification requires each robot to infinitely often visit their goal cells, while avoiding collision with each other, walls and the closed doors, i.e., the robots cannot occupy the same location simultanously, or switch locations in two following time steps, they cannot move to cells $\{4, 9, 17, 22\}$ (walls), and they cannot move to cells 10 or 16 if the corresponding door is closed. The doors are controlled by the environment and we assume that each door is always eventually open.

The global specification is realizable. We decompose the specification as follows. A local specification $\phi_1 = \phi_{e_1} \to \phi_{s_1}$ for R_1 where ϕ_{e_1} is the environment assumption on the doors and ϕ_{s_1} is a conjunction of R_1's guarantees which consist of its initial location, its transition rules, avoiding collision with walls and closed doors, and its goal to visit cell 5 infinitely often. A local specification $\phi_2 = \phi_{e_2} \to \phi_{s_2}$ for R_2 where ϕ_{e_2} includes assumptions on the doors, R_1's initial location, goal, and its transition rules, and ϕ_{s_2} consists of R_2's initial location, its transition rules, avoiding collision with R_1, walls and closed doors while fulfilling its goal. The specification ϕ_1 is realizable, but ϕ_2 is not. We use the algorithms outlined in Sect. 5 to find refinements for both components. We slightly modified the algorithms to find all refinements within the specified search depth. We use the variables corresponding to the location of R_1 for computing the abstraction and generating the candidate formulas. Furthermore, since the counter-strategies are large, computing all eventually and always eventually patterns is not feasible (may take years), and hence we only synthesize some of them.

Using the first approach along with abstraction, three refinements are found in 173 minutes which are conjunctions of safety and transition formulas. One of the computed refinements is $\psi_1 = \Box(Loc_{R_1} = 7 \rightarrow \bigcirc(Loc_{R_1} \notin \{7, 8, 12\})) \wedge \Box(Loc_{R_1} = 13 \rightarrow \bigcirc(Loc_{R_1} \notin \{12, 14\})) \wedge \Box(Loc_{R_1} = 11 \rightarrow \bigcirc(Loc_{R_1} \neq 16)) \wedge \Box(Loc_{R_1} = 2 \rightarrow \bigcirc(Loc_{R_1} \neq 7)) \wedge \Box(Loc_{R_1} \notin \{2, 12\})$. Intuitively, ψ_1 assumes some restrictions on how R_1 behaves, in which case a strategy for R_2 can be computed. Indeed, R_1 has a strategy that can guarantee ψ_1. Without using abstraction, four refinements are found within search depth 1 in 17 minutes. A suggested refinement is $\Box(Loc_{R_1} \notin \{7, 12, 16\})$, i.e., if R_1 avoids cells $\{7, 12, 16\}$, a strategy for R_2 can be computed. Using abstraction reduces the number of states of the counter-strategy from 576 to 12 states, however, not all the formulas that are satisfied by the counter-strategy, can be computed over its abstraction, as mentioned in Remark 1. Note that computing all the refinements within search depth 3 without using abstraction takes almost 5 times more time compared to when abstraction is used. Using the second approach (with and without abstraction) the refinement $\psi_2 = \Box(Loc_{R_1} = 10 \rightarrow Loc_{R_1} = 5)$ is found by infering fromulas from the strategy computed for R_1. Using abstraction slightly improves the process. Finally, using the third approach, providing either the full encoding or the abstract encoding of the strategy computed for ϕ_1 as assumptions for ϕ_2, makes the specification realizable. Therefore, no counter-strategy is produced, as knowing how R_1 behaves enables R_2 to find a strategy for itself.

Table 1 shows the experimental results for the case study. The columns specify the approach, whether abstraction is used or not, the total time for the experiment in minutes, number of strategies (counter-strategies) and number of states of the largest strategy (counter-strategy, respectively), the depth of the search,

Table 1. Evaluation of approaches on robot motion planning case study

Appr.	abstraction	time (min)	$\#_S$	max $|Q|_S$	$\#_{CS}$	max $|Q|_{CS}$	depth	$\#_{ref.}$	$\#_{candid.}$
1	yes	173.05	-	-	17	12	3	3	104
1	no	17.18	-	-	1	576	1	4	22
1	no	869.84	-	-	270	644	3	589	7911
2	yes	69.21	1	8	18	576	1	2	19
2	no	73.78	1	22	19	576	1	2	24
3	yes	0.01	1	8	0	0	1	1	0
3	no	0.02	1	22	0	0	1	1	0

number of refinements found, and number of candidate formulas generated during the search. As it can be seen from the table, knowing more about the strategy chosen for the realizable specification can significantly reduce the time needed to find suitable refinement (from hours for the first approach to seconds for the third approach). However, the improvement in time comes with the cost of introducing more coupling between the components, i.e., the strategy computed for C_2 can become too dependent on the strategy chosen for C_1.

7   Conclusion and Future Work

We showed how automated refinement of specifications can be used to refine the specifications of the components in the context of compositional synthesis. We proposed three different approaches for compositional refinement of specifications. The choice of the appropriate approach depends on the size of the problem (e.g., number of states in strategies and counter-strategies) and the level of acceptable coupling between components. Supplying more information about the strategies of the components with realizable local specifications to unrealizable specification under refinement, reduces the number of scenarios the game solver needs to consider, and facilitates the synthesis procedure, while increasing the coupling between components. Overall, patterns provide a tool for the designer to refine and complete temporal logic specifications. In future we plan to extend the methods to more general architectures.

References

1. Rosner, R.: Modular synthesis of reactive systems. Ann Arbor 1050, 41346–48106 (1991)
2. Bloem, R., Jobstmann, B., Piterman, N., Pnueli, A., Sa'ar, Y.: Synthesis of reactive (1) designs. Journal of Computer and System Sciences 78(3), 911–938 (2012)
3. Ozay, N., Topcu, U., Murray, R.: Distributed power allocation for vehicle management systems. In: CDC-ECC, pp. 4841–4848 (2011)
4. Alur, R., Moarref, S., Topcu, U.: Counter-strategy guided refinement of GR(1) temporal logic specifications. In: FMCAD, pp. 31–44 (2013)
5. Li, W., Dworkin, L., Seshia, S.: Mining assumptions for synthesis. In: MEMOCODE, pp. 43–50 (2011)
6. Chatterjee, K., Henzinger, T.A., Jobstmann, B.: Environment assumptions for synthesis. In: van Breugel, F., Chechik, M. (eds.) CONCUR 2008. LNCS, vol. 5201, pp. 147–161. Springer, Heidelberg (2008)
7. Pnueli, A., Rosner, R.: Distributed reactive systems are hard to synthesize. In: FoCS, pp. 746–757 (1990)
8. Finkbeiner, B., Schewe, S.: Uniform distributed synthesis. In: LICS, pp. 321–330. IEEE (2005)
9. Chatterjee, K., Henzinger, T.A.: Assume-guarantee synthesis. In: Grumberg, O., Huth, M. (eds.) TACAS 2007. LNCS, vol. 4424, pp. 261–275. Springer, Heidelberg (2007)
10. LaValle, S.M.: Planning algorithms. Cambridge University Press (2006)

11. Bloem, R., Cimatti, A., Greimel, K., Hofferek, G., Könighofer, R., Roveri, M., Schuppan, V., Seeber, R.: RATSY – A new requirements analysis tool with synthesis. In: Touili, T., Cook, B., Jackson, P. (eds.) CAV 2010. LNCS, vol. 6174, pp. 425–429. Springer, Heidelberg (2010)
12. Pnueli, A., Sa'ar, Y., Zuck, L.D.: JTLV: A framework for developing verification algorithms. In: Touili, T., Cook, B., Jackson, P. (eds.) CAV 2010. LNCS, vol. 6174, pp. 171–174. Springer, Heidelberg (2010)
13. McMillan, K.: Cadence SMV, http://www.kenmcmil.com/smv.html

Assume-Guarantee Synthesis for Concurrent Reactive Programs with Partial Information*

Roderick Bloem[1], Krishnendu Chatterjee[2], Swen Jacobs[1,3], and Robert Könighofer[1]

[1] IAIK, Graz University of Technology, Austria
[2] IST Austria, Institute of Science and Technology, Austria
[3] Reactive Systems Group, Saarland University, Germany

Abstract. Synthesis of program parts is particularly useful for concurrent systems. However, most approaches do not support common design tasks, like modifying a single process without having to re-synthesize or verify the whole system. Assume-guarantee synthesis (AGS) provides robustness against modifications of system parts, but thus far has been limited to the perfect information setting. This means that local variables cannot be hidden from other processes, which renders synthesis results cumbersome or even impossible to realize. We resolve this shortcoming by defining AGS under partial information. We analyze the complexity and decidability in different settings, showing that the problem has a high worst-case complexity and is undecidable in many interesting cases. Based on these observations, we present a pragmatic algorithm based on bounded synthesis, and demonstrate its practical applicability on several examples.

1 Introduction

Concurrent programs are notoriously hard to get right, due to unexpected behavior emerging from the interaction of different processes. At the same time, concurrency aspects such as mutual exclusion or deadlock freedom are easy to express declaratively. This makes concurrent programs an ideal subject for automatic synthesis. Due to the prohibitive complexity of synthesis tasks [33,34,17], the automated construction of *entire* programs from high-level specifications such as LTL is often unrealistic. More practical approaches are based on partially implemented programs that should be completed or refined automatically [17,16,39], or program repair, where suitable replacements need to be synthesized for faulty program parts [25]. This paper focuses on such applications, where parts of the system are already given.

When several processes need to be synthesized or refined simultaneously, a fundamental question arises: What are the assumptions about the behavior of other processes on which a particular process should rely? The classical synthesis approaches assume either completely adversarial or cooperative behavior, which leads to problems in both

---

* This work was supported by the Austrian Science Fund (FWF) through the research network RiSE (S11406-N23, S11407-N23) and grant nr. P23499-N23, by the European Commission through an ERC Start grant (279307: Graph Games) and project STANCE (317753), as well as by the German Research Foundation (DFG) through SFB/TR 14 AVACS and project ASDPS (JA 2357/2-1).

© Springer-Verlag Berlin Heidelberg 2015
C. Baier and C. Tinelli (Eds.): TACAS 2015, LNCS 9035, pp. 517–532, 2015.
DOI: 10.1007/978-3-662-46681-0_50

cases: adversarial components may result in unrealizability of the system, while cooperative components may rely on a specific form of cooperation, and therefore are not robust against even small changes in a single process. Assume-Guarantee Synthesis (AGS) [9] uses a more reasonable assumption: processes are adversarial, but will not violate their own specification to obstruct others. Therefore, a system constructed by AGS will still satisfy its overall specification if we replace or refine one of the processes, as long as the new process satisfies its local specification. Furthermore, AGS leads to the desired solutions in cases where the classical notions (of cooperative or completely adversarial processes) do not, for example in the synthesis of mutual exclusion protocols [9] or fair-exchange protocols for digital contract signing [13].

A drawback of existing algorithms for AGS [9,13] is that they only work in a perfect information setting. This means that each component can access and use the values of all variables of the other processes. This is a major restriction, as most concurrent implementations rely on variables that are *local* to one process, and should not be changed or observed by the other process. While classical notions of synthesis have been considered in such partial information settings before [28,17], we provide the first solution for AGS with partial information.

Contributions. In this work, we extend assume-guarantee synthesis to the synthesis of processes with partial information. In particular:

i) We analyze the complexity and decidability of AGS by reductions to games with three players. We distinguish synthesis problems based on informedness (perfect or partial) and resources (bounded or unbounded memory) of processes, and on specifications from different fragments of linear-time temporal logic (LTL).

ii) In light of the high complexity of many AGS problems, we propose a pragmatic approach, based on partially implemented programs and synthesis with bounded resources. We extend the bounded synthesis approach [18] to enable synthesis from partially defined, non-deterministic programs, and to the AGS setting.

iii) We provide the first implementation of AGS, integrated into a programming model that allows for a combined imperative-declarative programming style with fine-grained, user-provided restrictions on the exchange of information between processes. To obtain efficient and simple code, our prototype also supports optimization of the synthesized program with respect to some basic user-defined metrics.

iv) We demonstrate the value of our approach on a number of small programs and protocols, including Peterson's mutual exclusion protocol, a double buffering protocol, and synthesis of atomic sections in a concurrent device driver. We also demonstrate how the robustness of AGS solutions allows us to refine parts of the synthesized program without starting synthesis from scratch.

2 Motivating Example

We illustrate our approach using the running example of [9], a version of Peterson's mutual exclusion protocol.

Sketch. We use the term *sketch* for concurrent reactive programs with non-deterministic choices. Listing 1 shows a sketch for Peterson's protocol with processes P_1 and P_2.

Listing 1. Sketch of Peterson's mutual exclusion protocol. F=false, T=true.

```
 0                        turn:=F;  flag1:=F;  flag2:=F;
 1 cr1:=F;  wait1:=F;                     21 cr2:=F;  wait2:=F;
 2 do {  // Process P1:                   22 do {  // Process P2:
 3    flag1:=T;                           23    flag2:=T;
 4    turn:=T;                            24    turn:=F;
 5    while(?1,1) {}  // wait              25    while(?2,1) {}  // wait
 6    cr1:=T;                             26    cr2:=T;  // read:=?2,3
 7    cr1:=F;  flag1:=F;  wait1:=T;       27    cr2:=F;  flag2:=F;  wait2:=T;
 8    while(?1,2) {}  // local work        28    while(?2,2) {}  // local work
 9    wait1:=F;                           29    wait2:=F;
10 } while(T)                             30 } while(T)
```

Variable $\texttt{flag}i$ indicates that P_i wants to enter the critical section, and $\texttt{cr}i$ that P_i is in the critical section. The first $\texttt{while}$-loop waits for permission to enter the critical section, the second loop models some local computation. Question marks denote non-deterministic choices, and we want to synthesize expressions that replace question marks such that P_1 and P_2 never visit the critical section simultaneously.

Specification. The desired properties of both processes are that (1) whenever a process wants to enter the critical section, it will eventually enter it (starvation freedom), and (2) the two processes are never in the critical section simultaneously (mutual exclusion). In LTL[1], the specification is $\Phi_i = \mathsf{G}(\neg\texttt{cr1} \vee \neg\texttt{cr2}) \wedge \mathsf{G}(\texttt{flag}i \rightarrow \mathsf{F}\,\texttt{cr}i)$, for $i \in \{1,2\}$.

Failure of Classical Approaches. There are essentially two options for applying standard synthesis techniques. First, we may assume that both processes are cooperative, and synthesize all $?_{i,j}$ simultaneously. However, the resulting implementation of P_2 may only work for the computed implementation of P_1, i.e., changing P_1 may break P_2. For instance, the solution $?_{1,1} = \texttt{turn}$ & $\texttt{flag2}$, $?_{2,1} = \texttt{!turn}$ and $?_{1,2} = \texttt{F}$ satisfies the specification, but changing $?_{1,2}$ in P_1 to $\texttt{T}$ will make P_2 starve. Note that this is not just a hypothetical case; we got exactly this solution in our experiments. As a second option, we may assume that the processes are adversarial, i.e., P_2 must work for *any* P_1 and vice versa. However, under this assumption, the problem is unrealizable [9].

Success of Assume-Guarantee Synthesis (AGS) [9]. AGS fixes this dilemma by requiring that P_2 must work for *any* realization of P_1 that satisfies its local specification (and vice versa). An AGS solution for Listing 1 is $?_{1,1} = \texttt{turn}$ & $\texttt{flag2}$, $?_{2,1} = \texttt{!turn}$ & $\texttt{flag2}$ and $?_{i,2} = \texttt{F}$ for $i \in \{1,2\}$.

Added Advantage of AGS. If one process in an AGS solution is changed or extended, but still satisfies its original specification, then the other, unchanged process is guaranteed to remain correct as well. We illustrate this feature by extending P_2 with a new variable named $\texttt{read}$. It is updated in a yet unknown way (expressed by $?_{2,3}$) whenever P_2 enters the critical section in line 26 of Listing 1. Assume that we want to implement $?_{2,3}$ such that $\texttt{read}$ is true and false infinitely often. We take the solution from the previous paragraph and synthesize $?_{2,3}$ such that P_2 satisfies $\Phi_2 \wedge (\mathsf{G}\,\mathsf{F}\,\neg\texttt{read}) \wedge (\mathsf{G}\,\mathsf{F}\,\texttt{read})$, where Φ_2 is the original specification of P_2. The fact that the modified process still

---

[1] In case the reader is not familiar with LTL: G is a temporal operator meaning "in all time steps"; likewise F means "at some point in the future".

Listing 2. Result for Listing 1: turn is replaced by memory m in a clever way.

```
0                        flag1:=F; flag2:=F;  m:=F;
1  cr1:=F; wait1:=F;                          21  cr2:=F; wait2:=F;
2  do { // Process P1:                        22  do { // Process P2:
3    flag1:=T;                                23    flag2:=T;
4    while(!m) {} // wait                     24    while(m) {} // wait
5    cr1:=T;                                  25    cr2:=T;
6    cr1:=F; flag1:=F; wait1:=T;              26    cr2:=F; flag2:=F; wait2:=T;
7    while(input1()) // work                  27    while(input2()) // work
8      m:=F;                                  28      m:=T;
9    wait1:=F; m:=F;                          29    wait2:=F; m:=T;
10 } while(T)                                 30  } while(T)
```

satisfies Φ_2 implies that P_1 will still satisfy its original specification. We also notice that modular refinement saves overall synthesis time: our tool takes $19 + 55 = 74$ seconds to first synthesize the basic AGS solution for both processes and then refine P_2 in a second step to get the expected solution with $?_{2,3} = \neg read$, while direct synthesis of the refined specification for both processes requires 263 seconds.

Drawbacks of the Existing AGS Framework [9]. While AGS provides important improvements over classical approaches, it may still produce solutions like $?_{1,1} = $ turn $\wedge \neg$wait2 and $?_{2,1} = \neg$turn $\wedge \neg$wait1. However, wait2 is intended to be a *local* variable of P_2, and thus invisible for P_1. Solutions may also utilize modeling artifacts such as program counters, because AGS has no way to restrict the information visible to other processes. As a workaround, the existing approach [9] allows the user to define candidate implementations for each ?, and let the synthesis algorithm select one of the candidates. However, when implemented this way, a significant part of the problem needs to be solved by the user.

AGS with Partial Information. Our approach resolves this shortcoming by allowing the declaration of local variables. The user can write $f_{1,1}($turn, flag2$)$ instead of $?_{1,1}$ to express that the solution may only depend on turn and flag2. Including more variables of P_1 does not make sense for this example, because their value is fixed at the call site. When setting $?_{2,1} = f_{1,2}($turn, flag1$)$ (and $?_{i,2} = f_{i,2}()$), we get the solution proposed by Peterson: $?_{1,1} = $ turn $\wedge$ flag2 and $?_{2,1} = \neg$turn $\wedge$ flag1 (and $?_{i,2} = $ F). This is the only AGS solution with these dependency constraints.

AGS with Additional Memory and Optimization. Our approach can also introduce additional memory in form of new variables. As with existing variables, the user can specify which question mark may depend on the memory variables, and also which variables may be used to update the memory. For our example, this feature can be used to synthesize the entire synchronization from scratch, without using turn, flag1, and flag2. Suppose we remove turn, allow some memory m instead, and impose the following restrictions: $?_{1,1} = f_{1,1}($flag2, m$)$, $?_{2,1} = f_{2,1}($flag1, m$)$, $?_{i,2}$ is an uncontrollable input (to avoid overly simplistic solutions), and m can only be updated depending on the program counter and the old memory content. Our approach also supports cost functions over the result, and optimizes solutions iteratively. For our example, the user can assign costs for each memory update in order to obtain a simple solution with few memory updates. In this setup, our approach produces the solution presented in Listing 2. It is surprisingly simple: It requires only one bit of memory m, ignores both flags (although we did not force it to), and updates m only twice[2]. Our proof-of-concept implementation took only 74 seconds to find this solution.

3 Definitions

In this section we first define processes, refinement, schedulers, and specifications. Then we consider different versions of the co-synthesis problem, depending on *informedness* (partial or perfect), *cooperation* (cooperative, competitive, assume-guarantee), and *resources* (bounded or unbounded) of the players.

Variables, Valuations, Traces. Let X be a finite set of binary variables. A *valuation* on X is a function $v : X \to \mathbb{B}$ that assigns to each variable $x \in X$ a value $v(x) \in \mathbb{B}$. We write $\mathbb{B}^X$ for the set of valuations on X, and $u \circ v$ for the concatenation of valuations $u \in \mathbb{B}^X$ and $v \in \mathbb{B}^{X'}$ to a valuation in $\mathbb{B}^{X \cup X'}$. A *trace* on X is an infinite sequence $(v_0, v_1, \dots)$ of valuations on X. Given a valuation $v \in \mathbb{B}^X$ and a subset $X' \subseteq X$ of the variables, define $v\lceil_{X'}$ as the *restriction* of v to X'. Similarly, for a trace $\pi = (v_0, v_1, \dots)$ on X, write $\pi\lceil_{X'} = (v_0\lceil_{X'}, v_1\lceil_{X'}, \dots)$ for the restriction of π to the variables X'. The restriction operator extends naturally to sets of valuations and traces.

Processes and Refinement. We consider non-deterministic processes, where the non-determinism is modeled by variables that are not under the control of the process. We call these variables *input*, but they may also be internal variables with non-deterministic updates. For $i \in \{1, 2\}$, a *process* $P_i = (X_i, O_i, Y_i, \tau_i)$ consists of finite sets

- X_i of modifiable state variables,
- $O_i \subseteq X_{3-i}$ of observable (but not modifiable) state variables,
- Y_i of input variables,

and a *transition function* $\tau_i : \mathbb{B}^{X_i} \times \mathbb{B}^{O_i} \times \mathbb{B}^{Y_i} \to \mathbb{B}^{X_i}$. The transition function maps a current valuation of state and input variables to the next valuation for the state variables. We write $X = X_1 \cup X_2$ for the set of state variables of both processes, and similarly $Y = Y_1 \cup Y_2$ for the input variables. Note that some variables may be shared by both processes. Variables that are not shared between processes will be called *local* variables.

   We obtain a refinement of a process by resolving some of the non-determinism introduced by input variables, and possibly extending the sets of local state variables. Formally, let $C_i \subseteq Y_i$ be a set of *controllable variables*, let $Y_i' = Y_i \setminus C_i$, and let $X_i' \supseteq X_i$ be an extended (finite) set of state variables, with $X_1' \cap X_2' = X_1 \cap X_2$. Then a *refinement* of process $P_i = (X_i, O_i, Y_i, \tau_i)$ *with respect to* C_i is a process $P_i' = (X_i', O_i, Y_i', \tau_i')$ with a transition function $\tau_i' : \mathbb{B}^{X_i'} \times \mathbb{B}^{O_i} \times \mathbb{B}^{Y_i'} \to \mathbb{B}^{X_i'}$ such that for all $\overline{x} \in \mathbb{B}^{X_i'}, \overline{o} \in \mathbb{B}^{O_i}, \overline{y} \in \mathbb{B}^{Y_i'}$ there exists $\overline{c} \in \mathbb{B}^{C_i}$ with

$$\tau_i'(\overline{x}, \overline{o}, \overline{y})\lceil_{X_i} = \tau_i(\overline{x}\lceil_{X_i}, \overline{o}, \overline{y} \circ \overline{c}).$$

We write $P_i' \preceq P_i$ to denote that P_i' is a refinement of P_i.

---

[2] The memory m is updated whenever an input is read in line 7 or 27; we copied the update into both branches to increase readability.

Important Modeling Aspects. Local variables are used to model partial information: all decisions of a process need to be independent of the variables that are local to the other process. Furthermore, variables in $X_i' \setminus X_i$ are used to model additional memory that a process can use to store observed information. We say a refinement is *memoryless* if $X_i' = X_i$, and it is *b-bounded* if $|X_i' \setminus X_i| \leq b$.

Schedulers, Executions. A *scheduler* for processes P_1 and P_2 chooses at each computation step whether P_1 or P_2 can take a step to update its variables. Let $\mathcal{X}_1, \mathcal{X}_2$ be the sets of all variables (state, memory, input) of P_1 and P_2, respectively, and let $\mathcal{X} = \mathcal{X}_1 \cup \mathcal{X}_2$. Let furthermore $V = \mathbb{B}^{\mathcal{X}}$ be the set of global valuations. Then, the scheduler is a function sched $: V^* \to \{1, 2\}$ that maps a finite sequence of global valuations to a process index $i \in \{1, 2\}$. Scheduler sched is *fair* if for all traces $(v_0, v_1, \ldots) \in V^\omega$ it assigns infinitely many turns to both P_1 and P_2, i.e., there are infinitely many $j \geq 0$ such that sched$(v_0, \ldots, v_j) = 1$, and infinitely many $k \geq 0$ such that sched$(v_0, \ldots, v_k) = 2$.

Given two processes P_1, P_2, a scheduler sched, and a start valuation v_0, the set of possible *executions* of the parallel composition $P_1 \parallel P_2 \parallel$ sched is

$$[\![P_1 \parallel P_2 \parallel \text{sched}, v_0]\!] = \left\{ (v_0, v_1, \ldots) \in V^\omega \left| \begin{array}{l} \forall j \geq 0. \text{ sched}(v_0, v_1, \ldots, v_j) = i \\ \text{and } v_{j+1}\lceil_{(\mathcal{X} \setminus \mathcal{X}_i)} = v_j\lceil_{(\mathcal{X} \setminus \mathcal{X}_i)} \\ \text{and } v_{j+1}\lceil_{\mathcal{X}_i \setminus Y_i} \in \tau_i(v_j\lceil_{\mathcal{X}_i}) \end{array} \right. \right\}.$$

That is, at every turn the scheduler decides which of the processes makes a transition, and the state and memory variables are updated according to the transition function of that process. Note that during turns of process P_i, the values of local variables of the other process (in $\mathcal{X} \setminus \mathcal{X}_i$) remain unchanged.

Safety, GR(1), LTL. A specification Φ is a set of traces on $X \cup Y$. We consider ω-regular specifications, in particular the following fragments of LTL:[3]

- *safety properties* are of the form $\mathsf{G}\, B$, where B is a Boolean formula over variables in $X \cup Y$, defining a subset of valuations that are safe.
- *GR(1) properties* are of the form $\left(\bigwedge_i \mathsf{GF}\, L_e^i \right) \to \left(\bigwedge_j \mathsf{GF}\, L_s^j \right)$, where the L_e^i and L_s^j are Boolean formulas over $X \cup Y$.
- *LTL properties* are given as arbitrary LTL formulas over $X \cup Y$. They are a subset of the ω-regular properties.

Co-Synthesis. In all co-synthesis problems, the input to the problem is given as: two processes P_1, P_2 with $P_i = (X_i, O_i, Y_i, \tau_i)$, two sets C_1, C_2 of controllable variables with $C_i \subseteq Y_i$, two specifications Φ_1, Φ_2, and a start valuation $v_0 \in \mathbb{B}^{X \cup Y}$, where $Y = Y_1 \cup Y_2$.

Cooperative co-synthesis. The *cooperative co-synthesis problem* is to find out whether there exist two processes $P_1' \preceq P_1$ and $P_2' \preceq P_2$, and a valuation v_0' with $v_0'\lceil_{X \cup Y} = v_0$, such that for all fair schedulers sched we have

$$[\![P_1' \parallel P_2' \parallel \text{sched}, v_0']\!]\lceil_{X \cup Y} \subseteq \Phi_1 \wedge \Phi_2.$$

---

[3] For a definition of syntax and semantics of LTL, see e.g. [15].

Competitive co-synthesis. The *competitive co-synthesis problem* is to determine whether there exist two processes $P_1' \preceq P_1$ and $P_2' \preceq P_2$, and a valuation v_0' with $v_0' \lceil_{X \cup Y} = v_0$, such that for all fair schedulers sched we have

(i) $[\![P_1' \parallel P_2 \parallel \mathsf{sched}, v_0']\!] \lceil_{X \cup Y} \subseteq \Phi_1$, and
(ii) $[\![P_1 \parallel P_2' \parallel \mathsf{sched}, v_0']\!] \lceil_{X \cup Y} \subseteq \Phi_2$.

Assume-guarantee Synthesis. The *assume-guarantee synthesis (AGS)* problem is to determine whether there exist two processes $P_1' \preceq P_1$ and $P_2' \preceq P_2$, and a valuation v_0' with $v_0' \lceil_{X \cup Y} = v_0$, such that for all fair schedulers sched we have

(i) $[\![P_1' \parallel P_2 \parallel \mathsf{sched}, v_0']\!] \lceil_{X \cup Y} \subseteq \Phi_2 \to \Phi_1$,
(ii) $[\![P_1 \parallel P_2' \parallel \mathsf{sched}, v_0']\!] \lceil_{X \cup Y} \subseteq \Phi_1 \to \Phi_2$, and
(iii) $[\![P_1' \parallel P_2' \parallel \mathsf{sched}, v_0']\!] \lceil_{X \cup Y} \subseteq \Phi_1 \wedge \Phi_2$.

We refer the reader to [9] for more intuition and a detailed discussion of AGS.

Informedness and Boundedness. A synthesis problem is under *perfect information* if $X_i \cup O_i = X$ for $i \in \{1, 2\}$, and $Y_1 = Y_2$. That is, both processes have knowledge about all variables in the system. Otherwise, it is under *partial information*. A synthesis problem is *memoryless* (or b-bounded) if we additionally require that P_1', P_2' are memoryless (or b-bounded) refinements of P_1, P_2.

Optimization Criteria. Let $\mathcal{P}$ be the set of all processes. A cost function is a function $\mathsf{cost} : \mathcal{P} \times \mathcal{P} \to \mathbb{N}$ that assigns a cost to a tuple of processes. By requiring that the cost of solutions is minimal or below a certain threshold, we will use cost functions to optimize synthesis results.

Note on Robustness against Modifications. Suppose P_1', P_2' are the result of AGS on a given input, including specifications Φ_1, Φ_2. By the properties of AGS, this solution is robust against replacing one of the processes, say P_2, with a different solution: if a replacement P_2'' of P_2' satisfies Φ_2, then the overall system will still be correct. If we furthermore ensure that conditions (ii) and (iii) of AGS are satisfied by P_1' and P_2'', then this pair is again an AGS solution, i.e., we can go on and refine another process.

Co-synthesis of more than 2 Processes. The definitions above naturally extend to programs with more than 2 concurrent processes, cp. [13] for AGS with 3 processes.

4   Complexity and Decidability of AGS

We give an an overview of the complexity of AGS. The complexity results are with respect to the size of the input, where the input consists of the given non-deterministic state transition system and the specification formula (i.e., the size of the input is the size of the explicit state transition system and the length of the formula).

Theorem 1. *The complexity of AGS is given in the following table:*

	Bounded Memory		Unbounded Memory	
	Perfect Inf.	Partial Inf.	Perfect Inf.	Partial Inf.
Safety	P	NP-C	P	Undec
GR(1)	NP-C	NP-C	P	Undec
LTL	PSPACE-C	PSPACE-C	2EXP-C	Undec

Note that the complexity classes for memoryless AGS are the same as for AGS with bounded memory — the case of bounded memory reduces to the memoryless case, by considering a game that is larger by a constant factor: the given bound.

Also note that if we consider the results in the order given by the columns of the table, they form a non-monotonic pattern: (1) For safety objectives the complexity increases and then decreases (from PTIME to NP-complete to PTIME again); (2) for GR(1) objectives it remains NP-complete and finally decreases to PTIME; and (3) for LTL it remains PSPACE-complete and then increases to 2 EXPTIME-complete.

In the following, we give proof ideas for these complexity results. For formal definitions of three-player games, we refer the reader to [9].

Proof Ideas

First Column: Bounded Memory, Perfect Information

Safety: It was shown in [9] that AGS solutions can be obtained from the solutions of games with secure equilibria. It follows from the results of [10] that for games with safety objectives, the solution for secure equilibria reduces to solving games with safety and reachability objectives for which memoryless strategies suffice (i.e., memoryless strategies are as powerful as arbitrary strategies for safety objectives). It also follows from [10] that for safety objectives, games with secure equilibria can be solved in polynomial time.

GR(1): It follows from the results of [20] that even in a graph (not a game) the question whether there exists a memoryless strategy to visit two distinct states infinitely often is NP-hard (a reduction from directed subgraph homeomorphism). Since visiting two distinct states infinitely often is a conjunction of two Büchi objectives, which is a special case of GR(1) objectives, the lower bound follows. For the NP upper bound, the witness memoryless strategy can be guessed, and once a memoryless strategy is fixed, we have a graph, and the polynomial-time verification procedure is the polynomial-time algorithm for model checking graphs with GR(1) objectives [32].

LTL: In the special case of a game graph where every player-1 state has exactly one outgoing edge, the memoryless AGS problem is an LTL model checking problem, and thus the lower bound of LTL model checking [15] implies PSPACE-hardness. For the upper bound, we guess a memoryless strategy (as for GR(1)), and the verification problem is an LTL model checking question. Since LTL model checking is in PSPACE [15] and NPSPACE=PSPACE (by Savitch's theorem) [37,30], we obtain the desired result.

Second Column: Bounded Memory, Partial Information

Safety: The lower bound result was established in [12]. For the upper bound, again the witness is a memoryless strategy. Given the fixed strategy, we have a graph problem with safety and reachability objectives that can be solved in polynomial time (for the polynomial-time verification).

GR(1): The lower bound follows from the perfect-information case; for the upper bound, we can again guess and check a memoryless strategy.

LTL: Similar to the perfect information case, given above.

Third Column: Unbounded Memory, Perfect Information

Safety: As mentioned before, for AGS under perfect information and safety objectives, the memoryless and the general problem coincide, implying this result.

GR(1): It follows from results of [9,10] that solving AGS for perfect-information games requires solving games with implication conditions. Since games with implication of GR(1) objectives can be solved in polynomial time [21], the result follows.

LTL: The lower bound follows from standard LTL synthesis [33]. For the upper bound, AGS for perfect-information games requires solving implication games, and games with implication of LTL objectives can be solved in 2EXPTIME [33]. The desired result follows.

Fourth Column: Unbounded Memory, Partial Information

It was shown in [31] that three-player partial-observation games are undecidable, and it was also shown that the undecidability result holds for safety objectives too [11].

5 Algorithms for AGS

Given the undecidability of AGS in general, and its high complexity for most other cases, we propose a pragmatic approach that divides the general synthesis problem into a sequence of synthesis problems with a bounded amount of memory, and encodes the resulting problems into SMT formulas. Our encoding is inspired by the *Bounded Synthesis* approach [18], but supports synthesis from non-deterministic program sketches, as well as AGS problems. By iteratively deciding whether there exists an implementation for an increasing bound on the number of memory variables, we obtain a semi-decision procedure for AGS with partial information.

We first define the procedure for cooperative co-synthesis problems, and then show how to extend it to AGS problems.

5.1 SMT-Based Co-synthesis from Program Sketches

Consider a *cooperative* co-synthesis problem with inputs P_1 and P_2, defined as $P_i = (X_i, O_i, Y_i, \tau_i)$, two sets C_1, C_2 of controllable variables with $C_i \subseteq Y_i$, a specification $\Phi_1 \wedge \Phi_2$, and a start valuation $v_0 \in \mathbb{B}^{X \cup Y}$, where $Y = Y_1 \cup Y_2$.

In the following, we describe a set of SMT constraints such that a model represents refinements $P_1' \preceq P_1, P_2' \preceq P_2$ such that for all fair schedulers sched, we have $\llbracket P_1' \parallel P_2' \parallel \text{sched}, v_0 \rrbracket \subseteq \Phi_1 \wedge \Phi_2$. Assume we are given a bound $b \in \mathbb{N}$, and let Z_1, Z_2 be disjoint sets of additional memory variables with $|Z_i| = b$ for $i \in \{1, 2\}$.

Constraints on given Transition Functions. In the expected way, the transition functions τ_1 and τ_2 are declared as functions $\tau_i : \mathbb{B}^{X_i} \times \mathbb{B}^{O_i} \times \mathbb{B}^{Y_i} \rightarrow \mathbb{B}^{X_i}$, and directly encoded into SMT constraints by stating $\tau_i(\overline{x}, \overline{o}, \overline{y}) = \overline{x}'$ for every $\overline{x} \in \mathbb{B}^{X_i}, \overline{o} \in \mathbb{B}^{O_i}, \overline{y} \in \mathbb{B}^{Y_i}$, according to the given transition functions τ_1, τ_2.

Constraints for Interleaving Semantics, Fair Scheduling. To obtain an encoding for interleaving semantics, we add a scheduling variable s to both sets of inputs Y_1 and Y_2, and require that (i) $\tau_1(\overline{x}, \overline{o}, \overline{y}) = \overline{x}$ whenever $\overline{y}(s) = \text{false}$, and (ii) $\tau_2(\overline{x}, \overline{o}, \overline{y}) =$

$\overline{x}$ whenever $\overline{y}(s) = $ true. Fairness of the scheduler can then be encoded as the LTL formula $\mathsf{G}\,\mathsf{F}\,s \wedge \mathsf{G}\,\mathsf{F}\,\neg s$, abbreviated fair in the following.

Constraints on Resulting Strategy. Let $X_i' = X_i \cup Z_i$ be the extended state set, and $Y_i' = Y_i \setminus C_i$ the set of input variables of process P_i', reduced by its controllable variables. Then the resulting strategy of P_i' is represented by functions $\mu_i : \mathbb{B}^{X_i'} \times \mathbb{B}^{O_i} \times \mathbb{B}^{Y_i'} \to \mathbb{B}^{Z_i}$ to update the memory variables, and $f_i : \mathbb{B}^{X_i'} \times \mathbb{B}^{O_i} \times \mathbb{B}^{Y_i'} \to \mathbb{B}^{C_i}$ to resolve the non-determinism for controllable variables. Functions f_i and μ_i for $i \in \{1,2\}$ are constrained indirectly using constraints on an auxiliary annotation function that will ensure that the resulting strategy satisfies the specification $\Phi = (\text{fair} \to \Phi_1 \wedge \Phi_2)$. To obtain these constraints, first transform Φ into a universal co-Büchi automaton $\mathcal{U}_\Phi = (Q, q_0, \Delta, F)$, where

- Q is a set of states and $q_0 \in Q$ is the initial state,
- $\Delta \subseteq Q \times Q$ is a set of transitions, labeled with valuations $v \in \mathbb{B}^{X_1 \cup X_2 \cup Y_1 \cup Y_2}$, and
- $F \subseteq Q$ is a set of rejecting states.

The automaton is such that it rejects a trace if it violates Φ, i.e., if rejecting states are visited infinitely often. Accordingly, it accepts a concurrent program $(P_1 \parallel P_2 \parallel \text{sched}, v_0)$ if no trace in $[\![P_1 \parallel P_2 \parallel \text{sched}, v_0]\!]$ violates Φ. See [18] for more background.

Let $X' = X_1' \cup X_2'$. We constrain functions f_i and μ_i with respect to an additional annotation function $\lambda : Q \times \mathbb{B}^{X'} \to \mathbb{N} \cup \{\bot\}$. In the following, let $\tau_i'(\overline{x} \circ \overline{z}, \overline{o}, \overline{y})$ denote the combined update function for the original state variables and additional memory variables, explicitly written as

$$\tau_i(\overline{x} \circ \overline{z}, \overline{o}, \overline{y} \circ f_i(\overline{x}, \overline{z}, \overline{o}, \overline{y})) \circ \mu_i(\overline{x} \circ \overline{z}, \overline{o}, \overline{y}).$$

Similar to the original bounded synthesis encoding [18], we require that

$$\lambda(q_0, v_0 \restriction_{X'}) \in \mathbb{N}.$$

If (1) $(q, (\overline{x}_1, \overline{x}_2))$ is a composed state with $\lambda(q, (\overline{x}_1, \overline{x}_2)) \in \mathbb{N}$, (2) $\overline{y}_1 \in \mathbb{B}^{Y_1}, \overline{y}_2 \in \mathbb{B}^{Y_1}$ are inputs and $q' \in Q$ is a state of the automaton such that there is a transition $(q, q') \in \Delta$ that is labeled with $(\overline{y}_1, \overline{y}_2)$, and (3) q' is a non-rejecting state of $\mathcal{U}_\Phi$, then we require

$$\lambda(q', (\tau_1'(\overline{x}_1, \overline{o}_1, \overline{y}_1), \tau_2'(\overline{x}_2, \overline{o}_2, \overline{y}_2))) \geq \lambda(q, (\overline{x}_1, \overline{x}_2)),$$

where values of $\overline{o}_1, \overline{o}_2$ are determined by values of $\overline{x}_2$ and $\overline{x}_1$, respectively (and the subset of states of one process which is observable by the other process).

Finally, if conditions (1) and (2) above hold, and q' is rejecting in $\mathcal{U}_\Phi$, we require

$$\lambda(q', (\tau_1'(\overline{x}_1, \overline{o}_1, \overline{y}_1), \tau_2'(\overline{x}_2, \overline{o}_2, \overline{y}_2))) > \lambda(q, (\overline{x}_1, \overline{x}_2)).$$

Intuitively, these constraints ensure that in no execution starting from (q_0, v_0), the automaton will visit rejecting states infinitely often. Finkbeiner and Schewe [18] have shown that these constraints are satisfiable if and only if there exist implementations of P_1, P_2 with state variables X_1, X_2 that satisfy Φ. With our additional constraints on the original τ_1, τ_2 and the integration of the f_i and μ_i as new uninterpreted functions, they are satisfiable if there exist b-bounded refinements of P_1, P_2 (based on C_1, C_2) that satisfy Φ. An SMT solver can then be used to find interpretations of the f_i and μ_i, as well as the auxiliary annotation functions that witness correctness of the refinement.

Correctness. The proposed algorithm for bounded synthesis from program sketches is correct and will eventually find a solution if it exists:

Proposition 1. *Any model of the SMT constraints will represent a refinement of the program sketches such that their composition satisfies the specification.*

Proposition 2. *There exists a model of the SMT constraints if there exist b-bounded refinements $P_1' \preceq P_1, P_2' \preceq P_2$ that satisfy the specification.*

Proof ideas for correctness can be found in an extended version [3] of this paper.

Optimization of Solutions. Let cost : $\mathcal{P} \times \mathcal{P} \to \mathbb{N}$ be a user-defined cost function. We can synthesize an implementation $P_1', P_2' \in \mathcal{P}$ with *maximal cost c* by adding the constraint $\mathsf{cost}(P_1', P_2') \leq c$ (and a definition of the cost function), and we can *optimize* the solution by searching for implementations with incrementally smaller cost. For instance, a cost function could count the number of memory updates in order to optimize solutions for simplicity.

5.2   SMT-Based AGS

Based on the encoding from Section 5.1, this section presents an extension that solves the AGS problem. Recall that the inputs to AGS are two program sketches P_1, P_2 with $P_i = (X_i, O_i, Y_i, \tau_i)$, two sets C_1, C_2 of controllable variables with $C_i \subseteq Y_i$, two specifications Φ_1, Φ_2, and a start valuation $v_0 \in \mathbb{B}^{X \cup Y}$, where $Y = Y_1 \cup Y_2$. The goal is to obtain refinements $P_1' \preceq P_1$ and $P_2' \preceq P_2$ such that:

(i) $[\![P_1' \parallel P_2 \parallel \mathsf{sched}, v_0]\!] \subseteq (\mathsf{fair} \wedge \Phi_2 \to \Phi_1)$
(ii) $[\![P_1 \parallel P_2' \parallel \mathsf{sched}, v_0]\!] \subseteq (\mathsf{fair} \wedge \Phi_1 \to \Phi_2)$
(iii) $[\![P_1' \parallel P_2' \parallel \mathsf{sched}, v_0]\!] \subseteq (\mathsf{fair} \to \Phi_1 \wedge \Phi_2)$.

Using the approach presented above, we can encode each of the three items into a separate set of SMT constraints, using the same function symbols and variable identifiers in all three problems. In more detail, this means that we

1. encode (i), where we ask for a model of f_1 and μ_1 such that P_1' with τ_1' and P_2 with the given τ_2 satisfy the first property,
2. encode (ii), where we ask for a model of f_2 and μ_2 such that P_1 with the given τ_1 and P_2' with τ_2' satisfy the second property, and
3. encode (iii), where we ask for models of f_i and μ_i for $i \in \{1, 2\}$ such that P_1' and P_2' with τ_1' and τ_2' satisfy the third property.

Then, a solution for the conjunction of all of these constraints must be such that the resulting refinements of P_1 and P_2 satisfy all three properties simultaneously, and are thus a solution to the AGS problem. Moreover, a solution to the SMT problem exists if and only if there exists a solution to the AGS problem.

5.3   Extensions

While not covered by the definition of AGS in Section 3, we can easily extend our algorithm to the following cases:

1. If we allow the sets Z_1, Z_2 to be non-disjoint, then the synthesis algorithm can refine processes also by *adding shared variables*.
2. Also, our algorithms can easily be adapted to AGS with *more than 2 processes*, as defined in [13].

6   Experiments

We implemented[4] our approach as an extension to BoSY, the bounded synthesis backend of the parameterized synthesis tool PARTY [26]. The user defines the sketch in SMT-LIB format with a special naming scheme. The specification is given in LTL. The amount of memory is defined using an integer constant M, which is increased until a solution is found. To optimize solutions, the user can assert that some arbitrarily computed cost must be lower than some constant Opt. Our tool will find the minimal value of Opt such that the problem is still realizable. Our tool can also run cooperative co-synthesis and verify existing solutions. Due to space constraints, we can only sketch our experiments here. Details can be found in the extended version [3] of this paper.

For a simple **peer-to-peer file sharing protocol** [19], we synthesize conditions that define when a process uploads or downloads data. The specification requires that all processes download infinitely often, but a process can only download if the other one uploads. Without AGS, we obtain a brittle solution: if one process is changed to upload and download simultaneously, the other process will starve, i.e., will not download any more. The reason is that cooperative co-synthesis can produce solutions where the correctness of one process relies on a concrete realization of the other processes. With AGS, this problem does not exist. Synthesis takes only one second for this example.

Our next experiment is performed on a **double buffering** protocol, taken from [40]. There are two buffers. While one is read by P_1, the other one is written by P_2. Then, the buffers are swapped. We synthesize waiting conditions such that the two processes can never access the same buffer location simultaneously. The example is parameterized by the size N of the buffers. Table 1 lists the synthesis times for increasing N. We use bitvectors to encode the array indices, and observe that the computation time mostly depends on the bitwidth. This explains the jumps whenever N reaches the next power of two.

Table 1. Synthesis times [sec] for increasing N.

N	1	2	3	4	5	6	7	8	15
AGS	1	5	5	54	51	49	47	1097	877
non-AGS	1	4	4	38	35	32	31	636	447

Cooperative co-synthesis is only slightly faster than AGS on this example.

Finally, we use our tool to **synthesize atomic sections in** a simplified version of **the i2c Linux kernel driver** in order to fix a real bug[5]. This example has been taken

---

[4] Available at http://www.iaik.tugraz.at/content/research/
design_verification/others
[5] See http://kernel.opensuse.org/cgit/kernel/commit/
?id=7a7d6d9c5fcd4b674da38e814cfc0724c67731b2

from [6]. We synthesize two functions f_1 and f_2 that map the program counter value of the respective process to true or false. The value true means that the process cannot be interrupted at this point in the program, i.e., the two adjacent instructions are executed atomically. We also assign costs to active atomic sections, and let our tool minimize the total costs. A meaningful solution with minimal costs is computed in 54 seconds.

7   Related Work

Reactive Synthesis. Automatic synthesis of reactive programs from formal specifications, as defined by Church [14], is usually reduced either to games on finite graphs [5], or to the emptiness problem of automata over infinite trees [35]. Pnueli and Rosner [33] proposed synthesis from LTL specifications, and showed its 2EXPTIME complexity based on a doubly exponential translation of the specification into a tree automaton. We use extensions of the game-based approach (see below) to obtain new complexity results for AGS, while our implementation uses an encoding based on tree automata [18] that avoids one exponential blowup compared to the standard approaches [27].

We consider the synthesis of concurrent or distributed reactive systems with partial information, which has been shown to be undecidable in general [34], even for simple safety fragments of temporal logics [38]. Several approaches for distributed synthesis have been proposed, either by restricting the specifications to be local to each process [28], by restricting the communication graph to pipelines and similar structures [17], or by falling back to semi-decision procedures that will eventually find an implementation if one exists, but in general cannot detect unrealizability of a specification [18]. Our synthesis approach is based on the latter, and extends it with synthesis from program sketches [39], as well as the assume-guarantee paradigm [9].

Graph Games. Graph games provide a mathematical foundation to study reactive synthesis problems [14,5,22]. For the traditional perfect-information setting, the complexity of solving games has been deeply studied; e.g., for reachability and safety objectives the problem is PTIME-complete [23,1]; for GR(1) the problem can be solved in polynomial time [32]; and for LTL the problem is 2EXPTIME-complete [33]. For two player partial-information games with reachability objectives, EXPTIME-completeness was established in [36], and symbolic algorithms and strategy construction procedures were studied in [8,2]. However, in the setting of multi-player partial-observation games, the problem is undecidable even for three players [31] and for safety objectives as well [11]. While most of the previous work considers only the general problem and its complexity, the complexity distinction we study for memoryless strategies, and the practical SMT-based approach to solve these games has not been studied before.

Equilibria Notions in Games. In the setting of two-player games for reactive synthesis, the goals of the two players are complementary (i.e., games are zero-sum). For multi-player games there are various notions of equilibria studied for graph games, such as Nash equilibria [29] for graph games that inspired notions of rational synthesis [19]; refinements of Nash equilibria such as secure equilibria [10] that inspired assume-guarantee synthesis (AGS) [9], and doomsday equilibria [7]. An alternative to Nash equilibria and its refinements are approaches based on iterated admissibility [4].

Among the various equilibria and synthesis notions, the most relevant one for reactive synthesis is AGS, which is applicable for synthesis of mutual-exclusion protocols [9] as well as for security protocols [13]. The previous work on AGS is severely restricted by perfect information, whereas we consider the problem under the more general framework of partial information, the need of which was already advocated in applications in [24].

8   Conclusion

Assume-Guarantee Synthesis (AGS) is particularly suitable for concurrent reactive systems, because none of the synthesized processes relies on the concrete realization of the others. This feature makes a synthesized solution robust against changes in single processes. A major limitation of previous work on AGS was that it assumed perfect information about all processes, which implies that synthesized implementations may use local variables of other processes. In this paper, we resolved this shortcoming by (1) defining AGS in a partial information setting, (2) proving new complexity results for various sub-classes of the problem, (3) presenting a pragmatic synthesis algorithm based on the existing notion of bounded synthesis to solve the problem, (4) providing the first implementation of AGS, which also supports the optimization of solutions with respect to user-defined cost functions, and (5) demonstrating its usefulness by resolving sketches of several concurrent protocols. We believe our contributions can form an important step towards a mixed imperative/declarative programming paradigm for concurrent programs, where the user writes sequential code and the concurrency aspects are taken care of automatically.

In the future, we plan to work on issues such as scalability and usability of our prototype, explore applications for security protocols as mentioned in [24], and research restricted cases where the AGS problem with partial information is decidable.

References

1. Beeri, C.: On the membership problem for functional and multivalued dependencies in relational databases. ACM Trans. on Database Systems 5, 241–259 (1980)
2. Berwanger, D., Chatterjee, K., De Wulf, M., Doyen, L., Henzinger, T.A.: Strategy construction for parity games with imperfect information. I& C 208(10), 1206–1220 (2010)
3. Bloem, R., Chatterjee, K., Jacobs, S., Könighofer, R.: Assume-guarantee synthesis for concurrent reactive programs with partial information. CoRR, abs/1411.4604 (2014)
4. Brenguier, R., Raskin, J.F., Sassolas, M.: The complexity of admissibility in omega-regular games. In: CSL-LICS, ACM (2014)
5. Büchi, J.R., Landweber, L.H.: Solving sequential conditions by finite-state strategies. Transactions of the AMS 138, 295–311 (1969)
6. Černý, P., Henzinger, T.A., Radhakrishna, A., Ryzhyk, L., Tarrach, T.: Efficient synthesis for concurrency by semantics-preserving transformations. In: Sharygina, N., Veith, H. (eds.) CAV 2013. LNCS, vol. 8044, pp. 951–967. Springer, Heidelberg (2013)
7. Chatterjee, K., Doyen, L., Filiot, E., Raskin, J.-F.: Doomsday equilibria for omega-regular games. In: McMillan, K.L., Rival, X. (eds.) VMCAI 2014. LNCS, vol. 8318, pp. 78–97. Springer, Heidelberg (2014)

8. Chatterjee, K., Doyen, L., Henzinger, T.A., Raskin, J.-F.: Algorithms for omega-regular games of incomplete information. In: Logical Methods in Computer Science, vol. 3(3:4) (2007)
9. Chatterjee, K., Henzinger, T.A.: Assume-guarantee synthesis. In: Grumberg, O., Huth, M. (eds.) TACAS 2007. LNCS, vol. 4424, pp. 261–275. Springer, Heidelberg (2007)
10. Chatterjee, K., Henzinger, T.A., Jurdzinski, M.: Games with secure equilibria. Theor. Comput. Sci. 365(1-2), 67–82 (2006)
11. Chatterjee, K., Henzinger, T.A., Otop, J., Pavlogiannis, A.: Distributed synthesis for LTL fragments. In: FMCAD, pp. 18–25. IEEE (2013)
12. Chatterjee, K., Kößler, A., Schmid, U.: Automated analysis of real-time scheduling using graph games. In: HSCC, pp. 163–172. ACM (2013)
13. Chatterjee, K., Raman, V.: Assume-guarantee synthesis for digital contract signing. Formal Asp. Comput. 26(4), 825–859 (2014)
14. Church, A.: Logic, arithmetic, and automata. In: Proceedings of the International Congress of Mathematicians, pp. 23–35 (1962)
15. Clarke, E.M., Grumberg, O., Peled, D.: Model checking. MIT Press (2001)
16. Finkbeiner, B., Jacobs, S.: Lazy synthesis. In: Kuncak, V., Rybalchenko, A. (eds.) VMCAI 2012. LNCS, vol. 7148, pp. 219–234. Springer, Heidelberg (2012)
17. Finkbeiner, B., Schewe, S.: Uniform distributed synthesis. In: LICS, IEEE (2005)
18. Finkbeiner, B., Schewe, S.: Bounded synthesis. STTT 15(5-6), 519–539 (2013)
19. Fisman, D., Kupferman, O., Lustig, Y.: Rational synthesis. In: Esparza, J., Majumdar, R. (eds.) TACAS 2010. LNCS, vol. 6015, pp. 190–204. Springer, Heidelberg (2010)
20. Fortune, S., Hopcroft, J.E., Wyllie, J.: The directed subgraph homeomorphism problem. Theor. Comput. Sci, 111–121 (1980)
21. Grädel, E., Thomas, W., Wilke, T. (eds.): Automata, Logics, and Infinite Games. LNCS, vol. 2500. Springer, Heidelberg (2002)
22. Gurevich, Y., Harrington, L.: Trees, automata, and games. In: STOC, pp. 60–65. ACM (1982)
23. Immerman, N.: Number of quantifiers is better than number of tape cells. J. Comput. Syst. Sci. 22, 384–406 (1981)
24. Jamroga, W., Mauw, S., Melissen, M.: Fairness in non-repudiation protocols. In: Meadows, C., Fernandez-Gago, C. (eds.) STM 2011. LNCS, vol. 7170, pp. 122–139. Springer, Heidelberg (2012)
25. Jobstmann, B., Staber, S., Griesmayer, A., Bloem, R.: Finding and fixing faults. J. Comput. Syst. Sci. 78(2), 441–460 (2012)
26. Khalimov, A., Jacobs, S., Bloem, R.: PARTY parameterized synthesis of token rings. In: Sharygina, N., Veith, H. (eds.) CAV 2013. LNCS, vol. 8044, pp. 928–933. Springer, Heidelberg (2013)
27. Kupferman, O., Vardi, M.Y.: Safraless decision procedures. In: FOCS (2005)
28. Madhusudan, P., Thiagarajan, P.S.: Distributed controller synthesis for local specifications. In: Orejas, F., Spirakis, P.G., van Leeuwen, J. (eds.) ICALP 2001. LNCS, vol. 2076, pp. 396–407. Springer, Heidelberg (2001)
29. Nash, J.F.: Equilibrium points in n-person games. Proceedings of the National Academny of Sciences USA 36, 48–49 (1950)
30. Papadimitriou, C.H.: Computational complexity. Addison-Wesley (1994)
31. Peterson, G.L., Reif, J.H.: Multiple-person alternation. In: FOCS. IEEE (1979)
32. Piterman, N., Pnueli, A., Sa'ar, Y.: Synthesis of reactive(1) designs. In: Emerson, E.A., Namjoshi, K.S. (eds.) VMCAI 2006. LNCS, vol. 3855, pp. 364–380. Springer, Heidelberg (2006)
33. Pnueli, A., Rosner, R.: On the synthesis of a reactive module. In: POPL (1989)
34. Pnueli, A., Rosner, R.: Distributed reactive systems are hard to synthesize. In: FOCS, pp. 746–757. IEEE (1990)

35. Rabin, M.O.: Automata on Infinite Objects and Churchs Problem. American Mathematical Society (1972)
36. Reif, J.H.: The complexity of two-player games of incomplete information. J. Comput. Syst. Sci. 29(2), 274–301 (1984)
37. Savitch, W.J.: Relationships between nondeterministic and deterministic tape complexities. JCSS 4(2), 177–192 (1970)
38. Schewe, S.: Distributed synthesis is simply undecidable. IPL 114(4), 203–207 (2014)
39. Solar-Lezama, A.: Program sketching. STTT 15(5-6), 475–495 (2013)
40. Vechev, M.T., Yahav, E., Yorsh, G.: Abstraction-guided synthesis of synchronization. In: POPL, pp. 327–338. ACM (2010)

Shield Synthesis:

Runtime Enforcement for Reactive Systems*

Roderick Bloem[1], Bettina Könighofer[1], Robert Könighofer[1], and Chao Wang[2]

[1] IAIK, Graz University of Technology, Austria
[2] Department of ECE, Virginia Tech, Blacksburg, VA 24061, USA

Abstract. Scalability issues may prevent users from verifying critical properties of a complex hardware design. In this situation, we propose to synthesize a "safety shield" that is attached to the design to enforce the properties at run time. *Shield synthesis* can succeed where model checking and reactive synthesis fail, because it only considers a small set of critical properties, as opposed to the complex design, or the complete specification in the case of reactive synthesis. The shield continuously monitors the input/output of the design and corrects its erroneous output only if necessary, and as little as possible, so other non-critical properties are likely to be retained. Although runtime enforcement has been studied in other domains such as action systems, reactive systems pose unique challenges where the shield must act without delay. We thus present the first shield synthesis solution for reactive hardware systems and report our experimental results.

1 Introduction

Model checking [10,18] can formally verify that a design satisfies a temporal logic specification. Yet, due to scalability problems, it may be infeasible to prove all critical properties of a complex design. Reactive synthesis [17,4] is even more ambitious since it aims to generate a provably correct design from a given specification. In addition to scalability problems, reactive synthesis has the drawback of requiring a complete specification, which describes every aspect of the desired design. However, writing a complete specification can sometimes be as hard as implementing the design itself.

We propose *shield synthesis* as a way to complement model checking and reactive synthesis. Our goal is to enforce a small set of critical properties at runtime even if these properties may occasionally be violated by the design. Imagine a complex design and a set of properties that cannot be proved due to scalability issues or other reasons (e.g., third-party IP cores). In this setting, we are in good faith that the properties hold but we need to have certainty. We would like to automatically construct a component, called the *shield*, and attach it to the design as illustrated in Fig. 1. The shield monitors the input/output of the design and corrects the erroneous output values instantaneously, but only if necessary and as little as possible.

* This work was supported in part by the Austrian Science Fund (FWF) through the research network RiSE (S11406-N23) and by the European Commission through project STANCE (317753). Chao Wang was supported by the National Science Foundation grant CNS-1128903.

C. Baier and C. Tinelli (Eds.): TACAS 2015, LNCS 9035, pp. 533–548, 2015.
DOI: 10.1007/978-3-662-46681-0_51

The shield ensures both *correctness* and *minimum interference*. By correctness, we mean that the properties must be satisfied by the combined system, even if they are occasionally violated by the design. By minimum interference, we mean that the output of the shield deviates from the output of the design

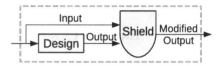

Fig. 1. Attaching a safety shield

only if necessary, and the deviation is kept minimum. The latter requirement is important because we want the design to retain other (non-critical) behaviors that are not captured by the given set of properties. We argue that shield synthesis can succeed even if model checking and reactive synthesis fail due to scalability issues, because it has to enforce only a small set of critical properties, regardless of the implementation details of a complex design.

This paper makes two contributions. First, we define a general framework for solving the shield synthesis problem for reactive hardware systems. Second, we propose a new synthesis method, which automatically constructs a shield from a set of safety properties. To minimize deviations of the shield from the original design, we propose a new notion called *k-stabilization*: When the design arrives at a state where a property violation becomes unavoidable for some possible future inputs, the shield is allowed to deviate for at most k consecutive steps. If a second violation happens during the k-step recovery phase, the shield enters a *fail-safe* mode where it only enforces correctness, but no longer minimizes the deviation. We show that the k-stabilizing shield synthesis problem can be reduced to *safety games* [15]. Following this approach, we present a proof-of-concept implementation and give the first experimental results.

Our work on shield synthesis can complement model checking by enforcing any property that cannot be formally proved on a complex design. There can be more applications. For example, we may not trust third-party IP components in our system, but in this case, model checking cannot be used because we do not have the source code. Nevertheless, a shield can enforce critical interface assumptions of these IP components at run time. Shields may also be used to simplify certification. Instead of certifying a complex design against critical requirements, we can synthesize a shield to enforce them, regardless of the behavior of the design. Then, we only need to certify this shield, or the synthesis procedure, against the critical requirements. Finally, shield synthesis is a promising new direction for synthesis in general, because it has the strengths of reactive synthesis while avoiding its weaknesses — the set of critical properties can be small and relatively easy to specify — which implies scalability and usability.

Related Work. Shield synthesis is different from recent works on reactive synthesis [17,4,12], which revisited Church's problem [9,8,19] on constructing correct systems from logical specifications. Although there are some works on runtime enforcement of properties in other domains [20,14,13], they are based on assumptions that do not work for reactive hardware systems. Specifically, Schneider [20] proposed a method that simply halts a program in case of a violation. Ligatti et al. [14] used edit automata to suppress or insert actions, and Falcone et al. [13] proposed to buffer actions and dump them once the execution is shown to be safe. None of these approaches is appropriate for reactive systems where the shield must act upon erroneous outputs on-the-fly, i.e., without delay and without knowing what future inputs/outputs are. In particular, our shield cannot insert or delete time steps, and cannot halt in the case of a violation.

Methodologically, our new synthesis algorithm builds upon the existing work on synthesis of robust systems [3], which aims to generate a complete design that satisfies as many properties of a specification as possible if assumptions are violated. However, our goal is to synthesize a shield component S, which can be attached to any design D, to ensure that the combined system $(S \circ D)$ satisfies a given set of critical properties. Our method aims at minimizing the ratio between shield deviations and property violations by the design, but achieves it by solving pure safety games. Furthermore, the synthesis method in [3] uses heuristics and user input to decide from which state to continue monitoring the environmental behavior, whereas we use a subset construction to capture all possibilities to avoid unjust verdicts by the shield. We use the notion of k-stabilization to quantify the shield deviation from the design, which has similarities to Ehlers and Topcu's notion of k-resilience in robust synthesis [12] for GR(1) specifications [4]. However, the context of our work is different, and our k-stabilization limits the length of the recovery period instead of tolerating bursts of up to k glitches.

Outline. The remainder of this paper is organized as follows. We illustrate the technical challenges and our solutions in Section 2 using an example. Then, we establish notation in Section 3. We formalize the problem in a general framework for shield synthesis in Section 4, and present our new method in Section 5. We present our experimental results in Section 6 and, finally, give our conclusions in Section 7.

2   Motivation

In this section, we illustrate the challenges associated with shield synthesis and then briefly explain our solution using an example. We start with a traffic light controller that handles a single crossing between a highway and a farm road. There are red (r) or green (g) lights for both roads. An input signal, denoted $p \in \{0, 1\}$, indicates whether an emergency vehicle is approaching. The controller takes p as input and returns h,f as output. Here, $h \in \{r, g\}$ and $f \in \{r, g\}$ are the lights for highway and farm road, respectively. Although the traffic light controller interface is simple, the actual implementation can be complex. For example, the controller may have to be synchronized with other traffic lights, and it can have input sensors for cars, buttons for pedestrians, and sophisticated algorithms to optimize traffic throughput and latency based on all sensors, the time of the day, and even the weather. As a result, the actual design may become too complex to be formally verified. Nevertheless, we want to ensure that a handful of safety critical properties are satisfied with certainty. Below are three example properties:

1. The output gg — meaning that both roads have green lights — is never allowed.
2. If an emergency vehicle is approaching (p = 1), the output must be rr.
3. The output cannot change from gr to rg, or vice versa, without passing rr.

We want to synthesize a safety shield that can be attached to any implementation of this traffic light controller, to enforce these properties at run time.

In a first exercise, we only consider enforcing Properties 1 and 2. These are simple invariance properties without any temporal aspects. Such properties can be represented by a truth table as shown in Fig. 2 (left). We use 0 to encode r, and 1 to encode g. Forbidden behavior is marked in bold red. The shield must ensure both correctness and minimum interference. That is, it should only change the output for red entries. In particular, it should not ignore the design and hard-wire the output to rr. When p = 1 but the output is not rr, the shield must correct the output to rr. When p = 0 but the output is gg, the shield must turn the original output gg into either rg, gr, or rr. Assume that gr is chosen. As illustrated in Fig. 2 (right), we can construct the transition functions $h' = \neg p \wedge h$ and $f' = \neg p \wedge \neg h \wedge f$, as well as the shield circuit accordingly.

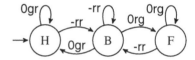

p	h	f	h'	f'
0	0	0	0	0
0	0	1	0	1
0	1	0	1	0
0	1	1	1	0
1	0	0	0	0
1	0	1	0	0
1	1	0	0	0
1	1	1	0	0

$$h' = \neg p \wedge h$$
$$f' = \neg p \wedge \neg h \wedge f$$

Fig. 2. Enforcing Properties 1 and 2

Next, we consider enforcing Properties 1–3 together. Property 3 brings in a temporal aspect, so a simple truth table does not suffice any more. Instead, we express the properties by an automaton, which is shown in Fig. 3. Edges are labeled by values of phf, where p ∈ {0, 1} is the controller's input and h, f are outputs for highway and farm road. There are three non-error states: H denotes the state where highway has the green light, F denotes the state where farm road has the green light, and B denotes the state where both have red lights. There is also an error state, which is not shown. Missing edges lead to this error state, denoting forbidden situa-

Fig. 3. Traffic light specification

tions, e.g., 1gr is not allowed in state H. Although the automaton still is not a complete specification, the corresponding shield can prevent catastrophic failures. By automatically generating a small shield as shown in Fig. 1, our approach has the advantage of combining the functionality and performance of the aggressively optimized implementation with guaranteed safety.

While the shield for Property 1 and 2 could be realized by purely combinational logic, this is not possible for the specification in Fig. 3. The reason is the temporal aspect brought in by Property 3. For example, if we are in state F and observe 0gg, which is not allowed, the shield has to make a correction in the output signals to avoid the violation. There are two options: changing the output from gg to either rg or rr. However, this fix may result in the next state being either B or F. The question is, without knowing what the future inputs/outputs are, how do we decide *from which state the shield should continue to monitor* the behavior of the design in order to best detect and correct future violations? If the shield makes a wrong guess now, it may lead to a suboptimal implementation that causes unnecessarily large deviation in the future.

To solve this problem, we adopt the most conservative approach. That is, we assume that the design $\mathcal{D}$ meant to give one of the allowed outputs, so either rr or rg. Thus, our shield continues to monitor the design from both F and B. Technically, this is achieved by a form of subset construction (see Sec. 5.2), which tracks all possibilities for now, and then gradually refines its knowledge with future observations. For example, if the next observation is Ogr, we assume that the design $\mathcal{D}$ meant rr earlier, and so it must be in B and traverse to H. If it were in F, we could only have explained Ogr by assuming a second violation, which is less optimistic than we would like to be. In this work, we assume that a second violation occurs only if an observation is inconsistent with *all* states that it could possibly be in. For example, if the next observation is not Ogr but 1rg, which is neither allowed in F nor in B, we know that a second violation occurs. Yet, after observing 1rg, we can be sure that we have reached the state B, because starting from both F and B, with input p = 1, the only allowed output is rr, and the next state is always B. In this sense, our construction implements an "innocent until proved guilty" philosophy, which is key to satisfy the *minimum interference* requirement.

To bound the deviation of the shield when a property violation becomes unavoidable, we require the shield to deviate for at most k consecutive steps after the initial violation. We shall formalize this notion of k-*stabilization* in subsequent sections and present our synthesis algorithm. For the safety specification in Fig. 3, our method would reduce the shield synthesis problem into a set of *safety games*, which are then solved using standard techniques (cf. [15]). We shall present the synthesis results in Section 6.

3   Preliminaries

We denote the Boolean domain by $\mathbb{B} = \{\text{true}, \text{false}\}$, denote the set of natural numbers by $\mathbb{N}$, and abbreviate $\mathbb{N} \cup \{\infty\}$ by $\mathbb{N}^\infty$. We consider a reactive system with a finite set $I = \{i_1, \ldots, i_m\}$ of Boolean inputs and a finite set $O = \{o_1, \ldots, o_n\}$ of Boolean outputs. The input alphabet is $\Sigma_I = 2^I$, the output alphabet is $\Sigma_O = 2^O$, and $\Sigma = \Sigma_I \times \Sigma_O$. The set of finite (infinite) words over Σ is denoted by Σ^* (Σ^ω), and $\Sigma^{*,\omega} = \Sigma^* \cup \Sigma^\omega$. We will also refer to words as *(execution) traces*. We write $|\overline{\sigma}|$ for the length of a trace $\overline{\sigma} \in \Sigma^{*,\omega}$. For $\overline{\sigma_I} = x_0 x_1 \ldots \in \Sigma_I^\omega$ and $\overline{\sigma_O} = y_0 y_1 \ldots \in \Sigma_O^\omega$, we write $\overline{\sigma_I} \| \overline{\sigma_O}$ for the composition $(x_0, y_0)(x_1, y_1) \ldots \in \Sigma^\omega$. A set $L \subseteq \Sigma^\omega$ of infinite words is called a *language*. We denote the set of all languages as $\mathcal{L} = 2^{\Sigma^\omega}$.

Reactive Systems. A *reactive system* $\mathcal{D} = (Q, q_0, \Sigma_I, \Sigma_O, \delta, \lambda)$ is a Mealy machine, where Q is a finite set of states, $q_0 \in Q$ is the initial state, $\delta : Q \times \Sigma_I \to Q$ is a complete transition function, and $\lambda : Q \times \Sigma_I \to \Sigma_O$ is a complete output function. Given the input trace $\overline{\sigma_I} = x_0 x_1 \ldots \in \Sigma_I^\omega$, the system $\mathcal{D}$ produces the output trace $\overline{\sigma_O} = \mathcal{D}(\overline{\sigma_I}) = \lambda(q_0, x_0)\lambda(q_1, x_1) \ldots \in \Sigma_O^\omega$, where $q_{i+1} = \delta(q_i, x_i)$ for all $i \geq 0$. The set of words produced by $\mathcal{D}$ is denoted $L(\mathcal{D}) = \{\overline{\sigma_I} \| \overline{\sigma_O} \in \Sigma^\omega \mid \mathcal{D}(\overline{\sigma_I}) = \overline{\sigma_O}\}$. We also refer to a reactive system $\mathcal{D}$ as a *(hardware) design*.

Let $\mathcal{D} = (Q, q_0, \Sigma_I, \Sigma_O, \delta, \lambda)$ and $\mathcal{D}' = (Q', q_0', \Sigma, \Sigma_O, \delta', \lambda')$ be reactive systems. Their serial composition is constructed by feeding the input and output of $\mathcal{D}$ to $\mathcal{D}'$ as input. We use $\mathcal{D} \circ \mathcal{D}'$ to denote such a composition $(\hat{Q}, \hat{q_0}, \Sigma_I, \Sigma_O, \hat{\delta}, \hat{\lambda})$, where $\hat{Q} = Q \times Q'$, $\hat{q_0} = (q_0, q_0')$, $\hat{\delta}((q, q'), \sigma_I) = (\delta(q, \sigma_I), \delta'(q', (\sigma_I, \lambda(q, \sigma_I))))$, and $\hat{\lambda}((q, q'), \sigma_I) = \lambda'(q', (\sigma_I, \lambda(q, \sigma_I)))$.

Specifications. A *specification* φ defines a set $L(\varphi) \subseteq \Sigma^\omega$ of allowed traces. A specification φ is *realizable* if there exists a design $\mathcal{D}$ that realizes it. $\mathcal{D}$ *realizes* φ, written $\mathcal{D} \models \varphi$, iff $L(\mathcal{D}) \subseteq L(\varphi)$. We assume that φ is a (potentially incomplete) set of *properties* $\{\varphi_1, \ldots, \varphi_l\}$ such that $L(\varphi) = \bigcap_i L(\varphi_i)$, and a design satisfies φ iff it satisfies all its properties. In this work, we are concerned with a *safety* specification φ^s, which is represented by an automaton $\varphi^s = (Q, q_0, \Sigma, \delta, F)$, where $\Sigma = \Sigma_I \cup \Sigma_O$, $\delta : Q \times \Sigma \to Q$, and $F \subseteq Q$ is a set of safe states. The *run* induced by trace $\overline{\sigma} = \sigma_0 \sigma_1 \ldots \in \Sigma^\omega$ is the state sequence $\overline{q} = q_0 q_1 \ldots$ such that $q_{i+1} = \delta(q_i, \sigma_i)$. Trace $\overline{\sigma}$ (of a design $\mathcal{D}$) *satisfies* φ^s if the induced run visits only the safe states, i.e., $\forall i \geq 0 . q_i \in F$. The *language* $L(\varphi^s)$ is the set of all traces satisfying φ^s.

Games. A (2-player, alternating) *game* is a tuple $\mathcal{G} = (G, g_0, \Sigma_I, \Sigma_O, \delta, \text{win})$, where G is a finite set of game states, $g_0 \in G$ is the initial state, $\delta : G \times \Sigma_I \times \Sigma_O \to G$ is a complete transition function, and win $: G^\omega \to \mathbb{B}$ is a winning condition. The game is played by two players: the system and the environment. In every state $g \in G$ (starting with g_0), the environment first chooses an input letter $\sigma_I \in \Sigma_I$, and then the system chooses some output letter $\sigma_O \in \Sigma_O$. This defines the next state $g' = \delta(g, \sigma_I, \sigma_O)$, and so on. The resulting (infinite) sequence $\overline{g} = g_0 g_1 \ldots$ of game states is called a *play*. A play is *won* by the system iff win$(\overline{g})$ is true.

A *safety game* defines win via a set $F^g \subseteq G$ of safe states: win$(g_0 g_1 \ldots)$ is true iff $\forall i \geq 0 . g_i \in F^g$, i.e., if only safe states are visited. A (memoryless) *strategy* for the system is a function $\rho : G \times \Sigma_I \to \Sigma_O$. A strategy is *winning* for the system if all plays $\overline{g}$ that can be constructed when defining the outputs using the strategy satisfy win$(\overline{g})$. The *winning region* is the set of states from which a winning strategy exists. We will use safety games to synthesize a shield, which implements the winning strategy in a new reactive system $\mathcal{S} = (G, q_0, \Sigma_I, \Sigma_O, \delta', \rho)$ with $\delta'(g, \sigma_I) = \delta(g, \sigma_I, \rho(g, \sigma_I))$.

4   The Shield Synthesis Framework

We define a general framework for shield synthesis in this section before presenting a concrete realization of this framework in the next section.

Definition 1 (Shield). *Let $\mathcal{D} = (Q, q_0, \Sigma_I, \Sigma_O, \delta, \lambda)$ be a design, φ be a set of properties, and $\varphi^v \subseteq \varphi$ be a valid subset such that $\mathcal{D} \models \varphi^v$. A reactive system $\mathcal{S} = (Q', q_0', \Sigma, \Sigma_O, \delta', \lambda')$ is a shield of $\mathcal{D}$ with respect to $(\varphi \setminus \varphi^v)$ iff $(\mathcal{D} \circ \mathcal{S}) \models \varphi$.*

Here, the design is known to satisfy $\varphi^v \subseteq \varphi$. Furthermore, we are in good faith that $\mathcal{D}$ also satisfies $\varphi \setminus \varphi^v$, but it is not guaranteed. We synthesize $\mathcal{S}$, which reads the input and output of $\mathcal{D}$ while correcting its erroneous output as illustrated in Fig. 1.

Definition 2 (Generic Shield). *Given a set $\varphi = \varphi^v \cup (\varphi \setminus \varphi^v)$ of properties. A reactive system $\mathcal{S}$ is a generic shield iff it is a shield of any design $\mathcal{D}$ such that $\mathcal{D} \models \varphi^v$.*

A generic shield must work for any design $\mathcal{D} \models \varphi^v$. Hence, the shield synthesis procedure does not need to consider the design implementation. This is a realistic assumption in many applications, e.g., when the design $\mathcal{D}$ comes from the third party. Synthesis of a generic shield also has a scalability advantage since the design $\mathcal{D}$, even if available, can be too complex to analyze, whereas φ often contains only a small set of critical properties. Finally, a generic shield is more robust against design changes, making it attractive for safety certification. In this work, we focus on the synthesis of generic shields.

Although the shield is defined with respect to φ (more specifically, $\varphi \setminus \varphi^v$), we must refrain from ignoring the design completely while feeding the output with a replacement circuit. This is not desirable because the original design may satisfy additional (non-critical) properties that are not specified in φ but should be retained as much as possible. In general, we want the shield to deviate from the design *only if necessary, and as little as possible*. For example, if $\mathcal{D}$ does not violate φ, the shield $\mathcal{S}$ should keep the output of $\mathcal{D}$ intact. This rationale is captured by our next definitions.

Definition 3 (Output Trace Distance Function). *An output trace distance function (OTDF) is a function $d^\sigma : \Sigma_O^{*,\omega} \times \Sigma_O^{*,\omega} \to \mathbb{N}^\infty$ such that*

1. $d^\sigma(\overline{\sigma_O}, \overline{\sigma_O}') = 0$ *when* $\overline{\sigma_O} = \overline{\sigma_O}'$*;*
2. $d^\sigma(\overline{\sigma_O}\sigma_O, \overline{\sigma_O}'\sigma_O') = d^\sigma(\overline{\sigma_O}, \overline{\sigma_O}')$ *when* $\sigma_O = \sigma_O'$*, and*
3. $d^\sigma(\overline{\sigma_O}\sigma_O, \overline{\sigma_O}'\sigma_O') > d^\sigma(\overline{\sigma_O}, \overline{\sigma_O}')$ *when* $\sigma_O \neq \sigma_O'$*.*

An OTDF measures the difference between two output sequences (of the design $\mathcal{D}$ and the shield $\mathcal{S}$). The definition requires monotonicity with respect to prefixes: when comparing trace prefixes with increasing length, the distance can only become larger.

Definition 4 (Language Distance Function). *A language distance function (LDF) is a function $d^L : \mathcal{L} \times \Sigma^\omega \to \mathbb{N}^\infty$ such that $\forall L \in \mathcal{L}, \overline{\sigma} \in \Sigma^\omega . \overline{\sigma} \in L \to d^L(L, \overline{\sigma}) = 0$.*

An LDF measures the severity of specification violations by the design by mapping a language (of φ) and a trace (of $\mathcal{D}$) to a number. Given a trace $\overline{\sigma} \in \Sigma^\omega$, its distance to $L(\varphi)$ is 0 if $\overline{\sigma}$ satisfies φ. Greater distances indicate more severe specification violations. An OTDF can (but does not have to) be defined via an LDF by taking the minimum output distance between $\overline{\sigma} = (\overline{\sigma_I} || \overline{\sigma_O})$ and any trace in the language L:

$$d^L(L, \overline{\sigma_I} || \overline{\sigma_O}) = \begin{cases} \min\limits_{\overline{\sigma_I} || \overline{\sigma_O}' \in L} d^\sigma(\overline{\sigma_O}', \overline{\sigma_O}) & \text{if } \exists \overline{\sigma_O}' \in \Sigma_O^\omega . (\overline{\sigma_I} || \overline{\sigma_O}') \in L \\ 0 & \text{otherwise.} \end{cases}$$

The input trace is ignored in d^σ because the design $\mathcal{D}$ can only influence the output. If no alternative output trace makes the word part of the language, the distance is set to 0 to express that it cannot be the design's fault. If L is defined by a realizable specification φ, this cannot happen anyway, since $\forall \overline{\sigma_I} \in \Sigma_I^\omega . \exists \overline{\sigma_O} \in \Sigma_O^\omega . (\overline{\sigma_I} || \overline{\sigma_O}) \in L(\varphi)$ is a necessary condition for the realizability of φ.

Definition 5 (Optimal Generic Shield). *Let φ be a specification, $\varphi^v \subseteq \varphi$ be the valid subset, d^σ be an OTDF, and d^L be an LDF. A reactive system $\mathcal{S}$ is an* optimal generic shield *if and only if for all $\overline{\sigma_I} \in \Sigma_I^\omega$ and $\overline{\sigma_O} \in \Sigma_O^\omega$,*

$$(\overline{\sigma_I} || \overline{\sigma_O}) \in L(\varphi^v) \to \left(d^L\left(L(\varphi), \overline{\sigma_I} || \mathcal{S}(\overline{\sigma_I} || \overline{\sigma_O}) \right) = 0 \wedge \right. \tag{1}$$

$$\left. d^\sigma(\overline{\sigma_O}, \mathcal{S}(\overline{\sigma_I} || \overline{\sigma_O})) \leq d^L(L(\varphi), \overline{\sigma_I} || \overline{\sigma_O}) \right). \tag{2}$$

The implication means that we only consider traces that satisfy φ^v since $\mathcal{D} \models \varphi^v$ is assumed. This can be exploited by synthesis algorithms to find a more succinct shield. Part (1) of the implied formula ensures correctness: $\mathcal{D} \circ \mathcal{S}$ must satisfy φ.[1] Part (2) ensures minimum interference: "small" violations result in "small" deviations. Def. 5 is designed to be flexible: Different notions of minimum interference can be realized with appropriate definitions of d^σ and d^L. One realization will be presented in Section 5.

---

[1] Applying d^L instead of "$\subseteq L(\varphi)$" adds flexibility: the user can define d^L in such a way that $d^L(L, \overline{\sigma}) = 0$ even if $\overline{\sigma} \notin L$ to allow such traces as well.

Proposition 1. *An optimal generic shield S cannot deviate from the design's output before a specification violation by the design $\mathcal{D}$ is unavoidable.*

Proof. If there has been a deviation $d^\sigma(\overline{\sigma_O}, S(\overline{\sigma_I}\|\overline{\sigma_O})) \neq 0$ on the finite input prefix $\overline{\sigma}$, but this prefix can be extended into an infinite trace $\overline{\sigma}'$ such that $d^L(L(\varphi), \overline{\sigma}') = 0$, meaning that a violation is avoidable, then Part (2) of Def. 5 is violated because of the (prefix-)monotonicity of d^σ (the deviation can only increase when the trace is extended), and the fact that $d^\sigma \leq d^L$ is false if $d^\sigma \neq 0$. □

5   Our Shield Synthesis Method

In this section, we present a concrete realization of the shield synthesis framework by defining OTDF and LDF in a practical way. We call the resulting shield a *k-stabilizing* generic shield. While our framework works for arbitrary specifications, our realization assumes safety specifications.

5.1 k-Stabilizing Generic Shields

A k-stabilizing generic shield is an optimal generic shield according to Def. 5, together with the following restrictions. When a property violation by the design $\mathcal{D}$ becomes unavoidable (in the worst case over future inputs), the shield S is allowed to deviate from the design's outputs for at most k consecutive time steps, including the current step. Only after these k steps, the next violation is tolerated. This is based on the assumption that specification violations are rare events. If a second violation happens within the k-step recovery period, the shield enters a *fail-safe* mode, where it enforces the critical properties, but stops minimizing the deviations. More formally, a k-stabilizing generic shield requires the following configuration of the OTDF and LDF functions:

1. The LDF $d^L(L(\varphi), \overline{\sigma})$ is defined as follows: Given a trace $\overline{\sigma} \in \Sigma^\omega$, its distance to $L(\varphi)$ is 0 initially, and increased to ∞ when the shield enters the *fail-safe* mode.
2. The OTDF function $d^\sigma(\overline{\sigma_O}, \overline{\sigma_O}')$ returns 0 initially, and is set to ∞ if $\sigma_{O_i} \neq \sigma_{O_i}'$ outside of a k-step recovery period.

To indicate whether the shield is in the fail-safe mode or a recovery period, we add a counter $c \in \{0, \ldots, k\}$. Initially, c is 0. Whenever there is a property violation by the design, c is set to k in the next step. In each of the subsequent steps, c decrements until it reaches 0 again. The shield can deviate if the next state has $c > 0$. If a second violation happens when $c > 1$, then the shield enters the fail-safe mode. A 1-stabilizing shield can only deviate in the time step of the violation, and can never enter the fail-safe mode.

5.2   Synthesizing k-Stabilizing Generic Shields

The flow of our synthesis procedure is illustrated in Fig. 4. Let $\varphi = \{\varphi_1, \ldots, \varphi_l\}$ be the critical safety specification, where each φ_i is represented as an automaton $\varphi_i = (Q_i, q_{0,i}, \Sigma, \delta_i, F_i)$. The synchronous product of these automata is again a safety automaton. We use three product automata: $\mathcal{Q} = (Q, q_0, \Sigma, \delta, F)$ is the product of all

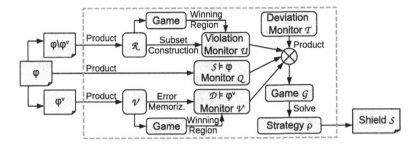

Fig. 4. Outline of our k-stabilizing generic shield synthesis procedure

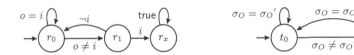

Fig. 5. The safety automaton $\mathcal{R}$ **Fig. 6.** The deviation monitor $\mathcal{T}$

properties in φ; $\mathcal{V} = (V, v_0, \Sigma, \delta^v, F^v)$ is the product of properties in $\varphi^v \subseteq \varphi$; and $\mathcal{R} = (R, r_0, \Sigma, \delta^r, F^r)$ is the product of properties in $\varphi \setminus \varphi^v$. Starting from these automata, our shield synthesis procedure consists of five steps.

Step 1. Constructing the Violation Monitor $\mathcal{U}$: From $\mathcal{R}$, which represents $\varphi \setminus \varphi^v$, we build $\mathcal{U} = (U, u_0, \Sigma, \delta^u)$ to monitor property violations by the design. The goal is to identify the latest point in time from which a specification violation can still be corrected with a deviation by the shield. This constitutes the start of the recovery period.

The first phase of this construction (Step 1-a) is to consider the automaton $\mathcal{R} = (R, r_0, \Sigma, \delta^r, F^r)$ as a *safety game* and compute its winning region $W^r \subseteq F^r$. The meaning of W^r is such that every reactive system $\mathcal{D} \models (\varphi \setminus \varphi^v)$ must produce outputs in such a way that the next state of $\mathcal{R}$ stays in W^r. Only when the next state of $\mathcal{R}$ would be outside of W^r, our shield will be allowed to interfere.

Example 1. Consider the safety automaton $\mathcal{R}$ in Fig. 5, where i is an input, o is an output, and r_x is unsafe. The winning region is $W = \{r_0\}$ because from r_1 the input i controls whether r_x is visited. The shield must be allowed to deviate from the original transition $r_0 \to r_1$ if $o \neq i$. In r_1 it is too late because visiting an unsafe state cannot be avoided any more, given that the shield can modify the value of o but not i. □

The second phase (Step 1-b) is to expand the state space from R to 2^R via a subset construction. The rationale behind it is as follows. If the design makes a mistake (i.e., picks outputs such that $\mathcal{R}$ enters a state $r \notin W^r$ from which the specification cannot be enforced), we have to "guess" what the design actually meant to do in order to find a state from which we can continue monitoring its behavior. We follow a generous approach in order not to treat the design unfairly: we consider all output letters that would have avoided falling out of W^r, and continue monitoring the design behavior from all the corresponding successor states in parallel. Thus, $\mathcal{U}$ is essentially a subset construction of $\mathcal{R}$, where a state $u \in U$ of $\mathcal{U}$ represents a set of states in $\mathcal{R}$.

The third phase (Step 1-c) is to expand the state space of $\mathcal{U}$ by adding a counter $c \in \{0, \ldots, k\}$ as described in the previous subsection, and adding a special fail-safe state u_E. The final violation monitor is $\mathcal{U} = (U, u_0, \Sigma, \delta^u)$, where $U = (2^R \times \{0, \ldots, k\}) \cup u_E$ is the set of states, $u_0 = (\{r_0\}, 0)$ is the initial state, Σ is the set of input letters, and δ^u is the next-state function, which obeys the following rules:

1. $\delta^u(u_E, \sigma) = u_E$ (meaning that u_E is a trap state),
2. $\delta^u((u, c), \sigma) = u_E$ if $c > 1$ and $\forall r \in u : \delta^r(r, \sigma) \notin W^r$,
3. $\delta^u((u, c), (\sigma_I, \sigma_O)) = (\{r' \in W^r \mid \exists r \in u, \sigma_O' \in \Sigma_O . \delta^r(r, (\sigma_I, \sigma_O')) = r'\}, k)$
   if $c \le 1$ and $\forall r \in u . \delta^r(r, (\sigma_I, \sigma_O)) \notin W^r$, and
4. $\delta^u((u, c), \sigma) = (\{r' \in W^r \mid \exists r \in u . \delta^r(r, \sigma) = r'\}, \mathsf{dec}(c))$ if $\exists r \in u . \delta^r(r, \sigma) \in W^r$,
   where $\mathsf{dec}(0) = 0$ and $\mathsf{dec}(c) = c - 1$ if $c > 0$.

Our construction sets $c = k$ whenever the design leaves the winning region, and not when it enters an unsafe state. Hence, the shield $\mathcal{S}$ can take remedial action as soon as the "the crime is committed", before the damage is detected, which would have been too late to correct the erroneous outputs of the design.

Example 2. We illustrate the construction of $\mathcal{U}$ using the specification from Fig. 3, which is a safety automaton if we make all missing edges point to an (additional) unsafe state. The winning region consists of all safe states, i.e., $W^r = \{H, B, F\}$. The resulting violation monitor is $\mathcal{U} = (\{H, B, F, HB, FB, HFB\} \times \{0, \ldots, k\} \cup u_E, (H, 0), \Sigma, \delta^u)$, where δ^u is illustrated in Fig. 7 as a table (the graph would be messy), which lists the next state for all possible present states as well as inputs and outputs by the design. Lightning bolts denote specification

	1g-	1rg	-rr	0gg	0gr	0rg
H	B↯	B↯	B	HB↯	H	HB↯
B	B↯	B↯	B	HFB↯	H	F
F	B↯	B↯	B	FB↯	FB↯	F
HB	B↯	B↯	B	HFB↯	H	F
FB	B↯	B↯	B	HFB↯	H	F
HFB	B↯	B↯	B	HFB↯	H	F

Fig. 7. δ^u for the spec from Fig. 3

violations. The update of the counter c, which is not included in Fig. 7, is as follows: whenever the design commits a violation (indicated by lightning) and $c \le 1$, then c is set to k. If $c > 1$ at the violation, the next state is u_E. Otherwise, c is decremented. □

Step 2. Constructing the Validity Monitor $\mathcal{V}'$: From $\mathcal{V} = (V, v_0, \Sigma, \delta^v, F^v)$, which represents φ^v, we build an automaton $\mathcal{V}'$ to monitor the validity of φ^v by solving a safety game on $\mathcal{V}$ and computing the winning region $W^v \subseteq F^v$. We will use W^v to increase the freedom for the shield: since we assume that $\mathcal{D} \models \varphi^v$, we are only interested in the cases where $\mathcal{V}$ never leaves W^v. If it does, our shield is allowed to behave arbitrarily from that point on. We extend the state space from V to V' by adding a bit to memorize if we have left the winning region W^v. Hence, the validity monitor is defined as $\mathcal{V}' = (V', v_0', \Sigma, \delta^{v'}, F^{v'})$, where $V' = \mathbb{B} \times V$ is the set of states, $v_0' = \{\text{false}, v_0\}$ is the initial state, $\delta^{v'}((b, v), \sigma) = (b', \delta^v(v, \sigma))$, where $b' = \text{true}$ if $b = \text{true}$ or $\delta^v(v, \sigma) \notin W^v$, and $b' = \text{false}$ otherwise, and $F^{v'} = \{(b, v) \in V' \mid b = \text{false}\}$.

Step 3. Constructing the Deviation Monitor $\mathcal{T}$: We build $\mathcal{T} = (T, t_0, \Sigma_O \times \Sigma_O, \delta^t)$ to monitor the deviation of the shield's output from the design's output. Here, $T = \{t_0, t_1\}$ and $\delta^t(t, (\sigma_O, \sigma_O')) = t_0$ iff $\sigma_O = \sigma_O'$. That is, $\mathcal{T}$ will be in t_1 if there was a deviation in the last time step, and in t_0 otherwise. This deviation monitor is shown in Fig. 6.

Step 4. Constructing the Safety Game $\mathcal{G}$: Given the monitors $\mathcal{U}, \mathcal{V}', \mathcal{T}$ and the automaton $\mathcal{Q}$, which represents φ, we construct a safety game $\mathcal{G} = (G, g_0, \Sigma_I \times \Sigma_O, \Sigma_O, \delta^g, F^g)$, which is the synchronous product of $\mathcal{U}, \mathcal{T}, \mathcal{V}'$ and $\mathcal{Q}$, such that $G = U \times T \times V' \times Q$ is the state space, $g_0 = (u_0, t_0, v'_0, q_0)$ is the initial state, $\Sigma_I \times \Sigma_O$ is the input of the shield, Σ_O is the output of the shield, δ^g is the next-state function, and F^g is the set of safe states, such that $\delta^g\big((u, t, v', q), (\sigma_I, \sigma_O), \sigma_O'\big) =$

$$\big(\delta^u(u, (\sigma_I, \sigma_O)), \delta^t(t, (\sigma_O, \sigma_O')), \delta^{v'}(v', (\sigma_I, \sigma_O)), \delta^q(q, (\sigma_I, \sigma_O'))\big),$$

and $F^g = \{(u, t, v', q) \in G \mid v' \notin F^{v'} \vee ((q \in F^q) \wedge (u = (w, 0) \rightarrow t = t_0))\}$.

In the definition of F^g, the term $v' \notin F^{v'}$ reflects our assumption that $\mathcal{D} \models \varphi^v$. If this assumption is violated, then $v' \notin F^{v'}$ will hold forever, and our shield is allowed to behave arbitrarily. This is exploited by our synthesis algorithm to find a more succinct shield by treating such states as *don't cares*. If $v' \in F^{v'}$, we require that $q \in F^q$, i.e., it is a safe state in $\mathcal{Q}$, which ensures that the shield output will satisfy φ. The last term ensures that the shield can only deviate in the k-step recovery period, i.e., while $c \neq 0$ in $\mathcal{U}$. If the design makes a second mistake within this period, $\mathcal{U}$ enters u_E and arbitrary deviations are allowed. Yet, the shield will still enforce φ in this mode (unless $\mathcal{D} \not\models \varphi^v$).

Step 5. Solving the Safety Game: We use standard algorithms for safety games (cf. e.g. [15]) to compute a winning strategy ρ for $\mathcal{G}$. Then, we implement this strategy in a new reactive system $\mathcal{S} = (G, g_0, \Sigma, \Sigma_O, \delta, \rho)$ with $\delta(g, \sigma) = \delta^g(g, \sigma, \rho(g, \sigma))$. $\mathcal{S}$ is the k-stabilizing generic shield. If no winning strategy exists, we increase k and try again. In our experiments, we start with $k = 1$ and then increase k by 1 at a time.

Theorem 1. *Let $\varphi = \{\varphi_1, \ldots, \varphi_l\}$ be a set of critical safety properties $\varphi_i = (Q_i, q_{0i}, \Sigma, \delta_i, F_i)$, and let $\varphi^v \subseteq \varphi$ be a subset of valid properties. Let $|V| = \prod_{\varphi_i \in \varphi^v} |Q_i|$ be the cardinality of the product of the state spaces of all properties of φ^v. Similarly, let $|R| = \prod_{\varphi_i \notin \varphi^v} |Q_i|$. A k-stabilizing generic shield with respect to $\varphi \setminus \varphi^v$ and φ^v can be synthesized in $O(k^2 \cdot 2^{2|R|} \cdot |V|^4 \cdot |R|^2)$ time (if one exists).*

Proof. Safety games can be solved in $O(x + y)$ time [15], where x is the number of states and y is the number of edges in the game graph. Our safety game $\mathcal{G}$ has at most $x = ((k + 1) \cdot 2^{|R|} + 1) \cdot (2 \cdot |V|) \cdot 2 \cdot (|R| \cdot |V|)$ states, so at most $y = x^2$ edges. □

Variations. The assumption that no second violation occurs within the recovery period increases the chances that a k-stabilizing shield exists. However, it can also be dropped with a slight modification of $\mathcal{U}$ in Step 1: if a violation is committed and $c > 1$, we set c to k instead of visiting u_E. This ensures that synthesized shields will handle violations within a recovery period normally. The assumption that the design meant to give one of the allowed outputs if a violation occurs can also be relaxed. Instead of continuing to monitor the behavior from the allowed next states, we can just continue from the set of all states, i.e., traverse to state (R, k) in $\mathcal{U}$. The assumption that $\mathcal{D} \models \varphi^v$, i.e., the design satisfies some properties, is also optional. By removing $\mathcal{V}$ and $\mathcal{V}'$, the construction can be simplified at the cost of less implementation freedom for the shield.

By solving a Büchi game (which is potentially more expensive) instead of a safety game, we can also eliminate the need to increase k iteratively until a solution is found. This is outlined in the appendix of an extended version [5] of this paper.

6 Experiments

We have implemented the k-stabilizing shield synthesis procedure in a proof-of-concept tool. Our tool takes as input a set of safety properties, defined as automata in a simple textual representation. The product of these automata, as well as the subset construction in Step 1 of our procedure is done on an explicit representation. The remaining steps are performed symbolically using Binary Decision Diagrams (BDDs). Synthesis starts with $k = 1$ and increments k in case of unrealizability until a user-defined bound is hit. Our tool is written in Python and uses CUDD [1] as the BDD library. Our tool can output shields in Verilog and SMV. It can also use the model checker VIS [6] to verify that the synthesized shield is correct.

We have conducted three sets of experiments, where the benchmarks are (1) selected properties for a traffic light controller from the VIS [6] manual, (2) selected properties for an ARM AMBA bus arbiter [4], and (3) selected properties from LTL specification patterns [11]. None of these examples makes use of φ^v, i.e., φ^v is always empty. The source code of our proof-of-concept synthesis tool as well as the input files and instructions to reproduce our experiments are available for download².

Traffic Light Controller Example. We used the safety specification in Fig. 3 as input, for which our tool generated a 1-stabilizing shield within a fraction of a second. The shield has 6 latches and 95 (2-input) multiplexers, which is then reduced by ABC [7] to 5 latches and 41 (2-input) AIG gates. However, most of the states are either unreachable or equivalent. The behavior of the shield is illustrated in Fig. 8. Edges are labeled with the inputs of the shield.

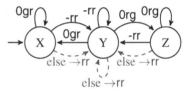

Fig. 8. Traffic light shield

Red dashed edges denote situations where the output of the shield is different from its inputs. The modified output is written after the arrow. For all non-dashed edges, the input is just copied to the output. Clearly, the states X, Y, and Z correspond to H, B, and F in Fig. 3.

We also tested the synthesized shield using the traffic light controller of [16], which also appeared in the user manual of VIS [6]. This controller has one input (car) from a car sensor on the farm road, and uses a timer to control the length of the different phases. We set the "short" timer period to one tick and the "long" period to two ticks.

The resulting behavior without preemption is visualized in Fig. 9, where nodes are labeled with names and outputs, and edges are labeled with conditions on the inputs. The red dashed arrow represents a subtle bug we introduced: if the last car on the farm road exits the crossing at a rare point in time, then the controller switches from rg to gr without passing rr. This bug only shows up in very special situations, so it can go unnoticed

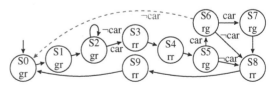

Fig. 9. Traffic light implementation

---

² http://www.iaik.tugraz.at/content/research/design_verification/others/

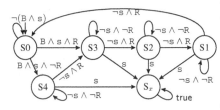

Fig. 10. Guarantee 3 from [4]

Step	3	4	5	6	7	8	9	10	11	12
State in Fig. 10	S0	S4	S3	S2	S1	S0	S0	S0	S0	...
State in Design	S0	S3	S2	S1	S0	S3	S2	S1	S0	...
B	1	1	1	1	1	1	1	1	1	...
R	0	1	1	1	1	1	1	1	1	...
s from Design	1	0	0	0	1½	0	0	0	0	...
s from Shield	1	0	0	0	0	0	0	0	0	...

Fig. 11. Shield execution results

easily. Preemption is implemented by modifying both directions to r without changing the state if $p = 1$. We introduced another bug here as well: only the highway is switched to r if $p = 1$, whereas the farm road is not. This bug can easily go unnoticed as well, because the farm road is mostly red anyway. The following trace illustrates how the synthesized shield handles these errors:

Step	0	1	2	3	4	5	6	7	8	9	10	11	12	13	14	15
State in Fig. 3 (safety spec.)	H	H	B	H	B	B	F	F	F,B	H	H	B	B	B	B	...
State in Fig. 9 (buggy design)	S0	S1	S2	S3	S4	S5	S6	S0	S1	S2	S3	S4	S5	S8	S9	...
State in Fig. 8 (shield)	X	X	Y	X	Y	Y	Z	Z	Y	X	X	Y	Y	Y	Y	...
Input (p,car)	00	11	01	01	01	01	00	00	00	01	01	00	10	00	00	...
Design output	gr	rr	gr	rr	rr	rg	rg	gr⁄	gr	gr	rr	rr	rg⁄	rr	rr	...
Shield output	gr	rr	gr	rr	rr	rg	rg	rr	gr	gr	rr	rr	rr	rr	rr	...

The first bug strikes at Step 7. The shield corrects it with output rr. A 2-stabilizing shield could also have chosen rg, but this would have made a second deviation necessary in the next step. Our shield is 1-stabilizing, i.e., it deviates only at the step of the violation. After this correction, the shield continues monitoring the design from both state F and state B of Fig. 3, as explained earlier, to detect future errors. Yet, this uncertainty is resolved in the next step. The second bug in Step 12 is simpler: outputting rr is the only way to correct it, and the next state in Fig. 3 must be B.

When only considering the properties 1 and 2 from Section 2, the synthesized shield has no latches and three AIG gates after optimization with ABC [7].

ARM AMBA Bus Arbiter Example. We used properties of an ARM AMBA bus arbiter [4] as input to our shield synthesis tool. Due to page limit, we only present the result on one example property, and then present the performance results for other properties. The property that we enforced was Guarantee 3 from the specification of [4], which says that if a length-four locked burst access starts, no other access can start until the end of this burst. The safety automaton is shown in Fig. 10, where B, s and R are short for hmastlock ∧ HBURST=BURST4, start, and HREADY, respectively. Lower case signal names are outputs, and upper-cases are inputs of the arbiter. S_x is unsafe. S0 is the idle state waiting for a burst to start (B ∧ s). The burst is over if input R has been true 4 times. State Si, where $i = 1, 2, 3, 4$, means that R must be true for i more times. The counting includes the time step where the burst starts, i.e., where S0 is left. Outside of S0, s is required to be false.

Our tool generated a 1-stabilizing shield within a fraction of a second. The shield has 8 latches and 142 (2-input) multiplexers, which is then reduced by ABC [7] to 4 latches and 77 AIG gates. We verified it against an arbiter implementation for 2 bus masters, where we introduced the following bug: the design does not check R when the burst starts, but behaves as if R was true. This corresponds to removing the transition from S0 to S4 in Fig. 10, and going to S3 instead. An execution trace is shown in Fig. 11. The first burst starts with s = true in Step 3. R is false, so the design counts wrongly. The erroneous output shows up in Step 7, where the design starts the next burst, which is forbidden, and thus blocked by the shield. The design now thinks that it has started a burst, so it keeps s = false until R is true 4 times. Actually, this burst start has been blocked by the shield, so the shield waits in S0. Only after the suppressed burst is over, the components are in sync again, and the next burst can start normally.

To evaluate the performance of our tool, we ran a stress test with increasingly larger sets of safety properties for the ARM AMBA bus arbiter in [4]. Table 1 summarizes the results. The columns list the number of states, inputs, and outputs, the minimum k for which a k-stabilizing shield exists, and the synthesis time in seconds. All experiments were performed on a machine with an Intel i5-3320M CPU@2.6 GHz, 8 GB RAM, and a 64-bit Linux. Time-outs (G2+3+4,

Table 1. Performance for AMBA [4]

Property	$|Q|$	$|I|$	$|O|$	k	Time [sec]
G1	3	1	1	1	0.1
G1+2	5	3	3	1	0.1
G1+2+3	12	3	3	1	0.1
G1+2+4	8	3	6	2	7.8
G1+3+4	15	3	5	2	65
G2+3+4	17	3	6	?	>3600
G1+2+3+5	18	3	4	2	242
G1+2+4+5	12	3	7	?	>3600
G1+3+4+5	23	3	6	?	>3600

G1+2+4+5 and G1+3+4+5) occurred only when the number of states and input/output signals grew large. However, this should not be a concern in practice because the set of critical properties of a system is usually much smaller, e.g., often consisting of invariance properties with a single state.

LTL Specification Patterns. Dwyer et al. [11] studied the frequently used LTL specification patterns in verification. As an exercise, we applied our tool to the first 10 properties from their list [2] and summarized the results in Table 2. For a property containing liveness aspects (e.g., something must happen eventually), we imposed a bound on the reaction time to obtain the safety (bounded-liveness) property. The bound on the reaction time is shown in Column 3. The last four columns list the number of states in the

Table 2. Synthesis results for the LTL patterns [11]

Nr.	Property	b	$|Q|$	Time [sec]	#Latches	#AIG-Gates
1	$G \neg p$	-	2	0.01	0	0
2	$F r \to (\neg p \, U \, r)$	-	4	0.34	2	6
3	$G(q \to G(\neg p))$	-	3	0.34	2	6
4	$G((q \wedge \neg r \wedge F r) \to (\neg p \, U \, r))$	-	4	0.34	1	9
5	$G(q \wedge \neg r \to (\neg p \, W \, r))$	-	3	0.01	2	14
6	$F p$	0	3	0.34	1	1
6	$F p$	256	259	33	18	134
7	$\neg r \, W \, (p \wedge \neg r)$	-	3	0.05	3	11
8	$G(\neg q) \vee F(q \wedge F p)$	0	3	0.04	3	11
8	$G(\neg q) \vee F(q \wedge F p)$	4	7	0.04	6	79
8	$G(\neg q) \vee F(q \wedge F p)$	16	19	0.03	10	162
8	$G(\neg q) \vee F(q \wedge F p)$	64	67	0.37	14	349
8	$G(\neg q) \vee F(q \wedge F p)$	256	259	34	18	890
9	$G(q \wedge \neg r \to (\neg r \, W \, (p \wedge \neg r)))$	-	3	0.05	2	12
10	$G(q \wedge \neg r \to (\neg r \, U \, (p \wedge \neg r)))$	12	14	5.4	14	2901
10	$G(q \wedge \neg r \to (\neg r \, U \, (p \wedge \neg r)))$	14	16	38	15	6020
10	$G(q \wedge \neg r \to (\neg r \, U \, (p \wedge \neg r)))$	16	18	377	18	13140

safety specification, the synthesis time in seconds, and the shield size (latches and AIG gates). Overall, our method runs sufficiently fast on all properties and the resulting shield size is small. We also investigated how the synthesis time increased with an increasingly larger bound b. For Property 8 and Property 6, the run time and shield size remained small even for large automata. For Property 10, the run time and shield size grew faster, indicating room for further improvement. As a proof-of-concept implementation, our tool has not yet been optimized specifically for speed or shield size – we leave such optimizations for future work.

7   Conclusions

We have formally defined the shield synthesis problem for reactive systems and presented a general framework for solving the problem. We have also implemented a new synthesis procedure that solves a concrete instance of this problem, namely the synthesis of k-stabilizing generic shields. We have evaluated our new method on two hardware benchmarks and a set of LTL specification patterns. We believe that our work points to an exciting new direction for applying synthesis, because the set of critical properties of a complex system tends to be small and relatively easy to specify, thereby making shield synthesis scalable and usable. Many interesting extensions and variants remain to be explored, both theoretically and experimentally, in the future.

References

1. CUDD: CU Decision Diagram Package, ftp://vlsi.colorado.edu/pub/
2. LTL Specification Patterns, http://patterns.projects.cis.ksu.edu/documentation/patterns/ltl.shtml
3. Bloem, R., Chatterjee, K., Greimel, K., Henzinger, T., Hofferek, G., Jobstmann, B., Könighofer, B., Könighofer, R.: Synthesizing robust systems. Acta Inf. 51, 193–220 (2014)
4. Bloem, R., Jobstmann, B., Piterman, N., Pnueli, A., Sa'ar, Y.: Synthesis of reactive(1) designs. J. Comput. Syst. Sci. 78(3), 911–938 (2012)
5. Bloem, R., Könighofer, B., Könighofer, R., Wang, C.: Shield synthesis: Runtime enforcement for reactive systems. CoRR, abs/1501.02573 02573 (2015)
6. Brayton, R.K., et al.: VIS: A system for verification and synthesis. In: Alur, R., Henzinger, T.A. (eds.) CAV 1996. LNCS, vol. 1102, pp. 428–432. Springer, Heidelberg (1996)
7. Brayton, R., Mishchenko, A.: ABC: An academic industrial-strength verification tool. In: Touili, T., Cook, B., Jackson, P. (eds.) CAV 2010. LNCS, vol. 6174, pp. 24–40. Springer, Heidelberg (2010)
8. Büchi, J.R., Landweber, L.H.: Solving sequential conditions by finite-state strategies. Trans. Amer. Math. Soc. 138, 367–378 (1969)
9. Church, A.: Logic, arithmetic, and automata. Int. Congr. Math, 23–35 (1962,1963)
10. Clarke, E.M., Emerson, E.A.: Design and synthesis of synchronization skeletons using branching time temporal logic. In: Kozen, D. (ed.) Logic of Programs 1981. LNCS, vol. 131, pp. 52–71. Springer, Heidelberg (1982)
11. Dwyer, M.B., Avrunin, G.S., Corbett, J.C.: Patterns in property specifications for finite-state verification. In: ICSE, pp. 411–420. ACM (1999)
12. Ehlers, R., Topcu, U.: Resilience to intermittent assumption violations in reactive synthesis. In: HSCC, pp. 203–212. ACM (2014)

13. Falcone, Y., Fernandez, J.-C., Mounier, L.: What can you verify and enforce at runtime? STTT 14(3), 349–382 (2012)
14. Ligatti, J., Bauer, L., Walker, D.: Run-time enforcement of nonsafety policies. ACM Trans. Inf. Syst. Secur. 12(3) (2009)
15. Mazala, R.: 2 infinite games. In: Grädel, E., Thomas, W., Wilke, T. (eds.) Automata, Logics, and Infinite Games. LNCS, vol. 2500, pp. 23–38. Springer, Heidelberg (2002)
16. Mead, C., Conway, L.: Introduction to VLSI systems. Addison-Wesley (1980)
17. Pnueli, A., Rosner, R.: On the synthesis of a reactive module. In: POPL, pp. 179–190. ACM (1989)
18. Quielle, J.P., Sifakis, J.: Specification and verification of concurrent systems in CESAR. In: Dezani-Ciancaglini, M., Montanari, U. (eds.) Programming 1982. LNCS, vol. 137, Springer, Heidelberg (1982)
19. Rabin, M.O.: Automata on Infinite Objects and Church's Problem. In: Regional Conference Series in Mathematics, American Mathematical Society (1972)
20. Schneider, F.B.: Enforceable security policies. ACM Trans. Inf. Syst. Secur. 3, 30–50 (2000)

Program and Runtime Verification

Verifying Concurrent Programs by Memory Unwinding*

Ermenegildo Tomasco[1], Omar Inverso[1], Bernd Fischer[2], Salvatore La Torre[3], and Gennaro Parlato[1]

[1] Electronics and Computer Science, University of Southampton, UK
[2] Division of Computer Science, Stellenbosch University, South Africa
[3] Università degli Studi di Salerno, Italy

Abstract. We describe a new sequentialization-based approach to the symbolic verification of multithreaded programs with shared memory and dynamic thread creation. Its main novelty is the idea of *memory unwinding* (MU), i.e., a sequence of write operations into the shared memory. For the verification, we nondeterministically guess an MU and then simulate the behavior of the program according to any scheduling that respects it. This approach is complementary to other sequentializations and explores an orthogonal dimension, i.e., the number of write operations. It also simplifies the implementation of several important optimizations, in particular the targeted exposure of individual writes. We implemented this approach as a code-to-code transformation from multithreaded into nondeterministic sequential programs, which allows the reuse of sequential verification tools. Experiments show that our approach is effective: it found all errors in the concurrency category of SV-COMP15.

1 Introduction

Concurrent programming is becoming more important as concurrent computer architectures such as multi-core processors are becoming more common. However, the automated verification of concurrent programs remains a difficult problem. The main cause of the difficulties is the large number of possible ways in which the different elements of a concurrent program can interact with each other, e.g., the number of different interleavings of a program's threads. In practice, however, we fortunately do not need to consider all possible interactions. For example, it is well known that many concurrency errors manifest themselves already after only a few context switches [20]; this observation gives rise to a variety of *context-bounded analysis* methods [16,19,13,5,8,6,9,11].

Recent empirical studies have pointed out other common features for concurrency errors, but these have not yet been exploited for practical verification algorithms. In particular, Lu et al. [17] observed that "almost all [...] concurrency bugs are guaranteed to manifest if certain partial order among *no more than 4 memory accesses* is enforced."

---

* Partially supported by EPSRC grant no. EP/M008991/1, INDAM-GNCS 2014 grant and MIUR-FARB 2012-2014 grants.

C. Baier and C. Tinelli (Eds.): TACAS 2015, LNCS 9035, pp. 551–565, 2015.
DOI: 10.1007/978-3-662-46681-0_52

In this paper we follow up on their observation that only a few memory accesses are relevant, and propose a corresponding new approach to the automated verification of concurrent programs, more specifically multithreaded programs with shared memory. Our approach simulates the executions of a multithreaded program but bounds the total number of write operations into the shared memory that can be read by threads other than the one performing the writing. It is related to context-bounded analyses [19,16,13] but the bounding parameter is different, which allows an orthogonal exploration of the search space.

The central concept in our approach is called *memory unwinding* (MU). This is a an explicit representation of the write operations as a sequence that contains for each write the writing thread, the variable or lock, and the written value. Our approach can then be seen as an *eager sequentialization* of the original concurrent program over the unwound memory. We first guess an MU and then simulate all program runs that are compatible with this guess. For the simulation, each thread is translated into a simulation function where write and read accesses over the shared memory are replaced by operations over the unwound memory. The simulation functions are executed sequentially; each thread creation is translated into a call to the corresponding simulation function. All context switches are implicitly simulated through the MU.

The approach allows us to vary which write operations are represented and thus exposed to the other threads. This leads to different strategies with different performance characteristics. In a *fine-grained* MU *every* write operation is represented explicitly and individually while *coarse-grained* MUs only represent a subset of the writes, but group together multiple writes. In an *intra-thread* MU the writes in one group are all executed by one thread; the writes not represented can thus be seen as having been superseded by subsequent writes in the same context. In an *inter-thread* MU the writes in one group can come from different threads, thus summarizing the effect of multiple context switches.

We have implemented in our MU-CSeq tool these strategies as code-to-code transformations for ANSI-C programs that use the POSIX threads API. We have evaluated MU-CSeq over the SV-COMP15 [3] concurrency benchmarks. It has found all errors and shown itself to be competitive with state-of-the-art tools for concurrent programs, in particular CBMC [7] and Lazy-CSeq [12].

In summary, in this paper we make the following main contributions:

- We describe in Section 3 a new sequentialization-based symbolic verification approach for multithreaded programs with shared memory based on the novel idea of memory unwinding.
- We describe in Section 4 different strategies to implement our approach as code-to-code translations that can be used with arbitrary sequential verification backends.
- We evaluate in Section 5 these implementations over the SV-COMP15 benchmark suite; the results are in line with those of the current best tools for concurrency handling.

In addition, we formalize in Section 2 the language we use to illustrate our approach, while we discuss related work in Section 6 and conclude in Section 7.

2 Concurrent Programs

We use a simple imperative language for multithreaded programs to illustrate our approach. It features shared variables, dynamic thread creation, and thread join and mutex locking and unlocking for thread synchronization. We adopt a C-like syntax, which is given in Fig. 1; here, terminal symbols are set in typewriter font, and $\langle n\ \mathtt{t}\rangle^*$ denotes a possibly empty list of non-terminals n that are separated by terminals $\mathtt{t}$. We further denote with x a local variable, y a shared variable, m a mutex, t a thread variable and p a procedure name.

A *concurrent* program consists of a list of *shared variable* declarations, followed by a list of procedures. Each procedure has a list of typed parameters, and its body has a declaration of *local* variables followed by a state-

$$
\begin{array}{lll}
P & ::= & (dec\,;)^*\ (type\ p\ (\langle dec\,,\rangle^*)\{(dec\,;)^*\,stm\})^* \\
dec & ::= & type\ z \\
type & ::= & \mathtt{bool}\mid\mathtt{int}\mid\mathtt{void} \\
stm & ::= & seq\mid conc\mid\{(stm\,;)^*\} \\
seq & ::= & \mathtt{assume}(b)\mid\mathtt{assert}(b)\mid x := e\mid p(\langle e,\rangle^*)\mid\mathtt{return}\ e \\
& & \mid\mathtt{if}(b)\,\mathtt{then}\ stm\ \mathtt{else}\ stm\mid\mathtt{while}(b)\ \mathtt{do}\ stm \\
conc & ::= & x := y\mid y := x\mid t := \mathtt{create}\ p(\langle e,\rangle^*)\mid\mathtt{join}\ t \\
& & \mid\mathtt{lock}\ m\mid\mathtt{unlock}\ m\mid\mathtt{atomic}\ stm
\end{array}
$$

Fig. 1. Syntax of concurrent programs

ment. A statement is either a sequential or concurrent statement, or a sequence of statements enclosed in braces. A *sequential statement* can be an **assume**- or **assert**-statement, an assignment, a procedure call with a call-by-value parameter passing semantics a **return**-statement, a conditional statement, or a **while**-loop. All variables involved in a sequential statement must be local. Note that we leave expressions e and Boolean expressions b undefined; we assume the usual constants and operations. We also use $*$ to denote the nondeterministic choice of any possible value of the corresponding type. A *concurrent statement* can be a concurrent assignment, a thread creation, a thread join, a mutex lock or unlock operation, or an atomic block. A concurrent assignment assigns a shared (resp. local) variable to a local (resp. shared) one. A thread creation statement $t := \mathtt{create}\ p(e_1,\ldots,e_n)$ creates a new thread by calling the starting procedure p with the expressions $e_1,\ldots,e_n$ as arguments and assigning the thread identifier to t. A thread join statement **join** t pauses the current thread until the thread identified by t terminates. Lock and unlock statements respectively acquire and release a mutex. If the mutex is already acquired, the lock operation is blocking for the thread, i.e., the thread waits until the mutex is released. Context switches to other threads are disallowed when a thread's control flow is within an atomic statement or block.

We assume that a valid program P satisfies the usual well-formedness and type-correctness conditions. We also assume that P contains a procedure **main**, which is the starting procedure of the only thread that exists in the beginning. We call this the *main thread*. To simplify the translation, we assume that there are no calls to **main** in P and that no other thread can be created that uses **main** as starting procedure.

The semantics is the obvious one: a configuration is a tuple of configurations of each thread that has been created and has not yet terminated, along with a valuation of the shared variables. A thread configuration consists of a *stack* which stores the history of positions at which calls were made, along with valuations for local variables, and the top of the stack contains the local and global valuations, and a pointer to the current statement being executed.

The behavioral semantics of a program P is obtained by interleaving the behaviors of its threads. At the beginning of any computation only the main thread is *available*. At any point of a computation, only one of the available threads is *active*. A step is either the execution of a step of the active thread or a context-switch that replaces the active thread with one of the available threads that thus becomes the active thread at the next step. A thread may become temporarily unavailable if it is waiting to acquire a mutex or waiting to join another thread. A thread will no longer be available when its execution is terminated, i.e., there are no more steps that it can take.

Fibonacci-example. Fig. 2(a) shows a multithreaded implementation of a nondeterministic Fibonacci-function. This example from the SV-COMP15 benchmark suite uses two threads $f1$ and $f2$ to repeatedly increment the shared variables i and j by j and i, respectively. With a round-robin schedule with context switches after each assignment the variables i and j take on the consecutive values from the Fibonacci-series, and the program terminates with $i = fib(11) = 89$ and $j = fib(12) = 144$ if this interleaving starts with $f1$. Any other schedule will lead to smaller values for i or j.

The **main** function first creates the two threads $f1$ and $f2$, then uses two join statements to ensure that both threads run to completion, and finally checks the outcome of the choosen interleaving. Note that each of the assignments contains three sequence points; our core language makes these explicit and thus "$i = i+j$;" becomes "$x = i$; $y = j$; $z = i + j$; $i = z$;" for local variables x, y, and z.

3   Sequentialization by Memory Unwinding

In this section we first give a general overview of the main concepts of our approach, namely the memory unwinding and the simulation of the read and write operations, before we describe the sequentialization translation. We use the Fibonacci-example above to illustrate the concepts. We describe different implementation alternatives for the concepts in Section 4.

High-level description.   Our approach is based on a code-to-code translation of any concurrent program P into a corresponding sequential program $P_{n,\tau}$ that captures all the executions of P involving at most n write operations in the shared memory and τ threads. We show that an assertion fails for such an execution of P if and only if a corresponding assertion fails in $P_{n,\tau}$.

A core concept in this translation is the *memory unwinding*. An *n-memory unwinding* M of P is a sequence of writes $w_1 \ldots w_n$ of P's shared variables; each w_i is a triple (t_i, var_i, val_i) where t_i is the identifier of the thread that has performed the write operation, var_i is the name of the written variable and val_i is the new value of var_i. A *position* in an n-memory unwinding M is an index in the interval $[1, n]$. An execution of P *conforms* to a memory unwinding M if the sequence of its writes in the shared memory exactly matches M. Fig. 2(c)

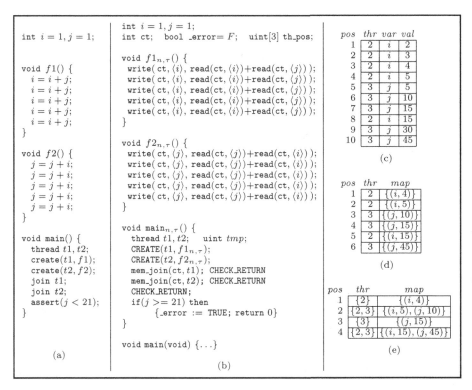

Fig. 2. Multithreaded Fibonacci: (a) code for 5 iterations, (b) translated code, and sample memory unwindings: (c) fine grained, (d) intra-thread and (e) inter-thread

gives a 10-memory unwinding. The following is an execution of the multithreaded program given in Fig. 2(a) that conforms to it (we omit the main thread): the first three assignments of $f1$, followed by a read of i by $f2$, then the fourth assignment of $f1$, the completion of the first two assignments of $f2$, the read of j by $f1$, the third assignment of $f2$, the last assignment of $f1$ and the remaining assignments of $f2$. Note that a memory unwinding can be *unfeasible* for a program, in the sense that no execution of the program conforms to it. Conversely, multiple executions can also conform to one memory unwinding, although this is not the case for the Fibonacci-example.

We use a memory unwinding M to explore the runs of P that conform to it by running each thread t separately. The idea is to use the MU for the concurrent statements (which involve the shared memory) and execute the sequential statements directly. In particular, when we execute a *write* of t in the shared memory, we check that it matches the next write of t in M. However, a *read* of t in the shared memory is more involved, since the sequence of reads is not explicitly stored in the MU. We therefore need to nondeterministically guess the position in the MU from which we read. Admissible values are all the positions that are in the range from the current position (determined by previous operations on the shared memory) to the position of t's next write in M. The nondeterministic guess ensures that we are accounting for all possible interleavings of thread executions that conform to the MU.

For example, consider again the 10-memory unwinding of Fig. 2(c). The execution of $f1$ is simulated over this as follows. The first four writes are matched with the first four positions of the MU; moreover, the related reads are positioned at the current index since they are each followed by the write which is at the next position in the MU. The fifth write is matched with position 8. The corresponding read operations can be assigned nondeterministically to any position from 4 to 7. However, in order to match the value 15 with the write, the read of j must be positioned at 6. Note that the read of i can be positioned anywhere in this range since it was written last time at position 4.

We stress that when simulating one thread we assume that the writes executed by the other threads, and stored in the memory unwinding, indeed all occur and, moreover, in the ordering shown in M. Thus, for the correctness of the simulation, for each thread t we must ensure not only that each of its writes involving the shared variables conforms to the write sequence in M, but also that all the writes claimed in the MU are actually executed. Further, t should not contribute to the computation before the statement that creates it has been simulated. This can be easily enforced by making the starting position of the child thread to coincide with the current position in M of the parent thread when its creation is simulated.

Construction of $P_{n,\tau}$. The program $P_{n,\tau}$ first guesses an n-memory unwinding M and then simulates a run of P that conforms to M. The simulation starts from the main thread (which is the only active thread when P starts) and then calls the other threads one by one, as soon as their thread creation statements are reached. Thus, the execution of the parent thread is suspended and then resumed after that the simulation of the child thread has completed. Essentially, dynamic thread creation in P is modeled by function calls in $P_{n,\tau}$.

$P_{n,\tau}$ is formed by a main, and a new procedure $p_{n,\tau}$ for each procedure p of P. It uses some additional global variables: _error is initialized to false and stores whether an assertion failure in P has occurred; ct stores the identifier of the current thread; the array th_pos stores the current position in the memory unwinding for each thread.

The main procedure of $P_{n,\tau}$ is given in Fig. 3. First, we call mem_init(V, n, τ) that guesses an n-memory unwinding with V variables and τ threads, and then mem_thread_create(0) that registers the main thread and returns its id. Note that we encode each of P's shared variables y with a different integer $\langle\langle y \rangle\rangle$ in the interval $[1, V]$ and each thread with a different integer in $[1, \tau]$; once τ threads are

```
void main(void) {
  mem_init(V, n, τ);
  ct := mem_thread_create(0);
  main_{n,τ}(x_1, …, x_k);
  mem_thread_terminate(ct);
  mem_allthreads_executed();
  assert(_error ≠ 1)  }
```

Fig. 3. $P_{n,\tau}$: main()

created mem_thread_create returns -1 (an invalid id) that causes the thread not to be simulated. The parameter passed to mem_thread_create is the id of the thread that is invoking the thread creation. For the creation of the main thread we thus pass 0 to denote that this is the first created thread.

```
1. [type p (par*){dec* stm}]  ::=  type p_{n,τ} (par*){dec*; uint tmp; [stm]}
2. [{(stm;)*}]  ::=  {([stm];)*}
```

Sequential statements:
```
3. [assume(b)]  ::=  CHECK_RETURN; assume(b)
4. [assert(b)]  ::=  CHECK_RETURN; if(¬b) then {_error:= TRUE; return 0}
5. [p(e_1,...,e_n)]  ::=  p_{n,τ}(e_1,...,e_n); CHECK_RETURN
6. [return e]  ::=  return e
7. [x := e]  ::=  x := e
8. [x := p(e_1,...,e_n)]  ::=  x := p_{n,τ}(e_1,...,e_n); CHECK_RETURN
9. [while(b) do stm]  ::=  while(b) do {CHECK_RETURN; [stm]}
10. [if (b) then stm else stm]  ::=  if (b) then [stm] else [stm]
```

Concurrent statements: (x is local, y is shared, ct contains the current tread id)
```
11. [y := x]  ::=  write(ct, ⟨⟨y⟩⟩, x); CHECK_RETURN
12. [x := y]  ::=  x :=read(ct, ⟨⟨y⟩⟩); CHECK_RETURN
13. [t := create p(e_1,...,e_n)]  ::=  tmp := ct;    t:= mem_thread_create(ct);
                                         if(t ≠ -1) then {
                                            ct := t;  p_{n,τ}(e_1,...,e_n);
                                            mem_thread_terminate(t);  };
                                         ct := tmp;
14. [join t]  ::=  mem_join(ct, t); CHECK_RETURN
15. [lock v]  ::=  var_lock(ct, ⟨⟨v⟩⟩); CHECK_RETURN
    [unlock v]  ::=  var_unlock(ct, ⟨⟨v⟩⟩); CHECK_RETURN
16. [atomic stm]  ::=  call mem_lock(ct); CHECK_RETURN;
                        [stm]; mem_unlock(ct); CHECK_RETURN
```

Fig. 4. Rewriting rules

The call to $main_{n,τ}$ starts the simulation of the main thread. Then, we check that all the write operations guessed for the main thread have been executed (by mem_thread_terminate), and all the threads involved in the guessed writes have indeed been simulated (by mem_allthreads_executed). If either one of the above checks fails, the simulation is infeasible and thus aborted. The global variable _error is used to check whether an assertion has been violated. It is set to TRUE in the simulation of the threads of P whenever an assertion gets violated and is never reset.

Each $p_{n,τ}$ is obtained from p according to the transformation function $[·]$ defined inductively over the program syntax by the rules given in Fig. 4. For example, Fig. 2(b) gives the transformations for the functions of the Fibonacci program from Fig. 2(a). There we use the macro CREATE as a shorthand for the code given in the translation rules for the create statement. Also, we have omitted the declaration of tmp in the functions $f1_{n,τ}$ and $f2_{n,τ}$ since it is not used there, and reported the translation of the assignments in a compact form.

The transformation adds a local variable tmp that is used to store the current thread id when a newly created thread is simulated. The sequential statements are left unchanged except for the injection of the macro CHECK_RETURN that is defined as "if(is_th_terminated()) then return 0;", where is_th_terminated is a function that checks if the simulation of the current thread is terminated. The macro is injected after each function call, as a first statement of a loop, and before any assume- and assert-statement; in this way, when the simulation of the current thread has finished or is aborted, we resume the simulation of the parent thread.

The concurrent statements are transformed as follows. A *write* of v into a shared variable x in thread t is simulated by a call to `write` that checks that the next write operation of t in the guessed MU (starting from the current position) writes x and that the guessed value coincides with v. Otherwise, the simulation of all threads must be aborted as the current execution does not conform to the MU. If t has already terminated its writes in the MU, we return immediately; otherwise we update t's current position to the index of its next write operation. A *read* of a shared variable x in thread t is simulated by a call to `read`. The read value is determined by nondeterministically guessing a position i between the current position for `ct` and the position prior to the next write operation of t in the memory unwinding. Thus, we return the value of the write operation involving x that is at the largest position $j \leq i$ and then update the stored position of t to i.

As above, we use `mem_thread_create` and `mem_thread_terminate` for the translation of thread creations but we check whether the thread creation was successful before calling the simulation function. Also, we save the current thread id in a temporary variable during the execution of the newly created thread.

The remaining concurrent statements are simulated by corresponding functions. A call `mem_join(ct, t)` returns if and only if the simulation of t is terminated at the current position of thread `ct` in the memory unwinding. Otherwise, the simulation of `ct` is aborted. A call `mem_lock(ct)` gives exclusive usage of the shared memory to thread `ct`. If the memory is already locked, the whole simulation is aborted. The unlocking is done by calling `mem_unlock`. Similarly, `var_lock` and `var_unlock` respectively lock and unlock an individual variable. Note that for join, lock, and unlock operations we choose to abort also computations that are still feasible, i.e., the lock could still be acquired later or we can wait for another thread to terminate. This is indeed correct for our purposes, in the sense that we are not missing bugs for this. In fact, we can capture those computations by scheduling the request to acquire the lock or to join exactly at the time when this will be possible, and by maintaining the rest of the computation unchanged. Due to space limitations we do not discuss the simulation of the locking mechanism in any detail, and omit it from the code fragments shown in the following section.

The correctness of our construction is quite straightforward to demonstrate. For *soundness*, assume any execution of P that does at most n writes in the shared memory, creates at most τ threads, and violates an assertion statement. We guess the exact sequence of writes in the MU, and simulate for each thread exactly the same steps as in P. This will allow us to execute all the writes for each thread and eventually reach the if-statement corresponding to the violated assertion of P. This will be properly propagated back to the main procedure of $P_{n,\tau}$; and since all threads have done all their writes, all the invocations of `mem_thread_terminate` will successfully return and thus the only assertion of $P_{n,\tau}$ will fail. For *completeness*, assume that there is an execution ρ of $P_{n,\tau}$ that violates the assertion in its main. This means that, along ρ we guess an n-memory unwinding M and simulate step by step a run ρ' of P that conforms to M and reaches an assertion failure. In fact, when on ρ we set _error to TRUE, ρ' reaches the corresponding if-statement that violates an assertion of P. Before reaching the assertion in the main of $P_{n,\tau}$, we have already checked that all the invocations of mem_thread_terminate in each thread and the only invocation of mem_allthreads_executed in the main thread have successfully returned; therefore all the writes of M have been simulated. Therefore, we get:

Theorem 1. *A concurrent program P violates an assertion in at least one of its executions with at most n writes in the shared memory and τ thread creations if and only if $P_{n,\tau}$ violates its only assertion.*

4   Memory Unwinding Implementations

In this section, we discuss different implementation strategies of the memory unwinding approach that are characterized by orthogonal choices. The first choice we make is either to store in the MU all the writes of the shared variables in a run (*fine-grained* MU) or to expose only some of them (*coarse-grained* MU). In either case, depending on how we store the values of the variables that are not written at a position of the MU, we have two implementation alternatives that we call *read-explicit* (where all the shared variables are duplicated to each position, not only those that are changed in the writes) and *read-implicit* (where only the modified variables are duplicated at each position).

In a coarse-grained MU we store at each position a partial mapping from the shared variables to values, with the meaning that the variables in the domain of the mapping are modified from the previous position and the value given by the mapping is their value at this position. A variable that is modified at position $i+1$ could also be modified between positions i and $i+1$ by other writes that are not exposed in the MU. We distinguish the implementations according to whether only one (*intra-thread coarse-grained* MU) or multiple (*inter-thread coarse-grained* MU) threads are entitled to modify the variables.

4.1   Fine-Grained Memory Unwinding

In this approach all writes are stored individually in the MU as described in Section 3. We use three arrays such that for each position i: thread[i] stores the thread id, var[i] stores the variable name, and value[i] stores the value of the i-th write. For an efficient implementation of the functions used in the translation described in Section 3, we use additional data such as variable last_wr_pos that stores the index of the last write performed in the simulation and table th_nxt_wr[t,i] that for each thread t and position i stores the position of the next write of t after i in the MU.

We describe the *read-explicit* and the *read-implicit* schemes only for this approach. It is not hard to extend them to the coarse-grained MU approach (discussed later) and thus we will omit this here.

Read-explicit scheme. We use a matrix mem to store for each variable v and each position i of the MU the value of v at i. mem is logically characterized as follows: for every memory position $i \in [1,n]$ and variable index $v \in [1,V]$, mem[i][v] is the valuation of variable v after the i-th write operation (assuming the values of arrays thread, var, and value). At memory position 1, all variables in $[1, V] \setminus \{v\}$ with $v = $ var$[1]$ have their initial value, i.e., 0, and mem$[1][v]$ coincides with value$[1]$. For all the other memory positions, mem has the same valuation for all variables as in the previous position except for the one written at that position.

In Fig. 5, we give an implementation of read for the read-explicit scheme. For the current thread t, Jump guesses a position $jump$ in the MU from the current position to the next write of t in the MU. If the simulation of t is deemed terminated, then consistently the read is not

```
int read(uint t, uint v) {
    if (is_th_terminated()) then return 0;
    th_pos[t]=Jump(t);
    return (mem[th_pos[t]][var_name]);  }
```

Fig. 5. Function read (explicit-read schema)

performed and the control returns (we recall that since we have injected the macro CHECK_RETURN at the end of each function call, all the calls to functions of t in the stack will immediately return and the simulation of t will actually end). Otherwise, the current position of t is updated to this value, and the valuation of the variable at position $jump$ obtained from mem is retuned.

Read-implicit scheme. Here, instead of replicating the valuations of the shared variables at each memory position, on reading a variable we get its value from the last relevant write. For this, we use two arrays var_nxt_wr and var_fst_wr s.t.: for each $i \in [1, n]$, var_nxt_wr$[i]$ is the smallest memory position $j > i$ s.t. var$[j]$ = var$[i]$ and for each variable v, var_fst_wr$[v]$ is the position of its first write in the MU.

```
int read(uint t, uint v) {
    uint pos = th_pos[t];
    uint jump = *;
    if (is_th_terminated()) then return 0;
    if (var_fst_wr[v]==0) then return 0;
    assume((jump <= last_wr_pos)
        && (jump < th_nxt_wr[t][pos]));
    assume( var[jump] == var_name );
    if (jump < pos) then
        assume(var_nxt_wr[jump] > pos);
    else { if (jump < var_fst_wr[v]) then
            return 0;
        th_pos[t]=jump;  }
    return (value[jump]);    }
```

Fig. 6. Function read (implicit-read schema)

In Fig. 6, we give an implementation of function read in the read-implicit scheme. The first if-statement (corresponding to the CHECK_RETURN macro) takes care of thread termination as usual. The following if-statement handles the case when variable v is never written in the MU, and thus its value is always the initial one, i.e., 0. The first assume-statement constraints $jump$ to a range of valid values similarly to as function Jump does in the previous scheme. Additionally, the second assume-statement requires that the guessed index indeed coincides with a write of variable v. Now, if $jump$ is less than the thread's current position pos, we finally ensure that $jump$ coincides with the last write operation involving v up to pos; otherwise we update the thread's current position to $jump$. In either case, the returned value is that at position $jump$ unless $jump$ precedes the index of the first write of v in the MU, and in this case the initial value is returned.

Mixing implicit and explicit read operations. We have also implemented a third schema that mixes the ideas of the above two. It uses an explicit representation for scalar variables and an implicit representation for arrays, in order to balance the translation's memory overhead against the complexity of the sequentialized program.

4.2   Coarse-Grained Memory Unwinding

The main idea of this approach is to expose only some of the writes of an MU. This has two main consequences in terms of explored runs of the original multithreaded program. On the one side, we restrict the number of possible runs that can match an MU. In fact, the unexposed writes cannot be read externally, and thus some possible interleavings of the threads are ruled out. On the other side, we can handle larger number of writes by nondeterministically deeming few of them as interesting for the other threads.

Intra-thread coarse-grained MU. We store a sequence of *clusters of writes* where each cluster is formed by a thread that is entitled to write and a partial mapping from the shared variables to values. The intended meaning is as follows. Consider the simulation of a thread t at a position i. If i is a position where t does not write into the shared memory, we are only allowed to read from the shared memory, and we reason similarly as to the approach given in the previous section. If i is a position of t (i.e., t is entitled to write into the shared memory), we ensure that all the writes in the shared memory only involve the variables that are annotated in the cluster at i and that all the writes in the cluster are matched before advancing to the next position in the simulation (some writes on the same variables can be processed before matching the value assigned in the cluster).

As an example, consider the intra-thread MU from Fig. 2(d). It is matched by the same execution as the MU from Fig. 2(c). Note that in this execution, the writes at the positions 1, 2, 5 and 9 are not used by the other thread and thus this is consistent with hiding them.

Inter-thread coarse-grained MU. The notion of cluster is extended with multiple threads assigned to each position. The idea is that all such *writing threads at i* can cooperate to match the writes exposed in the cluster. Thus, the unexposed writes are not local to a thread as in the alternative scheme but they can be exposed to the other writing threads. For this, in our implementation, we use for each position i in the sequence of clusters an additional copy of the shared variables that are modified at i (i.e., that are in the domain of the partial mapping at i). In the simulation of each writing thread at position i we treat them as local variables (thus we do not use the **read** and **write** functions, but we just use the name of the variable and the assignment). The intra-thread MU version of the MUs from Fig. 2(c) and (d) is given in Fig. 2(e).

5   Implementation and Evaluation

Implementation and Architecture. We have implemented in MU-CSeq (v0.3, http://users.ecs.soton.ac.uk/gp4/cseq/cseq.html) the different variants of the MU schema discussed in Section 4 as a code-to-code transformation for sequentially-consistent concurrent C programs with POSIX threads (**pthreads**). The output of MU-CSeq can, in principle, be processed by any analysis tool for sequential programs, but we primarily target BMC tools, in particular CBMC [7]. However, since the schema is very generic and the instrumentation for the different backends only differs in a few lines, backend integration is straightforward

Table 1. Performance comparison among different tools on the unsafe instances of the SV-COMP15 *Concurrency category*

sub-category	files	l.o.c.	CBMC 4.9 pass	fail	time	LR-CSeq 0.5a pass	fail	time	Lazy-CSeq 0.5 pass	fail	time	MU-CSeq 0.3 pass	fail	time
pthread	14	4381	12	2	33.4	6	8	76.5	11	3	134.2	14	0	19.9
pthread-atomic	2	202	2	0	0.3	2	0	3.0	2	0	6.1	2	0	2.0
pthread-ext	8	763	6	2	153.3	1	7	119.6	8	0	16.6	8	0	2.4
pthread-lit	3	117	2	1	166.8	2	1	166.9	3	0	7.0	3	0	2.7
pthread-wmm-mix	466	146448	466	0	57.2	466	0	8.9	466	0	6.3	466	0	21.8
pthread-wmm-podwr	16	4240	16	0	10.6	16	0	4.2	16	0	6.0	16	0	12.3
pthread-wmm-rfi	76	20981	76	0	9.3	76	0	4.1	76	0	6.2	76	0	12.7
pthread-wmm-safe	184	57391	184	0	27.3	184	0	6.6	184	0	6.2	184	0	18.6
pthread-wmm-thin	12	4008	12	0	9.6	12	0	6.2	12	0	6.1	12	0	29.3

and not fundamentally limited to any underlying technology. A wrapper script bundles up the translation and the call to the backend for the actual analysis.

MU-CSeq is implemented as a chain of modules within the CSeq framework [9,10]. The sequentialized program is obtained from the original program through transformations, which (*i*) insert boilerplate code for simulating the pthreads API; (*ii*) automatically generate control code for the bounded memory unwinding layer parameterized on n and τ; (*iii*) map the statements that in the original program correspond to read and write operations on shared variables to corresponding operations on the memory unwinding; (*iv*) insert code for the simulation of the pthreads API, concurrency simulation, and finalize the translation by adding backend-specific instrumentation.

Experiments. We have evaluated MU-CSeq with CBMC (v4.9) as a backend on the benchmark set from the Concurrency category of the TACAS Software Verification Competition (SV-COMP15) [3]. These are widespread benchmarks, and many state-of-the-art analysis tools have been trained on them; in addition, they offer a good coverage of the core features of the C programming language as well as of the basic concurrency mechanisms.

Since we use a BMC tool as a backend, and BMC can in general not prove correctness, but can only certify that an error is not reachable within the given bounds, we only evaluate our approach on the unsafe files. Our prototype does not fully support dynamic memory allocation of shared memory, so five of the test cases are excluded here. We thus use 781 of the 993 files in the whole benchmark set, with a total of approx. 240,000 lines of code.

We have performed the experiments on an otherwise idle machine with a Xeon W3520 2.6GHz processor and 12GB of memory, running a Linux operating system with 64-bit kernel 3.0.6. We set a 10GB memory limit and a 500s timeout for the analysis of each test case.

The experiments are summarized in Table 1. Each row corresponds to a sub-category of the SV-COMP15 benchmarks, where we report the number of files and the total number of lines of code. The table reports the evaluation of CBMC [7], LR-CSeq [9], Lazy-CSeq [12,11], and MU-CSeq on these benchmarks. For each tool and sub-category we consider the best parameters (i.e., minimal loop unrolling, number of rounds, etc.). Furthermore, we indicate with *pass* the number of correctly found bugs, with *miss* the number of unsuccessful analyses including tool crashes, backend crashes, memory limit hits, and timeouts, and with *time* the average time in seconds to find the bug.

The table shows that MU-CSeq is competitive with other tools based on BMC, and in particular it is able to find all bugs. However, as in other bounded methods the choice of the bounds (i.e., size of the unwinding and number of simulated threads) also influences MU-CSeq's performance. Here we have simply increased the unwinding bounds until we found all bugs. In the first four sub-categories, a 24-memory unwinding is sufficient; with this, the explicit-read fine-grained implementation has the best performance. For the remaining sub-categories an MU with at least 90 writes is required; here the performance of the fine-grained implementation degrades, and the inter-thread coarse-grained variant performs best. A more refined strategy selection is left for future work.

The MU-Cseq source code, static Linux binaries and benchmarks are available at http://users.ecs.soton.ac.uk/gp4/cseq/CSeq-MU-TACAS.tar.gz.

6   Related Work

The idea of sequentialization was originally proposed by Qadeer and Wu [20] but became popular with the first scheme for an arbitrary but bounded number of context switches given by Lal and Reps [16] (LR). This has been implemented and modified by several authors, e.g., in CSeq [9,10], and in STORM that also handles dynamic memory allocation [14]. Poirot [18,8] and Corral [15] are successors of STORM. Rek implements a sequentialization targeted to real-time systems [6].

The basic idea of the LR schemas is to simulate in the sequential program all round-robin schedules of the threads in the concurrent program, in such a way that (i) each thread is run to completion, and (ii) each simulated round works on its own copy of the shared global memory. The initial values of all memory copies are nondeterministically guessed in the beginning (*eager* exploration), while the context switch points are guessed during the simulation of each thread. At the end a checker prunes away all infeasible runs where the initial values guessed for one round do not match the values computed at the end of the previous round. This requires a second set of memory copies.

Similarly to LR, sequentialization by memory unwinding runs each thread only once and simulates it to completion; however, there are several differences. First, the threads are not scheduled in a fixed ordering and in rounds. Instead, any scheduling that matches the memory unwinding is taken into account, including schedules with unboundedly many context switches (although one can show that a subset of them using a bounded number of context-switches suffices to expose the same bugs). Second, the consistency check to prune away unfeasible computations is interleaved with the simulation, thus many unfeasible runs can be found earlier and not only at the end of the simulation. This can improve the performance, in particular for BMC backends. Third, it is possible to show that the assertion violations that can be exposed by our sequentialization is equivalent to those that can be exposed with LR, with different parameter values though. For example, for our intra-thread MU implementation, the exectutions that can be captured up to a size n in the memory unwinding can also be captured by LR with at most $2\,n-1$ rounds, and vice-versa all the computations of LR up to k context-switches (note that $k = r\,n - 1$ where n is the number of threads and r is the number of rounds) can be captured with at most k clusters.

MU can also be seen as a hybrid eager/lazy technique. It guesses the thread interactions at the beginning of the simulation, like the eager techniques in the Lal/Reps mould. However, it prunes away unfeasible computations incrementally, like Lazy-CSeq [12,11], but it calls the thread simulation function only once and runs it to completion, rather then repeatedly traversing it. Unlike the original lazy techniques [13], it also does not need to recompute the values of the local variables.

A parameter related to the memory unwinding bound has been considered in [4] for message passing programs where the bounded analysis is done on the number of "process communication cycles".

7   Conclusions and Future Work

We have presented a new approach to verify concurrent programs based on bounding the number of the shared-memory writes that are exposed in the interaction between threads. At its core it is a new *eager sequentialization* algorithm that uses the notion of *memory unwinding*, i.e., the sequence of the exposed writes, to synchronize the separate simulation of singular threads.

We have designed different strategies and implemented them as code-to-code transformations for ANSI-C programs that use the Pthreads API; our implementations support the full language, but the handling of dynamic memory allocation is still limited. We have evaluated them over the SV-COMP15 [3] concurrency benchmarks, finding all the errors and achieving performance on par with those of the current best BMC tools with built-in concurrency handling as well as other sequentializations.

We have found that in general our fine-grained MU implementations work well for most problem categories, thus confirming the good results we achieved last year with MU-CSeq [21], which is based on an initial version of the work presented here. However, for the problems in the weak memory model category the size of the fine-grained unwindings becomes too big; here, coarse-grained MUs work better.

The main future direction of this research is to extend our approach to weak memory models implemented in modern architectures (see for example [2,1]), and to other communication primitives such as MPI. For MPI programs, our memory unwinding approach can be rephrased for the sequence of *send operations* in a computation.

References

1. Alglave, J., Kroening, D., Tautschnig, M.: Partial Orders for Efficient Bounded Model Checking of Concurrent Software. In: Sharygina, N., Veith, H. (eds.) CAV 2013. LNCS, vol. 8044, pp. 141–157. Springer, Heidelberg (2013)
2. Atig, M.F., Bouajjani, A., Parlato, G.: Getting rid of store-buffers in TSO analysis. In: Gopalakrishnan, G., Qadeer, S. (eds.) CAV 2011. LNCS, vol. 6806, pp. 99–115. Springer, Heidelberg (2011)

3. Beyer, D.: SV-COMP home page, http://sv-comp.sosy-lab.org/
4. Bouajjani, A., Emmi, M.: Bounded phase analysis of message-passing programs. In: Flanagan, C., König, B. (eds.) TACAS 2012. LNCS, vol. 7214, pp. 451–465. Springer, Heidelberg (2012)
5. Bouajjani, A., Emmi, M., Parlato, G.: On Sequentializing Concurrent Programs. In: Yahav, E. (ed.) Static Analysis. LNCS, vol. 6887, pp. 129–145. Springer, Heidelberg (2011)
6. Chaki, S., Gurfinkel, A., Strichman, O.: Time-bounded analysis of real-time systems. In: FMCAD, pp. 72–80 (2011)
7. Clarke, E.M., Kroening, D., Lerda, F.: A Tool for Checking ANSI-C Programs. In: Jensen, K., Podelski, A. (eds.) TACAS 2004. LNCS, vol. 2988, pp. 168–176. Springer, Heidelberg (2004)
8. Emmi, M., Qadeer, S., Rakamaric, Z.: Delay-bounded scheduling. POPL, 411–422 (2011)
9. Fischer, B., Inverso, O., Parlato, G.: CSeq: A Concurrency Pre-Processor for Sequential C Verification Tools. In: ASE, pp. 710-713 (2013)
10. Fischer, B., Inverso, O., Parlato, G.: CSeq: A Sequentialization Tool for C (Competition Contribution). In: Piterman, N., Smolka, S.A. (eds.) TACAS 2013. LNCS, vol. 7795, pp. 616–618. Springer, Heidelberg (2013)
11. Inverso, O., Tomasco, E., Fischer, B., La Torre, S., Parlato, G.: Bounded model checking of multi-threaded C programs via lazy sequentialization. In: Biere, A., Bloem, R. (eds.) CAV 2014. LNCS, vol. 8559, pp. 585–602. Springer, Heidelberg (2014)
12. Inverso, O., Tomasco, E., Fischer, B., La Torre, S., Parlato, G.: Lazy-CSeq: A Lazy Sequentialization Tool for C - (Competition Contribution). In: Ábrahám, E., Havelund, K. (eds.) TACAS 2014. LNCS, vol. 8413, pp. 398–401. Springer, Heidelberg (2014)
13. La Torre, S., Madhusudan, P., Parlato, G.: Reducing context-bounded concurrent reachability to sequential reachability. In: Bouajjani, A., Maler, O. (eds.) CAV 2009. LNCS, vol. 5643, pp. 477–492. Springer, Heidelberg (2009)
14. Lahiri, S.K., Qadeer, S., Rakamaric, Z.: Static and precise detection of concurrency errors in systems code using SMT solvers. In: Bouajjani, A., Maler, O. (eds.) CAV 2009. LNCS, vol. 5643, pp. 509–524. Springer, Heidelberg (2009)
15. Lal, A., Qadeer, S., Lahiri, S.K.: A solver for reachability modulo theories. In: Madhusudan, P., Seshia, S.A. (eds.) CAV 2012. LNCS, vol. 7358, pp. 427–443. Springer, Heidelberg (2012)
16. Lal, A., Reps, T.W.: Reducing concurrent analysis under a context bound to sequential analysis. Formal Methods in System Design 35(1), 73–97 (2009)
17. Lu, S., Park, S., Seo, E., Zhou, Y.: Learning from mistakes: A comprehensive study on real world concurrency bug characteristics. SIGOPS Oper. Syst. Rev. 42(2), 329–339 (2008)
18. Qadeer, S.: Poirot - a concurrency sleuth. In: Qin, S., Qiu, Z. (eds.) ICFEM 2011. LNCS, vol. 6991, p. 15. Springer, Heidelberg (2011)
19. Qadeer, S., Rehof, J.: Context-bounded model checking of concurrent software. In: Halbwachs, N., Zuck, L.D. (eds.) TACAS 2005. LNCS, vol. 3440, pp. 93–107. Springer, Heidelberg (2005)
20. Qadeer, S., Wu, D.: Kiss: keep it simple and sequential. In: PLDI, pp. 14–24 (2004)
21. Tomasco, E., Inverso, O., Fischer, B., La Torre, S., Parlato, G.: MU-CSeq: Sequentialization of C Programs by Shared Memory Unwindings - (Competition Contribution). In: Ábrahám, E., Havelund, K. (eds.) TACAS 2014. LNCS, vol. 8413, pp. 402–404. Springer, Heidelberg (2014)

AutoProof: Auto-Active Functional Verification of Object-Oriented Programs

Julian Tschannen, Carlo A. Furia, Martin Nordio, and Nadia Polikarpova

Chair of Software Engineering, Department of Computer Science, ETH Zurich, Switzerland
{firstname,lastname}@inf.ethz.ch

Abstract. Auto-active verifiers provide a level of automation intermediate between fully automatic and interactive: users supply code with annotations as input while benefiting from a high level of automation in the back-end. This paper presents AutoProof, a state-of-the-art auto-active verifier for object-oriented sequential programs with complex functional specifications. AutoProof fully supports advanced object-oriented features and a powerful methodology for framing and class invariants, which make it applicable in practice to idiomatic object-oriented patterns. The paper focuses on describing AutoProof's interface, design, and implementation features, and demonstrates AutoProof's performance on a rich collection of benchmark problems. The results attest AutoProof's competitiveness among tools in its league on cutting-edge functional verification of object-oriented programs.

1 Auto-Active Functional Verification of Object-Oriented Programs

Program verification techniques differ wildly in their degree of automation and, correspondingly, in the kinds of properties they target. One class of approaches—which includes techniques such as abstract interpretation and model checking—is fully *automatic* or "push button", the only required input being a program to be verified; to achieve complete automation, these approaches tend to be limited to verifying simple or implicit properties such as absence of invalid pointer dereference. At the other end of the spectrum are *interactive* approaches to verification—which include tools such as KeY [3]—where the user is ultimately responsible for providing input to the prover on demand, whenever it needs guidance through a successful correctness proof; in principle, this makes it possible to verify arbitrarily complex properties, but it is approachable only by highly-trained verification experts.

In more recent years a new class of approaches have emerged that try to achieve an intermediate degree of automation in the continuum that goes from automatic to interactive—hence their designation [22] as the portmanteau *auto-active*[1]. Auto-active tools need no user input during verification, which proceeds autonomously until it succeeds or fails; however, the user is still expected to provide guidance indirectly through *annotations* (such as loop invariants) in the input program. The auto-active approach has the potential to better support *incrementality*: proving simple properties would require

---

[1] Although *inter-matic* would be as good a name.

© Springer-Verlag Berlin Heidelberg 2015
C. Baier and C. Tinelli (Eds.): TACAS 2015, LNCS 9035, pp. 566–580, 2015.
DOI: 10.1007/978-3-662-46681-0_53

little annotations and of the simple kinds that novice users may be able to provide; proving complex properties would still be possible by sustaining a heavy annotation burden.

This paper describes AutoProof, an auto-active verifier for functional properties of (sequential) object-oriented programs. In its latest development state, AutoProof offers a unique combination of features that make it a powerful tool in its category and a significant contribution to the state of the art. AutoProof targets a real complex object-oriented programming language (Eiffel)—as opposed to more abstract languages designed specifically for verification. It supports most language constructs, as well as a full-fledged verification methodology for heap-manipulating programs based on a flexible annotation protocol, sufficient to completely verify a variety of programs that are representative of object-oriented idioms as used in practice. AutoProof was developed with extensibility in mind: its annotation library can be augmented with new abstract models, and its implementation can accommodate changes in the input language. While Eiffel has a much smaller user base than other object-oriented languages such as C++, Java, and C#, the principles behind AutoProof are largely language independent; hence, they are relevant to a potentially large number of researchers and users—for whom this paper is written.

The verification challenges we use to evaluate AutoProof (Sect. 5) are emerging as the gold standard [17] to demonstrate the capabilities of program provers for functional correctness which, unlike fully automatic tools, use different formats and conventions for input annotations and support specifications of disparate expressiveness, and hence cannot directly be compared on standard benchmark implementations.

Previous work of ours, summarized in Sect. 2.2, described the individual techniques available in AutoProof. This paper focuses on presenting AutoProof's functionalities (Sect. 3), on describing significant aspects of its design and implementation (Sect. 4), and on outlining the results of experiments with realistic case studies, with the goal of showing that AutoProof's features and performance demonstrate its competitiveness among other tools in its league—auto-active verifiers for object-oriented programs.

AutoProof is available as part of the open-source Eiffel Verification Environment (EVE) as well as online in your browser; the page

http://se.inf.ethz.ch/research/autoproof/

contains source and binary distributions, detailed usage instructions, a user manual, an interactive tutorial, and the benchmarks solutions discussed in Sect. 5.

2 Related Work

2.1 Program Verifiers

In reviewing related work, we focus on the tools that are closer to AutoProof in terms of features, and design principles and goals. Only few of them are, like AutoProof, auto-active, work on real object-oriented programming languages, and support the verification of general functional properties. Krakatoa [10] belongs to this category, as it works on Java programs annotated with a variant of JML (the Java Modeling Language [18]). Since it lacks a full-fledged methodology for class invariants and framing, using Krakatoa to verify object-oriented idiomatic patterns—such as those we discuss in Sect. 5.1—would be quite impractical; in fact, the reference examples distributed with Krakatoa target the verification of algorithmic problems where object-oriented features are immaterial. Similar observations apply to the few other auto-active tools working on Java and JML, such as ESC/Java2 [5] or the more recent OpenJML [25,7]. Even when ESC/Java2 was used on industrial-strength case studies (such as the KOA e-voting system [16]), the emphasis was on modeling and correct-by-construction development, and verification was normally applied only to limited parts of the systems. By contrast, the Spec# system [1] was the forerunner in a new research direction, also followed by AutoProof, that focuses on the complex problems raised by object-oriented structures with sharing, object hierarchies, and collaborative patterns. Spec# works on an annotation-based dialect of the C# language and supports an ownership model which is suitable for hierarchical object structures, as well as visibility-based invariants to specify more complex object relations. Collaborative object structures as implemented in practice (Sect. 5.1) require, however, more flexible methodologies [27] not currently available in Spec#. Tools, such as VeriFast [15], based on separation logic provide powerful methodologies through abstractions different than class invariants, which may lead to a lower level of automation than tools such as AutoProof and a generally higher annotation overhead—ultimately targeting highly trained users.

The experience with the Spec# project suggested that targeting a real object-oriented programming language introduces numerous complications and may divert the focus away from fundamental problems in tool-supported verification. The Dafny program verifier [21] was developed based on this lesson: it supports a simple language expressly designed for verification, which eschews most complications of real object-oriented programming languages (such as inheritance and a complex memory model). Other auto-active verifiers target programming language paradigms other than object orientation. Leon [30] and Why3 [11], for example, work on functional programming languages—respectively, a subset of Scala and a dialect of ML; VCC [6] works on C programs and supports object invariants but with an emphasis on memory safety of low-level concurrent code.

AutoProof lies between automatic and interactive tools in the wide spectrum of verification tools. The CodeContract checker (formerly known as Clousot [24]) is a powerful static analyzer for .NET languages that belongs to the former category (and hence it is limited to properties expressible in its abstract domains). The KeY system [3] for Java belongs to the latter category: while it supports SMT solvers as back-ends to automatically discharge some verification conditions, its full-fledged usage requires explicit user interactions to guide the prover through the verification process.

2.2   Our Previous Work on AutoProof

In previous work, we formalized some critical object-oriented features as they are available in Eiffel, notably function objects (called "agents" in Eiffel) and inheritance and polymorphism [33]. An important aspects for usability is reducing annotation overhead; to this end, we introduced heuristics known as "two-step verification" [34] and demonstrated them on algorithmic challenges [31]. We recently presented the theory behind AutoProof's invariant methodology [27], which includes full support for class invariants, framing, and ghost code. The current paper discusses how these features are available in AutoProof, with a focus on advanced object-oriented verification challenges.

3   Using AutoProof

AutoProof is a static verifier for Eiffel programs which interacts with users according to the auto-active paradigm [22]: verification attempts are completely automated ("push button"), but users are expected in general to provide additional information in the form of *annotations* (loop invariants, intermediate assertions, etc.) for verification to succeed.

AutoProof targets the verification of functional correctness. Given a collection of Eiffel classes, it tries to establish that: routines satisfy their pre/post and frame specifications and maintain class invariants; routine calls take place in states satisfying the callee's precondition; loops and recursive calls terminate; integer variables do not overflow; there are no dereferences of **Void** (**null**) objects.

AutoProof's techniques are *sound*[2]: successful verification entails that the input program is correct with respect to its given specification. Since it deals with expressive specifications, AutoProof is necessarily *incomplete*: failed verification may indicate functional errors but also shortcomings of the heuristics of the underlying theorem prover (which uses such heuristics to reason in practice about highly-complex and undecidable logic fragments).

Dealing with inconclusive error reports in incomplete tools is a practical hurdle to usability that can spoil user experience—especially for novices. To improve user feedback in case of failed verification attempts, AutoProof implements a collection of heuristics known as "*two-step verification*" [34]. When they are enabled, each failed verification attempt is transparently followed by a second step that is in general unsound (as it uses under-approximations such as loop unrolling) but helps discern whether failed verification is due to real errors or just to insufficiently detailed annotations. Users see the combined output from the two steps in the form of suggestions to improve the program and its annotations. For example, if verification of a loop fails in the first step but succeeds with finite loop unrolling, the suggestion is that there are no obvious errors in the loop but the loop invariant should be strengthened to make it inductive.

3.1   User Interface (UI)

AutoProof offers its core functionalities both through a command line interface (CLI) and a library (API). End users normally interact with AutoProof through one of two graphical interfaces (GUI): a web-based GUI is available at `http://cloudstudio.ethz.ch/comcom/#AutoProof`; and AutoProof is fully integrated in EVE, the open-source research branch of the EiffelStudio development environment. The following presentation focuses on AutoProof in EVE, but most features are available in every UI.

Users launch AutoProof on the current project, or on specific classes or members thereof. Verification proceeds in the background until it terminates, is stopped, or times

---

[2] As usual, modulo bugs in the implementation.

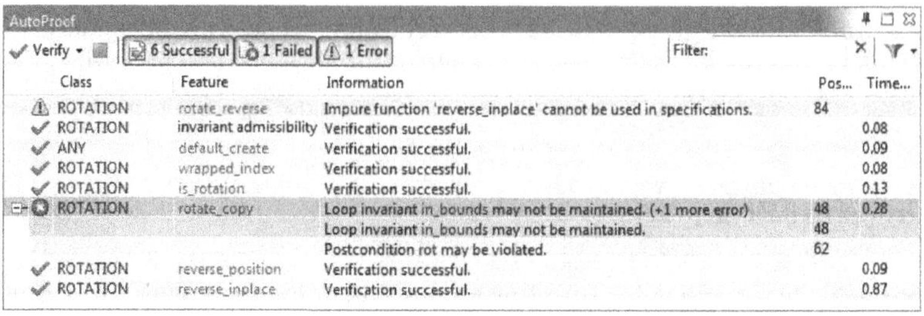

Fig. 1. The AutoProof output panel showing verification results in EVE

out. Results are displayed in a panel such as in Fig. 1: each entry corresponds to a routine of some class and is colored to summarize verification outcome. Green entries are successfully verified; red entries have failed verification; and yellow entries denote invalid input, which cannot be translated and verified (for example, impure functions with side effects used as specification elements determine invalid input). Red entries can be expanded into more detailed error messages or suggestions to fix them (when enabled, two-step verification helps provide more precise suggestions). For example, the failed verification entry for a routine may detail that its loop invariant may not be maintained, or that it may not terminate; and suggest that the loop invariant be strengthened, or a suitable variant be provided.

AutoProof's UI is deliberately kept simple with few options and sensible defaults. For advanced users, fine-grained control over AutoProof's behavior is still possible through program annotations, which we outline in the next section.

3.2 Input Language Support

AutoProof supports most of the Eiffel language as used in practice, obviously including Eiffel's native notation for contracts (specification elements) such as pre- and postconditions, class invariants, loop invariants and variants, and inlined assertions such as **check** (**assert** in other languages). Object-oriented features—classes and types, multiple inheritance, polymorphism—are fully supported [33], and so are imperative and procedural constructs.

Partially Supported and Unsupported Features. A few language features that AutoProof does not currently fully support have a semantics that violates well-formedness conditions required for verification: AutoProof doesn't support specification expressions with side effects (for example, a precondition that creates an object). It also doesn't support the semantics of **once** routines (similar to **static** in Java and C#), which would require global reasoning thus breaking modularity.

Other partially supported features originate in the distinction between machine and mathematical representation of types. Among primitive types, machine INTEGERs are fully supported (including overflows); floating-point REALs are modeled as infinite-precision mathematical reals; strings are not supported but for single-character operations. Array and list library containers with simplified interfaces are supported out of the box. Other container types require custom specification; we recently developed a fully verified full-fledged data structure library including sets, hash tables, and trees [9].

Agents (function objects) are partially supported, with some restrictions in their specifications [33]. The semantics of native **external** routines is reduced to their specification. We designed [33] a translation for exceptions based on the latest draft of the Eiffel language standard, but AutoProof doesn't support it yet since the Eiffel compiler still only implements the obsolete syntax for exceptions (and exceptions have very limited usage in Eiffel anyway).

Annotations for Verification. Supporting effective auto-active verification requires much more than translating the input language and specification into verification conditions. AutoProof supports *semantic collaboration*, a full-fledged framing methodology we designed to reason about class invariants of structures made of collaborating objects, integrated with a standard *ownership* model; both are described in detail in our previous work [27]. AutoProof's verification methodology relies on annotations that are not part of the Eiffel language. Annotations in assertions or other specification elements use predefined dummy features with empty implementation. Annotations of this kind include *modify* and *read* clauses (specifying objects whose state may be modified or read by a routine's body). For instance, a clause **modify (set)** in a routine's precondition denotes that executing the routine may modify objects in **set**.

Annotations that apply to whole classes or features are expressed by means of Eiffel's **note** clauses, which attach additional information that is ignored by the Eiffel compiler but is processed by AutoProof. Annotations of this kind include defining class members as *ghost* (only used in specifications), procedures as *lemmas* (outlining a proof using assertions and ghost-state manipulation), and which members of a class define its abstract *model* (to be referred to in interface specifications). For example **note status: ghost** tags as ghost the member it is attached to.

A distinctive trait of semantic collaboration, as available to AutoProof users, is the combination of flexible expressive annotations with useful defaults. Flexible annotations offer fine-grained control over the visibility of specification elements (for example, invariant clauses can be referenced individually); defaults reduce the amount of required manual annotations in many practical cases. The combination of the two is instrumental in making AutoProof usable on complex examples of realistic object-oriented programs.

Verifier's Options. AutoProof *verification options* are also expressed by means of **note** clauses: users can disable generating boilerplate implicit contracts, skip verification of a specific class, disable termination checking (only verify partial correctness), and define a custom mapping of a class's type to a Boogie theory file. See AutoProof's manual for a complete list of features, options, and examples of usage.

Specification Library. To support writing complex specifications, AutoProof provides a library—called MML for Mathematical Model Library—of pre-defined abstract types. These includes mathematical structures such as sets, relations, sequences, bags (multisets), and maps. The MML annotation style follows the model-based paradigm [26], which helps write abstract and concise, yet expressive, specifications. MML's features are fully integrated in AutoProof by means of effective mappings to Boogie background theories. A distinctive advantage of providing mathematical types as an annotated library is that MML is *extensible*: users can easily provide additional abstractions by writing annotated Eiffel classes and by linking them to background theories using custom **note** annotations—in the very same way existing MML classes are defined. This is not possible in most other auto-active verifiers, where mathematical types for specification are built into the language syntax.

```
binary_search (a: ARRAY [INTEGER]; value: INTEGER): INTEGER
    require sorted: is_sorted (a.sequence)
    local low, up, middle: INTEGER
    do
        from low := 1; up := a.count + 1
        invariant
            low_and_up_range: 1 ≤ low and low ≤ up and up ≤ a.count + 1
            result_range: Result = 0 or 1 ≤ Result and Result ≤ a.count
            not_left: across 1 |..| (low−1) as i all a.sequence[i] < value end
            not_right: across up |..| a.count as i all value < a.sequence[i] end
            found: Result > 0 implies a.sequence[Result] = value
        until low ≥ up or Result > 0
        loop
            middle := low + ((up − low) // 2)
            if a[middle] < value then low := middle + 1
            elseif a[middle] > value then up := middle
            else Result := middle end
        variant (a.count − Result) + (up − low) end
    ensure
        present: a.sequence.has (value) = (Result > 0)
        not_present: not a.sequence.has (value) = (Result = 0)
        found_if_present: Result > 0 implies a.sequence[Result] = value
    end
```

Fig. 2. Binary search implementation verified by AutoProof

Input Language Syntax. Fig. 2 shows an example of annotated input: an implementation of binary search (problem BINS in Tab. 1) that AutoProof can verify. From top to bottom, the routine binary_search includes signature, precondition (**require**), **local** variable declarations, body consisting of an initialization (**from**) followed by a **loop** that executes **until** its exit condition becomes true, and postcondition (**ensure**). The loop's annotations include loop **invariant** and **variant**. Each specification element consists of clauses, one per line, with a *tag* (such as *sorted* for the lone precondition clause) for identification in error reports. Quantified expressions in contracts use the **across** syntax, which corresponds to (bounded) first-order universal (**across ... all**) and existential (**across ... some**) quantification. For example, loop invariant clause *not_left* corresponds to $\forall i: 1 \leq i < \text{low} \implies \text{a.sequence}[i] < \text{value}$.

4 How AutoProof Works: Architecture and Implementation

As it is customary in deductive verification, AutoProof translates input programs into verification conditions (VCs): logic formulas whose validity entails correctness of the input programs. Following the approach pioneered by Spec# [1] and since adopted by numerous other tools, AutoProof does not generate VCs directly but translates Eiffel programs into Boogie programs [20] and calls the Boogie tool to generate VCs from the latter. Boogie is a simple procedural language tailored for verification, as well as a verification tool that takes programs written in the Boogie language, generates VCs for them, feeds the VCs to an SMT solver (Z3 by default), and interprets the solver's output in terms of elements of the input Boogie program. Using Boogie decouples VC generation from processing the source language (Eiffel, in AutoProof's case) and takes advantage of Boogie's efficient VC generation capabilities.

Fig. 3. Workflow of AutoProof with Boogie back-end

As outlined in Fig. 3, AutoProof implements the translation from Eiffel to Boogie in two stages. In the first stage, it processes an input Eiffel program and translates it into a Boogie-like abstract syntax tree (AST); in the second stage, AutoProof transcribes the AST into a textual Boogie program.

The rest of this section focuses on describing how AutoProof's architecture (Sect. 4.1) and implementation features (Sect. 4.2) make for a flexible and customizable translation process. An extended version of this paper [35] also outlines the mapping from Eiffel to Boogie. We focus on discussing the challenges tackled when developing AutoProof and the advantages of our implemented solutions.

4.1 Extensible Architecture

Top-level API. Class AUTOPROOF is the main entry point of AutoProof's API. It offers features to submit Eiffel code, and to start and stop the verification process. Objects of class RESULT store the outcome of a verification session, which can be queried by calling routines of the class. One can also register an Eiffel **agent** (function object) with an AUTOPROOF object; the outcome RESULT object is passed to the agent for processing as soon as it is available. This pattern is customary in reactive applications such as AutoProof's GUI in EVE.

Translation to Boogie. An abstract syntax tree (AST) expresses the same semantics as Eiffel source code but using elements reflecting Boogie's constructs. Type relations such as inheritance are explicitly represented (based on type checking) using axiomatic constraints, so that ASTs contain all the information necessary for verification. The transcription of the AST into a concrete Boogie program is implemented by a *visitor* of the AST. Modifying AutoProof in response to changes in Boogie's syntax would only require to modify the visitor.

Extension Points. AutoProof's architecture incorporates *extension points* where it is possible to programmatically modify and extend AutoProof's behavior to implement different verification processes. Each extension point maintains a number of *handlers* that take care of aspects of the translation from Eiffel to the Boogie-like AST. Multiple handlers are composed according to the *chain of responsibility* pattern; this means that a handler may only implement the translation of one specific source language element, while delegating to the default AutoProof handlers in all other cases. A new translation feature can thus be added by writing a handler and registering it at an extension point. Extension points target three program elements of different generality.

Across extension points handle the translation of Eiffel **across** expressions, which correspond to quantified expressions. Handlers can define a semantics of quantification over arbitrary data structures and domains. (AutoProof uses this extension point to translate quantifications over arrays and lists.)

Call extension points handle the translation of Eiffel calls, both in executable code and specifications. Handlers can define translations specific to certain data types. (AutoProof uses this extension point to translate functions on integers and dummy features for specification.)

Expression extension points handle the translation of expressions. Handlers can define translations of practically every Eiffel expression into a Boogie-like AST representation. This extension point subsumes the other two, which offer a simpler interface sufficient when only specific language elements require a different translation.

The flexibility provided for by extension points is particular to AutoProof: the architecture of other similar tools (Spec#, Dafny, and OpenJML) does not seem to offer comparable architectural features for straightforward extensibility in the object-oriented style.

4.2   Implementation Features

AutoProof's implementation consists of about 25'000 lines of Eiffel code in 160 classes.

Modular Translation. AutoProof performs *modular* reasoning: the effects of a call to p within routine r's body are limited to what is declared in p's specification (its pre- and postcondition and frame) irrespective of p's body (which is only used to verify p's correctness). To achieve modularity incrementally, AutoProof maintains a *translation pool* of references to Eiffel elements (essentially, routines and their specifications). Initially, it populates the pool with references to the routines of the classes specified as input to be verified. Then, it proceeds as follows: (1) select an element el from the pool that hasn't been translated yet; (2) translate el into Boogie-like AST and mark el as translated; (3) if el refers to (i.e., calls) any element p not in the pool, add a reference to p's specification to the pool; (4) if all elements in the pool are marked as translated stop, otherwise repeat (1). This process populates the pool with the transitive closure of the "calls" relation, whose second elements in relationship pairs are specifications, starting from the input elements to be verified.

Traceability of Results. The auto-active paradigm is based on interacting with users at the high level of the source language; in case of failed verification, reports must refer to the input Eiffel program rather than to the lower level (Boogie code). To this end, AutoProof follows the standard approach of adding structured comments to various parts of the Boogie code—most importantly to every assertion that undergoes verification: postconditions; preconditions of called routine at call sites; loop invariants; and other intermediate **assert**s. Comments may include information about the *type* of condition that is checked (postcondition, loop termination, etc.), the *tag* identifying the clause (in Eiffel, users can name each assertion clause for identification), a *line* number in the Eiffel program, the *called* routine's name (at call sites), and whether an assertion was *generated* by applying a default schema that users have the option to disable (such as in the case of default class invariant annotations [27]). For each assertion that fails verification, AutoProof reads the information in the corresponding comment and makes it available in a RESULT object to the **agent**s registered through the API to receive verification outcomes about some or all input elements. RESULT objects also include information about verification times. This *publish/subscribe* scheme provides fine-grained control on how results are displayed.

Bulk vs. Forked Feedback. AutoProof provides feedback to users in one of two modes. In *bulk* mode all input is translated into a single Boogie file; results are fed back to users when verification of the whole input has completed. Using AutoProof in bulk mode minimizes translation and Boogie invocation overhead but provides feedback synchronously, only when the whole batch has been processed. In contrast, AutoProof's *forked* mode offers asynchronous feedback: each input routine (and implicit proof obligations such as for class invariant admissibility checking) is translated into its own self-contained Boogie file; parallel instances of Boogie run on each file and results are fed back to users asynchronously as soon as any Boogie process terminates. AutoProof's UIs use the simpler bulk mode by default, but offer an option to switch to the forked mode when responsiveness and a fast turnaround are deemed important.

5 Benchmarks and Evaluation

We give capsule descriptions of benchmark problems that we verified using the latest version of AutoProof; the complete solutions are available at http://se.inf.ethz.ch/research/autoproof/repo through AutoProof's web interface.

5.1 Benchmarks Description

Our selection of problems is largely based on the verification challenges put forward during several scientific forums, namely the SAVCBS workshops [28], and various verification competitions [17,4,12,14] and benchmarks [36]. These challenges have recently emerged as the customary yardstick against which to measure progress and open challenges in verification of full functional correctness.

Tab. 1 presents a short description of verified problems. For complete descriptions see the references (and [27] for our solutions to problems 11–17). The table is partitioned in three groups: the first group (1–10) includes mainly *algorithmic* problems; the second group (11–17) includes object-oriented design challenges that require complex *invariant* and *framing* methodologies; the third group (18–27) targets *data-structure* related problems that combine algorithmic and invariant-based reasoning. The second and third group include cutting-edge challenges of reasoning about functional properties of objects in the heap; for example, PIP describes a data structure whose node invariants depend on objects not accessible in the physical heap.

5.2 Verified Solutions with AutoProof

Tab. 2 displays data about the verified solutions to the problems of Sect. 5.1; for each problem: the number of Eiffel classes (#C) and routines (#R), the latter split into *ghost* functions and lemma procedures and *concrete* (non-ghost) routines; the lines of executable Eiffel CODE and of Eiffel SPECIFICATION (a total of T specification lines, split into preconditions P, postconditions Q, frame specifications F, loop invariants L and

Table 1. Descriptions of benchmark problems

#	NAME	DESCRIPTION	FROM
1	Arithmetic (ARITH)	Build arithmetic operations based on the increment operation.	[36]
2	Binary search (BINS)	Binary search on a sorted array (iterative and recursive version).	[36]
3	Sum & max (S&M)	Sum and maximum of an integer array.	[17]
4	Search a list (SEARCH)	Find the index of the first zero element in a linked list of integers.	[17]
5	Two-way max (2-MAX)	Find the maximum element in an array by searching at both ends.	[4]
6	Two-way sort (2-SORT)	Sort a Boolean array in linear time using swaps at both ends.	[12]
7	Dutch flag (DUTCH)	Partition an array in three different regions (specific and general verions).	[8]
8	LCP (LCP)	Longest common prefix starting at given positions x and y in an array.	[14]
9	Rotation (ROT)	Circularly shift a list by k positions (multiple algorithms).	[13]
10	Sorting (SORT)	Sorting of integer arrays (multiple algorithms).	
11	Iterator (ITER)	Multiple iterators over a collection are invalidated when the content changes.	[28, '06]
12	Subject/observer (S/O)	Design pattern: multiple observers cache the content of a subject object.	[28, '07]
13	Composite (CMP)	Design pattern: a tree with consistency between parent and children nodes.	[28, '08]
14	Master clock (MC)	A number of slave clocks are loosely synchronized to a master.	[2]
15	Marriage (MAR)	Person and spouse objects with co-dependent invariants.	[23]
16	Doubly-linked list (DLL)	Linked list whose nodes have links to left and right neighbors.	[23]
17	PIP (PIP)	Graph structure with cycles where each node links to at most one parent.	[29]
18	Closures (CLOSE)	Various applications of function objects.	[19]
19	Strategy (STRAT)	Design pattern: a program's behavior is selected at runtime.	[19]
20	Command (COMMAND)	Design pattern: encapsulate complete information to execute a command.	[19]
21	Map ADT (MAP)	Generic map ADT with layered data.	[36]
22	Linked queue (QUEUE)	Queue implemented using a linked list.	[36]
23	Tree maximum (TMAX)	Find the maximum value in nodes of a binary tree.	[4]
24	Ring buffer (BUFF)	A bounded queue implemented using a circular array.	[12]
25	Hash set (HSET)	A hash set with mutable elements.	
26	Board game 1 (GAME1)	A simple board game application: players throw dice and move on a board.	
27	Board game 2 (GAME2)	A more complex board game application: different board-square types.	

variants V, auxiliary annotations including ghost code A, and class invariants C); the S/C specification to code ratio (measured in tokens)[3]; the lines of BOOGIE input (where *tr* is the problem-specific translation code and *bg* are the included background theory necessary for verification); the overall verification time (in bulk mode). AutoProof ran on a single core of a Windows 7 machine with a 3.5 GHz Intel i7-core CPU and 16 GB of memory, using Boogie v. 2.2.30705.1126 and Z3 v. 4.3.2 as backends.

Given that we target full functional verification, our specification to code ratios are small to moderate, which demonstrates that AutoProof's notation and methodology support concise and effective annotations for verification. Verification times also tend to be moderate, which demonstrates that AutoProof's translation to Boogie is effective.

To get an idea of the kinds of annotations required, we computed the ratio A/T of auxiliary to total annotations. On average, 2.8 out of 10 lines of specification are auxiliary annotations; the distribution is quite symmetric around its mean; auxiliary annotations are less than 58% of the specification lines in all problems. Auxiliary annotations tend to be lower level, since they outline intermediate proof goals which are somewhat specific to the way in which the proof is carried out. Thus, the observed range of A/T ratios seems to confirm how AutoProof supports incrementality: complex proofs are possible but require more, lower level annotations.

5.3 Open Challenges

The collection of benchmark problems discussed in the previous sections shows, by and large, that AutoProof is a state-of-the-art auto-active tool for the functional verifica-

---

[3] In accordance with common practices in verification competitions, we count *tokens* for the S/C ratio; but we provide other measures in *lines*, which are more naturally understandable.

Table 2. Verification of benchmark problems with AutoProof

#	NAME	#C	#R		CODE	SPECIFICATION								S/C	BOOGIE		TIME [s]
			co	gh		T	P	Q	F	L	V	A	C		tr	bg	
1	ARITH	1	6	0	99	44	11	12	0	12	9	0	0	0.4	927	579	3.1
2	BINS	1	4	1	62	48	11	12	0	6	3	16	0	1.6	965	1355	3.7
3	S&M	1	1	0	23	12	3	2	1	4	0	2	0	1.0	638	1355	3.9
4	SEARCH	2	5	1	57	62	2	12	2	6	2	27	11	2.3	931	1355	4.1
5	2-MAX	1	1	0	23	12	2	4	0	4	2	0	0	2.3	583	1355	3.0
6	2-SORT	1	2	0	35	28	5	7	2	6	2	6	0	1.8	683	1355	3.2
7	DUTCH	1	4	1	72	75	13	22	4	21	0	15	0	2.6	1447	1355	4.1
8	LCP	2	2	0	40	28	4	7	0	6	2	9	0	1.0	1138	1355	4.2
9	ROT	1	3	3	51	74	14	10	3	17	2	28	0	2.6	1138	1355	4.1
10	SORT	1	9	6	177	219	31	38	9	56	5	80	0	2.6	2302	1355	5.8
11	ITER	3	8	0	88	69	15	26	6	0	0	11	11	1.4	1461	1355	8.9
12	S/O	3	6	0	71	56	10	14	4	3	0	15	10	1.4	1156	1355	4.4
13	CMP	2	5	3	54	125	19	18	5	0	2	72	9	4.3	1327	1355	7.5
14	MC	3	7	0	63	61	9	14	5	0	0	26	7	1.8	956	579	3.7
15	MAR	2	5	0	45	50	12	11	3	0	0	19	5	2.3	755	579	3.3
16	DLL	2	8	0	69	76	12	14	4	0	0	39	7	2.0	891	579	4.4
17	PIP	2	5	1	54	111	23	18	6	0	1	56	7	3.9	988	1355	5.8
18	CLOSE	9	18	0	145	106	40	31	8	0	0	22	5	0.8	2418	688	5.7
19	STRAT	4	4	0	43	5	0	4	0	0	0	1	0	0.2	868	579	3.3
20	CMD	6	8	0	77	32	4	14	2	0	0	10	5	0.7	1334	579	3.3
21	MAP	1	8	0	78	67	6	29	2	6	4	15	5	2.3	1259	1355	4.1
22	QUEUE	4	13	1	121	101	11	26	1	0	0	48	15	1.5	2360	1355	7.4
23	TMAX	1	3	0	31	43	3	12	2	0	2	19	5	2.1	460	1355	3.2
24	BUFF	1	9	0	66	54	8	19	4	0	0	12	11	1.1	1256	1355	4.4
25	HSET	5	14	5	146	341	45	39	10	20	2	197	28	3.7	3546	1355	13.7
26	GAME1	4	8	0	165	93	16	13	4	31	3	10	16	1.2	4044	1355	26.6
27	GAME2	8	18	0	307	173	25	27	11	48	3	29	30	1.4	7037	1355	54.2
	total	72	184	22	2262	2165	354	455	98	246	44	784	184	1.9	43089	1355	203.8

tion of object-oriented programs. To our knowledge, no other auto-active verifier fully supports the complex reasoning about class invariants that is crucial to verify object-oriented pattern implementation such as S/O and PIP. It is important to remark that we're describing *practical* capabilities of tools: other auto-active verifiers may support logics sufficiently rich to express the semantics of object-oriented benchmarks, but this is a far cry from automated verification that is approachable idiomatically at the level of a real object-oriented language. Also, AutoProof's performance is incomparable against that of interactive tools, which may still offer some automation but always have the option of falling back to asking users when verification gets stuck.

The flip side of AutoProof's focus on supporting a real object-oriented language is that it may not be the most powerful tool to verify purely algorithmic problems. The benchmarks have shown that AutoProof still works quite well in that domain, and there are no intrinsic limitations that prevent from applying it to the most complex examples. However, algorithmic verification is often best approached at a level that abstracts from implementation details (such as pointers and objects) and can freely use high-level constructs such as infinite maps and nondeterminism. Verifiers such as Dafny [21] and Why3 [11], whose input languages have been explicitly designed to match such abstraction level, are thus best suited for algorithmic verification, which is instead not the primary focus of AutoProof.

Another aspect of the complexity vs. expressivity trade-off emerges when verifying realistic data structure implementations (or, more generally, object-oriented code as it is written in real-life projects). Tools such as Dafny offer a bare-bones framing methodology that is simple to learn (and to teach) and potentially very expressive; but it becomes unwieldy to reason about complicated implementations, which require to deal with an abundance of special cases by specifying each of them at a low level of detail—and annotational complexity easily leads to unfeasible verification. AutoProof's methodology is richer, which implies a steeper learning curve but also a variety of constructs and defaults that can significantly reduce the annotational overhead and whose custom Boogie translation offers competitive performance in many practical cases.

Given AutoProof's goal of targeting a real programming language, there are few domain-specific features of the Eiffel language that are not fully supported but are used in practice in a variety of programs: reasoning in AutoProof about strings and floating-point numbers is limited by the imprecision of the verification models of such features. For instance (see Sect. 3.2), floating point numbers are translated as infinite-precision reals; precise reasoning requires manually specifying properties of floating point operations. Another domain deliberately excluded from AutoProof so far is concurrent programming. As a long term plan, we envision extending AutoProof to cover these domains to the extent possible: precise functional verification of such features is still largely an open challenge for automated verification tools.

A related goal of AutoProof's research is verifying a fully-specified realistic data structure library—the first such verification carried out entirely with an auto-active tool. This effort—one of the original driving forces behind designing AutoProof's features—has been recently completed with the verification of the EiffelBase2 container library [9].

6   Discussion

How do AutoProof's techniques and implementation generalize to other domains? While Eiffel has its own peculiarities, it is clear that AutoProof's techniques are applicable with little changes to other mainstream object-oriented languages such as Java and C#; and that AutoProof's architecture uses patterns that lead to proper designs in other object-oriented languages too.

A practically important issue is the input language, namely how to reconcile the conflicting requirements of supporting Eiffel as completely as possible and of having a convenient notation for expressing annotations necessary for auto-active verification. While Eiffel natively supports fundamental specification elements (pre- and postconditions and invariants), we had to introduce ad hoc notations, using naming conventions and dummy features, to express modifies clauses, ghost code, and other verification-specific directives in a way that is backward compatible with Eiffel syntax. We considered different implementation strategies, such as using a pre-processor or extending Eiffel's parser, but we concluded that being able to reuse standard Eiffel tools without modifying them is a better option in terms of reusability and compatibility (as the language and its tools may evolve), albeit it sacrifices a bit of notational simplicity. This trade-off is reasonable whenever the goal is verifying programs in a real language used in practice; verifiers focused on algorithmic challenges would normally prefer ad hoc notations with an abstraction level germane to the tackled problems.

In future work, AutoProof's architecture could integrate translations to back-end verifiers other than Boogie. To this end, we could leverage verification systems such as Why3 [11], which generates verification conditions and discharges them using a variety of SMT solvers or other provers.

Supporting back-ends with different characteristics is one of the many aspects that affect the *flexibility* of AutoProof and similar tools. Another crucial aspect is the quality of feedback in case of failed verification attempts, when users have to change the input to fix errors and inconsistencies, work around limitations of the back-end, or both. As mentioned in Sect. 3, AutoProof incorporates heuristics that improve feedback. Another component of the EVE environment combines AutoProof with automatic random testing and integrates the results of applying both [32]. As future work we plan to further experiment with integrating the feedback of diverse code analysis tools (AutoProof being one of them) to improve usability of verification.

References

1. Barnett, M., Fähndrich, M., Leino, K.R.M., Müller, P., Schulte, W., Venter, H.: Specification and verification: the Spec# experience. Commun. ACM 54(6), 81–91 (2011), http://specsharp.codeplex.com/
2. Barnett, M., Naumann, D.A.: Friends need a bit more: Maintaining invariants over shared state. In: Kozen, D. (ed.) MPC 2004. LNCS, vol. 3125, pp. 54–84. Springer, Heidelberg (2004)
3. Beckert, B., Hähnle, R., Schmitt, P.H. (eds.): Verification of Object-Oriented Software. LNCS (LNAI), vol. 4334. Springer, Heidelberg (2007)
4. Bormer, T., et al.: The COST IC0701 verification competition 2011. In: Beckert, B., Damiani, F., Gurov, D. (eds.) FoVeOOS 2011. LNCS, vol. 7421, pp. 3–21. Springer, Heidelberg (2012), http://foveoos2011.cost-ic0701.org/verification-competition
5. Chalin, P., Kiniry, J.R., Leavens, G.T., Poll, E.: Beyond assertions: Advanced specification and verification with JML and eSC/Java2. In: de Boer, F.S., Bonsangue, M.M., Graf, S., de Roever, W.-P. (eds.) FMCO 2005. LNCS, vol. 4111, pp. 342–363. Springer, Heidelberg (2006), http://kindsoftware.com/products/opensource/ESCJava2/
6. Cohen, E., Dahlweid, M., Hillebrand, M.A., Leinenbach, D., Moskal, M., Santen, T., Schulte, W., Tobies, S.: VCC: a practical system for verifying concurrent C. In: Berghofer, S., Nipkow, T., Urban, C., Wenzel, M. (eds.) TPHOLs 2009. LNCS, vol. 5674, pp. 23–42. Springer, Heidelberg (2009), http://vcc.codeplex.com/
7. Cok, D.: The OpenJML toolset. In: NASA Formal Methods, vol. 6617 (2011)
8. Dijkstra, E.W.: A Discipline of Programming. Prentice Hall (1976)
9. EiffelBase2: A fully verified container library (2015), https://github.com/nadia-polikarpova/eiffelbase2
10. Filliâtre, J.-C., Marché, C.: The Why/Krakatoa/Caduceus platform for deductive program verification. In: Damm, W., Hermanns, H. (eds.) CAV 2007. LNCS, vol. 4590, pp. 173–177. Springer, Heidelberg (2007), http://krakatoa.lri.fr/
11. Filliâtre, J.-C., Paskevich, A.: Why3 – where programs meet provers. In: Felleisen, M., Gardner, P. (eds.) ESOP 2013. LNCS, vol. 7792, pp. 125–128. Springer, Heidelberg (2013), http://why3.lri.fr/
12. Filliâtre, J.-C., Paskevich, A., Stump, A.: The 2nd verified software competition: Experience report. In: COMPARE. CEUR Workshop Proceedings, vol. 873, CEUR-WS.org (2012), https://sites.google.com/site/vstte2012/compet
13. Furia, C.A.: Rotation of sequences: Algorithms and proofs (June 2014), http://arxiv.org/abs/1406.5453
14. Huisman, M., Klebanov, V., Monahan, R.: VerifyThis verification competition (2012), http://verifythis2012.cost-ic0701.org
15. Jacobs, B., Smans, J., Piessens, F.: A quick tour of the VeriFast program verifier. In: Ueda, K. (ed.) APLAS 2010. LNCS, vol. 6461, pp. 304–311. Springer, Heidelberg (2010), http://people.cs.kuleuven.be/~bart.jacobs/verifast/
16. Kiniry, J.R., Morkan, A.E., Cochran, D., Fairmichael, F., Chalin, P., Oostdijk, M., Hubbers, E.: The KOA remote voting system: A summary of work to date. In: Montanari, U., Sannella, D., Bruni, R. (eds.) TGC 2006. LNCS, vol. 4661, pp. 244–262. Springer, Heidelberg (2007)

17. Klebanov, V., et al.: The 1st verified software competition: Experience report. In: Butler, M., Schulte, W. (eds.) FM 2011. LNCS, vol. 6664, pp. 154–168. Springer, Heidelberg (2011), `https://sites.google.com/a/vscomp.org/main/`

18. Leavens, G.T., Cheon, Y., Clifton, C., Ruby, C., Cok, D.R.: How the design of JML accommodates both runtime assertion checking and formal verification. Sci. Comput. Program. 55(1-3), 185–208 (2005)

19. Leavens, G.T., Leino, K.R.M., Müller, P.: Specification and verification challenges for sequential object-oriented programs. Formal Aspects of Computing 19(2), 159–189 (2007)

20. Leino, K.R.M.: This is boogie 2. Technical report, Microsoft Research (June 2008), `http://research.microsoft.com/apps/pubs/default.aspx?id=147643`

21. Leino, K.R.M.: Dafny: An automatic program verifier for functional correctness. In: Clarke, E.M., Voronkov, A. (eds.) LPAR-16 2010. LNCS, vol. 6355, pp. 348–370. Springer, Heidelberg (2010), `http://research.microsoft.com/en-us/projects/dafny/`

22. Leino, K.R.M., Moskal, M.: Usable auto-active verification. In: Usable Verification Workshop (November 2010), `http://fm.csl.sri.com/UV10/`

23. Leino, K.R. M., Müller, P.: Object invariants in dynamic contexts. In: Odersky, M. (ed.) ECOOP 2004. LNCS, vol. 3086, pp. 491–515. Springer, Heidelberg (2004)

24. Logozzo, F.: Our experience with the CodeContracts static checker. In: Joshi, R., Müller, P., Podelski, A. (eds.) VSTTE 2012. LNCS, vol. 7152, pp. 241–242. Springer, Heidelberg (2012), `http://msdn.microsoft.com/en-us/devlabs/dd491992.aspx`

25. The OpenJML toolset (2013), `http://openjml.org/`

26. Polikarpova, N., Furia, C.A., Meyer, B.: Specifying reusable components. In: Leavens, G.T., O'Hearn, P., Rajamani, S.K. (eds.) VSTTE 2010. LNCS, vol. 6217, pp. 127–141. Springer, Heidelberg (2010)

27. Polikarpova, N., Tschannen, J., Furia, C.A., Meyer, B.: Flexible invariants through semantic collaboration. In: Jones, C., Pihlajasaari, P., Sun, J. (eds.) FM 2014. LNCS, vol. 8442, pp. 514–530. Springer, Heidelberg (2014)

28. SAVCBS workshop series (2010), `http://www.eecs.ucf.edu/~leavens/SAVCBS/`

29. Summers, J., Drossopoulou, S., Müller, P.: The need for flexible object invariants. In: IWACO, pp. 1–9. ACM (2009)

30. Suter, P., Köksal, A.S., Kuncak, V.: Satisfiability modulo recursive programs. In: Yahav, E. (ed.) Static Analysis. LNCS, vol. 6887, pp. 298–315. Springer, Heidelberg (2011), `http://leon.epfl.ch/`

31. Tschannen, J., Furia, C.A., Nordio, M.: AutoProof meets some verification challenges. International Journal on Software Tools for Technology Transfer, 1–11 (February 2014)

32. Tschannen, J., Furia, C.A., Nordio, M., Meyer, B.: Usable verification of object-oriented programs by combining static and dynamic techniques. In: Barthe, G., Pardo, A., Schneider, G. (eds.) SEFM 2011. LNCS, vol. 7041, pp. 382–398. Springer, Heidelberg (2011)

33. Tschannen, J., Furia, C.A., Nordio, M., Meyer, B.: Automatic verification of advanced object-oriented features: The AutoProof approach. In: Meyer, B., Nordio, M. (eds.) LASER 2011. LNCS, vol. 7682, pp. 133–155. Springer, Heidelberg (2012)

34. Tschannen, J., Furia, C.A., Nordio, M., Meyer, B.: Program checking with less hassle. In: Cohen, E., Rybalchenko, A. (eds.) VSTTE 2013. LNCS, vol. 8164, pp. 149–169. Springer, Heidelberg (2014)

35. Tschannen, J., Furia, C.A., Nordio, M., Polikarpova, N.: AutoProof: Auto-active functional verification of object-oriented programs (2015), `http://arxiv.org/abs/1501.03063`

36. Weide, B.W., Sitaraman, M., Harton, H.K., Adcock, B., Bucci, P., Bronish, D., Heym, W.D., Kirschenbaum, J., Frazier, D.: Incremental benchmarks for software verification tools and techniques. In: Shankar, N., Woodcock, J. (eds.) VSTTE 2008. LNCS, vol. 5295, pp. 84–98. Springer, Heidelberg (2008)

An LTL Proof System for Runtime Verification

Clare Cini and Adrian Francalanza

Computer Science, ICT, University of Malta, Malta
{clare.cini.08,adrian.francalanza}@um.edu.mt

Abstract. We propose a local proof system for LTL formalising deductions within the constraints of Runtime Verification (RV), and show how such a system can be used as a basis for the construction of online runtime monitors. Novel soundness and completeness results are proven for this system. We also prove decidability and incrementality properties for a monitoring algorithm constructed from it. Finally, we relate its expressivity to existing symbolic analysis techniques used in RV.

1 Introduction

Runtime verification (RV) is a lightweight verification technique that checks whether the current execution of a system under scrutiny satisfies or violates a given correctness property. It has its origins in model checking, as a more scalable (yet still formal) approach to program verification where state explosion problems (which are part and parcel of model checking) are mitigated [LS09]. Linear Temporal Logic, (LTL) [Pnu77] is prevalently used for formal expositions of RV [Gei01, SRA04, BLS07, BLS10, BLS11, BF12], because it has a pleasingly straightforward definition over strings, denoting execution traces.

Proof systems [Bus98, TS00] embody mechanical syntactic deductions similar to those made by monitors in RV. We propose a proof system for LTL attuned to the constraints of an RV setting, and show how it can be used as a basis for monitor construction. Although deductive systems for LTL exist, *c.g.*, [MP91, KI11, BL08] they are geared towards reasoning about the full statespace of a system. By contrast, our proof system is *local* [SW91] focussing on checking whether a specific point lies within a property set, instead of interpreting a formula *wrt.* a set of points; this mirrors closely the runtime analysis in RV.

RV settings pose further constraints on our symbolic analysis. In online settings, deductions are often performed on the *partial* traces generated thus far, while the program is still executing. This has two important consequences: (*a*) *conclusive* deductions must be *consistent with any extension* leading to a complete trace (*b*) in order to keep RV overheads low, *inconclusive* deductions must reusable, and contribute to deductions of subsequent extensions *i.e.*, the analysis must be *incremental*. In addition, monitors for partial traces typically reason about trace *satisfactions*, but also trace *violations* [BLS11, BLS10] so as to determine good/bad prefixes [KYV01]. Accordingly, proof system deductions should reason directly about both satisfactions and violations. Moreover, timely detections often require *synchronous* monitor instrumentation where monitored

© Springer-Verlag Berlin Heidelberg 2015
C. Baier and C. Tinelli (Eds.): TACAS 2015, LNCS 9035, pp. 581–595, 2015.
DOI: 10.1007/978-3-662-46681-0_54

system execute in lock-step with the respective monitor, producing a trace event and waiting for the monitor to terminate its (incremental) analysis before executing further. Thus, in order for such an instrumentation to be safe, it is important to ensure that incremental deductions are *decidable*.

We formally compare our system with other LTL symbolic techniques used in RV. In particular we consider Geilen's work [Gei01], based on informative prefixes [KYV01], as well as Sen *et al.*'s work [SRA04] which is based on derivatives [HR01]. Apart from enabling a better understanding of each approach, facilitating comparisons between seemingly different formalisations, this study enables cross fertilisation of techniques from one formalisation to the other.

The paper is structured as follows. After introducing the logic, §2, we present our proof system in §3. §4 presents the associated monitor algorithm. §5 details formal comparisons with other symbolic analyses and §6 concludes.

2   The Logic: An LTL Primer

Syntax. Fig. 1 defines the *core* syntax of LTL as used in [BLS11, EFH+03], parameterised by a set of predicates $p \in$ PRED. It consists of two base cases, *i.e.*, the true formula, tt, and a predicate formula, p, standard negation and conjunction constructors, $\neg\psi$ and $\psi_1 \wedge \psi_2$, and the characteristic *next* and *until* formulas, $X\psi$ and $\psi_1 \cup \psi_2$ resp. Other studies of LTL (*e.g.*, [Gei01, BL08]) prefer to work with formulas in *negation normal form* (nnf), where negations are pushed to the leaves of a formula. To accommodate this, we also consider an extended LTL syntax in Fig. 1, that also includes base formulas for falsity, ff, and constructors such as disjunctions, $\varphi_1 \vee \varphi_2$, and release formulas, $\varphi_1 \mathrel{R} \varphi_2$. Our extended syntax also employs an extended predicate notation that includes *co-predicates*, *i.e.*, for any predicate[1] $p = S \subseteq \Sigma$, its co-predicate, denoted as $\bar{p}$, represents its *dual* and is defined as $\Sigma \setminus S$. This allows us to eliminate negations from normalised formulas; because of this we sometimes refer to an nnf formula as *negation-free*. Fig. 1 also defines a translation function, $\langle - \rangle :: \text{LTL} \to \text{ELTL}$ from formulas of the core LTL to a negation-free formula in the extended syntax.

Model. The logic semantics is also given in Fig. 1. It assumes an alphabet, Σ (with element variables σ), over which predicates are defined, $p :: \Sigma \to \text{BOOL}$. As in other RV studies [Gei01, SRA04, BLS11], the logic is defined over *infinite* strings, $s \in \Sigma^\omega$; *finite* strings over the same alphabet are denoted by the variable $t \in \Sigma^*$. A string with element σ at its head is denoted as σs (resp. σt). For indexes $i, j \in$ NAT, s_i denotes the ith *element* in the string (starting from index 0) and $[s]^i$ denotes the *suffix* of s starting at index i; note that for any s, $[s]^0 = s$. Infinite strings with a regular (finite) pattern t are sometimes denoted as t^*, whereas the shorthand $t \ldots$ represents infinite strings with a (finite) prefix t.

Semantics. The denotational semantic function $[\![-]\!] :: \text{ELTL} \to \mathcal{P}(\Sigma^\omega)$ is defined by induction over the structure of LTL formulas; in Fig. 1 we define the

---

[1] Predicates are sometimes denoted as sets over Σ.

Core LTL Syntax

$$\psi \in \text{LTL} ::= \text{tt} \mid p \mid \neg\psi \mid \psi_1 \wedge \psi_2 \mid X\psi \mid \psi_1 \text{ U } \psi_2$$

Extended LTL Syntax

$$\varphi \in \text{ELTL} ::= \text{tt} \mid p \mid \varphi_1 \wedge \varphi_2 \mid \varphi_1 \text{ U } \varphi_2 \mid X\varphi \mid \neg\varphi$$
$$\mid \text{ff} \mid \overline{p} \mid \varphi_1 \vee \varphi_2 \mid \varphi_1 \text{ R } \varphi_2$$

Formula Translation (Normalisation)

$$\langle\text{tt}\rangle \overset{\text{def}}{=} \text{tt} \qquad \langle\neg\text{tt}\rangle \overset{\text{def}}{=} \text{ff} \qquad \langle p\rangle \overset{\text{def}}{=} p \qquad \langle\neg p\rangle \overset{\text{def}}{=} \overline{p}$$

$$\langle X\psi\rangle \overset{\text{def}}{=} X\langle\psi\rangle \qquad \langle\neg X\psi\rangle \overset{\text{def}}{=} X\langle\neg\psi\rangle \qquad \langle\neg\neg\psi\rangle \overset{\text{def}}{=} \langle\psi\rangle$$

$$\langle\psi_1 \wedge \psi_2\rangle \overset{\text{def}}{=} \langle\psi_1\rangle \wedge \langle\psi_2\rangle \qquad \langle\neg(\psi_1 \wedge \psi_2)\rangle \overset{\text{def}}{=} \langle\neg\psi_1\rangle \vee \langle\neg\psi_2\rangle$$

$$\langle\psi_1 \text{ U } \psi_2\rangle \overset{\text{def}}{=} \langle\psi_1\rangle \text{ U } \langle\psi_2\rangle \qquad \langle\neg(\psi_1 \text{ U } \psi_2)\rangle \overset{\text{def}}{=} \langle\neg\psi_1\rangle \text{ R } \langle\neg\psi_2\rangle$$

Semantics

$$[\![\text{tt}]\!] \overset{\text{def}}{=} \Sigma^\omega \qquad\qquad\qquad [\![\text{ff}]\!] \overset{\text{def}}{=} \emptyset$$
$$[\![p]\!] \overset{\text{def}}{=} \{s \mid p(s_0)\} \qquad\qquad [\![\overline{p}]\!] \overset{\text{def}}{=} \{s \mid \text{not } p(s_0)\}$$
$$[\![\varphi_1 \wedge \varphi_2]\!] \overset{\text{def}}{=} [\![\varphi_1]\!] \cap [\![\varphi_1]\!] \qquad [\![\varphi_1 \vee \varphi_2]\!] \overset{\text{def}}{=} [\![\varphi_1]\!] \cup [\![\varphi_1]\!]$$
$$[\![X\psi]\!] \overset{\text{def}}{=} \{s \mid [s]^1 \in [\![\psi]\!]\} \qquad\quad [\![\neg\varphi]\!] \overset{\text{def}}{=} (\Sigma^\omega) \setminus [\![\varphi]\!]$$
$$[\![\varphi_1 \text{ U } \varphi_2]\!] \overset{\text{def}}{=} \{s \mid \exists j \text{ such that } [s]^j \in [\![\varphi_2]\!] \text{ and } (i < j \text{ implies } [s]^i \in [\![\varphi_1]\!])\}$$
$$[\![\varphi_1 \text{ R } \varphi_2]\!] \overset{\text{def}}{=} \{s \mid \forall j \text{ we have } ([s]^j \in [\![\varphi_2]\!] \text{ or } (\exists i < j \text{ such that } [s]^i \in [\![\varphi_1]\!]))\}$$

Fig. 1. Linear Temporal Logic Syntax and Semantics

semantics for the extended LTL syntax (of which the core syntax is a subset). Most cases are standard. For instance, $[\![\text{tt}]\!]$ (*resp.* $[\![\text{ff}]\!]$) returns the universal (*resp.* empty) set of strings, $[\![\neg\varphi]\!]$ returns the dual of $[\![\varphi]\!]$, whereas $[\![\varphi_1 \wedge \varphi_2]\!]$ (*resp.* $[\![\varphi_1 \vee \varphi_2]\!]$) denotes the intersection (*resp.* union) of the meaning of its subformulas, $[\![\varphi_1]\!]$ and $[\![\varphi_2]\!]$. The meaning of $[\![p]\!]$ (*resp.* $[\![\overline{p}]\!]$) contains all strings whose *first element* satisfies the predicate p (*resp.* $\overline{p}$). The temporal formulas are more involving. The denotation of $[\![X\varphi]\!]$ contains all strings whose immediate suffix (*i.e.*, at index 1) is included in $[\![\psi]\!]$. Until formulas $[\![\varphi_1 \text{ U } \varphi_2]\!]$ contain all strings that contain a suffix (at *some* index j) satisfying $[\![\psi_2]\!]$, and *all* the suffixes preceding j satisfy $[\![\psi_1]\!]$. Finally, release formulas, $\varphi_1 \text{ R } \varphi_2$ contain strings whose suffixes *always* satisfy φ_2, as well as strings that contain a suffix satisfying both φ_1 and φ_2 and *all* the preceding suffixes satisfying φ_2.

The denotational semantics allows us to observe the duality between the formulas tt, $\varphi_1 \wedge \varphi_2$ and $\psi_1 \text{ U } \psi_2$, and their counterparts ff, $\varphi_1 \vee \varphi_2$ and $\psi_1 \text{ R } \psi_2$. It also helps us understand the mechanics of the translation function, pushing negation to the leaves of a formula using negation propagation identities (*e.g.*, DeMorgan's law), converting constructors to their dual constructor; at the leaves the function then performs direct translations from tt and p to ff and $\overline{p}$

resp. The semantics also allows us to prove Prop. 1, justifying the use of a corresponding negation-free formula instead of a core LTL formula, in order to reason exclusively in terms of positive interpretations. It states that (i) the translation function is *total* (otherwise the equality cannot be determined) but also that (ii) the translated formula *preserves the semantic meaning* of the original formula.

Proposition 1. *For any $\psi \in$ LTL, $[\![\psi]\!] = [\![\langle\psi\rangle]\!]$*

Example 1. The behaviour of a traffic-light system may be described by observing its states consisting of green, g, orange, o, and red, r. Complete executions may thus be represented as traces (strings) over the alphabet $\Sigma = \{g, o, r\}$. Predicate definitions may be defined as sets over this alphabet Σ *e.g.*, st $= \{o, r\}$ is true for *stopping* actions o and r; singleton-set predicates are denoted by single-letter names *e.g.*, g $= \{g\}$. We can specify the following properties:

- $(\neg r) \wedge$ Xr describes a trace where the system is not in a red state initially, but turns red at the next instant. *e.g.*, $gr \ldots$ or $or \ldots$;
- g U o describes traces that eventually switch to the orange state from a green state *e.g.*, $go \ldots$ or $gggo \ldots$;
- G st, *i.e.*, always st, which is shorthand for $\neg(\text{tt U } \neg\text{st})$, describes traces that contain only stopping states, *e.g.*, strings of the form $(or)^*$ or r^*.

To determine whether $r^* \in [\![G\,st]\!]$, we can use $[\![\neg(\text{tt U } \neg\text{st})]\!]$ for which we would need to calculate $[\![\text{tt U } \neg\text{st}]\!]$ and then take its dual. Alternatively, we can calculate the denotation of $\langle\neg(\text{tt U } \neg\text{st})\rangle$, which translates to ff R st, and check inclusion *wrt.* the translated negation-free formula, safe in the knowledge that $[\![\neg(\text{tt U } \neg\text{st})]\!] = [\![\text{ff R st}]\!]$. Using similar reasoning, to determine whether $r \ldots \notin [\![(\,\text{r}) \wedge \text{Xr}]\!]$, we can check whether $r \ldots \subset [\![r \vee \text{X}\bar{r}]\!]$ holds.   ■

3   An Online Monitoring Proof System

Online[2] runtime verification of LTL properties consist in determining whether the current execution satisfies (or violates) a property from *the trace generated thus far*. We present a local proof system [SW91, BS92] that characterises such runtime analysis, and allows us to determine whether any (complete) trace ts with *finite* prefix t is included in (or excluded from) $[\![\varphi]\!]$. The proof system is defined as the least relation satisfying the rules in Fig. 2. These rules employ two, mutually dependent, judgements: the sequent $t \vdash^+ \varphi$ denotes a *satisfaction* judgement, whereas $t \vdash^- \psi$ denotes a *violation* judgement; note the polarity differentiating the two judgements, *i.e.*, $+$ and $-$.

Fig. 2 includes three satisfaction axioms (PTRU, PPRD and PCOP) and three violation axioms (NFLS, NPRD and NCOP); the system is parametric *wrt.* the pre-computation of predicates and co-predicates, p and $\bar{p}$. The conjunction and disjunction rules, PAND, POR1 and POR2 (*resp.* NAND1, NAND2 and NOR) *decompose* the composite formula of the judgement for their premises. The negation

---

[2] By contrast, *offline* monitoring typically works on *complete* execution traces. [RH05]

Satisfaction Rules

$$\text{PTRU}\frac{}{t \vdash^+ tt} \qquad \text{PPRD}\frac{p(\sigma)}{\sigma t \vdash^+ p} \qquad \text{PCOP}\frac{\overline{p}(\sigma)}{\sigma t \vdash^+ \overline{p}} \qquad \text{PNEG}\frac{t \vdash^- \varphi}{t \vdash^+ \neg\varphi}$$

$$\text{PAND}\frac{t \vdash^+ \varphi_1 \quad t \vdash^+ \varphi_2}{t \vdash^+ \varphi_1 \wedge \varphi_2} \qquad \text{PNXT}\frac{t \vdash^+ \varphi}{\sigma t \vdash^+ \mathsf{X}\varphi}$$

$$\text{POR1}\frac{t \vdash^+ \varphi_1}{t \vdash^+ \varphi_1 \vee \varphi_2} \qquad \text{POR2}\frac{t \vdash^+ \varphi_2}{t \vdash^+ \varphi_1 \vee \varphi_2}$$

$$\text{PUNT1}\frac{t \vdash^+ \varphi_2}{t \vdash^+ \varphi_1 \mathsf{U} \varphi_2} \qquad \text{PUNT2}\frac{\sigma t \vdash^+ \varphi_1 \quad t \vdash^+ \varphi_1 \mathsf{U} \varphi_2}{\sigma t \vdash^+ \varphi_1 \mathsf{U} \varphi_2}$$

$$\text{PREL1}\frac{t \vdash^+ \varphi_1 \quad t \vdash^+ \varphi_2}{t \vdash^+ \varphi_1 \mathsf{R} \varphi_2} \qquad \text{PREL2}\frac{\sigma t \vdash^+ \varphi_2 \quad t \vdash^+ \varphi_1 \mathsf{R} \varphi_2}{\sigma t \vdash^+ \varphi_1 \mathsf{R} \varphi_2}$$

Violation Rules

$$\text{NFLS}\frac{}{t \vdash^- ff} \qquad \text{NPRD}\frac{\overline{p}(\sigma)}{\sigma t \vdash^- p} \qquad \text{NCOP}\frac{p(\sigma)}{\sigma t \vdash^- \overline{p}} \qquad \text{NNEG}\frac{t \vdash^+ \varphi}{t \vdash^- \neg\varphi}$$

$$\text{NOR}\frac{t \vdash^- \varphi_1 \quad t \vdash^- \varphi_2}{t \vdash^- \varphi_1 \vee \varphi_2} \qquad \text{NNXT}\frac{t \vdash^- \psi}{\sigma t \vdash^- \mathsf{X}\psi}$$

$$\text{NAND1}\frac{t \vdash^- \varphi_1}{t \vdash^- \varphi_1 \wedge \varphi_2} \qquad \text{NAND2}\frac{t \vdash^- \varphi_2}{t \vdash^- \varphi_1 \wedge \varphi_2}$$

$$\text{NUNT1}\frac{t \vdash^- \varphi_1 \quad t \vdash^- \varphi_2}{t \vdash^- \varphi_1 \mathsf{U} \varphi_2} \qquad \text{NUNT2}\frac{\sigma t \vdash^- \varphi_2 \quad t \vdash^- \varphi_1 \mathsf{U} \varphi_2}{\sigma t \vdash^- \varphi_1 \mathsf{U} \varphi_2}$$

$$\text{NREL1}\frac{t \vdash^- \varphi_2}{t \vdash^- \varphi_1 \mathsf{R} \varphi_2} \qquad \text{NREL2}\frac{\sigma t \vdash^- \varphi_1 \quad t \vdash^- \varphi_1 \mathsf{R} \varphi_2}{\sigma t \vdash^- \varphi_1 \mathsf{R} \varphi_2}$$

Fig. 2. Satisfaction and Violation Proof Rules

rules PNEG and NNEG also decompose the formula, but *switch the modality* of the sequents for their premises, *transitioning* from one judgement form to the other. Specifically, in the case of PNEG, the satisfaction sequent $t \vdash^+ \neg\varphi$ is defined in terms of the *violation* sequent $t \vdash^- \varphi$ (and dually for NNEG).

The rules for the temporal formulas may decompose judgement formulas, e.g., PUNT1, PREL1, NUNT1, NREL1, but may also analyse suffixes of the trace *in incremental fashion*. For instance, in order to prove $\sigma t \vdash^+ \mathsf{X}\varphi$, rule PNXT requires the satisfaction judgement to hold for the *immediate* suffix t and the subformula φ, i.e., $t \vdash^+ \varphi$. Similarly, to prove the satisfaction sequent $\sigma t \vdash^+ \varphi_1 \mathsf{U} \varphi_2$, rule PUNT2 requires a satisfaction proof of the current trace σt and the subformula φ_1, as well as a satisfaction proof of the immediate suffix t wrt. $\varphi_1 \mathsf{U} \varphi_2$. Since this suffix premise is wrt. to the same composite formula $\varphi_1 \mathsf{U} \varphi_2$, it may well be the case that PUNT2 is applied again for suffix t. In fact, satisfaction proofs for until formulas are characterised by a series of PUNT2 applications, followed by an application of rule PUNT1 (the satisfaction proofs for $\varphi_1 \mathsf{R} \varphi_2$ and violation proofs for $\varphi_1 \cup \varphi_2$ and $\varphi_1 \mathrel{R} \varphi_2$ follow an analogous structure). This incremental analysis structure mirrors that of RV algorithms for LTL [Gei01, SRA04, BLS11] and contrasts with the descriptive nature of the *resp.* semantic definition for $\varphi_1 \cup \varphi_2$ (Fig. 1) (which merely stipulates the *existence* of some index j at which point φ_2 holds without stating *how* to find this index).

We note the inherent symmetry between the satisfaction and violation rules, internalising the negation-propagation mechanism of the normalisation function $\langle - \rangle$ of §2 through rules PNEG and NNEG. For instance, there are no satisfaction (*resp.* violation) proof rules for the formula ff (*resp.* tt). The *resp.* predicate axioms for satisfactions and violations are dual to one another, as are the rules for conjunctions and disjunctions. More precisely, following $\langle \neg(\psi_1 \wedge \psi_2) \rangle \stackrel{\text{def}}{=} \langle \neg\psi_1 \rangle \vee \langle \neg\psi_2 \rangle$ from Fig. 1, the violation rules for conjunctions (NAND1 and NAND2) have the same structure as the satisfaction rules for the *resp.* disjunctions (POR1 and POR2). The symmetric structure carries over to the temporal proof rules as well, *e.g.*, violation rules NUNT1 and NUNT2 have an analogous structure to that of rules PREL1 and PREL2.

Example 2. Recall property g U o from Ex. 1. We can construct the satisfaction proof for trace *go* and the violation proof for trace *gr* below:

$$
\cfrac{\text{PUNT2} \cfrac{\text{PPRD}\cfrac{\mathsf{g}(g)}{go \vdash^+ \mathsf{g}} \quad \text{PUNT1}\cfrac{\text{PPRD}\cfrac{\mathsf{o}(o)}{o\vdash^+ \mathsf{o}}}{o\vdash^+ \mathsf{g}\, \mathsf{U}\, \mathsf{o}}}{go \vdash^+ \mathsf{g}\, \mathsf{U}\, \mathsf{o}}}
\qquad
\cfrac{\text{NUNT2}\cfrac{\text{NPRD}\cfrac{\overline{\mathsf{o}}(g)}{gr \vdash^- \mathsf{o}}}{} \quad \text{NUNT1}\cfrac{\text{NPRD}\cfrac{\overline{\mathsf{g}}(r)}{r\vdash^- \mathsf{g}} \quad \text{NPRD}\cfrac{\overline{\mathsf{o}}(r)}{r\vdash^- \mathsf{o}}}{r\vdash^+ \mathsf{g}\, \mathsf{U}\, \mathsf{o}}}{gr \vdash^- \mathsf{g}\, \mathsf{U}\, \mathsf{o}}
$$

Crucially, however, we are *unable* to construct *any* proof for the trace *gg*. For instance, attempting to construct a satisfaction proof fails because we hit the end-of-trace, ϵ, before completing the proof tree. Intuitively, we do not have enough information from the trace generated thus far to conclude that the complete trace satisfies the property. For instance, the next state may be o, in which case we can infer satisfaction for *ggo*, or it can be r, in which case we infer a violation for *ggr*; if it is g, we postpone any conclusive judgement once again.

$$
\cfrac{\text{PUNT2}\cfrac{\text{PPRD}\cfrac{\mathsf{g}(g)}{gg \vdash^+ \mathsf{g}}}{} \quad \text{PUNT2}\cfrac{\text{PPRD}\cfrac{\mathsf{g}(g)}{g \vdash^+ \mathsf{g}} \quad ??\cfrac{}{\epsilon \vdash^+ \mathsf{g}\, \mathsf{U}\, \mathsf{o}}}{g \vdash^+ \mathsf{g}\, \mathsf{U}\, \mathsf{o}}}{gg \vdash^+ \mathsf{g}\, \mathsf{U}\, \mathsf{o}} \qquad \blacksquare
$$

Properties. Our proof system is sound, in the following sense.

Theorem 1 (Soundness). *For arbitrary* t, φ:

$$(t \vdash^+ \varphi \ \text{implies} \ \forall s.\, ts \in [\![\varphi]\!]) \quad \text{and} \quad (t \vdash^- \varphi \ \text{implies} \ \forall s.\, ts \notin [\![\varphi]\!])$$

Proof. By rule induction on $t \vdash^+ \varphi$ and $t \vdash^- \varphi$. $\qquad\square$

Example 3. The satisfaction and violation proofs of Ex. 2 suffice to prove $gos \in [\![\mathsf{g}\, \mathsf{U}\, \mathsf{o}]\!]$ and $grs \notin [\![\mathsf{g}\, \mathsf{U}\, \mathsf{o}]\!]$ for any (infinite) suffix s. Moreover, to determine whether $r \ldots \notin [\![(\neg\mathsf{r}) \wedge \mathsf{X}\mathsf{r}]\!]$ from Ex. 1, it suffices to consider the prefix r and either construct a violation proof directly, or else normalise the negation of the formula, $\langle\neg((\neg r) \wedge X r)\rangle = r \vee X\bar{r}$ and construct a satisfaction proof:

$$\text{NAND1} \cfrac{\text{PNEG} \cfrac{\text{PPRE} \cfrac{r(r)}{r \vdash^+ r}}{r \vdash^- \neg r}}{r \vdash^- (\neg r) \wedge X r} \qquad \text{POR1} \cfrac{\text{PPRE} \cfrac{r(r)}{r \vdash^+ r}}{r \vdash^+ r \vee X\bar{r}} \qquad \blacksquare$$

Remark 1. The apparent redundancy (Ex. 3) allows us to use the proof system as a unifying framework that embeds other approaches (*cf.* §5), which may handle negation directly [SRA04], or work exclusively with formulas in nnf [Gei01].

Our proof system handles empty strings ϵ, as these arise naturally from the incremental analysis of finite traces discussed above.

Example 4. We can prove $oo \ldots \in [\![X X \text{tt}]\!]$ from the prefix oo, by constructing the proof tree below; the leaf node relies on being able to deduce $\epsilon \vdash^+ \text{tt}$:

$$\text{PNXT} \cfrac{\text{PNXT} \cfrac{\text{PTRU} \cfrac{}{\epsilon \vdash^+ \text{tt}}}{o \vdash^+ X \text{tt}}}{oo \vdash^+ X X \text{tt}} \qquad \blacksquare$$

Theorem 2 (Incompleteness). *For arbitrary* t, φ:

$$(\forall s. ts \in [\![\varphi]\!] \text{ does not imply } t \vdash^+ \varphi) \quad and \quad (\forall s. ts \notin [\![\varphi]\!] \text{ does not imply } t \vdash^- \varphi)$$

Proof. By counter example. For the positive case, consider $t = \epsilon$. We have $\forall s. ts \in [\![X \text{tt}]\!]$ but $t \not\vdash^+ X \text{tt}$, $\forall s. ts \in [\![p \vee \bar{p}]\!]$ but $t \not\vdash^+ p \vee \bar{p}$, and $\forall s. ts \in [\![\text{ff R tt}]\!]$ but $t \not\vdash^+ \text{ff R tt}$. Curiously, whenever $p(\sigma)$ holds for *all* $\sigma \in \Sigma$, we also have $\forall s. ts \in [\![p]\!]$ but $t \not\vdash^+ p$. Analogous examples can be drawn up for the negative case. □

We can however prove completeness for a syntactic subset of the logic, limiting ourselves to *discriminating* predicates[3], *i.e.*, predicates p where $\exists \sigma_1, \sigma_2 \in \Sigma$ such that $\sigma_1 \neq \sigma_2, p(\sigma_1)$ and $\neg p(\sigma_2)$. We define the following syntactic subset:

$$\phi \in \text{PLTL} ::= \text{tt} \mid \text{ff} \mid p \mid \bar{p} \mid \phi_1 \wedge \phi_2 \mid \phi_1 \cup \phi_2 \mid \neg \gamma$$
$$\gamma \in \text{NLTL} ::= \text{tt} \mid \text{ff} \mid p \mid \bar{p} \mid \gamma_1 \vee \gamma_2 \mid \gamma_1 \text{ R } \gamma_2 \mid \neg \phi$$

Theorem 3 (Partial Completeness). *For arbitrary* t, ϕ, γ:

$$(\forall s. ts \in [\![\phi]\!] \quad implies \quad t \vdash^+ \phi) \quad and \quad (\forall s. ts \notin [\![\gamma]\!] \quad implies \quad t \vdash^- \gamma)$$

Proof. By induction on the structure of ϕ and γ. □

4 An Automation

An automated proof search using the rules in Fig. 2 can be *syntax directed* by the formula (and the polarity) since, for most formulas, there is only *one* applicable rule. Moreover, the exception cases have *at most* two applicable rules.

---

[3] This does not decrease expressivity, since tt and ff can be used for the other cases. Note also that the co-predicate of a discrimination predicate is also discriminating.

$$\mathbf{exp}(d) \stackrel{\text{def}}{=} \begin{cases} \{( )\} & \text{if } ( ) \in d \\ \{\} & \text{if } d = \{\} \\ d & \text{if } c \in d \text{ implies } \mathbf{sat}(c) \\ \mathbf{exp}(\bigcup_{c \in d} \mathbf{expC}(c)) & \text{otherwise} \end{cases}$$

$$\mathbf{expC}(c) \stackrel{\text{def}}{=} \bigoplus_{o \in c} \mathbf{expO}(o)$$

$$\mathbf{expO}(o) \stackrel{\text{def}}{=} \begin{cases} \{c \mid r \in \mathbf{rls}(\varphi, q), c = \mathbf{prm}(r, t, \varphi)\} & \text{if } o = (t, \varphi)^q \\ \{(\lceil \epsilon, \varphi \rceil^q)\} & \text{if } o = \lceil \epsilon, \varphi \rceil^q \end{cases}$$

Fig. 3. A breadth-first incremental search algorithm

Notation. In what follows, $(t, \varphi)^+$ and *resp.* $(t, \varphi)^-$ denote the *resp.* outstanding proof obligations $t \vdash^+ \varphi$ and $t \vdash^- \varphi$. Since our algorithm works on partial traces, $\lceil \epsilon, \varphi \rceil^+$ and $\lceil \epsilon, \varphi \rceil^-$ are used to denote *saturated* proof obligations, where the string ϵ does not yield enough information to complete the proof search (*e.g.*, $\epsilon \vdash^+ g \ \mathsf{U} \ o$ in Ex. 2). A *conjunction set* $(o_1, \ldots, o_n)$ denotes a conjunction of proof obligations; metavariables o_i range over obligations of the form $(t, \varphi)^q$ or $\lceil t, \varphi \rceil^q$ for $q \in \{+, -\}$. A *disjunction set* $\{c_1, \ldots, c_n\}$, where c_i range over conjunction sets, denotes a disjunction of conjunction sets.[4] We employ a merge operation over disjunction sets, $\oplus$, defined below:

$$d \oplus d' \stackrel{\text{def}}{=} \{c \cup c' \mid c \in d, c' \in d'\}$$

The disjunction set $\{( )\}$ acts as the *identity,* , *i.e.*, $\{( )\} \oplus d = d \oplus \{( )\} = d$, whereas the disjunction set $\{\}$ *annihilates* such sets, *i.e.*, $\{\} \oplus d = d \oplus \{\} = \{\}$.

Algorithm. A breadth-first proof search algorithm is described in Fig. 3. Disjunction sets encode the alternative proof derivations that may lead to a completed proof-tree (resulting from multiple proof rules that can be applied at certain stages of the search), and conjunction sets represent the outstanding obligations within each potential derivation. Thus, a disjunction set with an element $( )$, denotes a *successful* search, whereas an empty disjunction set $\{\}$ represents a *failed* search. Another terminating condition for the search algorithm of Fig. 3 is when a disjunction set contains only *saturated* conjunction sets: these containing *only* saturated obligations of the form $\lceil \epsilon, \varphi \rceil^q$ (the predicate $\mathbf{sat}(c)$ denotes this).

To verify whether the judgement $t \vdash^q \varphi$ holds, we initiate the function $\mathbf{exp}(-)$ with the disjunction set $\{((t, \varphi)^q)\}$. If none of the terminating conditions in Fig. 3 are met, $\mathbf{exp}(-)$ expands each conjunction set using $\mathbf{expC}(-)$, and recurses. Conjunction set expansion consists in expanding and merging *every* proof obligation using $\mathbf{expO}(-)$ and $\oplus$. Obligation expansion returns a disjunction set, where each conjunction set denotes the proof obligations resulting from the premises of the rules applied. It uses two auxilliary functions:

---

[4] For clarity, conjunction set notation, $(-)$, differs from that of disjunction sets, $\{-\}$.

- **rls**(φ, q) returns a set of rule names r from Fig. 2 that can be applied to obligations with the formula φ and polarity qualifier q (e.g., **rls**$(\varphi_1 \ \mathsf{U} \ \varphi_2, +) = \{\text{PUNT1}, \text{PUNT2}\}$ and **rls**$(\mathsf{X}\varphi, -) = \{\text{NNXT}\}$).
- **prm**(r, t, φ) returns a conjunction set with the premises of rule r instantiated to the conclusion with string t and formula φ (e.g., **prm**$(\text{PUNT2}, go, \mathsf{g} \ \mathsf{U} \ \mathsf{o}) = (\!((go, \mathsf{g})^+, (o, \mathsf{g} \ \mathsf{U} \ \mathsf{o})^+)\!)$ and **prm**$(\text{PTRU}, go, \mathsf{tt}) = (\!( )\!)$). Importantly:
  (i) For cases such as **prm**$(\text{PUNT2}, \epsilon, \mathsf{g} \ \mathsf{U} \ \mathsf{o})$ the function returns $(\!(\lceil \epsilon, \mathsf{g} \ \mathsf{o} \rceil^+)\!)$ since the string ϵ prohibits the function from generating *all* the premises for the rule (one premise requires the string to be of length ≥ 1).
  (ii) The function is *undefined* when rule conditions are not satisfied (e.g., **prm**$(\text{PPRD}, g, \mathsf{o})$ is undefined since $\mathsf{o}(g)$ does not hold).

Example 5. Recall the inconclusive judgement $gg \vdash^+ \mathsf{g} \ \mathsf{U} \ \mathsf{o}$ from Ex. 2.

$$\mathbf{exp}(\{(\!((gg, \mathsf{g} \ \mathsf{U} \ \mathsf{o})^+)\!)\}) = \mathbf{exp}(\{(\!((gg, \mathsf{o})^+)\!), (\!((gg, \mathsf{g})^+, (g, \mathsf{g} \ \mathsf{U} \ \mathsf{o})^+)\!)\})$$
$$= \mathbf{exp}(\{\} \cup (\{(\!( )\!)\} \oplus \{(\!((g, \mathsf{o})^+)\!), (\!((g, \mathsf{g})^+, (\epsilon, \mathsf{g} \ \mathsf{U} \ \mathsf{o})^+)\!)\})$$
$$= \mathbf{exp}(\{(\!((g, \mathsf{o})^+)\!), (\!((g, \mathsf{g})^+, (\epsilon, \mathsf{g} \ \mathsf{U} \ \mathsf{o})^+)\!)\}) = \{(\!(\lceil \epsilon, \mathsf{g} \ \mathsf{U} \ \mathsf{o} \rceil^+)\!)\} \ \blacksquare$$

Properties. An execution of $\mathbf{exp}(\{(\!((t, \varphi)^q)\!)\})$ may yield either of *three* verdicts. Apart from success, $\{(\!( )\!)\}$, meaning that a full proof tree was derived, the algorithm partitions negative results as either a definite fail, $\{\}$, or an *inconclusive* verdict, consisting of a saturate disjunction set d (where $c \in d$ implies **sat**(c)).

Saturated disjunction sets make the algorithm *incremental*, in the following sense. When a further suffix t' is learnt to a judgement $t \vdash^q \varphi$ with an inconclusive verdict, we can *reuse* the saturated disjunction set returned for $t \vdash^q \varphi$, instead of processing $tt' \vdash^q \varphi$ from scratch. This is done by converting each obligation of the form $\lceil \epsilon, \varphi \rceil^q$ in each saturated conjunction set to the *active* obligation $(t', \varphi)^q$ using an auxilliary "append" function **app**$(-)$.

Example 6. To determine whether $ggo \vdash^+ \mathsf{g} \ \mathsf{U} \ \mathsf{o}$ holds, we can take the inconclusive outcome of $\mathbf{exp}(\{(\!((gg, \mathsf{g} \ \mathsf{U} \ \mathsf{o})^+)\!)\})$ from Ex. 5, convert the saturated obligations using suffix o, **app**$(\{(\!(\lceil \epsilon, \mathsf{g} \ \mathsf{U} \ \mathsf{o} \rceil^+)\!)\}, o) = \{(\!((o, \mathsf{g} \ \mathsf{U} \ \mathsf{o})^+)\!)\}$, and calculate from that point onwards, $\mathbf{exp}(\{(\!((o, \mathsf{g} \ \mathsf{U} \ \mathsf{o})^+)\!)\}) = \{(\!( )\!)\}$. $\blacksquare$

Theorem 4 (Incrementality). $\mathbf{sat}(\mathbf{exp}(\{(\!((t_1, \varphi)^q)\!)\}))$ *implies*

$$\mathbf{exp}(\{(\!((t_1 t_2, \varphi)^q)\!)\}) = \mathbf{exp}(\mathbf{app}(\mathbf{exp}(\{(\!((t_1, \varphi)^q)\!)\}), t_2))$$

Proof. By induction on t_2.   □

The algorithm of Fig. 3 is also *decidable* for the proof rules of Fig. 2. Intuitively, the main reason for this is because the proof system is *cut-free*, where rule premises are either defined in terms of string suffixes or subformula. Formally, we define a rank function $| - |$ mapping proof obligations to pairs of naturals, for which we assume a lexicographical ordering $(n_1, m_1) \geq (n_2, m_2) \overset{\text{def}}{=} n_1 \geq n_2 \vee (n_1 = n_2 \wedge m_1 \geq m_2)$ and the obvious function $\mathbf{max}(-)$ returning the greatest element from a set of such pairs. Apart from $|t|$, we also assume $|\varphi|$ returning the *maximal depth* of the formula (e.g., $|p \cup \neg(\bar{p} \vee p)| = 3$ and $|\bar{p}| = 0$).

$$|(t, \varphi)^q| \stackrel{\text{def}}{=} (|t|, |\varphi|) \qquad |\lceil t, \varphi \rceil^q| \stackrel{\text{def}}{=} (0, 0) \qquad |c| \stackrel{\text{def}}{=} \mathbf{max}(\{|o| \mid o \in c\} \cup \{(0,0)\})$$

$$|d| \stackrel{\text{def}}{=} \text{if } (\!|\,|\!) \in d \text{ then } (0,0) \text{ else } \mathbf{max}(\{|c| \mid c \in d\} \cup \{(0,0)\})$$

Above, the rank function maps saturated obligations to the bottom element $(0,0)$. We overload the function to conjunction sets, where we add $(0,0)$ to the $\mathbf{max}(-)$ calculation to cater for the case where c is empty. Following a similar pattern, we also extend the rank function to disjunction sets, but equate all sets with an empty conjunction set to the bottom element $(0,0)$; this mirrors the termination condition of the algorithm in Fig. 3 which terminates the search as soon as the shortest proof tree is detected.

Theorem 5 (Decidability). *$exp(\{(\!|\,(t, \varphi)^q\,|\!)\})$ always terminates.*

Proof. Follows from the fact that when $|d| = (0,0)$, $\mathbf{exp}(d)$ terminates immediately, and when $|d| \neq (0,0)$, we have $|d| > |\bigcup_{c \in d} \mathbf{expC}(c)|$.   □

Runtime Monitoring. We can obtain a setup akin to the three-valued monitors of [BLS11] with outcome **Y**, denoting satisfaction, outcome **N**, denoting violation, and outcome **?**, denoting an inconclusive outcome. Following [BLS11], given a finite trace t and a property φ, we attempt to construct a deduction for *both* the satisfaction, $t \vdash^+ \varphi$ and violation, $t \vdash^- \varphi$, by *concurrently* running $\mathbf{exp}(\{(\!|\,(t, \varphi)^+\,|\!)\})$ and $\mathbf{exp}(\{(\!|\,(t, \varphi)^-\,|\!)\})$ with the following possible outcomes:

1. We are able to construct a proof for $t \vdash^+ \psi$, corresponding to **Y**.
2. We are able to construct a proof for $t \vdash^- \psi$, corresponding to **N**.
3. We are unable to construct proofs for either case, corresponding to **?**.

Remark 2. The fourth possible outcome, *i.e.*, constructing a proof for *both* $t \vdash_3^+ \psi$ and $t \vdash_3^- \psi$, is ruled out by soundness (Thm. 1), which implicitly guarantees that our analysis is consistent (since the semantics is defined in terms of sets).

Like in most online RV setups, Thm. 4 allows for *incremental* monitor, as soon as individual trace elements are received. Moreover, Thm. 5 allows for a *safe synchronous* instrumentation, where the monitor and system execute in lock-step (*i.e.*, the system is paused after producing each monitored event so as to allow the monitor to carry out its analysis and perform timely detections). Since the monitoring analysis always terminates, the monitored system is guaranteed to be able to progress normally under a synchronous instrumentation.

5   Alternative RV Symbolic Techniques for LTL

We relate our deductive system to two prominent, but substantially distinct, symbolic techniques for LTL in the context of RV, namely [Gei01] and [SRA04].

5.1 Informative Prefixes

Intuitively, an *informative prefix* for a formula *explains* why a trace satisfies that formula [KYV01]. In [Gei01], trace satisfactions are monitored wrt. LTL *formulas in nnf*, by checking whether a trace contains an informative prefix.

Example 7. Recall $g \cup o$ (Ex. 1). Prefix go is informative because (i) although the head, g, does not satisfy $g \cup o$ in a definite manner, it allows the possibility of its suffix to satisfy the formula conclusively ($g(g)$ holds); (ii) the immediate suffix, o, satisfies $g \cup o$ conclusively ($o(o)$ holds). In [Gei01], both go and o are deemed to be *locally-informative* wrt. $g \cup o$ but go generates satisfaction obligations for the immediate suffix (*temporal informative successor*).   ■

The algorithm in [Gei01] formalises the notion of locally informative by converting formulas to their *informative normal forms*. Moreover, temporal informative successors are formalised through the function $next(-)$, returning a set of formulas from a given formula and a trace element. For instance, in Ex. 7 $next(g, g \cup o) = \{g \cup o\}$ whereas $next(o, g \cup o) = \{\}$. These functions are then used to construct automata that check for these properties over string prefixes.

$$\text{GTRU} \frac{}{linf(t, \text{tt}, \emptyset)} \qquad \text{GPRE1} \frac{p(\sigma)}{linf(\sigma t, p, \emptyset)} \qquad \text{GPRE2} \frac{\bar{p}(\sigma)}{linf(\sigma t, \bar{p}, \emptyset)}$$

$$\text{GOR1} \frac{linf(t, \varphi_1, m)}{linf(t, \varphi_1 \vee \varphi_2, m)} \qquad\qquad \text{GOR2} \frac{linf(t, \varphi_2, m)}{linf(t, \varphi_1 \vee \varphi_2, m)}$$

$$\text{GAND} \frac{linf(t, \varphi_1, m_1) \quad linf(t, \varphi_2, m_2)}{linf(t, \varphi_1 \wedge \varphi_2, m_1 \cup m_2)} \qquad \text{GNXT} \frac{}{linf(t, X\varphi, \{\varphi\})}$$

$$\text{GUNT1} \frac{linf(t, \varphi_2, m)}{linf(t, \varphi_1 \cup \varphi_2, m)} \qquad \text{GUNT2} \frac{linf(t, \varphi_1, m)}{linf(t, \varphi_1 \cup \varphi_2, m \cup \{\varphi_1 \cup \varphi_2\})}$$

$$\text{GREL1} \frac{linf(t, \varphi_1, m_1) \quad linf(t, \varphi_2, m_2)}{linf(t, \varphi_1 R \varphi_2, m_1 \cup m_2)} \qquad \text{GREL2} \frac{linf(t, \varphi_2, m)}{linf(t, \varphi_1 R \varphi_2, m \cup \{\varphi_1 R \varphi_2\})}$$

In this section, we express the locally-informative predicate and the associated temporal informative successors as the single judgement $linf(t, \varphi, m)$, defined as the least relation satisfying the rules above. It states that t is locally informative for φ with obligations $m \in \mathcal{P}(\text{ELTL})$ for the succeeding suffix. For example, for a formula $X\varphi$, *any* string t is locally informative, but requires the immediate suffix to satisfy φ (see GNXT); in the case of $\varphi_1 \cup \varphi_2$, if t is locally informative for ψ_1 with suffix obligations m, then t is also locally informative for $\varphi_1 \cup \varphi_2$ with obligations $m \cup \{\varphi_1 \cup \varphi_2\}$ (see GUNT2). Informative prefixes are formalised as the predicate $inf(t, \varphi)$ below. Note that recursion in $inf(t, \varphi)$ is employed on a substring of t and terminates when $m = \emptyset$.

$$inf(t, \varphi) \overset{\text{def}}{=} \exists m. \left(linf(t, \varphi, m) \quad \text{and} \quad (\varphi' \in m \text{ implies } (inf([t]^1, \varphi'))) \right)$$

Example 8. We can deduce that $inf(go, g \cup o)$ because $linf(go, g \cup o, \{g \cup o\})$ and then that $linf(o, g \cup o, \emptyset)$.   ■

We can formally show a correspondence between informative prefixes and our monitoring proof systems.

Theorem 6. *For all φ in nnf, $inf(t, \varphi)$ iff $t \vdash^+ \varphi$*

Proof. By structural induction on t, then by rule induction on $linf(t, \varphi, m)$ for the *only-if* case. By rule induction for the *if* case.   □

In the *only-if* direction, Thm. 6 ensures that our system is as expressive as [Gei01]. In the *if* direction, Thm. 6 shows that every derivation in our proof system corresponds to an informative prefix as defined in [KYV01][5]. This re-inforces existing justifications as to why our system is unable to symbolically process certain prefix and formula pairs.

Example 9. The proof system of §3 is unable to deduce $\epsilon \vdash^+$ Xtt (*cf.* proof for Thm. 2) even though, on a semantic level, this holds for any string continuation because ϵ in *not* an informative prefix of Xtt.   ■

Thm. 6 has another important implication. One justification of informative prefixes is that any bad/good prefixes detected can be accompanied by an expla-nation [BLS11]. However, whereas in [Gei01] this explanation is given in terms of the algorithm implementation, delineating the proof system from its imple-menting monitor (as in our case) allows for better separation of concerns, by giving the explanation as a derivation[6] in terms of the proof rules of Fig. 2.

5.2   Derivatives

In a derivatives approach [HR01, SRA04], LTL formulas are interpreted as *func-tions* that take a state *i.e.*, an element of the alphabet Σ, and return another LTL formula. The returned formula is then applied again to the next state in the trace, until either one of the *canonical* formulas tt or ff are reached; the trace analysis stops at canonical formulas, since tt (*resp.* ff) are idempotent, returning tt (*resp.* ff), irrespective of the state applied to. In [SRA04], coinductive deduc-tive techniques are used on derivatives to establish LTL formula equivalences, which are then used to obtain optimal monitors for good/bad prefixes.

Example 10. Recall $\epsilon \not\vdash^+$ Xtt from Ex. 9. In [SRA04], they establish that formu-las tt and Xtt are equivalent *wrt.* good prefixes, tt $\equiv_G$ Xtt, which allows them to reason symbolically about ϵ and Xtt in terms of ϵ and tt instead.   ■

Formally, a derivative is a rewriting operator $\_\{\_\}$ :: ALTL $\times \Sigma \longrightarrow$ ALTL (adapted from [SRA04]) defined on the structure of the formula as follows:

---

[5] As a corollary, we also establish a correspondence between $t \vdash^- \varphi$ and $inf(t, \neg\varphi)$ as used in [Gei01] for bad prefixes.

[6] The algorithm in §4 can be easily extended so as to record the rules used.

$$\mathsf{tt}\{\sigma\} \stackrel{\mathrm{def}}{=} \mathsf{tt} \qquad\qquad\qquad \mathsf{ff}\{\sigma\} \stackrel{\mathrm{def}}{=} \mathsf{ff}$$

$$\mathsf{p}\{\sigma\} \stackrel{\mathrm{def}}{=} \textit{if } \mathsf{p}(\sigma) \textit{ then } \mathsf{tt} \textit{ else } \mathsf{ff}$$

$$(\neg\psi)\{\sigma\} \stackrel{\mathrm{def}}{=} (\mathsf{tt} \oplus \psi)\{\sigma\} \qquad\qquad \psi_1 \oplus \psi_2\{\sigma\} \stackrel{\mathrm{def}}{=} \psi_1\{\sigma\} \oplus \psi_2\{\sigma\}$$

$$\psi_1 \wedge \psi_2\{\sigma\} \stackrel{\mathrm{def}}{=} \psi_1\{\sigma\} \wedge \psi_2\{\sigma\} \qquad\quad \psi_1 \vee \psi_2\{\sigma\} \stackrel{\mathrm{def}}{=} \psi_1\{\sigma\} \vee \psi_2\{\sigma\}$$

$$\mathsf{X}\psi\{\sigma\} \stackrel{\mathrm{def}}{=} \psi$$

$$\psi_1 \mathsf{U} \psi_2\{\sigma\} \stackrel{\mathrm{def}}{=} \psi_2\{\sigma\} \vee (\psi_1\{\sigma\} \wedge \psi_1\mathsf{U}\psi_2)$$

Above, we position rewriting definitions for core LTL formulas of Fig. 1 on the left; formula rewriting however also uses an *extended* set of formulas that include falsity, ff, disjunction, $\psi_1 \vee \psi_2$, and exclusive-or, $\psi_1 \oplus \psi_2$. The derivatives algorithm also works up to formula normalisations using the following equalities:

$$\mathsf{tt} \wedge \psi \equiv \psi \qquad \mathsf{ff} \wedge \psi \equiv \mathsf{ff} \qquad \mathsf{ff} \vee \psi \equiv \psi \qquad \mathsf{tt} \vee \psi \equiv \mathsf{tt}$$
$$\psi \wedge \psi \equiv \psi \qquad \psi \vee \psi \equiv \psi \qquad \mathsf{ff} \oplus \psi \equiv \psi \qquad (\psi_1 \wedge \psi_2) \oplus \psi_1 \oplus \psi_2 \equiv \psi_1 \vee \psi_2$$

Thus, for any finite trace t of the form $\sigma_1\sigma_2\dots\sigma_n$ we say:

- t is a good prefix for ψ iff $((\psi\{\sigma_1\})\{\sigma_2\})\{\dots\sigma_n\} \equiv \mathsf{tt}$;
- t is a bad prefix for ψ iff $((\psi\{\sigma_1\})\{\sigma_2\})\{\dots\sigma_n\} \equiv \mathsf{ff}$.

Example 11. The partial trace go is a *good prefix* for $\mathsf{gU o}$ (Ex. 1) because:

$$(\mathsf{gU o}\{g\})\{o\} \stackrel{\mathrm{def}}{=} o\{g\} \vee (\mathsf{g}\{g\} \wedge \mathsf{gU o})\{o\}$$
$$\stackrel{\mathrm{def}}{=} \mathsf{ff} \vee (\mathsf{g}\{g\} \wedge \mathsf{gU o})\{o\} \equiv (\mathsf{g}\{g\} \wedge \mathsf{gU o})\{o\}$$
$$\stackrel{\mathrm{def}}{=} (\mathsf{tt} \wedge \mathsf{gU o})\{o\} \equiv \mathsf{gU o}\{o\}$$
$$\stackrel{\mathrm{def}}{=} o\{o\} \vee (\mathsf{g}\{o\} \wedge \mathsf{gU o}) \stackrel{\mathrm{def}}{=} \mathsf{tt} \vee (\mathsf{g}\{o\} \wedge \mathsf{gU o}) \equiv \mathsf{tt} \qquad \blacksquare$$

Good (*resp.* bad) prefixes, as defined in[SRA04], correspond to finite traces with a satisfaction (*resp.* violation) proof in our system (§3), and vice-versa.

Theorem 7. *For any finite trace* $t = \sigma_1\dots\sigma_n$, *and core LTL formula* ψ:

$$((\psi\{\sigma_1\})\{\dots\sigma_n\} \equiv \mathsf{tt} \quad \textit{iff} \quad t \vdash^+ \psi) \quad \textit{and} \quad ((\psi\{\sigma_1\})\{\dots\sigma_n\} \equiv \mathsf{ff} \quad \textit{iff} \quad t \vdash^- \psi)$$

Proof. For the *only-if* case both statements are proved simultaneously by numerical induction on n and then by structural induction on ψ. For the *if* case both statements are proved simultaneously by rule induction. □

Apart from establishing a one-to-one correspondence between derivative prefixes and proof deductions for core LTL formulas in our system, Thm. 7 (together with Thm. 6) allows us to relate indirectly the informative prefixes of §5.1 to derivative prefixes. Moreover, Thm. 7 identifies from where the additional expressivity of the analysis in [SRA04] derives, namely through the deductive system for formula equivalence *wrt.* good/bad prefixed, $\vdash \psi_1 \equiv_G \psi_2$ and $\vdash \psi_1 \equiv_B \psi_2$. This opens up the possibility of merging the two approaches, perhaps by extending our deductive system with rules analogous to those show below:

$$\mathrm{PEQ}\frac{t \vdash^+ \varphi_1 \qquad \vdash \varphi_1 \equiv_G \varphi_2}{t \vdash^+ \varphi_2} \qquad\qquad \mathrm{NEQ}\frac{t \vdash^- \varphi_1 \qquad \vdash \varphi_1 \equiv_B \varphi_2}{t \vdash^- \varphi_2}$$

6   Conclusion

We presented a proof system and the respective monitor generation for runtime-verifying LTL properties. One novel aspect of our approach is that we tease apart the specification of the symbolic analysis from its automation. This allows us to localise correctness results e.g., soundness is determined for the proof system, independent of the subsequent automation. The higher level of abstraction used elucidates completeness studies, seldom tackled in other work in RV e.g., the syntactic subclass identified for Thm. 3 appears to be new. This separation of concerns also facilitates comparisons and cross-fertilisation with other symbolic techniques (§ 5) and leads to modular organisations that are easier to maintain e.g., more efficient monitor automation may be considered without changing the proof rules. The concrete contributions are:

1. A *sound, local* LTL proof system inferring complete trace inclusion from finite prefixes, Thm. 1, together with completeness results, Thm. 2 and Thm. 3.
2. A mechanisation of proof derivations for this system that is formally incremental, Thm. 4, and decidable, Thm. 5.
3. An exposition of how the proof system can be used as a unifying framework where to relate different runtime monitoring formalisms, Thm. 7 and Thm. 6.

Related Work. Apart from the deductive system for LTL formula equivalence in [SRA04], there are other LTL proof systems [GPSS80, MP91, KI11, BL08]. Each differ substantially from ours. For instance, the model used in [GPSS80, MP91] is different from ours, i.e., programs (*sets of traces*) instead of traces; the work in [GPSS80, KI11] is concerned with developing tableau methods for inferring the validity of a formula from a conjunction of formulas; [BL08] study cut-free sequent systems; importantly, none of these proof systems are local. In [MP91], they develop three *tailored* proof systems for separate classes of properties, namely safety, response and reactivity properties; crucially however, they do not consider aspects such as deductions from *partial* traces.

A substantial body of work studies alternative LTL semantics for partial traces [EFH$^+$03, BLS07, BLS11]; consult [BLS10] for a comprehensive survey. Although complementary, the aim and methodology of this work is substantially different from ours. In particular, we keep the LTL semantics *constant*, and explore the soundness, completeness and expressivity aspects of our symbolic analysis wrt. to this fixed semantics.

Future Work. It would be fruitful to relate other LTL symbolic analyses to the ones discussed in §5. Our work may also be used as a point of departure for developing proof systems for other interpretations of LTL. For instance, a different LTL model to that of §2, consisting of both *finite* and infinite traces, alters the negation propagation identities used for the translation function (*e.g.*, $\neg X \psi \equiv X \neg \psi$ does not hold) which, amongst other things, would require tweaking to the proof rules. Similar issues arise in distributed LTL interpretations such as [BF12] where instead of having one execution trace, we have a *set of traces* (one for each location). We also leave complexity analysis and the assessment of the runtime overheads introduced by our setup as future work.

References

[BF12]   Bauer, A., Falcone, Y.: Decentralised LTL Monitoring. In: Giannakopoulou, D., Méry, D. (eds.) FM 2012. LNCS, vol. 7436, pp. 85–100. Springer, Heidelberg (2012)

[BL08]   Brunnler, K., Lange, M.: Cut-free sequent systems for temporal logic. JLAP 76(2), 216–225 (2008)

[BLS07]   Bauer, A., Leucker, M., Schallhart, C.: The good, the bad, and the ugly, but how ugly is ugly? In: Sokolsky, O., Taşıran, S. (eds.) RV 2007. LNCS, vol. 4839, pp. 126–138. Springer, Heidelberg (2007)

[BLS10]   Bauer, A., Leucker, M., Schallhart, C.: Comparing LTL semantics for runtime verification. Logic and Comput. 20(3), 651–674 (2010)

[BLS11]   Bauer, A., Leucker, M., Schallhart, C.: Runtime verification for LTL and TLTL. TOSEM 20(4), 14 (2011)

[BS92]   Bradfield, J., Stirling, C.: Local model-checking for infinite state spaces. TCS 96, 157–174 (1992)

[Bus98]   Buss, S.R. (ed.): Handbook of Proof Theory. Elsevier (1998)

[EFH+03]   Eisner, C., Fisman, D., Havlicek, J., Lustig, Y., McIsaac, A., Van Campenhout, D.: Reasoning with temporal logic on truncated paths. In: Hunt Jr., W.A., Somenzi, F. (eds.) CAV 2003. LNCS, vol. 2725, pp. 27–39. Springer, Heidelberg (2003)

[Gei01]   Geilen, M.: On the construction of monitors for temporal logic properties. ENTCS 55(2), 181–199 (2001)

[GPSS80]   Gabbay, D., Pnueli, A., Shelah, S., Stavi, J.: On the temporal analysis of fairness. In: POPL, pp. 163–173. ACM, New York (1980)

[HR01]   Havelund, K., Rosu, G.: Monitoring programs using rewriting. In: ASE, pp. 135–143. IEEE, Wash., DC (2001)

[KI11]   Kojima, K., Igarashi, A.: Constructive linear-time temporal logic: Proof systems and kripke semantics. Inf. Comput. 209(12), 1491–1503 (2011)

[KYV01]   Kupferman, O., Vardi, M.Y.: Model checking of safety properties. Form. Methods Syst. Des. 19(3), 291–314 (2001)

[LS09]   Leucker, M., Schallhart, C.: A brief account of Runtime Verification. JLAP 78(5), 293–303 (2009)

[MP91]   Manna, Z., Pnueli, A.: Completing the Temporal Picture. Theoretical Computer Science 83(1), 97–130 (1991)

[Pnu77]   Pnueli, A.: The Temporal Logic of Programs. In: SFCS, pp. 46–57. IEEE, Wash., DC (1977)

[RH05]   Roşu, G., Havelund, K.: Rewriting-based techniques for runtime verification. Automated Software Engg. 12(2), 151–197 (2005)

[SRA04]   Sen, K., Roşu, G., Agha, G.: Generating optimal linear temporal logic monitors by coinduction. In: Saraswat, V.A. (ed.) ASIAN 2003. LNCS, vol. 2896, pp. 260–275. Springer, Heidelberg (2003)

[SW91]   Stirling, C., Walker, D.: Local model-checking in the modal mu-calculus. TCS 89, 161–177 (1991)

[TS00]   Troelstra, A.S., Schwichtenberg, H.: Basic Proof Theory. Cambridge University Press (2000)

MARQ: **Monitoring at Runtime with QEA**

Giles Reger, Helena Cuenca Cruz, and David Rydeheard

University of Manchester, Manchester, UK

Abstract. Runtime monitoring is the process of checking whether an execution trace of a running system satisfies a given specification. For this to be effective, monitors which run trace-checking algorithms must be efficient so that they introduce minimal computational overhead. We present the MARQ tool for monitoring properties expressed as Quantified Event Automata. This formalism generalises previous automata-based specification methods. MARQ extends the established parametric trace slicing technique and incorporates existing techniques for indexing and garbage collection as well as a new technique for optimising runtime monitoring: *structural specialisations* where monitors are generated based on structural characteristics of the monitored property. MARQ recently came top in two tracks in the 1st international Runtime Verification competition, showing that MARQ is one of the most efficient existing monitoring tools for both offline monitoring of trace logs and online monitoring of running systems.

1 Introduction

Runtime monitoring [14,17] is the process of checking whether an execution trace produced by a running system satisfies a given specification. Here we present MARQ, a new runtime monitoring tool that uses the QEA specification language. Over the past few years a number of runtime monitoring approaches have been developed [2,4,6,9,11,18,19] but there has been little comparison of the relative *efficiency* and *expressiveness* of runtime monitoring tools; mainly due to a lack of agreed benchmarks. This prompted the recently held 1st international Runtime Verification competition [5], where MARQ won the offline monitoring and online monitoring for `Java` tracks [1]. This paper makes use of specifications and benchmarks from this competition.

Runtime monitoring. Whilst techniques such as model checking are concerned with checking correctness against all possible runs of a system, runtime monitoring considers traces observed on individual runs of a system. Although incomplete, in the sense that only observed runs are checked, this approach has the advantage that actual behaviour is analysed. Scalability issues are then restricted to deciding which runs to analyse.

Typically runtime monitoring consists of three stages: firstly, a property denoting a set of valid traces is specified in a formal language. Secondly, the system of interest is *instrumented* to produce the required events recording information about the state of the system. Thirdly, a monitor is generated from the specification, which processes the trace to produce a verdict. This monitoring can occur *offline* on recorded executions or *online* whilst the monitored system is running. The offline case means that any system that produces logs can be monitored; whereas the online case requires specific mechanisms

© Springer-Verlag Berlin Heidelberg 2015
C. Baier and C. Tinelli (Eds.): TACAS 2015, LNCS 9035, pp. 596–610, 2015.
DOI: 10.1007/978-3-662-46681-0_55

for receiving events at runtime. The MARQ tool is suitable for offline monitoring and online monitoring of Java programs using AspectJ for instrumentation.

In both online and offline monitoring, *efficiency* is a key concern; monitoring a system online may introduce computational overheads and also interference with the monitored system. The aim is to produce monitors that minimise these effects. One advantage of online monitoring is that it can be included in production systems to guard against incorrect behaviour and potentially take corrective action. However, this becomes impractical if the monitoring tool introduces excessive overhead.

To illustrate the runtime monitoring process, consider a system where different services may be requested. A typical desired property is that every request should receive a response; in first-order Linear Temporal Logic this might be specified as $\forall s.\Box(\texttt{request}(s) \rightarrow \Diamond\texttt{response}(s))$. MARQ uses quantified event automata (QEA) [4,21] to specify such properties as they admit an efficient monitoring algorithm via the *parametric trace slicing* approach discussed later. Fig. 1 gives a QEA for this property:

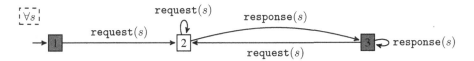

Fig. 1. A QEA describing a request-response property for services (see Sec. 2.1)

This uses an automaton to capture the allowed ordering of events and a quantification $\forall s$ to indicate the property should hold for all services s. The trace $\texttt{request}(A)$. $\texttt{request}(B).\texttt{response}(A)$ violates the property as service B has no response. As explained in Sec. 2.1, this verdict is computed by *slicing* the trace for values A and B and inspecting the subtraces separately.

This is an example of a *parametric* or *first-order* property as it deals with events containing data. QEA allows data to be treated in both a *quantified* and a *free* way (see Sec. 2). Runtime monitoring approaches for parametric properties tend to focus either on *efficiency* or *expressiveness*. Those focussing on efficiency typically employ the *parametric trace slicing* technique [8,23] illustrated above.

Contribution. As shown previously [4,21], QEA is more expressive than the underlying languages of comparably efficient monitoring tools i.e. those that make us of parametric trace slicing [2,8,18]. Therefore, MARQ can monitor properties that make use of these additional features e.g. existential quantification and free variables. As well as additional expressiveness, the MARQ tool implements a range of optimisations for efficient monitoring, including a novel technique which selects optimisations according to the structure of the specified property.

Availability. MARQ is available from

```
https://github.com/selig/qea
```

This includes instructions on how to perform online and offline monitoring and a collection of specifications used in the 1st international runtime verification competition.

Structure. We first describe how MARQ can be used to specify properties (Sec. 2) and perform monitoring (Sec. 3). This is followed by an overview of MARQ's implementation (Sec. 4). Then we look at how changing the way a specification is written can improve monitoring efficiency (Sec. 5). We finish by comparing MARQ with other tools (Sec. 6) and giving conclusions (Sec. 7).

2   Writing Specifications in QEA

We consider the problem of using QEA to write parametric specifications for MARQ. This presentation is example-led, omitting details which can be found in [4,21].

We are concerned with parametric properties in which events may carry data. A *parametric event* is a pair of an event name and a list of data values, and a parametric trace is a finite sequence of parametric events. A parametric property denotes a set of parametric traces. Quantified event automata (QEA) determine such sets of traces - those accepted by the automata.

A QEA is a list of quantified variables together with an event automata. An event automata is a finite state machine with transitions labelled with symbol parametric events, where data values can be replaced by variables. Transitions may also include guards and assignments over these variables.

2.1   The Slicing Approach

Let us revisit the QEA in Fig. 1. The event automaton consists of three states and five transitions. The shaded states are final states. The square states are *closed to failure* i.e. if no transition can be taken there is a transition to an implicit failure state; the alternative, seen below, is to have a circular state that is *closed to self* i.e. if no transition can be taken there is an implicit self-looping transition. The quantifier list ∀s means that the property must hold for *all* values that s takes in the trace i.e. the values obtained when matching the symbolic events in the specification with concrete events in the trace.

To decide the verdict given the trace

$$\mathtt{request}(A).\mathtt{request}(B).\mathtt{request}(C).\mathtt{response}(A).\mathtt{request}(C).\mathtt{response}(C)$$

we *slice* the trace based on the values that can match s, giving the slices

$$
\begin{array}{lcl}
[s \mapsto A] & \mapsto & \mathtt{request}(A).\mathtt{response}(A) \\
[s \mapsto B] & \mapsto & \mathtt{request}(B) \\
[s \mapsto C] & \mapsto & \mathtt{request}(C).\mathtt{request}(C).\mathtt{response}(C)
\end{array}
$$

Then we ask whether each slice is accepted by the event automaton *instantiated* with the binding i.e. with s replaced by the appropriate value. The slice for $[s \mapsto B]$ does not reach a final state, therefore the whole trace is not accepted.

2.2   Two Different Kinds of Variables

In QEA variables can either be quantified or free. This is an important distinction and we review the difference here. The variables of a QEA are those appearing in symbolic events labelling transitions. For example, the QEA in Fig. 1 has the single variable s.

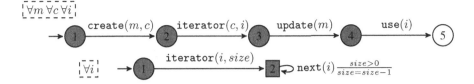

Fig. 2. Two QEAs demonstrating QEA features. **unsafemapiter** (top) specifies how iterators over collections created from maps should be used. **safeiter** (bottom) restricts the maximum number of calls to **next** on an iterator.

Quantified variables. A QEA may have zero or more variables that are universally or existentially quantified. Quantifications have their usual interpretation i.e. universal means *for all values in the domain* where the domain is determined by the trace (see above). A quantification may be associated with a guard (a predicate over previously quantified variables), which excludes some bindings of quantified variables from consideration. A quantification list may be negated, which inverts the verdict obtained.

As an example, the **unsafemapiter** property in Fig. 2 uses multiple quantified variables. The property is that an iterator over a collection created from a map cannot be used after the map is updated. The style of specification here is to specify the events that lead to failure i.e. for every map m, collection c and iterator i if we see $create(m, c).iterator(c, i).update(m).use(i)$ then the property has been violated. Note that the circular states are closed to self (see above) so any additional events are ignored.

Free variables. Any variables in a QEA that are not quantified are called *free*. Quantified variables indicate that the automaton should be instantiated for each binding of those variables; free variables are local to each of these instantiations and are rebound as the trace is processed. The purpose of free variables is to store data that can be accessed by *guards* and *assignments* on transitions. Guards are predicates that restrict the availability of transitions and assignments can modify the values given to free variables.

The **safeiter** property in Fig. 2 uses a free variable $size$ to track the size of a collection being iterated over. The property is that the **next** method may only be called on an Iterator object as many times as their are objects in the base collection. This is a generalisation of the standard HasNext property often used in runtime monitoring [2,18]. The value for $size$ is bound on the **iterator** event and then checked and updated in a loop on state 2; as this state is square if the guard is false there is an implicit failure.

2.3 Creating QEAs and Monitors in MARQ

To specify QEA as input to the MARQ system, we introduce a QEABuilder as illustrated in Fig. 3. A builder object is used to add transitions and record information about quantification and states. These are used to construct a QEA that is passed to the MonitorFactory as discussed below.

Fig. 4 shows how QEABuilder can be used to construct the **safeiter** property QEA seen in Fig. 2. First the builder object q is created. Then we declare the event names and variables as integers; quantified variables are negative, free variables are positive.

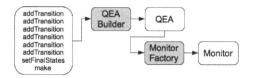

Fig. 3. Using the QEABuilder and MonitorFactory

```
QEABuilder q = new QEABuilder("safeiter");

int ITERATOR = 1; int NEXT = 2;
final int i = −1; final int size = 1;
q.addQuantification(FORALL, i)

q.addTransition(1,ITERATOR, i, size, 2);
q.addTransition(2,NEXT, i, isGreaterThanConstant(size,0), decrement(size), 2);

q.addFinalStates(1, 2); q.setSkipStates(1);

QEA qea = q.make();
```

Fig. 4. Using QEABuilder to construct the **safeiter** QEA in Fig. 2

We then declare the universal quantification for i. The two transitions are added using addTransition. For the first transition we specify only the start state, event name, parameters and end state. For the second transition we include the guard and assignment. MARQ includes a library of guards and assignments. Additionally, it is possible for the user to define a new guard or assignment by implementing a simple interface. Currently MARQ supports the guards and assignments for dealing with equality and integer arithmetic. The last stage of defining the QEA is to specify the final (accepting) and the types of states, which can skip (circular) or next (square) as explained above.

Once we have constructed a QEA we can create a monitor object by a call to the MonitorFactory. This will inspect the structure of the QEA and produce an optimised monitor as described in Sec. 4.3. Optionally, we can also specify garbage and restart modes on monitor creation.

```
Monitor monitor = MonitorFactory.create(qea);
Monitor monitor = MonitorFactory.create(qea, GarbageMode.LAZY, RestartMode.REMOVE);
```

Garbage mode determines how garbage objects should be treated. As explained in Sec. 4.2 it is sometimes possible to remove bindings related to *garbage* objects in online monitoring. The default is to not collect garbage as this allows us to use more streamlined data structures and is applicable to the offline case. Restart mode determines what happens when an ultimate verdict is detected e.g. violation of a safety property. There is the option to remove or rollback the status of the offending binding. Both achieve a *signal-and-continue* approach used by other systems. The default is not to restart.

3   Running MARQ **Online and Offline**

Here we demonstrate how our tool can be used for offline and online monitoring. Fig. 5 illustrates the two different monitoring settings. In the first case, offline monitoring, a

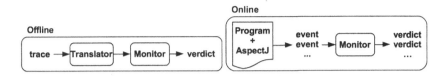

Fig. 5. Two different monitoring modes

trace is given as a log file and processed by a translator and the monitor to produce a verdict. In the second case, online monitoring, a program is instrumented to emit events which are consumed by the monitor. The monitor then produces a verdict on each event. In the following we discuss how MARQ can be used in both settings. For complete examples of how to run MARQ in either mode see the website.

3.1 Offline Monitoring

Offline monitoring can be performed in five lines of code that will take a trace and a translator to produce a verdict. MARQ can process traces in two different formats: CSV and XML. Alternatively, a custom parser for a new format could call the monitor directly as is done in online mode (see below).

The translator converts the string version of each event to the format used by the monitor. The default translator maps a list of strings to successive integers. If a different mapping is required, or it is necessary to ignore some parameters, a simple interface can be implemented to achieve this.

To monitor a trace we simply create the component parts, construct an appropriate `FileMonitor` (which reads in the trace) and call `monitor()` to produce a verdict.

```
String trace = ''trace_dir/trace.csv'';
QEA qea = builder.make(); //see Section 2
OfflineTranslator translator = new DefaultTranslator(''iterator'', ''next'');
CSVFileMonitor m = new CSVFileMonitor(trace_name, qea, translator);
Verdict v = m.monitor();
```

Calling `getStatus()` on the monitor after monitoring will print the final status of the monitor, giving the configurations associated with each binding of quantified variables.

3.2 Online Monitoring

For online monitoring it is necessary to submit each event to the monitor at the time it is generated by the running system. Here we show how this can be done using AspectJ [16] where *aspects* define code that is to be *weaved* into the object at specified points. Weaving can occur at compile or load time, both are useful for runtime monitoring.

Fig. 6 gives an example aspect to be used to monitor the **safeiter** property from Fig. 2. Firstly we specify the event names, ensuring they are the same as those used in the QEA definition. We then create the monitor as described in the previous section. Two pointcuts are used to relate the events of the QEA to concrete Java calls. Note how we call `size` on the base collection of the iterator call to provide this information in the event. Finally, we check the verdict returned by each `step` call for failure. It should

```
public aspect SafeIterAspect {

  private int ITERATOR = 1; private int NEXT = 2;
  private Monitor monitor;

  SafeIterAspect(){
    QEA qea = SafeIter.get ();
    monitor = MonitorFactory.create(qea);
  }

  pointcut iter(Collection c) : (call(Iterator Collection+.iterator()) && target(c));
  pointcut next(Iterator i) : (call(* Iterator.next()) && target(i));

  after (Collection c) returning (Iterator i) : iter(c) {
      synchronized(monitor){ check(monitor.step(ITERATOR,i,c.size())); }
  }
  before(Iterator i) : next(i) {
      synchronized(monitor){ check(monitor.step(NEXT,i)); }
  }

  private void check(Verdict verdict){
      if(verdict==Verdict.FAILURE){ <report error here> }
  }
}
```

Fig. 6. AspectJ for monitoring the **safeiter** property

be noted that MARQ is *not thread-safe*. We therefore synchronize on the monitor object for each call as we might be monitoring a concurrent program. One abstract event in the specification may relate to many different concrete events produced by the instrumentation, and vice versa. For example, in the **unsafemapiter** property in Fig. 2 we would relate the create event with the values and keySet methods from the Map interface. In the **withdrawal** specification given later (Fig. 8) there are different abstract events that would match with the same concrete event.

4   Efficient Monitoring

Details of the monitoring algorithm used in MARQ can be found in [21]. Here we highlight the major optimisations that ensure efficiency.

4.1   Indexing

Monitoring requires information to be attached to bindings of quantified variables. When an event occurs in the trace, we need to find the *relevant bindings* and update the information attached to them. The collection of bindings generated by runtime monitoring can be very large and so efficient techniques to identify relevant bindings are necessary. These often involve indexing.

Purandare et al. [20] discuss three different kinds of indexing that use different parts of a parametric event to lookup the monitor state *relevant* to that event. The first two - *value-based*, using the values of an event, and *state-based*, using the states of the underlying propositional monitor - are used by JavaMOP [18] and tracematches [2] respectively. MARQ implements the third, symbol-based. When a binding is created it is used to partially instantiate the alphabet of the automaton and each partially instantiated event is added to a map associating it with the binding. An observed concrete event is then *matched* against these partially instantiated events to locate the relevant bindings.

4.2   Garbage and Redundancy

Early work [3] showed that removing monitored objects that are no longer used in the monitored system can prevent memory leaks and improve performance. For example, in the case of the **safeiter** property, if the iterator object is garbage-collected the property cannot be violated for that iterator and the binding can be deleted. This can have a significant impact as millions of monitored short-lived objects can be generated in a typical run of a monitored system.

This idea belongs to a collection of optimisations for *redundancy elimination* - information about monitored objects can be safely omitted if it does not effect the outcome of the monitoring process. MARQ supports garbage collection in the same way as [15] i.e. when monitored objects are garbage collected it is checked whether the bindings they participate in can be removed. MARQ also implements a form of redundancy elimination that generalises the concept of *enable sets* [18]. Based on the automaton it is possible to conservatively precompute a reachability relationship that indicates whether recording a new binding will make an observable difference. This relationship is used to decide whether to create a new binding or not.

A further form of redundancy elimination is that of early detection of success or failure by identifying whether a certain verdict is *reachable* [7]. MARQ will return a verdict as soon as it is guaranteed that the verdict cannot change given any future events. To enable this the true and false verdicts are split into *weak* and *strong* variants.

4.3   Structural Specialisations

Many common forms of specification use only a subset of available features i.e. conform to a particular structural restriction. Properties can be categorised according to their structural characteristics and a custom monitor for each category can be built. At first it might seem that the improvements will be insignificant. However, most monitoring activities consist of the repeated execution of a small number of operations. Therefore, when processing large event traces the small improvements accumulate, resulting in a significant reduction in time overhead.

Specialisations. As detailed in [10], we implement a number of specialisations of the monitoring algorithm that make assumptions about the structure of the monitored QEA. The first assumption we make is about the **number of quantified variables**. If we assume that a single quantified variable is used we can directly index on this value. Currently specialisations are restricted to this setting.

The remaining specialisations simplify the monitoring algorithm by removing checks and replacing complex data structures with simpler versions. The structural assumptions are as follows:

– **Use of free variables:** if free variables are not used then the structures for storing these, and support for guards and assignments, can be removed.

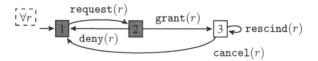

Fig. 7. A QEA giving the lifecycle of a resource object

- **Determinism/non-determinism:** when the monitored QEA is deterministic we only need to track a single state or configuration per binding.
- **Fixed quantified variable:** if the unique quantified variable (recall we only consider one) always appears in a fixed position the matching process is simplified.

Whilst currently restricted to a single quantification, these specialisations cover a large number of useful cases and commonly occurring specification patterns. Future work will look at extending these to multiple quantifications.

Example. Let us illustrate this approach using the **resourcelife** property given as a QEA in Fig. 7. This specifies the possible actions over a resource: it can be requested and then either denied or granted, and when granted it can be rescinded before it is cancelled. We randomly construct a valid trace of 1M events using 5k resources and measure monitoring time for different monitor specialisations.

Monitoring this trace with the naive incremental monitoring algorithm described in [4] takes 96k ms. By noticing that there is a single quantified variable and directly indexing on this we can reduce this to 202 ms, which is $477 \times$ faster. We expect this large speedup as we have gone from a case without indexing to one using indexing. Removing support for non-determinism we can reduce this further to 172 ms, $1.2 \times$ faster than the previous monitor. Removing support for free variables reduces this to 106 ms, $1.6 \times$ faster than the previous monitor. Overall we achieve a $913 \times$ speedup, and ignoring the vast speedup from moving to indexing we still achieve a $1.9 \times$ speedup.

5   Writing Specifications for Efficient Monitoring

Many different QEAs can specify the same property. However, choosing the right specification can determine the efficiency of the monitoring process.

The time complexity of MARQ's monitoring algorithm is dependent on characteristics of the trace (length, distribution of events) and of the specification (types of variables and transitions). One of the main factors is the number of quantified variables used in the specification. If there are n quantified variables there are a maximum of $\prod_i^n d_i$ bindings of quantified variables where d_i is the size of the domain of the ith quantified variable; this is exponential in n. Redundancy elimination can reduce this dramatically, but if it is possible to rewrite the specification to eliminate a quantified variable it can dramatically improve the performance of monitoring.

Here we discuss optimisations that eliminate quantified variables. In the future we plan to explore automatically simplifying a QEA to improve monitoring efficiency.

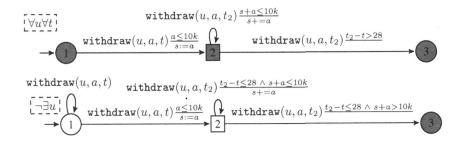

Fig. 8. Two QEAs for the property that a user must withdraw less than $10k in a 28 day period

5.1 Introducing Non-determinism

Consider the **withdrawal** property that states that a user does not withdraw more than $10k from an account in a 28 day period. Fig. 8 gives two equivalent QEAs for this property. The first QEA quantifies over a user u and a time point t that reflects the beginning of a 28-day period. The second QEA introduces non-determinism on the first state to remove the quantification over t. Whenever a withdraw event occurs this non-determinism records the start of a new 28-day period by making a transition to state 2 but also taking a transition to state 1, allowing another period to start on the next event.

To make the translation it was necessary to invert the automaton and extend the guards on transitions out of state 2. Adding the negation means that the event automaton now accepts incorrect, rather than correct traces. State 3 in the new QEA is the implicit failure state from the first QEA - the guard $t_2 - t \leq 28 \land s + a > 10k$ is the negation of the conjunction of guards labelling transitions out of state 2 in the old QEA. The $t_2 - t \leq 28$ conjunct in the guard of the looping transition on state 2 ensures that we discard the information for a time period when it exceeds 28 days; this is not necessary for correctness but important for efficiency.

Even though support for non-determinism adds some overhead (see Sec. 4.3), this is negligible in comparison to the savings made by removing bindings.

5.2 Introducing Counters

The next example we consider is the **persistenthash** property that states that the hashCode of an object should remain the same whilst it is inside a structure that uses hashing e.g. a HashMap or HashSet. Fig. 9 gives two equivalent QEAs for this property. The first QEA quantifies over the structure. To remove this quantification, the second QEA introduces a counter to track how many structures the object is inside.

5.3 Stripping Existential Quantification

Finally, we consider the **publishers** property that every publisher p that sends messages to subscribers s gets at least one reply. Fig. 10 gives two equivalent QEAs for this property. The second strips the tailing existential quantification, making the variable s a free variable. This has the same effect as any subscriber that led to a trace being accepted by the first QEA would cause the trace to be accepted by the second.

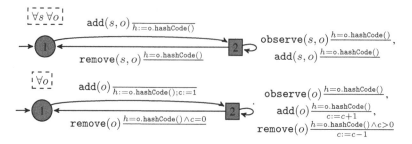

Fig. 9. Two equivalent QEAs for the persistence of hashes for objects in hashing structures

Fig. 10. Two equivalent QEAs for the property that every publisher has a subscriber

5.4 Performance Improvements

We briefly demonstrate that these translations achieve a significant performance improvement. Table 5.4 shows that this translation can speed monitoring up by an order of magnitude, demonstrating that the way in which a property is specified can have a dramatic impact on efficiency. It should be noted that the exponential dependence on the number of quantified variables is common to all tools that use parametric trace slicing.

Table 1. Performance improvements for translated QEAs

Property	Trace length	Runtime (milliseconds)		Speedup
		Original	Translated	
withdrawal	150k	3,050	2,106	1.44
persistenthash	4M	12,267	864	14.12
publishers	200k	355	37	9.59

6   Comparative Evaluation

In this section we compare MARQ with other runtime monitoring tools. We make use of benchmarks taken from the 1st international Runtime Verification competition [5]. We consider the performance of tools on selected benchmarks and reflect on the specification languages used by each tool. We also report the results of the competition [1].

6.1 Offline Monitoring

We evaluate MARQ for its use in offline monitoring i.e. the processing of recorded logs. We consider four properties, two previously introduced, and the two given in Fig. 11.

Table 2. Selected timing results for offline monitoring (in seconds)

Property	Trace length	RiTHM2	MonPoly	STePr	MARQ	Speedup Min	Avg.
maxchunk (Fig. 11)	1.4M	**0.59**	8.4	8.86	3.58	0.16	**1.66**
withdrawal (Fig. 8)	315k	-	**1.53**	3.67	2.57	0.6	**1.01**
processes (Fig. 11)	823k	2.39	2.0	2.91	**0.63**	3.17	**3.86**
resourcelife (Fig. 7)	10M	5.18	3405	9.96	**2.04**	2.54	**558.8**
Competition score		236.91	293.54	220.40	**339.15**		

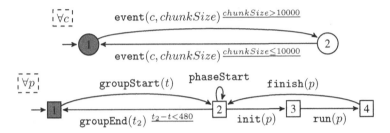

Fig. 11. Two QEAs used for evaluation. The first ensures that the chunk size eventually drops below 10k. The second captures a complex property about processes running in groups and phases.

We compare against three other competing tools in the offline track of the competition. MonPoly [6] monitors properties in Metric First-Order Temporal Logic and is designed to search for violating instantiations of a property. STePr is based on the LOLA language [11], which is a functional stream computation language. RiTHM2 [19] monitors properties in LTL and is designed with real-time systems in mind.

Table 2 gives the monitoring runtime with minimum and average speedup using MARQ. Firstly, note that these benchmarks involve very large traces, in some cases with millions of events. RiTHM2 cannot express the **withdrawal** property. MARQ always performs better on average. In the case of **maxchunk**, which has a very simple structure, the RiTHM2 tool performs the best. MonPoly struggled with the liveness elements of the **resourcelife** property.

The first three properties in Table. 2 were supplied by the teams behind RiTHM2, MonPoly and STePr respectively. We compare how these properties are specified in their native language with how they are specified in QEA. However, note that QEA graphical models must currently be represented using Java code as shown in Fig. 4.

In the RiTHM2 tool the **maxchunk** property is specified as

$$\text{For all Connections, } \Box((\text{Connection.Chunksize} > 10000) \Rightarrow \Diamond(\text{Connection.Chunksize} \leq 10000))$$

which is very similar to the QEA specification given in Fig. 11. Response properties of this kind are common specification patterns that most languages handle easily.

MonPoly specifies the **withdrawal** property as

ALWAYS FORALL s, u.
$\quad (s \leftarrow \text{SUM } a; u \text{ ONCE}[0, 28] \text{ withdraw}(u, a) \text{ AND } \text{tp}(i)) \text{ IMPLIES } s \leq 10000$

which makes use of SUM and ONCE to capture the property concisely. The SUM aggregate operator takes the sum of values for a for a given u over a specified period and ONCE[0,28] defines the 28 day window. It should be noted that MonPoly cannot handle true liveness, only finitely-bounded intervals. It deals with this by putting a very large bound in the place to simulate infinity.

STePr specifies the **processes** property as

```
G(
      groupStart ⇒ WY(¬groupStart WS groupEnd)
    ∧ groupEnd ⇒ Y(¬groupEnd S groupStart)
    ∧ phaseStart ⇒ ¬groupEnd S groupStart)
    ∧ phaseStart ⇒ ¬(init(x) ∨ run(x)) WS finish(x)
    ∧ run(x) ⇒ Y(¬run(x) S init(x))
    ∧ finish(x) ⇒ Y(¬finish(x) S run(x))
    ∧ init(x) ⇒ WY(¬(init(x) ∨ run(x)) WS finish(x))
    ∧ (¬groupStart WS groupEnd) ⇒ ¬finish(x) ∧ ¬init(x) ∧ ¬run(x)
    ∧ groupEnd ∧ (¬groupStart S (groupStart ∧ time = x)) ⇒ time − x < 480000
)
```

which is more complex than the QEA given in Fig. 11. MonPoly requires a similarly complicated formalisation as both tools use temporal logic where each subproperty must be specified separately; whereas QEA can capture the intuition of the property.

Table 2 also gives the scores from the competition (see `http://rv2014.imag.fr/monitoring-competition/results` for a breakdown). This shows that MARQ outperformed the other tools in this competition.

6.2 Online Monitoring

We consider MARQ's use in online monitoring for `Java`. We report the competition results and compare specification languages.

The other tools competing in this track of the competition were as follows. Larva [9] monitors properties specified as Dynamic Automata with Timers and Events. Java-MOP [18], like MARQ, is based on the parametric trace slicing approach. Both Larva and JavaMOP automatically generate `AspectJ` code. JUnitRV [12] extends the JUnit framework to perform monitoring where events are defined via a reflection library; they also include the monitoring modulo theories approach [13].

Table 3. Breakdown of results in CSRV14 online `Java` track (higher is better)

Tool	Correctness	Overhead	Memory	Total
Larva	165	7.79	38.43	211.22
JUnitRV	200	49.15	31.67	280.82
JavaMOP	230	88.56	77.89	396.45
MARQ	230	84.5	82.01	**396.51**

Table 3 gives a breakdown of the results from the CSRV14 competition. The correctness score reflects the properties that each tool was able to capture. On these benchmarks, Larva and JUnitRV struggled with expressiveness and running time (overhead). The results for MARQ and JavaMOP are similar, with JavaMOP running slightly faster and MARQ consuming slightly less memory. Although the scores put MARQ just ahead of JavaMOP the authors would argue that, given the variability in results, this shows that the tools are equally matched on the kinds of benchmarks used in the competition.

Both Larva and JavaMOP divide specifications into a part that defines events and a part that declares a property over these events. For each tool events are specified as AspectJ pointcuts. JUnitRV uses a reflection library to capture events.

Larva supports free variables in its language, making the specification of **safeiter** very similar to that of QEA. However, it has limited support for multiple quantifications meaning that to capture the **unsafemapiterator** property Larva uses a free variable to track the iterators created from each collection; although this could be seen as an optimisation. JavaMOP provides multiple *plugin* languages for giving properties over events. This means that the **unsafemapiterator** property can be specified using a regular expression as follows:

ere : createColl updateMap* createIter useIter* updateMap updateMap* useIter

The JavaMOP language has no native support for free variables, requiring programming in the AspectJ part of the language to capture properties such as **safeiter** and **persistenthash**. Both Larva and JavaMOP lack a natural way to relate a concrete event to multiple abstract events. JUnitRV can use at least future time LTL or explicit Mealy Machines but a description of the language is not available to the authors.

7   Conclusion

We have introduced the MARQ tool for runtime monitoring with QEA. We have shown how to use MARQ in both online and offline monitoring. Efficiency of the tool is discussed at length, both how to produce efficient QEA specification and how the tool performs relative to others that are available.

MARQ is an ongoing project and there is much work to be done. Firstly, we need to introduce an external language for specifying QEAs. Secondly, we aim to extend the notion of structural specialisations: considering properties with multiple quantifications and automatically translating properties to remove features where possible. It will be possible to use MARQ to continue research in specification mining for QEA [22].

References

1. http://rv2014.imag.fr/monitoring-competition/results
2. Allan, C., Avgustinov, P., Christensen, A.S., Hendren, L., Kuzins, S., Lhoták, O., de Moor, O., Sereni, D., Sittampalam, G., Tibble, J.: Adding trace matching with free variables to AspectJ. SIGPLAN Not. 40, 345–364 (2005)
3. Avgustinov, P., Tibble, J., de Moor, O.: Making trace monitors feasible. SIGPLAN Not. 42(10), 589–608 (2007)
4. Barringer, H., Falcone, Y., Havelund, K., Reger, G., Rydeheard, D.: Quantified event automata: Towards expressive and efficient runtime monitors. In: Giannakopoulou, D., Méry, D. (eds.) FM 2012. LNCS, vol. 7436, pp. 68–84. Springer, Heidelberg (2012)

5. Bartocci, E., Bonakdarpour, B., Falcone, Y.: First international competition on software for runtime verification. In: Bonakdarpour, B., Smolka, S.A. (eds.) RV 2014. LNCS, vol. 8734, pp. 1–9. Springer, Heidelberg (2014)
6. Basin, D.: Monpoly: Monitoring usage-control policies. In: Khurshid, S., Sen, K. (eds.) Runtime Verification. LNCS, vol. 7186, pp. 360–364. Springer, Heidelberg (2012)
7. Bauer, A., Leucker, M., Schallhart, C.: The good, the bad, and the ugly, but how ugly is ugly? In: Sokolsky, O., Taşıran, S. (eds.) RV 2007. LNCS, vol. 4839, pp. 126–138. Springer, Heidelberg (2007)
8. Chen, F., Roşu, G.: Parametric trace slicing and monitoring. In: Kowalewski, S., Philippou, A. (eds.) TACAS 2009. LNCS, vol. 5505, pp. 246–261. Springer, Heidelberg (2009)
9. Colombo, C., Pace, G.J., Schneider, G.: Larva — safer monitoring of real-time java programs (tool paper). In: Proceedings of the 2009 Seventh IEEE International Conference on Software Engineering and Formal Methods, SEFM 2009, pp. 33–37. IEEE Computer Society, Washington, DC (2009)
10. Cruz, H.C.: Optimisation techniques for runtime verification. Master's thesis, University of Manchester (2014)
11. D'Angelo, B., Sankaranarayanan, S., Sanchez, C., Robinson, W., Finkbeiner, B., Sipma, H.B., Mehrotra, S., Manna, Z.: Lola: Runtime monitoring of synchronous systems. In: 2013 20th International Symposium on Temporal Representation and Reasoning, pp. 166–174 (2005)
12. Decker, N., Leucker, M., Thoma, D.: Junitrv–adding runtime verification to junit. In: Brat, G., Rungta, N., Venet, A. (eds.) NASA Formal Methods. LNCS, vol. 7871, pp. 459–464. Springer, Heidelberg (2013)
13. Decker, N., Leucker, M., Thoma, D.: Monitoring modulo theories. In: Ábrahám, E., Havelund, K. (eds.) TACAS 2014. LNCS, vol. 8413, pp. 341–356. Springer, Heidelberg (2014)
14. Falcone, Y., Havelund, K., Reger, G.: A tutorial on runtime verification. In: Broy, M., Peled, D. (eds.) Summer School Marktoberdorf 2012 - Engineering Dependable Software Systems. IOS Press (2013) (to appear)
15. Jin, D., Meredith, P.O., Griffith, D., Rosu, G.: Garbage collection for monitoring parametric properties. SIGPLAN Not. 46(6), 415 424 (2011)
16. Kiczales, G., Hilsdale, E., Hugunin, J., Kersten, M., Palm, J., Griswold, W.G.: An overview of aspectj. In: Lindskov Knudsen, J. (ed.) ECOOP 2001. LNCS, vol. 2072, pp. 327–353. Springer, Heidelberg (2001)
17. Leucker, M., Schallhart, C.: A brief account of runtime verification. Journal of Logic and Algebraic Programming 78(5), 293–303 (2008)
18. Meredith, P., Jin, D., Griffith, D., Chen, F., Roşu, G.: An overview of the mop runtime verification framework. J. Software Tools for Technology Transfer, 1–41 (2011)
19. Navabpour, S., Joshi, Y., Wu, W., Berkovich, S., Medhat, R., Bonakdarpour, B., Fischmeister, S.: Rithm: A tool for enabling time-triggered runtime verification for c programs. In: Proceedings of the, 9th Joint Meeting on Foundations of Software Engineering, ESEC/FSE, pp. 603–606. ACM, New York (2013)
20. Purandare, R., Dwyer, M.B., Elbaum, S.: Monitoring finite state properties: Algorithmic approaches and their relative strengths. In: Khurshid, S., Sen, K. (eds.) RV 2011. LNCS, vol. 7186, pp. 381–395. Springer, Heidelberg (2012)
21. Reger, G.: Automata Based Monitoring and Mining of Execution Traces. PhD thesis, University of Manchester (2014)
22. Reger, G., Barringer, H., Rydeheard, D.: A pattern-based approach to parametric specification mining. In: Proceedings of the 28th IEEE/ACM International Conference on Automated Software Engineering (November 2013) (to appear)
23. Roşu, G., Chen, F.: Semantics and algorithms for parametric monitoring. TACAS 2009 8(1), 1–47 (2012); Short version presented at TACAS 2009

Temporal Logic and Automata

Parallel Explicit Model Checking for Generalized Büchi Automata

Etienne Renault[1,2,3], Alexandre Duret-Lutz[1],
Fabrice Kordon[2,3], and Denis Poitrenaud[3,4]

[1] LRDE, EPITA, Kremlin-Bicêtre, France
[2] Sorbonne Universités, UPMC Univ. Paris 06, France
[3] CNRS UMR 7606, LIP6, F-75005 Paris, France
[4] Université Paris Descartes, Paris, France

Abstract. We present new parallel emptiness checks for LTL model checking. Unlike existing parallel emptiness checks, these are based on an SCC enumeration, support generalized Büchi acceptance, and require no synchronization points nor repair procedures. A salient feature of our algorithms is the use of a global union-find data structure in which multiple threads share structural information about the automaton being checked. Our prototype implementation has encouraging performances: the new emptiness checks have better speedup than existing algorithms in half of our experiments.

1 Introduction

The automata-theoretic approach to explicit LTL model checking explores the product between two ω-automata: one automaton that represents the system, and the other that represents the negation of the property to check on this system. This product corresponds to the intersection between the executions of the system and the behaviors disallowed by the property. The property is verified if this product has no accepting executions (i.e., its language is empty).

Usually, the property is represented by a Büchi automaton (BA), and the system by a Kripke structure. Here we represent the property with a more concise Transition-based Generalized Büchi Automaton (TGBA), in which the Büchi acceptance condition is generalized to use multiple acceptance conditions. Furthermore, any BA can be represented by a TGBA without changing the transition structure: the TGBA-based emptiness checks we present are therefore compatible with BAs.

A BA (or TGBA) has a non-empty language iff it contains an accepting cycle reachable from the initial state (for model checking, this maps to a counterexample). An emptiness check is an algorithm that searches for such a cycle.

Most sequential explicit emptiness checks are based on a *Depth-First Search* (DFS) exploration of the automaton and can be classified in two families: those based on an enumeration of *Strongly Connected Components* (SCC), and those based on a *Nested Depth First Search* (NDFS) (see [26, 10, 24] for surveys).

Recently, parallel (or distributed) emptiness checks have been proposed [6, 2, 9, 7, 3, 4]: they are mainly based on a *Breadth First Search* (BFS) exploration

C. Baier and C. Tinelli (Eds.): TACAS 2015, LNCS 9035, pp. 613–627, 2015.
DOI: 10.1007/978-3-662-46681-0_56

which scales better than DFS [23]. Multicore adaptations of these algorithms with lock-free data structure have been discussed, but not evaluated, by Barnat et al. [5].

Recent publications show that NDFS-based algorithms combined with the *swarming* technique [16] scale better in practice [13, 18, 17, 14]. As its name implies, an NDFS algorithm uses two nested DFS: a first DFS explores a BA to search for accepting states, and a second DFS is started (in post order) to find cycles around these accepting states. In these parallel setups, each thread performs the same search strategy (an NDFS) and differs only in the search order (swarming). Because each thread shares some information about its own progress in the NDFS, synchronization points (if a state is handled by multiple threads in the nested DFS, its status is only updated after all threads have finished) or recomputing procedures (to resolve conflicts a posteriori using yet another DFS) are required. So far, attempts to design scalable parallel DFS-based emptiness check that does not require such mechanisms have failed [14].

This paper proposes new parallel emptiness checks for TGBA built upon two SCC-based strategies that do not require such synchronization points nor recomputing procedures. The reason no such mechanisms are necessary is that threads only share structural information about the automaton of the form *"states x and y are in the same SCC"* or *"state x cannot be part of a counterexample"*. Since threads do not share any information about the progress of their search, we can actually mix threads with different strategies in the same emptiness check. Because the shared information can be used to partition the states of the automaton, it is stored in a global and lock-free union-find data structure.

Section 2 defines TGBAs and introduces our notations. Section 3 presents our two SCC-based strategies. Finally, Section 4 compares emptiness checks based on these new strategies against existing algorithms.

2 Preliminaries

A *TGBA* is a tuple $A = \langle Q, q^0, \delta, \mathcal{F} \rangle$ where Q is a finite set of states, q^0 is a designated initial state, $\mathcal{F}$ is a finite set of acceptance marks, and $\delta \subseteq Q \times 2^{\mathcal{F}} \times Q$ is the (non-deterministic) transition relation where each transition is labelled by a subset of acceptance marks. Let us note that in a real model checker, transitions (or states) of the automata would be labeled by atomic propositions, but we omit this information as it is not pertinent to emptiness check algorithms.

A *path* between two states $q, q' \in Q$ is a finite and non-empty sequence of adjacent transitions $\rho = (s_1, \alpha_1, s_2)(s_2, \alpha_2, s_3) \ldots (s_n, \alpha_n, s_{n+1}) \in \delta^+$ with $s_1 = q$ and $s_{n+1} = q'$. We denote the existence of such a path by $q \rightsquigarrow q'$. When $q = q'$ the path is a *cycle*. This cycle is *accepting* iff $\bigcup_{0 < i \le n} \alpha_i = \mathcal{F}$.

A non-empty set $S \subseteq Q$ is a Strongly Connected Component (SCC) iff $\forall s, s' \in S, s \ne s' \Rightarrow s \rightsquigarrow s'$ and S is maximal w.r.t. inclusion. If S is not maximal we call it a *partial* SCC. An SCC is *accepting* iff it contains an accepting cycle. The language of a TGBA A is non-empty iff there is a path from q^0 to an accepting SCC, i.e. the language of A is non-empty ($\mathcal{L}(A) \ne \emptyset$).

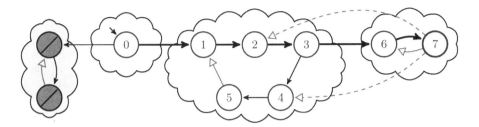

Fig. 1. LIVE states are numbered by their live number, dead states are stroke. Clouds represents SCC as discovered so far. The current state of the DFS is 7, and the DFS stack is represented by thick edges. All plain edges have already been explored while dashed edges are yet to be explored. Closing edges have white triangular tips.

3 Generalized Parallel Emptiness Checks

In a previous work [24] we presented sequential emptiness checks for generalized Büchi automata derived from the SCC enumeration algorithms of Tarjan [27] and Dijkstra [11], and a third one using a union-find data-structure. This section adapts these algorithms to a parallel setting.

The sequential versions of Tarjan-based and Dijkstra-based emptiness checks both have very similar structures: they explore the automaton using a single DFS to search for accepting SCCs and maintain a partition of the states into three classes. States that have not already been visited are UNKNOWN; a state is LIVE when it is part of an SCC that has not been fully explored (i.e., it is part of an SCC that contains at least one state on the DFS stack); the other states are called DEAD. A DEAD state cannot be part of an accepting SCC. Any LIVE state can reach a state on the DFS stack, therefore a transition from the DFS stack leading to a LIVE state is called a *closing edge*. Figure 1 illustrates some of these concepts.

These two algorithms differ in the way they propagate information about currently visited SCCs, and when they detect accepting SCCs. A Tarjan-based emptiness check propagates information during backtrack, and may only find accepting SCC when its *root* is popped. (The *root* of an SCC is the first state encountered by the DFS when entering it.) A Dijkstra-based emptiness check propagates information every time a closing edge is detected: when this happens, a partial SCC made of all states on the cycle closed by the closing edge is immediately formed. While we have shown these two emptiness checks to be comparable [24], the Dijkstra-based algorithm reports counterexamples earlier: as soon as all the transitions belonging to an accepting cycle have been seen.

A third algorithm was a variant of Dijkstra using a union-find data structure to manage the membership of each state to its SCC. Note that this data structure could be used as well for a Tarjan-based emptiness check.

Algorithm 1: Main procedure

---

1 **Shared Variables:**

2   A: TGBA of $\langle Q, q^0, \delta, \mathcal{F}\rangle$

3   *stop*: *boolean*

4   *uf*: *union-find* of $\langle Q \cup Dead, 2^{\mathcal{F}}\rangle$

5 **Global Structures:**

6   **struct** *Step* { *src*: Q,   *acc*: $2^{\mathcal{F}}$,

7   *pos*: *int*,   *succ*: 2^{δ} }

8   **struct** *Transition* { *src*: Q, *acc*: $2^{\mathcal{F}}$

9   *dst*: Q}

10   **enum** *Strategy* { Mixed,   Tarjan,

11   Dijkstra}

12   **enum** *Status* { LIVE,   DEAD,

13   UNKNOWN}

14 **Local Variables:**

15   *dfs*: *stack* of $\langle Step\rangle$

16   *live*: *stack* of $\langle Q\rangle$

17   *livenum*: *hashmap* of $\langle Q, int\rangle$

18   *pstack*: *stack* of $\langle P\rangle$

19 **main**(*str*: *Strategy*)

20   *stop* $\leftarrow \perp$

21   *uf*.make_set($\langle Dead, \emptyset\rangle$)

22   **if** str $\neq$ Mixed

23   EC(*str*, 1) $\|\ldots\|$ EC(*str*, n)

24   **else**

25   str $\leftarrow$ Dijkstra

26   EC(*str*, 1) $\|\ldots\|$ EC(*str*, $\lfloor\frac{n}{2}\rfloor$)

27   str $\leftarrow$ Tarjan

28   EC(*str*, $1+\lfloor\frac{n}{2}\rfloor$) $\|\ldots\|$ EC(*str*, n)

29   **Wait for all threads to finish**

30 GET_STATUS($q \in Q$) $\to$ *Status*

31   **if** *livenum*.contains(q)

32   **return** LIVE

33   **else if** *uf*.contains(varq) $\land$

34   *uf*.same_set(q, *Dead*)

35   **return** DEAD

36   **else**

37   **return** UNKNOWN

38 EC(*str*: *Strategy*, *tid*: *int*)

39   seed(*tid*) // Random Number Gen.

40   PUSH$_{str}$($\emptyset, q^0$)

41   **while** $\neg$ *dfs*.empty() $\land \neg$ *stop*

42   *Step step* $\leftarrow$ *dfs*.top()

43   **if** *step.succ* $\neq \emptyset$

44   *Transition t* $\leftarrow$ **randomly**

45   pick one off from *step.succ*

46   **switch** GET_STATUS(*t.dst*)

47   **case** DEAD

48   **skip**

49   **case** LIVE

50   UPDATE$_{str}$(*t.acc*, *t.dst*)

51   **case** UNKNOWN

52   PUSH$_{str}$(*t.acc*, *t.dst*)

53   **else**

54   POP$_{str}$(*step*)

55   *stop* $\leftarrow \top$

Here, we parallelize the Tarjan-based and Dijkstra-based algorithms and use a (lock-free) shared union-find data structure. We rely on the *swarming* technique: each thread execute the same algorithm, but explores the automaton in a different order [16]. Furthermore, threads will use the union-find to share information about membership to SCCs, acceptance of these SCCs, and DEAD states. Note that the shared information is stable: the fact that two states belong to the same SCC, or that a state is DEAD will never change over the execution of the algorithm. All threads may therefore reuse this information freely to accelerate their exploration, and to find accepting cycles collaboratively.

3.1   Generic Canvas

Algorithm 1 presents the structure common to the Tarjan-based and Dijkstra-based parallel emptiness checks.

All threads share the automaton A to explore, a *stop* variable used to stop all threads as soon an accepting cycle is found or one thread detects that the whole automaton has been visited, and the union-find data-structure [20]. The union-find maintains the membership of each state to the various SCCs of the automaton, or the set of DEAD states (a state is DEAD if it belongs to the same class as the artificial *Dead* state). Furthermore this data structure has been extended to store the acceptance marks occurring in an SCC.

The union-find structure partitions the set $Q' = Q \cup \{Dead\}$ labeled with an element of $2^{\mathcal{F}}$ and offers the following methods:

- make_set($s \in Q'$) creates a new class containing the state s if s is not already in the union-find.
- contains($s \in Q'$) checks whether s is already in the union-find.
- unite($s_1 \in Q'$, $s_2 \in Q'$, $acc \in 2^{\mathcal{F}}$) merges the classes of s_1 and s_2, and adds the acceptance marks acc to the resulting class. This method returns the set of acceptance marks of resulting class. However, when the class constructed by unite contains *Dead*, this method always returns $\emptyset$. An accepting cycle can therefore be reported as soon as unite returns $\mathcal{F}$.
- same_set($s_1 \in Q'$, $s_2 \in Q'$) checks whether two states are in the same class.

As suggested by Anderson and Woll [1], we implement a thread safe version of this union-find structure using *compare-and-swap* since it relies on linked lists and an hash table.

The original sequential algorithms maintain a stack of LIVE states in order to mark all states of an explored SCC as DEAD. In our previous work [24], we suggested to use a union-find data structure for this, allowing to mark all states of an SCC as dead by doing a single unite with an artificial *Dead* state. However, this notion of LIVE state (and closing edge detection) is obviously dependent on the traversal order, and will therefore be different in each thread. Consequently, each thread has to keep track locally of its own LIVE states. Thus, each thread maintains the following local variables:

- The *dfs* stack stores elements of type *Step* composed of the current state (*src*), the acceptance mark (*acc*) for the incoming transition (or $\emptyset$ for the initial state), an identifier *pos* (whose use is different in Dijkstra and Tarjan) and the set *succ* of unvisited successors of the *src* state.
- The *live* stack stores all the LIVE states that are not on the *dfs* stack (as suggested by Nuutila and Soisalon-Soininen [19]).
- The hash map *livenum* associates each LIVE state to a (locally) unique increasing identifier.
- *pstack* holds identifiers that are used differently in the emptiness checks of this paper.

With these data structures, a thread can decide whether a state is LIVE, DEAD, or UNKNOWN (i.e., new) by first checking *livenum* (a local structure), and then *uf* (a shared structure). This test is done by GET_STATUS. Note that a state marked LIVE locally may have already been marked DEAD by another thread, thus leading to redundant work. However, avoiding this extra work would require more queries to the shared *uf*.

The procedure EC shows the generic DFS that will be executed by all threads. The order of the successors is chosen randomly in each thread, and the DFS stops as soon as one thread sets the *stop* flag. GET_STATUS is called on each reached state to decide how it has to be handled: DEAD states are ignored, UNKNOWN states are pushed on the *dfs* stack, and LIVE states correspond to closing edges. This generic DFS is adapted to the Tarjan and Dijkstra strategies by calling PUSH$_{str}$ on new states, UPDATE$_{str}$ on closing edges, and POP$_{str}$ when all the successors of a state have been visited by this thread.

Several parallel instances of this EC algorithm are instantiated by the **main** procedure, possibly using different strategies. Each instance is parameterized by a unique identifier *tid* and a *Strategy* selecting either Dijkstra or Tarjan. If **main** is called with the Mixed strategy, it instantiates a mix of both emptiness-checks. When one thread reports an accepting cycle or ends the exploration of the entire automaton, it sets the *stop* variable, causing all threads to terminate. The **main** procedure therefore only has to wait for all threads to terminate.

3.2   The Tarjan Strategy

Strategy 1 shows how the generic canvas is refined to implement the Tarjan strategy. In this algorithm, each new LIVE state is numbered with the actual number of LIVE states during the PUSH$_{Tarjan}$ operation. Furthermore each state is associated to a *lowlink*, i.e., the smallest live number of any state known to be reachable from this state. These *lowlinks*, whose purpose is to detect the root of each SCC, are only maintained for the states on the *dfs* stack, and are stored on the *pstack*.

These *lowlinks* are updated either when a closing edge is detected in the UPDATE$_{Tarjan}$ method (in this case the current state and the destination of the closing edge are in the same SCC) or when a non-root state is popped in POP$_{Tarjan}$ (in this case the current state and its predecessor on the *dfs* stack are in the same SCC). Every time a *lowlink* is updated, we therefore learn that two states belong to the same SCC and can publish this fact to the shared *uf* taking into account any acceptance mark between those two states. If the *uf* detects that the union of these acceptance marks with those already known for this SCC is $\mathcal{F}$, then the existence of an accepting cycle can be reported immediately.

POP$_{Tarjan}$ has two behaviors depending on whether the state being popped is a root or not. At this point, a state is a root if its *lowlink* is equal to its live number. Non-root states are transferred from the *dfs* stack to the *live* stack. When a root state is popped, we first publish that all the SCC associated to this root is DEAD, and also locally we remove all these states from *live* and *livenum* using the **markdead** function.

If there is no accepting cycle, the number of calls to **unite** performed in a single thread by this strategy is always the number of transitions in each SCC

Strategy 1: Tarjan	**Strategy 2:** Dijkstra
struct $P \{p : int\}$	**struct** $P \{p : int, acc : 2^{\mathcal{F}}\}$

Strategy 1: Tarjan

```
1  PUSH_Tarjan (acc ∈ 2^F, q ∈ Q)
2    uf.make_set(q)
3    p ← livenum.size()
4    livenum.insert(⟨q, p⟩)
5    pstack.push(⟨p⟩)
6    dfs.push(⟨q, acc, p, succ(q)⟩)

7  UPDATE_Tarjan (acc ∈ 2^F, d ∈ Q)
8    pstack.top().p ←
9      min(pstack.top().p,
10         livenum.get(d))
11   a ← uf.unite(d, dfs.top().src,
12                acc)
13   if a = F
14     stop ← ⊤
15     report accepting cycle found
```

```
16 POP_Tarjan (s ∈ Step)
17   dfs.pop()
18   ⟨ll⟩ ← pstack.pop()
19   if ll = s.pos
20     markdead(s)

21   else
22     pstack.top().p ←
23       min(pstack.top().p, ll)
24     a ← uf.unite(s.src,
25                  dfs.top().src, s.acc)
26     if a = F
27       stop ← ⊤
28       report accepting cycle found

29     live.push(s.src)
```

Strategy 2: Dijkstra

```
1  PUSH_Dijkstra (acc ∈ 2^F, q ∈ Q)
2    uf.make_set(q)
3    p ← livenum.size()
4    livenum.insert(⟨q, p⟩)
5    pstack.push(⟨dfs.size(), ∅⟩)
6    dfs.push(⟨q, acc, p, succ(q)⟩)

7  UPDATE_Dijkstra (acc ∈ 2^F, d ∈ Q)
8    dpos ← livenum.get(d)
9    ⟨r,a⟩ ← pstack.top()
10   a ← a ∪ acc
11   while dpos < dfs[r].pos
12     ⟨r, la⟩ ← pstack.pop()
13     a ← a ∪ dfs[r].acc ∪ la
14     a ← uf.unite(d, dfs[r].src, a)
15   pstack.top().acc ← a
16   if a = F
17     stop ← ⊤
18     report accepting cycle found
```

```
19 POP_Dijkstra (s ∈ Step)
20   dfs.pop()
21   if pstack.top().p = dfs.size()
22     pstack.pop()
23     markdead(s)

24   else
25     live.push(s.src)
```

```
26 // Common to all strategies.
27 markdead(s ∈ Step)
28   uf.unite(s.src, Dead)
29   livenum.remove(s.src)
30   while livenum.size() > s.pos
31     q ← live.pop()
32     livenum.remove(q)
```

Fig. 2. Worst cases to detect accepting cycle using only one thread. The left automaton is bad for Tarjan since the accepting cycle is always found only after popping state 1. The right one disadvantages Dijkstra since the union of the states represented by dots can be costly.

(corresponding to the lowlink updates) plus the number of SCCs (corresponding to the calls to markdead). The next strategy performs fewer calls to unite.

3.3   The Dijkstra Strategy

Strategy 2 shows how the generic canvas is refined to implement the Dijkstra strategy. The way LIVE states are numbered and the way states are marked as DEAD is identical to the previous strategy. The difference lies in the way SCC information is encoded and updated.

This algorithm maintains *pstack*, a stack of potential roots, represented (1) by their positions p in the *dfs* stack (so that we can later retrieve the incoming acceptance marks and the live number of the potential roots), and (2) the union *acc* of all the acceptance marks seen in the cycles visited around the potential root.

Here *pstack* is updated only when a closing edge is detected, but not when backtracking a non-root as done in Tarjan. When a closing edge is detected, the live number *dpos* of its destination can be used to pop all the potential roots on this cycle (those whose live number are greater than *dpos*), and merge the sets of acceptance marks along the way: this happens in UPDATE$_{Dijkstra}$. Note that the *dfs* stack has to be addressable like an array during this operation.

As it is presented, UPDATE$_{Dijkstra}$ calls unite only when a potential root is discovered not be a root (lines 10–14). In the particular case where a closing edge does not invalidate any potential root, no unite operation is performed; still, the acceptance marks on this closing edge are updated locally line 15. For instance in Figure 1, when the closing edge $(7, 4)$ is explored, the root of the right-most SCC (containing state 7) will be popped (effectively merging the two right-most SCCs in *uf*) but when the closing edge $(7, 2)$ is later explored no pop will occur because the two states now belong to the same SCC. This strategy therefore does not share all its acceptance information with other threads. In this strategy, the acceptance accumulated in *pstack* locally are enough to detect accepting cycles. However the unite operation on line 14 will also return some acceptance marks discovered by other threads around this state: this additional information is also accumulated in *pstack* to speedup the detection of accepting cycles.

In this strategy, a given thread only calls unite to merge two disjoint sets of states belonging to the same SCC. Thus, the total number of unite needed to build an SCC of n states is necessarily equal to $n - 1$. This is better than the Tarjan-based version, but it also means we share less information between threads.

3.4   The Mixed Strategy

Figure 2 presents two situations on which Dijkstra and Tarjan strategies can clearly be distinguished.

The left-hand side presents a bad case for the Tarjan strategy. Regardless of the transition order chosen during the exploration, the presence of an accepting cycle is only detected when state 1 is popped. This late detection can be costly because it implies the exploration of the whole subgraph represented by a cloud.

The Dijkstra strategy will report the accepting cycle as soon as all the involved transitions have been visited. So if the transition $(1, 0)$ is visited before the transition going to the cloud, the subgraph represented by this cloud will not be visited since the counterexample will be detected before.

On the right-hand side of Fig. 2, the dotted transition represents a long path of m transitions, without acceptance marks. On this automaton, both strategies will report an accepting cycle when transition $(n, 0)$ is visited. However, the two strategies differ in their handling of transition $(m, 0)$: when Dijkstra visits this transition, it has to pop all the candidate roots $1 \ldots m$, calling unite m times; Tarjan however only has to update the *lowlink* of m (calling unite once), and it delays the update of the *lowlinks* of states $0 \ldots m - 1$ to when these states would be popped (which will never happen because an accepting cycle is reported).

In an attempt to get the best of both worlds, the strategy called "Mixed" in Algo. 1 is a kind of *collaborative portfolio* approach: half of the available threads run the Dijkstra strategy and the other half run the Tarjan strategy. These two strategies can be combined as desired since they share the same kind of information.

Discussion. All these strategies have one drawback since they use a local check to detect whether a state is alive or not: if one thread marks an SCC as DEAD, other threads already exploring the same SCC will not detect it and will continue to perform unite operations. Checking whether a state is DEAD in the global *uf* could be done for instance by changing the condition of line 43 of Algo. 1 into: $step.succ \neq \emptyset \land \neg uf.same\_set(step.src, Dead)$. However such a change would be costly, as it would require as many accesses to the shared structure as there are transitions in the automaton. To avoid these additional accesses to *uf*, we propose to change the interface of unite so it returns an additional Boolean flag indicating that one of the two states is already marked as DEAD in *uf*. Then whenever unite is called and the extra bit is set, the algorithm can immediately backtrack the *dfs* stack until it finds a state that is not marked as DEAD.

Moreover these strategies only report the existence of an accepting cycle but do not extract it. When a thread detects an accepting cycle, it can stop the others threads and can optionally launch a sequential counterexample computation [10]. Nonetheless, when performing a Dijkstra strategy the extraction can be limited to the states that are already in the union-find. The search of the accepting cycle can also be restricted to states whose projection are in the same SCC of the property automaton.

3.5   Sketch of Proof

Due to lack of space, and since the Tarjan strategy is really close to the Dijkstra strategy, we only give the scheme of a proof[1] that the latter algorithm will terminate and will report a counterexample if and only if there is an accepting cycle in the automaton.

---

[1] A complete proof can be found at:
   http://www.lrde.epita.fr/~renault/publis/TACAS15.pdf

Theorem 1. For all automata A the emptiness check terminates.

Theorem 2. The emptiness check reports an accepting cycle iff $\mathscr{L}(A) \neq \emptyset$.

The theorem 1 is obvious since the emptiness check performs a DFS on a finite graph. Theorem 2 ensues from the invariants below which use the following notations. For any thread, n denotes the size of its *pstack* stack. For $0 \leq i < n$, S_i denotes the set of states in the same partial SCC represented by *pstack*[i]:

$$S_i = \left\{ q \in livenum \left| \begin{array}{l} dfs[pstack[i].p].pos \leq livenum[q] \\ livenum[q] \leq dfs[pstack[i+1].p].pos \end{array} \right. \right\} \quad \text{for } i < n-1$$

$$S_{n-1} = \{ q \in livenum \mid dfs[pstack[n-1].p].pos \leq livenum[q] \}$$

The following invariants hold for all lines of algorithm 1:

Invariant 1. *pstack* contains a subset of positions in *dfs*, in increasing order.

Invariant 2. For all $0 \leq i < n - 1$, there is a transition with the acceptance marks $dfs[pstack[i+1].p].acc$ between S_i and S_{i+1}.

Invariant 3. For all $0 \leq i < n$, the subgraph induced by S_i is a partial SCC.

Invariant 4. If the class of a state inside the union-find is associated to $acc \neq \emptyset$, then the SCC containing this state has a cycle visiting acc. (Note: a state in the same class as *Dead* is always associated to $\emptyset$.)

Invariant 5. The first thread marking a state as DEAD has seen the full SCC containing this state.

Invariant 6. The set of DEAD states is a union a maximal SCC.

Invariant 7. If a state is DEAD it cannot be part of an accepting cycle.

These invariants establish both directions of Theorem 2: invariants 1–4 prove that when the algorithm reports a counterexample there exists a cycle visiting all acceptance marks; invariants 5–7 justify that when the algorithm exits without reporting anything, then no state can be part of a counterexample.

4   Implementation and Benchmarks

Table 1 presents the models we use in our benchmark and gives the average size of the synchronized products. The models are a subset of the BEEM benchmark [21], such that every type of model of the classification of Pelánek [22] is represented, and all synchronized products have a high number of states, transitions, and SCC. Because there are too few LTL formulas supplied by BEEM, we opted to generate random formulas to verify on each model. We computed a total number of 3268 formulas.[2]

The presented algorithms deal with any kind of generalized Büchi automata, but there exists specialized algorithms for subclasses of Büchi automata. For instance the verification of a safety property reduces to a reachability test. Similarly, persistent properties can be translated into automata where SCC cannot mix accepting cycles with non-accepting cycles [8] and for which a simpler

---

[2] For a description of our setup, including selected models, formulas, and detailed results, see
http://www.lrde.epita.fr/~renault/benchs/TACAS-2015/results.html

Table 1. Statistics about synchronized products having an empty language ($\checkmark$) and non-empty one ($\times$)

Model	Avg. States		Avg. Trans.		Avg. SCCs	
	($\checkmark$)	($\times$)	($\checkmark$)	($\times$)	($\checkmark$)	($\times$)
adding.4	5 637 711	7 720 939	10 725 851	14 341 202	5 635 309	7 716 385
bridge.3	1 702 938	3 114 566	4 740 247	8 615 971	1 701 048	3 106 797
brp.4	15 630 523	38 474 669	33 580 776	94 561 556	4 674 238	16 520 165
collision.4	30 384 332	101 596 324	82 372 580	349 949 837	347 535	22 677 968
cyclic-sched	724 400	1 364 512	6 274 289	12 368 800	453 547	711 794
elevator.4	2 371 413	3 270 061	7 001 559	9 817 617	1 327 005	1 502 808
elevator2.3	10 339 003	13 818 813	79 636 749	120 821 886	2 926 881	6 413 279
exit.3	3 664 436	8 617 173	11 995 418	29 408 340	3 659 550	8 609 674
leader-el.3	546 145	762 684	3 200 607	4 033 362	546 145	762 684
prod-cell.3	2 169 112	3 908 715	7 303 450	13 470 569	1 236 881	1 925 909

emptiness check exists. Our benchmark contains only non-persistent properties, requiring a general emptiness check.

Among the 3268 formulas, 1706 result in products with the model having an empty language (the emptiness check may terminate before exploring the full product). All formulas were selected so that the sequential NDFS emptiness check of Gaiser and Schwoon [15] would take between 15 seconds and 30 minutes on an four Intel(R) Xeon(R) CPUX7460@ 2.66GHz with 128GB of RAM. This 24-core machine is also used for the following parallel experiments.

All the approaches mentioned in Section 3 have been implemented in Spot [12]. The union-find structure is lock-free and uses two common optimizations: "Immediate Parent Check", and "Path Compression" [20].

The seed used to choose a successor randomly depends on the thread identifier *tid* passed to EC. Thus our strategies have the same exploration order when executed sequentially; otherwise this order may be altered by information shared by other threads.

Figure 3 presents the comparison of our prototype implementation in Spot against the cndfs algorithm implemented in LTSmin and the owcty algorithm implemented in DiVine 2.4. We selected owcty because it is reported to be the most efficient parallel emptiness check based on a non-DFS exploration, while cndfs is reported to be the most efficient based on a DFS [14].

We generate the corresponding system automata using the version of DiVinE 2.4 patched by the LTSmin team.[3] For each emptiness check, we limit the execution time to one hour: all the algorithms presented in this paper proceess the 3268 synchronized products within this limit while owcty fails over 11 cases and cndfs fails over 784 cases. DiVinE and LTSmin implement all sorts of optimizations (like state compression, caching of successors, dedicated memory allocator...) while our implementation in Spot is still at a prototype stage. So in

---

[3] http://fmt.cs.utwente.nl/tools/ltsmin/#divine

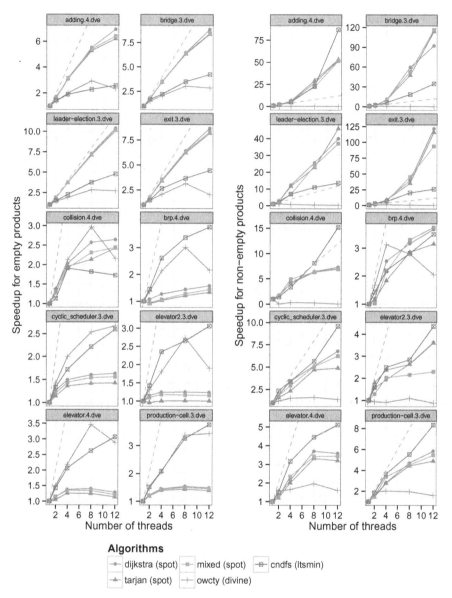

Fig. 3. Speedup of emptiness checks over the benchmark[4]

absolute time, the sequential version of `cndfs` is around 3 time faster[5] than our prototype implementation which is competitive to DiVinE.

---

[4] This figure can be zoomed in color in the electronic version.

[5] Note that the time measured for `cndfs` does not includes the on-the-fly generation of the product (it is precalculated because doing the on-the-fly product in LTSmin exhibits a bug) while the time measured for the others includes the generation of the product.

Since the implementations are different, we therefore compare the average speedup of the parallel version of each algorithm against its sequential version. The actual time can be found in the detailed results[2].

The left-hand side of Figure 3 shows those speedups, averaged for each model, for verified formulas (where the entire product has to be explored). First, it appears that the Tarjan strategy's speedup is always lower than those of Dijkstra or Mixed for empty products. These low speedups can be explained by contention on the shared union-find data structure during unite operations. In an SCC of n states and m edges, a thread applying the Tarjan strategy performs m unite calls while applying Dijkstra one needs only $n-1$ unite invocations before they both mark the whole SCC as DEAD with a unique unite call.

Second, for all strategies we can distinguish two groups of models. For adding.4, bridge.3, exit.3, and leader-election.3, the speedups are quasi-linear. However for the other six models, the speedups are much more modest: it seems that adding new threads quickly yield no benefits. A look to absolute time (for the first group) shows that the Dijkstra strategy is 25% faster than cndfs using 12 threads where it was two time slower with only one thread.

A more detailed analysis reveals that products of the first group have many small SCC (organized in a tree shape) while products of the second group have a few big SCC. These big SCC have more closing edges: the union-find data structure is stressed at every unite. This confirms what we observed for the Tarjan strategy about the impact of unite operations.

The right-hand side of Figure 3 shows speedups for violated formulas. In these cases, the speedup can exceed the number of threads since the different threads explore the product in different orders, thus increasing the probability to report an accepting cycle earlier. The three different strategies have comparable speedup for all models, however their profiles differ from cndfs on some models: they have better speedups on bridge.3, exit.3, and leader-election.3, but are worse on collision.4, elevator.4 and production-cell.3. The Mixed strategy shows speedups between those of Tarjan and Dijkstra strategies.

5   Conclusion

We have presented some first and new parallel emptiness checks based on an SCC enumeration. Our approach departs from state-of-the-art emptiness checks since it is neither BFS-based nor NDFS-based. Instead it parallelizes SCC-based emptiness checks that are built over a single DFS. Our approach supports generalized Büchi acceptance, and requires no synchronization points nor repair procedures. We therefore answer positively to the question raised by Evangelista et al. [14]: "Is the design of a scalable linear-time algorithm without repair procedures or synchronisation points feasible?". Our prototype implementation has encouraging performances: the new emptiness checks have better speedup than existing algorithms in half of our experiments, making them suitable for portfolio approaches.

The core of our algorithms relies on a union-find (lock-free) data structure to share structural information between multiple threads. The use of a union-find seems adapted to this problem, and yet it has never been used for parallel emptiness checks (and only recently for sequential emptiness checks [24]): we believe that this first use might stimulate other researchers to derive new emptiness checks or ideas from it.

In some future work, we would like to investigate different variations of our algorithms. For instance could the information shared in the union-find be used to better direct the DFS performed by the Dijkstra or Tarjan strategies and help to balance the exploration of the automaton by the various threads? We would also like to implement Gabow's algorithm that we presented in a sequential context [24] in this same parallel setup. Changing the architecture, we would like to explore how the union-find data structure could be adapted to develop asynchronous algorithms where one thread could call unite without waiting for an answer. Another topic is to explore the use of SCC strengths [25] to improve parallel emptiness checks.

References

1. Anderson, R.J., Woll, H.: Wait-free parallel algorithms for the union-find problem. In: Proc. 23rd ACM Symposium on Theory of Computing, pp. 370–380 (1994)
2. Barnat, J., Brim, L., Chaloupka, J.: Parallel breadth-first search LTL model-checking. In: ASE 2003, pp. 106–115. IEEE Computer Society (2003)
3. Barnat, J., Brim, L., Chaloupka, J.: From distributed memory cycle detection to parallel LTL model checking. In: FMICS 2004, vol. 133. ENTCS, pp. 21–39 (2005)
4. Barnat, J., Brim, L., Ročkai, P.: A time-optimal on-the-fly parallel algorithm for model checking of weak LTL properties. In: Breitman, K., Cavalcanti, A. (eds.) ICFEM 2009. LNCS, vol. 5885, pp. 407–425. Springer, Heidelberg (2009)
5. Barnat, J., Brim, L., Ročkai, P.: Scalable shared memory LTL model checking. STTT 12(2), 139–153 (2010)
6. Brim, L., Černá, I., Krčál, P., Pelánek, R.: Distributed LTL model checking based on negative cycle detection. In: Hariharan, R., Mukund, M., Vinay, V. (eds.) FSTTCS 2001. LNCS, vol. 2245, pp. 96–107. Springer, Heidelberg (2001)
7. Brim, L., Černá, I., Moravec, P., Šimša, J.: Accepting predecessors are better than back edges in distributed LTL model-checking. In: Hu, A.J., Martin, A.K. (eds.) FMCAD 2004. LNCS, vol. 3312, pp. 352–366. Springer, Heidelberg (2004)
8. Černá, I., Pelánek, R.: Relating hierarchy of temporal properties to model checking. In: Rovan, B., Vojtáš, P. (eds.) MFCS 2003. LNCS, vol. 2747, pp. 318–327. Springer, Heidelberg (2003)
9. Černá, I., Pelánek, R.: Distributed explicit fair cycle detection (set based approach). In: Ball, T., Rajamani, S.K. (eds.) SPIN 2003. LNCS, vol. 2648, pp. 49–73. Springer, Heidelberg (2003)
10. Couvreur, J.-M., Duret-Lutz, A., Poitrenaud, D.: On-the-fly emptiness checks for generalized Büchi automata. In: Godefroid, P. (ed.) SPIN 2005. LNCS, vol. 3639, pp. 143–158. Springer, Heidelberg (2005)
11. Dijkstra, E.W.: EWD 376: Finding the maximum strong components in a directed graph (May 1973), http://www.cs.utexas.edu/users/EWD/ewd03xx/EWD376.PDF
12. Duret-Lutz, A., Poitrenaud, D.: SPOT: an Extensible Model Checking Library using Transition-based Generalized Büchi Automata. In: MASCOTS 2004, pp. 76–83. IEEE Computer Society Press (October 2004)
13. Evangelista, S., Petrucci, L., Youcef, S.: Parallel nested depth-first searches for LTL model checking. In: Bultan, T., Hsiung, P.-A. (eds.) ATVA 2011. LNCS, vol. 6996, pp. 381–396. Springer, Heidelberg (2011)

14. Evangelista, S., Laarman, A., Petrucci, L., van de Pol, J.: Improved multi-core nested depth-first search. In: Chakraborty, S., Mukund, M. (eds.) ATVA 2012. LNCS, vol. 7561, pp. 269–283. Springer, Heidelberg (2012)

15. Gaiser, A., Schwoon, S.: Comparison of algorithms for checking emptiness on Büchi automata. In: MEMICS 2009. OASICS, vol. 13. Schloss Dagstuhl, Leibniz-Zentrum fuer Informatik, Germany (2009)

16. Holzmann, G.J., Joshi, R., Groce, A.: Swarm verification techniques. IEEE Transaction on Software Engineering 37(6), 845–857 (2011)

17. Laarman, A., van de Pol, J.: Variations on multi-core nested depth-first search. In: PDMC, pp. 13–28 (2011)

18. Laarman, A., Langerak, R., van de Pol, J., Weber, M., Wijs, A.: Multi-core nested depth-first search. In: Bultan, T., Hsiung, P.-A. (eds.) ATVA 2011. LNCS, vol. 6996, pp. 321–335. Springer, Heidelberg (2011)

19. Nuutila, E., Soisalon-Soininen, E.: On finding the strongly connected components in a directed graph. Information Processing Letters 49(1), 9–14 (1994)

20. Patwary, M.M.A., Blair, J.R.S., Manne, F.: Experiments on union-find algorithms for the disjoint-set data structure. In: Festa, P. (ed.) SEA 2010. LNCS, vol. 6049, pp. 411–423. Springer, Heidelberg (2010)

21. Pelánek, R.: BEEM: benchmarks for explicit model checkers. In: Bošnački, D., Edelkamp, S. (eds.) SPIN 2007. LNCS, vol. 4595, pp. 263–267. Springer, Heidelberg (2007)

22. Pelánek, R.: Properties of state spaces and their applications. International Journal on Software Tools for Technology Transfer (STTT) 10, 443–454 (2008)

23. Reif, J.H.: Depth-first search is inherently sequential. Information Processing Letters 20, 229–234 (1985)

24. Renault, E., Duret-Lutz, A., Kordon, F., Poitrenaud, D.: Three SCC-based emptiness checks for generalized Büchi automata. In: McMillan, K., Middeldorp, A., Voronkov, A. (eds.) LPAR-19 2013. LNCS, vol. 8312, pp. 668–682. Springer, Heidelberg (2013)

25. Renault, E., Duret-Lutz, A., Kordon, F., Poitrenaud, D.: Strength-based decomposition of the property büchi automaton for faster model checking. In: Piterman, N., Smolka, S.A. (eds.) TACAS 2013. LNCS, vol. 7795, pp. 580–593. Springer, Heidelberg (2013)

26. Schwoon, S., Esparza, J.: A note on on-the-fly verification algorithms. In: Halbwachs, N., Zuck, L.D. (eds.) TACAS 2005. LNCS, vol. 3440, pp. 174–190. Springer, Heidelberg (2005)

27. Tarjan, R.: Depth-first search and linear graph algorithms. SIAM Journal on Computing 1(2), 146–160 (1972)

Limit Deterministic and Probabilistic Automata for LTL\\GU

Dileep Kini and Mahesh Viswanathan

Department of Computer Science,
University of Illinois at Urbana-Champaign, Urbana, IL, USA

Abstract. LTL\\$GU$ is a fragment of linear temporal logic (LTL), where negations appear only on propositions, and formulas are built using the temporal operators X (next), F (eventually), G (always), and U (until, with the restriction that no until operator occurs in the scope of an always operator. Our main result is the construction of Limit Deterministic Büchi automata for this logic that are exponential in the size of the formula. One consequence of our construction is a new, improved EXPTIME model checking algorithm (as opposed to the previously known doubly exponential time) for Markov Decision Processes and LTL\\$GU$ formulae. Another consequence is that it gives us a way to construct exponential sized Probabilistic Büchi Automata for LTL\\$GU$.

1   Introduction

Starting with the seminal work of Vardi, Wolper, and Sistla [17], there has been a lot of interest in discovering efficient translations of Linear Temporal logic (LTL) formulae into small automata (see [16,7,10,14,13,11,2,6] for example). The reason for this is that logic to automata translations have a direct impact on algorithms of verification and synthesis of systems [18]. When verifying systems, one is often satisfied with constructing nondeterministic Büchi automata for LTL formulae. However, for a couple of applications, general nondeterministic automata don't suffice — when synthesizing reactive modules for LTL specifications, deterministic automata are necessary, and when model checking Markov Decision Processes with respect to almost sure satisfaction of LTL specifications, one needs either deterministic or limit deterministic automata. As a consequence, a series of papers recently present algorithms and tools for constructing deterministic automata from LTL specifications [10,14,13,11,12,2,6]; though in the worst case the size of the constructed automata are doubly exponential, these algorithms have been shown to construct small automata for a number of examples. In this paper, we investigate whether there are provable improvements in translating fragments of LTL to limit deterministic automata, and explore whether these can then be exploited to improve the asymptotic complexity of the MDP model checking problem.

We consider the fragment LTL\\GU, first introduced in [12]. In this logic, formulae are built from propositions and their negations using conjunction, disjunction, and the temporal operators X (next), F (eventually), G (always), and

© Springer-Verlag Berlin Heidelberg 2015
C. Baier and C. Tinelli (Eds.): TACAS 2015, LNCS 9035, pp. 628–642, 2015.
DOI: 10.1007/978-3-662-46681-0_57

U (until), with the restriction that no U operator appears in the scope of a G operator. Our main result is a translation of LTL\$GU$ formulae into nondeterministic Büchi automata of exponential size that is *deterministic in the limit* — an automaton is deterministic in the limit (or limit deterministic) if the transitions from any state that is reachable from an accepting state are deterministic. This construction should be contrasted with the observation that any translation from LTL\$GU$ to deterministic automata must in the worst case result in automata that are doubly exponential in size [1]; in fact, this lower bound applies to any fragment of LTL that has $\vee$, $\wedge$, and F.

Our construction of limit deterministic automata for LTL\$GU$ proceeds in two steps. First we construct limit deterministic automata for LTL(F,G) which is the LTL fragment without until, i.e., with just the temporal operators next, always, and eventually. Next, we observe that the automaton for $\varphi \in$ LTL\$GU$ can be seen as the composition of two limit deterministic automata: one automata for the formula ψ, where all the until-free subformulae of φ are replaced by propositions, and another automaton for the until-free subformulae of φ. This composition is reminiscent of the master-slave composition in [6] and the composition of temporal testers [15] but with some differences.

Our construction of exponentially sized limit deterministic automata for LTL\$GU$ has complexity theoretic consequences for model checking MDPs. Courcoubetis and Yannakakis [5] proved that the problem of model checking MDPs against LTL is 2EXPTIME-complete. Our automata construction, coupled with the algorithm outlined in [5], shows that model checking MDPs against LTL\$GU$ is in EXPTIME; we prove a matching lower bound in this paper as well. Thus, for a large, expressively rich subclass of LTL specifications, our results provide an exponential improvement to the complexity of model checking MDPs.

Another consequence of our main result is that it gives us a way to translate LTL\GU formulae to exponential sized probabilistic Büchi automata (PBA) [3]. Probabilistic Büchi automata are like Büchi automata, except that they probabilistically choose the next state on reading an input symbol. On input w, such a machine can be seen as defining a probability measure on the space of all runs on w. A PBA is said to accept a (infinite length) string w iff the set of all accepting runs (i.e., runs that visit some final state infinitely often) have measure > 0. We use the observation that any assignment of non-zero probabilities to the nondeterministic choices of a limit deterministic NBA, results in a PBA that accepts the same language [3]. This result also generalizes some of the results in [8] where exponential sized *weak probabilistic monitors* [1] are constructed for the LTL fragment with just the temporal operators X and G.

The rest of the paper is organized as follows. In Section 2 we introduce the notations and definitions we use in the paper. In Section 3 we present a translation from LTL(F,G) to limit deterministic NBAs. In Section 4 we give a compositional style construction for formulae in LTL\GU by using the construction in

---

[1] A weak finite state probabilistic monitor [4] is a PBA with the restriction that all states except a unique reject state are final, and all transitions from the unique rejecting state are self loops.

the previous section. In Section 5 we reflect on the consequences of our results and finally give concluding remarks in Section 6.

2   Preliminaries

First we introduce the notation we use throughout the paper. We use P to denote the set of propositions. An assignment ν is a function mapping all propositions to true or false. We use w to denote infinite words over a finite alphabet. We use $w[i]$ to denote the ith symbol in the sequence w, and use w_i to denote the suffix $w[i]w[i+1]\ldots$ of w starting at i. We use $[n]$ to denote all non-negative integers less than n that is $\{0, 1, \ldots, n-1\}$. We shall use Σ, Γ to denote finite sets of symbols.

Definition 1 (Syntax). *The formulae in the fragment* LTL(F,G) *over P is given by the following syntax*

$$\varphi \quad ::= \quad p \mid \neg p \mid \varphi \wedge \varphi \mid \varphi \vee \varphi \mid \boldsymbol{X}\varphi \mid \boldsymbol{F}\varphi \mid \boldsymbol{G}\varphi \qquad p \in P$$

and the formulae in the fragment LTL\GU *are given by the syntax*

$$\psi \quad ::= \quad \varphi \mid \psi \wedge \psi \mid \psi \vee \psi \mid \boldsymbol{X}\psi \mid \psi\boldsymbol{U}\psi \qquad \varphi \in \text{LTL}(F,G)$$

Let $\mathbb{F}_\varphi$ and $\mathbb{G}_\varphi$ denote the set of all $\boldsymbol{F}$ and $\boldsymbol{G}$ subformulae of φ respectively. We drop the subscript whenever the formula φ is clear from the context. For a temporal operator $Op \in \{\boldsymbol{G}, \boldsymbol{F}, \boldsymbol{U}\}$ we use LTL(Op) to denote the fragment consisting of formulae built using $Op, \boldsymbol{X}, \vee, \wedge$, and $\neg$ with negation allowed to appear only on propositions.

Definition 2 (Semantics). *LTL formulae over a set P are interpreted over words w in $(2^P)^\omega$. The semantics of the logic are given by the following rules*

$$
\begin{aligned}
w &\vDash p &&\iff p \in w[0] & w &\vDash \boldsymbol{X}\varphi &&\iff w_1 \vDash \varphi \\
w &\vDash \neg p &&\iff p \notin w[0] & w &\vDash \boldsymbol{F}\varphi &&\iff \exists\, i : w_i \vDash \varphi \\
w &\vDash \varphi \wedge \psi &&\iff w \vDash \varphi \text{ and } w \vDash \psi & w &\vDash \boldsymbol{G}\varphi &&\iff \forall\, i : w_i \vDash \varphi \\
w &\vDash \varphi \vee \psi &&\iff w \vDash \varphi \text{ or } w \vDash \psi & w &\vDash \varphi\boldsymbol{U}\psi &&\iff \exists\, i : w_i \vDash \psi, \text{ and} \\
& && & & && \qquad \forall\, j < i : w_j \vDash \varphi
\end{aligned}
$$

The semantics of φ, denoted by $[\![\varphi]\!]$, is defined as the set $\big\{w \in (2^P)^\omega \mid w \vDash \varphi\big\}$.

Definition 3 (Büchi Automata). *A nondeterministic Büchi automaton (NBA) over input alphabet Σ is a tuple (Q, δ, I, F) where Q is a finite set of states; $\delta \subseteq Q \times \Sigma \times Q$ is a set of transitions; $I \subseteq \delta$ is a set of initial transitions [2] and F is a set of final states. We say state $q \in Q$ is initial if $(q, \sigma, q') \in I$ for some σ and q'.*

---

[2] We use initial transitions instead of states for notational convenience. It can be easily converted into a state based definition.

A *run of a NBA over a word* $w \in \Sigma^\omega$ *is an infinite sequence of states* $q_0 q_1 q_2 \ldots$ *such that* $(q_0, w[0], q_1) \in I$ *and* $\forall i \geq 0$ $(q_i, w[i], q_{i+1}) \in \delta$. *A run is accepting if* $q_i \in F$ *for infinitely many* i.

The language accepted by an NBA $\mathcal{A}$, denoted by $L(\mathcal{A})$ is the set of all words $w \in \Sigma^\omega$ which have an accepting run on $\mathcal{A}$.

Definition 4 (Limit Determinism). *A NBA* (Q, δ, I, F) *over input alphabet* Σ *is said to be* limit deterministic *if for every state* q *reachable from a final state, it is the case that* $|\delta(q, \sigma)| \leq 1$ *for every* $\sigma \in \Sigma$.

We make note of the fact that any limit deterministic NBA translation for a fragment devoid of the $\boldsymbol{X}$ operator can be converted into translation for the fragment with $\boldsymbol{X}$ by incurring a multiplicative factor blow-up that is exponential in the number of nested $\boldsymbol{X}$s in the formula. A proof sketch of this result can be found in the companion technical report [9].

Proposition 5. *Let* LTL$'$ *be some fragment of* LTL. *If for every* $\varphi \in$ LTL$'\backslash \boldsymbol{X}$ *one can build a limit deterministic NBA* $\mathcal{A}_\varphi$ *such that it recognizes* $[\![\varphi]\!]$ *and is of size* $f(|\varphi|)$, *then for every* $\varphi' \in$ LTL$'$ *one can build a limit deterministic NBA* $\mathcal{A}'_{\varphi'}$ *such that it recognizes* $[\![\varphi']\!]$ *and has size* $\mathcal{O}(2^n f(|\varphi'|))$ *where* n *is the number of nested* $\boldsymbol{X}$s *appearing in* φ'.

The compositional construction for LTL*GU* requires we deal with automata with outputs. For this purpose we define Mealy automata with Büchi acceptance which we use in Section 4.

Definition 6 (Mealy Automata). *A nondeterministic Mealy machine with Büchi acceptance (NBM) with input alphabet* Σ *and output alphabet* Γ *is a tuple* (Q, δ, I, M, F) *where* (Q, δ, I, F) *is an NBA with input alphabet* Σ *and* $M : Q \times \Sigma \to \Gamma$ *is a partial function that is defined on all* (q, σ) *for which there is a* q' *such that* $(q, \sigma, q') \in \delta$.

The relation accepted by an NBM is the set of all pairs $(w, \lambda) \in \Sigma^\omega \times \Gamma^\omega$ such that w is accepted by the NBA (Q, δ, I, F) and λ is such that there is an accepting run of w of the form $q_0 q_1 q_2 \ldots$ where $M(q_i, w[i]) = \lambda[i]$ for all i.

In section 5 we describe our result regarding construction of probabilistic Büchi automata, which we define next.

Definition 7 (Probabilistic Automata). *A probabilistic Büchi automaton (PBA) over input alphabet* Σ *is a tuple* (Q, Δ, q_s, F) *where* Q *is a finite set of states;* $\Delta : Q \times \Sigma \times Q \to [0, 1]$ *specifies transition probabilities such that for every* $q \in Q$ *and* $\sigma \in \Sigma$ *we have* $\sum_{r \in Q} \Delta(q, \sigma, r) = 1$; $q_s \in Q$ *is an initial state;* $F \subseteq Q$ *is a set of final states.*

Given a word $w \in \Sigma^\omega$ a PBA $\mathcal{M}$ behaves as follows: it is initially at state $q_0 = q_s$. After having seen the first i symbols $w[0]w[1]\ldots w[i-1]$ it is in state q_i. On seeing $w[i]$ it chooses the next state q_{i+1} with probability $\Delta(q_i, w[i], q_{i+1})$. It continues this process to produce a run $\rho \in Q^\omega$. A run ρ is accepting if some final state appears infinitely often.

A word w produces a Markov chain C obtained by unfolding the PBA $\mathcal{M}$ along the symbols of w [3]. The probability measure induced by this Markov chain on runs in Q^ω is used to define the acceptance probability of the word w on $\mathcal{M}$ as

$$\Pr(w) = \Pr\{\rho \in Q^\omega \mid \rho \text{ is accepting for } w \text{ over } \mathcal{M}\}$$

The language accepted by a PBA over input Σ denoted by $L_{>0}(\mathcal{M})$ is the set of all words $w \in \Sigma^\omega$ with positive acceptance probability, i.e $\Pr(w) > 0$.

We conclude this section by observing a result from [3] that enables translation from limit deterministic automata to PBAs.

Lemma 8. *[3] Given a limit deterministic NBA $\mathcal{D} = (Q, \delta, I, F)$ there is a PBA $\mathcal{M}$ with $|Q| + 1$ states such that $L(\mathcal{D}) = L_{>0}(\mathcal{M})$.*

3   Automata for LTL(F,G) Formulae

In this section, we present a construction of exponential sized limit deterministic NBA for the fragment LTL(F,G). Thanks to Proposition 5 we ignore the $\boldsymbol{X}$ operator since we are aiming to construct exponential size automata.

The following proposition embodies the key idea behind our construction. A proof is provided in the technical report [9].

Proposition 9. *For any formula $\varphi \in$ LTL over P, and any word $w \in (2^P)^\omega$ exactly one of the following three holds*

$$w \vDash \neg\boldsymbol{F}\varphi, \quad w \vDash (\neg\boldsymbol{G}\varphi \wedge \boldsymbol{F}\varphi), \quad w \vDash \boldsymbol{G}\varphi$$

Furthermore, if φ is of the form $\boldsymbol{F}\psi$ or $\boldsymbol{G}\psi$ then we can deduce if $w \vDash \varphi$ holds from knowing which one of the above three holds.

The essence of our construction is in guessing which one of the three formulae in Proposition 9 holds for $\boldsymbol{F}$ and $\boldsymbol{G}$ subformulae. We define a *guess*, to be tripartition $\pi = \langle \pi^\tau \mid \pi^\upsilon \mid \pi^\kappa \rangle$ of $\mathbb{F}_\varphi \cup \mathbb{G}_\varphi$. Let Π denote the set of all tripartitions π of $\mathbb{F}_\varphi \cup \mathbb{G}_\varphi$. If a subformula $\boldsymbol{F}\psi$ is present in π^τ, our guess is that $\neg\boldsymbol{F}\psi(\equiv \neg\boldsymbol{F}\boldsymbol{F}\psi)$ holds for the input to be seen. If a subformula $\boldsymbol{G}\psi$ is in π^τ, our guess is that $\boldsymbol{G}\psi(\equiv \boldsymbol{G}\boldsymbol{G}\psi)$ holds for the input to be seen. Table 1 summarizes how we interpret a tripartition as one of three guesses for $\boldsymbol{F}$ and $\boldsymbol{G}$ subformulae.

Table 1. Guess corresponding to a tripartition π

	π^τ	π^υ	π^κ
$\boldsymbol{F}\psi$	$\neg\boldsymbol{F}\psi$	$\boldsymbol{F}\psi \wedge \neg\boldsymbol{G}\boldsymbol{F}\psi$	$\boldsymbol{G}\boldsymbol{F}\psi$
$\boldsymbol{G}\psi$	$\boldsymbol{G}\psi$	$\neg\boldsymbol{G}\psi \wedge \boldsymbol{F}\boldsymbol{G}\psi$	$\neg\boldsymbol{F}\boldsymbol{G}\psi$

From the second part of Proposition 9 we know exactly which formulae in $\mathbb{F}_\varphi \cup \mathbb{G}_\varphi$ are presently true according to $\pi \in \Pi$. This information along with the knowledge of the truth of propositions at present allows us to *evaluate* the truth of the formula φ according to π. We define what it means to evaluate a formula.

Definition 10 (Evaluation). *For any formula $\varphi \in$ LTL(F,G) over P, a partition $\pi \in \Pi$ and assignment ν on P we inductively define a boolean function $[\varphi]_\nu^\pi$, the evaluation of a formula φ, as follows:*

$$[p]_\nu^\pi = \nu(p) \qquad [\varphi \wedge \psi]_\nu^\pi = [\varphi]_\nu^\pi \wedge [\psi]_\nu^\pi \qquad [\boldsymbol{G}\psi]_\nu^\pi = true \ iff \ \boldsymbol{G}\psi \in \pi^\tau$$

$$[\neg p]_\nu^\pi = \neg\nu(p) \qquad [\varphi \vee \psi]_\nu^\pi = [\varphi]_\nu^\pi \vee [\psi]_\nu^\pi \qquad [\boldsymbol{F}\psi]_\nu^\pi = true \ iff \ \boldsymbol{F}\psi \notin \pi^\tau$$

Next, we observe that if π is sound in the sense that every formula $\boldsymbol{G}\psi \in \pi^\tau$ and $\boldsymbol{F}\psi \notin \pi^\tau$ is true at present then φ evaluates to true with respect to π indicates that φ is indeed true.

Proposition 11 (Soundness). *For any formula $\varphi \in$ LTL(F,G), a guess $\pi \in \Pi$ and word $w \in \Sigma^\omega$ if the following implications hold*

$$\boldsymbol{G}\psi \in \pi^\tau \implies w \vDash \boldsymbol{G}\psi \qquad \boldsymbol{F}\psi \notin \pi^\tau \implies w \vDash \boldsymbol{F}\psi$$

for every $\boldsymbol{G}\psi$, $\boldsymbol{F}\psi$ that is a subformula of φ then: $[\varphi]_{w[0]}^\pi = true$ implies $w \vDash \varphi$.

Proof. Induction on the structure of φ. □

Similarly, if π is complete in the sense that every $\boldsymbol{G}\psi$ that is true is in π^τ and every $\boldsymbol{F}\psi$ that is true is not in π^τ then φ is true implies it evaluates to true.

Proposition 12 (Completeness). *For any formula $\varphi \in$ LTL(F,G), a guess $\pi \in \Pi$ and a word $w \in \Sigma^\omega$ if the following implications holds*

$$w \vDash \boldsymbol{G}\psi \implies \boldsymbol{G}\psi \in \pi^\tau \qquad w \vDash \boldsymbol{F}\psi \implies \boldsymbol{F}\psi \notin \pi^\tau$$

for every $\boldsymbol{G}\psi$, $\boldsymbol{F}\psi$ that is a subformula of φ then: $w \vDash \varphi$ implies $[\varphi]_{w[0]}^\pi = true$.

Proof. Induction on the structure of φ. □

In our construction, every state of the automaton holds a tripartition that corresponds to a guess. According to this guess some subformulae may hold now, in the future, or never. Each initial transition is such that it enables the main formula to be true. Each transition ensures the propagation of temporal requirements to successive guesses. In an accepting run we ensure that each of our guesses is sound.

Since our formulae are in negation normal form, it only makes sense to take care of checking a guess (or a part of it) on a subformula φ if the guess claims φ to be true at present or some point in the future. If a guess claims that φ does not hold we don't need to bother checking it, because even if it did it could not make a superformula false that was otherwise true. For instance, if $\boldsymbol{F}\psi \in \pi^\tau$ we don't need to enforce that $\neg\boldsymbol{F}\psi$ holds, and if $\boldsymbol{F}\psi \in \pi^\upsilon$ we only need to ensure $\boldsymbol{F}\psi$ holds but don't need to enforce $\neg\boldsymbol{G}\boldsymbol{F}\psi$. Similarly if $\boldsymbol{G}\psi \in \pi^\kappa$ then we don't need to check $\neg \boldsymbol{F}\boldsymbol{G}\psi$, and if $\boldsymbol{G}\psi \in \pi^{\upsilon}$ then we only need to check $\boldsymbol{F}\boldsymbol{G}\psi$ but not $\neg \boldsymbol{F}\boldsymbol{G}\psi$.

Say $\boldsymbol{G}\psi \in \pi^{\tau}$, it requires that $\boldsymbol{G}\psi$ holds now. This can be checked by ensuring ψ holds now and $\boldsymbol{G}\psi$ holds at the next time step. We can check if ψ is true at present by evaluating ψ with respect to our guess and the incoming input symbol. We can ensure ψ holds at the next time step by propagating $\boldsymbol{G}\psi$ to the π^{τ} in the next guess. If $\boldsymbol{G}\psi \in \pi^{\upsilon}$, we need to check that $\boldsymbol{F}\boldsymbol{G}\psi$ holds by having $\boldsymbol{G}\psi$ either in π^{τ} or π^{υ} of the next guess. If $\boldsymbol{G}\psi$ is not moved to π^{τ} but kept in π^{υ} forever then $\boldsymbol{F}\boldsymbol{G}\psi$ might not hold. We overcome this by imposing an acceptance condition which requires the set π^{υ} to eventually become empty.

For $\boldsymbol{F}\psi \in \pi^{\upsilon}$ we need to ensure $\boldsymbol{F}\psi$ holds. That is either ψ should hold now or some point in the future. The former can be checked by evaluating ψ using the current guess and the incoming input symbol. If it does not evaluate to true we require $\boldsymbol{F}\psi$ to hold at the next time step, which can be ensured by having $\boldsymbol{F}\psi$ in π^{υ} in the next step. Like before, this creates a possibility for $\boldsymbol{F}\psi$ to be false if it keeps getting delayed by its presence in π^{υ} forever, but as mentioned above our acceptance condition will be such that π^{υ} is eventually empty. For $\boldsymbol{F}\psi \in \pi^{\kappa}$ we are claiming $\boldsymbol{G}\boldsymbol{F}\psi$, this can be ensured by evaluating ψ with the respect to the current guess and input symbol, and requiring the resulting valuation to be true infinitely often. This can be achieved by fixing $\boldsymbol{F}\psi$ to be in π^{κ} forever and using an appropriate Büchi condition to verify that for $\boldsymbol{F}\psi$ in π^{κ}, ψ holds infinitely often.

Before we present the formal details of the construction we illustrate the above ideas above using a simple example.

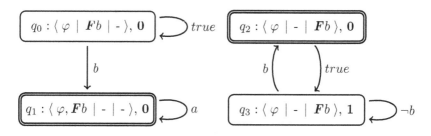

Fig. 1. The limit deterministic NBA for $\varphi = \boldsymbol{G}(a \vee \boldsymbol{F}b)$ obtained using our construction. Here states q_0, q_1, q_2 are initial with each transition going out of them being an initial transition. The final states q_1, q_2 are double bordered.

Example 13. Figure 1 shows the limit deterministic automaton constructed using our translation for the formula $\varphi = \boldsymbol{G}(a \vee \boldsymbol{F}b)$. Each state consists of a guess-counter pair (π, n). A guess here is a tripartition $\pi = \langle \pi^{\tau} \mid \pi^{\upsilon} \mid \pi^{\kappa} \rangle$ of $\{\varphi, \boldsymbol{F}b\}$, the set of all $\boldsymbol{G}, \boldsymbol{F}$ subformulae of φ. A dash '-' in the tripartition indicates that the corresponding part is empty. For simplicity the transitions are annotated by propositional formulae: a transition of the form (q, ϕ, q') indicates there is a transition from q to q' on each assignment that makes ϕ true.

(Example contd.) A transition $q \xrightarrow{\nu} q'$ is initial when the main formula φ evaluates to true on the guess in q and input ν, and the counter is 0 in q. The formula φ being a $\boldsymbol{G}$ subformula evaluates to true iff $\varphi \in \pi^\tau$ (see Definition 10). Hence every initial state is required to have $\varphi \in \pi^\tau$, and in this case because φ evaluates to true irrespective of the next input symbol every transition going out of an initial state is an initial transition.

For each $\boldsymbol{G}\psi$ formula in π^τ one needs to check $\boldsymbol{G}\psi$ holds for all accepting runs starting from that state. This is ensured by proceeding from guess π_1 to π_2 on input ν only if ψ evaluates to true on π_1 and ν (ensuring ψ holds now), and $\boldsymbol{G}\psi$ is present in π_2 (propagating the temporal requirement $\boldsymbol{G}\psi$ to the next state). In our example since $\varphi \in \pi^\tau$ for every initial state it is also propagated to every successive state, ensuring that $\varphi \in \pi^\tau$ for all states as shown in Figure 1. Therefore we have no freedom in the assignment of φ in our state space.

What remains is to assign the subformula $\boldsymbol{F}b$ to one of the three partitions. Consider q_0 in which it is assigned to π^υ. The automaton has to ensure $\boldsymbol{F}b$ holds for all accepting runs from q_0. If b holds now then it can either move to q_0 or q_1 depending upon whether it chooses to guess if $\boldsymbol{F}b$ holds again at the next time step. If b does not hold it has no choice but to remain in q_0 waiting for b to become true. The presence of $\boldsymbol{F}b \in \pi^\upsilon$ for q_0 ensures $(a \vee \boldsymbol{F}b)$ evaluates to true (independent of the input) thus the requirement of $\varphi \in \pi^\tau$ mentioned above is satisfied. Now consider q_1, here we assume that $\boldsymbol{F}b$ is false (since $\boldsymbol{F}b \in \pi^\tau$) and hence have to rely on a being true for $(a \vee \boldsymbol{F}b)$ to evaluate to true for the requirement of $\varphi \in \pi^\tau$, giving rise to the transition (q_1, a, q_1). In q_0 and q_1 the counter is not needed due to the fact that π^κ is empty. State q_1 is marked as final because π^υ is empty and the counter is 0. Now, consider q_2 and q_3 which have the same guess with $\boldsymbol{F}b \in \pi^\kappa$ but different counters. Since $\boldsymbol{F}b \in \pi^\kappa$ the formula $(a \vee \boldsymbol{F}b)$ evaluates to true irrespective of the input, thus satisfying the requirement of $\varphi \in \pi^\tau$. For $\boldsymbol{F}b \in \pi^\kappa$ we need to ensure that $\boldsymbol{G}\boldsymbol{F}b$ holds, this is done by the Büchi condition which requires q_2, a final state (where π^υ is empty and counter is 0), to be visited infinitely often thus making sure that b becomes true infinitely often.

Next we provide the formal details of our construction for an arbitrary LTL(F,G) formula.

Definition 14 (Construction). *Given a formula φ in LTL(F,G) defined over propositions P, let $\mathcal{D}(\varphi)$ be the NBA (Q, I, δ, F) over the alphabet 2^P defined as follows*

- *Q is the set $\Pi \times [z]$, consisting of guess-counter pairs where $z = |\mathbb{F}_\varphi| + 1$*
- *δ is the set of all transitions*

$$(\pi_1, m) \xrightarrow{\nu} (\pi_2, n)$$

such that
(A) for each $\boldsymbol{G}\psi \in \pi_1^\tau$, $[\psi]_\nu^{\pi_1}$ is true

(B) for each $\boldsymbol{F}\psi \in \pi_1^\upsilon$, $[\psi]_\nu^{\pi_1}$ is false implies $\boldsymbol{F}\psi \in \pi_2^\upsilon$.

(C) $\pi_1^\tau \subseteq \pi_2^\tau$ *and* $\pi_1^\kappa = \pi_2^\kappa$

(D) n *is updated as follows*

$$n = \begin{cases} m, & (|\pi_1^v| > 0) \vee (m > 0 \wedge \neg[\,\psi_m\,]_v^{\pi_1}) \\ m+1 \ (\mathrm{mod}\ k) & otherwise \end{cases}$$

where $k = |\pi^\kappa \cap \mathbb{F}_\varphi| + 1$ *and* ψ_m *be such that* $\boldsymbol{F}(\psi_m)$ *is the* m^{th} *formula in* $\pi^\kappa \cap \mathbb{F}_\varphi$

- *I is the set of transitions of the form* $(\pi, 0) \xrightarrow{v} (\pi', i)$ *where* $[\,\varphi\,]_v^\pi$ *is true*
- *F is the set of states* $(\pi, 0)$ *where* π^v *is empty.*

Next, we present the theorem that states the correctness of the above construction.

Theorem 15. *For any formula* $\varphi \in \mathrm{LTL}(F,G)$, *the NBA* $\mathcal{D}(\varphi)$ *is a limit deterministic automaton of size* $2^{\mathcal{O}(|\varphi|)}$ *such that* $L(\mathcal{D}(\varphi)) = [\![\varphi]\!]$.

Proof. The number of states in $\mathcal{D}(\varphi)$ is bounded by $3^{|\mathbb{F} \cup \mathbb{G}|} \times |\mathbb{F}|$ and so clearly the size of $\mathcal{D}(\varphi)$ is exponential in $|\varphi|$.

We can see that $\mathcal{D}(\varphi)$ is limit deterministic as follows: The final states are of the form $(\pi, 0)$ where π^v is empty. Note that according to condition (C), π^v remains empty once it becomes empty, and π^τ and π^κ remain fixed. Hence the guess π can never change after visiting a final state. And since the counter is updated deterministically we have that any state reachable from a final state chooses its next state deterministically.

The proof of the fact $L(\mathcal{D}(\varphi)) = [\![\varphi]\!]$ is provided in the companion technical report [9]. $\qquad\square$

4   Automata for LTL\GU Formulae

In this section, we present a construction of limit deterministic NBAs for the fragment LTL\GU of exponential size. We follow a compositional approach where we compose a *master* and a *slave* automata (terminology borrowed from [6]) to obtain the required one. The master automaton assumes that the truth values of the maximal until-free subformulae are known at each step and checks whether the top-level until formula holds true. The master automaton works over an extended set of propositions where the new propositions are introduced in place of the until-free subformulae. The slave automaton works over the original set of propositions and outputs at each step the truth value of the subformulae abstracted by the master in the form of the new propositions. The master and the slave are then composed such that they work together to check the entire formula. Once again we apply Proposition 5 to ignore $\boldsymbol{X}$ operators when presenting our construction.

We first clarify some notation we use in this section. For a finite set of formulae Φ we use P_Φ to denote a set of propositions p_ϕ indexed by formulae $\phi \in \Phi$. We will use $\varphi_{/\Phi}$ to denote the formula obtained from φ by replacing subformulae of φ appearing in Φ by their corresponding propositions in P_Φ.

Definition 16 (Characteristic Relation). *For a finite set of LTL formulae Φ over propositions P we define its characteristic relation $R_\Phi \subseteq (2^P)^\omega \times (2^{P_\Phi})^\omega$ as follows:*

$$(w, \lambda) \in R_\Phi \quad \textit{iff} \quad \lambda[i] = \{p_\varphi \mid \varphi \in \Phi, \ w_i \vDash \varphi\}$$

Given $w_1 \in 2^{P_1}$ and $w_2 \in 2^{P_2}$ define the join of w_1 and w_2 denoted by $w_1 \cup w_2$ as the word in $(2^{P_1 \cup P_2})^\omega$ whose i^{th} element $(w_1 \cup w_2)[i]$ is $w_1[i] \cup w_2[i]$. Given a relation $R \subseteq (2^{P_1})^\omega \times (2^{P_2})^\omega$ define the language $R^\circ \subseteq (2^{P_1 \cup P_2})^\omega$ as the set of words obtained by joining the pairs in R:

$$R^\circ = \{\rho \in (2^{P_1 \cup P_2})^\omega \mid \exists (w, \lambda) \in R, \ \rho = w \cup \lambda\}$$

Later on in this section (Proposition 23) we show how to construct a NBM for a set of LTL(F,G) formula which accepts a relation that is not the characteristic relation but is "subsumed" by the characteristic relation of the set. In that direction we define what it means for a relation to be subsumed by another.

Definition 17 (Subsumption). *For two relations $R, S \subseteq (2^{P_1})^\omega \times (2^{P_2})^\omega$ we say that R is* subsumed *by S, denoted by $R \triangleleft S$ iff $S \subseteq R$ and for every $(w, \lambda) \in R$ there exists $(w, \lambda') \in S$ such that $\forall i \ \lambda[i] \subseteq \lambda'[i]$.*

Next, we describe how to break an LTL\\GU formula into an until factor and an until-free factor which are going to be handled by the master and slave automata respectively.

Definition 18 (Factorization). *Given a formula $\varphi \in$ LTL\\GU over propositions P we identify the set of maximal subformulae of φ that do not contain U as the* until-free factor *of φ denoted by $\Upsilon(\varphi)$.*

$$\Upsilon(\boldsymbol{G}\varphi) = \{\boldsymbol{G}\varphi\} \qquad\qquad \Upsilon(\boldsymbol{F}\varphi) = \{\boldsymbol{F}\varphi\}$$

$$\Upsilon(\varphi_1 \wedge/\vee \varphi_2) = \begin{cases} \{\varphi_1 \wedge/\vee \varphi_2\} & \textit{if } \varphi_1 \in \Upsilon(\varphi_1) \textit{ and } \varphi_2 \in \Upsilon(\varphi_2) \\ \Upsilon(\varphi_1) \cup \Upsilon(\varphi_2) & \textit{otherwise} \end{cases}$$

$$\Upsilon(\varphi_1 \boldsymbol{U} \varphi_2) = \Upsilon(\varphi_1) \cup \Upsilon(\varphi_2) \qquad \Upsilon(\ell) = \ell \quad \textit{for literals } \ell$$

For a formula $\varphi \in$ LTL\\$GU$ we define its until factor *as the formula $\varphi_{/\Upsilon(\varphi)} \in$ LTL(U) simply written as χ_φ.*

The following proposition relates the semantics of an LTL\\GU formula with the semantics of its until and until-free factors.

Proposition 19. *For any $\varphi \in$ LTL\\$GU$ over propositions P and any relation $R \subseteq (2^P)^\omega \times (2^{P\Upsilon(\varphi)})^\omega$ such that $R \triangleleft R_{\Upsilon(\varphi)}$ we have*

$$\llbracket \varphi \rrbracket = (R^\circ \cap \llbracket \chi_\varphi \rrbracket) \upharpoonright_{2^P}$$

Proof. We prove our statement by proving the following equivalence

$$w \vDash \varphi \iff (w \cup \lambda(w)) \vDash \chi_\varphi \tag{1}$$

where $\lambda(w) \in (2^{P\Upsilon(\varphi)})^\omega$ is the unique word such that $(w, \lambda(w)) \in R_{\Upsilon(\varphi)}$. We do so by performing induction on φ:

i. $\varphi \in \Upsilon(\varphi)$: in which case $\chi_\varphi = p_\varphi$.

$$w \vDash \varphi$$
$$\Longleftrightarrow \qquad p_\varphi \in \lambda(w)[0] \qquad\qquad \text{(definition of } \lambda(w))$$
$$\Longleftrightarrow \qquad (w \cup \lambda(w)) \vDash p_\varphi$$

ii. $\varphi = (\varphi_1 \wedge/\vee \varphi_2) \notin \Upsilon(\varphi_1 \wedge/\vee \varphi_2)$: here $\chi_{\varphi_1 \wedge\!\!\!\wedge \varphi_2} = \chi_{\varphi_1} \wedge/\vee \chi_{\varphi_2}$

$$w \vDash \varphi_1 \wedge/\vee \varphi_2$$
$$\Longleftrightarrow \qquad w \vDash \varphi_1 \quad \text{and/or} \quad w \vDash \varphi_2$$
$$\Longleftrightarrow \qquad (w \cup \lambda(w)) \vDash \chi_{\varphi_1} \quad \text{and/or} \quad (w \cup \lambda(w)) \vDash \chi_{\varphi_2} \qquad \text{(inductive hypothesis)}$$
$$\Longleftrightarrow \qquad (w \cup \lambda(w)) \vDash (\chi_{\varphi_1} \wedge/\vee \chi_{\varphi_1}) = \chi_{\varphi_1 \wedge\!\!\!\wedge \varphi_2}$$

iii. $\varphi = (\varphi_1 \,\boldsymbol{U}\, \varphi_2)$: here $\chi_{\varphi_1 \boldsymbol{U} \varphi_2} = \chi_{\varphi_1} \boldsymbol{U} \chi_{\varphi_2}$

$$w \vDash \varphi_1 \,\boldsymbol{U}\, \varphi_2$$
$$\Longleftrightarrow \qquad \exists i \; w_i \vDash \varphi_2 \quad \text{and} \quad \forall j{<}i \; w_j \vDash \varphi_1$$
$$\Longleftrightarrow \qquad \exists i \; (w_i \cup \lambda(w_i)) \vDash \chi_{\varphi_2} \quad \text{and} \quad \forall j{<}i \; (w_j \cup \lambda(w_j)) \vDash \chi_{\varphi_1}$$
$$\text{(inductive hypothesis)}$$
$$\Longleftrightarrow \qquad (w \cup \lambda(w)) \vDash \chi_{\varphi_1} \,\boldsymbol{U}\, \chi_{\varphi_2} = \chi_{\varphi_1 \boldsymbol{U} \varphi_2}$$

Now we also have $(w \cup \lambda(w)) \in R^\circ$ due to the fact that $(w, \lambda(w)) \in R_{\Upsilon(\varphi)}$ and $R_{\Upsilon(\varphi)} \subseteq R$. This along with (1) gives us $[\![\varphi]\!] \subseteq (R^\circ \cap [\![\chi_\varphi]\!]) \restriction_{2^P}$.

Next we observe that if $\lambda_1 \subseteq \lambda_2$ then $w \cup \lambda_1 \vDash \chi_\varphi$ implies $w \cup \lambda_2 \vDash \chi_\varphi$ because the propositions in $P_{\Upsilon(\varphi)}$ appear positively in χ_φ. Consider $w \in (R^\circ \cap [\![\chi_\varphi]\!]) \restriction_{2^P}$, this implies there is a λ such that $(w, \lambda) \in R$ and $(w \cup \lambda) \vDash \chi_\varphi$. Since $R \triangleleft R_{\Upsilon(\varphi)}$ we have $\lambda \subseteq \lambda(w)$ where $(w, \lambda(w)) \in R_{\Upsilon(\varphi)} \subseteq R$. Now from our first observation in this paragraph we have that $(w \cup \lambda(w)) \vDash \chi_\varphi$, from which we can conclude $w \vDash \varphi$ using (1). This proves the other side of the containment $(R^\circ \cap [\![\chi_\varphi]\!]) \restriction_{2^P} \subseteq [\![\varphi]\!]$. $\qquad\square$

Let P_1 and P_2 be disjoint set of propositions. Let $\Sigma = 2^{P_1}$, $\Gamma = 2^{P_2}$ and by abusing notation let $\Sigma \times \Gamma = 2^{P_1 \cup P_2}$. Next we describe how to compose a master NBA $\mathcal{A}$ over input $\Sigma \times \Gamma$ and a slave NBM $\mathcal{B}$ over input alphabet Σ and output alphabet Γ to obtain an NBA $\mathcal{A} \times \mathcal{B}$ over input Σ.

Definition 20 (Composition). *Consider a NBA* $\mathcal{A} = (Q_\mathcal{A}, \delta_\mathcal{A}, I_\mathcal{A}, F_\mathcal{A})$ *over input alphabet* $\Sigma \times \Gamma$ *and a NBM* $\mathcal{B} = (Q_\mathcal{B}, \delta_\mathcal{B}, I_\mathcal{B}, M_\mathcal{B}, F_\mathcal{B})$ *over input alphabet* Σ *and output alphabet* Γ. *We define a NBA* $(Q_\mathcal{A} \times Q_\mathcal{B}, \delta_{\mathcal{A} \times \mathcal{B}}, I_{\mathcal{A} \times \mathcal{B}}, F_\mathcal{A} \times F_\mathcal{B})$ *over input* Σ *denoted by* $\mathcal{A} \times \mathcal{B}$ *where*

$$\delta_{\mathcal{A} \times \mathcal{B}}((a_1, b_1), \sigma) = \{(a_2, b_2) \mid q_2 \in \delta_\mathcal{B}(q_1, \sigma), \; a_2 \in \delta_\mathcal{A}(a_1, \sigma \cup M_\mathcal{B}(b_1, \sigma))\}$$

$$I_{\mathcal{A} \times \mathcal{B}} = \{(a_1, b_1) \xrightarrow{\nu} (a_2, b_2) \mid b_1 \xrightarrow{\nu} b_2 \in I_\mathcal{B}, \; a_1 \xrightarrow{\nu \cup M_\mathcal{B}(b_1, \nu)} a_2 \in I_\mathcal{A}\}$$

The proposition below relates the languages accepted by a master and a slave NBA to the language accepted by the product defined above. It requires the master to have final states such that on entering a final state it can never leave the set of final states. We shall refer to this property as absorbing final states. We provide a complete proof of this result in the technical report [9].

Proposition 21. *Given a NBA $\mathcal{A}$ with input alphabet $\Sigma \times \Gamma$ with absorbing final states, and a NBA $\mathcal{B}$ with input alphabet Σ and output alphabet Γ we have*

$$L(\mathcal{A} \times \mathcal{B}) = (R_{\mathcal{B}}^{\circ} \cap L(\mathcal{A})) \restriction_{\Sigma}$$

The following proposition shows that the composition of a master and slave is limit deterministic if both of them are limit deterministic. The proof is provided in the technical report [9].

Proposition 22. *Given a limit deterministic NBA $\mathcal{A}$ over input alphabet $\Sigma \times \Gamma$, and a limit deterministic NBM $\mathcal{B}$ with input alphabet Σ and output alphabet Γ it is the case that $\mathcal{A} \times \mathcal{B}$ is also limit deterministic.*

The next proposition illustrates how to construct a Mealy machine which recognizes a relation which is subsumed by the characteristic relation of an until-free factor, thus constructing a slave automaton of exponential size.

Proposition 23. *For any finite set $\Phi \subset$ LTL(F,G) over propositions P there is a NBM $\mathcal{B}_{\Phi}$ with input over 2^P and output over $2^{P_{\Phi}}$ such that $R_{\mathcal{B}_{\Phi}} \lhd R_{\Phi}$, $\mathcal{B}_{\Phi}$ is limit deterministic and of size $\mathcal{O}(2^{|\Phi|})$.*

Proof. Consider the construction of Theorem 15 with the following modifications to construct $\mathcal{B}_{\Phi}$:

– let Π be set of all three way partition of $\mathbb{G}_{\Phi} \cup \mathbb{F}_{\Phi}$ instead of $\mathbb{G}_{\varphi} \cup \mathbb{F}_{\varphi}$
– every transition of the form $(\pi, 0) \xrightarrow{\nu} (\pi', m)$ is initial
– define $M_{\mathcal{B}}((\pi, n), \nu)$ as $\{ p_{\varphi} \in P_{\Phi} \mid [\varphi]_{\nu}^{\pi} = true \}$

The proof of $R_{\mathcal{B}_{\Phi}} \lhd R_{\Phi}$ can be found in the technical report [9].   □

Next we observe that master automaton can be constructed using a standard approach of translating an alternating automaton for the until factor to an NBA.

Proposition 24. *[18] For any formula $\varphi \in$ LTL(U) there is a NBA $\mathcal{A}_{\varphi}$ with a single absorbing final state such that $L(\mathcal{A}_{\varphi}) = [\![\varphi]\!]$ and is of size $\mathcal{O}(2^{|\varphi|})$.*

Proof. As observed in Lemma 2 in [8], the construction follows from Theorem 22 and Proposition 20 of [18].   □

Finally we combine all the results in this section to show that the composition of the master and slave for the until and the until free components is as desired.

Theorem 25. *For any formula* $\varphi \in \text{LTL}\backslash GU$ *the NBA* $\mathcal{A}_{\chi_\varphi} \times \mathcal{B}_{\Upsilon(\varphi)}$ *recognizes* $[\![\varphi]\!]$, *is limit deterministic and is of size* $2^{\mathcal{O}(|\varphi|)}$.

Proof. First we look at the language recognized by $\mathcal{A}_{\chi_\varphi} \times \mathcal{B}_{\Upsilon(\varphi)}$:

$$
\begin{aligned}
&L(\mathcal{A}_{\chi_\varphi} \times \mathcal{B}_{\Upsilon(\varphi)}) \\
&= (R_{\mathcal{B}_{\Upsilon(\varphi)}}{}^\circ \cap L(\mathcal{A}_{\chi_\varphi})) \restriction_{2^P} && \text{(Proposition 21)} \\
&= (R_{\mathcal{B}_{\Upsilon(\varphi)}}{}^\circ \cap [\![\chi_\varphi]\!]) \restriction_{2^P} && \text{(Proposition 24)} \\
&= [\![\varphi]\!] && \text{(Proposition 19 \& 23)}
\end{aligned}
$$

We have $\mathcal{A}_{\chi_\varphi} \times \mathcal{B}_{\Upsilon(\varphi)}$ to be limit deterministic from Proposition 22. The automata $\mathcal{A}_{\chi_\varphi}$ and $\mathcal{B}_{\Upsilon(\varphi)}$ are both exponential in the size of φ as seen in Propositions 24 \& 23, and so the product is also of size $2^{\mathcal{O}(|\varphi|)}$. $\qquad\square$

5 Results and Applications

In this section, we summarize and reflect on some of the consequences of our results related to PBAs and model checking concurrent probabilistic programs.

5.1 Model Checking MDPs

MDPs are the prevalent models for concurrent probabilistic programs. Concurrency is modeled as nondeterministic states, where the transitions are chosen by a scheduler. We refer the reader to [5] for a complete definition of MDPs. The model checking problem can be formulated as follows.

Definition 26. *Given a MDP* $\mathcal{N}$ *and temporal logic formula* φ, *the model checking problem is to decide if there exists a scheduler* u *such that* $\text{Pr}_{\mathcal{N},u}([\![\varphi]\!]) > 0$.

Our construction of limit deterministic automata for $\text{LTL}\backslash GU$ leads to an improved EXPTIME model checking algorithm for MDPs and formulae in this logic which is matched by an EXPTIME-hard lower bound.

Theorem 27. *The model checking problem for MDPs and formulae in* $\text{LTL}\backslash GU$ *is* EXPTIME-*complete*.

Proof. Proposition 4.2.3 in [5] states one can decide the model checking problem of MDPs and limit deterministic NBAs by taking a product of the two and doing a linear time analysis of the resulting graph. Using this along with our result in Theorem 25 we obtain the required upper bound. Proof of the lower bound can be found in the technical report [9]. $\qquad\square$

We contrast this with the complexity of model checking MDPs and full LTL.

Proposition 28. *[5] The model checking problem for MDPs and formulae in* LTL *is* 2EXPTIME-*complete*.

5.2   PBAs for LTL

First, we observe that our construction of limit deterministic NBAs gives us an exponential upper-bound on the size of PBAs for LTL\GU.

Theorem 29. *For any formula $\varphi \in$ LTL\$GU$ there is a PBA $\mathcal{M}$ such that $L_{>0}(\mathcal{M}) = [\![\varphi]\!]$ and is of size $2^{\mathcal{O}(|\varphi|)}$.*

Proof. Follows from Lemma 8 and Theorem 25.   □

Next, we note that this upper-bound is the best one can achieve.

Proposition 30. *There exists a family of formulae $\varphi_n \in$ LTL(G) of size n such that any PBAs recognizing them have size at least 2^n.*

Proof. Consider the formula $\boldsymbol{G}(p \iff \boldsymbol{X}^n p)$. The language accepted by it is the set $\{u^\omega \mid u \in \Sigma^n\}$ where $\Sigma = \{\emptyset, \{p\}\}$. For each $u \in \Sigma^n$ there needs to be at least one state q_u such that u can reach q_u from the initial state with non-zero probability and no other $v \in \Sigma^n$ can reach q_u from the initial state with non-zero probability, because the word uv^ω should not be accepted with positive probability whereas u^ω should be accepted.   □

Next, we note that constructing deterministic automata can result in a double exponential blow-up.

Proposition 31. *[1] There exists a family of of formulae $\varphi_n \in$ LTL(F) such that any deterministic automata that recognize them have size $2^{2^{\Omega(n)}}$.*

6   Conclusions

In this paper, we have presented a translation of formulae in LTL\$GU$ to limit deterministic automata that are provably exponentially smaller than deterministic automata for this logic. This yields a new, improved exponential time algorithm for model checking MDPs and LTL\$GU$ as compared to the previously known double exponential time complexity for MDPs and full LTL. It also gives us a way to build PBAs of exponential size for LTL\$GU$. Our automata in addition to having better upper-bounds also have a well defined logical structure, which makes it amenable to several optimizations.

There are few questions that are still left open. While we have shown how to construct exponential sized probabilistic and limit deterministic automata for LTL\GU, it still remains open whether we can construct equally small probabilistic or limit deterministic automata for full LTL. In [8] we prove that translating the safety fragment of LTL to weak probabilistic monitors (which are special PBAs) can result in a double exponential blow-up. This might indicate that it is unlikely one will be able to give exponential sized PBAs for full LTL. While Proposition 28 excludes the possibility of constructing such automata in exponential time, it does not rule out the existence of exponential sized automata for full LTL which can potentially be built in double exponential time.

As a part of future work we intend to implement our construction and compare it with results for deterministic automata, and also see if our new algorithm for model checking yields better performance in practice.

Acknowledgments. Dileep Kini was partially supported by NSF grant CNS-1016791 and Mahesh Viswanathan by NSF grant CNS-1314485.

References

1. Alur, R., Torre, S.L.: Deterministic generators and games for ltl fragments. ACM Trans. Comput. Logic 5(1), 1–25 (2004)
2. Babiak, T., Blahoudek, F., Křetínský, M., Strejček, J.: Effective translation of LTL to deterministic Rabin automata: Beyond the (F,G)-fragment. In: Van Hung, D., Ogawa, M. (eds.) ATVA 2013. LNCS, vol. 8172, pp. 24–39. Springer, Heidelberg (2013)
3. Baier, C., Größer, M.: Recognizing omega-regular languages with probabilistic automata. In: LICS, pp. 137–146 (2005)
4. Chadha, R., Sistla, A.P., Viswanathan, M.: On the expressiveness and complexity of randomization in finite state monitors. J. ACM 56(5), 26:1–26:44 (2009)
5. Courcoubetis, C., Yannakakis, M.: The complexity of probabilistic verification. J. ACM 42(4), 857–907 (1995)
6. Esparza, J., Křetínský, J.: From LTL to deterministic automata: A safraless compositional approach. In: Biere, A., Bloem, R. (eds.) CAV 2014. LNCS, vol. 8559, pp. 192–208. Springer, Heidelberg (2014)
7. Gastin, P., Oddoux, D.: Fast LTL to büchi automata translation. In: Berry, G., Comon, H., Finkel, A. (eds.) CAV 2001. LNCS, vol. 2102, pp. 53–65. Springer, Heidelberg (2001)
8. Kini, D., Viswanathan, M.: Probabilistic automata for safety LTL specifications. In: McMillan, K.L., Rival, X. (eds.) VMCAI 2014. LNCS, vol. 8318, pp. 118–136. Springer, Heidelberg (2014)
9. Kini, D., Viswanathan, M.: Probabilistic büchi automata for LTL\GU. Technical Report University of Illinois at Urbana-Champaign (2015), http://hdl.handle.net/2142/72686
10. Klein, J., Baier, C.: Experiments with deterministic ω-automata for formulas of linear temporal logic. Theoretical Computer Science 363(2), 182–195 (2006)
11. Křetínský, J., Esparza, J.: Deterministic automata for the (F,G)-fragment of LTL. In: Madhusudan, P., Seshia, S.A. (eds.) CAV 2012. LNCS, vol. 7358, pp. 7–22. Springer, Heidelberg (2012)
12. Křetínský, J., Garza, R.L.: Rabinizer 2: Small deterministic automata for LTL\GU. In: Van Hung, D., Ogawa, M. (eds.) ATVA 2013. LNCS, vol. 8172, pp. 446–450. Springer, Heidelberg (2013)
13. Morgenstern, A., Schneider, K.: From LTL to symbolically represented deterministic automata. In: Logozzo, F., Peled, D.A., Zuck, L.D. (eds.) VMCAI 2008. LNCS, vol. 4905, pp. 279–293. Springer, Heidelberg (2008)
14. Piterman, N., Pnueli, A., Sa'ar, Y.: Synthesis of reactive(1) designs. In: Emerson, E.A., Namjoshi, K.S. (eds.) VMCAI 2006. LNCS, vol. 3855, pp. 364–380. Springer, Heidelberg (2006)
15. Pnueli, A., Zaks, A.: On the merits of temporal testers. In: 25 Years of Model Checking, pp. 172–195 (2008)
16. Somenzi, F., Bloem, R.: Efficient Büchi automata from LTL formulae. In: Emerson, E.A., Sistla, A.P. (eds.) CAV 2000. LNCS, vol. 1855, pp. 248–263. Springer, Heidelberg (2000)
17. Vardi, M., Wolper, P., Sistla, A.P.: Reasoning about infinite computation paths. In: FOCS (1983)
18. Vardi, M.Y.: An automata-theoretic approach to linear temporal logic. In: Moller, F., Birtwistle, G. (eds.) Logics for Concurrency. LNCS, vol. 1043, pp. 238–266. Springer, Heidelberg (1996)

Saturation-Based Incremental LTL Model Checking with Inductive Proofs

Vince Molnár[1], Dániel Darvas[1], András Vörös[1], and Tamás Bartha[2]

[1] Budapest University of Technology and Economics, Hungary
[2] Institute for Computer Science and Control, Hungarian Academy of Sciences

Abstract. Efficient symbolic and explicit model checking approaches have been developed for the verification of linear time temporal properties. Nowadays, advances resulted in the combination of on-the-fly search with symbolic encoding in a hybrid solution providing many results by now. In this work, we propose a new hybrid approach that leverages the so-called saturation algorithm both as an iteration strategy during the state space generation and in a new incremental fixed-point computation algorithm to compute strongly connected components (SCCs). In addition, our solution works on-the-fly during state space traversal and exploits the decomposition of the model as an abstraction to inductively prove the absence of SCCs with cheap explicit runs on the components. When a proof cannot be shown, the incremental symbolic fixed-point algorithm will find the SCC, if one exists. Evaluation on the models of the Model Checking Contest shows that our approach outperforms similar algorithms for concurrent systems.

1 Introduction

Linear temporal logic (LTL) specifications play an important role in the history of verification. Checking these properties is usually reduced to finding *strongly connected components* (SCCs) by checking language emptiness of the synchronous product of two Büchi automata: one characterizing the possible behaviors of the system and another accepting behaviors that violate the desired property. Two main approaches emerged during the history of model checking. *Explicit* methods process the state graph using proven graph algorithms. *Symbolic* model checking was introduced to address the problem of state space explosion. Symbolic approaches based on *decision diagrams* usually apply greatest fixed point computations on the set of states to compute an *SCC-hull* [14]. These approaches typically scale well, and they have improved considerably due to the extensive research in this area.

A considerable amount of effort was put in combining symbolic and explicit techniques [1,10–13]. The motivation is usually to introduce one of the main advantages of explicit approaches into symbolic model checking: the ability to look for SCCs on the fly, i.e., continuously during state space generation. Solutions typically include abstracting the state space into sets of states such as in the

© Springer-Verlag Berlin Heidelberg 2015
C. Baier and C. Tinelli (Eds.): TACAS 2015, LNCS 9035, pp. 643–657, 2015.
DOI: 10.1007/978-3-662-46681-0_58

case of multiple state tableaux or symbolic observation graphs. Explicit checks can then be run on the abstraction on the fly to look for potential SCCs.

The goal of this paper is to present a new hybrid LTL model checking algorithm that *1)* builds a symbolic state space representation, *2)* looks for SCCs on the fly, *3)* incrementally processes the discovered parts of the state space and *4)* uses explicit runs on multiple fine-grained abstractions to avoid unnecessary computations. Although example models are given as Petri nets, the algorithm can handle any discrete state model. The state space is encoded by decision diagrams, built using saturation. On-the-fly detection of SCCs is achieved by running searches over the discovered state space continuously during state space generation. In order to reduce the overhead of these searches, we present a new incremental fixed point algorithm that considers newly discovered parts of the state space when computing the SCC-hull. While this approach specializes on *finding* an SCC, a complementary algorithm maintains various abstractions of the state space to perform explicit searches in order to inductively prove the *absence* of SCCs.

The paper is structured as follows. Section 2 presents the background of this work. An overview of the proposed algorithm is given in Section 3, then Section 4 and 5 introduces the main components in detail. The whole algorithm is assembled in Section 6. A brief summary of related work is presented in Section 7, followed by an extensive evaluation of our approach and three other tools in Section 8. Finally, Section 9 summarizes the contributions of the paper.

2   Saturation

Saturation is an iteration strategy specifically designed to work with decision diagrams. It was originally used as a state space generation algorithm [5] to answer reachability queries on concurrent systems, but applications in branching-time model checking [17] and SCC computation [18] also proved to be successful.

Saturation works best if it can exploit the structure of high-level models. Therefore, it defines the input model on a finer level of granularity, introducing the concept of components and events into traditional discrete-state models. Formally, the input model of the algorithm is in the form $M = \langle \mathcal{S}, \mathcal{S}_{init}, \mathcal{E}, \mathcal{N} \rangle$. Provided that the model has K components, each with the set of possible *local states* $\mathcal{S}_k$, we call $\mathcal{S} = \mathcal{S}_1 \times \cdots \times \mathcal{S}_K$ the set of possible *global states*. A single global state $\mathbf{s}$ is then a K-tuple $(s_1, \ldots, s_K)$, where each $s_k \in \mathcal{S}_k$ is a state variable containing the local state of the kth component. The set of possible initial states of the system is $\mathcal{S}_{init} \subseteq \mathcal{S}$. Elements of set $\mathcal{E}$ are (asynchronous) *events* of the model, usually corresponding to transitions of the high-level system model. Events are used to decompose the next-state (or *transition*) relation $\mathcal{N} \subseteq \mathcal{S} \times \mathcal{S}$ into separate (but not necessarily disjoint) next-state relations: $\mathcal{N} = \bigcup_{\varepsilon \in \mathcal{E}} \mathcal{N}_\varepsilon$, where $\mathcal{N}_\varepsilon$ is the next state relation of event ε. We often use $\mathcal{N}$ as a function, defining $\mathcal{N}(\mathbf{s}) = \{\mathbf{s}' \mid (\mathbf{s}, \mathbf{s}') \in \mathcal{N}\}$ as the set of states that are reachable from $\mathbf{s}$ in one step (and also $\mathcal{N}(S)$ as an extension to sets of states). The inverse of a next state function is defined as $\mathcal{N}^{-1}(\mathbf{s}) = \{\mathbf{s}' \mid (\mathbf{s}', \mathbf{s}) \in \mathcal{N}\}$. In this paper, a state space will be denoted by a pair $(\mathcal{S}, \mathcal{N})$, where states of $\mathcal{S}$ and transitions of $\mathcal{N}$ are nodes and arcs of the state graph.

By introducing components and events, saturation can exploit the *locality* property of concurrent systems. Locality is the empirical assumption that high-level transitions of a concurrent model usually affect only a small number of components. An event ε is *independent* from component k if *1)* its firing does not change the state of the component, and *2)* its enabling does not depend on the state of the component. If ε depends on component k, then k is called a *supporting* component: $k \in supp(\varepsilon)$.

In order to map the components to variables of the underlying decision diagram, an ordering has to be defined. Without loss of generality, assume that every component is identified by its index in the ordering. Using these indices, it is possible to group events by defining $Top(\varepsilon) = k$ as the supporting component of ε with the highest index. The set of every event with a *Top* value of k is $\mathcal{E}_k = \{\varepsilon \in \mathcal{E} \mid Top(\varepsilon) = k\}$. For the sake of convenience, we use $\mathcal{N}_k$ to represent the next state function of all such events, formally $\mathcal{N}_k = \bigcup_{\varepsilon \in \mathcal{E}_k} \mathcal{N}_\varepsilon$. The notations $\mathcal{N}_{\leq k} = \bigcup_{i \leq k} \mathcal{N}_i$ and $\mathcal{N}_{<k} = \bigcup_{i<k} \mathcal{N}_i$ will also be used.

Symbolic encoding of the next state functions of events $\varepsilon \in \mathcal{E}_k$ relies on the following observation: $\mathcal{N}_\varepsilon((s_1, \ldots, s_K))$ and $\mathcal{N}_\varepsilon((s_1, \ldots, s_k)) \times \{(s_{k+1}, \ldots, s_K)\}$ are equivalent (i.e., $\mathcal{N}_\varepsilon$ does not change the local states of components above k). From this fact, two important properties of saturation follows: *1)* in the encoding of $\mathcal{N}_\varepsilon$ it is sufficient to encode the state changes of state variables $s_1, \ldots, s_k$, where $k = Top(\varepsilon)$, as well as *2)* it is possible to apply the individual $\mathcal{N}_\varepsilon$ functions in a finer granularity: $\mathcal{N}_\varepsilon$ is not only applicable on a set of global states, but also on sets of substates composed of state variables $s_1, \ldots, s_k$.

In order to reason about sets of substates encoded by decision diagram nodes, we will use the notations introduced in [4]. Let n_k be a single node in a decision diagram on the level representing the state variable of the kth component. Let $\mathcal{B}(n_k)$ represent the *below* substates encoded by n_k. Below substates can be regarded as the set of paths in the decision diagram that go from n_k to the terminal node $\mathbf{1}$. Throughout this paper, $n_k[i]$ will denote the *child node* of n_k on level $k - 1$ reachable through the arc corresponding to the local state $i \in \mathcal{S}_k$. With this notation, the set of substates $\mathcal{B}(n_k)$ encoded by node n_k is described with the following recursive definition:

$$\mathcal{B}(n_k) = \begin{cases} \{i \mid n_k[i] = \mathbf{1}\} & \text{if } k = 1 \\ \bigcup_{i \in \mathcal{S}_k} \mathcal{B}(n_k[i]) \times \{i\} & \text{otherwise.} \end{cases}$$

A possible interpretation of the definition is that the set of substates encoded by node n_k is composed of different instantiations of the sets of substates encoded by the children of n_k.

The goal of saturation as a state space generation algorithm is to compute the set of reachable states $\mathcal{S}_{rch} = \mathcal{N}^*(\mathcal{S}_{init})$ of model M, where $\mathcal{N}^*$ is the *transitive closure* of the next-state relation. To do this, it exploits the structure of decision diagrams and the aforementioned locality of concurrent systems by dividing the global fixed-point computation into smaller parts, computing local fixed-points with regard to a decision diagram node n_k and its corresponding next-state function $\mathcal{N}_k$. A node n_k is called *saturated*, if it is a terminal node, or its child nodes are saturated and it represents a set of substates computed as the fixed-point of the transitive closure of $\mathcal{N}_k$, formally: $\mathcal{B}(n_k) = \mathcal{N}_{\leq k}^*(\mathcal{B}(n_k))$. This definition yields a recursive algorithm that saturates nodes of the decision diagram in a bottom-up order, recursively saturating new nodes discovered when applying a next-state function on higher levels of the decision diagram.

3   Overview of the Algorithm

The goal of this paper is to present a new model checking solution that is *1)* symbolic, *2)* looks for SCCs on the fly during state space generation with an incremental fixed-point algorithm, and *3)* uses cheap explicit proofs to indicate the absence of SCCs when possible. The basis of the presented complex algorithm is saturation, which is highly efficient in the symbolic state space generation of large concurrent systems.

On-the-fly operation is achieved by performing fixed-point computations *when a node becomes saturated*. Processing saturated nodes has the advantage of handling a set of (sub)states that is closed with regard to events independent from higher levels. This means that the set will not change anymore during the exploration, i.e., each closed set has to be processed only once.

Even though a set with its related events will be processed only once, the recursive definition of saturation will cause such sets to appear again as part of larger sets encoded by the parent node in the decision diagram. The incremental fixed-point algorithm presented in Section 4 avoids redundant computations by restricting the search to SCCs containing at least one transition belonging to an event not considered before, causing the computation to converge faster.

It has been shown many times that symbolic model checking approaches can greatly benefit from explicit techniques [1, 10–13]. In this work, explicit checks are applied in two ways. First, the saturation algorithm is enhanced with a simple modification that is able to collect individual states appearing more than once during the exploration. As presented in Section 5.1, the absence of these *recurring* states indicates that no SCCs can be found in the set of explored states. Secondly, one of the main contributions of this paper is a cheap abstraction of the state space with regard to a single decision diagram node, on which explicit SCC computation algorithms can be run with a negligible overhead. A theorem presented in Section 5.2 gives an efficient method to inductively prove the absence of SCCs in the state space explored so far. Both methods are used to reduce the number of times a symbolic fixed-point computation is necessary, often making the overhead of on-the-fly searches to almost disappear.

4   Incremental Symbolic Fixed-point Computation

This section presents a symbolic fixed-point computation algorithm to look for SCCs incrementally in a growing state space. It can be regarded as a variation of traditional SCC-hull algorithms [14], but it is unique in the sense that it is optimized to run multiple times, each time on a superset of the previous input. SCC-hull algorithms usually start with a set of states and a transition relation and iteratively try to discard states to reach a fixed-point. Compared to this strategy, the main difference in our concept is that we specify *transitions* to discard. The reason for this design lies in the iteration strategy of saturation, but the algorithm itself is not restricted to any iteration strategy.

As noted in Section 2, the set of substates encoded by a node n_k can be written as $\mathcal{B}(n_k) = \bigcup_{i \in \mathcal{S}_k} \mathcal{B}(n_k[i]) \times \{i\}$, i.e., the union of the below substates of each child node instantiated with the corresponding value of the kth state variable. In case of a saturated node, each set in the union is closed with regard to the next-state function $\mathcal{N}_{<k}$, so no new SCCs can be found in $\mathcal{B}(n_k)$ using these transitions only. However, the sets of substates are connected by transitions in $\mathcal{N}_k$ that are not yet processed on $\mathcal{B}(n_k)$. Figure 1 shows an example: black arcs between sets of substates are transitions of $\mathcal{N}_k$. Constraining the search for SCCs to those that contain at least one transition from $\mathcal{N}_k$ can quickly discard parts of the state space to make the fixed point computation converge faster.

The main function of the algorithm, *DetectSCC*, does not have to know about saturation. It takes a set of states $(\mathcal{S})$, a next-state relation $(\mathcal{N})$, and a subset of this relation $(\mathcal{N}_{new} \subseteq \mathcal{N})$ as an input and returns a Boolean value indicating if there exists an SCC consisting of states and transitions from $\mathcal{S}$ and $\mathcal{N}$ that contains at least one transition from $\mathcal{N}_{new}$. The following observation provides a way to use this function as an incremental SCC computation algorithm.

Observation 1. *Consider a state space $(\mathcal{S}, \mathcal{N})$ containing an SCC and a subset of transitions $\mathcal{N}_{new} \subseteq \mathcal{N}$ considered to contain new transitions. If $\mathcal{S}$ does not contain any SCCs with only old transitions $\mathcal{N}_{old} = \mathcal{N} \setminus \mathcal{N}_{new}$, then the SCC contains at least one transition from $\mathcal{N}_{new}$.*

Let us assume that the function is called during state space exploration and the input is the current set of (sub)states, the set of transitions fired so far, and the set of transitions fired since the last time the algorithm was called. Then, the observation guarantees that by the end of the state space generation, the algorithm will have returned *true* at least once iff there exists an SCC in the reachable state space $(\mathcal{S}_{rch}, \mathcal{N}_{fired})$. The case of calling the function in a recursive setting is less obvious. To see that calling *DetectSCC* after a node is saturated gives a complete algorithm, consider the previous discussion. When a node n_k on level k becomes saturated, the only transitions that were fired but have never been input into the function yet are in $\mathcal{N}_k$. This way, the correct inputs when calling the function at that point are $\mathcal{B}(n_k)$ as the set of states, $\mathcal{N}_{\leq k}$ as the next-state relation and $\mathcal{N}_k$ as the subset of new transitions.

Algorithm 1 shows the pseudocode of *DetectSCC*. The function works by discarding transitions from $\mathcal{N}_{new}$ that cannot be closed with other transitions through the states in $\mathcal{S}$ to form a loop. Transitions are not processed directly: the set of their *source* states $\mathcal{S}^-$ and *target* states $\mathcal{S}^+$ represent them in the fixed-point computation. States of $\mathcal{S}^-$ that are not reachable from $\mathcal{S}^+$ and states of $\mathcal{S}^+$ that are not reachable from $\mathcal{S}^-$ *through transitions in $\mathcal{N}_{new}$* are discarded

input   : $\mathcal{S}, \mathcal{N}, \mathcal{N}_{new}$: set
  // $\mathcal{S}$: set of states,
  // $\mathcal{N}, \mathcal{N}_{new}$: set of transitions
output : bool

1   $\mathcal{S}^- \leftarrow \mathcal{N}_{new}^{-1}(\mathcal{S}); \quad \mathcal{S}^+ \leftarrow \mathcal{N}_{new}(\mathcal{S}^-);$
2   **if** $\mathcal{S}^+ = \emptyset$ **then return** *false*
3   **repeat**
4   $\quad\quad \mathcal{S}^- \leftarrow \mathcal{S}^- \cap \mathcal{N}^*(\mathcal{S}^+);$
5   $\quad\quad \mathcal{S}^+ \leftarrow \mathcal{S}^+ \cap \mathcal{N}_{new}(\mathcal{S}^-);$
6   **until** $\mathcal{S}^+$ *and* $\mathcal{S}^-$ *unchanged*;
7   **return** $\mathcal{S}^- \neq \emptyset \vee \mathcal{S}^+ \neq \emptyset$;

Algorithm 1. DetectSCC

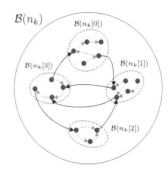

Fig. 1. Illustration of state space $(\mathcal{B}(n_k), \mathcal{N}_{\leq k})$

iteratively in lines 4 and 5. Checking reachability is performed using saturation. The iteration stops when no states can be discarded from the sets anymore, i. e., fixed point is reached. If $\mathcal{S}^-$ and $\mathcal{S}^+$ are empty, then no appropriate SCC could be found. Otherwise, the remaining states are part of an SCC containing at least one transition from $\mathcal{N}_{new}$. Since the goal of this algorithm is to quickly decide if an SCC exists in the input, it *will not* extract the SCC itself. However, remaining states in $\mathcal{S}^+$ and $\mathcal{S}^-$ can be used to aid the counterexample generation.

When looking for *fair SCCs*, i. e., SCCs containing at least one state from a set of states $\mathcal{F}$, the algorithm can be extended to involve $\mathcal{F}$ as the third set in the loop. States of $\mathcal{F}$ are then discarded if they are not reachable from $\mathcal{S}^+$ and states of $\mathcal{S}^-$ are discarded if they are not reachable from $\mathcal{F}$. When looking for accepting SCCs during LTL model checking, $\mathcal{F}$ is the set of accepting states.

5   Explicit Proofs

After presenting an incremental way to detect the presence of strongly connected components during state space generation, this section introduces methods to prove the absence of SCCs without performing symbolic fixed point computations. These methods are used to decide if a symbolic check should be performed when a node is saturated or it can be safely omitted.

When looking for accepting SCCs, checking the absence of accepting states is a usual optimization in similar algorithms, for example in the abstraction refinement approach presented in [16]. In this paper, we go two steps further. Section 5.1 introduces the use of recurring states, while Section 5.2 presents a new abstraction technique tailored to decision diagrams that allows the direct use of explicit algorithms to reason about the presence or absence of SCCs.

5.1   Using Recurring States for Explicit Proofs

Recurring states are those that have already been discovered before reaching them again during state space generation. In the context presented in Section

4, they are defined as follows: $\mathcal{R} = \mathcal{S}_{old} \cap \mathcal{N}_{new}(\mathcal{S}_{old})$, where $\mathcal{S}_{old}$ is the set of discovered states before applying $\mathcal{N}_{new}$ for the first time. Explicit SCC computation algorithms such as [15] primarily look for recurring states during graph traversal as they are suspects to constitute SCCs. Checking backward reachability from these states offers a simple algorithm to check the presence of an SCC [8]. Symbolic algorithms, on the other hand, execute many steps together, making the individual checking of the states inefficient. However, computing the set of recurring states during state space traversal can still be used to reason about SCCs.

Observation 2. *Given an SCC composed of a set of states $\mathcal{S}$ and a next-state relation $\mathcal{N}$, any traversal will yield at least one recurring state.*

According to the observation, recurring states offer a cheap way to distinguish situations where there is no chance of finding an SCC – situations that often arise during an on-the-fly algorithm. In addition, they can also be used to initialize the fixed-point computation algorithm with $\mathcal{S} := \mathcal{R}$ in Algorithm 1. This is useful if recurring states are collected between two subsequent *DetectSCC* calls, because *1)* only transitions of $\mathcal{N}_{new}$ can end in recurring states and *2)* this way, the function can also exploit Observation 2 and restrict the search for SCC candidates containing new recurring states.

5.2   Introducing Inductive Explicit Checks

Hybrid model checking algorithms usually use symbolic encoding to process huge state spaces, accompanied by clever abstraction techniques to produce an abstract model on which explicit graph algorithms can be used. In this context, the goal of abstraction is to reduce the size of a system's state space while preserving certain properties, such as the presence or absence of SCCs. In this work, we also use abstractions to reason about SCCs. However, unlike in most approaches in this domain, multiple abstract state graphs are used, ordered in a hierarchy matching the structure of the underlying decision diagram to build an inductive proof about strongly connected components of the state space.

In a symbolic setting, components of the model provide a convenient basis for abstraction. In LTL model checking, it is usual to use the Büchi automaton or its observable language to group states and build an abstraction from these aggregates. The abstraction framework presented in [16] goes beyond using only one kind of abstraction and explores strategies on a tableau of possible abstractions based on one or more components.

In addition to selecting the basis, there are multiple ways to define an abstraction based on a component. To illustrate this, two simple abstractions are presented before introducing a new approach of using the structure of a decision diagram to define a more powerful abstraction.

Simple Abstractions. Using abstractions to answer binary decisions has two potential goals. One can create an abstraction that can say a definite *yes* (these are called *must abstractions*), or one that can say a definite *no* (these are *may abstractions*). To construct an abstraction, the definition of an abstraction function is required for both the states and the transitions in the global state space. Abstracting states is straightforward, as the set of local states $\mathcal{S}_k$ of component k can be used directly.[1] Regarding may and must abstractions, different transformations have to be defined for the transitions of the state space.

Must abstraction of transitions $\mathcal{N}_k^\forall \subseteq \mathcal{S}_k \times \mathcal{S}_k$ for component k is defined as: $\mathcal{N}_k^\forall = \{(s_k, s_k') | \exists \varepsilon \in \mathcal{E}, supp(\varepsilon) = \{k\}, \exists(\mathbf{s}, \mathbf{s}') = ((\ldots, s_k, \ldots), (\ldots, s_k', \ldots)) \in \mathcal{N}_\varepsilon\}$. *May abstraction* of transitions $\mathcal{N}_k^\exists \subseteq S_k \times S_k$ for component k is defined as $\mathcal{N}_k^\exists = \{(s_k, s_k') | \exists \varepsilon \in \mathcal{E}, \ k \in supp(\varepsilon), \exists(\mathbf{s}, \mathbf{s}') = ((\ldots, s_k, \ldots), (\ldots, s_k', \ldots)) \in \mathcal{N}_\varepsilon\}$. The must abstraction of transitions is defined to keep only those transitions that correspond to events fully within the support of the chosen component. May abstraction preserves every local transition, but omits the synchronization constraints (i.e., assumes that if a transition is enabled in component k, it is globally enabled).

Due to this construction, it is sometimes possible to reason about the presence or absence of global SCCs. If there is an SCC in a single must abstraction, it is the direct representation of one or more SCCs of the global state space. Complementary, if there is no SCC in the may abstraction of *any* component, then the global state space cannot contain any SCCs either.

These abstractions usually yield small state graphs that can be represented explicitly. Running linear-time explicit algorithms on them gives a very cheap opportunity to possibly prove or refute the presence of SCCs before symbolic methods are used. Moreover, the definition of may and must abstractions implies $\mathcal{N}_k^\forall \subseteq \mathcal{N}_k^\exists$, so running the SCC computation on a may abstraction and then looking for a strongly connected subcomponent with transitions of $\mathcal{N}_k^\forall$ effectively considers both cases at the same time.

As an example, observe Figure 2 that illustrates the Petri net model of a producer-consumer system, also showing the explicit state graph. Transitions of the system are shown on Figure 3(a), with connected arcs representing a single transition affecting multiple components. In this case, every transition belongs to a separate event (events are related to transitions of the Petri net). Events affecting multiple components can be regarded as synchronization constraints between *local transitions*. Abstractions can be acquired by removing synchronizations and local transitions. Figure 3(b) and 3(c) depict the transitions transformed by must and may abstractions. If the goal is to find an SCC containing the state where only the places at the bottom of the Petri net are marked (depicted as a black state on Figure 2(b)), none of the abstractions can give an exact answer.

Node-wise Abstraction. As the example suggests, the simple abstractions presented so far may often be too general/specific, limiting their usefulness. Also, as before, the iteration strategy of saturation can be exploited when designing a special type of may abstraction that is stronger than its simple version. The goal

---

[1] It is assumed that local states in $\mathcal{S}_k$ actually appear in at least one reachable global state.

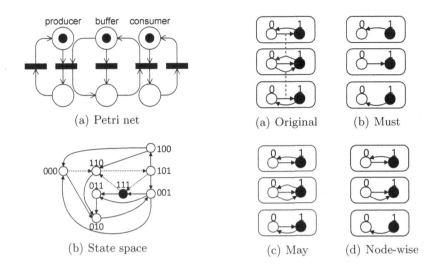

(a) Petri net

(b) State space

Fig. 2. Producer-consumer model with non-deterministic buffer

(a) Original   (b) Must

(c) May   (d) Node-wise

Fig. 3. The effect of the abstractions to the transitions

of the following construct is to match the order in which events are processed during saturation, as well as the structure of the underlying decision diagram.

Definition (Node-wise abstraction). *Node-wise abstraction of state space* $(\mathcal{S}, \mathcal{N})$ *with regard to node* n_k *is the pair* $\mathcal{A}^{\exists}_{n_k} = (\mathcal{S}_{n_k}, \mathcal{N}^{\exists}_{n_k})$, *where* $\mathcal{S}_{n_k} = \{i \mid n_k[i] \neq \mathbf{0}\}$, *i.e., the local states encoded by arcs of* n_k, *and* $\mathcal{N}^{\exists}_{n_k} = \{(s_k, s'_k) \mid s_k, s'_k \in \mathcal{S}_{n_k}, \exists(\mathbf{s}, \mathbf{s}') = ((\dots, s_k, \dots), (\dots, s'_k, \dots)) \in \mathcal{N}_k\}$, *i.e., the projections of events* $\mathcal{E}_k$ *to component* k.

By the time a node is saturated, the construction of its node-wise abstraction is permanently finished. This way, a single abstraction has to be analyzed only once. In addition, the set of node-wise abstractions corresponding to nodes of a sub-diagram rooted in n_k contains enough information to have the power of the simple may abstraction, that is, to clearly state if no SCC is present in the substate space $(\mathcal{B}(n_k), \mathcal{N}_{\leq k})$.

The following theorem gives the basis for an inductive method of using node-wise abstractions to prove the absence of SCCs.

Theorem. *Given a node-wise abstraction* $\mathcal{A}^{\exists}_{n_k}$ *with regard to a saturated node* n_k, *the substate space* $(\mathcal{B}(n_k), \mathcal{N}_{\leq k})$ *does not contain any SCC if 1) neither of the substate spaces* $(\mathcal{B}(n_k[s_i]), \mathcal{N}_{<k})$ *belonging to the children of* n_k *2) nor* $\mathcal{A}^{\exists}_{n_k}$ *contain an SCC.*

The main idea of the proof is that node-wise abstraction represents the effects of the events $\mathcal{E}_k$ exactly on the level of their *Top* value. At the time when a node n_k becomes saturated, the only transitions that can change the local states of component k are in $\mathcal{N}_k$. Node-wise abstractions contain the images of exactly these transitions, thus they describe the possible transitions between sets of substates encoded by the children of n_k, as seen on Figure 1. This is why they can be used to identify *one-way walls* that separate the possible spaces for SCCs. Figure 1 can be seen as a node-wise abstraction if gray sets are considered as states of $\mathcal{A}_{n_k}^{\exists}$, with black arcs between them being transitions of $\mathcal{N}_{n_k}^{\exists}$.

Note that it is not specified how to ensure assumption 1 of the theorem. Consequently even if the corresponding node-wise abstraction did contain an SCC (which only implies the *possible* presence of a global SCC), the symbolic fixed point computation algorithm of Section 4 can still be used to give a precise proof. This way, the series of saturated nodes give a full inductive proof by the end of the state space generation. In the previous example shown on Figure 3, node-wise abstraction *can* predict that SCC detection is unnecessary during saturation until the top level is processed.

The computation of node-wise abstractions is simple and cheap. It can be done on demand by projecting the next-state relation of corresponding events to the *Top* component, or on-the-fly during saturation by adding vertices and arcs each time a new local state is discovered or a new transition of the corresponding events is fired, respectively. A simple must abstraction can also be examined as part of computing SCCs of the node-wise abstraction by looking for a strongly connected subcomponent whose transitions belong to events having only the current component as a supporting one.

In addition to proving the absence of SCCs, the result of explicit computation on the abstraction can also be used to aid the incremental fixed point computation algorithm in finding them. Arcs of the *candidate SCCs* found in the node-wise abstraction correspond to a set of transitions in the state space ($\mathcal{N}_{SCC}$). Since these are the *only* transitions in $\mathcal{N}_k$ that can be part of an SCC, calling *DetectSCC* with $\mathcal{N}_{new} = \mathcal{N}_{SCC}$ helps the function to converge even faster.

6   Constructing the Algorithm

After getting familiar with the building blocks in Sections 2–5, this section assembles the main contribution of this work, the new saturation-based incremental LTL model checking algorithm. The algorithm uses saturation for state space generation. Recurring states are collected on the fly and vertices and arcs of node-wise abstractions may also be added continuously. Whenever a node becomes saturated, the following steps are executed:

1. The sets of encoded states and transitions are checked (shall be non-empty).
2. The set of collected recurring states is checked (shall be non-empty).
3. An explicit SCC computation algorithm is run on the current node-wise abstraction to obtain an SCC candidate (there shall be one).
4. Function *DetectSCC* is called with the set of recurring states and transitions in the candidate SCC to compute an SCC-hull.

If either of checks 1–3 fails, or *DetectSCC* returns *false*, saturation continues. If at any point *DetectSCC* returns *true*, the algorithm is stopped and the LTL

```
input    : s_k : node      // to saturate
output   : node
1  n_2k ← N_k as decision diagram;
2  t_k ← new node;   A^∃_{t_k} ← (S_k, ∅);
3  foreach i ∈ S_k : s_k[i] ≠ 0 do
4  |  t_k[i] ← Saturate(s_k[i]);
*  5  r_k ← new node;            // recurring states
6  repeat
7  |  foreach i, i' ∈ S_k : s_k[i] ≠ 0 ∧ n_2k[i][i'] ≠ 0 do
*  8  |  |  r'_{k-1} ← new node;      // temp for next call
9  |  |  u_k ← RelProd(t_k[i], n_2k[i][i'], t_k[i'], r'_{k-1});
◇10  |  |  if u_k ≠ 0 then add arc (i, i') to A^∃_{t_k};
11  |  |  t_k[i'] ← (t_k[i'] ∪ u_k);     // collect states
*12  |  |  r_k[i'] ← (r_k[i'] ∪ r'_{k-1}); // collect recurring
13  until t_k unchanged;
◇14  N_SCC ← TransitionsInSCC(A^∃_{t_k});
◇15  if DetectSCC(B(r_k), N_{≤k}, N_SCC) then
16  |  terminate with counterexample;
17  return CheckUnique(t_k);
```

Algorithm 2. Saturate

```
input    : s_k, n_2k, o_k : node
// s_k: node to be saturated,
// n_2k: next state node,
// o_k: old node
in-out   : r_k : node
// r_k: recurring states
output   : node
1  if s_k = 1 ∧ n_2k = 1 then
*  2  |  if o_k = 1 then
3  |  |  r_k ← 1;   // recurring state found
4  |  return 1;
5  t_k ← new node;
6  foreach s_k[i] ≠ 0 ∧ n_2k[i][i'] ≠ 0 do
*  7  |  r'_{k-1} ← new node;
8  |  t_k[i'] ← (t_k[i'] ∪
   |            RelProd(s_k[i], n_2k[i][i'], o_k[i'], r'_{k-1});
*  9  |  r_k[i'] ← (r_k[i'] ∪ r'_{k-1});
10  t_k ← Saturate(CheckUnique(t_k));
11  return t_k;
```

Algorithm 3. RelProd

formula is declared *invalid* in terms of the system. If saturation finishes and *DetectSCC* never returns *true*, the formula is declared *valid*.

Algorithm 2 and 3 presents the complete algorithm. Lines different from the original saturation algorithm are marked. Although it is crucial to implement, caching is now omitted for the sake of simplicity. *CheckUnique* is used to avoid the duplication of decision diagram nodes. If an equivalent node has already been registered, it returns that node, otherwise registers the input. The decision diagram representation of a next-state function has $2k$ levels. Even levels encode *from* states and odd levels encode *to* states. Custom functions are *TransitionsInSCC* and *DetectSCC*. The former performs an explicit SCC computation (e. g., [15]) on the abstraction and returns transitions of the state space corresponding to abstract arcs in an SCC. The latter is presented in Algorithm 1.

Lines marked with ∗ belong to the computation of recurring states. To identify recurring states, an additional node representing old states is passed to *RelProd*. Reached states that are also in the set of old states are collected similarly to the approach of *constrained saturation* [17]. Sign ◇ marks lines corresponding to explicit search. The node-wise abstraction is built on-the-fly, then *TransitionsInSCC* is used to extract candidate SCCs. Finally, on the line marked with ◇, *DetectSCC* is called with the set of recurring states, $N_{≤k}$, and transitions in the candidate SCC to perform the incremental fixed-point computation.

7   Related Work

This section briefly summarizes different approaches to SCC computation, from traditional SCC-hull algorithms to SAT-based solutions.

SCC-hull algorithms are usually variants of the algorithm of Emerson and Lei [14]. They solve the SCC computation problem by computing a least fixed point of the state space that is sure to contain at least one SCC. An SCC-hull is a superset of states belonging to an SCC, thus it proves only the *existence* of an SCC. The incremental SCC computation algorithm presented in Section 4 is also based on the idea of SCC-hull computation. However, our method is tuned to work on the fly, exploiting the results of previous runs to provide incrementality.

Saturation-based SCC computation has also been proposed. The algorithms implemented in [18] are different from SCC-hull algorithms, because both the algorithm of Xie and Beerel and the Transitive Closure method aim to compute exactly those states that belong to an SCC. Because of the caching mechanism of saturation, these algorithms can be very efficient to compute an exact counterexample detected by our algorithm.

An extensive approach to using abstraction in SCC computation has been proposed in [16]. By defining a lattice of abstractions based on one or more components of the model, the paper presents strategies of using some of the abstractions to discard uninteresting parts of the state space and search in relevant components. While node-wise abstraction can be interpreted in that context, the paper uses abstractions similar to the must abstraction presented in Section 5.2 and only accepting states are used to prove the lack of SCCs.

On-the-fly approaches to SCC computation and thus model checking also exist [1, 11–13]. One particularly interesting solution is described in [10]. The paper describes two types of abstractions used to achieve on-the-fly search, also using saturation as a state space generation algorithm.

A different approach in SAT-based model checking is the recent approach called IC3 [2]. By constructing a series of small intermediate lemmas, the k-liveness algorithm [7] identifies one-way walls that separate the possible spaces of SCCs. In this sense, the idea is similar to that of node-wise abstraction.

8   Evaluation

To demonstrate the efficiency of the presented new algorithm (referred to as *Hyb-MC*), models of the Model Checking Contest[2] have been used to compare it to three competitive tools. NuSMV2 [6] is a BDD-based model checker implementing traditional SCC-hull algorithms and is well-established in the industrial and academical community. Its successor, nuXmv [3] implements a k-liveness algorithm [7] based on IC3 for LTL model checking[3]. ITS-LTL is a powerful tool based on saturation that implements various optimizations both for symbolic encoding and on-the-fly SCC detection.

All four tools were run on 7 850 inputs: 27 scalable models of the Model Checking Contest were used to obtain a total of 157 different instances, each checked against 50 randomly generated LTL formulae produced by SPOT [9]. The models represent the behavior of mainly asynchronous, concurrent systems. Out of the successfully checked cases, properties were fulfilled 2 811 times, while 3 565 cases gave negative results. In 1 474 cases, all the tools exceeded the time limit.

---

[2] http://mcc.lip6.fr/

[3] nuXmv was executed with flag "-check_ltlspec_klive".

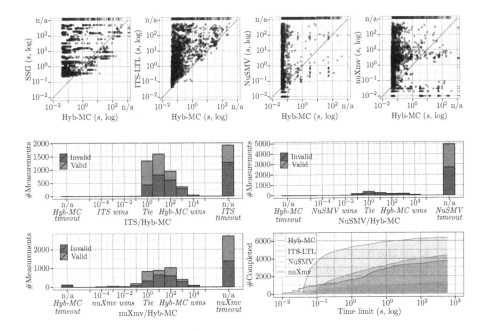

Fig. 4. Measurement results

Generated expressions contained a nearly equal number of safety and guarantee properties, as well as obligation formulae and more complex properties.

Measurements were done on identical server machines with Intel Xeon processors (4 cores, 2.2GHz) and 8 GB of RAM, with timeout set to 600 seconds. The decision diagram based tools used the same variable ordering produced by heuristics of the ITS toolset. Runtimes were measured internally by every tool, usually including every step of the model checking process (in case of NuSMV and nuXmv, internal transformation of the input was omitted from the result). A prototype of Hyb-MC was implemented in .NET to conduct the measurements.

Results can be seen on Figure 4. On the scatterplots, each point represents a single pair of model instance and property. The runtime of Hyb-MC is always on the x-axis, while the runtimes of state space generation, ITS-LTL, NuSMV and nuXmv are on the y-axis of the subfigures. A point above (below) the diagonal is a measurement where Hyb-MC solved the problem faster (slower). The borders of the diagrams represent the timeout of a measurement for one of the tools. As the plots show, Hyb-MC usually finishes the verification faster than the state space generation of the model, mainly because of on-the-fly operation and efficient incremental operation. State space generation could be finished for some models where model checking was unsuccessful, the overhead of model checking of these complex properties could not be compensated by the incremental operation. Comparing to the other model checking approaches, the vast majority of cases show the competitiveness of our algorithm. The three histograms depict the differences of runtimes: the bar in the middle shows cases where runtimes of the tools were in the same order of magnitude, while every bar to the left or right means an additional order of magnitude in the runtime of the corresponding tool compared to the other. The last diagram shows the number of cases in which a tool was able to finish the verification within the given time.

Analysis of collected data showed differences in the scalability of the algorithms. While Hyb-MC and ITS-LTL is better in handling a huge number of state variables, NuSMV and nuXmv performed much better on models with state variables of large domains. Only nuXmv's k-liveness algorithm proved to be sensitive to different classes of properties, the other tools did not show significant differences in the distribution of runtimes. During the measurements, Hyb-MC spent only 17% of the time computing SCCs. Overall, 359 084 symbolic fixed point computations were started, while abstraction and explicit algorithms prevented $1.22 \cdot 10^8$ runs of symbolic SCC computation, 99.7% of all the cases. 89% of these cases were prevented by the absence of recurring states (as a first check), while the remaining 11% were the cases where explicit runs on node-wise abstractions managed to find even more evidence.[4]

9   Conclusion and Future Work

In this paper, a new algorithm has been presented for LTL model checking. The described approach divides model checking into smaller tasks, and handles large state spaces by performing efficient local computations on the components. The absence of SCCs is proved with the help of a specialized abstraction function and inductive reasoning, while existing SCCs are discovered by a new incremental symbolic fixed point algorithm. These solutions constitute an efficient on-the-fly, hybrid model checking approach that combines the advantages of explicit and symbolic algorithms. Our solution uses saturation for state space traversal, which makes it suitable for concurrent systems. Extensive measurements justified this claim for the models of the Model Checking Contest.

The presented algorithm has a huge potential for future development. Following the idea of driving the symbolic algorithm with explicit runs, a promising direction is to combine partial order reduction with symbolic model checking. In addition, we also plan to use advanced representations of the properties to further improve the speed of model checking.

Acknowledgements. This work was partially supported by the ARTEMIS JU and the Hungarian Research and Technological Innovation Fund in the frame of the R5-COP project.

References

1. Biere, A., Zhu, Y., Clarke, E.: Multiple state and single state tableaux for combining local and global model checking. In: Olderog, E.-R., Steffen, B. (eds.) Correct System Design. LNCS, vol. 1710, pp. 163–179. Springer, Heidelberg (1999)

---

[4] For a detailed analysis of collected data, cf. http://inf.mit.bme.hu/en/tacas15.

2. Bradley, A.: Understanding IC3. In: Cimatti, A., Sebastiani, R. (eds.) SAT 2012. LNCS, vol. 7317, pp. 1–14. Springer, Heidelberg (2012)

3. Cavada, R., Cimatti, A., Dorigatti, M., Mariotti, A., Micheli, A., Mover, S., Griggio, A., Roveri, M., Tonetta, S.: The nuXmv symbolic model checker. Tech. rep., Fondazione Bruno Kessler (2014)

4. Ciardo, G., Lüttgen, G., Siminiceanu, R.: Saturation: an efficient iteration strategy for symbolic state space generation. In: Margaria, T., Yi, W. (eds.) TACAS 2001. LNCS, vol. 2031, pp. 328–342. Springer, Heidelberg (2001)

5. Ciardo, G., Marmorstein, R., Siminiceanu, R.: The saturation algorithm for symbolic state-space exploration. Int. J. on Softw. Tools for Technology Transfer 8(1), 4–25 (2006)

6. Cimatti, A., Clarke, E., Giunchiglia, E., et al.: NuSMV 2: An opensource tool for symbolic model checking. In: Brinksma, E., Larsen, K.G. (eds.) CAV 2002. LNCS, vol. 2404, pp. 359–364. Springer, Heidelberg (2002)

7. Claessen, K., Sorensson, N.: A liveness checking algorithm that counts. In: Formal Methods in Computer-Aided Design, 2012, pp. 52–59. IEEE (2012)

8. Courcoubetis, C., Vardi, M., Wolper, P., Yannakakis, M.: Memory efficient algorithms for the verification of temporal properties. In: Clarke, E., Kurshan, R.P. (eds.) CAV 1990. LNCS, vol. 531, pp. 233–242. Springer, Heidelberg (1991)

9. Duret-Lutz, A., Poitrenaud, D.: SPOT: An extensible model checking library using transition-based generalized Büchi automata. In: Proc. of the IEEE Int. Symp. on Modeling, Analysis, and Simulation of Computer and Telecommunications Systems, pp. 76–83 (2004)

10. Duret-Lutz, A., Klai, K., Poitrenaud, D., Thierry-Mieg, Y.: Combining explicit and symbolic approaches for better on-the-fly LTL model checking. arXiv:1106.5700 (cs) (2011)

11. Haddad, S., Ilié, J.M., Klai, K.: Design and evaluation of a symbolic and abstraction-based model checker. In: Wang, F. (ed.) ATVA 2004. LNCS, vol. 3299, pp. 196–210. Springer, Heidelberg (2004)

12. Klai, K., Poitrenaud, D.: MC-SOG: An LTL model checker based on symbolic observation graphs. In: van Hee, K.M., Valk, R. (eds.) PETRI NETS 2008. LNCS, vol. 5062, pp. 288–306. Springer, Heidelberg (2008)

13. Sebastiani, R., Tonetta, S., Vardi, M.: Symbolic systems, explicit properties: on hybrid approaches for LTL symbolic model checking. In: Etessami, K., Rajamani, S.K. (eds.) CAV 2005. LNCS, vol. 3576, pp. 350–363. Springer, Heidelberg (2005)

14. Somenzi, F., Ravi, K., Bloem, R.: Analysis of symbolic SCC hull algorithms. In: Aagaard, M.D., O'Leary, J.W. (eds.) FMCAD 2002. LNCS, vol. 2517, pp. 88–105. Springer, Heidelberg (2002)

15. Tarjan, R.: Depth first search and linear graph algorithms. SIAM Journal on Computing 1(2), 146–160 (1972)

16. Wang, C., Bloem, R., Hachtel, G.D., Ravi, K., Somenzi, F.: Compositional SCC analysis for language emptiness. Form. Method. Syst. Des. 28(1), 5–36 (2006)

17. Zhao, Y., Ciardo, G.: Symbolic CTL model checking of asynchronous systems using constrained saturation. In: Liu, Z., Ravn, A.P. (eds.) ATVA 2009. LNCS, vol. 5799, pp. 368–381. Springer, Heidelberg (2009)

18. Zhao, Y., Ciardo, G.: Symbolic computation of strongly connected components and fair cycles using saturation. Innov. Syst. Softw. Eng. 7(2), 141–150 (2011)

Nested Antichains for WS1S

Tomáš Fiedor, Lukáš Holík, Ondřej Lengál, and Tomáš Vojnar

FIT, Brno University of Technology, IT4Innovations Centre of Excellence, Czech Republic

Abstract. We propose a novel approach for coping with alternating quantification as the main source of nonelementary complexity of deciding WS1S formulae. Our approach is applicable within the state-of-the-art automata-based WS1S decision procedure implemented, e.g. in MONA. The way in which the standard decision procedure processes quantifiers involves determinization, with its worst case exponential complexity, for every quantifier alternation in the prefix of a formula. Our algorithm avoids building the deterministic automata—instead, it constructs only those of their states needed for (dis)proving validity of the formula. It uses a symbolic representation of the states, which have a deeply nested structure stemming from the repeated implicit subset construction, and prunes the search space by a nested subsumption relation, a generalization of the one used by the so-called antichain algorithms for handling nondeterministic automata. We have obtained encouraging experimental results, in some cases outperforming MONA by several orders of magnitude.

1 Introduction

Weak monadic second-order logic of one successor (WS1S) is a powerful, concise, and decidable logic for describing regular properties of finite words. Despite its nonelementary worst case complexity [1], it has been shown useful in numerous applications. Most of the successful applications were due to the tool MONA [2], which implements a finite automata-based decision procedure for WS1S and WS2S (a generalization of WS1S to finite binary trees). The authors of MONA list a multitude of its diverse applications [3], ranging from software and hardware verification through controller synthesis to computational linguistics, and further on. Among more recent applications, verification of pointer programs and deciding related logics [4,5,6,7,8] can be mentioned, as well as synthesis from regular specifications [9]. MONA is still the standard tool and the most common choice when it comes to deciding WS1S/WS2S. There are other related automata-based tools that are more recent, such as jMosel [10] for a logic M2L(Str), and other than automata-based approaches, such as [11]. They implement optimizations that allow to outperform MONA on some benchmarks, however, none provides an evidence of being consistently more efficient. Despite many optimizations implemented in MONA and the other tools, the worst case complexity of the problem sometimes strikes back. Authors of methods using the translation of their problem to WS1S/WS2S are then forced to either find workarounds to circumvent the complexity blowup, such as in [5], or, often restricting the input of their approach, give up translating to WS1S/WS2S altogether [12].

The decision procedure of MONA works with deterministic automata; it uses determinization extensively and relies on minimization of deterministic automata to

C. Baier and C. Tinelli (Eds.): TACAS 2015, LNCS 9035, pp. 658–674, 2015.
DOI: 10.1007/978-3-662-46681-0_59

suppress the complexity blow-up. However, the worst case exponential complexity of determinization often significantly harms the performance of the tool. Recent works on efficient methods for handling nondeterministic automata suggest a way of alleviating this problem, in particular works on efficient testing of language inclusion and universality of finite automata [13,14,15] and size reduction [16,22] based on a simulation relation. Handling nondeterministic automata using these methods, while avoiding determinization, has been shown to provide great efficiency improvements in [24] (abstract regular model checking) and also [23] (shape analysis). In this paper, we make a major step towards building the entire decision procedure of WS1S on nondeterministic automata using similar techniques. We propose a generalization of the antichain algorithms of [13] that addresses the main bottleneck of the automata-based decision procedure for WS1S, which is also the source of its nonelementary complexity: elimination of alternating quantifiers on the automata level.

More concretely, the automata-based decision procedure translates the input WS1S formula into a finite word automaton such that its language represents exactly all models of the formula. The automaton is built in a bottom-up manner according to the structure of the formula, starting with predefined atomic automata for literals and applying a corresponding automata operation for every logical connective and quantifier $(\wedge, \vee, \neg, \exists)$. The cause of the nonelementary complexity of the procedure can be explained on an example formula of the form $\varphi' = \exists X_m \forall X_{m-1} \ldots \forall X_2 \exists X_1 : \varphi_0$. The universal quantifiers are first replaced by negation and existential quantification, which results in $\varphi = \exists X_m \neg \exists X_{m-1} \ldots \neg \exists X_2 \neg \exists X_1 : \varphi_0$. The algorithm then builds a sequence of automata for the sub-formulae $\varphi_0, \varphi_0^\sharp, \ldots, \varphi_{m-1}, \varphi_{m-1}^\sharp$ of φ where for $0 \leq i < m$, $\varphi_i^\sharp = \exists X_{i+1} : \varphi_i$, and $\varphi_{i+1} = \neg \varphi_i^\sharp$. Every automaton in the sequence is created from the previous one by applying the automata operations corresponding to negation or elimination of the existential quantifier, the latter of which may introduce nondeterminism. Negation applied on a nondeterministic automaton may then yield an exponential blowup: given an automaton for ψ, the automaton for $\neg \psi$ is constructed by the classical automata-theoretic construction consisting of determinization by the subset construction followed by swapping of the sets of final and non-final states. The subset construction is exponential in the worst case. The worst case complexity of the procedure run on φ is then a tower of exponentials with one level for every quantifier alternation in φ; note that we cannot do much better—this non-elementary complexity is an inherent property of the problem.

Our new algorithm for processing alternating quantifiers in the prefix of a formula avoids the explicit determinization of automata in the classical procedure and significantly reduces the state space explosion associated with it. It is based on a generalization of the antichain principle used for deciding universality and language inclusion of finite automata [14,15]. It generalizes the antichain algorithms so that instead of being used to process only one level of the chain of automata, it processes the whole chain of quantifications with i alternations on-the-fly. This leads to working with automata states that are sets of sets of sets ... of states of the automaton representing φ_0 of the nesting depth i (this corresponds to i levels of subset construction being done on-the-fly). The algorithm uses nested symbolic terms to represent sets of such automata states and a generalized version of antichain subsumption pruning which descends recursively down the structure of the terms while pruning on all its levels.

Our nested antichain algorithm can be in its current form used only to process a quantifier prefix of a formula, after which we return the answer to the validity query, but not an automaton representing all models of the input formula. That is, we cannot use the optimized algorithm for processing inner negations and alternating quantifiers which are not a part of the quantifier prefix. However, despite this and the fact that our implementation is far less mature than that of MONA, our experimental results still show significant improvements over its performance, especially in terms of generated state space. We consider this a strong indication that using techniques for nondeterministic automata to decide WS1S (and WSkS) is highly promising. There are many more opportunities of improving the decision procedure based on nondeterministic automata, by using techniques such as simulation relations or bisimulation up-to congruence [17], and applying them to process not only the quantifier prefix, but all logical connectives of a formula. We consider this paper to be the first step towards a decision procedure for WS1S/WSkS with an entirely different scalability than the current state-of-the-art.

Plan of the paper. We define the logic WS1S in Section 2. In Sections 3 and 4, we introduce finite word automata and describe the classical decision procedure for WS1S based on finite word automata. In Section 5, we introduce our method for dealing with alternating quantifiers. Finally, we give an experimental evaluation and conclude the paper in Sections 6 and 7.

2   WS1S

In this section we introduce the *weak monadic second-order logic of one successor* (WS1S). We introduce only its minimal syntax here, for the full standard syntax and a more thorough introduction, see Section 3.3 in [18].

WS1S is a monadic second-order logic over the universe of discourse $\mathbb{N}_0$. This means that the logic allows second-order *variables*, usually denoted using upper-case letters $X, Y, \ldots$, that range over finite subsets of $\mathbb{N}_0$, e.g. $X = \{0, 3, 42\}$. Atomic formulae are of the form (i) $X \subseteq Y$, (ii) $\mathrm{Sing}(X)$, (iii) $X = \{0\}$, and (iv) $X = Y + 1$, where X and Y are variables. The atomic formulae are interpreted in turn as (i) standard set inclusion, (ii) the singleton predicate, (iii) X is a singleton containing 0, and (iv) $X = \{x\}$ and $Y = \{y\}$ are singletons and x is the successor of y, i.e. $x = y + 1$. Formulae are built from the atomic formulae using the logical connectives $\land, \lor, \neg$, and the quantifier $\exists X$ (for a second-order variable X).

Given a WS1S formula $\varphi(X_1, \ldots, X_n)$ with free variables $X_1, \ldots, X_n$, the assignment $\rho = \{X_1 \mapsto S_1, \ldots, X_n \mapsto S_n\}$, where $S_1, \ldots, S_n$ are finite subsets of $\mathbb{N}_0$, *satisfies* φ, written as $\rho \models \varphi$, if the formula holds when every variable X_i is replaced with its corresponding value $S_i = \rho(X_i)$. We say that φ is *valid*, denoted as $\models \varphi$, if it is satisfied by all assignments of its free variables to finite subsets of $\mathbb{N}_0$. Observe the limitation to *finite* subsets of $\mathbb{N}_0$ (related to the adjective *weak* in the name of the logic); a WS1S formula can indeed only have finite models (although there may be infinitely many of them).

3   Preliminaries and Finite Automata

For a set D and a set $\mathbb{S} \subseteq 2^D$ we use $\downarrow\mathbb{S}$ to denote the *downward closure* of $\mathbb{S}$, i.e. $\downarrow\mathbb{S} = \{R \subseteq D \mid \exists S \in \mathbb{S} : R \subseteq S\}$, and $\uparrow\mathbb{S}$ to denote the *upward closure* of $\mathbb{S}$, i.e. $\uparrow\mathbb{S} = \{R \subseteq D \mid \exists S \in \mathbb{S} : R \supseteq S\}$. The set $\mathbb{S}$ is in both cases called the set of *generators* of $\uparrow\mathbb{S}$ or $\downarrow\mathbb{S}$ respectively. A set $\mathbb{S}$ is *downward closed* if it equals its downward closure, $\mathbb{S} = \downarrow\mathbb{S}$, and *upward closed* if it equals to its upward closure, $\mathbb{S} = \uparrow\mathbb{S}$. The *choice* operator $\coprod$ (sometimes called the unordered Cartesian product) is an operator that, given a set of sets $\mathbb{D} = \{D_1, \ldots, D_n\}$, returns the set of all sets $\{d_1, \ldots, d_n\}$ obtained by taking one element d_i from every set D_i. Formally,

$$\coprod\mathbb{D} = \Big\{\{d_1, \ldots, d_n\} \mid (d_1, \ldots, d_n) \in \prod_{i=1}^{n} D_i\Big\} \tag{1}$$

where $\prod$ denotes the Cartesian product. Note that for a set D, $\coprod\{D\}$ is the set of all singleton subsets of D, i.e. $\coprod\{D\} = \{\{d\} \mid d \in D\}$. Further note that if any D_i is the empty set $\emptyset$, the result is $\coprod\mathbb{D} = \emptyset$.

Let $\mathbb{X}$ be a set of variables. A *symbol* τ over $\mathbb{X}$ is a mapping of all variables in $\mathbb{X}$ to either 0 or 1, e.g. $\tau = \{X_1 \mapsto 0, X_2 \mapsto 1\}$ for $\mathbb{X} = \{X_1, X_2\}$. An *alphabet* over $\mathbb{X}$ is the set of all symbols over $\mathbb{X}$, denoted as $\Sigma_{\mathbb{X}}$. For any $\mathbb{X}$ (even empty), we use $\overline{0}$ to denote the symbol which maps all variables from $\mathbb{X}$ to 0, $\overline{0} \in \Sigma_{\mathbb{X}}$.

A (nondeterministic) *finite* (word) *automaton* (abbreviated as FA) over a set of variables $\mathbb{X}$ is a quadruple $\mathcal{A} = (Q, \Delta, I, F)$ where Q is a finite set of states, $I \subseteq Q$ is a set of *initial* states, $F \subseteq Q$ is a set of *final* states, and Δ is a set of transitions of the form (p, τ, q) where $p, q \in Q$ and $\tau \in \Sigma_{\mathbb{X}}$. We use $p \xrightarrow{\tau} q \in \Delta$ to denote that $(p, \tau, q) \in \Delta$. Note that for an FA $\mathcal{A}$ over $\mathbb{X} = \emptyset$, $\mathcal{A}$ is a unary FA with the alphabet $\Sigma_{\mathbb{X}} = \{\overline{0}\}$.

A *run* r of $\mathcal{A}$ over a word $w = \tau_1\tau_2\ldots\tau_n \in \Sigma_{\mathbb{X}}^*$ from the state $p \in Q$ to the state $s \in Q$ is a sequence of states $r = q_0q_1\ldots q_n \in Q^+$ such that $q_0 = p$, $q_n = s$ and for all $1 \leq i \leq n$ there is a transition $q_{i-1} \xrightarrow{\tau_i} q_i$ in Δ. If $s \in F$, we say that r is an *accepting run*. We write $p \xRightarrow{w} s$ to denote that there exists a run from the state p to the state s over the word w. The *language* accepted by a state q is defined by $\mathcal{L}_{\mathcal{A}}(q) = \{w \mid q \xRightarrow{w} q_f, q_f \in F\}$, while the language of a set of states $S \subseteq Q$ is defined as $\mathcal{L}_{\mathcal{A}}(S) = \bigcup_{q \in S} \mathcal{L}_{\mathcal{A}}(q)$. When it is clear which FA $\mathcal{A}$ we refer to, we only write $\mathcal{L}(q)$ or $\mathcal{L}(S)$. The language of $\mathcal{A}$ is defined as $\mathcal{L}(\mathcal{A}) = \mathcal{L}_{\mathcal{A}}(I)$. We say that the state q accepts w and that the automaton $\mathcal{A}$ accepts w to express that $w \in \mathcal{L}_{\mathcal{A}}(q)$ and $w \in \mathcal{L}(\mathcal{A})$ respectively. We call a language $L \subseteq \Sigma_{\mathbb{X}}^*$ *universal* iff $L = \Sigma_{\mathbb{X}}^*$.

For a set of states $S \subseteq Q$, we define $post_{[\Delta,\tau]}(S) = \bigcup_{s \in S}\{t \mid s \xrightarrow{\tau} t \in \Delta\}$, $pre_{[\Delta,\tau]}(S) = \bigcup_{s \in S}\{t \mid t \xrightarrow{\tau} s \in \Delta\}$, and $cpre_{[\Delta,\tau]}(S) = \{t \mid post_{[\Delta,\tau]}(\{t\}) \subseteq S\}$.

The *complement* of $\mathcal{A}$ is the automaton $\mathcal{A}_{\mathcal{C}} = (2^Q, \Delta_{\mathcal{C}}, \{I\}, \downarrow\{Q \setminus F\})$ where $\Delta_{\mathcal{C}} = \{P \xrightarrow{\tau} post_{[\Delta,\tau]}(P) \mid P \subseteq Q\}$; this corresponds to the standard procedure that first determinizes $\mathcal{A}$ by the subset construction and then swaps its sets of final and non-final states, and $\downarrow\{Q \setminus F\}$ is the set of all subsets of Q that do not contain a final state of $\mathcal{A}$. The language of $\mathcal{A}_{\mathcal{C}}$ is the complement of the language of $\mathcal{A}$, i.e. $\mathcal{L}(\mathcal{A}_{\mathcal{C}}) = \overline{\mathcal{L}(\mathcal{A})}$.

For a set of variables $\mathbb{X}$ and a variable X, the *projection* of X from $\mathbb{X}$, denoted as $\pi_{[X]}(\mathbb{X})$, is the set $\mathbb{X} \setminus \{X\}$. For a symbol τ, the projection of X from τ, denoted

$\pi_{[X]}(\tau)$, is obtained from τ by restricting τ to the domain $\pi_{[X]}(\mathbb{X})$. For a transition relation Δ, the projection of X from Δ, denoted as $\pi_{[X]}(\Delta)$, is the transition relation $\left\{ p \xrightarrow{\pi_{[X]}(\tau)} q \mid p \xrightarrow{\tau} q \in \Delta \right\}$.

4   Deciding WS1S with Finite Automata

The classical decision procedure for WS1S [19] (as described in Section 3.3 of [18]) is based on a logic-automata connection and decides validity (satisfiability) of a WS1S formula $\varphi(X_1, \ldots, X_n)$ by constructing the FA $\mathcal{A}_\varphi$ over $\{X_1, \ldots, X_n\}$ which recognizes encodings of exactly the models of φ. The automaton is built in a bottom-up manner, according to the structure of φ, starting with predefined atomic automata for literals and applying a corresponding automata operation for every logical connective and quantifier ($\wedge, \vee, \neg, \exists$). Hence, for every sub-formula ψ of φ, the procedure will compute the automaton $\mathcal{A}_\psi$ such that $\mathcal{L}(\mathcal{A}_\psi)$ represents exactly all models of ψ, terminating with the result $\mathcal{A}_\varphi$.

The alphabet of $\mathcal{A}_\varphi$ consists of all symbols over the set $\mathbb{X} = \{X_1, \ldots, X_n\}$ of free variables of φ (for $a, b \in \{0, 1\}$ and $\mathbb{X} = \{X_1, X_2\}$, we use $\begin{smallmatrix} X_1 : a \\ X_2 : b \end{smallmatrix}$ to denote the symbol $\{X_1 \mapsto a, X_2 \mapsto b\}$). A word w from the language of $\mathcal{A}_\varphi$ is a sequence of these symbols, e.g. $\begin{smallmatrix} X_1 : \epsilon \\ X_2 : \epsilon \end{smallmatrix}$, $\begin{smallmatrix} X_1 : 011 \\ X_2 : 101 \end{smallmatrix}$, or $\begin{smallmatrix} X_1 : 01100 \\ X_2 : 10100 \end{smallmatrix}$. We denote the i-th symbol of w as $w[i]$, for $i \in \mathbb{N}_0$. An assignment $\rho : \mathbb{X} \to 2^{\mathbb{N}_0}$ mapping free variables $\mathbb{X}$ of φ to subsets of $\mathbb{N}_0$ is encoded into a word w_ρ of symbols over $\mathbb{X}$ in the following way: w_ρ contains 1 in the j-th position of the row for X_i iff $j \in X_i$ in ρ. Formally, for every $i \in \mathbb{N}_0$ and $X_j \in \mathbb{X}$, if $i \in \rho(X_j)$, then $w_\rho[i]$ maps $X_j \mapsto 1$. On the other hand, if $i \notin \rho(X_j)$, then either $w_\rho[i]$ maps $X_j \mapsto 0$, or the length of w is smaller than or equal to i. Notice that there exist an infinite number of encodings of ρ. The shortest one is w_ρ^s of the length $n + 1$, where n is the largest number appearing in any of the sets that is assigned to a variable of $\mathbb{X}$ in ρ, or -1 when all these sets are empty. The rest of the encodings are all those corresponding to w_ρ^s extended with an arbitrary number of $\overline{0}$ symbols appended to its end. For example, $\begin{smallmatrix} X_1 : 0 \\ X_2 : 1 \end{smallmatrix}$, $\begin{smallmatrix} X_1 : 00 \\ X_2 : 10 \end{smallmatrix}$, $\begin{smallmatrix} X_1 : 000 \\ X_2 : 100 \end{smallmatrix}$, $\begin{smallmatrix} X_1 : 000 \ldots 0 \\ X_2 : 100 \ldots 0 \end{smallmatrix}$ are all encodings of the assignment $\rho = \{X_1 \mapsto \emptyset, X_2 \mapsto \{0\}\}$. For the soundness of the decision procedure, it is important that $\mathcal{A}_\varphi$ always accepts either all encodings of ρ or none of them.

The automata $\mathcal{A}_{\varphi \wedge \psi}$ and $\mathcal{A}_{\varphi \vee \psi}$ are constructed from $\mathcal{A}_\varphi$ and $\mathcal{A}_\psi$ by standard automata-theoretic union and intersection operations, preceded by the so-called cylindrification which unifies the alphabets of $\mathcal{A}_\varphi$ and $\mathcal{A}_\psi$. Since these operations, as well as the automata for the atomic formulae, are not the subject of the contribution proposed in this paper, we refer the interested reader to [18] for details.

The part of the procedure which is central for this paper is processing negation and existential quantification; we will therefore describe it in detail. The FA $\mathcal{A}_{\neg\varphi}$ is constructed as the complement of $\mathcal{A}_\varphi$. Then, all encodings of the assignments that were accepted by $\mathcal{A}_\varphi$ are rejected by $\mathcal{A}_{\neg\varphi}$ and vice versa. The FA $\mathcal{A}_{\exists X : \varphi}$ is obtained from the FA $\mathcal{A}_\varphi = (Q, \Delta, I, F)$ by first projecting X from the transition relation Δ, yielding the FA $\mathcal{A}'_\varphi = (Q, \pi_{[X]}(\Delta), I, F)$. However, $\mathcal{A}'_\varphi$ cannot be directly used as $\mathcal{A}_{\exists X : \varphi}$. The reason is that $\mathcal{A}'_\varphi$ may now be inconsistent in accepting some encodings of an assignment

ρ while rejecting other encodings of ρ. For example, suppose that $\mathcal{A}_\varphi$ accepts the words $\begin{smallmatrix} X_1 : 010 \\ X_2 : 001 \end{smallmatrix}, \begin{smallmatrix} X_1 : 0100 \\ X_2 : 0010 \end{smallmatrix}, \begin{smallmatrix} X_1 : 0100\dots 0 \\ X_2 : 0010\dots 0 \end{smallmatrix}$ and we are computing the FA for $\exists X_2 : \varphi$. When we remove X_2 from all symbols, we obtain $\mathcal{A}'_\varphi$ that accepts the words $X_1 : 010$, $X_1 : 0100$, $X_1 : 0100\dots 0$, but does not accept the word $X_1 : 01$ that encodes the same assignment (because $\begin{smallmatrix} X_1 : 01 \\ X_2 : ?? \end{smallmatrix} \notin \mathcal{L}(A_\varphi)$ for any values in the places of "?"s). As a remedy for this situation, we need to modify $\mathcal{A}'_\varphi$ to also accept the rest of the encodings of ρ. This is done by enlarging the set of final states of $\mathcal{A}'_\varphi$ to also contain all states that can reach a final state of $\mathcal{A}'_\varphi$ by a sequence of $\overline{0}$ symbols. Formally, $\mathcal{A}_{\exists X : \varphi} = (Q, \pi_{[X]}(\Delta), I, F^\sharp)$ is obtained from $\mathcal{A}'_\varphi = (Q, \pi_{[X]}(\Delta), I, F)$ by computing $F^\sharp$ from F using the fixpoint computation $F^\sharp = \mu Z . F \cup pre_{[\pi_{[X]}(\Delta), \overline{0}]}(Z)$. Intuitively, the least fixpoint denotes the set of states backward-reachable from F following transitions of $\pi_{[X]}(\Delta)$ labelled by $\overline{0}$.

The procedure returns an automaton $\mathcal{A}_\varphi$ that accepts exactly all encodings of the models of φ. This means that the language of $\mathcal{A}_\varphi$ is (i) universal iff φ is valid, (ii) non-universal iff φ is invalid, (iii) empty iff φ is unsatisfiable, and (iv) non-empty iff φ is satisfiable. Notice that in the particular case of *ground* formulae (i.e. formulae without free variables), the language of $\mathcal{A}_\varphi$ is either $\mathcal{L}(\mathcal{A}_\varphi) = \{\overline{0}\}^*$ in the case φ is valid, or $\mathcal{L}(\mathcal{A}_\varphi) = \emptyset$ in the case φ is invalid.

5 Nested Antichain-Based Approach for Alternating Quantifiers

We now present our approach for dealing with alternating quantifiers in WS1S formulae. We consider a ground formula φ of the form

$$\varphi = \neg \exists \mathcal{X}_m \neg \dots \neg \exists \mathcal{X}_2 \underbrace{\neg \exists \mathcal{X}_1 : \varphi_0(\mathbb{X})}_{\varphi_1} \tag{2}$$
$$\underbrace{\phantom{\neg \exists \mathcal{X}_m \neg \dots \neg \exists \mathcal{X}_2 \neg \exists \mathcal{X}_1 : \varphi_0(\mathbb{X})}}_{\varphi_m}$$

where each $\mathcal{X}_i$ is a set of variables $\{X_a, \dots, X_b\}$, $\exists \mathcal{X}_i$ is an abbreviation for a nonempty sequence $\exists X_a \dots \exists X_b$ of consecutive existential quantifications, and φ_0 is an arbitrary formula called the *matrix* of φ. Note that the problem of checking validity or satisfiability of a formula with free variables can be easily reduced to this form.

The classical procedure presented in Section 4 computes a sequence of automata $\mathcal{A}_{\varphi_0}, \mathcal{A}_{\varphi_0^\sharp}, \dots, \mathcal{A}_{\varphi_{m-1}^\sharp}, \mathcal{A}_{\varphi_m}$ where for all $0 \leq i \leq m - 1$, $\varphi_i^\sharp = \exists \mathcal{X}_{i+1} : \varphi_i$ and $\varphi_{i+1} = \neg \varphi_i^\sharp$. The φ_i's are the subformulae of φ shown in Equation 2. Since eliminating existential quantification on the automata level introduces nondeterminism (due to the projection on the transition relation), every $\mathcal{A}_{\varphi_i^\sharp}$ may be nondeterministic. The computation of $\mathcal{A}_{\varphi_{i+1}}$ then involves subset construction and becomes exponential. The worst case complexity of eliminating the prefix is therefore the tower of exponentials of the height m. Even though the construction may be optimized, e.g. by minimizing every $\mathcal{A}_{\varphi_i}$ (which is implemented by MONA), the size of the generated automata can quickly become intractable.

The main idea of our algorithm is inspired by the antichain algorithms [13] for testing language universality of an automaton $\mathcal{A}$. In a nutshell, testing universality of $\mathcal{A}$ is testing whether in the complement $\overline{\mathcal{A}}$ of $\mathcal{A}$ (which is created by determinization via subset construction, followed by swapping final and non-final states), an initial state can reach a final state. The crucial idea of the antichain algorithms is based on the following: (i) The search can be done on-the-fly while constructing $\overline{\mathcal{A}}$. (ii) The sets of states that arise during the search are closed (upward or downward, depending on the variant of the algorithm). (iii) The computation can be done symbolically on the generators of these closed sets. It is enough to keep only the extreme generators of the closed sets (maximal for downward, minimal for upward closed). The generators that are not extreme (we say that they are *subsumed*) can be pruned away, which vastly reduces the search space.

We notice that individual steps of the algorithm for constructing $\mathcal{A}_\varphi$ are very similar to testing universality. Automaton $\mathcal{A}_{\varphi_i}$ arises by subset construction from $\mathcal{A}_{\varphi_{i-1}^\sharp}$, and to compute $\mathcal{A}_{\varphi_i^\sharp}$, it is necessary to compute the set of final states $F_i^\sharp$. Those are states backward reachable from the final states of $\mathcal{A}_{\varphi_i}$ via a subset of transitions of Δ_i (those labelled by symbols projected to $\overline{0}$ by π_{i+1}). To compute $F_i^\sharp$, the antichain algorithms could be actually taken off-the-shelf and run with $\mathcal{A}_{\varphi_{i-1}^\sharp}$ in the role of the input $\mathcal{A}$ and $\mathcal{A}_{\varphi_i^\sharp}$ in the role of $\overline{\mathcal{A}}$. However, this approach has the following two problems. First, antichain algorithms do not produce the automaton $\overline{\mathcal{A}}$ (here $\mathcal{A}_{\varphi_i^\sharp}$), but only a symbolic representation of a set of (backward) reachable states (here of $F_i^\sharp$). Since $\mathcal{A}_{\varphi_i^\sharp}$ is the input of the construction of $\mathcal{A}_{\varphi_{i+1}}$, the construction of $\mathcal{A}_\varphi$ could not continue. The other problem is that the size of the input $\mathcal{A}_{\varphi_{i-1}^\sharp}$ of the antichain algorithm is only limited by the tower of exponentials of the height $i - 1$, and this might be already far out of reach.

The main contribution of our paper is an algorithm that alleviates the two problems mentioned above. It is based on a novel way of performing not only one, but all the $2m$ steps of the construction of $\mathcal{A}_\varphi$ on-the-fly. It uses a nested symbolic representation of sets of states and a form of nested subsumption pruning on all levels of their structure. This is achieved by a substantial refinement of the basic ideas of antichain algorithms.

5.1 Structure of the Algorithm

Let us now start explaining our on-the-fly algorithm for handling quantifier alternation. Following the construction of automata in Section 4, the structure of the automata from the previous section, $\mathcal{A}_{\varphi_0}, \mathcal{A}_{\varphi_0^\sharp}, \dots, \mathcal{A}_{\varphi_{m-1}^\sharp}, \mathcal{A}_{\varphi_m}$, can be described using the following recursive definition. We use $\pi_i(C)$ for any mathematical structure C to denote projection of all variables in $\mathcal{X}_1 \cup \cdots \cup \mathcal{X}_i$ from C.

Let $\mathcal{A}_{\varphi_0} = (Q_0, \Delta_0, I_0, F_0)$ be an FA over $\mathbb{X}$. Then, for each $0 \leq i < m$, $\mathcal{A}_{\varphi_i^\sharp}$ and $\mathcal{A}_{\varphi_{i+1}}$ are FAs over $\pi_{i+1}(\mathbb{X})$ that have from the construction the following structure:

$$\mathcal{A}_{\varphi_i^\sharp} = (Q_i, \Delta_i^\sharp, I_i, F_i^\sharp) \text{ where} \qquad \mathcal{A}_{\varphi_{i+1}} = (Q_{i+1}, \Delta_{i+1}, I_{i+1}, F_{i+1}) \text{ where}$$

$$\Delta_i^\sharp = \pi_{i+1}(\Delta_i) \text{ and} \qquad \Delta_{i+1} = \left\{ R \xrightarrow{\tau} post[\Delta_i^\sharp, \tau](R) \,\middle|\, R \in Q_{i+1} \right\},$$

$$F_i^\sharp = \mu Z \,.\, F_i \cup pre[\Delta_i^\sharp, \overline{0}](Z). \qquad Q_{i+1} = 2^{Q_i}, \quad I_{i+1} = \{I_i\}, \quad \text{and} \quad F_{i+1} = \Downarrow\{Q_i \setminus F_i^\sharp\}.$$

We recall that $\mathcal{A}_{\varphi_i^\sharp}$ directly corresponds to existential quantification (cf. Section 4), and $\mathcal{A}_{\varphi_{i+1}}$ directly corresponds to the complement of $\mathcal{A}_{\varphi_i^\sharp}$ (cf. Section 3).

A crucial observation behind our approach is that, because φ is ground, $\mathcal{A}_\varphi$ is an FA over an empty set of variables, and, therefore, $\mathcal{L}(\mathcal{A}_\varphi)$ is either the empty set $\emptyset$ or the set $\{\overline{0}\}^*$. Therefore, we need to distinguish between these two cases only. To determine which of them holds, we do not need to explicitly construct the automaton $\mathcal{A}_\varphi$. Instead, it suffices to check whether $\mathcal{A}_\varphi$ accepts the empty string ϵ. This is equivalent to checking existence of a state that is at the same time final and initial, that is

$$\models \varphi \quad \text{iff} \quad I_m \cap F_m \neq \emptyset. \tag{3}$$

To compute I_m from I_0 is straightforward (it equals $\{\{\ldots\{\{I_0\}\}\ldots\}\}$ nested m-times). In the rest of the section, we will describe how to compute F_m (its symbolic representation), and how to test whether it intersects with I_m.

The algorithm takes advantage of the fact that to represent final states, one can use their complement, the set of non-final states. For $0 \leq i \leq m$, we write N_i and $N_i^\sharp$ to denote the sets of non-final states $Q_i \setminus F_i$ of $\mathcal{A}_i$ and $Q_i \setminus F_i^\sharp$ of $\mathcal{A}_i^\sharp$ respectively. The algorithm will then instead of computing the sequence of automata $\mathcal{A}_{\varphi_0}, \mathcal{A}_{\varphi_0^\sharp}, \ldots,$ $\mathcal{A}_{\varphi_{m-1}^\sharp}, \mathcal{A}_{\varphi_m}$ compute the sequence $F_0, F_0^\sharp, N_1, N_1^\sharp, \ldots$ up to either F_m (if m is even) or N_m (if m is odd), which suffices for testing the validity of φ. The algorithm starts with F_0 and uses the following recursive equations:

$$
\begin{array}{ll}
\text{(i) } F_{i+1} = \downarrow\{N_i^\sharp\}, & \text{(ii) } F_i^\sharp = \mu Z \,.\, F_i \cup pre_{[\Delta_i^\sharp, \overline{0}]}(Z), \\
\text{(iii) } N_{i+1} = \uparrow\coprod\{F_i^\sharp\}, & \text{(iv) } N_i^\sharp = \nu Z \,.\, N_i \cap cpre_{[\Delta_i^\sharp, \overline{0}]}(Z).
\end{array}
\tag{4}
$$

Intuitively, Equations (i) and (ii) are directly from the definition of $\mathcal{A}_i$ and $\mathcal{A}_i^\sharp$. Equation (iii) is a dual of Equation (i): N_{i+1} contains all subsets of Q_i that contain at least one state from $F_i^\sharp$. Finally, Equation (iv) is a dual of Equation (ii): in the k-th iteration of the greatest fixpoint computation, the current set of states Z will contain all states that cannot reach an F_i state over $\overline{0}$ within k steps. In the next iteration, only those states of Z are kept such that all their $\overline{0}$-successors are in Z. Hence, the new value of Z is the set of states that cannot reach F_i over $\overline{0}$ in $k+1$ steps, and the computation stabilises with the set of states that cannot reach F_i over $\overline{0}$ in any number of steps.

In the next two sections, we will show that both of the above fixpoint computations can be carried out symbolically on representatives of upward/downward closed sets. Particularly, in Sections 5.2 and 5.3, we show how the fixpoints from Equations (ii) and (iv) can be computed symbolically, using subsets of Q_{i-1} as representatives (generators) of upward/downward closed subsets of Q_i. Section 5.4 explains how the above symbolic fixpoint computations can be carried out using nested terms of depth i as a symbolic representation of computed states of Q_i. Section 5.5 shows how to test emptiness of $I_m \cap F_m$ on the symbolic terms, and Section 5.6 describes the subsumption relation used to minimize the symbolic term representation used within computations of Equations (ii) and (iv). Proofs of the lemmas and used equations can be found in [25].

5.2   Computing $N_i^\sharp$ on Representatives of $\uparrow\coprod\mathcal{R}$-sets

Computing $N_i^\sharp$ at each odd level of the hierarchy of automata is done by computing the greatest fixpoint of the function from Equation 4(iv):

$$f_{N_i^\sharp}(Z) = N_i \cap cpre_{[\Delta_i^\sharp,\overline{0}]}(Z). \tag{5}$$

We will show that the whole fixpoint computation from Equation 4(iv) can be carried out symbolically on the representatives of Z. We will explain that: (a) All intermediate values of Z have the form $\uparrow\coprod\mathcal{R}, \mathcal{R} \subseteq Q_i$, so the sets $\mathcal{R}$ can be used as their symbolic representatives. (b) $cpre$ and $\cap$ can be computed on such a representation efficiently.

Let us start with the computation of $cpre_{[\Delta_i^\sharp,\tau]}(Z)$ where $\tau \in \pi_{i+1}(\mathbb{X})$, assuming that Z is of the form $\uparrow\coprod\mathcal{R}$, represented by $\mathcal{R} = \{R_1,\ldots,R_n\}$. Observe that a set of symbolic representatives $\mathcal{R}$ stands for the intersection of denotations of individual representatives, that is

$$\uparrow\coprod\mathcal{R} = \bigcap_{R_j \in \mathcal{R}} \uparrow\coprod\{R_j\}. \tag{6}$$

Z can thus be written as the $cpre$-image $cpre_{[\Delta_i^\sharp,\tau]}(\bigcap\mathcal{S})$ of the intersection of the elements of a set $\mathcal{S}$ having the form $\uparrow\coprod\{R_j\}, R_j \in \mathcal{R}$. Further, because $cpre$ distributes over $\cap$, we can compute the $cpre$-image of an intersection by computing intersection of the $cpre$-images, i.e.

$$cpre_{[\Delta_i^\sharp,\tau]}(\bigcap\mathcal{S}) = \bigcap_{S\in\mathcal{S}} cpre_{[\Delta_i^\sharp,\tau]}(S). \tag{7}$$

By the definition of $\Delta_i^\sharp$ (where $\Delta_i^\sharp = \pi_{i+1}(\Delta_i)$), $cpre_{[\Delta_i^\sharp,\tau]}(S)$ can be computed using the transition relation Δ_i for the price of further refining the intersection. In particular,

$$cpre_{[\Delta_i^\sharp,\tau]}(S) = \bigcap_{\omega\in\pi_{i+1}^{-1}(\tau)} cpre_{[\Delta_i,\omega]}(S). \tag{8}$$

Intuitively, $cpre_{[\Delta_i^\sharp,\tau]}(S)$ contains states from which every transition labelled by *any* symbol that is projected to τ by π_{i+1} has its target in S. Using Equations 6, 7, and 8, we can write $cpre_{[\Delta_i^\sharp,\tau]}(Z)$ as $\bigcap_{S\in\mathcal{S},\omega\in\pi_{i+1}^{-1}(\tau)} cpre_{[\Delta_i,\omega]}(S)$.

To compute the individual conjuncts $cpre_{[\Delta_i,\omega]}(S)$, we take advantage of the fact that every S is in the special form $\uparrow\coprod\{R_j\}$, and that Δ_i is, by its definition (determinization via subset construction), *monotone* w.r.t. $\supseteq$. That is, if $P \xrightarrow{\omega} P' \in \Delta_i$ for some $P, P' \in Q_i$, then for every $R \supseteq P$, there is $R' \supseteq P'$ s.t. $R \xrightarrow{\omega} R' \in \Delta_i$. Due to monotonicity, the $cpre_{[\Delta_i,\omega]}$-image of an upward closed set is also upward closed. Moreover, we observe that it can be computed symbolically using pre on elements of its generators. Particularly, for a set of singletons $S = \uparrow\coprod\{R_j\}$, we get the following equation:

$$cpre_{[\Delta_i,\omega]}(\uparrow\coprod\{R_j\}) = \uparrow\coprod\{pre_{[\Delta_{i-1}^\sharp,\omega]}(R_j)\}. \tag{9}$$

Intuitively, the sets with *post*-images above a singleton set $\{p\} \in \{\{p\} \mid p \in R_j\} = \uparrow\coprod\{R_j\}$ are those that contain at least one state $q \in Q_{i-1}$ such that $q \xrightarrow{\omega} p \in$

$\Delta^\sharp_{i-1}$. Using Equation 9, the set $cpre[\Delta^\sharp_i, \tau](Z)$ can then be rewritten as the intersection $\bigcap_{R \in \mathcal{R}, \omega \in \pi^{-1}_{i+1}(\tau)} \uparrow \coprod \{ pre[\Delta^\sharp_{i-1}, \omega](R_j) \}$. By applying Equation 6, we get the final formula for $cpre[\Delta^\sharp_i, \tau]$ shown in the lemma below.

Lemma 1. $cpre[\Delta^\sharp_i, \tau](\uparrow \coprod \mathcal{R}) = \uparrow \coprod \{ pre[\Delta^\sharp_{i-1}, \omega](R_j) \mid \omega \in \pi^{-1}_{i+1}(\tau), R_j \in \mathcal{R} \}$.

To compute $f_{N^\sharp_i}(Z)$, it remains to intersect $cpre[\Delta^\sharp_i, \overline{0}](Z)$, computed using Lemma 1, with N_i. By Equation 4(iii), N_i equals $\uparrow \coprod \{ F^\sharp_{i-1} \}$, and, by Equation 6, the intersection can be done symbolically as

$$f_{N^\sharp_i}(Z) = \uparrow \coprod \left(\{ F^\sharp_{i-1} \} \cup \{ pre[\Delta^\sharp_{i-1}, \omega](R_j) \mid \omega \in \pi^{-1}_{i+1}(\overline{0}), R_j \in \mathcal{R} \} \right). \tag{10}$$

Finally, note that a symbolic application of $f_{N^\sharp_i}$ to $Z = \uparrow \coprod \mathcal{R}$ represented as the set $\mathcal{R}$ reduces to computing pre-images of the elements of $\mathcal{R}$, which are then put next to each other, together with $F^\sharp_{i-1}$. The computation starts from $N_i = \uparrow \coprod \{ F^\sharp_{i-1} \}$, represented by $\{ F^\sharp_{i-1} \}$, and each of its steps, implemented by Equation 10, preserves the form of sets $\uparrow \coprod \mathcal{R}$, represented by $\mathcal{R}$.

5.3 Computing $F^\sharp_i$ on Representatives of $\downarrow \mathcal{R}$-sets

Similarly as in the previous section, computation of $F^\sharp_i$ at each even level of the automata hierarchy is done by computing the least fixpoint of the function

$$f_{F^\sharp_i}(Z) = F_i \cup pre[\Delta^\sharp_i, \overline{0}](Z). \tag{11}$$

We will show that the whole fixpoint computation from Equation 4(ii) can be carried out symbolically. We will explain the following: (a) All intermediate values of Z are of the form $\downarrow \mathcal{R}$, $\mathcal{R} \subseteq Q_i$, so the sets $\mathcal{R}$ can be used as their symbolic representatives. (b) pre and $\cup$ can be computed efficiently on such a symbolic representation. The computation is a simpler analogy of the one in Section 5.2.

We start with the computation of $pre[\Delta^\sharp_i, \tau](Z)$ where $\tau \in \pi_{i+1}(\mathbb{X})$, assuming that Z is of the form $\downarrow \mathcal{R}$, represented by $\mathcal{R} = \{ R_1, \ldots, R_n \}$. A simple analogy to Equations 6 and 7 of Section 5.2 is that the union of downward closed sets is a downward closed set generated by the union of their generators, i.e. $\downarrow \mathcal{R} = \bigcup_{R_j \in \mathcal{R}} \downarrow \{ R_j \}$ and that pre distributes over union, i.e. $pre[\Delta^\sharp_i, \tau](\bigcup \mathcal{R}) = \bigcup_{R_j \in \mathcal{R}} pre[\Delta^\sharp_i, \tau](\downarrow \{ R_j \})$. An analogy of Equation 8 holds too:

$$pre[\Delta^\sharp_i, \tau](S) = \bigcup_{\omega \in \pi^{-1}_{i+1}(\tau)} pre[\Delta_i, \omega](S). \tag{12}$$

Intuitively, $pre[\Delta^\sharp_i, \tau](S)$ contains states from which *at least one* transition labelled by *any* symbol that is projected to τ by π_{i+1} leaves with the target in S. Using Equation 12, we can write $pre[\Delta^\sharp_i, \tau](Z)$ as $\bigcup_{R_j \in \mathcal{R}, \omega \in \pi^{-1}_{i+1}(\tau)} pre[\Delta_i, \omega](\downarrow \{ R_j \})$.

To compute the individual disjuncts $pre[\Delta_i, \omega](\downarrow \{ R_j \})$, we take advantage of the fact that every $\downarrow \{ R_j \}$ is downward closed, and that Δ_i is, by definition (determinization by subset construction), *monotone* w.r.t. $\subseteq$. That is, if $P \xrightarrow{\omega} P' \in \Delta_i$ for some $P, P' \in Q_i$, then for every $R \subseteq P$, there is $R' \subseteq P'$ s.t. $R \xrightarrow{\omega} R' \in \Delta_i$. Due to monotonicity, the $pre[\Delta_i, \omega]$-image of a downward closed set is downward closed. Moreover, we observe that it can be computed symbolically using *cpre* on elements of its generators. In particular, for a set $\downarrow\{R_j\}$, we get the following equation, which is a dual of Equation 9:

$$pre[\Delta_i, \omega](\downarrow\{R_j\}) = \downarrow\{cpre[\Delta^\sharp_{i-1}, \omega](R_j)\}. \tag{13}$$

Intuitively, the sets with the *post*-images below R_j are those which do not have an outgoing transition leading outside R_j. The largest such set is $cpre[\Delta^\sharp_{i-1}, \omega](R_j)$. Using Equation 13, $pre[\Delta^\sharp_i, \tau](Z)$ can be rewritten as $\bigcup_{R_j \in \mathcal{R}, \omega \in \pi^{-1}_{i+1}(\tau)} \downarrow\{cpre[\Delta^\sharp_{i-1}, \omega](R_j)\}$, which gives us the final formula for $pre[\Delta^\sharp_i, \tau]$ described in Lemma 2.

Lemma 2. $pre[\Delta^\sharp_i, \tau](\downarrow\mathcal{R}) = \downarrow\{cpre[\Delta^\sharp_{i-1}, \omega](R_j) \mid \omega \in \pi^{-1}_{i+1}(\tau), R_j \in \mathcal{R}\}$.

To compute $f_{F^\sharp_i}(Z)$, it remains to unite $pre[\Delta^\sharp_i, \bar{0}](Z)$, computed using Lemma 2, with F_i. From Equation 4(i), F_i equals $\downarrow\{N^\sharp_{i-1}\}$, so the union can be done symbolically as

$$f_{F^\sharp_i}(Z) = \downarrow\left(\{N^\sharp_{i-1}\} \cup \{cpre[\Delta^\sharp_{i-1}, \omega](R_j) \mid \omega \in \pi^{-1}_{i+1}(\bar{0}), R_j \in \mathcal{R}\}\right). \tag{14}$$

Therefore, a symbolic application of $f_{F^\sharp_i}$ to $Z = \downarrow\mathcal{R}$ represented using the set $\mathcal{R}$ reduces to computing *cpre*-images of elements of $\mathcal{R}$, which are put next to each other, together with $N^\sharp_{i-1}$. The computation starts from $F_i = \downarrow\{N^\sharp_{i-1}\}$, represented by $\{N^\sharp_{i-1}\}$, and each of its steps, implemented by Equation 14, preserves the form of sets $\downarrow\mathcal{R}$, represented by $\mathcal{R}$.

5.4 Computation of $F^\sharp_i$ and $N^\sharp_i$ on Symbolic Terms

Sections 5.2 and 5.3 show how sets of states arising within the fixpoint computations from Equations 4(ii) and 4(iv) can be represented symbolically using representatives which are sets of states of the lower level. The sets of states of the lower level will be again represented symbolically. When computing the fixpoint of level i, we will work with nested symbolic representation of states of depth i. Particularly, sets of states of $Q_k, 0 \leq k \leq i$, are represented by *terms of level* k where a term of level 0 is a subset of Q_0, a term of level $2j + 1$, $j \geq 0$, is of the form $\uparrow\coprod\{t_1, \ldots, t_n\}$ where $t_1, \ldots, t_n$ are terms of level $2j$, and a term of level $2j$, $j > 0$, is of the form $\downarrow\{t_1, \ldots, t_n\}$ where $t_1, \ldots, t_n$ are terms of level $2j - 1$.

The computation of *cpre* and $f_{N^\sharp_{2j+1}}$ on a term of level $2j + 1$ and computation of *pre* and $f_{F^\sharp_{2j}}$ on a term of level $2j$ then becomes a recursive procedure that descends via the structure of the terms and produces again a term of level $2j + 1$ or $2j$ respectively. In the case of *cpre* and $f_{N^\sharp_{2j+1}}$ called on a term of level $2j + 1$, Lemma 1 reduces the computation to a computation of *pre* on its sub-terms of level $2j$, which is again reduced by Lemma 2 to a computation of *cpre* on terms of level $2j - 1$, and so on until the bottom level where the algorithm computes *pre* on the terms of level 0 (subsets of Q_0). The case of *pre* and $f_{F^\sharp_{2j}}$ called on a term of level $2j$ is symmetrical.

Example. We will demonstrate the run of our algorithm on the following abstract example. Consider a ground WS1S formula $\varphi = \neg\exists\mathcal{X}_3\neg\exists\mathcal{X}_2\neg\exists\mathcal{X}_1 : \varphi_0$ and an FA $\mathcal{A}_0 = (Q_0, \Delta_0, I_0 = \{a\}, F_0 = \{a, b\})$ that represents φ_0. Recall that our method decides validity of φ by computing symbolically the sequence of sets $F_0^\sharp, N_1, N_1^\sharp, F_2, F_2^\sharp, N_3$, each of them represented using a symbolic term, and then checks if $I_3 \cap N_3 \neq \emptyset$. In the following paragraph, we will show how such a sequence is computed and interleave the description with examples of possible intermediate results.

The fixpoint computation from Equation 4(ii) of the first set in the sequence, $F_0^\sharp$, is an explicit computation of the set of states backward-reachable from F_0 via $\overline{0}$ transitions of $\Delta_0^\sharp$. It is done using Equation 11, yielding, e.g. the term

$$t_{[F_0^\sharp]} = F_0^\sharp = \{a, b, c\}.$$

The fixpoint computation of $N_1^\sharp$ from Equation 4(iv) is done symbolically. It starts from N_1 represented using Equation 4(iii) as the term $t_{[N_1]} = \uparrow\coprod\{\{a, b, c\}\}$, and each of its iterations is carried out using Equation 10. Equation 10 transforms the problem of computing $cpre_{[\Delta_1, \omega']}$-image of a term into a computation of a series of $pre_{[\Delta_0^\sharp, \omega]}$-images of its sub-terms, which is carried out using Equation 11 in the same way as when computing $t_{[F_0^\sharp]}$, ending with, e.g. the term

$$t_{[N_1^\sharp]} = \uparrow\coprod\{\{a, b, c\}, \{b, c\}, \{c, d\}\}.$$

The term representing F_2 is then $t_{[F_2]} = \downarrow\{t_{[N_1^\sharp]}\}$, due to Equation 4(i). The symbolic fixpoint computation of $F_2^\sharp$ from Equation 4(ii) then starts from $t_{[F_2]}$, in our example

$$t_{[F_2]} = \downarrow\left\{\uparrow\coprod\{\{a, b, c\}, \{b, c\}, \{c, d\}\}\right\}.$$

Its steps are computed using Equation 14, which transforms the computation of the image of $pre_{[\Delta_2^\sharp, \omega'']}$ into computations of a series of $cpre_{[\Delta_1^\sharp, \omega']}$-images of sub-terms. These are in turn transformed by Lemma 1 into computations of $pre_{[\Delta_0^\sharp, \omega]}$-images of sub-sub-terms, subsets of Q_0, in our example yielding, e.g. the term

$$t_{[F_2^\sharp]} = \downarrow\left\{\uparrow\coprod\{\{a, b, c\}, \{b, c\}, \{c, d\}\}, \uparrow\coprod\{\{b\}, \{d\}\}, \uparrow\coprod\{\{a\}, \{c, d\}\}\right\}.$$

Using Equation 4(iv), the final term representing N_3 is then

$$t_{[N_3]} = \uparrow\coprod\left\{\downarrow\left\{\uparrow\coprod\{\{a, b, c\}, \{b, c\}, \{c, d\}\}, \uparrow\coprod\{\{b\}, \{d\}\}, \uparrow\coprod\{\{a\}, \{c, d\}\}\right\}\right\}.$$

In the next section, we will describe how we check whether $I_3 \cap F_3 \neq \emptyset$ using the computed term $t_{[N_3]}$.

5.5 Testing $I_m \cap F_m \overset{?}{\neq} \emptyset$ on Symbolic Terms

Due to the special form of the set I_m (every $I_i, 1 \leq i \leq m$, is the singleton $\{I_{i-1}\}$), the test $I_m \cap F_m \neq \emptyset$ can be done efficiently over the symbolic terms representing F_m. Because $I_m = \{I_{m-1}\}$ is a singleton set, testing $I_m \cap F_m \neq \emptyset$ is equivalent to testing $I_{m-1} \in F_m$. If m is odd, our approach computes the symbolic representation of N_m instead of F_m. Obviously, since N_m is the complement of F_m, it holds that

$I_{m-1} \in F_m \iff I_{m-1} \notin N_m$. Our way of testing $I_{m-1} \in Y_m$ on a symbolic representation of the set Y_m of level m is based on the following equations:

$$\{x\} \in \downarrow\mathbb{Y} \qquad \iff \qquad \exists Y \in \mathbb{Y} : x \in Y \qquad (15)$$

$$\{x\} \in \uparrow\!\coprod\!\mathbb{Y} \qquad \iff \qquad \forall Y \in \mathbb{Y} : x \in Y \qquad (16)$$

and for $i = 0$, $\qquad I_0 \in \uparrow\!\coprod\!\mathbb{Y} \qquad \iff \qquad \forall Y \in \mathbb{Y} : I_0 \cap Y \neq \emptyset. \qquad (17)$

Given a symbolic term $t_{[X]}$ of level m representing a set $X \subseteq Q_m$, testing emptiness of $I_m \cap F_m$ or $I_m \cap N_m$ can be done over $t_{[X]}$ by a recursive procedure that descends along the structure of $t_{[X]}$ using Equations 15 and 16, essentially generating an AND-OR tree, terminating the descent by the use of Equation 17.

Example. In the example of Section 5.4, we would test whether $\{\{\{\{a\}\}\}\} \cap N_3 = \emptyset$ over $t_{[N_3]}$. This is equivalent to testing whether $I_2 = \{\{\{a\}\}\} \in N_3$. From Equation 16 we get that $I_2 \in N_3 \iff I_1 = \{\{a\}\} \in F_2^\sharp$ because $F_2^\sharp$ is the denotation of the only sub-term $t_{[F_2^\sharp]}$ of $t_{[N_3]}$. Equation 15 implies that $I_1 = \{\{a\}\} \in F_2^\sharp \iff \{a\} \in N_1^\sharp \vee \{a\} \in \uparrow\!\coprod\!\{\{b\}, \{d\}\} \vee \{a\} \in \uparrow\!\coprod\!\{\{a\}, \{c,d\}\}$. Each of the disjuncts could then be further reduced by Equation 16 into a conjunction of membership queries on the base level which would be solved by Equation 17. Since none of the disjuncts is satisfied, we conclude that $I_1 \notin F_2^\sharp$, so $I_2 \notin N_3$, implying that $I_2 \in F_3$ and thus obtain the result $\models \varphi$.

5.6 Subsumption of Symbolic Terms

Although the use of symbolic terms instead of an explicit enumeration of sets of states itself considerably reduces the searched space, an even greater degree of reduction can be obtained using subsumption inside the symbolic representatives to reduce their size, similarly as in the antichain algorithms [14]. For any set of sets $\mathbb{X}$ containing a pair of distinct elements $Y, Z \in \mathbb{X}$ s.t. $Y \subseteq Z$, it holds that

$$\downarrow\mathbb{X} = \downarrow(\mathbb{X} \setminus Y) \quad \text{and} \quad \uparrow\!\coprod\!\mathbb{X} = \uparrow\!\coprod(\mathbb{X} \setminus Z). \qquad (18)$$

Therefore, if $\mathbb{X}$ is used to represent the set $\downarrow\mathbb{X}$, the element Y is *subsumed* by Z and can be removed from $\mathbb{X}$ without changing its denotation. Likewise, if $\mathbb{X}$ is used to represent $\uparrow\!\coprod\!\mathbb{X}$, the element Z is *subsumed* by Y and can be removed from $\mathbb{X}$ without changing its denotation. We can thus simplify any symbolic term by pruning out its sub-terms that represent elements subsumed by elements represented by other sub-terms, without changing the denotation of the term.

Computing subsumption on terms can be done using the following two equations:

$$\downarrow\mathbb{X} \subseteq \downarrow\mathbb{Y} \qquad \iff \qquad \forall X \in \mathbb{X} \exists Y \in \mathbb{Y} : X \subseteq Y \qquad (19)$$

$$\uparrow\!\coprod\!\mathbb{X} \subseteq \uparrow\!\coprod\!\mathbb{Y} \qquad \iff \qquad \forall Y \in \mathbb{Y} \exists X \in \mathbb{X} : X \subseteq Y. \qquad (20)$$

Using Equations 19 and 20, testing subsumption of terms of level i reduces to testing subsumption of terms of level $i - 1$. The procedure for testing subsumption of two terms descends along the structure of the term, using Equations 19 and 20 on levels greater than 0, and on level 0, where terms are subsets of Q_0, it tests subsumption by set inclusion.

Example. In the example from Section 5.4, we can use the inclusion $\{b, c\} \subseteq \{a, b, c\}$ and Equation 18 to reduce $t_{[N_1^\sharp]} = {\uparrow}\coprod\{\{a, b, c\}, \{b, c\}, \{c, d\}\}$ to the term

$$t_{[N_1]}' = {\uparrow}\coprod\{\{b, c\}, \{c, d\}\}.$$

Moreover, Equation 20 implies that ${\uparrow}\coprod\{\{b, c\}, \{c, d\}\}$ is subsumed by the symbolic term ${\uparrow}\coprod\{\{b\}, \{d\}\}$, and, therefore, we can reduce the term $t_{[F_2^\sharp]}$ to the term

$$t_{[F_2^\sharp]}' = {\downarrow}\Big\{{\uparrow}\coprod\{\{b\}, \{d\}\}, {\uparrow}\coprod\{\{a\}, \{c, d\}\}\Big\}.$$

6   Experimental Evaluation

We implemented a prototype of the presented approach in the tool dWiNA [20] and evaluated it in a benchmark of both practical and generated examples. The tool uses the frontend of MONA to parse input formulae and also for the construction of the base automaton $\mathcal{A}_{\varphi_0}$, and further uses the MTBDD-based representation of FAs from the libvata [21] library. The tool supports the following two modes of operation.

In mode I, we use MONA to generate the deterministic automaton $\mathcal{A}_{\varphi_0}$ corresponding to the matrix of the formula φ, translate it to libvata and run our algorithm for handling the prefix of φ using libvata. In mode II, we first translate the formula φ into the formula φ' in prenex normal form (i.e. it consists of a quantifier prefix and a quantifier-free matrix) where the occurence of negation in the matrix is limited to literals, and then construct the nondeterministic automaton $\mathcal{A}_{\varphi_0}$ directly using libvata.

Our experiments were performed on an Intel Core i7-4770@3.4 GHz processor with 32 GiB RAM. The practical formulae for our experiments that we report on here were obtained from the shape analysis of [5] and evaluated using mode I of our tool; the results are shown in Table 1 (see [20] for additional experimental results). We measure the time of runs of the tools for processing only the prefix of the formulae. We can observe that w.r.t. the speed, we get comparable results; in some cases dWiNA is slower than MONA, which we attribute to the fact that our prototype implementation is, when compared with MONA, quite immature. Regarding space, we compare the sum of the number of states of all automata generated by MONA when processing the prefix of φ with the number of symbolic terms generated by dWiNA for processing the same. We can observe a significant reduction in the generated state space.

We also tried to run dWiNA on the modified formulae in mode II but ran into the problem that we were not able to construct the non-deterministic automaton for the quantifier-free matrix φ_0. This was because after transformation of φ into prenex normal form, if φ_0 contains

Table 1. Results for practical examples

Benchmark	Time [s]		Space [states]	
	MONA	dWiNA	MONA	dWiNA
reverse-before-loop	0.01	0.01	179	47
insert-in-loop	0.01	0.01	463	110
bubblesort-else	0.01	0.01	1 285	271
reverse-in-loop	0.02	0.02	1 311	274
bubblesort-if-else	0.02	0.23	4 260	1 040
bubblesort-if-if	0.12	1.14	8 390	2 065

many conjunctions, the sizes of the automata generated using intersection grow too large (one of the reasons for this is that libvata in its current version does not support efficient reduction of automata).

To better evaluate the scalability of our approach, we created several parameterized families of WS1S formulae. We start with basic formulae encoding interesting relations among subsets of $\mathbb{N}_0$, such as existence of certain transitive relations, singleton sets, or intervals (their full definition can be found in [20]). From these we algorithmically create families of formulae with

Table 2. Results for generated formulae

k	Time [s]		Space [states]	
	MONA	dWiNA	MONA	dWiNA
2	0.20	0.01	25 517	44
3	0.57	0.01	60 924	50
4	1.79	0.02	145 765	58
5	4.98	0.02	349 314	70
6	∞	0.47	∞	90

larger quantifier depth, regardless of the meaning of the created formulae (though their semantics is still nontrivial). In Table 2, we give the results for one of the families where the basic formula expresses existence of an ascending chain of n sets ordered w.r.t. $\subset$. The parameter k stands for the number of alternations in the prefix of the formulae:

$$\exists Y : \neg \exists X_1 \neg \ldots \neg \exists X_k, \ldots, X_n : \bigwedge_{1 \le i < n} \left(X_i \subseteq Y \wedge X_i \subset X_{i+1} \right) \Rightarrow X_{i+1} \subseteq Y.$$

We ran the experiments in mode II of dWiNA (the experiment in mode I was not successful due to a costly conversion of a large base automaton from MONA to libvata).

7 Conclusion and Future Work

We presented a new approach for dealing with alternating quantifications within the automata-based decision procedure for WS1S. Our approach is based on a generalization of the idea of the so-called antichain algorithm for testing universality or language inclusion of finite automata. Our approach processes a prefix of the formula with an arbitrary number of quantifier alternations on-the-fly using an efficient symbolic representation of the state space, enhanced with subsumption pruning. Our experimental results are encouraging (our tool often outperforms MONA) and show that the direction started in this paper—using modern techniques for nondeterministic automata in the context of deciding WS1S formulae—is promising.

An interesting direction of further development seems to be lifting the symbolic *pre*/*cpre* operators to a more general notion of terms that allow working with general sub-formulae (that may include logical connectives and nested quantifiers). The algorithm could then be run over arbitrary formulae, without the need of the transformation into the prenex form. This would open a way of adopting optimizations used in other tools as well as syntactical optimizations of the input formula such as anti-prenexing. Another way of improvement is using simulation-based techniques to reduce the generated automata as well as to weaken the term-subsumption relation (an efficient algorithm for computing simulation over BDD-represented automata is needed). We also plan to extend the algorithms to WSkS and tree-automata, and perhaps even further to more general inductive structures.

Acknowledgement. This work was supported by the Czech Science Foundation (projects 14-11384S and 202/13/37876P), the BUT FIT project FIT-S-14-2486, and the EU/Czech IT4Innovations Centre of Excellence project CZ.1.05/1.1.00/02.0070.

References

1. Meyer, A.R.: Weak monadic second order theory of successor is not elementary-recursive. In: Proc. of Logic Colloquium—Symposium on Logic Held at Boston. LNCS, vol. 453. Springer (1972)

2. Elgaard, J., Klarlund, N., Møller, A.: MONA 1.x: new techniques for WS1S and WS2S. In: Vardi, M.Y. (ed.) CAV 1998. LNCS, vol. 1427, pp. 516–520. Springer, Heidelberg (1998)

3. Klarlund, N., Møller, A.: MONA Ver. 1.4 Manual. http://www.brics.dk/mona/

4. Madhusudan, P., Parlato, G., Qiu, X.: Decidable logics combining heap structures and data. In: Proc. of POPL 2011. ACM (2011)

5. Madhusudan, P., Qiu, X.: Efficient decision procedures for heaps using STRAND. In: Yahav, E. (ed.) Static Analysis. LNCS, vol. 6887, pp. 43–59. Springer, Heidelberg (2011)

6. Iosif, R., Rogalewicz, A., Simacek, J.: The tree width of separation logic with recursive definitions. In: Bonacina, M.P. (ed.) CADE 2013. LNCS, vol. 7898, pp. 21–38. Springer, Heidelberg (2013)

7. Chin, W., David, C., Nguyen, H.H., Qin, S.: Automated verification of shape, size and bag properties via user-defined predicates in separation logic. Science of Computer Programing 77(9) (2012)

8. Zee, K., Kuncak, V., Rinard, M.C.: Full functional verification of linked data structures. In: Proc. of POPL 2008. ACM (2008)

9. Hamza, J., Jobstmann, B., Kuncak, V.: Synthesis for regular specifications over unbounded domains. In: Proc. of FMCAD 2010. IEEE (2010)

10. Topnik, C., Wilhelm, E., Margaria, T., Steffen, B.: jMosel: A stand-alone tool and jABC plugin for M2L(Str). In: Valmari, A. (ed.) SPIN 2006. LNCS, vol. 3925, pp. 293–298. Springer, Heidelberg (2006)

11. Ganzow, T., Kaiser, L.: New algorithm for weak monadic second-order logic on inductive structures. In: Dawar, A., Veith, H. (eds.) CSL 2010. LNCS, vol. 6247, pp. 366–380. Springer, Heidelberg (2010)

12. Wies, T., Muñiz, M., Kuncak, V.: An efficient decision procedure for imperative tree data structures. In: Bjørner, N., Sofronie-Stokkermans, V. (eds.) CADE 2011. LNCS, vol. 6803, pp. 476–491. Springer, Heidelberg (2011)

13. Doyen, L., Raskin, J.F.: Antichain algorithms for finite automata. In: Esparza, J., Majumdar, R. (eds.) TACAS 2010. LNCS, vol. 6015, pp. 2–22. Springer, Heidelberg (2010)

14. De Wulf, M., Doyen, L., Henzinger, T.A., Raskin, J.-F.: Antichains: A new algorithm for checking universality of finite automata. In: Ball, T., Jones, R.B. (eds.) CAV 2006. LNCS, vol. 4144, pp. 17–30. Springer, Heidelberg (2006)

15. Abdulla, P.A., Chen, Y.-F., Holík, L., Mayr, R., Vojnar, T.: When simulation meets antichains (on checking language inclusion of NFAs). In: Esparza, J., Majumdar, R. (eds.) TACAS 2010. LNCS, vol. 6015, pp. 158–174. Springer, Heidelberg (2010)

16. Bustan, D., Grumberg, O.: Simulation based minimization. In: McAllester, D. (ed.) CADE 2000. LNCS, vol. 1831, pp. 255–270. Springer, Heidelberg (2000)

17. Bonchi, F., Pous, D.: Checking NFA equivalence with bisimulations up to congruence. In: Proc. of POPL 2013. ACM (2013)

18. Comon, H., Dauchet, M., Gilleron, R., Löding, C., Jacquemard, F., Lugiez, D., Tison, S., Tommasi, M.: Tree Automata Techniques and Applications (2008)

19. Büchi, J.R.: Weak second-order arithmetic and finite automata. Technical report, The University of Michigan (1959, 2010), http://hdl.handle.net/2027.42/3930

20. Fiedor, T., Holík, L., Lengál, O., Vojnar, T.: dWiNA (2014). http://www.fit.vutbr.cz/research/groups/verifit/tools/dWiNA/

21. Lengál, O., Šimáček, J., Vojnar, T.: VATA: A library for efficient manipulation of nondeterministic tree automata. In: Flanagan, C., König, B. (eds.) TACAS 2012. LNCS, vol. 7214, pp. 79–94. Springer, Heidelberg (2012)
22. Abdulla, P.A., Bouajjani, A., Holík, L., Kaati, L., Vojnar, T.: Computing simulations over tree automata: Efficient techniques for reducing tree automata. In: Ramakrishnan, C.R., Rehof, J. (eds.) TACAS 2008. LNCS, vol. 4963, pp. 93–108. Springer, Heidelberg (2008)
23. Habermehl, P., Holík, L., Rogalewicz, A., Šimáček, J., Vojnar, T.: Forest automata for verification of heap manipulation. Formal Methods in System Design 41(1) (2012)
24. Bouajjani, A., Habermehl, P., Holík, L., Touili, T., Vojnar, T.: Antichain-based universality and inclusion testing over nondeterministic finite tree automata. In: Ibarra, O.H., Ravikumar, B. (eds.) CIAA 2008. LNCS, vol. 5148, pp. 57–67. Springer, Heidelberg (2008)
25. Fiedor, T., Holík, L., Lengál, O., Vojnar, T.: Nested Antichains for WS1S. Technical report FIT-TR-2014-06, http://www.fit.vutbr.cz/ ilengal/pub/FIT-TR-2014-06.pdf

Model Checking

Sylvan: Multi-core Decision Diagrams

Tom van Dijk* and Jaco van de Pol

Formal Methods and Tools, University of Twente, The Netherlands
{dijkt,vdpol}@cs.utwente.nl

Abstract Decision diagrams such as binary decision diagrams and multi-valued decision diagrams play an important role in various fields, including symbolic model checking. An ongoing challenge is to develop datastructures and algorithms for modern multi-core architectures. The BDD package Sylvan provides one contribution by implementing parallelized BDD operations and thus allowing sequential algorithms to exploit the power of multi-core machines.

We present several extensions to Sylvan. We implement parallel operations on list decision diagrams, a variant of multi-valued decision diagrams that is useful for symbolic model checking. We also substitute several core components of Sylvan by new designs, such as the work-stealing framework, the unique table and the operation cache. Furthermore, we combine parallel operations with parallelization on a higher level, by partitioning the transition relation. We show that this results in an improved speedup using the model checking toolset LTSMIN. We also demonstrate that the parallelization of symbolic model checking for explicit-state modeling languages with an on-the-fly next-state function, as supported by LTSMIN, scales well.

1 Introduction

A core problem in model checking is that space and time requirements increase exponentially with the size of the models. One method to alleviate this problem is symbolic model checking, where sets of states are stored in binary decision diagrams (BDDs). Another method uses parallel computation, e.g., in computer systems with multiple processors. In [9,11], we combined both approaches by parallelizing BDD operations in the parallel BDD library Sylvan.

In the literature, there is some early work involving parallel BDD operations [18,27,23]. Alternative approaches for parallel symbolic reachability use partitioning strategies [26,15]. Also saturation, an optimal iteration strategy, was parallelized using Cilk [7,13]. More recently, a thesis on JINC [24] describes a multi-threaded extension, but does not actually parallelize the BDD operations. Also, a recent BDD implementation in Java called BeeDeeDee [21] allows execution of BDD operations from multiple threads, but does not parallelize the BDD operations. See also [11] for an overview of earlier approaches to parallelizing symbolic model checking and/or binary decision diagrams.

---

* The first author is supported by the NWO project MaDriD, grant nr. 612.001.101.

C. Baier and C. Tinelli (Eds.): TACAS 2015, LNCS 9035, pp. 677–691, 2015.
DOI: 10.1007/978-3-662-46681-0_60

In the current paper, we present several extensions to Sylvan, in particular integration with the work-stealing framework Lace, an improved unique table, and the implementation of operations on list decision diagrams (LDDs), a variant of multi-valued decision diagrams (MDDs) useful in symbolic model checking.

We also investigate applying parallelism on a higher level than the BDD operations. Since calculating the full transition relation is expensive in symbolic model checking, our model checking toolset LTSMIN [3,20,10,17] has the notion of transition groups, which disjunctively partition the transition relations. We exploit the fact that partitioned transition relations can be applied in parallel and show that this strategy results in improved scalability.

In addition, LTSMIN supports learning transition relations on-the-fly, which enables the symbolic model checking of explicit-state models, such as Promela, DVE and mCRL2 models. We implement a specialized operation `collect`, which is a combination of `enumerate` and `union`, to perform parallel transition learning and we show that this results in good parallel performance.

This paper is organized as follows. We review background knowledge about BDDs, MDDs and LDDs in Section 2, as well as background information on symbolic model checking and LTSMIN. Section 3 discusses the design of our parallel library Sylvan, with an emphasis on the new unique table and the implementation of LDD operations. Section 4 introduces parallelism on the algorithmic level in the model checking toolset LTSMIN in order to run parallel symbolic on-the-fly reachability. Section 5 shows the results of several experiments using the BEEM database of explicit-state models to measure the effectiveness of our approach. Finally, Section 6 summarizes our findings and reflections.

2   Preliminaries

2.1   Symbolic Reachability

In model checking, we create abstractions of complex systems to verify that they function according to certain properties. Systems are modeled as a set of possible states of the system and a set of transitions between these states. A core component of model checking is state-space generation using a reachability algorithm, to calculate all states reachable from the initial state of the system.

One major problem in model checking is the size of the transition system. The memory required to store all explored states and transitions increases exponentially with the size of the models. One way to deal with this is symbolic model checking [6], which represents states as sets rather than storing them individually.

An efficient method to store sets of states uses Boolean functions $S: \mathbb{B}^N \to \mathbb{B}$. Every state for which the function S is `true` is in the set. Boolean functions can be stored efficiently using binary decision diagrams (BDDs). Similarly, states can also be represented using functions $S: \mathbb{N}^N \to \mathbb{B}$, which can be stored using multi-valued decision diagrams (MDDs) or list decision diagrams (LDDs).

2.2 Binary Decision Diagrams and Multi-valued Decision Diagrams

Binary decision diagrams (BDDs) were introduced by Akers [1] and developed by Bryant [5].

Definition 1 (Binary decision diagram). *An (ordered) BDD is a directed acyclic graph with the following properties:*

1. *There is a single root node and two terminal nodes 0 and 1.*
2. *Each non-terminal node p has a variable label x_i and two outgoing edges, labeled 0 and 1; we write $lvl(p) = i$ and $p[v] = q$, where $v \in \{0, 1\}$.*
3. *For each edge from node p to non-terminal node q, $lvl(p) < lvl(q)$.*
4. *There are no duplicate nodes, i.e.,*
   $\forall p \forall q \cdot (lvl(p) = lvl(q) \wedge p[0] = q[0] \wedge p[1] = q[1]) \rightarrow p = q.$

Furthermore, either of two reductions ensures canonicity:

Definition 2 (Fully-reduced/Quasi-reduced BDD). *Fully-reduced BDDs forbid redundant nodes, i.e., nodes with $p[0] = p[1]$. Quasi-reduced BDDs keep all redundant nodes, i.e., skipping levels is forbidden.*

Multi-valued decision diagrams (MDDs, also called multi-way decision diagrams) are a generalization of BDDs to the integer domain [16].

Definition 3 (Multi-valued decision diagram). *An (ordered) MDD is a directed acyclic graph with the following properties:*

1. *There is a single root node and terminal nodes 0 and 1.*
2. *Each non-terminal node p has a variable label x_i and n_i outgoing edges, labeled from 0 to $n_i - 1$; we write $lvl(p) = i$ and $p[v] = q$, where $0 \le v < n_i$.*
3. *For each edge from node p to non-terminal node q, $lvl(p) < lvl(q)$.*
4. *There are no duplicate nodes, i.e.,*
   $\forall p \forall q \cdot (lvl(p) = lvl(q) \wedge \forall v \cdot p[v] = q[v]) \rightarrow p = q.$

Similar to BDDs, fully-reduced and quasi-reduced MDDs can be defined:

Definition 4 (Fully-reduced/Quasi-reduced MDD). *Fully-reduced MDDs forbid redundant nodes, i.e., nodes where for all v, w, $p[v] = p[w]$. Quasi-reduced MDDs keep all redundant nodes, i.e., skipping levels is forbidden.*

See Fig. 1 for an example of an MDD representing a set.

In [8], Ciardo et al. mention advantages of quasi-reduced MDDs: edges that skip levels are more difficult to manage and quasi-reduced MDDs are cheaper than alternatives to keep saturation operations correct. In [2], Blom et al. prefer quasi-reduced MDDs since the set of possible values at each level is dynamic and extending the set of values requires an update of every diagram in a fully-reduced setting, while having no impact in the quasi-reduced setting.

A typical method to store MDDs in memory is to store the variable label x_i plus an array holding all n_i edges, e.g., in C: `struct node { int lvl; struct node* edges[0]; }` as in [22]. New nodes are dynamically allocated

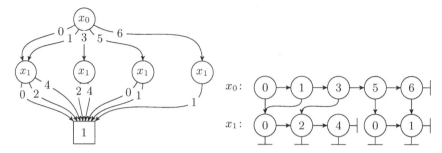

Fig. 1. Edge-labeled MDD hiding paths to 0 (left) and LDD (right) representing the set $\{\langle 0,0\rangle, \langle 0,2\rangle, \langle 0,4\rangle, \langle 1,0\rangle, \langle 1,2\rangle, \langle 1,4\rangle, \langle 3,2\rangle, \langle 3,4\rangle, \langle 5,0\rangle, \langle 5,1\rangle, \langle 6,1\rangle\}$. For simplicity, we hide paths to 0 and 1; the $p[x_i > v]$ edge of the last node in each "linked list" goes to 0, and every $p[x_i = v]$ edge on the last level goes to 1.

using `malloc` and a hash table ensures that no duplicate MDD nodes are created. Alternatively, one could use a large `int[]` array to store all MDDs (each MDD is represented by $n_i + 1$ consecutive integers) and represent edges to an MDD as the index of the first integer. In [8], the edges are stored in a separate `int[]` array to allow the number of edges n_i to vary.

2.3   List Decision Diagrams

Implementations of MDDs that use arrays to implement MDD nodes have two disadvantages. (1) For *sparse* sets (where only a fraction of the possible values are used) using arrays is a waste of memory. (2) MDD nodes typically have a variable size, complicating memory management. An alternative method uses list decision diagrams (LDDs), which can be understood as a linked-list representation of quasi-reduced MDDs. LDDs were initially described in [2, Sect. 5].

Definition 5 (List decision diagram). *A List decision diagram (LDD) is a directed acyclic graph with the following properties:*

1. *There is a single root node and two terminal nodes 0 and 1.*
2. *Each non-terminal node p is labeled with a value v, denoted by $val(p) = v$, and has two outgoing edges labeled $=$ and $>$ that point to nodes denoted by $p[x_i = v]$ and $p[x_i > v]$.*
3. *For all non-terminal nodes p, $p[x_i = v] \neq 0$ and $p[x_i > v] \neq 1$.*
4. *For all non-terminal nodes p, $val(p[x_i > v]) > v$.*
5. *There are no duplicate nodes.*

An LDD can be constructed from a quasi-reduced MDD by dropping all edges to 0 and creating an LDD node for each edge, using the edge label as the value in the LDD node. In a quasi-reduced BDD/MDD, every path from the root to a terminal encounters every variable (in the same order). Hence the variable label x_i follows implicitly from the depth of the node. We therefore do not store it in the LDD nodes either. The root node is at level 0, non-terminal nodes following

```
1 def reachable(initial, trans, K):
2     states = {initial}
3     next = states
4     while next != ∅:
5         for k in (0..K-1):
6             learn(next, k)
7             successors[k] = relprod(next, trans[k])
8             successors[k] = minus(successors[k], states)
9         next = union(successors[0], ..., successors[K-1])
10        states = union(states, next)
11    return states
```

Fig. 2. Symbolic on-the-fly reachability algorithm with transition groups: compute the set of all states reachable from the initial state. The transition relations are updated on-the-fly (line 6) and the algorithm relies on BDD operations `relprod` (relational product), `minus` ("diff") and `union` ("or"). See Fig. 9 for `learn`.

>-edges have the same level and non-terminal nodes following =-edges have the next level. See Fig. 1 for an example of an MDD and an LDD representing the same set of integer pairs.

2.4 LTSMIN and Partitioned Transition Relations

The model checking toolset LTSMIN[1] provides a language independent Partitioned Next-State Interface (PINS), which connects various input languages to model checking algorithms [3,20,10,17]. In PINS, states are vectors of N integer values. Furthermore, transitions are distinguished in disjunctive *transition groups*. The transition relation of each transition group is defined on a subset of the entire state vector, enabling efficient encoding of transitions that only affect a few integers of the state. For example, in a model of a software program, there could be a separate transition group for every line of source code.

Every language module implements a NEXTSTATE function, which computes the successors of a state for each transition group. Algorithms in LTSMIN thus learn new transitions on-the-fly. The reachability algorithm for symbolic model checking using BDD operations is given in Fig. 2.

3 Sylvan: Parallel BDD and LDD Operations

In [11], we implemented Sylvan[2], a parallel BDD package, which parallelizes BDD operations using lock-less data structures and work-stealing. Work-stealing [4] is a task-based load balancing method that involves breaking down a calculation into an (implicit) tree of (small) tasks. Independent subtasks are stored in queues and idle processors steal tasks from the queues of busy processors. Most BDD operations in Sylvan are implemented as recursive tasks, where operations are

---

[1] Available from https://github.com/utwente-fmt/ltsmin (open source).

[2] Available from https://github.com/utwente-fmt/sylvan (open source).

```
1 def ite(A,B,C):
2     if A = 1: return B
3     if A = 0: return C
4     result = cache_lookup(A,B,C)
5     if result = None:
6         x = min(var(A), var(B), var(C))
7         do in parallel:
8             Rlow = ite(low(A, x), low(B, x), low(C, x))
9             Rhigh = ite(high(A, x), high(B, x), high(C, x))
10        result = uniqueBDDnode(x, Rlow, Rhigh)
11        cache_store(A,B,C,result)
12    return result
```

Fig. 3. The ite algorithm calculating $(A \rightarrow B) \wedge (\overline{A} \rightarrow C)$ is used to implement binary operations like **and**, **or**. The recursive calls to **ite** are executed in parallel. BDDs are automatically fully-reduced by the **uniqueBDDnode** method using a hash table.

```
1 def uniqueBDDnode(var, edgelow, edgehigh):
2     if edgelow = edgehigh: return edgelow
3     node = {var, edgelow, edgehigh}
4     try:
5         return nodestable.insert-or-find(node)
6     catch TableFull:
7         garbagecollect()
8         return nodestable.insert-or-find(node)
```

Fig. 4. The **uniqueBDDnode** method creates a BDD node using the hash table **insert** method (Fig. 6) to ensure that there are no duplicate nodes. Line 2 ensures that there are no redundant nodes.

performed on the two subtasks in parallel, and the final result is computed using a hash table. See Fig. 3 for the **ite** algorithm. Other algorithms such as relational product and existential quantification are implemented similarly. To ensure that the results of BDD operations are canonical, reduced BDDs, they use a method **uniqueBDDnode** that employs a hash table as in Fig. 4.

We substituted the work-stealing framework Wool [14], that we used in the original version of Sylvan, by Lace [12], which we developed based on some ideas to minimize interactions between different workers and with memory. Lace is based around a novel work-stealing queue, which is described in detail in [12].

The parallel efficiency of a task-based parallelized algorithm depends in part on the contents of each task. If parallelized tasks mainly perform processor calculations and depend on many subtasks in a predictable or regular fashion, then they result in good speedups. However, if the number of subtasks is small and the subtasks are relatively shallow, i.e., the "task tree" has a low depth, then parallelization is more difficult. BDD tasks typically "spawn" only one or two subtasks for parallel execution, depending on the operation and the input BDDs.

BDD operations are also memory-intensive, since they consist mainly of operations on two data structures: a *unique table* that stores the unique BDD nodes and an *operation cache* that stores the results of BDD operations. The unique table is a hash table with support for garbage collection. The operation cache is a

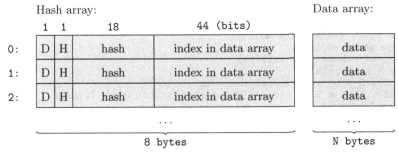

Fig. 5. Layout of the new lock-less hash table using a separate hash array **h** and data array **d**. **h**[n].D controls whether **d**[n] is used; **h**[n].H controls whether **h**[n] is used, i.e., the hash and index values correspond with an existing entry in the hash table. Every modification of **h**[n] must be performed using a compare_and_swap operation.

simplified hash table that overwrites on collision. Hence the design of concurrent scalable hash tables is crucial for a scalable BDD implementation.

3.1 Lock-Less Hash Table

In parallel programs, memory accesses are typically protected against race conditions using locking techniques. Locking severely cripples parallel performance, therefore Sylvan implements lock-less data structures that rely on the atomic compare_and_swap (cas) memory operation and short-lived local cas-locks to ensure parallel correctness as well as scalable performance.

Compared to [11], we implemented a new hash table based on the lock-less hash table presented in [19]. The new hash table consists of a *hash array* and a *data array*, as in Fig. 5. The data array simply stores fixed-sized data, such as BDD nodes and LDD nodes. We preallocate this data array to avoid losing scalability due to complex memory allocation management systems. Data can be stored at any position in the data array, and this position is recorded in the index field of the hash array. The advantage of storing data at any position is that this allows rehashing all BDD nodes without changing their position in the data array, which is important for efficient garbage collection.

The state of the buckets is manipulated using straight-forward cas-operations. Inserting data consists of three steps: searching whether the data is already in the table, claiming a bucket in the data array to store the data, and inserting the hash in the hash array. See Fig. 6.

First, the algorithm obtains a hash value of the data and a *probe sequence* similar to [19], which makes optimal use of memory management in modern systems. See further [19] for more details. The algorithm checks whether one of the hash buckets in the probe sequence already contains an entry with the same hash and with matching data in the data array. If so, it terminates.

If an empty hash bucket is reached, it searches for an empty data bucket (where D=0 in the hash array) and uses cas to set D=1, then writes the data. The position in the data array can be any position. In practice, we record the

```
 1 def insert-or-find(data):
 2   h = calculate_hash(data)
 3   ps = probe_sequence(data):
 4   while ps != empty:
 5     s, ps = head(ps), tail(ps)
 6     V = hasharr[s]
 7     if V.H = 0: goto EmptyBucketFound
 8     if V.hash = h && dataarr[V.index] = data: return V.index
 9   raise TableFull # abort: table full!

11 label EmptyBucketFound:
12   for d in (0..N): # note: traverse in smart order
13     W = hasharr[d]
14     if W.D=0:
15       if cas(hasharr[d],W,W[D=1]):
16         dataarr[idx]=data
17         goto EmptyDataSlotFound

19 label EmptyDataSlotFound:
20   while ps != empty: # note: continue same probe sequence
21     V = hasharr[s]
22     if V.H=0:
23       if cas(hasharr[s],V,V[H=1,hash=h,index=d]): return d
24     else:
25       if V.H = h && dataarr[V.index] = data:
26         W = hasharr[d]
27         while !cas(hasharr[d],W,W[D=0]): W = hasharr[d]
28         return V.index
29     s, ps = head(ps), tail(ps)
30   W = hasharr[d]
31   while !cas(hasharr[d],W,W[D=0]): W = hasharr[d]
32   raise TableFull # abort: table full!
```

Fig. 6. Algorithm for parallel **insert** of the lock-less hash table

empty data bucket of the previous **insert** call in a thread-specific variable, and continue from there. Initial values for this thread-specific variable are chosen such that all threads start at a different position in the data array.

After adding the entry in the data array, the algorithm continues with the probe sequence, starting where it found the empty hash bucket in the first step, to search either a matching hash with matching data (written by a concurrent thread), or an empty hash bucket. In the first case, the algorithm releases the data bucket by setting D=0 using **cas**. In the second case, it uses **cas** to set the values H, hash and index at once.

3.2   Sylvan API

Sylvan is released under the Apache 2.0 License, which means that anyone can freely use it and extend it. It comes with an example of a simple BDD-based reachability algorithm, which demonstrates how to use Sylvan to "automatically" parallelize sequential algorithms.

To use Sylvan, simply include **sylvan.h** or **lddmc.h** and initialize Lace and Sylvan. There is an API that exposes familiar BDD algorithms, such as **ite**,

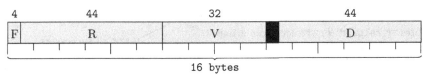

Fig. 7. Layout of an LDD node in memory. The F field is reserved for flags, such as "marked", and to indicate possible special node types. The R field contains the index of the LDD node $p[x_i > v]$ and the D field contains the index of the LDD node $p[x_i = v]$ in the LDD node table. The V field contains the 32-bit v value.

`exists`, `constrain`, `compose`, `satcount` and `relprod`, a specialized relational product for paired (x_i, x_i') variables. There is also functionality for drawing DOT graphs and writing/loading BDDs to/from disk. It is easy to add new algorithms by studying the implementation of current algorithms.

Sylvan is distributed with the work-stealing framework Lace. Lace can be integrated in other projects for out-of-the-box task-based parallelism. There are additional methods to integrate Lace worker threads with existing parallel approaches. Furthermore, we developed bindings for Java JNI[3] and Adam Walker developed bindings for Haskell[4], allowing parallelization of algorithms developed in those languages. Extending Sylvan with other types of decision diagrams requires copying files `sylvan.h` and `sylvan.c` and modifying the new files for the different algorithms, similar to what we did with LDDs.

3.3   LDDs in Sylvan

We extended Sylvan with an implementation of LDDs and various LDD algorithms. To represent LDD nodes in memory we use the layout described in Fig. 7. The size of each LDD node is 16 bytes and we allocate 32 bits to hold value v, i.e., the integer values of the state vector in PINS. In our design, 44 bits are reserved to store edges, which is sufficient for up to 2^{44} LDD nodes, i.e., 256 terabytes of just LDD nodes.

We implemented various LDD operations that are required for model checking in LTSMIN, especially `union`, `intersection`, `minus`, `project` (existential quantification), `enumerate` and `relprod` (relational product). These operations are all recursive and hence trivial to parallelize using the work-stealing framework Lace and the datastructures earlier developed for the BDD operations.

4   Parallelism in LTSMIN

4.1   Parallel Symbolic Reachability

Even with parallel operations, parallel scalability of model checking in LTSMIN is limited, especially in smaller models, when the size of "work units" (between

---

[3] Available from https://github.com/utwente-fmt/jsylvan
[4] Available from https://github.com/adamwalker/sylvan-haskell

states ⟶ `relprod` T_1 ⟶ successors group 1
states ⟶ `relprod` T_2 ⟶ successors group 2
states ⟶ `relprod` T_3 ⟶ successors group 3
states ⟶ `relprod` T_4 ⟶ successors group 4
⟩∪ ⟩∪ ⟶ all successors
⟩∪

Fig. 8. Schematic overview of parallel symbolic reachability. Note that the `relprod` and ∪ operations are also parallel operations internally.

```
1 def learn(states, i):
2     shorts = project(states, vars[i])
3     shorts = minus(shorts, visited[i])
4     visited[i] = union(visited[i], shorts)
5     enumerate(shorts, NextStateWrapper[i])
```

Fig. 9. On-the-fly learning in LTSMIN; `enumerate` calls NextStateWrapper[i] for each "short" state, which adds new transitions to `trans[i]`.

```
1 def learn_par(states, i):
2     shorts = project(states, vars[i])
3     shorts = minus(shorts, visited[i])
4     visited[i] = union(visited[i], shorts)
5     temp = collect(shorts, NextStateWrapperPar[i])
6     trans[i] = union(trans[i], temp)
```

Fig. 10. Parallel On-the-Fly Learning in LTSMIN. The `collect` method combines `enumerate` and `union`.

sequential points) is small and when the amount of parallelism in the work units is insufficient. Experiments in [11] demonstrate this limitation.

This is expected: if a parallel program consists of many small operations between sequential points, then we expect limited parallel scalability. If there are relatively few independent tasks in the "task tree" of a computation, then we also expect limited parallel scalability.

Since LTSMIN partitions the transition relation in transition groups (see Section 2.4), many small BDD operations are executed in sequence, for each transition group. We propose to calculate these operations in parallel and merge their results pairwise, as in Fig. 8. In Fig. 2, this corresponds to executing lines 7 and 8 in parallel. This strategy decreases the number of sequential points and thus increases the size of "work units". It also increases the amount of parallelism in the "task tree". We therefore expect improved parallel scalability.

4.2 Parallel On-the-Fly Learning

As described in Section 2.4, algorithms in LTSMIN learn new transitions on-the-fly, using a NextState function. The implementation of the `learn` algorithm used in Fig. 2, is given in Fig. 9. In LTSMIN, the transition relation of each transition group is only defined on a subset of the variables in the state vector. First the set of states is "projected" (using existential quantification) such that

```
1 def collect(states, callback, vec={}):
2    if states = 1: return callback(vec)
3    if states = 0: return ∅
4    do in parallel:
5        R0 = collect(follow-0(states), callback, vec+{0})
6        R1 = collect(follow-1(states), callback, vec+{1})
7    return union(R0, R1)
```

Fig. 11. The parallel `collect` algorithm (BDD version) combining `enumerate` and `union`. The callback is called for every state and the returned set is pairwise merged.

it is defined only on the variables relevant in transition group i. The `visited` set is used to remove all "short states" that were seen before. The `enumerate` method enumerates all states described by the BDD or LDD, i.e., all variable assignments that result in 1. For each state, it calls the supplied callback NEXTSTATEWRAPPER[i]. This method performs a `union` with `trans[i]` and every single discovered transition one by one. Note that this is not thread-safe.

Similar to calculating the relational product for every transition group in parallel, we can perform on-the-fly transition learning for every transition group in parallel. However, there are more opportunities for parallelism.

In Fig. 9, the `project` (existential quantification), `minus` ("diff") and `union` ("or") operations are already parallelized. The `enumerate` method is trivial to parallelize, but the callback wrappper is not thread-safe. We substituted this implementation by a new design that uses a method `collect`. See Fig. 10. The NEXTSTATEWRAPPERPAR callback in Fig. 10 adds all transitions for a state to a small temporary decision diagram and returns this decision diagram to the caller. The method `collect` (Fig. 11) performs enumeration in parallel (lines 4–6), and performs a `union` on the results of the two subtasks.

This method works in LTSMIN for all language modules that are thread-safe, and has been tested for mCRL2 and DVE models.

5   Experimental Evaluation

In the current section, we evaluate the presented LDD extension of Sylvan, and the application of parallelization to LTSMIN. As in [11], we base our experimental evaluation mostly on the BEEM model database [25], but in contrast to [11], we use the entire BEEM model database rather than a selection of models. We perform these experiments on a 48-core machine, consisting of 4 AMD Opteron[TM] 6168 processors with 12 cores each and 128 GB of internal memory.

5.1   Fully Parallel On-the-Fly Symbolic Model Checking

We perform symbolic reachability using the LTSMIN toolset using the following command: `dve2lts-sym --order=<order> --vset=lddmc -rgs <model>.dve`.

We also select as size of the unique table 2^{30} buckets and as size of the operation cache also 2^{30} buckets. Using parameter `--order` we either select the

Experiment	T_1	T_{16}	T_{24}	T_{32}	T_{48}	Speedup T_{48}/T_1
`blocks.4` (par)	629.54	41.61	29.26	23.04	16.58	38.0
`blocks.4` (bfs)	630.04	45.88	33.24	27.01	21.69	29.0
`telephony.8` (par)	843.70	58.17	41.17	32.76	24.68	34.2
`telephony.8` (bfs)	843.06	66.28	47.91	39.17	31.10	27.1
`lifts.8` (par)	377.52	25.92	18.68	15.18	12.03	31.4
`lifts.8` (bfs)	377.36	36.61	30.06	27.68	26.11	14.5
`firewire_tree.1` (par)	16.40	1.09	0.97	0.94	0.99	16.5
`firewire_tree.1` (bfs)	16.43	11.24	11.12	11.36	11.35	1.4
Sum of all `par-prev`	20756	1851	1552	1403	1298	16.0
Sum of all `bfs-prev`	20745	3902	3667	3625	3737	5.6

Fig. 12. Results of running symbolic reachability on 269 models of the BEEM database. Each value T_n is the result of at least 3 measurements and is in seconds.

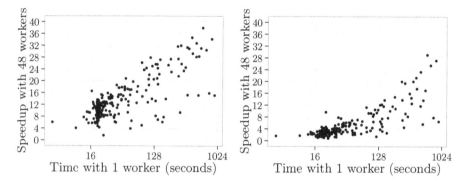

Fig. 13. Results of all models in the BEEM database that did not time out, with fully parallel learning and parallel transition groups (`par-prev`) on the left, and only parallel BDD operations (`bfs-prev`) on the right

`par-prev` variation or the `bfs-prev` variation. The `bfs-prev` variation does not have parallelism in LTSMIN, but it uses the parallelized LDD operations, including `collect`. This means that there is parallel learning, but only for one transition group at a time. In the `par-prev` variation, learning and calculating the successors are performed for all transition groups in parallel.

We measure the time spent to execute symbolic reachability, excluding time spent initializing LTSMIN. We use a timeout of 1200 seconds. Of all models in the BEEM database, only 7 timed out: `collision.6`, `driving_phils.3`, `driving_phils.5`, `elevator.5`, `frogs.4`, `hanoi.3`, and `public_subscribe.5`. We present here the results for the remaining 269 models. Each benchmark is performed at least 3 times.

See Fig. 12 for the results of this benchmark. Model `blocks.4` results in the highest speedup with `par-prev`, which is 38.0x. We also highlight the model

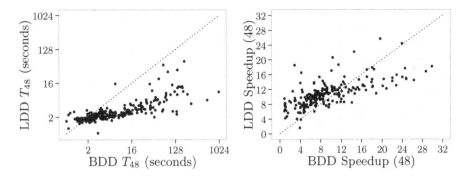

Fig. 14. Results of all models that did not time out for both BDDs and LDDs, comparing time with 48 workers (left) and obtained speedups (right)

`lifts.8` which has a speedup of 14.5x with `bfs-prev` and more than twice as high with `par-prev`. Fig. 13 shows that "larger" models are associated with a better parallel performance.

Fig. 13 also shows that adding parallellism on the algorithmic level benefits the parallel performance of many models. One of the largest improvements was obtained with the `firewire_tree.1` model, which went from 1.4x to 16.5x. We conclude that the bottleneck was the lack of parallelism.

In addition, Fig. 12 shows that the overhead between the "sequential" `bfs-prev` and "parallel" `par-prev` versions is negligible. Taking the time spent for the entire benchmark set, we see that the speedup of the entire benchmark is 16.0x for the fully parallelized version. For all models, the speedup improves with `par-prev`. The only exception is `peg_solitaire.1`, for which $T_{48} = 2.38$ with `par-prev`, and $T_{48} = 2.35$ with `bfs-prev`, which is within measurement error.

5.2 BDDs and LDDs

We now compare the performance of our multi-core BDD and LDD variants. We do this for the `par-prev` algorithm. Fig. 14 shows that the majority of models, especially larger models, are performed up to several orders of magnitude faster using LDDs. The most extreme example is model `frogs.3`, which has for BDDs $T_1 = 989.40$, $T_{48} = 1005.96$ and for LDDs $T_1 = 61.01$, $T_{48} = 9.36$. Some models are missing that timed out for BDDs but did not time out for LDDs, for example model `blocks.4`.

6   Conclusions

In the current paper we presented several modifications to Sylvan, such as a new hash table implementation for Sylvan and the replacement of the work-stealing framework by Lace. We also discussed how we extended Sylvan to implement parallel LDD operations and the specialized BDD/LDD method `collect` that parallelizes on-the-fly transition learning. We measured the performance of this implementation using symbolic reachability in LTSMIN applied to models from the BEEM model benchmark database. This resulted in a speedup of up to 38.0x when also applying parallelism on the algorithmic level in LTSMIN, or up to 29.0x when just using parallelized operations in an otherwise sequential symbolic reachability algorithm.

BDDs and other decision diagrams are also important in other domains. We conclude that sequential algorithms benefit from "automatic" parallelization using parallel BDD and LDD operations in Sylvan. We also conclude that additional parallelism at the algorithmic level results in significant improvements.

Our parallel BDD package is open-source and publicly available online and is easy to integrate with existing software, also using Java JNI bindings and Haskell bindings.

References

1. Akers, S.: Binary Decision Diagrams. IEEE Trans. Computers C-27(6), 509–516 (1978)
2. Blom, S., van de Pol, J.: Symbolic Reachability for Process Algebras with Recursive Data Types. In: Fitzgerald, J.S., Haxthausen, A.E., Yenigun, H. (eds.) ICTAC 2008. LNCS, vol. 5160, pp. 81–95. Springer, Heidelberg (2008)
3. Blom, S., van de Pol, J., Weber, M.: LTSmin: distributed and symbolic reachability. In: Touili, T., Cook, B., Jackson, P. (eds.) CAV 2010. LNCS, vol. 6174, pp. 354–359. Springer, Heidelberg (2010)
4. Blumofe, R.D.: Scheduling multithreaded computations by work stealing. In: FOCS, pp. 356–368. IEEE Computer Society (1994)
5. Bryant, R.E.: Graph-Based Algorithms for Boolean Function Manipulation. IEEE Trans. Computers C-35(8), 677–691 (1986)
6. Burch, J.R., Clarke, E.M., Long, D.E., McMillan, K.L., Dill, D.L.: Symbolic model checking for sequential circuit verification. IEEE Transactions on Computer-Aided Design of Integrated Circuits and Systems 13(4), 401–424 (1994)
7. Chung, M.Y., Ciardo, G.: Saturation NOW. In: QEST, pp. 272–281. IEEE Computer Society (2004)
8. Ciardo, G., Marmorstein, R.M., Siminiceanu, R.: Saturation Unbound. In: Garavel, H., Hatcliff, J. (eds.) TACAS 2003. LNCS, vol. 2619, pp. 379–393. Springer, Heidelberg (2003)
9. van Dijk, T.: The Parallelization of Binary Decision Diagram operations for model checking. Master's thesis, University of Twente, Dept. of C.S (April 2012)
10. van Dijk, T., Laarman, A.W., van de Pol, J.C.: Multi-core and/or Symbolic Model Checking. ECEASST 53 (2012)
11. van Dijk, T., Laarman, A.W., van de Pol, J.C.: Multi-Core BDD Operations for Symbolic Reachability. In: 11th International Workshop on Parallel and Distributed Methods in verification. ENTCS. Elsevier (2012)
12. van Dijk, T., van de Pol, J.C.: Lace: non-blocking split deque for work-stealing. In: Lopes, L., et al. (eds.) Euro-Par 2014, Part II. LNCS, vol. 8806, pp. 206–217. Springer, Heidelberg (2014)
13. Ezekiel, J., Lüttgen, G., Ciardo, G.: Parallelising symbolic state-space generators. In: Damm, W., Hermanns, H. (eds.) CAV 2007. LNCS, vol. 4590, pp. 268–280. Springer, Heidelberg (2007)

14. Faxén, K.F.: Efficient work stealing for fine grained parallelism. In: 39th International Conference on Parallel Processing (ICPP), pp. 313–322. IEEE Computer Society, Los Alamitos (2010)

15. Grumberg, O., Heyman, T., Schuster, A.: A work-efficient distributed algorithm for reachability analysis. Formal Methods in System Design 29(2), 157–175 (2006)

16. Kam, T., Villa, T., Brayton, R.K., Sangiovanni-vincentelli, A.L.: Multi-valued decision diagrams: theory and applications. Multiple-Valued Logic 4(1), 9–62 (1998)

17. Kant, G., Laarman, A.W., Meijer, J., van de Pol, J.C., Blom, S., van Dijk, T.: LTSmin: High-Performance Language-Independent Model Checking. In: TACAS 2015 (2015)

18. Kimura, S., Igaki, T., Haneda, H.: Parallel Binary Decision Diagram Manipulation. IEICE Transactions on Fundamentals of Electronics, Communications and Computer Science E75-A(10), 1255–1262 (1992)

19. Laarman, A.W., van de Pol, J.C., Weber, M.: Boosting multi-core reachability performance with shared hash tables. In: Formal Methods in Computer-Aided Design, pp. 247–255. IEEE (October 2010)

20. Laarman, A.W., van de Pol, J.C., Weber, M.: Multi-Core LTSmin: Marrying Modularity and Scalability. In: Bobaru, M., Havelund, K., Holzmann, G.J., Joshi, R. (eds.) NFM 2011. LNCS, vol. 6617, pp. 506–511. Springer, Heidelberg (2011)

21. Lovato, A., Macedonio, D., Spoto, F.: A Thread-Safe Library for Binary Decision Diagrams. In: Giannakopoulou, D., Salaün, G. (eds.) SEFM 2014. LNCS, vol. 8702, pp. 35–49. Springer, Heidelberg (2014)

22. Miller, D.M., Drechsler, R.: On the Construction of Multiple-Valued Decision Diagrams. In: 32nd IEEE International Symposium on Multiple-Valued Logic (ISMVL 2002), pp. 245–253. IEEE Computer Society (2002)

23. Milvang-Jensen, K., Hu, A.J.: BDDNOW: A parallel BDD package. In: Gopalakrishnan, G.C., Windley, P. (eds.) FMCAD 1998. LNCS, vol. 1522, pp. 501–507. Springer, Heidelberg (1998)

24. Ossowski, J.: JINC – A Multi-Threaded Library for Higher-Order Weighted Decision Diagram Manipulation. Ph.D. thesis, Rheinischen Friedrich-Wilhelms-Universität Bonn (October 2010)

25. Pelánek, R.: BEEM: benchmarks for explicit model checkers. In: Bošnački, D., Edelkamp, S. (eds.) SPIN 2007. LNCS, vol. 4595, pp. 263–267. Springer, Heidelberg (2007)

26. Sahoo, D., Jain, J., Iyer, S.K., Dill, D.L., Emerson, E.A.: Multi-threaded reachability. In: Proceedings of the 42nd Annual Design Automation Conference, DAC 2005, pp. 467–470. ACM, New York (2005)

27. Stornetta, T., Brewer, F.: Implementation of an efficient parallel BDD package. In: Proceedings of the 33rd Annual Design Automation Conference, DAC 1996, pp. 641–644. ACM, New York (1996)

LTSmin: High-Performance Language-Independent Model Checking

Gijs Kant[1,*], Alfons Laarman[1,2,§], Jeroen Meijer[1], Jaco van de Pol[1]
Stefan Blom[1,‡], and Tom van Dijk[1,‖]

[1] Formal Methods and Tools, University of Twente, The Netherlands
[2] Formal Methods in Systems Engineering, Vienna University of Technology, Austria

Abstract. In recent years, the LTSMIN model checker has been extended with support for several new modelling languages, including probabilistic (MAPA) and timed systems (UPPAAL). Also, connecting additional language front-ends or ad-hoc state-space generators to LTSMIN was simplified using custom C-code. From symbolic and distributed reachability analysis and minimisation, LTSMIN's functionality has developed into a model checker with multi-core algorithms for on-the-fly LTL checking with partial-order reduction, and multi-core symbolic checking for the modal μ-calculus, based on the multi-core decision diagram package SYLVAN.

In LTSMIN, the modelling languages and the model checking algorithms are connected through a Partitioned Next-State Interface (PINS), that allows to abstract away from language details in the implementation of the analysis algorithms and on-the-fly optimisations. In the current paper, we present an overview of the toolset and its recent changes, and we demonstrate its performance and versatility in two case studies.

1 Introduction

The LTSMIN model checker has a modular architecture which allows a number of modelling language front-ends to be connected to various analysis algorithms, through a common interface. It provides both symbolic and explicit-state analysis algorithms for many different languages, enabling multiple ways to attack verification problems. This connecting interface is called *Partitioned Next-State Interface* (PINS), the basis of which consists of a state-vector definition, an initial state, a *partitioned* successor function (NEXTSTATE), and labelling functions. PINS defines an implicit state space, abstracting away from modelling language details.

The main difference with other language interfaces, such as the OPEN/CÆSAR interface [21] of CADP [22] and the CESMI interface of DIVINE [3], is the structure that PINS exposes by exporting dependencies between the *partitioned* successor

* Supported by the NWO under grant 612.000.937 (VOCHS).

§ Supported by the Austrian National Research Network S11403-N23 (RiSE) of the Austrian Science Fund (FWF) and by the Vienna Science and Technology Fund (WWTF) grant VRG11-005.

‡ Partially funded by NWO under grant 612.063.817 (SYRUP).

‖ Supported by the NWO under grant 612.001.001 (MaDriD).

© Springer-Verlag Berlin Heidelberg 2015
C. Baier and C. Tinelli (Eds.): TACAS 2015, LNCS 9035, pp. 692–707, 2015.
DOI: 10.1007/978-3-662-46681-0_61

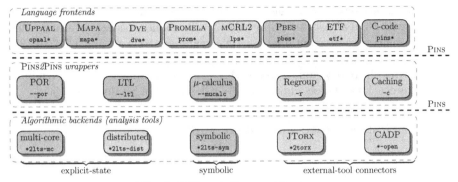

Fig. 1. LTSMIN's PINS architecture

function and the variables in the state vector in the form of *dependency matrices*. Our approach is also dissimilar from NUSMV's [9], where the transition *relation* is specified directly, imposing restrictions on the language. In the past, we have shown that these dependencies enable symbolic reachability using BDDs/MDDs with multiple orders of magnitude performance improvement [7,8] as well as (explicit-state) distributed reachability with state compression [6].

Recently, we extended PINS with separate read and write dependency matrices, special state labels for guards, and guard/transition dependency matrices. This extended interface, which we call PINS+, enables further performance improvements for the symbolic tools [40] and on-the-fly *partial-order reduction* (POR) [32] for the explicit-state tools. PINS+ will be presented in Section 2.

LTSMIN offers extensive analysis of implicit state spaces through PINS: reachability analysis, including deadlock detection, action detection and invariant/assertion checking, but since recently also verification of Linear Time (LTL) and modal μ-calculus properties. The toolset and its architecture have been previously presented in, e.g., [7], [5] and [8]. This article covers the changes since then. An up-to-date overview of LTSMIN is in Figure 1; this paper focuses on the pink (dark) boxes. The toolset is open source.[1]

The languages supported by LTSMIN are listed in Table 1, including newly added support for probabilistic (MAPA) and timed systems (UPPAAL) and for boolean equation systems with data types (PBES). New is also the possibility to add a new language front-end by providing a dynamically loaded .so-library implementing the PINS interface. These additions will be presented in Section 3.

Table 1. Languages supported by LTSMIN

UPPAAL	Timed automata.
MAPA	Process algebra for Markov automata from the SCOOP tool.
DVE	The modelling language of the DIVINE model checker.
PROMELA	The modelling language of the SPIN model checker.
MCRL2	Process algebra.
PBES	Parameterised Boolean Equation Systems.
ETF	Built-in symbolic format.

---

[1] Source code available at: `https://github.com/utwente-fmt/ltsmin`

In the explicit-state tools, new multi-core algorithms provide scalable LTL checking with POR and state compression. The symbolic tools have been extended with the multi-core *decision diagram* (DD) packages SYLVAN and LDDMC, enabling multi-core symbolic analysis algorithms by parallelising their DD operations. A symbolic parity game solver has been added, enabling multi-core symbolic μ-calculus checking. These additions will be described in Section 4 and 5.

2   The PINS-Architecture of LTSMIN

The starting point of our approach is a generalised implicit model of systems, called the *Partioned Next-State Interface* (PINS). An overview of PINS functions is in Table 2. The functions INITIALSTATE, NEXTSTATE and STATELABEL are mandatory, as well as the state vector length N, the number of transition groups K, and the names and types of labels, slots and actions. Together, these give rise to a transition system, see Section 2.1.

On top of this basic PINS interface, we distinguish several axes of extensions, A1 till A∞, which together form the extended PINS+ interface. These extensions allow to expose enough structure, in the form of information about dependency relations, to enable high-performance algorithms. The first axis of such information is provided by the functions labelled A1: the read and write dependency matrices (see [40]). LTSMIN's POR layer (see Section 4.3) requires guards, exported as special state labels, and the GUARDMATRIX, STATELABELM and DONOTACCORD dependency matrices – the functions labelled A2. The definitions of the dependencies and guards are given in Section 2.2.

The simulation relation over states provided by the COVEREDBY function, labelled A3, allows powerful *subsumption abstraction* [14] in our algorithms. Timed language formalisms allow such abstractions as described in Section 3.2. In the future, a symmetry-reduction layer, a la [17], could implement COVEREDBY.

Other named matrices, can be added to the generic GETMATRIX function, which we label A∞. This is used to increase POR's precision and facilitate statistical systems such as with MAPA (see Section 3.1).

We write MATRIX(x) as shorthand for $\{y \mid (x, y) \in \text{MATRIX}\}$.

Table 2. Functions in PINS+ are divided along multiple axes

Level	Function	Type	Description
B0	INITIALSTATE	$S_{\mathcal{P}}$	Initial state.
B0	NEXTSTATE$_i$	$S_{\mathcal{P}} \to \wp(\mathcal{A} \times S_{\mathcal{P}})$	Successors and action label for group i.
B0	STATELABEL	$S_{\mathcal{P}} \times \mathcal{L} \to \mathbb{N}$	State label.
A1	READMATRIX	$\mathbb{B}^{K \times N}$	Read dependency matrix (Definition 2).
A1	WRITEMATRIX	$\mathbb{B}^{K \times N}$	Write dependency matrix (Definition 3).
A2	GUARDMATRIX	$\mathbb{B}^{K \times G}$	Guard/transition group matrix (Definition 5).
A2	STATELABELM	$\mathbb{B}^{G \times N}$	State label dependency matrix (Definition 4).
A2	DONOTACCORD	$\mathbb{B}^{K \times K}$	Matrix for non-commutativity of groups [32].
A3	COVEREDBY	$S_{\mathcal{P}} \times S_{\mathcal{P}} \to \mathbb{B}$	State covering function.
A∞	GETMATRIX$_{Name}$	$\mathbb{B}^{X \times Y}$	Predefined $X \times Y$ matrix named *Name*.

2.1 Partitioned Transition Systems

In PINS, states are vectors of N values. We write $\langle s_1, \ldots, s_N \rangle$, for vector variables, or simply s for the state vector. Each position j in the vector ($1 \leq j \leq N$) is called a *slot* and has a unique identifier and a type, which are used in the language front-ends to specify conditions and updates. The NEXTSTATE function, which computes the successors of a state, is partitioned in K disjunctive *transition groups*, such that NEXTSTATE(s) $= \bigcup_{1 \leq i \leq K}$ NEXTSTATE$_i(s)$. We have action labels $a \in \mathcal{A}$ and a set of M state labels $\mathcal{L}$. A model, available through PINS, gives rise to a *Partitioned Transition System* (PTS).

Definition 1. *A PTS is a structure* $\mathcal{P} = \langle S_\mathcal{P}, \rightarrow_\mathcal{P}, s^0, L \rangle$, *where*

- $S_\mathcal{P} = S_1 \times \cdots \times S_N$ *is the set of states* $s \in S_\mathcal{P}$, *which are vectors of N values,*
- $\rightarrow_\mathcal{P} = \bigcup_{i=1}^{K} \rightarrow_i$ *is the labelled transition relation, which is a union of the K transition groups* $\rightarrow_i \subseteq S_\mathcal{P} \times \mathcal{A} \times S_\mathcal{P}$ *(for* $1 \leq i \leq K$*),*
- $s^0 = \langle s_1^0, \ldots, s_N^0 \rangle \in S_\mathcal{P}$ *is the initial state, and*
- $L : S_\mathcal{P} \times \mathcal{L} \rightarrow \mathbb{N}$ *is a state labelling function.*

We write $s \xrightarrow{a}_i t$ *when* $(s, a, t) \in \rightarrow_i$ *for* $1 \leq i \leq K$, *and* $s \xrightarrow{a}_\mathcal{P} t$ *when* $(s, a, t) \in \rightarrow_\mathcal{P}$. *Considering* $\mathcal{L}$ *as binary state labels,* $L(s)$ *denotes the set of labels that hold in state* s, *i.e. we define* $L(s) := \{\ell \mid L(s, \ell) \neq 0\}$.

When the LTL layer is used, the output PTS is interpreted as a *Büchi automaton*, where accepting states are marked using a special state label. When using the μ-calculus layer or the PBES front-end, the output PTS is interpreted as a *parity game*, where two state labels encode the *player* and the *priority*. When using the MAPA front-end, the output is a *Markov automaton*, where transitions are decorated with labels, representing hyperedges with rates. For all these interpretations, the same PINS interface is used.

2.2 Dependencies and Guards

The partitioning of the state vector into *slots* and of the transition relations into *transition groups*, enables to specify the *dependencies* between the two, i.e., which transition groups touch which slots of the vector.

Previously, we used a single notion of dependency; now we distinguish read, write and label dependencies [32, 40]. The read and write dependencies allow to *project* state vectors to relevant slots only, improving performance of both caching, state compression and the symbolic tools. Label dependencies enable POR. The following definitions apply to each PTS $\mathcal{P} = \langle S_\mathcal{P}, \rightarrow_\mathcal{P}, s^0, L \rangle$.

Definition 2 (Read independence). *Transition group i is* read-independent *from state slot j, if for all $s, t \in S_\mathcal{P}$ with $s \rightarrow_i t$, we have:*

$$\forall r_j \exists r_j' \in S_j : \langle s_1, \ldots, r_j, \ldots, s_N \rangle \rightarrow_i \langle t_1, \ldots, r_j', \ldots, t_N \rangle \wedge r_j' \in \{r_j, t_j\} \ ,$$

i.e., whatever value r_j we plug in, the transition is still possible, the values t_k ($k \neq j$) do not depend on the value of r_j, and the value of state slot j is either copied ($r_j' = r_j$) or overwritten ($r_j' = t_j$).

Definition 3 (Write independence). *Transition group i is* write-independent *from state slot j, if:*

$$\forall s, t \in S_{\mathcal{P}}\colon \langle s_1, \ldots, s_j, \ldots, s_N \rangle \rightarrow_i \langle t_1, \ldots, t_j, \ldots, t_N \rangle \Rightarrow (s_j = t_j) \ ,$$

i.e., state slot j is never modified in transition group i.

Definition 4 (Label independence). *Label $l \in \mathcal{L}$ is* independent *from state slot j, if:*

$$\forall s \in S_{\mathcal{P}}, t_j \in S_j\colon L(\langle s_1, \ldots, s_j, \ldots, s_N \rangle, l) = L(\langle s_1, \ldots, t_j, \ldots, s_N \rangle, l) \ .$$

Definition 5 (Guards). *Transition guards are represented as a subset of labels $\mathcal{G} \subseteq \mathcal{L}$. With each transition group we associate a set of guards. The guards associated with group i, denoted $\mathcal{G}(i)$, are evaluated conjunctively, i.e., transition group i is only enabled in state s if all guards $g \in \mathcal{G}(i)$ hold: if $s \rightarrow_i t$ then $\mathcal{G}(i) \subseteq L(s)$.*

We have provided semantic requirements for read, write and label independence relations. The language front-end must provide these dependency matrices. It can approximate dependencies using static analysis, for instance by checking occurrence of variables in expressions. Note that it is always safe to assume that groups/labels do depend on a state slot.

3   Language Front-Ends

LTSMIN already supported the languages MCRL2 [11], DIVINE [3], and SPIN's PROMELA [26] (through SPINS [4]). Since recently, also MAPA, UPPAAL and PBES are available, as well as the ability to load a model from a binary .so-file, all of which will be discussed in the current section.

3.1   MAPA: Markov Automata Process Algebra

For verification of quantitative aspects of systems, we support MAPA: *Markov Automata Process Algebra*. MA's are automata with non-deterministic choice, probabilistic choice and stochastic rates, generalising LTS, PA, MDP and CTMC. The SCOOP tool [43] offers state-space generation for MAPA specifications, applying several reduction techniques. It is part of the MAMA toolchain [25] for the quantitative analysis of Markov automata. LTSMIN has been extended with a MAPA language module based on SCOOP, allowing for high-performance state space generation for MAPA specifications. This language module uses PINS+ A∞ to add an *inhibit matrix* and a *confluence matrix*. The maximum progress assumption in the semantics of Markov automata forbids taking stochastic rate transitions when some action-labelled transition is enabled. This has been implemented using a *inhibit matrix*: when the higher priority transition is enabled, other transitions are inhibited. The distributed and symbolic tools of LTSMIN have been extended to handle inhibit matrices for MAPA. The distributed tool also includes confluence reduction.

3.2   Uppaal: Timed Automata

The langague frontend for UPPAAL timed automata is based on OPAAL [12]. The C-code generated by OPAAL implements the PINS+ A3 interface. Timed automata require symbolic states to handle time, for which OPAAL relies on the *difference bounds matrices* from the DBM-library. This is supported by PINS, by dedicating two reserved state slots for a pointer to a symbolic time abstraction.

Subsumption abstraction can prune large parts of the PTS on-the-fly. LTSMIN checks if two states subsume each other ($s \sqsubseteq t$) via the COVEREDBY-relation in PINS+, which is implemented by a call to the DBM-library. The reduced state space only consists of $\sqsubseteq$-maximal states. Since $\sqsubseteq$ is a simulation relation [14], the reduced PTS is a valid abstraction of the original PTS. The reachability algorithms in the multi-core tool perform this abstraction (`opaal2lts-mc -u2`). To maintain $\sqsubseteq$-maximal states, the pointers to the DBMs are stored in a separate lockless multi-map [12].

A new LTL model checking algorithm with subsumption [36] is also supported, by extending the multi-core CNDFS algorithm (see Section 5.1).

3.3   PBES: Parameterized Boolean Equation Systems

Parameterised Boolean Equation Systems (PBESs) extend Boolean equations with nested fixed points and data parameters [24, 39]. Several verification tasks are mapped to PBESs by the MCRL2 and CADP toolsets, such as model checking modal μ-calculus properties and equivalence checking. The MCRL2 toolset offers various tools for manipulating and solving PBESs. LTSMIN now provides high-performance generation of parity games from PBESs [29], by viewing them as PTSs with special labels for players and priorities. The PBES language module is available via the `pbes2lts-*` tools. The generated parity games can be solved by the means described in Section 5.

3.4   C-Code via the Dlopen Interface

The UNIX/POSIX dlopen-interface allows to specify a model or a language directly in C. We show an example of how this can be done for the Sokoban game board in Figure 2. The goal of sokoban is for the player (@) to move all boxes ($) in the room to destination locations (.) without hitting walls (#). This behaviour is implemented in the function `next_state` in Listing 1. For each place in the board, we reserve one slot in the state vector. We add a state label `goal`, to distinguish states where the game is finished. Finally, an `initial_state` function is defined, and functions returning dependency matrices. These need to be set using the `GBset*` functions in Listing 2. Setting the name of the plugin is also required. `sokoboard.c` is then compiled as shared library:

Fig. 2.
Example board

`gcc -shared -o sokoboard.so dlopen-impl.o sokoboard.o.`

To analyse the reachability of the goal label, call, e.g., the multi-core tool:

`pins2lts-mc sokoboard.so --invariant="!goal" --trace=solution.gcf.`

Listing 1. sokoboard.c

```
void next_state(int group, int* src,
    void (*callback)(int* dst, int action))
{ int dst[3]; int action;
  memcpy(dst, src, 3);
  if (group == 0
    && src[1] == EMPTY && src[2] == MAN)
  { dst[1] = MAN; dst[2] = EMPTY;
    action = WALK_LEFT;
    callback(dst, action);
  }
  else if (group == 1
    && src[1] == MAN && src[2] == EMPTY)
  { dst[1] = EMPTY; dst[2] = MAN;
    action = WALK_RIGHT;
    callback(dst, action);
  }
  else if (group == 2 && src[0] == EMPTY
    && src[1] == BOX && src[2] == MAN)
  { dst[0] = BOX; dst[1] = MAN;
    dst[2] = EMPTY; action = PUSH_LEFT;
    callback(dst, action);
  }
}

int state_label(int* src, int label)
{return label == LABEL_GOAL && src[0] == BOX;}
```

```
int* initial_state()
{ return {EMPTY, BOX, MAN}; }

int* read_matrix()
{ return {{0,1,1}, {0,1,1}, {1,1,1}}; }

int* write_matrix()
{ return {{0,1,1}, {0,1,1}, {1,1,1}}; }

int* label_matrix()
{ return {{1,0,0}}; }
```

Listing 2. dlopen-impl.c

```
#include <ltsmin/pins.h>
#include <ltsmin/dlopen-api.h>
#include <sokoboard.h>
char pins_plugin_name[] = "sokoban";
void pins_model_init(model_t m)
{ GBsetInitialState(m, initial_state());
  GBsetNextStateLong(m, next_state);
  GBsetStateLabelLong(m, state_label);
  GBsetDMInfoRead(m, read_matrix());
  GBsetDMInfoMustWrite(m, write_matrix());
  GBsetStateLabelInfo(m, label_matrix());
}
```

4   Intermediate Layers

Between language front-ends and the model checking back-ends, PINS2PINS-wrappers provide performance optimisations, state space reductions, and support for verification of LTL and μ-calculus properties. The *caching layer* reduces the number of next-state calls to the language module by storing the projected results of previous calls. The *regrouping layer* provides variable reordering, useful for the symbolic analysis tool, and reduces overhead by merging transition groups. The current section describes recent innovations in the intermediate layers, which are all language-independent and agnostic of the underlying model checking algorithm.

4.1   The LTL Layer

LTSMIN supports Linear Time Logic (LTL) formulae defined by the grammar:

$$\lambda ::= \texttt{true} \mid \texttt{false} \mid v\texttt{==}n \mid !\lambda \mid [\,]\lambda \mid <>\lambda \mid \texttt{X}\,\lambda \mid \lambda\texttt{\&\&}\lambda \mid \lambda||\lambda \mid \lambda\texttt{->}\lambda \mid \lambda\texttt{<->}\lambda \mid \lambda\texttt{U}\lambda \mid \lambda\texttt{R}\lambda$$

The negated formula is translated to a Büchi automaton using ltl2ba [23]. The product of the PTS and the Büchi automaton is computed on-the-fly, i.e., the layer does not perform reachability in advance. Instead, it wraps the NEXTSTATE function of a language module in its own NEXTSTATE function, which synchronises the translated Büchi automaton on the state labels or slot values of successor states (the expression $v == n$ can refer to a label or a slot named v). The synchronised successors are then passed to the analysis algorithm. A label added by the layer allows the algorithm to distinguish Büchi accepting states. On-the-fly accepting cycle detection algorithms are described in Section 5.1.

4.2 The μ-calculus Layer

The modal μ-calculus layer supports formulae defined by the grammar:

$$\varphi ::= \texttt{true} \mid \texttt{false} \mid \{v = e\} \mid !\{v = e\} \mid \varphi \ \&\& \ \varphi \mid \varphi \ || \ \varphi \mid Z \mid \sigma Z \,.\, \varphi \mid [\alpha]\varphi \mid <\alpha>\varphi \ ,$$

where v is a state variable, e is a value, $\sigma \in \{\texttt{mu}, \texttt{nu}\}$ is a minimal (mu) or maximal (nu) fixpoint operator, and α is an action label.

The μ-calculus PINS2PINS layer reads a modal μ-calculus property φ from a file, provided using the `--mucalc` option, and generates a parity game, which is the product $\mathcal{P} \times \varphi$ of the formula and a system $\mathcal{P}$ that is explored through PINS. Like the Büchi automaton, this game is generated on-the-fly. The explicit-state tools can write the parity game to a file which can be converted to a format that is readable by the tools `pgsolver` [20] and `pbespgsolve` (from MCRL2). The symbolic tools can write the game to a file, which can be solved by the new LTSMIN tool `spgsolver`. The symbolic tools also have an alternative implementation for μ-calculus model checking (available through the `--mu` option), which is a fixpoint algorithm applied to the system after reachability. This implementation also supports CTL* through the translation in [13] (the `--ctl-star` option).

4.3 The Partial-Order Reduction Layer

Partial-Order Reduction (POR, [30,44]) greatly reduces a PTS by pruning irrelevant interleavings. LTSMIN implements POR as an intermediate layer (cf. Figure 1). This POR layer (`--por`) wraps the next-state function of any language module, and provides a reduced state space to any analysis tool by replacing it with an *on-the-fly* reduction function: $\text{PORSTATE}(s) \subseteq \text{NEXTSTATE}(s)$.

We rephrased the stubborn set method [44] in terms of guards [32] to achieve language independence. For any state, a set of (enabled or disabled) stubborn transitions is computed, and $\text{PORSTATE}(s)$ corresponds to the enabled stubborn transitions. The stubborn set should (1) contain at least one enabled transition if one exists; (2) contain all non-commuting transitions for the *enabled* selected transitions; and (3) contain a *necessary-enabling set* of transitions for the *disabled* selected transitions.

To compute stubborn sets, LTSMIN needs structural model information via the PINS+ A2 interface. For effective POR, we extended PINS transitions with guards (Definition 5). In particular, a language module must declare when transitions commute, and the dependencies of guards (Definition 4). The former is declared with the $\text{DONOTACCORD} : \mathbb{B}^{K \times K}$-matrix. It should satisfy:

Definition 6 (Do-not-accord). *Transition groups i and j are according, if*

$$\forall s, s_i, s_j \in s : s \rightarrow_i s_i \wedge s \rightarrow_j s_j \Rightarrow \exists t \in s : s_i \rightarrow_j t \wedge s_j \rightarrow_i t$$

Otherwise, they must be declared conflicting in the DONOTACCORD matrix.

Next, the POR layer derives an enabling relation from the provided dependency information. A transition i can only enable guard g, if i writes to a variable that g depends on: $\text{ENABLEMATRIX}^{K \times G} \equiv \{(i,g) \mid \text{WRITEMATRIX}(i) \cap$

STATELABELM(g) $\neq \emptyset$}. A set of necessary-enabling transitions for a disabled transition j can then be found by selecting *one* disabled guard g of j and taking all transitions that may enable g: ENABLEMATRIX(g).

Optionally, these notions can be further refined by the language module for more reduction, by providing additional PINS+ A_∞ matrices. For example, the language module can compute a detailed ENABLEMATRIX by static analysis on assignment expressions and guards, or a DISABLEMATRIX and a CO-ENABLED-MATRIX on guards to leverage the power of *necessary disabling sets* [32].

LTSMIN contains heuristics to compute small stubborn sets efficiently. The user can select a fast heuristic search (`--por=heur`) or the subset-minimal deletion algorithm (`--por=del`). POR preserves at least all deadlock states. The multi-core algorithms in LTSMIN preserves all liveness properties, but this requires additional interaction with the LTL layer (to know the visible state properties) and the analysis algorithm (to avoid the so-called ignoring problem, see Section 5.1).

The POR layer is incompatible with the symbolic analysis tool, since after partial-order reduction all locality and dependence information is lost. The distributed analysis tool currently only supports POR for deadlock detection.

5   Algorithmic Back-Ends

LTSMIN has *distributed* [6], *multi-core* [12, 19, 35, 37], and *symbolic* [16] back-ends. Furthermore, connectors to the model-based testing tool JTORX, are available as the *2torx tools, and to the CADP toolset, through the OPEN/CÆSAR interface, as the *-open tools. Since its early origins, LTSMIN has a sequential (`ltsmin-reduce`) and a distributed (`ltsmin-reduce-dist`) reduction tool. Both provide strong and branching bisimulation minimisation, while the sequential tool also supports divergence sensitivity, cycle elimination and minimisation modulo lumping. In the current section, we highlight the multi-core algorithms for explicit-state and symbolic model checking, and the symbolic parity game solver.

5.1   Multi-core Reachability, POR and LTL Checking

Since [37], LTSMIN's multi-core tools were extended beyond reachability analysis, while improving state compression.

At the basis of our multi-core algorithms is still a lockless hash or tree table (`--state=table/tree`) for shared state storage coupled with a dynamic load balancer [33, 34]. However, state compression has been enhanced by extending the tree with a concurrent Cleary compact hash table [10, 45] (`--state=cleary-tree`), regularly yielding compressed sizes of 4 bytes per state [35, Tab. 11.4] without compromising completeness. *Incremental tree compression* [35, Sec. 3.3.4] uses the WRITEMATRIX from PINS+ to limit the number of hash computations, ensuring scalability and performance similar to that of plain hash tables [34].

LTSMIN's state storage provides ample flexibility for different search orders, enabling LTL verification by traditional linear-time algorithms, in particular nested depth-first search (NDFS). The CNDFS algorithm (`--strategy=cndfs`) runs multiple semi-independent DFS searches which are carefully synchronised in the backtrack [19]. DFS$_{fifo}$ (`--strategy=dfsfifo`) combines this with breadth-first search to find livelocks, an important subet of LTL [31]. The latter algorithm avoids the *ignoring problem* in POR [18], but the combination of POR and full LTL was until recently not possible in multi-core LTSMIN.

The ignoring problem occurs when POR consistently prunes the same relevant action infinitely often [18]. It can be solved by fully exploring one state s along each cycle in the PTS (PORSTATE(s) := NEXTSTATE(s)). The problem of detecting cycles while constructing the PTS on-the-fly is usually solved with DFS [18], which is hard to parallelise [2]. Exploiting the DFS-based parallel algorithms, this problem is efficiently solved with a new *parallel cycle proviso* [38] (`--proviso=cndfs`). Cycles are exchanged with the POR layer via PINS.

We have shown before [4, 31] that our multi-core reachability approach exhibits almost ideal scalability up to 48 cores, even for very fast NEXTSTATE implementations, like SPINS. CNDFS outperforms [4, 19] other algorithms for multi-core LTL model checking [1, 27]. For further information on multi-core algorithms and data structures, see [35].

5.2   Multi-core Decision Diagrams

The symbolic back-end of LTSMIN has been improved in several ways. *First*, it has been extended with the multi-core decision diagram packages SYLVAN and LDDMC [16] (`--vset=sylvan/lddmc`). *Second*, two parallel reachability algorithms have been added, based on the task-based parallelism framework LACE [15, 16]. *Third*, the distinction between read and write dependencies in PINS+ improves the symbolic algorithms by reducing the size of transitions relations [40].

5.3   Symbolic Parity Game Solving

We implemented Zielonka's recursive algorithm [46] using decision diagrams, which is available in the symbolic tools (`--pg-solve`) or stand-alone in `spgsolver`. The tool solves symbolic parity games, generated by the symbolic tool, and returns whether the game has a winning strategy for player **0**. When the game has been generated using the μ-calculus layer, this answer corresponds to whether $\mathcal{P} \models \varphi$.

6   Case Studies

The following two case studies demonstrate the use of having both explicit-state and symbolic approaches to attack problems. The second case also demonstrates the power of μ-calculus model checking for solving games.[2]

---

[2] Installation instructions and case-study data:
`https://github.com/utwente-fmt/ltsmin-tacas2015`. We used LTSMIN v2.1 on AMD Opterons with Ubuntu 14.04.

6.1   Attacking the RERS Challenge

LTSMIN participated in the RERS [28, 42] challenges of 2012, 2013 [41] and 2014, winning several first prizes. The flexibility of LTSMIN allowed us to address the RERS challenge problems from different angles. We will discuss three ways to connect LTSMIN to the challenge problems. We also demonstrate how LTSMIN's backend tools check for assertion errors and temporal properties.

Each RERS problem consists of a large C-program, encoding a system of Event-Condition-Action rules. The program operates in an infinite loop modifying the global state. In each iteration, the program gets an input from a small alphabet and checks for assertion errors. If the condition of one of the rules is met, it generates an output symbol and changes the state for the next iteration.

Linking LTSMIN *to RERS Programs.*   In the first approach, a RERS C-program is translated to a modelling language that is already supported by LTSMIN. We took this approach in 2012, by translating RERS programs to PROMELA and to MCRL2. The translations are rather straightforward, since the ECA-rules can be readily reverse-engineered from the C-programs.

A fundamentally different approach is to create a new language module for (a subclass of) C-programs. This was our approach in 2013 and 2014. In 2013, we just wrapped the body of the main-loop into a single, monolithic next-state function, compiled in a separate binary (.so file). This is a robust solution, since the original code is run during model checking.

This monolithic approach worked fine for multi-core model checking. However, it leads to a lack of "locality": there is only one transition, which reads and writes all state variables. In order to apply symbolic model checking, our 2014 approach was to adapt the C-language module, by providing a separate transition group for each ECA rule, checking its conditions and applying the state change. Edge labels are added, to indicate the input and output values and the assertion violations. In this partitioned view, every transition group only touches a couple of variables, enabling symbolic model checking. With SYLVAN linked to LTSMIN, RERS 2014 was the first large case to which we applied multi-core symbolic model checking.

Using LTSMIN *to Check Properties.*   We show here how LTSMIN can be used to check properties of Problem2.c from the RERS challenge 2014. The original C-code is optimized and transformed as indicated above. We assume that the transformed code is compiled and available in a shared object `Problem.so`.

In the following dialogue, we request the symbolic model checker to find all actions with prefix `error`. Flag `--no-exit` avoids that LTSMIN exits after finding the first error. We also request to store concrete error traces in a subdirectory and print one of them in human readable format. LTSMIN quickly finds 23 errors.

```
> pins2lts-sym Problem.so --action=error --trace=Error/ --no-exit
pins2lts-sym: writing to file: Error/error_6.gcf
pins2lts-sym: writing to file: Error/error_8.gcf
^C
> ltsmin-printtrace Error/error_6.gcf | grep action | cut -f3 -d=
"input_3" "output_20" ... "input_3" "output_26" "error_6"
```

Actually, the state space of this example is very big and LTSMIN keeps searching for more errors. In order to do an exhaustive search, we throw more power, by using the parallel BFS strategy and SYLVAN's (enlarged) multi-core multi-way decision diagrams [16]. We also request static variable reordering, to keep the MDDs small. With `--when`, we request timing information. The following experiments are run on a 48-core machine with 132 GB RAM. The parallel symbolic model checker of LTSMIN computes the full state space within 2 minutes. All 1.75 billion states, divided over 480 BFS levels, are stored in about 1 million MDD nodes.

```
> pins2lts-sym Problem.so --order=par-prev --regroup=gs --when \
   --vset=lddmc --lddmc-tablesize=30 --lddmc-cachesize=28
pins2lts-sym: Using 48 CPUs
pins2lts-sym, 28.076: level 90 is finished
pins2lts-sym, 113.768: level 480 is finished
pins2lts-sym: ... 1750528171 (~1.75e+09) states, 1158486 BDD nodes
```

Alternatively, we may decide to switch to the *explicit-state* multi-core reachability engine [33]. We request a strict breadth-first strategy, to facilitate comparison with the symbolic run. To squeeze the maximum out of our machine, we combine recursive tree compression [34] with Cleary's compact hashing [10, 45]. Within a minute we learn that there are no new errors up to depth 90. LTSMIN is able to traverse the full state space exhaustively within 5 minutes, generating over 1.75 billion states and 2.4 billion transitions.

```
> pins2lts-mc Problem.so --strategy=sbfs --state=cleary-tree --when
pins2lts-mc(23/48), 46.067: ~90 levels ~125829120 states ~191380560 trans
pins2lts-mc( 0/48), 296.759: Explored 1750528171 states 2445589869 trans
```

The explicit multi-core tool can also check LTL properties, using multi-core NDFS (`cndfs`, [19]). The LTL formula refers to integer variables in the original C-program a94 and a95. With `--ltl-semantics=ltsmin` we insist on checking infinite paths only, i.e., we don't consider traces that end in an assertion error. The violated trace can be printed as above, and will end in a lasso.

```
> pins2lts-mc Problem.so --ltl='a94==9 U a95==12' \
   --strategy=cndfs --ltl-semantics=ltsmin --trace=Error/ltl.gcf
pins2lts-mc( 0/48): Accepting cycle FOUND at depth 11!
pins2lts-mc( 3/48): Writing trace to ltl.gcf
```

6.2 Solving Connect Four

We explore the Connect Four game, originally played on a 7×6 board between two players: *yellow* and *red*, which is available in the examples directory of MCRL2. For the first run, we reduced the board size to 5×4, for which the model has 7,039,582 states.

The matrix is in Fig. 3a. LTS generation using `lps2lts` (mCRL2) takes 157 seconds and 540 MB. Using 64 cores, multi-core LTSmin takes 68 seconds and 63 MB. But symbolic LTSmin needs 80 seconds.

This is caused by the monolithic summands in the specification (the dense rows in Figure 3a), representing the winning condition. We split the condition in separate parts and let the game continue after a winning move has been done. The matrix of the problem becomes more sparse, see Figure 3b. Note that the four `r`'s in a row correspond to the four winning tiles. The symbolic tool now generates a different state space of the same game (5,464,758 states) in one second. mCRL2 takes 167 seconds for this version. The exploration time of LTSmin for a 6×5 board is 2.6 seconds, for 9.78×10^9 states in 41,239 MDD nodes.

```
rrrrrrrrrrrrrrrrrrrr+
rrrrrrrrrrrrrrrrrrrr+
+----+----+----+----+
--+----+----+----+--+
-+----+----+----+---+
----+----+----+----++
---+----+----+----+-+
+----+----+----+----+
--+----+----+----+--+
-+----+----+----+---+
----+----+----+----++
---+----+----+----+-+
```

(a) Monolithic.

```
+----+----+----+----+
--+----+----+----+--+
-+----+----+----+---+
----+----+----+----++
---+----+----+----+-+
rrrr-----------------
---r---r---r---r-----
r-----r-----r-----r--
r----r----r----r-----
-----------rrrr------
-----rrrr------------
-rrrr----------------
----r---r---r---r----
-r-----r-----r-----r-
--r----r----r----r---
-r----r----r----r----
---------------rrrr--
------------rrrr-----
------rrrr-----------
----r----r----r----r-
---r----r----r----r--
----------------rrrr-
```

(b) Separated

Fig. 3. Matrix

Next, we generate a PBES with mCRL2, to encode the μ-calculus property (in file `yellow_wins.mcl`) that player Yellow has a winning strategy, and solve it with LTSmin:

```
mu X . [Wins(Red)]false && <Move>(<Wins(Yellow)>true || [Move]X)
> lps2pbes -s -f yellow_wins.mcl four5x4.lps four5x4.pbes
> pbes2lts-sym --mcrl2=-rjitty --regroup=gs --pg-solve \
  --vset=lddmc --order=par-prev four5x4.pbes
```

For the 5×4-board mCRL2 takes 199 seconds, but the symbolic tool of LTSmin 8 seconds, to compute that the starting player has no winning strategy.

7 Discussion

There are several toolsets that take a similar approach, supporting a generic interface, or offer similar, multi-core or symbolic, analysis algorithms. The table below provides a brief qualitative comparison of the available types of algorithms and the supported logics. The last column indicates whether multiple input languages are supported, and if so, through which interface.

The Pins interface is the main differentiator of LTSmin. It is sufficiently general to support a wide range of modelling languages. At the same time, the dependency matrices provide sufficient structural model information to exploit locality in

Toolset	multi-core	distributed	symbolic	μ-calculus	LTL	POR	confluence	Language
LTSmin	yes	yes	yes	yes	yes	yes	yes	any (Pins)
mCRL2 [11]	no	no	no	yes	no	no	yes	`fixed`
CADP [22]	no	yes	no	yes*	no	no	yes	any (Open/C)
DiVinE [3]	yes	yes	no	no	yes	yes	no	any (CESMI)
Spin	yes	yes	no	no	yes	yes	no	`fixed`
NuSMV [9]	no	no	yes	no	yes	no	no	`fixed`

* CADP supports μ-calculus formulae up to alternation depth 2.

the analysis algorithms. As a consequence, LTSMIN is the only language-agnostic model checker that supports on-the-fly symbolic verification and full LTL model checking with POR. Due to the modular architecture, the user can freely choose a verification strategy depending on the problem at hand.

References

1. Barnat, J., Brim, L., Ročkai, P.: A Time-Optimal On-the-Fly Parallel Algorithm for Model Checking of Weak LTL Properties. In: Breitman, K., Cavalcanti, A. (eds.) ICFEM 2009. LNCS, vol. 5885, pp. 407–425. Springer, Heidelberg (2009)
2. Barnat, J., Brim, L., Ročkai, P.: Parallel Partial Order Reduction with Topological Sort Proviso. In: SEFM 2010, pp. 222–231. IEEE (2010)
3. Barnat, J., et al.: DiVinE 3.0 – An Explicit-State Model Checker for Multithreaded C & C++ Programs. In: Sharygina, N., Veith, H. (eds.) CAV 2013. LNCS, vol. 8044, pp. 863–868. Springer, Heidelberg (2013)
4. van der Berg, F.I., Laarman, A.W.: SpinS: Extending LTSmin with Promela through SpinJa. In: PDMC 2012. ENTCS, vol. 296, pp. 95–105 (2013)
5. Blom, S.C.C., van de Pol, J.C., Weber, M.: Bridging the Gap between Enumerative and Symbolic Model Checkers. University of Twente (2009)
6. Blom, S., Lisser, B., van de Pol, J., Weber, M.: A Database Approach to Distributed State-Space Generation. Journal of Logic and Computation 21(1), 45–62 (2009)
7. Blom, S., van de Pol, J.: Symbolic Reachability for Process Algebras with Recursive Data Types. In: Fitzgerald, J.S., Haxthausen, A.E., Yenigun, H. (eds.) ICTAC 2008. LNCS, vol. 5160, pp. 81–95. Springer, Heidelberg (2008)
8. Blom, S.C.C., van de Pol, J.C., Weber, M.: LTSmin: Distributed and Symbolic Reachability. In: Touili, T., Cook, B., Jackson, P. (eds.) CAV 2010. LNCS, vol. 6174, pp. 354–359. Springer, Heidelberg (2010)
9. Cimatti, A., et al.: NuSMV Version 2: An OpenSource Tool for Symbolic Model Checking. In: Brinksma, E., Larsen, K.G. (eds.) CAV 2002. LNCS, vol. 2404, pp. 359–364. Springer, Heidelberg (2002)
10. Cleary, J.G.: Compact Hash Tables Using Bidirectional Linear Probing. IEEE Transactions on Computers C-33(9), 828–834 (1984)
11. Cranen, S., others: An Overview of the mCRL2 Toolset and Its Recent Advances. In: Piterman, N., Smolka, S.A. (eds.) TACAS 2013. LNCS, vol. 7795, pp. 199–213. Springer, Heidelberg (2013)
12. Dalsgaard, A.E., others: Multi-core Reachability for Timed Automata. In: Jurdziński, M., Ničković, D. (eds.) FORMATS 2012. LNCS, vol. 7595, pp. 91–106. Springer, Heidelberg (2012)
13. Dam, M.: Translating CTL* into the modal μ-calculus. Report ECS-LFCS-90-123, LFCS, University of Edinburgh (1990)
14. Daws, C., Tripakis, S.: Model checking of real-time reachability properties using abstractions. In: Steffen, B. (ed.) TACAS 1998. LNCS, vol. 1384, pp. 313–329. Springer, Heidelberg (1998)
15. van Dijk, T., van de Pol, J.C.: Lace: non-blocking split deque for work-stealing. In: Lopes, L., et al. (eds.) Euro-Par 2014, Part II. LNCS, vol. 8806, pp. 206–217. Springer, Heidelberg (2014)
16. van Dijk, T., van de Pol, J.C.: Sylvan: Multi-core Decision Diagrams. In: TACAS 2015. Springer (2015)

17. Emerson, E.A., Wahl, T.: Dynamic symmetry reduction. In: Halbwachs, N., Zuck, L.D. (eds.) TACAS 2005. LNCS, vol. 3440, pp. 382–396. Springer, Heidelberg (2005)
18. Evangelista, S., Pajault, C.: Solving the Ignoring Problem for Partial Order Reduction. STTT 12, 155–170 (2010)
19. Evangelista, S., et al.: Improved Multi-core Nested Depth-First Search. In: Chakraborty, S., Mukund, M. (eds.) ATVA 2012. LNCS, vol. 7561, pp. 269–283. Springer, Heidelberg (2012)
20. Friedmann, O., Lange, M.: PGSolver (2008), https://github.com/tcsprojects/pgsolver
21. Garavel, H.: OPEN/CÆSAR: An open software architecture for verification, simulation, and testing. In: Steffen, B. (ed.) TACAS 1998. LNCS, vol. 1384, pp. 68–84. Springer, Heidelberg (1998)
22. Garavel, H., Lang, F., Mateescu, R., Serwe, W.: CADP 2011: a toolbox for the construction and analysis of distributed processes. STTT 15(2), 89–107 (2013)
23. Gastin, P., Oddoux, D.: Fast LTL to Büchi Automata Translation. In: Berry, G., Comon, H., Finkel, A. (eds.) CAV 2001. LNCS, vol. 2102, pp. 53–65. Springer, Heidelberg (2001)
24. Groote, J.F., Willemse, T.A.C.: Model-checking processes with data. Science of Computer Programming 56(3), 251–273 (2005)
25. Guck, D., et al.: Analysis of Timed and Long-Run Objectives for Markov Automata. Logical Methods in Computer Science 10(3) (2014)
26. Holzmann, G.J.: The model checker SPIN. IEEE TSE 23, 279–295 (1997)
27. Holzmann, G.J.: Parallelizing the SPIN Model Checker. In: Donaldson, A., Parker, D. (eds.) SPIN 2012. LNCS, vol. 7385, pp. 155–171. Springer, Heidelberg (2012)
28. Howar, F., et al.: Rigorous examination of reactive systems. STTT 16(5) (2014)
29. Kant, G., van de Pol, J.: Generating and Solving Symbolic Parity Games. In: GRAPHITE 2014. EPTCS, vol. 159, pp. 2–14 (2014)
30. Katz, S., Peled, D.: An efficient verification method for parallel and distributed programs. In: de Bakker, J.W., de Roever, W.-P., Rozenberg, G. (eds.) Linear Time, Branching Time and Partial Order in Logics and Models for Concurrency. LNCS, vol. 354, pp. 489–507. Springer, Heidelberg (1989)
31. Laarman, A., Faragó, D.: Improved On-The-Fly Livelock Detection. In: Brat, G., Rungta, N., Venet, A. (eds.) NFM 2013. LNCS, vol. 7871, pp. 32–47. Springer, Heidelberg (2013)
32. Laarman, A., Pater, E., van de Pol, J.C., Hansen, H.: Guard-based partial-order reduction. STTT (2014)
33. Laarman, A., van de Pol, J., Weber, M.: Boosting Multi-Core Reachability Performance with Shared Hash Tables. In: FMCAD 2010, pp. 247–255. IEEE (2010)
34. Laarman, A., van de Pol, J., Weber, M.: Parallel Recursive State Compression for Free. In: Groce, A., Musuvathi, M. (eds.) SPIN Workshops 2011. LNCS, vol. 6823, pp. 38–56. Springer, Heidelberg (2011)
35. Laarman, A.: Scalable Multi-Core Model Checking. Ph.D. thesis, University of Twente (2014)
36. Laarman, A., Olesen, M.C., Dalsgaard, A.E., Larsen, K.G., van de Pol, J.: Multi-core Emptiness Checking of Timed Büchi Automata Using Inclusion Abstraction. In: Sharygina, N., Veith, H. (eds.) CAV 2013. LNCS, vol. 8044, pp. 968–983. Springer, Heidelberg (2013)
37. Laarman, A., van de Pol, J., Weber, M.: Multi-Core LTSmin: Marrying Modularity and Scalability. In: Bobaru, M., Havelund, K., Holzmann, G.J., Joshi, R. (eds.) NFM 2011. LNCS, vol. 6617, pp. 506–511. Springer, Heidelberg (2011)

38. Laarman, A., Wijs, A.: Partial-Order Reduction for Multi-Core LTL Model Checking. In: Yahav, E. (ed.) HVC 2014. LNCS, vol. 8855, pp. 267–283. Springer, Heidelberg (2014)

39. Mateescu, R.: Local Model-Checking of an Alternation-Free Value-Based Modal Mu-Calculus. In: VMCAI 1998 (1998)

40. Meijer, J.J.G., Kant, G., van de Pol, J.C., Blom, S.C.C.: Read, Write and Copy Dependencies for Symbolic Model Checking. In: Yahav, E. (ed.) HVC 2014. LNCS, vol. 8855, pp. 204–219. Springer, Heidelberg (2014)

41. van de Pol, J., Ruys, T.C., te Brinke, S.: Thoughtful brute-force attack of the RERS 2012 and 2013 Challenges. STTT 16(5), 481–491 (2014)

42. RERS – Rigorous Examination of Reactive Systems, `http://rers-challenge.org/`

43. Timmer, M.: Efficient modelling, generation and analysis of Markov automata. Ph.D. thesis, University of Twente (2013)

44. Valmari, A.: Eliminating Redundant Interleavings During Concurrent Program Verification. In: Odijk, E., Rem, M., Syre, J.-C. (eds.) PARLE 1989. LNCS, vol. 366, pp. 89–103. Springer, Heidelberg (1989)

45. van der Vegt, S., Laarman, A.W.: A parallel compact hash table. In: Kotásek, Z., Bouda, J., Černá, I., Sekanina, L., Vojnar, T., Antoš, D. (eds.) MEMICS 2011. LNCS, vol. 7119, pp. 191–204. Springer, Heidelberg (2012)

46. Zielonka, W.: Infinite Games on Finitely Coloured Graphs with Applications to Automata on Infinite Trees. Theoretical Computer Science 200(1–2), 135–183 (1998)

Using a Formal Model to Improve Verification of a Cache-Coherent System-on-Chip

Abderahman Kriouile[1,2,3,4] and Wendelin Serwe[2,3,4]

[1] STMicroelectronics, 12, rue Jules Horowitz, BP 217, 38019 Grenoble, France
[2] Inria, Grenoble, France
[3] Univ. Grenoble Alpes, LIG, F-38000 Grenoble, France
[4] CNRS, LIG, F-38000 Grenoble, France

Abstract. In this paper we report about a case study on the functional verification of a System-on-Chip (SoC) with a formal system-level model. Our approach improves industrial simulation-based verification techniques in two aspects. First, we suggest to use the formal model to assess the sanity of an interface verification unit. Second, we present a two-step approach to generate clever semi-directed test cases from temporal logic properties: model-based testing tools of the CADP toolbox generate system-level abstract test cases, which are then refined with a commercial Coverage-Directed Test Generation tool into interface-level concrete test cases that can be executed at RTL level. Applied to an AMBA 4 ACE-based cache-coherent SoC, we found that our approach helps in the transition from interface-level to system-level verification, facilitates the validation of system-level properties, and enables early detection of bugs in both the SoC and the commercial test-bench.

1 Introduction

Due to increasing design complexity, functional verification continues to be one of the most expensive and time-consuming steps in a typical System-on-Chip (SoC) design flow. In practice, most widely used techniques are based on extensive simulation due to the related flexibility. However, the success of simulation-based verification, both in terms of total effort spent and final verification coverage achieved, depends heavily on the quality of the tests executed during simulation. Generating tests to achieve high coverage for complex designs has always been a challenging problem. In general, more constrained and less random tests reduce the overall validation effort, because the same verification coverage can be achieved with fewer and shorter tests [19]. We distinguish in this paper three types of test generation techniques with decreasing degree of randomness: fully random, constrained-random [26], and fully specified tests, hereafter called directed tests, i.e., without randomization.

Fully random tests are the easiest to automate, but require long simulation runs to obtain a reasonable coverage. In many situations, directed tests are the only tests that can thoroughly verify corner cases and important features of a design [2,15]. However, because directed tests are mostly written manually, it

© Springer-Verlag Berlin Heidelberg 2015
C. Baier and C. Tinelli (Eds.): TACAS 2015, LNCS 9035, pp. 708–722, 2015.
DOI: 10.1007/978-3-662-46681-0_62

is impractical to generate a comprehensive set of directed tests to achieve a coverage goal [19]. Automatic test generation using model checking is one of the most promising approaches for directed test generation. However, for large designs model checking rapidly faces state explosion, when considering hardware protocols in all their details.

Constrained-random testing uses constraint solvers to select tests satisfying a specified set of constraints; non-specified details are then filled in by randomization. The automation of the feedback from coverage analysis to constrained-random test generation led to *coverage-directed test generation* (CDTG) [22], which dynamically analyzes coverage results and automatically adapts the randomized test generation process to improve the coverage. CDTG is guided by different coverage metrics, such as state coverage and transition coverage [2] and shows various degrees of success [11]. For instance, it succeeds to achieve coverage goals for interface hardware protocols, but reaches its limits for complex system-level protocols, such as system-level cache coherency. Achieving good coverage for these recent protocols is a new challenge in the development of industrial test benches and calls for more directed and less random tests.

This paper is about the application of formal methods to improve the functional verification of a heterogeneous cache-coherent SoC for a commercial set-top-box supporting multiple Ultra HD flows on a single chip currently under development at STMicroelectronics. We use an extension of a previously developed system-level formal model of a cache-coherent SoC [16] and take advantage of equivalence checking, model checking, and test generation facilities offered by the CADP toolbox[1] [8].

The two principal contributions of this paper are the following.

1. A way to assess the sanity of an industrial *interface verification unit* (ivunit), consisting of a set of behaviors to cover. In our study, we focus on the complex behaviors expressed by so-called *checks* of a commercial ivunit.
2. A two-step approach to use model-based testing to generate clever semi-directed system level test cases from temporal logic properties. We use CADP to generate directed "abstract" system-level test cases, which are then refined with commercial CDTG tool into interface-level "concrete" test cases that can be executed at RTL level. Those tests concern system-level properties in the sense that several interfaces are activated. We propose the notion of a *system verification unit* (svunit) to measure the coverage and verdicts of system-level properties.

The rest of the paper is organized as follows: Section 2 presents related work. Section 3 recalls the main aspects of the considered SoC and its formal model [16]. Section 4 presents contribution 1 by describing the validation of an industrial ivunit using equivalence checking. Section 5 details contribution 2 by proposing our test generation methodology based on counterexamples generated by model checking. Section 6 presents experimental results and the industrial impact of our work. Finally, Section 7 concludes the paper.

---

[1] http://cadp.inria.fr/

2   Related Work

For instance, the specification-based test generation technique [21] uses a formal model to generate directed tests. Solutions based on model checking techniques are promising for functional verification and test generation for reasonably complex systems [10]. However, it is unrealistic to assume that a complete detailed model of a large SoC is tractable by a model checker. We address this issue by relying on a system-level model, abstracting from all irrelevant details. In this way, we succeed to model a complex industrial SoC and to extract relevant scenarios by model checking. The above approaches transform counterexamples produced by the model checker into test cases. In our approach, we use the counterexamples to produce smaller interesting configurations of the model that still do not satisfy a given property. We generate test cases from these smaller models, thus avoiding combinatorial explosion in many cases.

In the literature, it has already been proposed to mix model-based techniques and coverage-directed techniques. Coverage-directed techniques were used in property learning [4] ("reuse learned knowledge from one core to another"), which we do not use, and that relies on SAT-based BMC (whereas CADP implements totally different verification techniques). Some of those techniques [21] focus on homogeneous multicore architectures (exploiting symmetry between processors to reduce verification complexity), and only suggest how this could be extended to heterogeneous architectures (by grouping IPs into homogeneous groups to be studied separately). On the contrary, our approach was designed for heterogeneous SoCs and makes no symmetry assumption. Also, most of those techniques [4,5,21] remain at system level (SystemC-TLM level), whereas our approach starts from system level and goes down to RTL level.

Over the last two decades, the CADP toolbox has been used for verifying numerous complex hardware designs, including Bull supercomputers, STMicroelectronics multiprocessor architectures, Networks-on-Chip (CEA/Leti and University of Utah), and various asynchronous circuits. In this paper, we present an application of the latest languages and tools of CADP. Using the new generation formal language LNT [3] to describe the system and also the test purposes greatly facilitates the testing of complex behaviors. Similarly, the MCL language [17] provides a convenient way to express complex data-based temporal properties. We use a new prototype tool to generate tests on the fly. Finally, instead of a homogeneous system as in [9,14], we study the less symmetric and thus more complex case of an heterogeneous SoC.

3   Formal Model of an AMBA 4 ACE Based SoC

The recent AMBA 4 ACE (AXI Coherency Extension) protocol [1,23], proposed by ARM, extends the AMBA 3 AXI protocol in order to support system-level cache coherency in SoCs. AXI defines communication at interface-level between a pair of master/slave ports, which are connected by several read and write channels (AR, R, AW, W, B). AXI defines two transactions *Read* and *Write*, each of which consists of several transfers; each transfer is executed on an AXI channel. Thanks to the encapsulation mechanisms of AXI, a transfer on a channel can be considered to be atomic at higher levels.

ACE introduces system-level requirements on transaction ordering, adds coherency channels (AC, CR, CD), enriches existing channels with new coherency parameters (i.e., PassDirty, IsShared), and defines cache line states and several transactions (i.e., coherent transactions, cache maintenance transactions, memory update transactions, etc.). ACE introduces heterogeneity by defining two types of coherent masters: those with a cache are called *ACE masters*, and those without caches are called *ACE-Lite masters*. The latter can access data in the caches of the former, avoiding access to memory, which improves performance.

Example 1. The *ReadOnce* transaction is a coherent transaction (used in particular by an ACE-Lite master), which obtains the current contents of a memory line without keeping a copy into the cache. If an ACE-Lite master sends a *ReadOnce* transfer on the AR channel. The CCI then sends snoop requests to all ACE masters on the AC channels. Each ACE master answers on the CR channel with a Boolean indicating whether the data is in its cache, and a Boolean indicating if the master passes the responsibility of writing back the data in the memory (PassDirty). If the data is available, the ACE master sends also a data transfer on the CD channel. If none of the master has the data available, it is taken from the main memory. The CCI forwards the data to the ACE-Lite master using the R channel, to complete the transaction. If one of the ACE masters passed the responsibility to write back the data, the CCI must initiate a memory update, because an ACE-Lite master cannot take this responsibility.

We use an extension of a previously developed formal model [16] (about 3400 lines of LNT code) of an ACE-based SoC[2], consisting of a *cache-coherent interconnect* (CCI) connected to a non-cache-coherent Network-on-Chip (NoC). Figure 1 shows the overall architecture of the model in the configuration used in the present paper. Following the ARM® big.LITTLE™ solution [20], the two ACE masters are one big (powerful) and one little (lower-power) processor, enabling to dynamically adapt to changing computation load. The ACE-Lite master is a *Graphical Processing Unit* (GPU) that can access the caches of both processors. All three masters access the main memory through a non-cache-coherent NoC. The ACE protocol supports the coherency of data among the processors. Our formal model focuses on the cache-coherent part of the SoC.

The ACE specification contains some *global requirements*. Indeed, the ACE protocol does not guarantee system level cache coherency, but just provides support for it. Coherency has to be ensured by proprietary additional mechanisms on each implementation of a CCI. We model these global requirements in a constraint-oriented style by adding observer processes that prohibit incorrect executions. By omitting those observers, we obtain an *unconstrained model*, for which the global requirements are not necessarily satisfied.

---

[2] A large Petri net derived from our LNT model is available as Model Checking Contest 2014 benchmark (http://mcc.lip6.fr/pdf/ARMCacheCoherence-form.pdf).

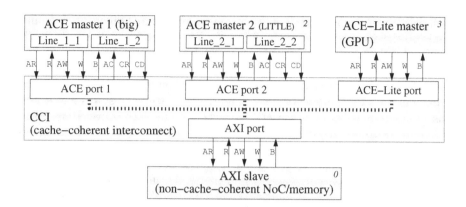

Fig. 1. Model architecture

A crucial feature of our formal model is that it is parametrized, in particular by the set of forbidden ACE transactions, the number of ACE masters, ACE-Lite masters, and cache lines per ACE master. Among the three masters, at most two initiate transactions at the same time. We will vary essentially one parameter, which is the set of forbidden ACE transactions; we refer to an instance of the model as Model($\mathcal{F}$), where $\mathcal{F}$ is the set of forbidden ACE transactions; thus, Model($\emptyset$) corresponds to the complete, unconstrained model.

4   Sanity of a Formal Check List

Industrial CDTG test benches are based on a so-called *verification plan*, i.e., a list of all behaviors to be covered by tests on the *Design Under Verification* (DUV). The coverage of the verification plan is collected to measure test progression.[3] In our work, we focus on the formal *checks*, which are grouped in so-called *interface verification units* (ivunit). Each check is an event sequence, e.g., expressed in *Property Specification Language* (PSL) [12]. Covering a check consists in activating the check and finishing correctly the specified sequence. Activating a check means to detect the first event of the sequence. It is a failure if a check is activated and not correctly finished.

In this section, we report about the use of our formal model to validate a commercial ivunit. To this end, we encode each check of the ivunit as a *Labeled Transition System* (LTS) (by means of an LNT model) and use equivalence checking techniques (hiding, minimization, and comparison operations on LTSs).

In fact, the ivunit considers only a single interface (i.e., a single master/slave pair), whereas the formal model describes the complete SoC. To obtain the LTS of the interface between ACE master 1 (big) and the CCI (upper left part of Fig. 1), we hide in the LTS of the whole system all labels except those of the

---

[3] There are two types of behaviors in a verification plan: simple behaviors, called *cover points* and complex behaviors, called (formal) *checks*.

selected interface and then minimize the resulting LTS according to *divergence-sensitive branching bisimulation* (divbranching) [25], which preserves the branching structure and livelocks (cycles of internal τ-transitions). Applying those steps reduces the LTS as generated from the model (498,197 states, 1,343,799 transitions) by two orders of magnitude (3,653 states, 8,924 transitions). We store the reduced LTS in a file named `interface.bcg`, where the extension `.bcg` stands for Binary Coded Graph, the compact binary format used to store LTSs in CADP.

We continue our study by identifying a subset of nine industrial checks (called C1 ... C9), which have a level of abstraction corresponding to our formal model. Then we verify that each check is an overapproximation of the model behavior. Last, we study if the list of checks covers all behaviors of the model.

4.1 Local Sanity of Each Check

We aim at verifying that each check is well specified. Because each check uses only a subset of interface channels, we generate a corresponding sub-interface by hiding all channels except those occurring in the check, and apply again divbranching reduction.

Example 2. Check C1 requires that the current read request address should not overlap with any of the outstanding write requests. C1 uses only three channels: address read (AR), address write (AW), and write response (B). Thus we obtain the corresponding sub-interface LTS (105 states, 474 transitions).

We verify that each sub-interface LTS is included in the corresponding check LTS modulo the preorder of the divbranching bisimulation. We conclude that the check is a correct overapproximation of the behavior of the subset of ACE channels.

4.2 Global Sanity of the List of Checks

To verify that the list of checks covers all the behaviors of the interface model, we compare the parallel composition of all the nine checks with the interface LTS. We use smart reduction [6] to automatically optimize the order of composing and minimizing the checks in the parallel composition: the complete composition process takes approximately five minutes. We express the parallel composition in SVL with an LNT-style parallel composition operation: each check is required to synchronize on all the gates (channels) it uses; synchronization is n-ary, i.e., *all* checks that have a given channel (e.g., AR) in their synchronization set (on the left of ->) synchronize on the channel (e.g., C1, C2, C3, C5 all together synchronize on AR).

```
"all_checks.bcg" = smart divbranching reduction of
        par   AR, AW, B      -> "C1.lnt"
          || AR, AW, R, B -> "C2.lnt"
          || AR, R           -> "C3.lnt"
          || AW, B           -> "C4.lnt"
```

```
    || AR, AW, R, B -> "C5.lnt"
    || AW, B, CD    -> "C6.lnt"
    || AC, CD       -> "C7.lnt"
    || AC, CR       -> "C8.lnt"
    || R            -> "C9.lnt"
  end par;
```

We compare the interface LTS and the checks LTS all_checks.bcg (11,773 states, 8,171,497 transitions) to verify if the interface LTS is included in the LTS all_checks.bcg modulo the preorder corresponding to the divbranching bisimulation. This verification fails, i.e., we detect a *missing check*; the counterexample (provided by CADP) shows a W label following an AW label.

According to the ACE specification, there must be the same number of W's and AW's. We express this constraint by a new check (C10), avoiding the use of counters, using asynchronous parallel composition (AW || W). Adding C10 to the parallel composition of the checks, yields a new LTS all_checks_bis.bcg (38,793 states, 27,200,587 transitions).

We compare all_checks_bis.bcg and interface.bcg and observe now that interface.bcg is included in all_checks_bis.bcg for divbranching bisimulation. Hence, the check list is now complete with respect to our formal model. Although the missing check could also be found manually by inspecting the list of channels in the checks (all channels but W are present), our approach has the additional benefits of illustrating the missing behavior and enabling to formally, and semi-automatically, establish the completeness of the check list.

5   From Temporal Logic Properties to Clever Test Cases

An interesting idea for the generation of directed tests is to focus on and derive tests from potential faults of the DUV [18]. For system-level protocols, in order to obtain a description of potential faults corresponding to the global requirements of the SoC, we suggest to use system-level properties together with a model containing faults. In our case, we use the unconstrained model (see Sec. 3). Applying the theory of conformance testing [24], we generate abstract test cases, which then have to be translated to the input language of a commercial CDTG solver to randomly complete interface-level details and finally to run the tests on the RTL test bench.

Because we found the generation of abstract test cases directly from the complete model to be impractical, we suggest to use information contained in counterexamples to select *interesting configurations* of the formal model, which still contain violations of the global requirements, and to extract abstract test cases from the selected configurations. Figure 2 gives an overview of our test generation flow.

5.1   System-Level Properties

We express properties in the *Model Checking Language* (MCL) [17], an extension of the modal μ-calculus with high-level operators to improve expressiveness and

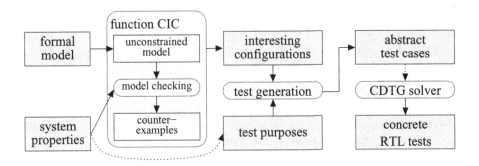

Fig. 2. Model-Based Test Generation flow

conciseness of formulæ. The main ingredients of MCL used in this paper are action patterns extracting data values from LTS transition labels, and modalities on transition sequences described by extended regular expressions. MCL formulæ are verified on the fly using the EVALUATOR 4.0 model checker of CADP.

Among the properties we considered[4], only the following two do not hold for the unconstrained model.

Data Integrity. The following property [16, φ_5], enforces correct order of write operations to the shared memory:

```
[ true * .
    {W !"WRITEBACK" ?m:Nat ?l:Nat ?d:Nat}.          (* memory update    *)
    (not {W !"WRITEBACK" !0 !l !d !m})*.
    {W !"WRITEBACK" !0 !l !d !m}.                    (* update written   *)
    (  (not {AC ... !m ?any of Nat !l}) and
       (not {W ?any of String !0 !l ?any of Nat ...}))*.
    {W ?any of String !0 !l ?h:Nat ... where h<>d}  (* different update *)
] false
```

The second line of this property matches an action corresponding to a rendezvous on gate W with four offers: the transaction ("WRITEBACK", i.e. a memory update), the initiating master (the id of which is stored in variable m), the memory line (the address of which is stored in variable l), and the data to be written (which is stored in variable d). When this update is effectively written to memory (2nd action on gate W), with as second offer the port number 0, i.e., the memory, the property forbids (last action on gate W) a data h different from d to be written to the same memory line l without previously receiving a snoop request (gate AC) concerning line l.

---

[4] We considered several properties, such as: absence of deadlocks, absence of livelocks, complete execution of read and write transactions, data integrity, and coherency of ACE-states and parameters of ACE transactions. All these properties are satisfied by our constrained model.

```
function CIC (φ: Property, F: Set of Transaction): Set of (Set of Transaction) is
    if Model(F) |= φ then
        return ∅
    else
        let Δ be a minimal-depth counterexample ;
        result := ∅ ;
        for each transaction T occuring in Δ do
            result := result ∪ CIC (φ, F ∪ {T} )
        end for ;
        if result = ∅ then result := { F } end if ;
        return result
    end if
end function
```

Fig. 3. Function CIC to compute a set of interesting configurations containing faults

Unique Dirty Coherency. To verify the coherency of the ACE states of all the caches of the system, we translated the state-based properties to action-based properties, using information about the ACE state added to transactions issued by cache lines. The following property [16, φ_3] requires that if a cache line is in the state ACE_UD (the cache line is unique and modified), then as long as the line does not change its status, all other cache lines containing the same memory line must be in the state ACE_I (the cache line is invalid)[5]:

```
[ true * .
    {?Ch:String ?op:String ?m1:Nat ?l:Nat !"ACE_UD"} .
    ( not ({?Ch:String ?op:String !m1 !l ?s:String
        where ace_state(s) and (s<>"ACE_UD")}))* .
    {?Ch:String ?op:String ?m2:Nat !l ?s:String
        where (m2<>m1) and ace_state(s) and (s<>"ACE_I")}
] false
```

5.2   Computation of Interesting Configurations Containing Faults

Counterexamples of a desired property provide interesting scenarios to test corner cases. To improve test coverage, it is interesting to have as many different counterexamples as possible. However, on-the-fly model checking provides at most *one* counterexample for each property φ and configuration of the model, because the model checker stops as soon as it detects a violation of the property. Therefore, we take advantage of the parametrization of our formal model, by varying the set $\mathcal{F}$ of forbidden ACE transactions, to compute with the recursive function CIC (*compute interesting configurations*) shown in Fig. 3 a comprehensive set of *interesting configurations* of the Model($\mathcal{F}$) containing faults.

Initially, all fifteen ACE transactions are allowed, i.e., we call CIC($\varphi, \emptyset$). Function CIC proceeds as follows. First, we configure the model to exclude the

---

[5] ace_state(s) is a macro predicate that holds iff the string s is an ACE state.

transactions in $\mathcal{F}$, and model check property φ. If φ is not satisfied, the model checker produces a counterexample Δ. We use the breadth-first search algorithm of EVALUATOR 4.0 to produce a counterexample of minimal depth, and avoid spurious actions in the counterexample. For each transaction T occurring in Δ, we call CIC recursively, deactivating T in addition to $\mathcal{F}$. Function CIC terminates, because the parameter $\mathcal{F}$ has an upper bound (the set of all transactions) and it strictly increases for each recursive call.

The set of interesting configurations $\{\text{Model}(\mathcal{F}_1), \ldots, \text{Model}(\mathcal{F}_n)\}$ corresponding to the set $\{\mathcal{F}_1, \ldots, \mathcal{F}_n\}$ computed by CIC has the following property: a configuration Model($\mathcal{F}'$) does not satisfy the property φ if and only if $\mathcal{F}'$ is smaller than or equal to at least one combination $\mathcal{F}_i$.

We applied CIC to the two properties that were invalid on the unconstrained model (see Sec. 5.1). Altogether, Data Integrity yields 21 interesting configurations (14 from an architecture with two ACE masters initiating transactions, and 7 from an architecture with one ACE-Lite master and one ACE master initiating transactions) and Unique Dirty Coherency yields 18 interesting configurations from an architecture with two ACE masters initiating transactions (with only one ACE master, i.e., a single cache, Unique Dirty Coherency holds trivially).

5.3 Abstract Test Generation

We aim at generating as many tests as possible leading to invalidation of the property for each interesting configuration. We call those tests *negative tests*, because if a test succeeds, we detect a failure of the system; but if the system is correct, all tests will fail.

Our test generation approach is based on the theory of conformance testing [24], i.e., we compute from a specification of a system and a so-called *test purpose* [13] a set of abstract test cases. Intuitively, a test purpose is a means to characterize those states (called ACCEPT states) of the specification that should be reached during test execution. To prune the search space for test cases, the test purpose can also contain so-called REFUSE states: if such a state is reached while testing the DUV, the test is stopped and declared inconclusive. Technically, a test purpose is provided as an LTS, e.g., an LNT model. Thus we express the negation of each property as a test purpose in LNT.

Example 3. The LNT code for the test purpose corresponding to the Unique Dirty Coherency is shown in Fig. 4. After an outgoing action (gates AR, AW, and W) from an ACE master m1 with a cache state ACE_UD (Unique Dirty), it monitors all outgoing actions of all ACE masters. If a different ACE master m2 has an ACE_UD state we ACCEPT the test (a coherency error has been detected). If m1 performs another action with a state other than ACE_UD, we REFUSE the test (the test is inconclusive).

We use two newly developed prototype tools for test generation. A first tool takes as input a model and a test purpose (both in LNT), and produces a *Complete Test Graph* (CTG), i.e., an intermediate LTS containing all information to

```
process main [AR, AW, CR, ACCEPT, REFUSE: any] is
var m1, m2: INDEX_MASTER, s: ACE_state_t in
  select
      AR (?any, ?m1, 1, ACE_UD)
  [] AW (?any, ?m1, 1, ACE_UD)
  [] CR (?any, ?any, ?m1, 1, ?any, ?any, ACE_UD)
  end select; -- cache line of m1 has unique dirty status
  select
    select
        AR (?any, ?m2, 1, ACE_UD) where (m2<>m1)
    [] AW (?any, ?m2, 1, ACE_UD) where (m2<>m1)
    [] CR (?any, ?any, ?m2, 1, ?any, ?any, ACE_UD) where (m2<>m1)
    end select;
    ACCEPT -- cache lines of both cpus have unique dirty status
  [] select
        AR (?any, m1, 1, ?s) where (s<>ACE_UD)
    [] AW (?any, m1, 1, ?s) where (s<>ACE_UD)
    [] CR (?any, ?any, m1, 1, ?any, ?any, ?s) where (s<>ACE_UD)
    end select;
    REFUSE -- cache line of m1 no longer has unique dirty status
  end select
end var end process
```

Fig. 4. Unique Dirty Coherency test purpose described in LNT

extract (all) abstract test cases. We use a second tool to extract a set of abstract test cases from the CTG. These test cases are abstract in the sense that they are system-level automata generated from the model. Thus, those abstract test cases have to be translated to the input language of the commercial coverage-based solver to randomly complete the interface-level details and to run the tests on the RTL test bench.

By extracting all test cases from each CTG and running each test case on the industrial test bench, we obtain a locally intensive test around corner cases specified by the global system-level properties.

Table 1 summarizes the results of our generation of abstract test cases for a test purpose encoding the negation of a property φ. The first two columns describe the property and the architecture. Columns 3 to 5 report the size of the global CTG (produced from the unconstrained model) and the time to extract test cases. The remaining columns give information about our approach based on individual CTGs (produced from the interesting configurations): column 6 presents the number of CTGs, each of which is extracted from an interesting configuration, columns 7 to 10 report the size of the largest and the smallest CTG, and the last column gives the time to extract test cases from all the individual CTGs. We see that the approach based on individual CTGs is much more efficient than the extraction of test cases directly from the global CTG, for which the extraction of test cases does not finish in half a year. Also our

Table 1. Experimental test case extraction results

prop.	masters	global CTG states	global CTG trans.	extr. time	nb. of CTGs	largest CTG states	largest CTG trans.	smallest CTG states	smallest CTG trans.	extr. time
φ_3	2ACE	6,402	14,323	>½ y	18	903	1,957	274	543	$\simeq$7h
φ_5	2ACE	23,032	48,543	>½ y	14	462	888	59	107	<1h
	1ACE/1Lite	2,815	7,071	>½ y	7	193	394	59	107	<1h

approach reduces the size of the largest CTG by a factor of 7 for φ_3 (Unique Dirty Coherency), a factor of 14 for φ_5 (Data Integrity) in the case of the architecture with one ACE master and one ACE-Lite master initiating transactions, and a factor of 49 for for φ_5 in the case of the architecture with two ACE masters.

6 Industrial Results and Impact

Our formal model is used inside STMicroelectronics as a reference in discussions with verification engineers and interconnect architects. It helps to understand the new aspects introduced by ACE and to define the verification strategy. In this context, the OCIS interactive step-by-step simulator with backtracking of CADP is found useful for exhibiting execution scenarios of interest.

We also used OCIS to extract the list of possible transaction initiations for each correct initial state of the system. A correct initial state of the system is a correct combination of initial ACE states of the caches. For example, if a memory line exists initially in two different caches, the state of these caches cannot be ACE_UD for both caches. So doing, we produce in less than one day 296 simple protocol tests, each of which consists of one single ACE transaction, from request to response, including all triggered snoop requests, if any.

Using some of the counterexamples generated during the computation of the interesting configurations (cf. Sec. 5.2), we produced also ten complex protocol tests containing concurrency between different ACE transactions.

6.1 Making the Test Bench Ready for System-Level Verification

The original test libraries developed by the verification engineers are interface tests. With a not so good coverage of system, new tests describing system scenarios are necessary. Because, system requirements cannot be verified on a single ivunit separately, we complete the verification infrastructure and introduce the notion of a *system verification unit* (svunit) connected to all ivunits, enabling to combine behaviors of different interfaces in order to validate system-level requirements. For the considered SoC, we defined an svunit consisting of 56 PSL sequences, 56 PSL basic cover points, and 36 PSL checks. This enables to verify on the RTL test bench that each coherent transaction produces the corresponding snoop transactions, and that each snoop transaction eventually receives a response from the snooped master.

Further modifications of the test bench are required to enable the execution of the concrete test cases derived from our abstract test cases. In particular, it is necessary to control the order of events. First, we added more synchronizations between different *Verification Intellectual Property* (VIP) events to enforce the desired order of the events. Second, we added speed-up randomization: by default the speed of a master for each of its channels is completely random. To express that a master is faster than another one or to enforce an order between two concurrent actions of a same master, we specify speed-up ranges (e.g., fast, slow, or very slow). So doing, the speed-up remains random, but in a limited range, ensuring the desired order.

6.2   Industrial Results

During the implementation of our abstract test cases on top of commercial VIPs, we detected ten bugs in those VIPs. This enabled the CAD supplier to correct the bugs before the use of these VIPs became critical in the development path of STMicroelectronics.

Because the VIPs and the coverage lists are provided by the same CAD supplier, some verification gaps may not be detected. In fact, the same misinterpretation of the ACE specification may find its way into both the VIPs and the coverage lists. Working with a different approach led us to validate the industrial checks (provided in the ivunits), and thanks to our directed tests we detected unverified behaviors.

In October 2014, STMicroelectronics architects detected a limitation in the IP implementation of the CCI. This limitation manifests in a subset of the counterexamples for the data integrity property we verified 20 months before. Precisely, when the CCI initiates a memory update (e.g., see Example 1), some parameters of this update are set to fixed values possibly loosing some important information, and disturbing the ACE-Lite flow in the non-coherent part of the SoC. This limitation corresponds to a gap that we have detected on the commercial VIPs one year before, when we started experimenting with the translation of abstract to concrete test cases. Our method for computing interesting faulty configurations (see Sec. 5.2) enabled us to provide all the scenarios triggering this limitation. In addition, we wrote new PSL checks to detect those corner cases. We should notice that our 306 extracted tests trigger those checks 16 times, whereas the other tests of the STMicroelectronics test library never trigger these checks.

Our generated tests have direct impact on the development flow of an industrial SoC of STMicroelectronics. We observe that the coverage of the verification plan increased significantly[6] and that the coverage of the svunit part of the verification plan is complete (100%), i.e., all the aspects corresponding to system-level behaviors are tested.

---

[6] The coverage of the verification plan increased from 30% to 68%. Notice that 100% coverage is not achievable for the considered SoC, because the verification plan, as defined by the VIPs, includes some features of ACE (e.g., distributed virtual memory), which are handled by the VIPs, but are not used by the considered SoC.

7   Conclusion

We used a system-level formal model of an SoC to improve functional verification in several aspects. First, we studied the sanity of a list of industrial formal checks. We also verified principal system properties with an explicit-state model checker. Using models containing faults, we computed a comprehensive set of interesting configurations, which are then used to generate negative abstract tests. Those tests were translated into RTL level through a coverage-directed test generation platform, thus intensively test the system around corner cases.

Our approach capitalizes on existing environments while solving their limitations for system-level protocols. This had an impact on an industrial SoC in production: It helped to improve the test bench and to increase test coverage. In addition, our approach contributed to the maturation of commercial VIPs.

Currently, we work on automating manual parts of our approach, in particular the translation of abstract test cases to the inputs of a CDTG solver. Given the success of our approach, it seems interesting to apply this approach to the system-level protocols in the next generation of SoCs.

Concerning reusability, our approach to assess the sanity of a check list against a formal model is akin to *crosschecking*, a technique widely used in the hardware community to improve confidence on the verification components. To apply our test generation approach, the formal model must be configurable, so as to violate a property. These preconditions seem acceptable, as we found modifying parts of the model (e.g., some data types) feasible using simple scripts, and the literature presents several techniques to automate the production of faulty models.

Acknowledgements. We are grateful to H. Garavel and R. Mateescu (Inria), G. Barthes and M. Zendri (STMicroelectronics) for their contributions and valuable remarks. We would also like to thank C. Chevallaz and G. Faux (STMicroelectronics) for helpful discussions, and the anonymous reviewers for their suggestions that contributed to improve the paper.

References

1. ARM. AMBA AXI and ACE Protocol Specification. version ARM IHI 0022E (February 2013),
   http://infocenter.arm.com/help/topic/com.arm.doc.ihi0022e
2. Benjamin, M., Geist, D., Hartman, A., Mas, G., Smeets, R.: A Study in Coverage-Driven Test Generation. In: Design Automation Conference, pp. 970–975. IEEE (1999)
3. Champelovier, D., Clerc, X., Garavel, H., Guerte, Y., McKinty, C., Powazny, V., Lang, F., Serwe, W., Smeding, G.: Reference manual of the LNT to LOTOS translator (version 6.1). INRIA/VASY – INRIA/CONVECS (December 2014)
4. Chen, M., Mishra, P.: Property learning techniques for efficient generation of directed tests. IEEE Transactions on Computers 60(6), 852–864 (2011)
5. Chen, M., Qin, X., Koo, H.-M., Mishra, P.: System-Level Validation: High-Level Modeling and Directed Test Generation Techniques. Springer (2013)

6. Crouzen, P., Lang, F.: Smart reduction. In: Giannakopoulou, D., Orejas, F. (eds.) FASE 2011. LNCS, vol. 6603, pp. 111–126. Springer, Heidelberg (2011)
7. Garavel, H., Lang, F.: SVL: a Scripting Language for Compositional Verification. In: Kim, M., Chin, B., Kang, S., Lee, D. (eds.) System Engineering and Automation. IFIP, vol. 69, pp. 377–392. Springer, Boston (2001)
8. Garavel, H., Lang, F., Mateescu, R., Serwe, W.: CADP 2011: A Toolbox for the Construction and Analysis of Distributed Processes. STTT 15(2), 89–107 (2013)
9. Garavel, H., Viho, C., Zendri, M.: System design of a CC-NUMA multiprocessor architecture using formal specification, model-checking, co-simulation, and test generation. STTT 3(3), 314–331 (2001)
10. Gargantini, A., Heitmeyer, C.: Using model checking to generate tests from requirements specifications. Software Engineering Notes 24, 146–162 (1999)
11. Guzey, O., Wang, L.-C.: Coverage-directed test generation through automatic constraint extraction. In: High Level Design Validation and Test Workshop, pp. 151–158. IEEE (2007)
12. IEEE standard for property Specification language (PSL). IEEE Std 1850-2010, pp. i–188 (2010), http://standards.ieee.org/findstds/standard/1850-2010.html
13. Jard, C., Jéron, T.: TGV: theory, principles and algorithms. STTT 7(4), 297–315 (2005)
14. Kahlouche, H., Viho, C., Zendri, M.: An industrial experiment in automatic generation of executable test suites for a cache coherency protocol. In: Petrenko, A., Yevtushenko, N. (eds.) Testing of Communicating Systems. IFIP, vol. 3, pp. 211–226. Springer, Boston (1998)
15. Koo, H.-M., Mishra, P., Bhadra, J., Abadir, M.: Directed micro-architectural test generation for an industrial processor: A case study. In: Microprocessor Test and Verification, pp. 33–36. IEEE (2006)
16. Kriouile, A., Serwe, W.: Formal Analysis of the ACE Specification for Cache Coherent Systems-on-Chip. In: Pecheur, C., Dierkes, M. (eds.) FMICS 2013. LNCS, vol. 8187, pp. 108–122. Springer, Heidelberg (2013)
17. Mateescu, R., Thivolle, D.: A model checking language for concurrent value-passing systems. In: Cuellar, J., Sere, K. (eds.) FM 2008. LNCS, vol. 5014, pp. 148–164. Springer, Heidelberg (2008)
18. Mathaikutty, D.A., Shukla, S.K., Kodakara, S.V., Lilja, D., Dingankar, A.: Design fault directed test generation for microprocessor validation. In: DATE, pp. 1–6. IEEE (2007)
19. Mishra, P., Chen, M.: Efficient techniques for directed test generation using incremental satisfiability. In: VLSI Design, pp. 65–70. IEEE (2009)
20. Greenhalgh, A.P.: Big. LITTLE Processing with ARM Cortex^{TM} -A15 & Cortex-A7 (2011)
21. Qin, X., Mishra, P.: Efficient directed test generation for validation of multicore architectures. In: Quality Electronic Design, pp. 276–283. IEEE (2011)
22. Shen, H., Wei, W., Chen, Y., Chen, B., Guo, Q.: Coverage directed test generation: Godson experience. In: Asian Test Symposium, pp. 321–326. IEEE (2008)
23. Stevens, A.: Introduction to AMBA 4 ACE. ARM whitepaper (June 2011)
24. Tretmans, J.: A formal approach to conformance testing. Twente University Press (1992)
25. Van Glabbeek, R.J., Weijland, W.P.: Branching time and abstraction in bisimulation semantics. Journal of the ACM 43(3), 555–600 (1996)
26. Yuan, J., Pixley, C., Aziz, A., Albin, K.: A framework for constrained functional verification. In: Computer Aided Design, pp. 142–145. IEEE (2003)

Author Index

Printed in the United States
By Bookmasters